DODGE | COLT/VISTA
1990-93 REPAIR MANUAL

D0841778

CHILTON'S

President	Dean F. Morgantini, S.A.E.
Vice President–Finance	Barry L. Beck
Vice President–Sales	Glenn D. Potere
Executive Editor	Kevin M. G. Maher
Production Manager	Ben Greisler, S.A.E.
Project Managers	Michael Abraham, George B. Heinrich III, S.A.E.
	Will Kessler, A.S.E., S.A.E., Richard Schwartz
Schematics Editor	Christopher G. Ritchie

CHILTON™ Automotive Books

PUBLISHED BY **W. G. NICHOLS, INC.**

Manufactured in USA
© 1993 Chilton Book Company
1020 Andrew Drive
West Chester, PA 19380
ISBN 0-8019-8418-1
Library of Congress Catalog Card No. 92-054893
4567890123 7654321098

™Chilton is a registered trademark of the Chilton Company and is licensed to W. G. Nichols, Inc.

Farmers Branch Manske Library
13613 Webb Chapel
Farmers Branch, TX 75234-3756

Contents

Contents

DRIVE TRAIN 7

SUSPENSION AND STEERING 8

BRAKES 9

BODY AND TRIM 10

GLOSSARY

MASTER INDEX

SAFETY NOTICE

Proper service and repair procedures are vital to the safe, reliable operation of all motor vehicles, as well as the personal safety of those performing repairs. This manual outlines procedures for servicing and repairing vehicles using safe, effective methods. The procedures contain many NOTES, CAUTIONS and WARNINGS which should be followed along with standard procedures to eliminate the possibility of personal injury or improper service which could damage the vehicle or compromise its safety.

It is important to note that the repair procedures and techniques, tools and parts for servicing motor vehicles, as well as the skill and experience of the individual performing the work vary widely. It is not possible to anticipate all of the conceivable ways or conditions under which vehicles may be serviced, or to provide cautions as to all of the possible hazards that may result. Standard and accepted safety precautions and equipment should be used when handling toxic or flammable fluids, and safety goggles or other protection should be used during cutting, grinding, chiseling, prying, or any other process that can cause material removal or projectiles.

Some procedures require the use of tools specially designed for a specific purpose. Before substituting another tool or procedure, you must be completely satisfied that neither your personal safety, nor the performance of the vehicle will be endangered.

Although information in this manual is based on industry sources and is complete as possible at the time of publication, the possibility exists that some vehicle manufacturers made later changes which could not be included here. While striving for total accuracy, W. G. Nichols, Inc. cannot assume responsibility for any errors, changes or omissions that may occur in the compilation of this data.

PART NUMBERS

Part numbers listed in this reference are not recommendations by Chilton for any product by brand name. They are references that can be used with interchange manuals and aftermarket supplier catalogs to locate each brand supplier's discrete part number.

SPECIAL TOOLS

Special tools are recommended by the vehicle manufacturer to perform their specific job. Use has been kept to a minimum, but where absolutely necessary, they are referred to in the text by the part number of the tool manufacturer. These tools can be purchased, under the appropriate part number, from your local dealer or regional distributor, or an equivalent tool can be purchased locally from a tool supplier or parts outlet. Before substituting any tool for the one recommended, read the SAFETY NOTICE at the top of this page.

ACKNOWLEDGMENTS

W. G. Nichols, Inc. expresses appreciation to the Chrysler Corporation for their generous assistance.

No part of this publication may be reproduced, transmitted or stored in any form or by any means, electronic or mechanical, including photocopy, recording, or by information storage or retrieval system without prior written permission from the publisher.

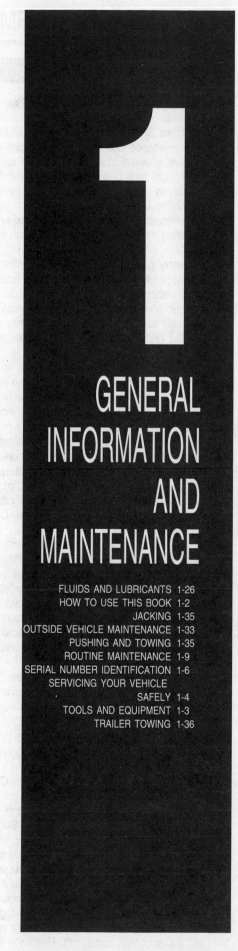

1

GENERAL INFORMATION AND MAINTENANCE

HOW TO USE THIS BOOK

This book covers all Colt and Vista models from 1990 through 1993.

The first two Sections will be the most used, since they contain maintenance and tune-up information and procedures. Studies have shown that a properly tuned and maintained car can get at least 10% better gas mileage (which translates into lower operating costs) and periodic maintenance will catch minor problems before they turn into major repair bills. The other Sections deal with the more complex systems of your car. Operating systems from engine through brakes are covered.

A secondary purpose of this book is a reference guide for owners who want to understand their car and/or their mechanics better. In this case, no tools at all are required. Knowing just what a particular repair job requires in parts and labor time will allow you to evaluate whether or not you're getting a fair price quote and help decipher itemized bills from a repair shop.

Before attempting any repairs or service on your car, read through the entire procedure outlined in the appropriate Section. This will give you the overall view of what tools and supplies will be required. There is nothing more frustrating than having to walk to the bus stop on Monday morning because you were short one gasket on Sunday afternoon. So read ahead and plan ahead. Each operation should be approached logically and all procedures thoroughly understood before attempting any work. Some special tools that may be required can often be rented from local automotive jobbers or places specializing in renting tools and equipment. Check the yellow pages of your phone book.

All Sections contain adjustments, maintenance, removal and installation procedures, and overhaul procedures. When overhaul is not considered practical, we tell you how to remove the failed part and then how to install the new or rebuilt replacement. In this way, you at least save the labor costs. Backyard overhaul of some components (such as the alternator or water pump) is just not practical, but the removal and installation procedure is often simple and well within the capabilities of the average car owner.

Two basic mechanic's rules should be mentioned here. First, whenever the LEFT side of the car or engine is referred to, it is meant to specify the DRIVER'S side of the car. Conversely, the RIGHT side of the car means the PASSENGER'S side. Second, all screws and bolts are removed by turning counterclockwise, and tightened by turning clockwise, unless otherwise noted.

Safety is always the most important rule. Constantly be aware of the dangers involved in working on or around an automobile and take proper precautions to avoid the risk of personal injury or damage to the vehicle. See the section in this Section, Servicing Your Vehicle Safely, and the SAFETY NOTICE on the acknowledgment page before attempting any service procedures and pay attention to the instructions provided. There are 3 common mistakes in mechanical work:

1. Incorrect order of assembly, disassembly or adjustment. When taking something apart or putting it together, doing things in the wrong order usually just costs you extra time; however it CAN break something. Read the entire procedure before beginning disassembly. Do everything in the order in which the instructions say you should do it, even if you can't immediately see a reason for it. When you're taking apart something that is very intricate (for example, a carburetor), you might want to draw a picture of how it looks when assembled at one point in order to make sure you get everything back in its proper position. We will supply exploded views whenever possible, but sometimes the job requires more attention to detail than an illustration provides. When making adjustments (especially tune-up adjustments), do them in order. One adjustment often affects another and you cannot expect satisfactory results unless each adjustment is made only when it cannot be changed by any other.

2. Overtorquing (or undertorquing) nuts and bolts. While it is more common for overtorquing to cause damage, undertorquing can cause a fastener to vibrate loose and cause serious damage, especially when dealing with aluminum parts. Pay attention to torque specifications and utilize a torque wrench in assembly. If a torque figure is not available remember that, if you are using the right tool to do the job, you will probably not have to strain yourself to get a fastener tight enough. The pitch of most threads is so slight that the tension you put on the wrench will be multiplied many times in actual force on what you are tightening. A good example of how critical torque is can be seen in the case of spark plug installation, especially where you are putting the plug into an aluminum cylinder head. Too little torque can fail to crush the gasket, causing leakage of combustion gases and consequent overheating of the plug and engine parts. Too much torque can damage the threads or distort the plug, which changes the spark gap at the electrode. Since more and more manufacturers are using aluminum in their engine and chassis parts to save weight, a torque wrench should be in any serious do-it-yourselfer's tool box.

There are many commercial chemical products available for ensuring that fasteners won't come loose, even if they are not torqued just right (a very common brand is Loctite®). If you're worried about getting something together tight enough to hold, but loose enough to avoid mechanical damage during assembly, one of these products might offer substantial insurance. Read the label on the package and make sure the product is compatible with the materials, fluids, etc. involved before choosing one.

3. Crossthreading. This occurs when a part such as a bolt is screwed into a nut or casting at the wrong angle and forced, causing the threads to become damaged. Crossthreading is more likely to occur if access is difficult. It helps to clean and lubricate fasteners, and to start threading with the part to be installed going straight in, using your fingers. If you encounter resistance, unscrew the part and start over again at a different angle until it can be inserted and turned several times without much effort. Keep in mind that many parts, especially spark plugs, use tapered threads so that gentle turning will automatically bring the part you're threading to the proper angle if you don't force it or resist a change in angle. Don't put a wrench on the part until it's been turned in a couple of times by hand. If you suddenly encounter resistance and the part has not seated fully, don't force it. Pull it back out and make sure it's clean and threading properly.

Always take your time and be patient; once you have some experience, working on your car will become an enjoyable hobby.

TOOLS AND EQUIPMENT

▶ **See Figures 1, 2, 3, 4 and 5**

Naturally, without the proper tools and equipment it is impossible to properly service your vehicle. It would be impossible to catalog each tool that you would need to perform each or every operation in this book. It would also be unwise for the amateur to rush out and buy an expensive set of tools an the theory that he may need one or more of them at sometime.

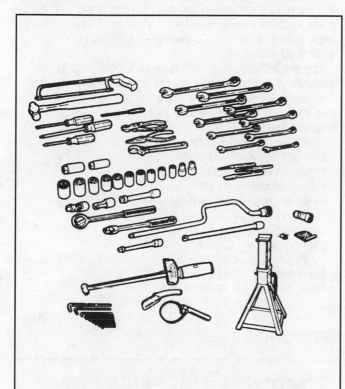

Fig. 1 A basic collection of hand tools is necessary for automotive service

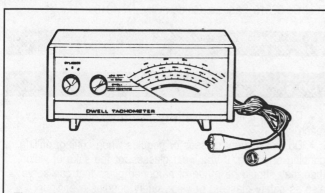

Fig. 2 A dwell/tach is useful for tune-up work

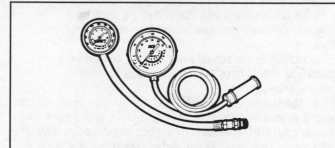

Fig. 3 A compression gauge and combination vacuum/fuel pressure gauge are helpful for troubleshooting and tune-up work

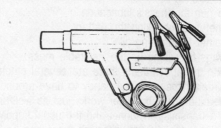

Fig. 4 An inductive pickup timing light is the best for checking timing. Some lights have an advance meter built in to check actual distributor advance at different engine rpm

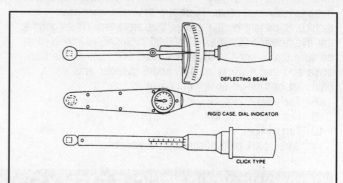

DEFLECTING BEAM

RIGID CASE, DIAL INDICATOR

CLICK TYPE

Fig. 5 Three different types of torque wrenches. The click-type is the best for all-around use

The best approach is to proceed slowly, gathering together a good quality set of those tools that are used most frequently. Don't be misled by the low cost of bargain tools. It is far better to spend a little more for better quality. Forged wrenches, 6- or 12-point sockets and fine tooth ratchets are by far preferable to their less expensive counterparts. As any good mechanic can tell you, there are few worse experiences than trying to work on a car with bad tools. Your monetary savings will be far outweighed by frustration and mangled knuckles.

Certain tools, plus a basic ability to handle tools, are required to get started. A basic mechanics tool set, a torque wrench, and a Torx bits set. Torx bits are hexlobular drivers which fit both inside and outside on special Torx head fasteners used in various places on your vehicles.

Begin accumulating those tools that are used most frequently; those associated with routine maintenance and tune-up.

In addition to the normal assortment of screwdrivers and pliers you should have the following tools for routine maintenance jobs:

1. Metric wrenches, sockets and combination open end/box end wrenches in sizes from 3mm to 22mm); and a spark plug socket ($^{13}/_{16}$ in.) If possible, buy various length socket drive extensions. One break in this department is that the metric sockets available in the U.S. will all fit the ratchet handles and extensions you may already have ($^{1}/_{4}$ in., $^{3}/_{8}$ in., and $^{1}/_{2}$ in. drive).
2. Jackstands for support
3. Oil filter wrench
4. Grease gun for chassis lubrication
5. Hydrometer for checking the battery
6. A container for draining oil
7. Many rags for wiping up the inevitable mess.

In addition to the above items there are several others that are not absolutely necessary, but handy to have around. These include oil-dry (cat box litter works just as well and may be cheaper), a transmission funnel and the usual supply of lubricants, antifreeze and fluids, although these can be purchased as needed. This is a basic list for routine maintenance, but only your personal needs and desires can accurately determine your list of necessary tools.

The second list of tools is for tune-ups. While the tools involved here are slightly more sophisticated, they need not be outrageously expensive. There are several inexpensive tach/dwell meters on the market that are every bit as good for the average mechanic as a $100.00 professional model. Just be sure that it goes to at least 1,200-1,500 rpm on the tach scale and that it works on 4, 6 and 8 cylinder engines. A basic list of tune-up equipment could include:

8. Tach-dwell meter
9. Spark plug wrench
10. Timing light
11. Wire spark plug gauge/adjusting tools

12. Set of feeler blades.

Here again, be guided by your own needs. In addition to these basic tools, there are several other tools and gauges you may find useful. These include:

13. A compression gauge. The screw-in type is slower to use, but eliminates the possibility of a faulty reading due to escaping pressure
14. A manifold vacuum gauge
15. A test light
16. An induction meter. This is used for determining whether or not there is current in a wire. These are handy for use if a wire is broken somewhere in a wiring harness.

As a final note, you will probably find a torque wrench necessary for all but the most basic work. The beam type models are perfectly adequate, although the click (breakaway) type are more precise, and you don't have to crane your neck to see a torque reading in awkward situations. The breakaway torque wrenches are more expensive and should be recalibrated periodically.

Torque specification for each fastener will be given in the procedure in any case that a specific torque value is required. If no torque specifications are given, use the following values as a guide, based upon fastener size:

Bolts marked 6T

6mm bolt/nut — 5-7 ft. lbs.
8mm bolt/nut — 12-17 ft. lbs.
10mm bolt/nut — 23-34 ft. lbs.
12mm bolt/nut — 41-59 ft. lbs.
14mm bolt/nut — 56-76 ft. lbs.

Bolts marked 8T

6mm bolt/nut — 6-9 ft. lbs.
8mm bolt/nut — 13-20 ft. lbs.
10mm bolt/nut — 27-40 ft. lbs.
12mm bolt/nut — 46-69 ft. lbs.
14mm bolt/nut — 75-101 ft. lbs.

SPECIAL TOOLS

Some repair procedures in this book call for the use of special factory tools. Although every effort is made to explain the repair job using your regular set of tools, sometimes the use of a special tool cannot be avoided. Special service tools for your vehicle can be ordered from:Miller Special Tools Utica Tool Co.32615 Park La.,Garden City, MI 48135

SERVICING YOUR VEHICLE SAFELY

It is virtually impossible to anticipate all of the hazards involved with automotive maintenance and service but care and common sense will prevent most accidents.

The rules of safety for mechanics range from DON'T smoke around gasoline, to use the proper tool for the job. The trick to avoiding injuries is to develop safe work habits and take every possible precaution.

Do's

• Do keep a fire extinguisher and first aid kit within easy reach.
• Do wear safety glasses or goggles when cutting, drilling, grinding or prying. If you wear glasses for the sake of vision, then they should be made of hardened glass that can serve also as safety glasses, or wear safety goggles over your regular glasses.
• Do shield your eyes whenever you work around the battery. Batteries contain sulfuric acid; in case of contact with

the eyes or skin, flush the area with water or a mixture of water and baking soda and get medical attention immediately.

• Do use safety stands for an under car service. Jacks are for raising vehicles; safety stands are for making sure the vehicle stays raised until you want it to come down. Whenever the vehicle is raised, block the wheels remaining on the ground and set the parking brake.

• Do use adequate ventilation when working with any chemicals. Asbestos dust resulting from brake lining wear can cause cancer.

• Do disconnect the negative battery cable when working on anything electrical, or when work around or near the electrical system.

• Do follow manufacturer's directions whenever working with potentially hazardous materials. Both brake fluid and antifreeze are poisonous if taken internally.

• Do properly maintain your tools. Loose hammerheads, mushroomed punches and chisels, frayed or poorly grounded electrical cords, excessively worn screwdrivers, spread wrenches (open end), cracked sockets, slipping ratchets, or faulty droplight sockets can cause accidents.

• Do use the proper size and type of tool for the job being done.

• Do when possible, pull on a wrench handle rather than push on it, and adjust your stance to prevent a fall.

• Do be sure that adjustable wrenches are tightly adjusted on the nut or bolt and pulled so that the face is on the side of the fixed jaw.

• Do select a wrench or socket that fits the nut or bolt. The wrench or socket should sit straight, not cocked.

• Do strike squarely with a hammer to avoid glancing blows.

• Do set the parking brake and block the drive wheels if the work requires that the engine be running.

Don'ts

• Don't run an engine in a garage or anywhere else without proper ventilation--LEVER! Carbon monoxide is poisonous; it is absorbed by the body 400 times faster than oxygen; it takes a long time to leave the human body and you can build up a deadly supply of it in your system by simply breathing in a little every day. You may not realize you are slowly poisoning yourself. Always use power vents, windows, fans or open the garage doors.

• Don't work around moving parts while wearing a necktie or other loose clothing. Short sleeves are much safer than long, loose sleeves. Hard-toed shoes with neoprene soles protect your toes and give a better grip on slippery surfaces. Jewelry such as watches, fancy belt buckles, beads or body adornment of any kind is not safe working around a car. Long hair should be hidden under a hat or cap.

• Don't use pockets for toolboxes. A fall or bump can drive a screwdriver deep into your body. Even a wiping cloth hanging from the back pocket can wrap around a spinning shaft or fan.

• Don't smoke when working around gasoline, cleaning solvent or other flammable material.

• Don't smoke when working around the battery. When the battery is being charged, it gives off explosive hydrogen gas.

• Don't use gasoline to wash your hands; there are excellent soaps available. Gasoline may contain lead, and lead can enter the body through a cut, accumulating in the body until you are very ill. Gasoline also removes all the natural oils from the skin so that bone dry hands will suck up oil and grease.

• Don't service the air conditioning system unless you are equipped with the necessary tools and training. The refrigerant, R-12 is extremely cold and when exposed to the air, will instantly freeze any surface it comes in contact with, including your eyes. Although the refrigerant is normally non-toxic, R-12 becomes a deadly poisonous gas in the presence of an open flame. One good whiff of the vapors from burning refrigerant can be fatal.

SERIAL NUMBER IDENTIFICATION

VEHICLE IDENTIFICATION CHART

It is important for servicing and ordering parts to be certain of the vehicle and engine identification. The VIN (vehicle identification number) is a 17 digit number visible through the windshield on the driver's side of the dash and contains the vehicle and engine identification codes. The tenth digit indicates model year and the eighth digit indicates engine code. It can be interpreted as follows:

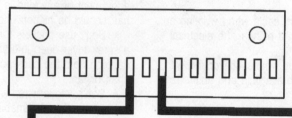

		Engine Code					Model Year	
Code	Liters	Cu. In. (cc)	Cyl.	Fuel Sys.	Eng. Mfg.	Code		Year
A	1.5	89.6 (1468)	4	MPI	Mitsubishi	L		1990
X	1.5	89.6 (1468)	4	MPI	Mitsubishi	M		1991
Y	1.6	97.0 (1595)	4	MPI	Mitsubishi	N		1992
T	1.8	107.1 (1775)	4	MPI	Mitsubishi	O		1993
V	2.0	121.9 (1997)	4	MPI	Mitsubishi			
C	1.8	111.9 (1834)	4	MPI	Mitsubishi			
G	2.4	143.4 (2350)	4	MPI	Mitsubishi			

ENGINE IDENTIFICATION

Year	Model	Engine Displacement Liters (cc)	Engine Series (ID/VIN)	Fuel System	No. of Cylinders	Engine Type
1990	Colt	1.5 (1468)	X	MPI	4	SOHC
		1.6 (1595)	Y	MPI	4	DOHC
	Colt Wagon	1.5 (1468)	X	MPI	4	SOHC
		1.8 (1755)	T	MPI	4	SOHC
	Vista	2.0 (1997)	V	MPI	4	SOHC
1991	Colt	1.5 (1468)	A	MPI	4	SOHC
	Vista	2.0 (1997)	V	MPI	4	SOHC
1992	Colt	1.5 (1468)	A	MPI	4	SOHC
	Vista	2.0 (1997)	V	MPI	4	SOHC
1993	Colt	1.5 (1468)	A	MPI	4	SOHC
		1.8 (1834)	C	MPI	4	SOHC
	Vista	1.8 (1834)	C	MPI	4	SOHC
		2.4 (2350)	G	MPI	4	SOHC

MPI—Multi-Point Fuel Injection
SOHC—Single Overhead Cam
DOHC—Dual Overhead Cam

TRANSAXLE APPLICATION CHART

Year	Model	Transaxle Identification	Transaxle Type
1990–92	Colt	F3A21	3-sp. auto.
		F4A21	4-sp. auto.
		F4M21	4-sp. man.
		F5M21	5-sp. man.
1990	Colt Wagon	F5M21	5-sp. man.
		W5M-31	5-sp. man./4WD
		F3A21-2	3-sp. auto.
1990–92	Vista	F5M22	5-sp. man.
		KM182	5-sp. man./4WD
		F3A22	3-sp. auto.
1993	Colt	F3A21	3-sp. auto.
		F5M21	5-sp. man.
		F5M22	5-sp. man.
		F4A22	4-sp. auto.
	Vista	F5M22	5-sp. man.
		F5M31	5-sp. man.
		W5M31	5-sp. man./4WD
		W5M33	5-sp. man./4WD
		F4A22	4-sp. auto.
		F4A23	4-sp. auto.
		W4A32	4-sp. auto./4WD

Vehicle Identification Number

The vehicle identification number plate is mounted on the instrument panel, adjacent to the lower corner of the windshield on the driver's side, and is visible through the windshield.

Engine Model Number

▶ See Figure 6

The engine model number is cast on the lower left side of the engine block or stamped near the engine serial number on the upper front side of the engine block.

Engine Serial Number

▶ See Figure 7

The engine serial number is stamped on a boss usually located on the right front top edge of the cylinder block.

Vehicle Body Number Location

▶ See Figures 8 and 9

The body number is located on the top center of the firewall in the engine compartment. The plate usually will also include, model, engine, transmission/transaxle and body paint color codes and identification.

Transaxle Serial Number

▶ See Figure 10

The manual transaxle serial number is stamped on housing of the transaxle case. On automatic transaxle models, the number is on a plate attached to the side of the transmission, or stamped on the boss of the oil pan flange.

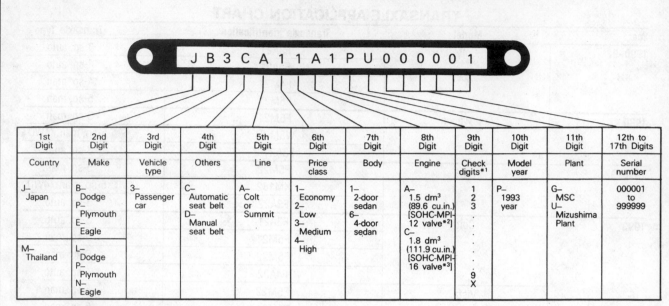

1st Digit	2nd Digit	3rd Digit	4th Digit	5th Digit	6th Digit	7th Digit	8th Digit	9th Digit	10th Digit	11th Digit	12th to 17th Digits
Country	Make	Vehicle type	Others	Line	Price class	Body	Engine	Check digits[1]	Model year	Plant	Serial number
J— Japan	B— Dodge P— Plymouth E— Eagle	3— Passenger car	C— Automatic seat belt D— Manual seat belt	A— Colt or Summit	1— Economy 2— Low 3— Medium 4— High	1— 2-door sedan 6— 4-door sedan	A— 1.5 dm³ (89.6 cu.in.) [SOHC-MPI-12 valve[2]]	1 2 3 . . . . . 9 X	P— 1993 year	G— MSC U— Mizushima Plant	000001 to 999999
M— Thailand	L— Dodge P— Plymouth N— Eagle						C— 1.8 dm³ (111.9 cu.in.) [SOHC-MPI-16 valve[3]]				

NOTE
[1]: "Check digit" means a single number or letter X used to verify the accuracy of transcription of vehicle identification number.
[2]: 2 intake valves and 1 exhaust valve per cylinder
[3]: 2 intake valves and 2 exhaust valves per cylinder

Fig. 6 VIN code explanation

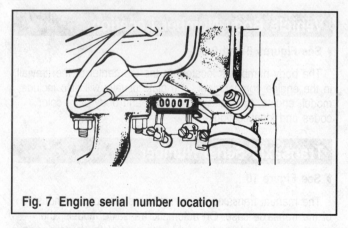

Fig. 7 Engine serial number location

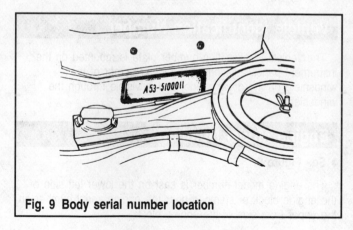

Fig. 9 Body serial number location

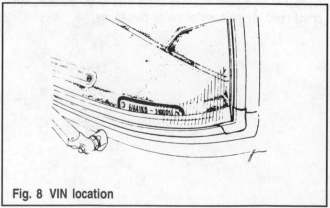

Fig. 8 VIN location

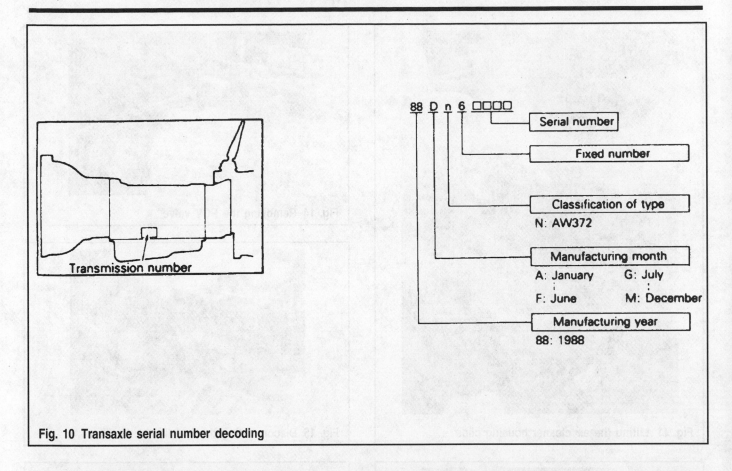

Fig. 10 Transaxle serial number decoding

ROUTINE MAINTENANCE

Routine maintenance and driver's preventive maintenance are the most important steps that can be taken to extend the life of your car and avoid many expensive repairs.

Driver's preventive maintenance consists of taking only a minute every day (or so) to check the various fluid levels, hoses, belts, tire pressures and general visual condition of the engine and car body.

Routine maintenance calls for periodical service or replacement of parts and systems according to a schedule.

Air Cleaner

▶ **See Figures 11 and 12**

The air cleaner contains a dry filter element that keeps most dirt and dust from entering the engine via the throttle body. Never run the engine (other than for adjusting) without a filter element. The dirt and dust entering the engine can cause expensive damage to the pistons, bearings, etc.

Proper maintenance of the air cleaner element is vital. A clogged filter element will fail to supply sufficient fresh air to induction system and engine, causing an over-rich fuel/air mixture. Such a condition will result in poor engine performance and economy. Periodical replacing of the filter element (refer to the maintenance chart) will help your car last longer and run better.

To replace the air cleaner filter element:

1. Loosen the side mounted spring clips.

2. Lift off the top of the air cleaner and remove the filter element. On some models a charcoal filter is also located in the air cleaner. This is for vapor control and is not to be disturbed.

3. If the element is not too clogged by dirt, use compressed air and clean the element. Hold the air nozzle at least 50mm from the inside screen (or the element).

4. Replace the filter element if mileage or dirt clogging is indicated.

5. Install the air cleaner element into position and secure the cover.

PCV Valve and Crankcase Vent Filter

▶ **See Figures 13 and 14**

A closed crankcase ventilation system is used on your car. The purpose of the closed system is to prevent blow-by gases, created by the engine, from escaping into the air.

Some models do not use a PCV Valve; blow-by gases are passed through a hose from the front of the valve cover to the air cleaner, and through another hose from the rear of the valve cover into the intake manifold. At part throttle, the blow-by gases are drawn from the rear of the valve cover into the intake manifold. At wide opened throttle, the blow-by gases are drawn through both the front and rear hose and returned to the engine.

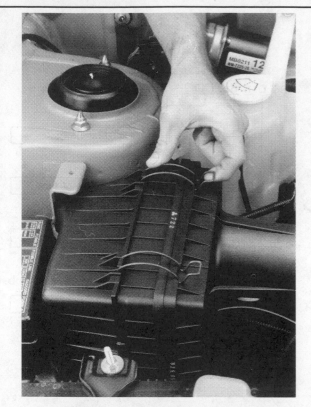

Fig. 11 Lifting the air cleaner housing clips

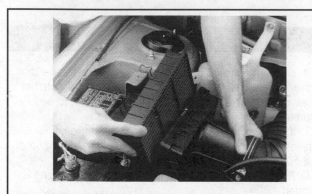

Fig. 12 Removing the air cleaner element

Fig. 13 Removing the PCV valve hose

Fig. 14 Removing the PCV valve

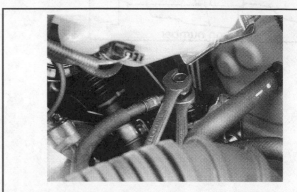

Fig. 15 Disconnecting the fuel line at the filter

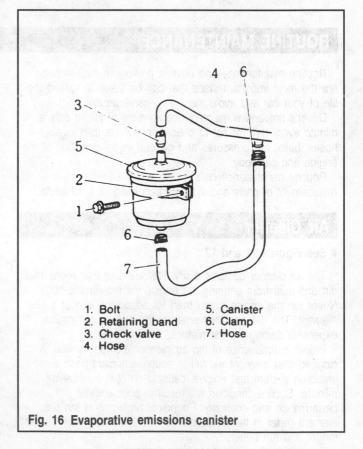

1. Bolt
2. Retaining band
3. Check valve
4. Hose
5. Canister
6. Clamp
7. Hose

Fig. 16 Evaporative emissions canister

Servicing the closed crankcase ventilation system on models without a PCV valve amounts to a periodic check of the hoses (cracked or hard hoses should be replaced) and the cleaning of the wire mesh in the air cleaner and the fixed orifice on the intake manifold. The wire mesh (resembles steel wool) acts as a filter for the crankcase ventilation system

On models equipped with a PCV valve, the PCV system supplies fresh air to the crankcase through the air cleaner. Inside the crankcase, the fresh air mixes with the blow-by gases. The mixture of fresh air and blow-by gases is then passed through the PCV valve and into the intake manifold. The PCV valve (usually mounted on the end of the valve cover) is a metered orifice that reacts to intake manifold vacuum, and has an adequate capacity for all normal driving conditions. However, under heavy engine loads or high speed driving there is less intake manifold vacuum and the blow-by gases exceed the PCV valve's capacity. When this happens, the blow-by gases back up into the air cleaner through the front hose, mix with fresh air and are reburned in the engine.

REMOVAL & INSTALLATION

1. Test the operation of the PCV valve, apply the parking brake, start the engine and allow it to operate at a normal idle speed.
2. Remove the PCV valve from the valve cover mounting. A hissing noise should be heard as air passes through the valve and a strong vacuum should be felt if you place a finger over the opened end of the valve.
3. To check the PCV valve with the engine not running, remove the PCV valve from the valve cover mounting. Shake the valve, if a rattling sound is heard, the valve is usually in operating condition.
4. If a rattling sound is not heard, or, suction is not felt when the engine is running, the valve is clogged.
5. Clean the valve and hose in solvent, check for air flow or rattle. Replace the valve and/or hose if necessary.

Fuel Filter

▶ See Figure 15

The fuel filter **must** be replaced at least every five years or 50,000 miles (80,000km). The is a maximum replacement period. Good preventive maintenance dictates that the fuel filter be replaced once a year, or every 10,000 miles (16,000km). However, since the amount of dirt and water in the fuel varies greatly, the filter should be replaced whenever you suspect it to be clogged. Typically, the symptoms of a clogged filter are a lack of engine performance under full throttle conditions, especially at high rpm, even though the engine operates normally under moderate driving conditions. With severe clogging, the filter may cause poor running under virtually every operating condition but idle. One way to check out the filter is to follow the steps below for removal and then drain the contents out of the filter through the inlet. Drain the filter into a tin can rather than a glass or styrofoam container. While it is normal for a light concentration of particles or a few drops of water to be trapped in the fuel on the inlet side of the filter, large amounts of water and heavy concentrations of dirt indicate dirty fuel and, probably, a clogged filter. If you find a

great deal of dirt trapped in the filter, it is a good idea not only to replace the filter, but to have the fuel tank drained or pumped out as well.

An electric fuel pump is used on these models and the filter is in the engine compartment. A connector, for checking the fuel function, is located under the battery tray. With the engine running, disconnect the connector. When the engine stops, no pressure will remain in the system.

REMOVAL & INSTALLATION

1. First, you MUST reduce the pressure in the system as follows:
   a. Open the trunk and pry up the lid located in the floor which covers the electric fuel pump.
   b. Start the engine and allow it to idle.
   c. Disconnect the fuel pump connector. Allow the engine to continue idling until it stalls. Then, turn off the ignition key.
   d. Disconnect the negative battery connector.
2. Remove the air cleaner assembly as required.
3. Using an open-end wrench to hold the fuel filter stationary, loosen the bolt for the banjo type connector on top of the fuel filter with a box wrench. Do exactly the same with the inlet connector on the bottom of the filter.
4. Remove the bolt or nuts attaching the filter to the bracket and remove it.
5. To install the new filter, reverse the above procedure. It's best to torque the bolts for the fuel line banjo fittings. If the banjo fitting washers are damaged, replace them. The outlet fitting is torqued to 18-25 ft. lbs. in all cases. The inlet fitting is torqued, to 25 ft. lbs.
6. Reconnect the fuel pump, start the engine and check for leaks.

Evaporative Emission Canister

▶ See Figure 16

The heart of this system is a charcoal canister located in the engine compartment. Fuel vapor that collects in the carburetor float bowl or gas tank and which would ordinarily be released to the atmosphere is stored in the canister because of the affinity of the charcoal for it.

In order to restore the ability of the charcoal to hold fuel, fresh air is drawn through the charcoal under certain operating conditions, thus drawing the fuel back out and burning it in the combustion chambers.

At idle speed, or when the engine is cold, the addition of any fuel vapor to the correct mixture would cause excessive emissions. A port in the carburetor or fuel injection system throttle body allows the fuel to be drawn out of the canister only after the throttle has been opened past the normal idle position (the port is located above the position of the throttle at idle). If there is no vacuum, the canister purge valve remains closed. The flow of air and fuel are prevented when the engine is cold via a thermal valve. This valve prevents the vacuum signal going to the canister purge valve from passing through it until the engine reaches a certain temperature. On turbocharged vehicles, two vacuum signals are sent to the purge valve so that the system will work only above idle speed and below full throttle.

When the canister purge valve opens, air is drawn under very slight vacuum from the air intake hose located between the air cleaner and carburetor or injection system.

REMOVAL & INSTALLATION

The canister or canisters should be replaced at specified intervals, as shown on the maintenance chart. Make sure all hoses are clamped and not dry rotted or broken. The canister filter, if equipped, should be inspected, cleaned or replaced at least every two years. Any clogging of the filter will inhibit air flow through the canister. Two different types of valves were used in the canister lines--refer to Section 4 for a detailed description of their function and necessary servicing. To replace the canister:

1. Remove the two connecting hoses from the canister.
2. Loosen and remove the canister retaining band bolt.
3. Remove the canister.
4. Check the hoses, replace any that are cracked, soft or collapsed. Install the new canister and connect the hoses.

Battery

▶ **See Figures 17, 18, 19 and 20**

❊❊CAUTION

Keep flame or sparks away from the battery! It gives off explosive hydrogen gas, while it is being charged.

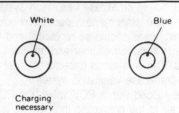

Fig. 19 The battery charge indicator is located on the top surface and changes blue or green, when adequately charged, to white or dark (check the label on the battery) when low on charge

GENERAL MAINTENANCE

Periodically, clean the top of the battery with a solution of baking soda and water using a stiff bristle brush.

❊❊CAUTION

Always wear goggle when cleaning the battery. Acid will splash into your eyes if they are not protected!

Make certain that none of this solution gets into the battery. If any acid has spilled onto the battery tray, clean this area in the same way. If paint has been removed from the tray, wire brush the area and paint it with a rust-resisting paint.

Remove the cable ends, clean the cable end clamps and battery posts, reconnect and tighten the clamps and apply a

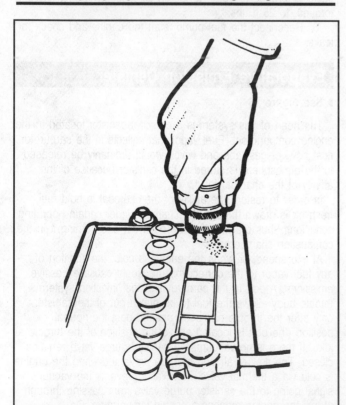

Fig. 17 Clean the posts with a wire brush or a terminal cleaner made for the purpose shown

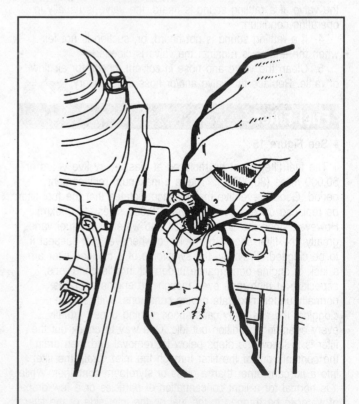

Fig. 18 Clean the inside of the cable clamps with a wire brush or special tool

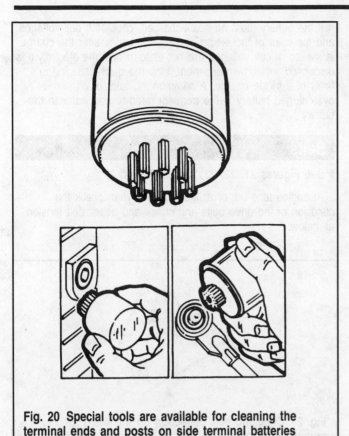

Fig. 20 Special tools are available for cleaning the terminal ends and posts on side terminal batteries

thin coat of petroleum jelly to the terminals. This will help to retard corrosion. The terminals can be cleaned with a staff wire brush or with an inexpensive terminal cleaner designed for this purpose.

Some batteries were equipped with a felt terminal washer. This should be saturated with engine oil approximately every 6,000 miles. This will also help to retard corrosion.

➡If the top of the battery is constantly wet, it a good sign that the voltage regulator is malfunctioning.

MAINTENANCE FREE BATTERIES

The factory-installed battery is a maintenance free type on all the cars covered by this book. That means that you'll never have to remove caps (there aren't any) to add water. But a yearly inspection and cleaning of the battery, connections, and battery mountings is recommended to guarantee maximum reliability.

Testing the Maintenance Free Battery

Maintenance-free batteries do not require normal attention as far as fluid level checks are concerned. However, the terminals require periodic cleaning, which should be performed at least once a year.

The sealed top battery cannot be checked for charge in the normal manner, since there is no provision for access to the electrolyte. To check the condition of the battery:

1. If the battery is equipped with an indicator eye on top of the battery check the color of the eye. If the eye is bright, the

battery has enough fluid. If the eye is dark, the electrolyte fluid is too low and the battery must be replaced.

2. If a green dot appears in the middle of the eye, the battery is sufficiently charged. Proceed to Step 4. If no green dot is visible, charge the battery as in Step 3.

3. Charge the battery at this rate:

✳✳WARNING

Do not charge the battery for more than 50 amp/hours! If the green dot appears, or if electrolyte squirts out of the vent hole, stop the charge and proceed to Step 4.

It may be necessary to tip the battery from side to side to get the green dot to appear after charging.

4. Connect a battery load tester and a voltmeter across the battery terminals (the battery cables should be disconnected from the battery). Apply a 300 amp load to the battery for 15 seconds to remove the surface charge. Remove the load.

5. Wait 15 seconds to allow the battery to recover. Apply the appropriate test load, as specified in the accompanying chart. Apply the load for 15 seconds while reading the voltage. Disconnect the load.

6. Check the results against the accompanying chart. If the battery voltage is at or above the specified voltage for the temperature listed, the battery is good. If the voltage falls below what's listed, the battery should be replaced.

REPLACEMENT BATTERIES

Many replacement batteries are of the maintenance free type. For these batteries, follow the procedures above. If the replacement battery you have purchased is not a maintenance free type, follow these easy maintenance procedures:

Check the battery fluid level at least once a month, more often in hot weather or during extended periods of travel. The electrolyte level should be up to the bottom of the split ring in each cell. If the level is low, add water. Distilled water is good for this purpose, but ordinary tap water can be used.

At least once a year, check the specific gravity of the battery with a hydrometer. It should be between 1.20-1.26 on the hydrometer's scale. Most importantly, all the cells should read approximately the same. If one or more cells read significantly lower than the others, it's an indication that these low cells are shorting out. Replace the battery.

If water is added during freezing weather, the vehicle should be driven several miles to allow the electrolyte and water to mix. Otherwise the battery could freeze.

Filling the Battery

Batteries should be checked for proper electrolyte level at least once a month or more frequently. Keep a close eye on any cell or cells that are unusually low or seem to constantly need water — this may indicate a battery on its last legs, a leak, or a problem with the charging system.

Top up each cell to the bottom of the split ring, or, if the battery has no split ring, about ⅜ in. (9.5mm) above the tops of the plates. Use distilled water where available, or ordinary tap water, if the water in your area isn't too hard. Hard water contains minerals that may slowly damage the plates of your battery.

CABLES AND CLAMPS

Twice a year, the battery terminal posts and the cable clamps should be cleaned. Loosen the clamp bolts (you may have to brush off any corrosion with a baking soda and water solution if they are really messy) and remove the cables, negative cable first. On batteries with posts on top, the use of a battery clamp puller is recommended. It is easy to break off a battery terminal if a clamp gets stuck without the puller. These pullers are inexpensive and available in most auto parts stores or auto departments. Side terminal battery cables are secured with a bolt.

The best tool for battery clamp and terminal maintenance is a battery terminal brush. This inexpensive tool has a female ended wire brush for cleaning terminals, and a male ended wire brush inside for cleaning the insides of battery clamps. When using this tool, make sure you get both the terminal posts and the insides of the clamps nice and shiny. Any oxidation, corrosion or foreign material will prevent a sound electrical connection and inhibit either starting or charging. If your battery has side terminals, there is also a cleaning tool available for these.

Before installing the cables, remove the battery hold-down clamp or strap and remove the battery. Inspect the battery casing for leaks or cracks (which unfortunately can only be fixed by buying a new battery). Check the battery tray, wash it off with warm soapy water, rinse and dry. Any rust on the tray should be sanded away, and the tray given at least two coats of a quality anti-rust paint. Replace the battery, and install the hold-down clamp or strap, but do not overtighten.

Reinstall your clean battery cables, negative cable last. Tighten the cables on the terminal posts snugly; do not overtighten. Wipe a thin coat of petroleum jelly or grease all over the outside of the clamps. This will help to inhibit corrosion.

Finally, check the battery cables themselves. If the insulation of the cables is cracked or broken, or if the ends are frayed, replace the cable with a new cable of the same length or gauge.

✳✳CAUTION

Batteries give off hydrogen gas, which is explosive. DO NOT SMOKE around the battery! The battery electrolyte contains sulfuric acid. If you should splash any into your eyes or skin, flush with plenty of clear water and get immediate medical help.

BATTERY CHARGING AND REPLACEMENT

Charging a battery is best done by the slow charging method (often called trickle charging), with a low amperage charger. Quick charging a battery can actually 'cook' the battery, damaging the plates inside and decreasing the life of the battery drastically. Any charging should be done in a well ventilated area away from the possibility of sparks or flame. The cell caps (not found on maintenance-free batteries) should be unscrewed from their cells, but not removed.

If the battery must be quick-charged, check the cell voltages and the color of the electrolyte a few minutes after the charge is started. If cell voltages are not uniform or if the electrolyte is discolored with brown sediment, stop the quick charging in favor of a trickle charge. A common indicator of an overcharged battery is the frequent need to add water to the battery.

Belts

▶ **See Figures 21, 22, 23, 24, 25, 26 and 27**

At engine tune-up, or at least once a year, check the condition of the drive belts and check and adjust belt tension as below:

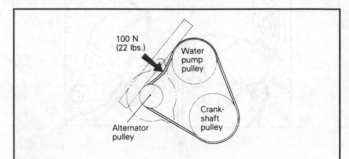

Fig. 21 Checking belt deflection on the water pump/alternator belt. Deflection should be 7-10mm at this point

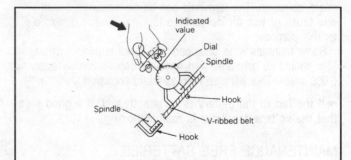

Fig. 22 Using a belt tension gauge to check belt adjustment. Standard tension should be 55-110 lbs. between any 2 pulleys

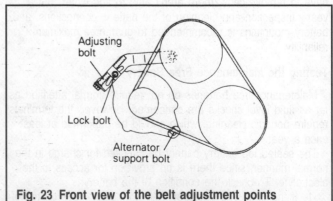

Fig. 23 Front view of the belt adjustment points

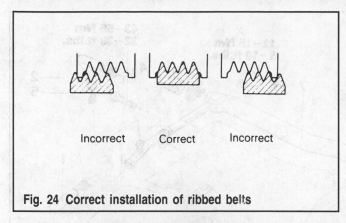

Fig. 24 Correct installation of ribbed belts

Incorrect   Correct   Incorrect

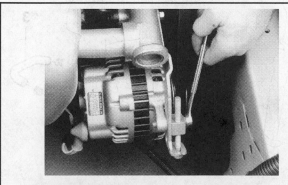

Fig. 25 Loosening the alternator lockdown bolt

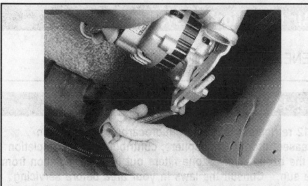

Fig. 26 Turning the alternator belt adjusting bolt

Fig. 27 Checking belt tension

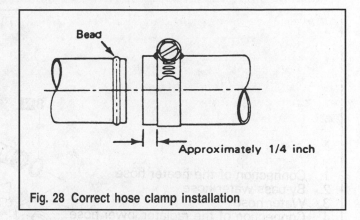

Fig. 28 Correct hose clamp installation

Bead

Approximately 1/4 inch

INSPECTION AND ADJUSTMENT

1. Inspect all belts for signs of glazing or cracking. A glazed belt will be perfectly smooth from slippage, while a good belt will have a slight texture of fabric visible. Cracks will usually start at the inner edge of the belt and run outward. Replace the belt at the first sign of cracking or if glazing is severe.

2. Belt tension does not refer to play or droop. By placing your thumb midway between the two pulleys, it should be possible to depress each belt about 10mm with about 20 lbs. (10 Kg) pressure. The air pump belt runs looser than this. You should be able to depress it about 15mm. If the belt can be depressed more than this, or cannot be depressed this much, adjust the tension. Inadequate tension will result in slippage and wear, while excessive tension will damage bearings and cause belts to fray and crack.

3. To adjust the tension on components, loosen the pivot and mounting bolts of the component, or idler pulley, which the belt is driving. Use a soft wooden hammer handle, a broomstick, or the like to pry the component toward or away from the engine until the proper tension is achieved. Do not use a screwdriver or other metal device, such as a prybar, as a lever.

4. Tighten the component mounting bolts securely. If a new belt has been installed, check the tension after about 200 miles of driving. Adjust if necessary.

5. If belt tension at the idler pulley bracket is incorrect, loosen the locknut, then turn the adjusting bolt to move the idler pulley up or down until the belt tension is correct. Tighten the locknut securely and recheck the adjustment.

Hoses

▶ **See Figures 28, 29 and 30**

Radiator hoses are generally of two constructions, the preformed (molded) type, which is custom made for a particular application, and the spring-loaded type, which is made to fit several different applications. Heater hoses are all of the same general construction.

Inspect the condition of the radiator and heater hoses periodically. Early spring and at the beginning of the fall or winter, when you are performing other maintenance, are good times. Make sure the engine and cooling system are cold. Visually inspect for cracking, rotting or collapsed hoses,

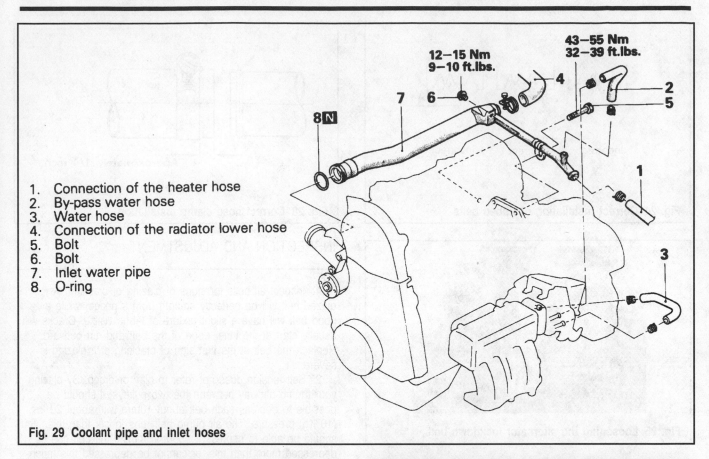

12—15 Nm
9—10 ft.lbs.

43—55 Nm
32—39 ft.lbs.

1. Connection of the heater hose
2. By-pass water hose
3. Water hose
4. Connection of the radiator lower hose
5. Bolt
6. Bolt
7. Inlet water pipe
8. O-ring

Fig. 29 Coolant pipe and inlet hoses

replace as necessary. Run your hand along the length of the hose. If a weak or swollen spot is noted when squeezing the hose wall, replace the hose.

REPLACEMENT

1. Remove the radiator cap.
2. Open the radiator petcock to drain the coolant. To replace the bottom hose drain all the radiator coolant. If only the top hose is to be replaced drain just enough fluid to bring the level down below the level of the top hose. If the coolant is over a year old discard it.
3. Remove the hose clamps and remove the hose.
4. Use new hose clamps if the old ones are badly rusted or damaged. Slide the hose clamps over each end of the new hose then slide the hose over the hose connections.
5. Position each clamp about 1/4 in. from the end of the hose and tighten.
6. Close the petcock and refill with the old fluid if it is less than a year old or with a new mixture of 50/50, coolant/water.
7. Start the engine and idle it for 15 minutes with the radiator cap off and check for leaks. Add coolant if necessary and install the radiator cap.

Air Conditioning System

GENERAL SERVICING PROCEDURES

✳✳CAUTION

R-12 refrigerant is a chlorofluorocarbon which, when released into the atmosphere, contributes to the depletion of the ozone layer. Ozone filters out harmful radiation from the sun. Consult the laws in your area before servicing any system containing R-12. In some states it is illegal to perform repairs involving refrigerant unless the work is done by a certified technician.

The most important aspect of air conditioning service is the maintenance of pure and adequate charge of refrigerant in the system. A refrigeration system cannot function properly if a significant percentage of the charge is lost. Leaks are common because the severe vibration encountered in an automobile can easily cause a sufficient cracking or loosening of the air conditioning fittings. As a result, the extreme operating pressures of the system force refrigerant out.

The problem can be understood by considering what happens to the system as it is operated with a continuous leak. Because the expansion valve regulates the flow of refrigerant to the evaporator, the level of refrigerant there is fairly constant. The receiver/drier stores any excess of refrigerant, and so a loss will first appear there as a reduction in the level of liquid. As this level nears the bottom of the vessel, some refrigerant vapor bubbles will begin to appear in

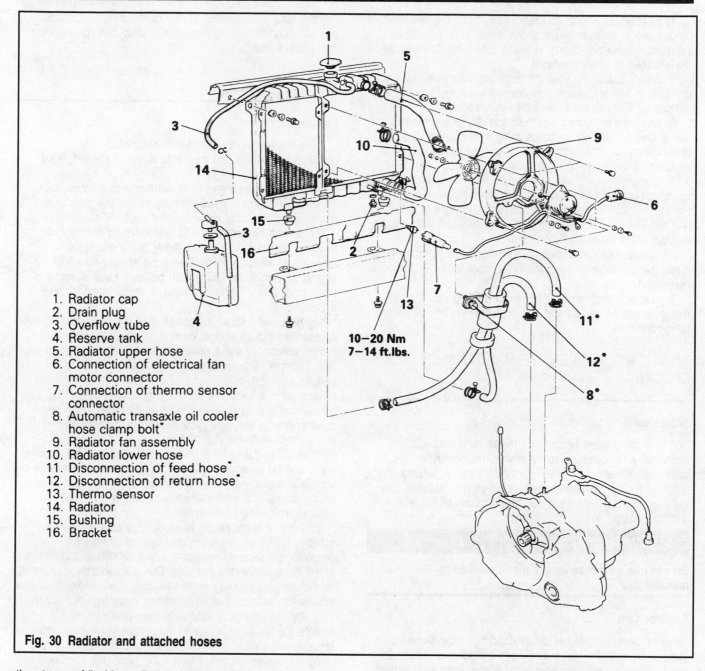

1. Radiator cap
2. Drain plug
3. Overflow tube
4. Reserve tank
5. Radiator upper hose
6. Connection of electrical fan motor connector
7. Connection of thermo sensor connector
8. Automatic transaxle oil cooler hose clamp bolt*
9. Radiator fan assembly
10. Radiator lower hose
11. Disconnection of feed hose*
12. Disconnection of return hose*
13. Thermo sensor
14. Radiator
15. Bushing
16. Bracket

10—20 Nm
7—14 ft.lbs.

Fig. 30 Radiator and attached hoses

the stream of liquid supplied to the expansion valve. This vapor decreases the capacity of the expansion valve very little as the valve opens to compensate for its presence. As the quantity of liquid in the condenser decreases, the operating pressure will drop there and throughout the high side of the system. As the R-12 continues to be expelled, the pressure available to force the liquid through the expansion valve will continue to decrease, and, eventually, the valve's orifice will prove to be too much of a restriction for adequate flow even with the needle fully withdrawn.

At this point, low side pressure will start to drop, and severe reduction in cooling capacity, marked by freeze-up of the evaporator coil, will result. Eventually, the operating pressure of the evaporator will be lower than the pressure of the atmosphere surrounding it, and air will be drawn into the system wherever there are leaks in the low side.

Because all atmospheric air contains at least some moisture, water will enter the system and mix with the R-12 and the oil. Trace amounts of moisture will cause sludging of the oil, and corrosion of the system. Saturation and clogging of the filter/drier, and freezing of the expansion valve orifice will eventually result. As air fills the system to a greater and greater extend, it will interfere more and more with the normal flows of refrigerant and heat.

A list of general precautions that should be observed while doing this follows:

1. Keep all tools as clean and dry as possible.

2. Thoroughly purge the service gauges and hoses of air and moisture before connecting them to the system. Keep them capped when not in use.

3. Thoroughly clean any refrigerant fitting before disconnecting it, in order to minimize the entrance of dirt into the system.

4. Plan any operation that requires opening the system beforehand in order to minimize the length of time it will be exposed to open air. Cap or seal the open ends to minimize the entrance of foreign material.

5. When adding oil, pour it through an extremely clean and dry tube or funnel. Keep the oil capped whenever possible. Do not use oil that has not been kept tightly sealed.

6. Use only refrigerant 12. Purchase refrigerant intended for use in only automotive air conditioning system. Avoid the use of refrigerant 12 that may be packaged for another use, such as cleaning, or powering a horn, as it is impure.

7. Completely evacuate any system that has been opened to replace a component, other than when isolating the compressor, or that has leaked sufficiently to draw in moisture and air. This requires evacuating air and moisture with a good vacuum pump for at least one hour.

If a system has been open for a considerable length of time it may be advisable to evacuate the system for up to 12 hours (overnight).

8. Use a wrench on both halves of a fitting that is to be disconnected, so as to avoid placing torque on any of the refrigerant lines.

ADDITIONAL PREVENTIVE MAINTENANCE CHECKS

Antifreeze

In order to prevent heater core freeze-up during A/C operation, it is necessary to maintain permanent type antifreeze protection of +15°F (-9°C) or lower. A reading of -15°F (-26°C) is ideal since this protection also supplies sufficient corrosion inhibitors for the protection of the engine cooling system.

❄❄WARNING

Do not use antifreeze longer than specified by the manufacturer.

Radiator Cap

For efficient operation of an air conditioned car's cooling system, the radiator cap should have a holding pressure which meets manufacturer's specifications. A cap which fails to hold these pressure should be replaced.

Condenser

Any obstruction of or damage to the condenser configuration will restrict the air flow which is essential to its efficient operation. It is therefore, a good rule to keep this unit clean and in proper physical shape.

➡**Bug screens are regarded as obstructions.**

Condensation Drain Tube

This single molded drain tube expels the condensation, which accumulates on the bottom of the evaporator housing, into the engine compartment.

If this tube is obstructed, the air conditioning performance can be restricted and condensation buildup can spill over onto the vehicle's floor.

SAFETY

Precautions

There are two particular hazards associated with air conditioning systems and they both relate to the refrigerant gas.

First, the refrigerant gas is an extremely cold substance. When exposed to air, it will instantly freeze any surface it comes in contact with, including your eyes.

The second hazard relates to fire. Although normally non-toxic, refrigerant gas becomes highly poisonous in the presence of an open flame. One good whiff of the vapor formed by burning refrigerant can be fatal. Keep all forms of fire (including cigarettes) well clear of the air conditioning system.

Any repair work to an air conditioning system should be approached with caution. If there is any doubt concerning correct servicing, have it done professional. Do not, under any circumstances, attempt to loosen or tighten any fittings or perform any work other than that outlined here.

Because of the importance of the necessary safety precautions that must be exercised when working with air conditioning systems and R-12 refrigerant, a recap of the safety precautions are outlined.

1. Avoid contact with a charged refrigeration system, even when working on another part of the air conditioning system or vehicle. If a heavy tool comes into contact with a section of copper tubing or a heat exchanger, it can easily cause the relatively soft material to rupture.

2. When it is necessary to apply force to a fitting which contains refrigerant, as when checking that all system couplings are securely tightened, use a wrench on both parts of the fitting involved, if possible. This will avoid putting torque on the refrigerant tubing. (It is advisable, when possible, to use tube or line wrenches when tightening these flare nut fittings.)

3. Do not attempt to discharge the system by merely loosening a fitting, or removing the service valve caps and cracking these valves. Precise control is possibly only when using the service gauges. Place a rag under the open end of the center charging hose while discharging the system to catch any drops of liquid that might escape. Wear protective gloves when connecting or disconnecting service gauge hoses.

4. Discharge the system only into a container made for the recovery of used refrigerant. When leak testing or soldering this is particularly important, as toxic gas is formed when R-12 contacts any flame.

5. Never start a system without first verifying that both service valves are backseated, if equipped, and that all fittings are throughout the system are snugly connected.

6. Avoid applying heat to any refrigerant line or storage vessel. Charging may be aided by using water heated to less than 125°F (52°C) to warm the refrigerant container. Never allow a refrigerant storage container to sit out in the sun, or near any other source of heat, such as a radiator.

7. Always wear goggles when working on a system to protect the eyes. If refrigerant contacts the eye, it is advisable in all cases to see a physician as soon as possible.

8. Frostbite from liquid refrigerant should be treated by first gradually warming the area with cool water, and then gently applying petroleum jelly. A physician should be consulted.

9. Always keep refrigerant can fittings capped when not in use. Avoid sudden shock to the can which might occur from dropping it, or from banging a heavy tool against it. Never carry a refrigerant can in the passenger compartment of a car.

10. Always completely discharge the system before painting the vehicle (if the paint is to be baked on), or before welding anywhere near the refrigerant lines.

SYSTEM INSPECTION

Refrigerant leaks show up as oil areas on the various components because the compressor oil is transported around the entire system along with the refrigerant. Look for oily spots on all the hoses and lines, and especially on the hose and tubing connections. If there are oily deposits, the system may have a leak, and you should have it checked by a qualified repairman.

➡**A small area of oil on the front of the compressor is normal and no cause for alarm.**

A lot of A/C problems can be avoided by simply running the air conditioner a least once a week, regardless of the season. Simply let the system run at least 5 minutes a week (even in the winter) and you'll keep the internal parts lubricated as well as preventing the hoses from hardening.

REFRIGERANT LEVEL CHECKS

You can safely make a few simple checks to determine if your air conditioning system needs service. The tests work best if the temperature is warm (about 70 F).

1. Place the automatic transmission in Park or the manual transmission in Neutral. Set the parking brake.

2. Run the engine at a fast idle (about 1,500 rpm) either with the help of a friend, or by temporarily readjusting the idle speed screw.

3. Set the controls for maximum cold with the blower on high.

4. Locate the sight glass in the head of the receiver/drier. Usually it is on the left alongside the top of the radiator.

5. If you see bubbles, the system must be recharged. Very likely there is a leak at some point.

6. If there are no bubbles, there is either no refrigerant at all or the system is fully charged. Feel the two hoses going to the belt-driven compressor. If they are both at the same temperature, the system is empty and must be recharged.

7. If one hose (high-pressure) is warm and the other (low-pressure) is cold, the system may be alright. However, you are probably making these tests because you think there is something wrong, so proceed to the next Step.

8. Have an assistant in the car turn the fan control on and off to operate the compressor clutch. Watch the sight glass.

9. If bubbles appear when the clutch is disengaged and disappear when it is engaged, the system is properly charged.

10. If the refrigerant takes more than 45 seconds to bubble when the clutch is disengaged, the system is overcharged. This usually causes poor cooling at low speeds.

GAUGE SETS

▶ **See Figures 31, 32, 33, 34 and 35**

Servicing, such as discharging and charging the system, and all other work that requires opening the sealed system requires the use of a set of two gauges. The required set consists of a high (head) pressure gauge, for the pressure side of the system; and a low (suction) pressure gauge for the low pressure side of the system.

The low side gauge records both pressure and vacuum. Vacuum readings are calibrated from 0 to 30 inches and the pressure graduations read from 0 to no less the 150 psi.

The high side gauge measures pressure from 0 to at least 300 psi.

Both gauges are threaded into a manifold that contains two hand shut-off valves. Proper manipulation of the valves, and the use of the attached hoses allow the user to perform the following services. Test high and low side pressures. Remove air, moisture, and contaminated refrigerant. Purge the system (of refrigerant). Charge the system (with refrigerant).

The manifold gauges are designed so they have no direct effect on gauge readings, but serve only to provide for, or cut off, flow of refrigerant through the manifold. During all testing and hook-up operations, the valves are kept in the closed position to avoid disturbing the refrigeration system. The valves are opened only to purge the system or to charge it.

When purging the system, the center hose is connected to a recovery tank at the lower end, and both valves are cracked open slightly. This allows refrigerant pressure to force the entire contents of the system out through the center hose. During charging, the valve on the high side is closed, and the valve on the low side is cracked open. Under these conditions, the low pressure in the evaporator will draw refrigerant from the relatively warm refrigerant storage container into the system.

DISCHARGING THE SYSTEM

1. Operate the A/C system for at least 10 minutes.

2. Shut off the engine and attach the gauge set.

3. Connect a recovery container to the outlet of the center manifold hose. The discharging refrigerant and system lubricating oil will be discharged through the hose into the container.

4. Open the low side manifold control slightly. Open the high side manifold control slightly.

➡**Too rapid a discharge process is identified by the appearance of oily foam, close both valves slightly until the foaming stops.**

5. Close both valves on the gauge set when the pressures read 0, all of the refrigerant should be discharged from the system.

Check item \ Amount of refrigerant	Almost no refrigerant	Insufficient	Suitable	Too much refrigerant
Temperature of high pressure and low pressure lines	Almost no difference between high pressure and low pressure side temperature	High pressure side is warm and low pressure side is fairly cold	High pressure side is hot and low pressure side is cold	High pressure side is abnormally hot
State in sight glass	Bubbles flow continuously. Bubbles will disappear and something like mist will flow when refrigerant is nearly gone	The bubbles are seen at intervals of 1-2 seconds	Almost transparent. Bubbles may appear when engine speed is raised and lowered. **No clear difference exists between these two conditions**	No bubbles can be seen
Pressure of system	High pressure side is abnormally low	Both pressure on high and low pressure sides are slightly low	Both pressure on high and low pressure sides are normal	Both pressure on high and low pressure sides are abnormally high
Repair	Stop compressor and conduct an overall check	Check for gas leakage, repair as required, replenish and charge system		Discharge refrigerant from service valve of low pressure side

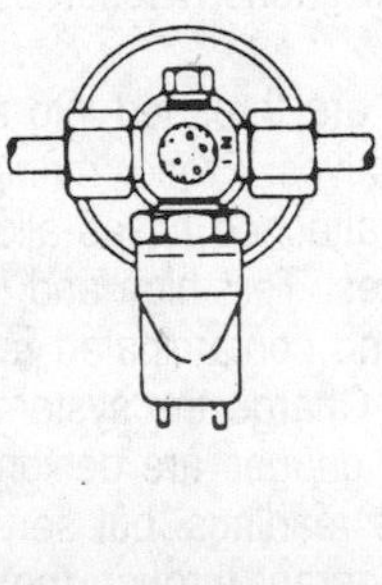

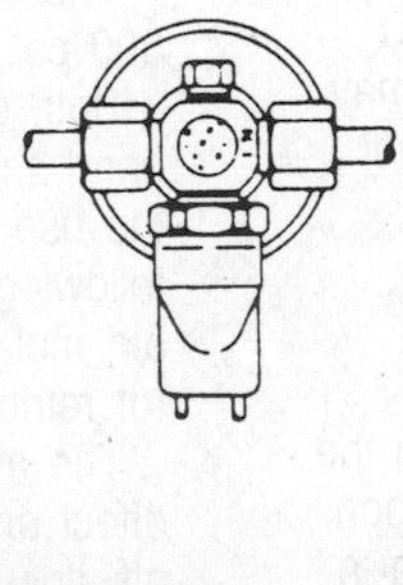

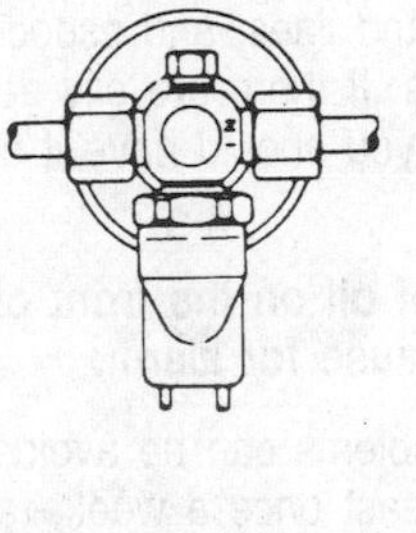

Fig. 31 Refrigerant level diagnosis chart

CHARGING THE SYSTEM

One pound cans of R12 refrigerant are available from auto parts and various retail stores. Always follow the manufacturer's instructions on the can when charging the systems.

❄❄CAUTION

Never use one pound cans to charge into the high pressure side of the system (compressor discharge side) or into a system that is at high pressure High system pressures could be transferred onto the charging can causing it to explode.

1. Attach the gauge set to the proper service port valves.

2. Install a R12 can dispensing valve to the center manifold hose (be sure the can puncturing needle is fully raised). Carefully attach a one pound can of refrigerant to the dispensing valve. The can of R12 MUST remain in the upright position so that gas and NOT liquid refrigerant enters the low side of the system.

3. Screw in the dispensing valve to puncture the can and then open the valve fully to permit the R12 to enter the center hose.

4. Loosen the center hose to gauge manifold slightly to purge the hose. Tighten the connector. Open the low side control valve slightly and loosen the low side connector at the service port slightly to purge the hose. Tighten the connector and close the manifold control valve.

5. Roll down the car windows, start the engine and place the A/C controls to the full maximum position(s).

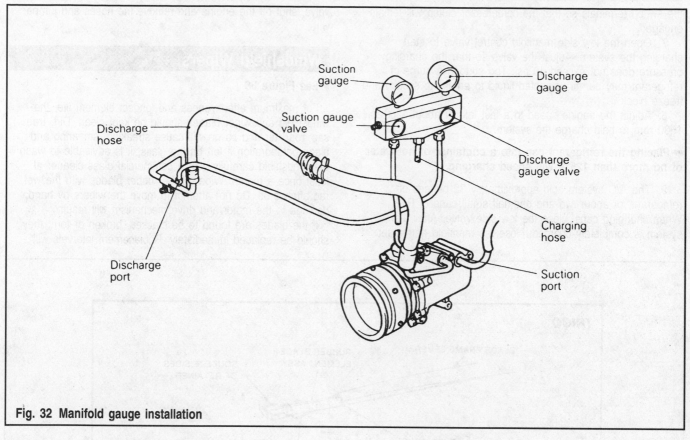

Fig. 32 Manifold gauge installation

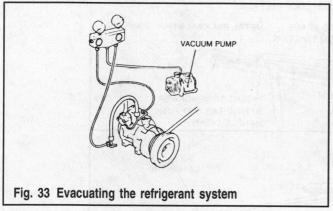

Fig. 33 Evacuating the refrigerant system

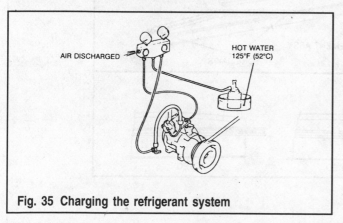

Fig. 35 Charging the refrigerant system

6. On models that are equipped with a low pressure cut-off switch mounted on the receiver-dryer, connect a jumper wire to

Fig. 34 Discharging the refrigerant system

the switch terminals so that the compressor clutch will remain engaged.

7. Open the low side manifold control valve to start charging the system. Adjust the valve so that the charging pressure does not exceed 40 psi. Too sudden a surge of refrigerant may permit unwanted liquid to enter the system and freeze block it.

8. Adjust the engine speed to a fast idle of about 1200 to 1500 rpm to help charge the system.

➡ **Placing the refrigerant can into a container of hot water of no more than 125°F will speed charging.**

9. The A/C system hold approximately 32 ounces of refrigerant, or about two and one-half small cans of R12. When changing cans, close the low side valve. After the system is completely charged, close the manifold gauge set

valve, shut off the engine and remove the hoses and jumper wire.

Windshield Wipers

▶ **See Figure 36**

For maximum effectiveness and longest element life, the windshield and wiper blades should be kept clean. Dirt, tree sap, road tar and so on will cause streaking, smearing and blade deterioration if left on the glass. It is advisable to wash the windshield carefully with a commercial glass cleaner at least once a month. Wipe off the rubber blades with the wet rag afterwards. Do not attempt to move the wipers by hand; damage to the motor and drive mechanism will result.

If the blades are found to be cracked, broken or torn, they should be replaced immediately. Replacement intervals will

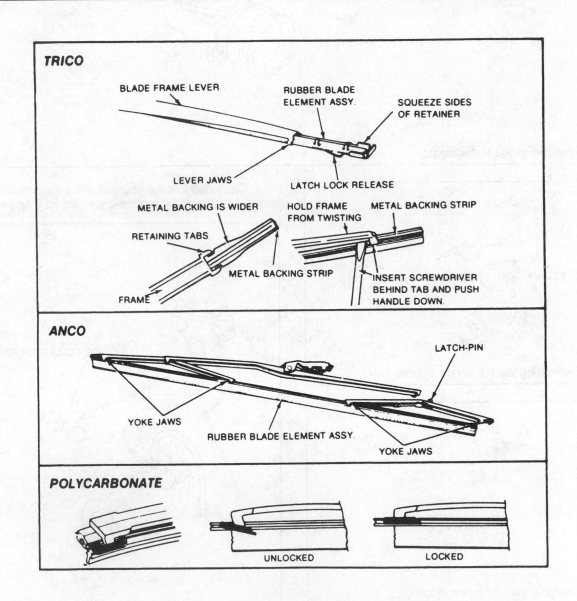

Fig. 36 The three common types of wiper blade refills

vary with usage, although ozone deterioration usually limits blade life to about one year. If the wiper pattern is smeared or streaked, or if the blade chatters across the glass, the elements should be replaced. It is easiest and most sensible to replace the elements in pairs.

There are basically three different types of refills, which differ in their method of replacement. One type has two release buttons, approximately one-third of the way up from the ends of the blade frame. Pushing the buttons down releases a lock and allows the rubber filler to be removed from the frame. The new filler slides back into the frame and locks in place.

The second type of refill has two metal tabs which are unlocked by squeezing them together. The rubber filler can then be withdrawn from the frame jaws. A new refill is installed by inserting the refill into the front frame jaws and sliding it rearward to engage the remaining frame jaws. There are usually four jaws; be certain when installing, that the refill is engaged in all of them. At the end of its travel, the tabs will lock into place on the front jaws of the wiper blade frame.

The third type is a refill made from polycarbonate. The refill has a simple locking device at one end which flexes downward out of the groove into which the jaws of the holder fit, allowing easy release. By sliding the new refill through all the jaws and pushing through the slight resistance when it reaches the end of its travel, the refill will lock into position. Regardless of the type of refill used, make sure that all of the frame jaws are engaged as the refill is pushed into place and locked. The metal blade holder and frame will scratch the glass if allowed to touch it.

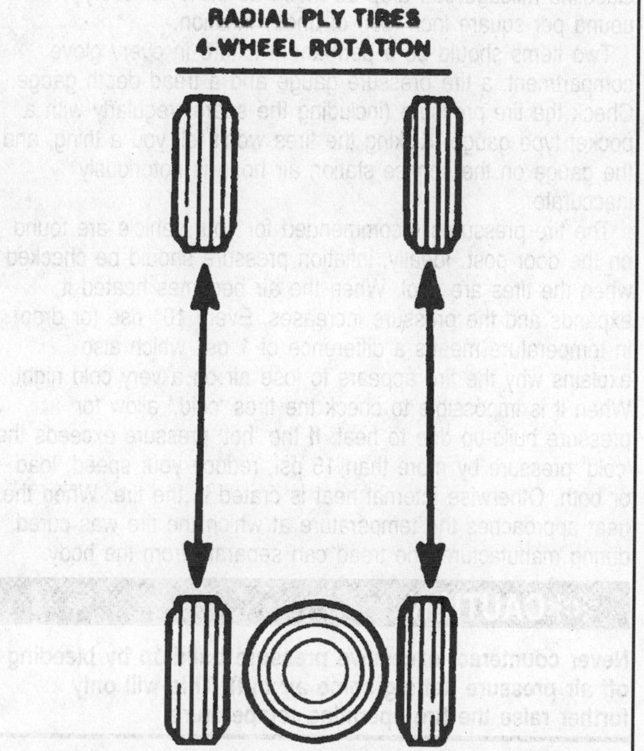

Tires and Wheels

TIRE ROTATION

Tire wear can be equalized by switching the position of the tires about every 6000 miles. Including a conventional spare in the rotation pattern can give up to 20% more tire life.

✳✳CAUTION

Do not include the new 'Spacesaver' or mini-spare tire in the rotation pattern.

There are certain exceptions to tire rotation, however. Studded snow tires should not be rotated, and radials should be kept on the same side of the vehicle (maintain the same direction of rotation). The belts on radial tires get set in a pattern. If the direction of rotation is reversed, it can cause rough ride and vibration.

➡ **When radials or studded snows are taken off the vehicle, mark them, so you can maintain the same direction of rotation.**

TIRE USAGE

▸ **See Figures 37, 38, 39, 40 and 41**

The tires on your car or truck were selected to provide the best all around performance for normal operation when inflated

RADIAL PLY TIRES
4-WHEEL ROTATION

Fig. 37 Tire rotation diagram

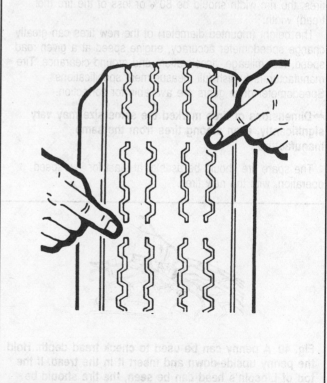

Fig. 38 Tread wear indicators will appear when the tire becomes worn to the point of replacement

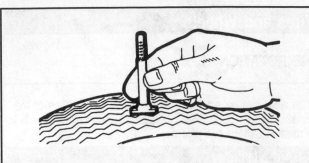

Fig. 39 Tread depth can be checked with an inexpensive tread depth gauge

as specified. On trucks, oversize tires (Load Range D) will not increase the maximum carrying capacity of the vehicle, although they will provide an extra margin of tread life. Be sure to check overall height before using larger size tires which may cause interference with suspension components or wheel wells. When replacing conventional tire sizes with other tire size designations, be sure to check the manufacturer's recommendations. Interchangeability is not always possible because of differences in load ratings, tire dimensions, wheel well clearances, and rim size. Also due to differences in handling characteristics, 70 Series and 60 Series tires should be used only in pairs on the same axle. Radial tires should be used only in sets of four.

The wheels must be the correct width for the tire. Tire dealers have charts of tire and rim compatibility. A mismatch can cause sloppy handling and rapid tread wear. The old rule of thumb is that the tread width should match the rim width (inside bead to inside bead) within 1 in. (25.4mm). For radial tires, the rim width should be 80% or less of the tire (not tread) width.

The height (mounted diameter) of the new tires can greatly change speedometer accuracy, engine speed at a given road speed, fuel mileage, acceleration, and ground clearance. Tire manufacturers furnish full measurement specifications. Speedometer drive gears are available for correction.

➡**Dimensions of tires marked the same size may vary significantly, even among tires from the same manufacturer.**

The spare tire should be usable, at least for low speed operation, with the new tires.

Fig. 40 A penny can be used to check tread depth. Hold the penny upside-down and insert it in the tread. If the top of Lincoln's head can be seen, the tire should be replaced

TIRE DESIGN

For maximum satisfaction, tires should be used in sets of five. Mixing or different types (radial, bias/belted, fiberglass belted) should be avoided. Conventional bias tires are constructed so that the cords run bead-to-bead at an angle. Alternate plies run at an opposite angle. This type of construction gives rigidity to both tread and sidewall. Bias/belted tires are similar in construction to conventional bias ply tires. Belts run at an angle and also at a 90° angle to the bead, as in the radial tire. Tread life is improved considerably over the conventional bias tire. The radial tire differs in construction, but instead of the carcass plies running at an angle of 90° to each other, they run at an angle of 90° to the bead. This gives the tread a great deal of rigidity and the sidewall a great deal of flexibility and accounts for the characteristic bulge associated with radial tires.

All Mitsubishi vehicles are capable of using radial tires and they are the recommended type for all years. If they are used, tire sizes and wheel diameters should be selected to maintain ground clearance and tire load capacity equivalent to the minimum specified tire. Radial tires should always be used in sets of five, but in an emergency radial tires can be used with caution on the rear axle only. If this is done, both tires on the rear should be of radial design.

➡**Radial tires should never be used on only the front axle.**

INFLATION PRESSURE

Tire inflation is the most ignored item of auto maintenance. Gasoline mileage can drop as much as 0.8% for every 1 pound per square inch (psi) of under inflation.

Two items should be a permanent fixture in every glove compartment; a tire pressure gauge and a tread depth gauge. Check the tire pressure (including the spare) regularly with a pocket type gauge. Kicking the tires won't tell you a thing, and the gauge on the service station air hose is notoriously inaccurate.

The tire pressures recommended for your vehicle are found on the door post. Ideally, inflation pressure should be checked when the tires are cool. When the air becomes heated it expands and the pressure increases. Every 10° rise (or drop) in temperature means a difference of 1 psi, which also explains why the tire appears to lose air on a very cold night. When it is impossible to check the tires 'cold,' allow for pressure build-up due to heat. If the 'hot' pressure exceeds the 'cold' pressure by more than 15 psi, reduce your speed, load or both. Otherwise internal heat is crated in the tire. When the heat approaches the temperature at which the tire was cured, during manufacture, the tread can separate from the body.

❋❋CAUTION

Never counteract excessive pressure build-up by bleeding off air pressure (letting some air out). This will only further raise the tire operating temperature.

Tire Size Comparison Chart

"Letter" sizes			Inch Sizes	Metric-Inch Sizes		
"60 Series"	"70 Series"	"78 Series"	1965–77	"60 Series"	"70 Series"	"80 Series"
			5.50-12, 5.60-12	165/60-12	165/70-12	155-12
		Y78-12	6.00-12			
		W78-13	5.20-13	165/60-13	145/70-13	135-13
		Y78-13	5.60-13	175/60-13	155/70-13	145-13
			6.15-13	185/60-13	165/70-13	155-13, P155/80-13
A60-13	A70-13	A78-13	6.40-13	195/60-13	175/70-13	165-13
B60-13	B70-13	B78-13	6.70-13	205/60-13	185/70-13	175-13
			6.90-13			
C60-13	C70-13	C78-13	7.00-13	215/60-13	195/70-13	185-13
D60-13	D70-13	D78-13	7.25-13			
E60-13	E70-13	E78-13	7.75-13			195-13
			5.20-14	165/60-14	145/70-14	135-14
			5.60-14	175/60-14	155/70-14	145-14
			5.90-14			
A60-14	A70-14	A78-14	6.15-14	185/60-14	165/70-14	155-14
	B70-14	B78-14	6.45-14	195/60-14	175/70-14	165-14
	C70-14	C78-14	6.95-14	205/60-14	185/70-14	175-14
D60-14	D70-14	D78-14				
E60-14	E70-14	E78-14	7.35-14	215/60-14	195/70-14	185-14
F60-14	F70-14	F78-14, F83-14	7.75-14	225/60-14	200/70-14	195-14
G60-14	G70-14	G77-14, G78-14	8.25-14	235/60-14	205/70-14	205-14
H60-14	H70-14	H78-14	8.55-14	245/60-14	215/70-14	215-14
J60-14	J70-14	J78-14	8.85-14	255/60-14	225/70-14	225-14
L60-14	L70-14		9.15-14	265/60-14	235/70-14	
	A70-15	A78-15	5.60-15	185/60-15	165/70-15	155-15
B60-15	B70-15	B78-15	6.35-15	195/60-15	175/70-15	165-15
C60-15	C70-15	C78-15	6.85-15	205/60-15	185/70-15	175-15
	D70-15	D78-15				
E60-15	E70-15	E78-15	7.35-15	215/60-15	195/70-15	185-15
F60-15	F70-15	F78-15	7.75-15	225/60-15	205/70-15	195-15
G60-15	G70-15	G78-15	8.15-15/8.25-15	235/60-15	215/70-15	205-15
H60-15	H70-15	H78-15	8.45-15/8.55-15	245/60-15	225/70-15	215-15
J60-15	J70-15	J78-15	8.85-15/8.90-15	255/60-15	235/70-15	225-15
	K70-15		9.00-15	265/60-15	245/70-15	230-15
L60-15	L70-15	L78-15, L84-15	9.15-15			235-15
	M70-15	M78-15				255-15
		N78-15				

NOTE: Every size tire is not listed and many size comaprisons are approximate, based on load ratings. Wider tires than those supplied new with the vehicle should always be checked for clearance

Before starting a long trip with lots of luggage, you can add about 2-4 psi to the tires to make them run cooler, but never exceed the maximum inflation pressure on the side of the tire.

TREAD DEPTH

All tires made since 1968, have 8 built-in tread wear indicator bars that show up as ½ in. wide smooth bands across the tire when 3/16 in. of tread remains. The appearance of tread wear indicators means that the tires should be replaced. In fact, many states have laws prohibiting the use of tires with less than 3/16 in. tread.

You can check your own tread depth with an inexpensive gauge or by using a Lincoln head penny. Slip the Lincoln penny into several tread grooves. If you can see the top of Lincoln's head in 2 adjacent grooves, the tires have less than 3/16 in. tread left and should be replaced. You can measure snow tires in the same manner by using the 'tails' side of the Lincoln penny. If you can see the top of the Lincoln memorial, it's time to replace the snow tires.

TIRE STORAGE

Store the tires at proper inflation pressure if they are mounted on wheels. All tires should be kept in a cool, dry place. If they are stored in the garage or basement, do not let them stand on a concrete floor; set them on strips of wood.

CARE OF ALUMINUM WHEELS

If your vehicle is equipped with aluminum wheels special attention should be paid to their care and maintenance. Aluminum is very susceptible to the action of alkalies often found in various detergents, road and sea salts. If the wheels have been exposed to these type of compounds, wash the wheels with water as soon as possible. After washing the vehicle, coat the wheels with body wax to prevent corrosion.

FLUIDS AND LUBRICANTS

Fluid Disposal

Used fluids, such as engine oil, antifreeze, transmission oils and brake fluid are hazardous as waste material and must be disposed of properly.

Before draining any fluids, consult with your local municipal government. In may areas, waste oils are being accepted as part of the recycling program. A number of service stations, repair facilities and auto parts stores are accepting these waste fluids.

Before draining and packaging your vehicle's waste fluids, be sure of the waste disposal facility's policy on mixing such fluids.

Fuel and Oil Recommendations

Unleaded fuel only must be used in all gasoline models. Leaded fuel will damage the catalytic converter almost immediately. This will increase emissions critically, and may cause the catalyst material to break up and clog the exhaust system.

Use a fuel with an octane rating of 87 (R+M/2). This is an average of the two methods of rating octane — Research and Motor. If a fuel is rated by the Research method only, the required rating is 91.

It always pays to buy a reputable brand of fuel. It is best to purchase fuel from a busy station where a large volume is pumped every day, as this helps protect you from dirt and water in the fuel. If you encounter engine ping or run-on, you might want to try a different brand or a slightly higher octane rated grade of fuel. If the engine exhibits a chronic knock problem which cannot be readily cured by changing the fuel you're using, it is wise to check the ignition timing and reset it, if necessary. If the timing is correct and the engine still exhibits severe knock, there may be internal mechanical problems. Persistent knock is severely damaging to the engine and should be corrected.

If the engine runs on, and changing to a different fuel does not cure the problem, routine checks of ignition timing and idle speed should be made. Persistent run-on can be damaging to such engine parts as the timing chain or belt.

Mitsubishi recommends against the 'indiscriminate use of fuel system cleaning agents.' Occasional use of solvents added to the fuel tank to remove gum and varnish from the fuel system is permissible; however, continuous use or extremely frequent use can damage gasket and diaphragm parts used in the system.

Gasohol, a mixture of 10% ethanol (or grain alcohol) and 90% unleaded gasoline, may be used in your Mitsubishi. You should switch back to unleaded gasoline or try another brand of gasohol if you experience driveability problems. Some brands may contain special fuel additives designed to overcome certain types of problems that may occur with gasohol use.

DO NOT use gasoline containing methanol (wood alcohol), as they may damage the fuel system.

If steam is used to the clean the vehicle, do not direct the steam at the wheels.

When changing an aluminum rimmed tire, observe the following precautions:
- Clean the surface of the hub first
- After the tire is in place, finger tighten the lug nuts and then torque them to the proper value
- DO NOT use an impact wrench to tighten the wheel nuts
- DO NOT use oil on either the nut or stud threads

Engine Oil Recommendations

Use only quality oils designated as shown in the chart above. Never use straight mineral or non-detergent oils — that is, oils not equipped with special cleaning agents. You must not only choose the grade of oil, but the viscosity number. Viscosity refers to the thickness of the oil. It's actually measured by how rapidly it flows though a hole of calibrated size. Thicker oil flows more slowly and has higher viscosity numbers — SAE 40 or 50. Thinner oil flows more easily and has lower numbers — SAE 10 or 20.

Mitsubishi recommends the use of what are called 'multigrade' oils. These are specially formulated to change their viscosity less with a change in temperature than straight grade oils. The oils are designated by the use of two numbers — the first referring to the thickness of the oil, relative to straight mineral oils, at a low temperature such as 0°F (-18°C); the second to the thickness relative to straight mineral oils at high temperatures typical of highway driving — in the neighborhood of 200°F (93°C). These numbers are preceded by the designation 'SAE' for the society which sets the viscosity standards. For example, use of an SAE 10W-40 oil would give nearly ideal engine operation under almost all operating conditions. The oil would be as thin as a straight 10 weight oil at cold cranking temperatures, and as thick as a straight 40 weight oil at hot running conditions.

Note that turbocharged engines and diesel engines require use of different oils. This is because the oil gets much hotter, partly due to running through the turbocharger bearing, and partly due to the higher frictional and thermal loads of a turbocharged engine. Be careful to adhere to all recommendations strictly for the longest possible engine life and best service. Recommendations are especially critical for turbocharged engines. Oil recommendations are as follows:

Normally Aspirated Engines

- Temperatures ranging from 32°F (0°C) to 120°F (49°C): SAE 20W-20, 20W-40, 20W-50
- Temperatures ranging from -10°F (-23°C) to 120°F (49°C): SAE 10W-30, 10W-40, 10W-50
- Temperatures ranging from -20°F (-29°C) up to 60°F (16°C): SAE 5W-20, 5W-30, 5W-40

➡ **5W-20 is not recommended for sustained high speed operation regardless of the weather.**

SYNTHETIC OIL

There are excellent synthetic and fuel-efficient oils available that, under the right circumstances, can help provide better fuel mileage and better engine protection. However, these advantages come at a price, which can be three or four times the cost per quart of conventional motor oils.

Before pouring any synthetic oils into your vehicle's engine, you should consider the condition of the engine and the type of driving you do. Also, check the manufacturer's warranty conditions regarding the use of synthetics.

Generally, it is best to avoid the use of synthetic oil in both brand new and older, high mileage engines. New engines require a proper break-in, and the synthetics are so slippery that they can prevent this. Most manufacturers recommend that you wait at least 5,000 miles before switching to a synthetic oil. Conversely, older engines are looser and tend to use more oil. Synthetics will slip past worn parts more readily than regular oil, and will be used up faster. If your truck already leaks and/or uses oil (due to worn parts and bad seals or gaskets), it will leak and use more with a slippery synthetic inside.

Consider your type of driving. If most of your accumulated mileage is on the highway at higher, steadier speeds, a synthetic oil will reduce friction and probably help deliver fuel mileage. Under such ideal highway conditions, the oil change interval can be extended, as long as the oil filter will operate effectively for the extended life of the oil. If the filter can't do its job for this extended period, dirt and sludge will build up in your engine's crankcase, sump, oil pump and lines, no matter what type of oil is used. If using synthetic oil in this manner, you should continue to change the oil filter at the recommended intervals.

Trucks used under harder, stop-and-go, short hop circumstances should always be serviced more frequently, and for these trucks, synthetic oil may not be a wise investment. Because of the necessary shorter change interval needed for this type of driving, you cannot take advantage of the long recommended change interval of most synthetic oils.

Finally, most synthetic oil are not compatible with conventional oils and cannot be added to them. This means you should always carry a couple of quarts of synthetic oil with you while on a long trip, as not all service stations carry this oil.

Engine

OIL LEVEL CHECK

▶ **See Figures 42, 43, 44, 45 and 46**

Checking the engine oil level at every full tank fuel stop is probably a good habit to have. Check the engine oil as follows:
1. Park the car on level ground.
2. The engine may be either hot or cold when checking oil level. However, if it is hot, wait for a few minutes after the engine has been shut off to allow the oil to drain back into the crankcase. If the engine is cold, do not start it before checking the oil level.
3. Open the hood and locate the dipstick. Pull the dipstick from its tube, wipe it clean, and reinsert it.
4. Pull the dipstick again and, holding it horizontally, read the oil level. The oil should be between the top and add mark. If the oil is below the add mark, add oil of the proper viscosity through the capped opening of the valve cover.

➡ **The dipstick may have a reading of 3.5 max. on it. That figure is the oil pan capacity in liters.**

5. Insert the dipstick, and check the level again after adding any oil. Be careful not to overfill the crankcase. Approximately one quart of oil will raise the level from the low mark to the high mark, Excess oil will generally be consumed at an accelerated rate even if no damage to the engine seals occurs.

OIL AND FILTER CHANGE

Oil changes should be performed at intervals as described in your owners manual. However, it is a good idea to change the oil and oil filter at least twice a year, and to change the filter each time the oil is changed. If your car is being used under dusty conditions, change the oil and filter sooner. The same thing goes for cars being driven in stop and go city traffic, where acid and sludge buildup is a problem. The oil should also be changed more frequently in cars which are constantly driven at high speeds on expressways. The relatively high engine speeds associated with turnpike driving mean higher operating temperatures and a greater instance of oil foaming.

Always drain the oil after the engine has been run long enough to bring it to the normal operating temperature. Hot oil will flow easier and more contaminants will be removed with the oil than if it were drained cold. A large capacity drain pan, which can be purchased at any automotive supply store, will be more than paid back by savings from do-it-yourself oil changes. Another necessity is containers for the used oil. You will find that plastic bleach containers make excellent storage bottles.

OIL CHANGE

1. Run the engine until it reaches the normal operating temperature. Raise and safely support the front of the car.
2. Slide a drain pan under the oil pan drain plug.

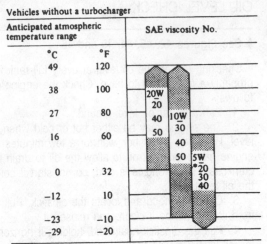
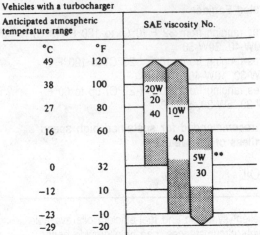

Vehicles without a turbocharger			
Anticipated atmospheric temperature range		SAE viscosity No.	
°C	°F		
49	120		
38	100	20W 20	
27	80	40	10W
16	60	50	30
		50	40
0	32		5W *20
			30
−12	10		40
−23	−10		
−29	−20		

*SAE 5W-20 Not recommended for sustained high speed vehicle operation.

Vehicles with a turbocharger			
Anticipated atmospheric temperature range		SAE viscosity No.	
°C	°F		
49	120		
38	100	20W 20	
27	80	40	10W
16	60		40
0	32		5W **
−12	10		30
−23	−10		
−29	−20		

** SAE 5W-30 oil should be used only in areas where extremely cold temperatures below −23°C (−10°F) are experienced.

Fig. 42 Oil viscosity recommendation chart

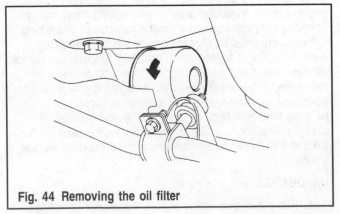

Fig. 43 Engine oil drain plug

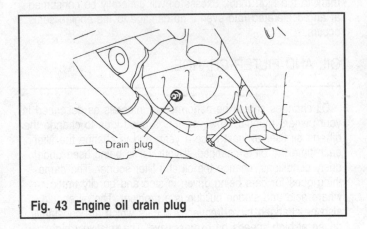

Fig. 44 Removing the oil filter

Fig. 45 Checking engine oil level on the dipstick

Fig. 46 Adding engine oil

3. Loosen the drain plug with a socket or box wrench, and then remove it by hand. Push in on the plug as you turn it out, so that no oil escapes until the plug is completely removed.

4. Allow the oil to drain into the pan.

5. Clean and install the drain plug , making sure that the gasket is still on the plug.

6. Refill the engine with oil. Start the engine and check for leaks.

OIL FILTER CHANGE

The car manufacturer recommends changing the oil filter at every other oil change, but it is more beneficial to replace the filter every time the oil is changed.

❋❋CAUTION

Prolonged and repeated skin contact with used engine oil, with no effort to remove the oil, may be harmful. Follow these simple precautions when handling used motor oil. Avoid prolonged skin contact with used motor oil. Remove oil from skin by washing thoroughly with soap and water or waterless hand cleaner. Do not use gasoline, thinners or solvents. Avoid prolonged skin contact with oil-soaked clothing.

1. Drain the oil as already described.

2. Remove the lower splash shield, if necessary for clearance.

3. Slide a drain pan under the oil filter. Slowly turn the filter off with an oil filter wrench.

4. Clean the oil filter adapter on the engine with a clean rag.

5. Oil the rubber seal on the replacement filter and install it. Tighten it until the seal is flush and then give it an additional ½ to ¾ turn.

➡On Colt with 1597cc engines, the oil filter mounting flange distorts as the temperature changes. As a result, leakage past the oil filter gasket may occur between the time the engine is started from cold and the time it reaches operating temperature. In most cases, the leakage stops when the engine is hot. The factory-supplied filter and replacement MoPar filters have a thick, wide gasket which compensates for this occurrence. Most aftermarket filters do not have such a gasket. The best idea on these cars is to coat the oil filter gasket and mounting flange mating surfaces with gasket sealer, such as Permatex® No.2, or its equivalent, not engine oil, prior to installation. Before applying the sealer, make certain that the mating surfaces are clean and free of oil. Screw the filter on in the normal manner.

6. Install the splash pan. Fill the engine with the proper amount of oil. Start the engine and check for leaks.

Manual Transaxle

FLUID RECOMMENDATIONS

▶ **See Figure 47**

A hypoid gear oil with an API classification of GL-4 or higher is required.

LEVEL CHECK

1. With the car parked on a level surface, or raised and supported safely and level, remove the filler plug from the right front of the case.

2. If lubricant begins to trickle out the hole, there is enough. Otherwise, carefully insert a finger (watch out for sharp threads) and check to see if the oil is up to the edge of the hole.

3. If not, add lubricant through the hole to raise the level to the edge of the filler hole. Most gear lubricants come in a plastic squeeze bottle with a nozzle, making additions easy. You can also use a squeeze bulb. Add gear oil GL4, Hypoid gear oil.

4. Replace the plug and check for leaks.

DRAIN AND REFILL

1. Jack up the front the car and support it safely on stands.

2. Slide a drain pan under the transaxle.

3. Remove the filler plug and then the drain plug.

4. When the oil has been completely drained, install the drain plug.

5. Using the suction gun, refill the transmission/transaxle up to the level of the filler plug.

6. Install and tighten the filler plug.

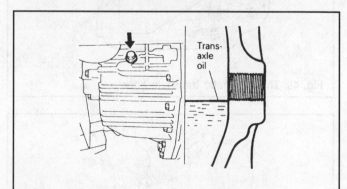

Fig. 47 Checking the oil level on manual transaxles

Automatic Transaxle

FLUID RECOMMENDATIONS

▶ **See Figures 48, 49 and 50**

Automatic transaxle fluid type Dexron®II is required.

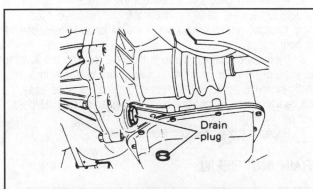

Fig. 48 Draining the automatic transaxle fluid

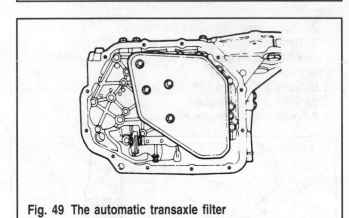

Fig. 49 The automatic transaxle filter

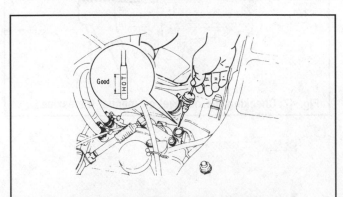

Fig. 50 Checking automatic transaxle fluid level

LEVEL CHECK

Check the level of the automatic transmission fluid every 2,000 miles.

✳✳CAUTION

The electric cooling fan may switch an any time the engine is running. Keep hands away.

The dipstick has a high and low mark which are accurate for level indications only when the transmission is hot (normal operating temperature). The transmission is considered hot after 15 miles of highway driving.

1. Park the car on a level surface with the engine idling. Apply the parking brake.
2. Shift the transmission through all ranges and return the lever to the PARK position.
3. Remove the dipstick wipe it clean, then reinsert it firmly. Be certain that it has been pushed fully home. Remove the dipstick and check the fluid level while holding the dipstick horizontally. The level should be at or near the high mark.
4. If the fluid level is below the low mark, add Dexron ®II type automatic transmission fluid through the dipstick tube. This is more easily accomplished with the aid of a funnel and hose. Check the level often between additions, being careful not to overfill the transmission. Overfilling will cause slippage, seal damage, and overheating. Approximately one pint of fluid will raise the level from low to high.

➡**The fluid on the dipstick should be a bright red color. It it is discolored (brown or black), or smells burnt, serious transmission troubles, probably due to overheating, should be suspected. The transmission should be inspected to locate the cause of the burnt fluid.**

DRAIN AND REFILL

1. Jack up the front of the car and support it on jackstands. Remove the lower cover.
2. Slide a drain pan under the differential and remove the drain plug. When the differential is completely drained, move the pan under the transmission. Remove the plug (on models equipped), or the transaxle oil pan (see the proceeding RWD section).
3. Install the drain plug(s) Clean all gasket mounting surfaces. Install the oil pan and new gasket. Tighten the mounting bolts to 8 ft. lbs. Fill the transmission with the required amount of Dexron®II fluid. Start the engine and allow to idle for at least two minutes. With the parking brake applied, move the selector to each position ending in PARK.
4. Add sufficient fluid to bring the level to the lower dipstick mark. Check the fluid level after the transmission is up to normal operating temperature.

PAN AND FILTER SERVICE

Drain the transaxle. With the oil pan removed, inspect the filter. If mileage servicing, or a clogged condition exists, remove the filter. Install a new filter and tighten the mounting bolts to 35 in. lbs. Install the oil pan and fill the transmission/transaxle with the proper amount of fluid.

Transfer Case

FLUID RECOMMENDATIONS

▶ **See Figures 51 and 52**

A hypoid gear oil with an API classification of GL-4 or higher is required.

LEVEL CHECK

A dipstick is provided for transfer case fluid level checks. Be sure the vehicle is parked on level ground. Remove the dipstick and wipe it clean. Insert the dipstick and remove it from the tube. If the level is between the upper and lower marks it is correct. Add fluid through the dipstick tube as required.

DRAIN AND REFILL

1. Place a suitable drain pan under the transfer case.
2. Remove the drain plug from the bottom of the transfer case.

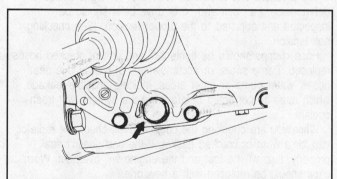

Fig. 51 Manual transaxle drain plug on vehicles with 4WD

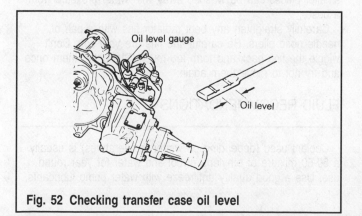

Fig. 52 Checking transfer case oil level

3. Drain the gear oil. Wipe the drain plug threads clean. Screw the plug into position and tighten it.
4. Fill the transfer case to the proper level on the dipstick (upper Mark) through the dipstick tube.

Rear Axle

FLUID RECOMMENDATIONS

▶ **See Figure 53**

A hypoid gear oil with an API classification of GL-5 or higher is required.

If the average ambient temperature is above -10°F (23°C), use SAE 85W-90.

If the average ambient temperature is -10°F to -30°F (-23°C to -34°C), use SAE 80W-90.

If the average ambient temperature is below -30°F (-34°C), use SAE 75W.

LEVEL CHECK

Rear axle lubricant level is checked at the filler plug in the rear of the differential housing. Use the proper size open end wrench (usually $^{15}/_{16}$ in.) to remove the filler plug. Insert your finger into the hole; the gear oil level should be right at the plug opening. Use an SAE 80 or 90 gear oil to bring up the differential oil level.

DRAIN AND REFILL

Place a drain pan under the rear axle housing and remove the lower drain plug. When the fluid has stopped draining, clean the threads on the drain plug and screw it into the housing. Tighten the drain plug and fill the housing to the proper level through the filler plug hole.

Cooling System

▶ **See Figures 54, 55, 56 and 57**

At least once every 2 years, the engine cooling system should be inspected, flushed, and refilled with fresh coolant. If the coolant is left in the system too long, it loses its ability to

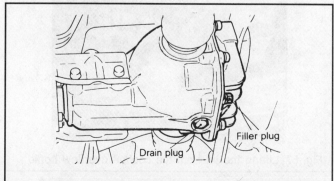

Fig. 53 Rear axle drain and fill plugs on 4WD vehicles

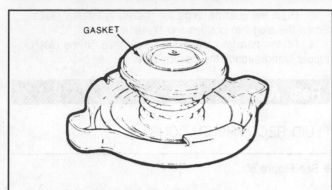

Fig. 54 Check the radiator cap gasket for cracks or leaks

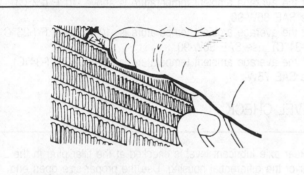

Fig. 55 Keep the radiator fins clear of debris for maximum cooling

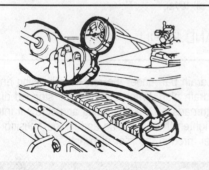

Fig. 56 The cooling system should be pressure tested once a year

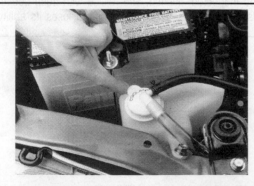

Fig. 57 Lifting the lid from the coolant overflow bottle

Fig. 58 Brake master cylinder reservoir

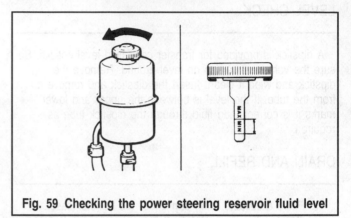

Fig. 59 Checking the power steering reservoir fluid level

prevent rust and corrosion. If the coolant has too much water, it won't protect against freezing.

The pressure cap should be looked at for signs of age or deterioration. Fan belt and other drive belts should be inspected and adjusted to the proper tension. (See checking belt tension.

Hose clamps should be tightened, and soft or cracked hoses replaced. Damp spots, or accumulations of rust or dye near hoses, water pump or other areas, indicate possible leakage, which must be corrected before filling the system with fresh coolant.

While you are checking the coolant level, check the radiator cap for a worn or cracked gasket. If the cap doesn't seal properly, fluid will be lost and the engine will overheat. Worn caps should be replaced with a new one.

Periodically clean any debris --leaves, paper, insects, etc.-- from the radiator fins. Pick the large pieces off by hand. The smaller pieces can be washed away with water pressure from a hose.

Carefully straighten any bent radiator fins with a pair of needle nose pliers. Be careful--the fins are very soft. Don't wiggle the fins back and forth too much. Straighten them once and try not to move them again.

FLUID RECOMMENDATIONS

Coolant used (depending on winter temperatures) is usually a 50-50 mixture of ethylene glycol and water for year round use. Use a good quality antifreeze with water pump lubricants, rust inhibitors and other corrosion inhibitors along with acid neutralizers.

LEVEL CHECKS

On models without an expansion tank, if the engine is hot, allow it to cool for several minutes to reduce the pressure in the system. Using a rag, turn the radiator cap ¼ turn to the stop and allow all pressure to escape. Then, remove the cap. On models equipped with an expansion tank, check the level visually in the tank. It should be above the low mark. Never fill the tank over the upper mark.

Fill the radiator until the level is within 25mm of the radiator cap. It is best to add a 50/50 mix of antifreeze and water to avoid diluting the coolant in the system. Use permanent type antifreeze only.

DRAINING, FLUSHING AND REFILLING THE COOLING SYSTEM

It's best to drain the cooling system when the engine is warm but has cooled to well below operating temperature to assist in complete removal of old coolant and any suspended material. Follow the procedure below to help ensure you will not be burned by hot coolant.

1. The first step is to loosen the drain cock or remove the drain plug located in the bottom radiator tank to begin the draining process and relieve pressure. DON'T START OUT BY REMOVING THE CAP! Just make sure you are well away from the direction coolant flow will take when you remove the plug, and then remove it.

2. Once coolant flow out of the bottom of the radiator has slowed, remove the radiator cap to vent the system. Then, remove the drain plug from the side of the engine block.

3. When all the coolant has drained, replace the plugs. If the hoses need attention, this would be an ideal time to relace them. Now, slowly fill the system with water until the water level reaches the top of the radiator tank. Start the engine and run it at idle. When the thermostat opens and water begins to flow through the top of the radiator, add more water as necessary until the engine is full. Now, shut the engine off and again carefully remove both drain plugs. Repeat the process of filling the system with water and draining it until drained water is clear. If the system cannot be cleaned out effectively this way, you may want to buy a reverse flushing kit at your local parts store and use it. An alternative is the use of a chemical cleaner; if you need to use one of these, just make sure it is

compatible with the use of aluminum engine parts and that you follow the directions on the can carefully to ensure that you do not damage your engine.

4. Now, coat both drain plugs with sealer and install them snugly. Look up the coolant capacity in the 'Capacities Chart'. Then, see the chart on the side of the antifreeze container in order to calculate just how much antifreeze is required to protect the system down to the lowest expected temperature in your area. Pour the antifreeze in first. Then, follow up with clean water until the level reaches the top of the radiator tank. Finally, follow the steps at the end of the procedure above for filling the system with coolant after checking the level.

Brake Master Cylinder

▶ **See Figure 58**

Check the levels of brake fluid in the brake master cylinder reservoir(s) every 2 weeks. The fluid should be maintained to a level not below the bottom line on the reservoirs and not above the top line. Any sudden decrease in the level in any of the reservoirs indicates a probable leak in that particular system and should be checked out immediately.

When making additions of fluid, use only fresh, uncontaminated brake fluid meeting or exceeding DOT 3 standards. Be careful not to spill any brake fluid on painted surfaces, because it eats paint. Do not allow the fluid container or master cylinder reservoirs to remain open any longer than necessary; brake fluid absorbs moisture from the air, reducing its effectiveness and causing brake and clutch line corrosion.

Power Steering Pump

FLUID RECOMMENDATIONS

Dexron®II automatic transmission fluid should be used.

LEVEL CHECK

▶ **See Figure 59**

Depending on the model, the power steering pump reservoir will be equipped with a cap mounted dipstick or a see through case. The level should be between the high and low marks provided. Add fluid as required, but no higher than the upper full mark.

OUTSIDE VEHICLE MAINTENANCE

Lock Cylinders

Apply graphite lubricant sparingly thought the key slot. Insert the key and operate the lock several times to be sure that the lubricant is worked into the lock cylinder.

Door Hinges and Hinge Checks

Spray a silicone lubricant on the hinge pivot points to eliminate any binding conditions. Open and close the door several times to be sure that the lubricant is evenly and thoroughly distributed.

Liftgate

Spray a silicone lubricant on all of the pivot and friction surfaces to eliminate any squeaks or binds. Work the tailgate to distribute the lubricant

Body Drain Holes

Be sure that the drain holes in the doors and rocker panels are cleared of obstruction. A small screwdriver can be used to clear them of any debris.

Chassis Greasing

Your car requires no regular chassis greasing. The lower ball joints are provided with plugged, threaded holes. A grease nipple can be installed and the ball joints lubricated, if necessary. No other lubrication points are provided or necessary.

Wheel Bearings

▶ See Figure 60

The following applies to the rear wheel bearings of front wheel drive cars.

The wheel bearings for the rear wheels should be repacked with Multipurpose Grease NLGI Grade #2 E.P. grease every 2 years or 30,000 miles. The best way to accomplish this is to combine the repacking operation with brake repairs. In other words, if brake linings require attention, always repack the

wheel bearings associated with the repair at the same time to avoid repeating the operation at the specified interval. Of course, if brake linings last longer than this interval, wheel bearings should be repacked as a discrete operation.

Before handling the bearings, there are a few things that you should remember to do and not to do. **Remember to DO the following:**

- Remove all outside dirt from the housing before exposing the bearing.
- Treat a used bearing as gently as you would a new one.
- Work with clean tools in clean surroundings.
- Use clean, dry canvas gloves, or at least clean, dry hands.
- Clean solvents and flushing fluids are a must.
- Use clean paper when laying out the bearings to dry.
- Protect disassembled bearings from rust and dirt. Cover them up.
- Use clean rags to wipe bearings.
- Keep the bearings in oil-proof paper when they are to be stored or are not in use.
- Clean the inside of the housing before replacing the bearing. **Do NOT do the following:**
- Don't work in dirty surroundings.
- Don't use dirty, chipped or damaged tools.
- Try not to work on wooden work benches or use wooden mallets.
- Don't handle bearings with dirty or moist hands.
- Do not use gasoline for cleaning; use a safe solvent.
- Do not spin-dry bearings with compressed air. They will be damaged.
- Do not spin dirty bearings.

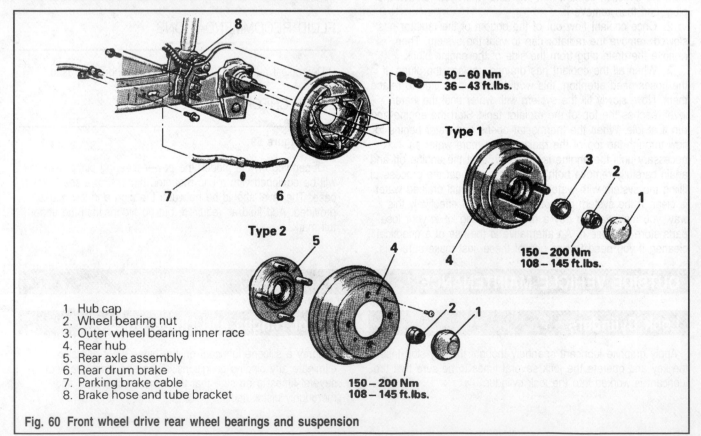

50 – 60 Nm
36 – 43 ft.lbs.

Type 1

150 – 200 Nm
108 – 145 ft.lbs.

Type 2

150 – 200 Nm
108 – 145 ft.lbs.

1. Hub cap
2. Wheel bearing nut
3. Outer wheel bearing inner race
4. Rear hub
5. Rear axle assembly
6. Rear drum brake
7. Parking brake cable
8. Brake hose and tube bracket

Fig. 60 Front wheel drive rear wheel bearings and suspension

- Avoid using cotton waste or dirty cloths to wipe bearings.
- Try not to scratch or nick bearing surfaces.
- Do not allow the bearing to come in contact with dirt or rust at any time.

1. Elevate and support the vehicle on jackstands. Make certain the parking brake is released and the rear wheels turn freely.

2. Remove the rear wheels.

3. Remove the small center cap, the cotter pin, the castellated nut and the lock nut.

4. Remove the drum, holding the outer bearing in place with a thumb as the drum comes off.

5. Remove the outer bearing. Turn the drum over and use a seal remover to remove the grease seal. After the seal is removed, the inner bearing may be lifted out.

6. If the bearings are in good condition, free of flats, gouges, scores etc., they may be cleaned, repacked and reused. If the bearings must be replaced, the bearing races must also be replaced. With a brass drift and hammer, knock out the outer races for both the inner and outer bearings. In doing this, work from above and knock the bearing out the bottom of the hub; then turn the hub over and repeat the process for the other bearing.

7. Use a bearing driver of the correct diameter and press each bearing race in from the top with the appropriate tool. The wider part of the race goes upward and the contour of the race fits that of the special tool. Races must be pressed in until the lower surface contacts the ridge in the hub designed to retain them.

8. Pack the bearing with grease meeting SAEJ310A NLGI grade #2 EPA standards. Use a liberal amount of grease and occasionally press the bearing into the palm of your hand to make sure that the grease passes all the way through. Also pack the inner contours of the hub. Fill the small cap about half full of grease.

9. Install the inner bearing into the race. Press fit a new seal into the inner diameter of the hub with the a seal driver of the correct diameter. Use the FLAT surface against the outer surface of the seal. The seal must end up flush with the inner surface of the hub. Apply grease to the lip of the oil seal.

10. Install the outer bearing in the race. Hold it in position with a thumb and fit the drum and bearing assembly onto the axle.

11. Install the slotted washer onto the axle and install the lock nut. As the lock nut contacts the washer, make certain that the bearing is firmly seated in the race.

12. Tighten the lock nut to 20 Nm (14 ft. lbs). Turn the drum 2 or 3 turns in each direction to seat the bearing.

13. Release the locknut to 0 Nm; then retighten it to 10 Nm (7 ft. lbs). Turn the drum 2 or 3 times.

14. Set the locknut to its final torque of 10 Nm (7 ft. lbs) and install the castle nut and a new cotter pin.

15. If the holes of the castle nut do not align with the holes in the axle, simply reposition the castle nut; the holes are not evenly spaced and should be able to align with the axle. In the unlikely event that no holes align, the lock not may be loosened by no more than 15° of rotation.

16. Reinstall the rear wheels.

17. Lower the vehicle to the ground.

PUSHING AND TOWING

Manual transmission equipped cars may be started by pushing, in the event of a dead battery. Ensure that the push car bumper doesn't override the bumper of your car. Depress the clutch pedal. Select Second or Third gear. Switch the ignition ON. When the car reaches a speed of approximately 10 mph, release the clutch to start the engine.

Front Wheel Drive cars should be flat-bedded, or towed with the front wheels off of the ground.

❋❋CAUTION

Do not attempt to push start in an automatic transmission equipped car.

JACKING

▶ **See Figure 61**

The vehicle is supplied with a scissors jack for emergency road repairs. The scissors jack may be used to raise the car via the notches on either side at the front and rear of the doors. Do not attempt to use the jack in any other places. Always block the diagonally opposite wheel when using a jack. When using a garage jack, support the car at the center of the front suspension member or at the differential carrier. Block both wheels at the opposite end of the car.

When using stands, use the side members at the front and the differential or trailing axle front mounting crossmember at the back for placement points. Whenever you plan to work under the car, you must support it on jackstands or ramps. Never use cinder blocks or stacks of wood to support the car, even if you're only going to be under it for a few minutes. Never crawl under the car when it is supported only by the tire-changing jack.

Small hydraulic, screw, or scissors jacks are satisfactory for raising the car. Drive-on trestles or ramps are also a handy and safe way to both raise and support the car. These can be bought or constructed from wood or steel. Never support the car on any suspension member or underbody panel.

TRAILER TOWING

If you are installing a trailer hitch and wiring on your car, there are a few thing that you ought to know.

Trailer Weight

Trailer weight is the first, and most important, factor in determining whether or not your vehicle is suitable for towing the trailer you have in mind. The horsepower-to-weight ratio should be calculated. The basic standard is a ratio of 35:1. That is, 35 pounds of GVW for every horsepower.

To calculate this ratio, multiply you engine's rated horsepower by 35, then subtract the weight of the vehicle, including passengers and luggage. The resulting figure is the ideal maximum trailer weight that you can tow. One point to consider: a numerically higher axle ratio can offset what appears to be a low trailer weight. If the weight of the trailer that you have in mind is somewhat higher than the weight you just calculated, you might consider changing your rear axle ratio to compensate.

Hitch Weight

There are three kinds of hitches: bumper mounted, frame mounted, and load equalizing.

Bumper mounted hitches are those which attach solely to the vehicle's bumper. Many states prohibit towing with this type of hitch, when it attaches to the vehicle's stock bumper, since it subjects the bumper to stresses for which it was not designed. Aftermarket rear step bumpers, designed for trailer towing, are acceptable for use with bumper mounted hitches.

Frame mounted hitches can be of the type which bolts to two or more points on the frame, plus the bumper, or just to several points on the frame. Frame mounted hitches can also be of the tongue type, for Class I towing, or, of the receiver type, for classes II and III.

Load equalizing hitches are usually used for large trailers. Most equalizing hitches are welded in place and use equalizing bars and chains to level the vehicle after the trailer is hooked up.

The bolt-on hitches are the most common, since they are relatively easy to install.

Check the gross weight rating of your trailer. Tongue weight is usually figured as 10% of gross trailer weight. Therefore, a trailer with a maximum gross weight of 2,000 lb. will have a maximum tongue weight of 200 lb. Class I trailers fall into this category. Class II trailers are those with a gross weight rating of 2,000-3,500 lb., while Class III trailers fall into the 3,500-6,000 lb. category. Class IV trailers are those over 6,000 lb. and are for use with fifth wheel trucks, only.

When you've determined the hitch that you'll need, follow the manufacturer's installation instructions, exactly, especially when it comes to fastener torques. The hitch will subjected to a lot of stress and good hitches come with hardened bolts. Never substitute an inferior bolt for a hardened bolt.

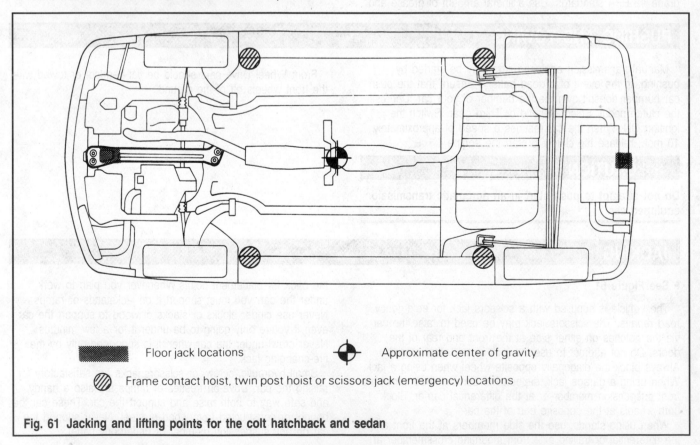

▰▰▰ Floor jack locations   ✛ Approximate center of gravity

▨ Frame contact hoist, twin post hoist or scissors jack (emergency) locations

Fig. 61 Jacking and lifting points for the colt hatchback and sedan

Wiring

Wiring the car for towing is fairly easy. There are a number of good wiring kits available and these should be used, rather than trying to design your own. All trailers will need brake lights and turn signals as well as tail lights and side marker lights. Most states require extra marker lights for overwide trailers. Also, most states have recently required back-up lights for trailers, and most trailer manufacturers have been building trailers with back-up lights for several years.

Additionally, some Class I, most Class II and just about all Class III trailers will have electric brakes.

Add to this number an accessories wire, to operate trailer internal equipment or to charge the trailer's battery, and you can have as many as seven wires in the harness.

Determine the equipment on your trailer and buy the wiring kit necessary. The kit will contain all the wires needed, plus a plug adapter set which included the female plug, mounted on the bumper or hitch, and the male plug, wired into, or plugged into the trailer harness.

When installing the kit, follow the manufacturer's instructions. The color coding of the wires is standard throughout the industry.

One point to note: some domestic vehicles, and most imported vehicles, have separate turn signals. On most domestic vehicles, the brake lights and rear turn signals operate with the same bulb. For those vehicles with separate turn signals, you can purchase an isolation unit so that the brake lights won't blink whenever the turn signals are operated, or, you can go to your local electronics supply house and buy four diodes to wire in series with the brake and turn signal bulbs. Diodes will isolate the brake and turn signals. The choice is yours. The isolation units are simple and quick to install, but far more expensive than the diodes. The diodes, however, require more work to install properly, since they require the cutting of each bulb's wire and soldering in place of the diode.

One, final point, the best kits are those with a spring loaded cover on the vehicle mounted socket. This cover prevent dirt and moisture from corroding the terminals. Never let the vehicle socket hang loosely; always mount it securely to the bumper or hitch.

Cooling

ENGINE

One of the most common, if not THE most common, problems associated with trailer towing is engine overheating.

With factory installed trailer towing packages, a heavy duty cooling system is usually included. Heavy duty cooling systems are available as optional equipment on some vehicles, with or without a trailer package. If you have one of these extra-capacity systems, you shouldn't have any overheating problems.

If you have a standard cooling system, without an expansion tank, you'll definitely need to get an aftermarket expansion tank kit, preferably one with at least a 2 quart capacity. These kits are easily installed on the radiator's overflow hose, and come with a pressure cap designed for expansion tanks.

Another helpful accessory is a Flex Fan. These fan are large diameter units are designed to provide more airflow at low speeds, with blades that have deeply cupped surfaces. The blades then flex, or flatten out, at high speed, when less cooling air is needed. These fans are far lighter in weight than stock fans, requiring less horsepower to drive them. Also, they are far quieter than stock fans.

If you do decide to replace your stock fan with a flex fan, note that if your car has a fan clutch, a spacer between the flex fan and water pump hub will be needed.

Aftermarket engine oil coolers are helpful for prolonging engine oil life and reducing overall engine temperatures. Both of these factors increase engine life.

While not absolutely necessary in towing Class I and some Class II trailers, they are recommended for heavier Class II and all Class III towing.

Engine oil cooler systems consist of an adapter, screwed on in place of the oil filter, a remote filter mounting and a multi-tube, finned heat exchanger, which is mounted in front of the radiator or air conditioning condenser.

TRANSMISSION

An automatic transmission is usually recommended for trailer towing. Modern automatics have proven reliable and, of course, easy to operate, in trailer towing.

The increased load of a trailer, however, causes an increase in the temperature of the automatic transmission fluid. Heat is the worst enemy of an automatic transmission. As the temperature of the fluid increases, the life of the fluid decreases.

It is essential, therefore, that you install an automatic transmission cooler.

The cooler, which consists of a multi-tube, finned heat exchanger, is usually installed in front of the radiator or air conditioning compressor, and hooked inline with the transmission cooler tank inlet line. Follow the cooler manufacturer's installation instructions.

Select a cooler of at least adequate capacity, based upon the combined gross weights of the car and trailer.

Cooler manufacturers recommend that you use an aftermarket cooler in addition to, and not instead of, the present cooling tank in your car's radiator. If you do want to use it in place of the radiator cooling tank, get a cooler at least two sizes larger than normally necessary.

One note: the transmission cooler can, sometimes, cause slow or harsh shifting in the transmission during cold weather, until the fluid has a chance to come up to normal operating temperature. Some coolers can be purchased with or retrofitted with a temperature bypass valve which will allow fluid flow through the cooler only when the fluid has reached operating temperature, or above.

CAPACITIES

Year	Model	Engine ID/VIN	Engine Displacement Liters (cc)	Engine Crankcase with Filter	Transmission (pts.)			Transfer Case (pts.)	Drive Axle		Fuel Tank (gal.)	Cooling System (qts.)
					4-Spd	5-Spd	Auto.		Front (pts.)	Rear (pts.)		
1990	Colt	X	1.5 (1468)	4.0	3.6	3.8	12.9	—	—	—	13.2	5.3
		Y	1.6 (1595)	5.0	—	3.8	—	—	—	—	13.2	5.3
	Colt Wagon	X	1.5 (1468)	4.0	—	3.8	12.2	—	—	—	12.4	5.3
		T	1.8 (1755)	4.0	—	3.8	—	1.3	—	—	12.4	5.3
	Vista	V	2.0 (1997)	5.0	—	4.4	12.9	1.5	—	1.5	14.5	7.4
1991	Colt	A	1.5 (1468)	4.0	3.6	3.8	12.9	—	—	—	13.2	5.3
	Vista	V	2.0 (1997)	5.0	—	4.4	12.2	1.5	—	1.5	14.5	7.4
1992	Colt	A	1.5 (1468)	4.0	3.6	3.8	12.9	—	—	—	13.2	5.3
	Vista	V	2.0 (1997)	5.0	—	4.4	12.2	1.5	—	1.5	14.5	7.4
1993	Colt	A	1.5 (1468)	4.0	—	3.8	12.6	—	—	—	13.2	5.3
		C	1.8 (1834)	4.2	—	3.8	12.6	—	—	—	13.2	6.3
	Vista	C	1.8 (1834)	4.2	—	3.8	12.8	—	—	—	14.5	6.3
		G	2.4 (2350)	4.7	—	4.8	13.8	1.2	—	1.5	14.5	6.8

SCHEDULED MAINTENANCE

Emission Control System Maintenance	Service Intervals	Kilometers in Thousands	24	48	72	80	96
		Mileage in Thousands	15	30	45	50	60
Change Engine Oil Every 12 Months	or	Every 12,000 Km (7,500 Miles)					
Replace Engine Oil Filter Every 12 Months	or		X	X	X		X
Check Valve Clearance; Adjust as Required	at		X	X	X		X
Check Engine Idle Speed[1]; Adjust as Required	at		X	X	X		X
Replace Fuel Filter Every 5 Years	or					X	
Check Fuel System (Tank, Line and Connections) for Leaks Every 5 Years	or					X	
Replace Vacuum Hoses, Secondary Air Hoses, Crankcase Ventilation Hoses and Water Hoses Every 5 Years	or						X
Replace Fuel Hoses, Vapor Hoses and Fuel Filler Cap Every 5 Years	or					X	
Replace Air Cleaner Element	at			X			X
Clean Crankcase Emission Control System (PCV Valve) Every 5 Years	or						X
Check Evaporative Emission Control System (Except Canister) for Leaks and Clogging Every 5 Years	or						X
Replace Canister	at			X			
Replace Spark Plugs	at			X			X
Replace Ignition Cables Every 5 Years	or						X
Replace Oxygen Sensor	at			X			

NOTE: 1: Recommended maintenance service item for California, and required maintenance service item except for California.

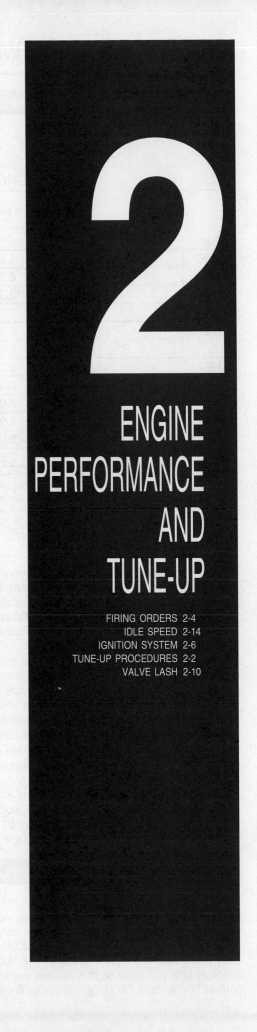

ENGINE PERFORMANCE AND TUNE-UP

TUNE-UP PROCEDURES

ENGINE TUNE-UP SPECIFICATIONS

Year	Engine ID/VIN	Engine Displacement Liters (cc)	Spark Plugs Gap (in.)	Ignition Timing (deg.) MT	Ignition Timing (deg.) AT	Fuel Pump (psi)	Idle Speed (rpm) MT	Idle Speed (rpm) AT	Valve Clearance In.	Valve Clearance Ex.
1990	X	1.5 (1468)	0.039–0.043	5B	5B	47.6	700	750	0.006	0.010
	Y	1.6 (1597)	0.039–0.043	5B	5B	47.6	700	750	Hyd.	Hyd.
	T	1.8 (1755)	0.039–0.043	5B	5B	47.6	700	700	0.006	0.010
	V	2.0 (1997)	0.039–0.043	5B	5B	47.6	700	700	Hyd.	Hyd.
1991	A	1.5 (1468)	0.039–0.043	5B	5B	47.6	750	750	0.006	0.010
	V	2.0 (1997)	0.039–0.043	5B	5B	47.6	700	700	Hyd.	Hyd.
1992	A	1.5 (1468)	0.039–0.043	5B	5B	47.6	750	750	0.006	0.010
	D	1.8 (1834)	0.039–0.043	5B	5B	47.6	750	750	0.008	0.012
	W	2.4 (2350)	0.039–0.043	5B	5B	47.6	750	750	Hyd.	Hyd.
1993	A	1.5 (1468)	0.039–0.043	5B	5B	47.6	750	750	0.008	0.010
	C	1.8 (1834)	0.039–0.043	5B	5B	47.6	700 ①	700 ①	0.008	0.012
	G	2.4 (2350)	0.039–0.043	5B	5B	47.6	700	700	Hyd.	Hyd.

NOTE: The lowest cylinder pressure should be within 75% of the highest cylinder pressure reading. For example, if the highest cylinder is 134 psi, the lowest should be 101. Engine should be at normal operating temperature with throttle valve in the wide open position.
The underhood specifications sticker often reflects tune-up specification changes in production. Sticker figures must be used if they disagree with those in this chart.
Hyd.—Hydraulic
① Calif. Vista: 750

In order to extract the full measure of performance and economy from your engine it is essential that it be properly tuned at regular intervals. A regular tune-up will keep your vehicle's engine running smoothly and will prevent the annoying minor breakdowns and poor performance associated with an untuned engine.

A complete tune-up should be performed every 24,000 miles or 24 months, whichever comes first. This interval should be halved if the vehicle is operated under severe conditions, such as trailer towing, prolonged idling, continual stop and start driving, or if starting or running problems are noticed. It is assumed that the routine maintenance described in Section 1 has been kept up, as this will have a decided effect on the results of a tune-up. All of the applicable steps of a tune-up should be followed in order, as the result is a cumulative one.

If the specifications on the tune-up sticker in the engine compartment disagree with the Tune-Up Specifications chart in this Section, the figures on the sticker must be used. The sticker often reflects changes made during the production run.

Spark Plugs

A typical spark plug consists of a metal shell surrounding a ceramic insulator. A metal electrode extends downward through the center of the insulator and protrudes a small distance. Located at the end of the plug and attached to the side of the outer metal shell is the side electrode. The side electrode bends in at a 90° angle so that its tip is even with, and parallel to, the tip of the center electrode. The distance between these two electrodes (measured in thousandths of an inch) is called the spark plug gap. The spark plug in no way produces a spark but merely provides a gap across which the current can arc. The coil produces anywhere from 20,000 to 40,000 volts which travels to the distributor where it is distributed through the spark plug wires to the spark plugs. The current passes along the center electrode and jumps the gap to the side electrode, and, in do doing, ignites the air/fuel mixture in the combustion chamber.

SPARK PLUG HEAT RANGE

Spark plug heat range is the ability of the plug to dissipate heat. The longer the insulator (or the farther it extends into the engine), the hotter the plug will operate; the shorter the insulator the cooler it will operate. A plug that absorbs little heat and remains too cool will quickly accumulate deposits of oil and carbon since it is not hot enough to burn them off. This leads to plug fouling and consequently to misfiring. A plug that absorbs too much heat will have no deposits, but, due to the excessive heat, the electrodes will burn away quickly and in some instances, preignition may result. Preignition takes place when plug tips get so hot that they glow sufficiently to ignite the fuel/air mixture before the actual spark occurs. This early ignition will usually cause a pinging during low speeds and heavy loads.

The general rule of thumb for choosing the correct heat range when picking a spark plug is: if most of your driving is long distance, high speed travel, use a colder plug; if most of your driving is stop and go, use a hotter plug. Original equipment plugs are compromise plugs, but most people never have occasion to change their plugs from the factory recommended heat range.

REPLACING SPARK PLUGS

▶ See Figures 1, 2, 3, 4, 5, 6, 7 and 8

A set of spark plugs usually requires replacement after about 20,000 to 30,000 miles, depending on your style of driving. In normal operation, plug gap increases about 0.001 in. for every 1,000-2,500 miles. As the gap increases, the plug's voltage

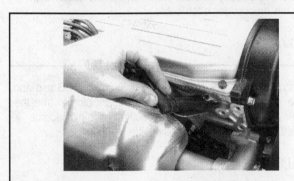

Fig. 1 Removing plug wires from routing clips

Fig. 2 Removing plug wires from plugs, pulling on the boot, not the wire

Fig. 3 Removing spark plugs

Fig. 4 Visually inspect the plugs

requirement also increases. It requires a greater voltage to jump the wider gap and about two to three times as much voltage to fire a plug at high speeds than at idle.

When you're removing spark plugs, you should work on one at a time. Don't start by removing the plug wires all at once, because unless you number them, they may become mixed up. Take a minute before you begin and number the wires with tape. The best location for numbering is near where the wires come out of the cap.

REMOVAL & INSTALLATION

1. If the spark plug wires are not numbered (by cylinder) place a piece of masking tape on each wire and number it.

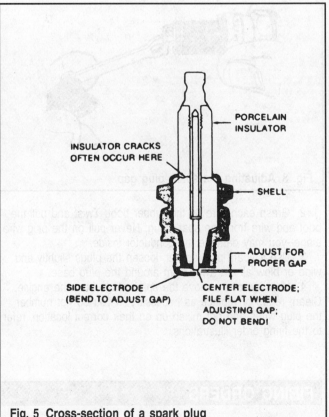

Fig. 5 Cross-section of a spark plug

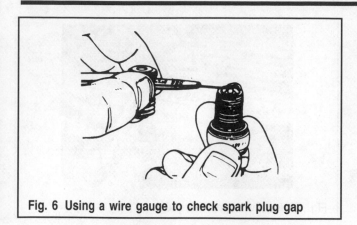

Fig. 6 Using a wire gauge to check spark plug gap

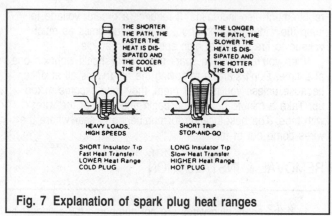

THE SHORTER THE PATH, THE FASTER THE HEAT IS DISSIPATED AND THE COOLER THE PLUG

THE LONGER THE PATH, THE SLOWER THE HEAT IS DISSIPATED AND THE HOTTER THE PLUG

HEAVY LOADS, HIGH SPEEDS

SHORT TRIP STOP-AND-GO

SHORT Insulator Tip
Fast Heat Transfer
LOWER Heat Range
COLD PLUG

LONG Insulator Tip
Slow Heat Transfer
HIGHER Heat Range
HOT PLUG

Fig. 7 Explanation of spark plug heat ranges

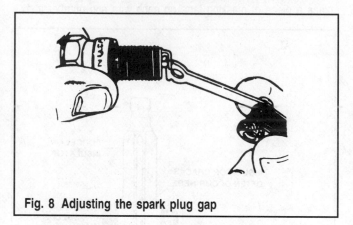

Fig. 8 Adjusting the spark plug gap

2. Grasp each wire by the rubber boot. Twist and pull the boot and wire from the spark plug. Never pull on the plug wire alone--you may damage the conductor inside.

3. Use a spark plug socket, loosen the plugs slightly and wipe or blow all dirt away from around the plug base.

4. Unscrew and remove the spark plugs from the engine. Clean, regap or replace as necessary. If you do not number the plug wires and get mixed up on their correct location, refer to the firing order illustrations.

5. If, after removing and examining the spark plugs you feel that cleaning and regapping them is all that is necessary; use a stiff wire brush and clean all the carbon deposits from the electrodes and insulator or take the plugs to a service center and have them cleaned in a plug cleaning machine. New spark plugs come pre-gapped, however different models require different size gaps. Always check the gap and reset if necessary.

6. To set the gap on new or cleaned spark plug, use a spark plug wire feeler gauge. The wire gauge should pass through the electrodes with just a slight drag. Use the electrode bending tool on the end of the gauge to adjust the gap. Never attempt to adjust the center electrode.

7. Put a drop of oil on the base threads of the plug. Start the spark plug into the cylinder head by hand. Use a socket and tighten to no more than 15 ft. lbs.

Spark Plug Wires

Visually inspect the spark plug cables for burns, cuts, or breaks in the insulation. Check the spark plug boots and the nipples on the distributor cap and coil. Replace any damaged wiring. If no physical damage is obvious, the wires can be checked with an ohmmeter for excessive resistance. (See the tune-up and troubleshooting section).

When installing a new set of spark plug cables, replace the cables on at a time so there will be no mix-up. Start by replacing the longest cable first. Install the boot firmly over the spark plug. Route the wire exactly the same as the original. Insert the nipple firmly into the tower on the distributor cap. Repeat the process for each cable.

REMOVAL

When removing spark plug wires, use great care. Grasp and twist the insulator back and forth on the spark plug to free the insulator. Do not pull on the wire directly as it may become separated from the connector inside the insulator.

INSTALLATION

1. Install each wire in or on the proper terminal of the distributor cap. Be sure the terminal connector inside the insulator is fully seated. The No. 1 terminal is identified on the cap.

2. Remove the brackets from the old spark plug wire set and install them on the new set in the same relative position. Install the wires in the brackets on the valve rocker arm covers. Connect the wires to the proper spark plugs. Install the coil high tension lead.

Wires must be positioned in the bracket in a special order to avoid cylinder cross-fire. Be sure to position the wire in the bracket in the order from front to rear.

FIRING ORDERS

▶ See Figures 9, 10, 11, 12, 13 and 14

To avoid confusion, replace spark plug wires one at a time.

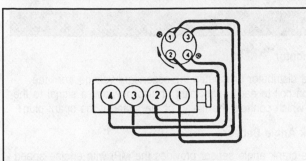

Fig. 9 1990 1.8L SOHC Engines
Firing order: 1-3-4-2
Rotation: clockwise

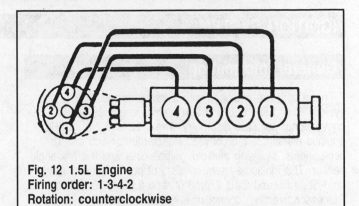

Fig. 12 1.5L Engine
Firing order: 1-3-4-2
Rotation: counterclockwise

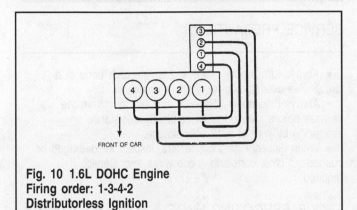

Fig. 10 1.6L DOHC Engine
Firing order: 1-3-4-2
Distributorless Ignition

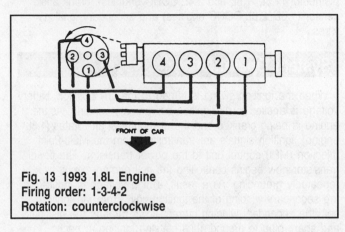

Fig. 13 1993 1.8L Engine
Firing order: 1-3-4-2
Rotation: counterclockwise

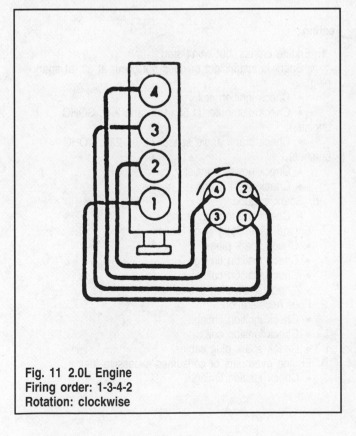

Fig. 11 2.0L Engine
Firing order: 1-3-4-2
Rotation: clockwise

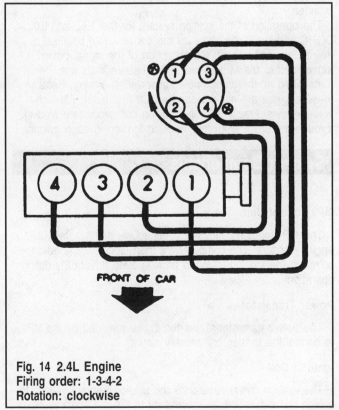

Fig. 14 2.4L Engine
Firing order: 1-3-4-2
Rotation: clockwise

IGNITION SYSTEM

General Information

These cars are equipped with a transistorized type ignition system. The 1.5L, 1.8L and 2.4L SOHC engines uses a conventional pointless distributor. The 1.6L and 2.0L DOHC engines eliminates the conventional distributor and all its components, by using multiple ignition coils and a crank angle sensor. The ignition system consists of power transistor(s) (1 on 1.5L, 1.8L and 2.4L, 2 on 1.6L and 2.0L), MPI (Micro-Processor Injection) control unit, ignition coil(s), pointless distributor (1.5L, 1.8L and 2.4L SOHC engines), crank angle sensor (1.6L, 2.0L DOHC engines) and secondary ignition wires.

System Operation

When the ignition switch is turned to the **ON** position, battery voltage is applied to the ignition coil primary winding. As the engine is being cranked and the distributor shaft rotates (1.8L engine), ignition signals are transmitted from the Multi-Point Injection (MPI) control unit to the power transistor. The power transistor now begins controlling the coil primary circuit by repeatedly grounding. As a result, a high voltage is induced in the secondary winding of the ignition coil. From the ignition coil, the secondary winding current flows through the distributor and spark plug to ground, thus causing ignition in each cylinder.

The operation of the ignition system for the 1.6L and 2.0L DOHC engines is the same as the conventional pointless distributor engines, with the exception of the signal being transmitted to the MPI control unit. These signals are transmitted as the crank angle sensor shaft rotates. Because these engines are not equipped with a distributor, the high voltage flows directly from the ignition coil secondary winding through the spark plug, thus causing ignition in each cylinder.

System Components

MPI Control Unit

The MPI (engine controller) continuously monitor various engine sensors. The computer will then electronically advance or retard the ignition timing to provide even driveability during operation.

Power Transistor

The power transistor(s) use the signal provided by the MPI to control the ignition coil primary circuit.

Ignition Coil

The ignition coil(s) transforms the ignition primary voltage to a high secondary voltage, necessary to fire the spark plugs.

Distributor

The distributor distributes the secondary voltage from the ignition coil to each spark plug. It also provides a signal to the MPI, which controls the timing of the spark at the spark plug.

Crank Angle Sensor

The crank angle sensor provides the MPI with engine speed and crank shaft position informations.

Diagnosis and Testing

SERVICE PRECAUTIONS

• Always turn the key **OFF** and isolate both ends of a circuit whenever testing for short or continuity.
• Always disconnect solenoids and switches from the harness before measuring for continuity, resistance or energizing by way of a 12 volts source.
• When disconnecting connectors, inspect for damaged or pushed-out pins, corrosion, loose wires, etc. Service if required.

TROUBLESHOOTING HINTS

Testing

1. Engine cranks, but won't start:
   a. Spark is insufficient or does not occur at all, at spark plug:
      • Check ignition coil.
      • Check distributor (1.5L, 1.8L and 2.4L SOHC engines).
      • Check crank angle sensor (1.6L, 2.0L DOHC engines).
      • Check power transistor.
      • Check spark plugs.
   b. Spark is good:
      • Check the ignition timing.
2. Engine Idles Roughly or Stalls:
   • Check spark plugs.
   • Check ignition timing.
   • Check ignition coil.
   • Check spark plug cables.
3. Poor Acceleration:
   • Check ignition timing.
   • Check ignition coil.
   • Check spark plug cables.
4. Engine overheats or consumes excessive fuel:
   • Check ignition timing.

Ignition Coil

TESTING

♦ **See Figures 15, 16, 17 and 18**

1.5L, 1.8L, 2.4L SOHC Engines

1. Disconnect the negative battery cable and ignition coil harness connector.

2. Measure the primary coil resistance between the positive (+) and negative (-) terminals of the coil. Should indicate a value of 0.72-0.88 ohms, except 1991-93 1.5L engine. On 1991-93 reading should indicate a value of 0.9-1.2 ohms.

3. Measure the coil secondary resistance between the positive (+) terminal and the high-voltage terminal. Should indicate a value of 10.3-13.9 kilo-ohms, except 1991-93 1.5L engine. On 1991-93 reading should indicate a value of 20-29 kilo-ohms.

4. If the readings are not within the specified value, replace the ignition coil.

1.6L and 2.0L DOHC Engines

1. Disconnect the negative battery cable and ignition coil harness connect

2. Measure the primary coil resistance.

3. On 1990 2.0L engine, measure the resistance between terminals 4 and 2 (coils at the No. 1 and No. 4 cylinder sides) of the ignition coil, and between terminals 4 and 1 (coils at the No. 2 and No. 3 cylinder sides).

4. On 1.6L engine and 1991-93 2.0L engine, measure the resistance between terminals 3 and 2 (coils at the No. 1 and No. 4 cylinder sides) of the ignition coil, and between terminals 3 and 1 (coils at the No. 2 and No. 3 cylinder sides).

5. The primary coil resistance should read 0.77-0.95 ohms.

6. Measure the coil secondary resistance.

7. Disconnect the connector of the ignition coil. Measure the resistance between the high-voltage terminals for the No. 1 and No. 4 cylinders, and between the high-voltage terminals for the No. 2 and No. 3 cylinders.

8. The secondary coil resistance should read 10.3-13.9 kilo-ohms.

9. If the readings are not within the specified value, replace the ignition coil.

Power Transistors

TESTING

♦ **See Figures 19, 20, 21 and 22**

➡ **When testing the power transistor(s), an analog-type circuit tester should be used.**

1.5L Engine

1990

1. Connect the negative (-) terminal of a 1.5 volts dry cell to terminal 2 of the power transistor; then check whether there is continuity between terminals 2 and 3 when terminal 1 and the positive (+) terminal are connected and disconnected.

2. If the results are not as indicated, replace the power transistor(s).

1991-93

1. Connect the negative (-) terminal of a 1.5 volts dry cell to terminal 7 of the power transistor; then check whether there is continuity between terminals 7 and 2 when terminal 8 and the positive (+) terminal are connected and disconnected.

2. If the results are not as indicated, replace the power transistor(s).

1.6L Engine

NO. 1-4 Coil Side

1. Connect the negative (-) terminal of a 1.5 volts dry cell to terminal 3 of the power transistor; then check whether there is continuity between terminals 7 and 3 when terminal 6 and the positive (+) terminal are connected and disconnected.

➡ **Connect the negative (-) probe of the tester to terminal 7 of the power transistor.**

NO. 2-3 Coil Side

2. Connect the negative (-) terminal of a 1.5 volts dry cell to terminal 3 of the power transistor; then check whether there is continuity between terminals 1 and 3 when terminal 2 and the positive (+) terminal are connected and disconnected.

➡ **Connect the negative (-) probe of the tester to terminal 1 of the power transistor.**

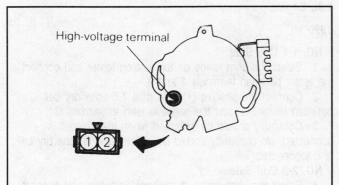

Fig. 15 Checking primary coil resistance, SOHC engines

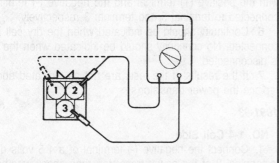

Fig. 16 Checking primary coil resistance, DOHC engines with a distributor

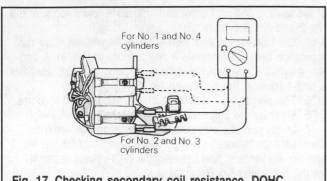

Fig. 17 Checking secondary coil resistance, DOHC engines with a distributor

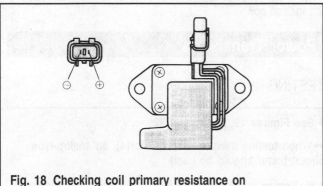

Fig. 18 Checking coil primary resistance on distributorless engines

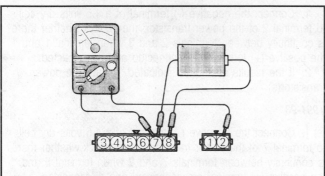

Fig. 19 Checking secondary coil resistance, SOHC engines

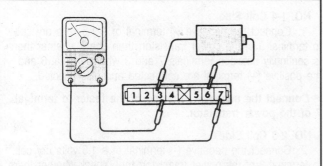

Fig. 20 Checking nos. 1 & 4 cylinders at the power transistor, on DOHC engines with a distributor

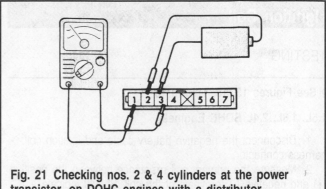

Fig. 21 Checking nos. 2 & 4 cylinders at the power transistor, on DOHC engines with a distributor

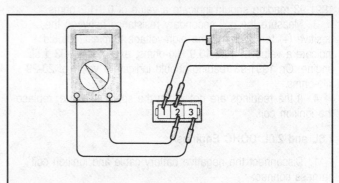

Fig. 22 Checking the power transistor for continuity on distributorless engines

3. If the results of the tests are not as indicated above, replace the power transistor(s).

2.0L Engine

1990

NO. 1-4 Coil Side

1. Select the ohm range on the analog tester and connect the tester between terminals 1 and 3.

2. Connect the positive (+) lead of a 1.5 volts dry cell between terminal 2 and the negative lead to terminal 3.

3. Continuity should be indicated when the dry cell is connected. No continuity should be indicated when the dry cell is disconnected.

NO. 2-3 Coil Side

4. Select the ohm range on the analog tester and connect the tester between terminals 6 and 3.

5. Connect a 1.5 volts dry cell between terminals 3 and 5, with the positive (+) terminal and the negative (-) terminal connected to terminal 5 and terminal 3 respectively.

6. Continuity should be indicated when the dry cell is connected. No continuity should be indicated when the dry cell is disconnected.

7. If the results of the tests are not as indicated above, replace the power transistor(s).

1991-93

NO. 1-4 Coil Side

1. Connect the negative (-) terminal of a 1.5 volts dry cell to terminal 3 of the power transistor; then check whether there

is continuity between terminals 7 and 3 when terminal 6 and the positive (+) terminal are connected and disconnected.

➡**Connect the negative (-) probe of the tester to terminal 7 of the power transistor.**

NO. 2-3 Coil Side

2. Connect the negative (-) terminal of a 1.5 volts dry cell to terminal 3 of the power transistor; then check whether there is continuity between terminals 1 and 3 when terminal 2 and the positive (+) terminal are connected and disconnected.

➡**Connect the negative (-) probe of the tester to terminal 1 of the power transistor.**

3. If the results of the tests are not as indicated above, replace the power transistor(s).

2.4L ENGINE

1. Connect the negative (-) terminal of a 1.5 volts dry cell to terminal 2 of the power transistor; then check whether there is continuity between terminals 3 and 2 when terminal 1 and the positive (+) terminal are connected and disconnect

2. If the results are not as indicated, replace the power transistor(s).

Ignition Timing

ADJUSTMENT

1.5L, 1.8L, 2.4L SOHC Engines
▶ **See Figures 25, 23, 24, 26, 27 and 28**

1. Apply the parking brake and block the wheels. Run the engine until it reach operating temperature.
2. Make certain all lights, cooling fan and accessories are **OFF.**
3. Position the steering wheel in straight ahead position and the gear selector lever in **P** or **N.**
4. Connect a timing light to the engine.
5. On 1.8L engine, insert a paper clip into the CRC filter connector (3-pole connector, 0.5-W cable). On 1.5L and 2.4L SOHC engines, insert a paper clip from behind the connector.
6. Connect a tachometer to the inserted clip. Do not separate the connector.
7. Check the curb idle speed. Should be 650-850 rpm (1.5L engine), 600-800 rpm (1.8L engine).
8. Stop the engine and jumper the terminal for ignition-timing adjustment to ground.
9. Start and run the engine at curb idle speed.
10. Check the basic ignition timing and adjust, if necessary. Basic ignition timing should be 5 degrees BTDC.
11. If the timing is not within specification, loosen the distributor hold-down bolt and turn the distributor to bring the timing within specs.
12. Tighten the hold-down bolt after adjustment. Recheck the timing and adjust if necessary.

13. Stop the engine and unground the ignition timing connector.

➡**Actual ignition timing may vary, depending on the control mode of the engine control unit. In such case, recheck the basic ignition timing. If there is no deviation, the ignition timing is functioning normally.**

14. Start the engine and run at curb idle. Check the actual ignition timing. Actual ignition timing should be 10 degrees BTDC for 1.5L and 1.8L engines, 8 degrees BTDC for 2.4L engine.

➡**At altitudes, more than approximately 2,300 ft. (701m) above sea level, the actual ignition timing is further advanced to ensure good combustion.**

Fig. 23 Loosening the distributor holddown bolt

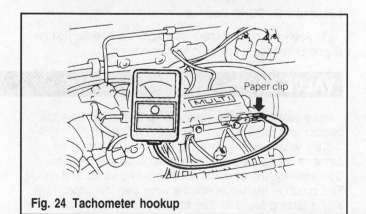

Fig. 24 Tachometer hookup

Fig. 25 Timing marks are on a scale attached to the front cover. A notch is provided on the pulley rim. It's a good idea to highlight the notch with a dab of white paint

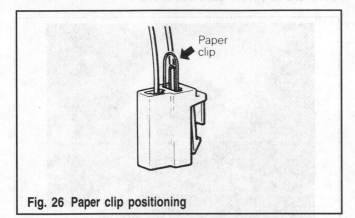

Fig. 26 Paper clip positioning

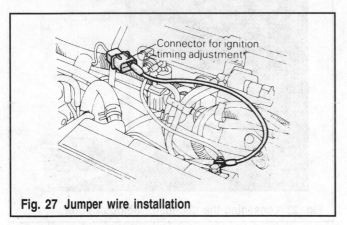

Fig. 27 Jumper wire installation

1.6L and 2.0L DOHC Engines

1. Apply the parking brake and block the wheels. Run the engine until it reach operating temperature.

2. Make certain all lights, cooling fan and accessories are **OFF**.

3. Position the steering wheel in straight ahead position and the gear selector lever in **P** or **N**.

4. Connect a timing light to the engine.

5. On 1.6L engine, insert a paper clip from behind the connector. On 2.0L engine, insert a paper clip into the engine revolution speed detection terminal (in engine compartment) and connect a tachometer to the inserted clip.

6. Check the curb idle speed. Should be 650-850 rpm.

7. Stop the engine and jumper the terminal for ignition-timing adjustment to ground.

8. Start and run the engine at curb idle speed.

9. Check the basic ignition timing and adjust, if necessary. Basic ignition timing should be 5 degrees BTDC.

10. If the timing is not within specification, loosen the crank angle sensor retaining nut and turn the crank angel sensor to bring the timing within specs.

11. Tighten the sensor retaining nut after adjustment. Recheck the timing and adjust if necessary.

12. Stop the engine and unground the ignition timing connector.

13. Start the engine and run at curb idle. Check the actual ignition timing. Actual ignition timing should be 8 degrees BTDC.

➡**Actual ignition timing may vary, depending on the control mode of the engine control unit. In such case, recheck the basic ignition timing. If there is no deviation, the ignition timing is functioning normally. At altitudes, more than approximately 2,300 ft. (701m) above sea level, the actual ignition timing is further advanced to ensure good combustion.**

VALVE LASH

Valve adjustment determines how far the valves enter the cylinder and how long they stay open and closed.

If the valve clearance is too large, part of the lift of the camshaft will be used in removing the excessive clearance. Consequently, the valve will not be opening as far as it should. This condition has two effects:the valve train components will emit a tapping sound as they take up the excessive clearance and the engine will perform poorly because the valves don't

open fully and allow the proper amount of gases to flow into and out of the engine.

If the valve clearance is too small, the intake valve and the exhaust valves will open too far and they will not fully seat on the cylinder head when they close. When a valve seats itself on the cylinder head, it does two things: it seals the combustion chamber so that none of the gases in the cylinder escape and it cools itself by transferring some of the heat it

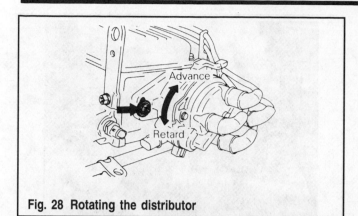

Fig. 28 Rotating the distributor

absorbs from the combustion in the cylinder to the cylinder head and to the engine's cooling system. If the valve clearance is too small, the engine will run poorly because of the gases escaping from the combustion chamber. The valves will also become overheated and will warp, since they cannot transfer heat unless they are touching the valve seat in the cylinder head.

➡ **While all valve adjustments must be made as accurately as possible, it is better to have the valve adjustment slightly loose than slightly tight as a burned valve may result from overly tight adjustments.**

ADJUSTMENT

◆ **See Figures 29, 30, 31, 32, 33, 34, 35, 36, 37, 38 and 39**

Except 2.4L

Valve lash must be adjusted on all engines not equipped with automatic lash adjusters. Some engines have a third valve of very small size called a jet valve. The jet valve must be adjusted, whether the engine uses automatic lash adjusters for the normal intake and exhaust valves or not. Thus, on some engines, there are 3 valves per cylinder that must be adjusted.

1. Run the engine until operating temperature is reached.
2. Turn off the engine and block the wheels.
3. Remove all necessary components in order to gain access to the rocker cover.

Fig. 29 Removing the upper part of the belt cover

4. Remove the spark plugs from the cylinder head for easy operations.

   a. On some engines it may be necessary to remove the air intake pipe.

   b. On some engines it may be necessary to disconnect the oxygen sensor connecting joint. Remove the engine bracket mounting, be sure to place a block of wood on the oil pan and jack it up into to place for the duration of the operation. Remove the upper front timing belt cover, remove the air cleaner assembly on the 2.0L engine and the air intake pipe on the 1.8L engine and remove the rocker cover.

   c. On all other vehicles, remove the air cleaner or air intake pipe assembly and remove the rocker cover.

5. Turn each cylinder head bolt, in sequence, back just until it is loose. Torque the cylinder head bolts in the proper sequence to specification.

6. Position the engine crankshaft at TDC with No. 1 cylinder at the firing position. Turn the engine by using a wrench on the bolt in the front of the crankshaft until the 0 degree timing mark on the timing cover lines up with the notch in the front pulley. On some engines, it may be necessary to turn the crankshaft clockwise until the notch on the pulley is lined up with the **T** mark on the timing belt lower cover.

7. Observe the valve rockers for No. 1 cylinder. If both are in identical positions with the valves up, the engine is in the right position. If not, rotate the engine exactly 360 degrees until the 0 degree timing mark is again aligned. Each jet valve is associated with an intake valve that is on the same rocker lever. In this position, adjust all the valves marked **A**, including associated jet valves which are located on the rockers, on the intake side only.

8. To adjust the appropriate jet valves, first loosen the regular (larger) intake valve adjusting stud by loosening the locknut and backing the stud off 2 turns. Note that this particular step is not required on engines that have automatic lash adjusters.

9. Loosen the jet valve (smaller) adjusting stud locknut, back the stud out slightly and insert the feeler gauge between the jet valve and stud. Make sure the gauge lies flat on the top of the jet valve. Be careful not to twist the gauge or otherwise depress the jet valve spring, rotate the jet valve adjusting stud back in until it just touches the gauge. Tighten the locknut. Make sure the gauge still slides very easily between the stud and jet valve and that they both are still just touching the gauge.

➡ **The clearances must not be too tight.**

10. Repeat the entire procedure for the other jet valves associated with rockers labeled **A** (Dark Arrow).

11. On engines without automatic lash adjusters, repeat the procedure for the intake valves labeled **A** (Dark Arrow).

12. Repeat the basic adjustment procedure for exhaust valves labeled **A** on engines without automatic lash adjusters.

13. Turn the engine exactly 360 degrees, until the timing marks are again aligned at **0** degrees BTDC.

14. On engines with automatic lash adjusters, after the jet valves and rockers on the intake side and labeled **B** (Light Arrow) are adjusted, the valve adjustment procedure is completed. On engines without automatic lash adjusters, adjust the regular intake and exhaust valves labeled **B** (Light Arrow).

15. Reinstall the cam cover. Run the engine to check for oil leaks.

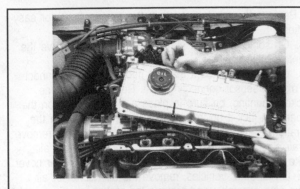

Fig. 30 Removing the camshaft cover

Fig. 31 Checking the gap with a feeler gauge

Fig. 32 Loosening the adjuster locknut

Fig. 33 Hold the locknut still while turning the adjuster

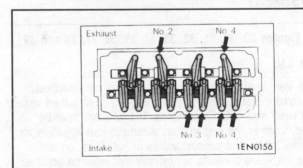

Fig. 35 Second rotation for valve adjustment — 1990-92 12 Valve engines

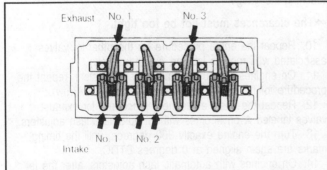

Fig. 34 First rotation for valve adjustment — 1990-92 12-valve engines

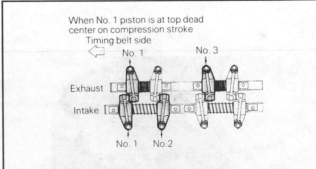

Fig. 36 First rotation for valve adjustment — 1990 8-valve engines

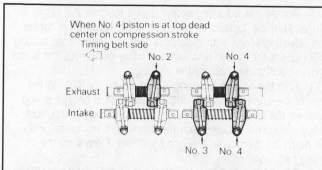

Fig. 37 Second rotation for valve adjustment — 1990 8-valve engines

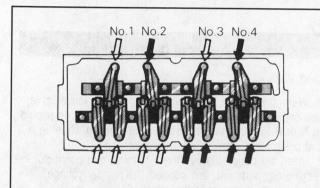

Fig. 38 Valve adjustment sequence for 1993 1.5L engines

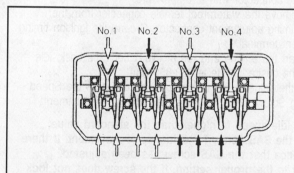

Fig. 39 Valve adjustment sequence for 1993 1.8L and 2.4L engines

2.4L

➡Incorrect valve clearances will cause unsteady engine operation, excessive noise and reduced engine output. Check the valve clearances and adjust as required while the engine is hot.

1. Adjust the valves with the engine cold. Disconnect the negative battery cable.

2. Remove all spark plugs so engine can be easily turned by hand.

3. Remove the valve cover.

4. Turn the crankshaft clockwise until the notch on the pulley is aligned with the **T** mark on the timing belt lower cover. This brings both No. 1 and No. 4 cylinder pistons to Top Dead Center (TDC).

5. Wiggle the rocker arms on No. 1 and No. 4 cylinders up and down to determine which cylinder is at TDC on the compression stroke. Both rocker arms should move if the piston in that cylinder is at TDC on the compression stroke.

6. Measure the valve clearance with a feeler gauge. When the No. 1 piston is at TDC on the compression stroke, check No. 1 intake and exhaust, No. 2 intake and No. 3 exhaust. Then turn the crankshaft clockwise 1 turn to bring No. 4 to TDC on its compression stroke. With No. 4 on TDC, compression stroke, check No. 2 exhaust, No. 3 intake and No. 4 intake and exhaust.

7. Valve lash specifications: Intake — 0.0035 in. (0.09mm) cold; Exhaust — 0.0079 in. (0.20mm) cold.

8. If the valve clearances are out of specification, loosen the rocker arm locknut and adjust the clearance using a feeler gauge while turning the adjusting screw. Be sure to hold the screw to prevent it from turning when tightening the locknut.

9. After adjusting the valves, install the valve cover and spark plugs, and connect the negative battery cable.

JET VALVE ADJUSTMENT

➡An incorrect jet valve clearance would affect the emission levels and could also cause engine troubles, so the jet valve clearance must be correctly adjusted. Adjust the jet valve clearance before adjusting the intake valve clearance. The cylinder head bolts should be retorqued before making this adjustment. The jet valve clearance should be adjusted with the adjusting screw on the intake valve side fully loosened.

1. Start the engine and let it run at idle until it reaches normal operating temperature.

2. Remove all spark plugs from the cylinder head for easy operation.

3. On some vehicles it may be necessary to remove the air intake pipe and remove the rocker cover.

4. It may be necessary to disconnect the oxygen sensor. Remove the engine bracket mounting, be sure to place a block of wood on the oil pan and jack it up into to place for the duration of the operation. Remove the upper front timing belt cover, remove the air cleaner assembly on the 1.8L and 2.0L engine.

5. Remove air intake pipe assembly and remove the rocker cover.

6. Set the engine at TDC with No. 1 cylinder at the firing position. Turn the engine by using a wrench on the bolt in the front of the crankshaft until the **0** degree timing mark on the timing cover lines up with the notch in the front pulley. On some engines, it may be necessary to turn the crankshaft clockwise until the notch on the pulley is lined up with the **T** mark on the timing belt lower cover. This will bring both No. 1 and No. 4 cylinder pistons up to TDC.

➡**Never turn the crankshaft counterclockwise.**

7. Move the rocker arms on the No. 1 and No. 4 cylinders up and down by hand to determine if the piston in that cylinder is at TDC center on the compression stroke. If the intake and exhaust rocker arms do not move, the piston in that cylinder is not at TDC on the compression stroke.

8. Measure the jet valve clearance at point **A**.

➡ **Measure the valve clearance when the No. 1 cylinder or the No. 4 cylinder pistons are at TDC on the compression stroke. Then give the crankshaft 1 clockwise turn to bring the other cylinder piston to TDC on compression stroke.**

9. If the jet valve clearance is not 0.010 in. (0.25mm) hot and 0.007 in. (0.18mm) cold, loosen the rocker arm locknut of the intake valve and loosen the adjusting screw at least 2 turns or more.

10. Loosen the jet valve locknut and adjust the clearance using a feeler gauge while turning the adjusting screw.

➡ **The jet valve spring has a small tension and the adjustment is somewhat delicate. Be careful not to push in the jet valve by turning the adjusting screw in too much.**

11. Tighten the adjusting screw until it touches the feeler gauge. Turn the locknut to secure it, while holding the rocker arm adjusting screw with a suitable tool to keep it from turning.

12. Check the intake and exhaust valve clearance, if it is not within specifications, adjust the valves.

13. Turn the engine by using a wrench on the bolt, in the front of the crankshaft, 360 degrees until the **0** degree timing mark on the timing cover lines up with the notch in the front pulley. On some vehicles turn the crankshaft clockwise until the notch on the pulley is aligned with the **T** mark on the timing belt lower cover.

14. Repeat Steps 9 through 13 on the other valves marked **B** for clearance adjustment.

IDLE SPEED

Idle Speed Adjustment

▶ **See Figure 40**

Colt and 1990-91 Vista

1. Slacken the accelerator cable, connect a tachometer, set the ignition switch to the **ON** position and turn the ignition **OFF**.

2. Disconnect the connectors from the idle speed control servo and lock the idle speed control plunger at the initial position.

3. Back out the speed adjusting screw SAS enough.

4. Start the engine and let idle. Check to see if the idle speed is 750 ± 50 for the Colt and 700 ± 100 for the Vista.

5. If not within specifications, adjust the fixed SAS until the engine speed rises. Then back out the SAS until the engine speed does not fall any longer (touch point). Back out the SAS an additional half a turn from the touch point.

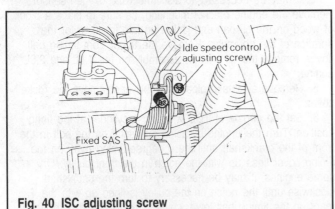

Fig. 40 ISC adjusting screw

1992-93 Vista

1. Warm the engine to operating temperature, leave lights, electric cooling fan and accessories **OFF**. The transaxle should be in **N** or **P** for automatic transaxle. The steering wheel in a neutral position for vehicles with power steering.

2. Insert the paper clip into the 1 terminal rpm connector in the engine compartment, and connect the primary voltage detection type tachometer to the paper clip.

3. Ground the self-diagnostic control terminal of the diagnostic connector with a jumper wire.

4. Remove the waterproof female connector from the ignition timing adjustment connector. Ground the ignition timing adjustment terminal.

5. Start the engine and run at idle. Check the basic idle speed, the desired value is 650-850 rpm.

6. If the value is not within specifications, turn the Speed Adjusting Screw (SAS) to make the necessary adjustment.

➡ **If the idle speed is higher than the standard value, inspect the SAS screw for evidence of movement. If there is evidence that the SAS screw has been adjusted, readjust to the proper setting. If the screw does not look as though it has been adjusted, it is possible that there is leakage as a result of deterioration of the Fast Idle Air Valve (FIAV), and, if so the throttle body should be replaced.**

7. Turn the ignition **OFF**. Disconnect and remove the jumper wires from the diagnosis control terminal and the ignition timing adjustment terminal.

8. Start the engine and let run at idle speed for about 10 minutes, check to be sure that the idling condition is normal.

3

ENGINE AND ENGINE REBUILDING

ENGINE ELECTRICAL

Understanding the Engine Electrical System

The engine electrical system can be broken down into three separate and distinct systems:
1. The starting system.
2. The charging system.
3. The ignition system.

BATTERY AND STARTING SYSTEM

Basic Operating Principles

The battery is the first link in the chain of mechanisms which work together to provide cranking of the automobile engine. In most modern cars, the battery is a lead/acid electrochemical device consisting of six 2v subsections connected in series so the unit is capable of producing approximately 12v of electrical pressure. Each subsection, or cell, consists of a series of positive and negative plates held a short distance apart in a solution of sulfuric acid and water. The two types of plates are of dissimilar metals. This causes a chemical reaction to be set up, and it is this reaction which produces current flow from the battery when its positive and negative terminals are connected to an electrical appliance such as a lamp or motor. The continued transfer of electrons would eventually convert the sulfuric acid in the electrolyte to water, and make the two plates identical in chemical composition. As electrical energy is removed from the battery, its voltage output tends to drop. Thus, measuring battery voltage and battery electrolyte composition are two ways of checking the ability of the unit to supply power. During the starting of the engine, electrical energy is removed from the battery. However, if the charging circuit is in good condition and the operating conditions are normal, the power removed from the battery will be replaced by the generator (or alternator) which will force electrons back through the battery, reversing the normal flow, and restoring the battery to its original chemical state.

The battery and starting motor are linked by very heavy electrical cables designed to minimize resistance to the flow of current. Generally, the major power supply cable that leaves the battery goes directly to the starter, while other electrical system needs are supplied by a smaller cable. During starter operation, power flows from the battery to the starter and is grounded through the car's frame and the battery's negative ground strap.

The starting motor is a specially designed, direct current electric motor capable of producing a very great amount of power for its size. One thing that allows the motor to produce a great deal of power is its tremendous rotating speed. It drives the engine through a tiny pinion gear (attached to the starter's armature), which drives the very large flywheel ring gear at a greatly reduced speed. Another factor allowing it to produce so much power is that only intermittent operation is required of it. This, little allowance for air circulation is required, and the windings can be built into a very small space.

The starter solenoid is a magnetic device which employs the small current supplied by the starting switch circuit of the ignition switch. This magnetic action moves a plunger which mechanically engages the starter and electrically closes the heavy switch which connects it to the battery. The starting switch circuit consists of the starting switch contained within the ignition switch, a transmission neutral safety switch or clutch pedal switch, and the wiring necessary to connect these in series with the starter solenoid or relay.

A pinion, which is a small gear, is mounted to a one-way drive clutch. This clutch is splined to the starter armature shaft. When the ignition switch is moved to the **start** position, the solenoid plunger slides the pinion toward the flywheel ring gear via a collar and spring. If the teeth on the pinion and flywheel match properly, the pinion will engage the flywheel immediately. If the gear teeth butt one another, the spring will be compressed and will force the gears to mesh as soon as the starter turns far enough to allow them to do so. As the solenoid plunger reaches the end of its travel, it closes the contacts that connect the battery and starter and then the engine is cranked.

As soon as the engine starts, the flywheel ring gear begins turning fast enough to drive the pinion at an extremely high rate of speed. At this point, the one-way clutch begins allowing the pinion to spin faster than the starter shaft so that the starter will not operate at excessive speed. When the ignition switch is released from the starter position, the solenoid is de-energized, and a spring contained within the solenoid assembly pulls the gear out of mesh and interrupts the current flow to the starter.

Some starter employ a separate relay, mounted away from the starter, to switch the motor and solenoid current on and off. The relay thus replaces the solenoid electrical switch, buy does not eliminate the need for a solenoid mounted on the starter used to mechanically engage the starter drive gears. The relay is used to reduce the amount of current the starting switch must carry.

THE CHARGING SYSTEM

Basic Operating Principles

The automobile charging system provides electrical power for operation of the vehicle's ignition and starting systems and all the electrical accessories. The battery services as an electrical surge or storage tank, storing (in chemical form) the energy originally produced by the engine driven generator. The system also provides a means of regulating generator output to protect the battery from being overcharged and to avoid excessive voltage to the accessories.

The storage battery is a chemical device incorporating parallel lead plates in a tank containing a sulfuric acid/water solution. Adjacent plates are slightly dissimilar, and the chemical reaction of the two dissimilar plates produces electrical energy when the battery is connected to a load such as the starter motor. The chemical reaction is reversible, so that when the generator is producing a voltage (electrical pressure) greater than that produced by the battery, electricity is forced into the battery, and the battery is returned to its fully charged state.

The vehicle's generator is driven mechanically, through V-belts, by the engine crankshaft. It consists of two coils of fine wire, one stationary (the stator), and one movable (the rotor). The rotor may also be known as the armature, and consists of fine wire wrapped around an iron core which is mounted on a shaft. The electricity which flows through the two coils of wire (provided initially by the battery in some cases) creates an intense magnetic field around both rotor and stator, and the interaction between the two fields creates voltage, allowing the generator to power the accessories and charge the battery.

There are two types of generators: the earlier is the direct current (DC) type. The current produced by the DC generator is generated in the armature and carried off the spinning armature by stationary brushes contacting the commutator. The commutator is a series of smooth metal contact plates on the end of the armature. The commutator is a series of smooth metal contact plates on the end of the armature. The commutator plates, which are separated from one another by a very short gap, are connected to the armature circuits so that current will flow in one directions only in the wires carrying the generator output. The generator stator consists of two stationary coils of wire which draw some of the output current of the generator to form a powerful magnetic field and create the interaction of fields which generates the voltage. The generator field is wired in series with the regulator.

Newer automobiles use alternating current generators or alternators, because they are more efficient, can be rotated at higher speeds, and have fewer brush problems. In an alternator, the field rotates while all the current produced passes only through the stator winding. The brushes bear against continuous slip rings rather than a commutator. This causes the current produced to periodically reverse the direction of its flow. Diodes (electrical one-way switches) block the flow of current from traveling in the wrong direction. A series of diodes is wired together to permit the alternating flow of the stator to be converted to a pulsating, but unidirectional flow at the alternator output. The alternator's field is wired in series with the voltage regulator.

The regulator consists of several circuits. Each circuit has a core, or magnetic coil of wire, which operates a switch. Each switch is connected to ground through one or more resistors. The coil of wire responds directly to system voltage. When the voltage reaches the required level, the magnetic field created by the winding of wire closes the switch and inserts a resistance into the generator field circuit, thus reducing the output. The contacts of the switch cycle open and close many times each second to precisely control voltage.

While alternators are self-limiting as far as maximum current is concerned, DC generators employ a current regulating circuit which responds directly to the total amount of current flowing through the generator circuit rather than to the output voltage. The current regulator is similar to the voltage regulator except that all system current must flow through the energizing coil on its way to the various accessories.

Distributor

REMOVAL & INSTALLATION

◢ **See Figures 1, 2, 3, 4, 5, 6, 7, 8, 9 and 10**

Although the distributor can be removed from the engine no matter which cylinder is about to fire, it is a good idea to have number one cylinder at TDC before distributor removal.

1.5L, 1.8L, 2.4L SOHC Engines

1. Disconnect the negative battery cable.
2. Disconnect and tag the spark plug wires from the distributor cap.
3. Disconnect the distributor harness connector.
4. Loosen the distributor retaining bolt and remove the distributor from the engine.

To install:

5. Rotate the engine until No. 1 cylinder is at TDC on its compression stroke.

➡**Be careful not to turn it to the No. 4 cylinder TDC on its compression stroke by mistake.**

6. Align the distributor housing and gear mating marks.
7. Install the distributor into the engine, while aligning the fine cut (groove or projection) on the distributor flange with the center of the distributor mounting stud.
8. Install and tighten the distributor retaining bolt.
9. Reconnect the distributor harness connector.
10. Install the distributor cap and spark plug wires.
11. Reconnect the negative battery cable.

Crank Angle Sensor

REMOVAL & INSTALLATION

◢ **See Figure 11**

1.6L Engines

1. Disconnect the negative battery cable.
2. Disconnect the crank angle sensor harness connector.
3. Remove the sensor retaining nut and remove the crank angle sensor.
4. Rotate the engine until No. 1 cylinder is at TDC on its compression stroke.
5. Align the punch mark on the crank angle sensor housing with the notch in plate or coupling.
6. Install the crank angle sensor.
7. Reconnect the crank angle sensor harness connector.
8. Reconnect the negative battery cable.

Alternator

The alternator charging system is a negative (-) ground system which consists of an alternator, a regulator, a charge indicator, a storage battery and wiring connecting the components, and fuse link wire.

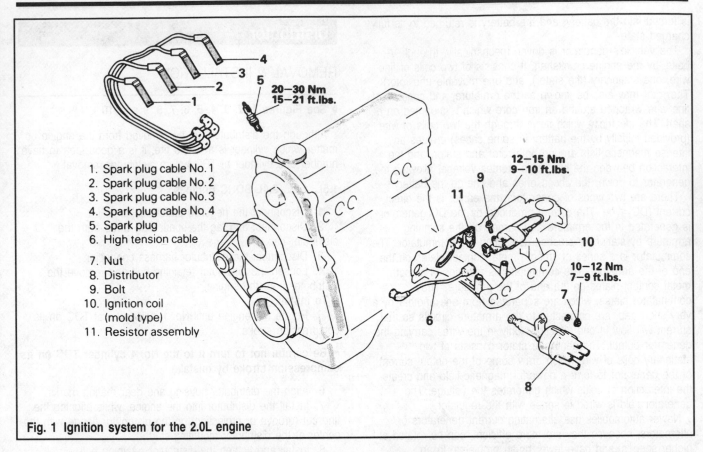

1. Spark plug cable No. 1
2. Spark plug cable No. 2
3. Spark plug cable No. 3
4. Spark plug cable No. 4
5. Spark plug
6. High tension cable

7. Nut
8. Distributor
9. Bolt
10. Ignition coil (mold type)
11. Resistor assembly

20–30 Nm
15–21 ft.lbs.

12–15 Nm
9–10 ft.lbs.

10–12 Nm
7–9 ft.lbs.

Fig. 1 Ignition system for the 2.0L engine

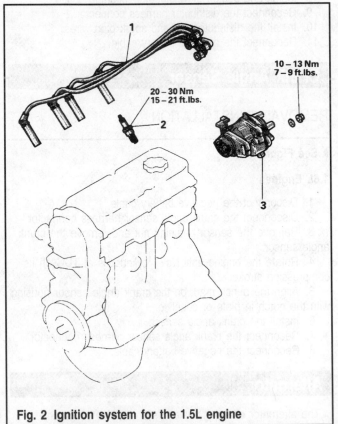

10 – 13 Nm
7–9 ft.lbs.

20 – 30 Nm
15 – 21 ft.lbs.

Fig. 2 Ignition system for the 1.5L engine

The alternator is belt-driven from the engine. Energy is supplied from the alternator/regulator system to the rotating field through two brushes to two slip-rings. The slip-rings are mounted on the rotor shaft and are connected to the field coil. This energy supplied to the rotating field from the battery is called excitation current and is used to initially energize the field to begin the generation of electricity. Once the alternator starts to generate electricity, the excitation current comes from its own output rather than the battery.

The alternator produces power in the form of alternating current. The alternating current is rectified by 6 diodes into direct current. The direct current is used to charge the battery and power the rest of the electrical system.

When the ignition key is turned on, current flows from the battery, through the charging system indicator light on the instrument panel, to the voltage regulator, and to the alternator. Since the alternator is not producing any current, the alternator warning light comes on. When the engine is started, the alternator begins to produce current and turns the alternator light off. As the alternator turns and produces current, the current is divided in two ways: part to the battery to charge the battery and power the electrical components of the vehicle, and part is returned to the alternator to enable it to increase its output. In this situation, the alternator is receiving current from the battery and from itself. A voltage regulator is wired into the current supply to the alternator to prevent it from receiving too much current which would cause it to put out too much current. Conversely, if the voltage regulator does not allow the alternator to receive enough current, the battery will not be fully charged and will eventually go dead.

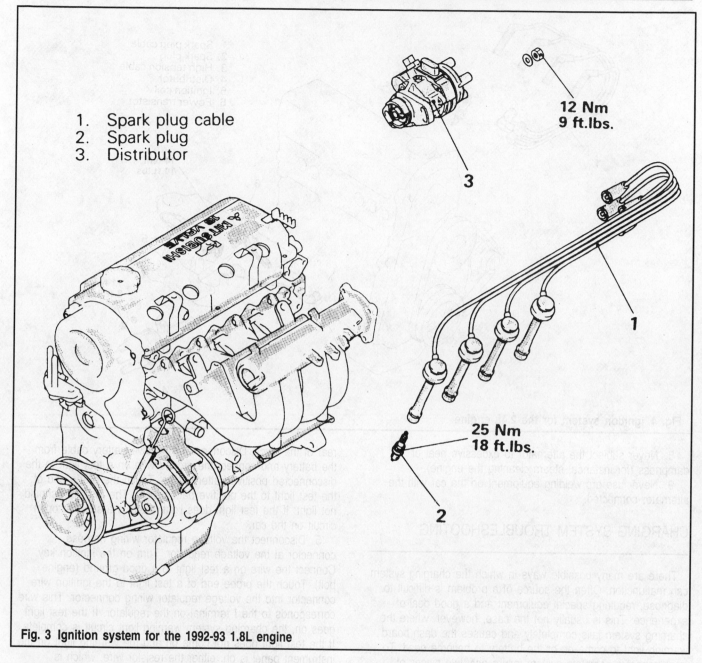

1. Spark plug cable
2. Spark plug
3. Distributor

**12 Nm
9 ft.lbs.**

**25 Nm
18 ft.lbs.**

Fig. 3 Ignition system for the 1992-93 1.8L engine

The battery is connected to the alternator at all times, whether the ignition key is turned on or not. If the battery were shorted to ground, the alternator would also be shorted. This would damage the alternator. To prevent this, a fuse link is installed in the wiring between the battery and the alternator. If the battery is shorted, the fuse link is melted, protecting the alternator.

PRECAUTIONS

Your car is equipped with an alternator. Unlike the direct current (DC) generators used on many old cars, there are several precautions which must be strictly observed in order to avoid damaging the unit. They are:

1. Always observe proper polarity of the battery connections: be especially careful when jump starting the car. (See chapter one for jump starting procedures).

2. Never ground or short out the alternator or alternator regulator terminals.

3. Never operate the alternator with any of its or the battery's lead wires disconnected.

4. Always remove the battery or at least disconnect the ground cable while charging.

5. Always disconnect the battery ground cable while repairing or replacing an electrical component.

6. Never use a fast battery charger to jump start a dead battery.

7. Never attempt to polarize an alternator.

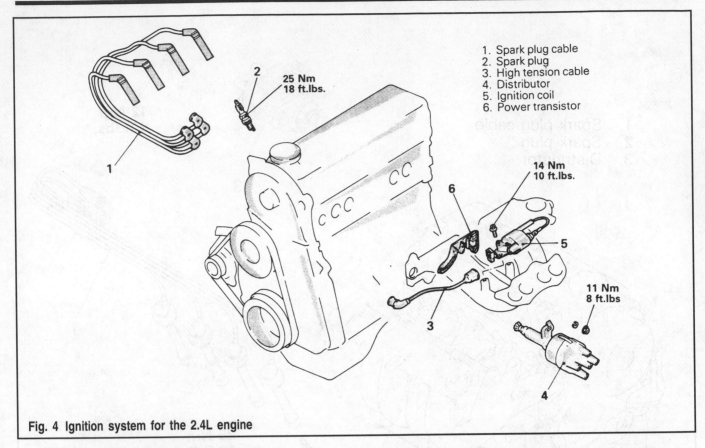

1. Spark plug cable
2. Spark plug
3. High tension cable
4. Distributor
5. Ignition coil
6. Power transistor

2 — 25 Nm 18 ft.lbs.

6 — 14 Nm 10 ft.lbs.

11 Nm 8 ft.lbs

Fig. 4 Ignition system for the 2.4L engine

8. Never subject the alternator to excessive heat or dampness (for instance, steam cleaning the engine).

9. Never use arc welding equipment on the car with the alternator connected.

CHARGING SYSTEM TROUBLESHOOTING

There are many possible ways in which the charging system can malfunction. Often the source of a problem is difficult to diagnose, requiring special equipment and a good deal of experience. This is usually not the case, however, where the charging system fails completely and causes the dash board warning light to come on or the battery to become dead. To troubleshoot a complete system failure only two pieces of equipment are needed: a test light, to determine that current is reaching a certain point; and a current indicator (ammeter), to determine the direction of the current flow and its measurement in amps.

This test works under three assumptions:

1. The battery is known to be good and fully charged.
2. The alternator belt is in good condition and adjusted to the proper tension.
3. All connections in the system are clean and tight.

➡**In order for the current indicator to give a valid reading, the car must be equipped with battery cables which are of the same gauge size and quality as original equipment battery cables.**

4. Turn off all electrical components on the car. Make sure the doors of the car are closed. If the car is equipped with a clock, disconnect the clock by removing the lead wire from the rear of the clock. Disconnect the positive battery cable from the battery and connect the ground wire on a test light to the disconnected positive battery cable. Touch the probe end of the test light to the positive battery post. The test light should not light. If the test light does light, there is a short or open circuit on the car.

5. Disconnect the voltage regulator wiring harness connector at the voltage regulator. Turn on the ignition key. Connect the wire on a test light to a good ground (engine bolt). Touch the probe end of a test light to the ignition wire connector into the voltage regulator wiring connector. This wire corresponds to the I terminal on the regulator. If the test light goes on, the charging system warning light circuit is complete. If the test light does not come on and the warning light on the instrument panel is on, either the resistor wire, which is parallel with the warning light, or the wiring to the voltage regulator, is defective. If the test light does not come on and the warning light is not on, either the bulb is defective or the power supply wire form the battery through the ignition switch to the bulb has an open circuit. Connect the wiring harness to the regulator.

6. Examine the fuse link wire in the wiring harness from the starter relay to the alternator. If the insulation on the wire is cracked or split, the fuse link may be melted. Connect a test light to the fuse link by attaching the ground wire on the test light to an engine bolt and touching the probe end of the light to the bottom of the fuse link wire where it splices into the alternator output wire. If the bulb in the test light does not light, the fuse link is melted.

7. Start the engine and place a current indicator on the positive battery cable. Turn off all electrical accessories and make sure the doors are closed. If the charging system is

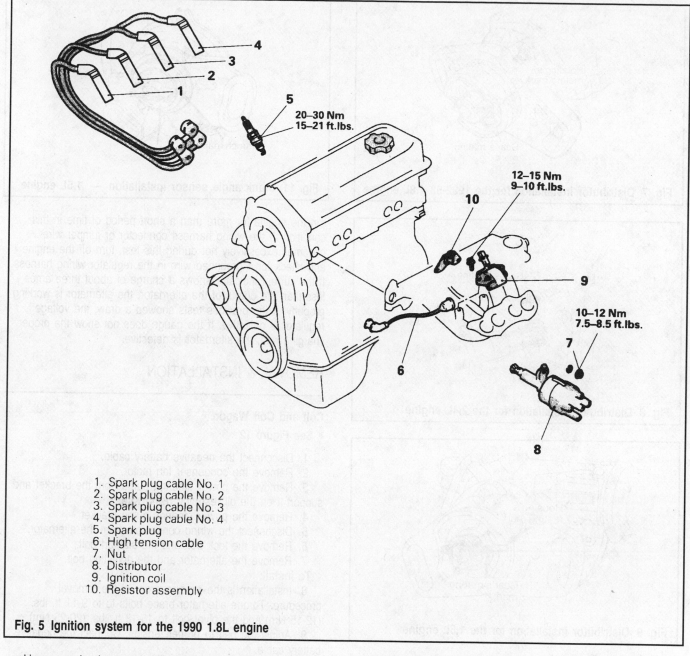

1. Spark plug cable No. 1
2. Spark plug cable No. 2
3. Spark plug cable No. 3
4. Spark plug cable No. 4
5. Spark plug
6. High tension cable
7. Nut
8. Distributor
9. Ignition coil
10. Resistor assembly

Fig. 5 Ignition system for the 1990 1.8L engine

working properly, the gauge will show a draw of less than 5 amps. If the system is not working properly, the gauge will

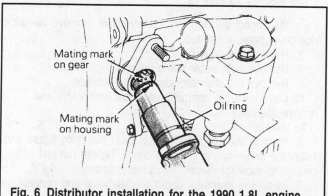

Fig. 6 Distributor installation for the 1990 1.8L engine

show a draw of more than 5 amps. A charge moves the needle toward the battery, a draw moves the needle away from the battery. Turn the engine off.

8. Disconnect the wiring harness from the voltage regulator at the regulator at the regulator connector. Connect a male spade terminal (solderless connector) to each end of a jumper wire. Insert one end of the wire into the wiring harness connector which corresponds to the **A** terminal on the regulator. Insert the other end of the wire into the wiring harness connector which corresponds to the **F** terminal on the regulator. Position the connector with the jumper wire installed so that it cannot contact any metal surface under the hood. Position a current indicator gauge on the positive battery cable. Have an assistant start the engine. Observe the reading on the current indicator. Have your assistant slowly raise the speed of the engine to about 2,000 rpm or until the current indicator needle stops moving, whichever comes first. Do not

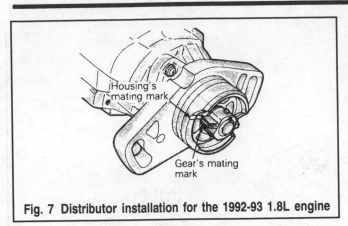

Fig. 7 Distributor installation for the 1992-93 1.8L engine

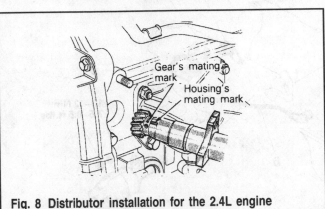

Fig. 8 Distributor installation for the 2.4L engine

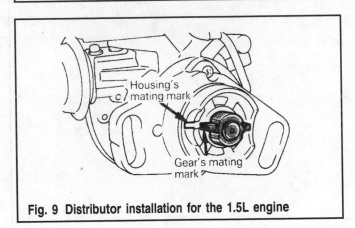

Fig. 9 Distributor installation for the 1.5L engine

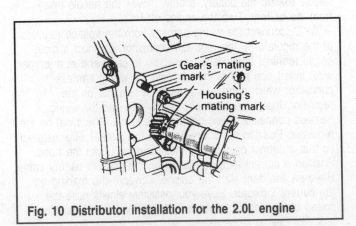

Fig. 10 Distributor installation for the 2.0L engine

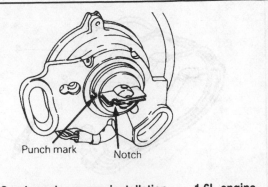

Fig. 11 Crank angle sensor installation — 1.6L engine

run the engine for more than a short period of time in this condition. If the wiring harness connector or jumper wire becomes excessively hot during this test, turn off the engine and check for a grounded wire in the regulator wiring harness. If the current indicator shows a charge of about three amps less than the output of the alternator, the alternator is working properly. If the previous tests showed a draw, the voltage regulator is defective. If the gauge does not show the proper charging rate, the alternator is defective.

REMOVAL & INSTALLATION

Colt and Colt Wagon

▶ See Figure 12

1. Disconnect the negative battery cable.
2. Remove the condenser fan motor.
3. Remove the power steering pump from the bracket and support it on the oil reservoir using wire.
4. Remove the power steering pump bracket.
5. Disconnect the wiring connectors from the alternator.
6. Remove the lock bolt and the support bolt.
7. Remove the alternator and the adjusting bolt.

To install:

8. Installation is the reverse order of the removal procedure. Torque alternator brace bolts to to 9-11 ft. lbs. (12-15 Nm) and the pivot bolt to 15-18 ft. lbs. (20-25 Nm).

9. Adjust the belt to proper tension. Connect the negative battery cable.

Vista

▶ See Figures 13 and 14

1. Disconnect the negative battery cable. Remove the left side cover panel if needed.
2. Remove the drive belts.
3. Remove both water pump pulleys.
4. Remove the alternator upper bracket/brace.
5. Disconnect the alternator electrical connectors and remove alternator.

To install:

6. Position the alternator on the lower mounting fixture and install the lower mounting bolt and nut. Tighten nut just enough to allow for movement of the alternator.

7. Install the alternator upper bracket/brace and connect the alternator electrical harness.

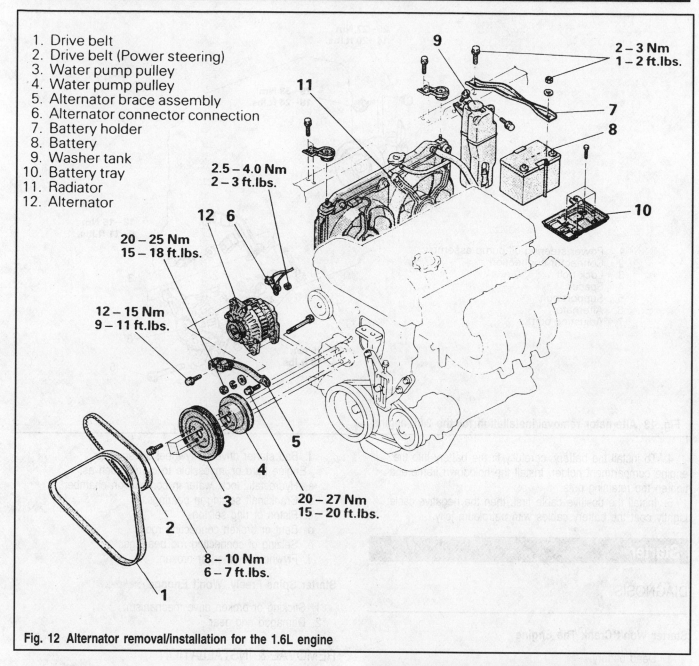

1. Drive belt
2. Drive belt (Power steering)
3. Water pump pulley
4. Water pump pulley
5. Alternator brace assembly
6. Alternator connector connection
7. Battery holder
8. Battery
9. Washer tank
10. Battery tray
11. Radiator
12. Alternator

2.5 – 4.0 Nm
2 – 3 ft.lbs.

20 – 25 Nm
15 – 18 ft.lbs.

12 – 15 Nm
9 – 11 ft.lbs.

2 – 3 Nm
1 – 2 ft.lbs.

20 – 27 Nm
15 – 20 ft.lbs.

8 – 10 Nm
6 – 7 ft.lbs.

Fig. 12 Alternator removal/installation for the 1.6L engine

8. Install the water pump pulleys.
9. Install the drive belts and adjust to the proper tension.
10. Install the left side cover panel under the vehicle as required.
11. Connect the negative battery cable and check for proper operation.

Regulator

A transistorized (electronic) voltage regulator is either built into the alternator, or mounted on top.

Battery

REMOVAL & INSTALLATION

1. Loosen the battery cable clamping nuts, negative (ground) cable first. Spread the battery cable terminals (or use a cable terminal puller). Remove the negative cable and then the positive cable.
2. Remove the battery holddown frame nuts and the frame.
3. Put on work gloves or use a battery carrier and lift the battery from the engine compartment. Be careful not to tip the battery and spill acid on yourself or the car during removal. Automotive batteries contain a sulfuric acid electrolyte which is harmful to skin, clothing and paint finishes.

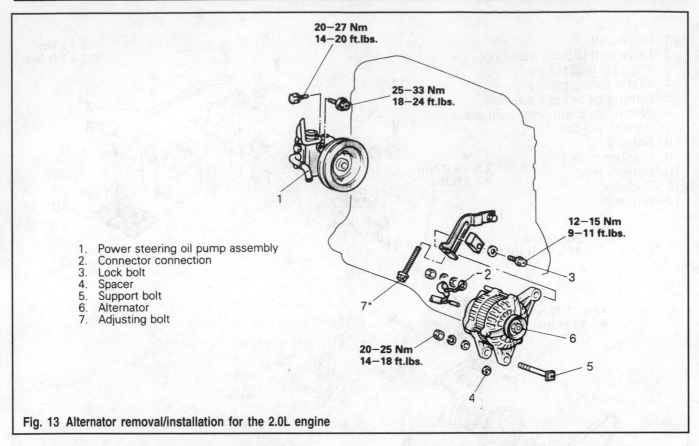

1. Power steering oil pump assembly
2. Connector connection
3. Lock bolt
4. Spacer
5. Support bolt
6. Alternator
7. Adjusting bolt

20—27 Nm
14—20 ft.lbs.

25—33 Nm
18—24 ft.lbs.

12—15 Nm
9—11 ft.lbs.

20—25 Nm
14—18 ft.lbs.

Fig. 13 Alternator removal/installation for the 2.0L engine

4. To install the battery: carefully fit the battery into the engine compartment holder. Install the holddown frame and tighten the retaining nuts.

5. Install the positive cable first, then the negative cable. Lightly coat the battery cables with petroleum jelly.

Starter

DIAGNOSIS

Starter Won't Crank The Engine

1. Dead battery.
2. Open starter circuit, such as:
   a. Broken or loose battery cables.
   b. Inoperative starter motor solenoid.
   c. Broken or loose wire from ignition switch to solenoid.
   d. Poor solenoid or starter ground.
   e. Bad ignition switch.
3. Defective starter internal circuit, such as:
   a. Dirty or burnt commutator.
   b. Stuck, worn or broken brushes.
   c. Open or shorted armature.
   d. Open or grounded fields.
4. Starter motor mechanical faults, such as:
   a. Jammed armature end bearings.
   b. Bad bearings, allowing armature to rub fields.
   c. Bent shaft.
   d. Broken starter housing.
   e. Bad starter drive mechanism.

   f. Bad starter drive or flywheel driven gear.
5. Engine hard or impossible to crank, such as:
   a. Hydrostatic lock, water in combustion chamber.
   b. Crankshaft seizing in bearings.
   c. Piston or ring seizing.
   d. Bent or broken connecting rod.
   e. Seizing of connecting rod bearings.
   f. Flywheel jammed or broken.

Starter Spins Freely, Won't Engage

1. Sticking or broken drive mechanism.
2. Damaged ring gear.

REMOVAL & INSTALLATION

▶ **See Figure 15**

1. Disconnect the battery negative battery cable and the starter motor wiring. Remove the air cleaner assembly.
2. Raise and support the vehicle safely.
3. Remove the intake manifold-to-engine support bracket (Colt and Colt Wagon).
4. Remove the 2 starter attaching bolts and remove the starter motor.
   To install:
5. Clean both surfaces of the starter motor flange and the rear plate.
6. Position the starter in the housing opening.
7. Install the manifold-to-engine support bracket (Colt and Colt Wagon).

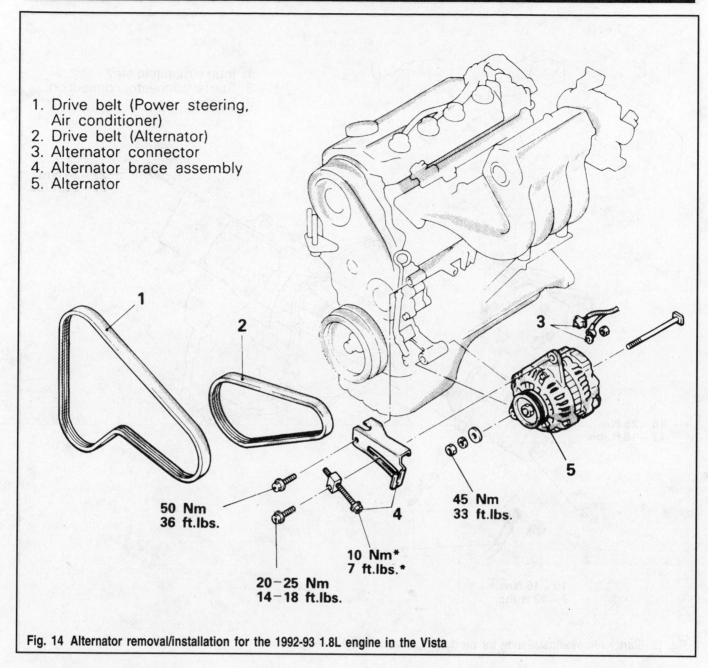

1. Drive belt (Power steering, Air conditioner)
2. Drive belt (Alternator)
3. Alternator connector
4. Alternator brace assembly
5. Alternator

50 Nm
36 ft.lbs.

20−25 Nm
14−18 ft.lbs.

10 Nm*
7 ft.lbs.*

45 Nm
33 ft.lbs.

Fig. 14 Alternator removal/installation for the 1992-93 1.8L engine in the Vista

8. Install the attaching bolts. Torque to 25 ft. lbs. (34 Nm) evenly to avoid binding.
9. Install the starter wiring and lower the vehicle.
10. Connect the negative battery cable and check operation.

SOLENOID REPLACEMENT

1. Disconnect the negative battery cable.
2. Remove the starter motor.

3. Disconnect the field coil wire from the terminal connector on the solenoid.
4. Remove the mounting crews and the solenoid from the starter motor.
5. Place the solenoid over the spring and into position on the starter motor. Secure the solenoid with the mounting screws. Connect the field coil wire to the solenoid terminal.
6. Install the starter motor and connect the negative battery cable.

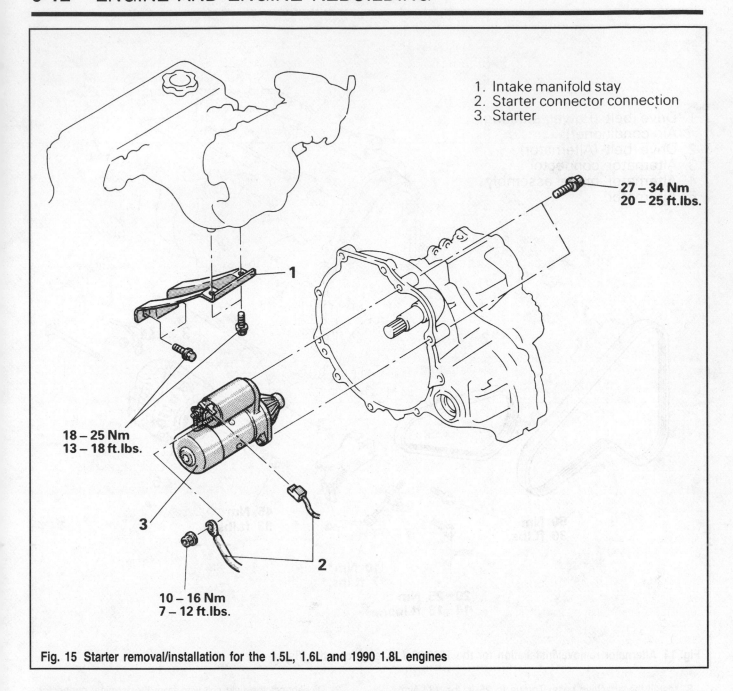

1. Intake manifold stay
2. Starter connector connection
3. Starter

27 – 34 Nm
20 – 25 ft.lbs.

18 – 25 Nm
13 – 18 ft.lbs.

10 – 16 Nm
7 – 12 ft.lbs.

Fig. 15 Starter removal/installation for the 1.5L, 1.6L and 1990 1.8L engines

ENGINE MECHANICAL

Engine Overhaul Tips

Most engine overhaul procedures are fairly standard. In addition to specific parts replacement procedures and complete specifications for your individual engine, this chapter also is a guide to accepted rebuilding procedures. Examples of standard rebuilding practice are shown and should be used along with specific details concerning your particular engine.

Competent and accurate machine shop services will ensure maximum performance, reliability and engine life. In most instances it is more profitable for the do-it-yourself mechanic to

remove, clean and inspect the component, buy the necessary parts and deliver these to a shop for actual machine work.

On the other hand, much of the rebuilding work (crankshaft, block, bearings, piston, rods, and other components) is still within the scope of the do-it-yourself mechanic.

TOOLS

The tools required for an engine overhaul or parts replacement will depend on the depth of your involvement. With a few exceptions, they will be the tools found in a mechanic's tool kit (see Chapter 1). More in-depth work will require any or all of the following: A dial indicator (reading in thousandths) mounted on a universal base. Micrometers and telescope gauges. Jaw and screw-type pullers. A scraper. A valve spring compressor. A ring groove cleaner. A piston ring expander and compressor. A ridge reamer. Cylinder hone or glaze breaker. Plastigage. An engine stand. Use of most of these tools is illustrated in this chapter. Many can be rented for a one-time use from a local parts jobber or tool supply house specializing in automotive work.

Occasionally, the use of special tools is called for. See the information on Special Tools and the Safety Notice in the front of this book before substituting another tool.

INSPECTION TECHNIQUES

Procedures and specifications are given in this chapter for inspecting, cleaning and assessing the wear limits of most major components. Other procedures such as Magnaflux® and Zyglo® can be used to locate material flaws and stress cracks. Magnaflux® a magnetic process applicable only to ferrous materials. The Zyglo® process coats the material with a fluorescent dye penetrant and can be used on any material. Check for suspected surface cracks can be more readily made using spot check dye. The dye is sprayed onto the suspected area, wiped off and area sprayed with a developer. Cracks will show up brightly.

Aluminum Engine Components

Aluminum has become extremely popular for use in engines, due to its low weight. Observe the following precautions when handling aluminum parts:

Never hot tank aluminum parts (the caustic hot-tank solution will eat the aluminum).

Remove all aluminum parts (identification tag, etc) from engine parts prior to hot-tanking.

Always coat threads lightly with engine oil or anti-seize compounds before installation, to prevent seizure.

Never over-torque bolts or spark plugs, especially in aluminum threads. Stripped threads in any component can be repaired using any of several commercial repair kits (Heli-Coil®, Microdot®, Keenserts®, etc)

When assembling the engine, any parts that will be in frictional contact must be prelubed to provide lubrication at initial start-up. Any product specifically formulated for this

purpose can be used, but engine oil is not recommended as a pre-lube.

When semi-permanent (locked, but removable) installation of bolts or nuts is desired, threads should be cleaned and coated with Loctite® or other similar, commercial non-hardening sealant.

Repairing Damaged Threads
▶ See Figures 16, 17, 18, 19 and 20

Several methods of repairing damaged threads are available. Heli-Coil® (shown here), Keenserts® and Microdot® are among the most widely used. All involve basically the same principle — drilling out stripped threads, tapping the hole and

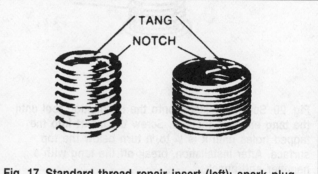

Fig. 17 Standard thread repair insert (left); spark plug hole thread repair insert (right)

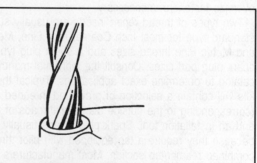

Fig. 18 Drill out the damaged threads with the specified drill bit. Drill completely through the hole or to the bottom of a blind hole

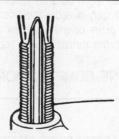

Fig. 19 With the tap supplied, tap the hole to receive the thread insert. Keep the tap well oiled and back it out frequently to avoid clogging the threads

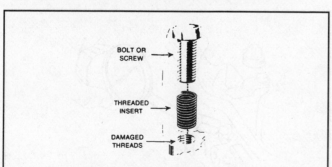

Fig. 16 Damaged bolt holes can be repaired with thread repair inserts

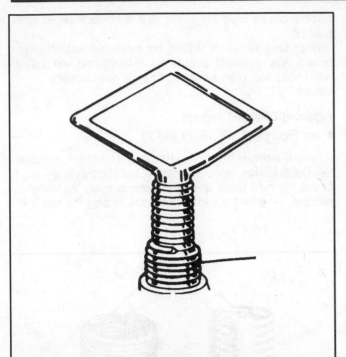

Fig. 20 Screw the insert onto the installation tool until the tang engages the slot. Screw the insert into the tapped holes until it is ¼ to ½ turn below the top surface. After installation, break off the tang with a hammer and punch

installing prewound insert — making welding, plugging and oversize fasteners unnecessary.

Two types of thread repair inserts are usually supplied: a standard type for most Inch Coarse, Inch Fine, Metric Coarse and Metric Fine thread sizes and a spark plug type to fit most spark plug port sizes. Consult the individual manufacturer's catalog to determine exact applications. Typical thread repair kits will contain a selection of prewound threaded inserts a tap (corresponding to the outside diameter threads of the insert) and an installation tool. Spark plug inserts usually differ because they require a tap equipped with pilot threads and combined reamer/tap section. Most manufacturers also supply blister-packed thread repair inserts separately in addition to a master kit containing a variety of taps and inserts plus installation tools.

Before effecting a repair to a threaded hole, remove any snapped, broken or damaged bolts or studs. Penetrating oil can be used to free frozen threads: the offending item can be removed with locking pliers or with a screw or stud extractor. After the hole is clear, the thread can be repaired, as follows:

CHECKING ENGINE COMPRESSION

▶ See Figure 21

A noticeable lack of engine power, excessive oil consumption and/or poor fuel mileage measured over an extended period are all indicators of internal engine wear. Worn piston rings, scored or worn cylinder bores, blown head gaskets, sticking or burnt valves and worn valve seats are all

possible culprits. here. A check of each cylinder's compression will help you locate the problems.

As mentioned in the Tools and equipment section of Chapter 1, a screw-in type compression gauge is more accurate than the type you simply hold against the spark plug hole, although it takes slightly longer to use. It's worth it to obtain a more accurate reading. Follow the procedures below.

1. Warm up the engine to normal operating temperature.
2. Remove all spark plugs.
3. Disconnect the high tension lead from the ignition coil.
4. Disconnect the cold start valve and all injector connections.
5. Screw the compression gauge into the No. 1 spark plug hold until the fitting is snug.

➡**Be careful not to crossthread the plug hold. On aluminum cylinder heads use extra care, as the threads in these heads are easily ruined.**

6. Ask an assistant to depress the accelerator pedal fully. Then, while you read the compression gauge, ask the assistant to crank the engine two or three times in short bursts using the ignition switch.
7. Read the compression gauge at the end of each series of cranks, and record the highest of these readings. Repeat this procedure for each of the engine's cylinders. Compare the highest reading of each cylinder to the compression pressure specifications in the Tune-Up Specifications chart in Chapter 2. The specs in this chart are maximum values.
8. A cylinder's compression pressure is usually acceptable if it is not less than 80% of maximum. The difference between each cylinder should be no more than 12-14 pounds.
9. If a cylinder is unusually low, pour a tablespoon of clean engine oil into the cylinder through the spark plug hold and repeat the compression test. If the compression comes up after adding the oil, it appears that that cylinder's piston rings or bore are damaged or worn. If the pressure remains low, the valves may not be seating properly (a valve job is needed), or the head gasket may be blown near that cylinder. If compression in any two adjacent cylinders is low, and if the addition of oil doesn't help the compression, there is leakage past the head gasket. Oil and coolant water in the combustion chamber can result from this problem. There may be evidence of water droplets on the engine dipstick when a head gasket has blown.

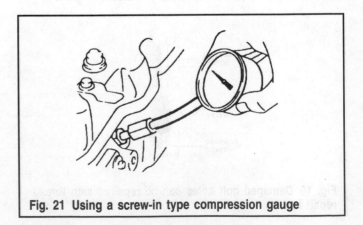

Fig. 21 Using a screw-in type compression gauge

GENERAL ENGINE SPECIFICATIONS

Year	Engine ID/VIN	Engine Displacement Liters (cc)	Fuel System Type	Net Horsepower @ rpm	Net Torque @ rpm (ft. lbs.)	Bore × Stroke (in.)	Compression Ratio	Oil Pressure @ 650 rpm
1990	X	1.5 (1468)	MPI	68 @ 5000	126 @ 3000	2.972 × 3.228	9.4:1	11.4
	Y	1.6 (1597)	MPI	92 @ 6500	134 @ 5000	3.240 × 2.950	9.2:1	11.4
	T	1.8 (1755)	MPI	65 @ 5000	138 @ 3000	3.173 × 3.386	9.0:1	11.4
	V	2.0 (1997)	MPI	72 @ 5000	153 @ 3500	3.350 × 3.460	8.5:1	11.4
1991	A	1.5 (1468)	MPI	92 @ 6000	93 @ 3000	2.972 × 3.228	9.2:1	11.4
	V	2.0 (1997)	MPI	96 @ 5000	115 @ 3000	3.350 × 3.460	8.5:1	11.4
1992	A	1.5 (1468)	MPI	92 @ 6000	93 @ 3000	2.972 × 3.228	9.2:1	11.4
	D	1.8 (1834)	MPI	113 @ 6000	116 @ 4500	3.189 × 3.504	8.5:1	11.4
	W	2.4 (2350)	MPI	116 @ 5000	134 @ 3500	3.406 × 3.937	8.5:1	11.4
1993	A	1.5 (1468)	MPI	92 @ 6000	93 @ 3000	2.972 × 3.228	9.2:1	11.4
	C	1.8 (1834)	MPI	113 @ 6000	116 @ 4500	3.189 × 3.504	9.5:1	11.4
	G	2.4 (2350)	MPI	116 @ 5000	134 @ 3500	3.406 × 3.937	9.5:1	11.4

MPI—Multi-Point Fuel Injection

VALVE SPECIFICATIONS

Year	Engine ID/VIN	Engine Displacement Liters (cc)	Seat Angle (deg.)	Face Angle (deg.)	Spring Test Pressure (lbs. to open)	Spring Installed Height (in.)	Stem-to-Guide Clearance (in.) Intake	Stem-to-Guide Clearance (in.) Exhaust	Stem Diameter (in.) Intake	Stem Diameter (in.) Exhaust
1990	X	1.5 (1468)	44	45	53	—	0.0008–0.0020	0.0020–0.0035	0.2598	0.2598
	Y	1.6 (1597)	44	45	66	—	0.0008–0.0019	0.0020–0.0033	0.2585–0.2591	0.2571–0.2579
	T	1.8 (1755)	45	45	65	—	0.0012–0.0024	0.0020–0.0035	0.3150	0.3150
	V	2.0 (1997)	45	45	73	—	0.0012–0.0024	0.0020–0.0035	0.3150	0.3150
1991	A	1.5 (1468)	44	45	①	—	0.0008–0.0020	0.0020–0.0035	0.2585–0.2591	0.2571–0.2579
	V	2.0 (1997)	45	45	73	—	0.0012–0.0024	0.0020–0.0035	0.3150	0.3150
1992	A	1.5 (1468)	44	45	①	—	0.0008–0.0020	0.0020–0.0035	0.2585–0.2591	0.2571–0.2579
	D	1.8 (1834)	44	45	132	—	0.0008–0.0020	0.0020–0.0035	0.2350–0.2354	0.2343–0.2350
	W	2.4 (2350)	44	45	73	—	0.0012–0.0024	0.0020–0.0035	0.3150	0.3150
1993	A	1.5 (1468)	44	45	①	—	0.0008–0.0020	0.0020–0.0035	0.2585–0.2591	0.2571–0.2579
	C	1.8 (1834)	44	45	132	—	0.0008–0.0016	0.0012–0.0024	0.2350–0.2354	0.2343–0.2350
	G	2.4 (2350)	44	45	60	—	0.0008–0.0020	0.0012–0.0028	0.2350–0.2354	0.2343–0.2350

① Int.: 51
Exh.: 64

CAMSHAFT SPECIFICATIONS

All measurements given in inches.

Year	Engine ID/VIN	Engine Displacement Liters (cc)	Journal Diameter 1	2	3	4	5	Cam Height In.	Ex.	Bearing Clearance	Camshaft End Play
1990	X	1.5 (1468)	1.8110	1.8110	1.8110	1.8110	—	1.5318	1.5344	0.0020–0.0079	0
	Y	1.6 (1597)	1.0236	1.0236	1.0236	1.0236	—	1.3858	1.3743	0.0020–0.0035	0
	T	1.8 (1755)	1.3363	1.3363	1.3363	1.3363	—	1.4138	1.4138	0.0020–0.0035	0
	V	2.0 (1997)	1.3386	1.3386	1.3386	1.3386	—	1.6567	1.6567	0.0020–0.0035	0
1991	A	1.5 (1468)	1.8110	1.8110	1.8110	1.8110	—	1.5256	1.5394	0.0024–0.0039	0
	V	2.0 (1997)	1.3386	1.3386	1.3386	1.3386	—	1.6567	1.6567	0.0020–0.0035	0
1992	A	1.5 (1468)	1.8110	1.8110	1.8110	1.8110	—	1.5256	1.5394	0.0024–0.0039	0
	D	1.8 (1834)	1.7691	1.7691	1.7691	1.7691	—	1.4876	1.4996	0.0020–0.0035	0
	W	2.4 (2350)	1.3364	1.3364	1.3364	1.3364	—	1.7531	1.7531	0.0020–0.0035	0
1993	A	1.5 (1468)	1.8110	1.8110	1.8110	1.8110	—	1.5268	1.5394	0.0024–0.0039	0
	C	1.8 (1834)	1.7691	1.7691	1.7691	1.7691	—	1.4876	1.4996	0.0020–0.0035	0
	G	2.4 (2350)	1.7691	1.7691	1.7691	1.7691	—	1.4720	1.4752	0.0020–0.0035	0

CRANKSHAFT AND CONNECTING ROD SPECIFICATIONS

All measurements are given in inches.

Year	Engine ID/VIN	Engine Displacement Liters (cc)	Crankshaft Main Brg. Journal Dia.	Main Brg. Oil Clearance	Shaft End-play	Thrust on No.	Connecting Rod Journal Diameter	Oil Clearance	Side Clearance
1990	X	1.5 (1468)	1.8900	0.0008–0.0018	0.002–0.007	3	1.6500	0.0006–0.0017	0.0039–0.0098
	Y	1.6 (1597)	2.2400	0.0008–0.0020	0.002–0.007	3	1.7700	0.0008–0.0020	0.0039–0.0098
	T	1.8 (1755)	2.2400	0.0008–0.0019	0.002–0.007	3	1.7700	0.0008–0.0020	0.0039–0.0098
	V	2.0 (1997)	2.2400	0.0008–0.0020	0.002–0.007	3	1.7700	0.0006–0.0020	0.0039–0.0098
1991	A	1.5 (1468)	1.8900	0.0008–0.0028	0.002–0.007	3	1.6500	0.0008–0.0024	0.0039–0.0098
	V	2.0 (1997)	2.2400	0.0008–0.0020	0.002–0.007	3	1.7700	0.0006–0.0020	0.0039–0.0098
1992	A	1.5 (1468)	1.8900	0.0008–0.0028	0.002–0.007	3	1.6500	0.0008–0.0024	0.0039–0.0098
	D	1.8 (1834)	1.9681	0.0008–0.0016	0.002–0.007	3	1.7712	0.0008–0.0020	0.0039–0.0098
	W	2.4 (2350)	2.2437	0.0008–0.0020	0.002–0.007	3	1.7712	0.0008–0.0020	0.0039–0.0098
1993	A	1.5 (1468)	1.8900	0.0008–0.0020	0.002–0.007	3	1.6500	0.0008–0.0020	0.0039–0.0098
	C	1.8 (1834)	1.9681	0.0008–0.0016	0.002–0.010	3	1.7712	0.0008–0.0020	0.0039–0.0098
	G	2.4 (2350)	2.2437	0.0008–0.0020	0.002–0.007	3	1.7712	0.0008–0.0020	0.0039–0.0098

PISTON AND RING SPECIFICATIONS
All measurements are given in inches.

Year	Engine ID/VIN	Engine Displacement Liters (cc)	Piston Clearance	Ring Gap			Ring Side Clearance		
				Top Compression	Bottom Compression	Oil Control	Top Compression	Bottom Compression	Oil Control
1990	X	1.5 (1468)	0.0008–0.0016	0.0079–0.0138	0.0079–0.0138	0.0079–0.0276	0.0012–0.0028	0.0008–0.0024	Snug
	Y	1.6 (1597)	0.0008–0.0016	0.0098–0.0157	0.0138–0.0197	0.0079–0.0276	0.0012–0.0028	0.0012–0.0028	Snug
	T	1.8 (1755)	0.0008–0.0016	0.0118–0.0177	0.0079–0.0138	0.0079–0.0276	0.0018–0.0033	0.0008–0.0024	Snug
	V	2.0 (1997)	0.0004–0.0012	0.0098–0.0157	0.0079–0.0138	0.0079–0.0276	0.0012–0.0028	0.0008–0.0024	Snug
1991	A	1.5 (1468)	0.0008–0.0016	0.0079–0.0157	0.0079–0.0138	0.0079–0.0276	0.0012–0.0028	0.0008–0.0024	Snug
	V	2.0 (1997)	0.0004–0.0012	0.0098–0.0157	0.0079–0.0138	0.0079–0.0276	0.0012–0.0028	0.0008–0.0024	Snug
1992	A	1.5 (1468)	0.0008–0.0016	0.0079–0.0157	0.0079–0.0138	0.0079–0.0276	0.0012–0.0028	0.0008–0.0024	Snug
	D	1.8 (1834)	0.0008–0.0016	0.0098–0.0157	0.0157–0.0217	0.0079–0.0236	0.0012–0.0028	0.0008–0.0024	Snug
	W	2.4 (2350)	0.0004–0.0012	0.0098–0.0157	0.0079–0.0157	0.0079–0.0276	0.0012–0.0028	0.0008–0.0024	Snug
1993	A	1.5 (1468)	0.0008–0.0016	0.0079–0.0157	0.0079–0.0138	0.0079–0.0276	0.0012–0.0028	0.0008–0.0024	Snug
	C	1.8 (1834)	0.0008–0.0016	0.0098–0.0157	0.0157–0.0217	0.0079–0.0276	0.0012–0.0028	0.0008–0.0024	Snug
	G	2.4 (2350)	0.0004–0.0012	0.0098–0.0138	0.0157–0.0217	0.0039–0.0157	0.0012–0.0028	0.0012–0.0028	Snug

TORQUE SPECIFICATIONS
All readings in ft. lbs.

Year	Engine ID/VIN	Engine Displacement Liters (cc)	Cylinder Head Bolts	Main Bearing Bolts	Rod Bearing Bolts	Crankshaft Damper Bolts	Flywheel Bolts	Manifold		Spark Plugs	Lug Nut
								Intake	Exhaust		
1990	X	1.5 (1468)	53	38	①	62	98	13	13	15	65
	Y	1.6 (1597)	65–72	47–51	36–38	80–94	98	22–30	18–22	15	65
	T	1.8 (1755)	51–54	37–39	25	80–94②	94–101	11–14	11–14	15	65
	V	2.0 (1997)	65–72	37–39	37–39	80–94②	94–101	11–15	11–15	15	65
1991	A	1.5 (1468)	53	38	①	62	98	13	13	15	65
	V	2.0 (1997)	65–72	37–39	37–39	80–94②	94–101	11–15	11–15	15	65
1992	A	1.5 (1468)	53	38	①	62	98	13	13	15	65
	D	1.8 (1834)	③	④	⑤	134	72	13	⑥	15	65
	W	2.4 (2350)	76–83	38	38	80–94②	94–101	13	22	15	65
1993	A	1.5 (1468)	53	38	①	62	98	13	13	15	65
	D	1.8 (1834)	③	④	⑤	134	72	13	⑥	15	65
	G	2.4 (2350)	⑦	⑧	⑤	80–94②	94–101	13	22	15	65

① 14.5 + ¼ turn + ¼ turn
② Sprocket bolt
③ 1. 54 ft. lbs.
  2. Loosen completely
  3. 14 ft. lbs.
  4. ¼ turn more
  5. ¼ turn more
④ 14 ft. lbs. + ¼ turn
⑤ 14.5 ft. lbs. + ¼ turn
⑥ Upper: 13
  Lower: 22
⑦ 1. 58 ft. lbs.
  2. Loosen completely
  3. 14.5 ft. lbs.
  4. ¼ turn more
  5. ¼ turn more
⑧ 18 ft. lbs. + ¼ turn

Engine

REMOVAL & INSTALLATION

1990-93 Colt w/1.5L Engine
▶ **See Figures 22, 23, 24, 25 and 26**

The factory recommends that the engine and transaxle be removed as a unit.

1. Disconnect the battery cables, negative cable first. Remove the battery and the tray.

2. Remove the air cleaner assembly. Disconnect the purge control valve. Remove the purge control valve mounting bracket. Remove the windshield washer reservoir, radiator tank and carbon canister.

3. Drain the coolant from the radiator. Remove the radiator assembly with the electric cooling fan attached. Be sure to disconnect the fan wiring harness and the transaxle cooler lines, if equipped.

4. Disconnect the following cables, hoses and wires from the engine and transaxle: clutch, accelerator, speedometer, heater hose, fuel lines, PCV vacuum line, high altitude compensator vacuum hose (California vehicles), bowl vent valve purge hose (U.S.A. vehicles), inhibitor switch (automatic transaxle), control cable (automatic transaxle), starter, engine ground cable, alternator, water temperature gauge, ignition coil, temperature sensor, back-up light (manual transaxle), oil pressure wires and the ISC cable.

➡**Release fuel system pressure before disconnecting any fuel lines.**

5. Remove the ignition coil. Be sure all wires and hoses are disconnected.

6. Raise the vehicle and support safely. Remove the splash shield, if equipped.

7. Drain the lubricant out of the transaxle.

8. Remove the right and left halfshafts from the transaxle and support them with wire. Plug the transaxle case holes so dirt cannot enter.

➡**The halfshaft retainer ring should be replaced whenever the shaft is removed.**

9. Disconnect the assist rod and the control rod from the transaxle. If the vehicle is equipped with a range selector, disconnect the selector cable.

10. Remove the mounting bolts from the front and rear roll control rods.

11. Disconnect the exhaust pipe from the engine and secure it with wire.

12. Loosen the engine and transaxle mounting bracket nuts. On turbocharged engines, disconnect the oil cooler tube.

13. Lower the vehicle.

14. Attach a lifting device to the engine. Apply slight lifting pressure to the engine. Remove the engine and transaxle mounting nuts and bolts.

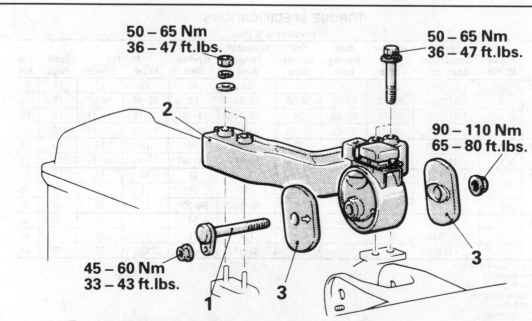

50 – 65 Nm
36 – 47 ft.lbs.

50 – 65 Nm
36 – 47 ft.lbs.

90 – 110 Nm
65 – 80 ft.lbs.

45 – 60 Nm
33 – 43 ft.lbs.

1. Engine mount bracket and body connection bolt
2. Engine mount bracket
3. Mounting stopper

Fig. 22 Engine mounting bracket — 1.5L engine

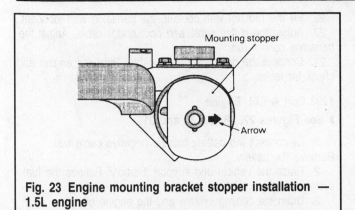

Fig. 23 Engine mounting bracket stopper installation — 1.5L engine

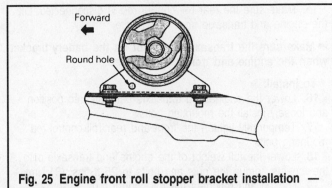

Fig. 25 Engine front roll stopper bracket installation — 1.5L engine

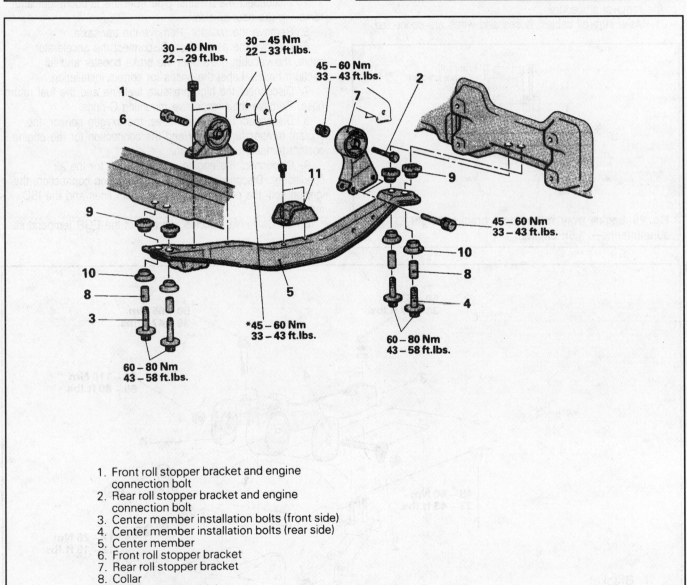

1. Front roll stopper bracket and engine connection bolt
2. Rear roll stopper bracket and engine connection bolt
3. Center member installation bolts (front side)
4. Center member installation bolts (rear side)
5. Center member
6. Front roll stopper bracket
7. Rear roll stopper bracket
8. Collar
9. Bushing (upper side)
10. Bushing (lower side)
11. Damper <Sedan>

Fig. 24 Engine roll stoppers and center member — 1.5L engine

15. Make sure the rear roll control rod is disconnected. Lift the engine and transaxle from the vehicle.

➡**Make sure the transaxle does not hit the battery bracket when the engine and transaxle are lifted.**

To install:

16. Lower the engine and transaxle carefully into position and loosely install the mounting bolts.

17. Temporarily tighten the front and rear roll control rod mounting bolts.

18. Lower the full weight of the engine and transaxle onto the mounts, torque the nuts and bolts to 25 ft. lbs. (34 Nm).

19. Loosen and retighten the roll control rods.

20. Complete the rest of the installation in the reverse order of the removal procedures.

21. Make sure all cables, hoses and wires are connected.

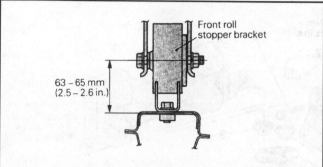

Fig. 26 Engine front roll stopper bracket height adjustment — 1.5L engine

22. Fill the radiator with coolant, the transaxle with lubricant.

23. Adjust the clutch cable and accelerator cable. Adjust the transaxle control rod.

24. Connect the negative battery cable. Start the engine and check for leaks.

1990 Colt w/1.6L Engine

▶ **See Figures 27, 28, 29, 30 and 31**

1. Disconnect the battery cables, negative cable first. Remove the battery.

2. Raise the vehicle and support it safely. Relieve the fuel system pressure.

3. Drain the cooling system and the engine oil.

4. Disconnect the exhaust pipe from the turbocharger after removing the heat shields.

5. Remove the radiator. Remove the transaxle.

6. Remove the air cleaner. Disconnect the accelerator cable, the vacuum hose from the brake booster and all vacuum hoses. Label the hoses for correct installation.

7. Disconnect the high pressure fuel line and the fuel return hose. Remove their respective mounting O-rings.

8. Disconnect the heater hoses, the oxygen sensor, the coolant temperature sensor and the connection for the engine coolant temperature gauge unit.

9. Disconnect the engine coolant switch for the air conditioner. Disconnect the fuel injector wiring connection, the ignition coil, the power transistor, vacuum lines and the ISC motor.

10. On California vehicles, disconnect the EGR temperature sensor.

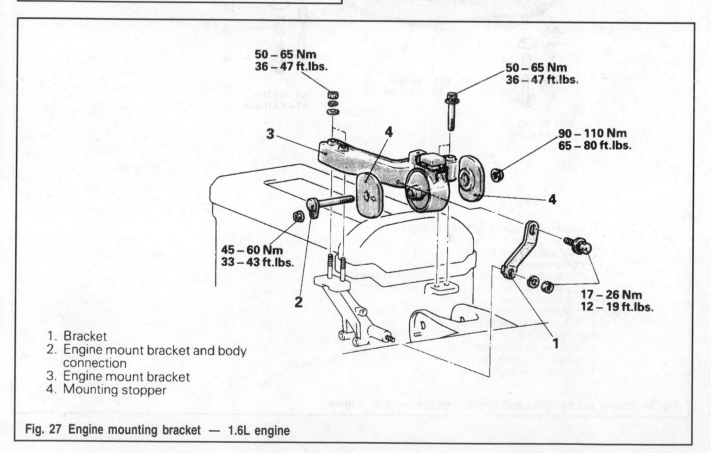

1. Bracket
2. Engine mount bracket and body connection
3. Engine mount bracket
4. Mounting stopper

Fig. 27 Engine mounting bracket — 1.6L engine

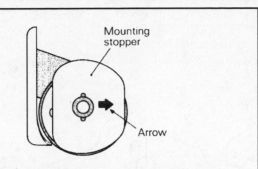

Fig. 28 Engine mounting bracket stopper installation — 1.6L engine

11. Disconnect the detonation sensor, the throttle position sensor, the crankshaft angle sensor and the control wiring harness connectors.

12. Disconnect the oil pressure switch for the power steering. Disconnect the alternator wiring. Remove the wiring harness mounting clamps. Disconnect the engine oil pressure switch.

13. Remove the air conditioning compressor, with lines attached and safely wire the assembly out of the way.

14. Remove the power steering pump, with hoses attached and safely wire it out of the way.

15. Connect a chain hoist to the engine with a suitable lifting bracket. Take up slack on the engine. Check to be sure all cables, hoses, harness connectors and vacuum hoses have been disconnected.

16. Remove the engine mounting bracket. Disconnect the front engine roll stopper and the rear roll stopper. Carefully raise and remove the engine assembly.

To install:

17. Installation is the reverse order of the removal procedure.

18. Make sure all cables, vacuum lines, hose and wire connectors are installed or attached.

19. Fill the radiator with the proper coolant mix. Fill the engine with the proper oil.

20. Adjust the clutch and accelerator cables.

21. Connect the negative battery cable. Start the engine and check for leaks.

22. Torque the lower engine mounts to 22-29 ft. lbs. (30-40 Nm), transaxle mount to 29-36 ft. lbs. (40-50 Nm), cylinder head mount to 43-58 ft. lbs. (60-80 Nm) and the exhaust pipe nuts to 14-22 ft. lbs. (20-30 Nm).

1990 Colt Wagon w/1.5L Engine

▶ **See Figures 32, 33, 34, 35 and 36**

1. Disconnect the battery cables, negative battery cable first. Remove the battery, battery tray and bracket.

2. Disconnect the engine oil pressure switch and power steering pump connectors.

3. Disconnect the alternator harness.

4. Remove the air cleaner.

5. Remove the high tension cable from the distributor.

6. Disconnect the engine ground wire at the firewall.

7. Remove the windshield washer bottle.

8. Disconnect the brake booster vacuum hose.

9. Disconnect and tag all other vacuum lines connected to the engine.

10. Drain the coolant.

11. Remove the coolant reservoir tank.

12. Remove the radiator.

13. Disconnect the heater hoses at the engine.

14. Disconnect the accelerator cable.

15. Disconnect the speed control cable.

16. Disconnect the speedometer cable at the transaxle.

17. If equipped with air conditioning, the system must be evacuated.

18. Disconnect the hose at the air conditioning compressor and cap all openings immediately.

19. Disconnect the hoses at the power steering pump.

20. Disconnect the fuel lines.

21. Disconnect the shift control cables at the transaxle.

22. Raise the vehicle and support it safely.

23. Remove the lower cover and skid plate.

24. Drain the transaxle and transfer case.

25. Disconnect the exhaust pipe from the manifold.

26. Remove the clutch slave cylinder.

27. Disconnect the halfshafts at the transaxle.

28. Remove the transfer case extension stopper bracket.

➡ **The 2 top stopper bracket bolts are easier to get at from the engine compartment, using a T-type box wrench.**

29. Lower the vehicle to the ground.

30. Remove the nuts only, from the engine mount-to-body bracket.

31. Remove the range select control valves from the transaxle insulator bracket.

32. Remove the nut only, from the transaxle mounting insulator.

33. Remove the front roll insulator nut.

34. Remove the rear insulator-to-engine nut.

35. Remove the grille and valance panel.

36. Remove the air conditioning condenser.

37. Take up the weight of the engine with a lifting device attached to the lifting eyes.

38. Remove all the mounting bolts.

39. Double check that all wiring, hoses and cables are disconnected from the engine, transaxle and transfer case have been disconnected. Move the assembly forward slightly, to a point at which it will clear the floor pan and lift the whole assembly clear of the vehicle.

To install:

40. Secure the engine to a suitable lifting device.

41. Carefully lower the engine and transaxle into position and loosely install the mounting bolts.

42. Temporarily tighten the front and rear roll control rod mounting bolts.

43. Lower the full weight of the engine and transaxle onto the mounts, tighten the nuts and bolts.

44. Loosen and retighten the roll control rods.

45. Complete the rest of the installation in the reverse order of the removal procedures.

46. Make sure all cables, hoses and wires are connected.

47. Fill the radiator with coolant, the transaxle with lubricant.

48. Adjust the clutch cable and accelerator cable. Adjust the transaxle control rod.

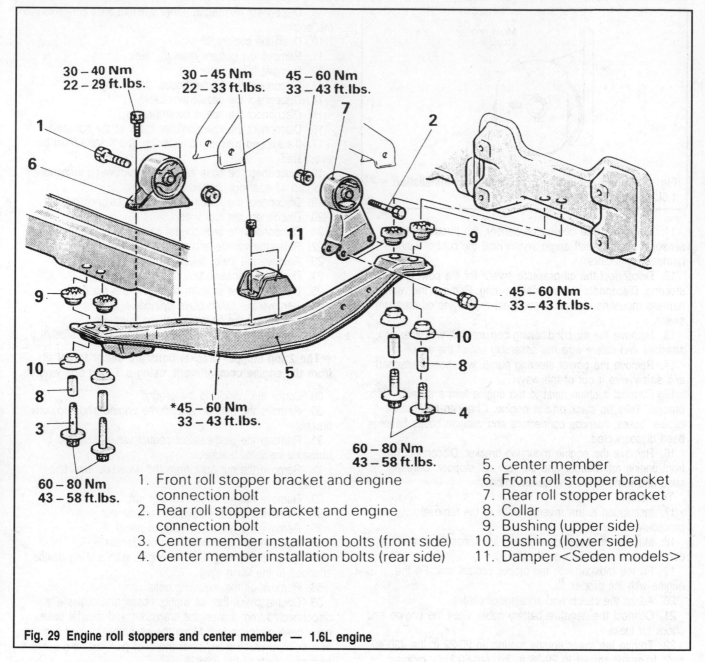

30 – 40 Nm
22 – 29 ft.lbs.

30 – 45 Nm
22 – 33 ft.lbs.

45 – 60 Nm
33 – 43 ft.lbs.

45 – 60 Nm
33 – 43 ft.lbs.

*45 – 60 Nm
33 – 43 ft.lbs.

60 – 80 Nm
43 – 58 ft.lbs.

60 – 80 Nm
43 – 58 ft.lbs.

1. Front roll stopper bracket and engine connection bolt
2. Rear roll stopper bracket and engine connection bolt
3. Center member installation bolts (front side)
4. Center member installation bolts (rear side)
5. Center member
6. Front roll stopper bracket
7. Rear roll stopper bracket
8. Collar
9. Bushing (upper side)
10. Bushing (lower side)
11. Damper <Seden models>

Fig. 29 Engine roll stoppers and center member — 1.6L engine

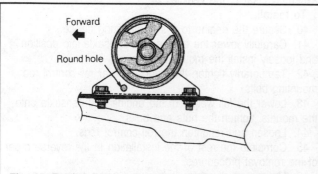

Forward

Round hole

Fig. 30 Engine front roll stopper bracket installation — 1.6L engine

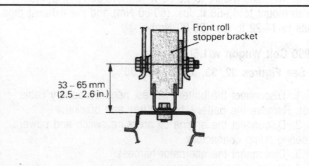

Front roll stopper bracket

63 – 65 mm
(2.5 – 2.6 in.)

Fig. 31 Engine front roll stopper bracket height adjustment — 1.6L engine

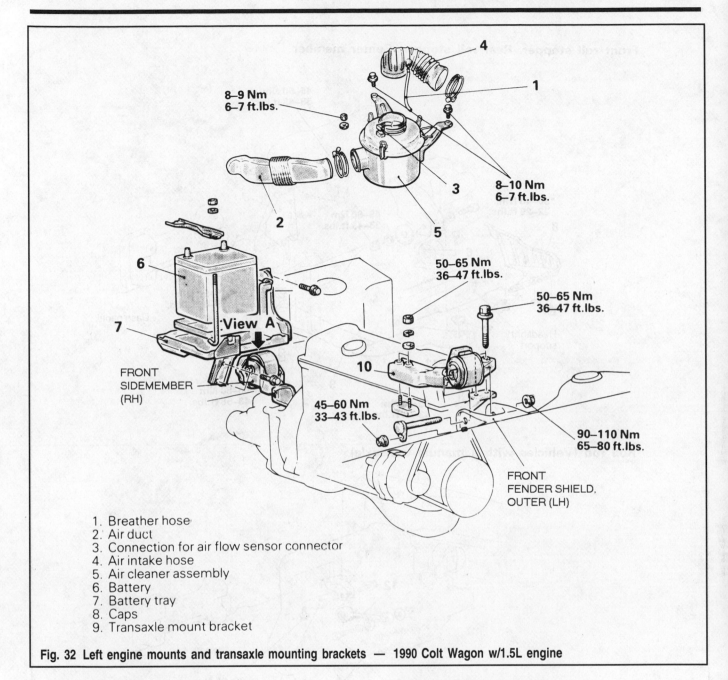

8–9 Nm
6–7 ft.lbs.

8–10 Nm
6–7 ft.lbs.

50–65 Nm
36–47 ft.lbs.

50–65 Nm
36–47 ft.lbs.

45–60 Nm
33–43 ft.lbs.

90–110 Nm
65–80 ft.lbs.

View A

FRONT
SIDEMEMBER
(RH)

FRONT
FENDER SHIELD,
OUTER (LH)

1. Breather hose
2. Air duct
3. Connection for air flow sensor connector
4. Air intake hose
5. Air cleaner assembly
6. Battery
7. Battery tray
8. Caps
9. Transaxle mount bracket

Fig. 32 Left engine mounts and transaxle mounting brackets — 1990 Colt Wagon w/1.5L engine

49. Observe the following torques:
Transaxle stopper — 58 ft. lbs. (79 Nm).
Engine-to-body bracket bolts — 47 ft. lbs. (64 Nm).
Rear insulator — 29 ft. lbs. (39 Nm).
Transaxle mount nuts — 58 ft. lbs. (79 Nm).
Heat shield — 7 ft. lbs. (9.5 Nm).
Front roll bracket nuts — 36 ft. lbs. (49 Nm).
50. Connect the negative battery cable. Start the engine and check for leaks.

1990 Colt Wagon w/1.8L Engine

▶ See Figures 37, 38 and 39

1. Disconnect the battery cables, negative battery cable first. Remove the battery, battery tray and bracket.
2. Disconnect the engine oil pressure switch and power steering pump connectors.

3. Disconnect the alternator harness.
4. Remove the air cleaner.
5. Remove the high tension cable from the distributor.
6. Disconnect the engine ground wire at the firewall.
7. Remove the windshield washer bottle.
8. Disconnect the brake booster vacuum hose.
9. Disconnect and tag all other vacuum lines connected to the engine.
10. Drain the coolant.
11. Remove the coolant reservoir tank.
12. Remove the radiator.
13. Disconnect the heater hoses at the engine.
14. Disconnect the accelerator cable.
15. Disconnect the speed control cable.
16. Disconnect the speedometer cable at the transaxle.
17. If equipped with air conditioning, the system must be evacuated.

Front roll stopper, Rear roll stopper, Center member

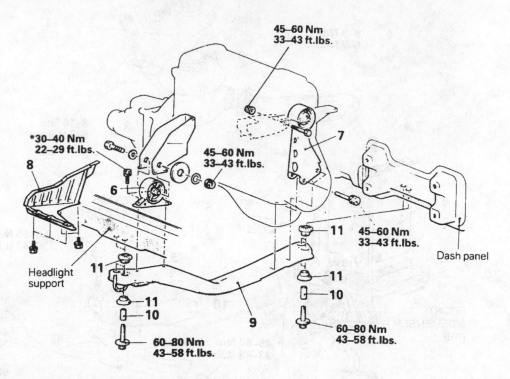

Roll rod (Vehicles with a manual transaxle)

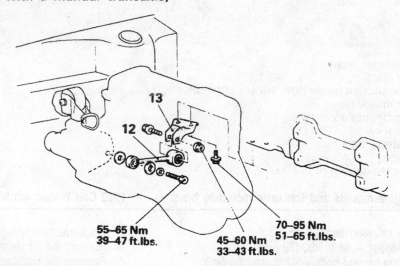

Front roll stopper removal

6. Front roll stopper

Rear roll stopper removal

7. Rear roll stopper

Center member removal steps

8. Under cover (R.H.)
9. Center member
10. Collars
11. Rubber bushings

Roll rod removal steps (Vehicles with a manual transaxle)

12. Roll rod
13. Roll rod bracket

Fig. 33 Front roll stopper, rear roll stopper and center member — 1990 Colt Wagon w/1.5L engine

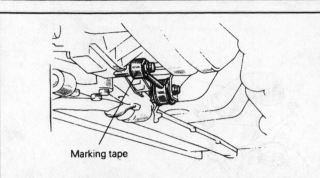

Fig. 34 Roll rod installation — 1990 Colt Wagon w.1.5L engine

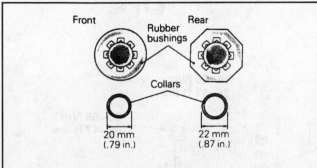

Fig. 35 Roll rod bushing installation — 1990 Colt Wagon w.1.5L engine

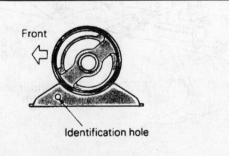

Fig. 36 Roll stopper installation — 1990 Colt Wagon w.1.5L engine

18. Disconnect the hose at the air conditioning compressor and cap all openings immediately.
19. Disconnect the hoses at the power steering pump.
20. Disconnect the fuel lines.
21. Disconnect the shift control cables at the transaxle.
22. Raise the vehicle and support it safely.
23. Remove the lower cover and skid plate.
24. Drain the transaxle and transfer case.
25. Disconnect the exhaust pipe from the manifold.
26. Remove the clutch slave cylinder.
27. Disconnect the halfshafts at the transaxle.
28. Remove the transfer case extension stopper bracket.

➡️**The 2 top stopper bracket bolts are easier to get at from the engine compartment, using a T-type box wrench.**

29. Lower the vehicle to the ground.
30. Remove the nuts only, from the engine mount-to-body bracket.
31. Remove the range select control valves from the transaxle insulator bracket.
32. Remove the nut only, from the transaxle mounting insulator.
33. Remove the front roll insulator nut.
34. Remove the rear insulator-to-engine nut.
35. Remove the grille and valance panel.
36. Remove the air conditioning condenser.
37. Take up the weight of the engine with a lifting device attached to the lifting eyes.
38. Remove all the mounting bolts.
39. Double check that all wiring, hoses and cables are disconnected from the engine, transaxle and transfer case have been disconnected. Move the assembly forward slightly, to a point at which it will clear the floor pan and lift the whole assembly clear of the vehicle.

To install:

40. Secure the engine to a suitable lifting device.
41. Carefully lower the engine and transaxle into position and loosely install the mounting bolts.
42. Temporarily tighten the front and rear roll control rod mounting bolts.
43. Lower the full weight of the engine and transaxle onto the mounts, tighten the nuts and bolts.
44. Loosen and retighten the roll control rods.
45. Complete the rest of the installation in the reverse order of the removal procedures.
46. Make sure all cables, hoses and wires are connected.
47. Fill the radiator with coolant, the transaxle with lubricant.
48. Adjust the clutch cable and accelerator cable. Adjust the transaxle control rod.
49. Observe the following torques:
Transaxle stopper — 58 ft. lbs. (79 Nm).
Engine-to-body bracket bolts — 47 ft. lbs. (64 Nm).
Rear insulator — 29 ft. lbs. (39 Nm).
Transaxle mount nuts — 58 ft. lbs. (79 Nm).
Heat shield — 7 ft. lbs. (9.5 Nm).
Front roll bracket nuts — 36 ft. lbs. (49 Nm).
50. Connect the negative battery cable. Start the engine and check for leaks.

1990-91 Vista w/2.0L

▶ **See Figure 40**

1. Disconnect the battery cables, negative battery cable first. Remove the battery, battery tray and bracket.
2. Disconnect the engine oil pressure switch and power steering pump connectors.
3. Disconnect the alternator harness.
4. Remove the air cleaner.
5. Remove the high tension cable from the distributor.
6. Disconnect the engine ground wire at the firewall.
7. Remove the windshield washer bottle.
8. Disconnect the brake booster vacuum hose.
9. Disconnect and tag all other vacuum lines connected to the engine.
10. Drain the coolant.
11. Remove the coolant reservoir tank.
12. Remove the radiator.

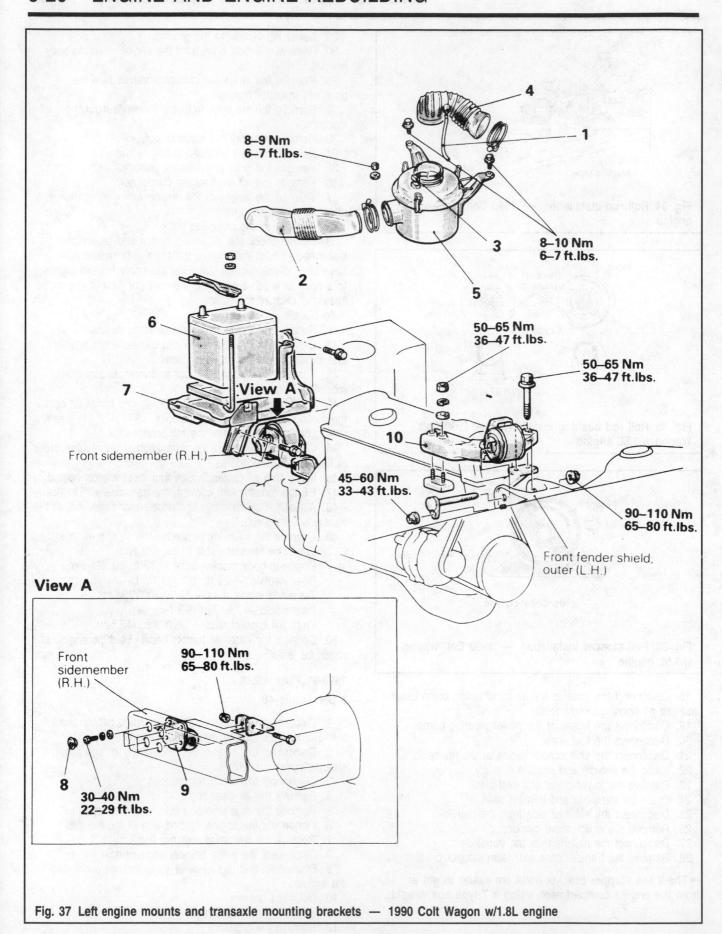

Fig. 37 Left engine mounts and transaxle mounting brackets — 1990 Colt Wagon w/1.8L engine

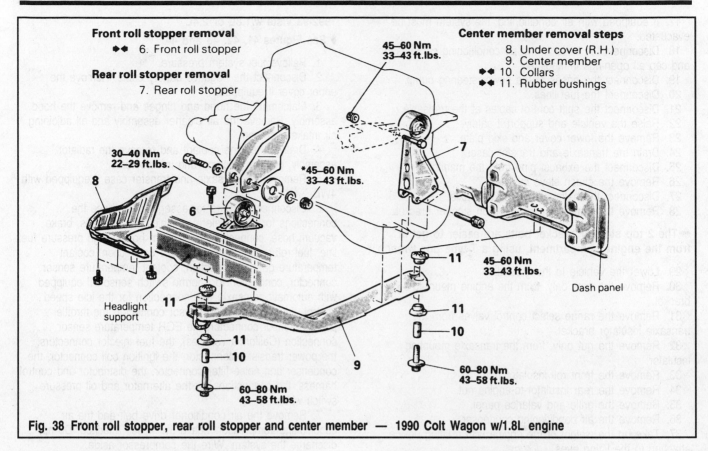

Front roll stopper removal

➤◆ 6. Front roll stopper

Rear roll stopper removal

7. Rear roll stopper

Center member removal steps

8. Under cover (R.H.)
9. Center member
➤◆ 10. Collars
➤◆ 11. Rubber bushings

45–60 Nm
33–43 ft.lbs.

30–40 Nm
22–29 ft.lbs.

*45–60 Nm
33–43 ft.lbs.

45–60 Nm
33–43 ft.lbs.

Dash panel

Headlight support

60–80 Nm
43–58 ft.lbs.

60–80 Nm
43–58 ft.lbs.

Fig. 38 Front roll stopper, rear roll stopper and center member — 1990 Colt Wagon w/1.8L engine

13. Disconnect the heater hoses at the engine.
14. Disconnect the accelerator cable.

15. Disconnect the speed control cable.
16. Disconnect the speedometer cable at the transaxle.

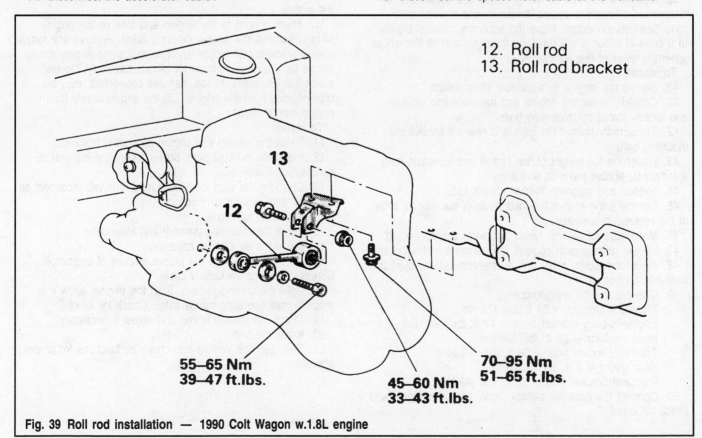

12. Roll rod
13. Roll rod bracket

55–65 Nm
39–47 ft.lbs.

45–60 Nm
33–43 ft.lbs.

70–95 Nm
51–65 ft.lbs.

Fig. 39 Roll rod installation — 1990 Colt Wagon w.1.8L engine

17. If equipped with air conditioning, the system must be evacuated.

18. Disconnect the hose at the air conditioning compressor and cap all openings immediately.

19. Disconnect the hoses at the power steering pump.

20. Disconnect the fuel lines.

21. Disconnect the shift control cables at the transaxle.

22. Raise the vehicle and support it safely.

23. Remove the lower cover and skid plate.

24. Drain the transaxle and transfer case.

25. Disconnect the exhaust pipe from the manifold.

26. Remove the clutch slave cylinder.

27. Disconnect the halfshafts at the transaxle.

28. Remove the transfer case extension stopper bracket.

➡The 2 top stopper bracket bolts are easier to get at from the engine compartment, using a T-type box wrench.

29. Lower the vehicle to the ground.

30. Remove the nuts only, from the engine mount-to-body bracket.

31. Remove the range select control valves from the transaxle insulator bracket.

32. Remove the nut only, from the transaxle mounting insulator.

33. Remove the front roll insulator nut.

34. Remove the rear insulator-to-engine nut.

35. Remove the grille and valance panel.

36. Remove the air conditioning condenser.

37. Take up the weight of the engine with a lifting device attached to the lifting eyes.

38. Remove all the mounting bolts.

39. Double check that all wiring, hoses and cables are disconnected from the engine, transaxle and transfer case have been disconnected. Move the assembly forward slightly, to a point at which it will clear the floor pan and lift the whole assembly clear of the vehicle.

To install:

40. Secure the engine to a suitable lifting device.

41. Carefully lower the engine and transaxle into position and loosely install the mounting bolts.

42. Temporarily tighten the front and rear roll control rod mounting bolts.

43. Lower the full weight of the engine and transaxle onto the mounts, tighten the nuts and bolts.

44. Loosen and retighten the roll control rods.

45. Complete the rest of the installation in the reverse order of the removal procedures.

46. Make sure all cables, hoses and wires are connected.

47. Fill the radiator with coolant, the transaxle with lubricant.

48. Adjust the clutch cable and accelerator cable. Adjust the transaxle control rod.

49. Observe the following torques:
    Transaxle stopper — 58 ft. lbs. (79 Nm).
    Engine-to-body bracket bolts — 47 ft. lbs. (64 Nm).
    Rear insulator — 29 ft. lbs. (39 Nm).
    Transaxle mount nuts — 58 ft. lbs. (79 Nm).
    Heat shield — 7 ft. lbs. (9.5 Nm).
    Front roll bracket nuts — 36 ft. lbs. (49 Nm).

50. Connect the negative battery cable. Start the engine and check for leaks.

1992-93 Vista w/1.8L or 2.4L

◗ See Figures 41, 42, 43 and 44

1. Relieve fuel system pressure.

2. Disconnect the negative battery cable. Remove the under cover if equipped.

3. Matchmark the hood and hinges and remove the hood assembly. Remove the air cleaner assembly and all adjoining air intake duct work.

4. Drain the engine coolant and remove the radiator assembly, coolant reservoir and intercooler.

5. Remove the transaxle and transfer case if equipped with 4WD.

6. Disconnect and tag for assembly reference the connections for the accelerator cable, heater hoses, brake vacuum hose, connection for vacuum hoses, high pressure fuel line, fuel return line, oxygen sensor connection, coolant temperature gauge connection, coolant temperature sensor connector, connection for thermo switch sensor, if equipped with automatic transaxle, the connection for the idle speed control, the motor position sensor connector, the throttle position sensor connector, the EGR temperature sensor connection (California vehicles), the fuel injector connectors, the power transistor connector, the ignition coil connector, the condenser and noise filter connector, the distributor and control harness, the connections for the alternator and oil pressure switch wires.

7. Remove the air conditioner drive belt and the air conditioning compressor. Leave the hoses attached. Do not discharge the system. Wire the compressor aside.

8. Remove the power steering pump and wire aside.

9. Remove the exhaust manifold to head pipe nuts. Discard the gasket.

10. Attach a hoist to the engine and take up the engine weight. Remove the engine mount bracket. Remove any torque control brackets (roll stoppers). Note that some engine mount pieces have arrows on them for proper assembly. Double check that all cables, hoses, harness connectors, etc., are disconnected from the engine. Lift the engine slowly from the engine compartment.

To install:

11. Install the engine and secure all control brackets.

12. Install the exhaust pipe, power steering pump and air conditioning compressor.

13. Checking the tags installed during removal, reconnect all electrical and vacuum connections.

14. Install the transaxle.

15. Install the radiator assembly and intercooler.

16. Install the air cleaner assembly.

17. Fill the engine with the proper amount of engine oil. Connect the negative battery cable.

18. Refill the cooling system. Start the engine, allow it to reach normal operating temperature. Check for leaks.

19. Check the ignition timing and adjust if necessary.

20. Install the hood.

21. Road test the vehicle and check all functions for proper operation.

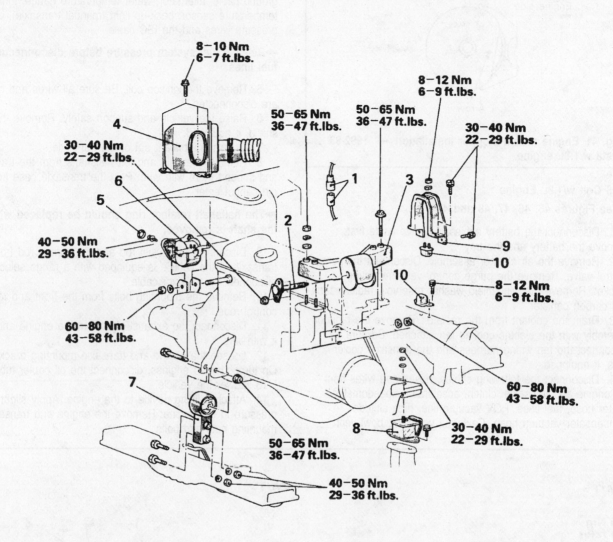

8—10 Nm
6—7 ft.lbs.

8—12 Nm
6—9 ft.lbs.

50—65 Nm
36—47 ft.lbs.

50—65 Nm
36—47 ft.lbs.

30—40 Nm
22—29 ft.lbs.

30—40 Nm
22—29 ft.lbs.

40—50 Nm
29—36 ft.lbs.

8—12 Nm
6—9 ft.lbs.

60—80 Nm
43—58 ft.lbs.

60—80 Nm
43—58 ft.lbs.

30—40 Nm
22—29 ft.lbs.

50—65 Nm
36—47 ft.lbs.

40—50 Nm
29—36 ft.lbs.

Engine mount bracket removal steps

1. Oxygen sensor connector
2. Bolt assembly
3. Engine mount bracket

Transaxle mount bracket removal steps

4. Air filter case
5. Cap
6. Transaxle mount bracket

Front roll stopper bracket removal steps

7. Front roll stopper bracket

Rear insulator removal steps

◆◆   8. Rear insulator

Transfer extension stopper removal steps

9. Transfer extension stopper bracket
10. Transfer extension stopper

Fig. 40 4-wheel drive 1990-91 Vista engine mounting

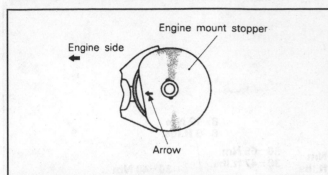

Fig. 41 Engine mount stopper installation — 1992-93 Vista w/1.8L engine

1993 Colt w/1.8L Engine

▶ See Figures 45, 46, 47, 48 and 49

1. Disconnect the battery cables, negative cable first. Remove the battery and the tray.

2. Remove the air cleaner assembly. Disconnect the purge control valve. Remove the purge control valve mounting bracket. Remove the windshield washer reservoir, radiator tank and carbon canister.

3. Drain the coolant from the radiator. Remove the radiator assembly with the electric cooling fan attached. Be sure to disconnect the fan wiring harness and the transaxle cooler lines, if equipped.

4. Disconnect the following cables, hoses and wires from the engine and transaxle: clutch, accelerator, speedometer, heater hose, fuel lines, PCV vacuum line, high altitude compensator vacuum hose (California vehicles), bowl vent valve purge hose (U.S.A. vehicles), inhibitor switch (automatic transaxle), control cable (automatic transaxle), starter, engine ground cable, alternator, water temperature gauge, ignition coil, temperature sensor, back-up light (manual transaxle), oil pressure wires and the ISC cable.

▶**Release fuel system pressure before disconnecting any fuel lines.**

5. Remove the ignition coil. Be sure all wires and hoses are disconnected.

6. Raise the vehicle and support safely. Remove the splash shield, if equipped.

7. Drain the lubricant out of the transaxle.

8. Remove the right and left halfshafts from the transaxle and support them with wire. Plug the transaxle case holes so dirt cannot enter.

▶**The halfshaft retainer ring should be replaced whenever the shaft is removed.**

9. Disconnect the assist rod and the control rod from the transaxle. If the vehicle is equipped with a range selector, disconnect the selector cable.

10. Remove the mounting bolts from the front and rear roll control rods.

11. Disconnect the exhaust pipe from the engine and secure it with wire.

12. Loosen the engine and transaxle mounting bracket nuts. On turbocharged engines, disconnect the oil cooler tube.

13. Lower the vehicle.

14. Attach a lifting device to the engine. Apply slight lifting pressure to the engine. Remove the engine and transaxle mounting nuts and bolts.

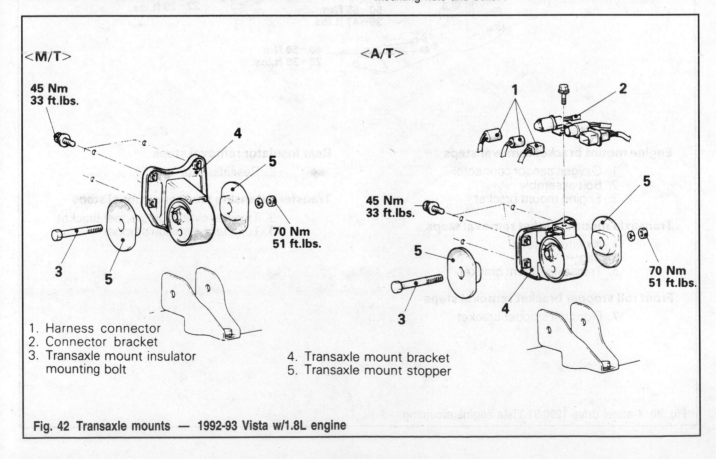

<M/T>

45 Nm
33 ft.lbs.

4

5

70 Nm
51 ft.lbs.

3

5

<A/T>

1

2

45 Nm
33 ft.lbs.

5

5

70 Nm
51 ft.lbs.

3

4

1. Harness connector
2. Connector bracket
3. Transaxle mount insulator mounting bolt

4. Transaxle mount bracket
5. Transaxle mount stopper

Fig. 42 Transaxle mounts — 1992-93 Vista w/1.8L engine

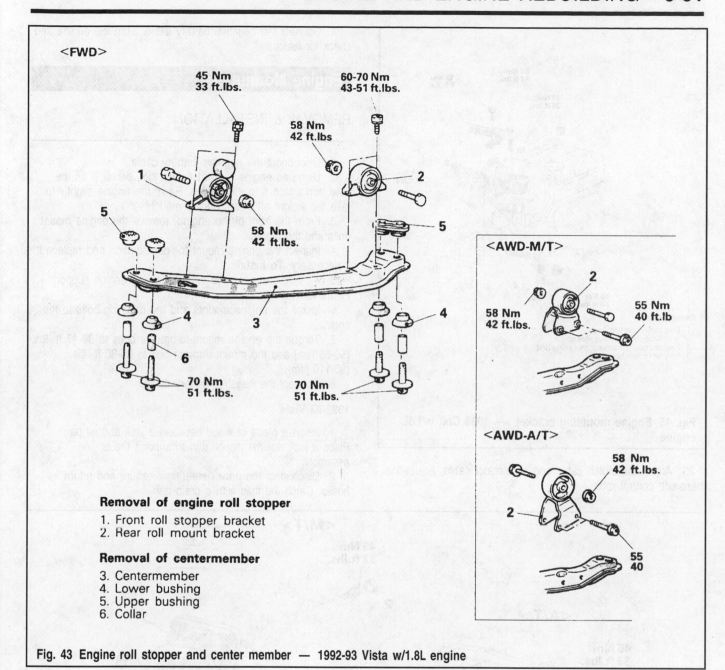

<FWD>

45 Nm
33 ft.lbs.

60-70 Nm
43-51 ft.lbs.

58 Nm
42 ft.lbs

1

2

5

5

58 Nm
42 ft.lbs.

3

4

4

6

70 Nm
51 ft.lbs.

70 Nm
51 ft.lbs.

<AWD-M/T>

58 Nm
42 ft.lbs.

2

55 Nm
40 ft.lb

<AWD-A/T>

58 Nm
42 ft.lbs.

2

55
40

Removal of engine roll stopper

1. Front roll stopper bracket
2. Rear roll mount bracket

Removal of centermember

3. Centermember
4. Lower bushing
5. Upper bushing
6. Collar

Fig. 43 Engine roll stopper and center member — 1992-93 Vista w/1.8L engine

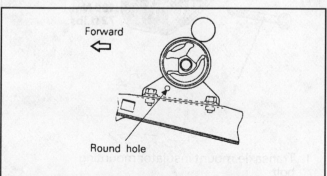

Forward

Round hole

Fig. 44 Engine roll stopper bracket installation —
1992-93 Vista w/1.8L engine

15. Make sure the rear roll control rod is disconnected. Lift the engine and transaxle from the vehicle.

➠Make sure the transaxle does not hit the battery bracket when the engine and transaxle are lifted.

To install:

16. Lower the engine and transaxle carefully into position and loosely install the mounting bolts.

17. Temporarily tighten the front and rear roll control rod mounting bolts.

18. Lower the full weight of the engine and transaxle onto the mounts, torque the nuts and bolts to 25 ft. lbs. (34 Nm).

19. Loosen and retighten the roll control rods.

20. Complete the rest of the installation in the reverse order of the removal procedures.

21. Make sure all cables, hoses and wires are connected.

22. Fill the radiator with coolant, the transaxle with lubricant.

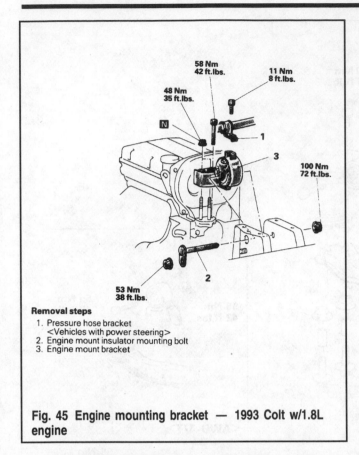

Removal steps

1. Pressure hose bracket
   <Vehicles with power steering>
2. Engine mount insulator mounting bolt
3. Engine mount bracket

Fig. 45 Engine mounting bracket — 1993 Colt w/1.8L engine

23. Adjust the clutch cable and accelerator cable. Adjust the transaxle control rod.

24. Connect the negative battery cable. Start the engine and check for leaks.

Engine Mounts

REMOVAL & INSTALLATION

1. Disconnect the negative battery cable.
2. Using an engine support fixture tool, center it on the cowl and attach it to the engine. Raise the engine slightly to take the weight off of the engine mounts.
3. From the front of the engine, remove the engine mount bolts and the mount.
4. Inspect the engine mount for deterioration and replace it, if necessary. **To install:**
5. To install, support the engine using a engine support fixture tool.
6. Install the engine mounts and the retaining bolts to the engine.
7. Torque the engine mount-to-bracket bolts to 36-47 ft. lbs. (50-65 Nm) and the mount through bolt to 65-80 ft. lbs. (90-110 Nm).
8. Connect the negative battery cable.

1992-93 Vista

1. Insert a piece of wood between a jack and oil pan. Place a jack against the oil pan to support the engine assembly.
2. Disconnect the power steering pressure and return hoses. Catch the fluid with a drain pan.

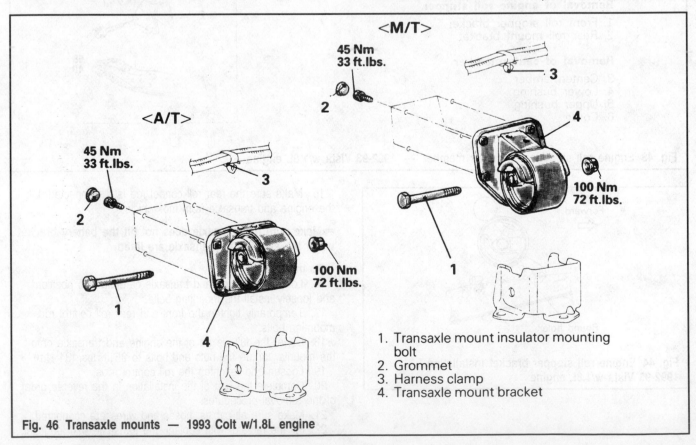

1. Transaxle mount insulator mounting bolt
2. Grommet
3. Harness clamp
4. Transaxle mount bracket

Fig. 46 Transaxle mounts — 1993 Colt w/1.8L engine

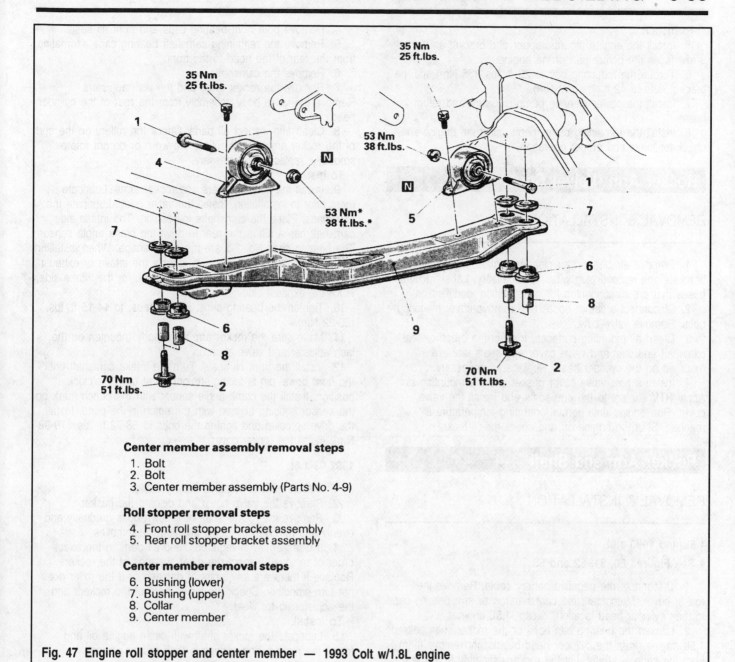

Center member assembly removal steps

1. Bolt
2. Bolt
3. Center member assembly (Parts No. 4-9)

Roll stopper removal steps

4. Front roll stopper bracket assembly
5. Rear roll stopper bracket assembly

Center member removal steps

6. Bushing (lower)
7. Bushing (upper)
8. Collar
9. Center member

Fig. 47 Engine roll stopper and center member — 1993 Colt w/1.8L engine

3. Remove the engine mount insulator bolt.
4. Remove the engine mount bracket and stopper.

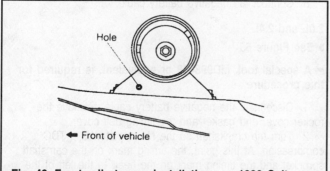

Fig. 49 Front roll stopper installation — 1993 Colt w/1.8L engine

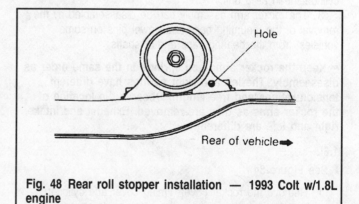

Fig. 48 Rear roll stopper installation — 1993 Colt w/1.8L engine

To install:

5. Install the engine mount stopper and bracket so the arrow faces the center part of the engine.

6. Torque the mounting bolt to 25 ft. lbs. (35 Nm) and the bracket nuts to 42 ft. lbs. (58 Nm).

7. Install the power steering pump pressure and return hoses.

8. Install the remaining components, start the engine and check for leaks and proper operation.

Rocker Arm (Valve) Cover

REMOVAL & INSTALLATION

1. Remove air cleaner, air cleaner snorkel, mounting brackets and remove plug wires, if necessary. Label vacuum hoses that are disconnected for reinstallation identification.

2. Disconnect breather hoses and remove cover mounting bolts. Remove valve cover.

3. Clean all mounting surfaces. Inspect the breather seal, camshaft end seal and valve cover end seals that are mounted on the cylinder head. Replace as necessary.

4. Install a new valve cover gasket into the mounting slot. Apply RTV sealant to the end seals and install the valve cover. Run engine until normal operating temperature is reached. Shut the engine off and check for oil leaks.

Rocker Arm and Shaft

REMOVAL & INSTALLATION

1.5L and 1990 1.8L

▶ **See Figures 50, 51, 52 and 53**

1. Disconnect the negative battery cable. Remove the rocker cover. Matchmark the camshaft/rocker arm bearing caps to their cylinder head location, except 1.5L engines.

2. Loosen the bearing cap bolts or the rocker shaft bolts on 1.5L engine, from the cylinder head but do not remove them from the caps or shafts. Lift the rocker assembly from the cylinder head as a unit.

3. The rocker arm assembly can be disassembled by the removal of the mounting bolts and dowel pins on some vehicles, from the bearing caps and/or shafts.

➡**Keep the rocker arms and springs in the same order as disassembly. The left and right springs have different tension ratings and free length. Observe the location of the rocker arms as they are removed. Exhaust and intake, right and left, are different.**

1.6L

▶ **See Figure 54**

1. Remove the rocker cover, timing cover and cylinder head from the vehicle. Remove the crank angle sensor.

2. Remove both camshaft drive sprockets.

3. Remove both rear (opposite end of the drive sprockets) camshaft bearing caps.

4. Remove both front bearing caps and front oil seals.

5. Remove the remaining camshaft bearing caps alternating from the rear of the head to the front.

6. Remove the camshafts.

7. Remove the rocker arms and the lash adjusters. Remove the valve body assembly from the rear of the cylinder head.

8. Clean and inspect all parts. Check the rollers on the end of the rocker arms. If the rollers are worn or do not rotate smoothly, replace, as necessary.

To install:

9. Install the lash adjusters and rocker arms. Lubricate them prior to installation. Install the valve body. Lubricate the camshafts. Place the camshafts in position. The intake side camshaft has a slit in the rear to drive the crank angle sensor. The bearing caps No. 2-5 are the same shape. When installing them, check the top markings to identify the intake or exhaust side. L or R is marked on the front caps, L for the intake side; R for the exhaust side.

10. Tighten the bearing caps, in 2-3 steps, to 14-15 ft. lbs. (20-22 Nm).

11. Make sure the rocker arm is properly mounted on the lash adjuster and valve stem tip.

12. Install the front oil seals. Turn the intake camshaft until the front dowel pin is facing straight up at the 12 o'clock position. Install the crank angle sensor with the punch mark on the sensor housing aligned with the notch in the plate. Install the drive sprocket and tighten the bolts to 58-72 ft. lbs. (79-98 Nm). Install the rocker cover.

1992-93 1.8L

1. Disconnect the negative battery cable.

2. Remove the valve cover and discard the gasket.

3. Remove the rocker shaft hold-down bolts gradually and evenly and remove the rocker shaft/arm assemblies.

4. If disassembly is required, keep all parts in the exact order of removal. Inspect the roller surfaces of the rockers. Replace if there are any signs of damage or if the roller does not turn smoothly. Check the inside bore of the rockers and the adjuster tip for wear.

To install:

5. Lubricate the rocker shaft with clean engine oil and install the rockers and springs in their proper places.

6. Install the rocker shaft assemblies on the engine and tighten the bolts gradually and evenly. Torque the rocker shaft bolts to 23 ft. lbs. (32 Nm).

7. Install the valve cover with a new gasket.

8. Connect the negative battery cable.

2.0L and 2.4L

▶ **See Figure 55**

➡**A special tool, MD998443 or equivalent, is required for this procedure.**

1. Disconnect the negative battery cable. Remove the rocker cover and gasket and the timing belt cover.

2. Turn the crankshaft so the No. 1 piston is a TDC compression. At this point, the timing mark on the camshaft sprocket and the timing mark on the head to the left of the sprocket will be aligned.

3. Remove the camshaft bearing cap bolts.

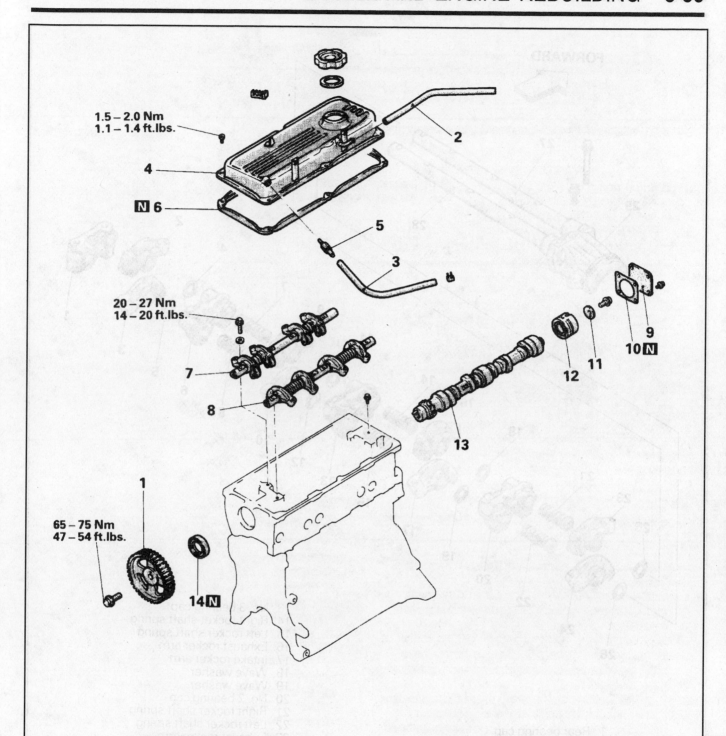

1.5 – 2.0 Nm
1.1 – 1.4 ft.lbs.

20 – 27 Nm
14 – 20 ft.lbs.

65 – 75 Nm
47 – 54 ft.lbs.

1. Camshaft sprocket
2. Breather hose
3. P.C.V. hose
4. Rocker cover
5. P.C.V. valve
6. Rocker cover gasket
7. Rocker arm assembly
8. Rocker arm assembly
9. Rear cover
10. Rear cover gasket
11. Thrust plate
12. Camshaft thrust case
13. Camshaft
14. Oil seal

Fig. 50 Rocker arms, shafts and camshaft — 1990 1.5L engine

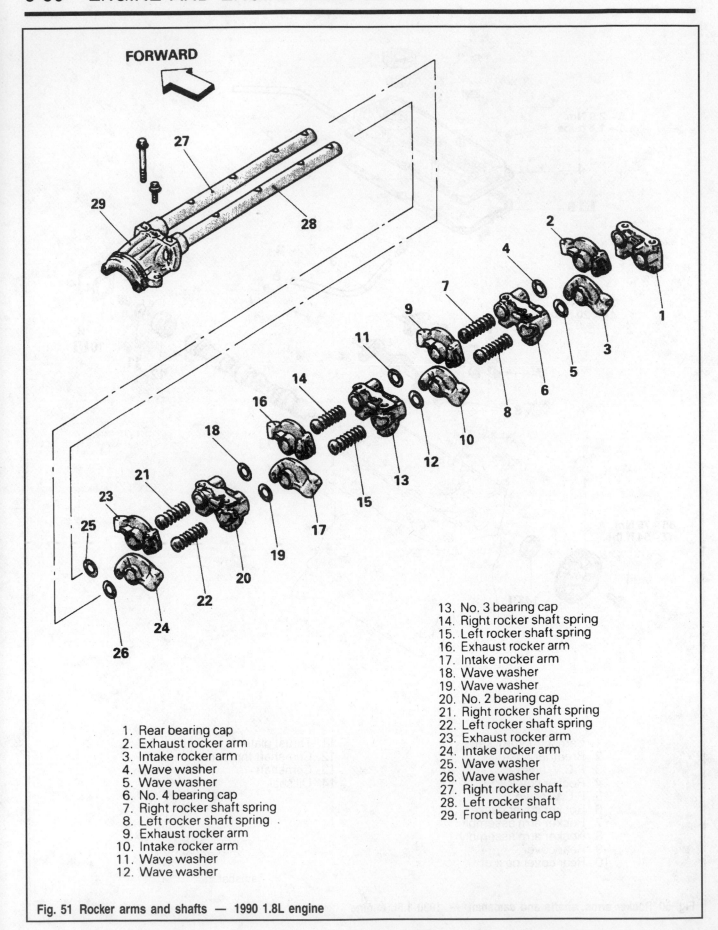

FORWARD

1. Rear bearing cap
2. Exhaust rocker arm
3. Intake rocker arm
4. Wave washer
5. Wave washer
6. No. 4 bearing cap
7. Right rocker shaft spring
8. Left rocker shaft spring
9. Exhaust rocker arm
10. Intake rocker arm
11. Wave washer
12. Wave washer
13. No. 3 bearing cap
14. Right rocker shaft spring
15. Left rocker shaft spring
16. Exhaust rocker arm
17. Intake rocker arm
18. Wave washer
19. Wave washer
20. No. 2 bearing cap
21. Right rocker shaft spring
22. Left rocker shaft spring
23. Exhaust rocker arm
24. Intake rocker arm
25. Wave washer
26. Wave washer
27. Right rocker shaft
28. Left rocker shaft
29. Front bearing cap

Fig. 51 Rocker arms and shafts — 1990 1.8L engine

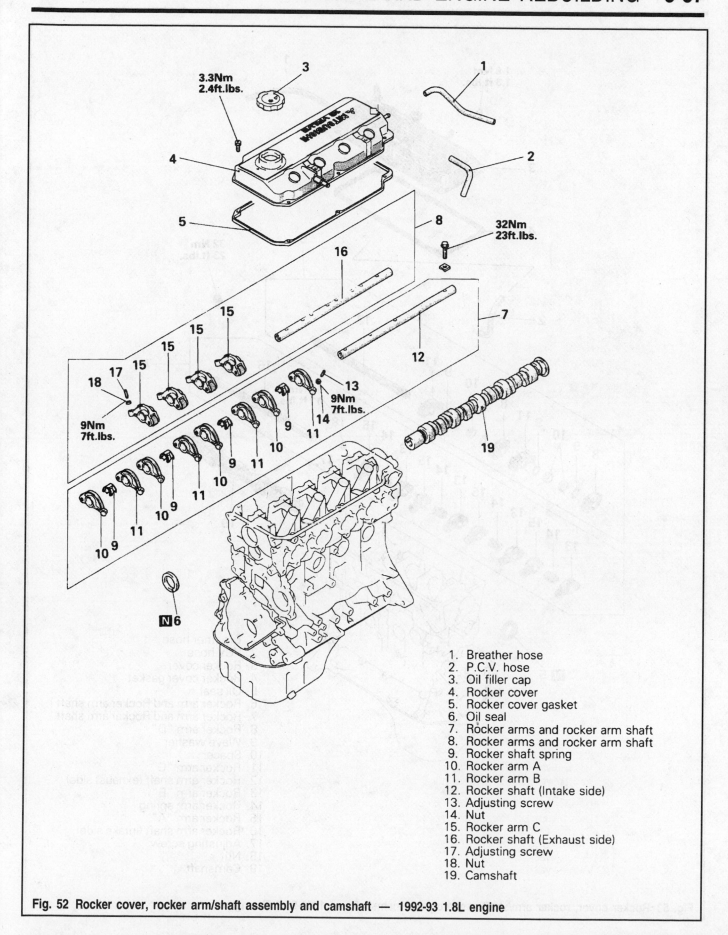

Fig. 52 Rocker cover, rocker arm/shaft assembly and camshaft — 1992-93 1.8L engine

1. Breather hose
2. P.C.V. hose
3. Oil filler cap
4. Rocker cover
5. Rocker cover gasket
6. Oil seal
7. Rocker arms and rocker arm shaft
8. Rocker arms and rocker arm shaft
9. Rocker shaft spring
10. Rocker arm A
11. Rocker arm B
12. Rocker shaft (Intake side)
13. Adjusting screw
14. Nut
15. Rocker arm C
16. Rocker shaft (Exhaust side)
17. Adjusting screw
18. Nut
19. Camshaft

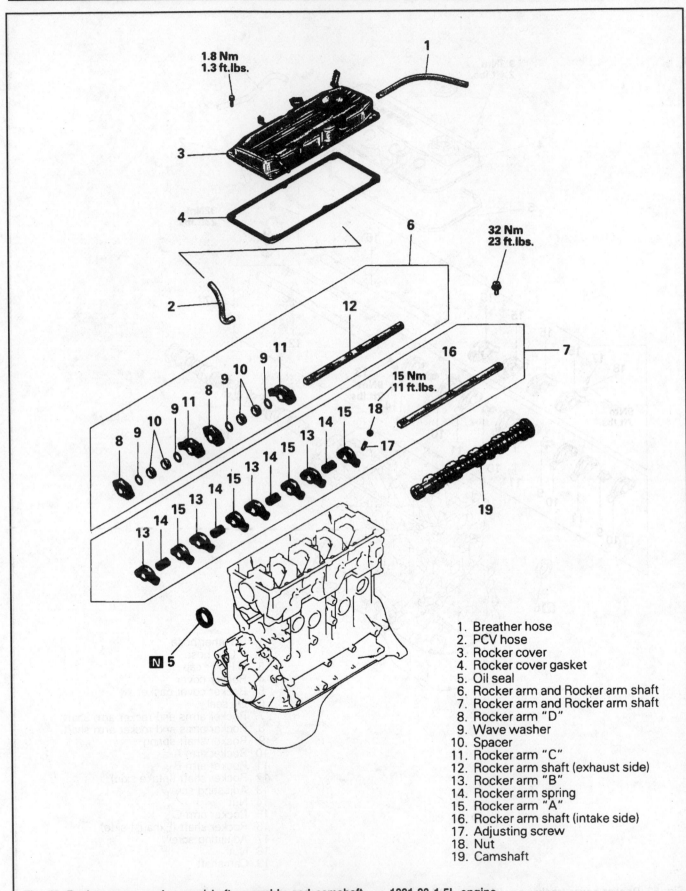

1.8 Nm
1.3 ft.lbs.

32 Nm
23 ft.lbs.

15 Nm
11 ft.lbs.

N 5

1. Breather hose
2. PCV hose
3. Rocker cover
4. Rocker cover gasket
5. Oil seal
6. Rocker arm and Rocker arm shaft
7. Rocker arm and Rocker arm shaft
8. Rocker arm "D"
9. Wave washer
10. Spacer
11. Rocker arm "C"
12. Rocker arm shaft (exhaust side)
13. Rocker arm "B"
14. Rocker arm spring
15. Rocker arm "A"
16. Rocker arm shaft (intake side)
17. Adjusting screw
18. Nut
19. Camshaft

Fig. 53 Rocker cover, rocker arm/shaft assembly and camshaft — 1991-93 1.5L engine

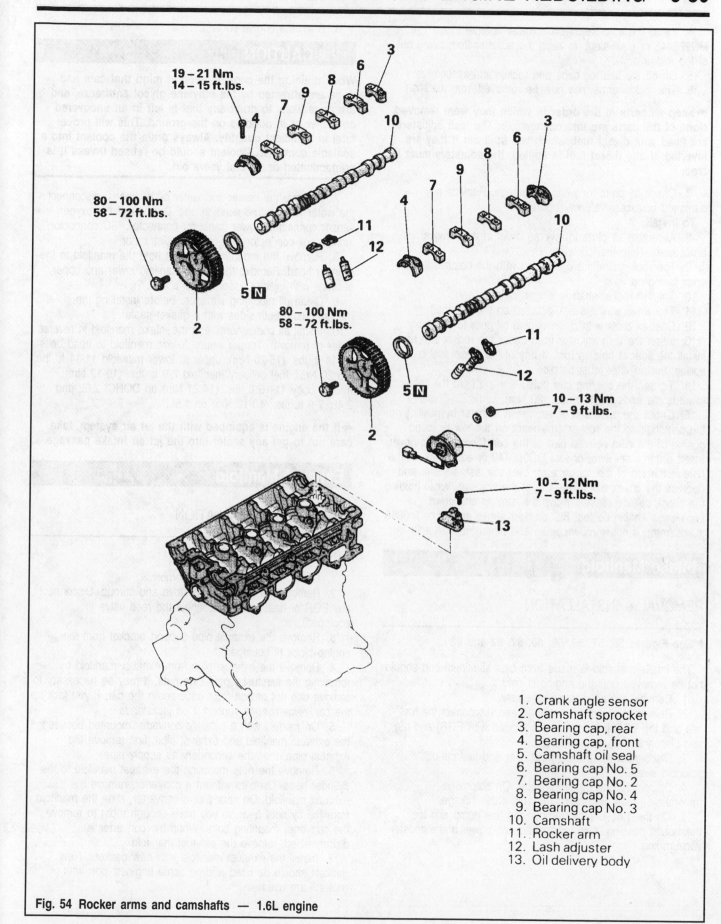

19 – 21 Nm
14 – 15 ft.lbs.

80 – 100 Nm
58 – 72 ft.lbs.

80 – 100 Nm
58 – 72 ft.lbs.

10 – 13 Nm
7 – 9 ft.lbs.

10 – 12 Nm
7 – 9 ft.lbs.

1. Crank angle sensor
2. Camshaft sprocket
3. Bearing cap, rear
4. Bearing cap, front
5. Camshaft oil seal
6. Bearing cap No. 5
7. Bearing cap No. 2
8. Bearing cap No. 4
9. Bearing cap No. 3
10. Camshaft
11. Rocker arm
12. Lash adjuster
13. Oil delivery body

Fig. 54 Rocker arms and camshafts — 1.6L engine

4. Install the automatic lash adjuster retainer tool MD998443 or equivalent, to keep the adjuster from falling out of the rocker arms.

5. Lift off the bearing caps and rocker arm assemblies.

6. The rocker arms may now be removed from the shaft.

➡ **Keep all parts in the order in which they were removed. None of the parts are interchangeable. The lash adjusters are filled with diesel fuel, which will spill out if they are inverted. If any diesel fuel is spilled, the adjusters must be bled.**

7. Check all parts for wear or damage. Replace any damaged or excessively worn parts.

To install:

8. Assemble all parts in reverse order of the removal procedures. Note the following:

9. The rocker shafts are installed with the notches in the ends facing up.

10. The left rocker shaft is longer than the right.

11. The wave washers are installed on the left shaft.

12. Coat all parts with clean engine oil prior to assembly.

13. Insert the lash adjuster from under the rocker arm and install the special holding tool. If any of the diesel fuel is spilled, the adjuster must be bled.

14. Tighten the bearing cap bolts, working from the center towards the ends to 15 ft. lbs. (20 Nm).

15. Check the operation of each lash adjuster by positioning the camshaft so the rocker arm bears on the low or round portion of the cam pointed part of the can faces straight down. Insert a thin steel wire, or tool MD998442 or equivalent, in the hole in the top of the rocker arm, over the lash adjuster and depress the check ball at the top of the adjuster. While holding the check ball depressed, move the arm up and down. Looseness should be felt. Full plunger stroke should be 0.0866 in. (2.2mm). If not, remove, clean and bleed the lash adjuster.

Intake Manifold

REMOVAL & INSTALLATION

▶ **See Figures 56, 57, 58, 59, 60, 61, 62 and 63**

The intake manifold is made from cast aluminum and should not he removed until the engine is cold.

1. Remove the air cleaner assembly.

2. Release fuel system pressure and disconnect the fuel line and the EGR lines (models equipped with EGR) and tag and disconnect all vacuum hoses.

3. Disconnect the throttle positioner and fuel cut-off solenoid wires.

4. Disconnect the throttle linkage. On automatic transmission cars disconnect the shift cable linkage.

5. On the 1.6L engine, remove the fuel pump and the thermostat housing. Also, disconnect the power brake booster vacuum line.

6. Drain the engine coolant.

❋❋CAUTION

When draining the coolant, keep in mind that cats and dogs are attracted by the ethylene glycol antifreeze, and are quite likely to drink any that is left in an uncovered container or in puddles on the ground. This will prove fatal in sufficient quantity. Always drain the coolant into a sealable container. Coolant should be reused unless it is contaminated or several years old.

7. Remove the heater and water outlet hoses, disconnect the water temperature sending unit. Disconnect the oxygen sensor connector, power transistor connector, ISC connector, ignition coil connector, etc., and the distributor.

8. Remove the mounting nuts that hold the manifold to the cylinder head. Remove the intake manifold lower and upper sections with injector assembly as a unit.

9. Clean all mounting surfaces. Before installing the manifold, coat both sides with a gasket sealer.

10. Install all components and the intake manifold in reverse order of removal. Torque values follow: manifold to head bolts 11-14 ft. lbs. (15-20 Nm); upper to lower manifold 11-14 ft. lbs. (15-20 Nm); fuel delivery manifold 7-9 ft. lbs. (10-12 Nm); throttle body 11-16 ft. lbs. (14-21 Nm) on DOHC, 2.0L and 2.4L; 7-9 ft. lbs. (10-12 Nm) on 1.5L.

➡ **If the engine is equipped with the jet air system, take care not to get any sealer into the jet air intake passage.**

Exhaust Manifold

REMOVAL & INSTALLATION

▶ **See Figures 64, 65, 66 and 67**

1. Remove the air cleaner assembly.

2. Remove the air duct-heat stove and shroud. Disconnect any EGR or heat lines. Disconnect the reed valve (if equipped).

3. Remove the exhaust pipe support bracket from the engine block (if equipped).

4. Remove the exhaust pipe from exhaust manifold by removing the exhaust pipe flange nuts. It may be necessary to remove one nut or bolt from underneath the car. If you jack up the car, remember to support it on jackstands.

5. On models with a catalytic converter mounted between the exhaust manifold and exhaust pipe: first remove the exhaust pipe, then the secondary air supply pipe.

6. Remove the nuts mounting the exhaust manifold to the cylinder head. On cars without a converter, remove the exhaust manifold. On cars with a converter, slide the manifold from the cylinder hear so you have enough room to remove the converter mounting bolts. When the converter is disconnected, remove the exhaust manifold.

7. Install the exhaust manifold with new gaskets. New gaskets should be used and on some engines, port liner gaskets are used.

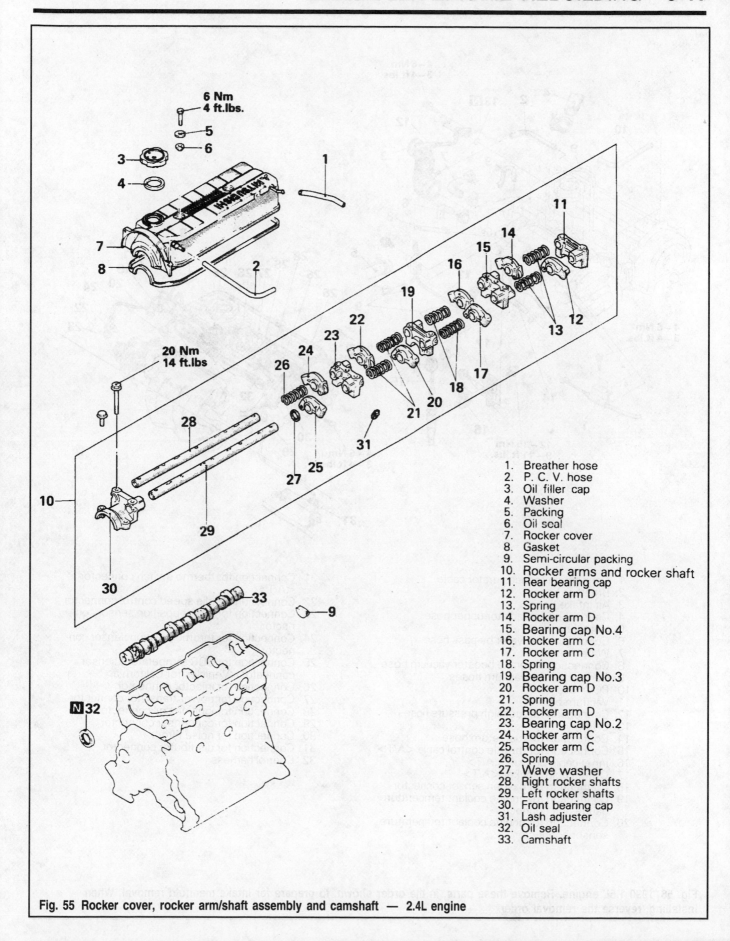

1. Breather hose
2. P. C. V. hose
3. Oil filler cap
4. Washer
5. Packing
6. Oil seal
7. Rocker cover
8. Gasket
9. Semi-circular packing
10. Rocker arms and rocker shaft
11. Rear bearing cap
12. Rocker arm D
13. Spring
14. Rocker arm D
15. Bearing cap No.4
16. Rocker arm C
17. Rocker arm C
18. Spring
19. Bearing cap No.3
20. Rocker arm D
21. Spring
22. Rocker arm D
23. Bearing cap No.2
24. Rocker arm C
25. Rocker arm C
26. Spring
27. Wave washer
28. Right rocker shafts
29. Left rocker shafts
30. Front bearing cap
31. Lash adjuster
32. Oil seal
33. Camshaft

Fig. 55 Rocker cover, rocker arm/shaft assembly and camshaft — 2.4L engine

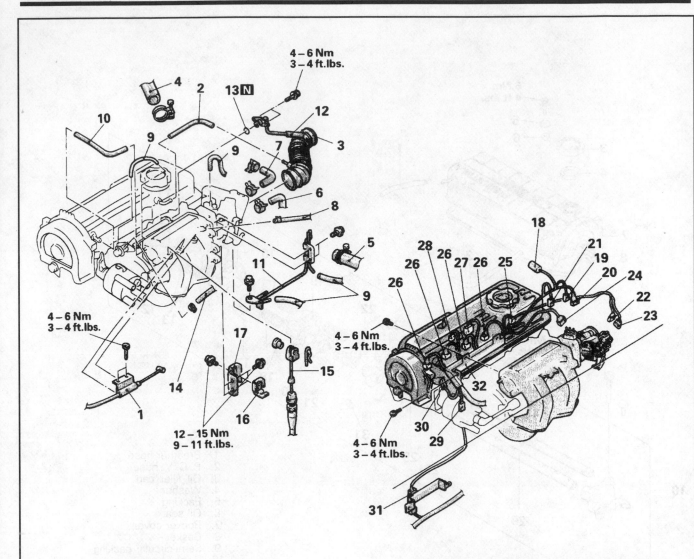

1. Connection for accelerator cable
2. Breather hose
3. Air intake hose
4. Connection for radiator upper hose
5. Heater hose
6. Connection for water by-pass hose
7. Water hose
8. Connection for brake booster vacuum hose
9. Connection for vacuum hoses
10. PCV hose
11. Vacuum pipe
12. Connection for fuel high pressure hose
13. O-ring
14. Connection for fuel return hose
15. Connection for throttle control cable <A/T>
16. Inner cable bracket <A/T>
17. Outer cable bracket <A/T>
18. Connection for oxygen sensor connector
19. Connection for engine coolant temperature gauge unit connector
20. Connection for engine coolant temperature sensor connector

21. Connection for thermo switch connector <A/T>
22. Connection for idle speed control connector
23. Connection for motor position sensor connector
24. Connection for throttle position sensor connector
25. Connection for EGR temperature sensor connector <Vehicles for California>
26. Connection for injector connector
27. Connection for power transistor connector
28. Connection for ignition coil connector
29. Connection for condenser connector
30. Connection for noise filter
31. Connection for distributor connector
32. Control harness

Fig. 56 1990 1.5L engine. Remove these parts, in the order shown, to prepare for intake manifold removal. When installing, reverse the removal order

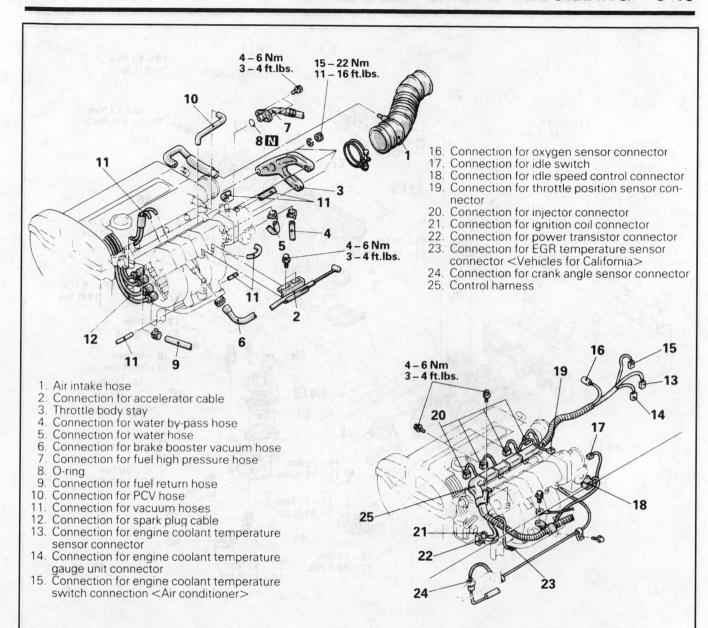

16. Connection for oxygen sensor connector
17. Connection for idle switch
18. Connection for idle speed control connector
19. Connection for throttle position sensor connector
20. Connection for injector connector
21. Connection for ignition coil connector
22. Connection for power transistor connector
23. Connection for EGR temperature sensor connector <Vehicles for California>
24. Connection for crank angle sensor connector
25. Control harness

1. Air intake hose
2. Connection for accelerator cable
3. Throttle body stay
4. Connection for water by-pass hose
5. Connection for water hose
6. Connection for brake booster vacuum hose
7. Connection for fuel high pressure hose
8. O-ring
9. Connection for fuel return hose
10. Connection for PCV hose
11. Connection for vacuum hoses
12. Connection for spark plug cable
13. Connection for engine coolant temperature sensor connector
14. Connection for engine coolant temperature gauge unit connector
15. Connection for engine coolant temperature switch connection <Air conditioner>

Fig. 57 1.6L engine. Remove these parts, in the order shown, to prepare for intake manifold removal. When installing, reverse the removal order

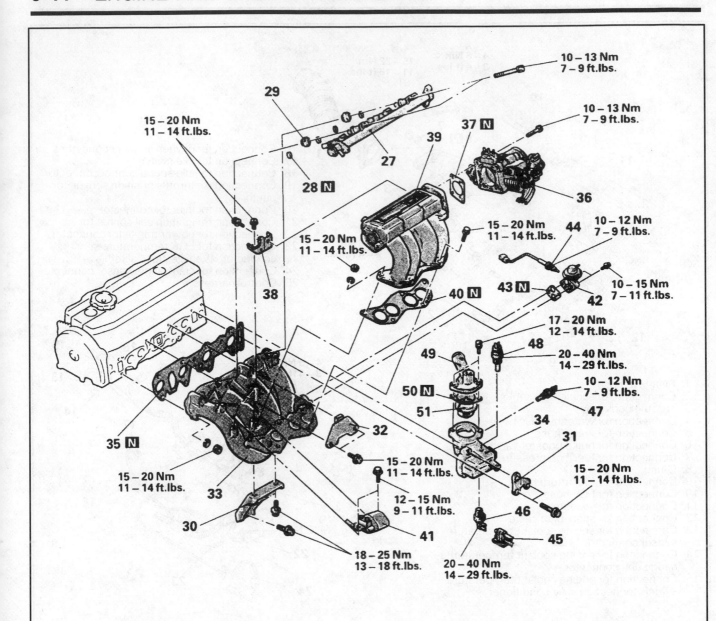

27. Delivery pipe, fuel injector and pressure regulator
28. Insulator
29. Insulator
30. Intake manifold stay
31. Engine hanger
32. Power transistor bracket
33. Intake manifold
34. Thermostat housing
35. Intake manifold gasket
36. Throttle body assembly
37. Gasket
38. Air intake plenum stay
39. Air intake plenum
40. Air intake plenum gasket
41. Ignition coil
42. EGR valve
43. EGR gasket
44. EGR temperature sensor <Vehicles for California>
45. Vacuum hose
46. Thermo valve
47. Engine coolant temperature gauge unit
48. Engine coolant temperature sensor
49. Water outlet fitting
50. Gasket
51. Thermostat

Fig. 58 1990 1.8L engine. To remove the upper and lower intake manifolds, proceed in the order illustrated. When installing the manifolds, reverse the removal sequence

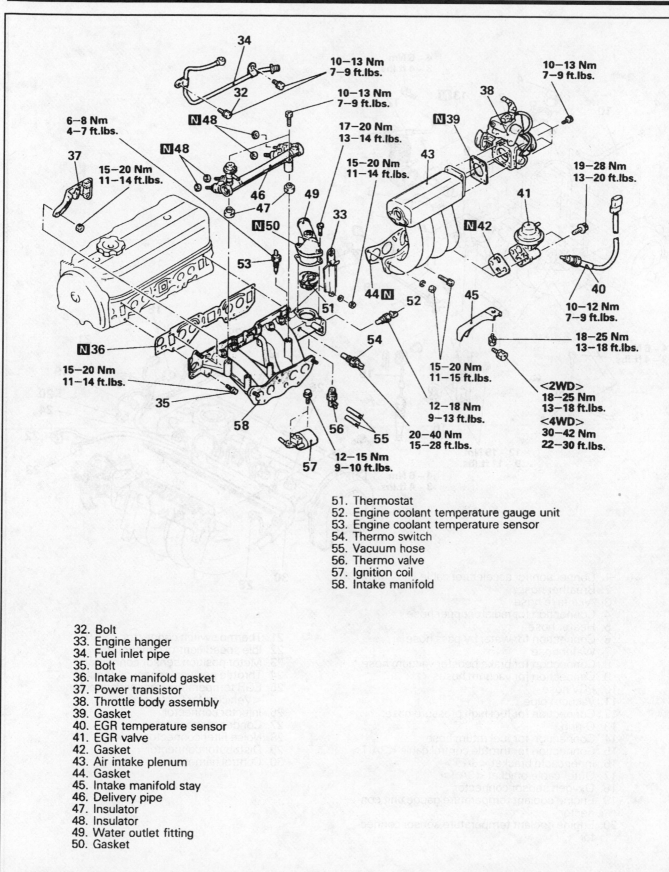

51. Thermostat
52. Engine coolant temperature gauge unit
53. Engine coolant temperature sensor
54. Thermo switch
55. Vacuum hose
56. Thermo valve
57. Ignition coil
58. Intake manifold

32. Bolt
33. Engine hanger
34. Fuel inlet pipe
35. Bolt
36. Intake manifold gasket
37. Power transistor
38. Throttle body assembly
39. Gasket
40. EGR temperature sensor
41. EGR valve
42. Gasket
43. Air intake plenum
44. Gasket
45. Intake manifold stay
46. Delivery pipe
47. Insulator
48. Insulator
49. Water outlet fitting
50. Gasket

Fig. 59 2.0L engine. To remove the upper and lower intake manifolds, proceed in the order illustrated. When installing the manifolds, reverse the removal sequence

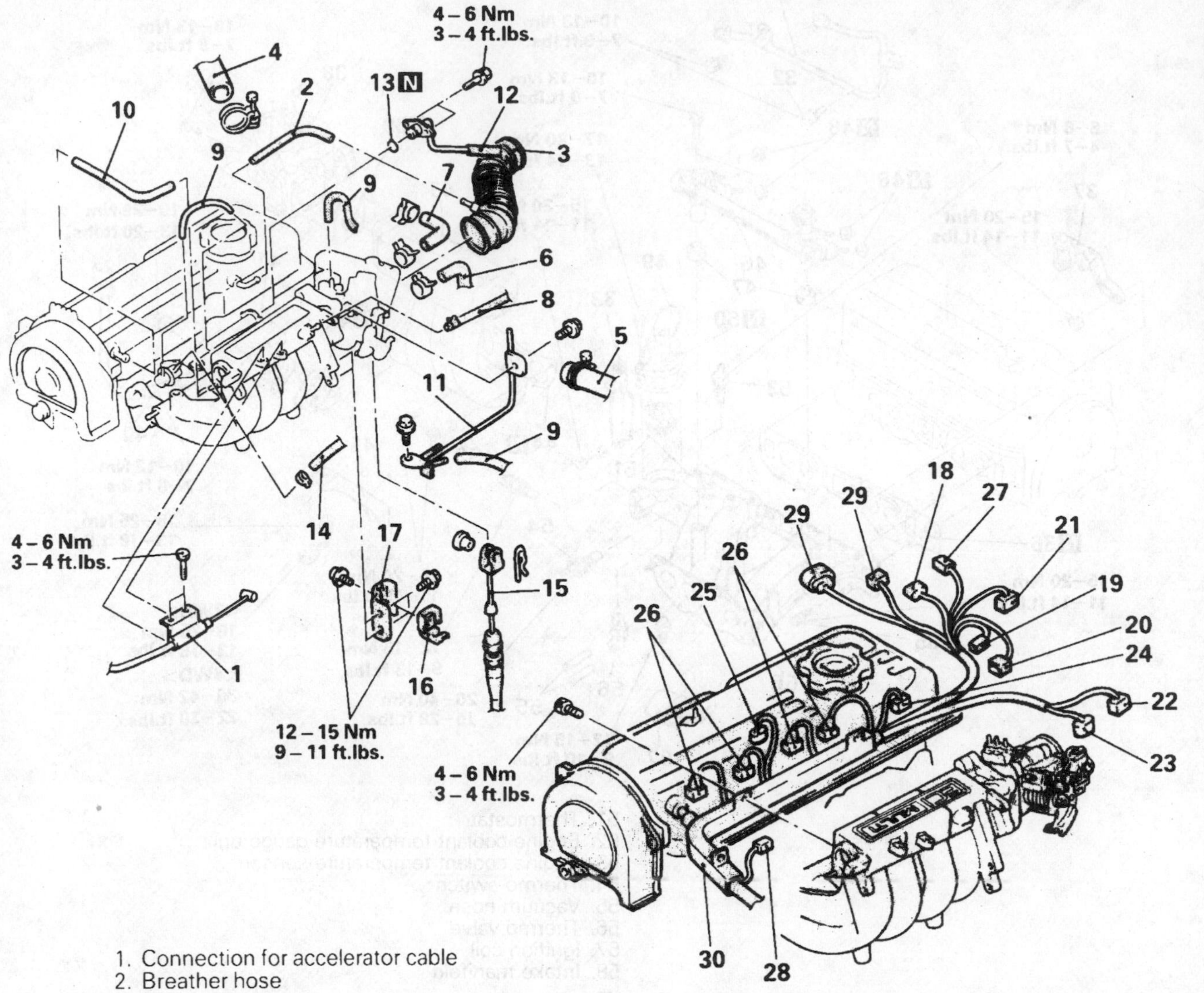

1. Connection for accelerator cable
2. Breather hose
3. Air intake hose
4. Connection for radiator upper hose
5. Heater hose
6. Connection for water by-pass hose
7. Water hose
8. Connection for brake booster vacuum hose
9. Connection for vacuum hoses
10. PCV hose
11. Vacuum pipe
12. Connection for fuel high pressure hose
13. O-ring
14. Connection for fuel return hose
15. Connection for throttle control cable <3A/T>
16. Inner cable bracket <3A/T>
17. Outer cable bracket <3A/T>
18. Oxygen sensor connector
19. Engine coolant temperature gauge unit connector
20. Engine coolant temperature sensor connector

21. Thermo switch connector <3A/T>
22. Idle speed control connector
23. Motor position sensor connector
24. Throttle position sensor connector
25. EGR temperature sensor connector <Vehicles for California>
26. Injector connector
27. Condenser connector
28. Noise filter connector
29. Distributor connector
30. Control harness

Fig. 60 1991-92 1.5L engine. Remove these parts, in the order shown, to prepare for intake manifold removal. When installing, reverse the removal order

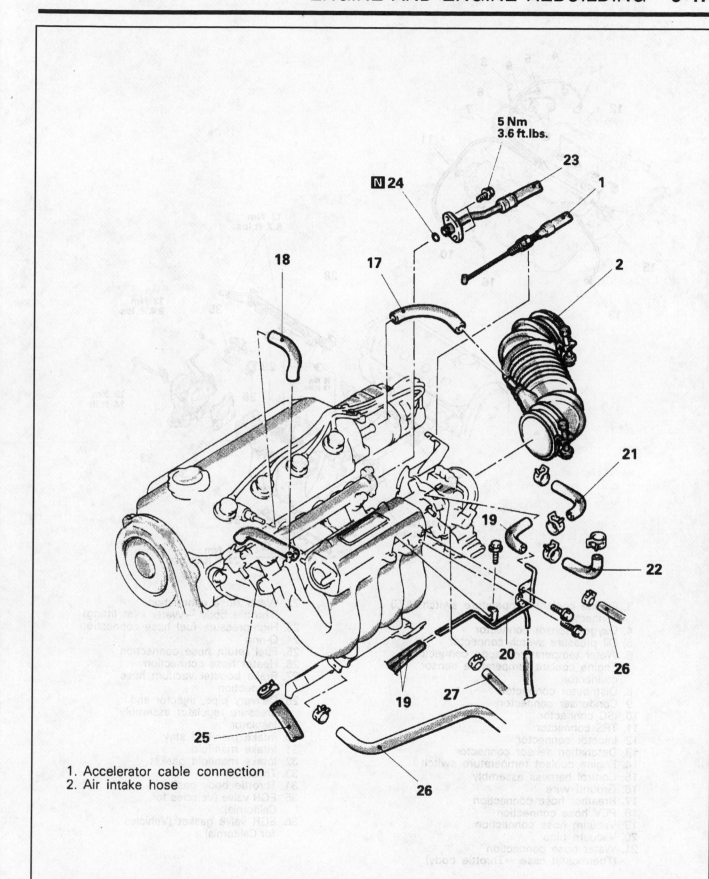

5 Nm
3.6 ft.lbs.

1. Accelerator cable connection
2. Air intake hose

Fig. 61 1992-93 1.8L engine. Remove these parts, in the order shown, to prepare for intake manifold removal. When installing, reverse the removal order

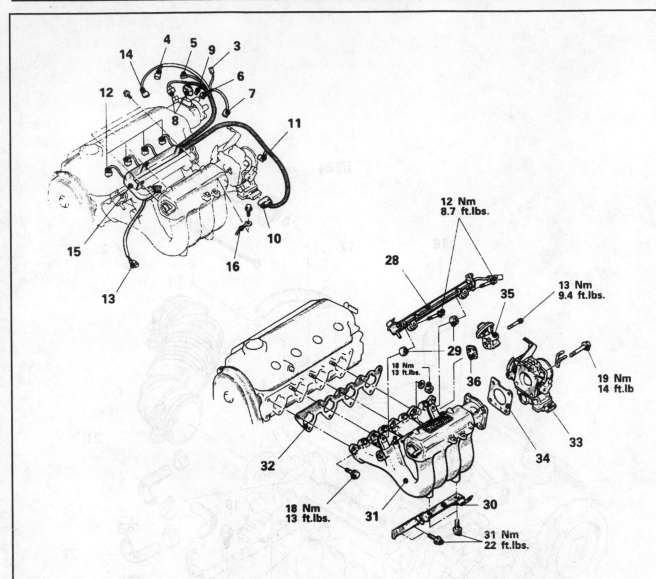

3. Engine coolant temperature switch (A/C) connector
4. Oxygen sensor connector
5. Oil pressure switch connector
6. Water temperature gauge connector
7. Engine coolant temperature sensor connector
8. Distributor connector
9. Condenser connector
10. ISC connector
11. TPS connector
12. Injector connector
13. Detonation sensor connector
14. Engine coolant temperature switch
15. Control harness assembly
16. Ground wire
17. Breather hose connection
18. PCV hose connection
19. Vacuum hose connection
20. Vacuum pipe
21. Water hose connection (Thermostat case →Throttle body)

22. Water hose connection (Throttle body →Water inlet fitting)
23. High-pressure fuel hose connection
24. O-ring
25. Fuel return hose connection
26. Heater hose connection
27. Brake booster vacuum hose connection
28. Delivery pipe, injector and pressure regulator assembly
29. Insulator
30. Intake manifold stay
31. Intake manifold
32. Intake manifold gasket
33. Throttle body
34. Throttle body gasket
35. EGR valve (Vehicles for California)
36. EGR valve gasket (Vehicles for California)

Fig. 62 1992-93 1.8L engine. To remove the intake manifold, proceed in the order illustrated. When installing the manifold, reverse the removal sequence

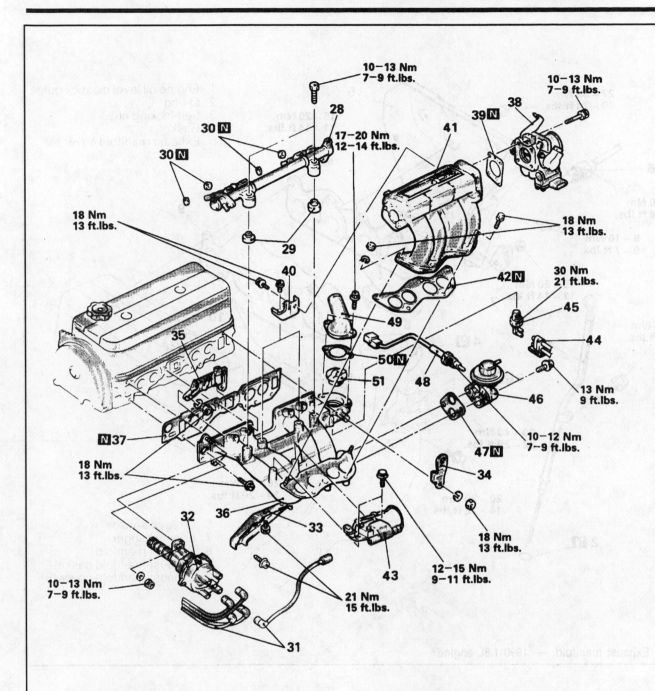

10—13 Nm
7—9 ft.lbs.

10—13 Nm
7—9 ft.lbs.

17—20 Nm
12—14 ft.lbs.

18 Nm
13 ft.lbs.

18 Nm
13 ft.lbs.

30 Nm
21 ft.lbs.

18 Nm
13 ft.lbs.

13 Nm
9 ft.lbs.

10—12 Nm
7—9 ft.lbs.

18 Nm
13 ft.lbs.

10—13 Nm
7—9 ft.lbs.

12—15 Nm
9—11 ft.lbs.

21 Nm
15 ft.lbs.

28. Delivery pipe, fuel injector and pressure
    regulator
29. Insulator
30. Insulator
31. High tension cable and spark plug cable
32. Distributor
33. Intake manifold stay
34. Engine hanger
35. Power transistor bracket
36. Intake manifold
37. Intake manifold gasket
38. Throttle body assembly
39. Gasket

40. Air intake plenum stay
41. Air intake plenum
42. Air intake plenum gasket
43. Ignition coil
44. Vacuum hose <Vehicles for Federal>
45. Thermo valve <Vehicles for Federal>
46. EGR valve
47. EGR gasket
48. EGR temperature sensor <Vehicles for California>
49. Water outlet fitting
50. Gasket
51. Thermostat

Fig. 63 2.4L engine. To remove the upper and lower intake manifolds, proceed in the order illustrated. When installing the manifolds, reverse the removal sequence

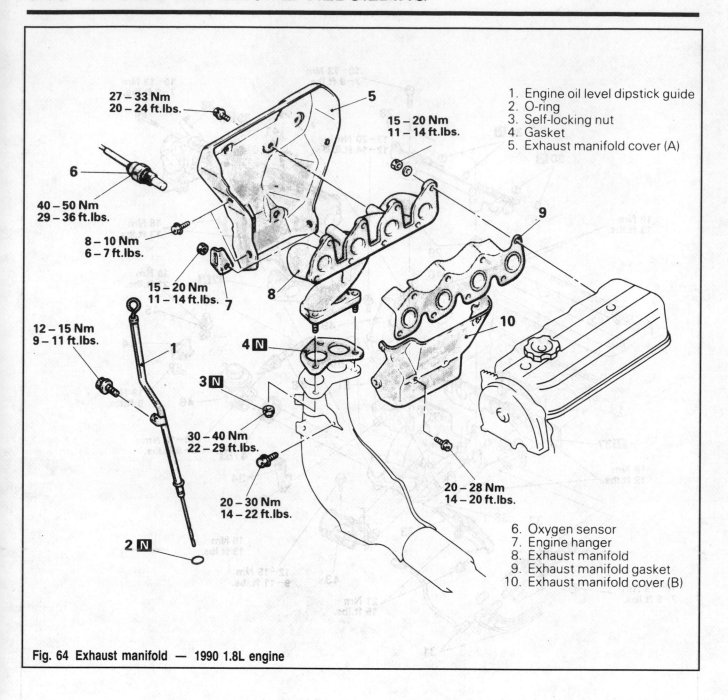

27 – 33 Nm
20 – 24 ft.lbs.

15 – 20 Nm
11 – 14 ft.lbs.

40 – 50 Nm
29 – 36 ft.lbs.

8 – 10 Nm
6 – 7 ft.lbs.

15 – 20 Nm
11 – 14 ft.lbs.

12 – 15 Nm
9 – 11 ft.lbs.

30 – 40 Nm
22 – 29 ft.lbs.

20 – 30 Nm
14 – 22 ft.lbs.

20 – 28 Nm
14 – 20 ft.lbs.

1. Engine oil level dipstick guide
2. O-ring
3. Self-locking nut
4. Gasket
5. Exhaust manifold cover (A)

6. Oxygen sensor
7. Engine hanger
8. Exhaust manifold
9. Exhaust manifold gasket
10. Exhaust manifold cover (B)

Fig. 64 Exhaust manifold — 1990 1.8L engine

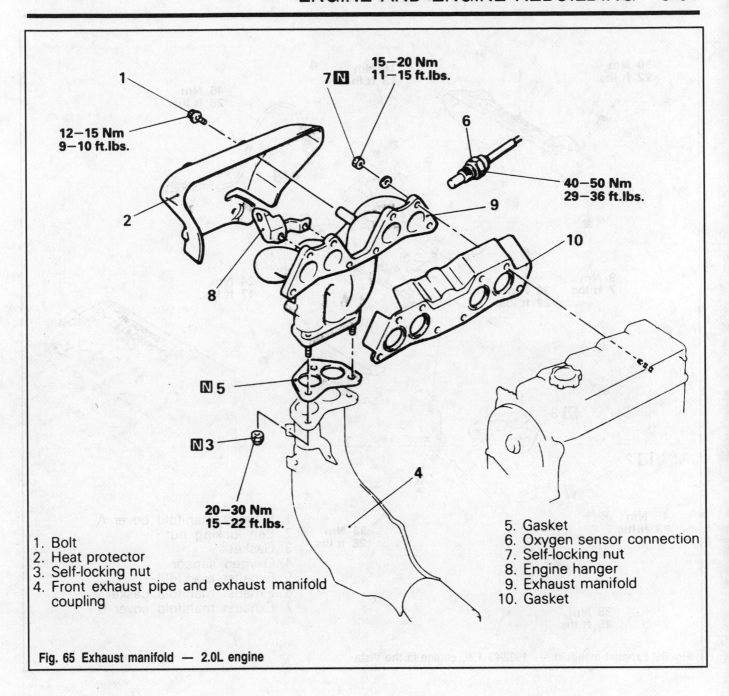

1. Bolt
2. Heat protector
3. Self-locking nut
4. Front exhaust pipe and exhaust manifold coupling

5. Gasket
6. Oxygen sensor connection
7. Self-locking nut
8. Engine hanger
9. Exhaust manifold
10. Gasket

Fig. 65 Exhaust manifold — 2.0L engine

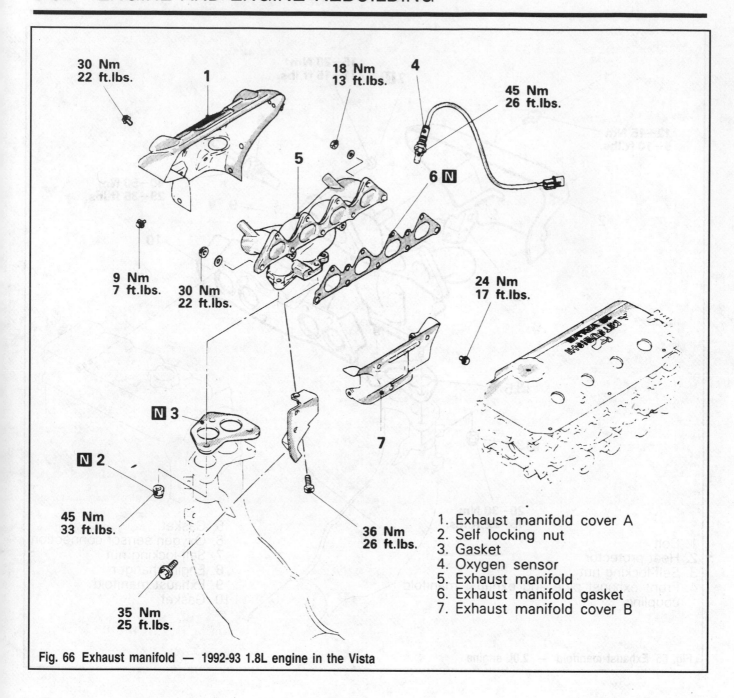

30 Nm
22 ft.lbs.

1

18 Nm
13 ft.lbs.

4

45 Nm
26 ft.lbs.

5

6

9 Nm
7 ft.lbs.

30 Nm
22 ft.lbs.

24 Nm
17 ft.lbs.

7

3

2

45 Nm
33 ft.lbs.

36 Nm
26 ft.lbs.

35 Nm
25 ft.lbs.

1. Exhaust manifold cover A
2. Self locking nut
3. Gasket
4. Oxygen sensor
5. Exhaust manifold
6. Exhaust manifold gasket
7. Exhaust manifold cover B

Fig. 66 Exhaust manifold — 1992-93 1.8L engine in the Vista

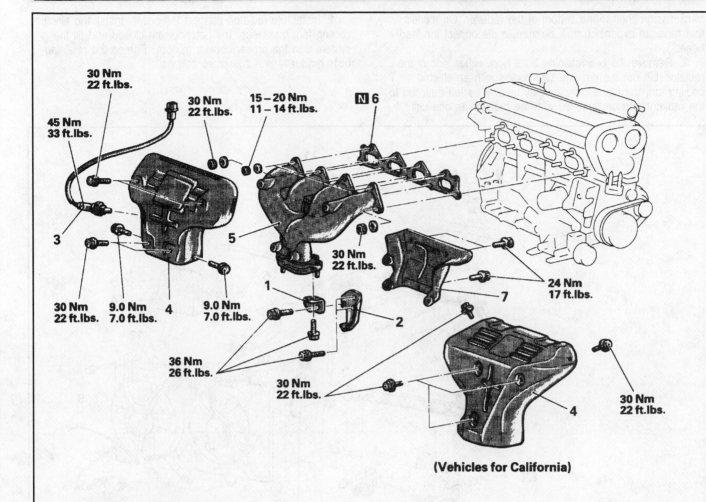

30 Nm
22 ft.lbs.

30 Nm
22 ft.lbs.

15 – 20 Nm
11 – 14 ft.lbs.

45 Nm
33 ft.lbs.

3

5

1

2

6

7

30 Nm
22 ft.lbs.

24 Nm
17 ft.lbs.

30 Nm
22 ft.lbs.

9.0 Nm
7.0 ft.lbs.

4

9.0 Nm
7.0 ft.lbs.

36 Nm
26 ft.lbs.

30 Nm
22 ft.lbs.

4

30 Nm
22 ft.lbs.

(Vehicles for California)

1. Bracket exhaust manifold B
2. Bracket exhaust manifold A
3. Oxygen sensor
4. Exhaust manifold cover A
5. Exhaust manifold
6. Exhaust manifold gasket
7. Exhaust manifold cover B

Fig. 67 Exhaust manifold — 1993 1.8L engine in the Colt

Radiator

REMOVAL & INSTALLATION

▶ See Figures 68, 69, 70, 71 and 72

※※CAUTION

The electric cooling fan may operate when the engine is turned off, or at various times when the engine is running. Be careful when working around the fan. Disconnect the negative battery cable when servicing the cooling system components.

1. Disconnect the negative battery cable. Remove the splash panel from the bottom of the car. Drain the radiator by opening the petcock. Remove the shroud on models so equipped. Disconnect the fan motor wiring harness.

※※CAUTION

When draining the coolant, keep in mind that cats and dogs are attracted by the ethylene glycol antifreeze, and are quite likely to drink any that is left in an uncovered container or in puddles on the ground. This will prove fatal in sufficient quantity. Always drain the coolant into a sealable container. Coolant should be reused unless it is contaminated or several years old.

2. Disconnect the radiator hoses at the engine. On automatic transmission cars, disconnect and plug the

transmission lines to the bottom of the radiator. On models that have an expansion tank be sure to disconnect the feed hose.

3. Remove the two retaining bolts from either side of the radiator. Lift out the radiator. On models with an electric cooling fan, the fan and motor may usually be left attached to the radiator and be removed with the radiator as one unit.

4. Install the radiator, connect the hoses, install the electric cooling fan, make sure the petcocks are closed and fill the system with the proper coolant mixture. Tighten the retaining bolts gradually in a crisscross pattern.

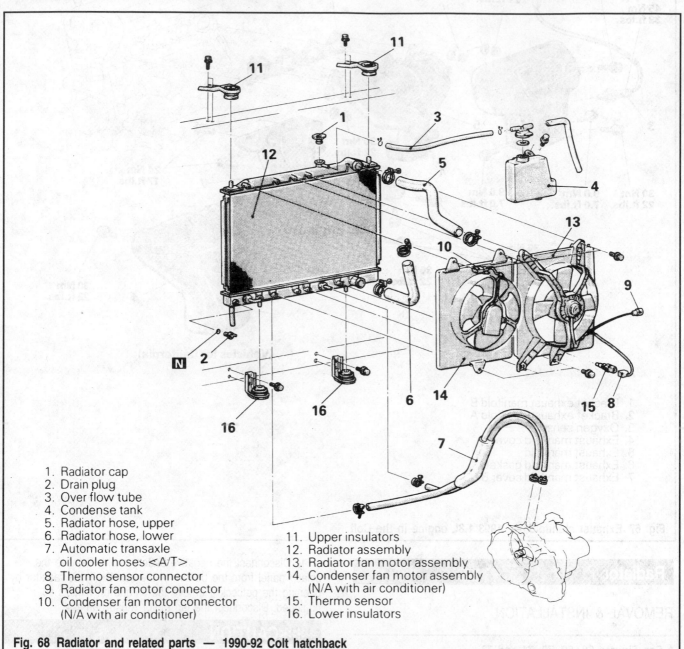

1. Radiator cap
2. Drain plug
3. Over flow tube
4. Condense tank
5. Radiator hose, upper
6. Radiator hose, lower
7. Automatic transaxle
   oil cooler hoses <A/T>
8. Thermo sensor connector
9. Radiator fan motor connector
10. Condenser fan motor connector
    (N/A with air conditioner)
11. Upper insulators
12. Radiator assembly
13. Radiator fan motor assembly
14. Condenser fan motor assembly
    (N/A with air conditioner)
15. Thermo sensor
16. Lower insulators

Fig. 68 Radiator and related parts — 1990-92 Colt hatchback

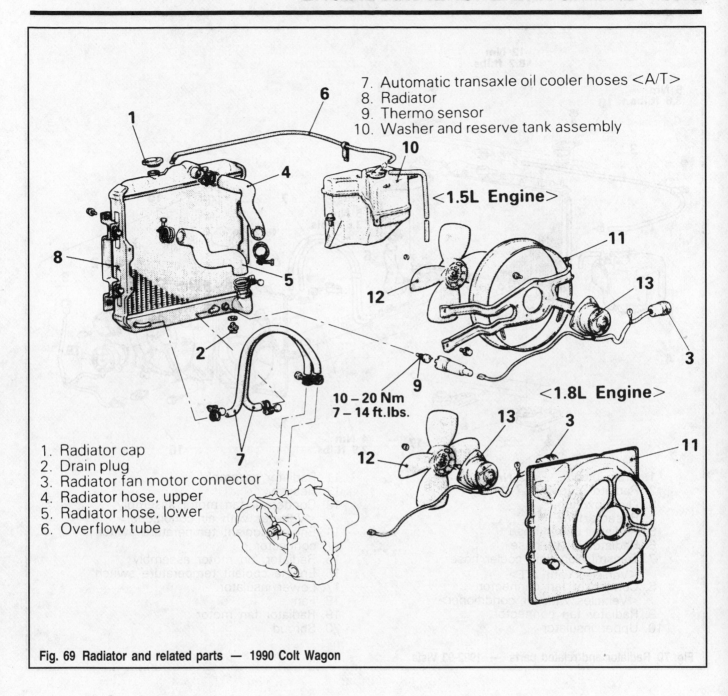

7. Automatic transaxle oil cooler hoses <A/T>
8. Radiator
9. Thermo sensor
10. Washer and reserve tank assembly

<1.5L Engine>

<1.8L Engine>

10 – 20 Nm
7 – 14 ft.lbs.

1. Radiator cap
2. Drain plug
3. Radiator fan motor connector
4. Radiator hose, upper
5. Radiator hose, lower
6. Overflow tube

Fig. 69 Radiator and related parts — 1990 Colt Wagon

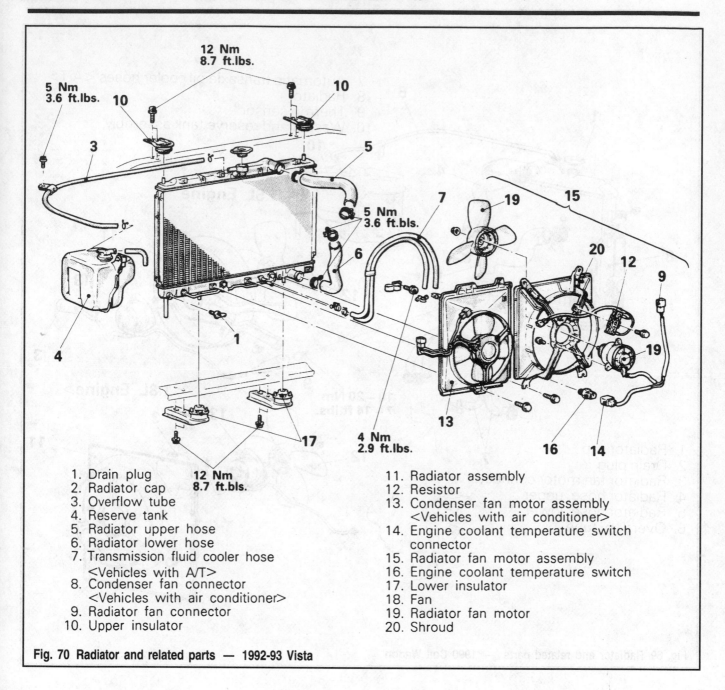

1. Drain plug
2. Radiator cap
3. Overflow tube
4. Reserve tank
5. Radiator upper hose
6. Radiator lower hose
7. Transmission fluid cooler hose
   <Vehicles with A/T>
8. Condenser fan connector
   <Vehicles with air conditioner>
9. Radiator fan connector
10. Upper insulator

11. Radiator assembly
12. Resistor
13. Condenser fan motor assembly
    <Vehicles with air conditioner>
14. Engine coolant temperature switch
    connector
15. Radiator fan motor assembly
16. Engine coolant temperature switch
17. Lower insulator
18. Fan
19. Radiator fan motor
20. Shroud

Fig. 70 Radiator and related parts — 1992-93 Vista

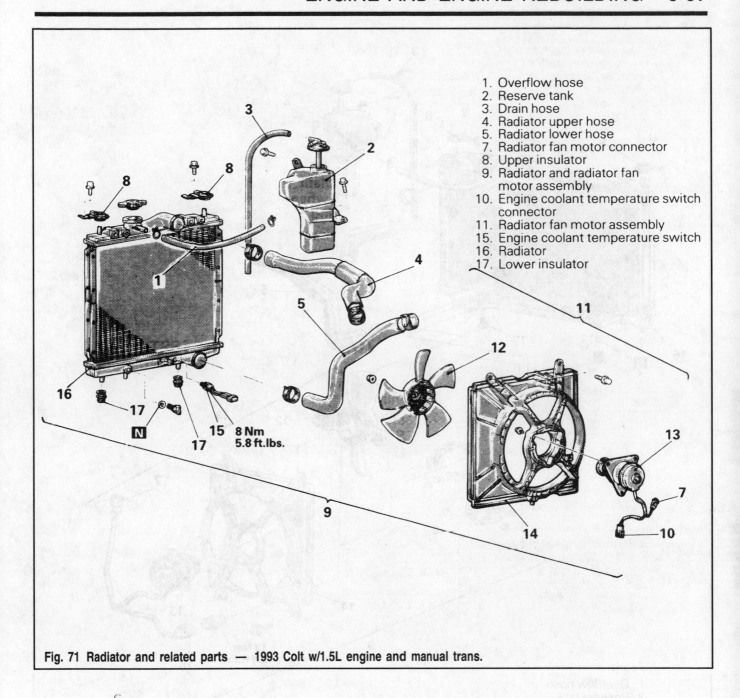

1. Overflow hose
2. Reserve tank
3. Drain hose
4. Radiator upper hose
5. Radiator lower hose
7. Radiator fan motor connector
8. Upper insulator
9. Radiator and radiator fan motor assembly
10. Engine coolant temperature switch connector
11. Radiator fan motor assembly
15. Engine coolant temperature switch
16. Radiator
17. Lower insulator

8 Nm
5.8 ft.lbs.

Fig. 71 Radiator and related parts — 1993 Colt w/1.5L engine and manual trans.

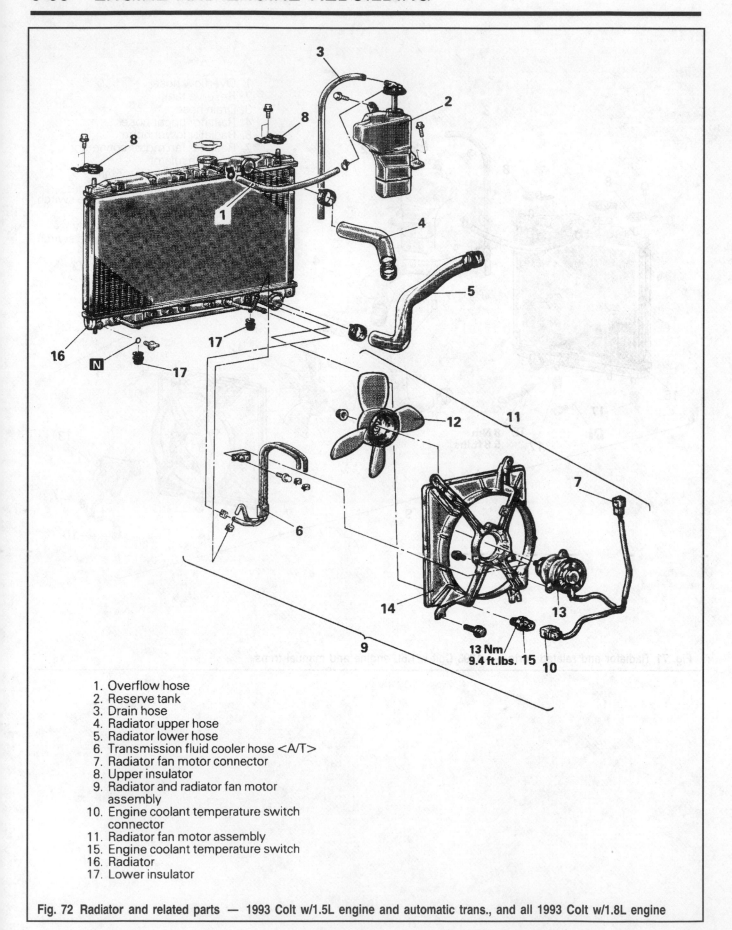

1. Overflow hose
2. Reserve tank
3. Drain hose
4. Radiator upper hose
5. Radiator lower hose
6. Transmission fluid cooler hose <A/T>
7. Radiator fan motor connector
8. Upper insulator
9. Radiator and radiator fan motor assembly
10. Engine coolant temperature switch connector
11. Radiator fan motor assembly
15. Engine coolant temperature switch
16. Radiator
17. Lower insulator

Fig. 72 Radiator and related parts — 1993 Colt w/1.5L engine and automatic trans., and all 1993 Colt w/1.8L engine

Water Pump

REMOVAL & INSTALLATION

▶ **See Figures 73, 74, 75, 76 and 77**

Colt and 1990-91 Vista

1. Drain the cooling system.
2. Remove the drive belt and water pump pulley.
3. Remove the timing belt covers and timing belt tensioner.
4. Remove the water pump bolts and alternator bracket.
5. Remove the water pump retaining bolts, it is important to observe the location of each bolt, they are different lengths.
6. Remove the water pump.

➡**The pump is not rebuildable. Check for driveshaft side to side play, if excessive replace the pump. If there are signs of damage or leakage from the seals or vent hole, the unit must be replaced.**

To install:

7. Discard the O-ring in the front end of the water pipe. Install a new O-ring coated with water.
8. Using a new gasket, mount the water pump and alternator bracket on the engine. Torque the bolts with a head marked '4' to 9-11 ft. lbs. (12-15 Nm); the bolts with a head marked '7' to 14-20 ft. lbs. (20-27 Nm).
9. Complete the remainder of installation in the reverse order of removal procedure. Fill the system with coolant and check for leaks.

1992-93 Vista

1. Disconnect the negative battery cable and drain the engine coolant.
2. Remove the drive belts and move the accessories out of the way, if necessary. Remove the alternator bracket.
3. Align the crankshaft timing mark to TDC of No. 1 cylinder. Remove the timing belt cover and timing belt as outlined in this section.
4. Remove the water pump.

To install:

5. Clean the gasket mating surfaces.
6. Install the water pump with a new gasket. The water pump bolts are different sizes. Make sure they are properly installed before tightening. Torque the bolts to 18 ft. lbs. (24 Nm). Install a new O-ring for the 2.4L engine.
7. Install the timing belt and cover.
8. Install the accessories and belts.
9. Install the remaining components.
10. Fill the engine with coolant, start the engine and check for leaks.

Thermostat

REMOVAL & INSTALLATION

▶ **See Figures 78 and 79**

Colt and 1990-91 Vista

1. Disconnect the negative battery cable.
2. Drain the cooling system to a point below the thermostat level.
3. Remove the air cleaner.
4. Disconnect the hose at the thermostat water pipe.
5. Remove the water pipe support bracket nut.

➡**This nut is also an intake manifold nut. It is very difficult to get to. A deep offset 12mm box wrench is used to remove or replace it.**

6. Unbolt and remove the thermostat housing and pipe.
7. Lift out the thermostat. Discard the gasket.

To install:

8. Clean the mating surfaces of the housing and manifold thoroughly.
9. Install the thermostat with the spring facing downward and position a new gasket. The jiggle valve in the thermostat should be on the manifold side.
10. Install the housing and pipe assembly. Torque the housing bolts to 11 ft. lbs. (14 Nm); the intake manifold nut to 14 ft. lbs. (19 Nm).
11. Refill the system with coolant. Connect the negative battery cable.
12. Start the engine and check for leaks.

1992-93 Vista

1. Drain the engine coolant to a level below the thermostat.
2. Remove the connection for the radiator upper hose.
3. Remove the water outlet fitting.
4. Remove the thermostat.

To install:

5. The thermostat should be closed tightly at room temperature and open 0.31 in. (8mm) when fully open. The opening temperature is 170°F (77°C) for the 1.8L engine and 190°F (88°C) for the 2.4L engine
6. Clean the gasket mating surfaces.
7. Install the thermostat with a new gasket.

➡**The jiggle valve should be aligned with the mark on the thermostat housing. If there is no mark, position the valve facing up. The main body of the thermostat should face the engine.**

8. Install the remaining components. Torque the housing bolts to 14 ft. lbs. (19 Nm).
9. Refill the engine with coolant, start the engine and check for leaks.

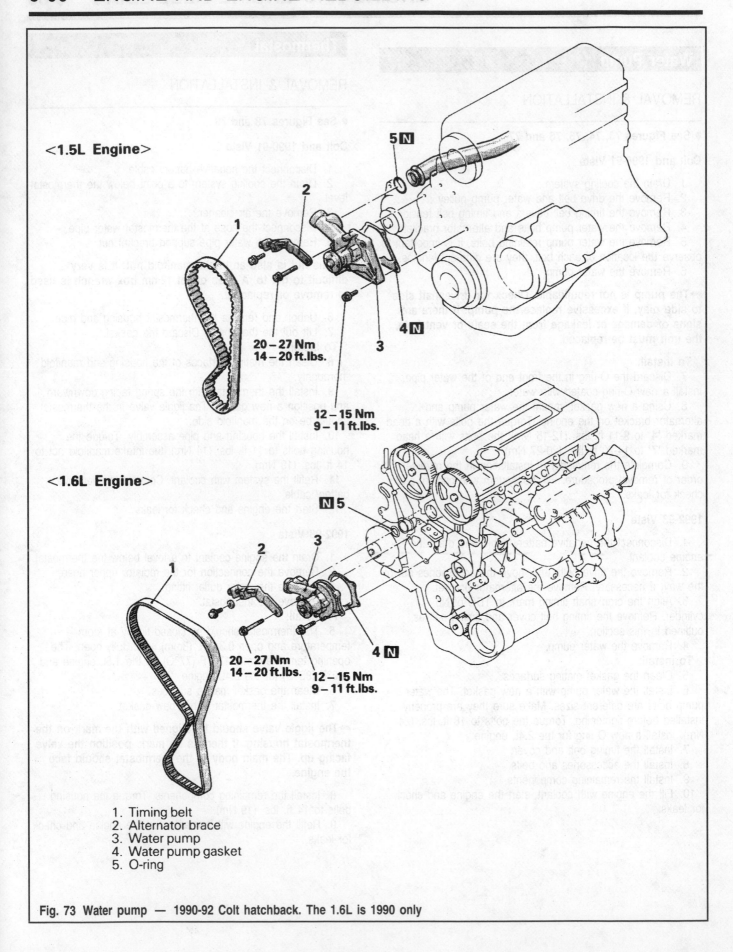

<1.5L Engine>

5

20 – 27 Nm
14 – 20 ft.lbs.

4

12 – 15 Nm
9 – 11 ft.lbs.

<1.6L Engine>

N 5

20 – 27 Nm
14 – 20 ft.lbs.

12 – 15 Nm
9 – 11 ft.lbs.

4 N

1. Timing belt
2. Alternator brace
3. Water pump
4. Water pump gasket
5. O-ring

Fig. 73 Water pump — 1990-92 Colt hatchback. The 1.6L is 1990 only

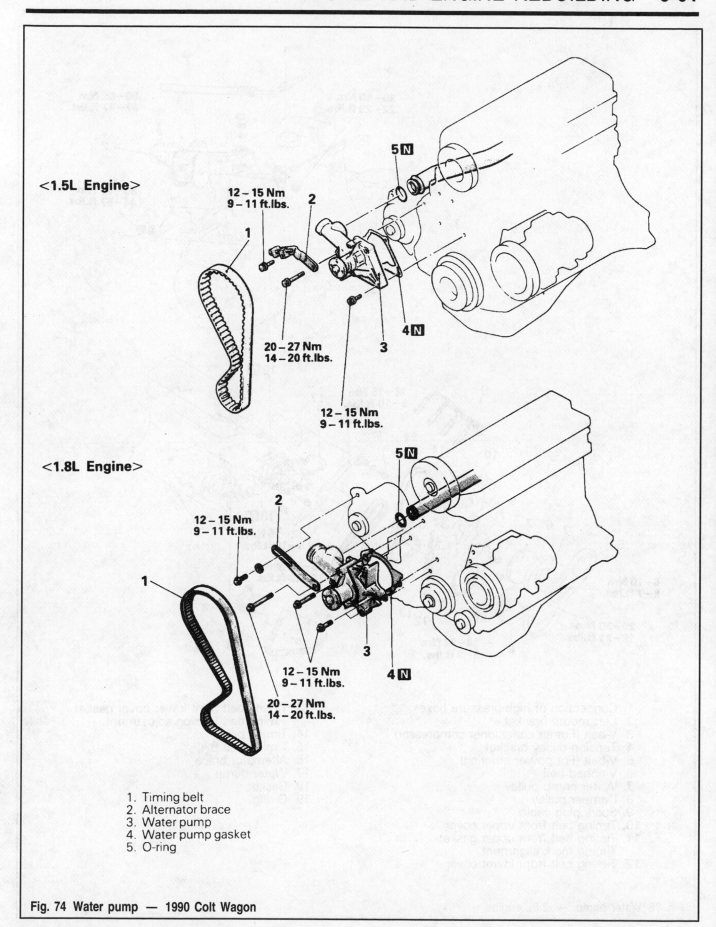

<1.5L Engine>

12 – 15 Nm
9 – 11 ft.lbs.

20 – 27 Nm
14 – 20 ft.lbs.

12 – 15 Nm
9 – 11 ft.lbs.

<1.8L Engine>

12 – 15 Nm
9 – 11 ft.lbs.

12 – 15 Nm
9 – 11 ft.lbs.

20 – 27 Nm
14 – 20 ft.lbs.

1. Timing belt
2. Alternator brace
3. Water pump
4. Water pump gasket
5. O-ring

Fig. 74 Water pump — 1990 Colt Wagon

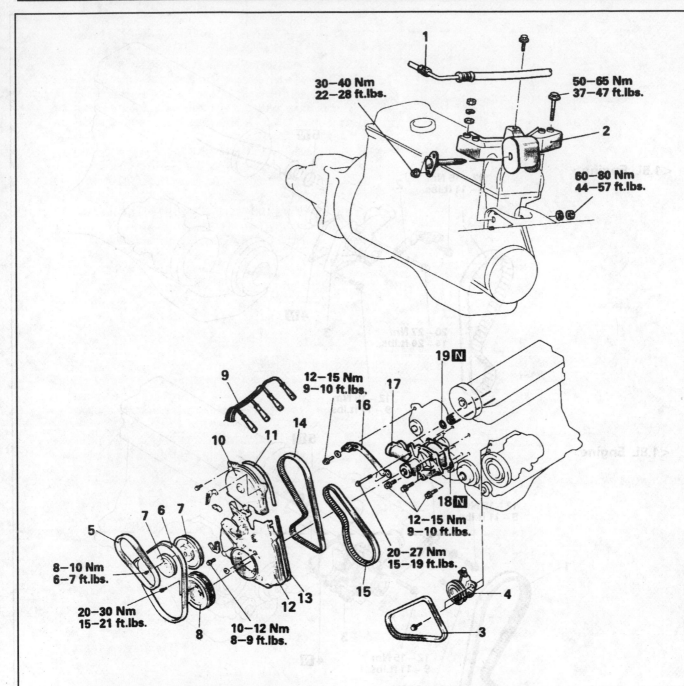

30—40 Nm
22—28 ft.lbs.

50—65 Nm
37—47 ft.lbs.

60—80 Nm
44—57 ft.lbs.

12—15 Nm
9—10 ft.lbs.

19 N

18 N

12—15 Nm
9—10 ft.lbs.

20—27 Nm
15—19 ft.lbs.

8—10 Nm
6—7 ft.lbs.

20—30 Nm
15—21 ft.lbs.

10—12 Nm
8—9 ft.lbs.

1. Connection of high-pressure hose
2. Left mount bracket
3. V-belt (For air conditioner compressor)
4. Tension pulley bracket
5. V-belt (For power steering)
6. V-ribbed belt
7. Water pump pulley
8. Damper pulley
9. Spark plug cable
10. Timing belt front upper cover
11. Timing belt front upper gasket
    Timing mark alignment
12. Timing belt front lower cover

13. Timing belt front lower cover gasket
    Timing belt tension adjustment
14. Timing belt
15. Timing belt B
16. Alternator brace
17. Water pump
18. Gasket
19. O-ring

Fig. 75 Water pump — 2.0L engine

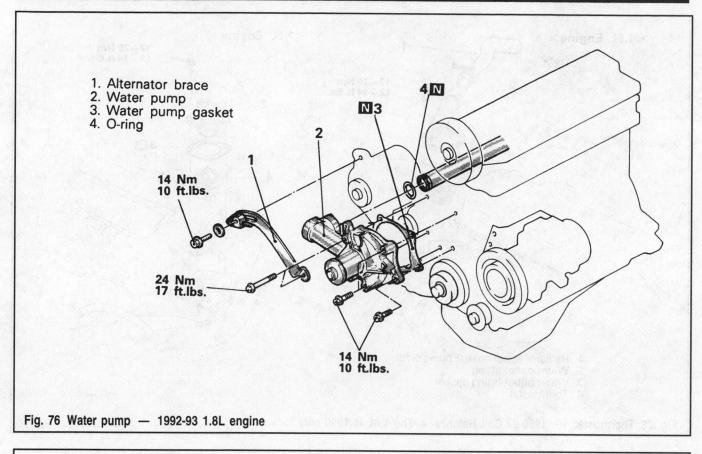

1. Alternator brace
2. Water pump
3. Water pump gasket
4. O-ring

14 Nm
10 ft.lbs.

24 Nm
17 ft.lbs.

14 Nm
10 ft.lbs.

Fig. 76 Water pump — 1992-93 1.8L engine

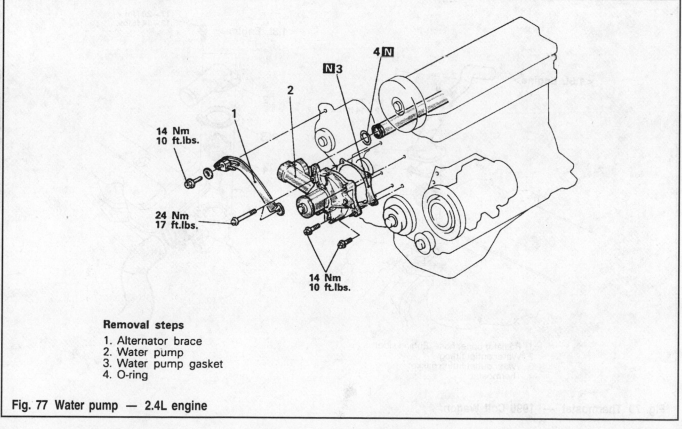

14 Nm
10 ft.lbs.

24 Nm
17 ft.lbs.

14 Nm
10 ft.lbs.

Removal steps

1. Alternator brace
2. Water pump
3. Water pump gasket
4. O-ring

Fig. 77 Water pump — 2.4L engine

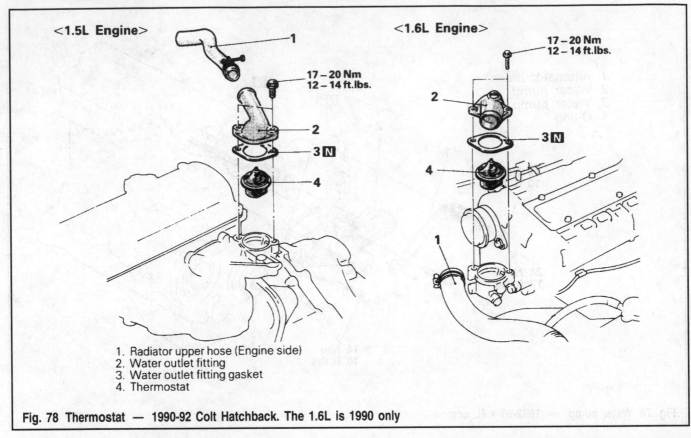

1. Radiator upper hose (Engine side)
2. Water outlet fitting
3. Water outlet fitting gasket
4. Thermostat

Fig. 78 Thermostat — 1990-92 Colt Hatchback. The 1.6L is 1990 only

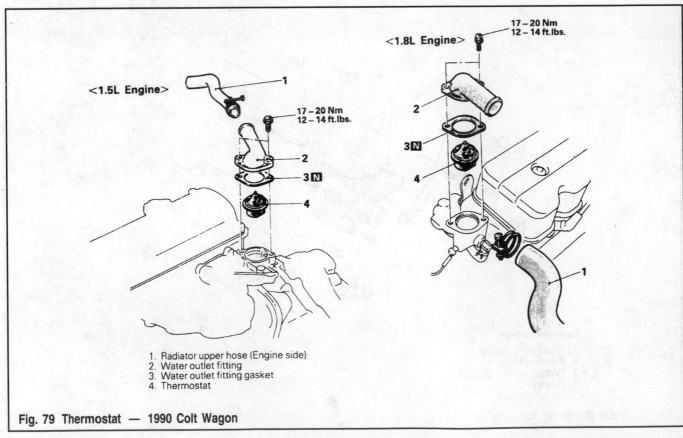

1. Radiator upper hose (Engine side)
2. Water outlet fitting
3. Water outlet fitting gasket
4. Thermostat

Fig. 79 Thermostat — 1990 Colt Wagon

Cylinder Head

REMOVAL & INSTALLATION

➡**Never remove the cylinder head unless the engine is absolutely cold; the cylinder head could warp.**

1990 1.5L

▶ **See Figures 80, 81, 82 and 83**

1. Disconnect the battery ground cable, remove the air cleaner assembly and the attached hoses.

2. Drain the coolant, remove the upper radiator hose and the heater hoses.

3. Release the fuel system pressure. Remove the fuel line, disconnect the accelerator linkage, distributor vacuum lines, purge valve and water temperature gauge wire.

4. Remove the spark plug wires and the fuel pump. Remove the distributor, where necessary.

5. Disconnect the exhaust pipe from the exhaust manifold flange.

6. Remove the exhaust manifold assembly.

7. Remove the intake manifold.

8. Turn the crankshaft to No. 1 piston at TDC on the compression stroke.

➡**During the following procedure, do not turn the crankshaft after locating TDC.**

9. Remove the timing belt cover. Be sure the knockout pin is at 12 o'clock and the cam sprocket mark and cylinder head pointer are aligned at 3 o'clock. Loosen the timing belt

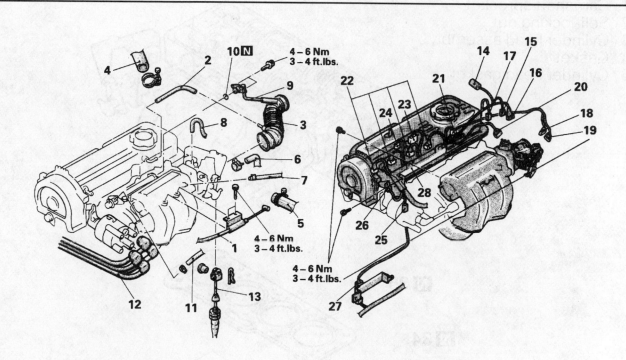

1. Connection for accelerator cable
2. Breather hose
3. Air intake hose
4. Connection for radiator upper hose
5. Connection for heater hose
6. Connection for water by-pass hose
7. Connection for brake booster vacuum hose
8. Connection for vacuum hoses
9. Connection for high pressure hose
10. O-ring
11. Connection for fuel return hose
12. Spark plug cable
13. Connection for throttle control cable <A/T>
14. Connection for oxygen sensor connector
15. Connection for engine coolant temperature gauge unit connector
16. Connection for engine coolant temperature sensor connector
17. Connection for thermo switch connector <A/T>
18. Connection for idle speed control connector
19. Connection for motor position sensor connector
20. Connection for throttle position sensor connector
21. Connection for EGR temperature sensor connector <Vehicles for California>
22. Connection for injector connector
23. Connection for power transistor connector
24. Connection for ignition coil connector
25. Connection for condenser connector
26. Connection for noise filter
27. Connection for distributor connector
28. Control harness

Fig. 80 1990 1.5L engine. Remove these parts, in the order shown, in preparation for cylinder head removal. When installing the head, reverse the removal sequence

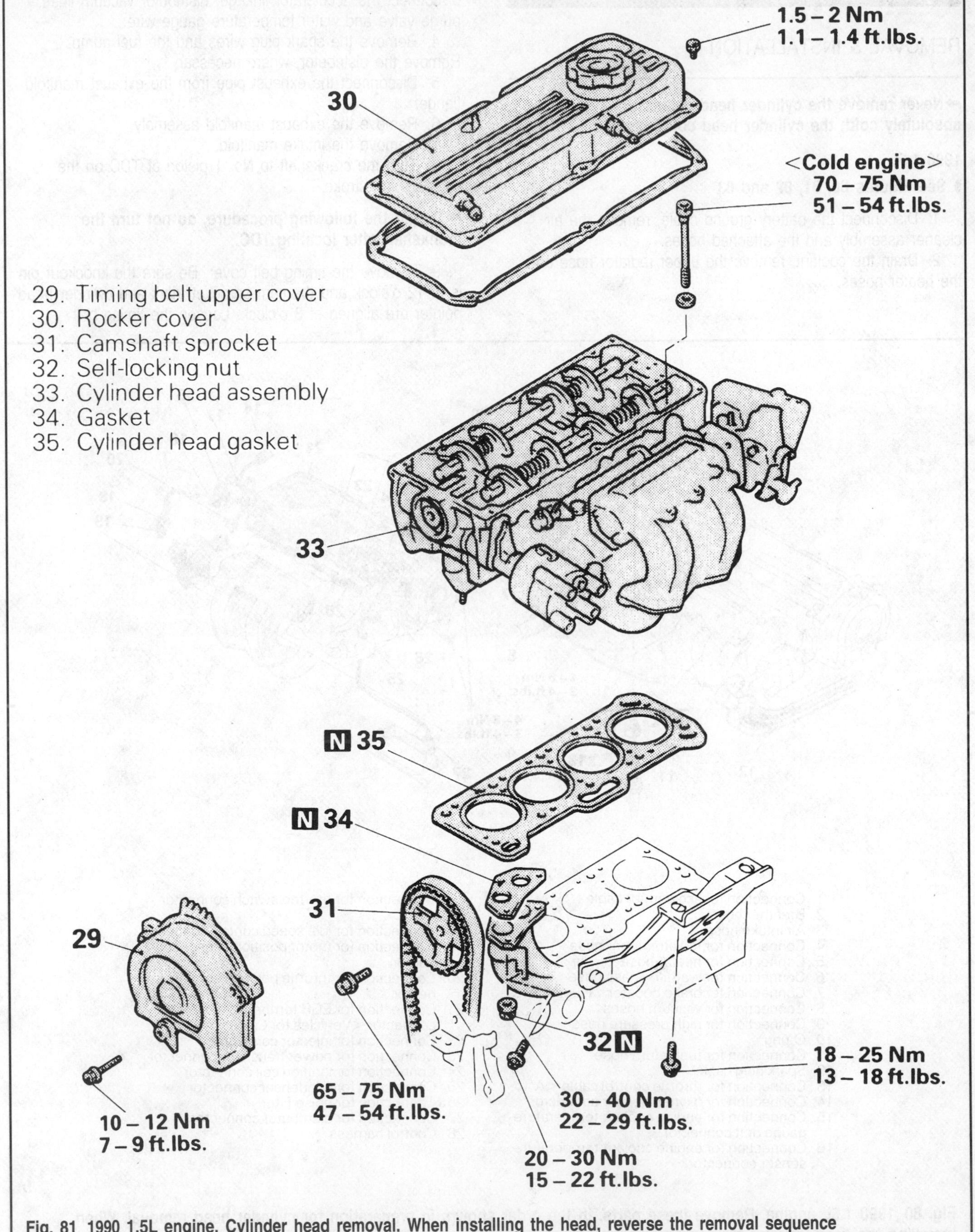

1.5 – 2 Nm
1.1 – 1.4 ft.lbs.

30

<Cold engine>
70 – 75 Nm
51 – 54 ft.lbs.

29. Timing belt upper cover
30. Rocker cover
31. Camshaft sprocket
32. Self-locking nut
33. Cylinder head assembly
34. Gasket
35. Cylinder head gasket

33

N 35

N 34

31

29

32 N

18 – 25 Nm
13 – 18 ft.lbs.

65 – 75 Nm
47 – 54 ft.lbs.

30 – 40 Nm
22 – 29 ft.lbs.

10 – 12 Nm
7 – 9 ft.lbs.

20 – 30 Nm
15 – 22 ft.lbs.

Fig. 81 1990 1.5L engine. Cylinder head removal. When installing the head, reverse the removal sequence

tensioner mounting. Move the tensioner toward the water pump and secure it in that position. Remove the rocker arm cover.

➡**The cam pulley need not be removed.**

10. Loosen and remove the cylinder head bolts in sequence, 2-3 stages to avoid cylinder head warpage.

11. Remove the cylinder head from the engine block.

To install:

12. Clean the cylinder head and block mating surfaces and install a new cylinder head gasket.

13. Position the cylinder head on the engine block, engage the dowel pins front and rear and install the cylinder head bolts.

14. Tighten the head bolts in, 3 stages, to 50-54 ft. lbs. (68-73 Nm).

15. Locate the camshaft in original position. Pull the camshaft sprocket and belt or chain upward and install on the camshaft.

➡**If the dowel pin and the dowel pin hole does not line up between the sprocket and the spacer or camshaft, move the camshaft by bumping either of the 2 projections provided at the rear of the No. 2 cylinder exhaust cam of the camshaft, with a light hammer or other tool, until the hole and pin align. Be certain the crankshaft does not turn.**

16. Install the camshaft sprocket bolt and the distributor gear and tighten.

17. Install the timing belt upper front cover and spark plug cable support.

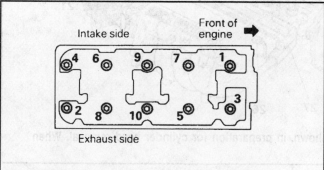

Fig. 82 1990 1.5L engine cylinder head loosening sequence

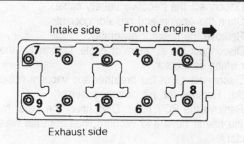

Fig. 83 1990 1.5L engine cylinder head tightening sequence

18. Apply sealant to the intake manifold gasket on both sides. Position the gasket and install the intake manifold.

➡**Be sure no sealant enters the jet air passages when equipped.**

19. Install the exhaust manifold gaskets and the manifold assembly.

20. Connect the exhaust pipe to the exhaust manifold and install the fuel pump. Install the purge valve.

21. Install the water temperature gauge wire, heater hoses and the upper radiator hose.

22. Connect the fuel lines, accelerator linkage, vacuum hoses and the spark plug wires.

23. Fill the cooling system and connect the battery ground cable. Install the distributor.

24. Temporarily adjust the valve clearance to the cold engine specifications.

25. Install the gasket on the rocker arm cover and temporarily install the cover on the engine.

26. Connect the negative battery cable.

27. Start the engine and bring it to normal operating temperature. Stop the engine and remove the rocker arm cover.

28. Adjust the valves to hot engine specifications.

29. Install the rocker arm cover and tighten securely.

30. Install the air cleaner, hoses, purge valve hose and any other removed unit.

1991-93 1.5L

▶ **See Figures 84 and ?**

1. Disconnect the negative battery cable and drain the engine coolant.

2. Disconnect the accelerator cable, breather hose, air intake hose and radiator hoses.

3. Label and disconnect the brake booster hose, EGR vacuum hoses and spark plug cables.

4. Relieve the fuel pressure. Disconnect the fuel hoses.

5. Disconnect the distributor connector, oxygen sensor, condenser connector, coolant temperature connectors, motor position sensor connector, idle speed control connector, TPS connector, injector connectors, EGR temperature sensor connector and control harness.

6. Remove the upper timing belt cover. Rotate the crankshaft clockwise and align the timing marks. Remove the camshaft sprocket and hold the sprocket and timing belt with a piece of wire. Remove the rocker cover and gasket.

7. Remove the exhaust manifold-to-pipe nuts.

8. Remove the cylinder head bolts using a special socket TW-10B or equivalent. Remove the cylinder head and gasket.

To install:

9. Clean the gasket mating surfaces and check for warpage.

10. Match the old gasket with the new and install the gasket with the identification mark facing upward and to the front of the engine.

11. Install the cylinder head and bolts. Using the spe[cial] head bolt tool TW-10B and torque the bolts in 3 ste[ps in] sequence. 1st step to 20 ft. lbs. (27 Nm), 2nd ste[p to] lbs. (54 Nm) and the 3rd step to 51-54 ft. lbs.

12. Install the exhaust manifold-to-pipe nut[s to] ft. lbs. (46 Nm).

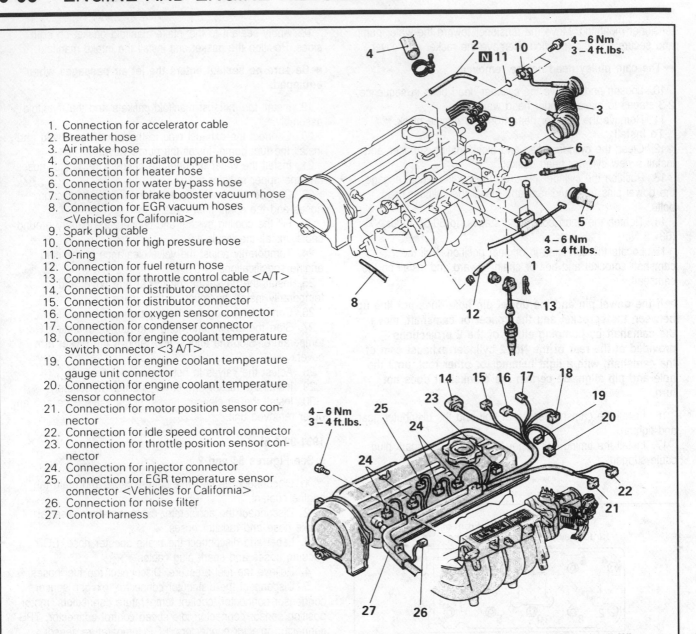

1. Connection for accelerator cable
2. Breather hose
3. Air intake hose
4. Connection for radiator upper hose
5. Connection for heater hose
6. Connection for water by-pass hose
7. Connection for brake booster vacuum hose
8. Connection for EGR vacuum hoses <Vehicles for California>
9. Spark plug cable
10. Connection for high pressure hose
11. O-ring
12. Connection for fuel return hose
13. Connection for throttle control cable <A/T>
14. Connection for distributor connector
15. Connection for distributor connector
16. Connection for oxygen sensor connector
17. Connection for condenser connector
18. Connection for engine coolant temperature switch connector <3 A/T>
19. Connection for engine coolant temperature gauge unit connector
20. Connection for engine coolant temperature sensor connector
21. Connection for motor position sensor connector
22. Connection for idle speed control connector
23. Connection for throttle position sensor connector
24. Connection for injector connector
25. Connection for EGR temperature sensor connector <Vehicles for California>
26. Connection for noise filter
27. Control harness

Fig. 84 1991-92 1.5L engine. Remove these parts, in the order shown, in preparation for cylinder head removal. When installing the head, reverse the removal sequence

13. Install the rocker cover, camshaft sprocket and upper timing belt cover.

14. Connect the distributor connector, oxygen sensor, condenser connector, coolant temperature connectors, motor position sensor connector, idle speed control connector, TPS connector, injector connectors, EGR temperature sensor connector and control harness.

15. Connect the fuel hoses.

16. Connect the brake booster hose, EGR vacuum hoses and spark plug cables.

17. Connect the accelerator cable, breather hose, air intake hose and radiator hoses.

18. Connect the negative battery cable and refill the engine coolant. Adjust the timing and idle if needed.

1.6L

▶ See Figures 86 and 87

1. Disconnect the negative battery cable.
2. Drain the engine and radiator coolant.
3. Remove the radiator assembly.
4. Disconnect the accelerator cable. Disconnect the air flow sensor wiring connector.
5. Disconnect all of the breather and vacuum hoses to the air intake. Remove the air cleaner assembly.
6. Remove the PCV hose. Disconnect the water bypass hose, the heater hose and vacuum lines from the water inlet connector.
7. Disconnect the vacuum hose to the power brake booster.

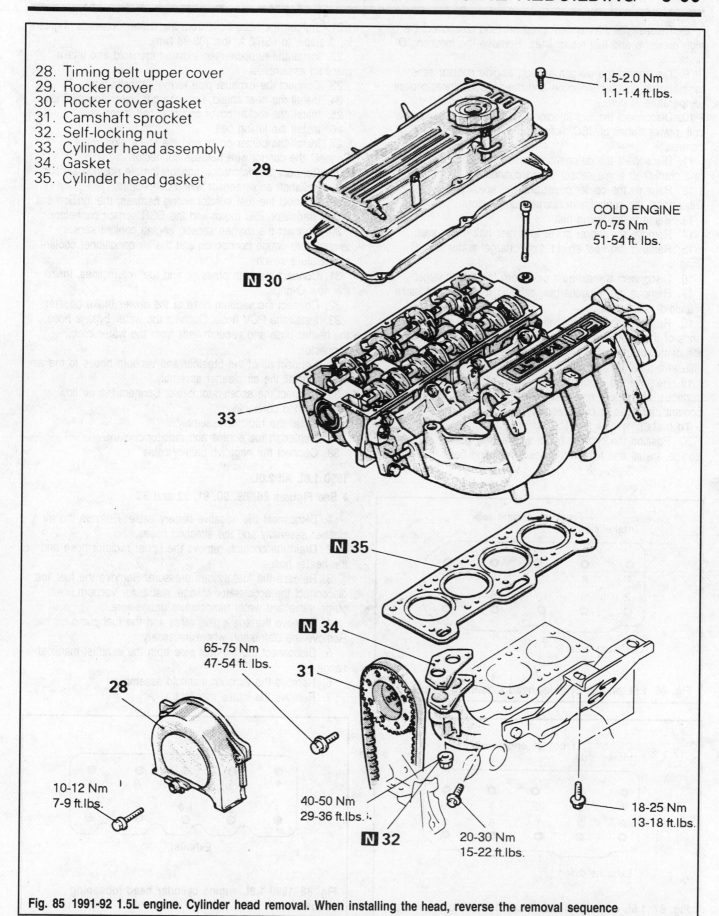

28. Timing belt upper cover
29. Rocker cover
30. Rocker cover gasket
31. Camshaft sprocket
32. Self-locking nut
33. Cylinder head assembly
34. Gasket
35. Cylinder head gasket

1.5-2.0 Nm
1.1-1.4 ft.lbs.

COLD ENGINE
70-75 Nm
51-54 ft. lbs.

65-75 Nm
47-54 ft. lbs.

40-50 Nm
29-36 ft.lbs.

20-30 Nm
15-22 ft.lbs.

18-25 Nm
13-18 ft.lbs.

10-12 Nm
7-9 ft.lbs.

Fig. 85 1991-92 1.5L engine. Cylinder head removal. When installing the head, reverse the removal sequence

8. Release the fuel system pressure and disconnect the high pressure and fuel return lines. Remove the mounting O-rings.

9. Disconnect the oxygen sensor, engine coolant sensor, temperature gauge connection and the air conditioner coolant temperature switch.

10. Disconnect the fuel injector wiring harness, the ignition coil, power transistor, ISC motor and the EGR sensor connector.

11. Disconnect the detonation sensor, throttle position sensor and crankshaft angle sensor wiring connectors.

12. Remove the center cover and the spark plug wires. Disconnect the control wire harness connector.

13. Remove the timing belt.

14. Remove the rocker cover and rear half moon seal.

15. Remove the heat shield, turbocharger water and oil lines.

16. Disconnect the exhaust pipe from the turbocharger.

17. Remove the turbocharger, exhaust manifold and intake manifold assemblies.

18. Remove the head mounting bolts. Start at the outer ends of the head and loosen, in a crisscross manner, toward the center of the head. Make 2-3 passes to loosen the bolts, a little at a time, in sequence.

19. Remove the cylinder head. Clean all gasket mounting surfaces. Make sure no gasket material gets into the cylinders, coolant passages or oil passages.

To install:

20. Position the cylinder head, with a new gasket, on the engine. Install and tighten the head mounting bolts.

21. Tighten the head bolts from the center outwards. Tighten in, 3 steps, to 65-72 ft. lbs. (88-98 Nm).

22. Install the turbocharger, exhaust manifold and intake manifold assemblies.

23. Connect the exhaust pipe to the turbocharger.

24. Install the heat shield, turbocharger water and oil lines.

25. Install the rocker cover and rear half moon seal.

26. Install the timing belt.

27. Install the center cover and the spark plug wires. Connect the control wire harness connector.

28. Connect the detonation sensor, throttle position sensor and crankshaft angle sensor wiring connectors.

29. Connect the fuel injector wiring harness, the ignition coil, power transistor, ISC motor and the EGR sensor connector.

30. Connect the oxygen sensor, engine coolant sensor, temperature gauge connection and the air conditioner coolant temperature switch.

31. Connect the high pressure and fuel return lines. Install the new O-rings.

32. Connect the vacuum hose to the power brake booster.

33. Install the PCV hose. Connect the water bypass hose, the heater hose and vacuum lines from the water inlet connector.

34. Connect all of the breather and vacuum hoses to the air intake. Install the air cleaner assembly.

35. Connect the accelerator cable. Connect the air flow sensor wiring connector.

36. Install the radiator assembly.

37. Replenish the engine and radiator coolant.

38. Connect the negative battery cable.

1990 1.8L All 2.0L

▶ See Figures 88, 89, 90, 91, 92 and 93

1. Disconnect the negative battery cable. Remove the air cleaner assembly and the attached hoses.

2. Drain the coolant, remove the upper radiator hose and the heater hoses.

3. Release the fuel system pressure. Remove the fuel line, disconnect the accelerator linkage, distributor vacuum lines, purge valve and water temperature gauge wire.

4. Remove the spark plug wires and the fuel pump. Remove the distributor, where necessary.

5. Disconnect the exhaust pipe from the exhaust manifold flange.

6. Remove the exhaust manifold assembly.

7. Remove the intake manifold.

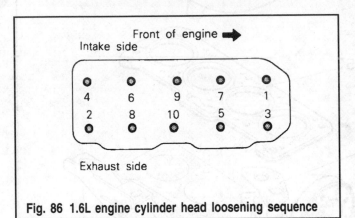

Fig. 86 1.6L engine cylinder head loosening sequence

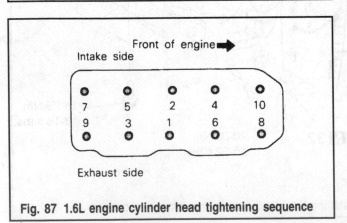

Fig. 87 1.6L engine cylinder head tightening sequence

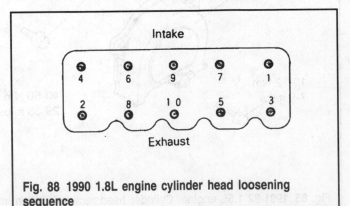

Fig. 88 1990 1.8L engine cylinder head loosening sequence

Timing belt side ➡️

Head bolt tightening sequence

Fig. 89 1990 1.8L engine cylinder head tightening sequence

8. Turn the crankshaft to No. 1 piston at TDC on the compression stroke.

➡️**During the following procedure, do not turn the crankshaft after locating TDC.**

9. Align the timing mark on the upper under cover of the timing belt with that of the camshaft sprocket. Matchmark the timing belt and the timing mark on the camshaft sprocket with a felt tip pen. Remove the sprocket and insert a 2 in. (51mm) piece of timing belt or other material between the bottom of the camshaft sprocket and the sprocket holder, on the timing belt lower front cover, to hold the sprocket and belt so the valve timing will not be changed. Remove the timing belt upper under cover and rocker arm cover.

10. Loosen and remove the cylinder head bolts in 2-3 stages to avoid cylinder head warpage.

11. Remove the cylinder head from the engine block.

1. Oxygen sensor connector
2. Bolt assembly
3. Engine mounting bracket
4. Air intake hose
5. Radiator upper hose
6. Heater hose
7. Water bypass hose
8. Engine narness (A)
9. Connection for ISC servo
10. Connection for injectors
11. Connection for power transister
12. Connection for condenser
13. Connection for ignition coil

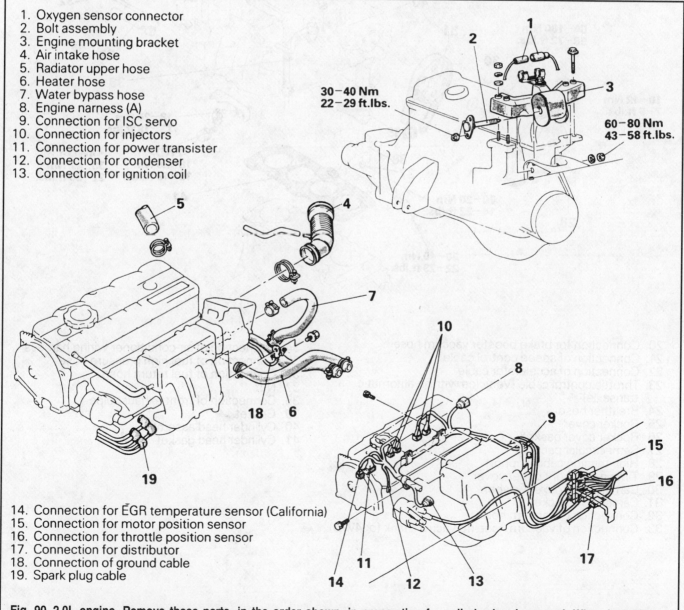

14. Connection for EGR temperature sensor (California)
15. Connection for motor position sensor
16. Connection for throttle position sensor
17. Connection for distributor
18. Connection of ground cable
19. Spark plug cable

Fig. 90 2.0L engine. Remove these parts, in the order shown, in preparation for cylinder head removal. When installing the head, reverse the removal sequence

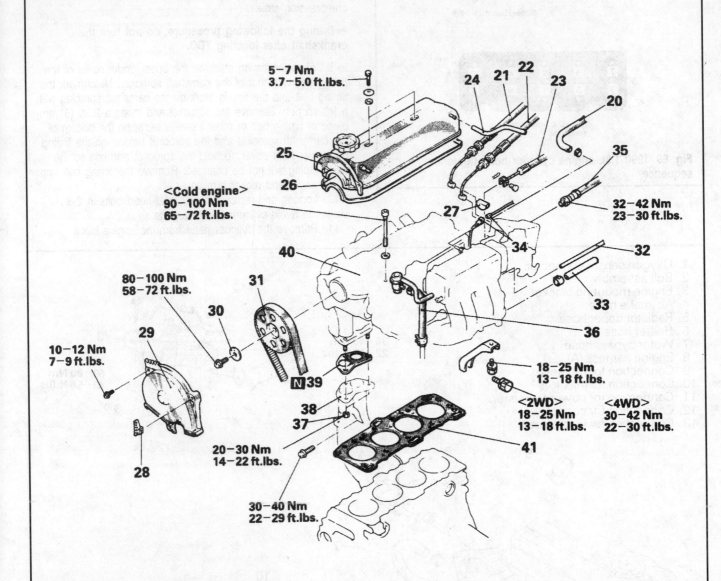

5−7 Nm
3.7−5.0 ft.lbs.

<Cold engine>
90−100 Nm
65−72 ft.lbs.

80−100 Nm
58−72 ft.lbs.

10−12 Nm
7−9 ft.lbs.

20−30 Nm
14−22 ft.lbs.

30−40 Nm
22−29 ft.lbs.

32−42 Nm
23−30 ft.lbs.

18−25 Nm
13−18 ft.lbs.

<2WD>
18−25 Nm
13−18 ft.lbs.

<4WD>
30−42 Nm
22−30 ft.lbs.

20. Connection for brake booster vaccum hose
21. Connection of speed control cable*
22. Connection of accelerator cable
23. Throttle control cable (Vehicles with an automatic transaxle)
24. Breather hose
25. Rocker cover
26. Rocker cover gasket
27. Semi-circular packing
28. High tension cable support
29. Timing belt front upper cover
30. Camshaft sprocket washer
31. Camshaft sprocket
32. Connection of vacuum hose
33. Connection of vacuum hose (to vacuum tank for 4WD)

34. Connection of air-conditioner wiring harness
35. Connection of fuel high pressure hose
36. Connection of fuel return hose
37. Nut
38. Connection of front exhaust pipe
39. Gasket
40. Cylinder head assembly
41. Cylinder head gasket

Fig. 91 2.0L engine. Cylinder head removal. When installing the head, reverse the removal sequence

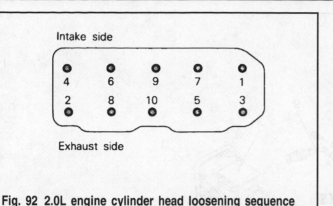

Fig. 92 2.0L engine cylinder head loosening sequence

To install:

12. Clean the cylinder head and block mating surfaces and install a new cylinder head gasket.

13. Position the cylinder head on the engine block, engage the dowel pins front and rear and install the cylinder head bolts.

14. Tighten the head bolts in 3 stages and then torque to:
   1.8L engine — 50-54 ft. lbs. (68-73 Nm).
   2.0L engine — 65-72 ft. lbs. (88-97 Nm).

15. Install the timing belt upper under cover.

16. Locate the camshaft in original position. Pull the camshaft sprocket and belt or chain upward and install on the camshaft.

➡If the dowel pin and the dowel pin hole does not line up between the sprocket and the spacer or camshaft, move the camshaft by bumping either of the 2 projections provided at the rear of the No. 2 cylinder exhaust cam of the camshaft, with a light hammer or other tool, until the hole and pin align. Be certain the crankshaft does not turn.

17. Install the camshaft sprocket bolt and the distributor gear and tighten.

18. Install the timing belt upper front cover and spark plug cable support.

19. Apply sealant to the intake manifold gasket on both sides. Position the gasket and install the intake manifold. Torque the nuts to 11-14 ft. lbs. (15-20 Nm).

➡Be sure no sealant enters the jet air passages when equipped.

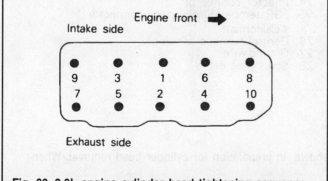

Fig. 93 2.0L engine cylinder head tightening sequence

20. Install the exhaust manifold gaskets and the manifold assembly. Tighten the nuts to 11-14 ft. lbs. (15-20 Nm).

21. Connect the exhaust pipe to the exhaust manifold and install the fuel pump. Install the purge valve.

22. Install the water temperature gauge wire, heater hoses and the upper radiator hose.

23. Connect the fuel lines, accelerator linkage, vacuum hoses and the spark plug wires.

24. Fill the cooling system and connect the battery ground cable. Install the distributor.

25. Temporarily adjust the valve clearance to the cold engine specifications.

26. Install the gasket on the rocker arm cover and temporarily install the cover on the engine.

27. Start the engine and bring it to normal operating temperature. Stop the engine and remove the rocker arm cover.

28. Adjust the valves to hot engine specifications.

29. Install the rocker arm cover and tighten securely.

30. Install the air cleaner, hoses, purge valve hose and any other removed unit.

1992-93 1.8L

▶ **See Figures 94, 95, 96 and 97**

1. Relieve fuel system pressure. Disconnect the negative battery cable.

2. Drain the cooling system. Disconnect the brake booster vacuum hose and PVC valve connection.

3. Remove the upper radiator hose, overflow tube and the water hose from the thermostat to the throttle body.

4. Disconnect the air flow sensor connector. Remove the air cleaner case cover and the air intake hose.

5. Wrap the connection with a shop towel and disconnect the high pressure fuel line at the fuel rail.

6. Disconnect the fuel return hose and remove the O-ring.

7. Disconnect the accelerator cable connection from the throttle body and position aside.

8. Disconnect the electrical harnesses at the oil pressure switch, oxygen sensor, water temperature sensor connector, distributor, condenser, ISC, TPS, detonation sensor and the fuel injectors.

9. Disconnect the spark plug cables from each spark plug.

10. Unbolt the control harness assembly and position aside.

11. Remove the thermostat housing, thermostat and the thermostat case with O-ring from the engine.

12. Remove the rocker cover.

13. Remove the timing belt upper cover.

14. Rotate the crankshaft in the forward (right) direction to align the camshaft timing marks. Matchmark the camshaft sprocket and the timing belt. Tie the camshaft sprocket and the timing belt together so the sprocket will not move with respect to the timing belt.

15. While holding the camshaft sprocket in position using the appropriate wrench, remove the camshaft sprocket and with the belt attached. Wire the sprocket and belt aside making sure constant tension is maintained on the belt. Do not allow the belt to slacken or engine timing may be altered.

➡When removing the camshaft sprocket, do not allow the crankshaft to rotate. If crankshaft rotation did occur, the engine timing may have been changed. Confirm proper engine timing during installation.

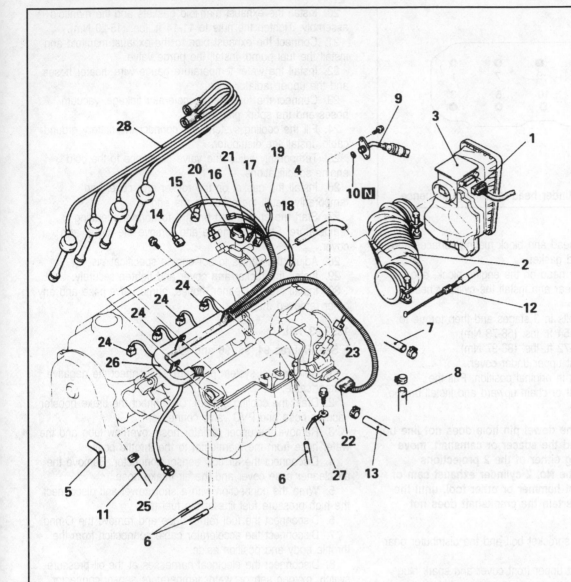

1. Air flow sensor connector
2. Air intake hose
3. Air cleaner case cover
4. Breather hose connection
5. PCV hose
6. Vacuum hose connection
7. Water hose connection
   (Thermostat case → throttle body)
8. Water hose connection
   (Throttle body → water inlet fitting)
9. Fuel high pressure hose connection
10. O-ring
11. Fuel return hose connection
12. Accelerator cable connection
13. Brake booster vacuum hose connection
14. Engine coolant temperature switch connector

15. Oxygen sensor connector
16. Oil pressure switch connector
17. Water temperature gauge unit connector
18. Engine coolant temperature sensor connector
19. Engine coolant temperature switch connector
    <for condenser fan>
20. Distributor connector
21. Condenser connector
22. Idle speed control connector
23. TPS connector
24. Injector connector
25. EGR temperature sensor connector
    <California>
26. Control harness assembly
27. Ground wire
28. Spark plug cable

Fig. 94 1992-93 1.8L engine. Remove these parts, in the order shown, in preparation for cylinder head removal. When installing the head, reverse the removal sequence

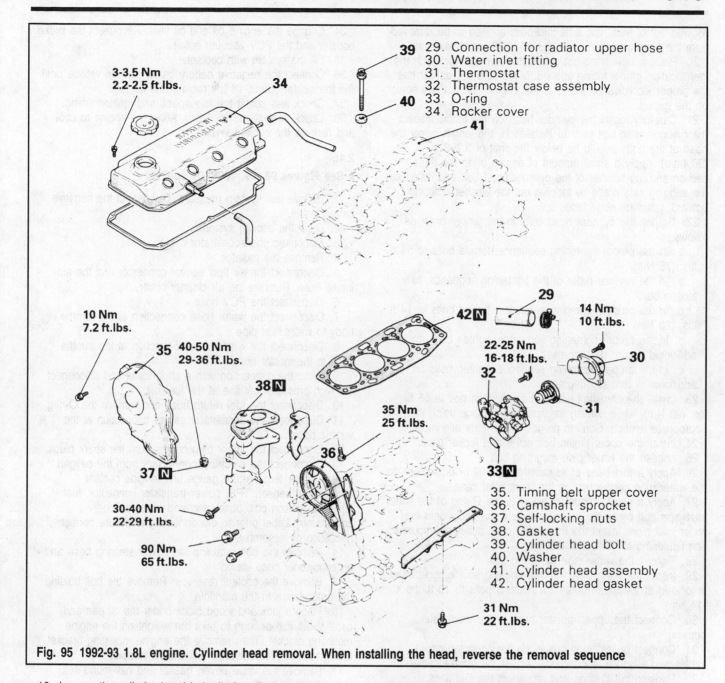

29. Connection for radiator upper hose
30. Water inlet fitting
31. Thermostat
32. Thermostat case assembly
33. O-ring
34. Rocker cover

3-3.5 Nm
2.2-2.5 ft.lbs.

14 Nm
10 ft.lbs.

22-25 Nm
16-18 ft.lbs.

10 Nm
7.2 ft.lbs.

40-50 Nm
29-36 ft.lbs.

35 Nm
25 ft.lbs.

30-40 Nm
22-29 ft.lbs.

90 Nm
65 ft.lbs.

31 Nm
22 ft.lbs.

35. Timing belt upper cover
36. Camshaft sprocket
37. Self-locking nuts
38. Gasket
39. Cylinder head bolt
40. Washer
41. Cylinder head assembly
42. Cylinder head gasket

Fig. 95 1992-93 1.8L engine. Cylinder head removal. When installing the head, reverse the removal sequence

16. Loosen the cylinder head bolts in 2 or 3 steps in the appropriate order and remove from the cylinder head.

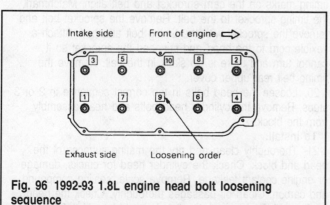

Intake side   Front of engine ⇨

Exhaust side   Loosening order

Fig. 96 1992-93 1.8L engine head bolt loosening sequence

17. Remove the cylinder head from the engine.

✳✳CAUTION

When placing the removed cylinder head upside down, take care not to bend or damage the plug guide. The plug guide can not be replaced.

18. Remove the cylinder head gasket from the block.
To install:
19. Thoroughly clean and dry the mating surfaces of the head and block. Check the cylinder head for cracks, damage or engine coolant leakage. Remove scale, sealing compound and carbon. Clean oil passages thoroughly. Check the head for flatness. End to end, the head should be within 0.002 in. (0.05mm) normally with 0.008 in. (0.200mm) the maximum

allowed out of true. The total thickness allowed to be removed from the head and block is 0.008 in. (0.200mm) maximum.

20. Place a new head gasket on the cylinder block with the identification marks facing upward. Make sure the gasket has the proper identification mark for the engine. Do not use sealer on the gasket.

21. Carefully install the cylinder head on the block. Inspect the cylinder head bolt prior to installation, the length below the head of the bolts should be below the limit of 3.795 in. (96.4mm). Apply a small amount of engine oil to the thread section and the washer of the cylinder head bolt and install so the sagging side made by tapping out the washer is facing upward. (chamfer edge faces up).

22. Tighten the cylinder head bolts in the proper order as follows:

    a. In the proper tightening sequence, torque bolts to 54 ft. lbs. (75 Nm).

    b. In the reverse order of the tightening sequence, fully loosen bolts.

    c. In the proper tightening sequence, torque bolts to 14 ft. lbs. (20 Nm).

    d. In the proper tightening sequence, tighten bolts an additional 1/4 turn (90 degrees).

    e. In the proper tightening sequence, tighten bolts an additional 1/4 turn (90 degrees).

23. Install the camshaft sprocket and tighten bolt to 65 ft. lbs. (90 Nm), while holding the sprocket in place using the appropriate wrench. Confirm proper timing mark alignment.

24. Install the upper timing belt cover and rocker cover.

25. Loosen the water pipe mounting bolt.

26. Apply a thin bead of sealant MD970389 or equivalent, to the water tube connection on the thermostat case.

27. Apply a small amount of water to the O-ring of the water inlet pipe and press the thermostat case assembly onto the water inlet pipe. Install the thermostat case assembly mounting bolt tightening to 16 ft. lbs. (22 Nm).

28. Tighten the water pipe mounting bolt.

29. Install the thermostat into the housing so the jiggle valve is located at the top. Tighten the housing bolts to 10 ft. lbs. (14 Nm).

30. Connect the upper radiator hose to the thermostat housing.

31. Connect or install all previously disconnected hoses, cables and electrical connections. Adjust the throttle cable(s).

32. Replace the O-rings and reconnect the fuel lines.

33. Install the air intake hose. Connect the breather hose, air cleaner case cover and air flow sensor connector.

34. Change the engine oil and oil filter. Reconnect the brake booster and the PCV vacuum hoses.

35. Fill the system with coolant.

36. Connect the negative battery cable, run the vehicle until the thermostat opens, fill the radiator completely.

37. Check and adjust the idle speed and ignition timing.

38. Check all systems for leaks. Allow the engine to cool and recheck the coolant level.

2.4L

▶ **See Figures 98, 99, 100, 101 and 102**

1. Relieve fuel system pressure. Disconnect the negative battery cable.

2. Drain the cooling system.

3. Disconnect the accelerator cable.

4. Remove the radiator.

5. Disconnect the air flow sensor connector and the air intake hose. Remove the air cleaner cover.

6. Disconnect the PCV hose.

7. Disconnect the water hose connection at the throttle body to water inlet pipe.

8. Disconnect the water hose connection at the throttle body to thermostat hose.

9. Wrap the connection with a shop towel and disconnect the high pressure fuel line at the fuel rail.

10. Disconnect the fuel return hose and remove the O-ring.

11. Disconnect the accelerator cables connection at the throttle body.

12. Disconnect the spark plug cables from the spark plugs.

13. Disconnect the electrical connectors from the oxygen sensor, water temperature gauge unit, engine coolant temperature sensor, TPS, power transistor connector, fuel injectors, ignition coil, distributor, and air conditioner compressor. Label prior to disconnecting to assure correct relocation on assembly.

14. Remove the bolt retaining the power steering hose and air conditioner hose clamp.

15. Remove the coolant reservoir. Remove the bolt holding the ground wire to the manifold.

16. Place a jack and wood block under the oil pan and carefully lift just enough to take the weight off the engine mounting bracket. Then remove the engine mounting bracket taking note of the position of the mount stopper.

17. Remove the valve cover, gasket and half-round seal.

18. Remove the timing belt front upper cover.

19. If possible, rotate the crankshaft clockwise until the timing marks on the cam sprocket and belt align. Matchmark the timing sprocket to the belt. Remove the sprocket bolt and remove the sprocket with the timing belt attached. Attach a flexible cord to the hood and suspend the sprocket so it cannot turn and there is no slack in the belt. Remove the timing belt rear upper cover.

20. Loosen the head bolts in the correct sequence in 2 or 3 steps. Remove the cylinder head bolts and head assembly from the block.

To install:

21. Thoroughly clean and dry the mating surfaces of the head and block. Check the cylinder head for cracks, damage or engine coolant leakage. Remove scale, sealing compound and carbon. Clean oil passages thoroughly. Check the head for flatness. End to end, the head should be within 0.002 in.

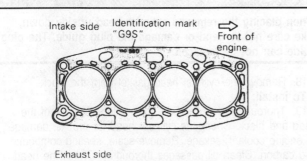

Fig. 97 1992-93 1.8L engine head bolt tightening sequence

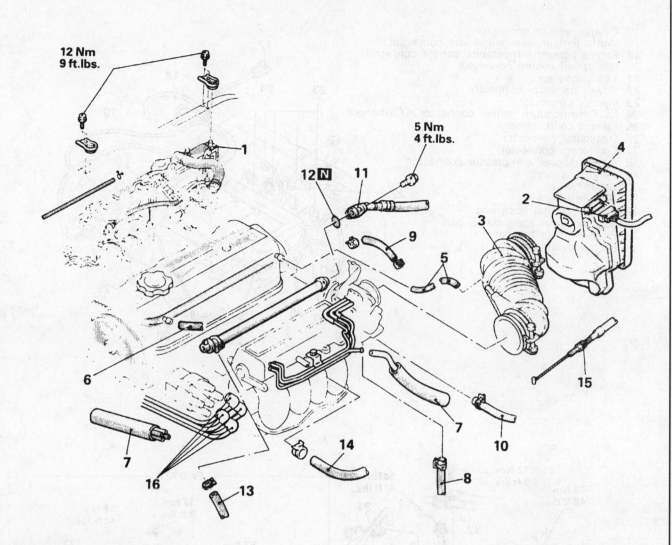

1. Radiator assembly
2. Air flow sensor connector
3. Air intake hose
4. Air cleaner case cover
5. Breather hose connection
6. PCV hose
7. Vacuum hose connection
8. Water hose connection
   (Throttle body → water inlet pipe)
9. Water hose connection
   (Throttle body → thermostat)
10. Water hose connection
    (Heater unit → thermostat)
11. Fuel high pressure hose connection
12. O-ring
13. Fuel return hose connection
14. Brake booster vacuum hose connection
15. Accelerator cable connection
16. Spark plug cable

Fig. 98 2.4L engine. Remove these parts, in the order shown, in preparation for cylinder head removal. When installing the head, reverse the removal sequence

17. Oxygen sensor connector
18. Water temperature gauge unit connector
19. Engine coolant temperature sensor connector
20. Idle speed control connector
21. TPS connector
22. Power transistor connector
23. Injector connector
24. EGR temperature sensor connector <California>
25. Ignition coil connector
26. Distributor connector
27. Condenser connector
28. Air conditioner compressor connector
29. Control harness
30. Ground wire
31. Condense tank
32. Power steering hose and
    air conditioner hose clamp part
33. Engine mount bracket
34. Engine mount stopper

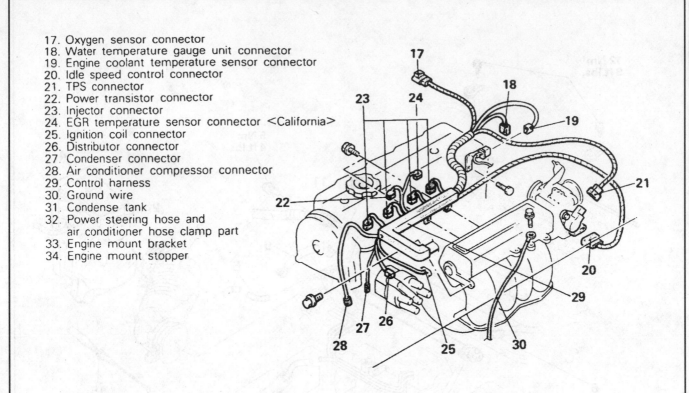

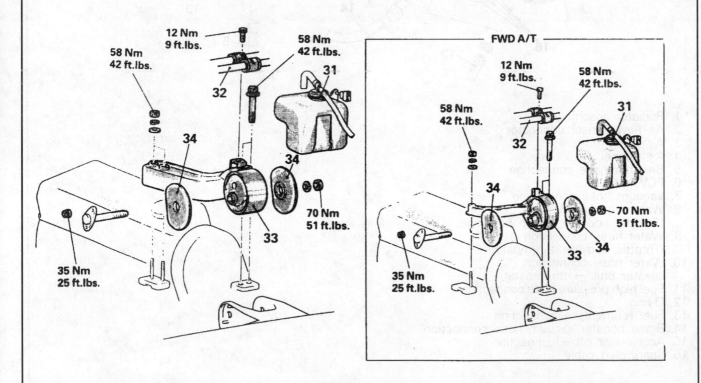

Fig. 99 2.4L engine. Remove these parts, in the order shown, in preparation for cylinder head removal. When installing the head, reverse the removal sequence

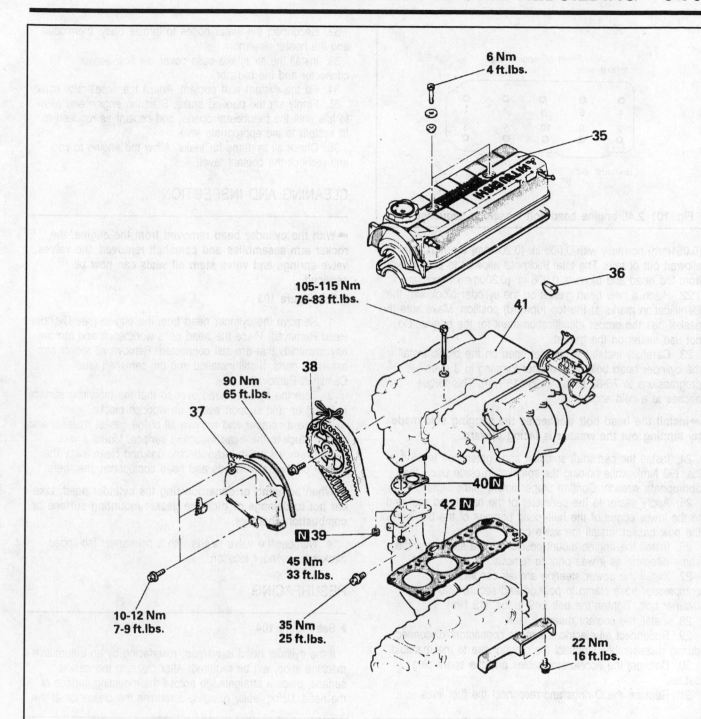

6 Nm
4 ft.lbs.

35

105-115 Nm
76-83 ft.lbs.

36

41

38

90 Nm
65 ft.lbs.

37

40

42

39

45 Nm
33 ft.lbs.

10-12 Nm
7-9 ft.lbs.

35 Nm
25 ft.lbs.

22 Nm
16 ft.lbs.

35. Rocker cover
36. Semi-circular packing
37. Timing belt front upper cover
38. Camshaft sprocket
39. Self-locking nuts
40. Gasket
41. Cylinder head assembly
42. Cylinder head gasket

Fig. 100 2.4L engine. Cylinder head removal. When installing the head, reverse the removal sequence

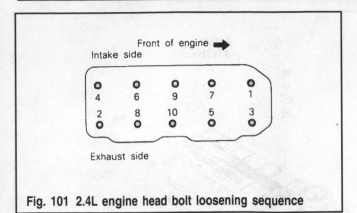

Fig. 101 2.4L engine head bolt loosening sequence

(0.051mm) normally with 0.008 in. (0.200mm) the maximum allowed out of true. The total thickness allowed to be removed from the head and block is 0.008 in. (0.200mm) maximum.

22. Place a new head gasket on the cylinder block with the identification marks at the top (upward) position. Make sure the gasket has the proper identification mark for the engine. Do not use sealer on the gasket.

23. Carefully install the cylinder head on the block. Install the cylinder head bolts and washer torquing in 3 even progressions to 76-83 ft. lbs. (105-115 Nm). This torque applies to a cold engine.

➡**Install the head bolt washer so the sagging side made by tapping out the washer is facing upward.**

24. Install the camshaft sprocket and tighten bolt to 65 ft. lbs. (90 Nm), while holding the sprocket in place using the appropriate wrench. Confirm proper timing mark alignment.

25. Apply sealer to the perimeter of the half-round seal and to the lower edges of the half-round portions of the belt-side of the new gasket. Install the valve cover.

26. Install the engine mount positioning the stopper in the same direction as it was prior to removal.

27. Install the power steering and air conditioning compressor hose clamp in position and secure with the retainer bolt. Tighten the bolt to 9 ft. lbs. (12 Nm).

28. Install the coolant reservoir tank.

29. Reconnect all electrical harness connectors disconnect during disassembly. Connect the ground wire to the manifold.

30. Connect the accelerator cables and the spark plug cables.

31. Replace the O-rings and reconnect the fuel lines.

32. Reconnect the water hoses to throttle body, thermostat and the heater assembly.

33. Install the air intake case cover, air flow sensor connector and the radiator.

34. Fill the system with coolant. Adjust the accelerator cable.

35. Firmly set the parking brake. Start the engine and allow to idle until the thermostat opens, add coolant as required to fill system to the appropriate level.

36. Check all systems for leaks. Allow the engine to cool and recheck the coolant level.

CLEANING AND INSPECTION

➡**With the cylinder head removed from the engine, the rocker arm assemblies and camshaft removed, the valves, valve springs and valve stem oil seals can now be serviced.**

▶ **See Figure 103**

1. Remove the cylinder head from the engine (see Cylinder Head Removal). Place the head on a workbench and remove any manifolds that are still connected. Remove all rocker arm assembly parts, if still installed and the camshaft (see Camshaft Removal).

2. Turn the cylinder head over so that the mounting surface is facing up and support evenly on wooden blocks.

3. Use a scraper and remove all of the gasket material and carbon stuck to the head mounting surface. Mount a wire carbon removal brush in an electric drill and clean away the carbon on the valve heads and head combustion chambers.

➡**When scraping or decarbonizing the cylinder head, take car not to damage or nick the gasket mounting surface or combustion chamber.**

4. Number the valve heads with a permanent felt-tipped marker for cylinder location.

RESURFACING

▶ **See Figure 104**

If the cylinder head is warped, resurfacing by an automotive machine shop, will be required. After cleaning the gasket surface, place a straightedge across the mounting surface of the head. Using feeler gauges, determine the clearance at the

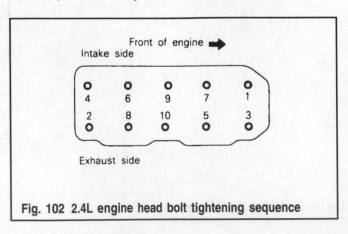

Fig. 102 2.4L engine head bolt tightening sequence

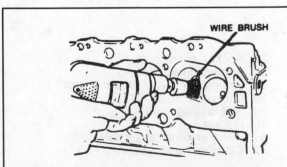

Fig. 103 Cleaning the head with a drill-mounted wire brush

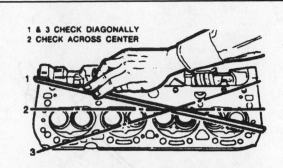

Fig. 104 Checking cylinder head flatness

center and along the length between the head and straightedge. Measure clearance at the center and along the lengths of both diagonals. If warpage exceeds 0.08mm in a 152mm span, or 0.15mm over the total length the cylinder head must be resurfaced.

Valves and Springs

▶ See Figures 105, 106, 107, 108, 109, 110, 111, 112, 113 and 114

REMOVAL & INSTALLATION

1. Block the head on its side, or install a pair of head-holding brackets made especially for valve removal.

2. Use a socket slightly larger than the valve stem and keepers, place the socket over the valve stem and gently hit the socket with a plastic hammer to break loose any varnish buildup.

3. Remove the valve keepers, retainer, spring shield (if equipped) and valve spring using a valve spring compressor (the locking C-clamp type is the easiest to use).

4. Do not mix removed parts. Place the parts from each valve in a separate container, numbered and identified for the valve and cylinder.

5. Remove and discard the valve stem oil seal, a new seal will be used at assembly time.

6. Remove the valve from the cylinder head and place, in order, through holes punched in a stiff piece of cardboard or stick in case the numbers marked on the valve head gets rubbed off.

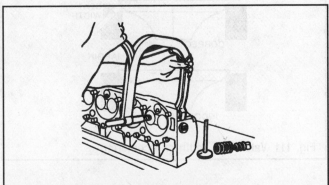

Fig. 105 Compressing valve springs

7. Use an electric drill and rotary wire brush to clean the intake and exhaust valve ports, combustion chamber and valve seats. In some cases, the carbon build-up will have to be chipped away. Use a blunt pointed drift for carbon chipping, be careful around valve seat areas.

➡**When using a wire brush to clean carbon on the valve parts, valves,etc., be sure the deposits are actually removed, rather than burnished.**

8. Use a valve guide cleaning brush and safe solvent to clean the valve guides.

9. Clean the valves with a revolving wire brush. Heavy carbon deposits may be removed with blunt drift.

10. Wash and clean all valve springs, keepers, retaining caps etc., in safe solvent. Remember to keep parts from each valve separate.

11. Check the cylinder head for cracks. Cracks usually start around the exhaust valve seat because it is the hottest part of the combustion chamber. If a crack is suspected but cannot be detected visually, have the area checked with a dye penetrant or other method by the machine shop.

12. After all cylinder head parts are reasonably clean check the valve stem-to-guide clearance. If a dial indicator is not on hand, a visual inspection can give you a fairly good idea if the guide, valve stem or both are worn.

13. Insert the valve into the guide until slightly away from the valve seat. Wiggle the valve sideways. A small amount of wobble is normal, excessive wobble means a worn guide and/or valve stem. If a dial indicator is on hand, mount the indicator so that gauge stem is 90° to the valve stem as close to the top of the valve guide as possible. Move the valve from the seat, and measure the valve guide-to-stem clearance by rocking the stem back and forth to actuate the dial indicator. Measure the valve stem using a micrometer and compare to specifications to determine whether stem or guide is causing excessive clearance.

14. The valve guide, if worn, must be repaired before the valve seats can be resurfaced. A new valve guide should be installed or, in some cases, knurled. Consult the automotive machine shop.

15. Valve faces and valve seats should be machined to specifications: the machine shop can handle the job for you. Only enough material to clean up any pits or grooves should be removed. The valve seat should not be too wide or too narrow. The valve face should contact the seat on their respective centers. The valve seat can be narrowed or widened as required.

16. After the valves and valve seats have been machined, they should be hand lapped. Use valve grinding compound and a small suction cupped valve stick. Place a small amount of compound on the valve face. Install the valve and rotate the valve face against the seat with the valve stick. Remove the valve and clean the compound from the valve face and seat. If the contact ring is too close to the outer edge of the valve face, narrow the seat: if too close to the inner edge widen the seat. If the edge of a valve head, after machining, is $1/32$ in. or less replace the valve. The tip of the valve stem should also be dressed on the valve grinding machine, however do not remove too much material.

17. After all valve and valve seats have been machined, check the remaining valve train parts (springs, retainers,

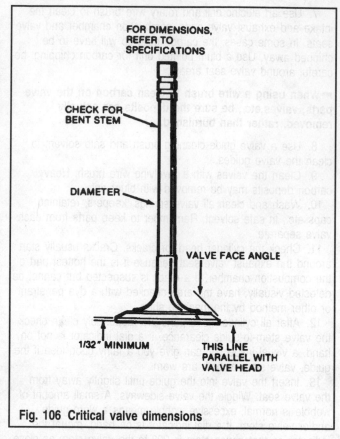

FOR DIMENSIONS, REFER TO SPECIFICATIONS

CHECK FOR BENT STEM

DIAMETER

VALVE FACE ANGLE

1/32" MINIMUM

THIS LINE PARALLEL WITH VALVE HEAD

Fig. 106 Critical valve dimensions

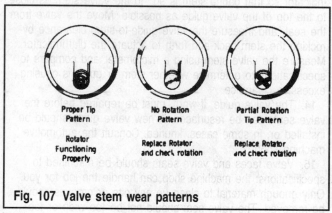

Proper Tip Pattern

Rotator Functioning Properly

No Rotation Pattern

Replace Rotator and check rotation

Partial Rotation Tip Pattern

Replace Rotator and check rotation

Fig. 107 Valve stem wear patterns

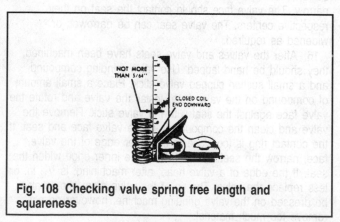

NOT MORE THAN 5/64"

CLOSED COIL END DOWNWARD

Fig. 108 Checking valve spring free length and squareness

Fig. 109 Checking valve spring test pressure

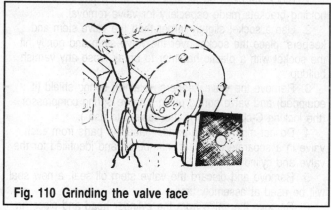

Fig. 110 Grinding the valve face

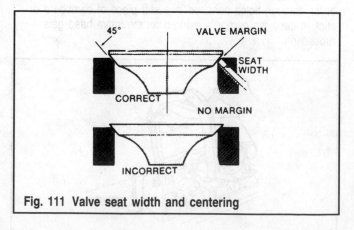

45°

VALVE MARGIN

SEAT WIDTH

CORRECT

NO MARGIN

INCORRECT

Fig. 111 Valve seat width and centering

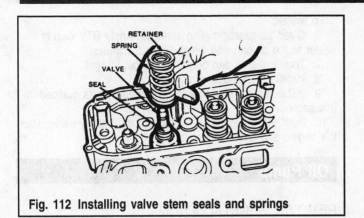

Fig. 112 Installing valve stem seals and springs

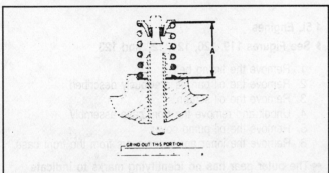

Fig. 113 Checking valve spring installed height with a modified steel ruler

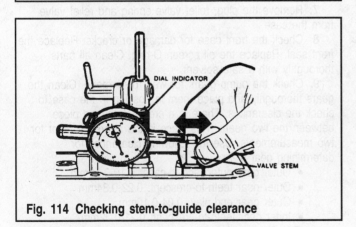

Fig. 114 Checking stem-to-guide clearance

keepers, etc) for wear. Check the valve springs for straightness and tension.

18. Assemble the head using new valve stem guide seals. Lubricate the valve stems before installation. Check the valve spring installed height, shim or replace necessary.

CHECKING VALVE SPRINGS

Place the valve spring on a flat surface next to a carpenters square. Measure the height of the spring, and rotate the spring against the edge of the square to measure distortion. If the spring height varies (by comparison) by more than 1.5mm or if the distortion exceeds 1.5mm, replace the spring.

Have the valve springs tested for spring pressure at the installed and compressed (installed height minus valve lift) height using a valve spring tester. Springs should be within one pound, plus or minus each other. Replace springs as necessary.

VALVE SPRING INSTALLED HEIGHT

After installing the valve spring, measure the distance between the spring mounting pad and the lower edge of the spring retainer. Compare the measurement to specifications. If the installed height is incorrect, add shim washers between the mounting pad and the base of the spring. Use only washers designed for spring shimming: available at parts houses.

VALVE STEM OIL SEALS

Positive valves seals are used. The seal fits over to top of the valve guide. Always install new valve stem seals when reassembling the cylinder head.

Valve Seats

▶ See Figure 115

The valve seat inserts are replaceable on all these engines.

1. With the valve removed, check the seat for wear, cracks, damage or uneven contact with the valve. If the damage or contact problem is slight, the valve may be refaced with a lapping compound and lapping tool. The compound is spread on the seat face and the valve inserted. The valve is then ground against the seat with the lapping tool, removing a small amount of metal and creating a polished surface.

2. If the damage or contact problem cannot be rectified by lapping, the insert can be cut with a special seat cutter which will remove the damaged material and cut the correct angle.

3. If the seat insert is cracked, too thin, or burnt, it must be replaced. An automotive machine shop can handle the job for you.

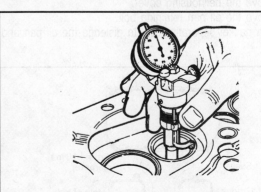

Fig. 115 Checking valve seat concentricity

Oil Pan

REMOVAL & INSTALLATION

▶ **See Figures 116, 117 and 118**

Except 1992-93 Vista

1. Raise the vehicle and support it safely. Remove the underbody splash shield. On 1993 Colt w/1.5L, remove the bellhousing cover. On 1993 Colt w/1.8L, remove the bellhousing cover and the front exhaust pipe section.
2. Remove the oil pan retaining bolts and remove the oil pan.

To install:

3. Installation is the reverse order of removal procedure.
4. These engines use no oil pan gasket. Rather, they use RTV silicone gasket material. See figure for proper gasket material application.
5. Torque the oil pan retaining bolts to 4-6 ft. lbs. (6-8 Nm).

1992-93 2WD Vista

1. Raise the vehicle and support it safely. Remove the underbody splash shield.
2. Remove the front exhaust pipe section.
3. Remove the oil pan retaining bolts and remove the oil pan.

To install:

4. Installation is the reverse order of removal procedure.
5. These engines use no oil pan gasket. Rather, they use RTV silicone gasket material. See figure for proper gasket material application.
6. Torque the oil pan retaining bolts to 4-6 ft. lbs. (6-8 Nm).

1992-93 4WD Vista

1. Disconnect the negative battery cable. Raise the vehicle and support safely. Drain the engine oil.
2. Remove the transfer case assembly and left halfshaft as outlined in this section.
3. Remove the bellhousing cover.
4. Remove the oil pan retaining bolt.
5. Use a gasket separating tool to dislodge the oil pan and remove.

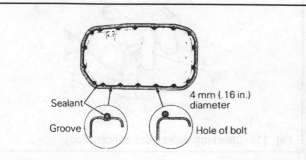

Fig. 116 Oil pan sealant coverage — 1990 1.8L and 1.6L engines; 1990-93 1.5L engines; 2.0L engines are similar

To install:

6. Clean all gasket mating surfaces. Apply RTV gasket sealer to the oil pan and install within 5 minutes.
7. Torque the oil pan bolts to 5 ft. lbs. (7 Nm).
8. Install the bellhousing cover.
9. Install the transfer case and left halfshaft as outlined in this section.
10. Refill the engine with oil, connect the battery cable, start the engine and check for leaks.

Oil Pump

REMOVAL & INSTALLATION

1.5L Engines

▶ **See Figures 119, 120, 121, 122 and 123**

1. Remove the timing belt.
2. Remove the oil pan as previously described.
3. Remove the oil screen.
4. Unbolt and remove the front case assembly.
5. Remove the oil pump cover.
6. Remove the inner and outer gears from the front case.

➡ **The outer gear has no identifying marks to indicate direction of rotation. Clean the gear and mark it with an indelible marker.**

7. Remove the plug, relief valve spring and relief valve from the case.
8. Check the front case for damage or cracks. Replace the front seal. Replace the oil screen O-ring. Clean all parts thoroughly with a safe solvent.
9. Check the pump gears for wear or damage. Clean the gears thoroughly and place them in position in the case to check the clearances. There is a crescent-shaped piece between the two gears. This piece is the reference point for two measurements. Use the following clearances for determining gear wear.
   - Outer gear outer face-to-case: 0.10-0.20mm
   - Outer gear teeth-to-crescent: 0.22-0.34mm
   - Outer gear end-play: 0.04-0.10mm
   - Inner gear teeth-to-crescent: 0.21-0.32mm
   - Inner gear end-play: 0.04-0.10mm
10. Check that the relief valve can slide freely in the case.
11. Check the relief valve spring for damage. The relief valve free length should be 47mm. Load/length should be 9.5-13 lbs. at 40mm.
12. Thoroughly coat both oil pump gears with clean engine oil and install them in the correct direction of rotation.
13. Install the pump cover and torque the bolts to 7-10 ft. lbs.
14. Coat the relief valve and spring with clean engine oil, install them and tighten the plug to 30-36 ft. lbs.
15. Position a new front case gasket, coated with sealer, on the engine and install the front case. Torque the bolts to 10 ft. lbs. Note that the bolts have different shank lengths. Use the following guide and figure to determine which bolts go where. Bolts marked **A**: 20mm. **B**: 30mm. **C**: 60mm.

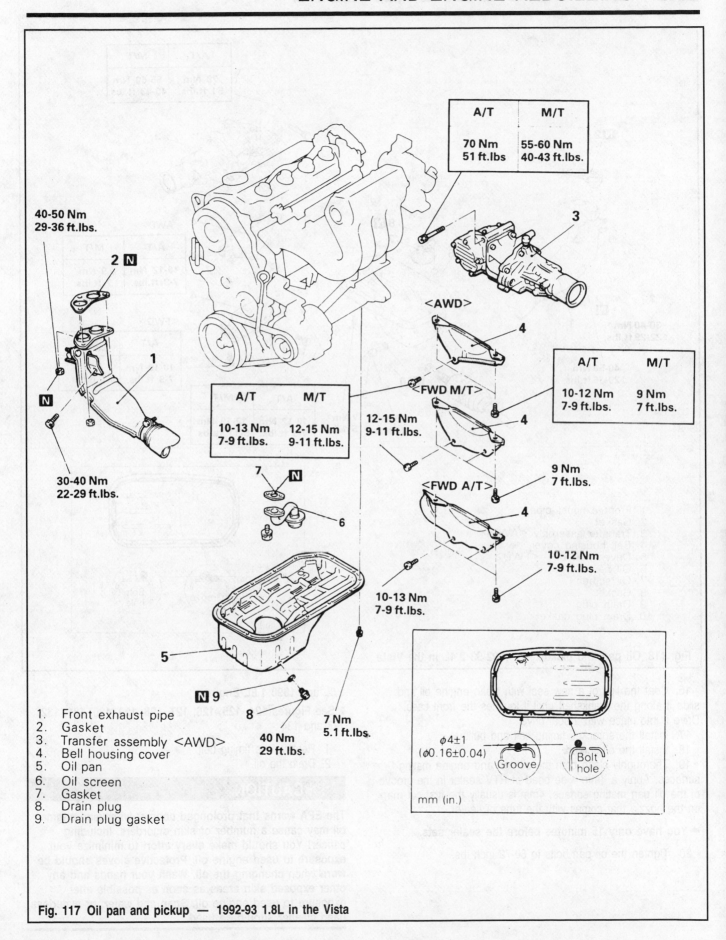

	A/T	M/T
	70 Nm	55-60 Nm
	51 ft.lbs.	40-43 ft.lbs.

40-50 Nm
29-36 ft.lbs.

2

30-40 Nm
22-29 ft.lbs.

3

<AWD>

4

	A/T	M/T
	10-13 Nm	12-15 Nm
	7-9 ft.lbs.	9-11 ft.lbs.

<FWD M/T>

12-15 Nm
9-11 ft.lbs.

4

	A/T	M/T
	10-12 Nm	9 Nm
	7-9 ft.lbs.	7 ft.lbs.

9 Nm
7 ft.lbs.

<FWD A/T>

4

7
6

5

9

8

10-13 Nm
7-9 ft.lbs.

10-12 Nm
7-9 ft.lbs.

7 Nm
5.1 ft.lbs.

40 Nm
29 ft.lbs.

1. Front exhaust pipe
2. Gasket
3. Transfer assembly <AWD>
4. Bell housing cover
5. Oil pan
6. Oil screen
7. Gasket
8. Drain plug
9. Drain plug gasket

φ4±1
(φ0.16±0.04)   Groove

Bolt hole

mm (in.)

Fig. 117 Oil pan and pickup — 1992-93 1.8L in the Vista

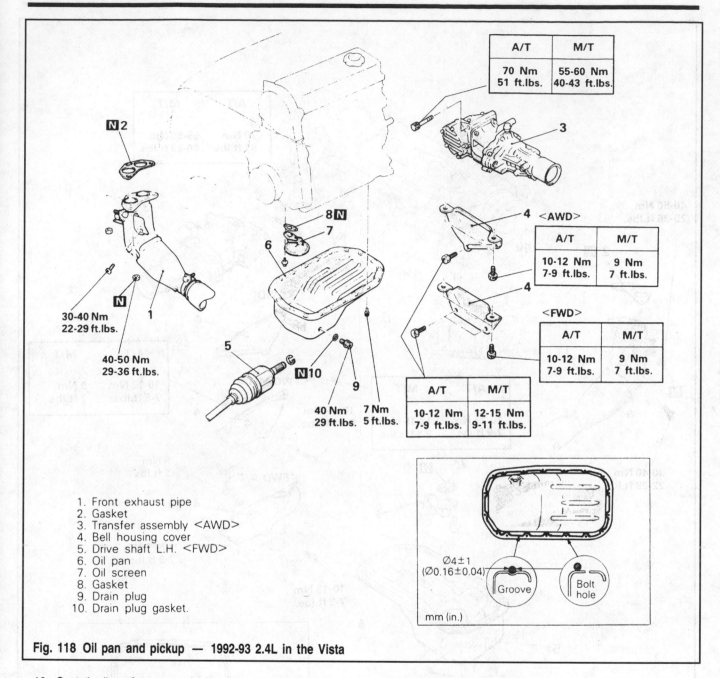

A/T	M/T
70 Nm 51 ft.lbs.	55-60 Nm 40-43 ft.lbs.

<AWD>	
A/T	M/T
10-12 Nm 7-9 ft.lbs.	9 Nm 7 ft.lbs.

<FWD>	
A/T	M/T
10-12 Nm 7-9 ft.lbs.	9 Nm 7 ft.lbs.

A/T	M/T
10-12 Nm 7-9 ft.lbs.	12-15 Nm 9-11 ft.lbs.

30-40 Nm
22-29 ft.lbs.

40-50 Nm
29-36 ft.lbs.

40 Nm   7 Nm
29 ft.lbs. 5 ft.lbs.

Ø4±1
(Ø0.16±0.04)

Groove   Bolt hole

mm (in.)

1. Front exhaust pipe
2. Gasket
3. Transfer assembly <AWD>
4. Bell housing cover
5. Drive shaft L.H. <FWD>
6. Oil pan
7. Oil screen
8. Gasket
9. Drain plug
10. Drain plug gasket.

Fig. 118 Oil pan and pickup — 1992-93 2.4L in the Vista

16. Coat the lips of a new seal with clean engine oil and slide it along the crankshaft until it touches the front case. Drive it into place with a seal drive.

17. Install the sprocket, timing belt and pulley.

18. Install the oil screen.

19. Thoroughly clean both the oil pan and engine mating surfaces. Apply a 4mm wide bead of RTV sealer in the groove of the oil pan mating surface. 4mm is usually the first cut mark on the nozzle that comes with the tube of sealer.

➡**You have only 15 minutes before the sealer sets.**

20. Tighten the oil pan bolts to 60-72 inch lbs.

1.6L and 1990 1.8L Engines

▶ **See Figures 124, 125, 126, 127, 128, 129, 130, 131, 132, 133 and 134**

1. Remove the timing belt.
2. Drain the oil.

✳✳CAUTION

The EPA warns that prolonged contact with used engine oil may cause a number of skin disorders, including cancer! You should make every effort to minimize your exposure to used engine oil. Protective gloves should be worn when changing the oil. Wash your hands and any other exposed skin areas as soon as possible after exposure to used engine oil. Soap and water, or waterless hand cleaner should be used.

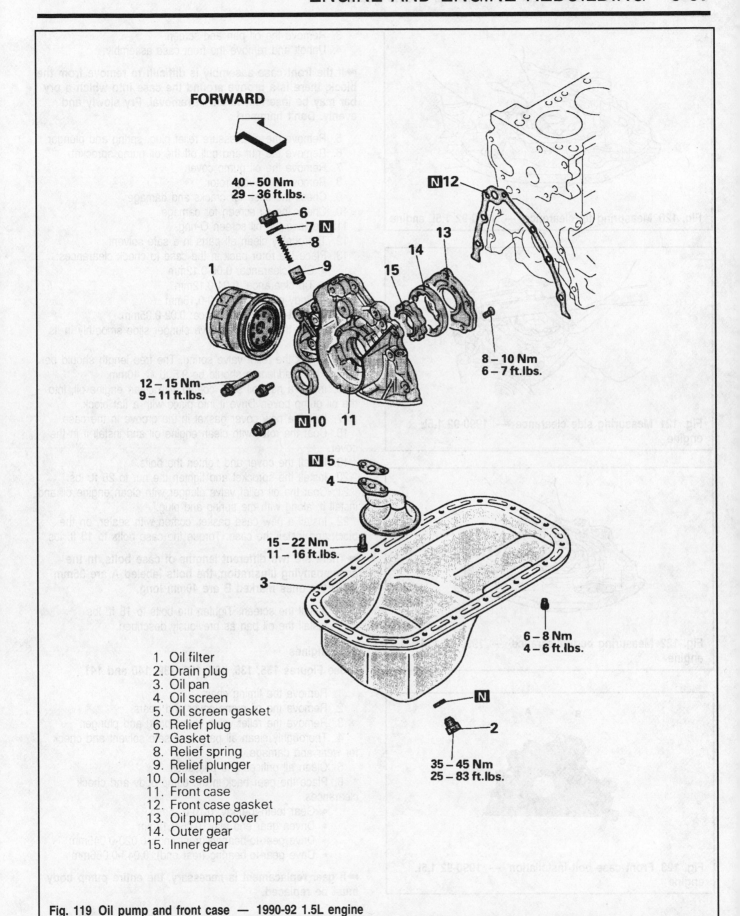

FORWARD

40 – 50 Nm
29 – 36 ft.lbs.

12 – 15 Nm
9 – 11 ft.lbs.

8 – 10 Nm
6 – 7 ft.lbs.

15 – 22 Nm
11 – 16 ft.lbs.

6 – 8 Nm
4 – 6 ft.lbs.

35 – 45 Nm
25 – 83 ft.lbs.

1. Oil filter
2. Drain plug
3. Oil pan
4. Oil screen
5. Oil screen gasket
6. Relief plug
7. Gasket
8. Relief spring
9. Relief plunger
10. Oil seal
11. Front case
12. Front case gasket
13. Oil pump cover
14. Outer gear
15. Inner gear

Fig. 119 Oil pump and front case — 1990-92 1.5L engine

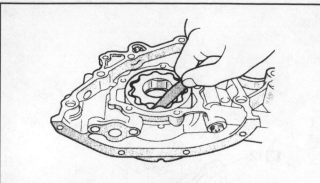

Fig. 120 Measuring tip clearance — 1990-92 1.5L engine

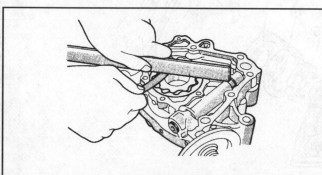

Fig. 121 Measuring side clearance — 1990-92 1.5L engine

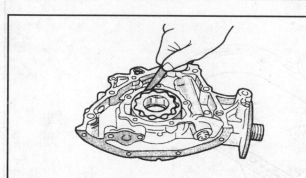

Fig. 122 Measuring body clearance — 1990-92 1.5L engine

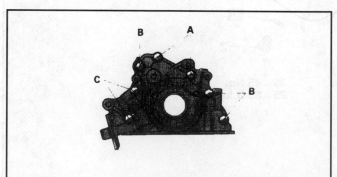

Fig. 123 Front case bolt installation — 1990-92 1.5L engine

3. Remove the oil pan and screen.
4. Unbolt and remove the front case assembly.

➡ If the front case assembly is difficult to remove from the block, there is a groove around the case into which a pry bar may be inserted, to aid in removal. Pry slowly and evenly. Don't hammer!

5. Remove the oil pressure relief plug, spring and plunger.
6. Remove the nut and pull off the oil pump sprocket.
7. Remove the oil pump cover.
8. Remove the pump rotor.
9. Check the case for cracks and damage.
10. Check the oil screen for damage.
11. Replace the oil screen O-ring.
12. Thoroughly clean all parts in a safe solvent.
13. Place the rotor back in the case to check clearances:
    • Side clearance: 0.06-0.12mm
    • Tip clearance: 0.04-0.12mm
    • Body clearance: 0.10-0.16mm
    • Shaft-to-cover clearance: 0.02-0.05mm.
14. Check that the relief valve plunger slide smoothly in its bore.
15. Check the relief valve spring. The free length should be 47mm; the load/length should be 9.5 lb @ 40mm.
16. Install a new oil seal, coated with clean engine oil, into the oil pump cover. Drive it into place with a flat block.
17. Install a new cover gasket in the groove in the case.
18. Coat the rotor with clean engine oil and install it in the cover.
19. Install the cover and tighten the bolts.
20. Install the sprocket and tighten the nut to 28 ft. lbs.
21. Coat the oil relief valve plunger with clean engine oil and install it, along with the spring and plug.
22. Install a new case gasket, coated with sealer, on the block and install the case. Torque the case bolts to 13 ft. lbs.

➡ There are two different lengths of case bolts. In the accompanying illustration, the bolts labeled A are 35mm long: the ones marked B are 40mm long.

23. Install the screen. Tighten the bolts to 18 ft. lbs.
24. Install the oil pan as previously described.

2.0L Engines

▶ See Figures 135, 136, 137, 138, 139, 140 and 141

1. Remove the timing chain.
2. Remove the oil pump cover and gears.
3. Remove the relief valve plug, spring and plunger.
4. Thoroughly clean all parts in a safe solvent and check for wear and damage.
5. Clean all orifices and passages.
6. Place the gear back in the pump body and check clearances.
    • Gear teeth-to-body: 0.10-0.15mm
    • Driven gear end play: 0.06-0.12mm
    • Drive gear-to-bearing (front end): 0.020-0.045mm
    • Drive gear-to-bearing (rear end): 0.043-0.066mm

➡ If gear replacement is necessary, the entire pump body must be replaced.

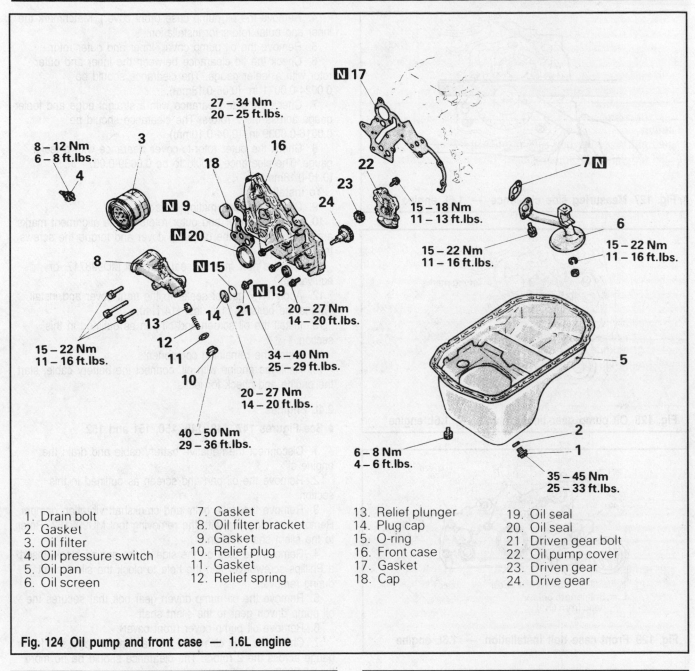

8 – 12 Nm
6 – 8 ft.lbs.

27 – 34 Nm
20 – 25 ft.lbs.

15 – 18 Nm
11 – 13 ft.lbs.

15 – 22 Nm
11 – 16 ft.lbs.

15 – 22 Nm
11 – 16 ft.lbs.

15 – 22 Nm
11 – 16 ft.lbs.

20 – 27 Nm
14 – 20 ft.lbs.

34 – 40 Nm
25 – 29 ft.lbs.

20 – 27 Nm
14 – 20 ft.lbs.

40 – 50 Nm
29 – 36 ft.lbs.

6 – 8 Nm
4 – 6 ft.lbs.

35 – 45 Nm
25 – 33 ft.lbs.

1. Drain bolt	7. Gasket	13. Relief plunger
2. Gasket	8. Oil filter bracket	14. Plug cap
3. Oil filter	9. Gasket	15. O-ring
4. Oil pressure switch	10. Relief plug	16. Front case
5. Oil pan	11. Gasket	17. Gasket
6. Oil screen	12. Relief spring	18. Cap

19. Oil seal	
20. Oil seal	
21. Driven gear bolt	
22. Oil pump cover	
23. Driven gear	
24. Drive gear	

Fig. 124 Oil pump and front case — 1.6L engine

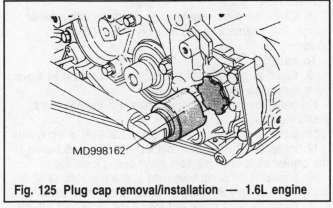

MD998162

Fig. 125 Plug cap removal/installation — 1.6L engine

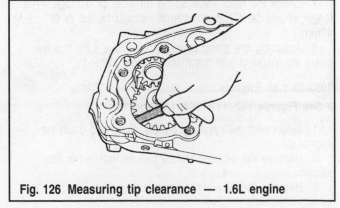

Fig. 126 Measuring tip clearance — 1.6L engine

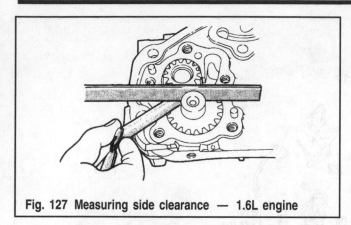

Fig. 127 Measuring side clearance — 1.6L engine

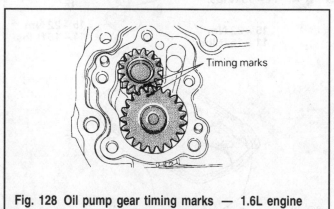

Timing marks

Fig. 128 Oil pump gear timing marks — 1.6L engine

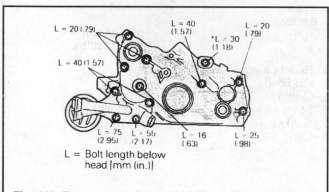

L = 20 (.79)
L = 40 (1.57)
L = 20 (.79)
*L = 30 (1.18)
L = 40 (1.57)
L = 75 (2.95)
L = 55 (2.17)
L - 16 (.63)
L = 25 (.98)
L = Bolt length below head [mm (in.)]

Fig. 129 Front case bolt installation — 1.6L engine

7. Check the relief valve spring for wear or damage. Free length should be 47mm; load/length should be 9.5 lb @ 40mm.

8. Assembly the pump components. Make sure that the gears are installed with the mating marks aligned.

1992-93 1.8L Engines

▶ See Figures 142, 143, 144, 145 and 146

1. Disconnect the negative battery cable and drain the engine oil.

2. Remove the oil filter and oil pan as outlined in this section.

3. Remove the oil pump screen and gasket.

4. Remove the oil pump case (front cover). Matchmark the inner and outer rotors for installation.

5. Remove the oil pump cover, inner and outer rotor.

6. Check the tip clearance between the inner and outer rotor with a feeler gauge. The clearance should be 0.0024-0.0071 in. (0.06-0.18mm).

7. Check the side clearance with a straight edge and feeler gauge across the 2 rotors. The clearance should be 0.0016-0.0039 in. (0.04-0.10mm).

8. Check the outer rotor-to-cover clearance with a feeler gauge. The clearance should to be 0.0039-0.0071 in. (0.10-0.18mm).

To install:

9. Clean all gasket mating surfaces.

10. Install the inner and outer rotors so the alignment marks are together. Install the oil pump cover and torque the screws to 7 ft. lbs. (10 Nm).

11. Install a new front oil seal with tool MD998717, or equivalent.

12. Apply RTV gasket sealer to the front cover and install. Torque the bolts to 11 ft. lbs. (14 Nm).

13. Install the oil screen and oil pan as outlined in this section.

14. Install the remaining components.

15. Refill the engine with oil, connect the battery cable, start the engine and check for leaks.

2.4L Engines

▶ See Figures 147, 148, 149, 150, 151 and 152

1. Disconnect the negative battery cable and drain the engine oil.

2. Remove the oil pan and screen as outlined in this section.

3. Remove the drive belts and crankshaft vibration damper. Remove the plug cap with the removing tool MD998162. Refer to the silent shaft section.

4. Remove the plug on the side of the engine block. Insert a Phillips screwdriver into the hole to block the silent shaft during removal.

5. Remove the oil pump driven gear bolt that secures the oil pump driven gear to the silent shaft.

6. Remove oil pump cover (front cover).

7. Check the side clearance with a straight edge and feeler gauge across the 2 rotors. The clearance should be no more than 0.0098 in. (0.25mm).

8. Check the outer rotor-to-cover clearance with a feeler gauge. The clearance should no more than 0.0098 in. (0.25mm).

To install:

9. Clean all gasket mating surfaces and lubricate all moving parts with clean engine oil.

10. Install the driven and drive gears with the alignment marks together.

11. Install a new front seal using tool C3095A, or equivalent.

12. Install an oil seal guide tool MD998285, or equivalent to the crankshaft to align the front cover during installation.

13. Install the oil pump cover and torque the bolts to 12 ft. lbs. (17 Nm). Apply RTV gasket sealer to the front cover.

14. Install the front cover and torque the bolts to 17 ft. lbs. (23 Nm).

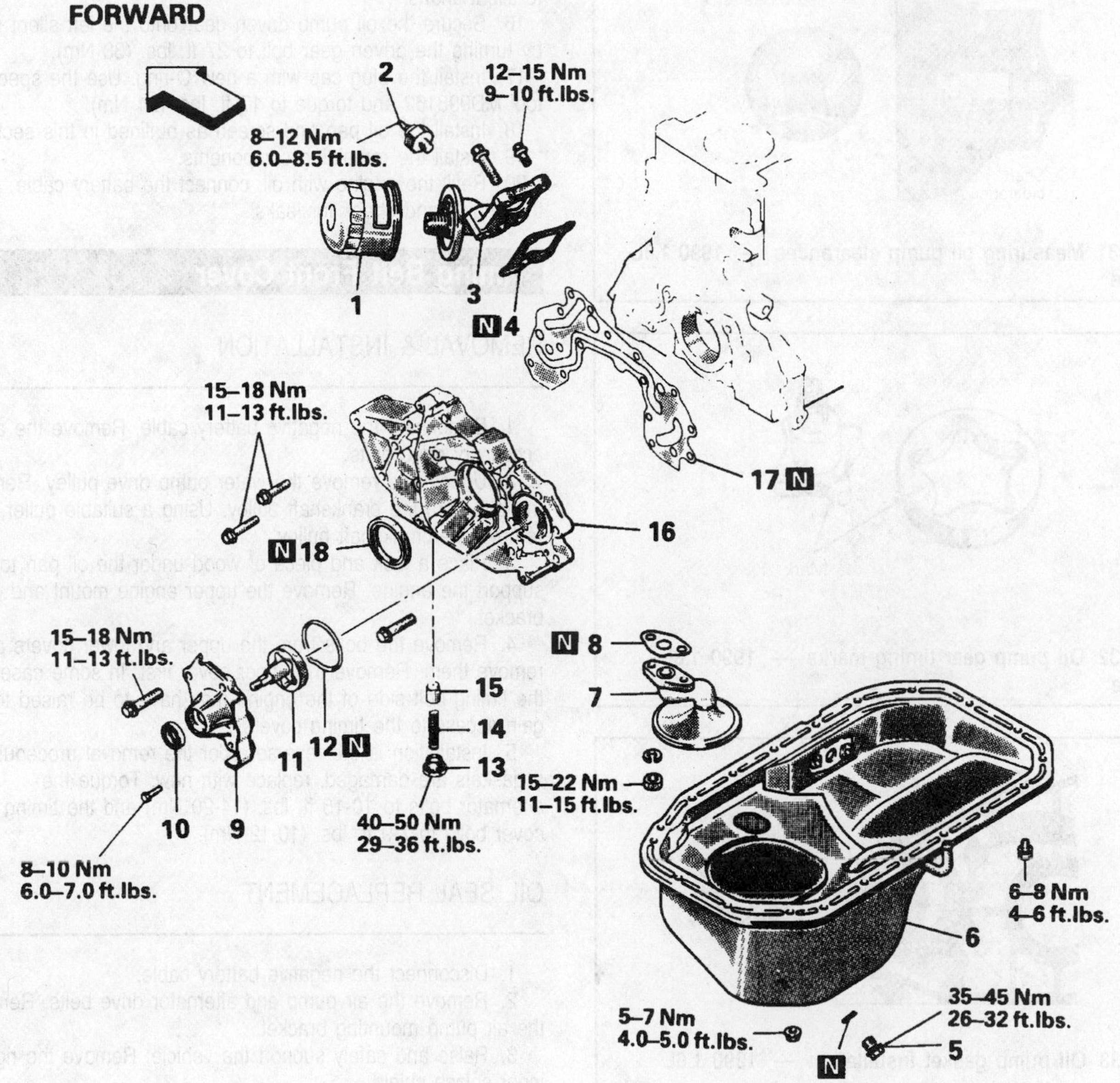

FORWARD

2. Oil pressure switch — 8–12 Nm / 6.0–8.5 ft.lbs.

12–15 Nm
9–10 ft.lbs.

1. Oil filter

3. Oil filter bracket

N 4. Gasket

17 N

15–18 Nm
11–13 ft.lbs.

N 18

16. Front case

15–18 Nm
11–13 ft.lbs.

N 8

7

15. Relief plunger

14. Relief spring

13. Plug

15–22 Nm
11–15 ft.lbs.

11. Oil pump rotor assembly

12 N

10. Oil seal

9. Oil pump cover

40–50 Nm
29–36 ft.lbs.

8–10 Nm
6.0–7.0 ft.lbs.

6–8 Nm
4–6 ft.lbs.

6. Oil pan

35–45 Nm
26–32 ft.lbs.

5–7 Nm
4.0–5.0 ft.lbs.

5. Drain plug

N

1. Oil filter
2. Oil pressure switch
3. Oil filter bracket
4. Gasket
5. Drain plug
6. Oil pan
7. Oil screen
8. Oil screen gasket
9. Oil pump cover
10. Oil seal
11. Oil pump rotor assembly
12. Oil pump gasket
13. Plug
14. Relief spring
15. Relief plunger
16. Front case
17. Front case gasket
18. Crankshaft oil seal

Fig. 130 Oil pump and front case — 1990 1.8L engine

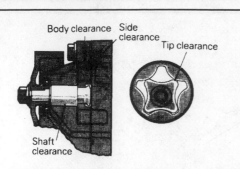

Fig. 131 Measuring oil pump clearances — 1990 1.8L engine

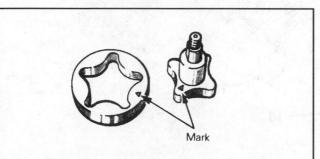

Fig. 132 Oil pump gear timing marks — 1990 1.8L engine

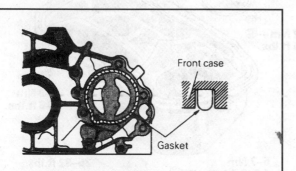

Fig. 133 Oil pump gasket installation — 1990 1.6L engine

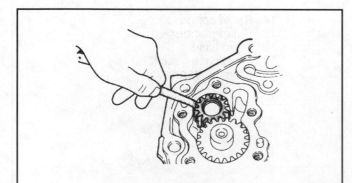

Fig. 134 Front case bolt installation — 1990 1.8L engine

15. Insert a Phillips screwdriver into the silent shaft hole in the left side of the engine block to lock the silent shaft. Refer to silent shafts.

16. Secure the oil pump driven gear onto the left silent shaft by turning the driven gear bolt to 27 ft. lbs. (38 Nm).

17. Install the plug cap with a new O-ring. Use the special tool MD998162 and torque to 17 ft. lbs. (24 Nm).

18. Install the oil pan and screen as outlined in this section.

19. Install the remaining components.

20. Refill the engine with oil, connect the battery cable, start the engine and check for leaks.

Timing Belt Front Cover

REMOVAL & INSTALLATION

1. Disconnect the negative battery cable. Remove the all accessory drive belts.

2. Unbolt and remove the water pump drive pulley. Remove the bolt from the crankshaft pulley. Using a suitable puller, remove the crankshaft pulley.

3. Place a jack and piece of wood under the oil pan to support the engine. Remove the upper engine mount and bracket.

4. Remove the bolts from the upper and lower covers and remove them. Remove the upper cover first. In some cases, the timing belt side of the engine may have to be raised to gain access to the timing covers.

5. Installation is the reverse order the removal procedures. If gaskets are damaged, replace with new. Torque the alternator bolts to 10-15 ft. lbs. (14-20 Nm) and the timing cover bolts to 7-9 ft. lbs. (10-12 Nm).

OIL SEAL REPLACEMENT

1. Disconnect the negative battery cable.

2. Remove the air pump and alternator drive belts. Remove the air pump mounting bracket.

3. Raise and safely support the vehicle. Remove the right inner splash shield.

4. Remove the crankshaft pulley bolt and washer and remove the pulley.

5. Install a seal remover tool over crankshaft nose and turn it tightly into the seal.

6. Tighten the thrust screw to remove the seal.

➡If the front cover is removed from the engine, tap the side of the thrust screw to remove the seal.

To install:

7. Using a oil seal installation tool, drive the new seal into the front cover.

8. Install the crankshaft pulley, washer and retaining bolt.

9. Install the right inner splash shield and lower the vehicle.

10. Install the air pump mounting bracket, air pump and alternator drive belts. Torque the crankshaft pulley bolt to 51-72 ft. lbs. (70-100 Nm).

11. Connect the negative battery cable.

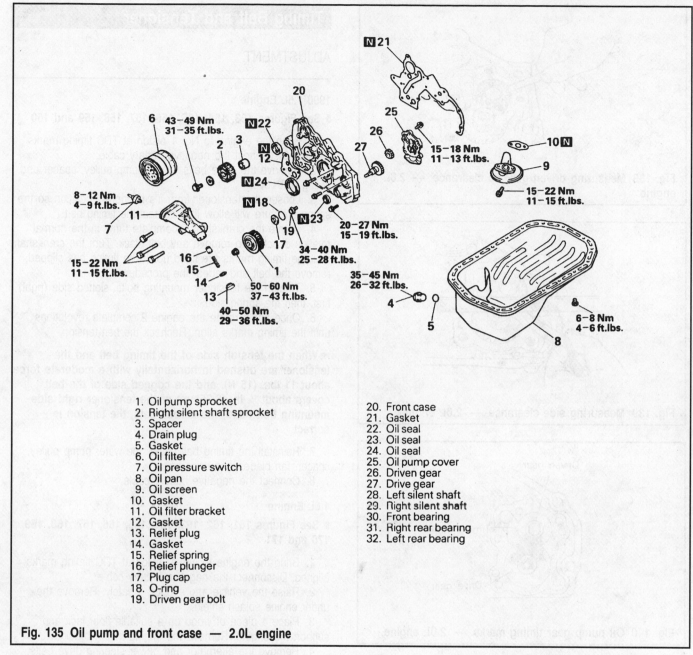

1. Oil pump sprocket
2. Right silent shaft sprocket
3. Spacer
4. Drain plug
5. Gasket
6. Oil filter
7. Oil pressure switch
8. Oil pan
9. Oil screen
10. Gasket
11. Oil filter bracket
12. Gasket
13. Relief plug
14. Gasket
15. Relief spring
16. Relief plunger
17. Plug cap
18. O-ring
19. Driven gear bolt

20. Front case
21. Gasket
22. Oil seal
23. Oil seal
24. Oil seal
25. Oil pump cover
26. Driven gear
27. Drive gear
28. Left silent shaft
29. Right silent shaft
30. Front bearing
31. Right rear bearing
32. Left rear bearing

Fig. 135 Oil pump and front case — 2.0L engine

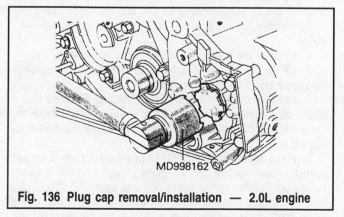

Fig. 136 Plug cap removal/installation — 2.0L engine

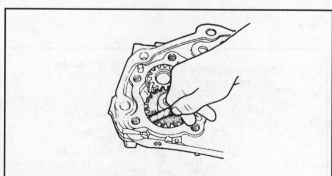

Fig. 137 Measuring drive gear tip clearance — 2.0L engine

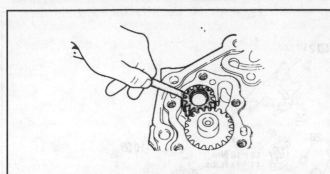

Fig. 138 Measuring driven gear tip clearance — 2.0L engine

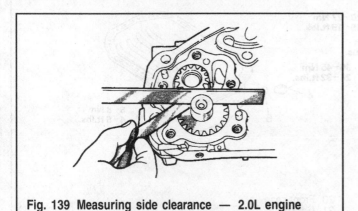

Fig. 139 Measuring side clearance — 2.0L engine

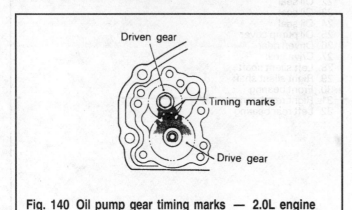

Fig. 140 Oil pump gear timing marks — 2.0L engine

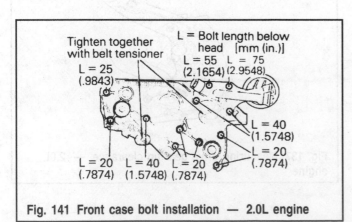

Fig. 141 Front case bolt installation — 2.0L engine

Timing Belt and Tensioner

ADJUSTMENT

1990 1.5L Engine

▶ **See Figures 153, 154, 155, 156, 157, 158, 159 and 160**

1. Bring the engine to No. 1 piston at TDC timing marks aligned. Disconnect the negative battery cable.
2. Remove the drive belts, water pump pulley, spacer and timing belt cover.
3. Loosen the tensioner from it's temporary position so the spring pressure will allow it to contact the timing belt.
4. Rotate the crankshaft 2 complete turns in the normal rotation direction to remove any belt slack. Turn the crankshaft until the timing marks are lined up. If the timing has slipped, remove the belt and repeat the procedure.
5. Tighten the tensioner mounting bolts, slotted side (right) first, then the spring side.
6. Once again rotate the engine 2 complete revolutions until the timing marks align. Recheck the belt tension.

➡ **When the tension side of the timing belt and the tensioner are pushed in horizontally with a moderate force, about 11 lbs. (15 N). and the cogged side of the belt covers about ¼ in. (6.35mm) of the tensioner right side mounting bolt head, the across flats, the tension is correct.**

7. Reinstall the timing belt cover, the water pump pulley, spacer, fan blades and drive belt.
8. Connect the negative battery cable.

1.6L Engine

▶ **See Figures 161, 162, 163, 164, 165, 166, 167, 168, 169, 170 and 171**

1. Bring the engine to No. 1 piston at TDC timing marks aligned. Disconnect the negative battery cable.
2. Raise the vehicle and support it safely. Remove the under engine splash shield.
3. Place a piece of wood on a suitable floor jack and support the engine. Remove the engine mount bracket.
4. Remove the alternator and power steering drive belts. Remove the air conditioner drive belt and tensioner assembly.
5. Remove the water pump pulley and the crankshaft pulley.
6. Remove the upper and lower timing belt covers.
7. Lift up the tensioner pulley against the belt and tighten the center bolt to hold it in position.
8. Make sure the timing marks are aligned. Remove the binder clips. Rotate the crankshaft a ¼ turn counter-clockwise. Then turn the crankshaft clockwise until the timing marks are aligned.
9. Place special tool MD998752 or equivalent, on a torque wrench. Insert the tool into the place provided on the tension pulley. Loosen the center pulley bolt and apply 2.2 ft. lbs. (3.1 Nm) of pressure against the timing belt with the tension pulley. While holding the required torque, tighten the center bolt. Screw in special tool MD998738 or equivalent, through the left engine support bracket until it contacts the tensioner arm

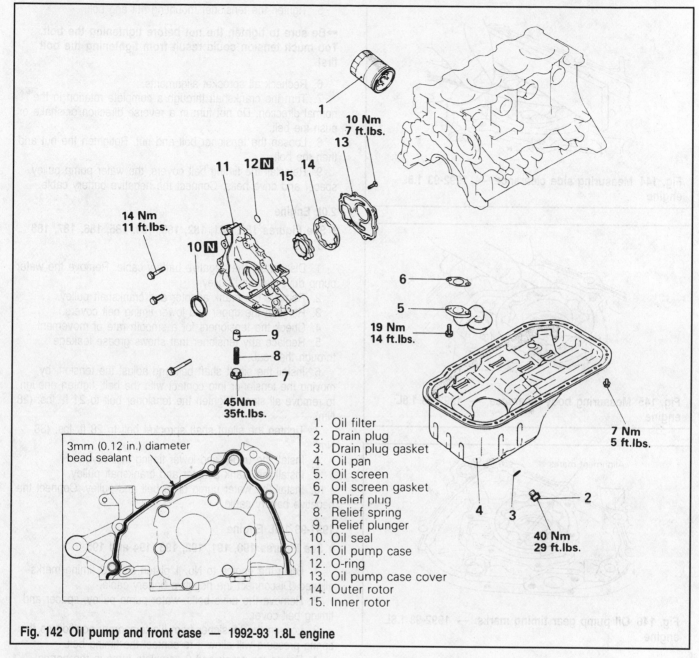

10 Nm
7 ft.lbs.

14 Nm
11 ft.lbs.

10

45Nm
35ft.lbs.

19 Nm
14 ft.lbs.

7 Nm
5 ft.lbs.

40 Nm
29 ft.lbs.

3mm (0.12 in.) diameter
bead sealant

1. Oil filter
2. Drain plug
3. Drain plug gasket
4. Oil pan
5. Oil screen
6. Oil screen gasket
7. Relief plug
8. Relief spring
9. Relief plunger
10. Oil seal
11. Oil pump case
12. O-ring
13. Oil pump case cover
14. Outer rotor
15. Inner rotor

Fig. 142 Oil pump and front case — 1992-93 1.8L engine

bracket. Turn the tool a little more to secure the tensioner and remove the locking wire placed into the automatic adjuster when it was reset.

10. Remove the special tool. Rotate the crankshaft 2 complete turns clockwise and allow it to set, for about 15 minutes. Then measure the protrusion of the automatic adjuster. It should be 3.8-4.5mm. If the proper amount of protrusion is not present, repeat the tensioning process.

11. Install the upper and lower timing belt covers.

12. Install the crankshaft pulley and water pump pulley.

13. Install the alternator and power steering drive belts. Install the air conditioner drive belt and tensioner assembly.

14. Install the engine mount bracket and lower the engine.

15. Install the under engine splash shield.

16. Connect the negative battery cable.

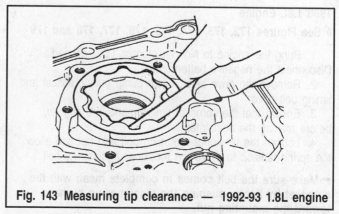

Fig. 143 Measuring tip clearance — 1992-93 1.8L engine

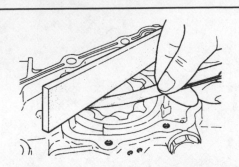

Fig. 144 Measuring side clearance — 1992-93 1.8L engine

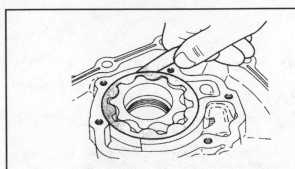

Fig. 145 Measuring body clearance — 1992-93 1.8L engine

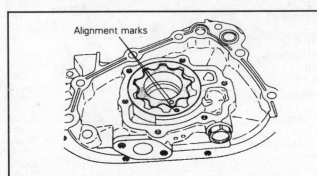

Fig. 146 Oil pump gear timing marks — 1992-93 1.8L engine

1990 1.8L Engine

▶ **See Figures 172, 173, 174, 175, 176, 177, 178 and 179**

1. Bring the engine to No. 1 piston at TDC, aligned. Disconnect the negative battery cable.
2. Remove the drive belts, water pump pulley, spacer and timing belt cover.
3. Ensure that the sprocket timing marks are aligned, before making the adjustment.
4. Loosen the tensioner mounting bolt and nut and allow the spring tension to move the tensioner against the belt.

➡**Make sure the belt comes in complete mesh with the sprocket by lightly pushing the tensioner up by hand toward the mounting nut.**

5. Tighten the tensioner mounting nut and bolt.

➡**Be sure to tighten the nut before tightening the bolt. Too much tension could result from tightening the bolt first.**

6. Recheck all sprocket alignments.
7. Turn the crankshaft through a complete rotation in the normal direction. Do not turn in a reverse direction or shake or push the belt.
8. Loosen the tensioner bolt and nut. Retighten the nut and then the bolt.
9. Reinstall the timing belt covers, the water pump pulley, spacer and drive belts. Connect the negative battery cable.

2.0L Engine

▶ **See Figures 180, 181, 182, 183, 184, 185, 186, 187, 188 and 189**

1. Disconnect the negative battery cable. Remove the water pump drive belt and pulley.
2. Remove the crank adapter and crankshaft pulley.
3. Remove the upper and lower timing belt covers.
4. Check the tensioners for a smooth rate of movement.
5. Replace any tensioner that shows grease leakage through the seal.
6. Install the silent shaft belt and adjust the tension, by moving the tensioner into contact with the belt, tighten enough to remove all slack. Tighten the tensioner bolt to 21 ft. lbs. (28 Nm).
7. Tighten the silent shaft sprocket bolt to 28 ft. lbs. (38 Nm)
8. Install the upper and lower timing belt covers.
9. Install the crank adapter and crankshaft pulley.
10. Install the water pump drive belt and pulley. Connect the negative battery cable.

1991-93 1.5L Engine

▶ **See Figures 190, 191, 192, 193, 194 and 195**

1. Bring the engine to No. 1 piston at TDC timing marks aligned. Disconnect the negative battery cable.
2. Remove the drive belts, water pump pulley, spacer and timing belt cover.
3. Loosen the tensioner from it's temporary position so the spring pressure will allow it to contact the timing belt.
4. Rotate the crankshaft 2 complete turns in the normal rotation direction to remove any belt slack. Turn the crankshaft until the timing marks are lined up. If the timing has slipped, remove the belt and repeat the procedure.
5. Tighten the tensioner mounting bolts, slotted side (right) first, then the spring side.
6. Once again rotate the engine 2 complete revolutions until the timing marks align. Recheck the belt tension.

➡**When the tension side of the timing belt and the tensioner are pushed in horizontally with a moderate force, about 11 lbs. (15 N). and the cogged side of the belt covers about 1/4 in. (6.35mm) of the tensioner right side mounting bolt head, the across flats, the tension is correct.**

7. Reinstall the timing belt cover, the water pump pulley, spacer, fan blades and drive belt.

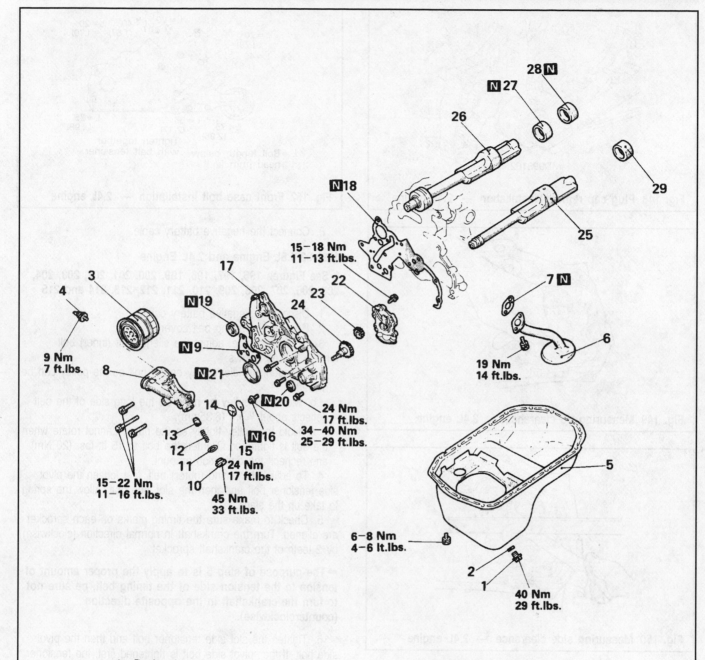

15—18 Nm
11—13 ft.lbs.

9 Nm
7 ft.lbs.

19 Nm
14 ft.lbs.

24 Nm
17 ft.lbs.
34—40 Nm
25—29 ft.lbs.

15—22 Nm
11—16 ft.lbs.

24 Nm
17 ft.lbs.

45 Nm
33 ft.lbs.

6—8 Nm
4—6 lt.lbs.

40 Nm
29 ft.lbs.

1. Drain plug
2. Gasket
3. Oil filter
4. Oil pressure switch
5. Oil pan
6. Oil screen
7. Gasket
8. Oil filter bracket
9. Gasket
10. Relief plug
11. Gasket
12. Relief spring
13. Relief plunger
14. Plug cap
15. O-ring

16. Driven gear bolt
17. Front case
18. Gasket
19. Oil seal
20. Oil seal
21. Crankshaft front oil seal
22. Oil pump cover
23. Oil pump driven gear
24. Oil pump drive gear
25. Left silent shaft
26. Right silent shaft
27. Silent shaft front bearing
28. Right silent shaft rear bearing
29. Left silent shaft rear bearing

Fig. 147 Oil pump and front case — 2.4L engine

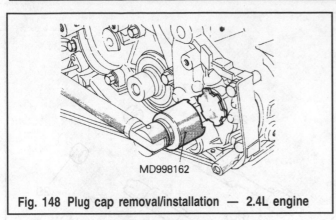

Fig. 148 Plug cap removal/installation — 2.4L engine

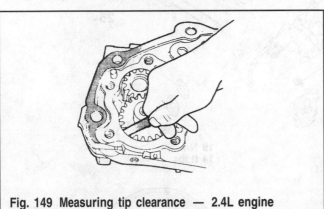

Fig. 149 Measuring tip clearance — 2.4L engine

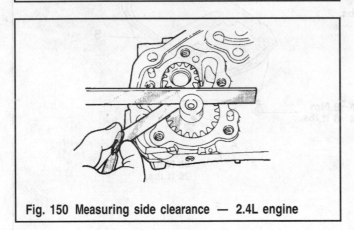

Fig. 150 Measuring side clearance — 2.4L engine

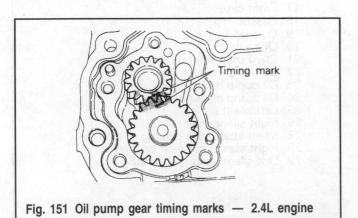

Fig. 151 Oil pump gear timing marks — 2.4L engine

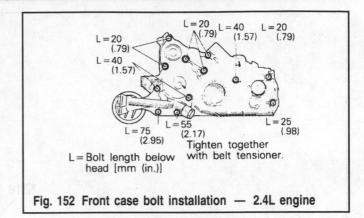

L = Bolt length below head [mm (in.)]

Tighten together with belt tensioner.

Fig. 152 Front case bolt installation — 2.4L engine

8. Connect the negative battery cable.

1992-93 1.8L Engine and 2.4L Engine

▶ See Figures 196, 197, 198, 199, 200, 201, 202, 203, 204, 205, 206, 207, 208, 209, 210, 211, 212, 213, 214 and 215

1. Disconnect negative battery cable.
2. Remove the timing belt covers.
3. On 2.4L engine, adjust the silent shaft (inner) belt tension first as follows:

   a. Loosen the idler pulley center bolt so the pulley can be moved.

   b. Move the pulley by hand so the long side of the belt deflects about ¼ in. (6.35mm).

   c. Hold the pulley tightly so the pulley cannot rotate when the bolt is tightened. Tighten the bolt to 15 ft. lbs. (20 Nm) and recheck the deflection amount.

4. To adjust the timing (outer) belt, first loosen the pivot side tensioner bolt and then the slot side bolt. Allow the spring to take up the slack.

5. Check to make sure the timing marks on each sprocket are aligned. Turn the crankshaft in normal direction (clockwise), by 2 teeth of the crankshaft sprocket.

➡The purpose of step 5 is to apply the proper amount of tension to the tension side of the timing belt, be sure not to turn the crankshaft in the opposite direction (counterclockwise).

6. Tighten the slot side tensioner bolt and then the pivot side bolt. If the pivot side bolt is tightened first, the tensioner could turn with bolt, causing over tension.

7. Lightly clamp the center of the span between the camshaft sprocket and the water pump sprocket on the belt tension side with a thumb and forefinger. Check to be sure the clearance between the reverse surface of the belt and the inside of the undercover seal line is at the standard value.

   a. 1.8L engine — 1.18 in. (30mm).

   b. 2.4L engine — 0.55 in. (14mm).

8. Install the timing belt covers and all related items.
9. Connect the negative battery cable.

REMOVAL & INSTALLATION

➡The timing chain case is cast aluminum, so exercise caution when handling this part.

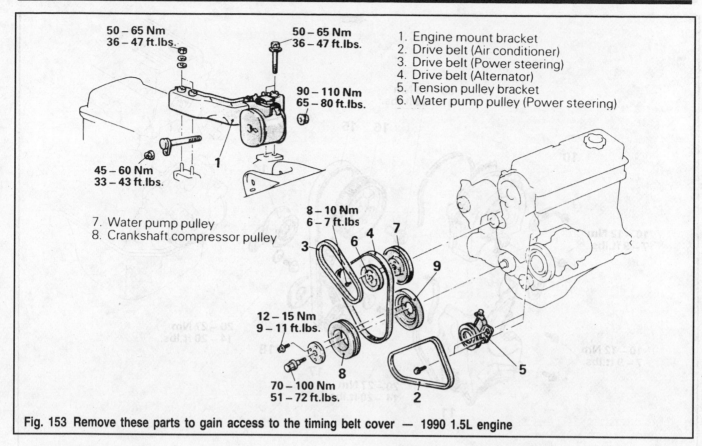

1. Engine mount bracket
2. Drive belt (Air conditioner)
3. Drive belt (Power steering)
4. Drive belt (Alternator)
5. Tension pulley bracket
6. Water pump pulley (Power steering)
7. Water pump pulley
8. Crankshaft compressor pulley

50 – 65 Nm
36 – 47 ft.lbs.

50 – 65 Nm
36 – 47 ft.lbs.

90 – 110 Nm
65 – 80 ft.lbs.

45 – 60 Nm
33 – 43 ft.lbs.

8 – 10 Nm
6 – 7 ft.lbs

12 – 15 Nm
9 – 11 ft.lbs.

70 – 100 Nm
51 – 72 ft.lbs.

Fig. 153 Remove these parts to gain access to the timing belt cover — 1990 1.5L engine

1.5L Engine

1. Turn the engine until the No. 1 piston is on TDC with the timing marks aligned.

2. Disconnect the negative battery cable.

3. Remove the fan drive belt, the fan blades, spacer and water pump pulley.

4. Remove the timing belt cover.

5. Loosen the timing belt tensioner mounting bolt and move the tensioner toward the water pump. Temporarily secure the tensioner.

6. Remove the crankshaft pulley and slide the belt off of the camshaft and crankshaft drive sprockets.

7. Inspect the drive sprockets for abnormal wear, cracks or damage and replace, if necessary. Remove and inspect the tensioner. Check for smooth pulley rotation, excessive play or noise. Replace tensioner, if necessary.

To install:

8. Reinstall the tensioner, if removed and temporarily secure it close to the water pump.

9. Make sure the timing mark on the camshaft sprocket is aligned with the pointer on the cylinder head and that the crankshaft sprocket mark is aligned with the mark on the engine case.

10. Install the timing belt on the crankshaft sprocket.

11. Install the belt counterclockwise over the camshaft sprocket making sure there is no play on the tension side of the belt. Adjust the belt fore and aft so it is centered on the sprockets.

12. Loosen the tensioner from it's temporary position so the spring pressure will allow it to contact the timing belt.

13. Rotate the crankshaft 2 complete turns in the normal rotation direction to remove any belt slack. Turn the crankshaft until the timing marks are lined up. If the timing has slipped, remove the belt and repeat the procedure.

14. Tighten the tensioner mounting bolts, slotted side (right) first, then the spring side.

15. Once again rotate the engine 2 complete revolutions until the timing marks line up. Recheck the belt tension.

➡ **When the tension side of the timing belt and the tensioner are pushed in horizontally with a moderate force, about 11 lbs. (15 N) and the cogged side of the belt covers about ¼ in. (6.35mm) of the tensioner right side mounting bolt head the across flats, the tension is correct.**

16. Reinstall the timing belt cover, the water pump pulley, spacer, fan blades and drive belt.

17. Connect the negative battery cable.

1.6L Engine

➡ **Special tools MD998752 tension pulley torque adapter and MD998738 tension pulley locker or equivalents, are required.**

1. Bring the engine to No. 1 piston at TDC (top dead center) timing marks aligned. Disconnect the negative battery cable.

2. Raise the vehicle and support it safely. Remove the under engine splash shield.

3. Place a piece of wood on a suitable floor jack and support the engine. Remove the engine mount bracket.

4. Remove the alternator and power steering drive belts. Remove the air conditioner drive belt and tensioner assembly.

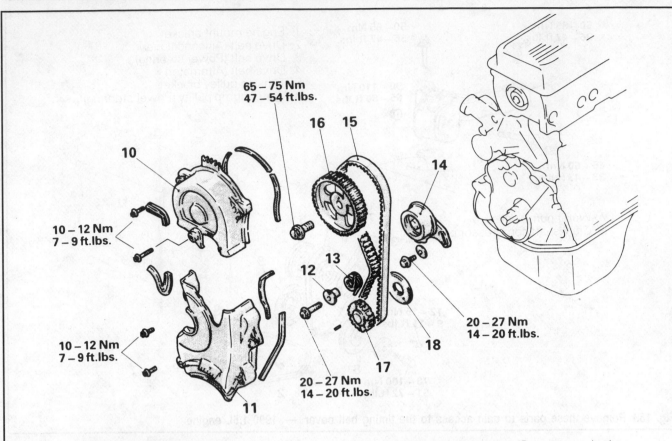

65 – 75 Nm
47 – 54 ft.lbs.

10 – 12 Nm
7 – 9 ft.lbs.

10 – 12 Nm
7 – 9 ft.lbs.

20 – 27 Nm
14 – 20 ft.lbs.

20 – 27 Nm
14 – 20 ft.lbs.

18. Flange
17. Crankshaft sprocket
16. Camshaft sprocket
14. Tensioner
13. Tensioner spring
12. Tensioner spacer
15. Timing belt
    Adjustment of timing belt tension
11. Timing belt lower cover
10. Timing belt upper cover
 9. Crankshaft pulley
 8. Crankshaft compressor pulley
 7. Water pump pulley

6. Water pump pulley (Power steering)
5. Tension pulley bracket
4. Drive belt (Alternator)
3. Drive belt (Power steering)
2. Drive belt (Air conditioner)
1. Engine mount bracket

Fig. 154 Timing belt cover and timing belt — 1990 1.5L engine

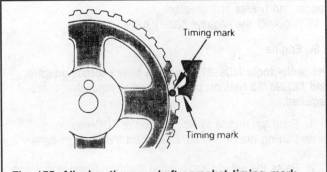

Fig. 155 Aligning the camshaft sprocket timing mark — 1990 1.5L engine

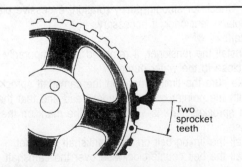

Fig. 156 Rotate the crankshaft until the timing mark on the camshaft advances by 2 teeth — 1990 1.5L engine

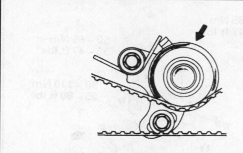

Fig. 157 Push the timing tensioner in the direction of the belt — 1990 1.5L engine

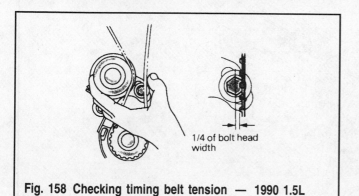

1/4 of bolt head width

Fig. 158 Checking timing belt tension — 1990 1.5L engine

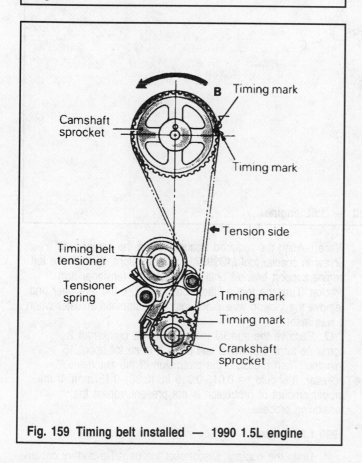

Camshaft sprocket

B — Timing mark

Timing mark

Tension side

Timing belt tensioner

Tensioner spring

Timing mark

Timing mark

Crankshaft sprocket

Fig. 159 Timing belt installed — 1990 1.5L engine

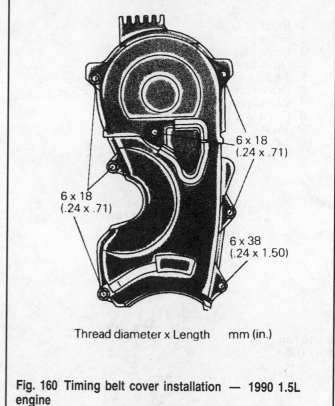

6 x 18 (.24 x .71)

6 x 18 (.24 x .71)

6 x 38 (.24 x 1.50)

Thread diameter x Length   mm (in.)

Fig. 160 Timing belt cover installation — 1990 1.5L engine

5. Remove the water pump pulley and the crankshaft pulley.

6. Remove the upper and lower timing belt covers.

7. Remove the engine center cover. Remove the breather hose from the rear of the rocker cover. Remove the PCV hose. Disconnect the spark plug cables from the plugs.

8. Remove the rocker cover and rear half-moon seal.

9. Confirm the engine is still at No. 1 TDC. The timing marks on the camshaft sprocket and the upper surface of the cylinder head should coincide. The dowel pin on the front of the camshafts should be in the 12 o'clock position. Remove the automatic belt tensioner. Loosen the tensioner pulley center bolt.

10. If the timing belt is to be reused, mark an arrow, on the belt, in the direction of rotation, for installation reference. Remove the timing belt.

To install:

11. Install the automatic tensioner, after reset.

➡**To reset the tensioner: Keep the adjuster level and clamp it in a soft jawed vise. Clamp with the extended adjuster on one side and the end mounting a plug on the other side. If the plug extends out of the adjuster body, place a suitable hole sized washer over the plug so the vise jaw pushes on the washer, not the plug. Close the vise slowly, forcing the adjuster back into the body. When the hole in the adjuster boss aligns with the adjuster rod, insert a snug fitting pin or wire into the holes to keep the rod in the compressed position. With the locking pin or wire in place, install the tensioner.**

12. Align the timing marks on the camshaft sprockets. Align the crankshaft timing marks. Align the oil pump timing marks.

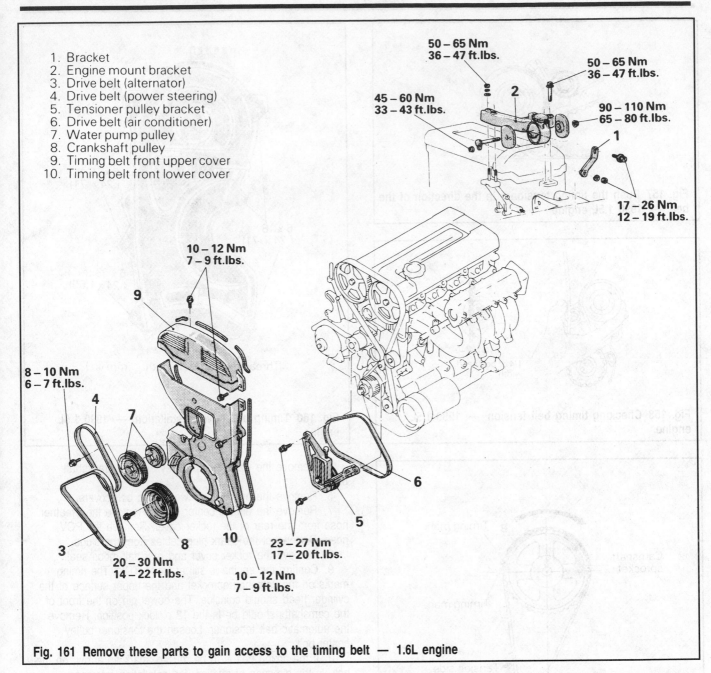

1. Bracket
2. Engine mount bracket
3. Drive belt (alternator)
4. Drive belt (power steering)
5. Tensioner pulley bracket
6. Drive belt (air conditioner)
7. Water pump pulley
8. Crankshaft pulley
9. Timing belt front upper cover
10. Timing belt front lower cover

50 – 65 Nm
36 – 47 ft.lbs.

50 – 65 Nm
36 – 47 ft.lbs.

45 – 60 Nm
33 – 43 ft.lbs.

90 – 110 Nm
65 – 80 ft.lbs.

17 – 26 Nm
12 – 19 ft.lbs.

10 – 12 Nm
7 – 9 ft.lbs.

8 – 10 Nm
6 – 7 ft.lbs.

20 – 30 Nm
14 – 22 ft.lbs.

23 – 27 Nm
17 – 20 ft.lbs.

10 – 12 Nm
7 – 9 ft.lbs.

Fig. 161 Remove these parts to gain access to the timing belt — 1.6L engine

Place the timing belt around the intake camshaft and secure it to the sprocket with a stationary binder spring clip. Install the timing belt around the exhaust camshaft sprocket, check sprocket marks for alignment and secure the belt with a second binder clip on the exhaust sprocket.

13. Install the timing belt around the idler pulley, oil pump sprocket, crankshaft sprocket and the tensioner pulley.

14. Lift up the tensioner pulley against the belt and tighten the center bolt to hold it in position.

15. Check to see that all of the timing marks are aligned. Remove the binder clips. Rotate the crankshaft a quarter turn counter clockwise. Then turn the crankshaft clockwise until the timing marks are aligned.

16. Place special tool MD998752 or equivalent, on a torque wrench. Insert the tool into the place provided on the tension pulley. Loosen the center pulley bolt and apply 2.2 ft. lbs. (3.0 Nm) of pressure against the timing belt with the tension pulley.

While holding the required torque, tighten the center bolt. Screw in special tool MD998738 or equivalent, through the left engine support bracket until it contacts the tensioner arm bracket. Turn the tool a little more to secure the tensioner and remove the locking wire place into the automatic adjuster when it was reset.

17. Remove the special tool. Rotate the crankshaft 2 complete turns clockwise and allow it to sit for about 15 minutes. Then measure the protrusion of the automatic adjuster. It should be 0.015-0.018 in. (0.381-0.457mm). If the proper amount of protrusion is not present, repeat the tensioning process.

1990 1.8L Engine

1. Drain the coolant. Disconnect the negative battery cable.
2. Remove the alternator and accessory belts. Remove the belt cover.

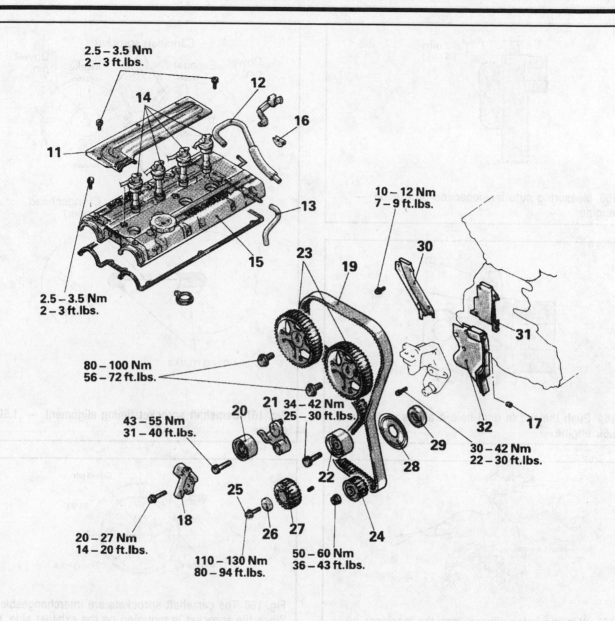

2.5 – 3.5 Nm
2 – 3 ft.lbs.

14

11

12

16

13

15

2.5 – 3.5 Nm
2 – 3 ft.lbs.

10 – 12 Nm
7 – 9 ft.lbs.

30

23

19

31

80 – 100 Nm
56 – 72 ft.lbs.

34 – 42 Nm
25 – 30 ft.lbs.

21

32

17

43 – 55 Nm
31 – 40 ft.lbs.

20

29

28

22

30 – 42 Nm
22 – 30 ft.lbs.

24

18

25

26

27

20 – 27 Nm
14 – 20 ft.lbs.

110 – 130 Nm
80 – 94 ft.lbs.

50 – 60 Nm
36 – 43 ft.lbs.

32. Timing belt rear left cover (lower)
31. Timing belt rear left cover (upper)
30. Timing belt rear right cover
29. Spacer
28. Flange
27. Crankshaft sprocket
26. Special washer
25. Crankshaft sprocket bolt
24. Oil pump sprocket
23. Camshaft sprocket
22. Idler pulley
18. Auto tensioner
21. Tensioner arm
20. Tensioner pulley
19. Timing belt
    Adjustment of timing belt tension
17. Plug rubber
16. Semi-circular packing

15. Rocker cover
14. Connection for spark plug cables
13. PCV hose
12. Breather hose
11. Center cover
10. Timing belt front lower cover
 9. Timing belt front upper cover
 8. Crankshaft pulley
 7. Water pump pulley
 6. Drive belt (air conditioner)
 5. Tensioner pulley bracket
 4. Drive belt (power steering)
 3. Drive belt (alternator)
 2. Engine mount bracket
 1. Bracket

Fig. 162 Timing belt and related parts — 1.6L engine

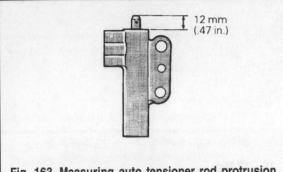

Fig. 163 Measuring auto tensioner rod protrusion — 1.6L engine

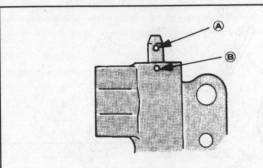

Fig. 164 Push the rod in until hole A aligns with hole B — 1.6L engine

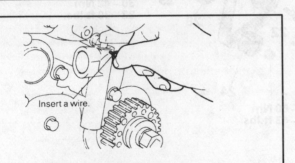

Fig. 165 With the holes aligned, lock the tensioner by inserting a 1.4mm dia. wire through the holes — 1.6L engine

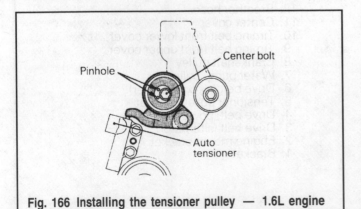

Fig. 166 Installing the tensioner pulley — 1.6L engine

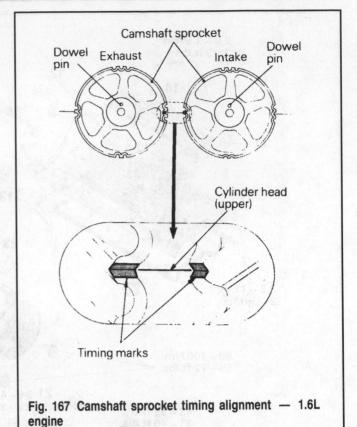

Fig. 167 Camshaft sprocket timing alignment — 1.6L engine

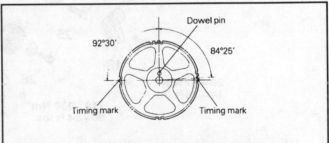

Fig. 168 The camshaft sprockets are interchangeable. When the sprocket is mounted on the exhaust side, use the timing mark on the right and vice-versa — 1.6L engine

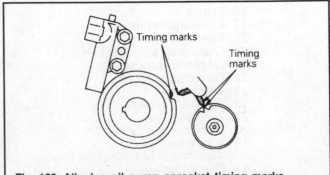

Fig. 169 Aligning oil pump sprocket timing marks — 1.6L engine

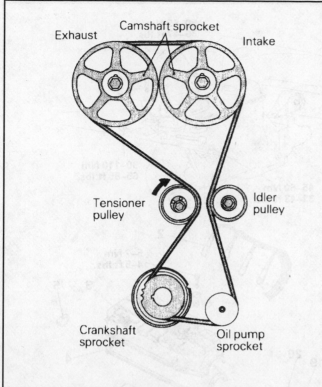

Fig. 170 Timing belt installed — 1.6L engine — 1.6L engine

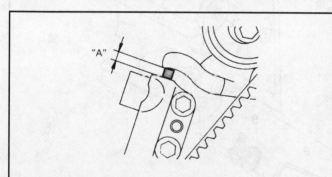

Fig. 171 After 2 complete revolutions, auto tensioner rod protrusion (A) should be 3.8-4.5mm — 1.6L engine

3. Rotate the crankshaft to bring No. 1 piston to TDC on the compression stroke. Align the notch on the crankshaft pulley with the T mark on the timing indicator scale and the timing mark on the upper under cover of the timing belt with the mark on the camshaft sprocket. Mark and remove the distributor.

4. Remove the crankshaft pulley and bolt.

5. Remove the lower splash shield, if necessary.

6. Remove the timing belt covers, upper front and lower front.

7. Remove the crankshaft sprocket bolt.

8. Loosen the tensioner mounting nut and bolt. Move the tensioner away from the belt and retighten the nut to keep the tensioner in the off position. Remove the belt.

9. Remove the camshaft sprocket, crankshaft sprocket, flange and tensioner.

10. The water pump or cylinder head may be removed at this point, depending upon the type of repairs needed.

11. Raise the vehicle and support it safely. Remove any interfering splash pans.

12. Drain the oil pan and remove the pan from the block.

13. Remove the oil pump sprocket and cover.

14. Remove the front cover and oil pump as a unit.

To install:

15. Install a new front seal in the cover. Install a new gasket on the front of the cylinder block and install the front cover.

16. Tighten the front cover bolts to 11-13 ft. lbs. (15-18 Nm). Install the oil screen and oil pan. Tighten the bolts to 5 ft. lbs. (7 Nm).

17. If the cylinder head and/or water pump had been removed, reinstall them, using new gaskets.

18. Install the upper and lower under covers.

19. Install the spacer, flange and crankshaft sprocket and tighten the bolt to 43.5-50 ft. lbs. (58-68 Nm).

20. Align the timing mark on the crankshaft sprocket with the timing mark on the front case.

21. Align the camshaft sprocket timing mark with the upper undercover timing mark.

22. Install the tensioner spring and tensioner. Temporarily tighten the nut. Install the front end of the tensioner spring (bent at right angles) on the projection of the tensioner and the other end (straight) on the water pump body.

23. Loosen the nut and move the tensioner in the direction of the water pump. Lock it by tightening the nut.

24. Ensure that the sprocket timing marks are aligned and install the timing belt. The belt should be installed on the crankshaft sprocket, the oil pump sprocket and then the camshaft sprocket, in that order, while keeping the belt tight.

25. Loosen the tensioner mounting bolt and nut and allow the spring tension to move the tensioner against the belt.

➡**Make sure the belt comes in complete mesh with the sprocket by lightly pushing the tensioner up by hand toward the mounting nut.**

26. Tighten the tensioner mounting nut and bolt.

➡**Be sure to tighten the nut before tightening the bolt. Too much tension could result from tightening the bolt first.**

27. Recheck all sprocket alignments.

28. Turn the crankshaft through a complete rotation in the normal direction. Do not turn in a reverse direction or shake or push the belt.

29. Loosen the tensioner bolt and nut. Retighten the nut and then the bolt.

30. Install the lower and upper front outer covers.

31. Install the crankshaft pulley and tighten the bolts to 7.5-8.5 ft. lbs. (10-11 Nm).

32. Install the alternator and belt and adjust. Install the distributor.

33. Install the radiator, fill the cooling system and inspect for leaks.

1992-93 1.8L Engine

1. Disconnect the negative battery cable. Remove the engine under cover.

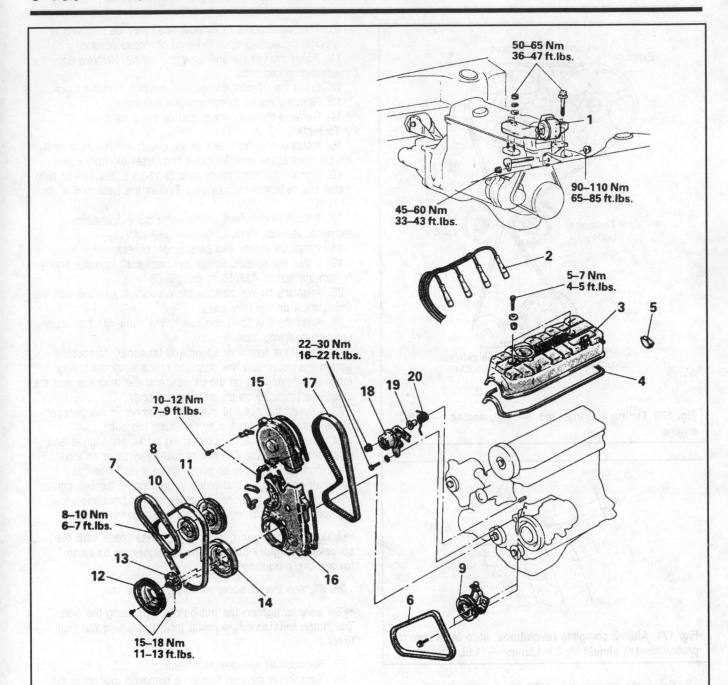

50–65 Nm
36–47 ft.lbs.

90–110 Nm
65–85 ft.lbs.

45–60 Nm
33–43 ft.lbs.

5–7 Nm
4–5 ft.lbs.

22–30 Nm
16–22 ft.lbs.

10–12 Nm
7–9 ft.lbs.

8–10 Nm
6–7 ft.lbs.

15–18 Nm
11–13 ft.lbs.

1. Left mount bracket
2. Spark plug cable
3. Rocker cover
4. Rocker cover gasket
5. Semi-circular packing
6. Drive belt (Air conditioner)
7. Drive belt (Power steering)
8. Drive belt (Alternator)
9. Tensioner pulley bracket
10. Water pump pulley
11. Water pump pulley
12. Damper pulley
13. Adapter
14. Crankshaft pulley
    Adjustment of the valve clearance
15. Timing belt front upper cover
16. Timing belt front lower cover
    Adjustment of timing belt
17. Timing belt
18. Timing belt tensioner
19. Tensioner spacer
20. Tensioner spring

Fig. 172 Timing belt cover, belt and related components — 1990 1.8L engine

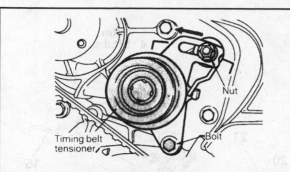

Fig. 173 Releasing timing belt tension — 1990 1.8L engine

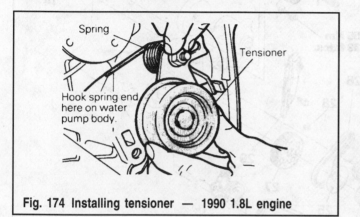

Fig. 174 Installing tensioner — 1990 1.8L engine

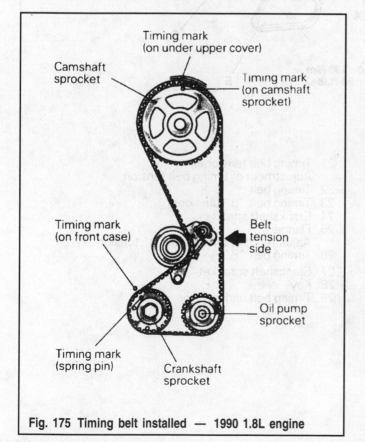

Fig. 175 Timing belt installed — 1990 1.8L engine

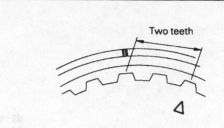

Fig. 176 Rotate the crankshaft clockwise until the timing mark on the camshaft sprocket is 2 teeth past the timing mark on the cover — 1990 1.8L engine

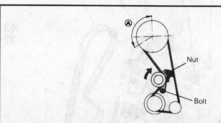

Fig. 177 To properly tension the belt, apply force to the tensioner, in the direction of the arrow, so that the belt meshes completely with the camshaft sprocket, without floating over portion A. Tighten first the nut, then the bolt — 1990 1.8L engine

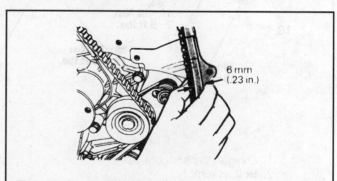

Fig. 178 Check the belt-to-cover clearance — 1990 1.8L engine

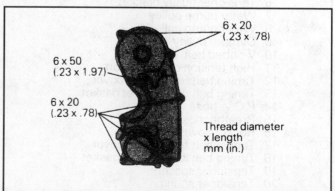

Fig. 179 Timing cover installation — 1990 1.8L engine

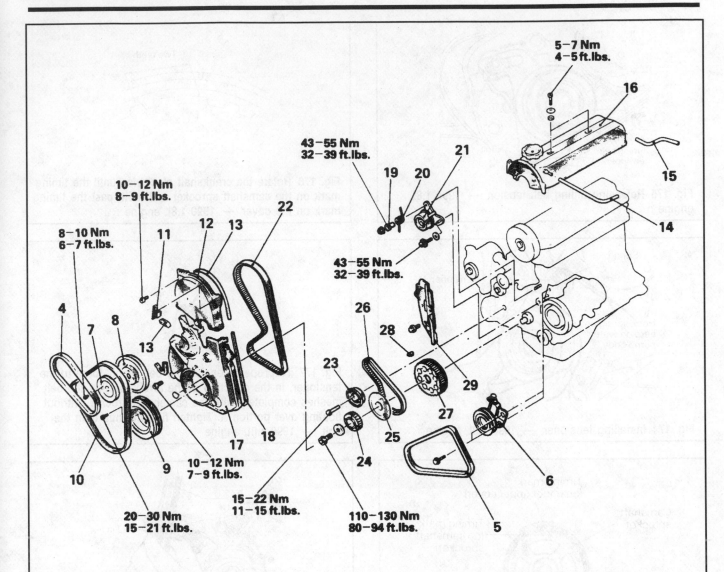

1. Oxygen sensor connector
2. Bolt assembly
3. Engine mounting bracket
4. V-belt (Power steering)
5. V-belt (Air conditioning)
6. Tensioner pulley bracket
7. Water pump pulley
8. Water pump pulley
9. Damper pulley
10. V-ribbed belt
11. High tension cable support
12. Timing belt front upper cover
13. Timing belt upper cover gasket
14. P.C.V. hose
15. Breather hose
16. Rocker cover
17. Timing belt front lower cover
18. Timing belt lower cover gasket
19. Tensioner spacer
20. Tensioner spring

21. Timing belt tensioner
    Adjustment of timing belt tension
22. Timing belt
23. Timing belt "B" tensioner
24. Crankshaft sprocket
25. Flange
    Adjustment of timing belt "B" tension
26. Timing belt "B"
27. Crankshaft sprocket "B"
28. Key
29. Timing belt under cover

Fig. 180 Timing belts and related parts — 2.0L engine

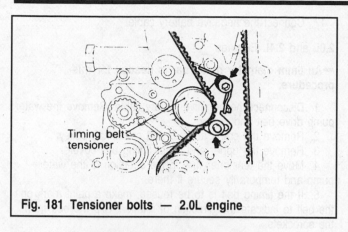

Fig. 181 Tensioner bolts — 2.0L engine

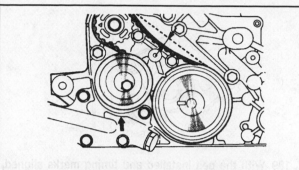

Fig. 185 After adjustment, check the timing belt deflection. Deflection should be 5-7mm — 2.0L engine

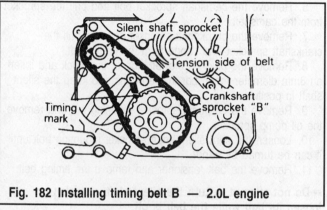

Fig. 182 Installing timing belt B — 2.0L engine

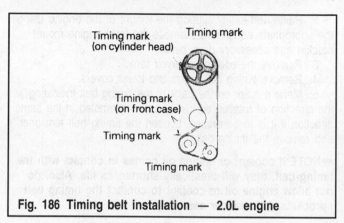

Fig. 186 Timing belt installation — 2.0L engine

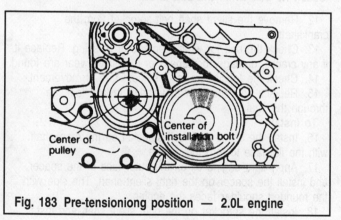

Fig. 183 Pre-tensioniong position — 2.0L engine

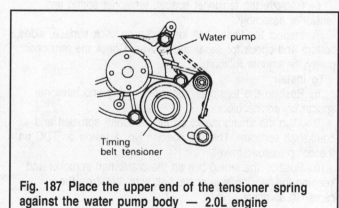

Fig. 187 Place the upper end of the tensioner spring against the water pump body — 2.0L engine

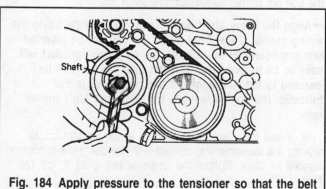

Fig. 184 Apply pressure to the tensioner so that the belt is taut — 2.0L engine

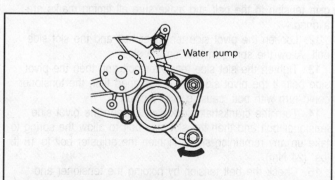

Fig. 188 Position the tensioner away from the belt prior to belt installation — 2.0L engine

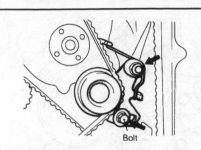

Fig. 189 With the belt installed and timing marks aligned, release the tensioner and let it rest on the belt — 2.0L engine

2. Raise and safely support the weight of the engine using the appropriate equipment. Remove the front engine mount bracket and accessory drive belts.

3. Remove the coolant reservoir tank.

4. Remove timing belt upper and lower covers.

5. Make a mark on the back of the timing belt indicating the direction of rotation so it may be reassembled in the same direction if it is to be reused. Loosen the timing belt tensioner and remove the timing belt.

➡NOTE:If coolant or engine oil comes in contact with the timing belt, they will drastically shorten its life. Also, do not allow engine oil or coolant to contact the timing belt sprockets or tensioner assembly.

6. Remove the tensioner spacer, tensioner spring and tensioner assembly.

7. Inspect the timing belt for cracks on back surface, sides, bottom and check for separated canvas. Check the tensioner pulley for smooth rotation.

To install:

8. Position the tensioner, tensioner spring and tensioner spacer on engine block.

9. Align the timing marks on the camshaft sprocket and crankshaft sprocket. This will position No. 1 piston on TDC on the compression stroke.

10. Position the timing belt on the crankshaft sprocket and keeping the tension side of the belt tight, set it on the camshaft sprocket.

11. Apply counterclockwise force to the camshaft sprocket to give tension to the belt and make sure all timing marks are aligned.

12. Loosen the pivot side tensioner bolt and the slot side bolt. Allow the spring to take up the slack.

13. Tighten the slot side tensioner bolt and then the pivot side bolt. If the pivot side bolt is tightened first, the tensioner could turn with bolt, causing over tension.

14. Turn the crankshaft clockwise. Loosen the pivot side tensioner bolt and then the slot side bolt to allow the spring to take up any remaining slack. Tighten the adjuster bolt to 18 ft. lbs. (24 Nm).

15. Check the belt tension by holding the tensioner and timing belt together by hand and give the belt a slight thumb pressure at a point level with tensioner center. Make sure the belt cog crest comes as deep as about ¼ of the width of the slot side tensioner bolt head. Do not manually overtighten the belt or it will howl.

16. Install the timing belt covers and all related items.

17. Connect the negative battery cable.

2.0L and 2.4L Engines

➡An 8mm diameter metal bar is needed for this procedure.

1. Disconnect the negative battery cable. Remove the water pump drive belt and pulley.

2. Remove the crank adapter and crankshaft pulley.

3. Remove the upper and lower timing belt covers.

4. Move the tensioner fully in the direction of the water pump and temporarily secure it there.

5. If the timing belt is to be reused, make a paint mark on the belt to indicate the direction of rotation. Slip the belt from the sprockets.

6. Remove the camshaft sprocket bolt and pull the sprocket from the camshaft.

7. Remove the crankshaft sprocket bolt and pull the crankshaft sprocket and flange from the crankshaft.

8. Remove the plug on the left side of the block and insert an 8mm diameter metal bar in the opening to keep the silent shaft in position.

9. Remove the oil pump sprocket retaining nut and remove the oil pump sprocket.

10. Loosen the right silent shaft sprocket mounting bolt until it can be turned by hand.

11. Remove the belt tensioner and remove the timing belt.

➡Do not attempt to turn the silent shaft sprocket or loosen its bolt while the belt is off.

12. Remove the silent shaft belt sprocket from the crankshaft.

13. Check the belt for wear, damage or glossing. Replace it if any cracks, damage, brittleness or excessive wear are found.

14. Check the tensioners for a smooth rate of movement.

15. Replace any tensioner that shows grease leakage through the seal.

To install:

16. Install the silent shaft belt sprocket on the crankshaft, with the flat face toward the engine.

17. Apply light engine oil on the outer face of the spacer and install the spacer on the right silent shaft. The side with the rounded shoulder faces the engine.

18. Install the sprocket on the right silent shaft and install the bolt but do not tighten completely at this time.

➡Align the silent shaft and oil pump sprockets using the timing marks. If the 8mm metal bar can not be inserted into the hole 2.36 in. (60mm), the oil pump sprocket will have to be turned 1 full rotation until the bar can be inserted to the full length. If this procedure is not followed, the engine will run but vibrate at high engine rpm.

19. Install the silent shaft belt and adjust the tension, by moving the tensioner into contact with the belt, tight enough to remove all slack. Tighten the tensioner bolt to 21 ft. lbs. (28 Nm).

20. Tighten the silent shaft sprocket bolt to 28 ft. lbs. (38 Nm).

21. Install the flange and crankshaft sprocket on the crankshaft. The flange conforms to the front of the silent shaft

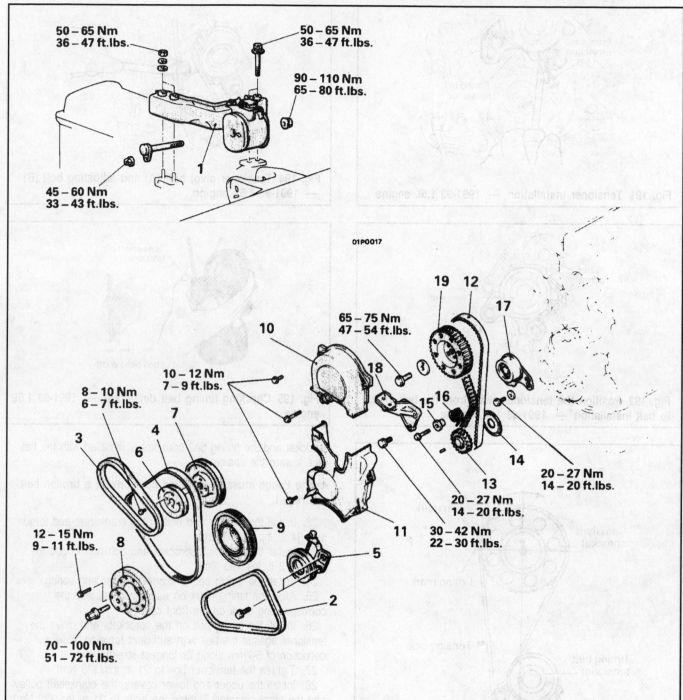

50 – 65 Nm
36 – 47 ft.lbs.

50 – 65 Nm
36 – 47 ft.lbs.

90 – 110 Nm
65 – 80 ft.lbs.

45 – 60 Nm
33 – 43 ft.lbs.

01P0017

65 – 75 Nm
47 – 54 ft.lbs.

10 – 12 Nm
7 – 9 ft.lbs.

8 – 10 Nm
6 – 7 ft.lbs.

20 – 27 Nm
14 – 20 ft.lbs.

12 – 15 Nm
9 – 11 ft.lbs.

20 – 27 Nm
14 – 20 ft.lbs.

30 – 42 Nm
22 – 30 ft.lbs.

70 – 100 Nm
51 – 72 ft.lbs.

1. Engine mount bracket
2. Drive belt (Air conditioner)
3. Drive belt (Power steering)
4. Drive belt (Alternator)
5. Tension pulley bracket
6. Water pump pulley (Power steering)
7. Water pump pulley
8. Crankshaft compressor pulley
9. Crankshaft pulley
10. Timing belt upper cover
11. Timing belt lower cover
12. Timing belt
13. Crankshaft sprocket
14. Flange
15. Tensioner spacer
16. Tensioner spring
17. Tensioner
18. Left engine support bracket
19. Camshaft sprocket

Fig. 190 Timing belt and related parts — 1991-93 1.5L engine

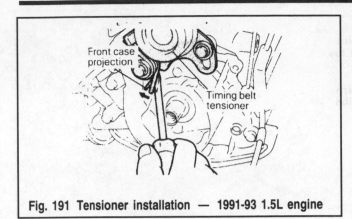

Fig. 191 Tensioner installation — 1991-93 1.5L engine

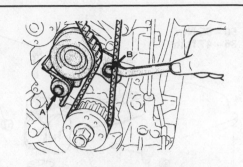

Fig. 194 Tensioner pivot bolt (A) and adjusting bolt (B) — 1991-93 1.5L engine

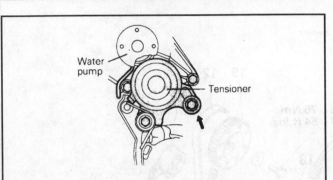

Fig. 192 Position the tensioner away from the belt, prior to belt installation — 1991-93 1.5L engine

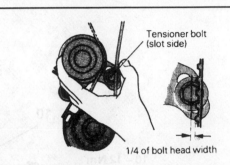

Fig. 195 Checking timing belt deflection — 1991-93 1.5L engine

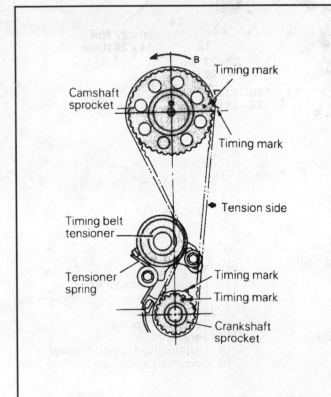

Fig. 193 Timing belt installation — 1991-93 1.5L engine

sprocket and the timing belt sprocket is installed with the flat face toward the engine.

➡The flange must be installed correctly or a broken belt will result.

22. Install the washer and bolt in the crankshaft and torque it to 94 ft. lbs. (127 Nm).

23. Install the camshaft sprocket and bolt and torque the bolt to 72 ft. lbs. (98 Nm).

24. Install the timing belt tensioner, spacer and spring.

25. Align the timing mark on each sprocket with the corresponding mark on the front case.

26. Install the timing belt on the sprockets and move the tensioner against the belt with sufficient force to allow a deflection of 5-7mm along its longest straight run.

27. Tighten the tensioner bolt to 21 ft. lbs. (28 Nm).

28. Install the upper and lower covers, the crankshaft pulley and the crank adapter. Tighten the bolts to 21 ft. lbs. (28 Nm).

29. Remove the 8mm bar and install the plug. Connect the negative battery cable.

SILENT SHAFT BELT REPLACEMENT

2.0L and 2.4L Engines

➡When replacing the timing belt, the manufacturer recommends to replace the silent shaft belt.

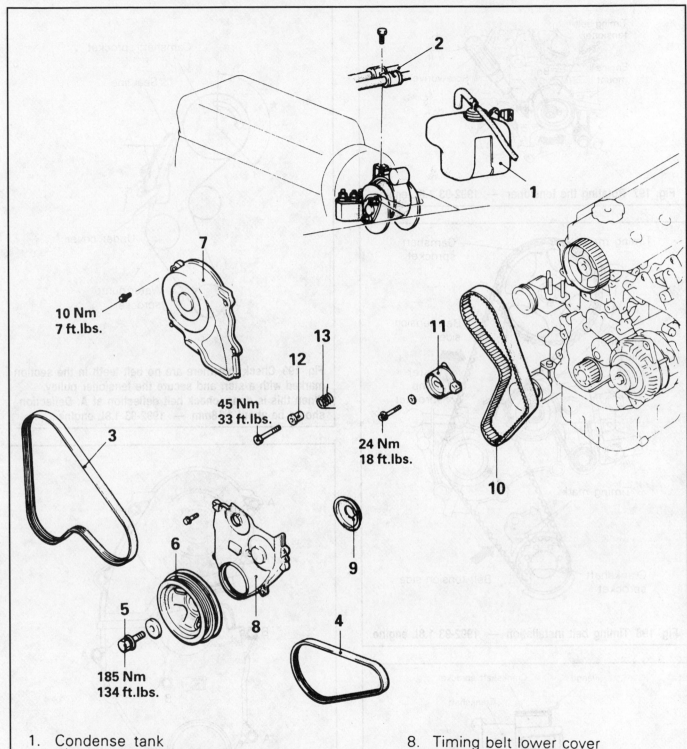

**10 Nm
7 ft.lbs.**

**45 Nm
33 ft.lbs.**

**24 Nm
18 ft.lbs.**

**185 Nm
134 ft.lbs.**

1. Condense tank
2. Clamp section of Air conditioner and Power steering hose
3. Drive belt (Power steering, Air conditioner)
4. Drive belt (Alternator)
5. Crankshaft bolt
6. Crankshaft pulley
7. Timing belt upper cover
8. Timing belt lower cover
9. Flange
•. Adjustment of timing belt tension
10. Timing belt
11. Timing belt tensioner
12. Tensioner spacer
13. Tensioner spring

Fig. 196 Timing belt and related parts — 1992-93 1.8L engine

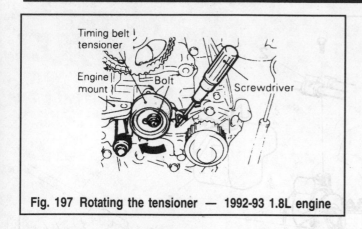

Fig. 197 Rotating the tensioner — 1992-93 1.8L engine

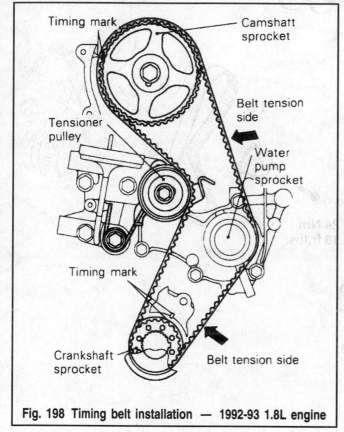

Fig. 198 Timing belt installation — 1992-93 1.8L engine

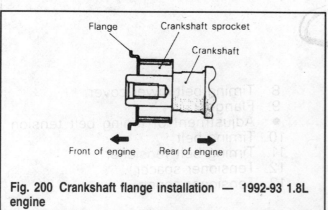

Fig. 200 Crankshaft flange installation — 1992-93 1.8L engine

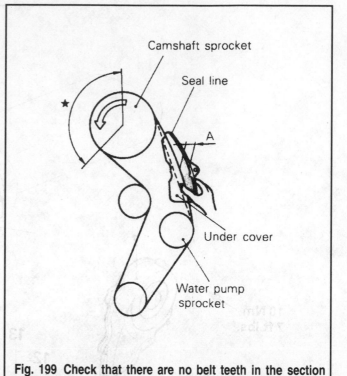

Fig. 199 Check that there are no belt teeth in the section marked with a star, and secure the tensioner pulley. When this is done, check belt deflection at A. Deflection should be about 1.18mm — 1992-93 1.8L engine

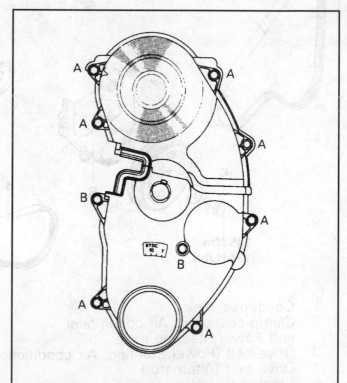

Fig. 201 Cover installation; bolts marked A are 6mm x 18mm and bolts marked B are 6mm x 30mm — 1992-93 1.8L engine

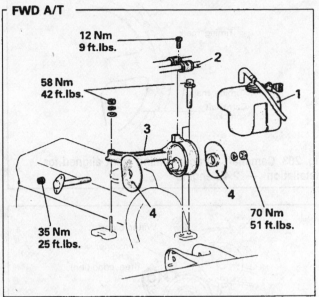

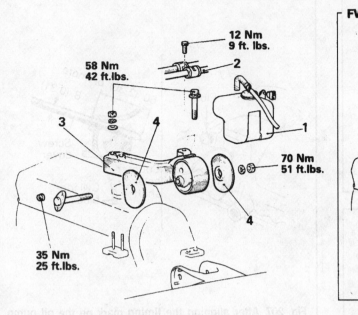

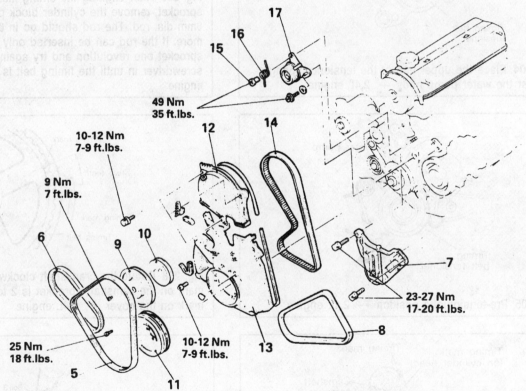

1. Condense tank
2. Power steering hose and air conditioner hose clamp part
3. Engine mount bracket
4. Engine mount stopper
5. Drive belt (Alternator)
6. Drive belt (Power steering oil pump)
7. Tension pulley bracket
8. Drive belt (Air conditioner compressor)
9. Water pump pulley
10. Water pump pulley for power steering
11. Crankshaft pulley
12. Timing belt front upper cover
13. Timing belt front lower cover
● Adjustment of timing belt tension
14. Timing belt
15. Tension spacer
16. Tension spring
17. Timing belt tensioner

Fig. 202 Timing belts and related parts — 2.4L engine

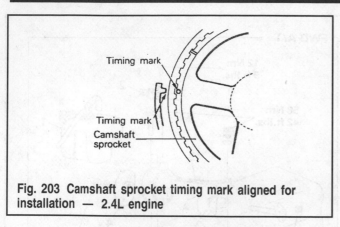

Fig. 203 Camshaft sprocket timing mark aligned for installation — 2.4L engine

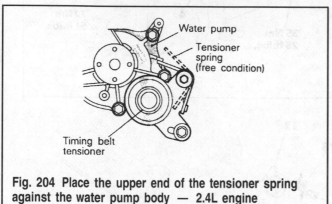

Fig. 204 Place the upper end of the tensioner spring against the water pump body — 2.4L engine

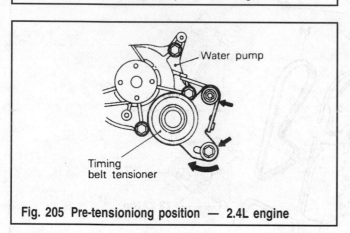

Fig. 205 Pre-tensioniong position — 2.4L engine

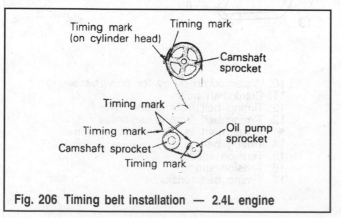

Fig. 206 Timing belt installation — 2.4L engine

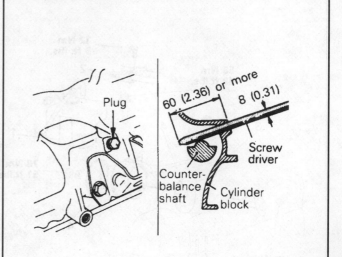

Fig. 207 After aligning the timing mark on the oil pump sprocket, remove the cylinder block plug and install an 8mm dia. rod. The rod should go in 60mm deep, or more. If the rod can be inserted only 20-25mm, turn the sprocket one revolution and try again. Leave the screwdriver in until the timing belt is installed — 2.4L engine

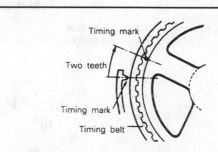

Fig. 208 Rotate the crankshaft clockwise until the timing mark on the camshaft sprocket is 2 teeth past the timing mark on the cover — 2.4L engine

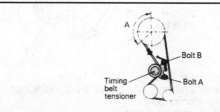

Fig. 209 To properly tension the belt, apply force to the tensioner, in the direction of the arrow, so that the belt meshes completely with the camshaft sprocket, without floating over portion A. Tighten first bolt A, then bolt B — 2.4L engine

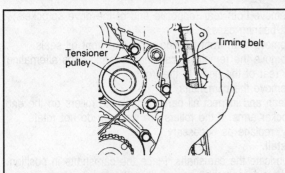

Fig. 210 After adjustment, check the timing belt deflection. Deflection should be 14mm — 2.4L engine

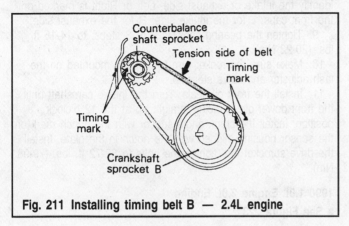

Fig. 211 Installing timing belt B — 2.4L engine

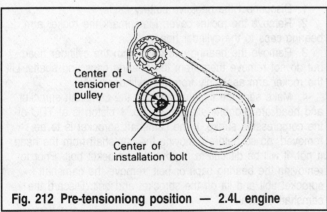

Fig. 212 Pre-tensioniong position — 2.4L engine

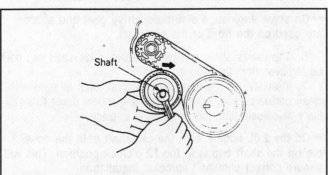

Fig. 213 Apply pressure to the tensioner so that the belt is taut — 2.4L engine

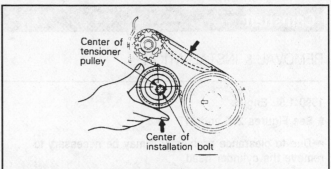

Fig. 214 After adjustment, check the belt deflection. Deflection should be 5-7mm — 2.4L engine

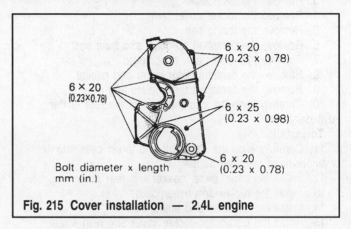

Fig. 215 Cover installation — 2.4L engine

1. After removing the timing belt, mark arrows on the belt to indicate direction of rotation (clockwise).

➡If the silent shaft belt is not installed properly, the engine will run but with a vibration. Align the silent shaft and oil pump sprockets using the timing marks. If the 8mm metal bar can not be inserted into the hole 2.36 inch (60mm), the oil pump sprocket will have to turned 1 full rotation until the bar can be inserted to the full length.

2. Align the timing marks before removal. Loosen the belt tensioner and remove the belt.

To install:

3. Make sure the crankshaft and silent shaft sprocket timing marks are aligned.

4. Fit the belt over the sprockets. Make sure there is no slack in the belt.

5. Temporarily fix the timing belt tensioner so that the center of the tensioner pulley is to the left and above the center of the installation bolt. Temporarily attach the tensioner pulley so that the flange is toward the front of the engine.

6. Adjust the belt so that the slack between the 2 sprockets is within 0.20-0.28 inch (5-7mm).

Camshaft

REMOVAL & INSTALLATION

1990 1.5L Engine

▶ **See Figures 216 and 217**

➡**Due to clearance problems, it may be necessary to remove the cylinder head.**

1. Disconnect the negative battery cable.
2. Tag and remove the spark plug wires.
3. Remove the distributor.
4. Remove the rocker cover.
5. Remove the timing belt.
6. Remove the camshaft sprocket and front seal.
7. Remove the rocker arm assemblies.
8. Remove the camshaft rear cover and gasket.
9. Remove the camshaft thrust plate and case.
10. Carefully slide the camshaft out of the rear of the cylinder head.

To install:

11. Carefully slide the camshaft and thrust case into the cylinder head from the front.
12. Install the thrust plate, gasket and rear cover.
13. Install the rocker arm assemblies.
14. Install the sprocket and timing belt.
15. Install the distributor, rocker cover and plug wires.
16. Connect the negative battery cable. Start the engine and test engine performance and check for leaks.

1991-93 1.5L Engine

➡**Due to clearance problems, it may be necessary to remove the cylinder head.**

1. Disconnect the negative battery cable.
2. Remove the rocker cover.
3. Remove the timing belt.
4. Remove the camshaft sprocket and front seal.
5. Remove the rocker arm assemblies.
6. Carefully slide the camshaft out of the cylinder head.

To install:

7. Carefully install the camshaft in the head with the dowel pin at the 12 o'clock position.
8. Install the rocker arm assemblies.
9. Coat a new seal with oil and install the seal, with the lip facing out.
10. Install the sprocket and timing belt.
11. Install the rocker cover.
12. Connect the negative battery cable. Start the engine and test engine performance and check for leaks.

1.6L Engine

▶ **See Figures 218, 219, 220, 221 and 222**

1. Disconnect the negative battery cable. Remove the cylinder head.
2. Remove the crank angle sensor. Remove both camshaft drive sprockets.

3. Remove both rear (opposite end of the drive sprockets) camshaft bearing caps.
4. Remove both front bearing caps and front oil seals.
5. Remove the remaining camshaft bearing caps alternating from the rear of the head to the front.
6. Remove the camshafts.
7. Clean and inspect all parts. Check the rollers on the end of the rocker arms. If the rollers are warn on do not rotate smoothly, replace as necessary.

To install:

8. Lubricate the camshafts. Place the camshafts in position. The intake side camshaft has a slit in the rear to drive the crank angle sensor. The bearing caps No. 2-5 are the same shape. When installing them, check the top markings to identify the intake or exhaust side. Left or Right is marked on the front caps, L for the intake side; R for the exhaust side.
9. Tighten the bearing caps, in 2 or 3 steps, to 14-15 ft. lbs. (20-22 Nm).
10. Make sure the rocker arm is properly mounted on the lash adjuster and valve stem tip.
11. Install the front oil seals. Turn the intake camshaft until the front dowel pin is facing straight up at the 12 o'clock position. Install the crank angle sensor with the punch mark on the sensor housing aligned with the notch in the plate. Install the drive sprocket and tighten the bolts to 58-72 ft. lbs. (79-98 Nm).

1990 1.8L Engine 2.0L Engine

▶ **See Figure 223**

1. Disconnect the negative battery cable.
2. Remove the rocker cover. Matchmark the rocker arm bearing caps to the cylinder head.
3. Remove the bearing cap bolts from the cylinder head, but do not remove them from the bearing caps and shafts. Lift the rocker arm assembly from the cylinder head.
4. Make sure the timing marks on the camshaft sprocket and head are properly aligned, so No. 1 piston is at TDC of the compression stroke. If the camshaft sprocket is to be removed, do so before removing the camshaft from the head. If not, it will be difficult to remove the sprocket bolt. Prior to removing the bearing caps or belt, remove the camshaft sprocket bolt and lift off the sprocket and belt. Discard the camshaft oil seal.
5. Remove the camshaft from the bearing saddles.

➡**On some engines, a distributor drive gear and spacer are used on the front of the camshaft.**

6. The valves, valve springs and valve guide seals can now be removed from the cylinder head.
7. Installation is the reverse of removal. Coat all parts with clean engine oil prior to installation. Use a seal driver to install the new oil seal after the camshaft is in place.

➡**On the 2.0L engine, turn the camshaft until the dowel pin on the shaft end is in the 12 o'clock position. This will ensure correct camshaft sprocket installation.**

8. Tighten the sprocket bolt to 50-60 ft. lbs. (68-81 Nm). on the 2.0L and 44-55 ft. lbs. (60-75 Nm). on the 1.8L engines. Tighten the rocker cover bolts to 5 ft. lbs. (7 Nm).

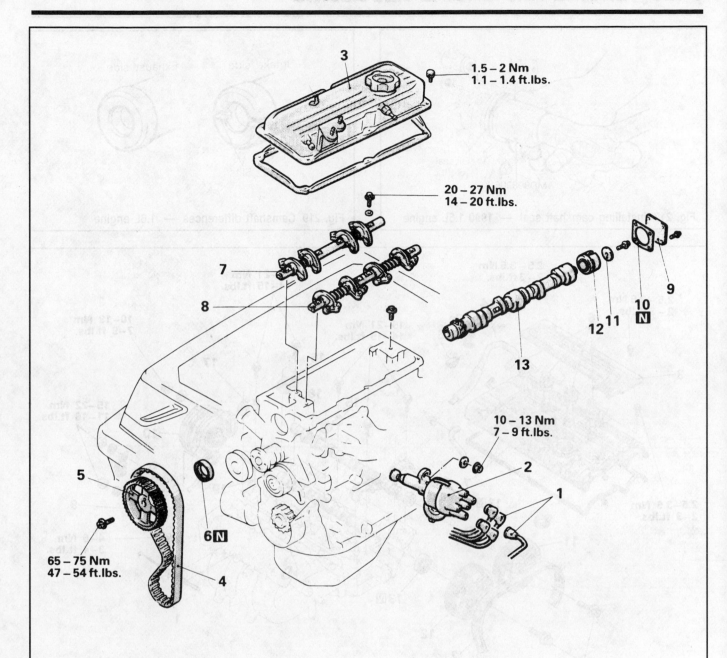

1.5 – 2 Nm
1.1 – 1.4 ft.lbs.

20 – 27 Nm
14 – 20 ft.lbs.

10 – 13 Nm
7 – 9 ft.lbs.

65 – 75 Nm
47 – 54 ft.lbs.

1. Spark plug cable and high tension cable
2. Distributor
3. Rocker cover
4. Timing belt
5. Camshaft sprocket
6. Oil seal
7. Rocker arm assembly
8. Rocker arm assembly
9. Rear cover
10. Rear cover gasket
11. Thrust plate
12. Camshaft thrust case
13. Camshaft

Fig. 216 Camshaft and related parts — 1990 1.5L engine

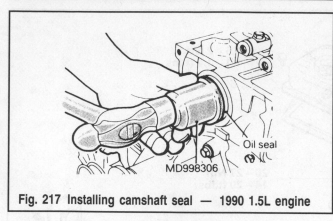

Fig. 217 Installing camshaft seal — 1990 1.5L engine

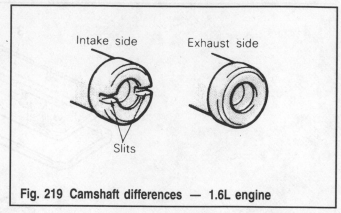

Fig. 219 Camshaft differences — 1.6L engine

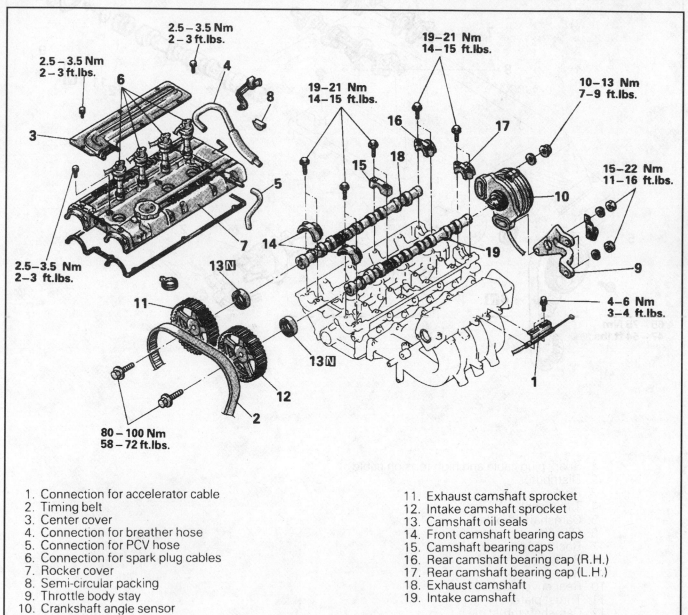

1. Connection for accelerator cable
2. Timing belt
3. Center cover
4. Connection for breather hose
5. Connection for PCV hose
6. Connection for spark plug cables
7. Rocker cover
8. Semi-circular packing
9. Throttle body stay
10. Crankshaft angle sensor
11. Exhaust camshaft sprocket
12. Intake camshaft sprocket
13. Camshaft oil seals
14. Front camshaft bearing caps
15. Camshaft bearing caps
16. Rear camshaft bearing cap (R.H.)
17. Rear camshaft bearing cap (L.H.)
18. Exhaust camshaft
19. Intake camshaft

Fig. 218 Camshaft and related parts — 1.6L engine

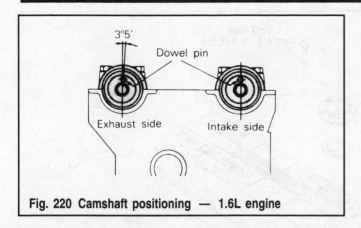

Fig. 220 Camshaft positioning — 1.6L engine

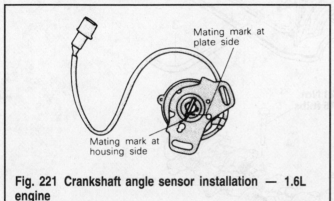

Fig. 221 Crankshaft angle sensor installation — 1.6L engine

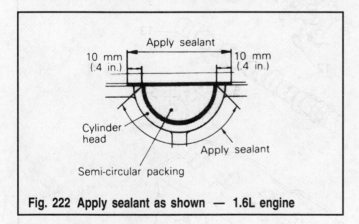

Fig. 222 Apply sealant as shown — 1.6L engine

1992-93 1.8L Engine 2.4L Engine
▶ See Figures 224, 225 and 226

1. Disconnect the negative battery cable.
2. On the 1.8L engine, remove the battery and battery cover. Disconnect the air flow sensor connector and remove the air cleaner case cover.
3. Remove the breather hose. Disconnect the PCV hose.
4. Label and disconnect the spark plug cables.
5. On the 1.8L engine, remove the distributor assembly.
6. Remove the rocker cover and the timing belt.
7. Remove the camshaft sprocket retainer bolt while holding shaft stationary with appropriate spanner wrench. Remove the sprocket from the shaft.
8. Remove the camshaft oil seal.

9. Install lash adjuster retainers on the 2.4L engine. Remove both rocker arm shaft assemblies from the head. Do not disassembly rocker arms and rocker arm shaft assemblies.
10. Remove the camshaft from the cylinder.
11. Inspect the bearing journals on the camshaft, cylinder head, and bearing caps.

To install:
12. Lubricate the camshaft journals and camshaft with clean engine oil and install the camshaft in the cylinder head.
13. Install the rocker arm and shaft assemblies. On the 1.8L engine, tighten the rocker arm shaft retainer bolts to 21-25 ft. lbs. (29-35 Nm). On 2.4L engine, tighten the rocker arm, bearing caps and shaft assembly to 14 ft. lbs. (20 Nm).
14. Remove the lash adjuster retainers. Install new camshaft oil seal.
15. Install camshaft sprocket and retainer bolt torquing to 65 ft. lbs. (90 Nm).
16. Install the timing belt.
17. On the 1.8L engine, install the distributor.
18. On the 1.8L engine, check the valve lash adjustment using specifications for a cold engine. Install the rocker cover.
19. Connect the spark plug cables.
20. Install the breather hose and connect the PCV hose.
21. Connect the air flow sensor connector and install the air cleaner case cover.
22. On the 1.8L engine, install the battery and battery cover.
23. Connect the negative battery cable. Run the engine at idle until normal operating temperature is reached. Check idle speed and ignition timing and adjust as required.

Silent Shafts

REMOVAL & INSTALLATION

2.0L and 2.4L Engines
▶ See Figures 227, 228, 229, 230 and 231

1. Disconnect the negative battery cable. Remove the engine from the vehicle.
2. Remove the drive belts, accessories, crankshaft pulley and timing belts.
3. Drain the engine oil and remove the filter. Remove the oil pump sprocket, right silent shaft sprocket and spacer.
4. Remove the oil pan, screen and filter bracket.
5. Using a special tool MD998162 or equivalent, remove the plug cap from the right silent.
6. Remove the plug from the cylinder block left side and insert a screwdriver or rod with an 8mm dia. shaft (at least 77mm long) into the plug hole. The rod must be inserted at least 60mm. If it can't be, rotate the shaft.
7. Remove the front case, oil pump cover, drive and driven gears.
8. Remove the left and right silent shafts, being careful not to damage the bearings.

To install:
9. Install the left and right silent shafts, being careful not to damage the bearings.
10. Install the front case, oil pump cover, drive and driven gears. Remove the rod.
11. Install the plug to the cylinder block left side silent shaft.

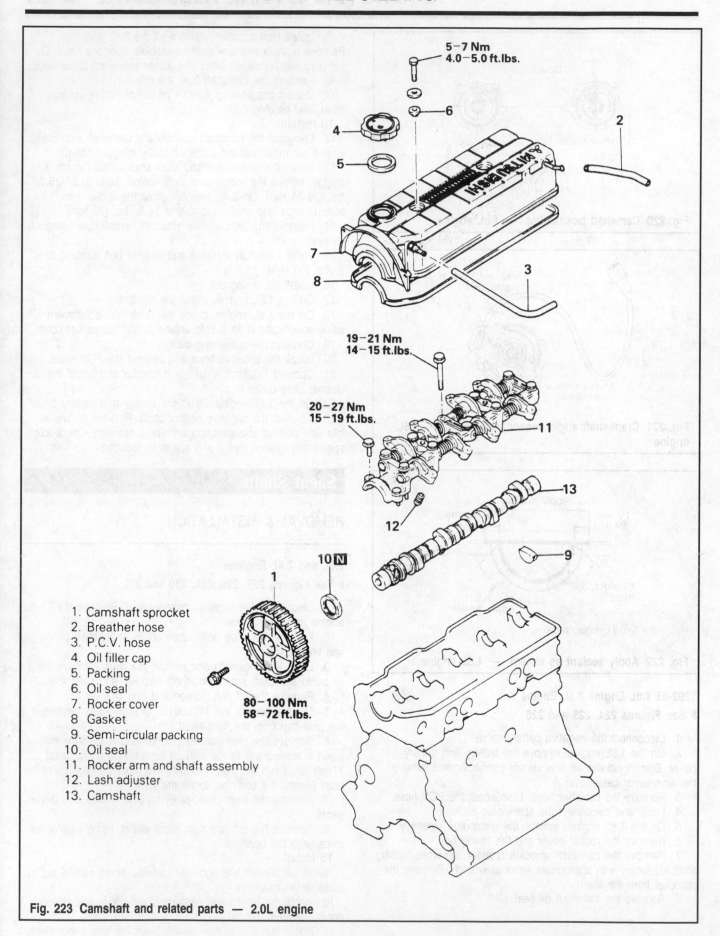

**5−7 Nm
4.0−5.0 ft.lbs.**

**19−21 Nm
14−15 ft.lbs.**

**20−27 Nm
15−19 ft.lbs.**

10 **N**

**80−100 Nm
58−72 ft.lbs.**

1. Camshaft sprocket
2. Breather hose
3. P.C.V. hose
4. Oil filler cap
5. Packing
6. Oil seal
7. Rocker cover
8 Gasket
9. Semi-circular packing
10. Oil seal
11. Rocker arm and shaft assembly
12. Lash adjuster
13. Camshaft

Fig. 223 Camshaft and related parts — 2.0L engine

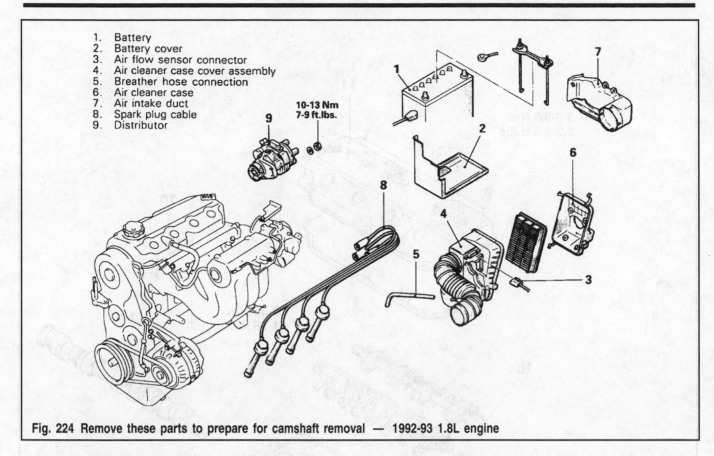

1. Battery
2. Battery cover
3. Air flow sensor connector
4. Air cleaner case cover assembly
5. Breather hose connection
6. Air cleaner case
7. Air intake duct
8. Spark plug cable
9. Distributor

10-13 Nm
7-9 ft.lbs.

Fig. 224 Remove these parts to prepare for camshaft removal — 1992-93 1.8L engine

12. Using a special tool MD998162 or equivalent, install the plug cap to the right silent.

13. Install the screen, filter bracket and oil pan.

14. Refill the engine oil and install the filter. Install the oil pump sprocket, right silent shaft sprocket and spacer.

15. Install the drive belts, accessories, crankshaft pulley and timing belts.

16. Install the engine into the vehicle. Connect the negative battery cable.

Pistons and Connecting Rods

REMOVAL & INSTALLATION

▶ See Figures 232, 233, 234, 235, 236, 237, 238, 239, 240, 241, 242, 243, 244, 245, 246 and 247

➡**Although, in most cases, the pistons and connecting rods can be removed from the engine (after the cylinder head and oil pan are removed) while the engine is still in the car: it is far easier to work on the engine when removed from the car.**

If removing pistons with the engine still installed, disconnect the radiator hoses, automatic transmission cooler lines and radiator shroud. Unbolt front mounts before jacking up the engine and block the engine in position with wooden blocks between the mounts.

1. Remove the engine from the car. Remove cylinder head, oil pan and front cover.

2. Because the top piston ring does not travel to the very top of the cylinder bore, a ridge is built up between the end of the travel and the top of the cylinder. Pushing the piston and connecting rod assembly past the ridge is difficult and may cause damage to the piston. If new rings are installed the ridge has not been removed, ring breakage and piston damage can occur when the ridge is encountered at engine speed.

3. Turn the crankshaft to position the piston at the bottom of the cylinder bore. Cover the top of the piston with a rag. Install a ridge reamer in the bore and follow the manufacture's instructions to remove the ridge. Use caution, avoid cutting too deeply. Remove the rag and cutting from the top of the piston. Remove the ridge from all cylinders.

4. Check the edges of the connecting rod and bearing cap for numbers or matchmarks, if none are present mark the rod and cap numerically and in sequence from front to back of engine. The numbers or marks not only tell from which cylinder the piston came from but also helps ensure that the rod caps are installed in the correct matching position.

5. Turn the crankshaft until the connecting rod is at the bottom of travel. Remove the two attaching nuts and the bearing cap. Take two pieces of rubber tubing and cover the rod bolts to prevent crank or cylinder scoring. Use a wooden hammer handle to help push the piston and rod up and out of the cylinder. Reinstall the rod cap in proper position. Remove all pistons and connecting rods. Inspect cylinder walls and deglaze or hone as necessary.

6. Lubricate each piston, rod bearing and cylinder wall. Install a ring compressor over the piston, position the piston with mark toward front of engine and carefully install it into engine. Tap the piston into the bore with a wooden hammer handle or rubber hammer. Position connecting rod with bearing

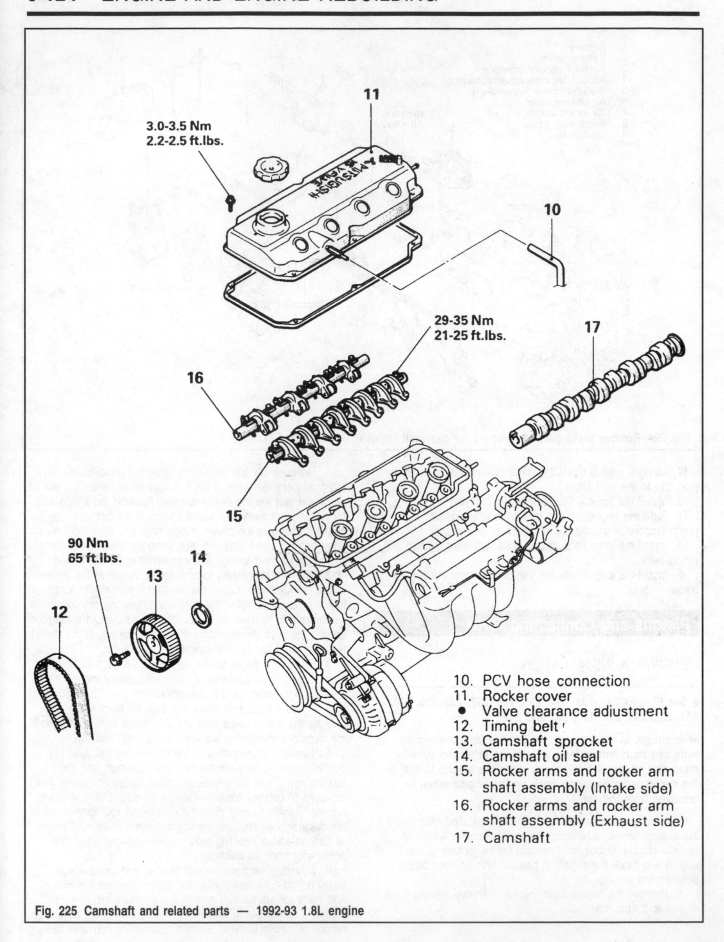

3.0-3.5 Nm
2.2-2.5 ft.lbs.

11

10

29-35 Nm
21-25 ft.lbs.

16

17

15

90 Nm
65 ft.lbs.

13

14

12

10. PCV hose connection
11. Rocker cover
● Valve clearance adjustment
12. Timing belt
13. Camshaft sprocket
14. Camshaft oil seal
15. Rocker arms and rocker arm
shaft assembly (Intake side)
16. Rocker arms and rocker arm
shaft assembly (Exhaust side)
17. Camshaft

Fig. 225 Camshaft and related parts — 1992-93 1.8L engine

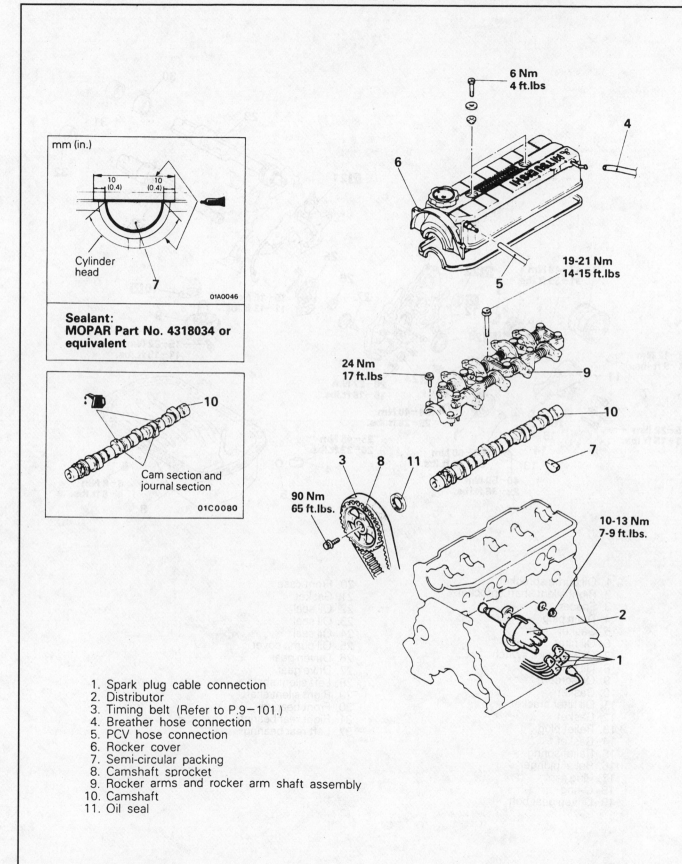

mm (in.)

Cylinder head

7

01A0046

**Sealant:
MOPAR Part No. 4318034 or
equivalent**

10

Cam section and
journal section

01C0080

6 Nm
4 ft.lbs

4

6

19-21 Nm
14-15 ft.lbs

5

24 Nm
17 ft.lbs

9

10

7

3   8   11

90 Nm
65 ft.lbs.

10-13 Nm
7-9 ft.lbs.

2

1

1. Spark plug cable connection
2. Distributor
3. Timing belt (Refer to P.9—101.)
4. Breather hose connection
5. PCV hose connection
6. Rocker cover
7. Semi-circular packing
8. Camshaft sprocket
9. Rocker arms and rocker arm shaft assembly
10. Camshaft
11. Oil seal

Fig. 226 Camshaft and related parts — 2.4L engine

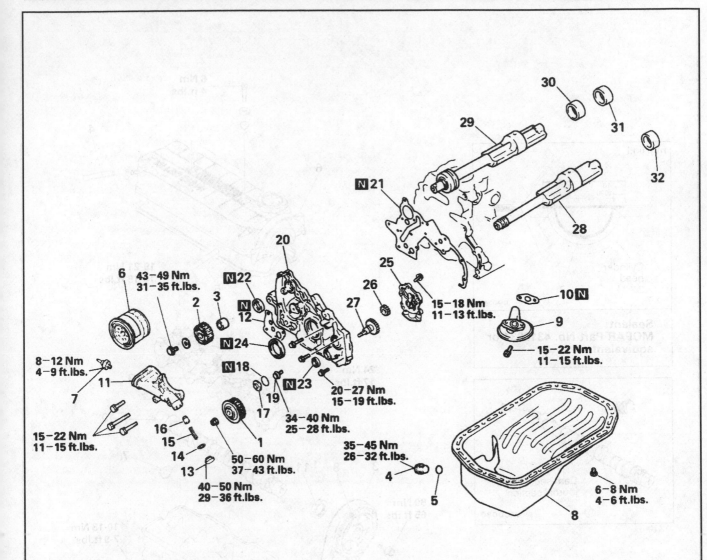

1. Oil pump sprocket
2. Right silent shaft sprocket
3. Spacer
4. Drain plug
5. Gasket
6. Oil filter
7. Oil pressure switch
8. Oil pan
9. Oil screen
10. Gasket
11. Oil filter bracket
12. Gasket
13. Relief plug
14. Gasket
15. Relief spring
16. Relief plunger
17. Plug cap
18. O-ring
19. Driven gear bolt
20. Front case
21. Gasket
22. Oil seal
23. Oil seal
24. Oil seal
25. Oil pump cover
26. Driven gear
27. Drive gear
28. Left silent shaft
29. Right silent shaft
30. Front bearing
31. Right rear bearing
32. Left rear bearing

Fig. 227 Silent shafts and related parts — 2.0L engine

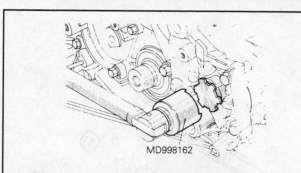

Fig. 228 Plug cap removal/installation — 2.0L or 2.4L engine

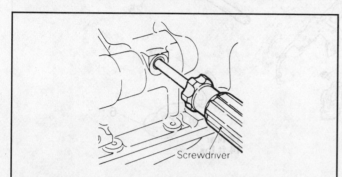

Fig. 229 Rod or screwdriver inserted in plug hole — 2.0L or 2.4L engine

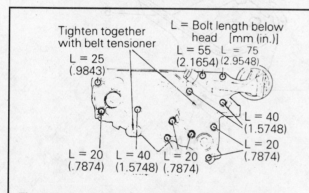

Fig. 230 Front case installation — 2.0L engine

insert installed over the crank journal. Install the rod cap with bearing in proper position. Secure with rod nuts and torque to proper specifications. Install all of the remaining piston assemblies.

CLEANING AND INSPECTION

1. Use a piston ring expander and remove the rings from the piston.

2. Clean the ring grooves using an appropriate cleaning tool, exercise care to avoid cutting too deeply.

3. Clean all varnish and carbon from the piston with a safe solvent. Do not use a wire brush or caustic solution on the pistons.

4. Inspect the pistons for scuffing, scoring, cracks, pitting or excessive ring groove wear. If wear is evident, the piston must be replaced.

5. Have the piston and connecting rod assembly checked by a machine shop for correct alignment, piston pin wear and piston diameter. If the piston had Collapsed it will have to be replaced or knurled to restore original diameter. Connecting rod bushing replacement, piston pin fitting and piston changing can be handled by the machine shop.

CYLINDER BORE

Check the cylinder bore for wear using a telescope gauge and a micrometer, measure the cylinder bore diameter perpendicular to the piston pin at a point 63.5mm below the top of the engine block. Measure the piston skirt perpendicular to the piston pin. The difference between the two measurements is the piston clearance. If the clearance is within specifications, finish honing or glaze breaking is all that is required. If clearance is excessive a slightly oversize piston may be required. If greatly oversize, the engine will have to be bored and 0.25mm or larger oversized pistons installed.

PISTON PINS

The pin connecting the piston and connecting rod is press fitted. If too much free play develops take the piston assemblies to the machine shop and have oversize pins installed. Installing new rods or pistons requires the use of a press. Have the machine shop handle the job for you.

FITTING AND POSITIONING PISTON RINGS

1. Take the new piston rings and care install, one at a time into the cylinder that they will be used in. Push the ring about 25mm below the top of the cylinder block using an inverted piston.

2. Use a feeler gauge and measure the distance between the ends of the ring, this is called measuring the ring end-gap. Compare the reading to the one called for in the specifications table. File the ends of the ring with a fine file to obtain necessary clearance.

➡**If inadequate ring end-gap is utilized, ring breakage will result.**

3. Inspect the ring grooves on the piston for excessive wear or taper. If necessary have the grooves recut for use with a standard ring and spacer. The machine shop can handle the job for you.

4. Check the ring groove by rolling the new piston ring around the groove to check for burrs or carbon deposits. If any are found, remove with a fine file. Hold the ring in the groove and measure side clearance with a feeler gauge. If clearance is excessive, spacer(s) will have to be added.

➡**Always add spacers above the piston ring.**

5. Install the rings on the piston, lower ring first using a ring installing tool. Consult the instruction sheet that comes

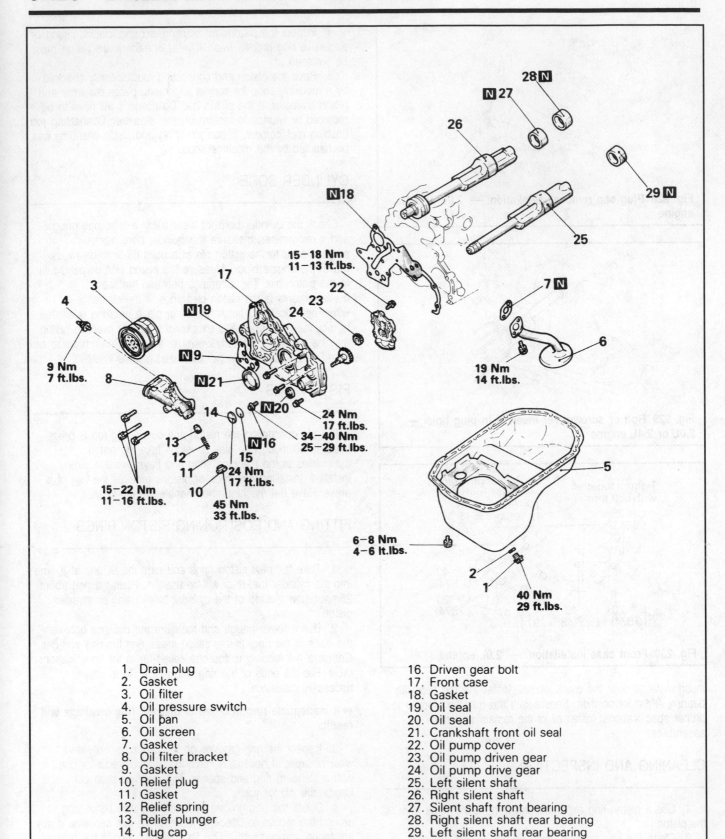

1. Drain plug
2. Gasket
3. Oil filter
4. Oil pressure switch
5. Oil pan
6. Oil screen
7. Gasket
8. Oil filter bracket
9. Gasket
10. Relief plug
11. Gasket
12. Relief spring
13. Relief plunger
14. Plug cap
15. O-ring
16. Driven gear bolt
17. Front case
18. Gasket
19. Oil seal
20. Oil seal
21. Crankshaft front oil seal
22. Oil pump cover
23. Oil pump driven gear
24. Oil pump drive gear
25. Left silent shaft
26. Right silent shaft
27. Silent shaft front bearing
28. Right silent shaft rear bearing
29. Left silent shaft rear bearing

Fig. 231 Silent shafts and related parts — 2.4L engine

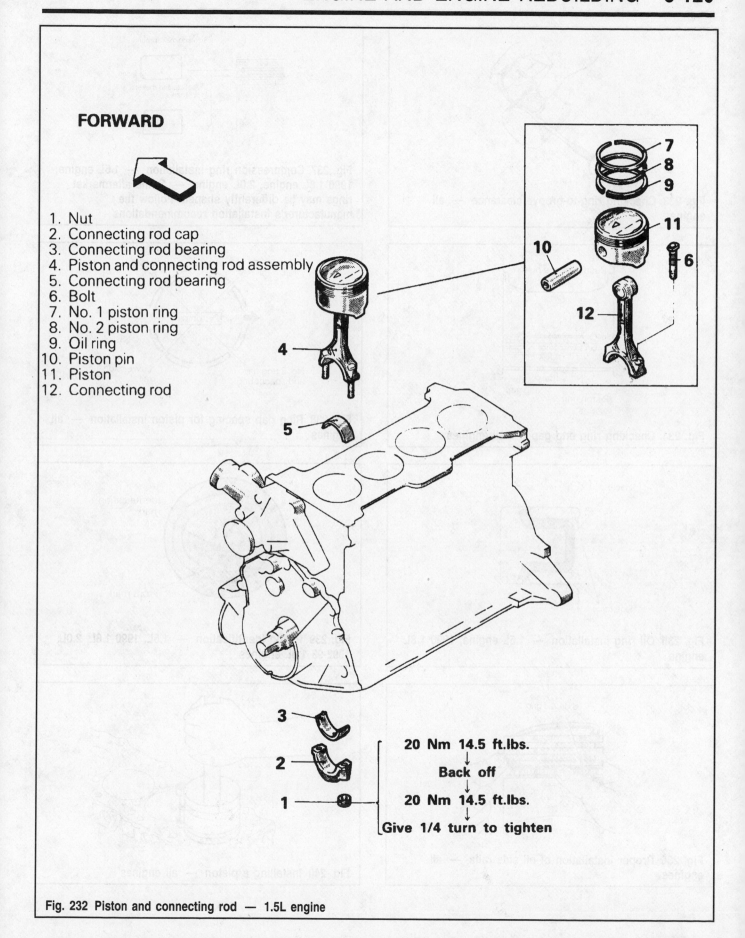

FORWARD

1. Nut
2. Connecting rod cap
3. Connecting rod bearing
4. Piston and connecting rod assembly
5. Connecting rod bearing
6. Bolt
7. No. 1 piston ring
8. No. 2 piston ring
9. Oil ring
10. Piston pin
11. Piston
12. Connecting rod

20 Nm 14.5 ft.lbs.
Back off
20 Nm 14.5 ft.lbs.
Give 1/4 turn to tighten

Fig. 232 Piston and connecting rod — 1.5L engine

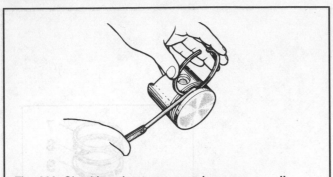

Fig. 233 Checking ring-to-groove clearance — all engines

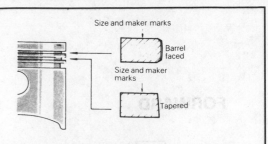

Fig. 237 Compression ring installation — 1.5L engine, 1990 1.8L engine, 2.0L engine — Some aftermarket rings may be differently shaped. Follow the manufacturer's installation recommendations

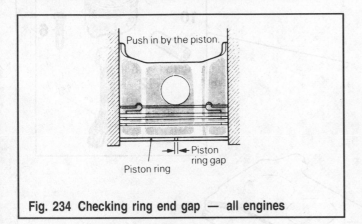

Fig. 234 Checking ring end gap — all engines

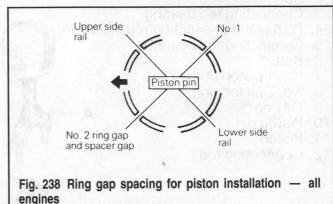

Fig. 238 Ring gap spacing for piston installation — all engines

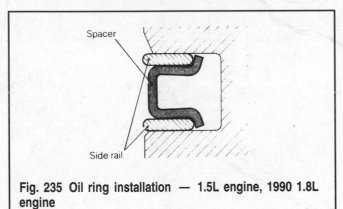

Fig. 235 Oil ring installation — 1.5L engine, 1990 1.8L engine

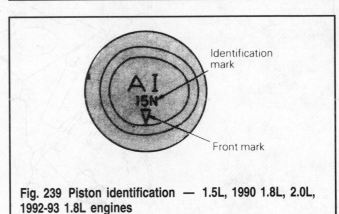

Fig. 239 Piston identification — 1.5L, 1990 1.8L, 2.0L, 1992-93 1.8L engines

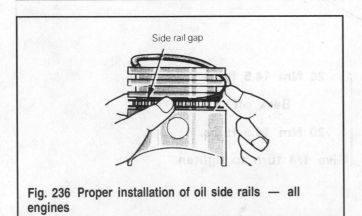

Fig. 236 Proper installation of oil side rails — all engines

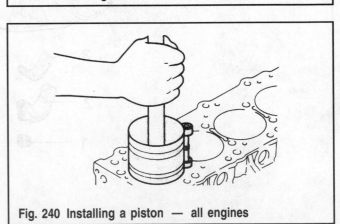

Fig. 240 Installing a piston — all engines

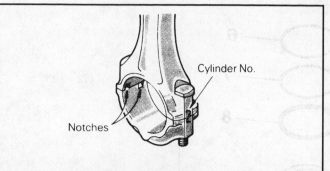

Fig. 241 When installing the rod bearings, the notches should mate like this — all engines

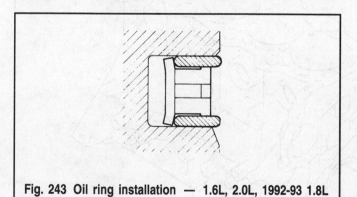

Fig. 242 Connecting rod side clearance — all engines

Fig. 243 Oil ring installation — 1.6L, 2.0L, 1992-93 1.8L and 2.4L engines

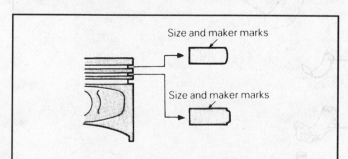

Fig. 244 Compression ring installation — 1.6L engine — Some aftermarket rings may be differently shaped. Follow the manufacturer's installation recommendations

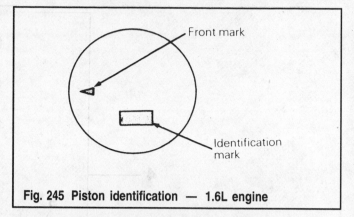

Fig. 245 Piston identification — 1.6L engine

with the rings to be sure they are installed with the correct side up. A mark on the ring usually faces upward.

6. When installing oil rings: install the center spreader (ring) in the groove. Hold the ends of the ring butted together (they must not overlap) and install the bottom rail (scraper) with the end about 25mm away from the butted end of the control ring. Install the top rail about 25mm away from the butted end of the control but on the opposite side from the lower rail.

7. Install the two compression rings (the rings usually have a stamped marked that faces up).

8. Consult the illustration with piston ring set instruction sheet for ring positioning, arrange the rings as shown, install a ring compressor and insert the piston and rod assembly into the engine.

ROD BEARING REPLACEMENT

1. Rod bearings can be installed when the pistons have been removed for servicing (rings etc) or, in most cases, while the engine is still in the car. Bearing replacement, however, is far easier with the engine out of the car and disassembled.

2. For in car service, remove the oil pan, spark plugs and front cover if necessary, Turn the engine until the connecting rod to be serviced is at the bottom of its travel. Remove the bearing cap, place two pieces of rubber hose over the rod cap bolts and push the piston and rod assembly up the cylinder bore until enough room is gained for bearing insert removal. Take care not to push the rod assembly up too far or the top ring will engage the cylinder ridge or come out of the cylinder and require head removal for reinstallation.

3. Clean the rod journal, the connecting rod end and the bearing cap after removing the old bearing inserts. Install the new inserts in the rod and bearing cap, lubricate them with oil. Position the rod over the crankshaft journal and install the rod cap. Make sure the cap and rod numbers match, torque the rod nuts to specifications.

4. Install the front cover, oil pan, etc.

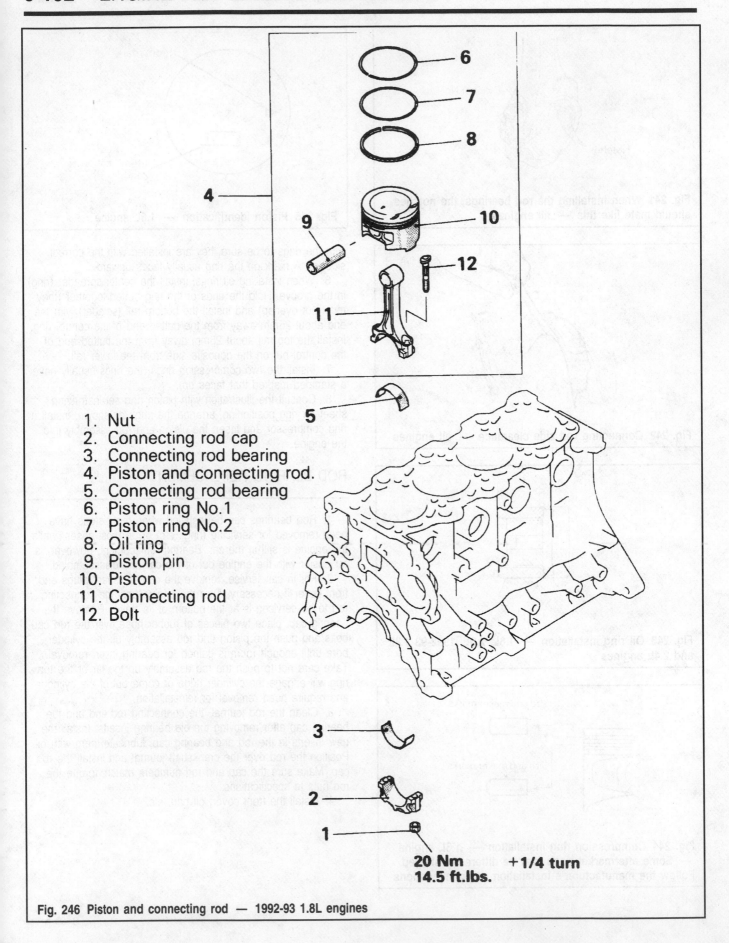

1. Nut
2. Connecting rod cap
3. Connecting rod bearing
4. Piston and connecting rod.
5. Connecting rod bearing
6. Piston ring No.1
7. Piston ring No.2
8. Oil ring
9. Piston pin
10. Piston
11. Connecting rod
12. Bolt

20 Nm   **+1/4 turn**
14.5 ft.lbs.

Fig. 246 Piston and connecting rod — 1992-93 1.8L engines

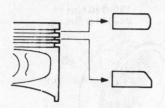

Fig. 247 Compression ring installation — 1992-93 1.8L and 2.4L engines — Some aftermarket rings may be differently shaped. Follow the manufacturer's installation recommendations

Rear Main Oil Seal

REMOVAL & INSTALLATION

➡**The factory recommends that the engine be removed from the car.**

1. Unscrew the retaining bolts and remove the housing from the block.
2. Remove the separator from the housing.
3. Using a small pry bar, pry out the old seal.
4. Clean the housing and the separator.
5. Lightly oil the replacement seal. Tap the seal into housing using a canister top or other circular piece of metal. The oil seal should be installed so that the seal plate fits into the inner contact surface of the seal case.
6. Install the separator into the housing so that the oil hole faces down.
7. Oil the lips of the seal and install the housing on the rear of the engine block.

Crankshaft and Main Bearings

REMOVAL & INSTALLATION

▶ **See Figures 248, 249, 250, 251, 252, 253, 254, 255, 256, 257, 258, 259, 260, 261, 262, 263, 264, 265, 266 and 267**

1. With the engine out of the car, remove the intake manifold, cylinder head, front cover, timing gears and/or chain, oil pan, oil pump and flywheel.
2. Remove the piston and rod assemblies. Remove the main bearing caps after marking them for position and direction.
3. Remove the crankshaft, bearing inserts and a rear main oil seal. Clean the engine block and cap bearing saddles. Clean the crankshaft and inspect for wear. Check the bearing journals with a micrometer for out-of-round condition and to determine what size rod and main bearing inserts to install.
4. Install the main bearing upper inserts and rear main oil seal half into the engine block.
5. Lubricate the bearing inserts and the crankshaft journals. Slowly and carefully lower the crankshaft into position.

6. Install the bearing inserts and rear main seal into the bearing caps, install the caps working from the middle out. Torque cap bolts to specifications in stages, rotate the crankshaft after each torque stage.
7. Remove the bearing caps, one at a time and check the oil clearance with Plastigage. Reinstall if clearance is within specifications. Check the crankshaft end-play, if within specifications install connecting rod and piston assemblies with new rod bearing inserts. Check connecting rod bearing oil clearance and rod side play, if correct, assemble the rest of the engine.

BEARING OIL CLEARANCE

Remove the cap from the bearing to be checked. Using a clean, dry rag, thoroughly clean all of the oil from the crankshaft journal and bearing insert.

➡**Plastigage is soluble in oil: therefore, oil on the journal or bearing could result in erroneous readings.**

Place a piece of Plastigage along the width of the bearing insert, install the cap, and torque to specifications.

Remove the bearing cap, and determine the bearing clearance by comparing the squashed width of Plastigage to the scale on the Plastigage envelope. Journal taper is determined by comparing the width of the Plastigage strip near its ends. Rotate the crankshaft 90° by hand, to determine journal eccentricity.

➡**Do not rotate the crankshaft with the Plastigage installed. If bearing insert and journal appear intact, and are within tolerances, no further main bearing service is required. If bearing or journal appear defective, cause of failure should be determined before replacement.**

CRANKSHAFT END-PLAY/CONNECTING ROD SIDE PLAY

Place a pry bar between a main bearing cap and crankshaft casting taking care not to damage any journals. Pry backward and forward measure the distance between the thrust bearing (center main) and crankshaft with a feeler gauge. Compare reading with specifications. If too great a clearance is determined, a larger thrust bearing or crank machining may be required. Check with an automotive machine shop for their advice.

Connecting rod clearance between the rod and crank throw casting can be checked with a feeler gauge. Pry the rod carefully to one side as far as possible and measure the distance on the other side of the rod.

CRANKSHAFT REPAIRS

If a journal is damaged on the crankshaft, repair is possible by having the crankshaft machined, after removal from engine to a standard undersize. Consult the machine shop for their advice.

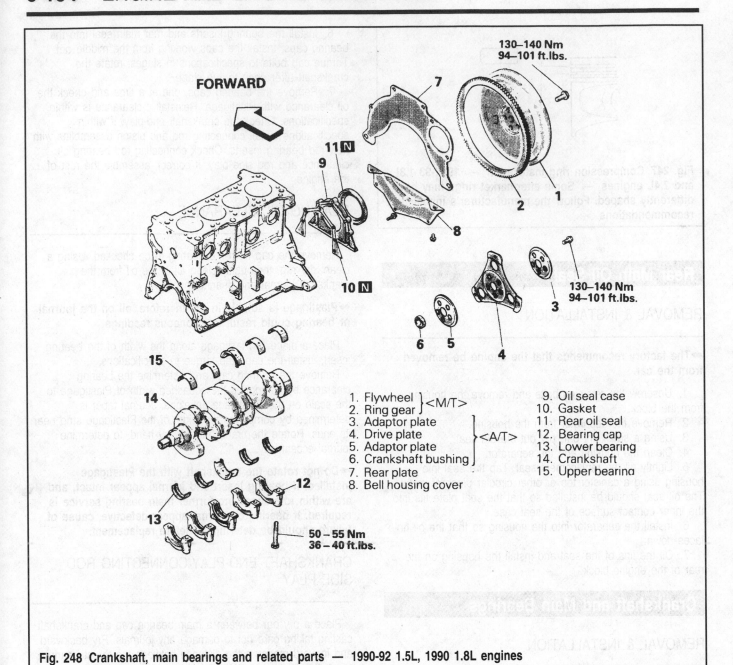

FORWARD

130–140 Nm
94–101 ft.lbs.

11

130–140 Nm
94–101 ft.lbs.

50–55 Nm
36–40 ft.lbs.

1. Flywheel   } <M/T>
2. Ring gear
3. Adaptor plate
4. Drive plate   } <A/T>
5. Adaptor plate
6. Crankshaft bushing
7. Rear plate
8. Bell housing cover
9. Oil seal case
10. Gasket
11. Rear oil seal
12. Bearing cap
13. Lower bearing
14. Crankshaft
15. Upper bearing

Fig. 248 Crankshaft, main bearings and related parts — 1990-92 1.5L, 1990 1.8L engines

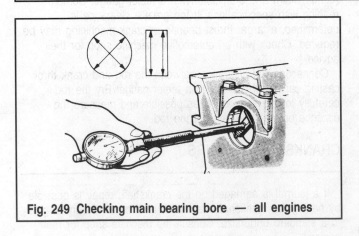

Fig. 249 Checking main bearing bore — all engines

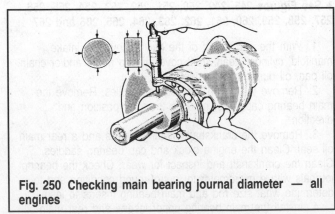

Fig. 250 Checking main bearing journal diameter — all engines

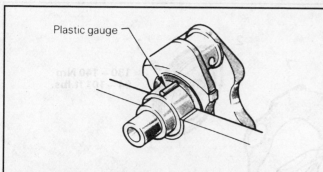

Fig. 251 Placing Plastigage® on the journal — all engines

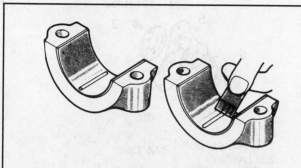

Fig. 252 Checking smashed Plastigage® width in the bearing cap — all engines

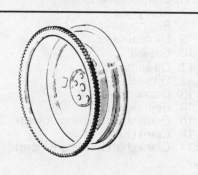

Fig. 253 Ring gear installation — all engines with manual transaxle

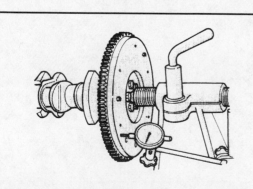

Fig. 254 Checking flywheel runout — all engines

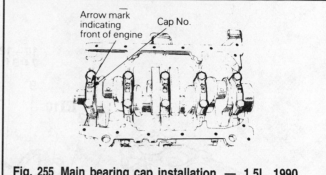

Fig. 255 Main bearing cap installation — 1.5L, 1990 1.8L, and 2.4L engines

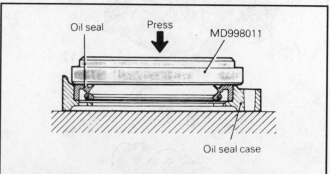

Fig. 256 Rear main seal installation — 1990-92 1.5L, 1990 1.8L engines

COMPLETING THE REBUILDING PROCESS

Fill the oil pump with oil, to prevent cavitating (sucking air) on initial engine start up. Install the oil pump and the pickup tube on the engine. Coat the oil pan gasket as necessary, and install the gasket and the oil pan. Mount the flywheel and the crankshaft vibration damper or pulley on the crankshaft.

➡Always use new bolts when installing the flywheel. Inspect the clutch shaft pilot bushing in the crankshaft. If the bushing is excessively worn, remove it with an expanding puller and a slide hammer, and tap a new bushing into place.

Position the engine, cylinder head side up. Lubricate the lifters, and install them into their bores. Install the cylinder head, and torque it as specified. Insert the pushrods (where applicable), and install the rocker shaft(s) (if so equipped) or position the rocker.

Install the intake and exhaust manifolds, the distributor and spark plugs. Mount all accessories and install the engine in the car. Fill the radiator with coolant, and the crankcase with high quality engine oil.

BREAK-IN PROCEDURE

Start the engine, and allow it to run at low speed for a few minutes, while checking for leaks. Stop the engine, check the oil level, and fill as necessary. Restart the engine, and fill the cooling system to capacity. Check and adjust the ignition

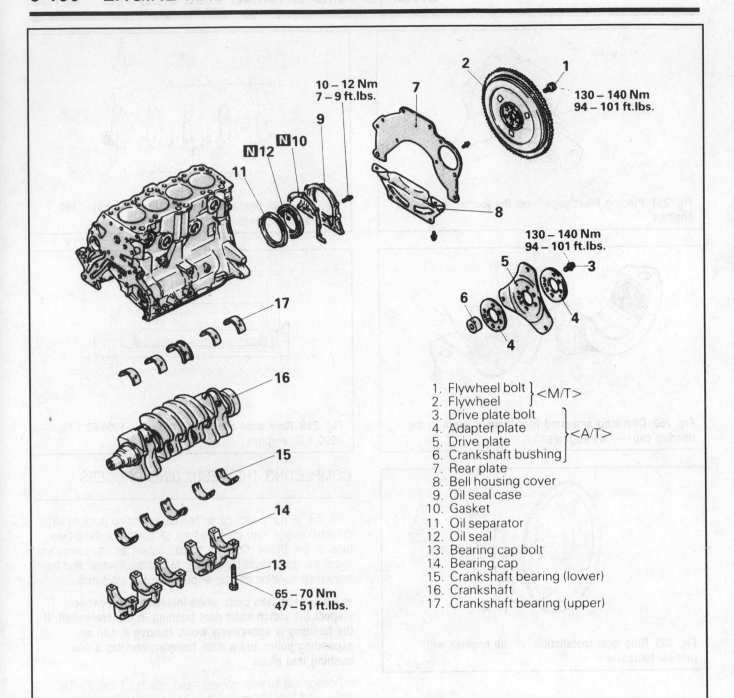

10 – 12 Nm
7 – 9 ft.lbs.

130 – 140 Nm
94 – 101 ft.lbs.

130 – 140 Nm
94 – 101 ft.lbs.

65 – 70 Nm
47 – 51 ft.lbs.

1. Flywheel bolt } <M/T>
2. Flywheel
3. Drive plate bolt
4. Adapter plate
5. Drive plate   <A/T>
6. Crankshaft bushing
7. Rear plate
8. Bell housing cover
9. Oil seal case
10. Gasket
11. Oil separator
12. Oil seal
13. Bearing cap bolt
14. Bearing cap
15. Crankshaft bearing (lower)
16. Crankshaft
17. Crankshaft bearing (upper)

Fig. 257 Crankshaft, main bearings and related parts — 1.6L engine

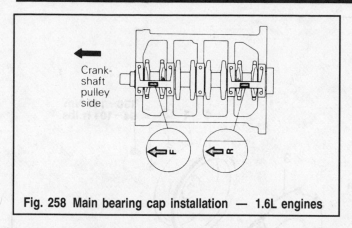

Fig. 258 Main bearing cap installation — 1.6L engines

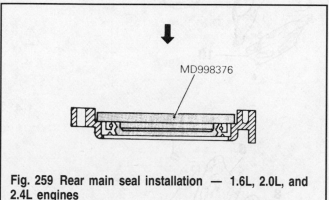

Fig. 259 Rear main seal installation — 1.6L, 2.0L, and 2.4L engines

timing. Run the engine at low to medium speed (800-2,500 rpm) for approximately ½ hour, and retorque the cylinder head bolts. Road test the car, and check again for leaks.

➡**Some gasket manufacturers recommend not retorquing the cylinder head(s) due to the composition of the head gasket. Follow the directions in the gasket set.**

Flywheel/Flex Plate and Ring Gear

➡**Flex plate is the term for a flywheel mated with an automatic transmission.**

REMOVAL & INSTALLATION

All Engines

➡**The ring gear is replaceable only on engines mated with a manual transmission. Engine with automatic transmissions have ring gears which are welded to the flex plate.**

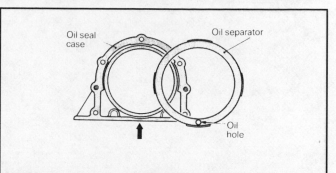

Fig. 260 Oil separator installation — 1.6L, 2.0L, and 2.4L engines

1. Remove the transmission and, on 4WD Vistas, the transfer case.

2. Remove the clutch, if equipped, or torque converter from the flywheel. The flywheel bolts should be loosened a little at a time in a cross pattern to avoid warping the flywheel. On trucks with manual transmission, replace the pilot bearing in the end of the crankshaft if removing the flywheel.

3. The flywheel should be checked for cracks and glazing. It can be resurfaced by a machine shop.

4. If the ring gear is to be replaced, drill a hole in the gear between two teeth, being careful not to contact the flywheel surface. Using a cold chisel at this point, crack the ring gear and remove it.

5. Polish the inner surface of the new ring gear and heat it in an oven to about 600°F (315°C). Quickly place the ring gear on the flywheel and tap it into place, making sure that it is fully seated.

➡**Never heat the ring gear past 800°F (426°C), or the tempering will be destroyed.**

6. Installation is the reverse of removal. Torque the bolts a little at a time in a cross pattern, to the torque figure shown in the Torque Specifications Chart.

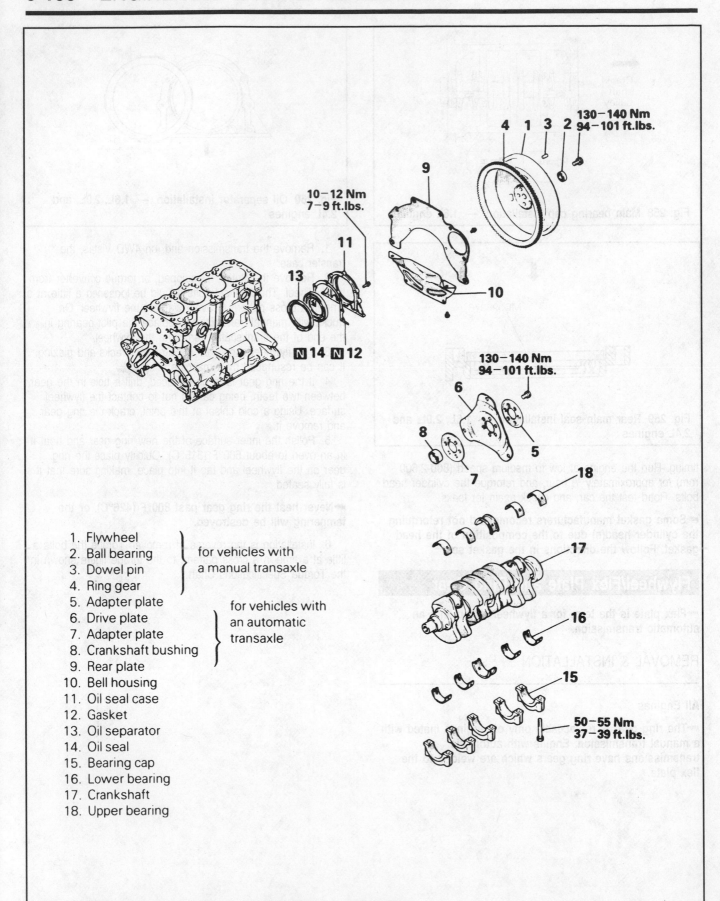

130–140 Nm
94–101 ft.lbs.

10–12 Nm
7–9 ft.lbs.

130–140 Nm
94–101 ft.lbs.

50–55 Nm
37–39 ft.lbs.

1. Flywheel
2. Ball bearing
3. Dowel pin
4. Ring gear
} for vehicles with a manual transaxle

5. Adapter plate
6. Drive plate
7. Adapter plate
8. Crankshaft bushing
} for vehicles with an automatic transaxle

9. Rear plate
10. Bell housing
11. Oil seal case
12. Gasket
13. Oil separator
14. Oil seal
15. Bearing cap
16. Lower bearing
17. Crankshaft
18. Upper bearing

Fig. 261 Crankshaft, main bearings and related parts — 2.0L engine

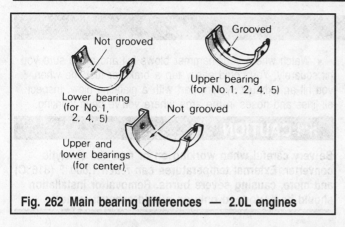

Fig. 262 Main bearing differences — 2.0L engines

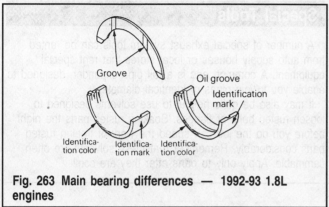

Fig. 263 Main bearing differences — 1992-93 1.8L engines

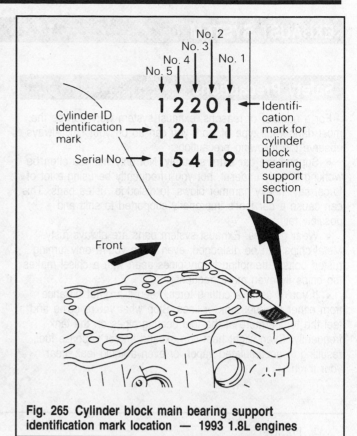

Fig. 265 Cylinder block main bearing support identification mark location — 1993 1.8L engines

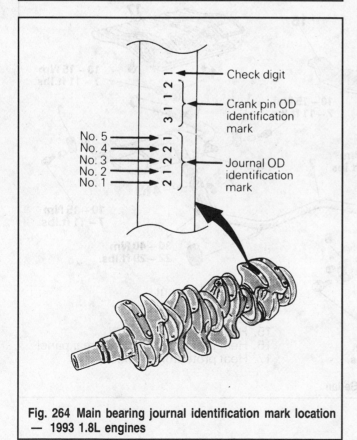

Fig. 264 Main bearing journal identification mark location — 1993 1.8L engines

Journal OD identification mark	Identification mark for cylinder block bearing support section ID	Crankshaft bearing	
		Identification mark	Identification color
1	0	S1	Brown
	1	S2	Black
	2	S3	Green
2	0	S2	Black
	1	S3	Green
	2	S4	Yellow
3	0	S3	Green
	1	S4	Yellow
	2	S5	Red

Fig. 266 Crankshaft bearing identification chart — 1993 1.8L engines

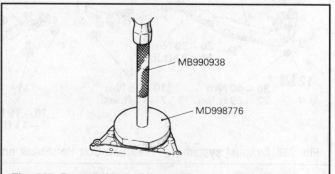

Fig. 267 Rear main seal installation — 1992-93 1.8L engines

EXHAUST SYSTEM

Safety Precautions

For a number of reasons, exhaust system work can be the most dangerous type of work you can do on your car. Always observe the following precautions:

• Support the car extra securely. Not only will you often be working directly under it, but you'll frequently be using a lot of force, say, heavy hammer blows, to dislodge rusted parts. This can cause a car that's improperly supported to shift and possibly fall.

• Wear goggles. Exhaust system parts are always rusty. Metal chips can be dislodged, even when you're only turning rusted bolts. Attempting to pry pipes apart with a chisel makes the chips fly even more frequently.

• If you're using a cutting torch, keep it a great distance from either the fuel tank or lines. Stop what you're doing and feel the temperature of the fuel bearing pipes on the tank frequently. Even slight heat can expand and/or vaporize fuel, resulting in accumulated vapor, or even a liquid leak, near your torch.

• Watch where your hammer blows fall and make sure you hit squarely. You could easily tap a brake or fuel line when you hit an exhaust system part with a glancing blow. Inspect all lines and hoses in the area where you've been working.

✳✳CAUTION

Be very careful when working on or near the catalytic converter. External temperatures can reach 1,500°F (816°C) and more, causing severe burns. Removal or installation should be performed only on a cold exhaust system.

Special Tools

A number of special exhaust system tools can be rented from auto supply houses or local stores that rent special equipment. A common one is a tail pipe expander, designed to enable you to join pipes of identical diameter.

It may also be quite helpful to use solvents designed to loosen rusted bolts or flanges. Soaking rusted parts the night before you do the job can speed the work of freeing rusted parts considerably. Remember that these solvents are often flammable. Apply only to parts after they are cool!

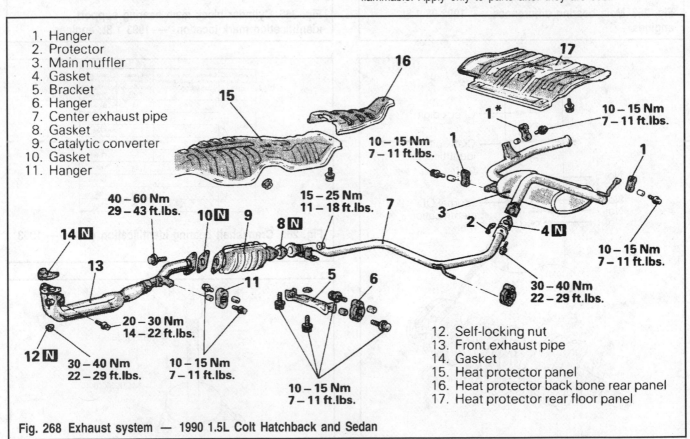

1. Hanger
2. Protector
3. Main muffler
4. Gasket
5. Bracket
6. Hanger
7. Center exhaust pipe
8. Gasket
9. Catalytic converter
10. Gasket
11. Hanger
12. Self-locking nut
13. Front exhaust pipe
14. Gasket
15. Heat protector panel
16. Heat protector back bone rear panel
17. Heat protector rear floor panel

10 – 15 Nm
7 – 11 ft.lbs.

10 – 15 Nm
7 – 11 ft.lbs.

10 – 15 Nm
7 – 11 ft.lbs.

15 – 25 Nm
11 – 18 ft.lbs.

40 – 60 Nm
29 – 43 ft.lbs.

30 – 40 Nm
22 – 29 ft.lbs.

20 – 30 Nm
14 – 22 ft.lbs.

30 – 40 Nm
22 – 29 ft.lbs.

10 – 15 Nm
7 – 11 ft.lbs.

10 – 15 Nm
7 – 11 ft.lbs.

Fig. 268 Exhaust system — 1990 1.5L Colt Hatchback and Sedan

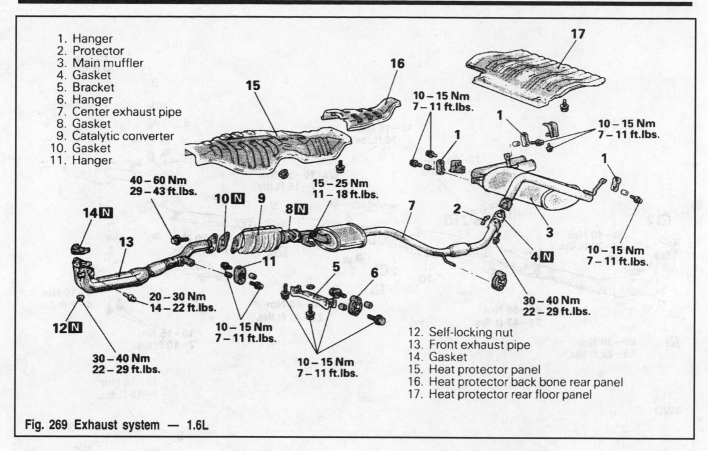

1. Hanger
2. Protector
3. Main muffler
4. Gasket
5. Bracket
6. Hanger
7. Center exhaust pipe
8. Gasket
9. Catalytic converter
10. Gasket
11. Hanger

12. Self-locking nut
13. Front exhaust pipe
14. Gasket
15. Heat protector panel
16. Heat protector back bone rear panel
17. Heat protector rear floor panel

10 – 15 Nm
7 – 11 ft.lbs.

10 – 15 Nm
7 – 11 ft.lbs.

40 – 60 Nm
29 – 43 ft.lbs.

15 – 25 Nm
11 – 18 ft.lbs.

10 – 15 Nm
7 – 11 ft.lbs.

20 – 30 Nm
14 – 22 ft.lbs.

30 – 40 Nm
22 – 29 ft.lbs.

10 – 15 Nm
7 – 11 ft.lbs.

10 – 15 Nm
7 – 11 ft.lbs.

30 – 40 Nm
22 – 29 ft.lbs.

Fig. 269 Exhaust system — 1.6L

REPAIR

▶ **See Figures 268, 269, 270, 271 and 272**

Once or twice a year, check the muffler(s) and pipes for signs of corrosion and damage. Check the hangers and, or O-ring suspensions for wear, cracks or hardening. Check the heat shields (models equipped) for corrosion or damage. Replace components as necessary.

The exhaust system is usually bolted together. Replacement parts are usually the same as the original system, with the exception of some mufflers. The original system usually has the muffler and the inlet and tailpipe welded together. Some replacement companies supply the system in three pieces that are clamped together during installation. Splash shield removal will be required, in some cases, for removal and installation clearance.

Care should be taken when working on the exhaust system. Allow the muffler and pipes, and especially the converter to cool completely. Wear protective eye glasses or goggles to prevent rust or metal chips from falling in your eyes.

Use only the proper size sockets or wrenches when unbolting system components. Do not tighten completely until all components are attached, aligned, and suspended. Check the system for leaks after the installation is completed.

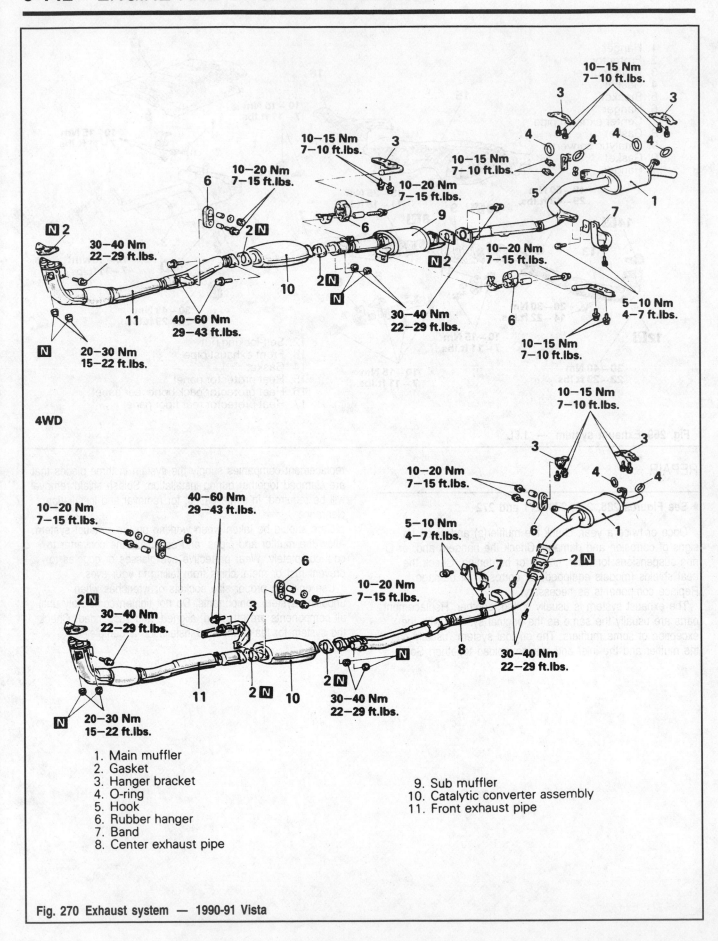

4WD

1. Main muffler
2. Gasket
3. Hanger bracket
4. O-ring
5. Hook
6. Rubber hanger
7. Band
8. Center exhaust pipe
9. Sub muffler
10. Catalytic converter assembly
11. Front exhaust pipe

Fig. 270 Exhaust system — 1990-91 Vista

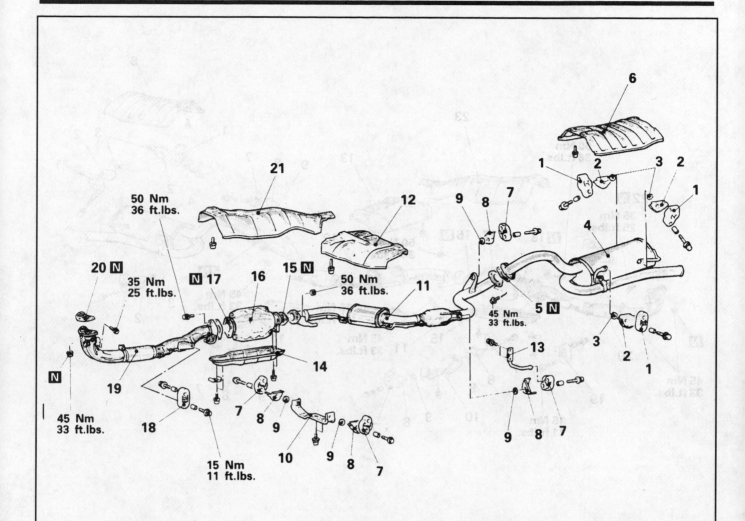

Fig. 271 Exhaust system — 1992 Vista

1. Hanger
2. Protector
3. Seat
4. Main muffler
5. Gasket
6. Rear floor heat protection panel
7. Hanger
8. Protector
9. Seat
10. Bracket
11. Center exhaust pipe
12. Center heat protection panel (AWD)
13. Hanger bracket
14. Catalytic converter heat protection panel
15. Gasket
16. Catalytic converter
17. Gasket
18. Hanger
19. Front exhaust pipe
20. Gasket
21. Front floor heat protector

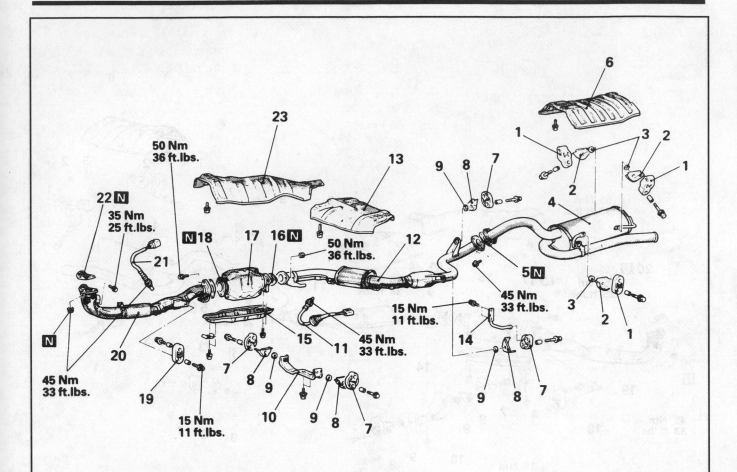

1. Hanger
2. Protector
3. Seat
4. Main muffler
5. Gasket
6. Rear floor heat protection panel
7. Hanger
8. Protector
9. Seat
10. Bracket
11. Connection for heated oxygen sensor <Vehicles for California>
12. Center exhaust pipe
13. Center heat protection panel (AWD)
14. Hanger bracket
15. Catalytic converter heat protection panel
16. Gasket
17. Catalytic converter
18. Gasket
19. Hanger
20. Front exhaust pipe
21. Connection for heated oxygen sensor <Vehicles for California>
22. Gasket
23. Front floor heat protection panel

Fig. 272 Exhaust system — 1993 Vista

ENGINE MECHANICAL SPECIFICATIONS

Component	U.S.	Metric
	1990 1.5L	
Cylinder Head		
Overall height	4.209-4.217 in.	106.9-107.1mm
Gasket surface flatness	0.0020 in.	0.05mm
Manifold mounting surface flatness	0.0059 in.	0.15mm
Valve seat location machining		
Intake		
0.012 in. (0.3mm) OS	1.4291-1.4301 in.	36.300-36.325mm
0.024 in. (0.6mm) OS	1.4409-1.4419 in.	36.600-26.625mm
Exhaust		
0.012 in. (0.3mm) OS	1.2717-1.2726 in.	32.300-33.325mm
0.024 in. (0.6mm) OS	1.2835-1.2844 in.	32.600-32.625mm
Valve guide machining		
Intake or Exhaust		
0.002 in. (0.05mm) OS	0.4744-0.4751 in.	12.05-12.07mm
0.010 in. (0.25mm) OS	0.4823-0.4830 in.	12.25-12.27mm
0.020 in. (0.50mm) OS	0.4921-0.4928 in.	12.50-12.52mm
Camshaft		
Cam height		
Intake	1.5318 in.	38.91mm
Exhaust	1.5344 in.	38.97mm
Journal OD	1.8110 in.	46.00mm
Bearing oil clearance	0.0020-0.0079 in.	0.05-0.20mm
Rocker Arm		
Inside dia.	0.7441 in.	18.9mm
Clearance to shaft	0.0004-0.0016 in.	0.01-0.04mm
Rocker shaft		
Outside dia.	0.7440 in.	18.9mm
Valve Timing		
Intake		
Opens	18.5° BTDC	
Closes	51.5° ABDC	
Exhaust		
Opens	51.5° BBDC	
Closes	18.5° ATDC	
Valves		
Valve length		
Intake	4.0197 in.	102.10mm
Exhaust	3.9724 in.	100.90mm
Stem OD	0.2598 in.	6.6mm
Face angle	45-45.5°	
Valve head margin		
Intake	0.020-0.039 in.	0.05-1.00mm
Exhaust	0.039-0.059 in.	1.00-1.50mm
Stem-to-guide clearance		
Intake	0.0008-0.0020 in.	0.02-0.05mm
Exhaust	0.0020-0.0035 in.	0.05-0.09mm
Valve Guides		
Length		
Intake	1.732 in.	44.0mm
Exhaust	1.949 in.	49.5mm
Service limits OS	0.002 in.	0.05mm
	0.010 in.	0.25mm
	0.020 in.	0.50mm

ENGINE MECHANICAL SPECIFICATIONS

Component	U.S.	Metric
Valve Seats		
Seat contact width	0.035-0.051 in.	0.9-1.3mm
Seat angle	44-44.5°	
Oversize valve seat height		
Intake		
0.012 in. (0.30mm) OS	0.276-0.283 in.	7.0-7.2mm
0.024 in. (0.60mm) OS	0.287-0.295 in.	7.3-7.5mm
Exhaust		
0.012 in. (0.30mm) OS	0.291-0.299 in.	7.4-7.6mm
0.024 in. (0.60mm) OS	0.303-0.311 in.	7.7-7.9mm
Valve Springs		
Free length	1.717-1.756 in.	43.6-44.6mm
Load (closed)	53 lbs.	242N
Out of square	2°	
Cylinder Block		
Cylinder bore	2.9724-2.9736 in.	75.47-75.50mm
Bore taper/out-of-round	0.0008 in.	0.02mm
Gasket surface flatness	0.0020 in.	0.05mm
Overall height	10.075-10.083 in.	255.9-256.1mm
Pistons		
Outside dia.	2.9713-2.9724 in.	75.47-75.50mm
Clearance-to-cyl.	0.0008-0.0016 in.	0.02-0.04mm
Ring groove width		
No. 1	0.0598-0.0606 in.	1.52-1.54mm
No. 2	0.0594-0.0602 in.	1.51-1.53mm
Oil	0.1581-0.1593 in.	4.015-4.045mm
Service OS	0.10 in.	0.25mm
	0.02 in.	0.50mm
	0.03 in.	0.75mm
	0.039 in.	1.00mm
Piston pin press load	1100-3300 lbs.	5000-15000 N
Piston Rings		
Side clearance		
No. 1	0.0012-0.0028 in.	0.03-0.07mm
No. 2	0.0008-0.0024 in.	0.02-0.06mm
Oil control	snug	
End gap		
No. 1	0.0079-0.0138 in.	0.20-0.35mm
No. 2	0.0079-0.0138 in.	0.20-0.35mm
Oil control	0.0079-0.0276 in.	0.20-0.70mm
Service OS	0.10 in.	0.25mm
	0.02 in.	0.50mm
	0.03 in.	0.75mm
	0.039 in.	1.00mm
Connecting Rods		
Bend	0.0020 in. per 3.937 in.	0.05mm per 100mm
Twist	0.0039 in. per 3.937 in.	0.10mm per 100mm
Lower end side clearance	0.0039-0.0098 in.	0.10-0.25mm
Bearing oil clearance	0.0006-0.0017 in.	0.014-0.044mm
Crankshaft		
Main bearing oil clearance	0.0008-0.0018 in.	0.021-0.045mm
Connecting rod journal OD	1.6535 in.	42.00mm
Main bearing journal OD	1.8898 in.	48.00mm
Journal out-of-round	0.0006 in.	0.015mm
Journal taper	0.0006 in.	0.015mm
End play	0.002-0.007 in.	0.05-0.18mm
Flywheel		
Runout	0.0051 in.	0.13mm

ENGINE MECHANICAL SPECIFICATIONS

Component	U.S.	Metric
Oil Pump		
Pressure @ idle & 167-194°F (75-90°C)	11.6 psi	80 kPa
Tip clearance	0.0024-0.0071 in.	0.06-0.18mm
Side clearance	0.0016-0.0039 in.	0.04-0.10mm
Body clearance	0.0039-0.0070 in.	0.10-0.18mm
Relief spring		
Free length	1.8346 in.	46.6mm
Load	13.4 lbs. @ 1.5787 in.	60 N @ 40.1mm

1991-93 1.5L

Component	U.S.	Metric
Cylinder Head		
Overall height	4.209-4.217 in.	106.9-107.1mm
Gasket surface flatness	0.0020 in.	0.05mm
Manifold mounting surface flatness	0.0059 in.	0.15mm
Valve seat location machining		
Intake		
Primary		
0.012 in. (0.3mm) OS	1.0796-1.0804 in.	27.421-27.441mm
0.024 in. (0.6mm) OS	1.0914-1.0922 in.	27.721-27.741mm
Secondary		
0.012 in. (0.3mm) OS	1.2766-1.2774 in.	32.425-32.445mm
0.024 in. (0.6mm) OS	1.2884-1.2892 in.	32.725-32.745mm
Exhaust		
0.012 in. (0.3mm) OS	1.3947-1.3955 in.	35.425-35.445mm
0.024 in. (0.6mm) OS	1.4065-1.4073 in.	35.725-35.745mm
Valve guide machining		
Intake or Exhaust		
0.002 in. (0.05mm) OS	0.4744-0.4751 in.	12.05-12.07mm
0.010 in. (0.25mm) OS	0.4823-0.4830 in.	12.25-12.27mm
0.020 in. (0.50mm) OS	0.4921-0.4928 in.	12.50-12.52mm
Camshaft		
Cam height		
Intake		
1991-92	1.5256 in.	38.75mm
1993	1.5268 in.	38.78mm
Exhaust	1.5394 in.	39.10mm
Journal OD	1.8110 in.	46.00mm
Bearing oil clearance	0.0024-0.0039 in.	0.06-0.10mm
Rocker Arm		
Inside dia.		
1991-92	0.7441 in.	18.9mm
1993	0.7445-0.7453 in.	18.91-18.93mm
Clearance to shaft	0.0004-0.0016 in.	0.01-0.04mm
Rocker shaft		
Outside dia.		
1991-92	0.7440 in.	18.9mm
1993	0.7437-0.7441 in.	18.89-18.90mm
Valve Timing		
Intake		
1991-92		
Opens	14.5° BTDC	
Closes	51.5° ABDC	
1993		
Opens	15° BTDC	
Closes	53° ABDC	
Exhaust		
1991-92		
Opens	51.5° BBDC	
Closes	14.5° ATDC	
1993		
Opens	57° BBDC	
Closes	15° ATDC	

ENGINE MECHANICAL SPECIFICATIONS

Component	U.S.	Metric
Valves		
Valve length		
Intake	3.9665 in.	100.75mm
Exhaust	3.9783 in.	101.05mm
Stem OD		
Intake	0.2585-0.2591 in.	6.565-6.580mm
Exhaust	0.2571-0.2579 in.	6.53-6.55mm
Face angle	45-45.5°	
Valve head margin		
Intake	0.020-0.039 in.	0.05-1.00mm
Exhaust	0.039-0.059 in.	1.00-1.50mm
Stem-to-guide clearance		
Intake	0.0008-0.0020 in.	0.02-0.05mm
Exhaust	0.0020-0.0035 in.	0.05-0.09mm
Valve Guides		
Length		
Intake	1.732 in.	44.0mm
Exhaust	1.949 in.	49.5mm
Service limits OS	0.002 in.	0.05mm
	0.010 in.	0.25mm
	0.020 in.	0.50mm
Valve Seats		
Seat contact width	0.035-0.051 in.	0.9-1.3mm
Seat angle	44-44.5°	
Oversize valve seat height		
Intake		
0.012 in. (0.30mm) OS	0.276-0.283 in.	7.0-7.2mm
0.024 in. (0.60mm) OS	0.287-0.295 in.	7.3-7.5mm
Exhaust		
0.012 in. (0.30mm) OS	0.291-0.299 in.	7.4-7.6mm
0.024 in. (0.60mm) OS	0.303-0.311 in.	7.7-7.9mm
Valve Springs		
Free length		
Intake	1.776-1.815 in.	45.1-46.1mm
Exhaust	1.803-1.843 in.	45.8-46.8mm
Load (closed)		
Intake	51 lbs.	230N
Exhaust	64 lbs.	290N
Out of square	2°	
Cylinder Block		
Cylinder bore	2.9724-2.9736 in.	75.47-75.50mm
Bore taper/out-of-round		
1991-92	0.0008 in.	0.02mm
1993	0.0004 in.	0.01mm
Gasket surface flatness	0.0020 in.	0.05mm
Overall height	10.075-10.083 in.	255.9-256.1mm

ENGINE MECHANICAL SPECIFICATIONS

Component	U.S.	Metric
Pistons		
Outside dia.		
1991-92	2.9713-2.9724 in.	75.47-75.50mm
1993	2.9716-2.9724 in.	75.48-75.50mm
Clearance-to-cyl.	0.0008-0.0016 in.	0.02-0.04mm
Ring groove width		
1991-92		
No. 1	0.0598-0.0606 in.	1.52-1.54mm
No. 2	0.0594-0.0602 in.	1.51-1.53mm
Oil	0.1581-0.1593 in.	4.015-4.045mm
1993		
No. 1	0.0480-0.0488 in.	1.22-1.24mm
No. 2	0.0594-0.0602 in.	1.51-1.53mm
Oil control	0.1187-0.1199 in.	3.015-3.045mm
Service OS	0.10 in.	0.25mm
	0.02 in.	0.50mm
	0.03 in.	0.75mm
	0.039 in.	1.00mm
Piston pin press load	1100-3300 lbs.	5000-15000 N
Piston Rings		
Side clearance		
No. 1	0.0012-0.0028 in.	0.03-0.07mm
No. 2	0.0008-0.0024 in.	0.02-0.06mm
Oil control	snug	
End gap		
No. 1	0.0079-0.0157 in.	0.20-0.40mm
No. 2	0.0079-0.0138 in.	0.20-0.35mm
Oil control	0.0079-0.0276 in.	0.20-0.70mm
Service OS	0.10 in.	0.25mm
	0.02 in.	0.50mm
	0.03 in.	0.75mm
	0.039 in.	1.00mm
Connecting Rods		
Bend	0.0020 in. per 3.937 in.	0.05mm per 100mm
Twist	0.0039 in. per 3.937 in.	0.10mm por 100mm
Lower end side clearance	0.0039-0.0098 in.	0.10-0.25mm
Bearing oil clearance		
1991-92	0.0008-0.0024 in.	0.02-0.06mm
1993	0.0008-0.0020 in.	0.02-0.05mm
Crankshaft		
Main bearing oil clearance		
1991-92	0.0008-0.0028 in.	0.02-0.07mm
1993	0.0008-0.0020 in.	0.02-0.05mm
Connecting rod journal OD	1.6500 in.	42.00mm
Main bearing journal OD	1.8900 in.	48.00mm
Journal out-of-round		
1991-92	0.0006 in.	0.015mm
1993	0.0002 in.	0.005mm
Journal taper		
1991-92	0.0006 in.	0.015mm
1993	0.0002 in.	0.005mm
End play	0.002-0.007 in.	0.05-0.18mm
Flywheel		
Runout	0.0051 in.	0.13mm
Oil Pump		
Pressure @ idle & 167-194°F (75-90°C)	11.4 psi	80 kPa
Tip clearance	0.0024-0.0071 in.	0.06-0.18mm
Side clearance	0.0016-0.0039 in.	0.04-0.10mm
Body clearance	0.0039-0.0070 in.	0.10-0.18mm
Relief spring		
Free length	1.8346 in.	46.6mm
Load	13.4 lbs. @ 1.5787 in.	60 N @ 40.1mm

ENGINE MECHANICAL SPECIFICATIONS

Component	U.S.	Metric
	1.6L	
Cylinder Head		
Overall height	5.193-5.201 in.	131.9-132.1mm
Gasket surface flatness	0.0020 in.	0.05mm
Manifold mounting surface flatness	0.0059 in.	0.15mm
Valve seat location machining		
Intake		
0.012 in. (0.3mm) OS	1.3898-1.3907 in.	35.300-35.325mm
0.024 in. (0.6mm) OS	1.4016-1.4026 in.	35.600-35.625mm
Exhaust		
0.012 in. (0.3mm) OS	1.3110-1.3120 in.	33.300-33.325mm
0.024 in. (0.6mm) OS	1.3228-1.3238 in.	33.600-33.625mm
Valve guide machining		
Intake or Exhaust		
0.002 in. (0.05mm) OS	0.4744-0.4751 in.	12.05-12.07mm
0.010 in. (0.25mm) OS	0.4823-0.4830 in.	12.25-12.27mm
0.020 in. (0.50mm) OS	0.4921-0.4928 in.	12.50-12.52mm
Camshaft		
Cam height		
Intake	1.3858 in.	35.20mm
Exhaust	1.3743 in.	34.91mm
Journal OD	1.02 in.	26.00mm
Bearing oil clearance	0.0020-0.0035 in.	0.05-0.09mm
Valve Timing		
Intake		
Man. Trans.		
Opens	16° BTDC	
Closes	48° ABDC	
Auto. Trans.		
Opens	26° BTDC	
Closes	38° ABDC	
Exhaust		
Man. Trans.		
Opens	43° BBDC	
Closes	17° ATDC	
Auto. Trans.		
Opens	53° BBDC	
Closes	7° ATDC	
Valves		
Valve length		
Intake	4.311 in.	109.5mm
Exhaust	3.319 in.	109.7mm
Stem OD		
Intake	0.2585-0.2586 in.	6.565-6.568mm
Exhaust	0.2571-0.2579 in.	6.53-6.55mm
Face angle	45-45.5°	
Valve head margin		
Intake	0.028-0.039 in.	0.07-1.00mm
Exhaust	0.039-0.059 in.	1.00-1.50mm
Stem-to-guide clearance		
Intake	0.0008-0.0019 in.	0.020-0.047mm
Exhaust	0.0020-0.0033 in.	0.050-0.085mm
Valve Guides		
Length		
Intake	1.791 in.	45.5mm
Exhaust	1.988 in.	50.5mm
Service limits OS	0.002 in.	0.05mm
	0.010 in.	0.25mm
	0.020 in.	0.50mm
Valve Seats		
Seat contact width	0.035-0.051 in.	0.9-1.3mm
Seat angle	44-44.5°	

ENGINE MECHANICAL SPECIFICATIONS

Component	U.S.	Metric
Valve Springs		
Free length	1.902 in.	48.3mm
Load (closed)	66 lbs.	300N
Out of square	2°	
Cylinder Block		
Cylinder bore	3.2402-3.2413 in.	82.30-82.33mm
Bore taper/out-of-round	0.0004 in.	0.01mm
Gasket surface flatness	0.0020 in.	0.05mm
Pistons		
Outside dia.	3.2390-3.2404 in.	82.27-82.30mm
Clearance-to-cyl.	0.0008-0.0016 in.	0.02-0.04mm
Ring groove width		
No. 1	0.0480-0.0488 in.	1.52-1.24mm
No. 2	0.0598-0.0606 in.	1.52-1.54mm
Oil	0.1185-0.1193 in.	3.010-3.030mm
Service OS	0.10 in.	0.25mm
	0.02 in.	0.50mm
	0.03 in.	0.75mm
	0.039 in.	1.00mm
Piston pin press load	1653-3858 lbs.	7350-17,160 N
Piston Rings		
Side clearance		
No. 1	0.0012-0.0028 in.	0.03-0.07mm
No. 2	0.0012-0.0028 in.	0.03-0.07mm
Oil control	snug	
End gap		
No. 1	0.0098-0.0157 in.	0.25-0.40mm
No. 2	0.0138-0.0197 in.	0.35-0.50mm
Oil control	0.0079-0.0276 in.	0.20-0.70mm
Service OS	0.10 in.	0.25mm
	0.02 in.	0.50mm
	0.03 in.	0.75mm
	0.039 in.	1.00mm
Connecting Rods		
Bend	0.0020 in. per 3.937 in.	0.05mm per 100mm
Twist	0.0039 in. per 3.937 in.	0.10mm per 100mm
Lower end side clearance	0.0039-0.0098 in.	0.10-0.25mm
Bearing oil clearance	0.0008-0.0020 in.	0.02-0.05mm
Crankshaft		
Main bearing oil clearance	0.0008-0.0020 in.	0.02-0.05mm
Connecting rod journal OD	1.7717 in.	45.00mm
Main bearing journal OD	2.2441 in.	57.00mm
Journal out-of-round	0.0006 in.	0.015mm
Journal taper	0.0002 in.	0.005mm
End play	0.002-0.007 in.	0.05-0.18mm
Flywheel		
Runout	0.0051 in.	0.13mm
Oil Pump		
Pressure @ idle & 167-194°F (75-90°C)	11.4 psi	80 kPa
Tip clearance		
Drive gear	0.0063-0.0083 in.	0.16-0.21mm
Driven gear	0.0051-0.0071 in.	0.13-0.18mm
Side clearance		
Drive gear	0.0031-0.0055 in.	0.08-0.14mm
Driven gear	0.0024-0.0047 in.	0.06-0.12
Relief spring		
Free length	1.8346 in.	46.6mm
Load	13.4 lbs. @ 1.5787 in.	60 N @ 40.1mm

ENGINE MECHANICAL SPECIFICATIONS

Component	U.S.	Metric
1990 1.8L		
Cylinder Head		
Overall height	3.484 in.	88.5mm
Gasket surface flatness	0.0020 in.	0.05mm
Manifold mounting surface flatness	0.0060 in.	0.15mm
Valve seat location machining		
Intake		
0.012 in. (0.3mm) OS	1.7047-1.7057 in.	43.300-43.325mm
0.024 in. (0.6mm) OS	1.7165-1.7175 in.	43.600-43.625mm
Exhaust		
0.012 in. (0.3mm) OS	1.4685-1.4695 in.	37.300-37.325mm
0.024 in. (0.6mm) OS	1.4803-1.4813 in.	37.600-37.625mm
Valve guide machining		
Intake or Exhaust		
0.002 in. (0.05mm) OS	0.5138-0.5145 in.	13.05-13.07mm
0.010 in. (0.25mm) OS	0.5216-0.5224 in.	13.25-13.27mm
0.020 in. (0.50mm) OS	0.5315-0.5322 in.	13.50-13.52mm
Camshaft		
Cam height		
Intake	1.4138 in.	35.91mm
Exhaust	1.4138 in.	35.91mm
Journal OD	1.3360-1.3366 in.	33.935-33.950mm
Bearing oil clearance	0.0020-0.0035 in.	0.05-0.09mm
Rocker Arm		
Inside dia.	0.7441 in.	18.9mm
Clearance to shaft	0.0004-0.0016 in.	0.01-0.04mm
Rocker shaft		
Outside dia.	0.7440 in.	18.9mm
Valve Timing		
Intake		
Opens	20° BTDC	
Closes	52° ABDC	
Exhaust		
Opens	55° BBDC	
Closes	17° ATDC	
Valves		
Valve length		
Intake	4.071 in.	103.4mm
Exhaust	3.937 in.	100.0mm
Stem OD	0.3150 in.	8.00mm
Face angle	45-45.5°	
Valve head margin		
Intake	0.039 in.	1.00mm
Exhaust	0.028 in.	0.7mm
Stem-to-guide clearance		
Intake	0.0012-0.0024 in.	0.03-0.06mm
Exhaust	0.0020-0.0035 in.	0.05-0.09mm
Valve Guides		
Length		
Intake	1.7323 in.	44mm
Exhaust	1.8898 in.	48mm
Service limits OS	0.002 in.	0.05mm
	0.010 in.	0.25mm
	0.020 in.	0.50mm
Valve Seats		
Seat contact width	0.035-0.051 in.	0.9-1.3mm
Seat angle	45°	
Valve Springs		
Free length	1.937 in.	49.2mm
Out of square	2°	

ENGINE MECHANICAL SPECIFICATIONS

Cylinder Block

Cylinder bore	3.173 in.	80.6mm
Bore taper/out-of-round	0.0008 in.	0.02mm

Pistons

Outside dia.	3.1732 in.	80.6mm
Clearance-to-cyl.	0.0008-0.0016 in.	0.02-0.04mm
Service OS	0.10 in.	0.25mm
	0.02 in.	0.50mm
	0.03 in.	0.75mm
	0.039 in.	1.00mm
Piston pin press load	112-337 lbs.	500-1500 N

Piston Rings

Side clearance		
No. 1	0.0018-0.0033 in.	0.045-0.085mm
No. 2	0.0008-0.0024 in.	0.02-0.06mm
Oil control	snug	
End gap		
No. 1	0.0118-0.0177 in.	0.30-0.45mm
No. 2	0.0079-0.0138 in.	0.20-0.35mm
Oil control	0.0079-0.0276 in.	0.20-0.70mm
Service OS	0.10 in.	0.25mm
	0.02 in.	0.50mm
	0.03 in.	0.75mm
	0.039 in.	1.00mm

Connecting Rods

Bend	0.0020 in. per 3.937 in.	0.05mm per 100mm
Twist	0.0039 in. per 3.937 in.	0.10mm per 100mm
Lower end side clearance	0.0039-0.0098 in.	0.10-0.25mm
Bearing oil clearance	0.0008-0.0020 in.	0.02-0.05mm

Crankshaft

Main bearing oil clearance	0.0008-0.0019 in.	0.02-0.05mm
Connecting rod journal OD	1.770 in.	45mm
Main bearing journal OD	2.2400 in.	57mm
Journal out-of-round	0.0006 in.	0.015mm
Journal taper	0.0006 in.	0.015mm
End play	0.002-0.007 in.	0.05-0.18mm

Flywheel

Runout	0.0051 in.	0.13mm

Oil Pump

Pressure @ idle & 167-194°F (75-90°C)	11.6 psi	80 kPa
Tip clearance	0.0016-0.0047 in.	0.04-0.12mm
Side clearance	0.0024-0.0047 in.	0.06-0.12mm
Body clearance	0.0039-0.0063 in.	0.10-0.16mm
Relief spring		
Free length	1.724 in.	43.8mm
Load	8.2 lbs. @ 1.5787 in.	37 N @ 40.1mm

1992-93 1.8L

Cylinder Head

Overall height	4.720-4.728 in.	119.9-120.1mm
Gasket surface flatness	0.0012 in.	0.03mm
Manifold mounting surface flatness	0.0039 in.	0.10mm
Valve seat location machining		
Intake		
0.012 in. (0.3mm) OS	1.2520-1.2531 in.	31.80-31.83mm
0.024 in. (0.6mm) OS	1.2638-1.2650 in.	32.10-32.13mm
Exhaust		
0.012 in. (0.3mm) OS	1.1535-1.1543 in.	29.30-29.32mm
0.024 in. (0.6mm) OS	1.1654-1.1661 in.	29.60-29.62mm
Valve guide machining		
Intake or Exhaust		
0.002 in. (0.05mm) OS	0.4300-0.4358 in.	11.05-11.07mm
0.010 in. (0.25mm) OS	0.4429-0.4598 in.	11.25-11.68mm
0.020 in. (0.50mm) OS	0.4528-0.4535 in.	11.50-11.52mm

ENGINE MECHANICAL SPECIFICATIONS

Component	U.S.	Metric
Camshaft		
Cam height		
Intake	1.4876 in.	37.78mm
Exhaust	1.4996 in.	38.09mm
Journal OD	1.7689-1.7693 in.	44.93-44.94mm
Bearing oil clearance	0.0020-0.0035 in.	0.05-0.09mm
Rocker Arm		
Inside dia.	0.7882-0.7890 in.	20.02-20.04mm
Clearance to shaft	0.0004-0.0020 in.	0.01-0.05mm
Rocker shaft		
Outside dia.	0.7870-0.7874 in.	19.99-20.00mm
Valve Timing		
Intake		
Opens	18° BTDC	
Closes	50° ABDC	
Exhaust		
Opens	58° BBDC	
Closes	10° ATDC	
Valves		
Valve length		
Intake	4.3366 in.	110.15mm
Exhaust	4.4764 in.	113.7mm
Stem OD		
Intake	0.2350-0.2354 in.	5.97-5.98mm
Exhaust	0.2343-0.2350 in.	5.95-5.97mm
Face angle	45-45.5°	
Valve head margin		
Intake	0.051-0.039 in.	0.02-1.00mm
Exhaust	0.039-0.051 in.	1.00-1.30mm
Stem-to-guide clearance		
Intake		
1992	0.0008-0.0020 in.	0.02-0.05mm
1993	0.0008-0.0016 in.	0.02-0.04mm
Exhaust		
1992	0.0020-0.0035 in.	0.05-0.09mm
1993	0.0012-0.0024 in.	0.03-0.06mm
Valve Guides		
Length		
Intake	1.791 in.	45.5mm
Exhaust	1.988 in.	50.5mm
Service limits OS	0.002 in.	0.05mm
	0.010 in.	0.25mm
	0.020 in.	0.50mm
Valve Seats		
Seat contact width	0.0354-0.0512 in.	0.9-1.3mm
Seat angle	43.5-44°	
Valve Springs		
Free length	1.965-2.004 in.	49.9-50.9mm
Load (closed)	132 lbs.	600N
Out of square	2°	
Cylinder Block		
Cylinder bore		
1992	3.1894-3.1898 in.	81.01-81.02mm
1993	3.1890-3.1902 in.	81.00-81.03mm
Bore taper/out-of-round	0.0004 in.	0.01mm
Gasket surface flatness	0.0020 in.	0.05mm
Overall height	10.37	263.5mm

ENGINE MECHANICAL SPECIFICATIONS

Component	U.S.	Metric
Pistons		
Outside dia.	3.1882-3.1886 in.	80.98-80.99mm
Clearance-to-cyl.	0.0008-0.0016 in.	0.02-0.04mm
Service OS	0.10 in.	0.25mm
	0.02 in.	0.50mm
	0.03 in.	0.75mm
	0.039 in.	1.00mm
Piston pin press load	112-337 lbs.	500-1500 N
Piston Rings		
Side clearance		
No. 1	0.0012-0.0028 in.	0.03-0.07mm
No. 2	0.0008-0.0024 in.	0.02-0.06mm
Oil control	snug	
End gap		
No. 1	0.0098-0.0157 in.	0.25-0.40mm
No. 2	0.0157-0.0217 in.	0.40-0.55mm
Oil control	0.0079-0.0236 in.	0.20-0.60mm
Service OS	0.10 in.	0.25mm
	0.02 in.	0.50mm
	0.03 in.	0.75mm
	0.039 in.	1.00mm
Connecting Rods		
Bend	0.0020 in. per 3.937 in.	0.05mm per 100mm
Twist	0.0039 in. per 3.937 in.	0.10mm per 100mm
Lower end side clearance	0.0039-0.0098 in.	0.10-0.25mm
Bearing oil clearance	0.0008-0.0020 in.	0.02-0.05mm
Crankshaft		
Main bearing oil clearance	0.0008-0.0016 in.	0.02-0.04mm
Connecting rod journal OD	1.7709-1.7715 in.	44.980-44.995mm
Main bearing journal OD	1.9678-1.9683 in.	49.982-49.994mm
Journal out-of-round	0.0006 in.	0.015mm
Journal taper	0.0002 in.	0.005mm
End play		
1992	0.0020-0.0070 in.	0.05-0.18mm
1993	0.0020-0.0098 in.	0.05-0.25mm
Flywheel		
Runout	0.0051 in.	0.13mm
Oil Pump		
Pressure @ idle & 167-194°F (75-90°C)	11.6 psi	80 kPa
Tip clearance	0.0012-0.0032 in.	0.03-0.08mm
Side clearance	0.0016-0.0039 in.	0.04-0.10mm
Body clearance	0.0039-0.0070 in.	0.10-0.18mm
Relief spring		
Free length	1.8346 in.	46.6mm
Load	13.4 lbs. @ 1.5787 in.	60 N @ 40.1mm
	2.0L	
Cylinder Head		
Overall height	3.540 in.	90mm
Gasket surface flatness	0.0020 in.	0.05mm
Manifold mounting surface flatness	0.0059 in.	0.15mm
Valve seat location machining		
Intake		
0.012 in. (0.3mm) OS	1.7441-1.7451 in.	44.300-44.325mm
0.024 in. (0.6mm) OS	1.7559-1.7569 in.	44.600-44.625mm
Exhaust		
0.012 in. (0.3mm) OS	1.5079-1.5089 in.	38.300-38.325mm
0.024 in. (0.6mm) OS	1.5197-1.5207 in.	38.600-38.625mm
Valve guide machining		
Intake or Exhaust		
0.002 in. (0.05mm) OS	0.4300-0.4358 in.	11.05-11.07mm
0.010 in. (0.25mm) OS	0.4429-0.4598 in.	11.25-11.68mm
0.020 in. (0.50mm) OS	0.4528-0.4535 in.	11.50-11.52mm

ENGINE MECHANICAL SPECIFICATIONS

Component	U.S.	Metric
	1990 1.5L	
Camshaft		
Cam height		
Intake	1.6567 in.	42.08mm
Exhaust	1.6567 in.	42.08mm
Journal OD	1.3386 in.	34.00mm
Bearing oil clearance	0.0020-0.0035 in.	0.05-0.09mm
Rocker Arm		
Inside dia.	0.7441 in.	18.9mm
Clearance to shaft	0.0004-0.0016 in.	0.01-0.04mm
Rocker shaft		
Outside dia.	0.7440 in.	18.9mm
Rocker Shaft Spring		
Free length	2.098 in.	53.3mm
Valve Timing		
Intake		
Opens	19° BTDC	
Closes	57° ABDC	
Exhaust		
Opens	57° BBDC	
Closes	19° ATDC	
Valves		
Valve length		
Intake	4.3230 in.	109.8mm
Exhaust	4.2800 in.	108.7mm
Stem OD	0.3150 in.	8.0mm
Face angle	45-45.5°	
Valve head margin		
Intake	0.047 in.	1.2mm
Exhaust	0.080 in.	2.00mm
Stem-to-guide clearance		
Intake	0.0012-0.0024 in.	0.03-0.06mm
Exhaust	0.0020-0.0035 in.	0.05-0.09mm
Valve Guides		
Length		
Intake	1.850 in.	47.0mm
Exhaust	2.050 in.	52.0mm
Service limits OS	0.002 in.	0.05mm
	0.010 in.	0.25mm
	0.020 in.	0.50mm
Valve Seats		
Seat contact width	0.0354-0.0512 in.	0.9-1.3mm
Seat angle	45°	
Valve Springs		
Free length	1.961 in.	49.8mm
Load (closed)	73 lbs.	329N
Out of square	2°	
Cylinder Block		
Cylinder bore	3.3460 in.	85.0mm
Bore taper/out-of-round	0.0008 in.	0.02mm
Gasket surface flatness	0.0020 in.	0.05mm
Right Silent Shaft		
Front journal dia.	1.650 in.	42.0mm
Rear journal dia.	1.610 in.	41.0mm
Oil clearance		
Front journal	0.0011-0.0024 in.	0.03-0.06mm
Rear journal	0.0020-0.0036	0.05-0.09mm

ENGINE MECHANICAL SPECIFICATIONS

Component	U.S.	Metric
Left Silent Shaft		
Front journal dia.	0.728 in.	18.5mm
Rear journal dia.	1.610 in.	41.0mm
Oil clearance		
Front journal	0.0011-0.0024 in.	0.03-0.06mm
Rear journal	0.0020-0.0036 in.	0.05-0.09mm
Pistons		
Outside dia.	3.3460 in.	85.0mm
Clearance-to-cyl.	0.0004-0.0012 in.	0.01-0.03mm
Ring groove width		
No. 1	0.06 in.	1.5mm
No. 2	0.06 in.	1.5mm
Oil control	0.157 in.	4.0mm
Service OS	0.10 in.	0.25mm
	0.02 in.	0.50mm
	0.03 in.	0.75mm
	0.039 in.	1.00mm
Piston pin press load	1653-3858 lbs.	7500-17,500 N
Piston Rings		
Side clearance		
No. 1	0.0012-0.0028 in.	0.03-0.07mm
No. 2	0.0008-0.0024 in.	0.02-0.06mm
Oil control	snug	
End gap		
No. 1	0.0098-0.0157 in.	0.25-0.40mm
No. 2	0.0079-0.0138 in.	0.20-0.35mm
Oil control	0.0079-0.0276 in.	0.20-0.70mm
Service OS	0.10 in.	0.25mm
	0.02 in.	0.50mm
	0.03 in.	0.75mm
	0.039 in.	1.00mm
Connecting Rods		
Bend	0.0020 in. per 3.937 in.	0.05mm per 100mm
Twist	0.0039 in. per 3.937 in.	0.10mm per 100mm
Lower end side clearance	0.0039-0.0098 in.	0.10-0.25mm
Bearing oil clearance	0.0006-0.0020 in.	0.014-0.050mm
Service OS	0.10 in.	0.25mm
	0.02 in.	0.50mm
	0.03 in.	0.75mm
Crankshaft		
Main bearing oil clearance	0.0008-0.0020 in.	0.02-0.05mm
Service OS	0.10 in.	0.25mm
	0.02 in.	0.50mm
	0.03 in.	0.75mm
Connecting rod journal OD	1.770 in.	45.0mm
Main bearing journal OD	2.2400 in.	57.0mm
Journal out-of-round	0.0006 in.	0.015mm
Journal taper	0.0005 in.	0.002mm
End play	0.002-0.007 in.	0.05-0.18mm
Flywheel		
Runout	0.0051 in.	0.13mm
Oil Pump		
Pressure @ idle & 167-194°F (75-90°C)	11.4 psi	80 kPa
Tip clearance		
Drive gear	0.0063-0.0083 in.	0.16-0.21mm
Driven gear	0.0051-0.0071 in.	0.13-0.18mm
Side clearance		
Drive gear	0.0031-0.0055 in.	0.08-0.14mm
Driven gear	0.0024-0.0047 in.	0.06-0.12mm
Relief spring		
Free length	1.8346 in.	46.6mm
Load	13.4 lbs. @ 1.5787 in.	60 N @ 40.1mm

ENGINE MECHANICAL SPECIFICATIONS

Component	U.S.	Metric
	1992 2.4L	
Cylinder Head		
Overall height	3.539-3.547 in.	89.9-90.1mm
Gasket surface flatness	0.0019 in.	0.05mm
Manifold mounting surface flatness	0.0059 in.	0.15mm
Valve seat location machining		
Intake		
0.012 in. (0.3mm) OS	1.8622-1.8634 in.	47.30-47.33mm
0.024 in. (0.6mm) OS	1.8740-1.8752 in.	47.60-47.63mm
Exhaust		
0.012 in. (0.3mm) OS	1.5866-1.5878 in.	40.30-40.33mm
0.024 in. (0.6mm) OS	1.5984-1.5996 in.	40.60-40.63mm
Valve guide machining		
Intake or Exhaust		
0.002 in. (0.05mm) OS	0.5138-0.5146 in.	13.05-13.07mm
0.010 in. (0.25mm) OS	0.5217-0.5224 in.	13.25-13.27mm
0.020 in. (0.50mm) OS	0.5315-0.5323 in.	13.50-13.57mm
Camshaft		
Cam height		
Intake	1.7531 in.	44.53mm
Exhaust	1.7531 in.	44.53mm
Journal OD	1.3362-1.3366 in.	33.94-33.95mm
Bearing oil clearance	0.0020-0.0035 in.	0.05-0.09mm
Rocker Arm		
Inside dia.	0.7445-0.7453 in.	18.91-18.93mm
Clearance to shaft	0.0004-0.0016 in.	0.01-0.04mm
Rocker shaft		
Outside dia.	0.7437-0.7441 in.	18.89-18.90mm
Rocker Shaft Spring		
Free length	2.098 in.	53.3mm
Valve Timing		
Intake		
Opens	19° BTDC	
Closes	57° ABDC	
Exhaust		
Opens	57° BBDC	
Closes	19° ATDC	
Valves		
Valve length		
Intake	4.321 in.	109.8mm
Exhaust	4.280 in.	108.7mm
Stem OD		
Intake	0.3150 in.	8.00mm
Exhaust	0.3150 in.	8.00mm
Face angle	45-45.5°	
Valve head margin		
Intake	0.028-0.047 in.	0.07-1.20mm
Exhaust	0.059-0.079 in.	1.50-2.00mm
Stem-to-guide clearance		
Intake	0.0012-0.0024 in.	0.03-0.06mm
Exhaust	0.0020-0.0035 in.	0.05-0.09mm
Valve Guides		
Length		
Intake	1.85 in.	47mm
Exhaust	2.05 in.	52mm
Service limits OS	0.002 in.	0.05mm
	0.010 in.	0.25mm
	0.020 in.	0.50mm
Valve Seats		
Seat contact width	0.0354-0.0512 in.	0.9-1.3mm
Seat angle	44-44.5°	

ENGINE MECHANICAL SPECIFICATIONS

Component	U.S.	Metric
Valve Springs		
Free length	1.921-1.961 in.	48.8-49.8mm
Load (closed)	73 lbs.	329N
Out of square	2°	
Cylinder Block		
Cylinder bore	3.4055-3.4067 in.	86.50-86.53mm
Bore taper/out-of-round	0.0004 in.	0.01mm
Gasket surface flatness	0.0020 in.	0.05mm
Right Silent Shaft		
Front journal dia.	1.6512-1.6528 in.	41.96-41.98mm
Rear journal dia.	1.6122-1.6130 in.	40.95-40.97mm
Journal oil clearance		
Front	0.0009-0.0024 in.	0.02-0.06mm
Rear	0.0020-0.0036 in.	0.05-0.09mm
Left Silent Shaft		
Front journal dia.	0.7272-0.7276 in.	18.47-18.48mm
Rear journal dia.	1.6122-1.6130 in.	40.95-40.97mm
Journal oil clearance		
Front	0.0008-0.0020 in.	0.02-0.05mm
Rear	0.0020-0.0036 in.	0.05-0.09mm
Pistons		
Outside dia.	3.4040-3.4055 in.	86.47-86.50mm
Clearance-to-cyl.	0.0004-0.0012 in.	0.01-0.03mm
Service OS	0.10 in.	0.25mm
	0.02 in.	0.50mm
	0.03 in.	0.75mm
	0.039 in.	1.00mm
Ring groove width		
No. 1	0.0598-0.0606 in.	1.52-1.54mm
No. 2	0.0594-0.0602 in.	1.51-1.53mm
Oil	0.1581-0.1593 in.	4.015-4.045mm
Piston pin press load	1653-3858 lbs.	7500-17,500 N
Piston Rings		
Side clearance		
No. 1	0.0012-0.0028 in.	0.03-0.07mm
No. 2	0.0008-0.0024 in.	0.02-0.06mm
Oil control	snug	
End gap		
No. 1	0.0098-0.0157 in.	0.25-0.40mm
No. 2	0.0079-0.0157 in.	0.20-0.40mm
Oil control	0.0079-0.0276 in.	0.20-0.70mm
Service OS	0.10 in.	0.25mm
	0.02 in.	0.50mm
	0.03 in.	0.75mm
	0.039 in.	1.00mm
Connecting Rods		
Bend	0.0020 in. per 3.937 in.	0.05mm per 100mm
Twist	0.0039 in. per 3.937 in.	0.10mm per 100mm
Lower end side clearance	0.0039-0.0098 in.	0.10-0.25mm
Bearing oil clearance	0.0008-0.0020 in.	0.02-0.05mm
Connecting rod bearing undersizes		
	0.010 in.	0.25mm
	0.020 in.	0.50mm
	0.030 in.	0.75mm

ENGINE MECHANICAL SPECIFICATIONS

Component	U.S.	Metric
Crankshaft		
Main bearing oil clearance	0.0008-0.0020 in.	0.02-0.05mm
Main bearing undersizes		
	0.010 in.	0.25mm
	0.020 in.	0.50mm
	0.030 in.	0.75mm
Connecting rod journal OD	1.7709-1.7717 in.	44.98-45.00mm
Main bearing journal OD	2.2433-2.2441 in.	56.98-57.00mm
Journal out-of-round	0.0006 in.	0.015mm
Journal taper	0.0002 in.	0.005mm
End play	0.002-0.007 in.	0.05-0.18mm
Connecting rod journal machining		
0.010 in. (0.25mm) US	1.7612-1.7617 in.	44.735-44.745mm
0.020 in. (0.50mm) US	1.7514-1.7518 in.	44.485-44.595mm
0.030 in. (0.75mm) US	1.7415-1.7419 in.	44.235-44.245mm
Main bearing journal machining		
0.010 in. (0.25mm) US	2.2337-2.2341 in.	56.735-56.745mm
0.020 in. (0.50mm) US	2.2238-2.2242 in.	56.485-56.595mm
0.030 in. (0.75mm) US	2.2140-2.2144 in.	56.235-56.245mm
Flywheel		
Runout	0.0051 in.	0.13mm
Oil Pump		
Pressure @ idle & 167-194°F (75-90°C)	11.6 psi	80 kPa
Tip clearance		
Drive gear	0.0063-0.0083 in.	0.16-0.21mm
Driven gear	0.0051-0.0071 in.	0.13-0.18mm
Side clearance		
Drive gear	0.0031-0.0055 in.	0.08-0.14mm
Driven gear	0.0024-0.0047 in.	0.06-0.12mm
Relief spring		
Free length	1.8346 in.	46.6mm
Load	13.4 lbs. @ 1.5787 in.	60 N @ 40.1mm

1993 2.4L

Component	U.S.	Metric
Cylinder Head		
Overall height	4.720-4.728 in.	119.9-120.1mm
Gasket surface flatness	0.0019 in.	0.05mm
Manifold mounting surface flatness	0.0059 in.	0.15mm
Valve seat location machining		
Intake		
0.012 in. (0.3mm) OS	1.3405-1.3416 in.	34.30-34.33mm
0.024 in. (0.6mm) OS	1.3622-1.3634 in.	34.60-34.63mm
Exhaust		
0.012 in. (0.3mm) OS	1.2520-1.2531 in.	31.80-31.83mm
0.024 in. (0.6mm) OS	1.2638-1.2650 in.	32.10-32.13mm
Valve guide machining		
Intake or Exhaust		
0.002 in. (0.05mm) OS	0.4350-0.4360 in.	11.05-11.07mm
0.010 in. (0.25mm) OS	0.4430-0.4440 in.	11.25-11.27mm
0.020 in. (0.50mm) OS	0.4530-0.4540 in.	11.50-11.52mm
Camshaft		
Cam height		
Intake	1.4720 in.	37.39mm
Exhaust	1.4752 in.	37.47m
Journal OD	1.7689-1.7693 in.	44.93-44.94mm
Bearing oil clearance	0.0020-0.0035 in.	0.05-0.09mm
Rocker Arm		
Inside dia.	0.7882-0.7890 in.	20.02-20.04mm
Clearance to shaft	0.0008-0.0020 in.	0.02-0.05mm
Rocker shaft		
Outside dia.	0.7870-0.7874 in.	19.99-20.00mm

ENGINE MECHANICAL SPECIFICATIONS

Component	U.S.	Metric
Valve Timing		
Intake		
Opens	18° BTDC	
Closes	58° ABDC	
Exhaust		
Opens	58° BBDC	
Closes	18° ATDC	
Valves		
Valve length		
Intake	4.420 in.	112.3mm
Exhaust	4.492 in.	114.1mm
Stem OD		
Intake	0.2350-0.2354 in.	5.97-5.98mm
Exhaust	0.2343-2350 in.	5.95-5.97mm
Face angle	45-45.5°	
Valve head margin		
Intake	0.020-0.039 in.	0.05-1.00mm
Exhaust	0.028-0.047 in.	0.07-1.20mm
Stem-to-guide clearance		
Intake	0.0008-0.0020 in.	0.02-0.05mm
Exhaust	0.0012-0.0028 in.	0.03-0.07mm
Valve Guides		
Length		
Intake	1.79 in.	45.5mm
Exhaust	1.99 in.	50.5mm
Service limits OS	0.002 in.	0.05mm
	0.010 in.	0.25mm
	0.020 in.	0.50mm
Valve Seats		
Seat contact width	0.0354-0.0512 in.	0.9-1.3mm
Seat angle	43.5-44°	
Valve Springs		
Free length	1.862-2.008 in.	47.3-51.0mm
Load (closed)	60 lbs.	272N
Out of square	2°	
Cylinder Block		
Cylinder bore	3.4055-3.4067 in.	86.50-86.53mm
Bore taper/out-of-round	0.0004 in.	0.01mm
Gasket surface flatness	0.0020 in.	0.05mm
Right Silent Shaft		
Front journal dia.	1.6512-1.6528 in.	41.96-41.98mm
Rear journal dia.	1.6122-1.6130 in.	40.95-40.97mm
Journal oil clearance		
Front	0.0009-0.0024 in.	0.02-0.06mm
Rear	0.0020-0.0036 in.	0.05-0.09mm
Left Silent Shaft		
Front journal dia.	0.7272-0.7276 in.	18.47-18.48mm
Rear journal dia.	1.6122-1.6130 in.	40.95-40.97mm
Journal oil clearance		
Front	0.0008-0.0020 in.	0.02-0.05mm
Rear	0.0020-0.0036 in.	0.05-0.09mm
Pistons		
Outside dia.	3.4040-3.4055 in.	86.47-86.50mm
Clearance-to-cyl.	0.0004-0.0012 in.	0.01-0.03mm
Service OS	0.10 in.	0.25mm
	0.02 in.	0.50mm
	0.03 in.	0.75mm
	0.039 in.	1.00mm
Ring groove width		
No. 1	0.0598-0.0606 in.	1.52-1.54mm
No. 2	0.0594-0.0602 in.	1.51-1.53mm
Oil	0.1581-0.1593 in.	4.015-4.045mm
Piston pin press load	1653-3858 lbs.	7500-17,500 N

ENGINE MECHANICAL SPECIFICATIONS

Component	U.S.	Metric
Piston Rings		
Side clearance		
No. 1	0.0012-0.0028 in.	0.03-0.07mm
No. 2	0.0012-0.0028 in.	0.03-0.07mm
Oil control	snug	
End gap		
No. 1	0.0098-0.0138 in.	0.25-0.35mm
No. 2	0.0157-0.0217 in.	0.40-0.55mm
Oil control	0.0039-0.0157 in.	0.10-0.40mm
Service OS	0.10 in.	0.25mm
	0.02 in.	0.50mm
	0.03 in.	0.75mm
	0.039 in.	1.00mm
Connecting Rods		
Bend	0.0020 in. per 3.937 in.	0.05mm per 100mm
Twist	0.0039 in. per 3.937 in.	0.10mm per 100mm
Lower end side clearance	0.0039-0.0098 in.	0.10-0.25mm
Bearing oil clearance	0.0008-0.0020 in.	0.02-0.05mm
Connecting rod bearing undersizes		
	0.010 in.	0.25mm
	0.020 in.	0.50mm
	0.030 in.	0.75mm
Crankshaft		
Main bearing oil clearance	0.0008-0.0020 in.	0.02-0.05mm
Main bearing undersizes		
	0.010 in.	0.25mm
	0.020 in.	0.50mm
	0.030 in.	0.75mm
Connecting rod journal OD	1.7709-1.7717 in.	44.98-45.00mm
Main bearing journal OD	2.2433-2.2441 in.	56.98-57.00mm
Journal out-of-round	0.0004 in.	0.01mm
Journal taper	0.0004 in.	0.01mm
End play	0.002-0.007 in.	0.05-0.18mm
Connecting rod journal machining		
0.010 in. (0.25mm) US	1.7612-1.7617 in.	44.735-44.745mm
0.020 in. (0.50mm) US	1.7514-1.7518 in.	44.485-44.595mm
0.030 in. (0.75mm) US	1.7415-1.7419 in.	44.235-44.245mm
Main bearing journal machining		
0.010 in. (0.25mm) US	2.2337-2.2341 in.	56.735-56.745mm
0.020 in. (0.50mm) US	2.2238-2.2242 in.	56.485-56.595mm
0.030 in. (0.75mm) US	2.2140-2.2144 in.	56.235-56.245mm
Flywheel		
Runout	0.0051 in.	0.13mm
Oil Pump		
Pressure @ idle & 167-194°F (75-90°C)	11.6 psi	80 kPa
Tip clearance		
Drive gear	0.0063-0.0083 in.	0.16-0.21mm
Driven gear	0.0051-0.0071 in.	0.13-0.18mm
Side clearance		
Drive gear	0.0031-0.0055 in.	0.08-0.14mm
Driven gear	0.0024-0.0047 in.	0.06-0.12mm
Relief spring		
Free length	1.8346 in.	46.6mm
Load	13.4 lbs. @ 1.5787 in.	60 N @ 40.1mm

TORQUE SPECIFICATIONS

Component	U.S.	Metric
1.5L		
Camshaft sprocket bolt	51 ft. lbs.	70 Nm
Connecting rod cap nuts	14.5 ft. lbs. + ¼ turn	20 Nm + ¼ turn
Coolant temperature senders		
Auto. trans. sender	60 inch lbs.	7.5 Nm
Condenser fan sender	8 ft. lbs.	11 Nm
Engine control unit sender	14-29 ft. lbs	20-40 Nm
Gauge sender	8 ft. lbs.	11 Nm
Crankshaft damper bolt	62 ft. lbs.	85 Nm
Crankshaft pulley bolts	10 ft. lbs.	13 Nm
Crossmember-to-frame bolts	51 ft. lbs.	70 Nm
Cylinder head bolts	53 ft. lbs.	73 Nm
Engine mount-to-engine bolts	42 ft. lbs.	58 Nm
Engine mount-to-frame bolt	72 ft. lbs.	100 Nm
Engine rear plate bolts	8 ft. lbs.	11 Nm
Engine roll stoppers-to-crossmember bolts	25 ft. lbs.	35 Nm
Engine roll stoppers-to-engine bolts	38 ft. lbs.	53 Nm
Engine support brackets-to-engine bolts	26 ft. lbs.	36 Nm
Exhaust manifold cover bolts		
Inner	22 ft. lbs.	30 Nm
Outer	7 ft. lbs.	9 Nm
Exhaust manifold-to-head bolts/nuts	13 ft. lbs.	18 Nm
Exhaust pipe-to-manifold nuts	36 ft. lbs.	50 Nm
Flywheel/flexplate bolts	98 ft. lbs.	135 Nm
Front case bolts	10 ft. lbs.	14 Nm
Front cover bolts	96 inch lbs.	11 Nm
Intake manifold-to-head bolts/nuts	13 ft. lbs.	18 Nm
Intake manifold support bolts	16 ft. lbs.	22 Nm
Main bearing cap bolts	38 ft. lbs.	53 Nm
Oil pan bolts	60 inch lbs.	40 Nm
Oil pan drain plug	29 ft. lbs.	40 Nm
Oil pan stud nuts	52 inch lbs.	6 Nm
Oil pressure switch	14 ft. lbs.	19 Nm
Oil pump cover bolts	84 inch lbs.	10 Nm
Oil pump pickup bolts	14 ft. lbs.	19 Nm
Oil pump relief plug	33 ft. lbs.	45 Nm
Power steering pump bracket bolts	29 ft. lbs.	40 Nm
Rear main seal case bolts	8 ft. lbs.	11 Nm
Rocker cover bolts	16 inch lbs.	1.8 Nm
Rocker shaft bolts		
1990	14-20 ft. lbs.	20-23 Nm
1991-93	23 ft. lbs.	32 Nm
Thermostat cover bolts	16 ft. lbs.	22 Nm
Timing belt tensioner center bolt	17 ft. lbs.	24 Nm
Timing belt tensioner lockbolt	17 ft. lbs.	24 Nm
Water inlet pipe bolts		
Long bolt	35 ft. lbs.	49 Nm
Short bolt	10 ft. lbs.	14 Nm
Water pump bolts	10 ft. lbs.	14 Nm

	1.6L	
Camshaft bearing cap bolts	15 ft. lbs.	21 Nm
Camshaft cover bolts	24-36 inch lbs.	2.5-3.5 Nm
Camshaft sprocket bolt	58-72 ft. lbs.	80-100 Nm
Connecting rod cap nuts	36-38 ft. lbs.	50-53 Nm
Coolant temperature senders		
Engine control unit sender	14-29 ft. lbs	20-40 Nm
Gauge sender	8 ft. lbs.	11 Nm
Crankshaft angle sensor nut	8 ft. lbs.	11 Nm
Crankshaft damper bolt	80-94 ft. lbs.	110-130 Nm
Crankshaft pulley bolts	14-22 ft. lbs.	20-30 Nm
Crossmember-to-frame bolts	51 ft. lbs.	70 Nm
Cylinder head bolts	65-72 ft. lbs.	90-100 Nm
Engine mount-to-engine bolts	42 ft. lbs.	58 Nm
Engine mount-to-frame bolt	72 ft. lbs.	100 Nm
Engine rear plate bolts	8 ft. lbs.	11 Nm
Engine roll stoppers-to-crossmember bolts	25 ft. lbs.	35 Nm
Engine roll stoppers-to-engine bolts	38 ft. lbs.	53 Nm
Engine support brackets-to-engine bolts	12-19 ft. lbs.	17-26 Nm
Exhaust manifold cover bolts	9-11 ft. lbs.	12-15 Nm
Exhaust manifold-to-head nuts	18-22 ft. lbs.	25-30 Nm
Exhaust pipe-to-manifold nuts	22-29 ft. lbs.	30-40 Nm
Flywheel/flexplate bolts	98 ft. lbs.	135 Nm
Front case bolts		
M8 × 30	20-26 ft. lbs.	27-34 Nm
Except M8 × 30	14-20 ft. lbs.	20-27 Nm
Front cover bolts	96 inch lbs.	11 Nm
Ignition coil bolts	14-24 ft. lbs.	20-27 Nm
Intake manifold-to-head bolts/nuts	22-30 ft. lbs.	30-42 Nm
Intake manifold support bolts	18-22 ft. lbs.	25-30 Nm
Main bearing cap bolts	47-51 ft. lbs.	65-70 Nm
Oil pan bolts	60 inch lbs.	40 Nm
Oil pan drain plug	29 ft. lbs.	40 Nm
Oil pan stud nuts	52 inch lbs.	6 Nm
Oil pressure switch	6-8 ft. lbs.	8-12 Nm
Oil pump cover bolts	11-13 inch lbs.	15-18 Nm
Oil pump pickup bolts	14 ft. lbs.	19 Nm
Oil pump relief plug	14-20 ft. lbs.	20-27 Nm
Oil pump sprocket bolt	36-43 ft. lbs.	50-60 Nm
Power steering pump bracket bolts	29 ft. lbs.	40 Nm
Power transistor unit bolts	8 ft. lbs.	11 Nm
Rear main seal case bolts	8 ft. lbs.	11 Nm
Thermostat cover bolts	16 ft. lbs.	22 Nm
Timing belt tensioner center bolt	17 ft. lbs.	24 Nm
Timing belt tensioner lockbolt	17 ft. lbs.	24 Nm
Water inlet pipe bolts		
Long bolt	35 ft. lbs.	49 Nm
Short bolt	10 ft. lbs.	14 Nm
Water pump bolts	10 ft. lbs.	14 Nm

	1990 1.8L	
A/C compressor lockbolt	17-20 ft. lbs.	23-27 Nm
Camshaft bearing cap bolts		
8mm × 65mm bolts	15 ft. lbs.	21 Nm
6mm × 20 mm bolts	9 ft. lbs.	12 Nm
Camshaft sprocket bolt	58-72 ft. lbs.	80-100 Nm
Connecting rod bearing cap nuts	24-25 ft. lbs.	32-35 Nm
Coolant temperature sending units		
Auto. trans. sender	48-84 inch lbs.	6-9 Nm
Control unit sender	14-29 ft. lbs.	20-40 Nm
Gauge sender	84-108 inch lbs.	10-12 Nm
Crankshaft pulley bolts	11-13 ft. lbs.	15-18 Nm
Crankshaft sprocket bolt	80-94 ft. lbs.	110-130 Nm
Cylinder head bolts	51-54 ft. lbs.	70-75 Nm
Engine crossmember-to-frame bolts	43-58 ft. lbs.	60-80 Nm
Engine front roll insulator nut	33-43 ft. lbs.	45-60 Nm
Engine front roll stopper-to-crossmember bolts	22-29 ft. lbs.	30-40 Nm
Engine front roll stopper bracket bolts	40-54 ft. lbs.	55-75 Nm
Engine front support bracket bolts	37-50 ft. lbs.	50-70 Nm
Engine left mount bracket-to-engine bolts/nuts	36-47 ft. lbs.	50-65 Nm
Engine left mount insulator nuts		
Large	65-80 ft. lbs.	90-110 Nm
Small	33-43 ft. lbs.	45-60 Nm
Engine left support bracket bolts	22-30 ft. lbs.	30-42 Nm
Engine rear roll insulator nut	33-43 ft. lbs.	45-60 Nm
Engine rear roll stopper bracket bolts	80-94 ft. lbs.	110-130 Nm
Engine rear roll stopper-to-crossmember bolts	33-43 ft. lbs.	45-60 Nm
Exhaust manifold-to-head bolts	11-14 ft. lbs.	15-20 Nm
Exhaust manifold inner cover bolts	14-20 ft. lbs.	20-28 Nm
Exhaust manifold outer cover bolts		
Front bolts	20-24 ft. lbs.	27-33 Nm
Side bolts	84 inch lbs.	10 Nm
Exhaust pipe-to-manifold nuts	22-29 ft. lbs.	30-40 Nm
Exhaust pipe support bracket bolts	14-22 ft. lbs.	20-30 Nm
Flywheel/flexplate bolts	94-101 ft. lbs.	130-140 Nm
Front case bolts	11-13 ft. lbs.	15-18 Nm
Main bearing cap bolts	37-39 ft. lbs.	50-55 Nm
Intake manifold-to-head bolts/nuts	11-14 ft. lbs.	15-20 Nm
Intake manifold-to-support bolts	15-22 ft. lbs.	21-31 Nm
Intake plenum-to-manifold nuts	11-14 ft. lbs.	15-20 Nm
Oil filter bracket bolts	9-11 ft. lbs.	12-15 Nm
Oil pan		
Bolts	48-72 inch lbs.	6-8 Nm
Nuts	48-60 inch lbs.	5-7 Nm
Oil pan drain plug	26-32 ft. lbs.	35-45 Nm
Oil pickup tube nuts	11-15 ft. lbs.	15-22 Nm
Oil pressure switch	84-108 inch lbs.	8-12 Nm
Oil pump cover bolts	72-84 inch lbs.	8-10 Nm
Oil pump relief valve plug	29-36 ft. lbs.	40-50 Nm
Oil pump sprocket nut	25-28 ft. lbs.	34-40 Nm
Oil return pipe bolts	72-84 inch lbs.	8-10 Nm
Rocker cover bolts	48-60 inch lbs.	5-7 Nm
Roll rod-to-bracket bolt/nut	33-43 ft. lbs.	45-60 Nm
Roll rod-to-engine bolt	39-47 ft. lbs.	55-65 Nm
Thermostat housing bolts	12-14 ft. lbs.	17-20 Nm
Timing belt cover bolts	84-96 inch lbs.	10-12 Nm
Timing belt tensioner bolts/nuts	16-22 ft. lbs.	22-30 Nm
Water inlet pipe bolts		
Long bolt	31-40 ft. lbs.	43-55 Nm
Short bolt	84-108 inch lbs.	10-12 Nm
Water pump bolts		
Head mark "4"	9-11 ft. lbs.	12-15 Nm
Head mark "7"	14-20 ft. lbs.	20-27 Nm
Water pump pulley bolts	72-84 inch lbs.	8-10 Nm

	1992-93 1.8L	
Alternator lockbolt	17 ft. lbs.	23 Nm
Alternator pivot bolt	33 ft. lbs.	45 Nm
Camshaft sprocket bolt	65 ft. lbs.	90 Nm
Connecting rod cap bolts	14.5 ft. lbs. + ¼ turn	20 Nm + ¼ turn
Crankshaft damper bolt	134 ft. lbs.	185 Nm
Cylinder head bolts	(1)	(1)
Distributor holddown bolt	9 ft. lbs.	12 Nm
Engine lifting eye	9 ft. lbs.	12 Nm
Engine mounts		
Colt		
Engine mount-to-engine bolts	42 ft. lbs.	58 Nm
Engine mount-to-frame bolt	72 ft. lbs.	100 Nm
Engine rear plate bolts	8 ft. lbs.	11 Nm
Engine roll stoppers-to-crossmember bolts	25 ft. lbs.	35 Nm
Engine roll stoppers-to-engine bolts	38 ft. lbs.	53 Nm
Engine support brackets-to-engine bolts	26 ft. lbs.	36 Nm
Vista		
Engine mount insulator bolt	25 ft. lbs.	35 Nm
Engine mount bracket nuts	42 ft. lbs.	58 Nm
Engine mount stopper nuts	51 ft. lbs.	70 Nm
Exhaust Manifold		
Upper nuts	13 ft. lbs.	18 Nm
Lower nuts	22 ft. lbs.	30 Nm
Exhaust manifold cover bolts		
Front cover outer bolts	22 ft. lbs.	30 Nm
Front cover side bolts	7 ft. lbs.	9 Nm
Inner cover bolts	17 ft. lbs.	24 Nm
Exhaust pipe bracket bolts		
Colt	18 ft. lbs.	25 Nm
Vista	22-29 ft. lbs.	30-40 Nm
Exhaust pipe-to-manifold nuts	29-36 ft. lbs.	40-50 Nm
Flywheel/flexplate bolts	72 ft. lbs.	100 Nm
Intake manifold bolts/nuts	13 ft. lbs.	18 Nm
Main bearing cap bolts	14 ft. lbs. + ¼ turn	20 Nm + ¼ turn
Oil drain plug	29 ft. lbs.	40 Nm
Oil pan bolts	60 inch lbs.	7 Nm
Oil pump case	11 ft. lbs.	14 Nm
Oil pump case cover	84 inch lbs.	10 Nm
Oil pump pickup tube bolts	14 ft. lbs.	19 Nm
Oil pump relief plug	35 ft. lbs.	45 Nm
Oil pressure switch	84 inch lbs.	10 Nm
Power steering pump front bolt	17 ft. lbs.	24 Nm
Power steering pump rear bolt	29 ft. lbs.	40 Nm
Radiator support bolts	9 ft. lbs.	12 Nm
Rear main seal case bolts	96 inch lbs.	11 Nm
Rear plate bolts	96 inch lbs.	11 Nm
Rocker arm shaft bolts	21-25 ft. lbs.	29-35 Nm
Rocker cover bolts	26-30 inch lbs.	3.0-3.5 Nm
Roll stopper bolts	40 ft. lbs.	55 Nm
Temperature gauge sending unit	96 inch lbs.	11 Nm
Thermostat case housing bolts	16-18 ft. lbs.	22-25 Nm
Thermostat housing bolts	10 ft. lbs.	14 Nm
Timing belt cover bolts	84 inch lbs.	10 Nm
Timing belt tensioner bolt	18 ft. lbs.	24 Nm
Timing belt tensioner spring bolt	33 ft. lbs.	45 Nm
Water pump bolts	18 ft. lbs.	24 Nm

(1) 1. Tighten to 54 ft. lbs. (75 Nm)
     2. Fully loosen all bolts in reverse order
     3. Tighten to 14 ft. lbs. (20 Nm)
     4. Tighten an additional ¼ turn
     5. Tighten an additional ¼ turn

	2.0L	
Camshaft bearing cap bolts	15-19 ft. lbs.	20-27 Nm
Camshaft sprocket bolt	58-72 ft. lbs.	80-100 Nm
Connecting rod cap nuts	37-38 ft. lbs.	50-53 Nm
Coolant temperature sending units		
Control unit sender	15-28 ft. lbs.	20-40 Nm
Cooling fan sender	60-84 inch lbs.	6-8 Nm
Gauge sender	9-13 ft. lbs.	12-18 Nm
Crankshaft pulley bolts	15-21 ft. lbs.	20-30 Nm
Crankshaft sprocket bolt	80-94 ft. lbs.	110-130 Nm
Cylinder head bolts	65-72 ft. lbs.	90-100 Nm
Engine mount bracket bolts	22-30 ft. lbs.	30-42 Nm
Engine mount insulator		
Large bolt	44-57 ft. lbs.	60-80 Nm
Small bolts	22-28 ft. lbs.	30-40 Nm
Exhaust manifold-to-head nuts	11-15 ft. lbs.	15-20 Nm
Exhaust manifold cover bolts	10 ft. lbs.	15 Nm
Exhaust pipe clamp bolts		
2WD	15-21 ft. lbs.	20-30 Nm
4WD	22-28 ft. lbs.	30-40 Nm
Exhaust pipe-to-manifold	15-21 ft. lbs.	20-30 Nm
Exhaust pipe support bracket bolts	22-30 ft. lbs.	30-42 Nm
Flywheel/flexplate bolts	94-101 ft. lbs.	130-140 Nm
Front case bolts	15-19 ft. lbs.	20-27 Nm
Front engine support bracket bolts	37-50 ft. lbs.	50-70 Nm
Front roll stopper bracket bolts	40-54 ft. lbs.	55-75 Nm
Front roll stopper bracket-to-crossmember bolts	29-36 ft. lbs.	40-50 Nm
Intake manifold-to-head bolts/nuts	11-15 ft. lbs.	15-20 Nm
Intake manifold support-to-engine bolts		
2WD	13-18 ft. lbs.	18-25 Nm
4WD	22-30 ft. lbs.	30-42 Nm
Intake manifold support-to-manifold bolts	13-18 ft. lbs.	18-25 Nm
Intake plenum-to-manifold bolts/nuts	11-15 ft. lbs.	15-20 Nm
Left engine support bracket bolts	22-30 ft. lbs.	30-42 Nm
Main bearing cap bolts	37-39 ft. lbs.	50-55 Nm
Oil filter bracket bolts	11-15 ft. lbs.	15-22 Nm
Oil pan bolts	48-72 inch lbs.	6-8 Nm
Oil pan drain plug	26-32 ft. lbs.	35-45 Nm
Oil pickup bolts	11-15 ft. lbs.	15-22 Nm
Oil pressure switch	9 ft. lbs.	12 Nm
Oil pump cover bolts	11-13 ft. lbs.	15-18 Nm
Oil pump driven gear bolt	25-28 ft. lbs.	34-40 Nm
Oil pump relief plug	29-36 ft. lbs.	40-50 Nm
Oil pump sprocket bolt/nut	37-43 ft. lbs.	50-60 Nm
Radiator support bolts	7-14 ft. lbs.	10-20 Nm
Rear insulator-to-crossmember bolts (4WD)	22-28 ft. lbs.	30-40 Nm
Rear insulator-to-engine bracket (4WD)	22-28 ft. lbs.	30-40 Nm
Rear main seal case bolts	9 ft. lbs.	12 Nm
Rear roll stopper bracket bolt	80-94 ft. lbs.	110-130 Nm
Rear roll stopper bracket-to-crossmember (2WD)	44-57 ft. lbs.	60-80 Nm
Rear roll stopper insulator bolt (2WD)	22-28 ft. lbs.	30-40 Nm
Rear roll stopper support-to-bracket (2WD)	22-28 ft. lbs.	30-40 Nm
Rocker cover bolts	48-60 inch lbs.	5-7 Nm
Rocker shaft bolts	14-15 ft. lbs.	19-21 Nm
Silent shaft belt tensioner bolt	11-15 ft. lbs.	15-22 Nm
Silent shaft sprocket bolt	31-35 ft. lbs.	43-49 Nm
Thermostat housing bolts	14 ft. lbs.	20 Nm
Timing belt cover bolts	9 ft. lbs.	12 Nm
Timing belt tensioner bolt/nut	32-39 ft. lbs.	43-55 Nm
Water inlet pipe bolts		
Long bolt	32-39 ft. lbs.	43-55 Nm
Short bolt	10 ft. lbs.	15 Nm
Water pump bolts	10 ft. lbs.	15 Nm
Water pump pulley bolts	84 inch lbs.	10 Nm

	1992 2.4L	
A/C compressor mounting bolts	36 ft. lbs.	50 Nm
Camshaft front bearing cap bolts	17 ft. lbs.	23 Nm
Camshaft sprocket bolt	65 ft. lbs.	90 Nm
Connecting rod cap nuts	38 ft. lbs.	52 Nm
Crankshaft sprocket bolt	80-94 ft. lbs.	110-130 Nm
Cylinder head bolts	76-83 ft. lbs.	105-115 Nm
Engine mounts		
Left	22-30 ft. lbs.	30-34 Nm
Front	36-51 ft. lbs.	50-70 Nm
Engine roll stopper bracket bolts		
Front	40-54 ft. lbs.	55-75 Nm
Rear	80-94 ft. lbs.	110-130 Nm
Exhaust manifold nuts	22 ft. lbs.	30 Nm
Exhaust manifold cover bolts	10 ft. lbs.	13 Nm
Exhaust pipe bracket bolts	22-30 ft. lbs.	30-34 Nm
Exhaust pipe-to-manifold nuts	29-36 ft. lbs.	40-50 Nm
Flywheel/flexplate bolts	94-101 ft. lbs.	130-140 Nm
Front case bolts	14-20 ft. lbs.	20-27 Nm
Front cover bolts	84-108 inch lbs.	10-12 Nm
Intake manifold bolts/nuts	13 ft. lbs.	18 Nm
Main bearing cap bolts	38 ft. lbs.	53 Nm
Oil filter bracket bolts	11-16 ft. lbs.	15-22 Nm
Oil pan bolts	48-72 inch lbs.	6-8 ft. lbs.
Oil pan drain plug	25-33 ft. lbs.	35-45 Nm
Oil pressure switch	72-108 inch lbs.	8-12 Nm
Oil pump cover bolts	11-13 ft. lbs.	15-18 Nm
Oil pump driven gear bolt	25-29 ft. lbs.	34-40 Nm
Oil pump pickup bolts	14 ft. lbs.	19 Nm
Oil pump relief plug	29-36 ft. lbs.	40-50 Nm
Power steering pump mounting bolts	29 ft. lbs.	40 Nm
Radiator support bolts	9 ft. lbs.	12 Nm
Rear main seal case bolts	84-108 inch lbs.	10-12 Nm
Rocker cover bolts	48 inch lbs.	6 Nm
Rocker shaft bolts	15 ft. lbs.	21 Nm
Silent shaft belt tensioner bolt	11-16 ft. lbs.	15-22 Nm
Temperature gauge sending unit	96 inch lbs.	11 Nm
Tensioner pulley bracket bolts	17-20 ft. lbs.	23-27 Nm
Timing belt tensioner bolts	35 ft. lbs.	49 Nm
Water pump bolts	10 ft. lbs.	14 Nm
Water pump pulley bolts	84 inch lbs.	9 Nm

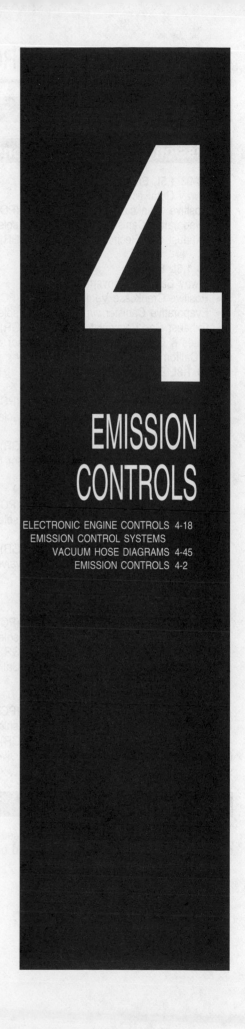

4

EMISSION
CONTROLS

EMISSION CONTROLS

Emission Control Applications

1990-93 1.5L Engine
- 3-way Catalytic Converter
- Positive Crankcase Ventilation Valve (PCV)
- Evaporative Canister w/purge control solenoid
- Exhaust Gas Recirculation system (EGR) — California only

1990 1.6L Engine
- 3-way Catalytic Converter
- Positive Crankcase Ventilation Valve (PCV)
- Evaporative Canister w/purge control solenoid
- Exhaust Gas Recirculation system (EGR) w/thermo valve (49 states & Canada, or temperature sensor & control solenoid valve (California)

1990 1.8L Engine
- 3-way Catalytic Converter
- Positive Crankcase Ventilation Valve (PCV)
- Evaporative Canister w/purge control solenoid & 2-way valve
- Exhaust Gas Recirculation system (EGR) w/thermo valve (49 states & Canada, or temperature sensor (California)

1990-91 2.0L Engine
- 3-way Catalytic Converter
- Positive Crankcase Ventilation Valve (PCV)
- Evaporative Canister w/purge control solenoid & 2-way valve
- Exhaust Gas Recirculation system (EGR) w/thermo valve (49 states & Canada, or control solenoid valve & temperature sensor (California)

1992-93 1.8L Engine
- 3-way Catalytic Converter
- Positive Crankcase Ventilation Valve (PCV)
- Evaporative Canister w/purge control solenoid
- Exhaust Gas Recirculation system (EGR) w/control solenoid valve & temperature sensor — California only

1992-93 2.4L Engine
- 3-way Catalytic Converter
- Positive Crankcase Ventilation Valve (PCV)
- Evaporative Canister w/purge control solenoid
- Exhaust Gas Recirculation system (EGR) w/thermo valve (49 states & Canada, or control solenoid valve & temperature sensor (California)

Catalytic Converter

The converter acts together with the closed-loop air/fuel ratio control system (See Section 5), and, based on the oxygen sensor signal, reduces the level of nitrogen oxide (NOx), hydrocarbons (HC) and carbon monoxide (CO).

This unit is filled with a catalyst to oxidize hydrocarbons and carbon monoxide in the exhaust gasses.

MAINTENANCE

1. Check the core for cracks and damages.
2. If the idle carbon monoxide and hydrocarbon content exceeds specifications and the ignition timing and idle mixture are correct, the converter must be replaced.

REPLACEMENT

See Section 3.

Crankcase Ventilation System

▶ **See Figures 1, 2, 3, 4, 5, 6, 7, 8 and 9**

OPERATION

A closed type crankcase ventilation system is used to prevent engine blow-by gases from escaping into the atmosphere.

See the accompanying illustrations for PCV valve location.

SERVICE

To check for a clogged PCV valve with the engine running, remove the valve from its mounting. A hissing sound should be heard and vacuum should be felt from the inlet (bottom) side of the valve. Turn off the engine, shake the valve. A clicking sound should come from the valve when it is shaken. If the valve fails either of these tests, replace it.

REMOVAL & INSTALLATION

Remove the valve from its mounting. Disconnect the hose from the valve. Install a new valve into the hose and push the valve into the mounting.

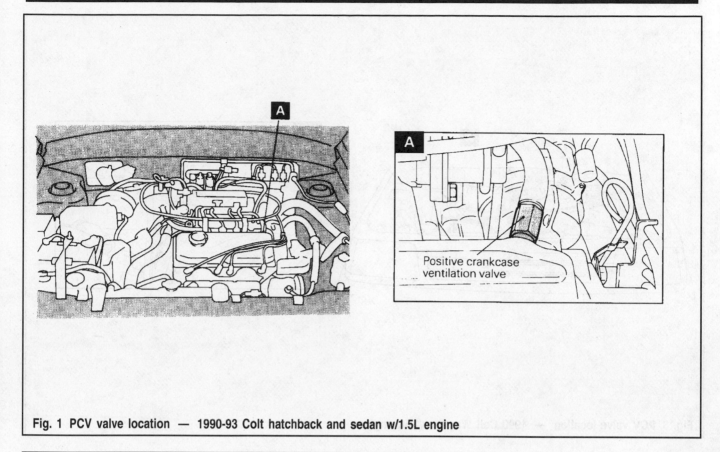

Fig. 1 PCV valve location — 1990-93 Colt hatchback and sedan w/1.5L engine

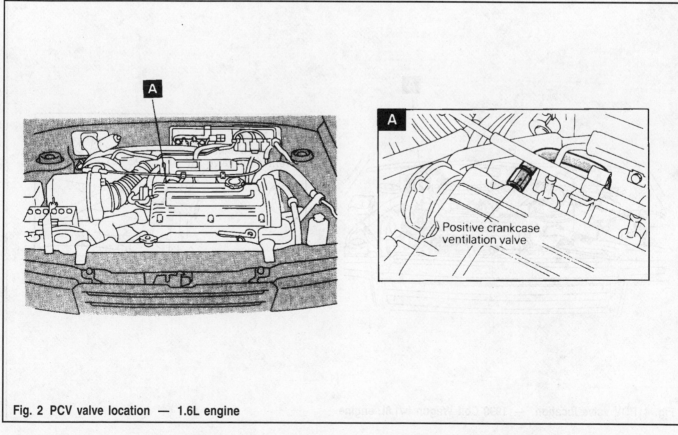

Fig. 2 PCV valve location — 1.6L engine

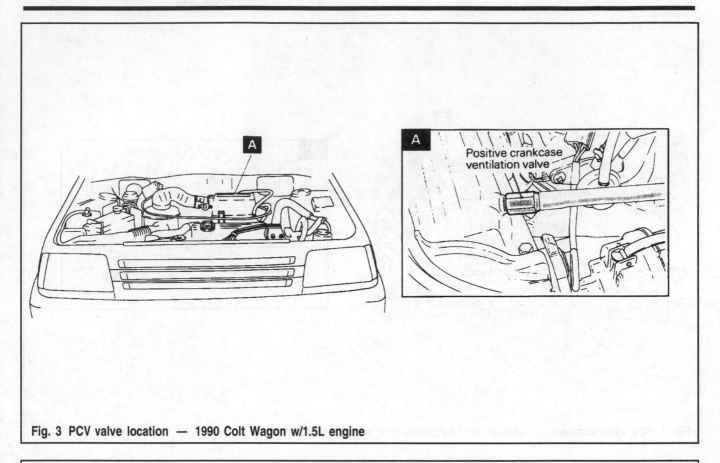

Fig. 3 PCV valve location — 1990 Colt Wagon w/1.5L engine

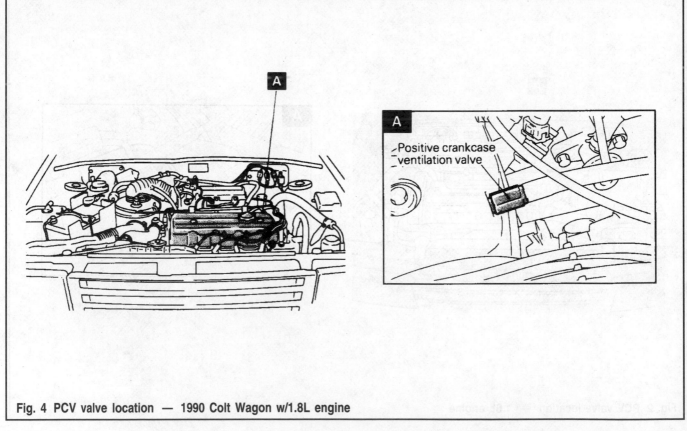

Fig. 4 PCV valve location — 1990 Colt Wagon w/1.8L engine

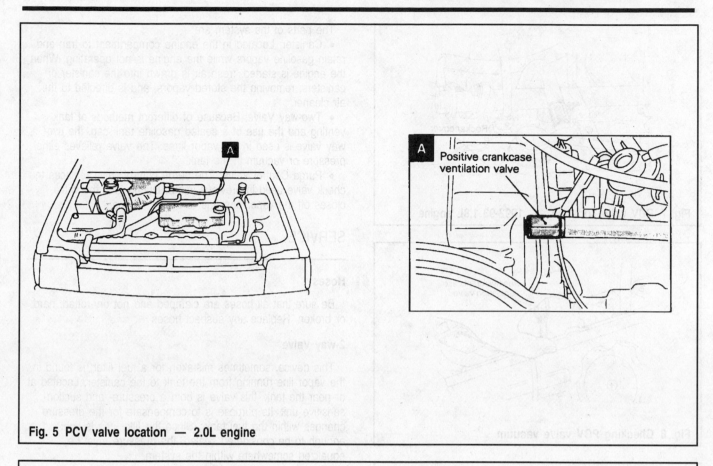

Fig. 5 PCV valve location — 2.0L engine

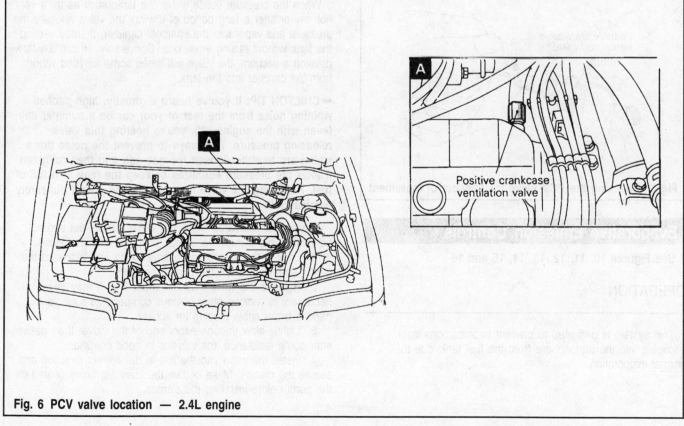

Fig. 6 PCV valve location — 2.4L engine

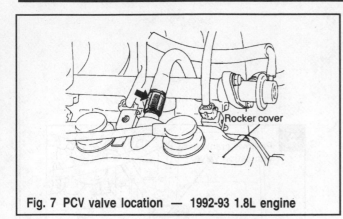

Fig. 7 PCV valve location — 1992-93 1.8L engine

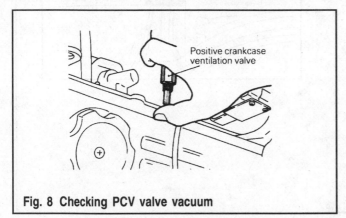

Fig. 8 Checking PCV valve vacuum

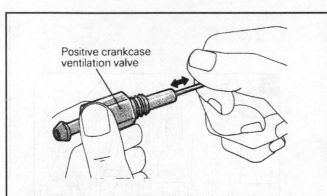

Fig. 9 Checking the PCV valve for freedom of movement

Evaporative Emission Controls

▶ **See Figures 10, 11, 12, 13, 14, 15 and 16**

OPERATION

This system is designed to prevent hydrocarbons from escaping into the atmosphere from the fuel tank, due to normal evaporation.

The parts of the system are:
- Canister: Located in the engine compartment to trap and retain gasoline vapors while the engine is not operating. When the engine is started, fresh air is drawn into the canister or canisters, removing the stored vapors, and is directed to the air cleaner.
- Two-way Valve: Because of different methods of tank venting and the use of a sealed gasoline tank cap, the two-way valve is used in the vapor lines. The valve relieves either pressure or vacuum in the tank.
- Purge Control Valve: The purge control valve replaces the check valve used in previous years. During idle, the valve closes off the vapor passage to the air cleaner.

SERVICE

Hoses

Be sure that all hoses are clamped and not dry-rotted, hard or broken. Replace any suspect hoses

2-way Valve

This device, sometimes mistaken for a fuel filter, is found in the vapor line running from the tank to the canister. Located at or near the tank, this valve is both a pressure- and suction-sensitive unit. Its purpose is to compensate for the pressure changes within the fuel tank. (Since the filler cap is tight enough to be considered sealed, the pressure must be equalized somewhere within the system.

When the pressure builds within the tank, such as on a very hot day or after a long period of driving, the valve releases the pressure and vapor into the charcoal canister, thereby venting the tank without raising emissions. Conversely, should the tank develop a vacuum, the valve will bleed some air (and vapor) from the canister into the tank.

➡**CHILTON TIP: If you've heard a ghostly, high-pitched whining noise from the rear of your car on a summer day (even with the engine off), you're hearing this valve releasing pressure. Two ways to prevent the noise (for a while) are to either loosen the gas cap and then retighten it after the pressure equalizes or keep the tank 1/2-3/4 full of fuel. Replacing the valve may change the sound but rarely eliminates it.**

The control pressures within the valve are pre-set and not adjustable, but a quick check can be performed as follows:
1. Look at the valve and observe which end is toward the tank. Label or diagram the correct position.
2. Remove the valve from the vapor line. It may be necessary to remove other obvious components such as a parking brake cable bracket for access.
3. Lightly blow through either end of the valve. If air passes after some resistance, the valve is in good condition.
4. Install the valve into the line in the correct direction and secure the clamps. Make certain the lines are firmly seated on the ports before installing the clamps.

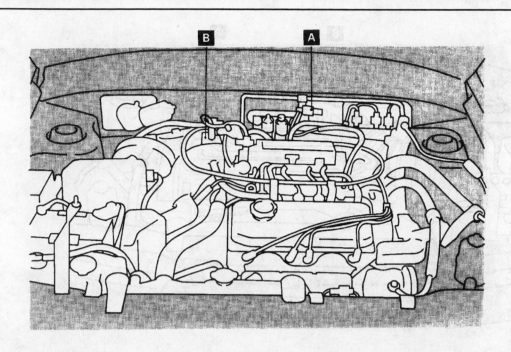

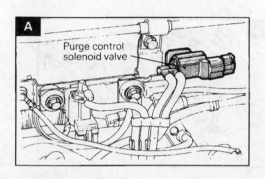

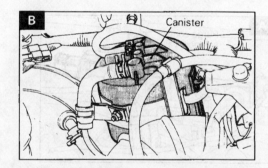

Fig. 10 Evaporative Emission Control System — 1990-92 Colt hatchback and sedan w/1.5L engine

Purge Control Solenoid Valve

▶ See Figures 17, 18, 19, 20, 21, 22, 23, 24, 25, 26, 27 and 28

First check all the hoses and connections for proper attachment, cracks, bends and leaks. Many problems relate simply to poor mechanical connections within the system or restricted hoses.

VACUUM TEST

1. Disconnect the vacuum hose (red stripes) from the throttle body and connect it to a hand-held vacuum pump. Plug the nipple from which the hose was removed.

2. Allow the engine to cool completely, or, with a cold engine, apply 14.8 in.Hg vacuum. The vacuum should hold.

3. Start the engine and allow it to idle. Increase engine speed to 3,00 rpm. Vacuum should hold throughout this range.

The engine temperature should not exceed 140°F (60°C) for this test.

4. Allow the engine to idle until engine temperature exceeds 158°F (70°C). Vacuum should hold at idle. Shut the engine off.

5. With 14.8 in.Hg vacuum applied and the engine temperature still above 158°F (70°C), start the engine and increase engine speed to 3,000 rpm within 3 minutes. A vacuum leakdown should occur. Return the engine to idle.

6. Reapply vacuum and, after 3 minutes, return the engine to 3,000 rpm. Vacuum should be held momentarily, then leakdown.

➡ At altitudes above 7,200 ft. (2,200 m), Step 6 does not apply.

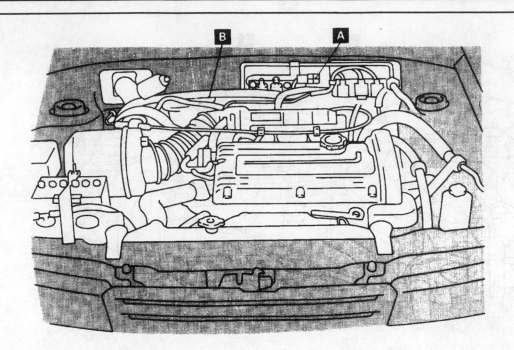

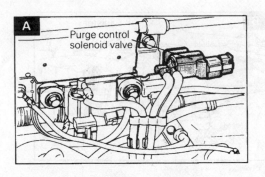

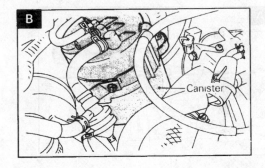

Fig. 11 Evaporative Emission Control System — 1.6L engine

ELECTRICAL TEST

1. Disconnect the vacuum hoses from the valve.
2. Disconnect the wiring harness from the valve
3. Connect a hand-held vacuum pump to the nipple from which the red striped hose was removed and apply 14.8 in.Hg vacuum. Vacuum should hold.
4. Using a jumper wire connected to a 12 volt source, apply battery voltage as shown in the accompanying illustration. Vacuum should leakdown.
5. With an ohmmeter, check the resistance between the valve's terminals. Resistance should be 36-44ω @ 68°F (20°C).
6. If the valve fails any test, it should be replaced.

REMOVAL & INSTALLATION

Charcoal Canister

The canister or canisters used on these models is replaced periodically. No other maintenance is necessary except for an occasional check of connecting hose condition. To replace the canister:

1. Remove the two connecting hoses from the canister.
2. Loosen and remove the canister retaining band bolt.
3. Remove the canister.
4. Install the canister and connect the hoses. Replace any brittle hoses.

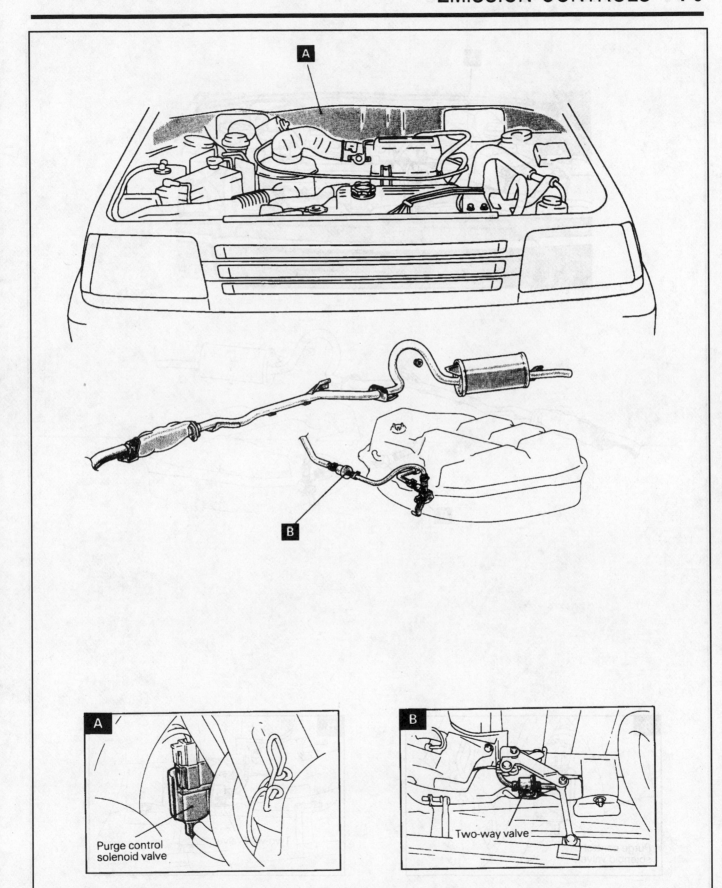

Fig. 12 Evaporative Emission Control System — 1990 Colt Wagon w/1.5L engine

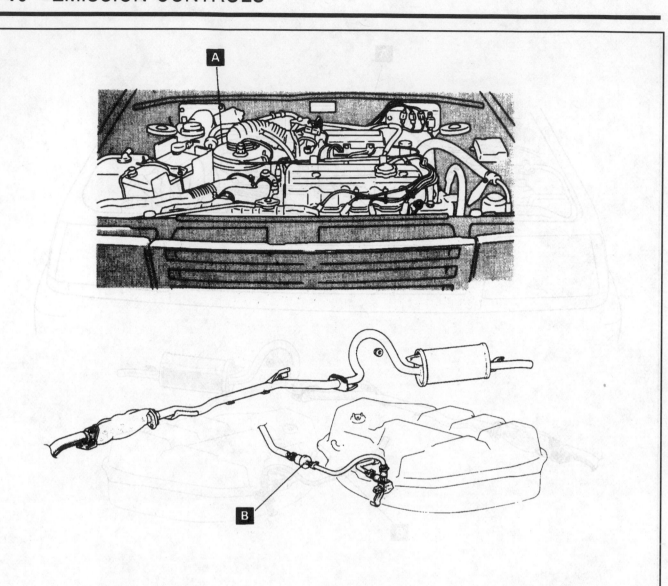

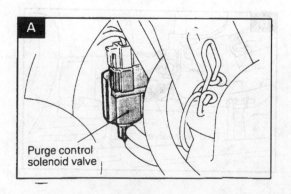

Purge control
solenoid valve

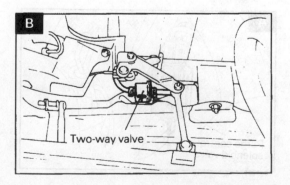

Two-way valve

Fig. 13 Evaporative Emission Control System — 1990 Colt Wagon w/1.8L engine

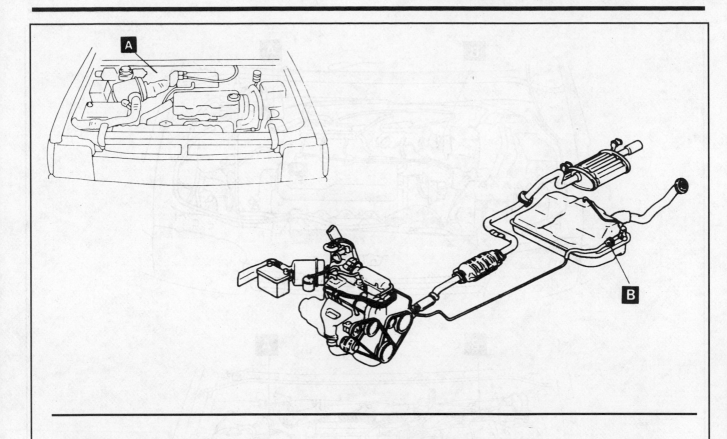

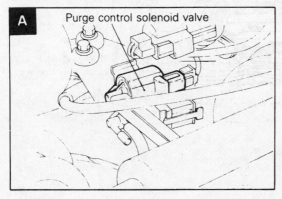

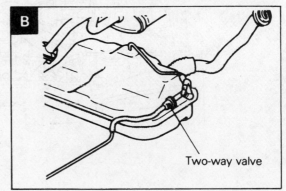

Fig. 14 Evaporative Emission Control System — 2.0L engine

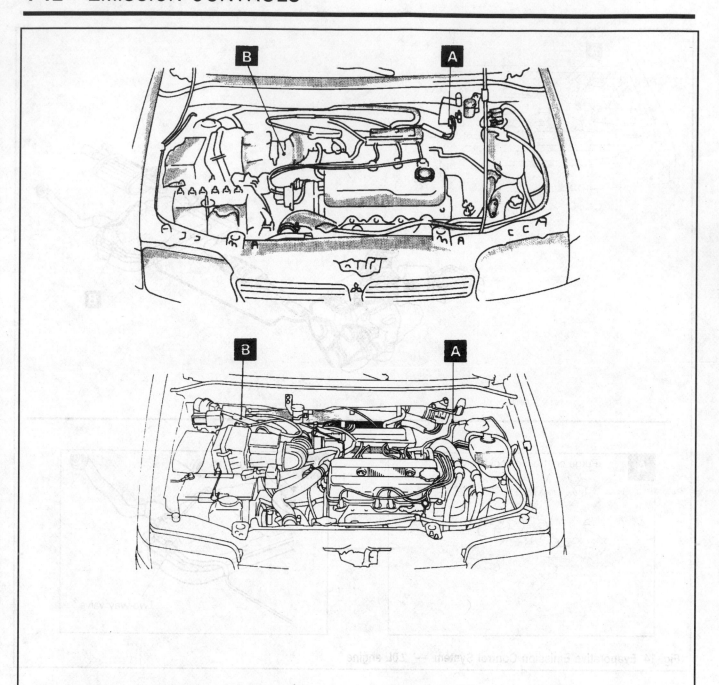

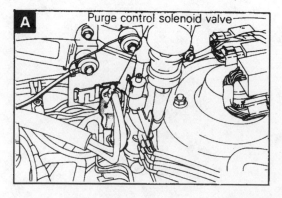

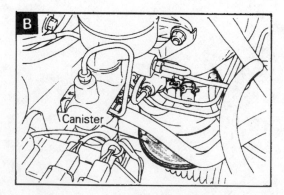

Fig. 15 Evaporative Emission Control System — 1992-93 Vista — 1.8L top; 2.4L bottom

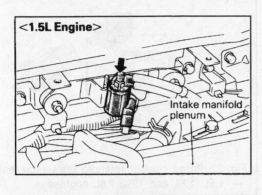

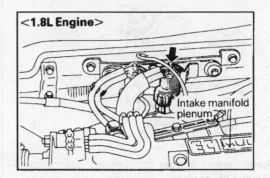

Evaporative emission (EVAP) canister

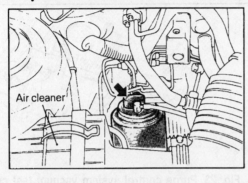

Fig. 16 Evaporative Emission Control System — 1993 Colt hatchback

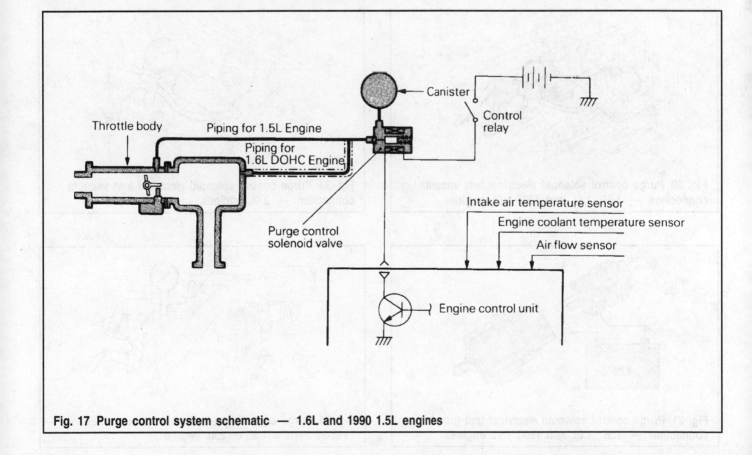

Fig. 17 Purge control system schematic — 1.6L and 1990 1.5L engines

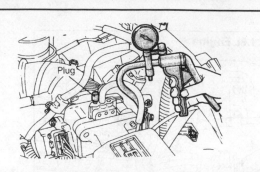

Fig. 18 Purge control system vacuum test connection — 1.5L and 1990 1.8L engines

Fig. 19 Purge control system vacuum test connection — 1.6L engine

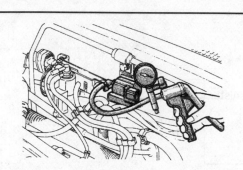

Fig. 20 Purge control solenoid electrical test vacuum connection — 1.5L, 1.6L and 1990 1.8L engines

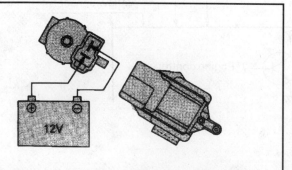

Fig. 21 Purge control solenoid electrical test jumper connection — 1.5L, 1.6L and 1990 1.8L engines

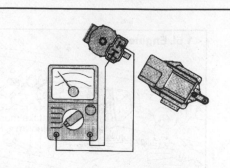

Fig. 22 Purge control solenoid resistance test connection — 1.5L, 1.6L and 1990 1.8L engines

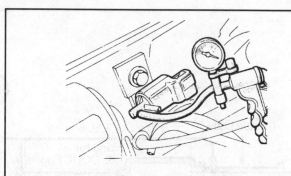

Fig. 23 Purge control system vacuum test connection — 2.0L engine

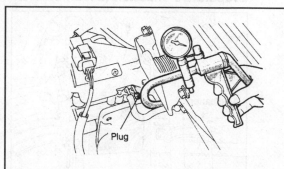

Fig. 24 Purge control solenoid electrical test vacuum connection — 2.0L engines

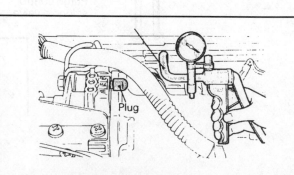

Fig. 25 Purge control system vacuum test connection — 1992-93 Vista w/1.8L or 2.4L engine

Fig. 26 Purge control solenoid electrical test vacuum connection — 1992-93 Vista w/1.8L or 2.4L engine

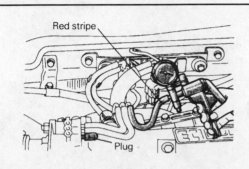

Red stripe

Plug

Fig. 27 Purge control system vacuum test connection — 1993 Colt

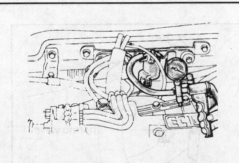

Fig. 28 Purge control solenoid electrical test vacuum connection — 1993 Colt

Exhaust Gas Recirculation System (EGR)

▶ See Figures 29, 30, 31 and 32

OPERATION

Exhaust Gas Recirculation is used to reduce peak flame temperatures in the combustion chamber. A small amount of exhaust gas is diverted from the exhaust manifold and re-entered into the intake manifold, where it mixes with the air/fuel charge and enters the cylinder to be burned. Cooler combustion reduces the formation of Nitrogen Oxide (NO_2) emissions.

The system consists of the EGR valve, controlling the flow of exhaust gas and various vacuum and/or electric controls to keep the EGR from working at the incorrect time.

No EGR is required when the engine is cold due to lower flame temperatures in the engine. EGR under these conditions would produce rough running so EGR function is cut off either by a thermo valve or by the fuel injection computer (which is monitoring coolant temperature.) Additionally, EGR flow is cut off at warm idle to eliminate any roughness or stumble on initial acceleration.

Cooler combustion temperatures also result in slightly reduced power output. This isn't felt during normal, part-throttle driving and the emission benefits outweigh the slight loss. However, in a wide-open throttle situation a power reduction is not desirable; full power could be the margin of success in a passing or accident avoidance situation. For this reason, EGR function is eliminated when the engine goes on wide-open throttle. Normally, the vacuum to the EGR valve can overcome the spring tension within the valve and hold it open. When the throttle opens fully, vacuum to the EGR is reduced and the spring closes the valve.

A common symptom of EGR malfunction is light engine ping at part throttle, particularly noticeable under load such as going uphill or carrying several passengers. An EGR valve which fails to close properly can also cause a rough or uneven idle. If the engine is correctly tuned and other common causes (vacuum leaks, bad plug wires, etc.) are eliminated, EGR function should considered as a potential cause when troubleshooting a rough idle.

Since the majority of EGR components do not require routine maintenance and should not clog or corrode if unleaded gas is used, you should check all other reasonable causes of a problem before checking this system.

TESTING

System Test

ALL EXCEPT CALIFORNIA

1. Allow the engine to cool overnight. Since the EGR system works differently for warm and cold engines, a completely cold engine is required for testing.

2. Disconnect the vacuum hose with the green stripe from the throttle body. Attach the end of the hose to vacuum pump.

3. Plug the port from which the hose was removed. Start the engine and attempt to draw a vacuum with the hand pump. The system should NOT hold vacuum with the engine cold and running at idle.

4. Allow the engine to run at idle until an engine temperature of 176°F (80°C), or higher, is reached. Draw a vacuum of 1.6 in.Hg and listen to the engine idle. There should be no change in the engine. Increase the vacuum to 7.9 in.Hg. As the correct vacuum is reached, the idle should roughen, become uneven, or possibly stall as the EGR valve opens and admits exhaust gas. The system should hold vacuum while the valve is open.

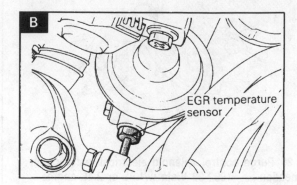

Fig. 29 EGR system — 1990-92 Colt hatchback and sedan w/1.5L — California only

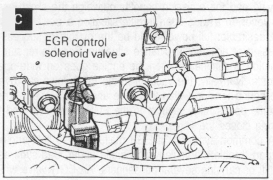

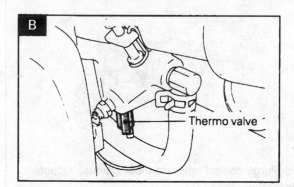

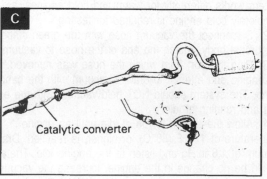

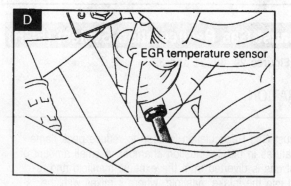

Fig. 30 EGR system — 2.0L engine

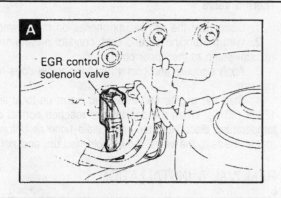

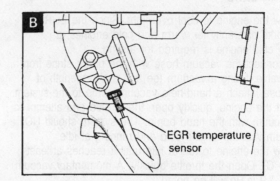

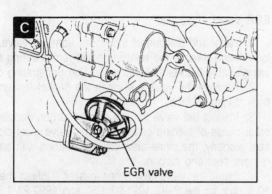

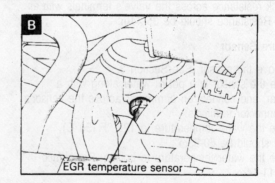

Fig. 31 EGR system — 1992-93 Vista w/1.8L engine

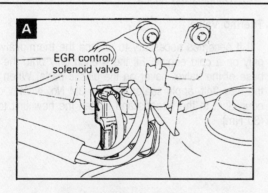

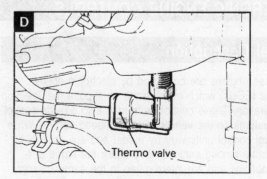

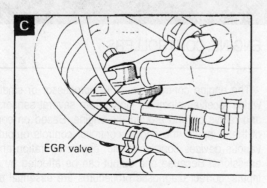

Fig. 32 EGR system — 2.4L engine

CALIFORNIA CARS

1. Allow the engine to cool overnight. Since the EGR system works differently for warm and cold engines, a completely cold engine is required for testing.

2. Disconnect the vacuum hose with the green stripe from the EGR valve. Using a vacuum tee and a short length of vacuum hose, attach a hand-held vacuum pump to the system.

3. Start the engine, quickly open the throttle and attempt to draw a vacuum with the hand pump. The system should NOT hold vacuum with the engine cold and running at idle.

4. Allow the engine to run at idle until it reaches at least 158°F (70°C). Open the throttle quickly. A momentary vacuum reading of 3.9 in.Hg will be noted.

EGR Valve

1. Disconnect the vacuum line from the EGR valve.
2. Connect a hand-held vacuum pump directly to the valve nipple.
3. Apply 20 in.Hg vacuum. Vacuum should be held.

Control Solenoid Valve

1. Disconnect the vacuum hose (yellow stripe/green stripe) from the control solenoid valve.
2. Disconnect the wiring harness from the valve.
3. Connect a hand-held vacuum pump to the valve's nipple.
4. Apply vacuum and check valve operation. The vacuum should not be held.
5. Apply battery voltage to the valve. Vacuum should be held.
6. Check resistance across the valve's terminals with an ohmmeter. Resistance should be 36-44ω.

Temperature Sensor

1. Remove the sensor. See Section 3.
2. Place the sensor in a pot of water along with a thermometer, and connect an ohmmeter across the sensor's harness connector terminals.
3. Raise the water temperature to 122 °F (50°C). Resistance should be 60-83ω.
4. Raise the water temperature to boiling. Resistance should be 11-14ω.

Thermo Valve

1. Disconnect the two vacuum hoses on the thermo valve.
2. With the engine off and cold, connect a hand-held vacuum pump to the upper port.
3. Apply vacuum and confirm that the valve does NOT hold vacuum.
4. Start the engine and allow it to warm up to at least 176°F (80°C). When the coolant has reached normal operating temperature, disconnect the appropriate hose as before and repeat the test; the valve should hold vacuum and not leak.

REMOVAL & INSTALLATION

EGR Valve

1. Label and disconnect the hoses from the valve. Carefully loosen and remove the retaining bolts, remembering that they are probably heat-seized and rusty. Use penetrating oil freely.
2. Remove the valve and clean the gasket remains from both mating surfaces.
3. Inspect the valve for any sign of carbon deposits or other cause of binding or sticking. The valve must close and seal properly; the pintle area may be cleaned with solvent to remove soot and carbon.
4. Install the valve with a new gasket. Tighten the bolts to 10 ft. lbs. for the 2.4L, 1991-93 1.5L and 1992-93 1.8L; 13 ft. lbs. for the 1990 1.5L and 1990 1.8L; 16 ft. lbs. for the 1.6L and 2.0L.
5. Connect the hoses.

Thermo Valve

If it becomes necessary to replace the thermovalve, do so only on a cold engine. Fit the wrench only onto the faceted base of the valve, never on the plastic parts. When installing the new unit, apply sealer such as 3M No. 4171® or equivalent to the threads and tighten the new unit to 22 ft.lbs. (30 Nm)

ELECTRONIC ENGINE CONTROLS

General Description

All of these engines are controlled by electronic engine control units (ECUs) which oversee the multi-point fuel injection system operation. These control units may also provide control for other systems on the vehicle such as speed control. While the individual control units vary by model and are not interchangeable among engines, they share the same self-diagnostic abilities and are interrogated in the same manner. Fault codes will vary by engine or engine/chassis combination.

ENGINE CONTROLLERS

The engine controller is a microprocessor or small computer which receives electrical inputs from several sensors, switches and relays on and around the engine. Based on combinations of these inputs, the engine controller controls outputs to various devices concerned with engine operation and emissions. Because one output can be affected by many inputs, correct diagnostic procedures are essential on these systems.

One part of the engine controller is devoted to monitoring both input and output functions within the system. This ability forms the core of the self-diagnostic system. When the monitor or self-check portion of the ECU notices either a loss of signal or a signal out of range — high or low — for a period of time, a fault code is assigned. The fault is stored in the ECU memory and will be held for later retrieval.

The memory is non-volatile; that is, it is retained by battery power when the ignition is turned **OFF**. The fault code(s) stored in the memory will be erased if either the battery or ECU is disconnected.

DASHBOARD WARNING LAMP

The CHECK ENGINE warning lamp is controlled by an output from the ECU. When an emissions related fault is detected, the warning lamp is turned on to advise the operator. Should the fault self-correct and re-establish the proper signal to the control unit, the dash warning lamp will turn off; a code may remain in the memory even though the lamp is off. The dash lamp will not light again until another fault is detected.

The CHECK ENGINE lamp should illuminate for approximately 5 seconds each time the engine is started. After this period, the lamp should extinguish and remain out during vehicle operation.

➡**The dash warning lamp will illuminate when the ignition timing adjustment terminal is grounded. This is a normal controller function and should not be taken to mean a fault has been detected while adjusting the engine timing.**

Tools and Equipment

The use of an analog (needle type) voltmeter is required if codes are to be read without a scan tool. Although the analog meter may be used for some component testing, the use of a high-impedance digital volt-ohmmeter is recommended for its accurate readout without affecting the circuit being tested.

The digital voltmeter or multimeter must be a high impedance unit, with 10 megohms of impedance in the voltmeter. This type of meter will not place an additional load on the circuit it is testing; this is extremely important in low voltage circuits. The multimeter must be of high quality in all respects. It should be handled carefully and protected from impact or damage. Replace the batteries frequently in the unit.

Other necessary tools include a quality tachometer with inductive (clip-on) pickup and a fuel pressure gauge with system adapters. A vacuum gauge may be required for certain test procedures.

Diagnosis and Testing

▶ **See Figures 33, 34, 35, 36, 37, 38, 39, 40, 41, 42, 43, 44, 45, 46, 47, 48, 49, 50, 51, 52, 53, 54, 55, 56, 57 and 58**

Diagnosis of a driveability problem requires attention to detail and following the diagnostic procedures in the correct order. Resist the temptation to begin extensive testing before completing the preliminary diagnostic steps. The preliminary or visual inspection must be completed in detail before diagnosis begins. In many cases this will shorten diagnostic time and often cure the problem without electronic testing.

VISUAL INSPECTION

This is possibly the most critical step of diagnosis. Many fault codes or apparent failures are caused by loose, damaged or corroded electrical connectors. A detailed examination of all connectors, wiring and vacuum hoses can often lead to a repair without further diagnosis. Performance of this step relies on the skill of the technician performing it; a careful inspector will check the undersides of hoses as well as the integrity of hard-to-reach hoses blocked by the air cleaner or other components. Wiring should be checked carefully for any sign of strain , burning, crimping or terminal pull-out from a connector.

Checking connectors at components or in harnesses is required; usually, pushing them together will reveal a loose fit. Pay particular attention to ground circuits, making sure they are not loose or corroded. Remember to inspect connectors and hose fittings at components not mounted on the engine, such as the evaporative canister or relays mounted on the fender aprons. Any component or wiring in the vicinity of a fluid leak or spillage should be given extra attention during inspection.

Additionally, inspect maintenance items such as belt condition and tension, battery charge and condition and the radiator cap carefully. Any of these very simple items may affect the system enough to set a fault. The self-diagnostic system will not operate if the battery is low on charge.

READING FAULT CODES

All stored codes are read through connections at the diagnostic connector. The DRB-II or equivalent may be used to read stored codes; the Mitsubishi Adapter must be used as an interface between the scan tool and the vehicle. The DRB-II may be used to read codes and observe the signal values being sent to and from the ECU. Fault codes stored within the system may be cleared through the DRB-II.

In the absence of a scan tool and/or adapter, codes may be read directly from the diagnostic connector. All stored fault codes are read through an analog (needle type) voltmeter after the system enters self-diagnostics. The codes are transmitted as pulses which cause the needle to sweep repeatedly. To enter the self-diagnostic mode:

1. The self-diagnostic connector is located either next to or below the fuse panel, under the left dash. The only exception is the Colt Wagon, which locates the connector under the left side of the glove box, behind the center console. Remove the cover if one is fitted.

2. With the ignition switch **OFF**, connect the ground probe of the voltmeter to the ground terminal (terminal No. 12) of the diagnostic connector.

3. Connect the voltage probe of the voltmeter to the MPI diagnostic terminal (terminal No. 1) of the connector.

4. Turn the ignition switch **ON** but do not start the engine. The codes will be transmitted immediately. Each two-digit code will be sent as groups of electrical pulses; these pulses will cause needle sweeps on the voltmeter. The codes are sent in place value groups. For example, Code 23 is sent as a group of 2 long pulses followed by a group of 3 shorter pulses.

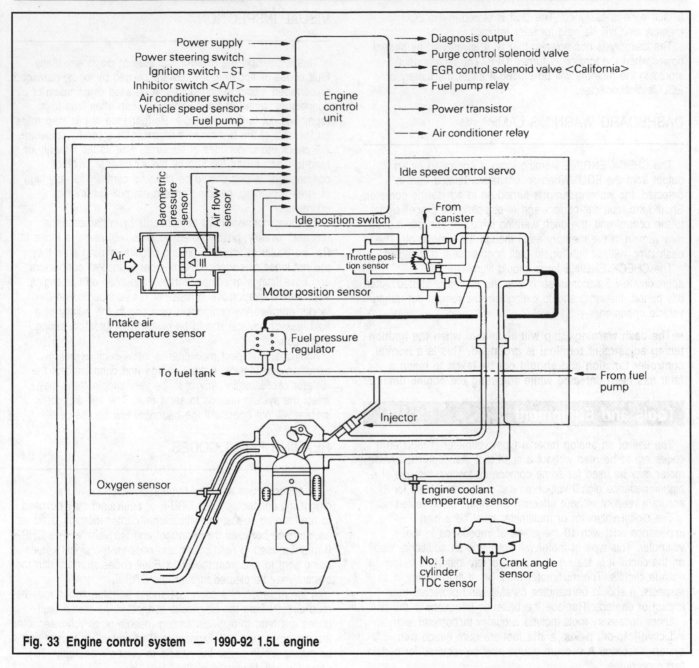

Power supply →
Power steering switch →
Ignition switch – ST →
Inhibitor switch <A/T> →
Air conditioner switch →
Vehicle speed sensor →
Fuel pump →

Engine control unit

→ Diagnosis output
→ Purge control solenoid valve
→ EGR control solenoid valve <California>
→ Fuel pump relay
→ Power transistor
→ Air conditioner relay

Barometric pressure sensor

Air flow sensor

Idle speed control servo

Idle position switch

From canister

Air →

Throttle position sensor

Motor position sensor

Intake air temperature sensor

Fuel pressure regulator

To fuel tank ←

← From fuel pump

Injector

Oxygen sensor

Engine coolant temperature sensor

No. 1 cylinder TDC sensor

Crank angle sensor

Fig. 33 Engine control system — 1990-92 1.5L engine

There is a short pause between place value groups and a longer pause between code groups.

➡️**If multiple codes are stored in the memory they will be transmitted in numerical order from lowest to highest, not in the order of occurrence.**

5. If the ECU detects an internal error, the needle on the voltmeter will show constant voltage instead of sweeping on and off. When this signal is received, the ECU must be replaced.

6. If no faults are stored within the memory, the Normal State signal will be displayed. This is a constant, rapid needle sweep with no pauses or groups. This signal shows that the system understands the request for stored data but has nothing to report.

7. Record the codes transmitted for use during repairs. Once the codes are recorded, switch the ignition **OFF**. Based

on the codes, perform diagnostic and test procedures on the individual components and circuits.

➡️**If, during testing or repair, a sensor is disconnected with the ignition ON, the fault code for that sensor or circuit will be set. For this reason, having the original codes written down will eliminate confusion about additional codes appearing during testing or repair.**

CLEARING STORED CODES

After all diagnosis has been completed and the needed repairs performed, the stored fault codes must be erased from the ECU memory.

Codes may be cleared using the DRB-II. When properly connected through the Mitubishi Adapter, select

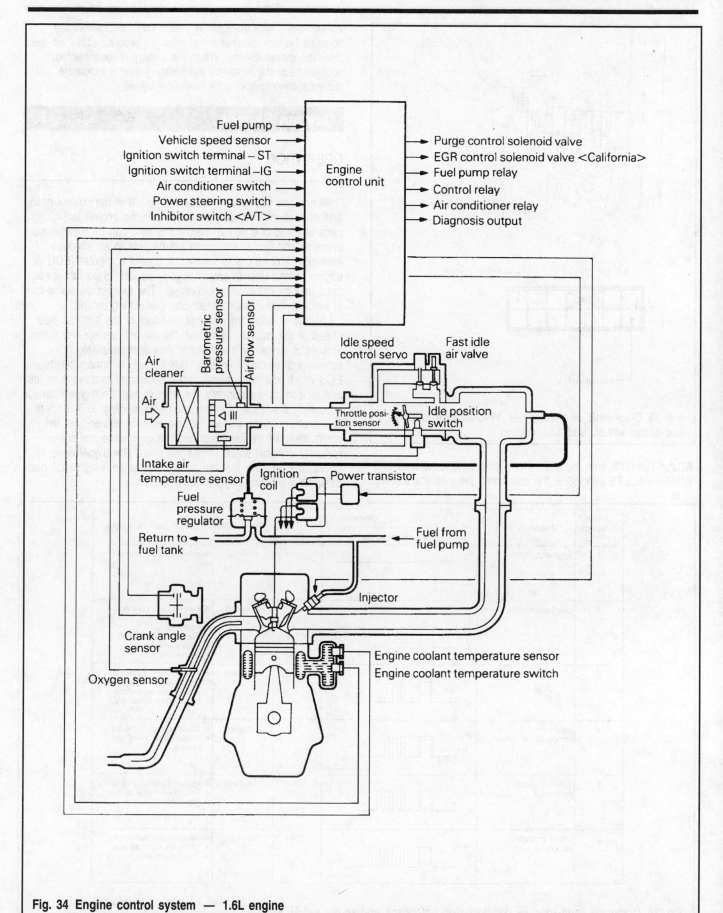

Fig. 34 Engine control system — 1.6L engine

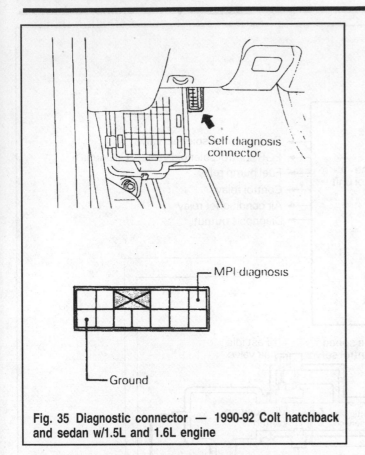

Fig. 35 Diagnostic connector — 1990-92 Colt hatchback and sedan w/1.5L and 1.6L engine

ADJUSTMENTS from the Main Menu screen. Choose item 1, ERASE FAULTS and follow the directions given on the screen.

Alternately, with the ignition switch **OFF**, disconnect the negative battery terminal for at least 10 seconds. This will also clear the stored codes. When the battery is reconnected, double check the repair by road testing over a moderate distance, then checking for newly-set codes.

Oxygen Sensor

OPERATION

All engines use an oxygen sensor to aid in the control of the air/fuel mixture. The ideal mixture within the engine is 14.7 parts of air to one part of fuel. If this ratio can be maintained under all conditions, emissions will be kept to an absolute minimum. The trick is to inform the control computer (ECU or engine control unit) of any change in conditions so that it can react and make necessary changes. The oxygen sensor is one of many sensors which detect changes during driving.

Located in either the exhaust manifold or the exhaust pipe ahead of the catalytic converter, the oxygen sensor reads the amount of oxygen in the exhaust flow and generates a proportional electrical voltage. This voltage is transmitted to ECU which interprets it and sends necessary messages to fuel and air control components. Remember that the oxygen sensor is reading the result of combustion and reacting to it. If there is a problem in the air/fuel mixture entering the engine, the combustion will be imperfect and the oxygen sensor will generate a signal which shows the error. The signal does not necessarily indicate that the sensor has failed, only that it has detected a different oxygen concentration.

Output preference order	Diagnosis item	Diagnosis code			Check item (Remedy)
		Output signal pattern	No.	Memory	
1	Engine control unit	H / L 12A0104	–	–	(Replace engine control unit)
2	Oxygen sensor	H / L 12A0104	11	Retained	• Harness and connector • Fuel pressure • Injectors (Replace if defective) • Intake air leaks • Oxygen sensor
3	Air flow sensor	H / L 12A0104	12	Retained	• Harness and connector (If harness and connector are normal, replace air flow sensor assembly.)
4	Intake air temperature sensor	H / L 12A0104	13	Retained	• Harness and connector • Intake air temperature sensor
5	Throttle position sensor	H / L 12A0104	14	Retained	• Harness and connector • Throttle position sensor • Idle position switch
6	Motor position sensor	H / L 12A0104	15	Retained	• Harness and connector • Motor position sensor • Throttle position sensor

Fig. 36 Diagnosis fault tree — 1990-92 Colt hatchback and sedan w/1.5L engine

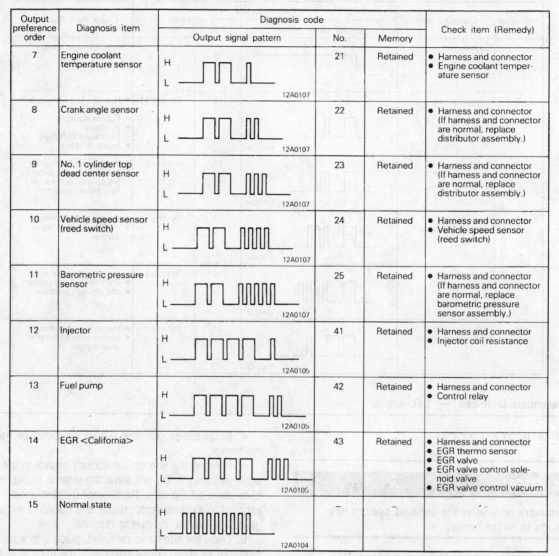

Output preference order	Diagnosis item	Diagnosis code			Check item (Remedy)
		Output signal pattern	No.	Memory	
7	Engine coolant temperature sensor	H L 12A0107	21	Retained	• Harness and connector • Engine coolant temperature sensor
8	Crank angle sensor	H L 12A0107	22	Retained	• Harness and connector (If harness and connector are normal, replace distributor assembly.)
9	No. 1 cylinder top dead center sensor	H L 12A0107	23	Retained	• Harness and connector (If harness and connector are normal, replace distributor assembly.)
10	Vehicle speed sensor (reed switch)	H L 12A0107	24	Retained	• Harness and connector • Vehicle speed sensor (reed switch)
11	Barometric pressure sensor	H L 12A0107	25	Retained	• Harness and connector (If harness and connector are normal, replace barometric pressure sensor assembly.)
12	Injector	H L 12A0105	41	Retained	• Harness and connector • Injector coil resistance
13	Fuel pump	H L 12A0105	42	Retained	• Harness and connector • Control relay
14	EGR <California>	H L 12A0105	43	Retained	• Harness and connector • EGR thermo sensor • EGR valve • EGR valve control solenoid valve • EGR valve control vacuum
15	Normal state	H L 12A0104	—	—	

NOTE
Replace the engine control unit if a malfunction code is output although the inspection reveals that there is no problem with the check items.

Fig. 37 Diagnosis fault tree — 1990-92 Colt hatchback and sedan w/1.5L engine cont.

Since the oxygen sensor is the furthest 'downstream' in the combustion process, it essential to check all other sensors and controls on the engine before assuming this sensor to be bad. Obviously, if the engine is running inefficiently, replacing the oxygen sensor won't cure the problem; the new sensor will continue to correctly read the imperfect exhaust content. About the only failure common to all oxygen sensors is loose or corroded connectors in the electrical wires. If a trouble code indicates an oxygen sensor malfunction, the first place to look is at the connector, making sure the pins are clean and fit tightly together. The low voltages flowing in this system can be changed or blocked by a high resistance (poor) connection.

TESTING

➡An accurate digital voltmeter is required for this test.

1. Before testing, warm the engine to normal operating temperature. Coolant temperature must be 80-85°C (175-185°F) or more.

2. Shut the engine off. Disconnect the oxygen sensor connector and connect the positive probe of the voltmeter to the sensor connector. If the connector has two terminals (California spec), use the terminal on the left.

3. Ground the negative probe of the meter to the body or the engine as convenient but do not ground it back to the sensor or connect it to the second terminal.

4. Place the meter where it can be seen from the driver's seat. Start the engine.

5. Race the engine to about 4000 rpm and observe the meter; it should show about 1 volt (600-1000 mV).

6. Shut the engine off, remove the test equipment and reconnect the sensor harness.

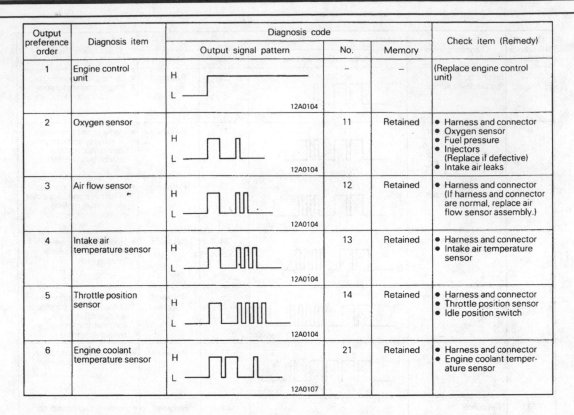

Output preference order	Diagnosis item	Diagnosis code			Check item (Remedy)
		Output signal pattern	No.	Memory	
1	Engine control unit	12A0104	–	–	(Replace engine control unit)
2	Oxygen sensor	12A0104	11	Retained	• Harness and connector • Oxygen sensor • Fuel pressure • Injectors (Replace if defective) • Intake air leaks
3	Air flow sensor	12A0104	12	Retained	• Harness and connector (If harness and connector are normal, replace air flow sensor assembly.)
4	Intake air temperature sensor	12A0104	13	Retained	• Harness and connector • Intake air temperature sensor
5	Throttle position sensor	12A0104	14	Retained	• Harness and connector • Throttle position sensor • Idle position switch
6	Engine coolant temperature sensor	12A0107	21	Retained	• Harness and connector • Engine coolant temperature sensor

Fig. 38 Diagnosis fault tree — 1.6L engine

REMOVAL & INSTALLATION

❈❈CAUTION

Perform this work only after the exhaust system has cooled enough to avoid burns.

It is more common to remove the oxygen sensor for protection or access during other repairs than to replace it because of failure. Once the sensor is removed, it must be protected from impact and/or chemical contact. Never attempt to clean the tip with solvent and never allow the tip to contact grease, oil or other chemicals. The zirconia element in the tip will be polluted and the sensor will function poorly, if at all.

1. Locate the oxygen sensor. It will be located in the exhaust manifold, usually mounted either underneath or from the side.
2. Follow the wiring from the sensor to the first connector and disconnect it. Do not attempt to disconnect the wiring at the sensor.
3. The sensor may be obstructed by heat shields on the exhaust manifold. Remove them as necessary.

4. Install the proper size wrench or socket on the flats of the sensor.
5. Keeping the wrench (or socket) square to the sensor while removing it. Do not allow the wrench to become crooked or to come off the flats. Remember that the sensor has been exposed to extreme temperature and corrosive exhaust gasses. It may be difficult to remove.
6. Once the sensor is removed, place it in a clean, protected location. For reinstallation, the threads of the sensor may be lightly coated with an anti-seize compound but extreme care must be taken to protect the tip and shield area of the sensor from even the slightest contamination.
7. Handle the oxygen sensor carefully, protecting it from impact, and install it in place. Start the threads by hand and hand tighten it as far as possible.
8. Tighten the sensor to 33 ft. lbs.
9. Install the heat shields if any were removed. Tighten the bolts to 12 ft. lbs. (16 Nm).
10. Connect the sensor wiring to the harness connector. Make certain the wiring is correctly run and out of the way of hot or moving components.

Output preference order	Diagnosis item	Malfunction code			Check item (Remedy)
		Output signal pattern	No.	Memory	
7	Crank angle sensor	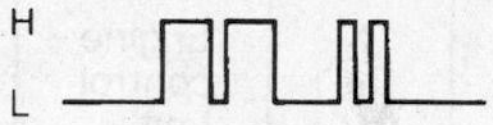 H ⎍⎍⎍ L 12A0107	22	Retained	• Harness and connector (If harness and connector are normal, replace crank angle sensor assembly.)
8	Top dead center sensor	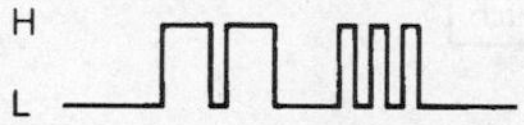 H ⎍⎍⎍ L 12A0107	23	Retained	• Harness and connector (If harness and connector are normal, replace crank angle sensor assembly.)
9	Vehicle speed sensor (reed switch)	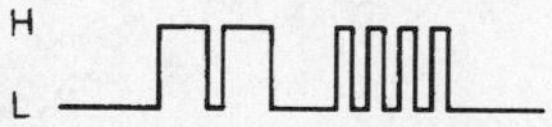 H ⎍⎍⎍⎍ L 12A0107	24	Retained	• Harness and connector • Vehicle speed sensor (reed switch)
10	Barometric pressure sensor	 H ⎍⎍⎍⎍ L 12A0107	25	Retained	• Harness and connector (If harness and connector are normal, replace barometric pressure sensor assembly.)
11	Injector	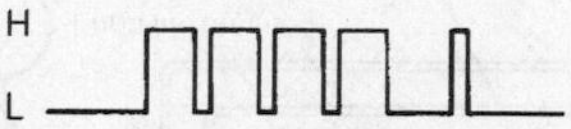 H ⎍⎍⎍⎍ L 12A0105	41	Retained	• Harness and connector • Injector coil resistance
12	Fuel pump	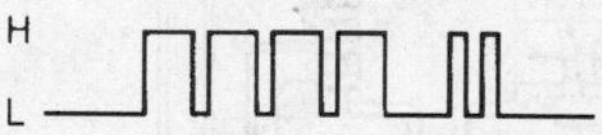 H ⎍⎍⎍⎍ L 12A0105	42	Retained	• Harness and connector • Control relay
13	EGR <California>	 H ⎍⎍⎍⎍ L 12A0105	43	Retained	• Harness and connector • EGR temperature sensor • EGR valve • EGR valve control solenoid valve • EGR valve control vacuum
14	Ignition coil	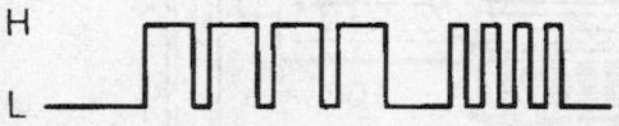 H ⎍⎍⎍⎍ L 12A0105	44	Retained	• Harness and connector • Ignition coil • Power transistor
15	Normal state	 H ⎍⎍⎍⎍⎍ L 12A0104			

NOTE
Replace the engine control unit if a malfunction code is output although the inspection reveals that there is no problem with the check items.

Fig. 39 Diagnosis fault tree — 1.6L engine cont.

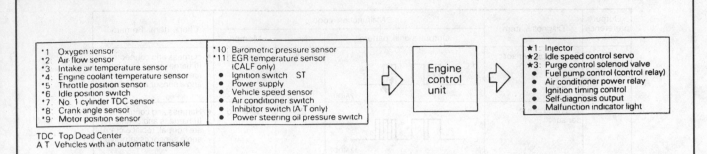

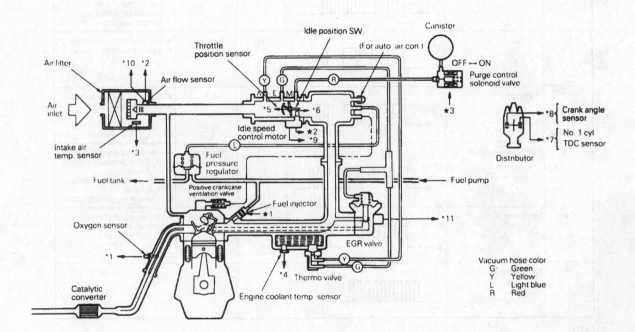

Fig. 40 Engine control system — 1990 1.8L engine

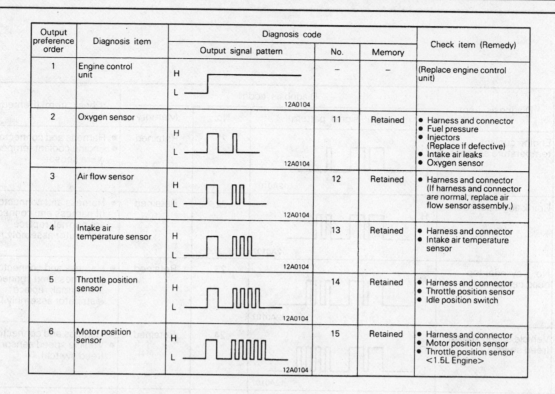

Output preference order	Diagnosis item	Diagnosis code			Check item (Remedy)
		Output signal pattern	No.	Memory	
1	Engine control unit	H L 12A0104	–	–	(Replace engine control unit)
2	Oxygen sensor	H L 12A0104	11	Retained	• Harness and connector • Fuel pressure • Injectors (Replace if defective) • Intake air leaks • Oxygen sensor
3	Air flow sensor	H L 12A0104	12	Retained	• Harness and connector (If harness and connector are normal, replace air flow sensor assembly.)
4	Intake air temperature sensor	H L 12A0104	13	Retained	• Harness and connector • Intake air temperature sensor
5	Throttle position sensor	H L 12A0104	14	Retained	• Harness and connector • Throttle position sensor • Idle position switch
6	Motor position sensor	H L 12A0104	15	Retained	• Harness and connector • Motor position sensor • Throttle position sensor <1.5L Engine>

Fig. 41 Diagnosis fault tree — 1990 Colt Wagon w/1.5L or 1.8L engine

Output preference order	Diagnosis item	Diagnosis code			Check item (Remedy)
		Output signal pattern	No.	Memory	
7	Engine coolant temperature sensor	 H L 12A0107	21	Retained	• Harness and connector • Engine coolant temperature sensor
8	Crank angle sensor	 H L 12A0107	22	Retained	• Harness and connector (If harness and connector are normal, replace distributor assembly.)
9	No. 1 cylinder top dead center sensor	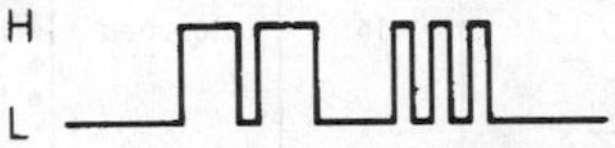 H L 12A0107	23	Retained	• Harness and connector (If harness and connector are normal, replace distributor assembly.)
10	Vehicle speed sensor (reed switch)	 H L 12A0107	24	Retained	• Harness and connector • Vehicle speed sensor (reed switch)
11	Barometric pressure sensor	 H L 12A0107	25	Retained	• Harness and connector (If harness and connector are normal, replace barometric pressure sensor assembly.)
12	Injector	 H L 12A0105	41	Retained	• Harness and connector • Injector coil resistance
13	Fuel pump	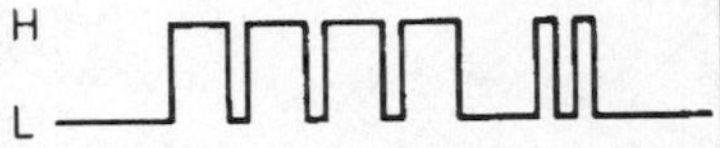 H L 12A0105	42	Retained	• Harness and connector • Control relay
14	EGR <California>	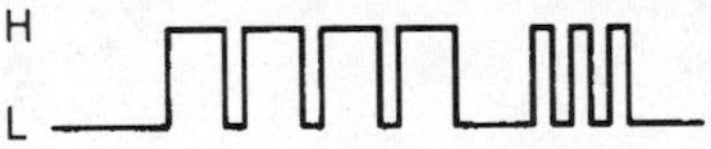 H L 12A0105	43	Retained	• Harness and connector • EGR temperature sensor • EGR valve • Thermo valve <1.8L engine> • EGR valve control solenoid valve <1.5L engine> • EGR valve control vacuum
15	Normal state	 H L 12A0104	–	–	–

NOTE
1. Replace the engine control unit if a malfunction code is output although the inspection reveals that there is no problem with the check items.

Fig. 42 Diagnosis fault tree — 1990 Colt Wagon w/1.5L or 1.8L engine cont.

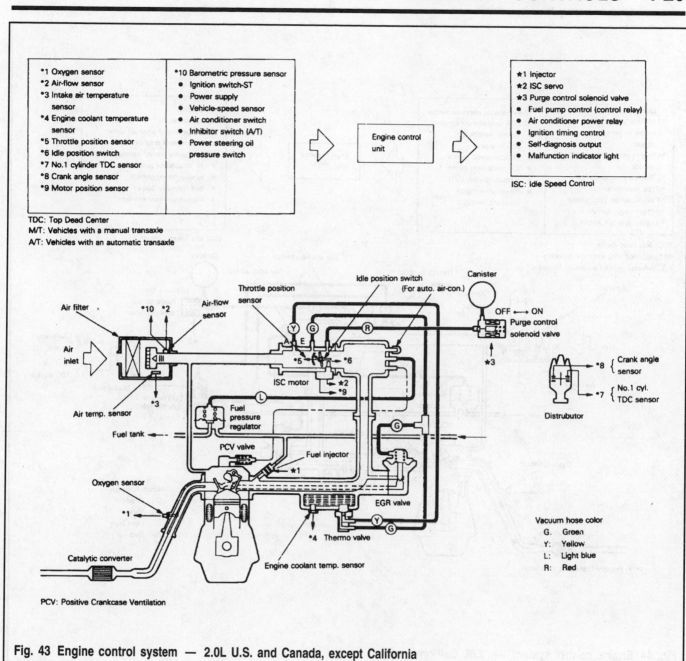

*1 Oxygen sensor
*2 Air-flow sensor
*3 Intake air temperature sensor
*4 Engine coolant temperature sensor
*5 Throttle position sensor
*6 Idle position switch
*7 No.1 cylinder TDC sensor
*8 Crank angle sensor
*9 Motor position sensor

*10 Barometric pressure sensor
● Ignition switch-ST
● Power supply
● Vehicle-speed sensor
● Air conditioner switch
● Inhibitor switch (A/T)
● Power steering oil pressure switch

Engine control unit

★1 Injector
★2 ISC servo
★3 Purge control solenoid valve
● Fuel pump control (control relay)
● Air conditioner power relay
● Ignition timing control
● Self-diagnosis output
● Malfunction indicator light

ISC: Idle Speed Control

TDC: Top Dead Center
M/T: Vehicles with a manual transaxle
A/T: Vehicles with an automatic transaxle

Air filter
Air inlet
*10 *2
Air-flow sensor
*3
Air temp. sensor
Throttle position sensor
Idle position switch
(For auto. air-con.)
Canister
OFF ← → ON
Purge control solenoid valve
★3
*5
*6
ISC motor
★2
*9
Fuel pressure regulator
Fuel tank
PCV valve
Oxygen sensor
*1
Fuel injector
★1
EGR valve
Crank angle sensor *8
No.1 cyl. TDC sensor *7
Distrubutor
Catalytic converter
*4 Thermo valve
Engine coolant temp. sensor

Vacuum hose color
G. Green
Y: Yellow
L: Light blue
R: Red

PCV: Positive Crankcase Ventilation

Fig. 43 Engine control system — 2.0L U.S. and Canada, except California

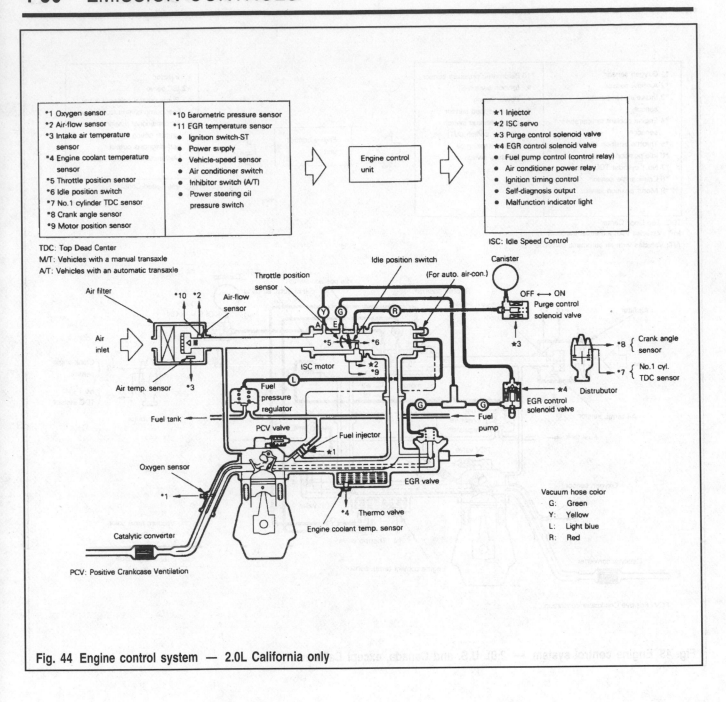

*1 Oxygen sensor
*2 Air-flow sensor
*3 Intake air temperature sensor
*4 Engine coolant temperature sensor
*5 Throttle position sensor
*6 Idle position switch
*7 No.1 cylinder TDC sensor
*8 Crank angle sensor
*9 Motor position sensor
*10 Barometric pressure sensor
*11 EGR temperature sensor
● Ignition switch-ST
● Power supply
● Vehicle-speed sensor
● Air conditioner switch
● Inhibitor switch (A/T)
● Power steering oil pressure switch

Engine control unit

★1 Injector
★2 ISC servo
★3 Purge control solenoid valve
★4 EGR control solenoid valve
● Fuel pump control (control relay)
● Air conditioner power relay
● Ignition timing control
● Self-diagnosis output
● Malfunction indicator light

ISC: Idle Speed Control

TDC: Top Dead Center
M/T: Vehicles with a manual transaxle
A/T: Vehicles with an automatic transaxle

Air filter
Air inlet
*10 *2 Air-flow sensor
Air temp. sensor *3
Throttle position sensor
Idle position switch
(For auto. air-con.)
Canister
OFF ← → ON
Purge control solenoid valve
*3
Y G R
A E
*5 *6
ISC motor
*2 *9
Fuel pressure regulator
Fuel tank
PCV valve
L
Fuel injector
★1
Oxygen sensor
*1
G G
Fuel pump
EGR control solenoid valve
★4
Distrubutor
*8 { Crank angle sensor
*7 { No.1 cyl. TDC sensor
EGR valve
*4 Thermo valve
Engine coolant temp. sensor
Catalytic converter
PCV: Positive Crankcase Ventilation

Vacuum hose color
G: Green
Y: Yellow
L: Light blue
R: Red

Fig. 44 Engine control system — 2.0L California only

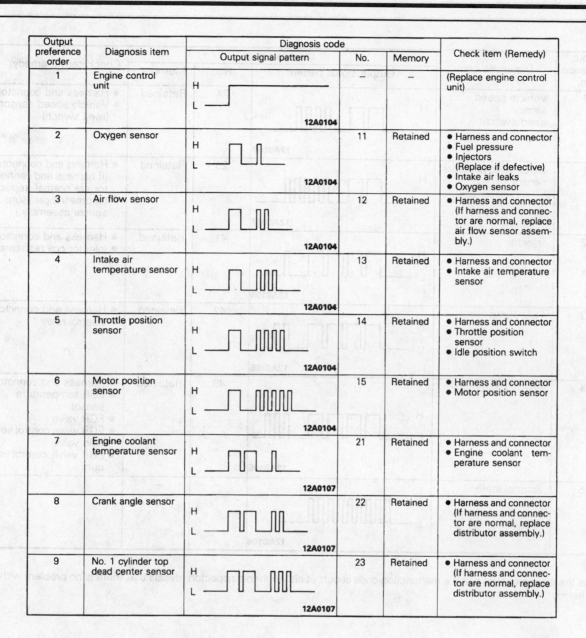

Output preference order	Diagnosis item	Diagnosis code			Check item (Remedy)
		Output signal pattern	No.	Memory	
1	Engine control unit	H L 12A0104	—	—	(Replace engine control unit)
2	Oxygen sensor	H L 12A0104	11	Retained	• Harness and connector • Fuel pressure • Injectors (Replace if defective) • Intake air leaks • Oxygen sensor
3	Air flow sensor	H L 12A0104	12	Retained	• Harness and connector (If harness and connector are normal, replace air flow sensor assembly.)
4	Intake air temperature sensor	H L 12A0104	13	Retained	• Harness and connector • Intake air temperature sensor
5	Throttle position sensor	H L 12A0104	14	Retained	• Harness and connector • Throttle position sensor • Idle position switch
6	Motor position sensor	H L 12A0104	15	Retained	• Harness and connector • Motor position sensor
7	Engine coolant temperature sensor	H L 12A0107	21	Retained	• Harness and connector • Engine coolant temperature sensor
8	Crank angle sensor	H L 12A0107	22	Retained	• Harness and connector (If harness and connector are normal, replace distributor assembly.)
9	No. 1 cylinder top dead center sensor	H L 12A0107	23	Retained	• Harness and connector (If harness and connector are normal, replace distributor assembly.)

Fig. 45 Diagnosis fault tree — 1990-91 Vista

Output preference order	Diagnosis item	Diagnosis code			Check item (Remedy)
		Output signal pattern	No.	Memory	
10	Vehicle speed sensor (reed switch)	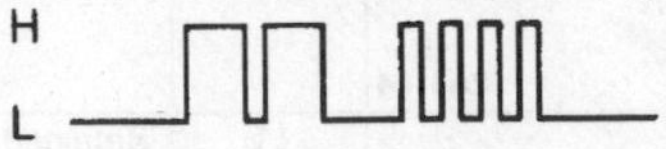 H L 12A0107	24	Retained	• Harness and connctor • Vehicle speed sensor (reed switch)
11	Barometric pressure sensor	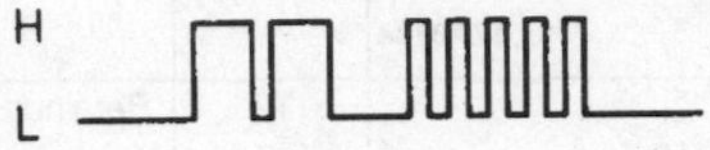 H L 12A0107	25	Retained	• Harness and connector (If harness and connector are normal, replace barometric pressure sensor assembly.)
12	Injector	 H L 12A0105	41	Retained	• Harness and connctor • Injector coil resistance
13	Fuel pump	 H L 12A0105	42	Retained	• Harness and connctor • Control relay
14	EGR <California>	 H L 12A0105	43	Retained	• Harness and connctor • EGR temperature sensor • EGR valve • EGR valve control solenoid valve • EGR valve control vacuum
15	Normal state	 H L 12A0104	–	–	–

NOTE
Replace the engine control unit if a malfunction code is output although the inspecton reveals that there is no problem with the check items.

Fig. 46 Diagnosis fault tree — 1990-91 Vista cont.

Name	Symbol	Name	Symbol
Air conditioner relay	A	Idle speed control servo	L
Air conditioner switch	B	Ignition coil (power transistor)	M
Air flow sensor (with incorporated intake air temperature sensor and barometric pressure sensor)	C	Ignition timing adjustment terminal	N
		Inhibitor switch (A/T)	O
Control relay	D	Injector	P
Diagnosis connector	E	Oxygen sensor	Q
EGR control solenoid valve <California>	F	Power steering fluid pressure switch	R
EGR temperature sensor <California>	G	Purge control solenoid valve	S
Engine control unit	H	Throttle position sensor (with idle position switch)	T
Engine coolant temperature sensor	I	Top dead centre sensor and crank angle sensor	U
Engine warning light (check engine light)	J	Vehicle speed sensor (reed switch)	V
Fuel pump check terminal	K		

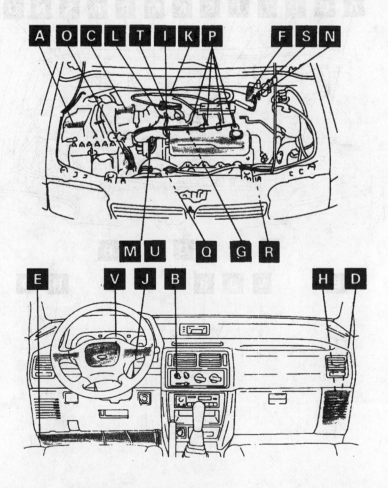

Fig. 47 Engine control system — 1992-93 Vista w/1.8L engine

Name	Symbol	Name	Symbol
Air conditioner relay	A	Ignition timing adjustment terminal	N
Air conditioner switch	B		
Air flow sensor (with incorporated intake air temperature sensor and barometric pressure sensor)	C	Inhibitor switch <A/T>	O
		Injector	P
Control relay	D	Oxygen sensor	Q
Diagnosis connecter	E	Power steering fluid pressure switch	R
EGR control solenoid valve <California>	F		
EGR temperature sensor <California>	G	Purge control solenoid valve	S
Engine control unit	H	Throttle position sensor (with idle position switch)	T
Engine coolant temperature sensor	I		
Engine warning light (check engine light)	J	Top dead centre sensor and crank angle sensor	U
Fuel pump check terminal	K		
Idle speed control servo	L	Vehicle speed sensor (reed switch)	V
Ignition coil (power transistor)	M		

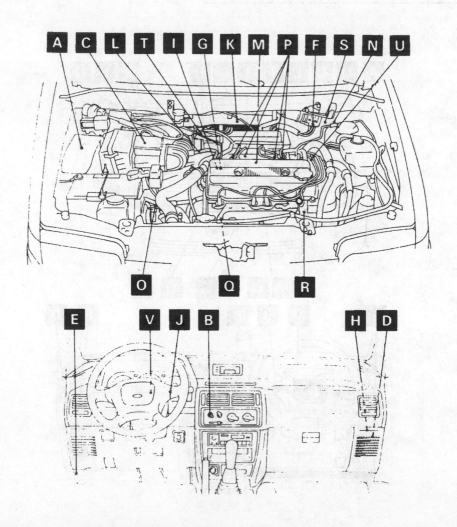

Fig. 48 Engine control system — 1992-93 Vista w/2.4L engine

Output preference order	Diagnosis item	Malfunction code			Check items (Remedy)
		Output signal pattern	No.	Memory	
1	Engine control unit	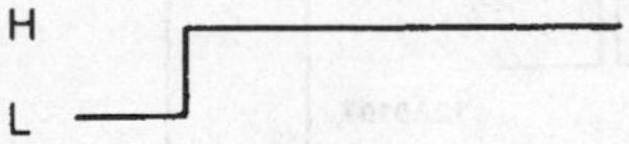 H / L 12A0104	–	–	(Replace engine control unit)
2	Oxygen sensor	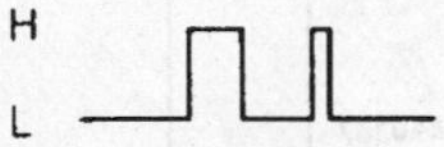 H / L 12A0104	11	Retained	• Harness and connector • Fuel pressure • Injectors (Replace if defective.) • Intake air leaks • Oxygen sensor
3	Air flow sensor	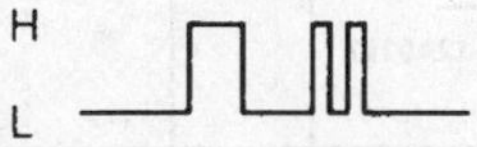 H / L 12A0104	12	Retained	• Harness and connector (If harness and connector are normal, rplace air flow sensor assembly)
4	Intake air temperature sensor	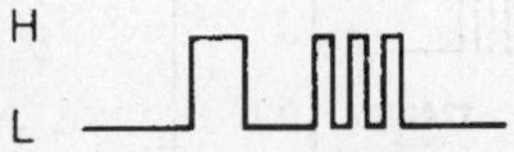 H / L 12A0104	13	Retained	• Harness and connector • Intake air temperature sensor
5	Throttle position sensor	 H / L 12A0104	14	Retained	• Harness and connector • Throttle position sensor • Idle position switch
6	Engine coolant temperature sensor	 H / L 12A0107	21	Retained	• Harness and connector • Engine coolant temperature sensor
7	Crank angle sensor	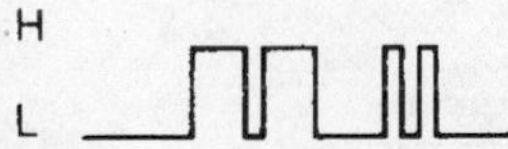 H / L 12A0107	22	Retained	• Harness and connector (If harness and connector are normal, replace distributor assembly.)
8	No.1 cylinder top dead center sensor	 H / L 12A0107	23	Retained	• Harness and connector (If harness and connector are normal, replace distributor assembly.)
9	Vehicle speed sensor (reed switch)	 H / L 12A0107	24	Retained	• Harness and connector • Vehicle speed sensor (reed switch)
10	Barometric pressure sensor	 H / L 12A0107	25	Retained	• Harness and connector (If harness and connector are normal, replace barometric pressure sensor assembly.)
11	Ignition timing adjustment signal	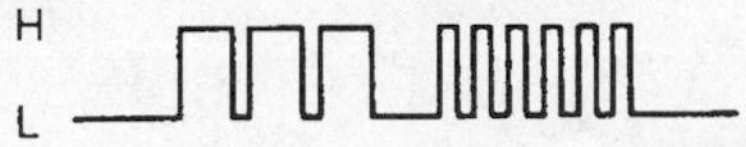 H / L 12A0107	36	–	• Harness and connector

Fig. 49 Diagnosis fault tree — 1992-93 Vista w/1.8L or 2.4L engine

Output preference order	Diagnosis item	Malfunction code			Check items (Remedy)
		Output signal pattern	No.	Memory	
12	Injector	 H ⎍⎍⎍⎍ L 12A0107	41	Retained	• Harness and connector • Injector coil resistance
13	Fuel pump <2.4L Engine>	 H ⎍⎍⎍ ⎍⎍ L 12A0107	42	Retained	• Harness and connector • Control relay
14	EGR <California>	 H ⎍⎍⎍⎍ ⎍⎍ L 12A0107	43	Retained	• Harness and connector • EGR valve • EGR control solenoid valve • EGR valve control vacuum • EGR temperature sensor
15	Servo valve position sensor	 H ⎍⎍⎍⎍⎍ ⎍⎍⎍⎍ L 12A0107	55	Retained	• Harness and connector • Servo valve position sensor • Idle speed control servo (DC motor)
16	Normal state	 H ⎍⎍⎍⎍⎍⎍⎍ L 12A0107	–	–	–

NOTE
1. Replace the engine control unit if a malfunction code is output although the inspection reveals that there is no problem with the check items.
2. The code numbers will be displayed in order, starting from the lowest.

Fig. 50 Diagnosis fault tree — 1992-93 Vista w/1.8L or 2.4L engine cont.

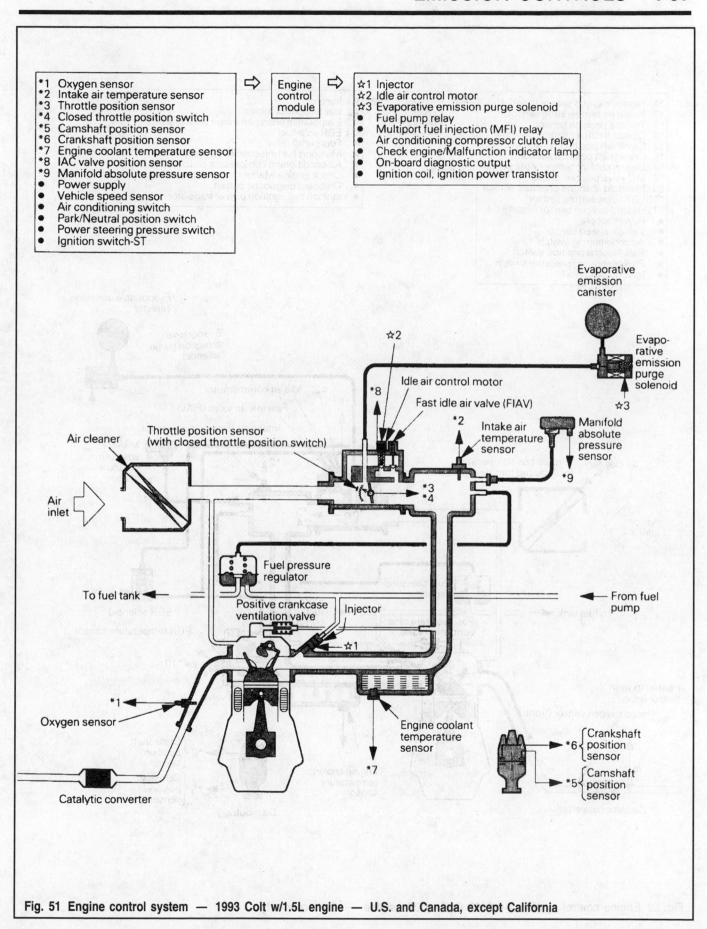

*1 Oxygen sensor
*2 Intake air temperature sensor
*3 Throttle position sensor
*4 Closed throttle position switch
*5 Camshaft position sensor
*6 Crankshaft position sensor
*7 Engine coolant temperature sensor
*8 IAC valve position sensor
*9 Manifold absolute pressure sensor
• Power supply
• Vehicle speed sensor
• Air conditioning switch
• Park/Neutral position switch
• Power steering pressure switch
• Ignition switch-ST

Engine control module

☆1 Injector
☆2 Idle air control motor
☆3 Evaporative emission purge solenoid
• Fuel pump relay
• Multiport fuel injection (MFI) relay
• Air conditioning compressor clutch relay
• Check engine/Malfunction indicator lamp
• On-board diagnostic output
• Ignition coil, ignition power transistor

Evaporative emission canister

Evaporative emission purge solenoid ☆3

☆2

Idle air control motor

Fast idle air valve (FIAV)

*8

*2 Intake air temperature sensor

Manifold absolute pressure sensor

*9

Throttle position sensor (with closed throttle position switch)

Air cleaner

Air inlet

*3
*4

Fuel pressure regulator

To fuel tank

From fuel pump

Positive crankcase ventilation valve

Injector

☆1

*1

Oxygen sensor

Engine coolant temperature sensor

*7

Crankshaft position sensor *6

Camshaft position sensor *5

Catalytic converter

Fig. 51 Engine control system — 1993 Colt w/1.5L engine — U.S. and Canada, except California

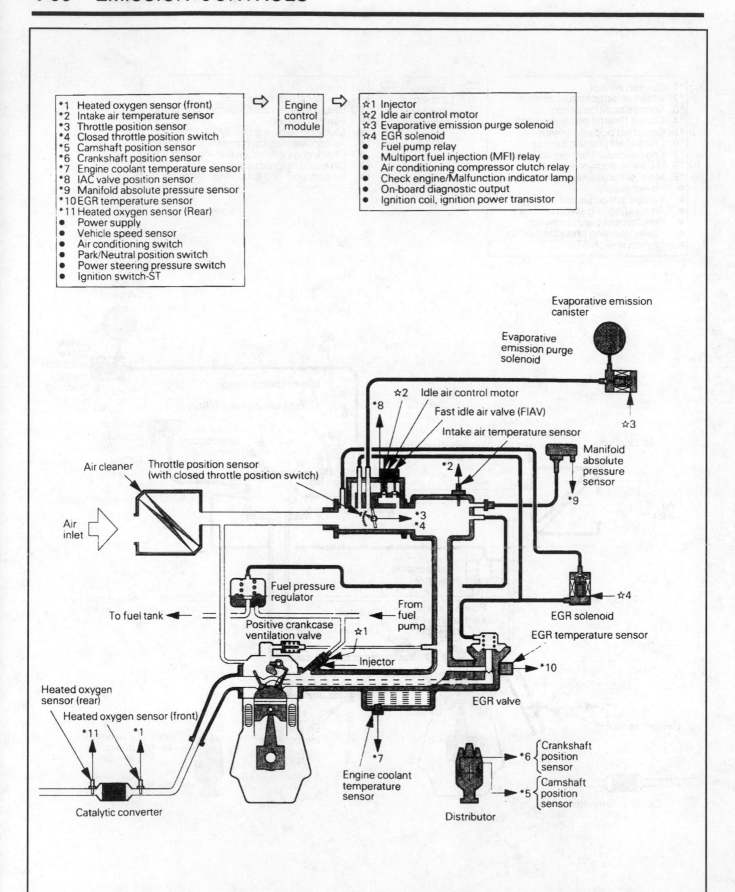

*1 Heated oxygen sensor (front)
*2 Intake air temperature sensor
*3 Throttle position sensor
*4 Closed throttle position switch
*5 Camshaft position sensor
*6 Crankshaft position sensor
*7 Engine coolant temperature sensor
*8 IAC valve position sensor
*9 Manifold absolute pressure sensor
*10 EGR temperature sensor
*11 Heated oxygen sensor (Rear)
●   Power supply
●   Vehicle speed sensor
●   Air conditioning switch
●   Park/Neutral position switch
●   Power steering pressure switch
●   Ignition switch-ST

Engine control module

☆1 Injector
☆2 Idle air control motor
☆3 Evaporative emission purge solenoid
☆4 EGR solenoid
●   Fuel pump relay
●   Multiport fuel injection (MFI) relay
●   Air conditioning compressor clutch relay
●   Check engine/Malfunction indicator lamp
●   On-board diagnostic output
●   Ignition coil, ignition power transistor

Evaporative emission canister

Evaporative emission purge solenoid

☆3

☆2 Idle air control motor

*8

Fast idle air valve (FIAV)

Intake air temperature sensor

*2

Manifold absolute pressure sensor

*9

Air cleaner

Throttle position sensor (with closed throttle position switch)

Air inlet

*3
*4

Fuel pressure regulator

From fuel pump

☆4

EGR solenoid

EGR temperature sensor

To fuel tank

Positive crankcase ventilation valve

☆1

Injector

*10

EGR valve

Heated oxygen sensor (rear)

Heated oxygen sensor (front)

*11   *1

Catalytic converter

*7

Engine coolant temperature sensor

Crankshaft position sensor

*6

Camshaft position sensor

*5

Distributor

Fig. 52 Engine control system — 1993 Colt w/1.5L engine — California only

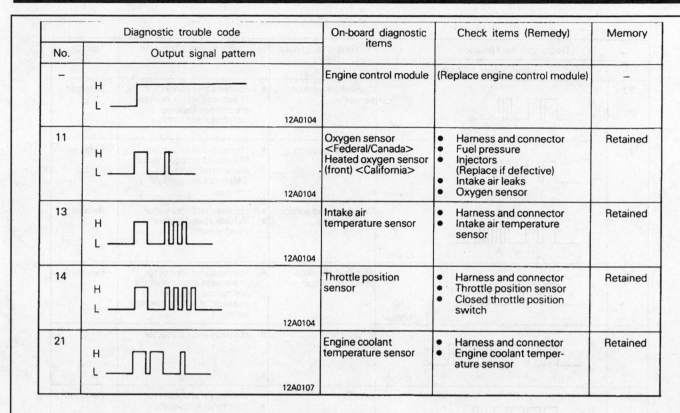

Diagnostic trouble code		On-board diagnostic items	Check items (Remedy)	Memory
No.	Output signal pattern			
–	H ⎍ L 12A0104	Engine control module	(Replace engine control module)	–
11	H ⎍ L 12A0104	Oxygen sensor <Federal/Canada> Heated oxygen sensor (front) <California>	• Harness and connector • Fuel pressure • Injectors (Replace if defective) • Intake air leaks • Oxygen sensor	Retained
13	H ⎍ L 12A0104	Intake air temperature sensor	• Harness and connector • Intake air temperature sensor	Retained
14	H ⎍ L 12A0104	Throttle position sensor	• Harness and connector • Throttle position sensor • Closed throttle position switch	Retained
21	H ⎍ L 12A0107	Engine coolant temperature sensor	• Harness and connector • Engine coolant temper- ature sensor	Retained

Fig. 53 Diagnosis fault tree — 1993 Colt w/1.5 engine

Diagnostic trouble code		On-board diagnostic items	Check items (Remedy)	Memory
No.	Output signal pattern			
22	 12A0107	Crankshaft position sensor	• Harness and connector (If harness and connector are normal, replace distributor assembly.)	Retained
23	 12A0107	Camshaft position sensor	• Harness and connector (If harness and connector are normal, replace distributor assembly.)	Retained
24	 12A0107	Vehicle speed sensor (reed switch)	• Harness and connector • Vehicle speed sensor (reed switch)	Retained
32	 12A0107	Manifold absolute pressure sensor	• Harness and connector (If harness and connector are normal, replace manifold absolute pressure sensor.)	Retained
36	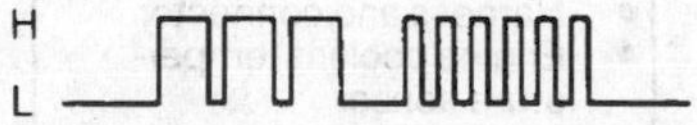 12A0107	Ignition timing adjustment signal	• Harness and connector	–
41	 12A0107	Injector	• Harness and connector • Injector coil resistance	Retained
43	 12A0107	EGR <California>	• Harness and connector • EGR valve • EGR solenoid • EGR valve control vacuum • EGR temperature sensor	Retained
55	 12A0107	IAC valve position sensor	• Harness and connector • IAC valve movement (If harness, connector and IAC valve movement are normal, replace Idle air control motor assembly)	Retained
59	 12A0106	Heated oxygen sensor (rear) <California>	• Harness and connector • Heated oxygen sensor	Retained
–	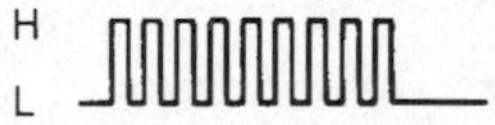 12A0107	Normal state	–	–

NOTE
1. Replace the engine control module if a diagnostic trouble code is output although the inspection reveals that there is no problem with the check items.
2. The code numbers will be displayed in order, starting from the lowest.

Fig. 54 Diagnosis fault tree — 1993 Colt w/1.5 engine cont.

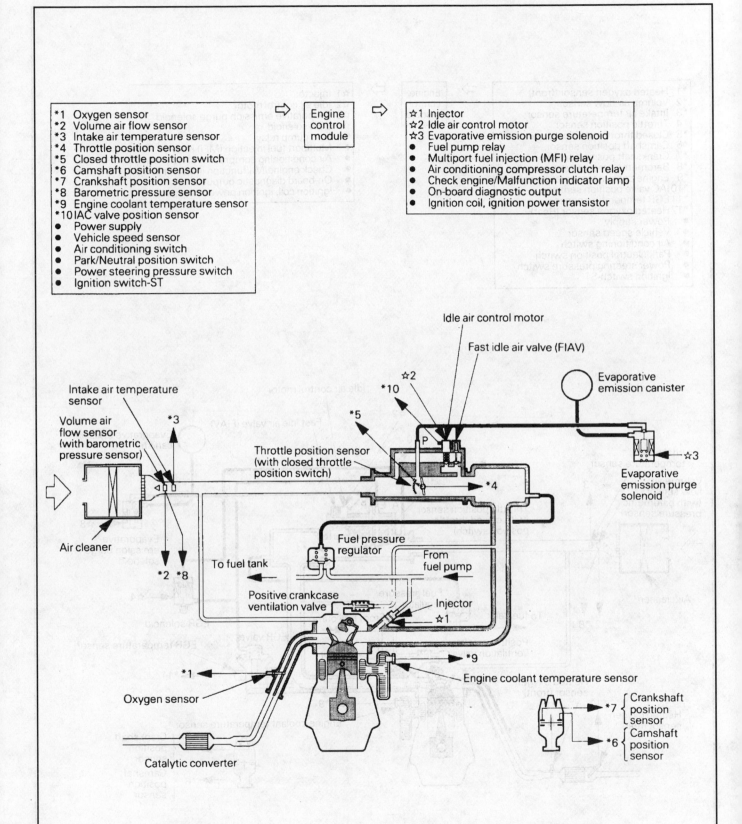

*1 Oxygen sensor
*2 Volume air flow sensor
*3 Intake air temperature sensor
*4 Throttle position sensor
*5 Closed throttle position switch
*6 Camshaft position sensor
*7 Crankshaft position sensor
*8 Barometric pressure sensor
*9 Engine coolant temperature sensor
*10 IAC valve position sensor
• Power supply
• Vehicle speed sensor
• Air conditioning switch
• Park/Neutral position switch
• Power steering pressure switch
• Ignition switch-ST

Engine control module

☆1 Injector
☆2 Idle air control motor
☆3 Evaporative emission purge solenoid
• Fuel pump relay
• Multiport fuel injection (MFI) relay
• Air conditioning compressor clutch relay
• Check engine/Malfunction indicator lamp
• On-board diagnostic output
• Ignition coil, ignition power transistor

Idle air control motor

Fast idle air valve (FIAV)

Evaporative emission canister

Intake air temperature sensor

Volume air flow sensor (with barometric pressure sensor)

*3

*10

*5

☆2

P

☆3

Evaporative emission purge solenoid

Throttle position sensor (with closed throttle position switch)

*4

Air cleaner

*2 *8

To fuel tank

Fuel pressure regulator

From fuel pump

Positive crankcase ventilation valve

Injector

☆1

*1

Oxygen sensor

*9

Engine coolant temperature sensor

Catalytic converter

*7 Crankshaft position sensor

*6 Camshaft position sensor

Fig. 55 Engine control system — 1993 Colt w/1.8L engine — U.S. and Canada, except California

*1 Heated oxygen sensor (front)
*2 Volume air flow sensor
*3 Intake air temperature sensor
*4 Throttle position sensor
*5 Closed throttle position switch
*6 Camshaft position sensor
*7 Crankshaft position sensor
*8 Barometric pressure sensor
*9 Engine coolant temperature sensor
*10 IAC valve position sensor
*11 EGR temperature sensor
*12 Heated oxygen sensor (Rear)
● Power supply
● Vehicle speed sensor
● Air conditioning switch
● Park/Neutral position switch
● Power steering pressure switch
● Ignition switch-ST

⇒   Engine control module   ⇒

☆1 Injector
☆2 Idle air control motor
☆3 Evaporative emission purge solenoid
☆4 EGR solenoid
● Fuel pump relay
● Multiport fuel injection (MFI) relay
● Air conditioning compressor clutch relay
● Check engine/Malfunction indicator lamp
● On-board diagnostic output
● Ignition coil, ignition power transistor

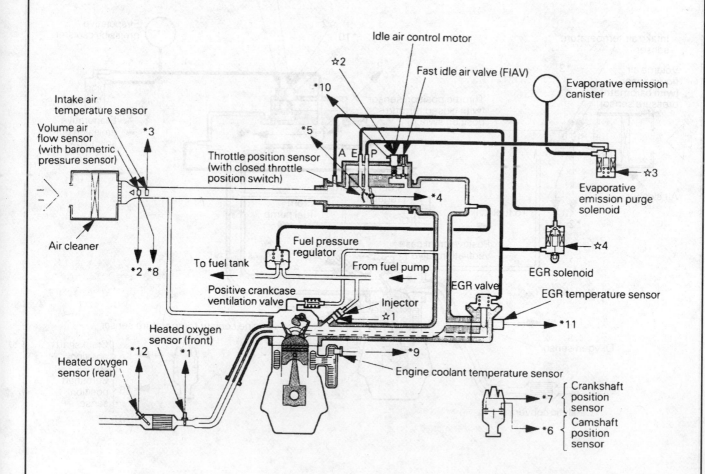

Fig. 56 Engine control system — 1993 Colt w/1.8L engine — California only

Diagnostic trouble code		On-board diagnostic items	Check items (Remedy)	Memory
No.	Output signal pattern			
–	H ⎍ L (12A0104)	Engine control module	(Replace engine control module)	–
11	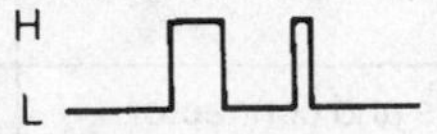 H ⊓⊓ L (12A0104)	Oxygen sensor <Federal/Canada> Heated oxygen sensor (front) <California>	• Harness and connector • Fuel pressure • Injectors (Replace if defective) • Intake air leaks • Oxygen sensor	Retained
12	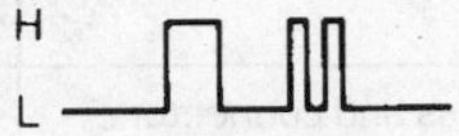 H ⊓⊓⊓ L (12A0104)	Volume air flow sensor	• Harness and connector (If harness and connector are normal, replace volume air flow sensor assembly.)	Retained
13	 H ⊓⊓⊓⊓ L (12A0104)	Intake air temperature sensor	• Harness and connector • Intake air temperature sensor	Retained
14	 H ⊓⊓⊓⊓⊓ L (12A0104)	Throttle position sensor	• Harness and connector • Throttle position sensor • Closed throttle position switch	Retained

Fig. 57 Diagnosis fault tree — 1993 Colt w/1.8 engine

Diagnostic trouble code		On-board diagnostic items	Check items (Remedy)	Memory
No.	Output signal pattern			
21	H L  12A0107	Engine coolant temperature sensor	• Harness and connector • Engine coolant temperature sensor	Retained
22	H L 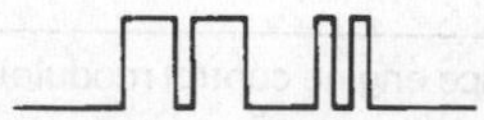 12A0107	Crankshaft position sensor	• Harness and connector (If harness and connector are normal, replace distributor assembly.)	Retained
23	H L  12A0107	Camshaft position sensor	• Harness and connector (If harness and connector are normal, replace distributor assembly.)	Retained
24	H L 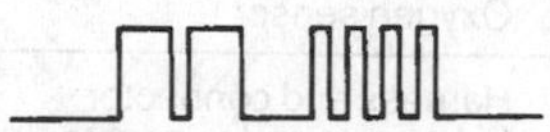 12A0107	Vehicle speed sensor (reed switch)	• Harness and connector • Vehicle speed sensor (reed switch)	Retained
25	H L 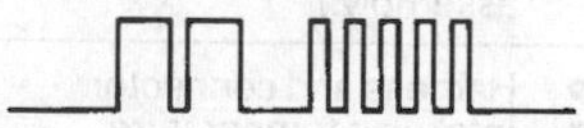 12A0107	Barometric pressure sensor	• Harness and connector (If harness and connector are normal, replace volume air flow sensor assembly.)	Retained
36	H L  12A0107	Ignition timing adjustment signal	• Harness and connector	··
41	H L  12A0107	Injector	• Harness and connector • Injector coil resistance	Retained
43	H L  12A0107	EGR <California>	• Harness and connector • EGR valve • EGR solenoid • EGR valve control vacuum • EGR temperature sensor	Retained
55	H L  12A0107	IAC valve position sensor	• Harness and connector • IAC valve movement (If harness, connector and IAC valve movement are normal, replace Idle air control motor assembly)	Retained
59	H L 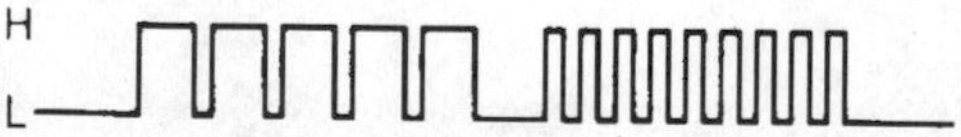 12A0106	Heated oxygen sensor (rear) <California>	• Harness and connector • Heated oxygen sensor	Retained
	H L  12A0107	Normal state		

NOTE
1. Replace the engine control module if a diagnostic trouble code is output although the inspection reveals that there is no problem with the check items.
2. The code numbers will be displayed in order, starting from the lowest.

Fig. 58 Diagnosis fault tree — 1993 Colt w/1.8 engine cont.

EMISSION CONTROL SYSTEMS VACUUM HOSE DIAGRAMS

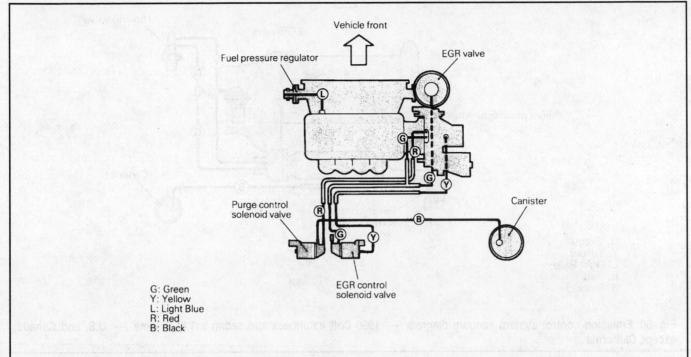

G: Green
Y: Yellow
L: Light Blue
R: Red
B: Black

Fig. 59 Emission control system vacuum diagram — 1990 Colt hatchback and sedan w/1.5L engine — California only

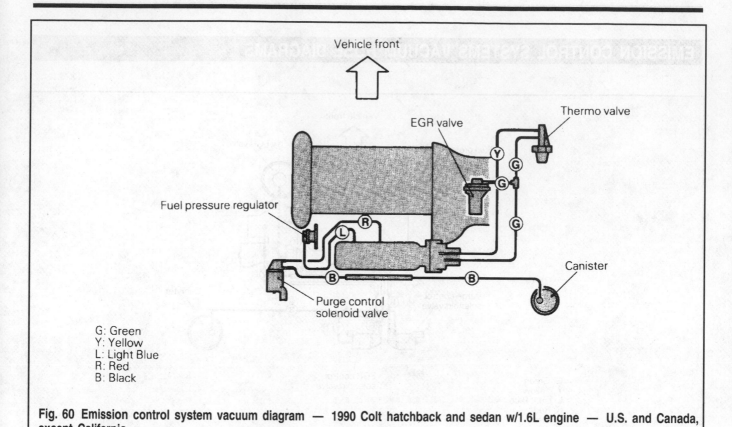

G: Green
Y: Yellow
L: Light Blue
R: Red
B: Black

Fig. 60 Emission control system vacuum diagram — 1990 Colt hatchback and sedan w/1.6L engine — U.S. and Canada, except California

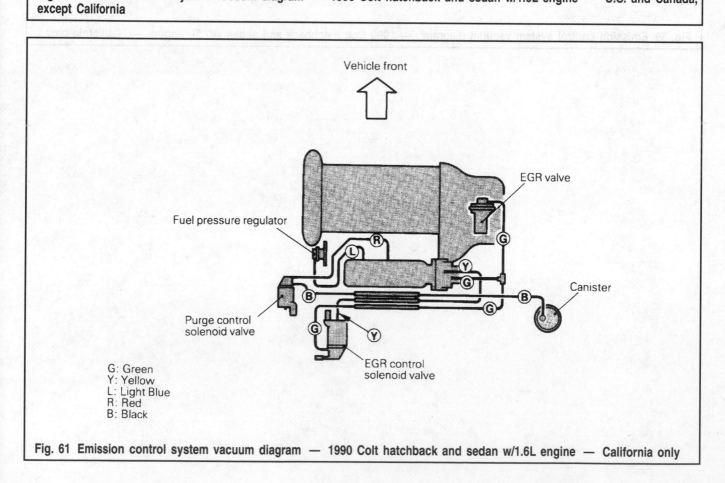

G: Green
Y: Yellow
L: Light Blue
R: Red
B: Black

Fig. 61 Emission control system vacuum diagram — 1990 Colt hatchback and sedan w/1.6L engine — California only

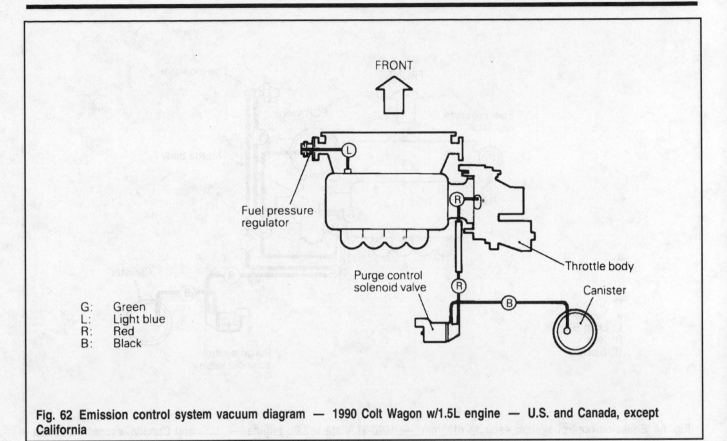

Fig. 62 Emission control system vacuum diagram — 1990 Colt Wagon w/1.5L engine — U.S. and Canada, except California

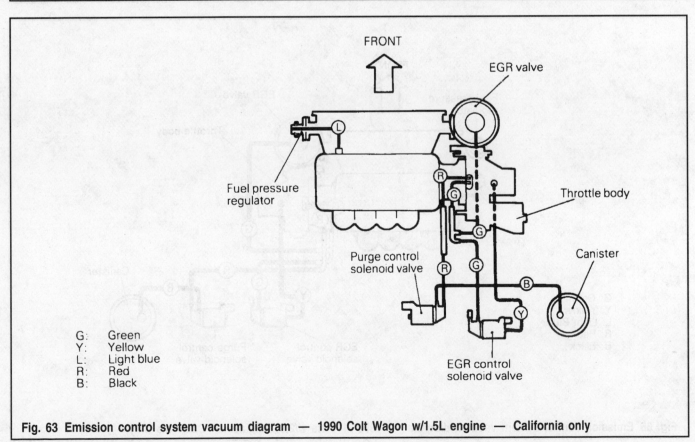

Fig. 63 Emission control system vacuum diagram — 1990 Colt Wagon w/1.5L engine — California only

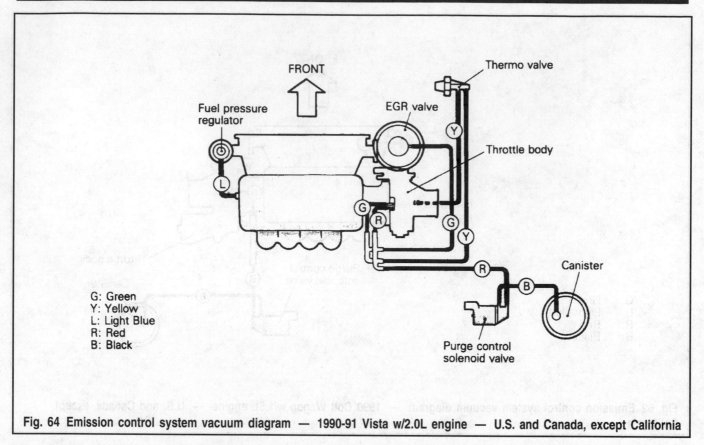

G: Green
Y: Yellow
L: Light Blue
R: Red
B: Black

Fig. 64 Emission control system vacuum diagram — 1990-91 Vista w/2.0L engine — U.S. and Canada, except California

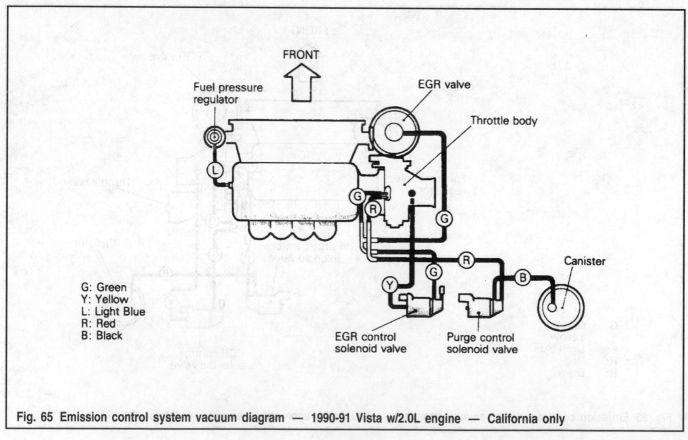

G: Green
Y: Yellow
L: Light Blue
R: Red
B: Black

Fig. 65 Emission control system vacuum diagram — 1990-91 Vista w/2.0L engine — California only

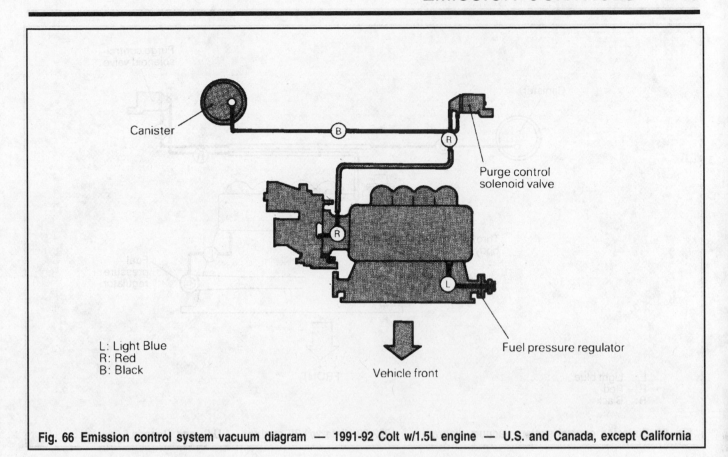

L: Light Blue
R: Red
B: Black

Fig. 66 Emission control system vacuum diagram — 1991-92 Colt w/1.5L engine — U.S. and Canada, except California

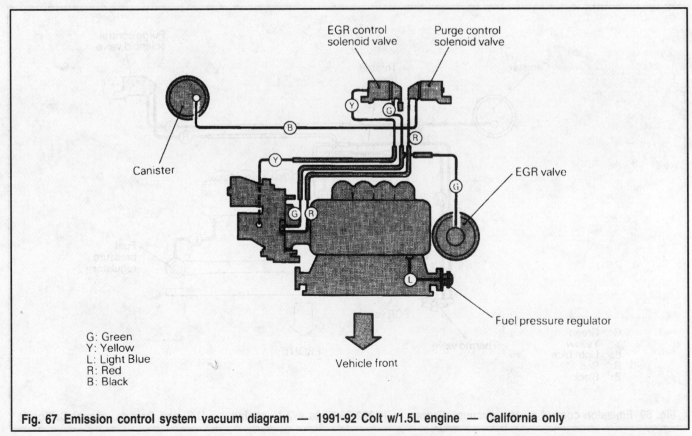

G: Green
Y: Yellow
L: Light Blue
R: Red
B: Black

Fig. 67 Emission control system vacuum diagram — 1991-92 Colt w/1.5L engine — California only

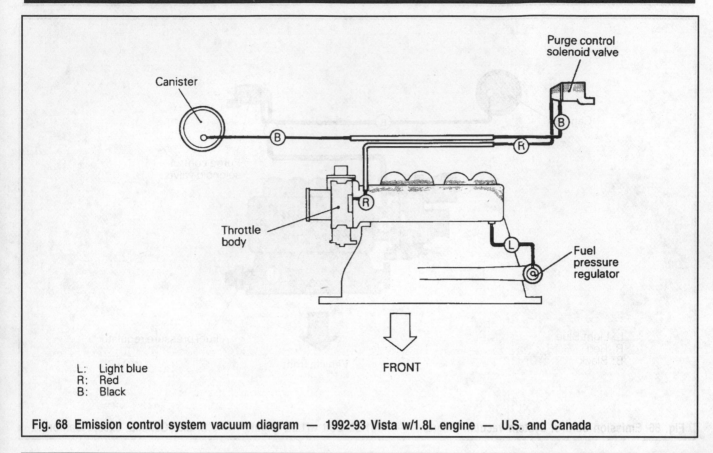

L: Light blue
R: Red
B: Black

FRONT

Fig. 68 Emission control system vacuum diagram — 1992-93 Vista w/1.8L engine — U.S. and Canada

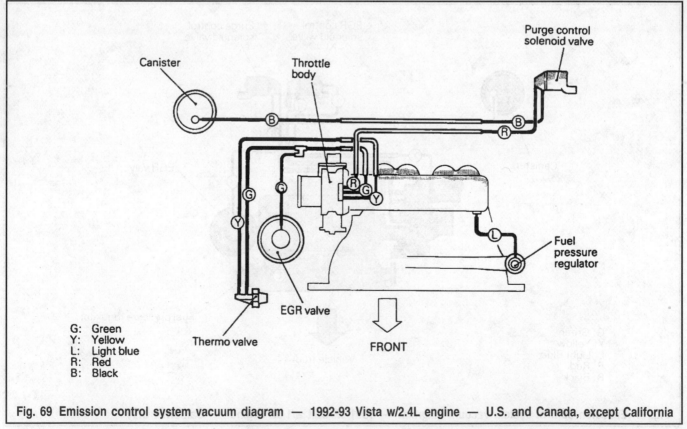

G: Green
Y: Yellow
L: Light blue
R: Red
B: Black

FRONT

Fig. 69 Emission control system vacuum diagram — 1992-93 Vista w/2.4L engine — U.S. and Canada, except California

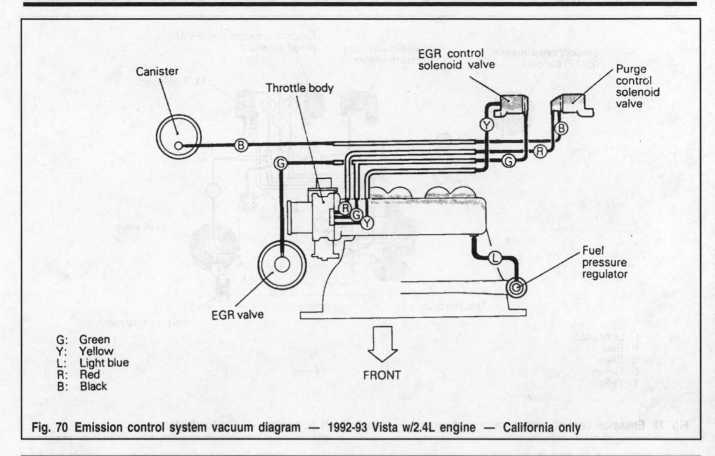

G: Green
Y: Yellow
L: Light blue
R: Red
B: Black

FRONT

Fig. 70 Emission control system vacuum diagram — 1992-93 Vista w/2.4L engine — California only

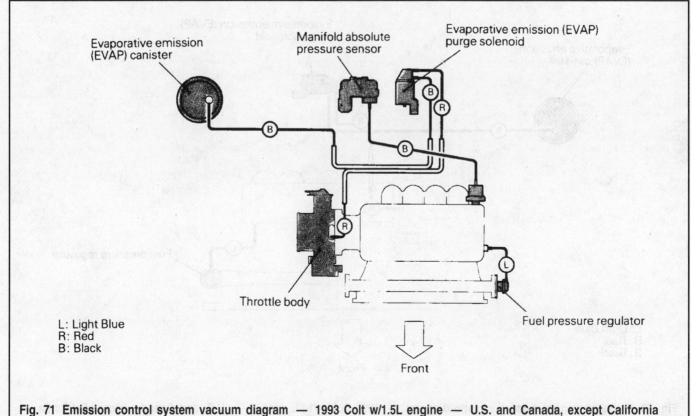

L: Light Blue
R: Red
B: Black

Front

Fig. 71 Emission control system vacuum diagram — 1993 Colt w/1.5L engine — U.S. and Canada, except California

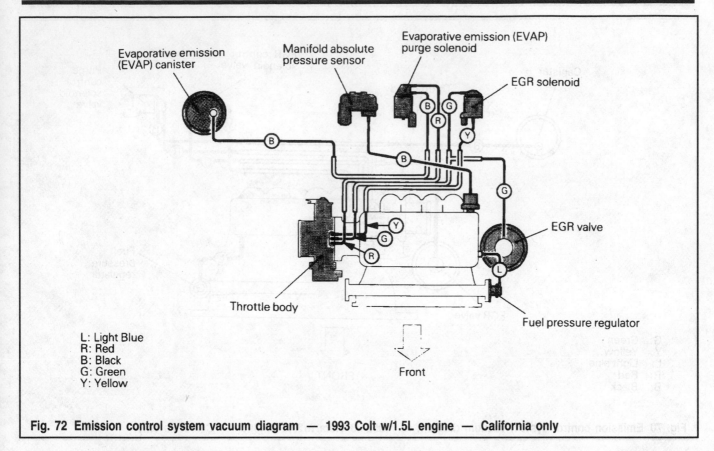

L: Light Blue
R: Red
B: Black
G: Green
Y: Yellow

Fig. 72 Emission control system vacuum diagram — 1993 Colt w/1.5L engine — California only

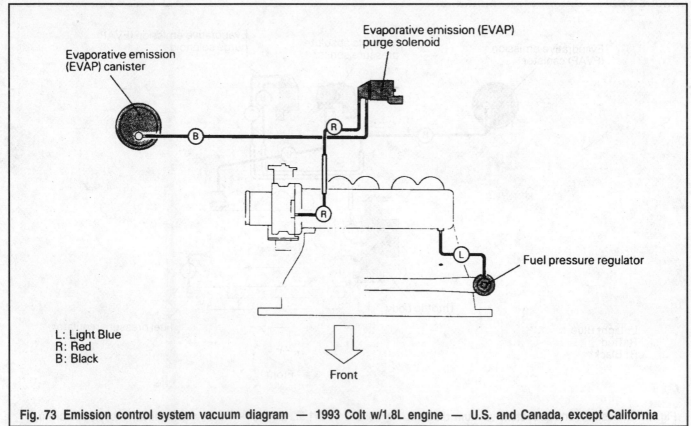

L: Light Blue
R: Red
B: Black

Fig. 73 Emission control system vacuum diagram — 1993 Colt w/1.8L engine — U.S. and Canada, except California

5

FUEL SYSTEM

GENERAL FUEL SYSTEM SERVICE

Fuel System Service Precautions

Safety is the most important factor when performing not only fuel system maintenance but any type of maintenance. Failure to conduct maintenance and repairs in a safe manner may result in serious personal injury or death. Maintenance and testing of the vehicle's fuel system components can be accomplished safely and effectively by adhering to the following rules and guidelines.

• To avoid the possibility of fire and personal injury, always disconnect the negative battery cable unless the repair or test procedure requires that battery voltage be applied.

• Always relieve the fuel system pressure prior to disconnecting any fuel system component (injector, fuel rail, pressure regulator, etc.), fitting or fuel line connection. Exercise extreme caution whenever relieving fuel system pressure to avoid exposing skin, face and eyes to fuel spray. Please be advised that fuel under pressure may penetrate the skin or any part of the body that it contacts.

• Always place a shop towel or cloth around the fitting or connection prior to loosening to absorb any excess fuel due to spillage. Ensure that all fuel spillage (should it occur) is quickly removed from engine surfaces. Ensure that all fuel soaked cloths or towels are deposited into a suitable waste container.

• Always keep a dry chemical (Class B) fire extinguisher near the work area.

• Do not allow fuel spray or fuel vapors to come into contact with a spark or open flame.

• Always use a backup wrench when loosening and tightening fuel line connection fittings. This will prevent unnecessary stress and torsion to fuel line piping. Always follow the proper torque specifications.

• Always replace worn fuel fitting O-rings with new. Do not substitute fuel hose or equivalent where fuel pipe is installed.

Relieving Fuel System Pressure

1. Disconnect the fuel pump harness connector located near the fuel tank. To access this connector it may be necessary, depending on year and model, to remove the rear seat cushion and carpet. Note the fuel pump wire running along the floor. It has an inwire connector in it.

2. Start the engine and uncouple the connector in the wire. Let the engine stop by itself.

3. Turn the key to OFF. Disconnect the negative battery cable.

MULTI-POINT FUEL INJECTION SYSTEM (MPI)

Electric Fuel Pump

All cars are equipped with an electric fuel pump. The fuel pump is in the gas tank.

PRESSURE TESTING

▶ **See Figures 1, 2, 3 and 4**

1. Install a suitable fuel pressure gauge to the fuel delivery pipe, be sure to tighten the bolt at 18-25 ft. lbs. (25-34 Nm).

2. Apply voltage to the terminal for the fuel pump drive and activate the fuel pump; then, with fuel pressure applied, check that there is no fuel leakage from the pressure gauge or the special tool connection pipe.

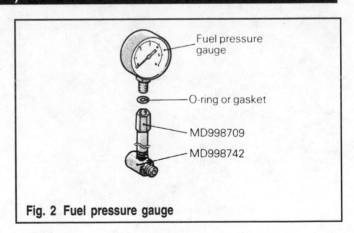

Fuel pressure gauge

O-ring or gasket

MD998709

MD998742

Fig. 2 Fuel pressure gauge

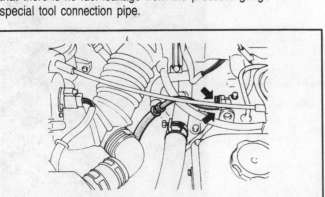

Fig. 1 Fuel pressure gauge connection points

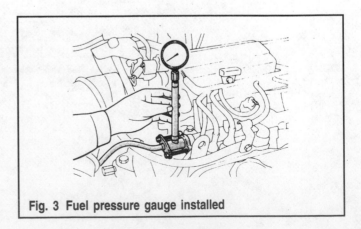

Fig. 3 Fuel pressure gauge installed

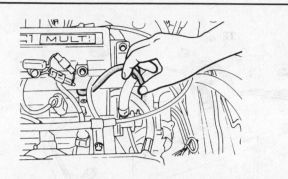

Fig. 4 Plugging the vacuum regulator hose

3. Disconnect and plug the vacuum hose at the pressure regulator. Measure the fuel pressure during idling. The standard value is 47-50 psi (330-350 kPa).

4. Measure the fuel pressure when the vacuum hose is connected to the pressure regulator. The standard value is 38 psi (270 kPa).

5. If the fuel pressure readings are not within specifications, determine the probable cause and make the necessary repairs.

6. Remove all test equipment, use a new gasket and tighten the bolt on the delivery pipe to 18-25 ft. lbs. (25-34). Start the engine and check for fuel leaks.

REMOVAL & INSTALLATION

▶ **See Figures 5, 6, 7, 8, 9, 10, 11, 12 and 13**

❋❋CAUTION

The electric fuel pump supplies fuel under high pressure. The system pressure must be relieved before servicing the fuel system. Working around gasoline is extremely dangerous unless precautions are taken! NEVER smoke! Make sure the electrical system is disconnected. Avoid prolonged contact of gasoline with the skin. Wear safety glasses. Avoid prolonged breathing of gasoline vapors.

1. Relieve the fuel system pressure.
2. Remove the fuel tank as described at the end of this Section.
3. Disconnect the hoses at the pump.
4. Unbolt and remove the pump.
5. Install the new pump. Use a new gasket. Connect the fuel lines, inline connector and battery cable.

TROUBLESHOOTING

If the fuel pump doesn't work:
1. Check the fuse.
2. Check all wiring connections.
3. Check the control relay which is located in the engine compartment, next to the ignition coil. If the engine starts when the ignition switch is turned to START but stops when it is turned to ON, the relay is defective. Jumper terminals 1 and 2 of the test connector, the fuel pump should operate. If the

pump fails to operate when the the jumper is connected, the pump is probably defective.

Throttle Body

▶ **See Figures 14, 15 and 16**

REMOVAL & INSTALLATION

❋❋CAUTION

Gasoline in either liquid or vapor state is EXTREMELY explosive. Take great care to contain spillage. Work in an open or well-ventilated area. Do not connect or disconnect electrical connectors while fuel hoses are removed or loosened. Observe smoking/no open flame rules during repairs. Have a dry-chemical fire extinguisher (type B-C) within arm's reach at all times and know how to use it.

➡**The throttle body for each of the engines is slightly different. The procedure below is general and may require slight alteration of sequence depending on the engine.**

1. Disconnect the negative battery cable.
2. Drain the coolant, at least to a level below the intake manifold.

❋❋CAUTION

When draining the coolant, keep in mind that cats and dogs are attracted by the ethylene glycol antifreeze, and are quite likely to drink any that is left in an uncovered container or in puddles on the ground. This will prove fatal in sufficient quantity. Always drain the coolant into a sealable container. Coolant should be reused unless it is contaminated or several years old.

3. Disconnect the main air intake duct from the throttle body.
4. Label and disconnect the vacuum and breather hoses running to the throttle body. Take care that clamps are not bent or distorted during removal.
5. Disconnect the accelerator cable and the cruise control cable if so equipped. On some engines, the bracket holding the cable to the intake manifold must be removed.
6. Label and disconnect the coolant hoses running to the throttle body.
7. Follow each wire running from the throttle body. Label and disconnect each at its connector. Most of the wiring harnesses have connectors at some distance from the throttle body. Loosen, release or remove any clips or brackets holding the throttle body harnesses in place.
8. Carefully remove the four nuts and bolts holding the throttle body to the manifold. On 1.6L, the throttle body is supported by a bracket which must be removed before the throttle body can be removed.

➡**Some throttle bodies have the idle speed control servo assembly mounted on the top of the unit. The large bracket may appear to be holding the throttle body in place. It should not be removed from the throttle body.**

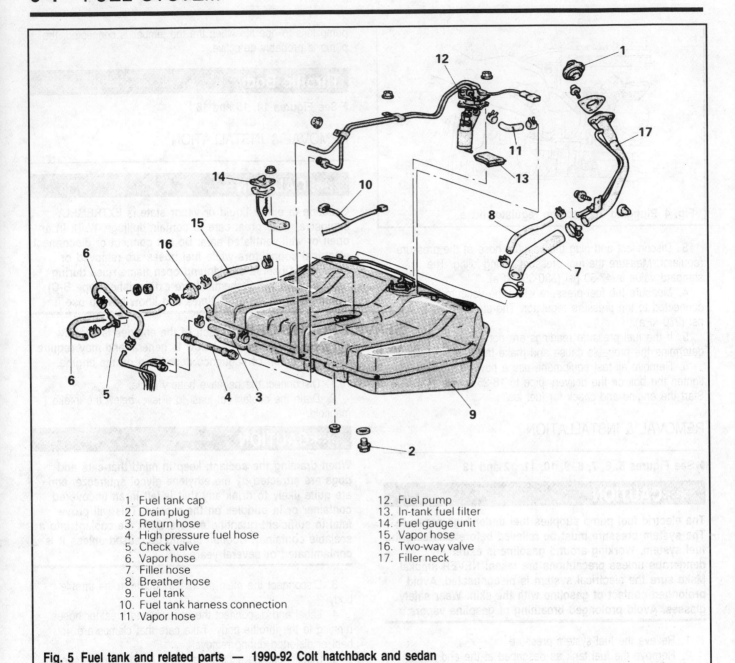

1. Fuel tank cap
2. Drain plug
3. Return hose
4. High pressure fuel hose
5. Check valve
6. Vapor hose
7. Filler hose
8. Breather hose
9. Fuel tank
10. Fuel tank harness connection
11. Vapor hose
12. Fuel pump
13. In-tank fuel filter
14. Fuel gauge unit
15. Vapor hose
16. Two-way valve
17. Filler neck

Fig. 5 Fuel tank and related parts — 1990-92 Colt hatchback and sedan

9. Lift the throttle body away from the manifold and handle it carefully. Place it in a protected location.

10. If the unit is being replaced, compare the old and the new ones. Look for any components which need to be transferred from the old unit. The throttle plate area may be cleaned with a spray cleaner, but must be completely dry before installation. Disassembly of the throttle body is not recommended.

To install:

11. Before reinstalling, make sure that all remains of the old gasket are removed from both the manifold flange and the base of the throttle body. Place a new gasket on the manifold and hold the throttle body in place. Don't forget the support bracket on the twin cam engines.

12. Install the four nuts and bolts finger tight. Tighten the bolts evenly, alternating from bolt to bolt, in small increments.

The bolts must draw down evenly, creating an airtight seal against the gasket.

13. Tighten the nuts and bolts to 11 Nm (8 ft. lbs.). The bracket bolt or nut is tightened to the same figure.

14. Reconnect the wiring connectors to the harnesses. Secure, tighten or reinstall any wire clips or retainers. The harnesses must be kept clear of moving or hot surfaces.

15. Install the coolant hoses, making sure each is properly clamped to its port.

16. Install the accelerator cable and cruise control cable if so equipped. Adjust the cable to the correct tension and make certain the lock nuts or bracket bolts are secure.

17. Connect the vacuum hoses. Examine the end of each and replace any showing signs of cracking or hardening.

18. Install the main air duct and connect the breather tubes.

19. Refill the coolant to the proper level.

20. Connect the negative battery cable.

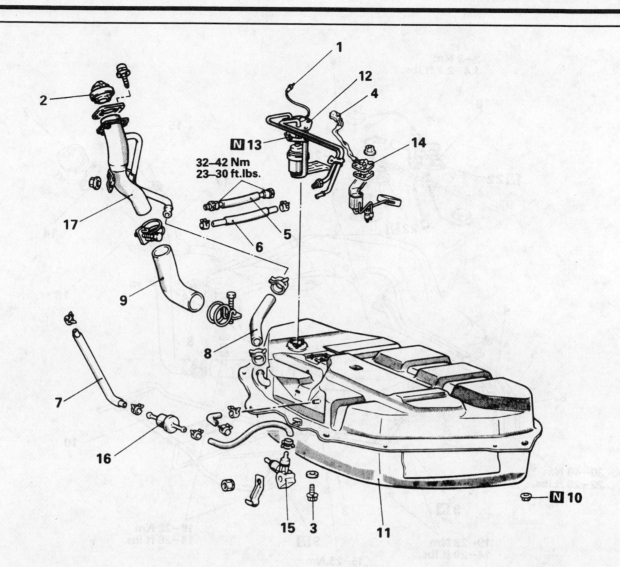

32–42 Nm
23–30 ft.lbs.

1. Connection for fuel pump
2. Fuel tank cap
3. Drain plug
4. Connection for fuel gauge unit
5. Fuel high pressure hose
6. Return hose
7. Vapor hose
8. Leveling hose
9. Filler hose
10. Self-locking nut
11. Fuel tank
12. Electrical fuel pump
13. Gasket
14. Fuel gauge unit
15. Fuel check valve
16. Overfill limiter (two-way valve)
17. Filler neck

Fig. 6 Fuel tank and related parts — 1990 Colt Wagon

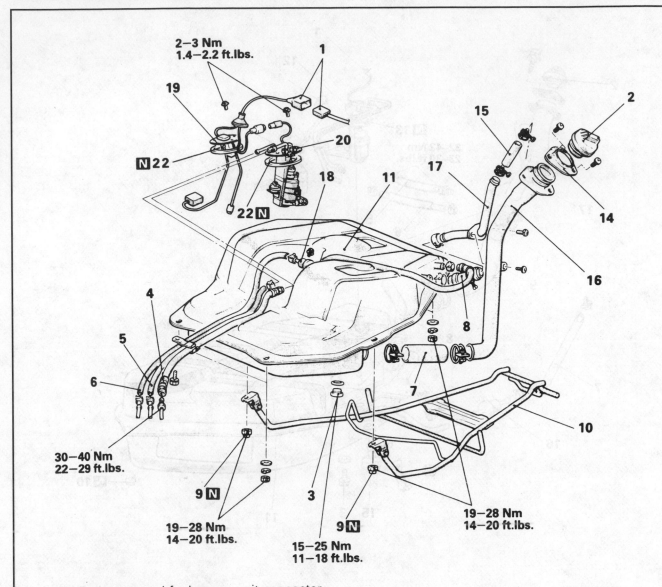

1. Fuel pump and fuel gauge unit connector
2. Fuel tank cap
3. Drain plug
4. Connection of fuel high-pressure hose
5. Fuel return hose
6. Fuel vapor hose
7. Fuel filler hose
8. Breather hose
9. Self-locking nuts
10. Spare tire carrier
11. Fuel tank
14. Packing
15. Breather hose
16. Fuel filler neck
17. Breather pipe
18. Overfill limiter (two-way valve)
19. Fuel gauge unit
20. Electric fuel pump
22. Packing

Fig. 7 Fuel tank and related parts — 1990-91 2WD Vista

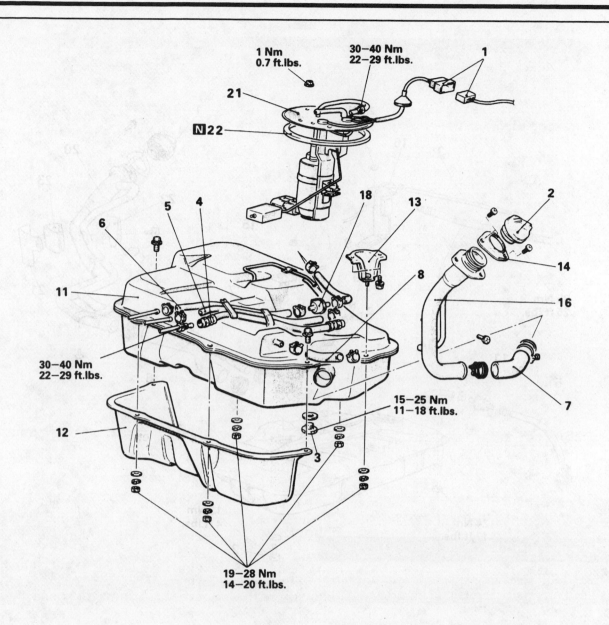

1 Nm
0.7 ft.lbs.

30—40 Nm
22—29 ft.lbs.

21

N 22

18

13

2

14

16

5

4

6

11

8

30—40 Nm
22—29 ft.lbs.

7

15—25 Nm
11—18 ft.lbs.

12

3

19—28 Nm
14—20 ft.lbs.

1. Fuel pump and fuel gauge unit connector
2. Fuel tank cap
3. Drain plug
4. Connection of fuel high-pressure hose
5. Fuel return hose
6. Fuel vapor hose
7. Fuel filler hose
8. Breather hose
11. Fuel tank
12. Fuel tank protector
13. Tank bracket
14. Packing
16. Fuel filler neck
18. Overfill limiter (two-way valve)
21. Fuel pump and fuel gauge unit assembly
22. Packing

Fig. 8 Fuel tank and related parts — 1990-91 4WD Vista

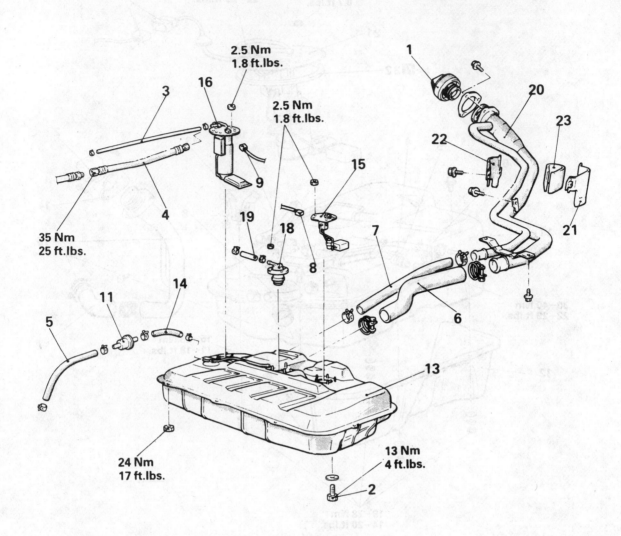

1. Fuel tank cap
2. Drain plug
3. Return hose
4. Fuel high-pressure hose
5. Vapor hose
6. Filler hose
7. Vapor hose
8. Fuel gauge unit connector
9. Fuel pump connector
11. Two-way valve
13. Fuel tank
14. Vapor hose
15. Fuel gauge unit
16. Fuel pump
18. Fuel cut off valve
19. Vapor hose
20. Filler neck
21. Protector (A)
22. Protector (B)
23. Insulator

Fig. 9 Fuel tank and related parts — 1992-93 2WD Vista

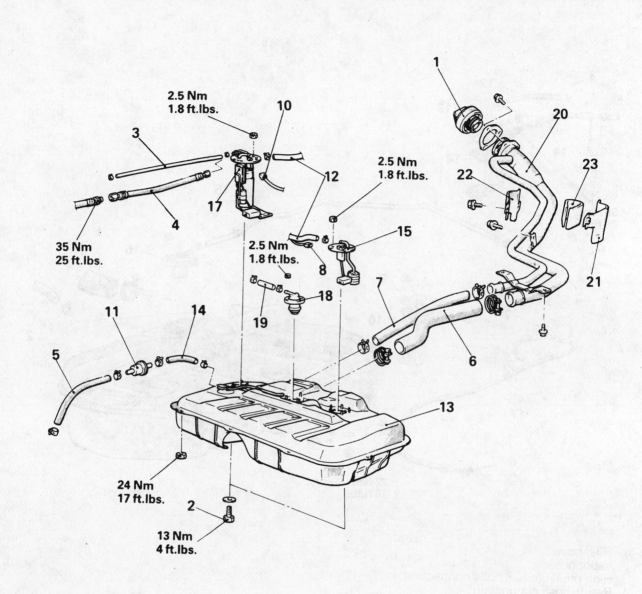

2.5 Nm
1.8 ft.lbs.

35 Nm
25 ft.lbs.

2.5 Nm
1.8 ft.lbs.

2.5 Nm
1.8 ft.lbs.

24 Nm
17 ft.lbs.

13 Nm
4 ft.lbs.

1. Fuel tank cap
2. Drain plug
3. Return hose
4. Fuel high-pressure hose
5. Vapor hose
6. Filler hose
7. Vapor hose
8. Fuel gauge unit connector
10. Fuel gauge and pump assembly connector
11. Two-way valve
12. Suction hose

13. Fuel tank
14. Vapor hose
15. Fuel gauge unit
17. Fuel gauge and pump assembly
18. Fuel cut off valve
19. Vapor hose
20. Filler neck
21. Protector (A)
22. Protector (B)
23. Insulator

Fig. 10 Fuel tank and related parts — 1992-93 4WD Vista

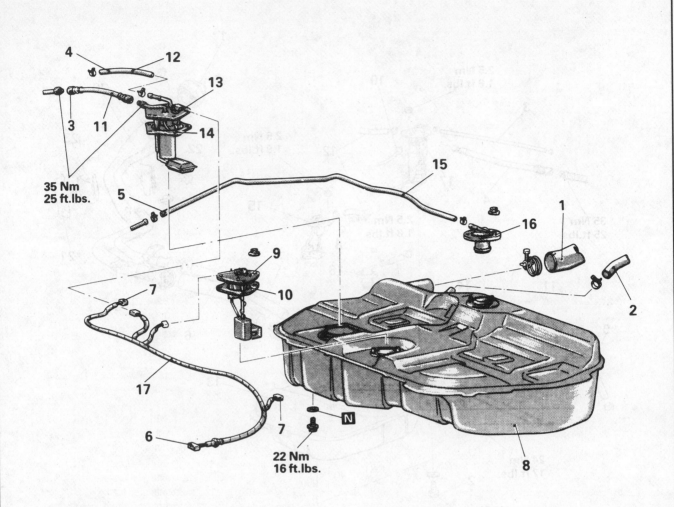

1. Filler hose
2. Vapor hose
3. High-pressure fuel hose connection
4. Return hose connection
5. Vapor hose connection
6. Fuel gauge and pump connector
7. Rear speed sensor connector
   <Vehicles with ABS>
8. Fuel tank assembly
9. Fuel gauge unit
10. Packing
11. High-pressure fuel hose
12. Return hose
13. Fuel pump
14. Packing
15. Vapor hose
16. Fuel cut off valve
17. Fuel gauge and pump wiring harness

Fig. 11 Fuel tank and related parts — 1993 Colt hatchback and sedan

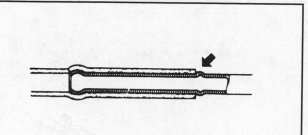

Fig. 12 The vapor hoses must be pushed onto the pipes until they touch the second bulge

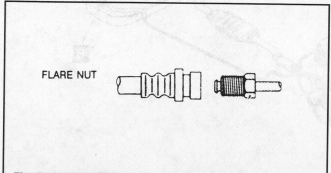

FLARE NUT

Fig. 13 Use great care when tightening the high pressure fuel connections

Fuel Injectors

REMOVAL & INSTALLATION

❋❋WARNING

The injectors are extremely sensitive to dirt and impact. They must be handled gently and protected at all times. The entire work area must be as clean as possible. Any particle of dirt entering the system can foul an injector or change its operation. Any gaskets or O-rings removed with the injector MUST be replaced with new ones at reassembly. Do not attempt to reuse these seals; high pressure fuel leaks may result.

Except 1.6L Engines
▶ See Figures 17 and 18

1. Safely relieve the pressure within the fuel system.

❋❋CAUTION

The fuel system is under pressure. Release pressure slowly and contain spillage. Observe no smoking/no open flame precautions. Have a Class B-C (dry powder) fire extinguisher within arm's reach at all times.

2. Disconnect the negative battery cable.

3. Disconnect the high pressure fuel line at the delivery pipe (rail). The O-ring inside the fitting is not reusable.

❋❋WARNING

Wrap the connection in a clean towel or cloth before disconnecting. Some pressure will remain within the system.

4. Disconnect the fuel return hose and remove its O-ring.
5. Disconnect the electrical connector to each injector. Label each at the time of removal.
6. Remove the bolts holding the injector rail; remove the rubber grommets or insulators below the rail mounting points.
7. Lift the rail with the injectors attached up and away from the engine. Take great care not to drop any of the injectors during this removal.

❋❋WARNING

If an injector should fall and hit the floor or other hard surface, it must be considered unusable.

8. The injectors may be removed from the rail with a gentle pull. Both the grommet and O-ring on the top of the injector must be discarded and replaced. The lower insulator or seat must also be removed and replaced.
9. Reassembly begins by installing a new grommet and O-ring (in that order) onto the injector. Coat the O-ring with a light coating of gasoline. Do not use grease or oil.
10. Install each injector into the rail, making sure that the injector turns freely when in place. If it does not turn under finger pressure, remove it, inspect the O-ring and reinsert the injector. (While the injector does not turn during its operation, its ability to turn is an indicator of correct installation).
11. Replace the seats in the intake manifold. Install the delivery pipe and the injectors onto the manifold without dropping an injector. Make certain the rubber bushings are in place under the delivery pipe brackets.
12. Tighten the fuel rail bolts to 11 Nm (8 ft. lbs or 72 INCH lbs.).
13. Connect each electrical connector to the proper injector.
14. Replace the O-ring, coat it lightly with gasoline and connect the fuel pressure regulator. Tighten the connection to 8 Nm (6 ft. lbs or 72 INCH lbs.).
15. Connect the fuel return hose.
16. Replace the O-ring, coat it lightly with gasoline and install the high pressure fuel line. Make certain the O-ring is not damaged during installation. Tighten the bolts to 4 Nm (3 ft. lbs. or 36 INCH lbs.).
17. Connect the negative battery cable.

1.6L Engines
▶ See Figure 19

1. Safely relieve the pressure within the fuel system.

❋❋CAUTION

The fuel system is under pressure. Release pressure slowly and contain spillage. Observe no smoking/no open flame precautions. Have a Class B-C (dry powder) fire extinguisher within arm's reach at all times.

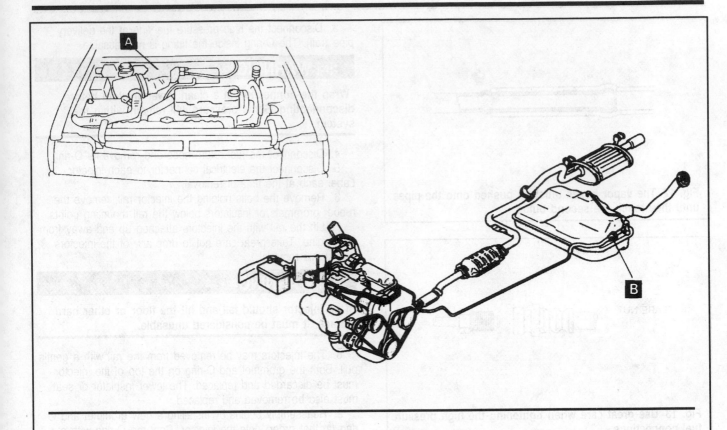

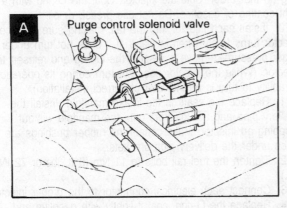

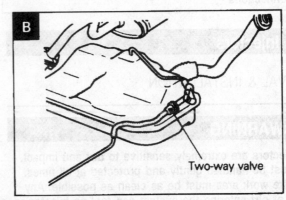

Fig. 14 Throttle body and related parts — 1990-92 1.5L and 1990 1.8L engines

2. Disconnect the negative battery cable.

3. Disconnect the high pressure fuel line at the delivery pipe (rail). The O-ring inside the fitting is not reusable.

❈❈WARNING

Wrap the connection in a clean towel or cloth before disconnecting. Some pressure will remain within the system.

4. Disconnect the fuel return hose and remove its O-ring. Disconnect the vacuum hose from the fuel pressure regulator.

5. Remove the fuel pressure regulator and its O-ring.

6. Disconnect the PCV hose.

7. Remove the electrical connector from each injector.

8. Remove the bolts holding the delivery pipe to the engine. Note that the accelerator cable retaining brackets will come off.

9. Lift the rail with the injectors attached up and away from the engine. Take great care not to drop any of the injectors during this removal.

❈❈WARNING

If an injector should fall and hit the floor or other hard surface, it must be considered unusable.

10. The injectors may be removed from the rail with a gentle pull. Both the grommet and O-ring on the top of the injector must be discarded and replaced. The lower insulator or seat must also be removed and replaced.

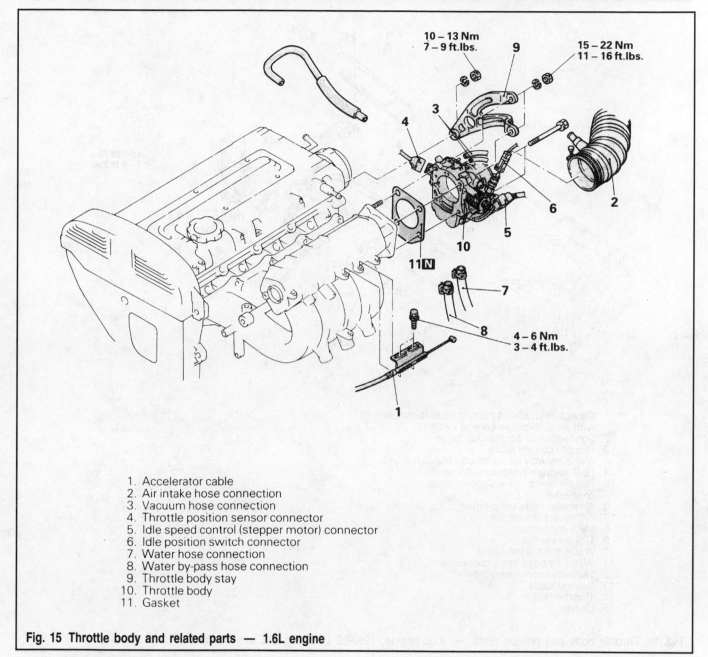

10 – 13 Nm
7 – 9 ft.lbs.

15 – 22 Nm
11 – 16 ft.lbs.

4 – 6 Nm
3 – 4 ft.lbs.

1. Accelerator cable
2. Air intake hose connection
3. Vacuum hose connection
4. Throttle position sensor connector
5. Idle speed control (stepper motor) connector
6. Idle position switch connector
7. Water hose connection
8. Water by-pass hose connection
9. Throttle body stay
10. Throttle body
11. Gasket

Fig. 15 Throttle body and related parts — 1.6L engine

11. Reassembly begins by installing a new grommet and O-ring (in that order) onto the injector. Coat the O-ring with a light coating of gasoline. Do not use grease or oil.

12. Install each injector into the rail, making sure that the injector turns freely when in place. If it does not turn under finger pressure, remove it, inspect the O-ring and reinsert the injector. (While the injector does not turn during its operation, its ability to turn is an indicator of correct installation).

13. Replace the seats in the intake manifold. Install the delivery pipe and the injectors onto the manifold without dropping an injector. Make certain the rubber bushings are in place under the delivery pipe brackets.

14. Tighten the fuel rail bolts to 11 Nm (8 ft. lbs or 72 INCH lbs.) Remember to include the accelerator cable brackets under the bolt.

15. Connect each electrical connector to the proper injector.

16. Connect the PCV hose.

17. Replace the O-ring, coat it lightly with gasoline and install the fuel pressure regulator. Tighten the fasteners to 8 Nm (6 ft. lbs or 72 INCH lbs.).

18. Connect the fuel return hose.

19. Replace the O-ring, coat it lightly with gasoline and install the high pressure fuel line. Make certain the O-ring is not damaged during installation. Tighten the bolts to 4 Nm (36 INCH lbs.).

20. Connect the negative battery cable.

FUEL INJECTOR TESTING

▶ See Figure 20

The simplest way to test the injectors is simply to listen to them with the engine running. Use a mechanic's stethoscope, touch each injector while the engine is idling. You should hear

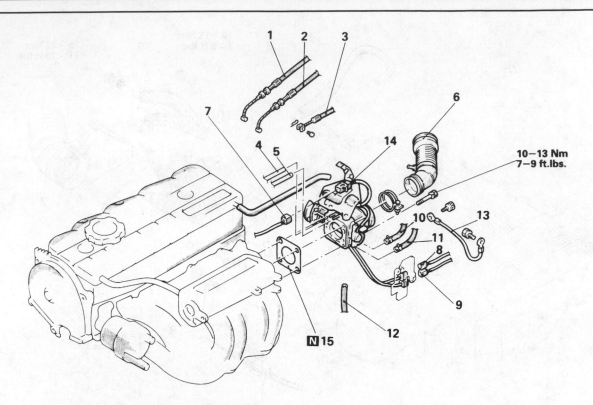

1. Connction of speed control cable (Vehicles with an auto-cruise control system)
2. Connection of accelerator cable
3. Throttle control cable (Vehicles with an automatic transaxle)
4. EGR vacuum hose connection
5. Purge control valve vacuum hose connection
6. Air intake hose connection
7. ISC motor connector
8. MPS connector
9. TPS connector
10. Water hose connection
11. Water by-pass hose connection
12. Vacuum hose connection
13. Ground cable
14. Throttle body
15. Gasket

Fig. 16 Throttle body and related parts — 2.0L engine; 1992-93 1.8L and 2.4L are similar

a distinct clicking as each injector opens and closes. Check that the operating sound increases as the engine speed is increased.

➡**The sounds of the other injector(s) may be heard, even though the one being checked is not operating. Listen to each injector to get a feel for normal sounds; the one with the abnormal sound is the problem.**

Additionally, the resistance of the injector can be easily checked. Disconnect the negative battery cable and remove the electrical connector from the injector to be tested. Use an ohmmeter to check the resistance across the terminals of the injector. Correct resistance at 68°F (20°C) is 13-16ω.

Slight variations are acceptable due to temperature conditions.

Bench testing of the injectors can only be done using expensive special equipment. Generally this equipment can be found at a dealership and sometimes at a well-equipped machine shop or performance shop. There is no provision for field testing the injectors by the owner/mechanic. DO NOT attempt to test the injector by removing it from the engine and making it spray into a jar.

Never attempt to check a removed injector by hooking it directly to the battery. The injector runs on a much smaller voltage and the 12 volts from the battery will destroy it internally. Since this happens at the speed of electricity, you don't get a second chance.

TESTING THE INJECTION SYSTEM AND SENSORS

For complete fuel injection testing, see the Engine Controls part of Section 4.

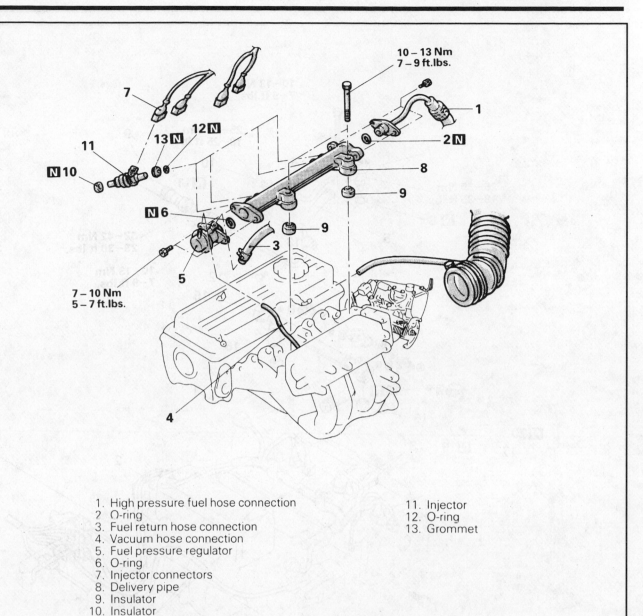

1. High pressure fuel hose connection
2. O-ring
3. Fuel return hose connection
4. Vacuum hose connection
5. Fuel pressure regulator
6. O-ring
7. Injector connectors
8. Delivery pipe
9. Insulator
10. Insulator
11. Injector
12. O-ring
13. Grommet

Fig. 17 Fuel injectors and related parts — 1990-93 1.5L, 1990 1.8L and 1992-93 1.8L engines

As stated before, the heart of any fuel injection system is the computer or ECU. Besides reacting to the changing signals from various sensors and controlling various relays, switches and injectors, the ECU can serve an important diagnostic function. It 'knows' what characteristics to look for in the signal from each unit. If any irregularity is detected (improper voltage, improper time duration, etc) the ECU notes the problem and assigns it a predetermined identifying number. if two of more faults are sensed, the codes are stored in numeric order. In some cases a light on the dashboard will come on to show a fault has occurred. Even without a dash light, the fault code is stored in the computer until someone asks for it.

If you're going to read these codes, certain conditions must be observed. Since the codes are maintained by battery voltage, the battery must be fully charged. If the battery is low on charge, the codes may be lost. The codes will be lost (erased) if the battery cable is disconnected or if the ECU is

disconnected before the codes are read. Additionally, the engine should be fully warmed up and driven a good distance before retrieving the codes; this allows the sensors and the oxygen sensor to enter their proper ranges.

Mitsubishi, like most manufacturers, has a diagnostic tool which plugs into the system between the wire harness and the ECU. This tester allows the operator to read out trouble codes and check the operation of various components during operation. Think of the tester as a window through which you can see the voltages change as they are transmitted to or from the ECU. If the normal values are known, a faulty item can be quickly found.

Unfortunately, these diagnostic tools are extremely expensive. The cost far exceeds the need of the owner/mechanic who is occasionally servicing one or two cars. If you suspect a fuel injection system problem that cannot be found through more common diagnostic means, take the car to

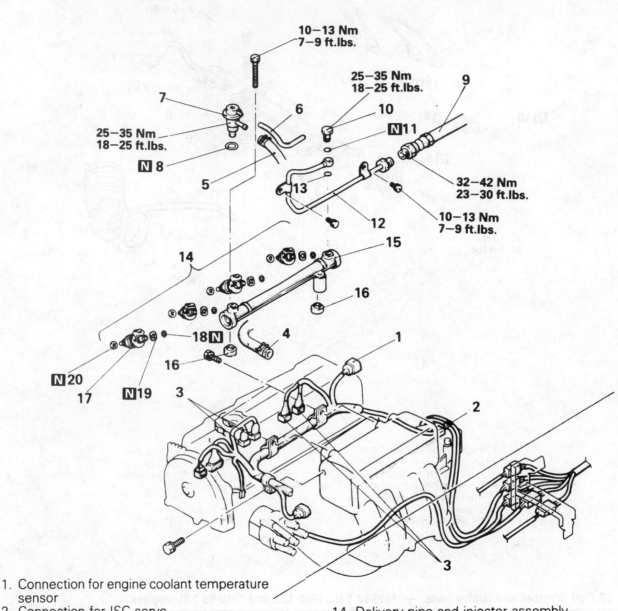

10—13 Nm
7—9 ft.lbs.

25—35 Nm
18—25 ft.lbs.

25—35 Nm
18—25 ft.lbs.

32—42 Nm
23—30 ft.lbs.

10—13 Nm
7—9 ft.lbs.

7

6

10

9

5

8

13

12

11

14

15

16

18

16

4

1

20

17

19

3

2

3

1. Connection for engine coolant temperature sensor
2. Connection for ISC servo
3. Connection for injectors
4. Connection of brake booster vacuum hose
5. Connection of fuel return hose
6. Connection of vacuum hose (to air intake plenumn)
7. Fuel pressure regulator
8. O-ring
9. Connection of fuel high pressure hose
10. Eye bolt
11. Gasket
12. Fuel inlet pipe
13. Gasket
14. Delivery pipe and injector assembly
15. Delivery pipe
16. Insulator
17. Injector
18. O-ring
19. Grommet
20. Insulator

Fig. 18 Fuel injectors and related parts — 2.0L and 2.4L engines

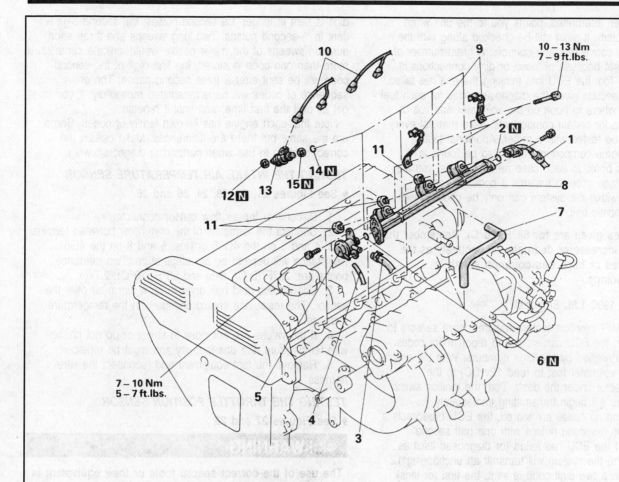

10 – 13 Nm
7 – 9 ft.lbs.

7 – 10 Nm
5 – 7 ft.lbs.

1. High pressure fuel hose connection
2. O-ring
3. Fuel return hose connection
4. Vacuum hose connection
5. Fuel pressure regulator
6. O-ring
7. PCV hose
8. Delivery pipe
9. Accelerator cable clamp
10. Injector connectors

11. Insulator
12. Insulator
13. Injector
14. O-ring
15. Grommet

Fig. 19 Fuel injectors and related parts — 1.6L engines

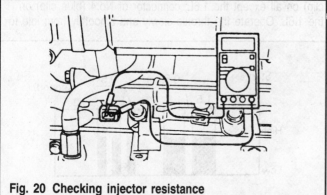

Fig. 20 Checking injector resistance

either a dealer or a reputable diagnostic shop. The cost will be well repaid by the speed of diagnosis.

The stored codes may also be read on an analog (dial type) voltmeter hooked into the system. Since the output from the ECU is electrical, the meter needle will deflect or sweep as the pulses are generated. Recording the number of sweeps and their time duration will yield the numeric code involved. (For example: Two ½-second sweeps followed by a 2 second pause followed by three ½-sweeps might indicate code 23 or code 2 and code 3, depending on the system.).

✳✳WARNING

The order of the fault codes does NOT indicate the order of occurrence. Multiple codes are stored in numerical order, regardless of which occurred first.

The code, when interpreted, points you to the unit which may be the problem. It must still be checked along with the attendant wiring, connectors and controls. A great number of fault codes are set because of loose or dirty connections in the wiring which fool the ECU into thinking the unit has failed.

The following section gives the diagnosis codes for each fuel injected engine, where to hook up the voltmeter and volt or ohmmeter testing for certain components. Note that not every component can be tested with a meter. Additional testing information for some components may also be found in Section 4 in this book. In each case remember that you are only reading voltage used to transmit a code; the actual voltage running within the system can only be checked with the factory diagnostic unit.

➡**All resistances given are for 68°F (20°C). Remember that resistance will increase or decrease respectively as the temperature rises or falls. Use common sense in interpreting readings.**

1.5L, 1.6L, and 1990 1.8L Engines

Because the MPI injection system requires more sensors to operate properly, the ECU can store and report more codes. The codes are identified by two digit numbers. With the engine off, connect the voltmeter (set to read 12v DC) to the diagnostic connector under the dash. Turn the ignition switch to **ON**; the codes will begin transmitting immediately.

If all is well and no codes are stored, the ECU broadcasts a steady stream of ½-second pulses with one half second between each. If the ECU has failed (or diagnosed itself as having a problem) the system will transmit an unchanging 12 volt signal. When a two digit code is sent, the first (or tens)

digit is sent in longer 1½ second pulses; the second digit is sent in ½-second pulses. Two long sweeps and three short duration sweeps of the meter needle would indicate code 23. If more than one code is stored, the first digit of the second code will be sent after a three second pause. The entire sequence of codes will be retransmitted repeatedly; if you don't get all of it the first time, wait until it repeats.

Note that each engine has its own family of codes. Some are the same but there are differences. Make certain the correct chart is in use when performing diagnostic work.

TESTING THE INTAKE AIR TEMPERATURE SENSOR

▶ **See Figures 21, 22, 23, 24, 25 and 26**

1. Disconnect the air flow sensor connector.
2. Connect the terminals of the ohmmeter between terminal Nos. 4 and 6 on the 4G15 or Nos. 6 and 8 on the 4G61. Resistance will depend on air temperature. Two reference points are: 32°F (0°C), 6kω and 68°F (20°C), 2.7kω.
3. Use a hand-held hair dryer to blow warm air over the sensor. The resistance should change with the temperature increase.
4. If the values are not close to target or do not change with temperature, the unit is faulty and must be replaced.
5. Remove the test equipment and reconnect the wire harness.

TESTING THE THROTTLE POSITION SENSOR

▶ **See Figures 27 and 28**

✳✳WARNING

The use of the correct special tools or their equivalent is REQUIRED for this procedure. Wiring harness adapter MD 998478 (998464 for 1.6L) is highly recommended to prevent damage to the wiring and connectors.

1. With the engine off, disconnect the TPS wiring connector.
2. Install the special wiring device between the connectors.
3. On all except the 1.6L, connect the ohmmeter across terminal Nos. 1 (ground; the black clip on the adapter) and 2 (the red clip on the adapter). On the 1.6L, connect the ohmmeter to terminal No. 2 (red clip) and 3 (white clip). In both cases, the resistance should be 3.5-6.5 kω;.
4. Move the positive ohmmeter lead to terminal No.3 (blue clip) on all except the 1.6L; connector or No.4 (blue clip) on the 1.6L. Operate the throttle slowly and smoothly from idle to

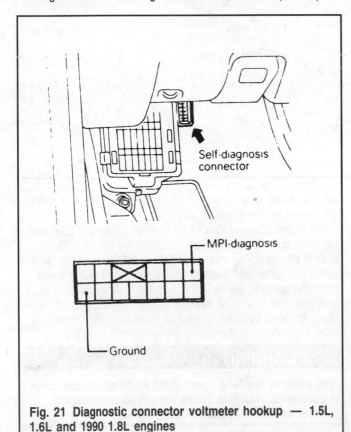

Fig. 21 Diagnostic connector voltmeter hookup — 1.5L, 1.6L and 1990 1.8L engines

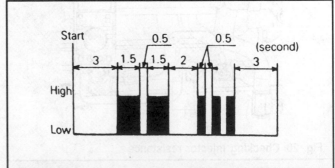

Fig. 22 Pulse duration indicates place value for each 2-digit code

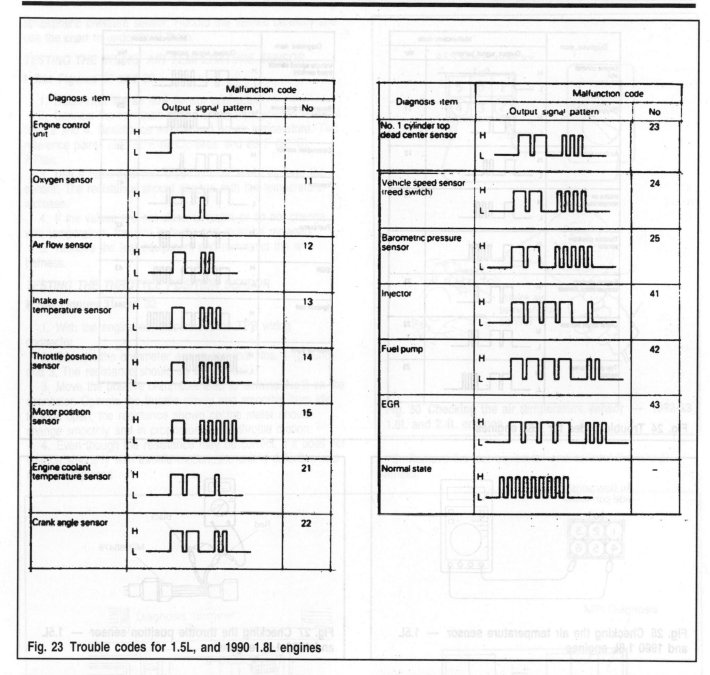

Diagnosis item	Malfunction code	
	Output signal pattern	No
Engine control unit	H ___/‾‾‾‾‾‾‾‾ L	
Oxygen sensor	H ___/‾__/‾___ L	11
Air flow sensor	H ___/‾__/‾_/‾_ L	12
Intake air temperature sensor	H ___/‾__/‾_/‾_/‾_ L	13
Throttle position sensor	H ___/‾__/‾_/‾_/‾_/‾_ L	14
Motor position sensor	H ___/‾__/‾_/‾_/‾_/‾_/‾_ L	15
Engine coolant temperature sensor	H ___/‾_/‾__/‾___ L	21
Crank angle sensor	H ___/‾_/‾__/‾_/‾_ L	22

Diagnosis item	Malfunction code	
	Output signal pattern	No
No. 1 cylinder top dead center sensor	H _/‾_/‾__/‾_/‾_/‾_ L	23
Vehicle speed sensor (reed switch)	H _/‾_/‾__/‾_/‾_/‾_/‾_ L	24
Barometric pressure sensor	H _/‾_/‾__/‾_/‾_/‾_/‾_/‾_ L	25
Injector	H _/‾_/‾_/‾_/‾__/‾_ L	41
Fuel pump	H _/‾_/‾_/‾_/‾__/‾_/‾_ L	42
EGR	H _/‾_/‾_/‾_/‾__/‾_/‾_/‾_ L	43
Normal state	H _/\/\/\/\/\/\/\/\/_ L	–

Fig. 23 Trouble codes for 1.5L, and 1990 1.8L engines

wide open; the resistance shown on the meter should change smoothly and in proportion to the throttle motion. Even though the resistance may be correct, if it does not change smoothly with throttle motion, the unit is defective and must be replaced.

5. Remove the test equipment and connect the wiring harness.

RESETTING THE SYSTEM

After recording the fault code and making repairs based on diagnosis, disconnect the negative battery cable for at least 15 seconds. Reconnect the cable and check for fault codes after running the engine. If the repair cured the problem, the original fault code should not reappear. The fault code will remain stored (even after repair) if the battery cable is not disconnected.

1992-93 1.8L and 2.4L Engines

With the ignition switch off, open the glovebox and pull out the diagnostic connector located behind the glovebox. It may be easier to remove the glovebox completely; the diagnostic connector is not on a very long harness. Connect the voltmeter (set to read 12v DC) to the diagnostic connector, observing the correct polarity. The codes will be transmitted when the ignition is turned **ON**.

The codes will be transmitted as a series of long and short duration pulses which you will see as needle motion on the meter. A short pulse translates as a zero and a long pulse as a one. These binary codes are are 5 digits long and all must be read before knowing the code. An example would be: short-short-long-short-short or 00100. This is not code 100; it is the designation — in binary code — for trouble code 4 or the

Malfunction No.	Diagnosis item	Self-diagnosis output pattern and output code
0	Normal	H / L — 0 0 0 0 0
1	Oxygen sensor	H / L — 1 0 0 0 0
2	Crank angle sensor	H / L — 0 1 0 0 0
3	AFS	H / L — 1 1 0 0 0
4	Atmospheric pressure sensor	H / L — 0 0 1 0 0

Malfunction No.	Diagnosis item	Self-diagnosis output pattern and output code
5	TPS	H / L — 1 0 1 0 0
6	MPS	H / L — 0 1 1 0 0
7	Coolant temperature sensor	H / L — 1 1 1 0 0
8	No. 1 cylinder TDC sensor	H / L — 0 0 0 1 0

Fig. 31 The binary codes are not difficult but may be confusing. Record the needle sweeps carefully

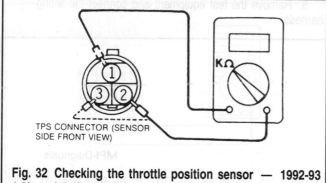

Fig. 32 Checking the throttle position sensor — 1992-93 1.8L and 2.4L engines

RESETTING THE SYSTEM

After recording the fault code and making repairs based on diagnosis, disconnect the negative battery cable for at least 15 seconds. Reconnect the cable and check for fault codes after running the engine. If the repair cured the problem, the original fault code should not reappear. The fault code will remain stored (even after repair) if the battery cable is not disconnected.

2.0L Engines

This engine incorporates several additional sensors to improve engine control and driveability. The ECU can store and report more codes. The codes are identified by two digit numbers. With the engine off, connect the voltmeter (set to read 12v DC) to the diagnostic connector under the dash. Turn the ignition switch to **ON**; the codes will begin transmitting immediately.

If all is well and no codes are stored, the ECU broadcasts a steady stream of ½-second pulses with one half second between each. If the ECU has failed (or diagnosed itself as having a problem) the system will transmit an unchanging 12 volt signal. When a two digit fault code is sent, the first (or tens) digit is sent in longer 1½ second pulses; the second digit is sent in ½-second pulses. Two long sweeps and three short-duration sweeps of the meter needle would indicate code 23. If more than one code is stored, the first digit of the second code will be sent after a three second pause. The entire sequence of codes will be retransmitted repeatedly; if you don't get all of it the first time, wait until it repeats.

Note that each engine has its own family of codes. Some are the same but there are differences. Make certain the correct chart is in use when performing diagnostic work.

TESTING THE INTAKE AIR TEMPERATURE SENSOR
▶ See Figure 33

1. Disconnect the air flow sensor connector.
2. Connect the terminals of the ohmmeter between terminal Nos. 4 and 6 on either engine. Resistance will depend on air temperature. Two reference points are: 32°F (0°C), 6kω; and 68°F (20°C), 2.7kω;.
3. Use a hand-held hair dryer to blow warm air over the sensor. The resistance should change with the temperature increase.
4. If the values are not close to target or do not change with temperature, the unit is faulty and must be replaced.
5. Remove the test equipment and reconnect the wire harness.

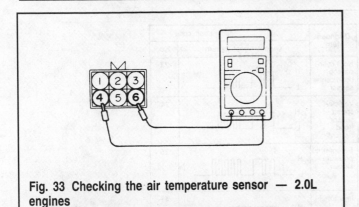

Fig. 33 Checking the air temperature sensor — 2.0L engines

TESTING THE THROTTLE POSITION SENSOR

▶ See Figures 34 and 35

✳✳WARNING

The use of the correct special tools or their equivalent is REQUIRED for this procedure. Wiring harness adapter MD 998478 for the SOHC or 998464 for the DOHC is highly recommended to prevent damage to the wiring and connectors.

1. With the engine off, disconnect the TPS wiring connector.
2. Install the special wiring device between the connectors.
3. On the SOHC, connect the ohmmeter across terminal Nos. 1 (ground; the black clip on the adapter) and 2 (the red

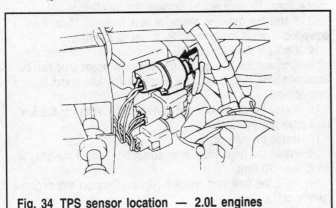

Fig. 34 TPS sensor location — 2.0L engines

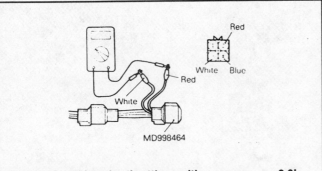

Fig. 35 Checking the throttle position sensor — 2.0L engines

clip on the adapter). On the DOHC, connect the ohmmeter to terminal No. 2 (red clip) and 3 (white clip). In both cases, the resistance should be 3.5-6.5 kω;.

4. Move the positive ohmmeter lead to terminal No.3 (blue clip) on the SOHC connector or No.4 (blue clip) on the DOHC. Operate the throttle slowly and smoothly from idle to wide open; the resistance shown on the meter should change smoothly and in proportion to the throttle motion.

5. Even though the resistance may be correct, if it does not change smoothly with throttle motion, the unit is defective and must be replaced.

6. Remove the test equipment and connect the wiring harness.

RESETTING THE SYSTEM

▶ See Figures 36 and 37

After recording the fault code and making repairs based on diagnosis, disconnect the negative battery cable for at least 15 seconds. Reconnect the cable and check for fault codes after running the engine. If the repair cured the problem, the original fault code should not reappear. The fault code will remain stored (even after repair) if the battery cable is not disconnected.

Fuel Tank

REMOVAL & INSTALLATION

▶ See Figures 5, 6, 7, 8, 9, 10, 11, 12 and 13

✳✳CAUTION

When working on fuel tanks, be sure to disconnect the battery ground (negative) cable. The fuel system pressure must be relieved. See the Fuel Pump procedures, above.

1. Disconnect the negative battery cable.
2. Drain the fuel tank using an approved tank pump and container. Remove and drain the remaining fuel using the drain plug, if so equipped.
3. Remove the fuel cap.
4. Remove the spare tire and carrier (2WD Vista) or the fuel tank protector (4WD Vista).

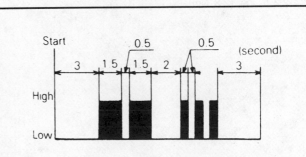

Fig. 36 Pulse duration indicates place value for each 2-digit code

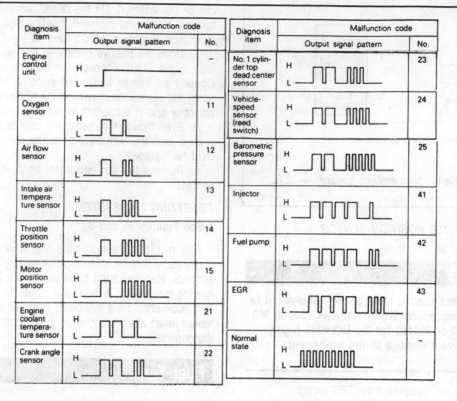

Diagnosis item	Malfunction code		Diagnosis item	Malfunction code	
	Output signal pattern	No.		Output signal pattern	No.
Engine control unit		—	No. 1 cylinder top dead center sensor		23
Oxygen sensor		11	Vehicle-speed sensor (reed switch)		24
Air flow sensor		12	Barometric pressure sensor		25
Intake air temperature sensor		13	Injector		41
Throttle position sensor		14	Fuel pump		42
Motor position sensor		15	EGR		43
Engine coolant temperature sensor		21	Normal state		—
Crank angle sensor		22			

Fig. 37 Trouble codes for 2.0L engines

5. Disconnect the fuel gauge unit and fuel hoses that can be accessed before lowering the tank. Disconnect the fuel pump connectors.

6. Disconnect the filler hose.

7. Place a floor jack and a piece of wood under the tank before removing the straps or retaining bolts.

8. Remove the retaining straps and the tank retaining bolts, if so equipped.

9. Slowly lower the tank and disconnect any electrical or fuel connections. Be care not to damage the fuel fittings.

10. Remove all hardware from the old tank if installing a new tank. Remove the fuel pump nuts and remove the pump.

To install:

11. Install all hardware to the tank, if installing a new tank. Always use new gaskets around the fuel pump and gauge unit. Install the pump and gauge unit. Torque the nuts or bolts to 1.4-2.2 ft. lbs. (2-3 Nm).

12. Slowly raise the tank and connect any electrical or fuel connections. Be care not to damage the fuel fittings.

13. Install the retaining straps or tank retaining bolts, if so equipped. Torque the bolts to 20 ft. lbs. (27 Nm).

14. Connect the filler hose.

15. Connect the fuel gauge unit and fuel hoses that can be accessed after raising the tank. Connect the fuel pump connectors.

16. Install the spare tire and carrier (2WD Vista) or the fuel tank protector (4WD Vista).

17. Install the fuel cap.

18. Install the drain plug, if so equipped. Torque the plug to 15 ft. lbs. (20 Nm).

19. Refill the tank and check for leaks. Connect the negative battery cable.

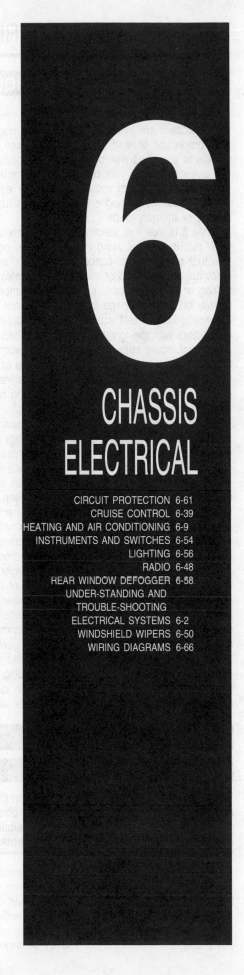

6

CHASSIS ELECTRICAL

UNDER-STANDING AND TROUBLE-SHOOTING ELECTRICAL SYSTEMS

With the rate at which both import and domestic manufacturers are incorporating electronic control systems into their production lines, it won't be long before every new vehicle is equipped with one or more on-board computer, like the unit installed on your car. These electronic components (with no moving parts) should theoretically last the life of the vehicle, provided nothing external happens to damage the circuits or memory chips.

While it is true that electronic components should never wear out, in the real world malfunctions do occur. It is also true that any computer-based system is extremely sensitive to electrical voltages and cannot tolerate careless or haphazard testing or service procedures. An inexperienced individual can literally do major damage looking for a minor problem by using the wrong kind of test equipment or connecting test leads or connectors with the ignition switch ON. When selecting test equipment, make sure the manufacturers instructions state that the tester is compatible with whatever type of electronic control system is being serviced. Read all instructions carefully and double check all test points before installing probes or making any test connections.

The following section outlines basic diagnosis techniques for dealing with computerized automotive control systems. Along with a general explanation of the various types of test equipment available to aid in servicing modern electronic automotive systems, basic repair techniques for wiring harnesses and connectors is given. Read the basic information before attempting any repairs or testing on any computerized system, to provide the background of information necessary to avoid the most common and obvious mistakes that can cost both time and money. Although the replacement and testing procedures are simple in themselves, the systems are not, and unless one has a thorough understanding of all components and their function within a particular computerized control system, the logical test sequence these systems demand cannot be followed. Minor malfunctions can make a big difference, so it is important to know how each component affects the operation of the overall electronic system to find the ultimate cause of a problem without replacing good components unnecessarily. It is not enough to use the correct test equipment; the test equipment must be used correctly.

Safety Precautions

✳✳CAUTION

Whenever working on or around any computer based microprocessor control system, always observe these general precautions to prevent the possibility of personal injury or damage to electronic components.

• Never install or remove battery cables with the key ON or the engine running. Jumper cables should be connected with the key OFF to avoid power surges that can damage electronic control units. Engines equipped with computer controlled systems should avoid both giving and getting jump starts due to the possibility of serious damage to components

from arcing in the engine compartment when connections are made with the ignition ON.

• Always remove the battery cables before charging the battery. Never use a high output charger on an installed battery or attempt to use any type of 'hot shot' (24 volt) starting aid.

• Exercise care when inserting test probes into connectors to insure good connections without damaging the connector or spreading the pins. Always probe connectors from the rear (wire) side, NOT the pin side, to avoid accidental shorting of terminals during test procedures.

• Never remove or attach wiring harness connectors with the ignition switch ON, especially to an electronic control unit.

• Do not drop any components during service procedures and never apply 12 volts directly to any component (like a solenoid or relay) unless instructed specifically to do so. Some component electrical windings are designed to safely handle only 4 or 5 volts and can be destroyed in seconds if 12 volts are applied directly to the connector.

• Remove the electronic control unit if the vehicle is to be placed in an environment where temperatures exceed approximately 176°F (80°C), such as a paint spray booth or when arc or gas welding near the control unit location in the car.

ORGANIZED TROUBLESHOOTING

When diagnosing a specific problem, organized troubleshooting is a must. The complexity of a modern automobile demands that you approach any problem in a logical, organized manner. There are certain troubleshooting techniques that are standard:

1. Establish when the problem occurs. Does the problem appear only under certain conditions? Were there any noises, odors, or other unusual symptoms?

2. Isolate the problem area. To do this, make some simple tests and observations; then eliminate the systems that are working properly. Check for obvious problems such as broken wires, dirty connections or split or disconnected vacuum hoses. Always check the obvious before assuming something complicated is the cause.

3. Test for problems systematically to determine the cause once the problem area is isolated. Are all the components functioning properly? Is there power going to electrical switches and motors? Is there vacuum at vacuum switches and/or actuators? Is there a mechanical problem such as bent linkage or loose mounting screws? Doing careful, systematic checks will often turn up most causes on the first inspection without wasting time checking components that have little or no relationship to the problem.

4. Test all repairs after the work is done to make sure that the problem is fixed. Some causes can be traced to more than one component, so a careful verification of repair work is important to pick up additional malfunctions that may cause a problem to reappear or a different problem to arise. A blown fuse, for example, is a simple problem that may require more than another fuse to repair. If you don't look for a problem that

caused a fuse to blow, for example, a shorted wire may go undetected.

Experience has shown that most problems tend to be the result of a fairly simple and obvious cause, such as loose or corroded connectors or air leaks in the intake system; making careful inspection of components during testing essential to quick and accurate troubleshooting. Special, hand held computerized testers designed specifically for diagnosing the system are available from a variety of aftermarket sources, as well as from the vehicle manufacturer, but care should be taken that any test equipment being used is designed to diagnose that particular computer controlled system accurately without damaging the control unit (ECU) or components being tested.

➡Pinpointing the exact cause of trouble in an electrical system can sometimes only be accomplished by the use of special test equipment. The following describes commonly used test equipment and explains how to put it to best use in diagnosis. In addition to the information covered below, the manufacturer's instructions booklet provided with the tester should be read and clearly understood before attempting any test procedures.

TEST EQUIPMENT

Jumper Wires

Jumper wires are simple, yet extremely valuable, pieces of test equipment. Jumper wires are merely wires that are used to bypass sections of a circuit. The simplest type of jumper wire is merely a length of multistrand wire with an alligator clip at each end. Jumper wires are usually fabricated from lengths of standard automotive wire and whatever type of connector (alligator clip, spade connector or pin connector) that is required for the particular vehicle being tested. The well equipped tool box will have several different styles of jumper wires in several different lengths. Some jumper wires are made with three or more terminals coming from a common splice for special purpose testing. In cramped, hard-to-reach areas it is advisable to have insulated boots over the jumper wire terminals in order to prevent accidental grounding, sparks, and possible fire, especially when testing fuel system components.

Jumper wires are used primarily to locate open electrical circuits, on either the ground (-) side of the circuit or on the hot (+) side. If an electrical component fails to operate, connect the jumper wire between the component and a good ground. If the component operates only with the jumper installed, the ground circuit is open. If the ground circuit is good, but the component does not operate, the circuit between the power feed and component is open. You can sometimes connect the jumper wire directly from the battery to the hot terminal of the component, but first make sure the component uses 12 volts in operation. Some electrical components, such as fuel injectors, are designed to operate on about 4 volts and running 12 volts directly to the injector terminals can burn out the wiring. By inserting an inline fuseholder between a set of test leads, a fused jumper wire can be used for bypassing open circuits. Use a 5 amp fuse to provide protection against voltage spikes. When in doubt, use a voltmeter to check the voltage input to the component and measure how much

voltage is being applied normally. By moving the jumper wire successively back from the lamp toward the power source, you can isolate the area of the circuit where the open is located. When the component stops functioning, or the power is cut off, the open is in the segment of wire between the jumper and the point previously tested.

✳✳CAUTION

Never use jumpers made from wire that is of lighter gauge than used in the circuit under test. If the jumper wire is of too small gauge, it may overheat and possibly melt. Never use jumpers to bypass high resistance loads (such as motors) in a circuit. Bypassing resistances, in effect, creates a short circuit which may, in turn, cause damage and fire. Never use a jumper for anything other than temporary bypassing of components in a circuit.

12 Volt Test Light

The 12 volt test light is used to check circuits and components while electrical current is flowing through them. It is used for voltage and ground tests. Twelve volt test lights come in different styles but all have three main parts; a ground clip, a probe, and a light. The most commonly used 12 volt test lights have pick-type probes. To use a 12 volt test light, connect the ground clip to a good ground and probe wherever necessary with the pick. The pick should be sharp so that it can penetrate wire insulation to make contact with the wire, without making a large hole in the insulation. The wrap-around light is handy in hard to reach areas or where it is difficult to support a wire to push a probe pick into it. To use the wrap around light, hook the wire to probed with the hook and pull the trigger. A small pick will be forced through the wire insulation into the wire core.

✳✳CAUTION

Do not use a test light to probe electronic ignition spark plug or coil wires. Never use a pick-type test light to probe wiring on computer controlled systems unless specifically instructed to do so. Any wire insulation that is pierced by the test light probe should be taped and sealed with silicone after testing.

Like the jumper wire, the 12 volt test light is used to isolate opens in circuits. But, whereas the jumper wire is used to bypass the open to operate the load, the 12 volt test light is used to locate the presence of voltage in a circuit. If the test light glows, you know that there is power up to that point; if the 12 volt test light does not glow when its probe is inserted into the wire or connector, you know that there is an open circuit (no power). Move the test light in successive steps back toward the power source until the light in the handle does glow. When it does glow, the open is between the probe and point previously probed.

➡The test light does not detect that 12 volts (or any particular amount of voltage) is present; it only detects that some voltage is present. It is advisable before using the test light to touch its terminals across the battery posts to make sure the light is operating properly.

Self-Powered Test Light

The self-powered test light usually contains a 1.5 volt penlight battery. One type of self-powered test light is similar in design to the 12 volt test light. This type has both the battery and the light in the handle and pick-type probe tip. The second type has the light toward the open tip, so that the light illuminates the contact point. The self-powered test light is dual purpose piece of test equipment. It can be used to test for either open or short circuits when power is isolated from the circuit (continuity test). A powered test light should not be used on any computer controlled system or component unless specifically instructed to do so. Many engine sensors can be destroyed by even this small amount of voltage applied directly to the terminals.

Open Circuit Testing

To use the self-powered test light to check for open circuits, first isolate the circuit from the vehicle's 12 volt power source by disconnecting the battery or wiring harness connector. Connect the test light ground clip to a good ground and probe sections of the circuit sequentially with the test light. (start from either end of the circuit). If the light is out, the open is between the probe and the circuit ground. If the light is on, the open is between the probe and end of the circuit toward the power source.

Short Circuit Testing

By isolating the circuit both from power and from ground, and using a self-powered test light, you can check for shorts to ground in the circuit. Isolate the circuit from power and ground. Connect the test light ground clip to a good ground and probe any easy-to-reach test point in the circuit. If the light comes on, there is a short somewhere in the circuit. To isolate the short, probe a test point at either end of the isolated circuit (the light should be on). Leave the test light probe connected and open connectors, switches, remove parts, etc., sequentially, until the light goes out. When the light goes out, the short is between the last circuit component opened and the previous circuit opened.

➡ **The 1.5 volt battery in the test light does not provide much current. A weak battery may not provide enough power to illuminate the test light even when a complete circuit is made (especially if there are high resistances in the circuit). Always make sure that the test battery is strong. To check the battery, briefly touch the ground clip to the probe; if the light glows brightly the battery is strong enough for testing. Never use a self-powered test light to perform checks for opens or shorts when power is applied to the electrical system under test. The 12 volt vehicle power will quickly burn out the 1.5 volt light bulb in the test light.**

Voltmeter

A voltmeter is used to measure voltage at any point in a circuit, or to measure the voltage drop across any part of a circuit. It can also be used to check continuity in a wire or circuit by indicating current flow from one end to the other. Voltmeters usually have various scales on the meter dial and a selector switch to allow the selection of different voltages. The voltmeter has a positive and a negative lead. To avoid damage to the meter, always connect the negative lead to the negative (-) side of circuit (to ground or nearest the ground side of the circuit) and connect the positive lead to the positive (+) side of the circuit (to the power source or the nearest power source). Note that the negative voltmeter lead will always be black and that the positive voltmeter will always be some color other than black (usually red). Depending on how the voltmeter is connected into the circuit, it has several uses.

A voltmeter can be connected either in parallel or in series with a circuit and it has a very high resistance to current flow. When connected in parallel, only a small amount of current will flow through the voltmeter current path; the rest will flow through the normal circuit current path and the circuit will work normally. When the voltmeter is connected in series with a circuit, only a small amount of current can flow through the circuit. The circuit will not work properly, but the voltmeter reading will show if the circuit is complete or not.

Available Voltage Measurement

Set the voltmeter selector switch to the 20V position and connect the meter negative lead to the negative post of the battery. Connect the positive meter lead to the positive post of the battery and turn the ignition switch ON to provide a load. Read the voltage on the meter or digital display. A well charged battery should register over 12 volts. If the meter reads below 11.5 volts, the battery power may be insufficient to operate the electrical system properly. This test determines voltage available from the battery and should be the first step in any electrical trouble diagnosis procedure. Many electrical problems, especially on computer controlled systems, can be caused by a low state of charge in the battery. Excessive corrosion at the battery cable terminals can cause a poor contact that will prevent proper charging and full battery current flow.

Normal battery voltage is 12 volts when fully charged. When the battery is supplying current to one or more circuits it is said to be 'under load'. When everything is off the electrical system is under a 'no-load' condition. A fully charged battery may show about 12.5 volts at no load; will drop to 12 volts under medium load; and will drop even lower under heavy load. If the battery is partially discharged the voltage decrease under heavy load may be excessive, even though the battery shows 12 volts or more at no load. When allowed to discharge further, the battery's available voltage under load will decrease more severely. For this reason, it is important that the battery be fully charged during all testing procedures to avoid errors in diagnosis and incorrect test results.

Voltage Drop

When current flows through a resistance, the voltage beyond the resistance is reduced (the larger the current, the greater the reduction in voltage). When no current is flowing, there is no voltage drop because there is no current flow. All points in the circuit which are connected to the power source are at the same voltage as the power source. The total voltage drop always equals the total source voltage. In a long circuit with many connectors, a series of small, unwanted voltage drops due to corrosion at the connectors can add up to a total loss of voltage which impairs the operation of the normal loads in the circuit.

INDIRECT COMPUTATION OF VOLTAGE DROPS

1. Set the voltmeter selector switch to the 20 volt position.
2. Connect the meter negative lead to a good ground.
3. Probe all resistances in the circuit with the positive meter lead.
4. Operate the circuit in all modes and observe the voltage readings.

DIRECT MEASUREMENT OF VOLTAGE DROPS

1. Set the voltmeter switch to the 20 volt position.
2. Connect the voltmeter negative lead to the ground side of the resistance load to be measured.
3. Connect the positive lead to the positive side of the resistance or load to be measured.
4. Read the voltage drop directly on the 20 volt scale.

Too high a voltage indicates too high a resistance. If, for example, a blower motor runs too slowly, you can determine if there is too high a resistance in the resistor pack. By taking voltage drop readings in all parts of the circuit, you can isolate the problem. Too low a voltage drop indicates too low a resistance. If, for example, a blower motor runs too fast in the MED and/or LOW position, the problem can be isolated in the resistor pack by taking voltage drop readings in all parts of the circuit to locate a possibly shorted resistor. The maximum allowable voltage drop under load is critical, especially if there is more than one high resistance problem in a circuit because all voltage drops are cumulative. A small drop is normal due to the resistance of the conductors.

HIGH RESISTANCE TESTING

1. Set the voltmeter selector switch to the 4 volt position.
2. Connect the voltmeter positive lead to the positive post of the battery.
3. Turn on the headlights and heater blower to provide a load.
4. Probe various points in the circuit with the negative voltmeter lead.
5. Read the voltage drop on the 4 volt scale. Some average maximum allowable voltage drops are:

    FUSE PANEL — 7 volts
    IGNITION SWITCH — 5 volts
    HEADLIGHT SWITCH — 7 volts
    IGNITION COIL (+) — 5 volts
    ANY OTHER LOAD — 1.3 volts

➡**Voltage drops are all measured while a load is operating; without current flow, there will be no voltage drop.**

Ohmmeter

The ohmmeter is designed to read resistance (ohms) in a circuit or component. Although there are several different styles of ohmmeters, all will usually have a selector switch which permits the measurement of different ranges of resistance (usually the selector switch allows the multiplication of the meter reading by 10, 100, 1000, and 10,000). A calibration knob allows the meter to be set at zero for accurate measurement. Since all ohmmeters are powered by an internal battery (usually 9 volts), the ohmmeter can be used as a self-powered test light. When the ohmmeter is connected, current from the ohmmeter flows through the circuit or component

being tested. Since the ohmmeter's internal resistance and voltage are known values, the amount of current flow through the meter depends on the resistance of the circuit or component being tested.

The ohmmeter can be used to perform continuity test for opens or shorts (either by observation of the meter needle or as a self-powered test light), and to read actual resistance in a circuit. It should be noted that the ohmmeter is used to check the resistance of a component or wire while there is no voltage applied to the circuit. Current flow from an outside voltage source (such as the vehicle battery) can damage the ohmmeter, so the circuit or component should be isolated from the vehicle electrical system before any testing is done. Since the ohmmeter uses its own voltage source, either lead can be connected to any test point.

➡**When checking diodes or other solid state components, the ohmmeter leads can only be connected one way in order to measure current flow in a single direction. Make sure the positive (+) and negative (-) terminal connections are as described in the test procedures to verify the one-way diode operation.**

In using the meter for making continuity checks, do not be concerned with the actual resistance readings. Zero resistance, or any resistance readings, indicate continuity in the circuit. Infinite resistance indicates an open in the circuit. A high resistance reading where there should be none indicates a problem in the circuit. Checks for short circuits are made in the same manner as checks for open circuits except that the circuit must be isolated from both power and normal ground. Infinite resistance indicates no continuity to ground, while zero resistance indicates a dead short to ground.

RESISTANCE MEASUREMENT

The batteries in an ohmmeter will weaken with age and temperature, so the ohmmeter must be calibrated or 'zeroed' before taking measurements. To zero the meter, place the selector switch in its lowest range and touch the two ohmmeter leads together. Turn the calibration knob until the meter needle is exactly on zero.

➡**All analog (needle) type ohmmeters must be zeroed before use, but some digital ohmmeter models are automatically calibrated when the switch is turned on. Self-calibrating digital ohmmeters do not have an adjusting knob, but its a good idea to check for a zero readout before use by touching the leads together. All computer controlled systems require the use of a digital ohmmeter with at least 10 megohms impedance for testing. Before any test procedures are attempted, make sure the ohmmeter used is compatible with the electrical system or damage to the on-board computer could result.**

To measure resistance, first isolate the circuit from the vehicle power source by disconnecting the battery cables or the harness connector. Make sure the key is OFF when disconnecting any components or the battery. Where necessary, also isolate at least one side of the circuit to be checked to avoid reading parallel resistances. Parallel circuit resistances will always give a lower reading than the actual resistance of either of the branches. When measuring the resistance of parallel circuits, the total resistance will always be lower than the smallest resistance in the circuit. Connect the meter leads to both sides of the circuit (wire or component) and read the actual measured ohms on the meter scale. Make sure the selector switch is set to the proper ohm scale for the circuit being tested to avoid misreading the ohmmeter test value.

❋❋CAUTION

Never use an ohmmeter with power applied to the circuit. Like the self-powered test light, the ohmmeter is designed to operate on its own power supply. The normal 12 volt automotive electrical system current could damage the meter.

Ammeters

An ammeter measures the amount of current flowing through a circuit in units called amperes or amps. Amperes are units of electron flow which indicate how fast the electrons are flowing through the circuit. Since Ohms Law dictates that current flow in a circuit is equal to the circuit voltage divided by the total circuit resistance, increasing voltage also increases the current level (amps). Likewise, any decrease in resistance will increase the amount of amps in a circuit. At normal operating voltage, most circuits have a characteristic amount of amperes, called 'current draw' which can be measured using an ammeter. By referring to a specified current draw rating, measuring the amperes, and comparing the two values, one can determine what is happening within the circuit to aid in diagnosis. An open circuit, for example, will not allow any current to flow so the ammeter reading will be zero. More current flows through a heavily loaded circuit or when the charging system is operating.

An ammeter is always connected in series with the circuit being tested. All of the current that normally flows through the circuit must also flow through the ammeter; if there is any other path for the current to follow, the ammeter reading will not be accurate. The ammeter itself has very little resistance to current flow and therefore will not affect the circuit, but it will measure current draw only when the circuit is closed and electricity is flowing. Excessive current draw can blow fuses and drain the battery, while a reduced current draw can cause motors to run slowly, lights to dim and other components to not operate properly. The ammeter can help diagnose these conditions by locating the cause of the high or low reading.

Multimeters

Different combinations of test meters can be built into a single unit designed for specific tests. Some of the more common combination test devices are known as Volt/Amp testers, Tach/Dwell meters, or Digital Multimeters. The Volt/Amp tester is used for charging system, starting system or battery tests and consists of a voltmeter, an ammeter and a variable resistance carbon pile. The voltmeter will usually have at least two ranges for use with 6, 12 and 24 volt systems. The ammeter also has more than one range for testing various levels of battery loads and starter current draw and the carbon pile can be adjusted to offer different amounts of resistance. The Volt/Amp tester has heavy leads to carry large amounts of current and many later models have an inductive ammeter pickup that clamps around the wire to simplify test

connections. On some models, the ammeter also has a zero-center scale to allow testing of charging and starting systems without switching leads or polarity. A digital multimeter i s a voltmeter, ammeter and ohmmeter combined in an instrument which gives a digital readout. These are often used when testing solid state circuits because of their high input impedance (usually 10 megohms or more).

The tach/dwell meter combines a tachometer and a dwell (cam angle) meter and is a specialized kind of voltmeter. The tachometer scale is marked to show engine speed in rpm and the dwell scale is marked to show degrees of distributor shaft rotation. In most electronic ignition systems, dwell is determined by the control unit, but the dwell meter can also be used to check the duty cycle (operation) of some electronic engine control systems. Some tach/dwell meters are powered by an internal battery, while others take their power from the car battery in use. The battery powered testers usually require calibration much like an ohmmeter before testing.

Special Test Equipment

A variety of diagnostic tools are available to help troubleshoot and repair computerized engine control systems. The most sophisticated of these devices are the console type engine analyzers that usually occupy a garage service bay, but there are several types of aftermarket electronic testers available that will allow quick circuit tests of the engine control system by plugging directly into a special connector located in the engine compartment or under the dashboard. Several tool and equipment manufacturers offer simple, hand held testers that measure various circuit voltage levels on command to check all system components for proper operation. Although these testers usually cost about $300-$500, consider that the average computer control unit (or ECM) can cost just as much and the money saved by not replacing perfectly good sensors or components in an attempt to correct a problem could justify the purchase price of a special diagnostic tester the first time it's used.

These computerized testers can allow quick and easy test measurements while the engine is operating or while the car is being driven. In addition, the on-board computer memory can be read to access any stored trouble codes; in effect allowing the computer to tell you where it hurts and aid trouble diagnosis by pinpointing exactly which circuit or component is malfunctioning. In the same manner, repairs can be tested to make sure the problem has been corrected. The biggest advantage these special testers have is their relatively easy hookups that minimize or eliminate the chances of making the wrong connections and getting false voltage readings or damaging the computer accidentally.

➡**It should be remembered that these testers check voltage levels in circuits; they don't detect mechanical problems or failed components if the circuit voltage falls within the preprogrammed limits stored in the tester PROM unit. Also, most of the hand held testers are designed to work only on one or two systems made by a specific manufacturer.**

A variety of aftermarket testers are available to help diagnose different computerized control systems. Owatonna Tool Company (OTC), for example, markets a device called the OTC Monitor which plugs directly into the assembly line diagnostic link (ALDL). The OTC tester makes diagnosis a simple matter of pressing the correct buttons and, by changing the internal PROM or inserting a different diagnosis cartridge, it will work on any model from full size to subcompact, over a wide range of years. An adapter is supplied with the tester to allow connection to all types of ALDL links, regardless of the number of pin terminals used. By inserting an updated PROM into the OTC tester, it can be easily updated to diagnose any new modifications of computerized control systems.

Wiring Harnesses

The average automobile contains about ½ mile of wiring, with hundreds of individual connections. To protect the many wires from damage and to keep them from becoming a confusing tangle, they are organized into bundles, enclosed in plastic or taped together and called wire harnesses. Different wiring harnesses serve different parts of the vehicle. Individual wires are color coded to help trace them through a harness where sections are hidden from view.

A loose or corroded connection or a replacement wire that is too small for the circuit will add extra resistance and an additional voltage drop to the circuit. A ten percent voltage drop can result in slow or erratic motor operation, for example, even though the circuit is complete. Automotive wiring or circuit conductors can be in any one of three forms:

1. Single strand wire
2. Multistrand wire
3. Printed circuitry

Single strand wire has a solid metal core and is usually used inside such components as alternators, motors, relays and other devices. Multistrand wire has a core made of many small strands of wire twisted together into a single conductor. Most of the wiring in an automotive electrical system is made up of multistrand wire, either as a single conductor or grouped together in a harness. All wiring is color coded on the insulator, either as a solid color or as a colored wire with an identification stripe. A printed circuit is a thin film of copper or other conductor that is printed on an insulator backing. Occasionally, a printed circuit is sandwiched between two sheets of plastic for more protection and flexibility. A complete printed circuit, consisting of conductors, insulating material and connectors for lamps or other components is called a printed circuit board. Printed circuitry is used in place of individual wires or harnesses in places where space is limited, such as behind instrument panel s.

Wire Gauge

Since computer controlled automotive electrical systems are very sensitive to changes in resistance, the selection of properly sized wires is critical when systems are repaired. The wire gauge number is an expression of the cross section area of the conductor. The most common system for expressing wire size is the American Wire Gauge (AWG) system.

Wire cross section area is measured in circular mils. A mil is $1/_{1000}$" (0.001"); a circular mil is the area of a circle one mil in diameter. For example, a conductor ¼" in diameter is 0.250 in. or 250 mils. The circular mil cross section area of the wire is 250 squared (250^2)or 62,500 circular mils. Imported car models usually use metric wire gauge designations, which is simply the cross section area of the conductor in square millimeters (mm^2).

Gauge numbers are assigned to conductors of various cross section areas. As gauge number increases, area decreases and the conductor becomes smaller. A 5 gauge conductor is smaller than a 1 gauge conductor and a 10 gauge is smaller than a 5 gauge. As the cross section area of a conductor decreases, resistance increases and so does the gauge number. A conductor with a higher gauge number will carry less current than a conductor with a lower gauge number.

➡**Gauge wire size refers to the size of the conductor, not the size of the complete wire. It is possible to have two wires of the same gauge with different diameters because one may have thicker insulation than the other.**

12 volt automotive electrical systems generally use 10, 12, 14, 16 and 18 gauge wire. Main power distribution circuits and larger accessories usually use 10 and 12 gauge wire. Battery cables are usually 4 or 6 gauge, although 1 and 2 gauge wires are occasionally used. Wire length must also be considered when making repairs to a circuit. As conductor length increases, so does resistance. An 18 gauge wire, for example, can carry a 10 amp load for 10 feet without excessive voltage drop; however if a 15 foot wire is required for the same 10 amp load, it must be a 16 gauge wire.

An electrical schematic shows the electrical current paths when a circuit is operating properly. It is essential to understand how a circuit works before trying to figure out why it doesn't. Schematics break the entire electrical system down into individual circuits and show only one particular circuit. In a schematic, no attempt is made to represent wiring and components as they physically appear on the vehicle; switches and other components are shown as simply as possible. Face views of harness connectors show the cavity or terminal locations in all multi-pin connectors to help locate test points.

If you need to backprobe a connector while it is on the component, the order of the terminals must be mentally reversed. The wire color code can help in this situation, as well as a keyway, lock tab or other reference mark.

➡**Wiring diagrams are not included in this book. As trucks have become more complex and available with longer option lists, wiring diagrams have grown in size and complexity. It has become almost impossible to provide a readable reproduction of a wiring diagram in a book this size. Information on ordering wiring diagrams from the vehicle manufacturer can be found in the owner's manual.**

WIRING REPAIR

Soldering is a quick, efficient method of joining metals permanently. Everyone who has the occasion to make wiring repairs should know how to solder. Electrical connections that are soldered are far less likely to come apart and will conduct electricity much better than connections that are only 'pig-tailed' together. The most popular (and preferred) method of soldering is with an electrical soldering gun. Soldering irons are available in many sizes and wattage ratings. Irons with higher wattage ratings deliver higher temperatures and recover lost heat faster. A small soldering iron rated for no more than

50 watts is recommended, especially on electrical systems where excess heat can damage the components being soldered.

There are three ingredients necessary for successful soldering; proper flux, good solder and sufficient heat. A soldering flux is necessary to clean the metal of tarnish, prepare it for soldering and to enable the solder to spread into tiny crevices. When soldering, always use a resin flux or resin core solder which is non-corrosive and will not attract moisture once the job is finished. Other types of flux (acid core) will leave a residue that will attract moisture and cause the wires to corrode. Tin is a unique metal with a low melting point. In a molten state, it dissolves and alloys easily with many metals. Solder is made by mixing tin with lead. The most common proportions are 40/60, 50/50 and 60/40, with the percentage of tin listed first. Low priced solders usually contain less tin, making them very difficult for a beginner to use because more heat is required to melt the solder. A common solder is 40/60 which is well suited for all-around general use, but 60/40 melts easier, has more tin f or a better joint and is preferred for electrical work.

Soldering Techniques

Successful soldering requires that the metals to be joined be heated to a temperature that will melt the solder — usually 360-460°F (182-238°C). Contrary to popular belief, the purpose of the soldering iron is not to melt the solder itself, but to heat the parts being soldered to a temperature high enough to melt the solder when it is touched to the work. Melting flux-cored solder on the soldering iron will usually destroy the effectiveness of the flux.

➡**Soldering tips are made of copper for good heat conductivity, but must be 'tinned' regularly for quick transference of heat to the project and to prevent the solder from sticking to the iron. To 'tin' the iron, simply heat it and touch the flux-cored solder to the tip; the solder will flow over the hot tip. Wipe the excess off with a clean rag, but be careful as the iron will be hot.**

After some use, the tip may become pitted. If so, simply dress the tip smooth with a smooth file and 'tin' the tip again. An old saying holds that 'metals well cleaned are half soldered.' Flux-cored solder will remove oxides but rust, bits of insulation and oil or grease must be removed with a wire brush or emery cloth. For maximum strength in soldered parts, the joint must start off clean and tight. Weak joints will result in gaps too wide for the solder to bridge.

If a separate soldering flux is used, it should be brushed or swabbed on only those areas that are to be soldered. Most solders contain a core of flux and separate fluxing is unnecessary. Hold the work to be soldered firmly. It is best to solder on a wooden board, because a metal vise will only rob the piece to be soldered of heat and make it difficult to melt the solder. Hold the soldering tip with the broadest face against the work to be soldered. Apply solder under the tip close to the work, using enough solder to give a heavy film between the iron and the piece being soldered, while moving slowly and making sure the solder melts properly. Keep the work level or the solder will run to the lowest part and favor the thicker parts, because these require more heat to melt the

solder. If the soldering tip overheats (the solder coating on the face of the tip burns up), it should be retinned. Once the soldering is completed, let the soldered joint stand until cool. Tape and seal all soldered wire splices after the repair has cooled.

Wire Harness and Connectors

The on-board computer (ECM) wire harness electrically connects the control unit to the various solenoids, switches and sensors used by the control system. Most connectors in the engine compartment or otherwise exposed to the elements are protected against moisture and dirt which could create oxidation and deposits on the terminals. This protection is important because of the very low voltage and current levels used by the computer and sensors. All connectors have a lock which secures the male and female terminals together, with a secondary lock holding the seal and terminal into the connector. Both terminal locks must be released when disconnecting ECM connectors.

These special connectors are weather-proof and all repairs require the use of a special terminal and the tool required to service it. This tool is used to remove the pin and sleeve terminals. If removal is attempted with an ordinary pick, there is a good chance that the terminal will be bent or deformed. Unlike standard blade type terminals, these terminals cannot be straightened once they are bent. Make certain that the connectors are properly seated and all of the sealing rings in place when connecting leads. On some models, a hinge-type flap provides a backup or secondary locking feature for the terminals. Most secondary locks are used to improve the connector reliability by retaining the terminals if the small terminal lock tangs are not positioned properly.

Molded-on connectors require complete replacement of the connection. This means splicing a new connector assembly into the harness. All splices in on-board computer systems should be soldered to insure proper contact. Use care when probing the connections or replacing terminals in them as it is possible to short between opposite terminals. If this happens to the wrong terminal pair, it is possible to damage certain components. Always use jumper wires between connectors for circuit checking and never probe through weatherproof seals.

Open circuits are often difficult to locate by sight because corrosion or terminal misalignment are hidden by the connectors. Merely wiggling a connector on a sensor or in the wiring harness may correct the open circuit condition. This should always be considered when an open circuit or a failed sensor is indicated. Intermittent problems may also be caused by oxidized or loose connections. When using a circuit tester for diagnosis, always probe connections from the wire side. Be careful not to damage sealed connectors with test probes.

All wiring harnesses should be replaced with identical parts, using the same gauge wire and connectors. When signal wires are spliced into a harness, use wire with high temperature insulation only. With the low voltage and current levels found in the system, it is important that the best possible connection at all wire splices be made by soldering the splices together. It is seldom necessary to replace a complete harness. If replacement is necessary, pay close attention to insure proper harness routing. Secure the harness with suitable plastic wire clamps to prevent vibrations from causing the harness to wear in spots or contact any hot components.

➡Weatherproof connectors cannot be replaced with standard connectors. Instructions are provided with replacement connector and terminal packages. Some wire harnesses have mounting indicators (usually pieces of colored tape) to mark where the harness is to be secured.

In making wiring repairs, it's important that you always replace damaged wires with wires that are the same gauge as the wire being replaced. The heavier the wire, the smaller the gauge number. Wires are color-coded to aid in identification and whenever possible the same color coded wire should be used for replacement. A wire stripping and crimping tool is necessary to install solderless terminal connectors. Test all crimps by pulling on the wires; it should not be possible to pull the wires out of a good crimp.

Wires which are open, exposed or otherwise damaged are repaired by simple splicing. Where possible, if the wiring harness is accessible and the damaged place in the wire can be located, it is best to open the harness and check for all possible damage. In an inaccessible harness, the wire must be bypassed with a new insert, usually taped to the outside of the old harness.

When replacing fusible links, be sure to use fusible link wire, NOT ordinary automotive wire. Make sure the fusible segment is of the same gauge and construction as the one being replaced and double the stripped end when crimping the terminal connector for a good contact. The melted (open) fusible link segment of the wiring harness should be cut off as close to the harness as possible, then a new segment spliced in as described. In the case of a damaged fusible link that feeds two harness wires, the harness connections should be replaced with two fusible link wires so that each circuit will have its own separate protection.

➡Most of the problems caused in the wiring harness are due to bad ground connections. Always check all vehicle ground connections for corrosion or looseness before performing any power feed checks to eliminate the chance of a bad ground affecting the circuit.

Repairing Hard Shell Connectors

Unlike molded connectors, the terminal contacts in hard shell connectors can be replaced. Weatherproof hard-shell connectors with the leads molded into the shell have non-replaceable terminal ends. Replacement usually involves the use of a special terminal removal tool that depress the locking tangs (barbs) on the connector terminal and allow the connector to be removed from the rear of the shell. The connector shell should be replaced if it shows any evidence of burning, melting, cracks, or breaks. Replace individual terminals that are burnt, corroded, distorted or loose.

➡The insulation crimp must be tight to prevent the insulation from sliding back on the wire when the wire is pulled. The insulation must be visibly compressed under the crimp tabs, and the ends of the crimp should be turned in for a firm grip on the insulation.

The wire crimp must be made with all wire strands inside the crimp. The terminal must be fully compressed on the wire strands with the ends of the crimp tabs turned in to make a firm grip on the wire. Check all connections with an ohmmeter to insure a good contact. There should be no measurable resistance between the wire and the terminal when connected.

Mechanical Test Equipment

Vacuum Gauge

Most gauges are graduated in inches of mercury (in.Hg), although a device called a manometer reads vacuum in inches of water (in. H_2O). The normal vacuum reading usually varies between 18 and 22 in.Hg at sea level. To test engine vacuum, the vacuum gauge must be connected to a source of manifold vacuum. Many engines have a plug in the intake manifold which can be removed and replaced with an adapter fitting. Connect the vacuum gauge to the fitting with a suitable rubber hose or, if no manifold plug is available, connect the vacuum gauge to any device using manifold vacuum, such as EGR valves, etc. The vacuum gauge can be used to determine if enough vacuum is reaching a component to allow its actuation.

Hand Vacuum Pump

Small, hand-held vacuum pumps come in a variety of designs. Most have a built-in vacuum gauge and allow the component to be tested without removing it from the vehicle. Operate the pump lever or plunger to apply the correct amount of vacuum required for the test specified in the diagnosis routines. The level of vacuum in inches of Mercury (in.Hg) is indicated on the pump gauge. For some testing, an additional vacuum gauge may be necessary.

Intake manifold vacuum is used to operate various systems and devices on late model vehicles. To correctly diagnose and solve problems in vacuum control systems, a vacuum source is necessary for testing. In some cases, vacuum can be taken from the intake manifold when the engine is running, but vacuum is normally provided by a hand vacuum pump. These hand vacuum pumps have a built-in vacuum gauge that allow testing while the device is still attached to the component. For some tests, an additional vacuum gauge may be necessary.

HEATING AND AIR CONDITIONING

➡If a procedure requires that an air conditioning connection be loosened or disconnected, refer to Section 1 for the correct and safe way to discharge the system of refrigerant.

Blower Motor

REMOVAL & INSTALLATION

▶ See Figures 1, 2, 3, 4 and 5

Colt wo/Air Conditioning

1. Disconnect the negative battery cable. Remove the glove box and parcel tray.
2. Disconnect the changeover control wire and duct.
3. Remove the blower case.
4. Unbolt and remove the blower motor from the case.
5. The fan is removable from the motor shaft.
6. Install the fan to the blower motor shaft. Install the blower motor and case. Connect the control wire and duct.

Install the glove box and parcel tray. Connect the battery cable.

Colt w/Air Conditioning

1. Disconnect the negative battery cable.
2. Remove the glove box assembly and pry off the speaker cover to the lower right of the glove box.
3. Remove the passenger side lower cowl side trim kick panel.
4. Remove the passenger side knee protector, which is the panel surrounding the glove box opening.
5. Remove the glove box frame along the top of glove box opening.
6. Remove the lap heater duct. This is a small piece on vehicles without a rear heater and much larger on vehicles with a rear heater.

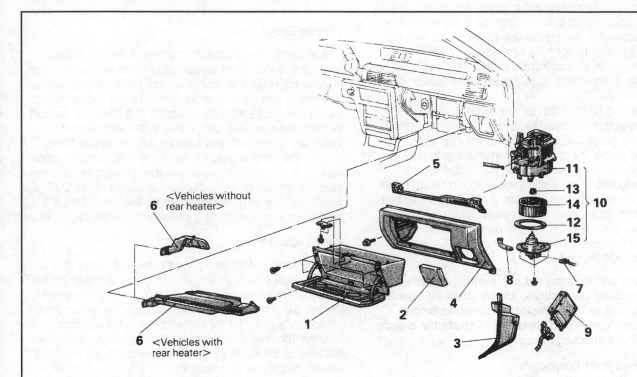

1. Glove box
2. Speaker cover
3. Cowl side trim, R.H.
4. Knee protector, R.H.
5. Glove box frame
6. Lap heater duct <vehicles without rear heater> or shower duct <vehicles with rear heater>
7. Connection of the connector for blower motor
8. Hose
9. MPI control unit
10. Blower motor assembly
11. Blower case
12. Packing
13. Fan installation nut
14. Fan
15. Blower motor

Fig. 1 Blower motor removal/installation — 1990-92 Colt hatchback and sedan

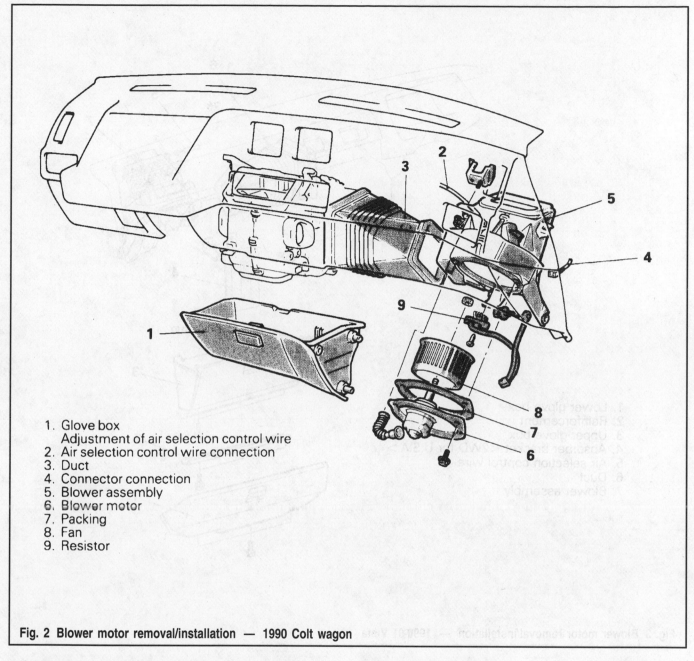

1. Glove box
   Adjustment of air selection control wire
2. Air selection control wire connection
3. Duct
4. Connector connection
5. Blower assembly
6. Blower motor
7. Packing
8. Fan
9. Resistor

Fig. 2 Blower motor removal/installation — 1990 Colt wagon

7. Disconnect the electrical connector from the blower motor.

8. Remove the cooling tube from the blower assembly.

9. Remove the MPI computer from the lower side of the cowl.

10. Remove the blower motor assembly and disassemble on a workbench.

To install:

11. Assemble the motor and fan. Install the blower motor assembly and connect the wiring and cooling tube.

12. Install the MPI computer.

13. Install the lap heater duct.

14. Install the glove box frame, interior trim pieces and glove box assembly.

15. Connect the negative battery cable and check the entire climate control system for proper operation.

Vista wo/Air Conditioning

1. Disconnect the negative battery cable. Remove the upper and lower glove boxes.

2. Disconnect the wiring and duct from the blower assembly.

3. Remove the blower motor mounting bolts and lift out the motor. If the entire blower case is to be removed, the instrument panel will have to be removed first.

4. Install the blower motor. Connect the wiring and duct. Install the glove boxes and connect the battery cable.

Vista w/Air Conditioning

1. Disconnect the negative battery cable.

2. Remove the instrument panel under cover and glove box assembly(s).

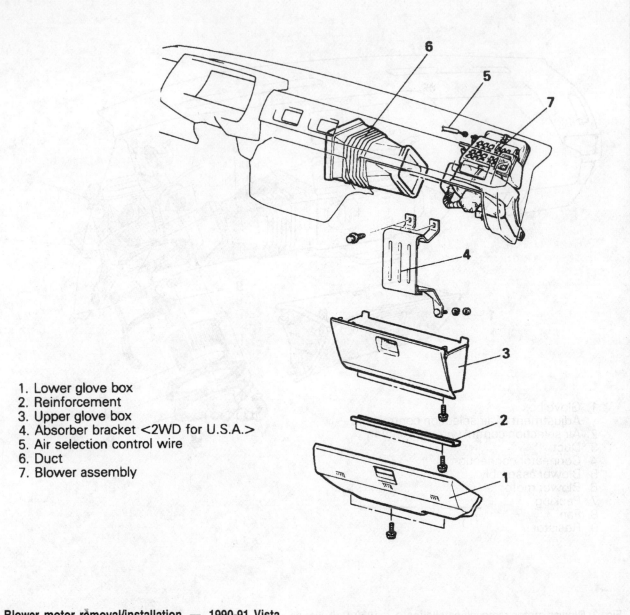

1. Lower glove box
2. Reinforcement
3. Upper glove box
4. Absorber bracket <2WD for U.S.A.>
5. Air selection control wire
6. Duct
7. Blower assembly

Fig. 3 Blower motor removal/installation — 1990-91 Vista

3. Disconnect the resistor and blower motor wire connectors, if necessary.

4. Remove the motor cooling tube. Remove the absorber bracket.

5. Remove the attaching screws and remove the blower assembly from the blower case and disassemble.

To install:

6. Position the blower motor onto the blower case and install the attaching screws.

7. Install the absorber bracket, if removed. Install the cooling tube.

8. Connect the resistor and blower motor wire connector.

9. Install the glove box(s) and instrument panel under cover.

10. Connect the negative battery cable and check the blower for proper operation.

Blower Motor Resistor or Power Transistor

REMOVAL & INSTALLATION

1. Disconnect the negative battery cable.

2. Remove the glove box assembly. The resistor or power transistor is accessible through the glove box opening and is mounted to the blower or evaporator case.

3. Disconnect the wire harness from the resistor.

4. Remove the mounting screws and remove the resistor.

5. The installation is the reverse of the removal procedure. Make sure the seal is intact when installing.

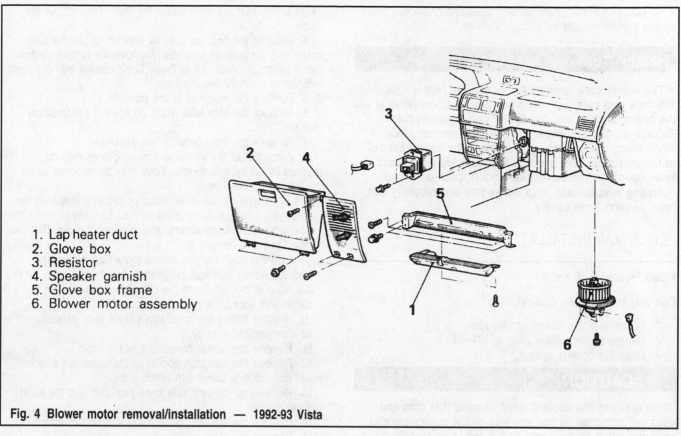

1. Lap heater duct
2. Glove box
3. Resistor
4. Speaker garnish
5. Glove box frame
6. Blower motor assembly

Fig. 4 Blower motor removal/installation — 1992-93 Vista

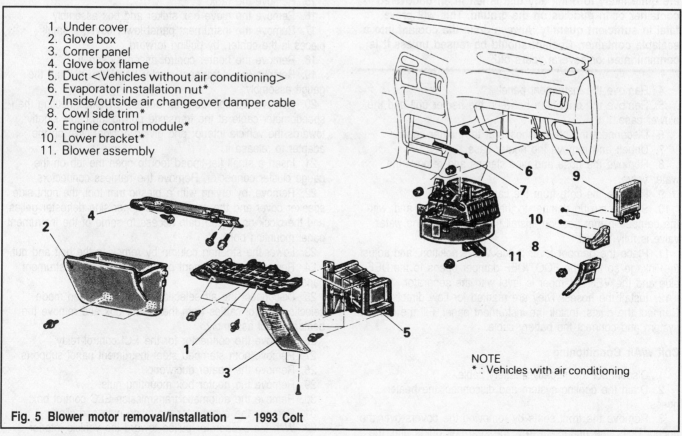

1. Under cover
2. Glove box
3. Corner panel
4. Glove box flame
5. Duct <Vehicles without air conditioning>
6. Evaporator installation nut*
7. Inside/outside air changeover damper cable
8. Cowl side trim*
9. Engine control module*
10. Lower bracket*
11. Blower assembly

NOTE
* : Vehicles with air conditioning

Fig. 5 Blower motor removal/installation — 1993 Colt

6. Connect the negative battery cable and check the entire climate control system for proper operation.

Heater Core

→The heater core is contained within the heater case unit. The core and case are remove as a unit. Upon removal of the heater control box, the heater core is removable. Replace all gaskets and insulation in its proper place. When filling the cooling system, place the heater control to the maximum heat position to insure full water control valve opening. Run the engine until it reaches normal operating temperature, stop the engine and carefully add more coolant if necessary.

REMOVAL & INSTALLATION

▶ **See Figures 6, 7 and 8**

Colt and Vista wo/Air Conditioning

1. Disconnect the battery ground cable.
2. Set the heater control lever to WARM.
3. Drain the cooling system.

❋❋CAUTION

When draining the coolant, keep in mind that cats and dogs are attracted by the ethylene glycol antifreeze, and are quite likely to drink any that is left in an uncovered container or in puddles on the ground. This will prove fatal in sufficient quantity. Always drain the coolant into a sealable container. Coolant should be reused unless it is contaminated or several years old.

4. Remove the instrument panel.
5. Remove the duct from between the heater unit and the blower case.
6. Disconnect the coolant hoses at the heater case.
7. Unbolt and remove the heater case.
8. Remove the hose and pipe clamps and remove the water valve.
9. Remove the core from the case.
10. Set the mixing damper to the closed position, and, with the damper in that position, install the rod so that the water valve is fully closed.
11. Place the damper lever in the VENT position, and adjust the linkage so that the FOOT/DEF damper opens to the DEF side and the VENT damper is level with the separator.
12. Install the hoses. They are marked for flow direction. Connect the ducts. Install the instrument panel. Fill the cooling system and connect the battery cable.

Colt w/Air Conditioning

1. Disconnect the negative battery cable.
2. Drain the cooling system and disconnect the heater hoses.
3. Remove the front seats by removing the covers over the anchor bolts, the underseat tray, the seat belt guide ring, the seat mounting nuts and bolts and disconnect the seat belt switch wiring harness from under the seat. Then lift out the seats.

4. Remove the floor console by first taking out the coin holder and the console box tray. Remove the remote control mirror switch or cover. All of these items require only a plastic trim tool to carefully pry them out.
5. Remove the rear half of the console.
6. Remove the shift lever knob on manual transmission vehicles.
7. Remove the front console box assembly.
8. A number of the instrument panel pieces may be retained by pin type fasteners. They may be removed using the following procedure:
   a. This type of clip is removed by pressing down on the center pin with a suitable blunt pointed tool. Press down a little more than $1/16$ in. (2mm); this releases the clip. Pull the clip outward to remove it.
   b. Do not push the pin inward more than necessary because it may damage the grommet or the pin may fall in if pushed in too far. Once the clips are removed, use a plastic trim stick to pry the piece loose.
9. Remove both lower cowl trim panels (kick panels).
10. Remove the ashtray.
11. Remove the center panel around the radio.
12. Remove the sunglass pocket at the upper left side of panel and the side panel into which it mounts.
13. Remove the driver's side knee protector and the hood release handle.
14. Remove the steering column top and bottom covers.
15. Remove the radio.
16. Remove the glove box striker and box assembly.
17. Remove the instrument panel lower cover, 2 small pieces in the center, by pulling forward.
18. Remove the heater control assembly screw.
19. Remove the instrument cluster bezel and pull out the gauge assembly.
20. Remove the speedometer adapter by disconnecting the speedometer cable at the transaxle pulling the cable sightly towards the vehicle interior and giving a slight twist on the adapter to release it.
21. Insert a small flat-tipped tool to open the tab on the gauge cluster connector. Remove the harness connectors.
22. Remove, by prying with a plastic trim tool, the right side speaker cover and the speaker, the upper side defroster grilles and the clock or plug to gain access to some of the instrument panel mounting bolts.
23. Lower the steering column by removing the bolt and nut.
24. Remove the instrument panel bolts and the instrument panel.
25. Disconnect the air selection, temperature and mode selection control cables from the heater box and remove the heater control assembly.
26. Remove the connector for the ECI control relay.
27. Remove both stamped steel instrument panel supports.
28. Remove the heater ductwork.
29. Remove the heater box mounting nuts.
30. Remove the automatic transmission ELC control box.
31. Remove the evaporator mounting nuts and clips.
32. With the evaporator pulled toward the vehicle interior, remove the heater unit. Be careful not to damage the heater tubes or to spill coolant.

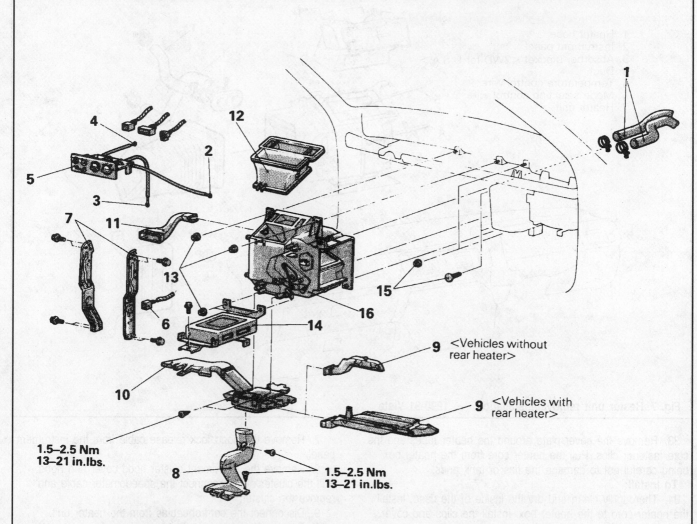

1. Connection for the heater hoses
2. Connection for the air selection control wire
3. Connection for the temperature control wire
4. Connection for the mode selection control wire
5. Heater control assembly
6. Connection of the connector [8P <1500> or 10P <1600>] for ECI control relay
7. Instrument panel center stay assembly
8. Rear heater duct A
9. Lap heater duct <vehicles without rear heater> or shower duct <vehicles with rear heater>
10. Foot duct
11. Lap duct
12. Center ventilation duct
13. Heater unit mounting nuts
14. ELC-4 A/T control unit
15. Evaporator mounting nuts, clips
16. Heater unit

Fig. 6 Heater unit removal/installation — 1990-92 Colt hatchback and sedan

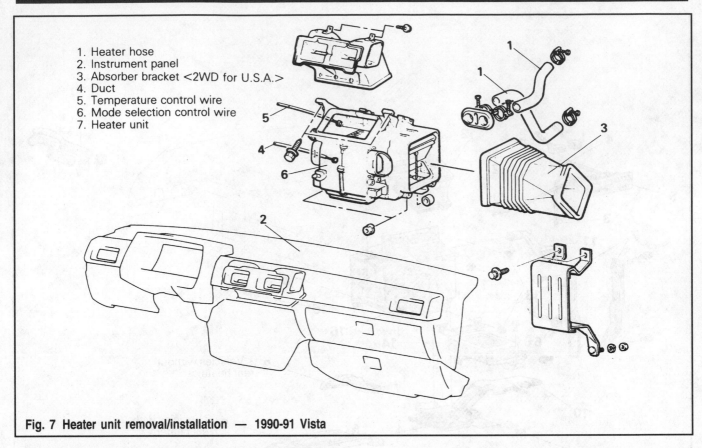

1. Heater hose
2. Instrument panel
3. Absorber bracket <2WD for U.S.A.>
4. Duct
5. Temperature control wire
6. Mode selection control wire
7. Heater unit

Fig. 7 Heater unit removal/installation — 1990-91 Vista

33. Remove the cover plate around the heater tubes and the core fastener clips. Pull the heater core from the heater box, being careful not to damage the fins or tank ends.

To install:

34. Thoroughly clean and dry the inside of the case. Install the heater core to the heater box. Install the clips and cover.

35. Install the evaporator and the automatic transmission ELC box.

36. Install the heater box and connect the duct work.

37. Connect all wires and control cables.

38. Install the instrument panel assembly and the console by reversing their removal procedures.

39. Install the seats.

40. Refill the cooling system.

41. Evacuate and recharge the air conditioning system. Add 2 oz. of refrigerant oil during the recharge if the evaporator was replaced.

42. Connect the negative battery cable and check the entire climate control system for proper operation. Check the system for leaks.

Vista w/Air Conditioning

1. Disconnect the negative battery cable.

2. Drain the coolant and disconnect the heater hoses from the core tubes.

3. Remove the steering column under covers. Remove the steering column. This can be accomplished by removing the pinch bolt at the U-joint below the instrument, disconnecting all connectors and pulling the column from the U-joint yoke.

4. Remove the entire glove box assemblies.

5. Remove the lap heater duct.

6. Remove the ashtray.

7. Remove the hood lock release cable from the instrument panel.

8. Remove the instrument cluster hood cover and hood. Pull the cluster out, disconnect the speedometer cable and remove the cluster.

9. Disconnect the control cables from the heater unit.

10. Remove the upper air ducts.

11. Disconnect the blower motor harness.

12. Remove the trim panels along the top of the instrument panel.

13. Disconnect the antenna feeder wire.

14. Remove the instrument panel retaining hardware and remove the assembly.

15. Remove the instrument panel absorber bracket, if equipped.

16. Remove the duct to the right of the heater unit.

17. Remove the mounting nuts and remove the heater unit from the vehicle.

18. To disassemble the heater unit, remove the water valve link, hose clamps and hoses. Remove the retaining screw and remove the heater core from the case.

To install:

19. Thoroughly clean and dry the inside of the case. Install the heater core to the case and assemble the unit.

20. Install the heater case to the vehicle and install the retaining nuts.

21. Install the duct on the right side of the unit.

22. Install the instrument panel absorber bracket, if equipped.

23. Install the instrument panel by reversing its removal procedure.

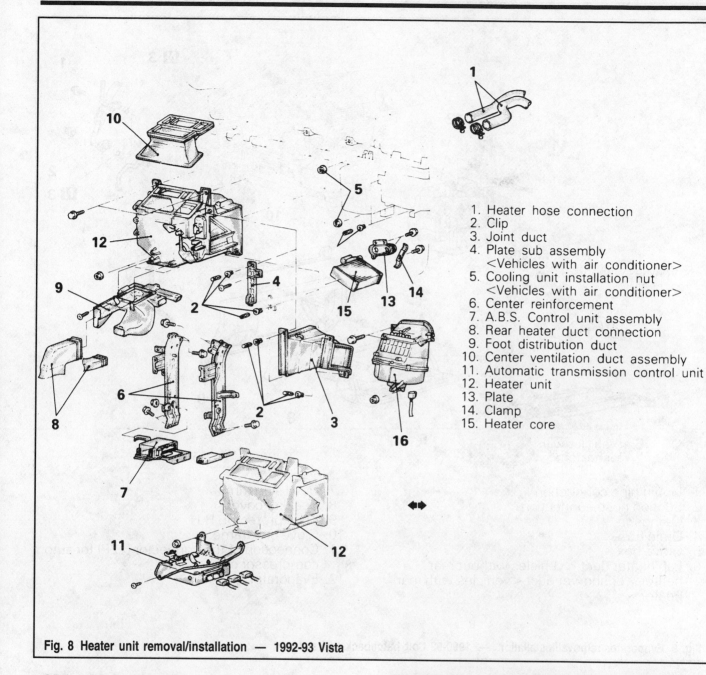

1. Heater hose connection
2. Clip
3. Joint duct
4. Plate sub assembly
   <Vehicles with air conditioner>
5. Cooling unit installation nut
   <Vehicles with air conditioner>
6. Center reinforcement
7. A.B.S. Control unit assembly
8. Rear heater duct connection
9. Foot distribution duct
10. Center ventilation duct assembly
11. Automatic transmission control unit
12. Heater unit
13. Plate
14. Clamp
15. Heater core

Fig. 8 Heater unit removal/installation — 1992-93 Vista

24. Install the hood lock release cable to the instrument panel.
25. Install the ashtray.
26. Install the lap heater duct.
27. Install the glove boxes.
28. Install the steering column and under covers.
29. Connect the heater hoses to the heater core tubes.
30. Fill the cooling system.
31. Connect the negative battery cable and check the entire climate control system for proper operation and leaks.

Evaporator Core

REMOVAL & INSTALLATION

▶ **See Figures 9, 10 and 11**

Colt and Vista

1. Discharge the A/C refrigerant system safely (see Section 1).
2. Disconnect the negative battery cable.
3. Remove the evaporator drain hose.
4. Disconnect the liquid and suction refrigerant lines from the evaporator (engine side). Remove the firewall insulator O-rings.
5. Remove the glove box and dash trim insert.

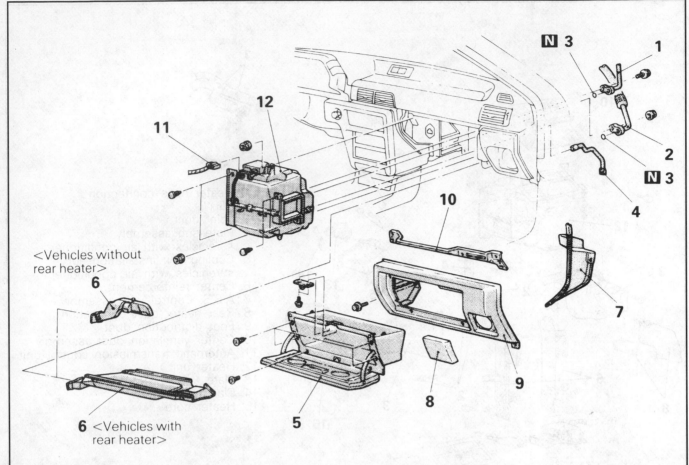

1. Liquid pipe connection
2. Suction hose connection
3. O-rings
4. Drain hose
5. Glove box
6. Lap heater duct <vehicles without rear heater> or shower duct <vehicles with rear heater>
7. Cowl side trim
8. Speaker cover
9. Knee protector, R.H.
10. Glove box frame
11. Connection of the connector (12P) for auto compressor control unit
12. Evaporator

Fig. 9 Evaporator removal/installation — 1990-92 Colt hatchback and sedan

6. Remove the heater ducts and disconnect the duct joints from the heater case.

7. Disconnect the switch and main wire harness connections from the evaporator.

8. Remove the evaporator case mounting nuts and bolts, lower the case assembly and remove it from the vehicle.

9. Separate the case halves by removing the spring clips. Remove the expansion valve and other components to free the evaporator core from the case mounting.

10. Install the evaporator, connect components and the expansion valve.

11. Assemble the evaporator case and mount in under the dash.

12. Connect the wiring harness, duct connections to the heater and install the ducts.

13. Install the glove box and trim panel.

14. Install the firewall insulators. Connect the refrigerant lines using new O-rings lubricated with refrigerant oil.

15. Connect the evaporator drain hose. Connect the negative battery cable. Charge the A/C refrigerant system.

Refrigerant Lines

REMOVAL & INSTALLATION

1. Disconnect the negative battery cable.

2. Properly discharge the air conditioning system.

3. Remove the nuts or bolts that attach the refrigerant lines sealing plates to the adjoining components. If the line is not equipped with a sealing plate, separate the flare connection.

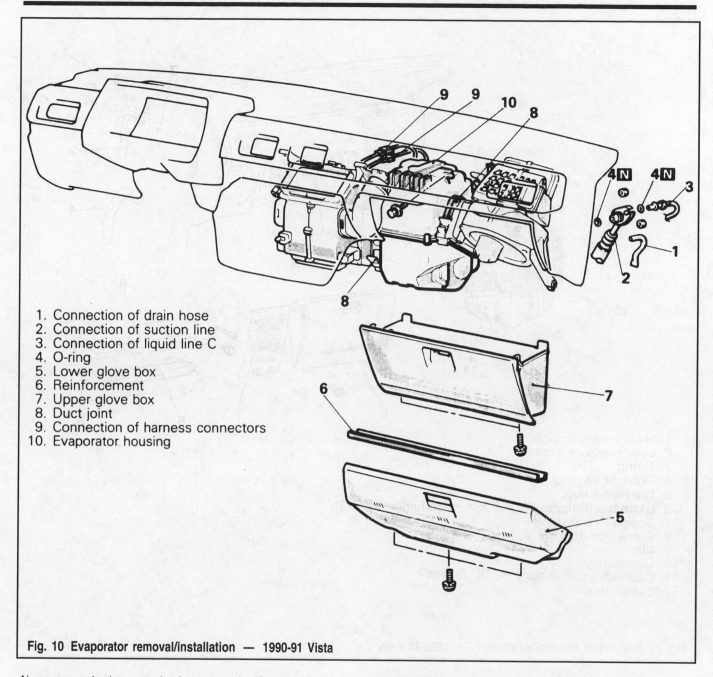

1. Connection of drain hose
2. Connection of suction line
3. Connection of liquid line C
4. O-ring
5. Lower glove box
6. Reinforcement
7. Upper glove box
8. Duct joint
9. Connection of harness connectors
10. Evaporator housing

Fig. 10 Evaporator removal/installation — 1990-91 Vista

Always use a backup wrench when separating flare connections.

4. Remove the line and discard the O-rings.

To install:

5. Coat the new O-rings refrigerant oil and install. Connect the refrigerant lines to the adjoining components and tighten the nuts, bolts or flare connections.

6. Evacuate and recharge the air conditioning system.

7. Connect the negative battery cable and check the entire climate control system for proper operation. Check the system for leaks.

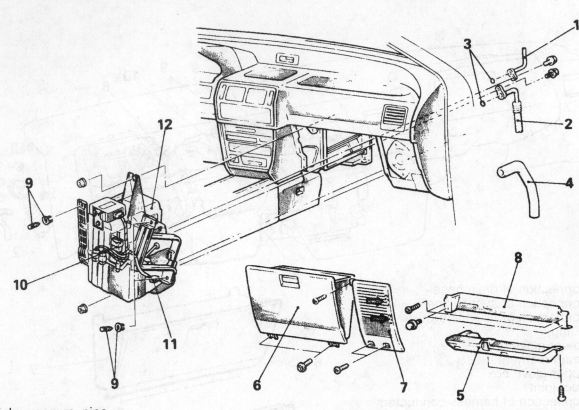

1. High pressure pipe
2. Low pressure pipe
3. O-ring
4. Drain hose
5. Lap heater duct
6. Glove box (Refer to GROUP 23A — Instrument Panel.)
7. Speaker garnish
8. Glove box frame
9. Clip
10. Connector
11. Connector connections <1.8L Engine>
12. Evaporator

Fig. 11 Evaporator removal/installation — 1992-93 Vista

Control Unit

REMOVAL & INSTALLATION

▶ See Figures 12, 13, 14 and 15

Colt

1. Disconnect the negative battery cable.
2. Remove the glove box and ashtray assembly.
3. Remove the heater control/radio bezel.
4. Remove the radio assembly.
5. Disconnect the air, temperature and mode selection control cables from the heater housing.
6. Remove the 3 control head mounting screws.

7. Separate the control head from the left side first, then press out the lower and upper mounting brackets from behind the instrument panel.
8. Pull the control head out and disconnect the 3 connectors. Remove the control head assembly.

To install:
9. Feed the control cable through the instrument panel, connect the connectors, install the control head assembly and secure with the screws.
10. Install the radio and bezel.
11. Move the mode selection lever to the **PANEL** position. Move the mode selection damper lever fully forward and connect the cable to the lever. Install the clip.
12. Move the temperature control lever to its coolest position. Move the blend air damper lever fully downward and connect the cable to the lever. Install the clip.

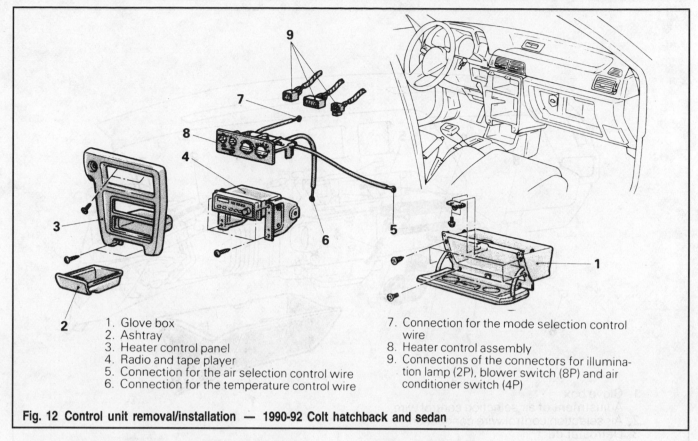

1. Glove box
2. Ashtray
3. Heater control panel
4. Radio and tape player
5. Connection for the air selection control wire
6. Connection for the temperature control wire
7. Connection for the mode selection control wire
8. Heater control assembly
9. Connections of the connectors for illumination lamp (2P), blower switch (8P) and air conditioner switch (4P)

Fig. 12 Control unit removal/installation — 1990-92 Colt hatchback and sedan

13. Move the air selection control lever to the **RECIRC** position. Move the air selection damper fully inward and connect the cable to the lever. Install the clip.

14. Connect the negative battery cable and check the entire climate control system for proper operation.

15. If everything is satisfactory, install the ashtray and glove box.

Vista

1. Disconnect the negative battery cable.

2. Remove the lever knobs and remove the control head bezel.

3. Remove the glove box and the defroster duct.

4. Disconnect the control cables from the heater housing.

5. Remove the control head mounting screws and pull the unit out of the instrument panel. Disconnect the electrical connectors and remove the control head.

6. The installation is the reverse of the removal procedure.

7. Connect the negative battery cable and check the entire climate control system for proper operation and leaks.

Control Cables

ADJUSTMENT

All control cables are self-adjusting. If any cable is not functioning properly, try to move the affected lever to either extreme position, observe what may be binding and reposition the connecting link if possible. Also, check for proper routing

and lubricate all moving parts. These cables cannot be disassembled. Replace if faulty.

Condenser Cooling Fan

REMOVAL & INSTALLATION

▶ See Figures 16, 17, 18 and 19

Colt

1. Disconnect the negative battery cable.

2. Unplug the connector(s). Most of these connectors employ a waterproof connector. When disconnecting, make sure all parts of the connectors remain intact.

3. Remove the upper radiator hose if necessary.

4. Remove the mounting screws. The radiator and condenser cooling fans are separately removable.

5. Remove the fan assembly and disassemble as required.

6. The installation is the reverse of the removal procedure.

7. Check the coolant level and refill as required.

8. Connect the negative battery cable and check the fan for proper operation.

Vista

The condenser fan is mounted between the condenser and grille, requiring grille and possibly bumper disassembly for removal. Remove the grille very carefully, since it is made of easily breakable plastic.

1. Disconnect the negative battery cable.

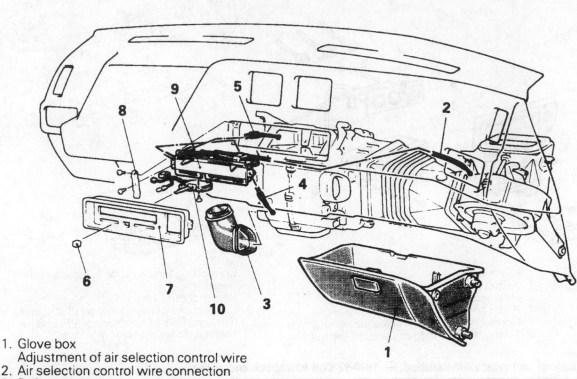

1. Glove box
   Adjustment of air selection control wire
2. Air selection control wire connection
3. Defroster duct
   Adjustment of temperature control wire
4. Temperature control wire connection
   Adjustment of mode selection control wire
5. Mode selection control wire connection
6. Knobs
7. Heater control panel
8. Heater control bracket
9. Heater control assembly
10. Blower switch

Fig. 13 Control unit removal/installation — 1990 Colt wagon

2. Remove the grille assembly. The grille is held in place with 1 or 2 screws and 5 or 6 clips that may require the use of a flat-tipped tool against the tab for release.

3. Unplug the connector. Most of these connectors employ a waterproof connector. When disconnecting, make sure all parts of the connectors remain intact.

4. Remove the mounting screws.

5. Remove the fan assembly through the grille opening.

To install:

6. Install the fan and secure with mounting screws.

7. Connect the connector. Connect the negative battery cable and check the fan for proper operation before assembling the remaining parts. Disconnect the negative battery cable before continuing.

8. Install the grille.

9. Connect the negative battery cable and recheck the system.

Condenser

REMOVAL & INSTALLATION

Colt

1. Disconnect the negative battery cable.

2. Properly discharge the air conditioning system.

3. Remove the battery, battery tray and windshield washer reservoir.

4. Remove the upper radiator mounts to allow the radiator to be moved toward the engine. Remove the fans if they do not allow enough radiator movement.

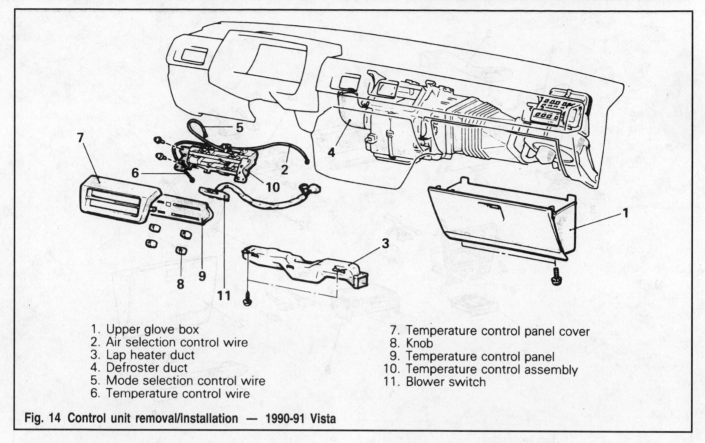

1. Upper glove box
2. Air selection control wire
3. Lap heater duct
4. Defroster duct
5. Mode selection control wire
6. Temperature control wire
7. Temperature control panel cover
8. Knob
9. Temperature control panel
10. Temperature control assembly
11. Blower switch

Fig. 14 Control unit removal/installation — 1990-91 Vista

5. Disconnect the refrigerant lines from the condenser. Cover the exposed ends of the lines to minimize contamination.

6. Remove the condenser mounting bolts.

7. Move the radiator toward the engine and lift the condenser from the vehicle. Inspect the lower rubber mounting insulators and replace, if necessary.

To install:

8. Lower the condenser into position and align the dowels with the lower mounting insulators. Install the bolts.

9. Replace the O-rings, lubricate and connect the refrigerant lines.

10. Install the radiator mounts and cooling fans.

11. Install remaining parts that were removed during the removal procedure.

12. Evacuate and recharge the air conditioning system. If the condenser was replaced, add 2 oz. of refrigerant oil during the recharge.

13. Connect the negative battery cable and check the entire climate control system for proper operation. Check the system for leaks.

Vista

1. Disconnect the negative battery cable.

2. Properly discharge the air conditioning system.

3. Remove the grille assembly. The grille is held in place with 1 or 2 screws and 5 or 6 clips that may require the use of a flat-tipped tool against the tab for release.

4. Unplug the fan connector. Most of these connectors employ a waterproof connector. When disconnecting, make sure all parts of the connectors remain intact.

5. Remove the mounting screws and remove the cooling fan assembly.

6. Disconnect the refrigerant lines from the condenser. Cover the exposed ends of the lines to minimize contamination.

7. Remove the condenser mounting bolts and remove the condenser.

To install:

8. Install the condenser and mounting bolts.

9. Replace the O-rings, lubricate and connect the refrigerant lines to the condenser.

10. Install automatic transmission oil cooling components, if removed.

11. Install the cooling fan and secure with mounting screws.

12. Connect the fan connector. Connect the negative battery cable and check the fan for proper operation before assembling the remaining parts. Disconnect the negative battery cable before continuing.

13. Install the grille.

14. Evacuate and recharge the air conditioning system. If the condenser was replaced, add 2 oz. of refrigerant oil during the recharge.

15. Connect the negative battery cable and check the entire climate control system for proper operation and leaks.

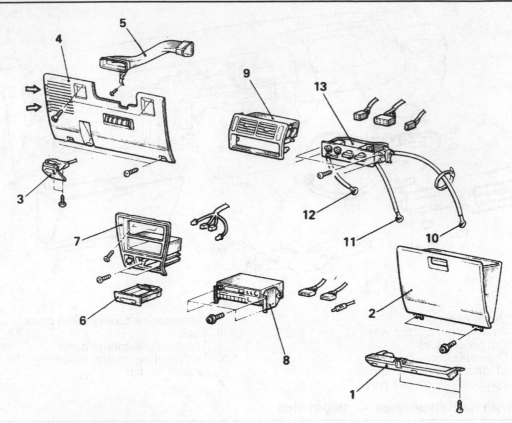

1. Lap heater duct
2. Glove box
3. Hood lock release handle
4. Instrument under cover
5. Lap duct
6. Ashtray
7. Center panel
8. Radio and tape player
9. Center air outlet assembly
10. Connection for inside/outside air changeover damper cable
11. Connection for air-mixing damper cable
12. Connection for air outlet changeover damper cable
13. Heater control assembly

Fig. 15 Control unit removal/installation — 1992-93 Vista

Compressor

REMOVAL & INSTALLATION

▶ **See Figures 20, 21, 22, 23, 24 and 25**

Colt and Vista

1. Disconnect the negative battery cable.
2. Properly discharge the air conditioning system.
3. Remove the distributor cap and wires so the compressor may be lifted from the engine compartment.
4. If equipped with 1.6L engine, remove the tensioner pulley assembly.
5. Remove the compressor drive belt. Disconnect the clutch coil connector.

6. Disconnect the refrigerant lines from the compressor and discard the O-rings. Cover the exposed ends of the lines to minimize contamination.
7. Remove the compressor mounting bolts and the compressor.

To install:

8. Install the compressor and torque the mounting bolts to 18 ft. lbs. (25 Nm). Connect the clutch coil connector.
9. Using new lubricated O-rings, connect the refrigerant lines to the compressor.
10. Install the belt and tensioner pulley, if removed. Adjust the belt to specifications.
11. Install the distributor cap and wires.
12. Evacuate and recharge the air conditioning system.
13. Connect the negative battery cable and check the entire climate control system for proper operation. Check the system for leaks.

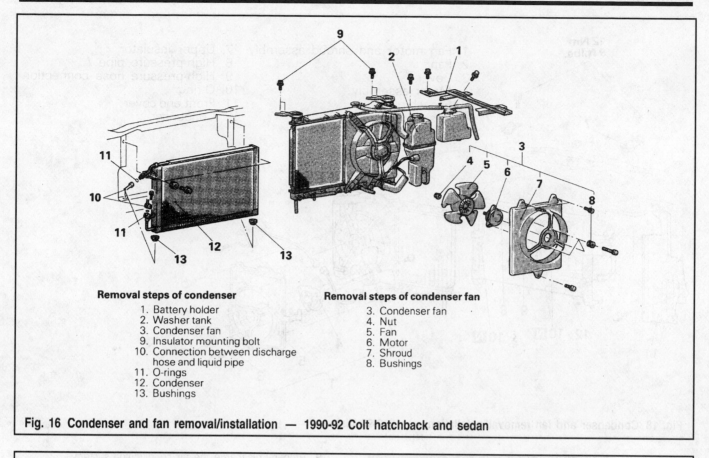

Removal steps of condenser
1. Battery holder
2. Washer tank
3. Condenser fan
9. Insulator mounting bolt
10. Connection between discharge hose and liquid pipe
11. O-rings
12. Condenser
13. Bushings

Removal steps of condenser fan
3. Condenser fan
4. Nut
5. Fan
6. Motor
7. Shroud
8. Bushings

Fig. 16 Condenser and fan removal/installation — 1990-92 Colt hatchback and sedan

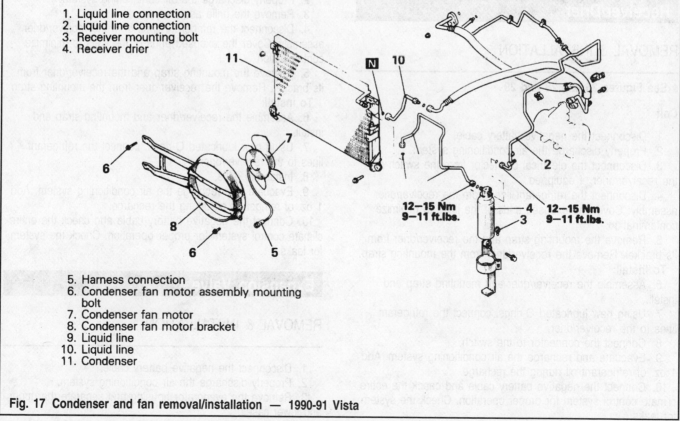

1. Liquid line connection
2. Liquid line connection
3. Receiver mounting bolt
4. Receiver drier

5. Harness connection
6. Condenser fan motor assembly mounting bolt
7. Condenser fan motor
8. Condenser fan motor bracket
9. Liquid line
10. Liquid line
11. Condenser

12–15 Nm
9–11 ft.lbs.

12–15 Nm
9–11 ft.lbs.

Fig. 17 Condenser and fan removal/installation — 1990-91 Vista

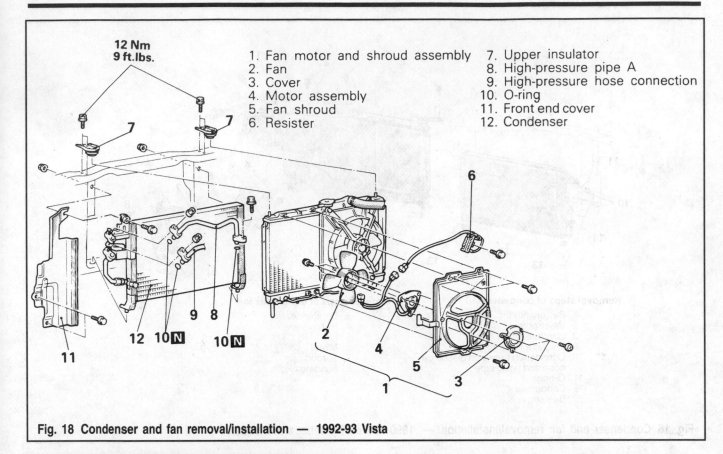

12 Nm
9 ft.lbs.

1. Fan motor and shroud assembly
2. Fan
3. Cover
4. Motor assembly
5. Fan shroud
6. Resister
7. Upper insulator
8. High-pressure pipe A
9. High-pressure hose connection
10. O-ring
11. Front end cover
12. Condenser

Fig. 18 Condenser and fan removal/installation — 1992-93 Vista

Receiver/Drier

REMOVAL & INSTALLATION

▶ **See Figures 26, 27, 28 and 29**

Colt

1. Disconnect the negative battery cable.
2. Properly discharge the air conditioning system.
3. Disconnect the electrical connector from the switch on the receiver/drier, if equipped.
4. Disconnect the refrigerant lines from the receiver/drier assembly. Cover the exposed ends of the lines to minimize contamination.
5. Remove the mounting strap and the receiver/drier from its bracket. Remove the receiver/drier from the mounting strap.
   To install:
6. Assemble the receiver/drier and mounting strap and install.
7. Using new lubricated O-rings. connect the refrigerant lines to the receiver/drier.
8. Connect the connector to the switch.
9. Evacuate and recharge the air conditioning system. Add 1 oz. of refrigerant oil during the recharge.
10. Connect the negative battery cable and check the entire climate control system for proper operation. Check the system for leaks.

Vista

1. Disconnect the negative battery cable.

2. Properly discharge the air conditioning system.
3. Remove the grille assembly.
4. Disconnect the refrigerant lines from the receiver/drier assembly. Cover the exposed ends of the lines to minimize contamination.
5. Remove the mounting strap and the receiver/drier from its bracket. Remove the receiver/drier from the mounting strap.
   To install:
6. Assemble the receiver/drier and mounting strap and install.
7. Using new lubricated O-rings. connect the refrigerant lines to the receiver/drier.
8. Install the grille.
9. Evacuate and recharge the air conditioning system. Add 1 oz. of refrigerant oil during the recharge.
10. Connect the negative battery cable and check the entire climate control system for proper operation. Check the system for leaks.

Expansion Valve

REMOVAL & INSTALLATION

1. Disconnect the negative battery cable.
2. Properly discharge the air conditioning system.
3. Remove the evaporator housing and separate the upper and lower cases.
4. Remove the expansion valve from the evaporator lines.
5. The installation is the reverse of the removal installation. Use new lubricated O-rings when assembling.

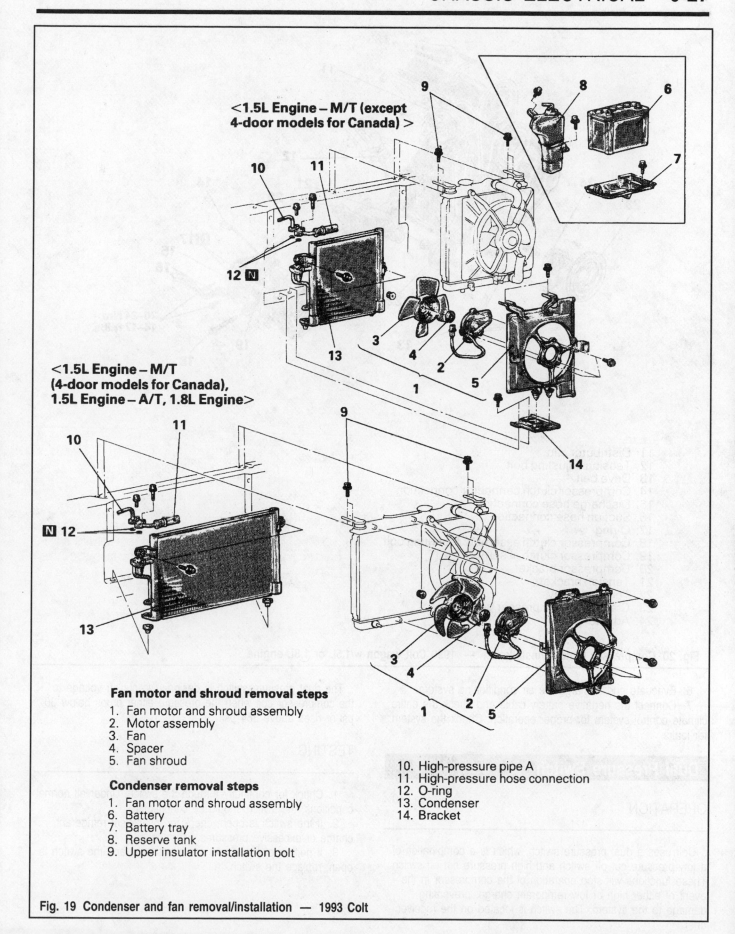

<1.5L Engine – M/T (except
4-door models for Canada) >

<1.5L Engine – M/T
(4-door models for Canada),
1.5L Engine – A/T, 1.8L Engine>

Fan motor and shroud removal steps

1. Fan motor and shroud assembly
2. Motor assembly
3. Fan
4. Spacer
5. Fan shroud

Condenser removal steps

1. Fan motor and shroud assembly
6. Battery
7. Battery tray
8. Reserve tank
9. Upper insulator installation bolt

10. High-pressure pipe A
11. High-pressure hose connection
12. O-ring
13. Condenser
14. Bracket

Fig. 19 Condenser and fan removal/installation — 1993 Colt

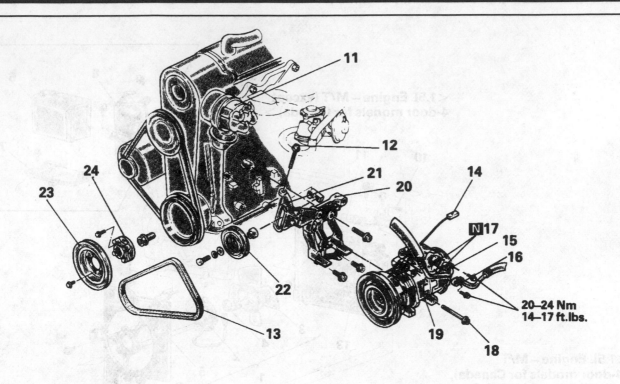

11. Distributor cap
12. Tension adjusting bolt
13. Drive belt
14. Compressor clutch connector connection
15. Discharge hose connection
16. Suction hose connection
17. O-ring
18. Compressor clutch assembly mounting bolt
19. Compressor clutch assembly
20. Compressor bracket
21. Tension bracket
22. Tension pulley
23. Crankshaft compressor pulley
24. Adapter

Fig. 20 Compressor removal/installation — 1990 Colt wagon w/1.5L or 1.8L engine

6. Evacuate and recharge the air conditioning system.

7. Connect the negative battery cable and check the entire climate control system for proper operation. Check the system for leaks.

Dual Pressure Switch

OPERATION

Colt uses a dual pressure switch, which is a combination of a low pressure cut off switch and high pressure cut off switch. These functions will stop operation of the compressor in the event of either high or low refrigerant charge, preventing damage to the system. The switch is located on the receiver drier.

The dual pressure switch is designed to cut off voltage to the compressor coil when the pressure either drops below 30 psi or rises above 384 psi.

TESTING

1. Check for continuity through the switch. Under all normal conditions, the switch should be continuous.

2. If the switch is open, check for insufficient refrigerant charge or excessive pressures.

3. If neither of the above conditions exist and the switch is open, replace the switch.

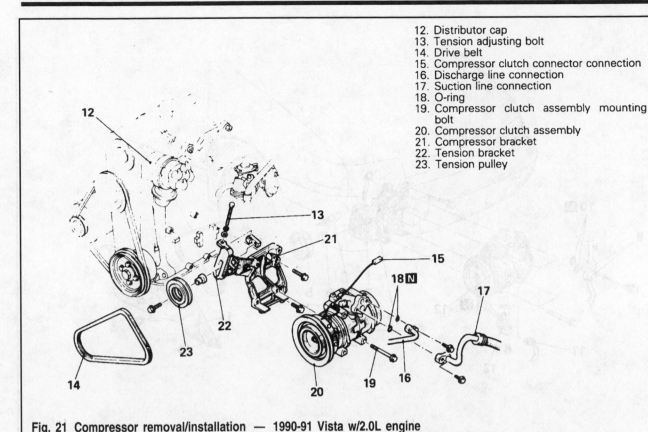

12. Distributor cap
13. Tension adjusting bolt
14. Drive belt
15. Compressor clutch connector connection
16. Discharge line connection
17. Suction line connection
18. O-ring
19. Compressor clutch assembly mounting bolt
20. Compressor clutch assembly
21. Compressor bracket
22. Tension bracket
23. Tension pulley

Fig. 21 Compressor removal/installation — 1990-91 Vista w/2.0L engine

REMOVAL & INSTALLATION

1. Disconnect the negative battery cable.
2. Properly discharge the air conditioning system.
3. Remove the switch from the refrigerant line or receiver/drier.
4. The installation is the reverse of the removal installation.
5. Evacuate and recharge the air conditioning system.
6. Connect the negative battery cable and check the entire climate control system for proper operation. Check the system for leaks.

Low Pressure Cut Off Switch

OPERATION

On Vista, the low pressure cut off switch monitors the refrigerant gas pressure on the suction side of the system. The switch is connected in series with the compressor and will turn off voltage to the compressor clutch coil when the monitored pressure drops to levels that could damage the compressor. The switch is located on the receiver/drier and is a sealed unit that must be replaced if faulty.

TESTING

1. Start the engine and allow to idle. Turn the air conditioner **ON**.

2. Disconnect the switch connector and use a jumper wire to jump between terminals inside the connector boot.
3. If the compressor clutch does not engage, inspect the system for an open circuit.
4. If the clutch engages, connect an air conditioning manifold gauge to the system.
5. Read the low pressure gauge. The low pressure cut off switch should complete the circuit at pressures of at least 30 psi. Check the system for leaks if the pressures are too low.
6. If the pressures are nominal and the system works when the terminals are jumped, the cut off switch is faulty and should be replaced.

REMOVAL & INSTALLATION

1. Disconnect the negative battery cable.
2. Properly discharge the air conditioning system.
3. Unplug the boot connector from the switch.
4. Using an oil pressure sending unit socket, remove the switch from the receiver/drier.
To install:
5. Seal the threads of the new switch with teflon tape.
6. Install the switch to the receiver/drier and connect the boot connector.
7. Evacuate and recharge the system. Check for leaks.
8. Check the switch for proper operation.

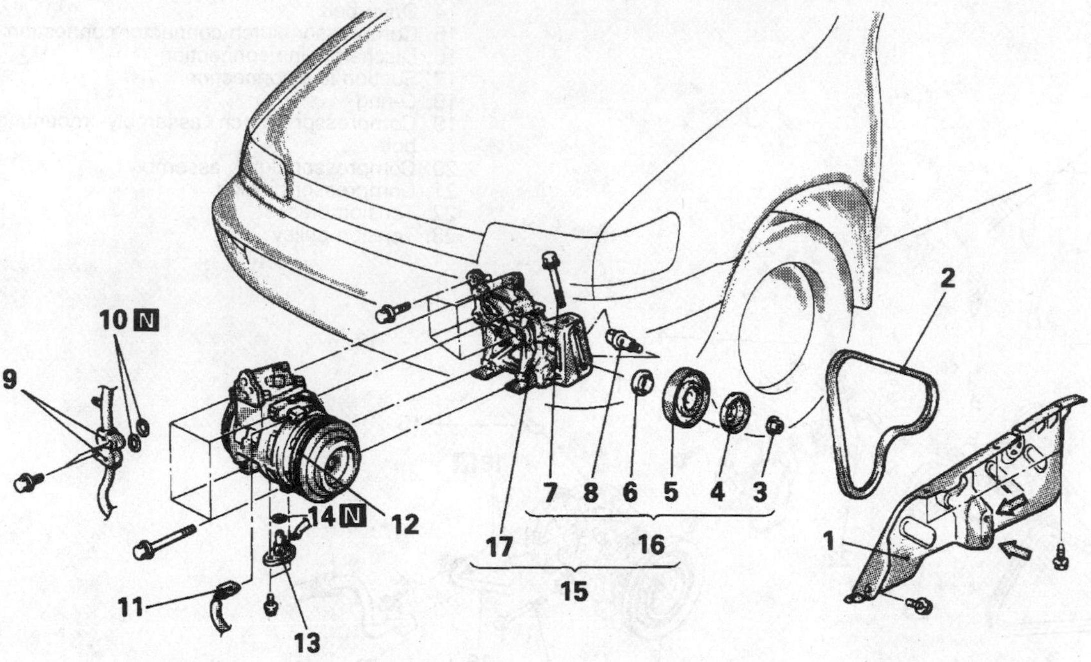

1. Under cover panel (LH)
2. Drive belt
3. Nut
4. Plate
5. Tension pulley
6. Collar
7. Bolt
8. Tension pulley bolt

Removal steps of compressor

1. Under cover panel (LH)
2. Drive belt
9. Connection for high-/low-pressure pipe
10. O-ring
11. Connector
12. Compressor
13. Revolution pick-up sensor
14. O-ring
15. Compressor bracket assembly
16. Tension pulley assembly
17. Compressor bracket

Fig. 22 Compressor removal/installation — 1992-93 Vista w/1.8L engine

High Pressure Cut Off Switch

OPERATION

On Vista, the high pressure cut off switch is located on the liquid line near the receiver/drier. The function of the switch is to disengage the compressor clutch by monitoring the discharge pressure when levels reach dangerously high levels, usually due to condenser restrictions. This switch is connected in series with the compressor clutch and is located on the liquid line near the receiver/drier.

TESTING

1. Start the engine and allow to idle. Turn the air conditioner **ON**.
2. Connect an air conditioning manifold gauge to the system. The system should operate at high gauge pressure below 300 psi.
3. Without allowing the engine to overheat, block the flow of air to the condenser with a cover. When the high pressure reaches the specified pressure, the clutch should disengage.
4. Remove the cover. When the gauge reading falls below about 230 psi, the clutch should cycle back on.
5. If faulty, replace the switch.

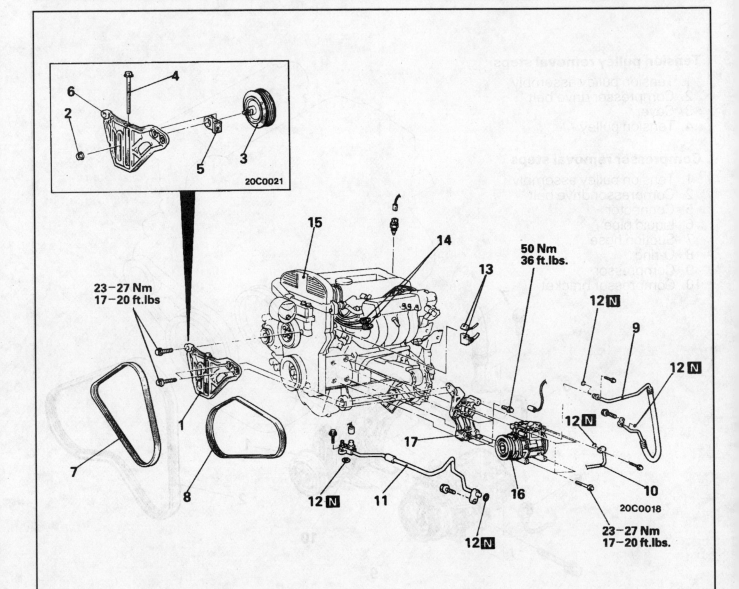

23—27 Nm
17—20 ft.lbs

50 Nm
36 ft.lbs.

23—27 Nm
17—20 ft.lbs.

20C0021

20C0018

1. Tension pulley assembly
2. Nut
3. Tension pulley
4. Bolt
5. Adjust plate
6. Tension pulley bracket
7. Drive belt (Alternator)
8. Drive belt (For air conditioning)
9. Low pressure hose
10. High pressure hose connection
11. High pressure pipe B
12. O-ring
13. Ignition coil connector
14. High tension cable connection (two)
15. Timing belt upper cover
16. Compressor
17. Compressor bracket

Fig. 23 Compressor removal/installation — 1992-93 Vista w/2.4L engine

Tension pulley removal steps

1. Tension pulley assembly
2. Compressor drive belt
3. Cover
4. Tension pulley

Compressor removal steps

1. Tension pulley assembly
2. Compressor drive belt
5. Connector
6. Liquid pipe
7. Suction hose
8. O-ring
9. Compressor
10. Compressor bracket

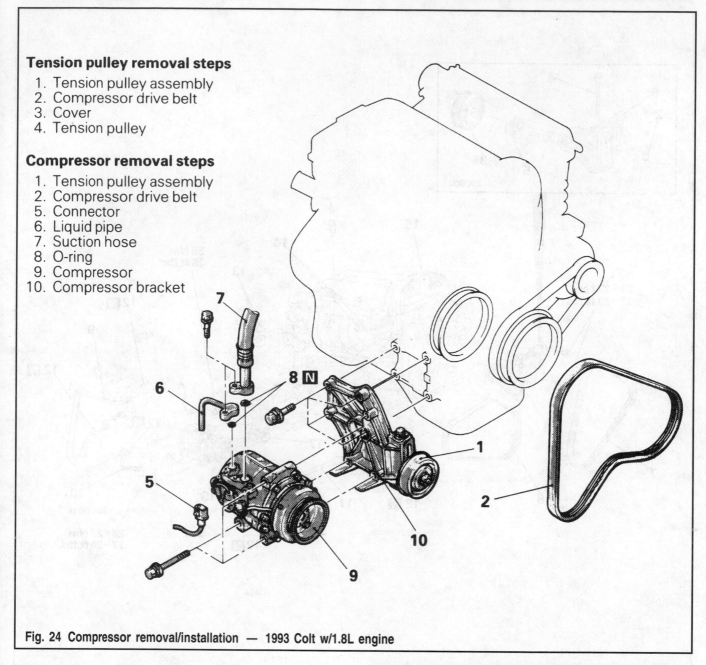

Fig. 24 Compressor removal/installation — 1993 Colt w/1.8L engine

REMOVAL & INSTALLATION

1. Disconnect the negative battery cable.
2. Properly discharge the air conditioning system.
3. Unplug the boot connector from the switch.
4. Remove the switch from the liquid line.

To install:

5. Seal the threads of the new switch with teflon tape.
6. Install the switch to the line and connect the boot connector.
7. Evacuate and recharge the system. Check for leaks.
8. Check the switch for proper operation.

Pressure Switch

OPERATION

The pressure switch, used on Colt with 1.6L engine, is used to control the 2-speed condenser cooling fan. The switch is normally located on the high pressure line near the left front of the engine compartment.

TESTING

1. Install a manifold gauge set to the air conditioning system.

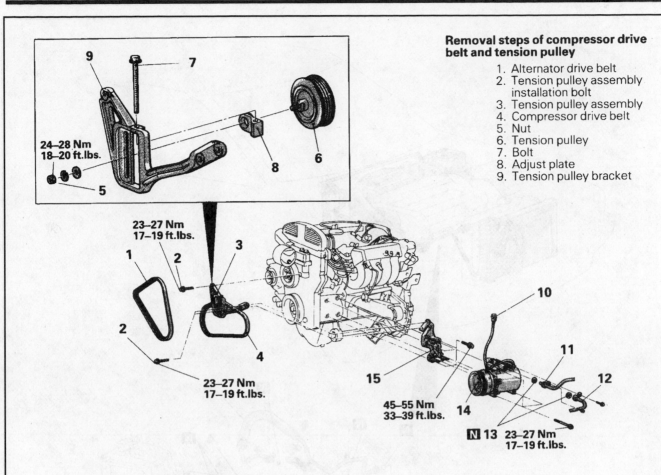

1. Alternator drive belt
2. Tension pulley assembly installation bolt
3. Tension pulley assembly
4. Compressor drive belt
5. Nut
6. Tension pulley
7. Bolt
8. Adjust plate
9. Tension pulley bracket

9
7
6
8
5

24–28 Nm
18–20 ft.lbs.

23–27 Nm
17–19 ft.lbs.

1
2
3
2
4

23–27 Nm
17–19 ft.lbs.

10
11
12
15
14
45–55 Nm
33–39 ft.lbs.
13   23–27 Nm
17–19 ft.lbs.

1. Alternator drive belt
2. Tension pulley assembly installation bolt
3. Tension pulley assembly
4. Compressor drive belt
10. Connector (3 pin) for the magnetic clutch
11. Connection for suction hose
12. Connection for liquid hose
13. O-rings
14. Compressor
15. Compressor bracket

Fig. 25 Compressor removal/installation — 1990 Colt w/1.6L engine

2. Check the continuity of the switch at different pressures. The switch should be open a pressures below 213 psi and closed at 256 psi or higher.

3. For the purpose of testing, the pressures can be lowered by using an auxiliary fan to cool the condenser and raised by placing a cover over the condenser to prevent air flow.

4. If faulty, replace the switch if faulty.

REMOVAL & INSTALLATION

1. Disconnect the negative battery cable.
2. Properly discharge the air conditioning system.
3. Remove the switch from the refrigerant line.
4. The installation is the reverse of the removal procedure.
5. Evacuate and recharge the air conditioning system.

6. Connect the negative battery cable and check the entire climate control system for proper operation. Check the system for leaks.

Refrigerant Temperature Sensor

OPERATION

Located on the rear of the compressor on Colt, the refrigerant temperature sensor detects the temperature of the refrigerant delivered from the compressor during operation. The switch is designed to cut off the compressor when the temperature of the refrigerant exceeds 347°F (175°C), preventing overheating.

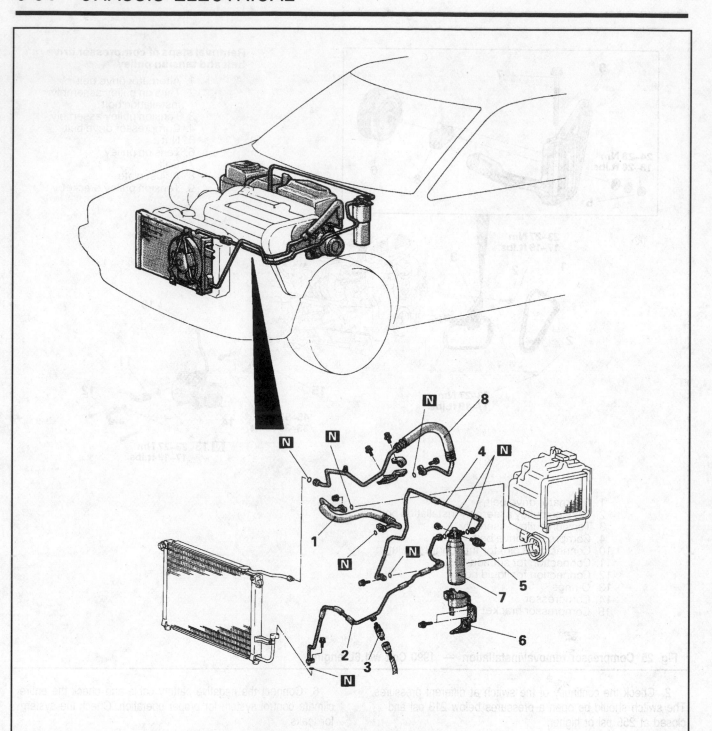

1. Suction hose
2. Liquid pipe
3. Pressure switch
4. Liquid pipe
5. Dual pressure switch
6. Receiver bracket
7. Receiver
8. Discharge hose

Fig. 26 Refrigerant line and receiver/drier removal/installation — 1990 Colt hatchback and sedan w/1.5L or 1.6L engine

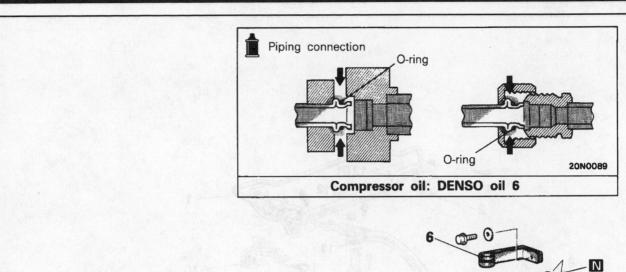

Piping connection

O-ring

O-ring

20N0089

Compressor oil: DENSO oil 6

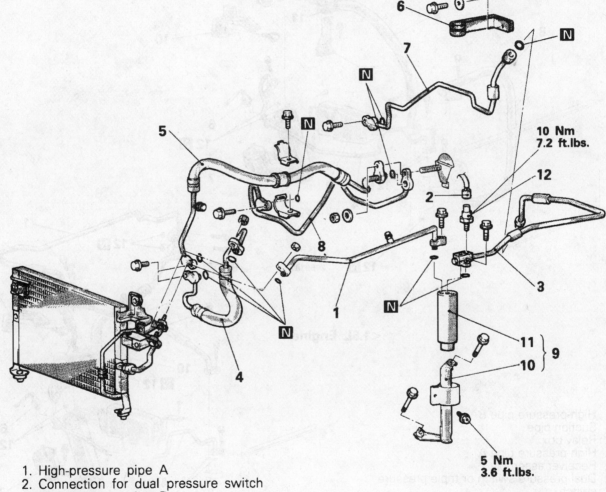

10 Nm
7.2 ft.lbs.

5 Nm
3.6 ft.lbs.

1. High-pressure pipe A
2. Connection for dual pressure switch
3. High-pressure pipe B
4. High-pressure hose
5. Low-pressure hose
6. Bracket
7. High-pressure pipe C
8. Low-pressure pipe
9. Receiver assembly
10. Receiver assembly
11. Receiver
12. Triple pressure switch

Fig. 27 Refrigerant line and receiver/drier removal/installation — 1992-93 Vista w/1.8L engine

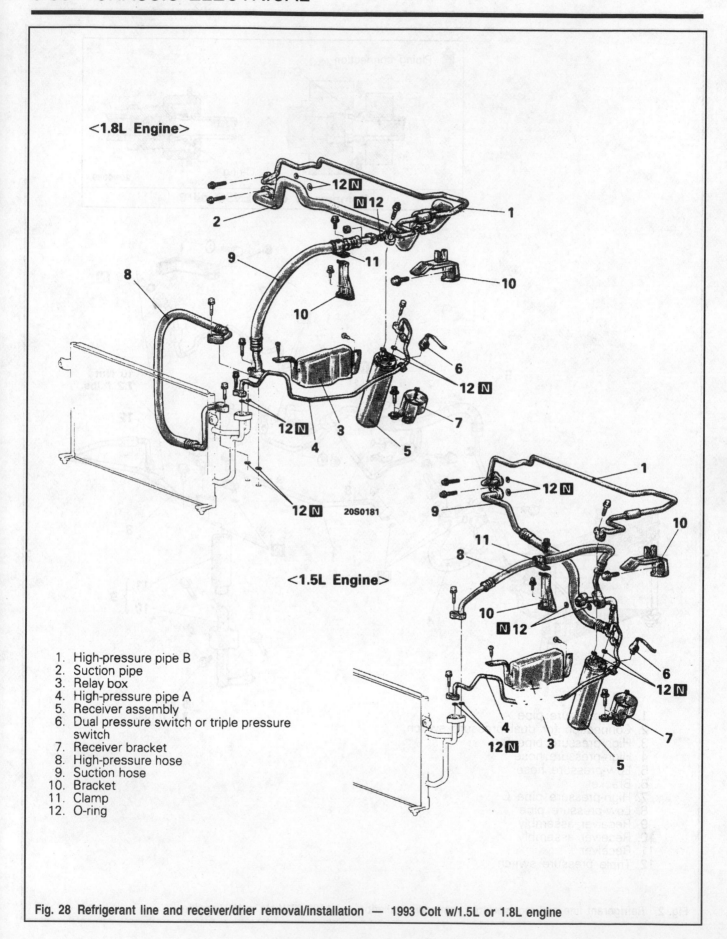

1. High-pressure pipe B
2. Suction pipe
3. Relay box
4. High-pressure pipe A
5. Receiver assembly
6. Dual pressure switch or triple pressure switch
7. Receiver bracket
8. High-pressure hose
9. Suction hose
10. Bracket
11. Clamp
12. O-ring

Fig. 28 Refrigerant line and receiver/drier removal/installation — 1993 Colt w/1.5L or 1.8L engine

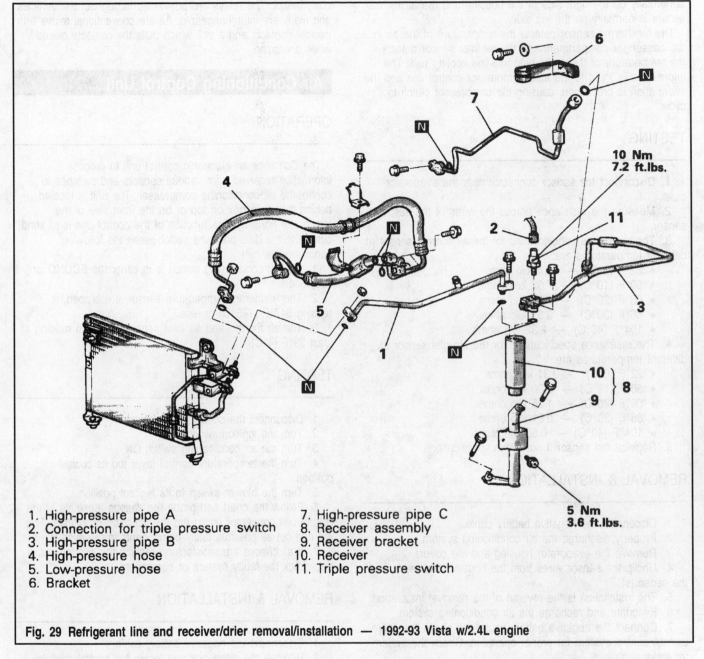

1. High-pressure pipe A
2. Connection for triple pressure switch
3. High-pressure pipe B
4. High-pressure hose
5. Low-pressure hose
6. Bracket
7. High-pressure pipe C
8. Receiver assembly
9. Receiver bracket
10. Receiver
11. Triple pressure switch

Fig. 29 Refrigerant line and receiver/drier removal/installation — 1992-93 Vista w/2.4L engine

TESTING

1. Measure the resistance between the yellow-with-green-tracer wire and the black-with-yellow-tracer wire.
2. At 75-80°F, the resistance specification is about 80 kilo ohms.
3. If the reading deviates greatly from the specification, replace the sensor.

REMOVAL & INSTALLATION

1. Disconnect the negative battery cable.
2. Properly discharge the air conditioning system.
3. Disconnect the connector.

4. Remove the mounting screws and the sensor from the compressor.
5. The installation is the reverse of the removal installation. Use a new lubricated O-ring when installing.
6. Evacuate and recharge the air conditioning system.
7. Connect the negative battery cable and check the entire climate control system for proper operation. Check the system for leaks.

Air Thermo and Air Inlet Sensors

OPERATION

These sensors function as cycling switches. Both sensors are located inside the evaporator housing. The air inlet sensor is normally on the right side of the housing and the air thermo sensor is normally on the left side.

The air thermo sensor detects the temperature of the air in the passenger compartment and the air inlet sensor detects the temperature of the air coming into the cooling unit. The information is input to the auto compressor control unit and the information is processed, causing the compressor clutch to cycle.

TESTING

1. Disconnect the sensor connector near the evaporator case.

2. Measure the resistance across the wires of the suspect sensor.

3. The resistance specifications for the air thermo sensor at different temperatures are:
- 32°F (0°C) — 11.4 kilo ohms
- 50°F (10°C) — 7.32 kilo ohms
- 68°F (20°C) — 4.86 kilo ohms
- 86°F (30°C) — 3.31 kilo ohms
- 104°F (40°C) — 2.32 kilo ohms

4. The resistance specifications for the air inlet sensor at different temperatures are:
- 32°F (0°C) — 3.31 kilo ohms
- 50°F (10°C) — 2.00 kilo ohms
- 68°F (20°C) — 1.25 kilo ohms
- 86°F (30°C) — 0.81 kilo ohms
- 104°F (40°C) — 0.53 kilo ohms

5. Replace the sensor if not within specifications.

REMOVAL & INSTALLATION

1. Disconnect the negative battery cable.
2. Properly discharge the air conditioning system.
3. Remove the evaporator housing and the covers.
4. Unclip the sensor wires from the housing and remove the sensor(s).
5. The installation is the reverse of the removal installation.
6. Evacuate and recharge the air conditioning system.
7. Connect the negative battery cable and check the entire climate control system for proper operation. Check the system for leaks.

System Relays

OPERATION

Many of the systems within the air conditioning systems use relays to send current on its way and energize various components. The relays are positioned throughout the vehicles and many are interchangeable. All are conventional relays with internal contacts and a coil which pulls the contacts closed when energized.

Air Conditioning Control Unit

OPERATION

The Colt uses an electronic control unit to process information received from various sensors and switches to control the air conditioning compressor. The unit is located behind the glove box on top or on the front side of the evaporator housing. The function of the control unit is to send current to the dual pressure switch when the following conditions are met:

1. The air conditioning switch is in either the **ECONO** or **A/C** mode.

2. The refrigerant temperature sensor, if equipped, is reading 347°F (175°C) or less.

3. The air thermo and air inlet sensors are both reading at least 39°F (4°C).

TESTING

1. Disconnect the control unit connector.
2. Turn the ignition switch **ON**.
3. Turn the air conditioning switch **ON**.
4. Turn the temperature control lever too its coolest position.
5. Turn the blower switch to its highest position.
6. Follow the chart and probe the various terminals of the control unit connector under the the specified conditions. This will rule out all possible faulty components in the system.
7. If all checks are satisfactory, replace the control unit. If not, check the faulty system or component.

REMOVAL & INSTALLATION

1. Disconnect the negative battery cable.
2. Remove the glove box and locate the control module.
3. Disconnect the connector to the module and remove the mounting screws.
4. Remove the module from the evaporator housing.
5. The installation is the reverse of the removal installation.
6. Connect the negative battery cable and check the entire climate control system for proper operation.

CRUISE CONTROL

General Description

The cruise control, which is a speed control system, maintains a desired speed of the vehicle under normal driving conditions. The cruise control system's main parts are the control switches, control unit, actuator, speed sensor, electrical release switches, electrical harness, vacuum pump, switch, pump relay and tank.

➡**The use of the speed control is not recommended when driving conditions do not permit maintaining a constant speed, such as in heavy traffic or on roads that are winding, icy, snow covered or slippery.**

Diagnosis and Testing

SERVICE PRECAUTIONS

• Never disconnect any electrical connection with the ignition switch **ON** unless instructed to do so in a test.

• Always wear a grounded wrist static strap when servicing any control module or component labeled with a Electrostatic Discharge (ESD) sensitive device symbol.

• Avoid touching module connector pins.

• Leave new components and modules in the shipping package until ready to install them.

• Always touch a vehicle ground after sliding across a vehicle seat or walking across vinyl or carpeted floors to avoid static charge damage.

• Never allow welding cables to lie on, near or across any vehicle electrical wiring.

• Do not allow extension cords for power tools or drop lights to lie on, near or across any vehicle electrical wiring.

• Do not operate the cruise control or the engine with the drive wheels off the ground unless specifically instructed to do so by a test procedure.

SELF DIAGNOSIS FUNCTION

The cruise control system can display trouble codes from the cruise control unit through the diagnostic connector. The codes can be read by using a voltmeter or. Be sure to turn the main switch **ON** before trying to read the codes.

Connect a voltmeter between the ground terminal and the terminal of for the cruise control of the diagnosis connector. It is possible to discover which circuit is the cause of the cancellation by verifying the indication shown on the voltmeter with the display patterns.

➡**The display of the trouble codes starts if the vehicle speed decreases to less than approximately 12 mph after the cancellation of the cruise control system function and stops if the vehicle speed increases to approximately 12 mph or higher.**

INPUT CHECK

Input checks should be made when the cruise control system cannot be set and when it is necessary to check (when a malfunction related to the cruise control system occurs) whether or not the input signals are normal.

1. If inspection of the self-diagnosis is necessary, confirm diagnosis code first and conduct the input check.

2. The input check can be conducted by set operations. Self-diagnosis terminal outputs display pattern.

3. Display codes are displayed only if the circuit is normal.

4. The voltmeter is set in the same way as for the self-diagnosis check.

5. Turn the ignition switch to the **ON** position.

6. Switch **ON** the main/cruise switch while pressing and holding the set and resume control switches at the same time.

7. With the set switch in the **ON** position, turn the main/cruise switch **ON** position.

8. With the set switch in the **ON** position, turn the main/cruise switch **ON** position. Then, within 1 second, place the resume switch in the **ON** position.

9. Perform each input operation according to the input check chart.

10. Turn the main/cruise switch to the **OFF** position.

BEFORE TROUBLESHOOTING

The cruise control system performs control functions for the setting or cancellation of the fixed speed driving speed based upon the data provided by input signals. As a result, when the cruise control system is canceled, the cause of cancellation is memorized in a separate circuit by the ECU, regardless of whether or not the cruise control system condition is normal or abnormal, thus providing the ECU with the self diagnosis function by certain fixed patterns as well as the function of being able to check whether or not the ECU's input switches or sensor are normal. Thus, by effectively using these functions, the time required checking and repairing the system can be shortened.

➡**When the ECU power supply (ignition switch and main switch) is switched OFF, the memorized trouble codes are erased, and so for this reason the power supply must be left ON until the checking is completed.**

SELF DIAGNOSIS CHECKING

The self diagnosis checking is performed when there has been an automatic cancellation, without cancel switch operation. The following method can be used for checking the diagnosis. Note that the diagnosis check connector is located under the driver's side instrument panel.

Connect a voltmeter between the ground terminal and the terminal of for the cruise control of the diagnosis connector. It is possible to discover which circuit is the cause of the cancellation by verifying the indication shown on the voltmeter with the display patterns.

When trouble codes number 11, 12, 15 or 16 are displayed, check the troubleshooting symptom applicable to that number.

➡Code number 16 is entered in the memory as cancel switch ON signal input if the system is canceled by depressing the brake pedal, and code number 13 or 14 is entered when there is an automatic cancellation because the vehicle speed drops when the vehicle is driven up a steep slope with the preset speed setting left set etc., when however, there is a cancellation not intentionally made by the driver, the cause might be damaged or disconnected stop lamp switch input wiring, a malfunction of the stop lamp switch ON, etc., even though the same code number 16 is displayed.

Component Testing

CRUISE CONTROL SWITCH

Inspection

▸ **See Figures 30 and 31**

1. Remove the knee protector (or lower panel assembly) and the steering column over.
2. Disconnect the steering column switch connector and check the continuity between the terminals.
3. When the switch is in the **OFF** position there should be no continuity between the terminals.
4. When the set switch is in the **ON** position there should be continuity between terminals 7 and 9.
5. When the set switch is in the **ON** position there should be continuity between terminals 7, 9 and 8.

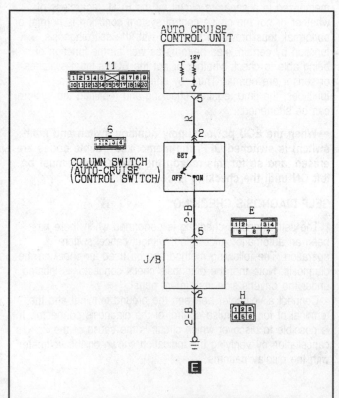

Fig. 30 Test connectors for control switch testing — 1990-92 Colt

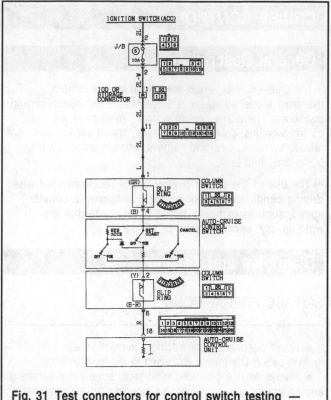

Fig. 31 Test connectors for control switch testing — 1993 Colt

6. If the switch fails any portion of this inspection, replace it with a new one.

BRAKE LAMP SWITCH

Inspection
COLT

▸ **See Figure 32**

1. Using a suitable ohmmeter, check for continuity between the terminals.
2. While depressing the brake pedal, there should be continuity between terminals 2 and 3 of the brake lamp switch connector.
3. While not depressing the brake pedal, there should be continuity between terminals 1 and 4 of the brake lamp switch connector.

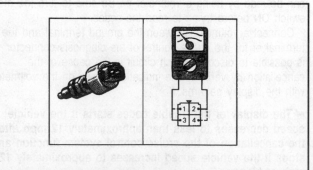

Fig. 32 Test connection for brake lamp switch testing — Colt

4. If the brake lamp switch fails any portion of this test, replace it with a new one.

VISTA

▶ **See Figure 33**

5. Using a suitable ohmmeter, check for continuity between the terminals.

6. While depressing the brake pedal, there should be continuity between terminals 1 and 2 of the brake lamp switch connector.

7. While not depressing the brake pedal, there should be continuity between terminals 3 and 4 of the brake lamp switch connector.

8. If the brake lamp switch fails any portion of this test, replace it with a new one.

CLUTCH SWITCH

Inspection

1. Using a suitable ohmmeter, check for continuity between the terminal.

2. While depressing the clutch pedal, there should be continuity between terminals of the clutch switch connect.

3. While not depressing the clutch pedal, there should be no continuity between the terminals of the clutch switch connect.

4. If the clutch switch fails any portion of this test, replace it with a new one.

INHIBITOR SWITCH

Inspection

COLT

▶ **See Figure 34**

1. Disconnect the inhibitor switch connector.

2. Using a suitable ohmmeter, check that there is continuity between connector terminals 8 and 9 when the shift lever is moved from the **N** range and the **P** range.

3. If the inhibitor switch fails any portion of this test, replace it with a new one.

VISTA

▶ **See Figure 35**

4. Disconnect the inhibitor switch connector.

5. Using a suitable ohmmeter, check that there is continuity between connector terminals **BY** and **BY** when the shift lever is moved from the **N** range and the **P** range.

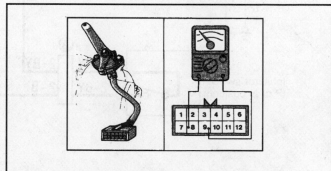

Fig. 34 Test connection for inhibitor switch testing — Colt

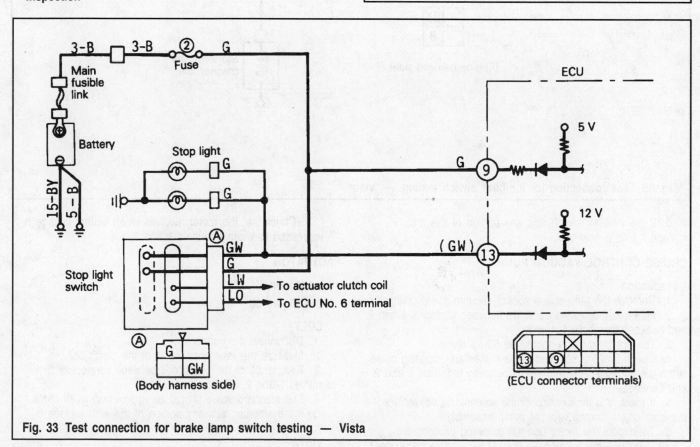

Fig. 33 Test connection for brake lamp switch testing — Vista

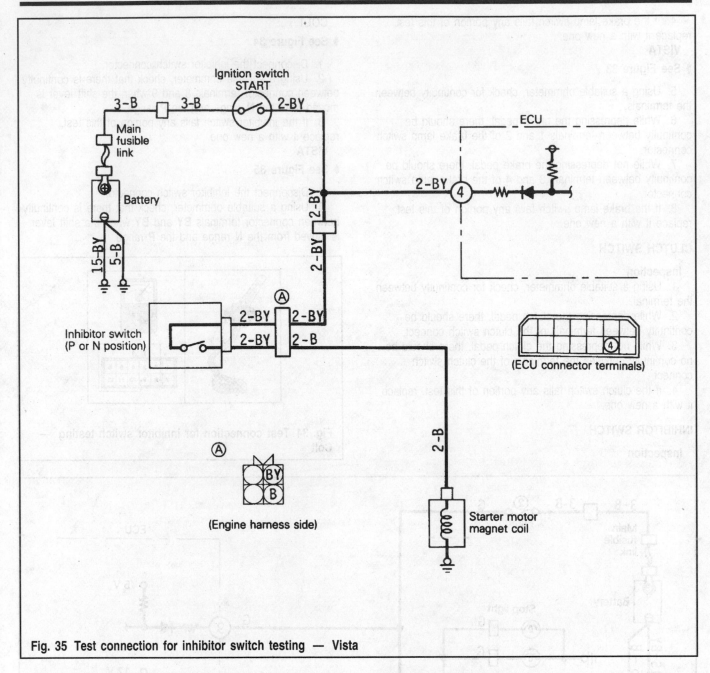

Fig. 35 Test connection for inhibitor switch testing — Vista

6. If the inhibitor switch fails any portion of this test, replace it with a new one.

CRUISE CONTROL VACUUM PUMP

Inspection

1. Remove the auto cruise control vacuum pump connector.

2. Measure the resistance value between terminals 1 and 2 and between terminals 1 and 3.

3. The standard value should be 50-60 ohms.

4. Check that the solenoid valve makes an operating noise when battery voltage is impressed between terminals 1 and 2 and between terminals 1 and 3.

5. If there is a malfunction of the solenoid valve, replace the auto cruise control vacuum pump assembly.

6. To inspect the motor use the following procedure:

    a. Remove the auto cruise control vacuum pump connect

b. Check that the motor revolves when battery voltage is impressed between terminals 1 and 4.

ACTUATOR

Inspection

▶ See Figure 36

COLT

1. Disconnect the connector.

2. Measure the resistance value of the clutch coil.

3. Resistance of the clutch coil between connector terminals 1 and 2.

4. The standard value should be approximately 20 ohms.

5. If the actuator fails any portion of this test, replace it with a new one.

VISTA

6. Disconnect the connect

Fig. 36 Actuator test connector

7. Measure the resistance value of the clutch cover.

8. Resistance of the clutch coil between connector terminals 1 and 4.

9. The standard value should be approximately 20 ohm.

10. If the actuator fails any portion of this test, replace it with a new one.

VEHICLE SPEED SENSOR

Inspection

▶ See Figure 37

1. Remove the combination meter from the instrument panel.

2. Connector the tester (resistance X 100 ohm range) to terminal 3 (negative side) and terminal 4 (reed switch positive side), or lead connector terminal and then slowly turn the shaft of the speedometer cable (turn by using a thin rod or similar tool). Note that the lead terminal is connected to terminal 4.

3. There should be 4 changes of continuity/non-continuity between terminals for each turn of the shaft.

4. Replace the speedometer assembly if there is a malfunction.

Component Replacement

▶ See Figures 38, 39, 40 and 41

ACCELERATOR CABLE, THROTTLE CABLE AND AUTO CRUISE CONTROL CABLE

Adjustment

1990 COLT

1. Check the inner cables for correct slack.

2. If there is too much slack or no slack, adjust the play by the following procedures:

   a. Remove the air cleaner assembly.

   b. Adjust the accelerator cable on the throttle valve side. After loosening the adjustment bolts at the air intake plenum side and freeing the inner cable use the adjustment bolts to secure the plate so that the free lay of the inner cable becomes the standard value of 0.04-0.08 in. (1-2mm).

➡**NOTE:If there is excessive play of the accelerator cable, the vehicle speed drop (undershoot) when climbing a slope will be large. If there is no play (excessive tension) of the accelerator cable, the idling speed will increase.**

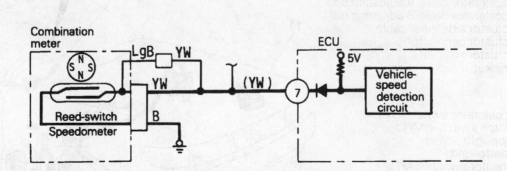

Fig. 37 Checking speed sensor

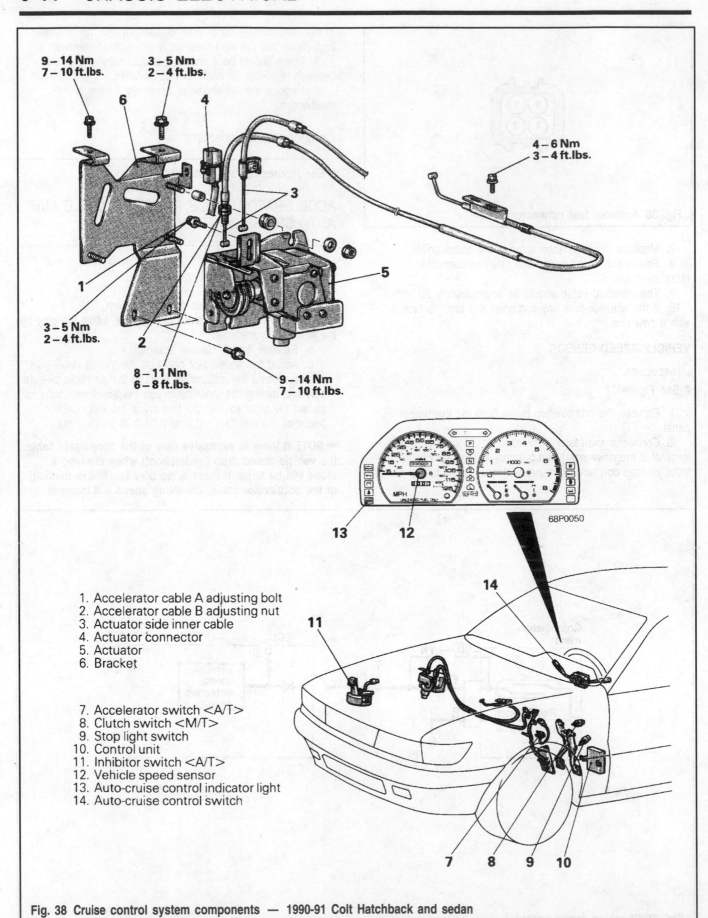

9 – 14 Nm
7 – 10 ft.lbs.

3 – 5 Nm
2 – 4 ft.lbs.

4 – 6 Nm
3 – 4 ft.lbs.

3 – 5 Nm
2 – 4 ft.lbs.

8 – 11 Nm
6 – 8 ft.lbs.

9 – 14 Nm
7 – 10 ft.lbs.

68P0050

1. Accelerator cable A adjusting bolt
2. Accelerator cable B adjusting nut
3. Actuator side inner cable
4. Actuator connector
5. Actuator
6. Bracket

7. Accelerator switch <A/T>
8. Clutch switch <M/T>
9. Stop light switch
10. Control unit
11. Inhibitor switch <A/T>
12. Vehicle speed sensor
13. Auto-cruise control indicator light
14. Auto-cruise control switch

Fig. 38 Cruise control system components — 1990-91 Colt Hatchback and sedan

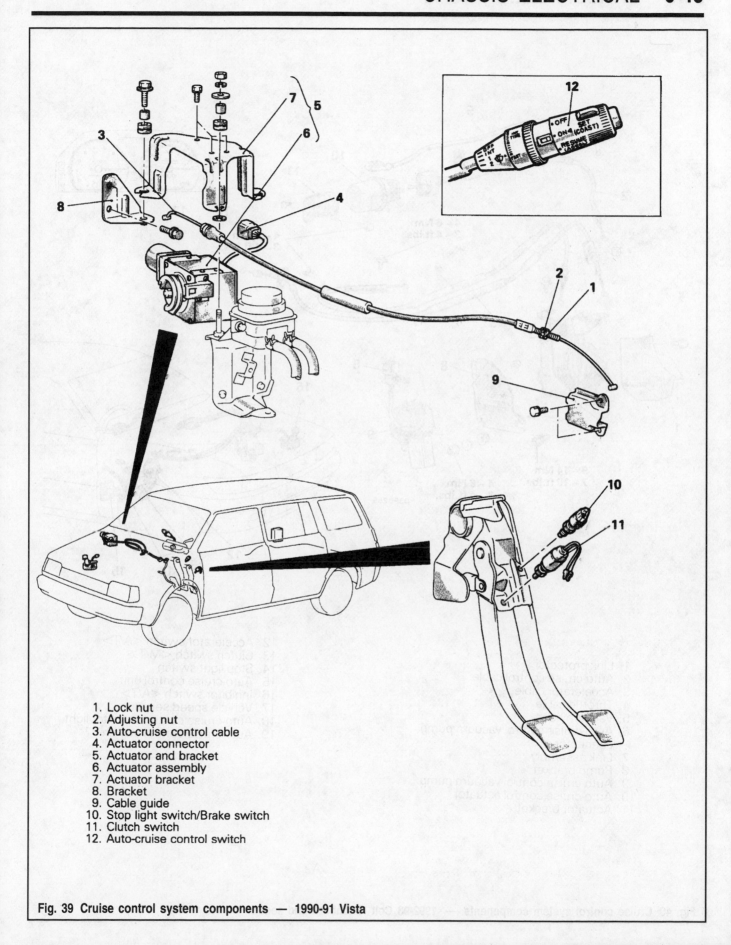

1. Lock nut
2. Adjusting nut
3. Auto-cruise control cable
4. Actuator connector
5. Actuator and bracket
6. Actuator assembly
7. Actuator bracket
8. Bracket
9. Cable guide
10. Stop light switch/Brake switch
11. Clutch switch
12. Auto-cruise control switch

Fig. 39 Cruise control system components — 1990-91 Vista

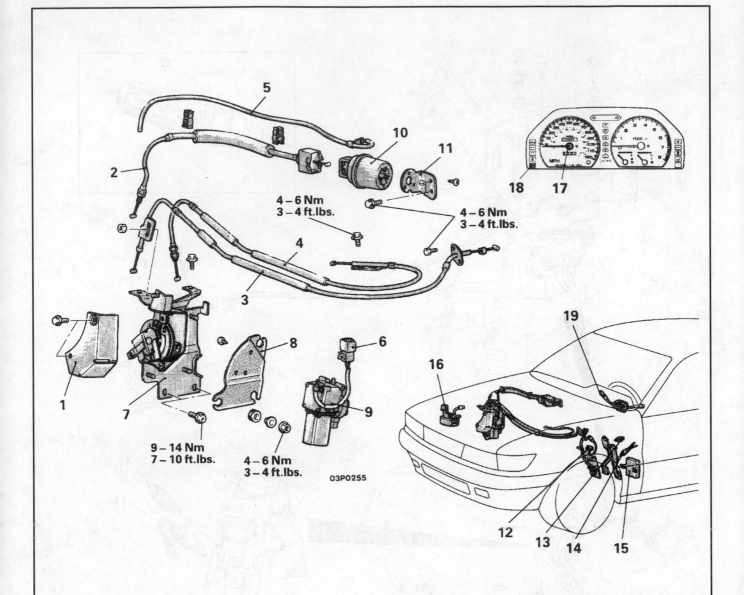

1. Link protector
2. Auto-cruise control cable
3. Accelerator cable
4. Throttle cable
5. Vacuum hose
6. Auto-cruise control vacuum pump connector
7. Link assembly
8. Pump bracket
9. Auto-cruise control vacuum pump
10. Auto-cruise control actuator
11. Actuator bracket
12. Accelerator switch <A/T>
13. Clutch switch <M/T>
14. Stop light switch
15. Auto-cruise control unit
16. Inhibitor switch <A/T>
17. Vehicle speed sensor
18. Auto-cruise control indicator light
19. Auto-cruise control switch

Fig. 40 Cruise control system components — 1992-93 Colt Hatchback and sedan

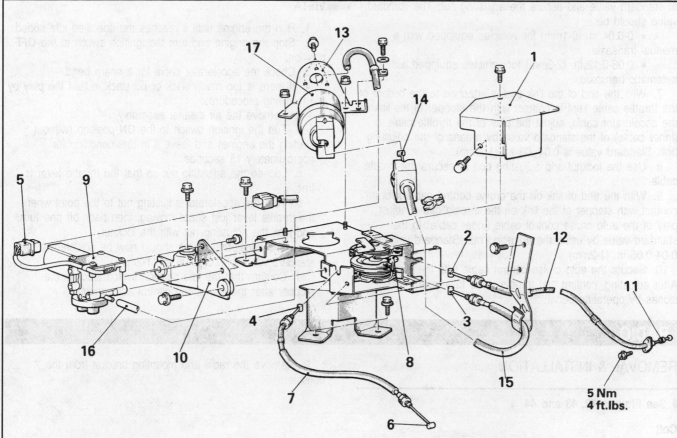

1. Link protector
2. Connection of accelerator cable and link assembly
3. Connection of cruise control cable and link assembly
4. Connection of throttle cable link assembly
5. Vacuum pump connector
6. Connection of throttle cable and throttle body
7. Throttle cable
8. Link assembly
9. Vacuum pump
10. Pump bracket
11. Bush connection
12. Accelerator cable
13. Actuator bracket
14. Connection of cruise control cable and actuator.
15. Cruise control cable
16. Vacuum hose
17. Actuator

Fig. 41 Cruise control system components — 1992-93 Vista

c. After adjusting the accelerator cable, confirm that the throttle lever touches the idle position switch.

d. Adjust the accelerator cable on the accelerator pedal side. Loosen the adjusting bolt. While keeping the intermediate link of the actuator in close contact with the stopper, adjust the inner cable play of the accelerator cable to specifications and tighten the adjusting bolt. The standard value should be:

   0-0.04 in. (0-1mm) for vehicles equipped with a manual transaxle.

   0.08-0.12 in. (2-3mm) for vehicles equipped with a automatic transaxle.

3. After making the adjustment of the cable, check to be sure that the throttle lever at the engine side is caused to move a distance of 0.04-0.08 in. (1-2mm) when the actuator link is turned.

4. Confirm that the throttle valve fully opens and closes by operating the pedal.

5. Install the air cleaner.

1991-93 COLT

1. Remove the air cleaner.
2. Remove the link protector.
3. Make sure that the accelerator cable, throttle cable and auto cruise control cable are free of sharp bends and folds.
4. Turn the ignition switch to the **ON** position (without starting the engine) and leave it in that condition for approximately 15 seconds.
5. Provide each cable with sufficient play and temporarily install the adjusting nuts as well as the adjusting bolt.
6. Move the plate so that when lower link is in contact with the stopper, play of the accelerator cable (inner cable) may be

of standard value and secure the adjusting nut. The standard value should be:

- 0-0.04 in. (0-1mm) for vehicles equipped with a manual transaxle.
- 0.08-0.12 in. (2-3mm) for vehicles equipped with a automatic transaxle.

7. With the end of the link that is attached to the bottom of the throttle cable kept in contact with the stopper of the link on the accelerator cable, adjust the play of the throttle cable (inner cable) of the standard value by means of the adjusting bolt. Standard value is 0.04-.08 in. (1-2mm).

8. Use the locknut and adjusting bolt to secure the throttle cable.

9. With the end of link on the cruise control cable kept in contact with stopper of the link on the throttle cable, adjust play of the auto cruise control cable (inner cable) to the standard value by using the adjusting nut. Standard value is 0.04-0.08 in. (1-2mm).

10. Secure the auto cruise control cable with the locknut. After adjusting, confirm that throttle valve fully opens and closes by operating pedal.

VISTA

1. Run the engine until it reaches the specified idle speed.

2. Stop the engine and turn the ignition switch to the **OFF** position.

3. Check the accelerator cable for a sharp bend.

4. If there is too much slack or no slack, adjust the play by the following procedures:

a. Remove the air cleaner assembly.

b. Tun the ignition switch to the **ON** position (without starting the engine) and leave it in that condition for approximately 15 seconds.

c. Loosen the adjusting nut so that the throttle lever is free.

d. Turn the accelerator adjusting nut to the point where the throttle lever just starts moving, then back off one turn and lock the adjusting nut with the locknut.

e. The accelerator cable should now be adjusted to the standard value of 0.04-0.08 in. (1-2mm).

f. Confirm that the idle position switch touches the stopper after the idle speed control adjustment.

RADIO

REMOVAL & INSTALLATION

▶ **See Figures 42, 43 and 44**

Colt

1. Remove the floor console. Disconnect the radio wiring harness and antenna.

2. Remove the radio and mounting bracket from the console.

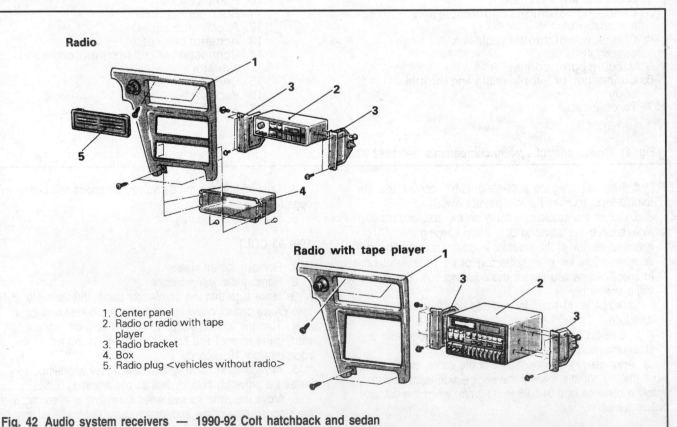

1. Center panel
2. Radio or radio with tape player
3. Radio bracket
4. Box
5. Radio plug <vehicles without radio>

Fig. 42 Audio system receivers — 1990-92 Colt hatchback and sedan

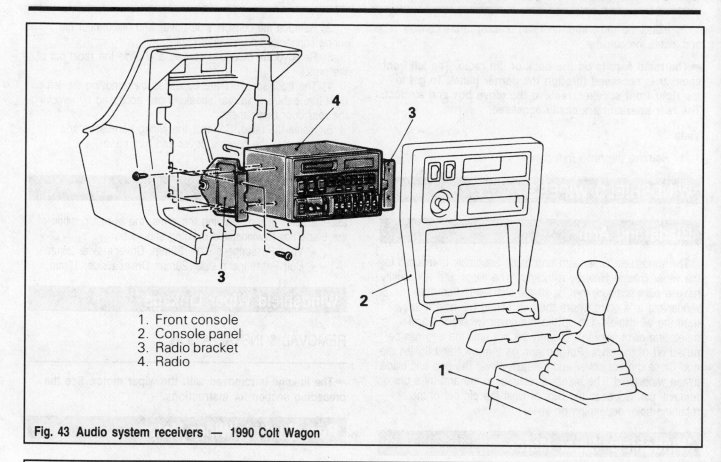

1. Front console
2. Console panel
3. Radio bracket
4. Radio

Fig. 43 Audio system receivers — 1990 Colt Wagon

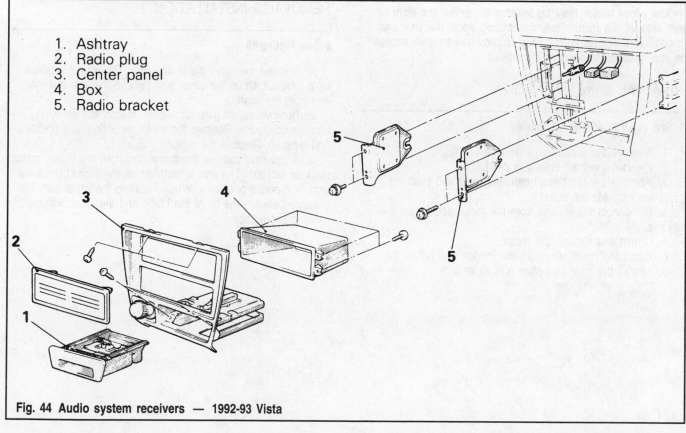

1. Ashtray
2. Radio plug
3. Center panel
4. Box
5. Radio bracket

Fig. 44 Audio system receivers — 1992-93 Vista

3. Install the radio and mounting bracket to the console and install the console.

➡**The radio fuse is on the back of the radio. The left front speaker is accessed through the corner panel. To get to the right front speaker, remove the glove box and air duct. The rear speakers are easily accessed.**

Vista

1. Remove the radio trim panel.

WINDSHIELD WIPERS

Blade and Arm

The windshield wiper arm and blade assembly is retained to the wiper linkage pivot by a locknut. The wiper arm will usually have a park position, that is, lift the arm away from the windshield to a point where the arm spring will hold it away from the windshield. Lift up the nut cover (where the arm meets the pivot linkage). Loosen the nut until the arm can be pulled off of the pivot. Put the arm on the pivot and tighten the nut. Close the nut cover and carefully lower the arm and blade to the windshield. The blade is retained to the arm by a clip or removal pin. Squeeze the clip, or twist the pin out of the retaining hole, depending on style.

Windshield Wiper Motor

➡**The wiper motor may be located on either the right or left side of the front deck, depending upon the year and model. A wiper removing hole is provided to gain access to the linkage for removal purposes.**

REMOVAL & INSTALLATION

▶ **See Figures 45, 46, 47 and 48**

1. Remove the wiper arm assemblies.
2. Remove the front cowl trim plate.
3. Remove the pivot shaft mounting nuts and push the pivot shaft toward the inside.
4. Disconnect the linkage from the motor and lift out the linkage.
5. Unbolt and remove the motor.
6. Install the motor. Connect the linkage and mount the pivots. Install the cowl trim plate and wiper arm

2. Remove the console side cover and disconnect the wiring connector and antenna cable.
3. Remove the mounting screws and slide the radio out of the panel.
4. The front speakers are accessed by removing the left or right trim panels. The rear speakers are accessed by removing the rear door trim panels.
5. Install the radio. Connect the wiring harnesses and antenna. Install the console cover and trim panel.

assemblies. When installing the arms, the at-rest position of the blade tips-to-windshield molding should be:
- Vista Passenger's side: 30mm; Driver's side: 25mm
- Colt Passenger's side: 20mm; Driver's side: 15mm

Windshield Wiper Linkage

REMOVAL & INSTALLATION

➡**The linkage is removed with the wiper motor. See the preceding section for instructions.**

Rear Window Wiper Motor

REMOVAL & INSTALLATION

▶ **See Figure 49**

1. Remove the wiper blade and arm. The arm is retained by a lock nut, lift up the cover and remove the nut: pull the arm from the shaft.
2. Remove the lift gate trim panel, disconnect the wiring harness connector. Remove the motor mounting nuts (inside and outside). Remove the motor.
3. If you must remove the crank arm from the motor, match mark its location. The arm is installed so the wiper blades will stop at a preset position. When installing the wiper arm, the distance between the tip of the blade and the lower window molding should be:
- Colt: 60mm
- Vista: 20mm

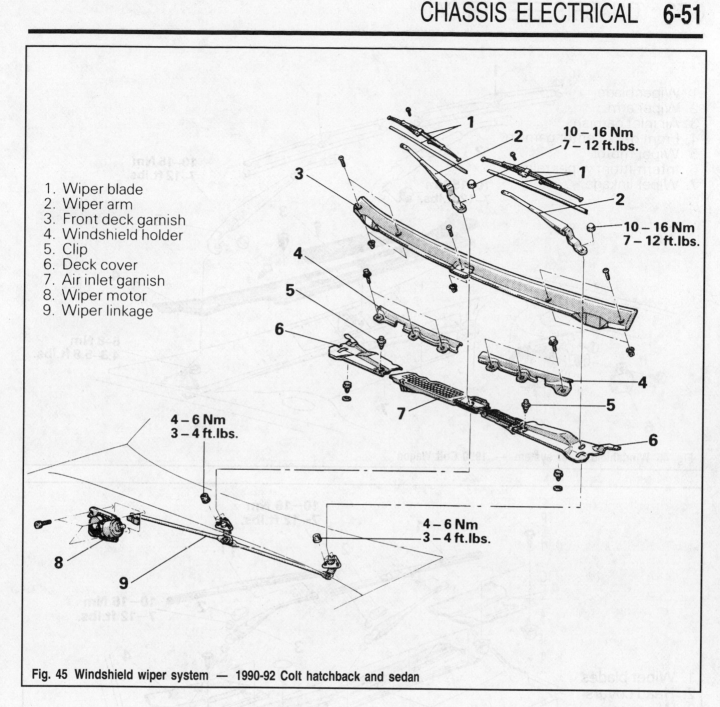

1. Wiper blade
2. Wiper arm
3. Front deck garnish
4. Windshield holder
5. Clip
6. Deck cover
7. Air inlet garnish
8. Wiper motor
9. Wiper linkage

10 – 16 Nm
7 – 12 ft.lbs.

10 – 16 Nm
7 – 12 ft.lbs.

4 – 6 Nm
3 – 4 ft.lbs.

4 – 6 Nm
3 – 4 ft.lbs.

Fig. 45 Windshield wiper system — 1990-92 Colt hatchback and sedan

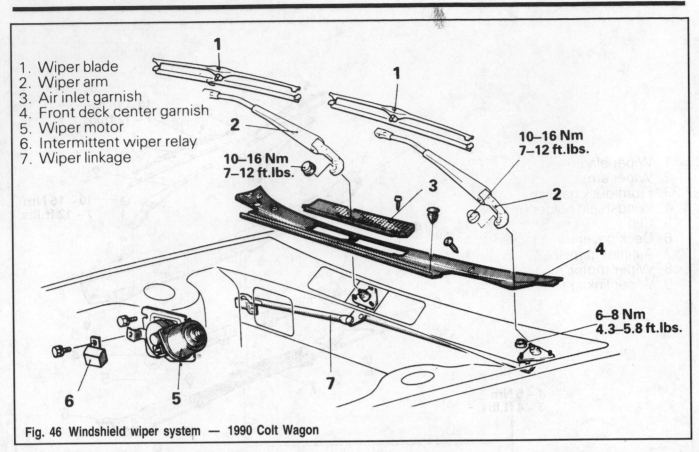

1. Wiper blade
2. Wiper arm
3. Air inlet garnish
4. Front deck center garnish
5. Wiper motor
6. Intermittent wiper relay
7. Wiper linkage

10–16 Nm
7–12 ft.lbs.

10–16 Nm
7–12 ft.lbs.

6–8 Nm
4.3–5.8 ft.lbs.

Fig. 46 Windshield wiper system — 1990 Colt Wagon

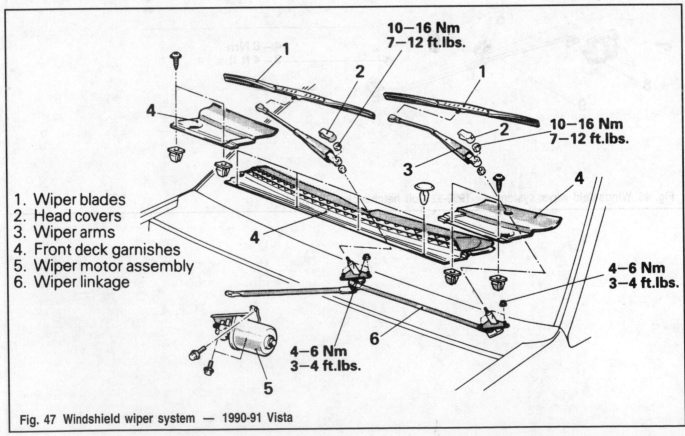

10–16 Nm
7–12 ft.lbs.

10–16 Nm
7–12 ft.lbs.

4–6 Nm
3–4 ft.lbs.

4–6 Nm
3–4 ft.lbs.

1. Wiper blades
2. Head covers
3. Wiper arms
4. Front deck garnishes
5. Wiper motor assembly
6. Wiper linkage

Fig. 47 Windshield wiper system — 1990-91 Vista

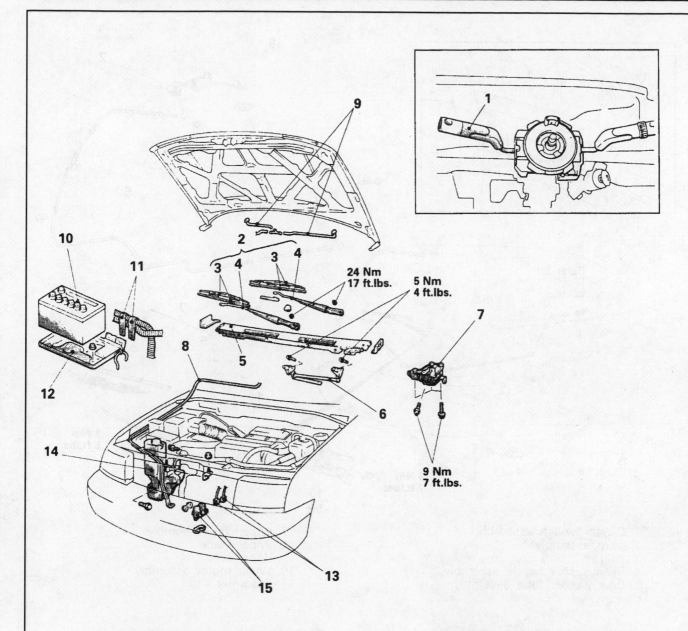

Fig. 48 Windshield wiper system — 1992-93 Vista

1. Column switch (with built-in wiper switch, washer switch and intermittent wiper relay)

Motor and bracket assembly removal steps

2. Wiper arm assembly
3. Wiper blade
4. Wiper arm
5. Front deck garnish
6. Link assembly
7. Wiper motor

Washer tube assembly and nozzle assembly removal steps

8. Washer tube assembly
9. Nozzle

Windshield washer tank assembly removal steps

10. Battery
11. Harness clip
12. Battery tray
13. Harness connector
14. Windshield washer tank assembly

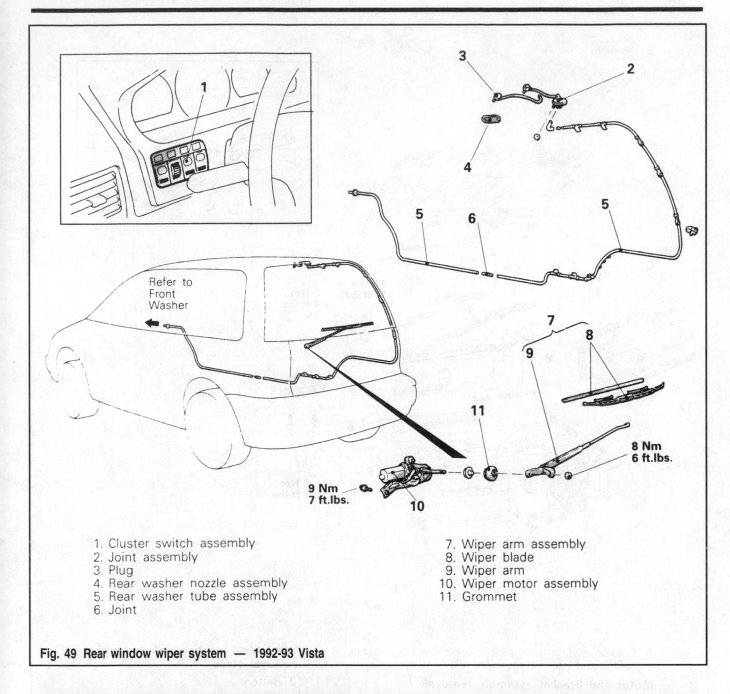

1. Cluster switch assembly
2. Joint assembly
3. Plug
4. Rear washer nozzle assembly
5. Rear washer tube assembly
6. Joint

7. Wiper arm assembly
8. Wiper blade
9. Wiper arm
10. Wiper motor assembly
11. Grommet

Fig. 49 Rear window wiper system — 1992-93 Vista

INSTRUMENTS AND SWITCHES

Instrument Cluster

REMOVAL & INSTALLATION

Colt

▶ **See Figure 50**

1. Disconnect the negative battery cable. Remove the steering wheel.
2. Remove the glove box.
3. Remove the instrument panel heater duct.

4. Remove the parcel tray.
5. Remove the steering column lower cover.
6. Disconnect the light switch and wiper switch connectors.
7. Remove the steering column upper cover.
8. Remove the instrument cluster hood screws and lift off the hood.
9. Remove the cluster mounting screws and pull the cluster slightly forward. Disconnect the speedometer cable and electrical connectors and lift out the cluster.
10. Install the cluster after connecting the wiring harness and speedometer cable. Install the steering column cover, parcel tray heater duct and glove box. Install the steering wheel and connect the battery cable.

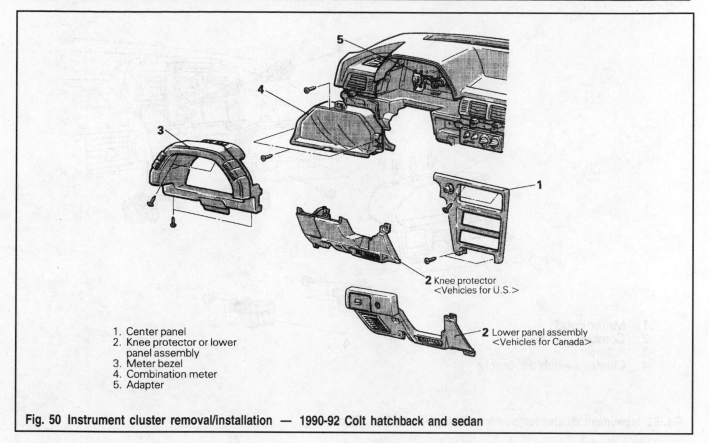

1. Center panel
2. Knee protector or lower
   panel assembly
3. Meter bezel
4. Combination meter
5. Adapter

Fig. 50 Instrument cluster removal/installation — 1990-92 Colt hatchback and sedan

Vista

▶ **See Figures 51 and 52**

1. Disconnect the negative battery cable. Remove the steering wheel.
2. Remove the ashtray.
3. Pry off (carefully) the cluster hood cover.
4. Remove the cluster hood mounting screws.
5. Pull the hood slightly toward you and release the connectors, Lift the hood off.
6. Remove the 4 cluster mounting screws, pull the cluster slightly toward you and disconnect the speedometer cable and electrical connectors.
7. Lift out the cluster.
8. Install the cluster after connecting the wiring harnesses and speedometer cable. Install the cluster hood and cover.

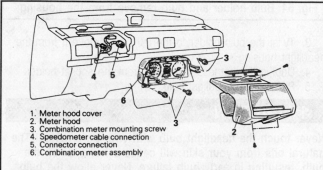

1. Meter hood cover
2. Meter hood
3. Combination meter mounting screw
4. Speedometer cable connection
5. Connector connection
6. Combination meter assembly

Fig. 51 Instrument cluster removal/installation — 1990-91 Vista

Install the ashtray. Install the steering wheel and connect the battery cable.

Windshield Wiper Switch

➡The wiper switch is integral with the turn signal switch. For wiper switch service, follow the procedures under **Turn Signal Switch, in Section 8.**

Rear Window Wiper Switch

REMOVAL & INSTALLATION

Vista

1. Pry the switch bezel from the panel.
2. Reach behind the panel and disconnect the wiring from the switch.
3. Depress the two retainers and pull the switch from the panel.
4. Install the switch. Connect the wiring harness and install the bezel.

Colt

The switch is integral with the windshield wiper switch.

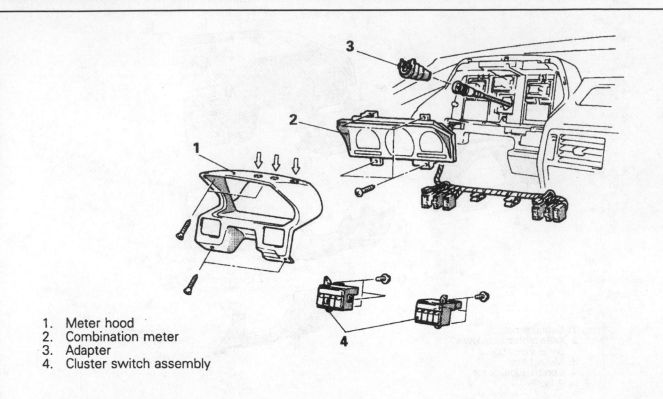

1. Meter hood
2. Combination meter
3. Adapter
4. Cluster switch assembly

Fig. 52 Instrument cluster removal/installation — 1992-93 Vista

LIGHTING

Headlights

BULB REPLACEMENT

1990-93 Colt Hatchback and Sedan

▶ **See Figures 53, 54 and 55**

1. Lift the hood.
2. For the right side bulb, remove the windshield washer reservoir and radiator overflow bottle.

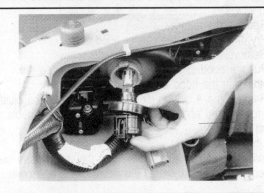

Fig. 54 Bulb holder and bulb remove from the housing

3. Twist the bulb holder to the left and remove it from the headlight housing.
4. Unplug the harness connector from the socket holder.
5. Pull out the headlight bulb.

※※CAUTION

Never touch the headlight bulb with your bare hands! The natural oils from your skin will cause a hot spot on the bulb, resulting in early bulb failure. Never allow the bulb to become dirty! If you are at doubt as to the cleanliness of the bulb, clean the glass thoroughly with rubbing alcohol.

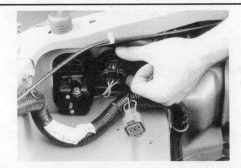

Fig. 53 Twist and remove the bulb holder from the housing

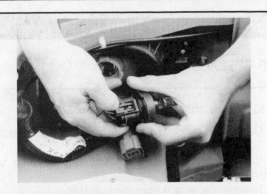

Fig. 55 Separating the bulb holder from the bulb.

6. Installation is the reverse of removal.

1990 Colt Wagon 1990-91 Vista

1. Reach behind the lamp assembly and disconnect the wiring harness.
2. Turn the bulb holder to the left and remove it from the housing.
3. Pull the bulb from the holder.

✳✳CAUTION

Never touch the headlight bulb with your bare hands! The natural oils from your skin will cause a hot spot on the bulb, resulting in early bulb failure. Never allow the bulb to become dirty! If you are at doubt as to the cleanliness of the bulb, clean the glass thoroughly with rubbing alcohol.

4. Installation is the reverse of removal.

1992-93 Vista

1. Reach behind the lamp assembly and disconnect the wiring harness.
2. Remove the bulb cover.
3. Remove the bulb retaining spring.
4. Remove the bulb.

✳✳CAUTION

Never touch the headlight bulb with your bare hands! The natural oils from your skin will cause a hot spot on the bulb, resulting in early bulb failure. Never allow the bulb to become dirty! If you are at doubt as to the cleanliness of the bulb, clean the glass thoroughly with rubbing alcohol.

5. Installation is the reverse of removal.

High Mounted Stop Light

BULB REPLACEMENT

1. Remove the cover screws and lift off the cover.
2. Remove the bulb from the housing.
3. Installation is the reverse of removal.

Front Combination Light

HOUSING REMOVAL & INSTALLATION BULB REPLACEMENT

Colt

▶ **See Figures 56, 57, 58 and 59**

1. Open the hood.
2. Reach behind the light and disconnect the retaining spring.
3. Slowly pull the housing assembly from the front of the car and twist and remove the bulb carrier.

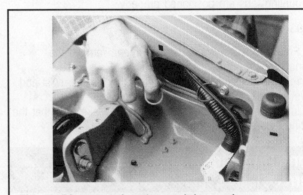

Fig. 56 Disconnecting the retaining spring

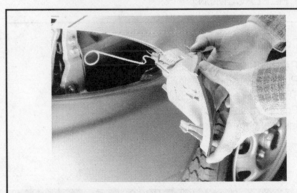

Fig. 57 Pulling the housing from the car

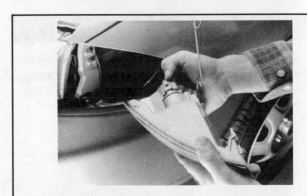

Fig. 58 Twisting the bulb holder from the housing

Fig. 59 Pull the bulb from the bulb holder

4. Remove the bulb from the carrier.
5. Installation is the reverse of removal. Make sure that all the mounting tabs are positioned properly.

1992-93 Vista

1. From inside the engine compartment, remove the combination light housing screws.
2. Pull the housing from the front of the vehicle, twist and remove the bulb holder, and remove the bulb.
3. Installation is the reverse of removal. Make sure that the mounting tabs are positioned properly.

Front Turn Signal and Side Marker Lights

BULB REPLACEMENT

1990 Colt Wagon 1990-91 Vista

1. Remove the light housing screws.
2. Pull the housing out slowly.
3. Twist and remove the bulb holder.
4. Pull the bulb from the holder.
5. Installation is the reverse of removal.

REAR WINDOW DEFOGGER

General Description

The rear window defogger system consists of a rear window with 2 vertical bus bars and a series of electrically connected grid lines baked on the inside surface. A control switch and a timer relay combined into a single assembly is used on all models.

Rear Combination Light

BULB REPLACEMENT

1990-93 Colt Hatchback and Sedan 1992-93 Vista

1. On the hatchback and Vista, pry off the light housing cover from inside the car.
2. Remove the socket assembly screws and pull the socket from the housing.
3. Remove the bulb(s) from the bulb holder.
4. Installation is the reverse of removal.

Rear Turn Signal and Side Marker Lights

BULB REPLACEMENT

1990 Colt Wagon 1990-91 Vista

1. Remove the light housing screws.
2. Pull the housing out slowly.
3. Twist and remove the bulb holder.
4. Pull the bulb from the holder.
5. Installation is the reverse of removal.

Turn Signal and Hazard Flashers

The flashers are located under the left side of the instrument panel. If the turn signals operate in only one direction, a bulb is probably burned out. If they operate in neither direction, a bulb on each side may be burned out, or the flasher may be defective.

REMOVAL & INSTALLATION

1. Pull the flasher from its spring clip mounting.
2. Unplug and discard the flasher. Plug in the new flasher.
3. Replace the flasher in the spring clip and check operation.

All circuit protection is provided by a fusible link, located in the charging circuit, for the heater grid circuit and by a fuse for the relay control circuit.

➡ **NOTE:Since the grid lines can be damaged or scraped off with sharp instruments, caution should be used when cleaning the glass or removing foreign materials, decals or stickers. Normal glass cleaning solvents or hot water used with rags or toweling is recommended.**

DIAGNOSIS & TESTING

Defogger System

The rear window defogger system operation can be checked in the vehicle using the following test procedure:

1. Turn the ignition switch to the **ON** position, also turn the rear window defogger control switch to the **ON** position.

2. Monitor the vehicle ammeter. With the control switch in the **ON** position, a distinct needle deflection should be noted.

➡ **NOTE:If the vehicle is not equipped with a voltmeter or a ammeter, the rear window defogger operation can be checked by feeling the glass in the rear windshield. A distinct difference in temperature between the grid lines and adjacent clear glass can be detected in 3-4 minutes of operation.**

3. Using a DC voltmeter, connect the vertical bus bar on the passenger side of the vehicle with the positive lead and the driver side of the vehicle with the negative lead. The voltmeter should read between 10-14 volts.

4. Only Steps 1, 2 and 3 will confirm the system is operational. The indicator or pilot light illumination means that there is power available at the output of the relay only and does not necessarily prove the system is operational.

5. If the rear window defogger system does not operate properly, the problem should be isolated as outlined in the following procedure:

a. Check to be sure the ignition switch is in the **ON** position. Be sure that the rear defogger feed (HOT) wire is connected to the terminal or pigtail and that the ground wire has a good ground.

b. Be sure the fusible link and control circuit fuse is operational and all electrical connections are secure. If all of these things have been completely checked out, then the following may be defective: the control switch/timer relay module or the rear window defogger grid lines.

c. If the grid lines were to blame, either all the grid lines would have to be broken, or the feed (HOT) wires are not connected for the system to be inoperative.

6. If turning the control switch procedures give severe voltmeter (ammeter) deflections, check the system for a shorting condition. If the systems check out but the indicator bulb does not light, check and or replace the bulb.

Defogger Grid

TESTING

When a grid is inoperable due to an open circuit, the area of glass normally cleared by that grid will remained fogged or iced until cleared by the adjacent grids. Use the following procedure to located a broken grid.

➡**The ground wire is connected to the driver's side of the window and the feed wire connection is located on the passenger side of the window.**

1. With the engine running at idle, place the rear defogger switch in the **ON** position. The pilot lamp is the switch lever should light up indicating the defogger is operating.

2. Using a 12 volt voltmeter, connect the positive lead of the voltmeter to the hot side of the vertical bus element on the inside surface of the glass.

3. Connect the negative lead of the voltmeter to the ground side of the bus element. The voltage drop indicated on the meter should be 11-13 volts. Connect the negative lead of the voltmeter to a good ground, the meter reading should stay constant.

4. Keep the negative lead connected to the ground and carefully use the positive lead to contact each grid at the approximate centerline of the window. A voltage drop of approximately 6 volts. indicates a good grid or a closed circuit.

5. No voltage indicated a broken grid wire. To located the exact location of the break, move the voltmeter lead along the grid wire. The voltage should decrease gradually. If the voltage drops suddenly, there is a break at that location.

➡**A grid repair kit 4106356, or equivalent is available from the manufacturer and the enclosed manufactures instruction should be followed for a proper grid repair.**

TESTING GRID RESISTANCE

1. Turn the defogger switch **OFF**. Use a ohmmeter (with a scale ranging from 0-100 ohms) to measure the resistance at each grid line between the center and the end, left and right separately.

2. The section involving a broken grid line indicates resistance twice that in other sections.

3. Once in the affected area, move the tester bar for a position where the resistance sharply changes. Mark the broken grid line and repair as necessary.

Defogger Timer

TESTING

Vista

▶ **See Figure 60**

1. Disconnect the the electrical connector from the defogger timer.

2. Use a suitable voltmeter and check for 12 volts at the middle terminal on the top row of terminals in the connector when the ignition and defogger switch is turned **ON**.

3. The timer should operate for approximately 11 minutes and then stop. If the defogger switch is pressed once again or the ignition switch is turned **OFF** while the timer is operating, the voltage at the same terminal should be 0 volts.

4. If the timer does not show the correct voltage during this test, replace the timer.

Colt

▶ **See Figure 61**

1. Disconnect the defogger timer.

2. Connect battery ground to terminal 4.

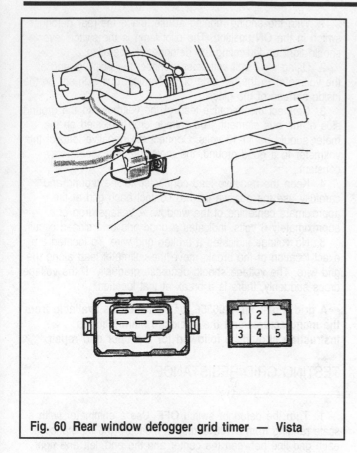

Fig. 60 Rear window defogger grid timer — Vista

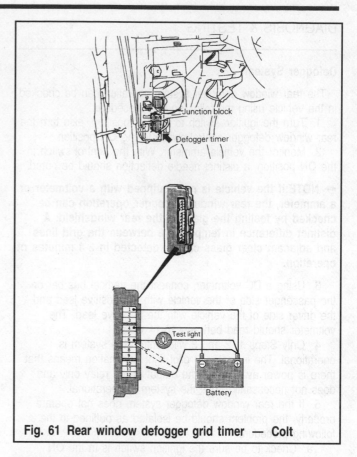

Fig. 61 Rear window defogger grid timer — Colt

3. Connect battery positive to terminal 1.

4. Connect a test light between battery positive and terminal 6.

5. The test light should light for 10 seconds when battery voltage is applied to terminal 7 for a few seconds.

6. Check that the test light goes off, when battery voltage is again applied to the terminal 7.

Defogger Switch

TESTING

Colt

1. Remove the switch.

2. Using an ohmmeter, turn the switch **ON** and check for continuity. Continuity should exist between terminals 1 & 5 and 2 & 4. With the switch **OFF**, there should be continuity between terminals **3** & **6** only.

Vista

1. Remove the switch.

2. Using an ohmmeter, turn the switch **ON** and check for continuity. Continuity should exist between terminals 2 & 5 and 1 & 4. With the switch **OFF**, there should be continuity between terminals 1 & 4 only.

REMOVAL & INSTALLATION

Colt and Vista

▶ **See Figure 62**

1. Disconnect the negative battery cable. Using a suitable tool, slip the tool behind the liftgate switch far enough to depress the locking tab. Repeat this procedure for the opposite side of the switch. Be careful not to damage the instrument panel.

2. Disconnect the electrical connector and remove the switch from the dash panel.

3. Installation is the reverse order of the removal procedure.

Relay

TESTING

1. Remove the relay.

2. Connect a 12v source to terminals 2. There should be continuity between terminals 1 & 2 only. Without power, there should be continuity between 3 & 4 only

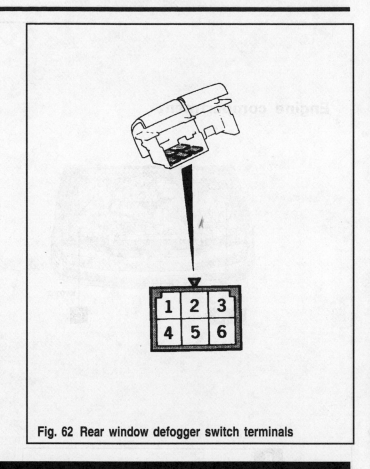

Fig. 62 Rear window defogger switch terminals

CIRCUIT PROTECTION

Fuses and Fusible Links

▶ **See Figures 63, 64, 65 and 66**

To locate the fuses or fusible links for your vehicle, refer to figures.

REPLACEMENT

Fuses

To replace a fuse, simply unplug it and plug in a new one.

Fusible Link

1. Disconnect the battery ground cable.

2. Disconnect the fusible link from the junction block or starter solenoid.

3. Cut the harness directly behind the connector to remove the damaged fusible link.

4. Strip the harness wire approximately 12mm.

5. Connect the new fusible link to the harness wire using a crimp on connector. Solder the connection using rosin core solder.

6. Tape all exposed wires with plastic electrical tape.

7. Connect the fusible link to the junction block or starter solenoid and reconnect the battery ground cable.

Engine compartment

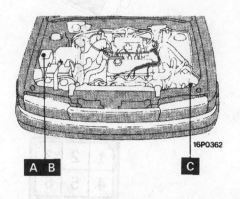

16P0362

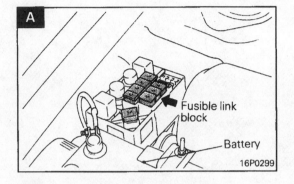

A

Fusible link block

Battery

16P0299

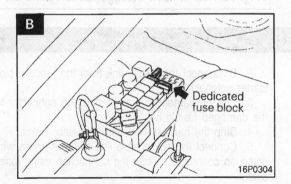

B

Dedicated fuse block

16P0304

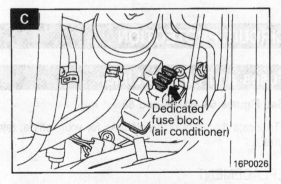

C

Dedicated fuse block (air conditioner)

16P0026

Interior

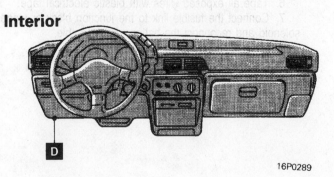

D

16P0289

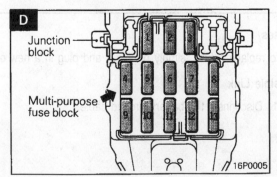

D

Junction block

Multi-purpose fuse block

16P0005

Fig. 63 Fuses and fusible links — 1990-93 Colt hatchback and sedan

ENGINE COMPARTMENT

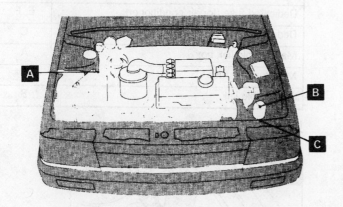

INSTRUMENT PANEL

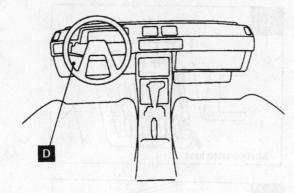

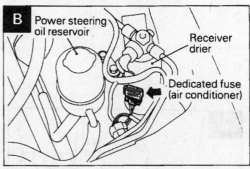

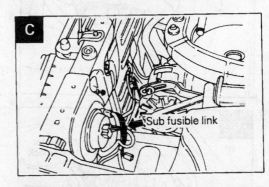

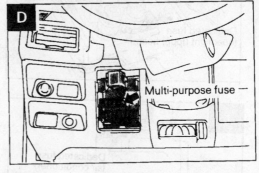

Fig. 64 Fuses and fusible links — 1990 Colt Wagon

<Engine Compartment>

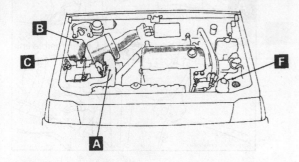

<Interior>

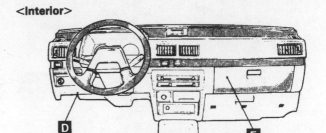

Name	Symbol
Dedicated fuse (for air conditioner)	E, F
Dedicated fuse (for headlight upper beam)	C
Main fusible link box	A
Multipurpose fuse	D
Sub fusible link	B

NOTE
The "Name" column is arranged in alphabetical order.

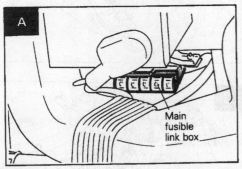

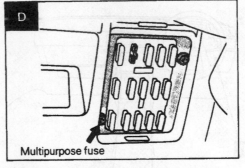

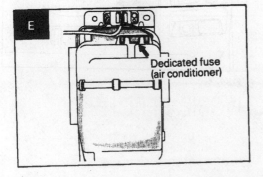

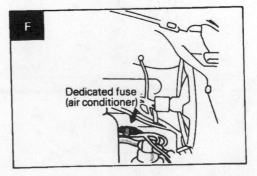

Fig. 65 Fuses and fusible links — 1990-91 Vista

\<Engine compartment\>

1.8L Engine

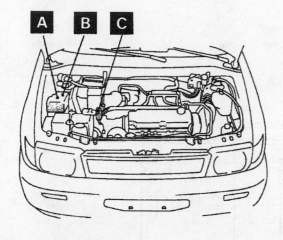

2.4L Engine

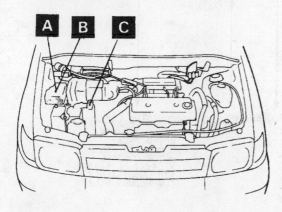

\<Interior\>

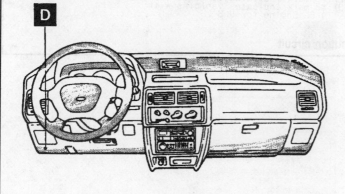

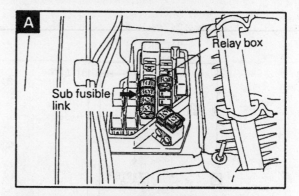

A — Sub fusible link, Relay box

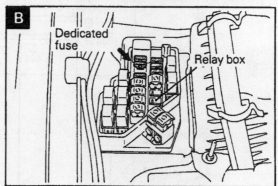

B — Dedicated fuse, Relay box

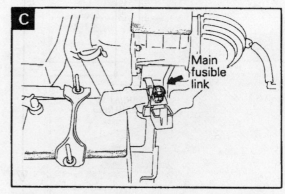

C — Main fusible link

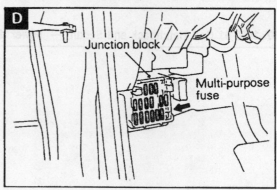

D — Junction block, Multi-purpose fuse

Fig. 66 Fuses and fusible links — 1992-93 Vista

WIRING DIAGRAMS

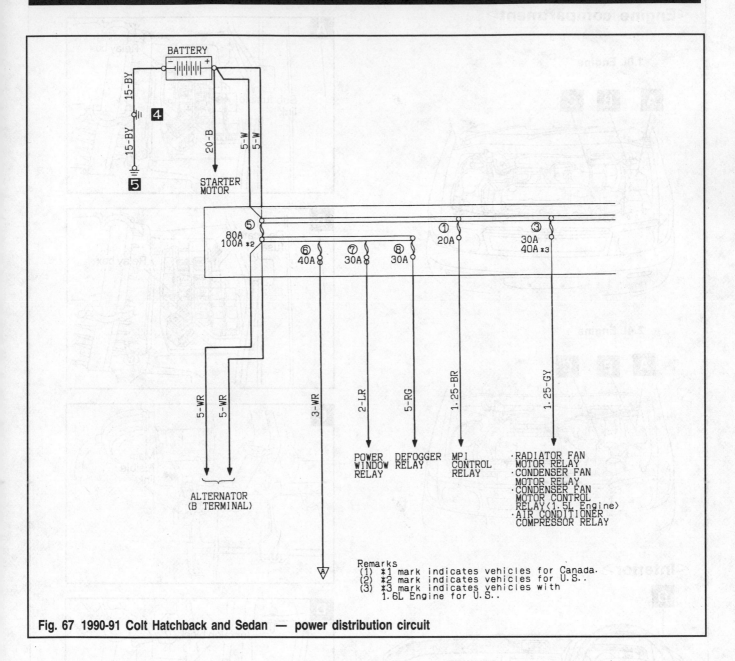

Fig. 67 1990-91 Colt Hatchback and Sedan — power distribution circuit

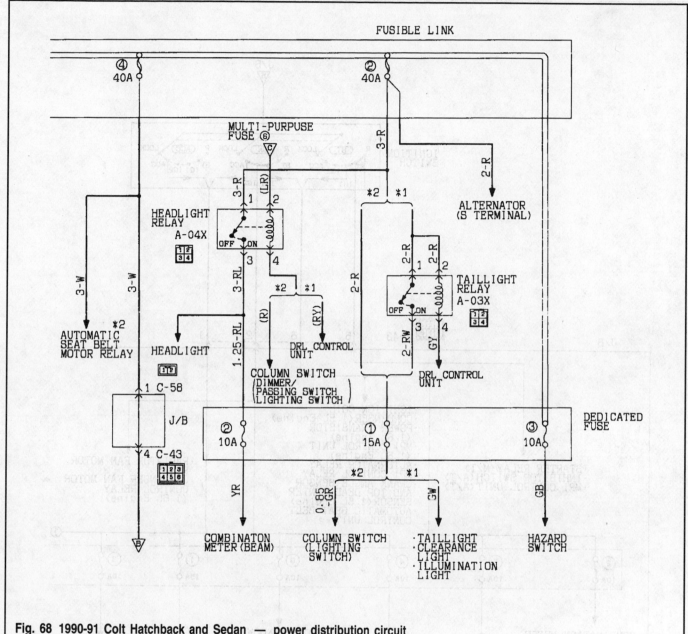

Fig. 68 1990-91 Colt Hatchback and Sedan — power distribution circuit

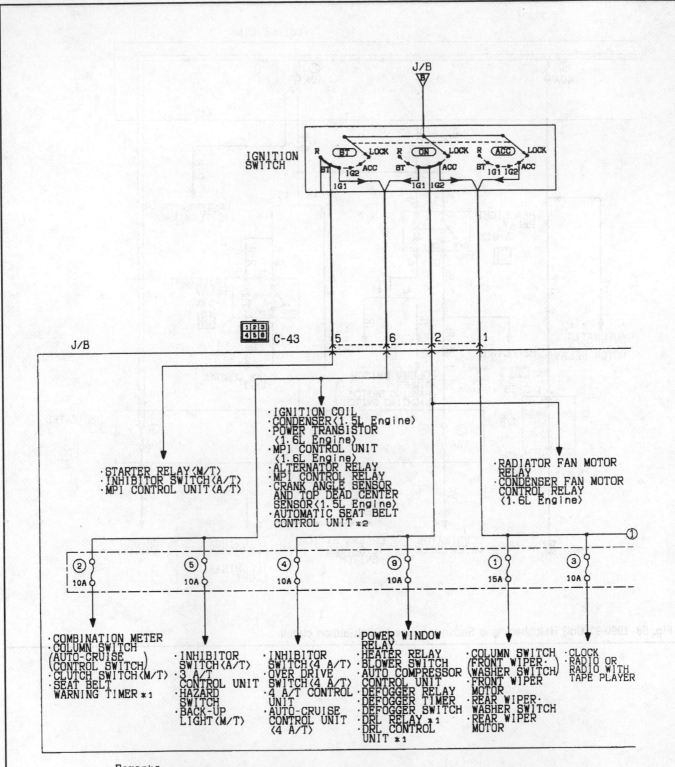

Fig. 69 1990-91 Colt Hatchback and Sedan — power distribution circuit

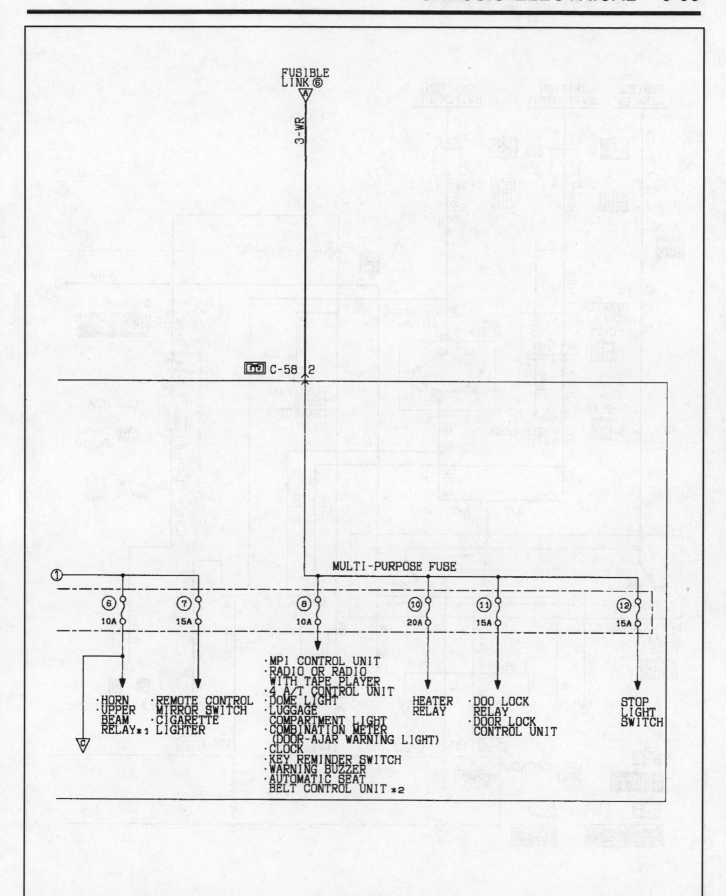

Fig. 70 1990-91 Colt Hatchback and Sedan — power distribution circuit

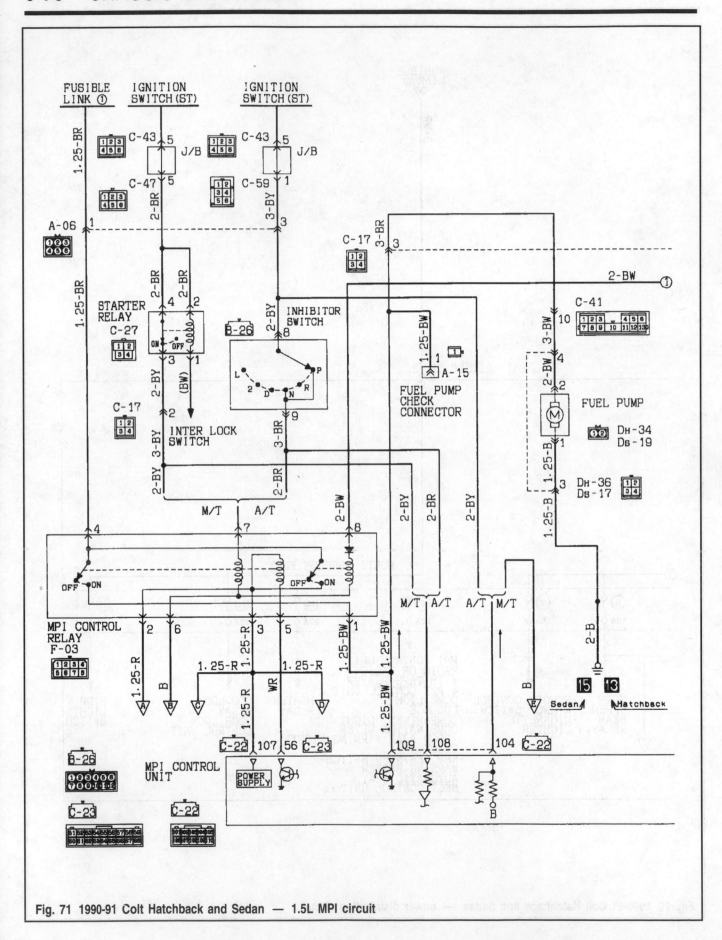

Fig. 71 1990-91 Colt Hatchback and Sedan — 1.5L MPI circuit

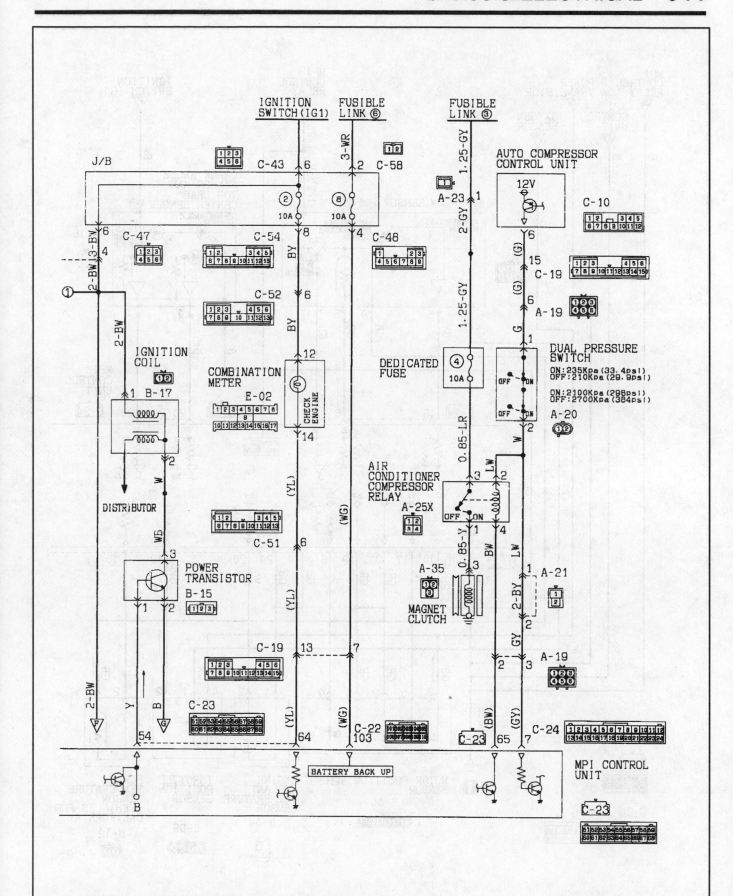

Fig. 72 1990-91 Colt Hatchback and Sedan — 1.5L MPI circuit

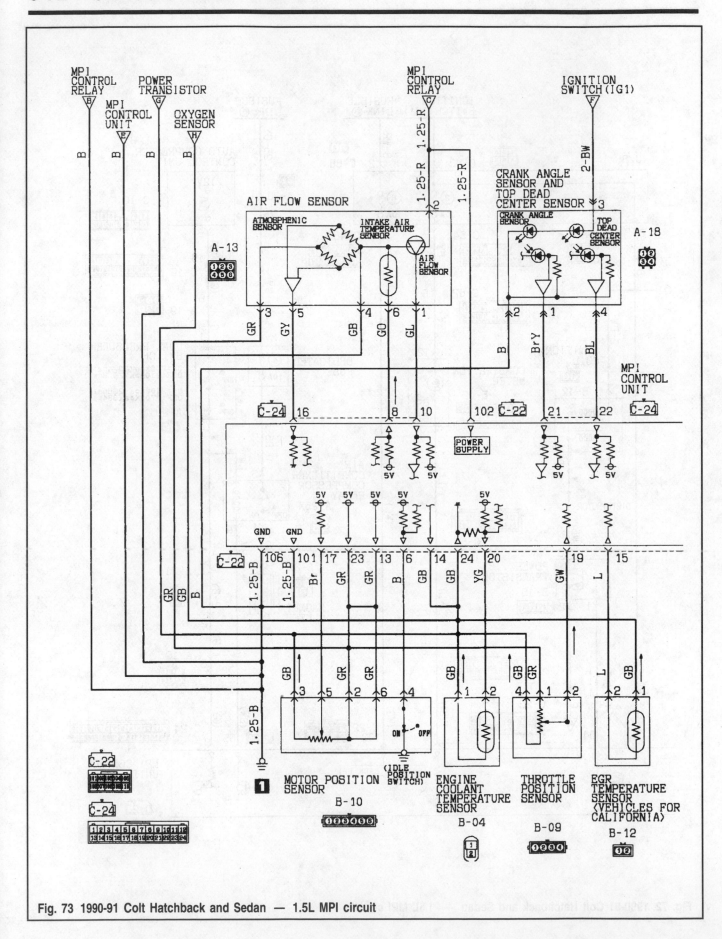

Fig. 73 1990-91 Colt Hatchback and Sedan — 1.5L MPI circuit

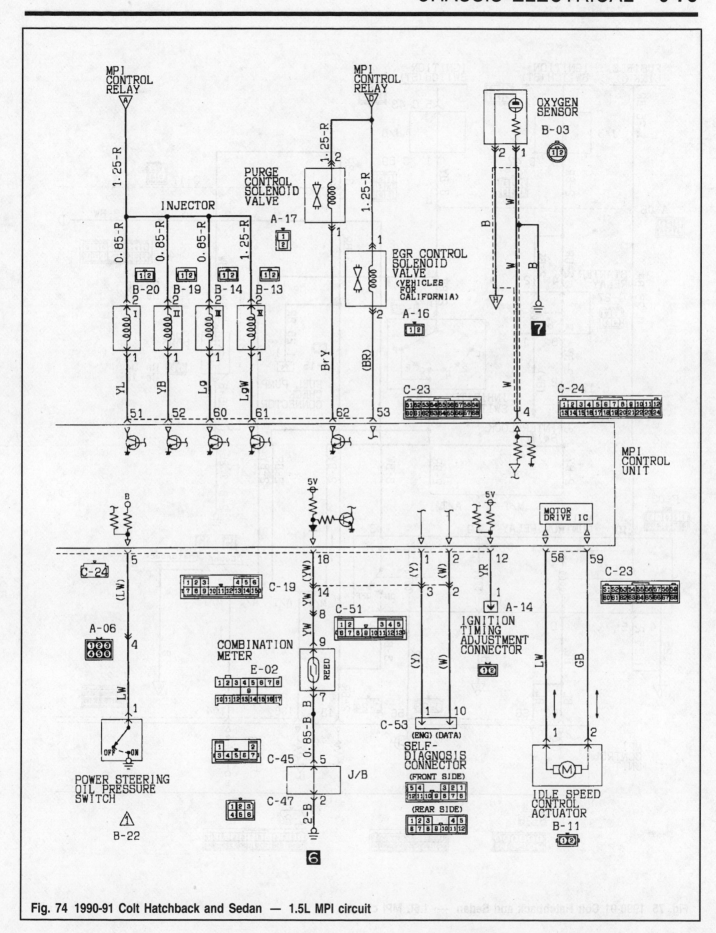

Fig. 74 1990-91 Colt Hatchback and Sedan — 1.5L MPI circuit

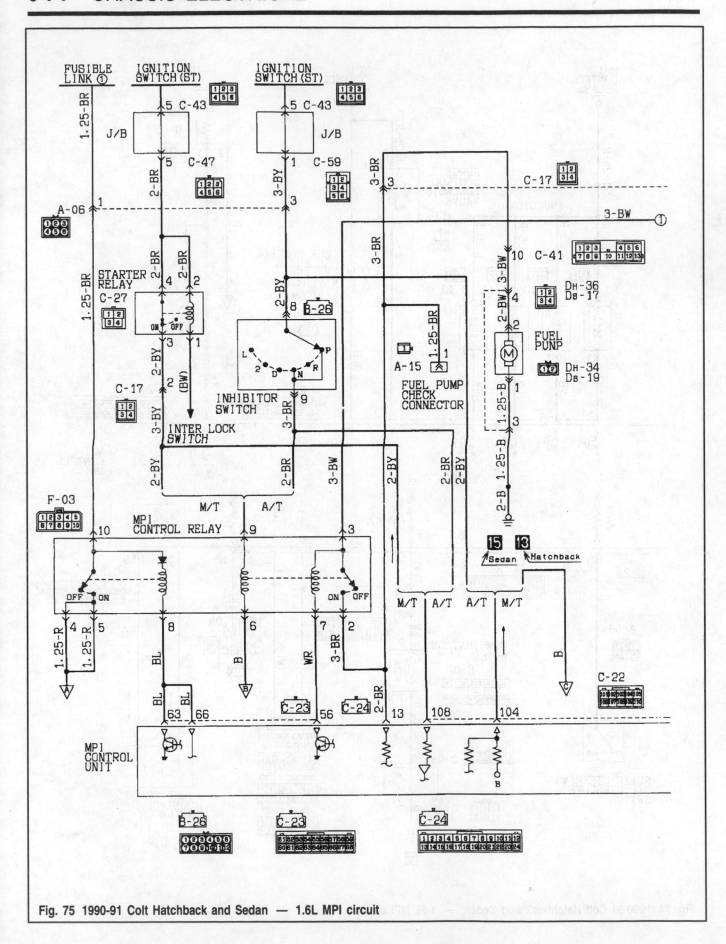

Fig. 75 1990-91 Colt Hatchback and Sedan — 1.6L MPI circuit

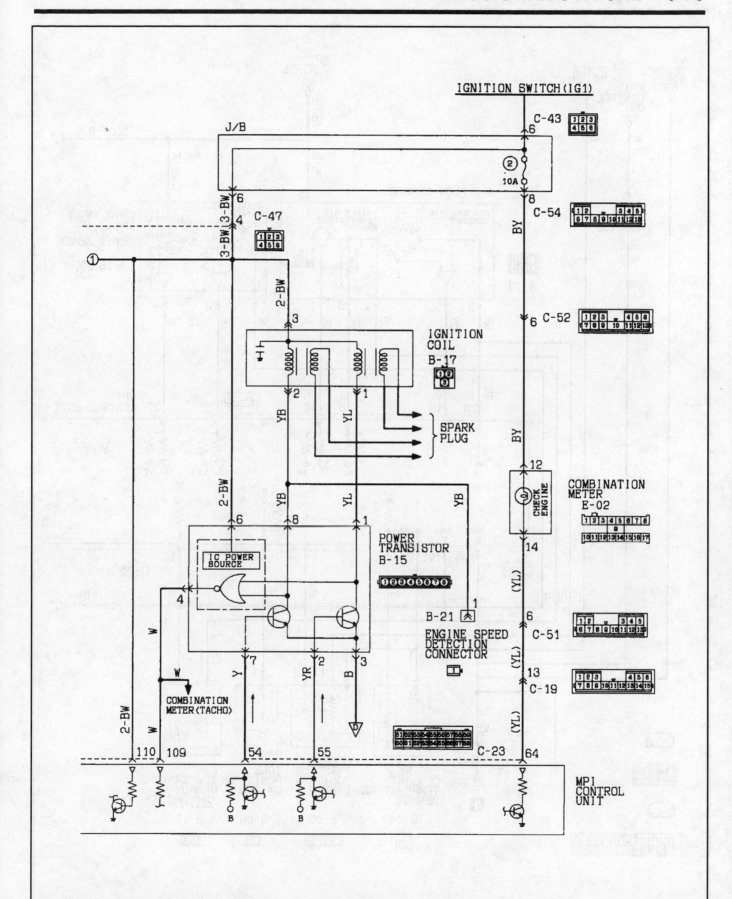

Fig. 76 1990-91 Colt Hatchback and Sedan — 1.6L MPI circuit

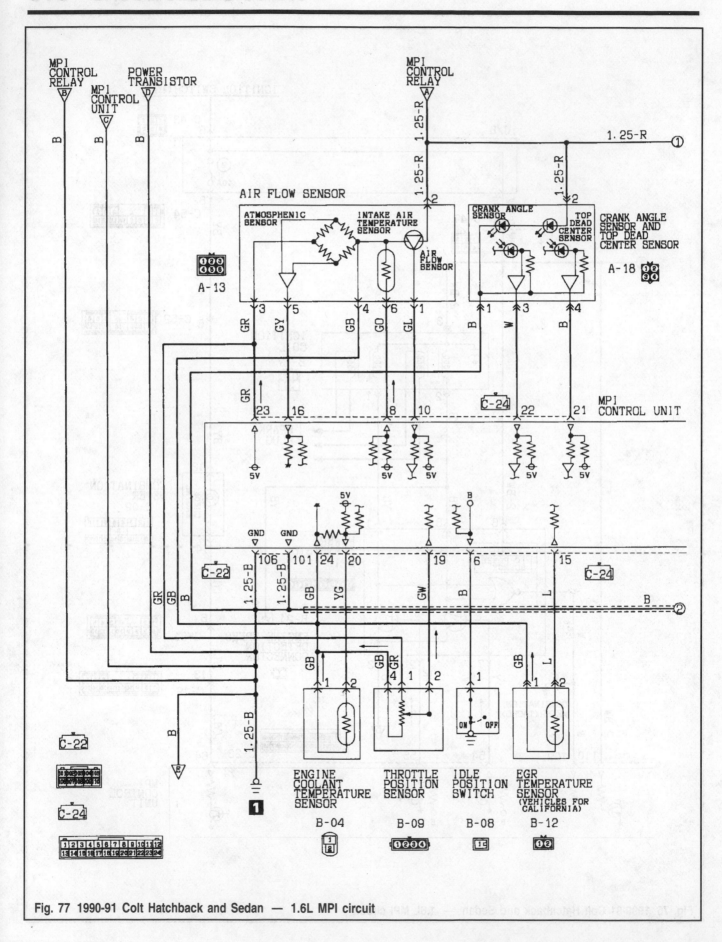

Fig. 77 1990-91 Colt Hatchback and Sedan — 1.6L MPI circuit

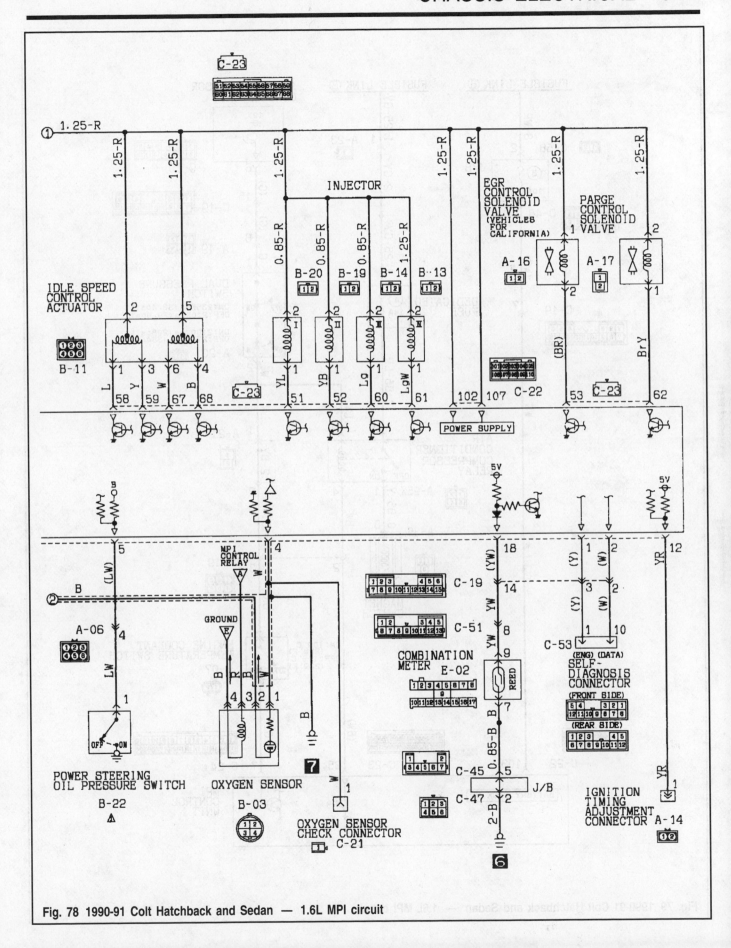

Fig. 78 1990-91 Colt Hatchback and Sedan — 1.6L MPI circuit

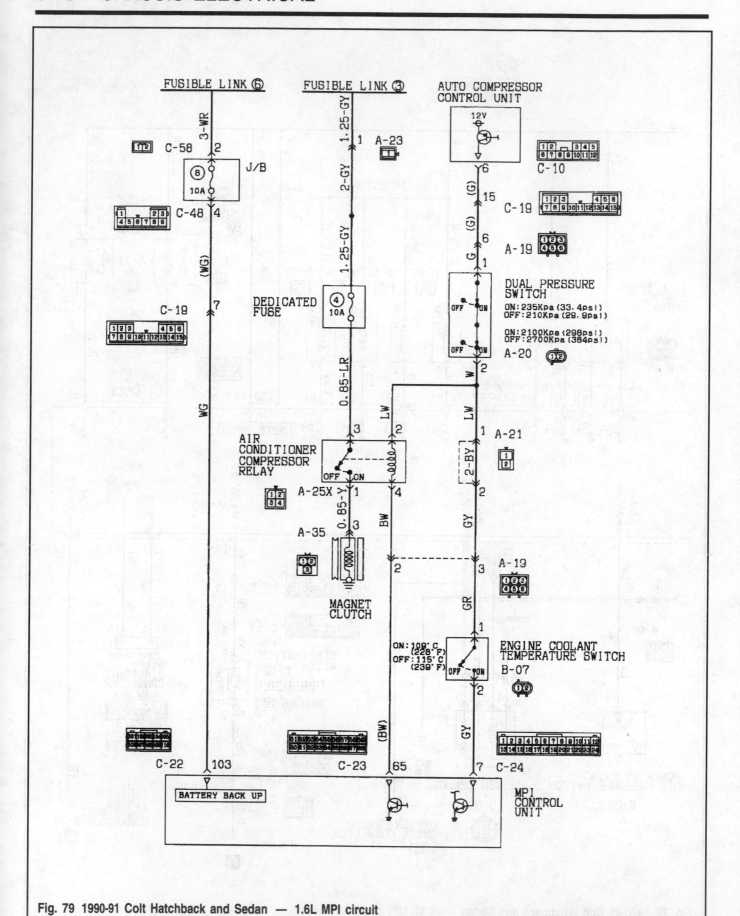

Fig. 79 1990-91 Colt Hatchback and Sedan — 1.6L MPI circuit

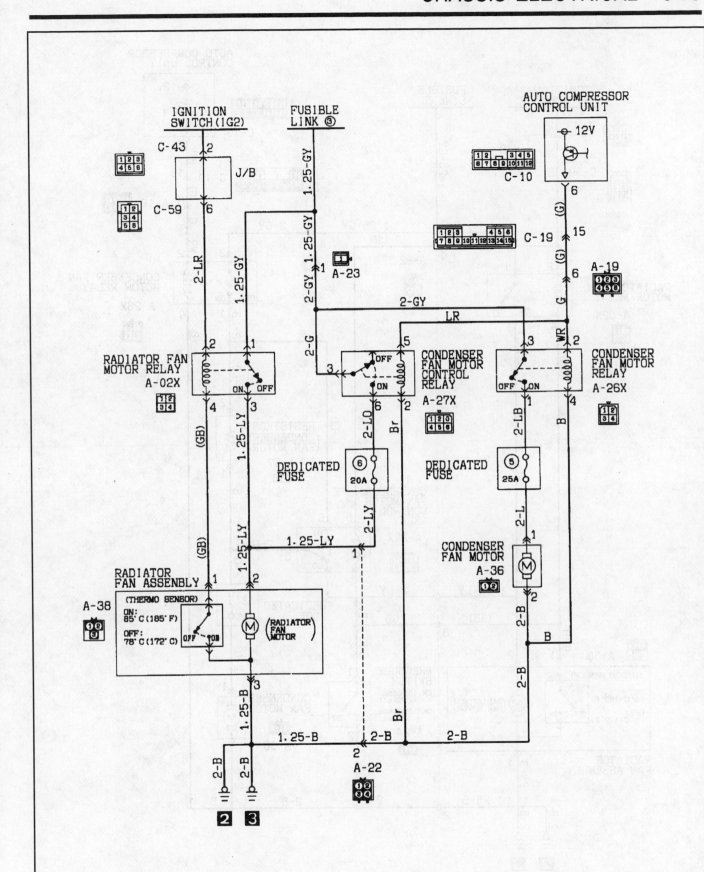

Fig. 80 1990-91 Colt Hatchback and Sedan — 1.5L cooling fan circuit

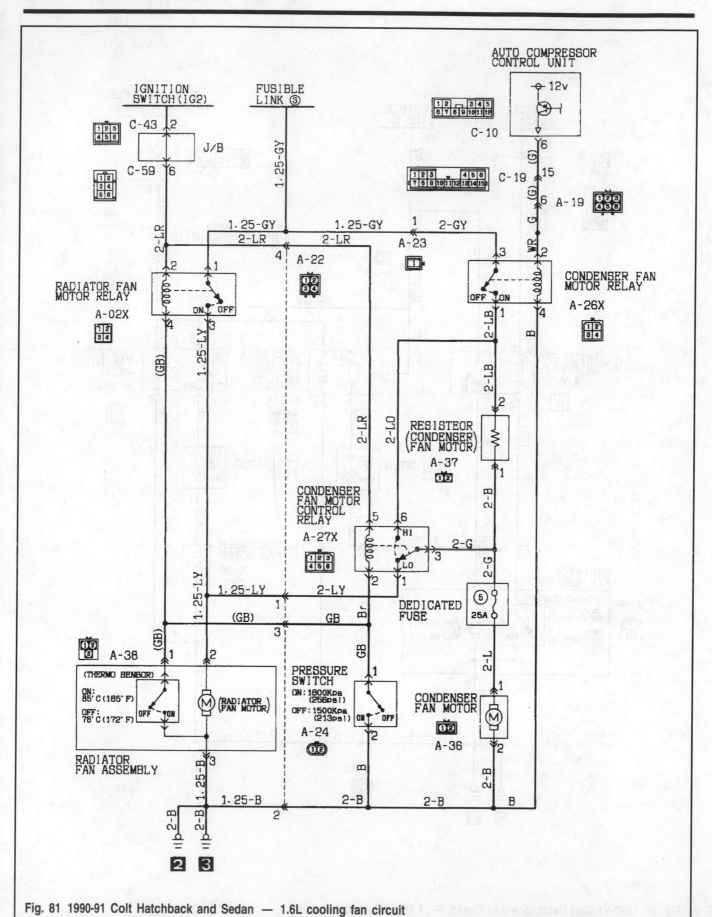

Fig. 81 1990-91 Colt Hatchback and Sedan — 1.6L cooling fan circuit

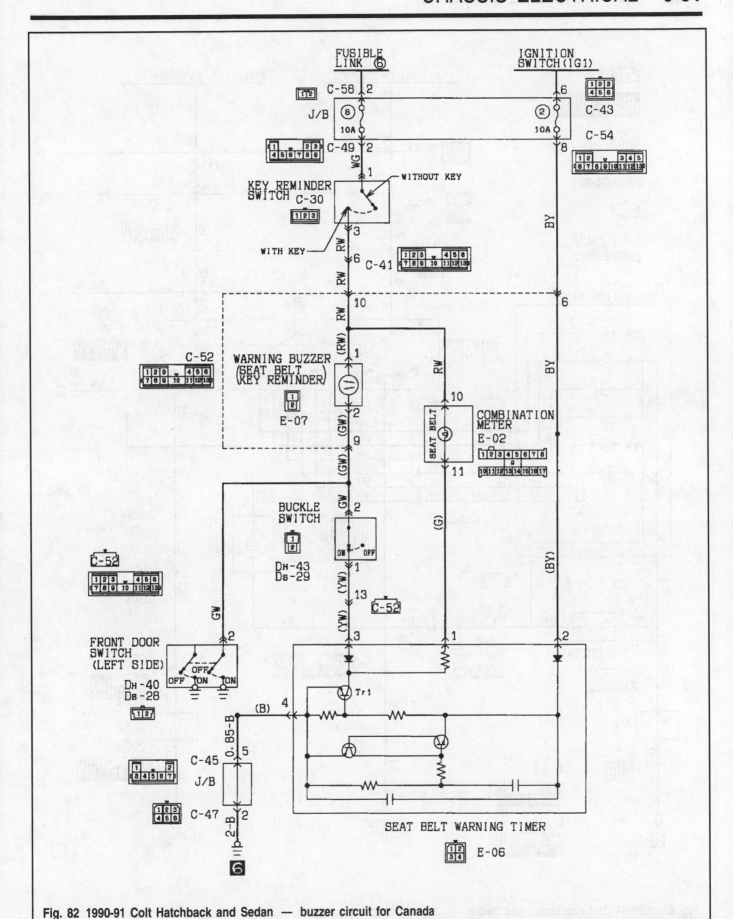

Fig. 82 1990-91 Colt Hatchback and Sedan — buzzer circuit for Canada

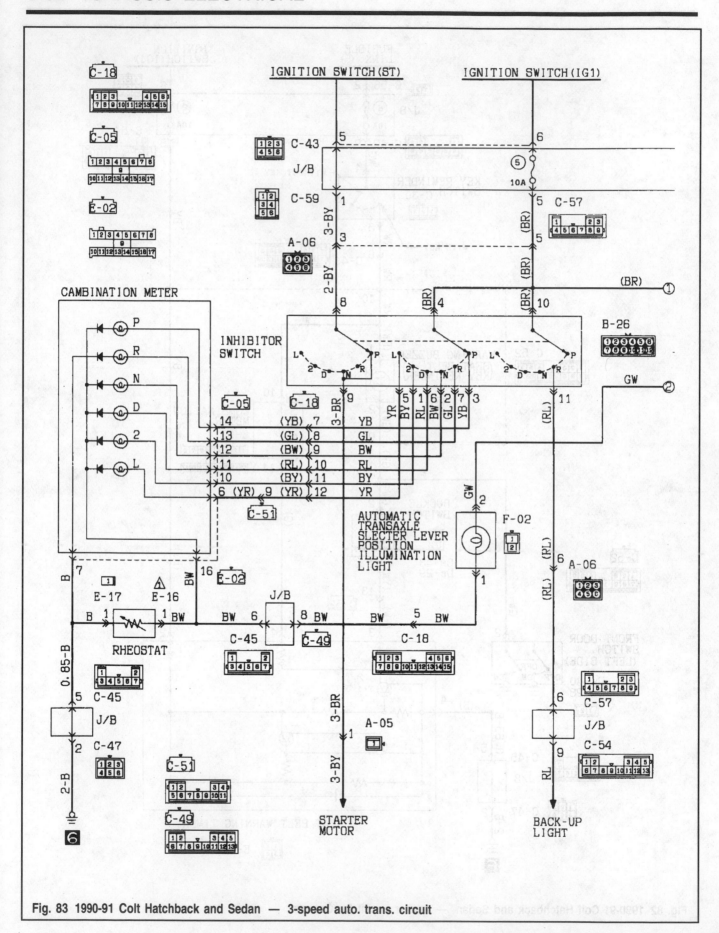

Fig. 83 1990-91 Colt Hatchback and Sedan — 3-speed auto. trans. circuit

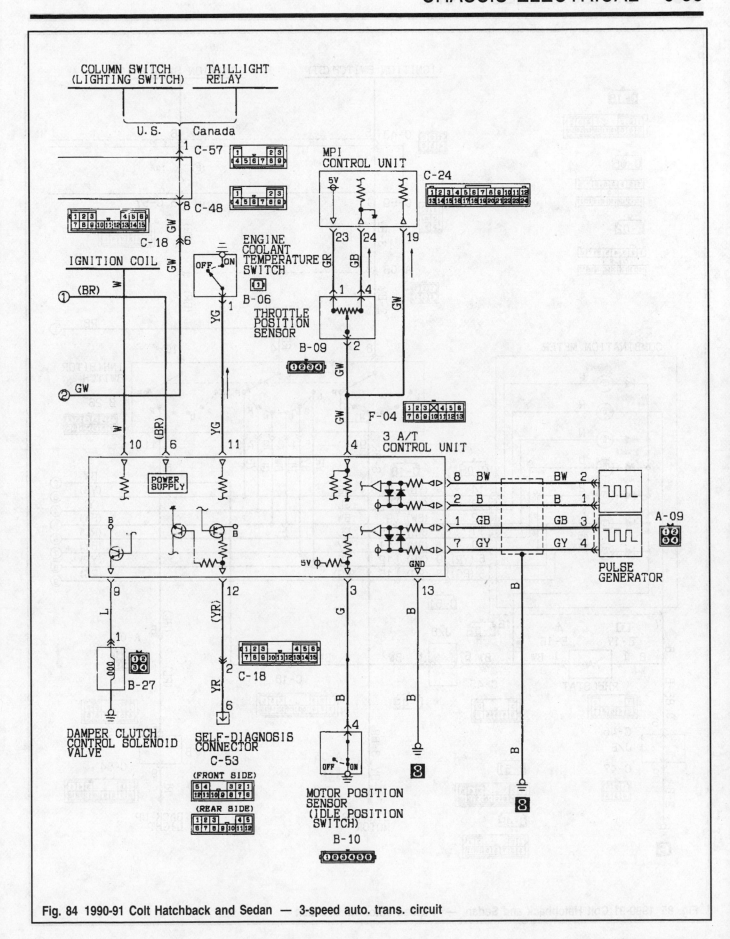

Fig. 84 1990-91 Colt Hatchback and Sedan — 3-speed auto. trans. circuit

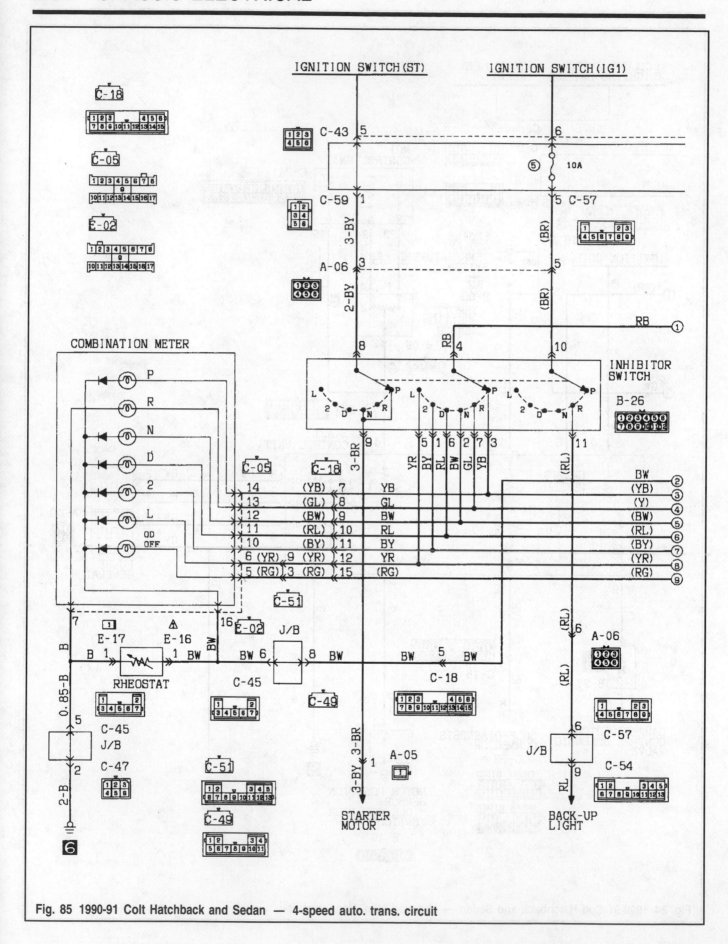

Fig. 85 1990-91 Colt Hatchback and Sedan — 4-speed auto. trans. circuit

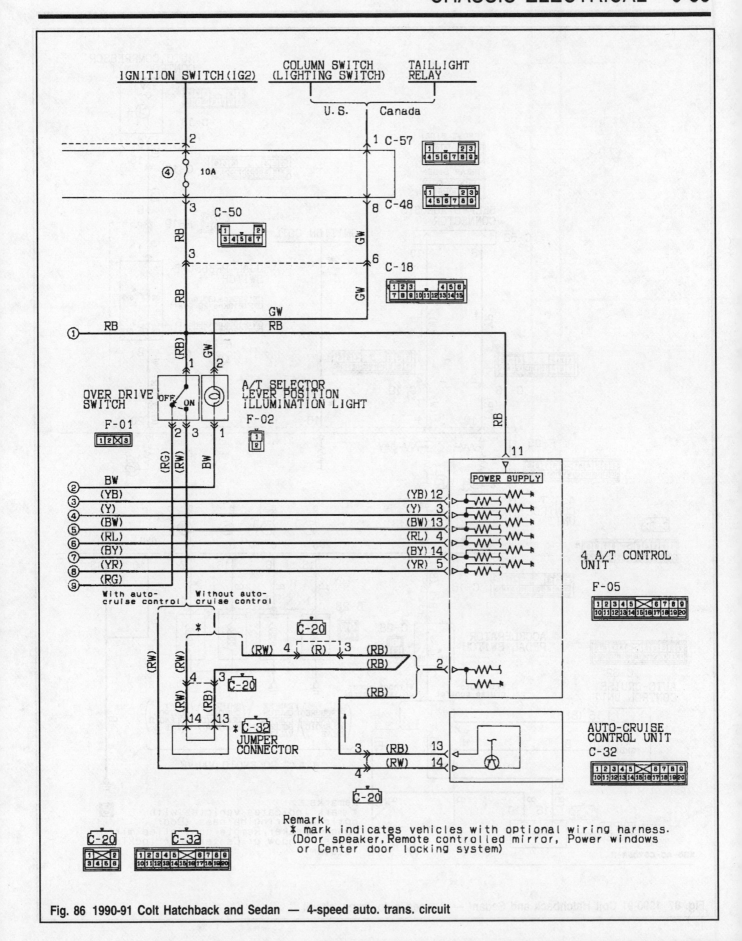

Fig. 86 1990-91 Colt Hatchback and Sedan — 4-speed auto. trans. circuit

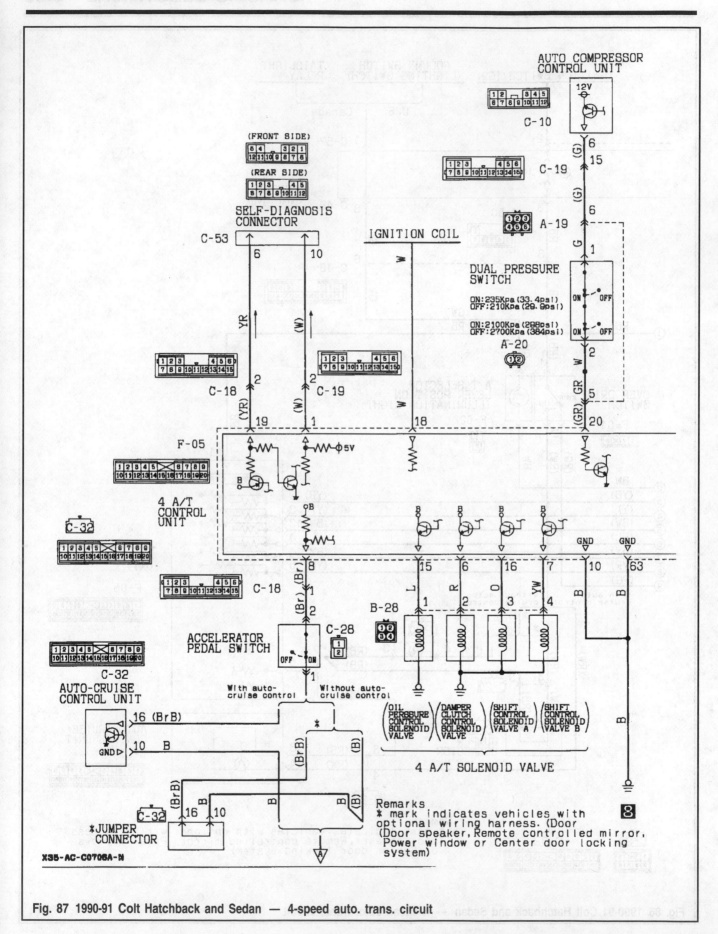

Fig. 87 1990-91 Colt Hatchback and Sedan — 4-speed auto. trans. circuit

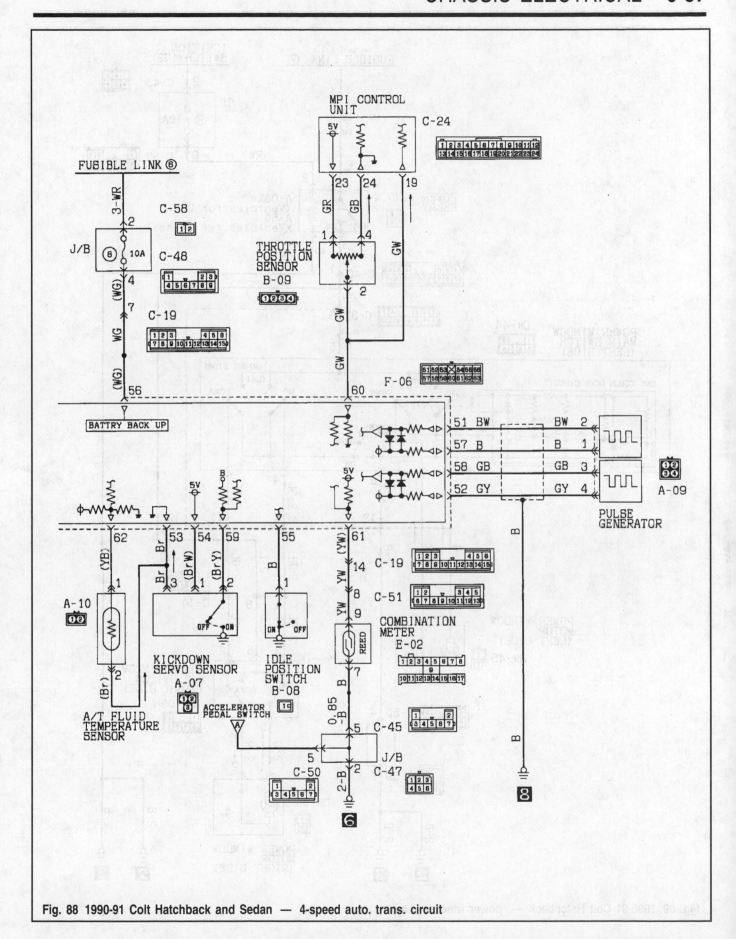

Fig. 88 1990-91 Colt Hatchback and Sedan — 4-speed auto. trans. circuit

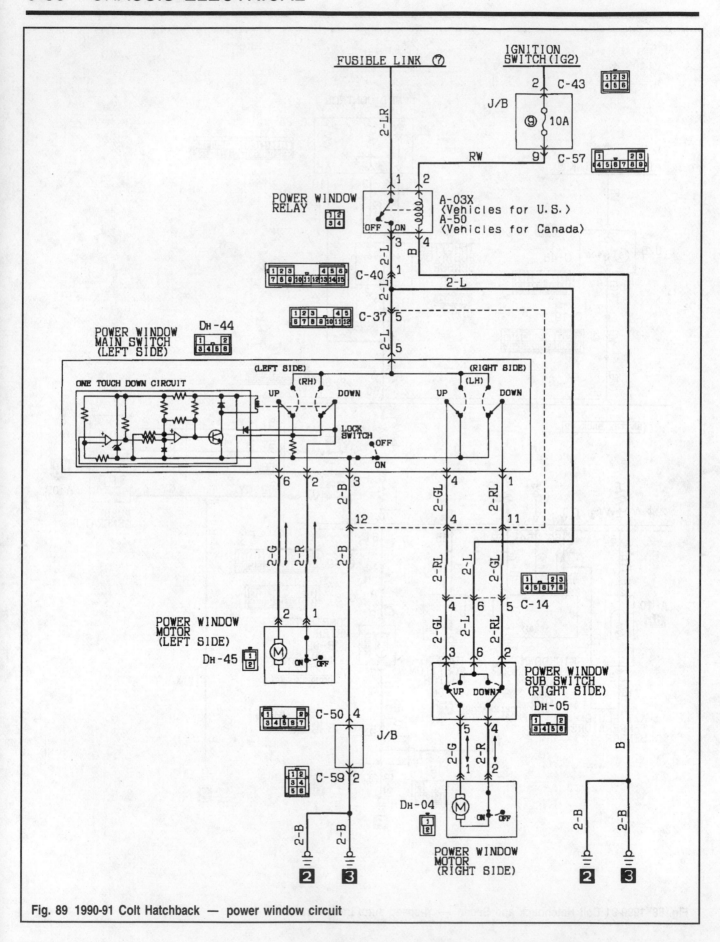

Fig. 89 1990-91 Colt Hatchback — power window circuit

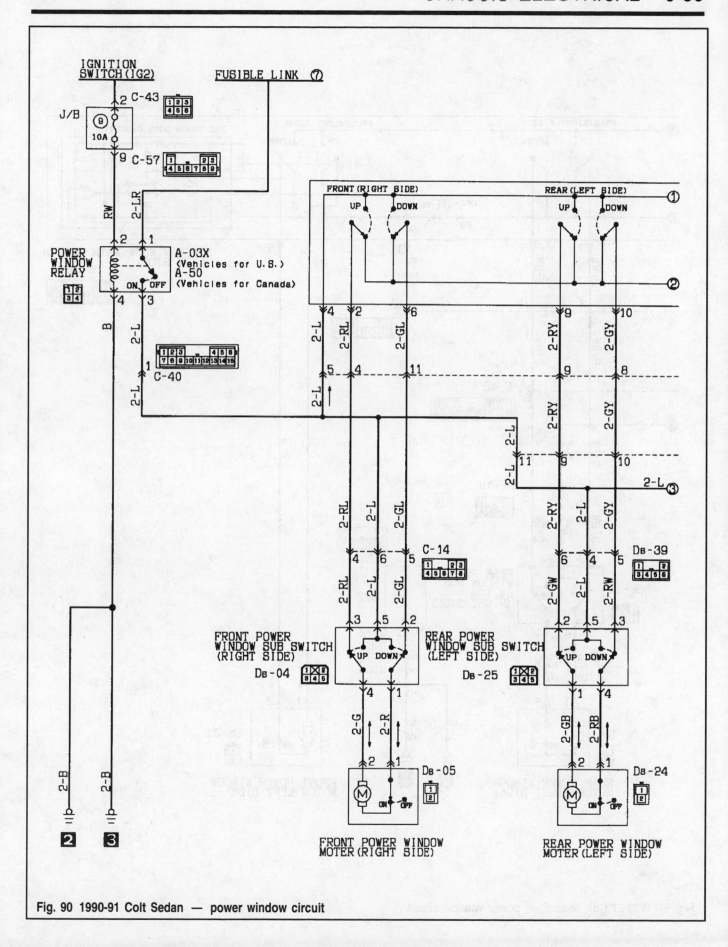

Fig. 90 1990-91 Colt Sedan — power window circuit

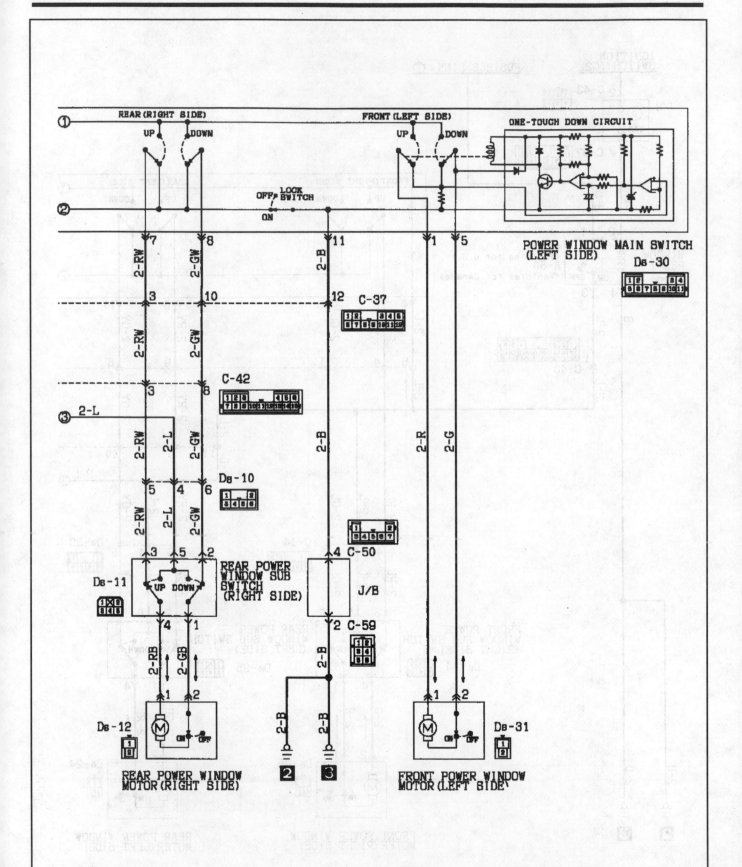

Fig. 91 1990-91 Colt Sedan — power window circuit

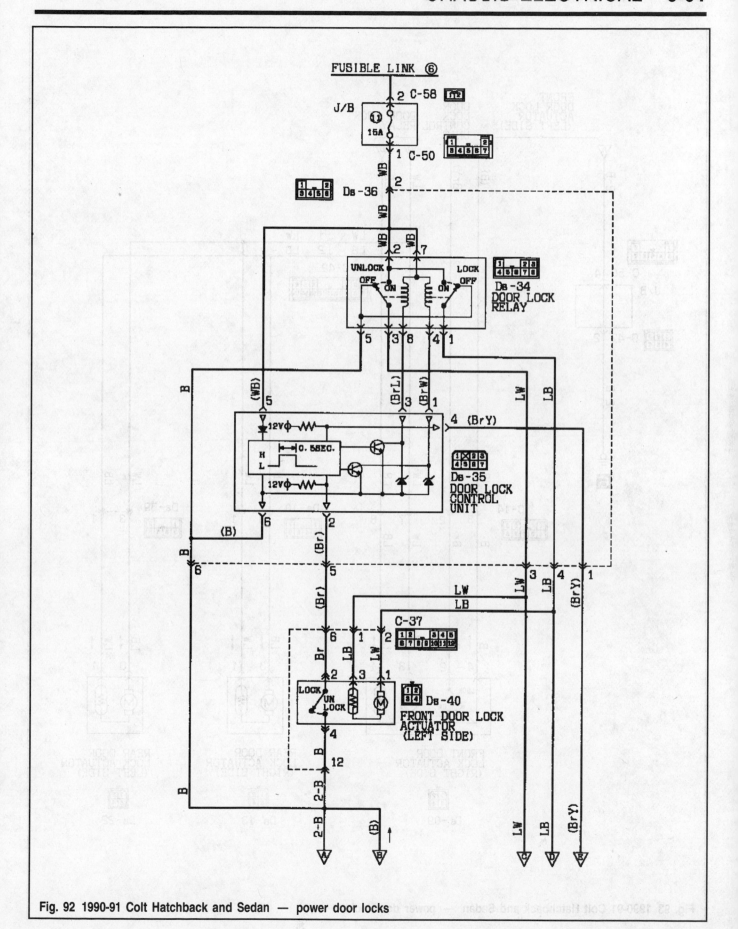

Fig. 92 1990-91 Colt Hatchback and Sedan — power door locks

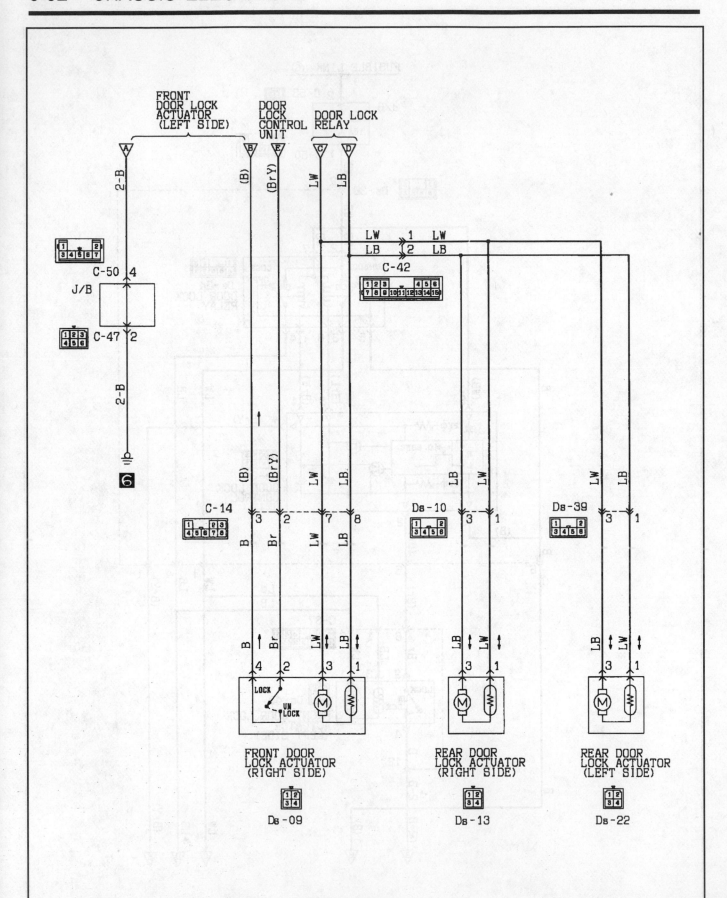

Fig. 93 1990-91 Colt Hatchback and Sedan — power door locks

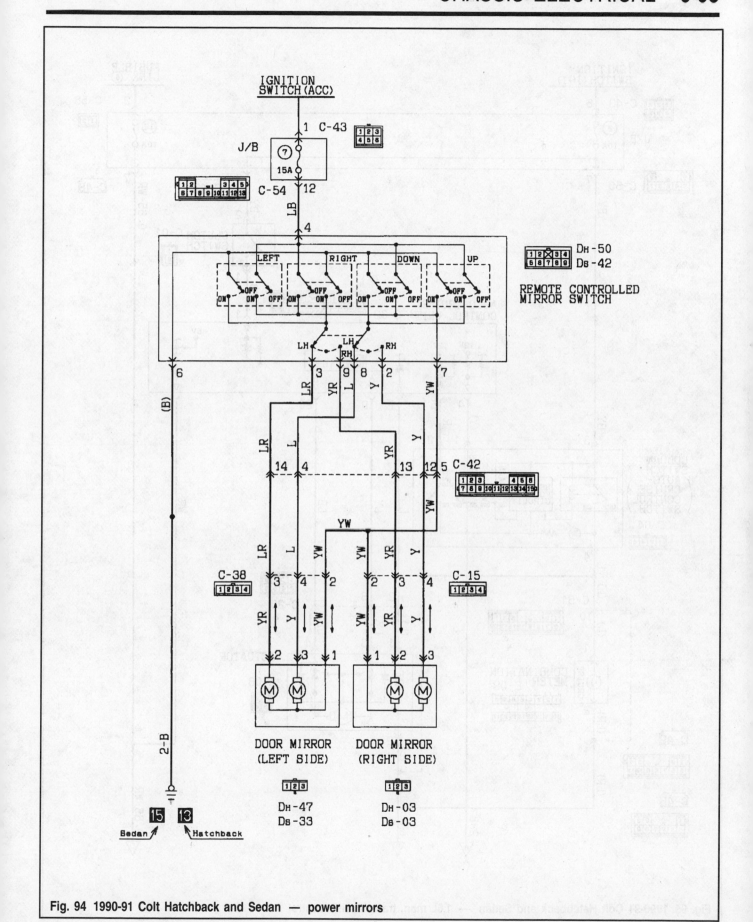

Fig. 94 1990-91 Colt Hatchback and Sedan — power mirrors

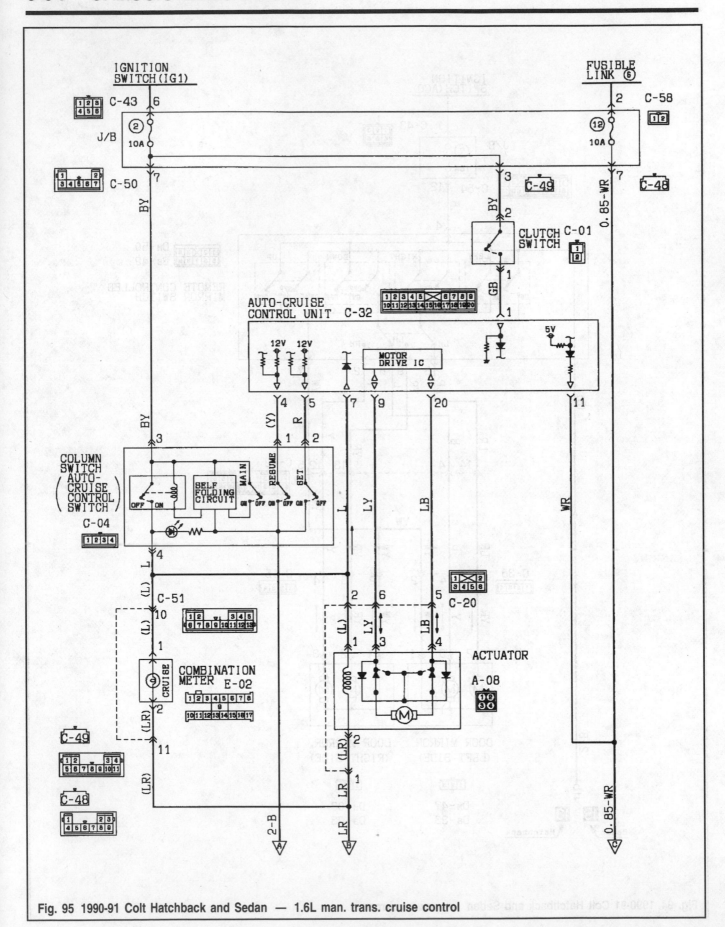

Fig. 95 1990-91 Colt Hatchback and Sedan — 1.6L man. trans. cruise control

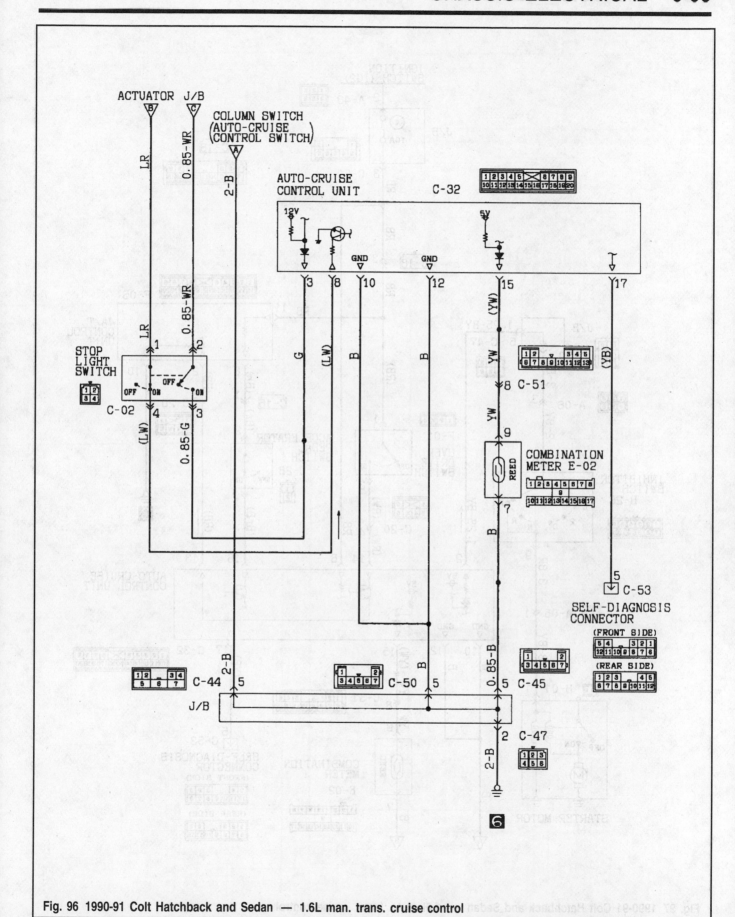

Fig. 96 1990-91 Colt Hatchback and Sedan — 1.6L man. trans. cruise control

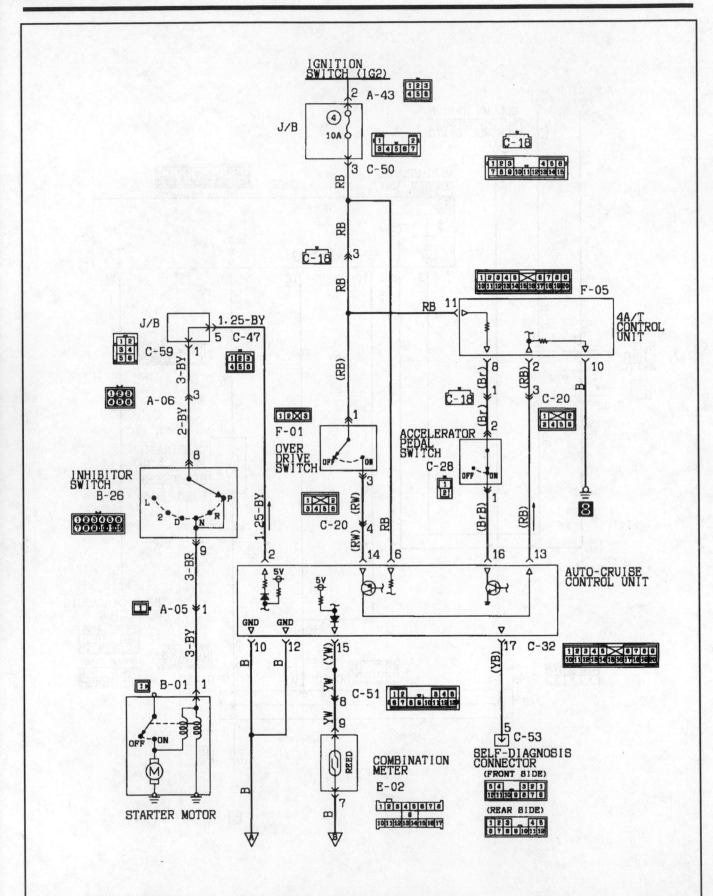

Fig. 97 1990-91 Colt Hatchback and Sedan — 1.6L auto. trans. cruise control

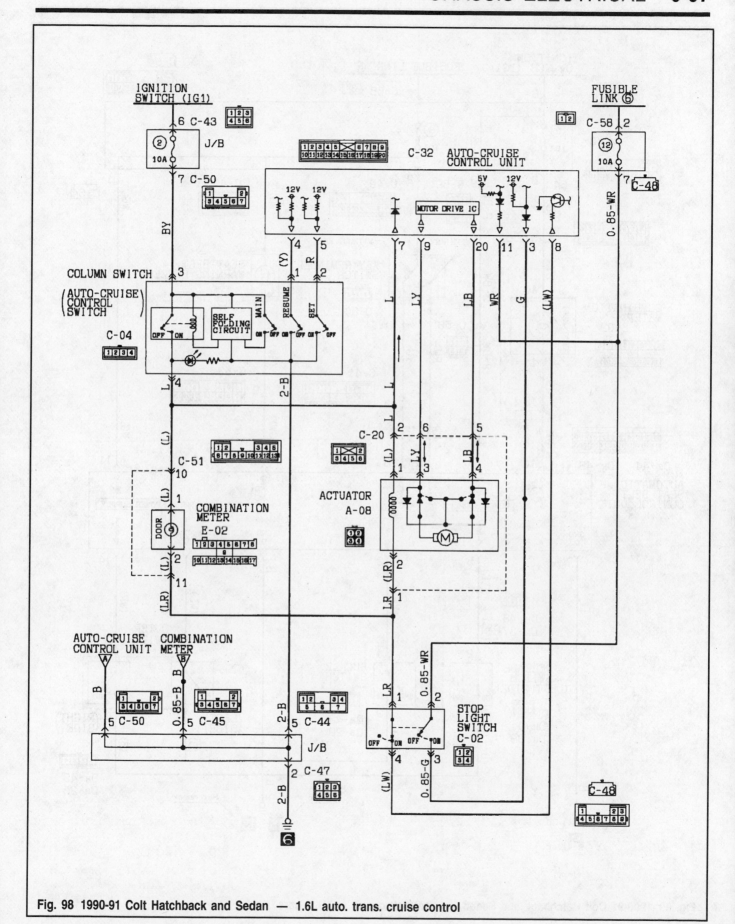

Fig. 98 1990-91 Colt Hatchback and Sedan — 1.6L auto. trans. cruise control

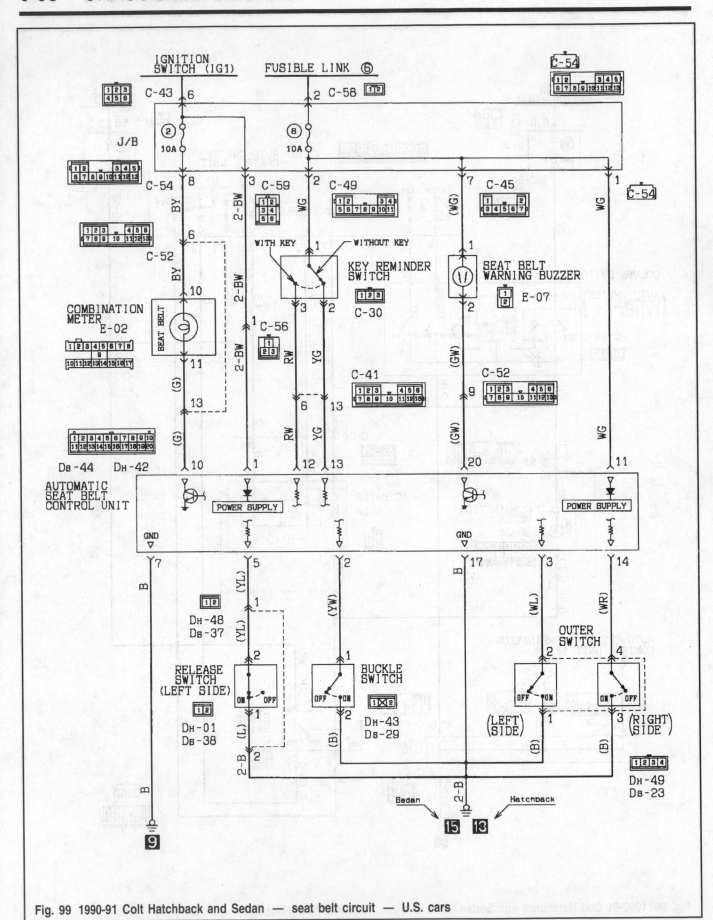

Fig. 99 1990-91 Colt Hatchback and Sedan — seat belt circuit — U.S. cars

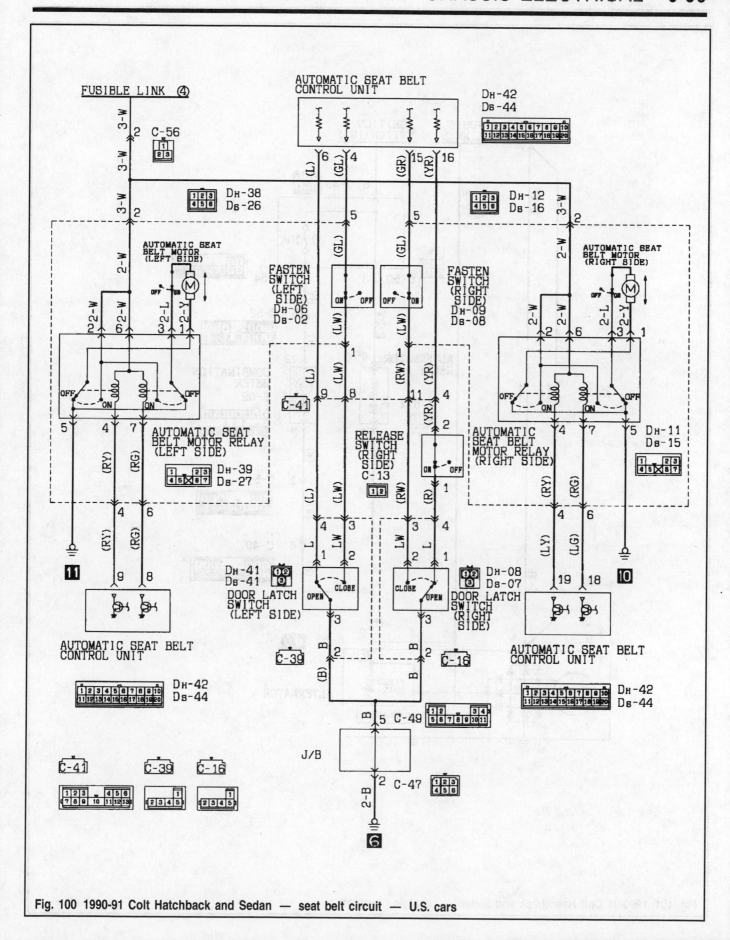

Fig. 100 1990-91 Colt Hatchback and Sedan — seat belt circuit — U.S. cars

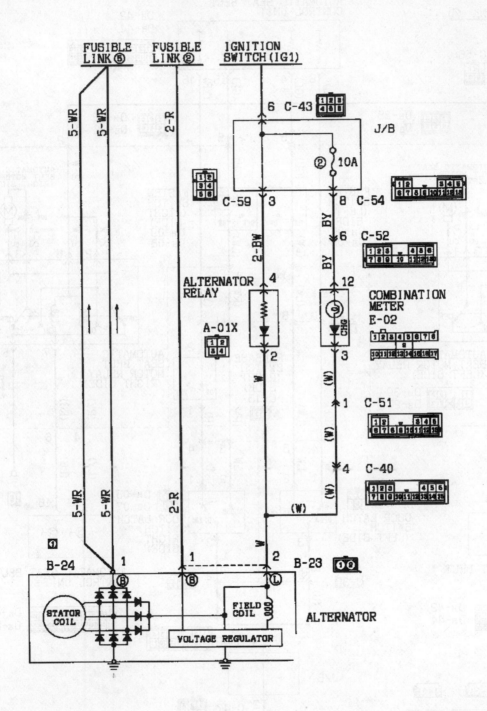

Fig. 101 1990-91 Colt Hatchback and Sedan — charging system

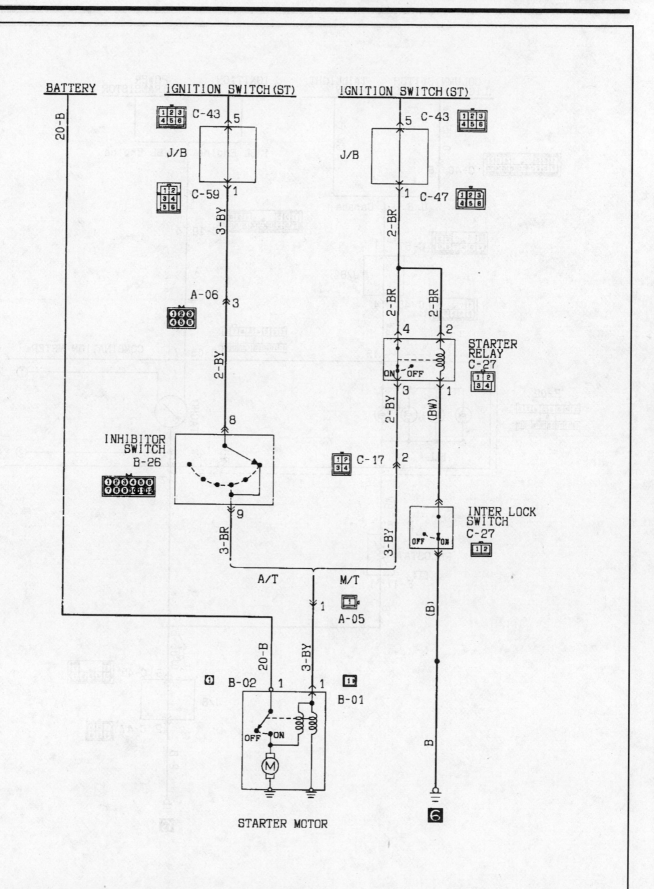

Fig. 102 1990-91 Colt Hatchback and Sedan — starting system

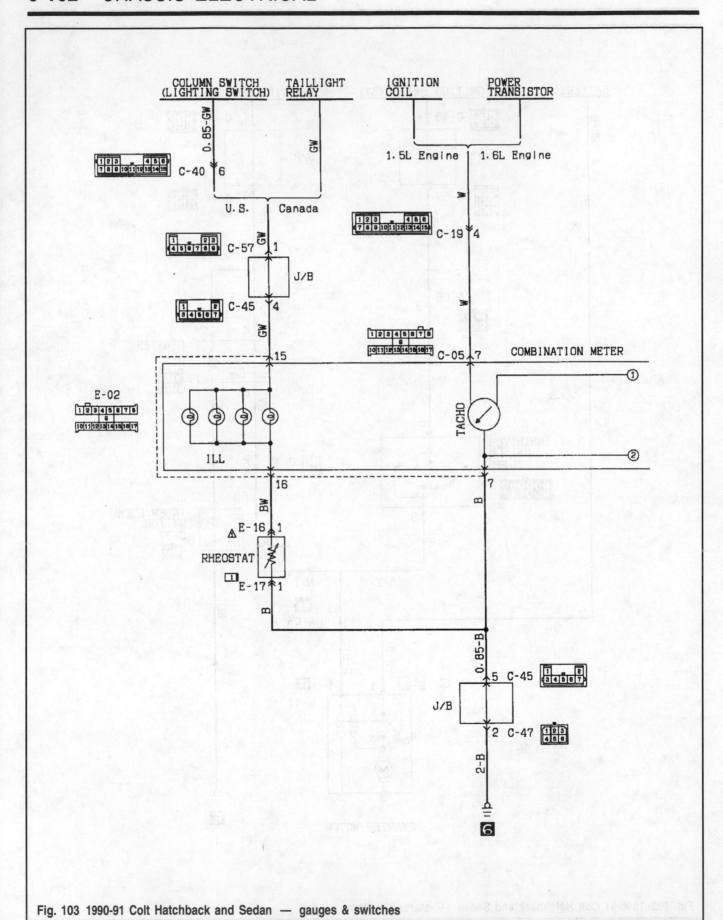

Fig. 103 1990-91 Colt Hatchback and Sedan — gauges & switches

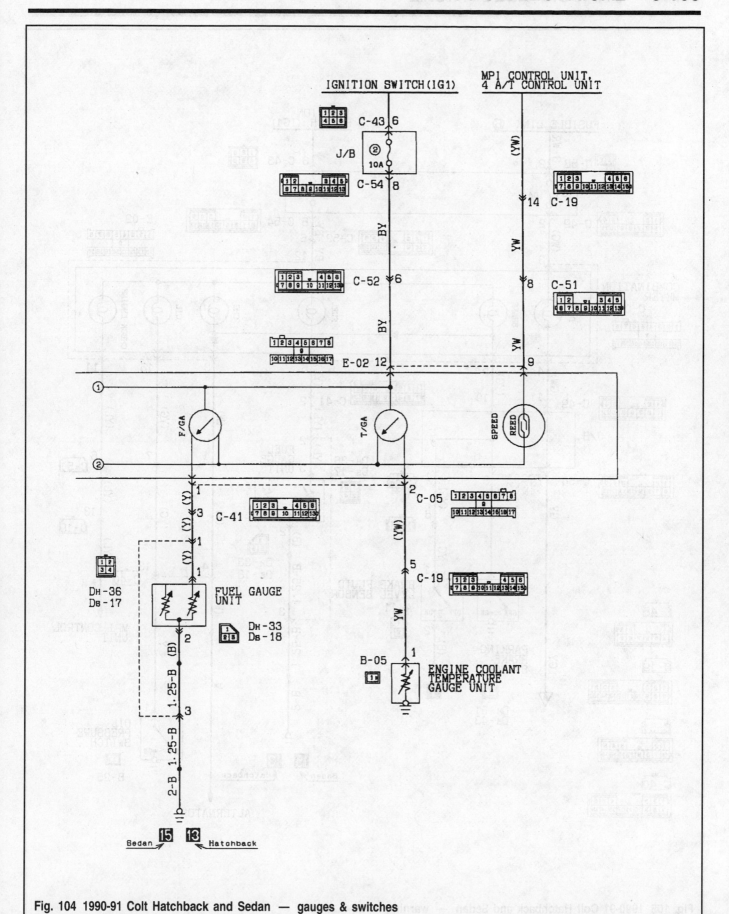

Fig. 104 1990-91 Colt Hatchback and Sedan — gauges & switches

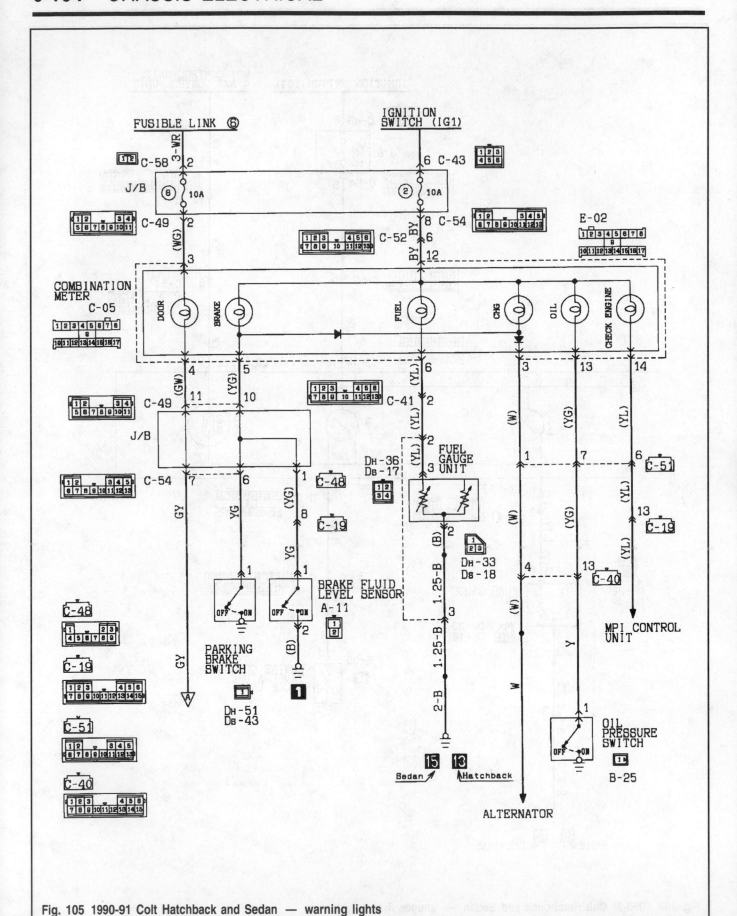

Fig. 105 1990-91 Colt Hatchback and Sedan — warning lights

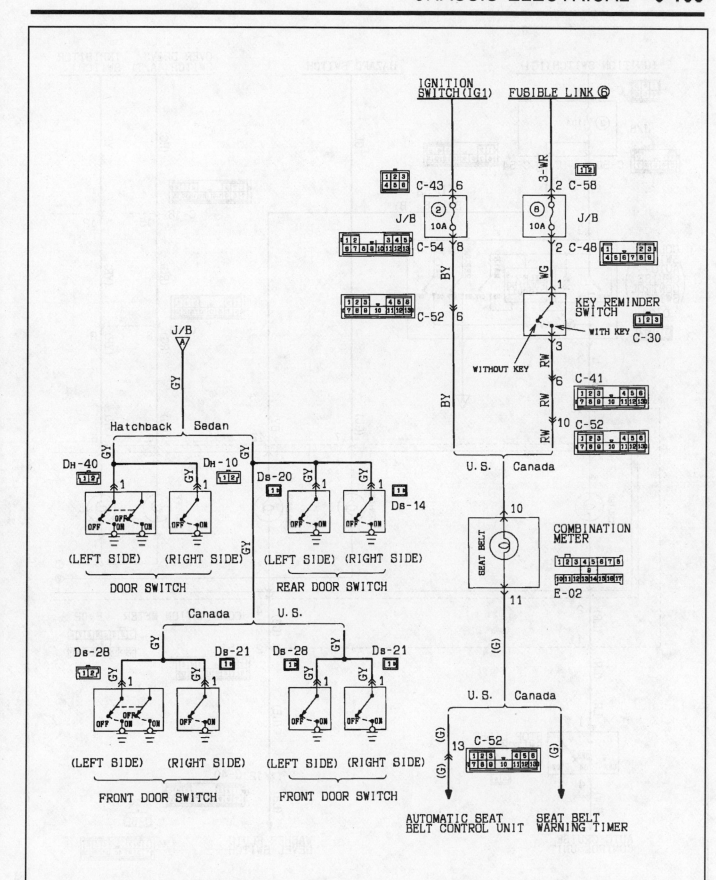

Fig. 106 1990-91 Colt Hatchback and Sedan — warning lights

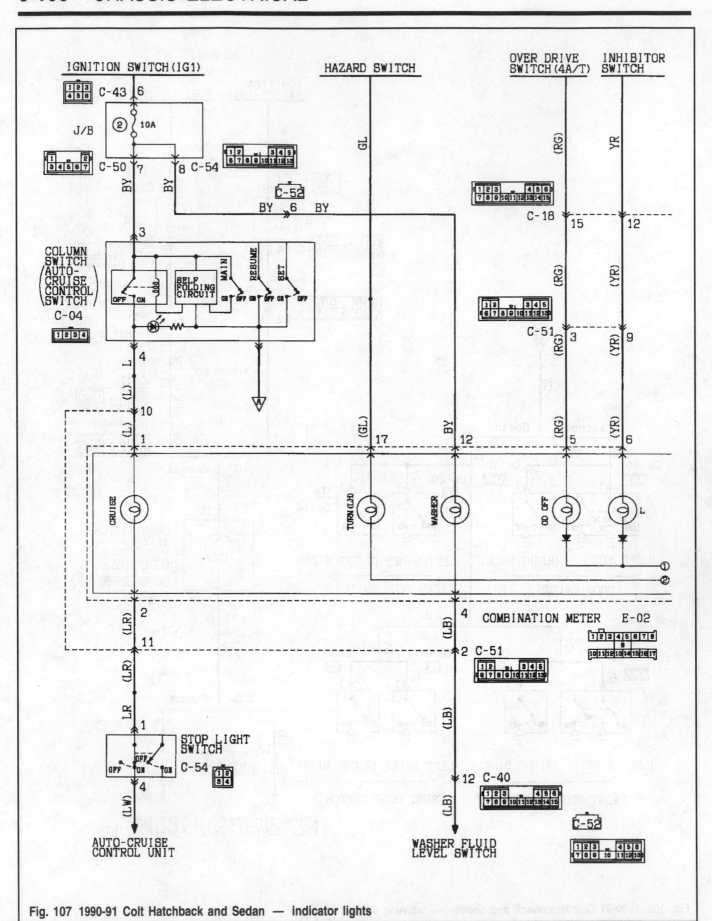

Fig. 107 1990-91 Colt Hatchback and Sedan — indicator lights

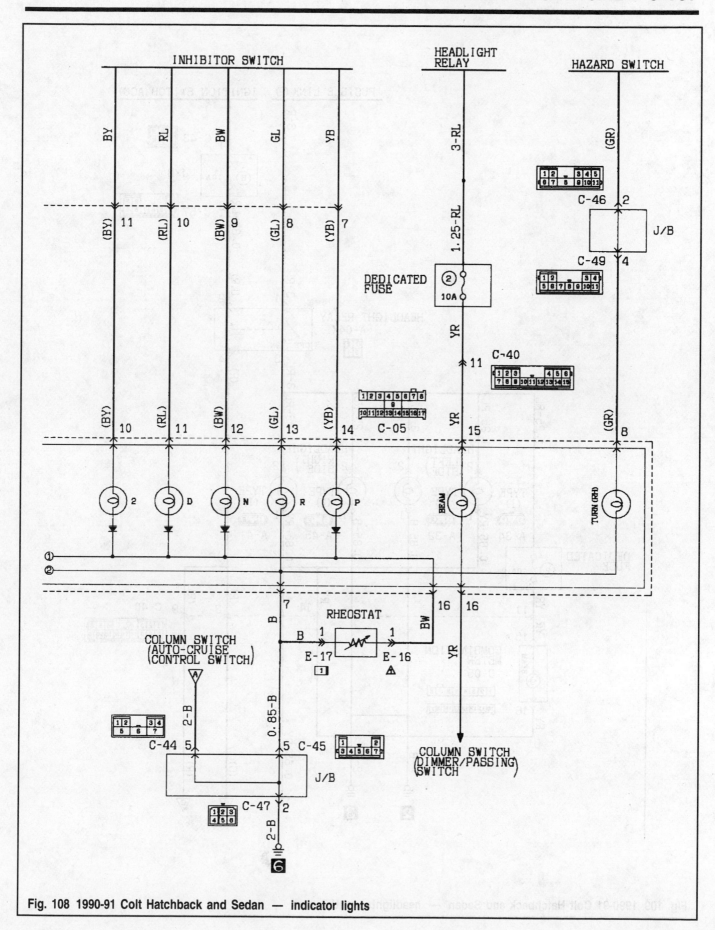

Fig. 108 1990-91 Colt Hatchback and Sedan — indicator lights

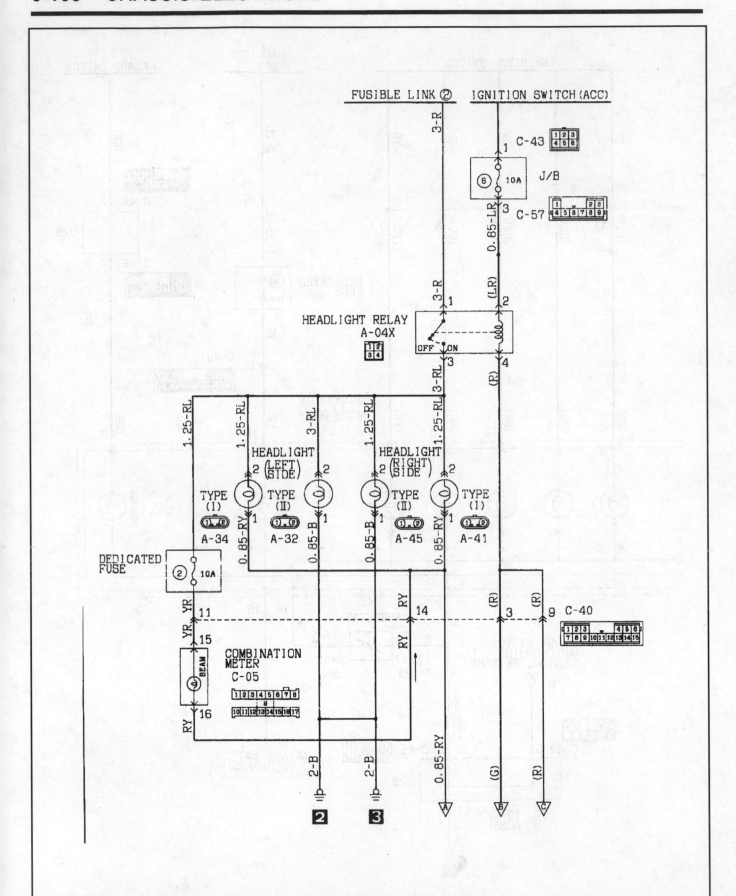

Fig. 109 1990-91 Colt Hatchback and Sedan — headlights — U.S. cars

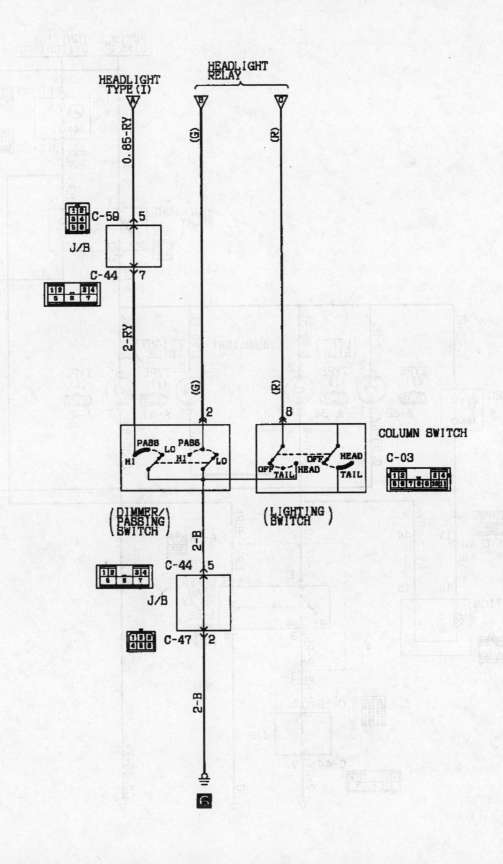

Fig. 110 1990-91 Colt Hatchback and Sedan — headlights — U.S. cars

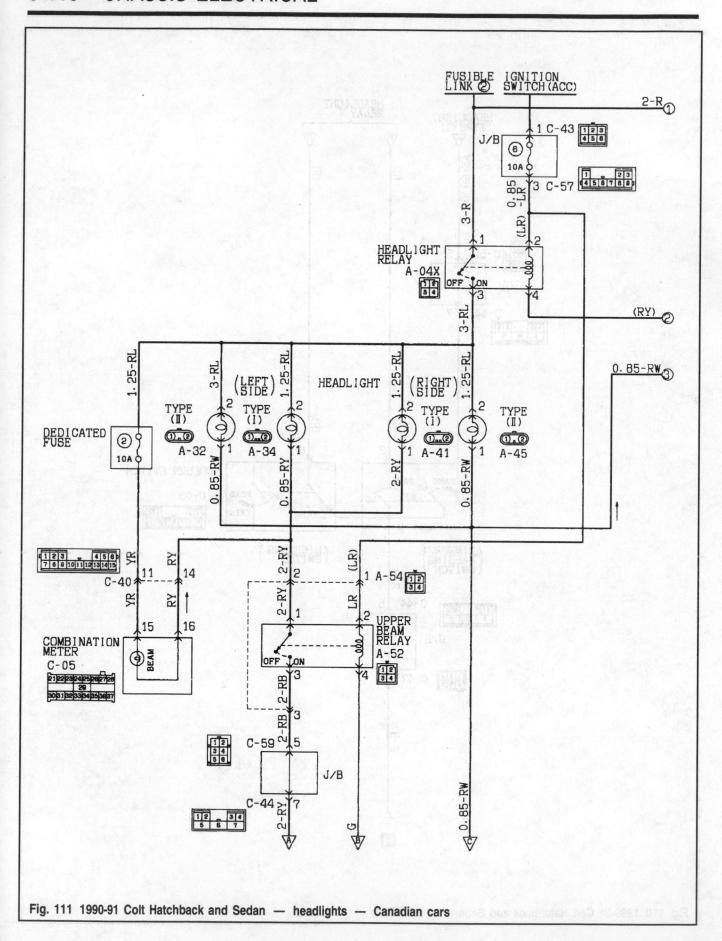

Fig. 111 1990-91 Colt Hatchback and Sedan — headlights — Canadian cars

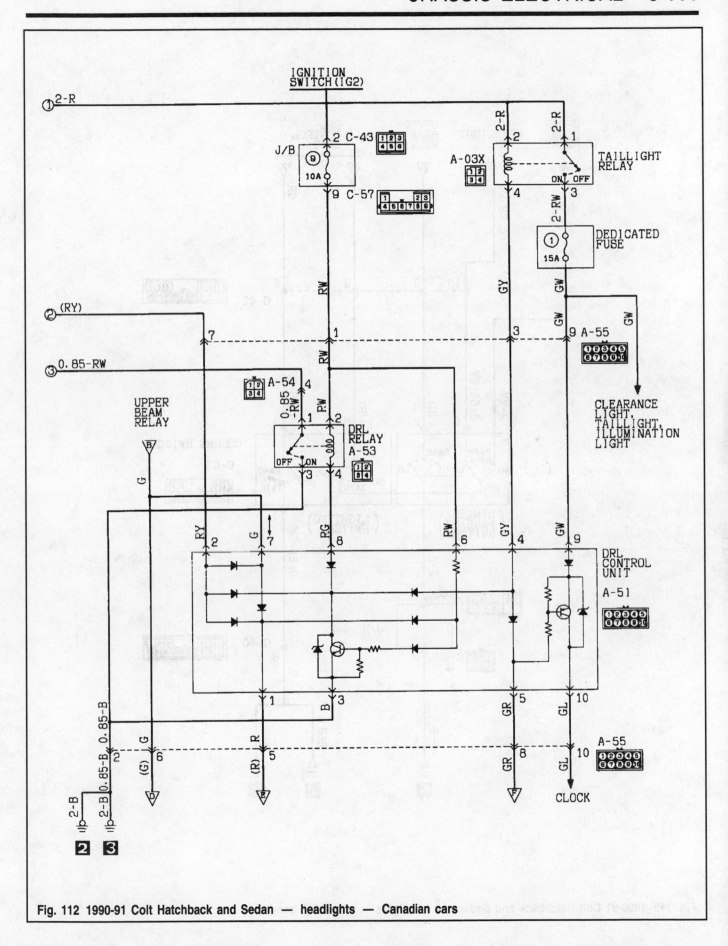

Fig. 112 1990-91 Colt Hatchback and Sedan — headlights — Canadian cars

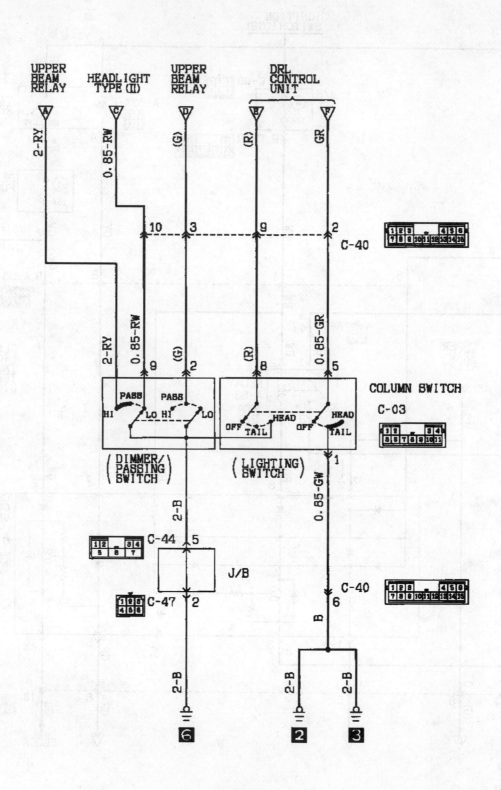

Fig. 113 1990-91 Colt Hatchback and Sedan — headlights — Canadian cars

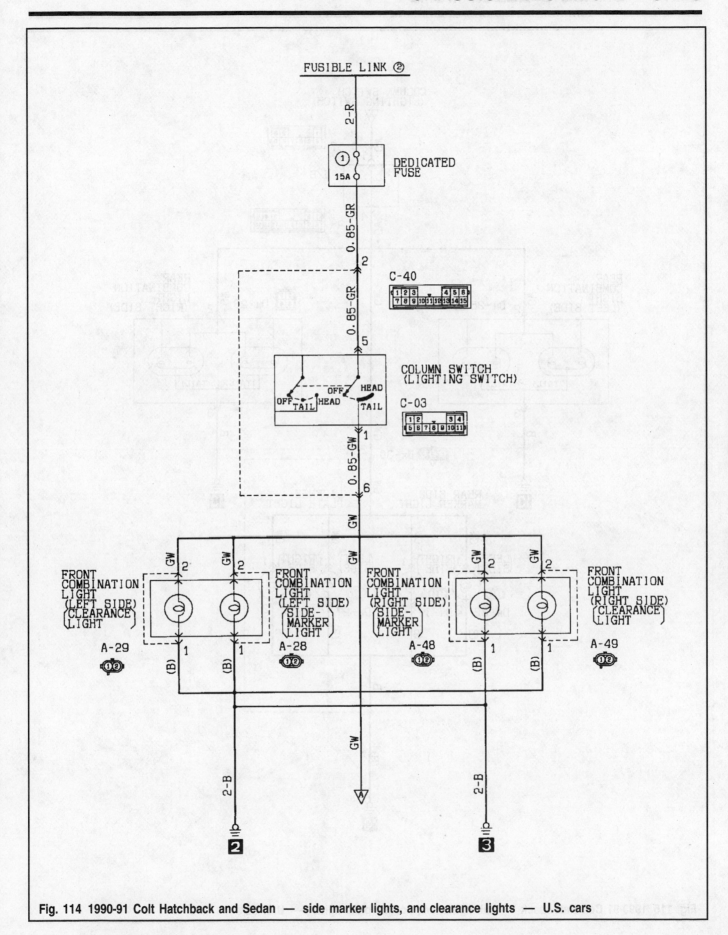

Fig. 114 1990-91 Colt Hatchback and Sedan — side marker lights, and clearance lights — U.S. cars

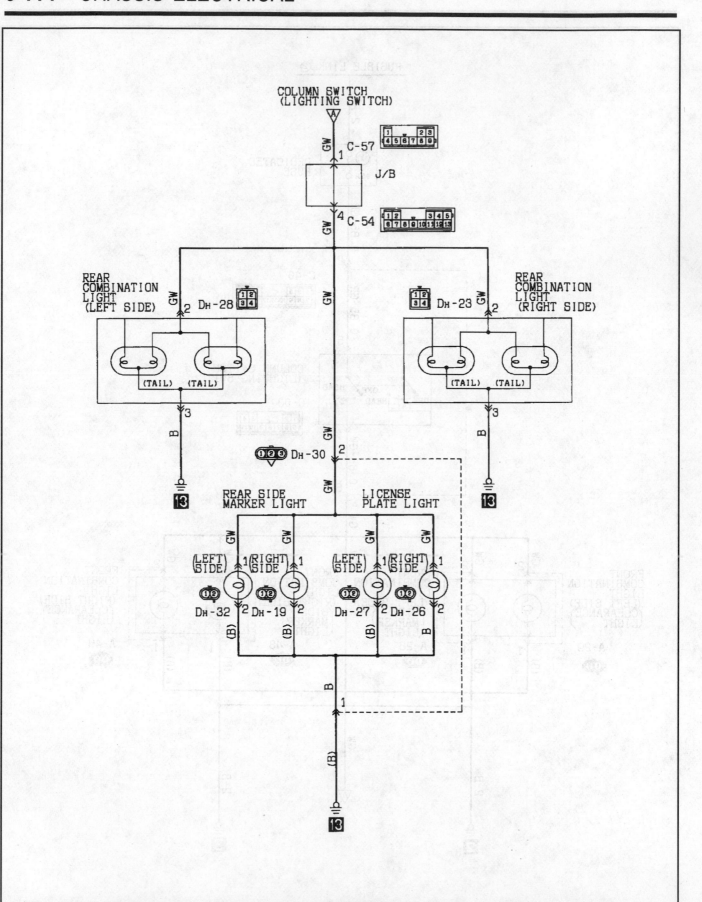

Fig. 115 1990-91 Colt Hatchback — tail lights, and license plate lights — U.S. cars

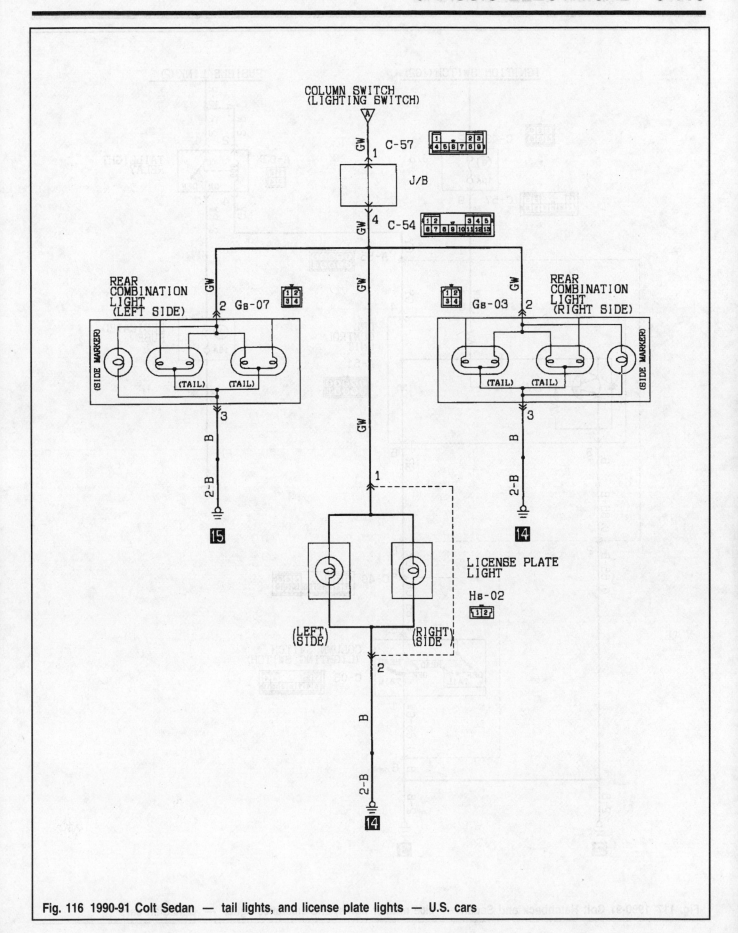

Fig. 116 1990-91 Colt Sedan — tail lights, and license plate lights — U.S. cars

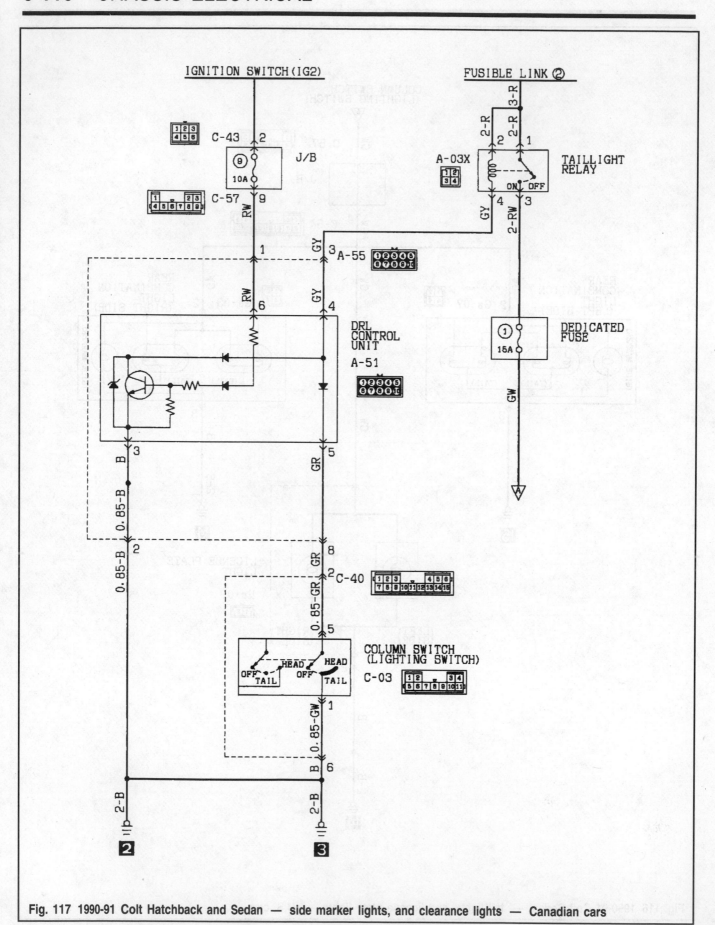

Fig. 117 1990-91 Colt Hatchback and Sedan — side marker lights, and clearance lights — Canadian cars

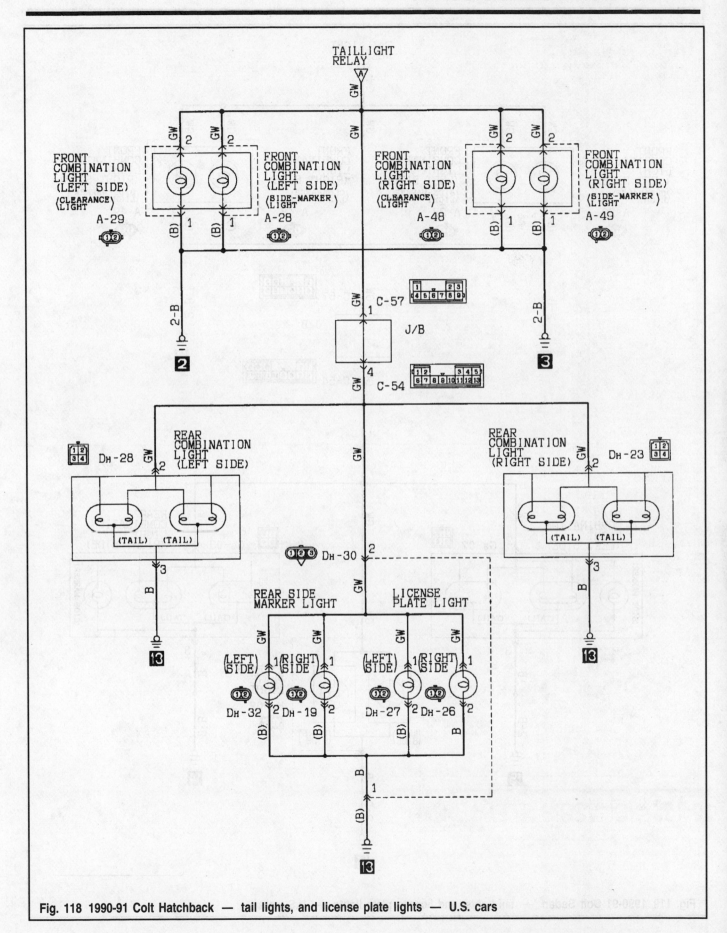

Fig. 118 1990-91 Colt Hatchback — tail lights, and license plate lights — U.S. cars

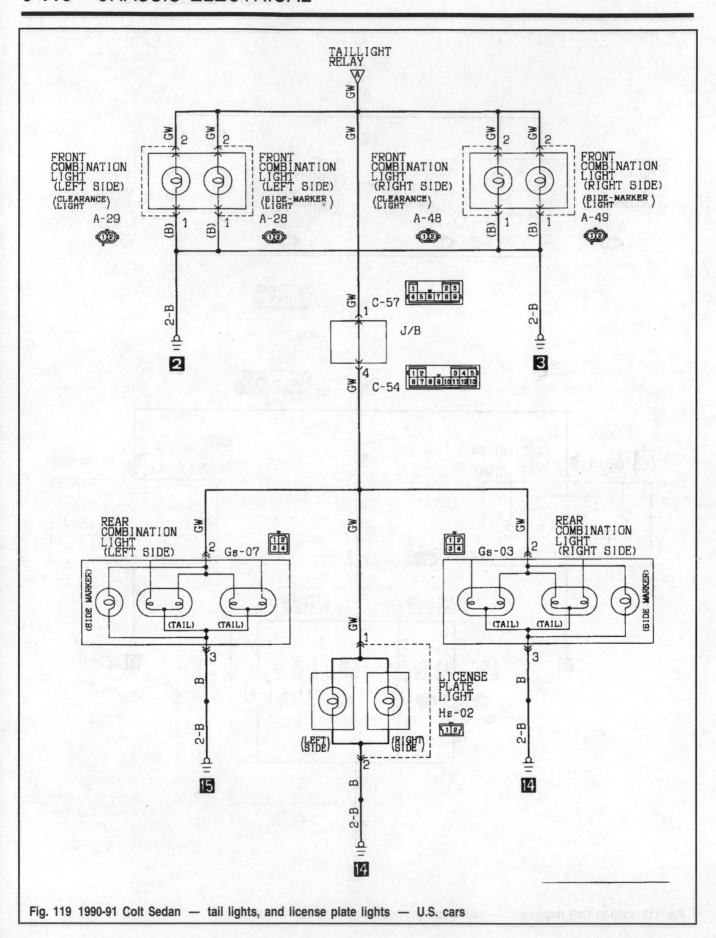

Fig. 119 1990-91 Colt Sedan — tail lights, and license plate lights — U.S. cars

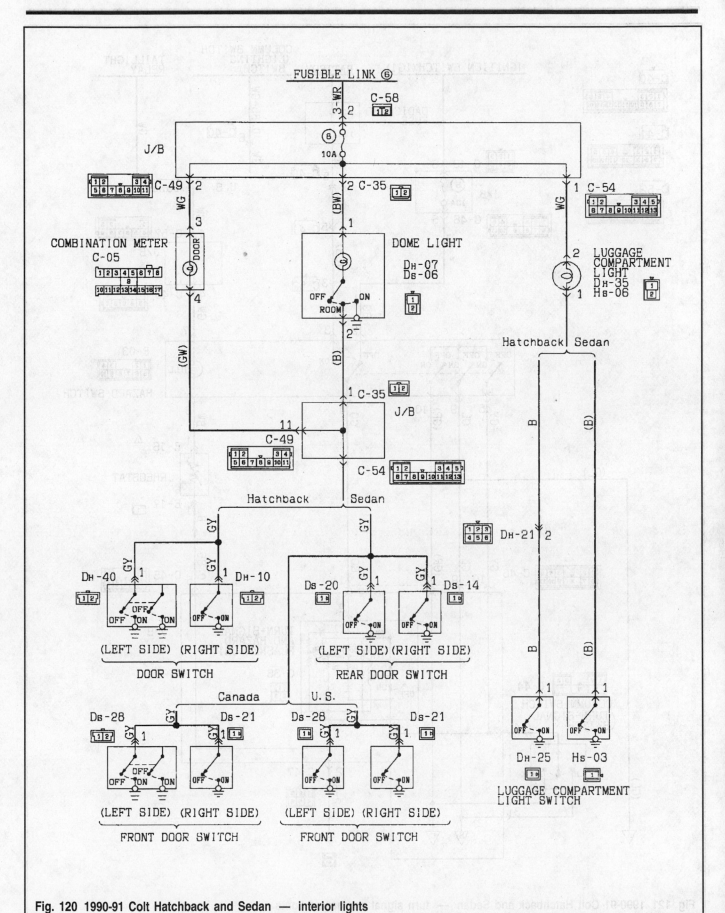

Fig. 120 1990-91 Colt Hatchback and Sedan — interior lights

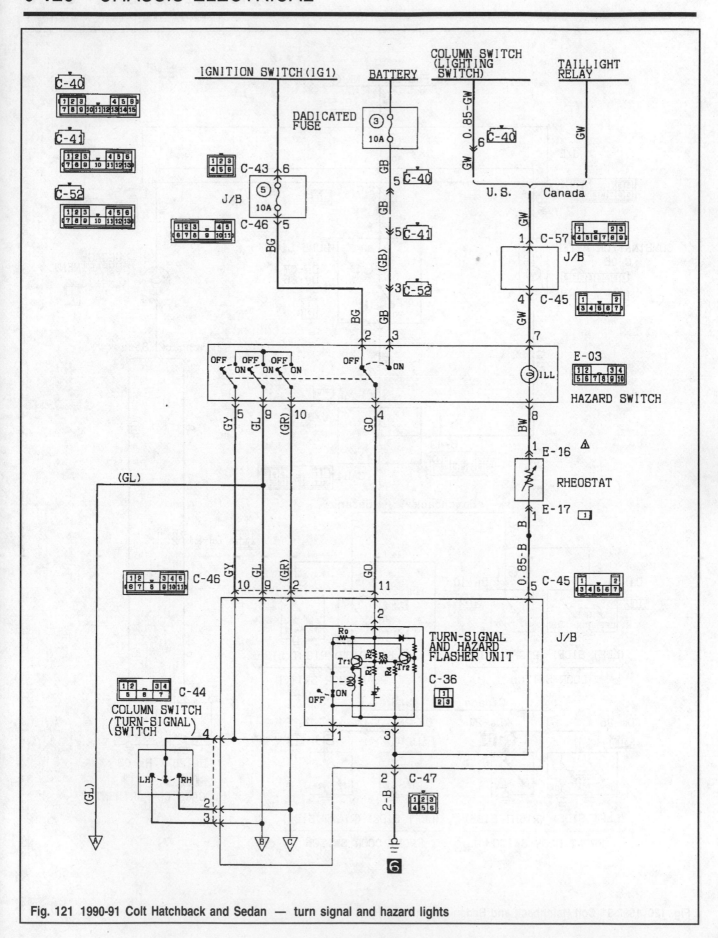

Fig. 121 1990-91 Colt Hatchback and Sedan — turn signal and hazard lights

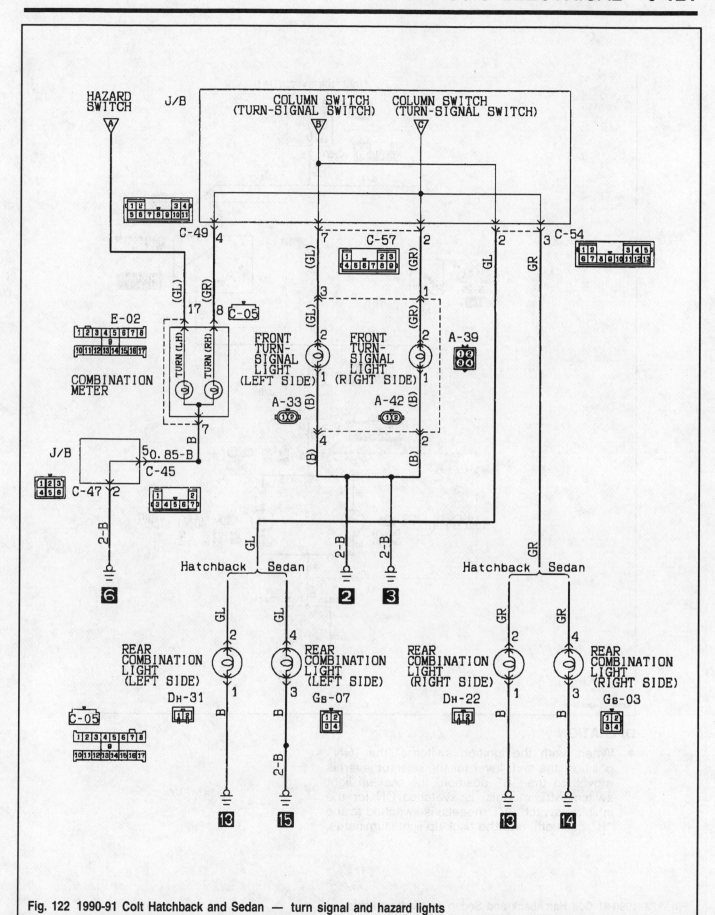

Fig. 122 1990-91 Colt Hatchback and Sedan — turn signal and hazard lights

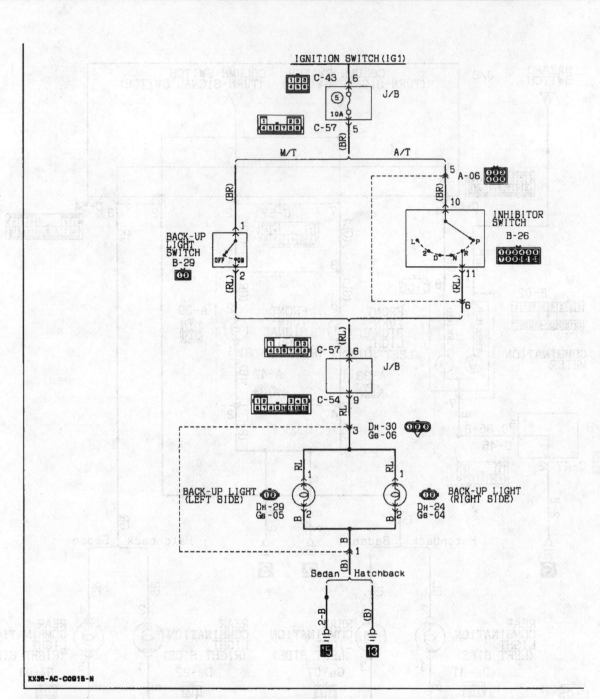

OPERATION

- When, with the ignition switch at the "ON" position, the shift lever (or the selector lever) is moved to the "R" position, the back-up light switch (M/T models) is switched ON [or the inhibitor switch (A/T models) is switched to the "R" position], and the back-up light illuminates.

Fig. 123 **1990-91 Colt Hatchback and Sedan — back-up lights**

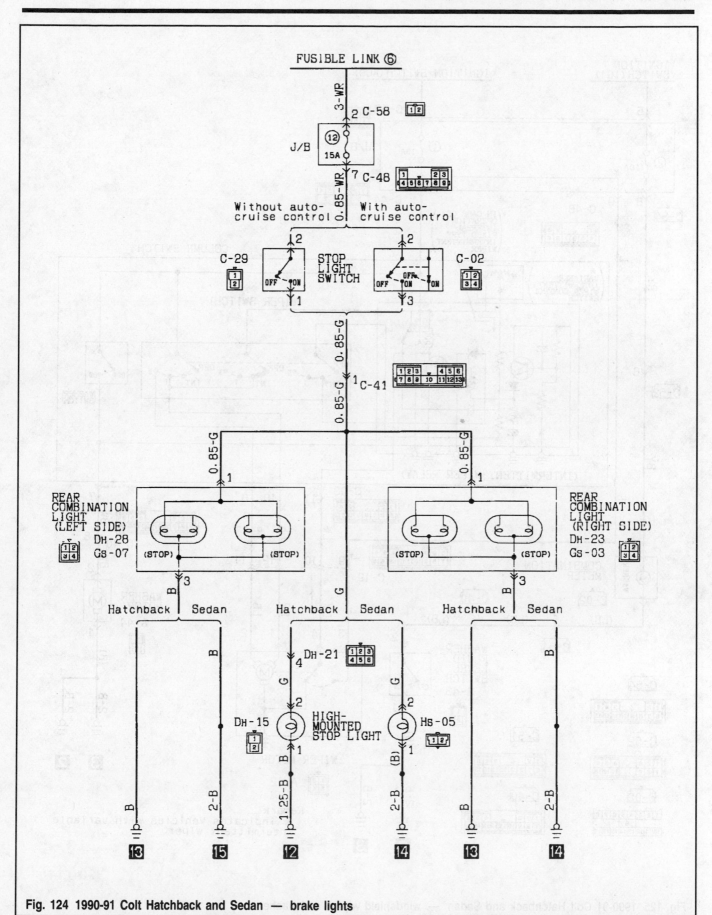

Fig. 124 1990-91 Colt Hatchback and Sedan — brake lights

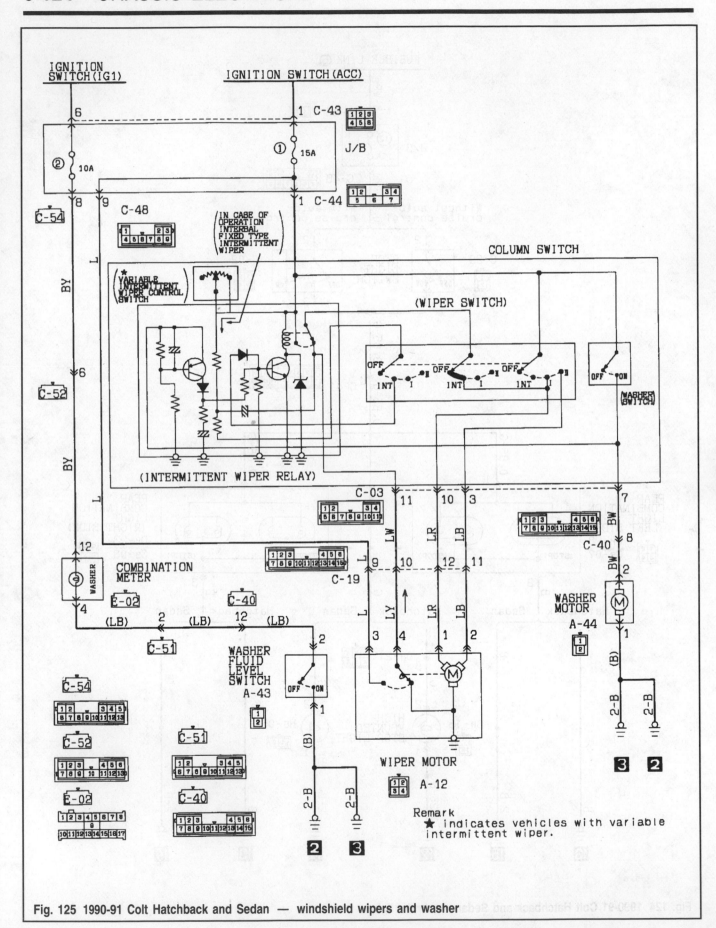

Fig. 125 1990-91 Colt Hatchback and Sedan — windshield wipers and washer

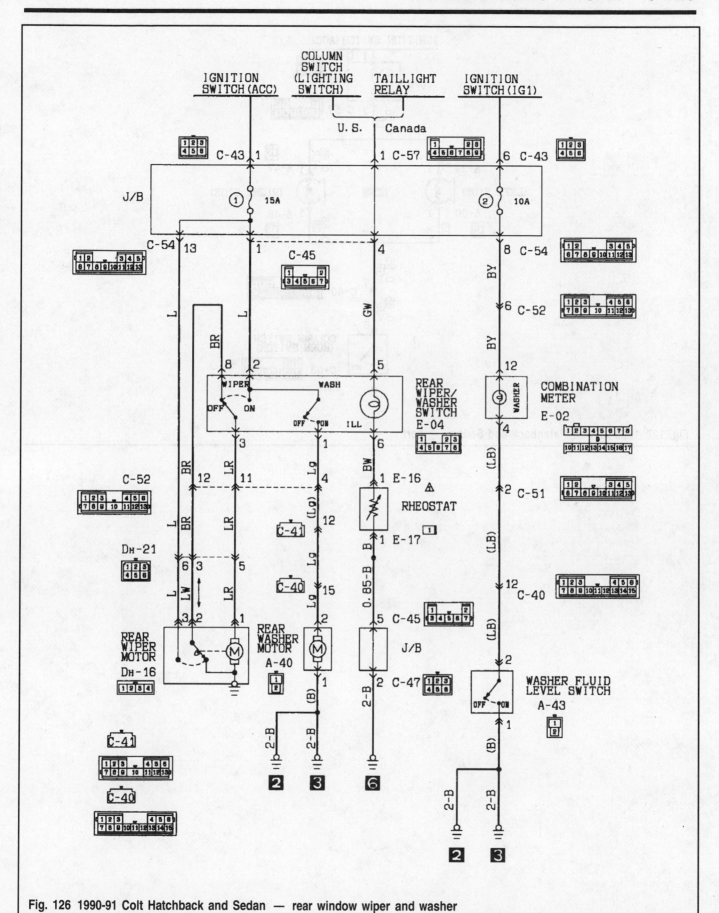

Fig. 126 1990-91 Colt Hatchback and Sedan — rear window wiper and washer

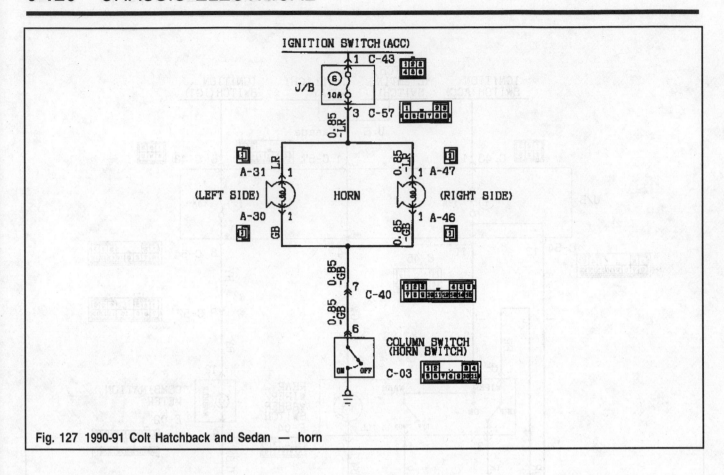

Fig. 127 1990-91 Colt Hatchback and Sedan — horn

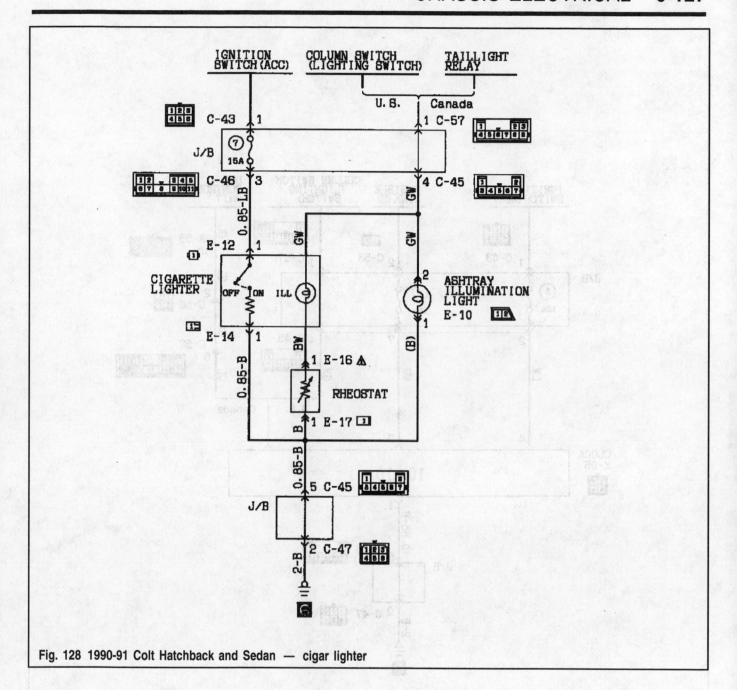

Fig. 128 1990-91 Colt Hatchback and Sedan — cigar lighter

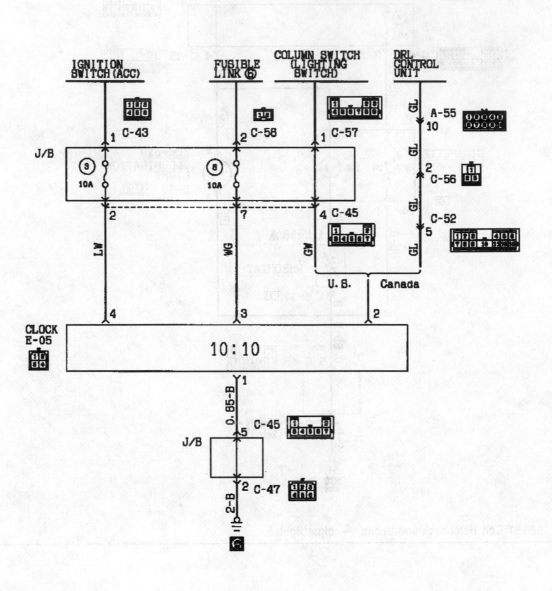

Fig. 129 1990-91 Colt Hatchback and Sedan — clock

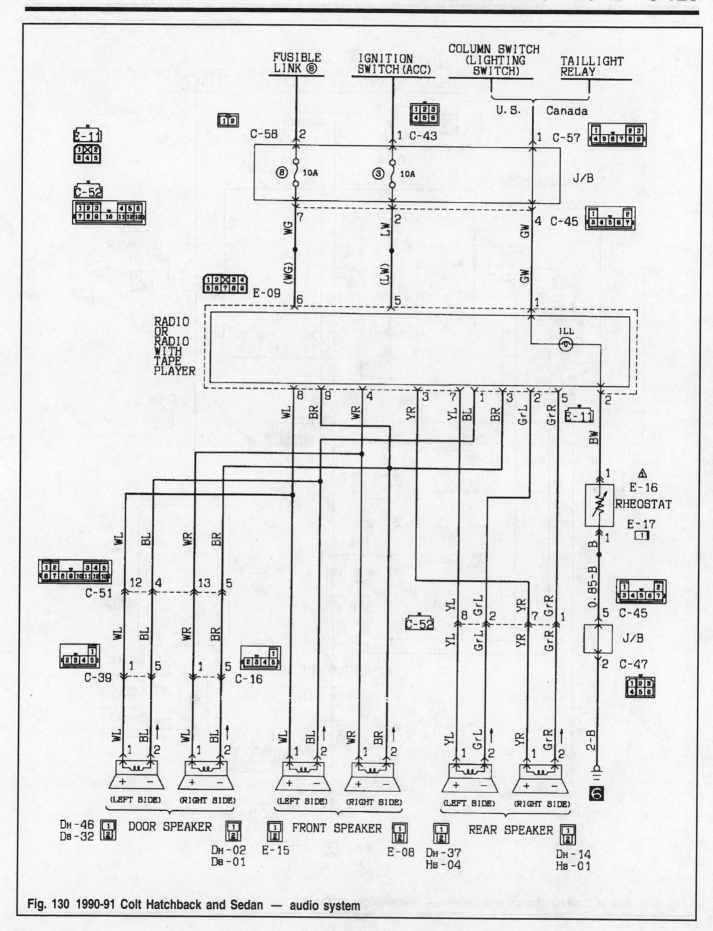

Fig. 130 1990-91 Colt Hatchback and Sedan — audio system

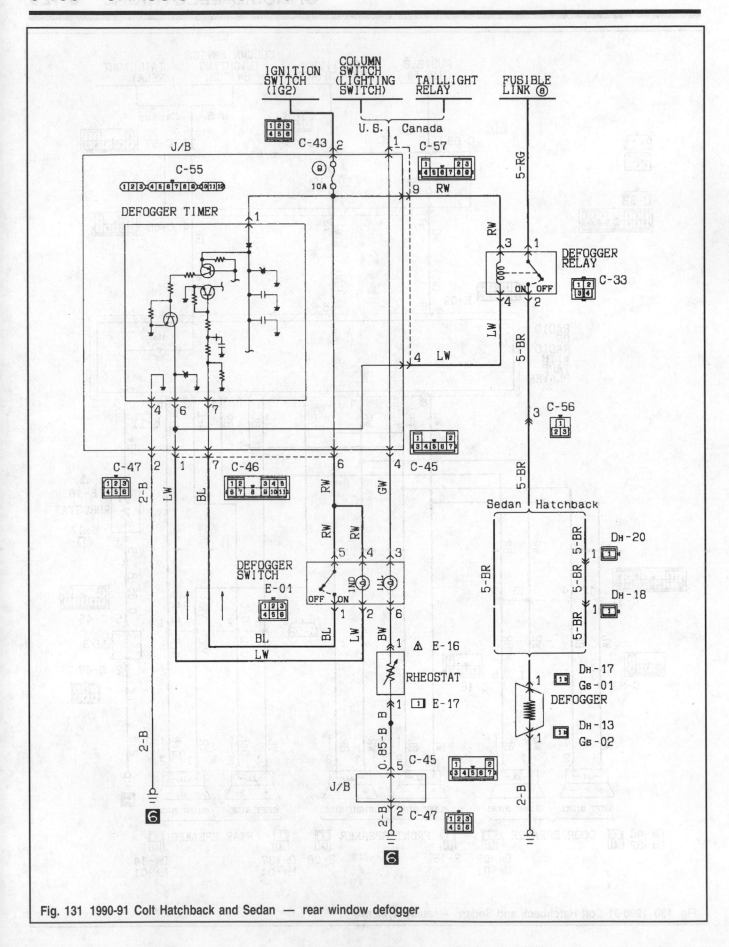

Fig. 131 1990-91 Colt Hatchback and Sedan — rear window defogger

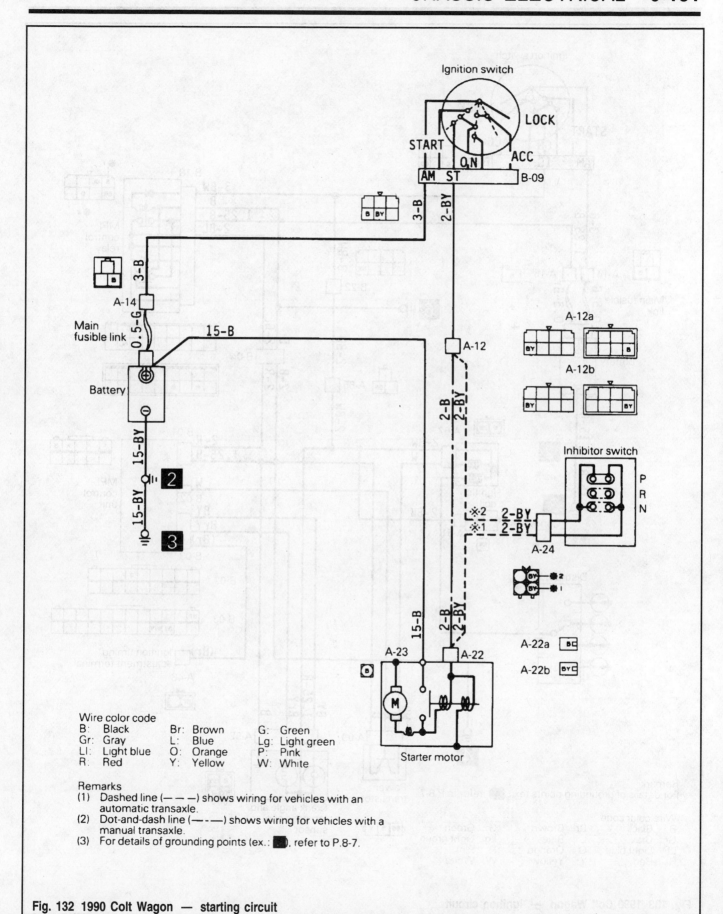

Fig. 132 1990 Colt Wagon — starting circuit

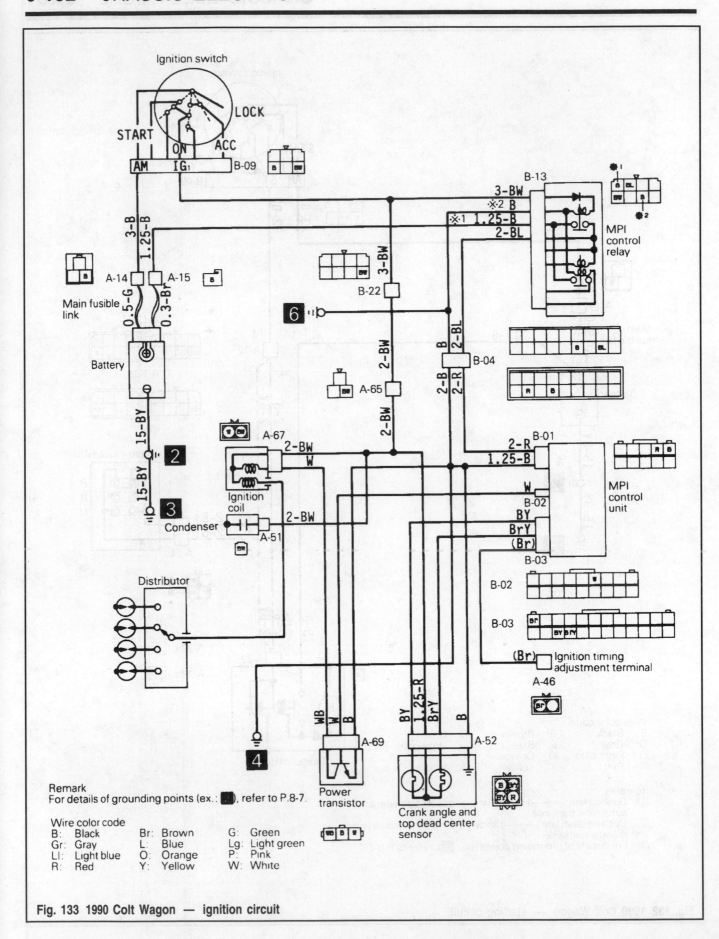

Fig. 133 1990 Colt Wagon — ignition circuit

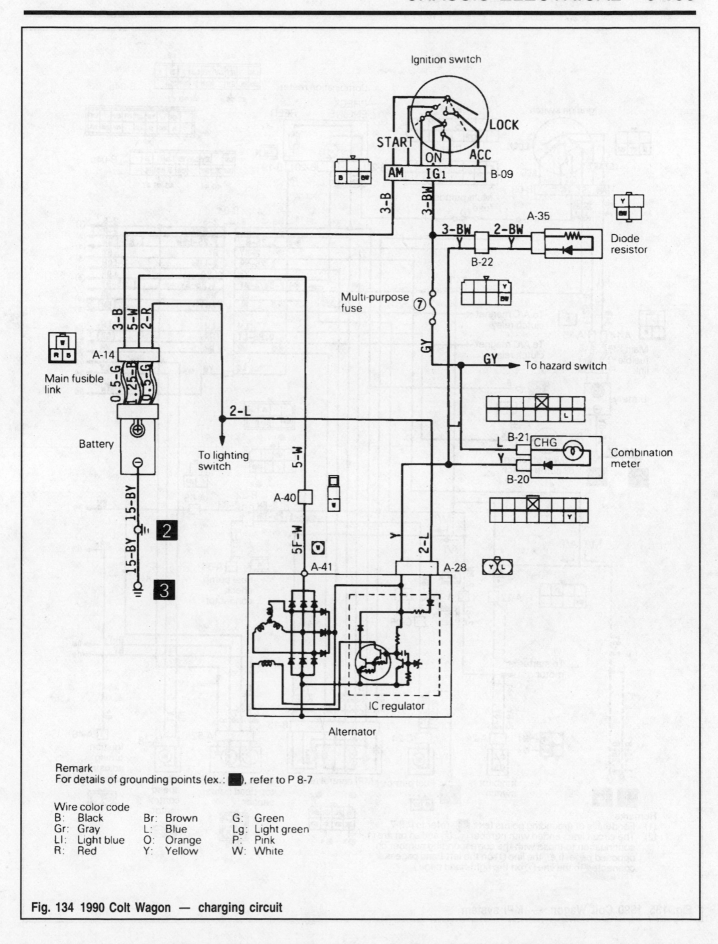

Fig. 134 1990 Colt Wagon — charging circuit

Remark
For details of grounding points (ex.: ■), refer to P 8-7

Wire color code
B: Black   Br: Brown   G: Green
Gr: Gray   L: Blue   Lg: Light green
Ll: Light blue   O: Orange   P: Pink
R: Red   Y: Yellow   W: White

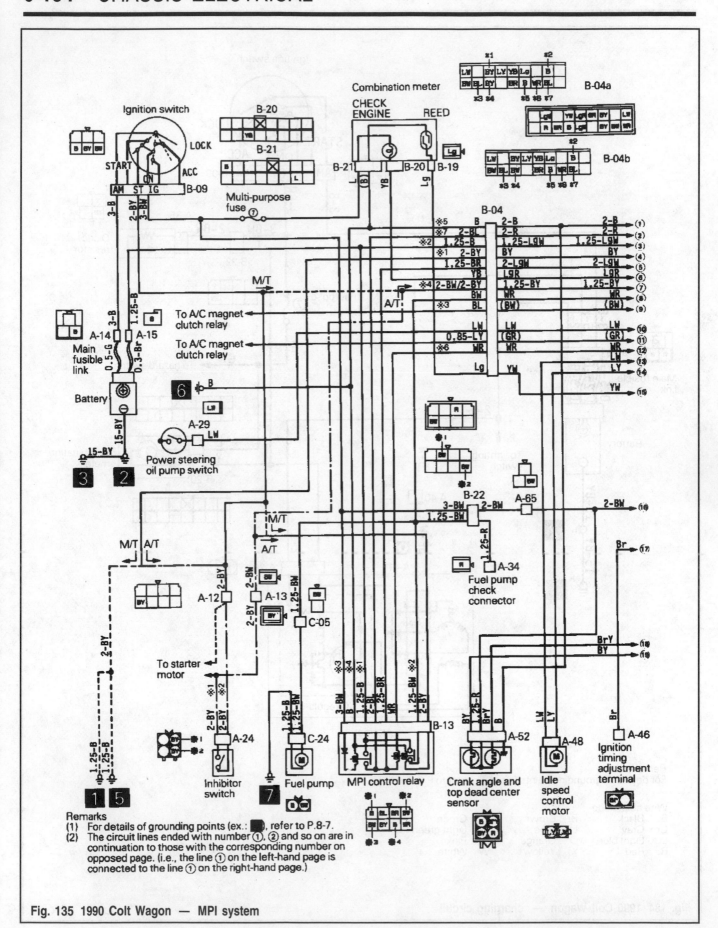

Fig. 135 1990 Colt Wagon — MPI system

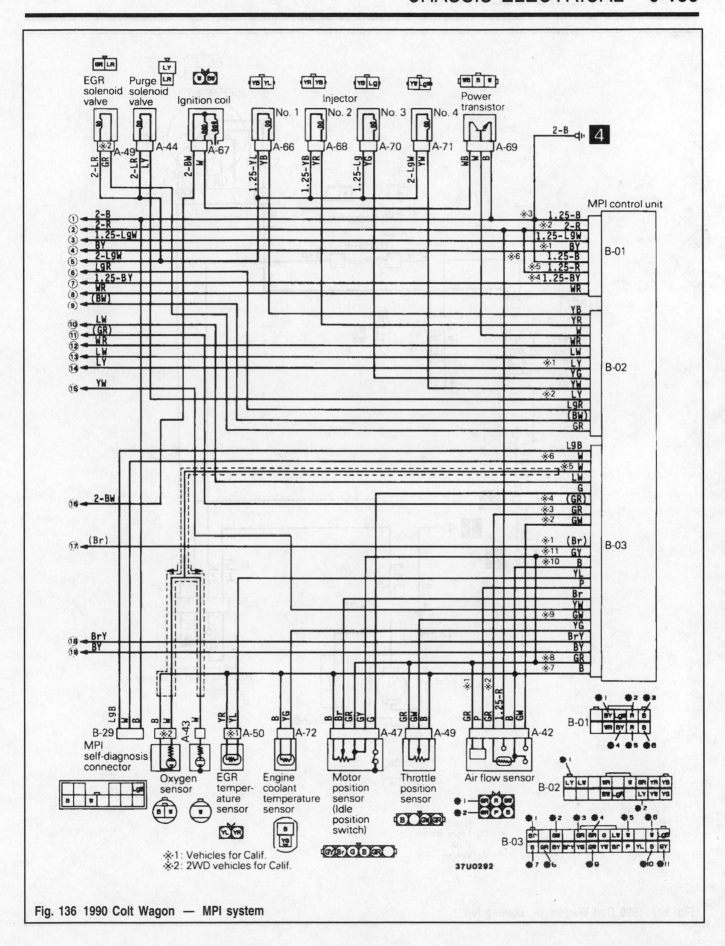

Fig. 136 1990 Colt Wagon — MPI system

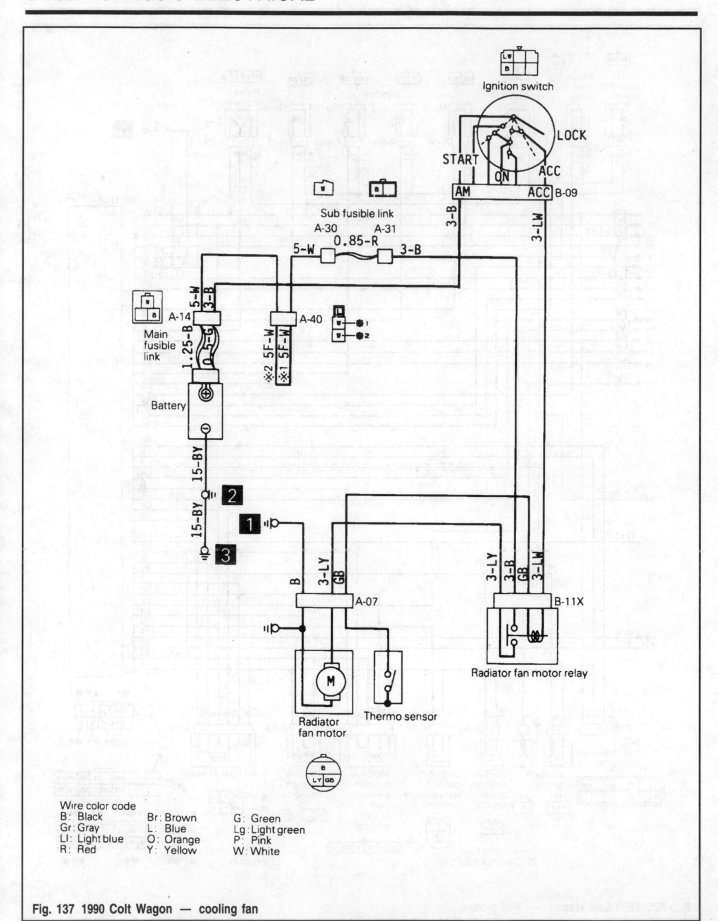

Fig. 137 1990 Colt Wagon — cooling fan

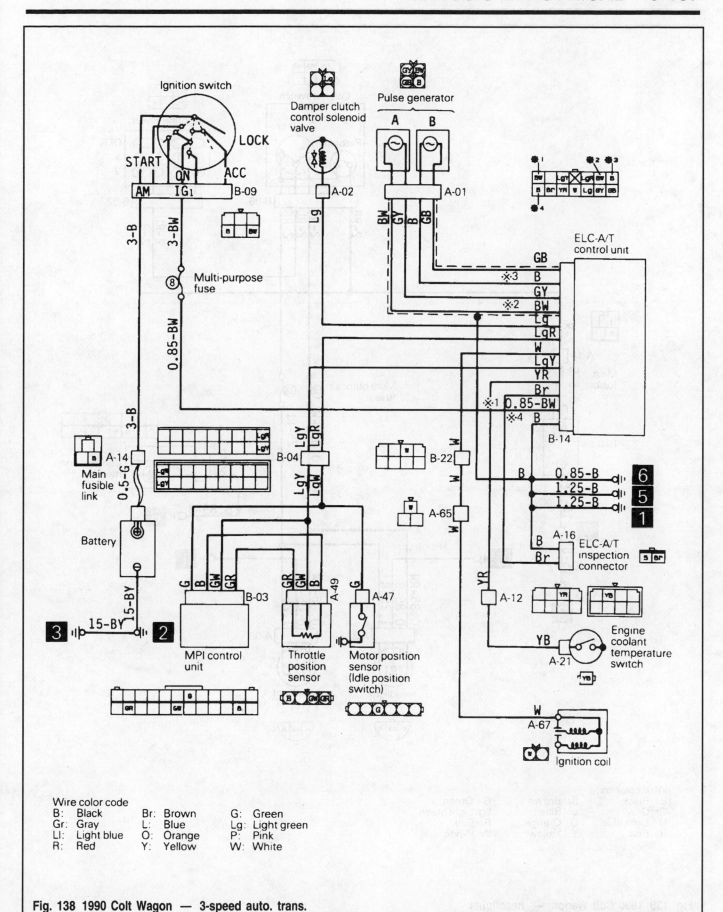

Fig. 138 1990 Colt Wagon — 3-speed auto. trans.

Wire color code
B: Black   Br: Brown   G: Green
Gr: Gray   L: Blue   Lg: Light green
Ll: Light blue O: Orange   P: Pink
R: Red   Y: Yellow   W: White

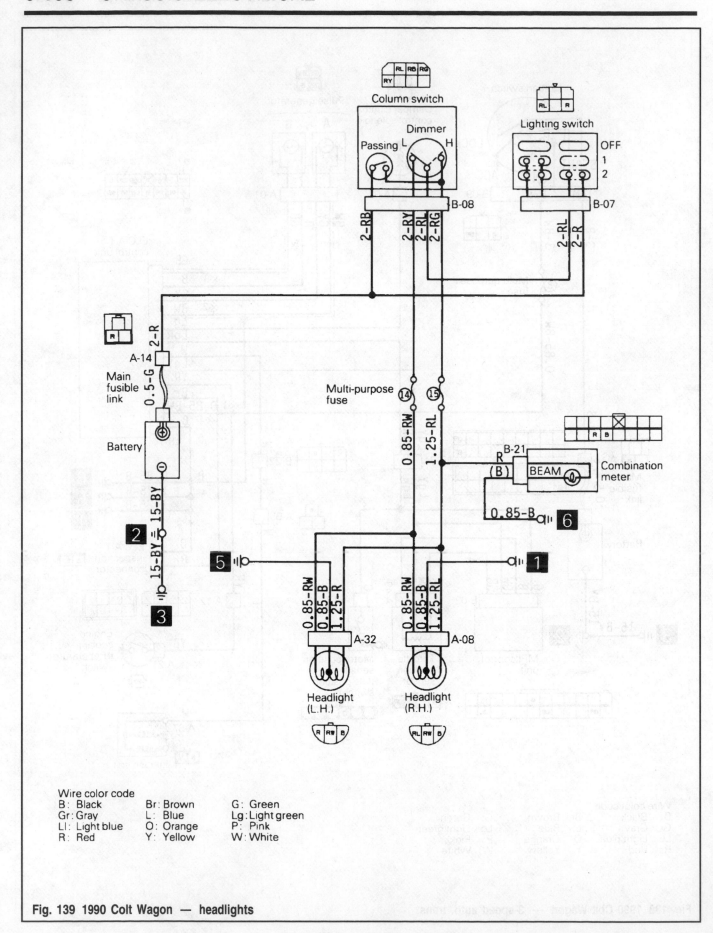

Fig. 139 1990 Colt Wagon — headlights

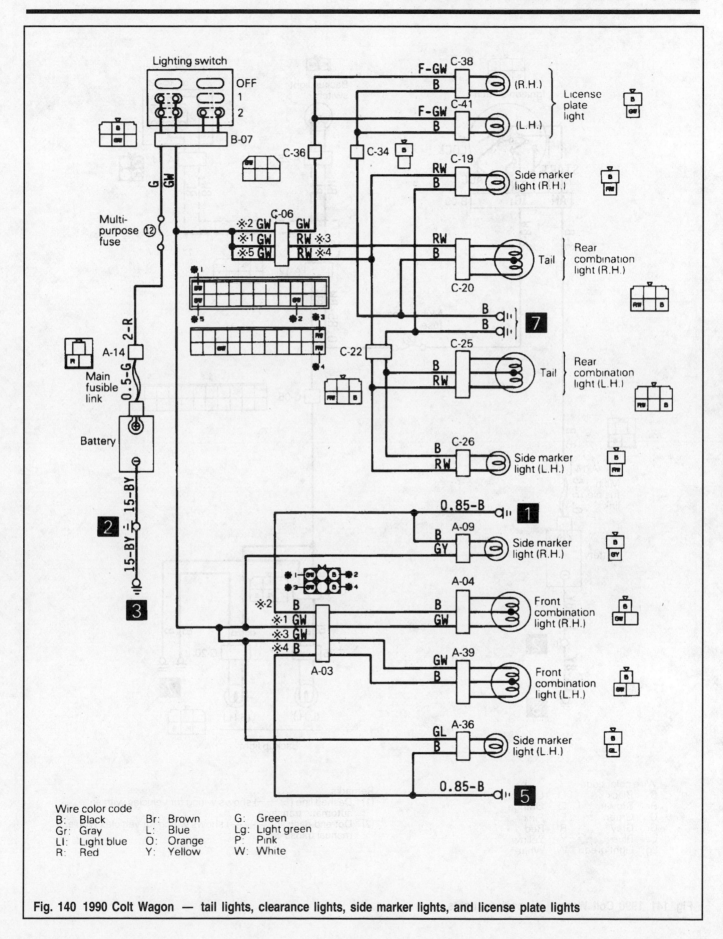

Fig. 140 1990 Colt Wagon — tail lights, clearance lights, side marker lights, and license plate lights

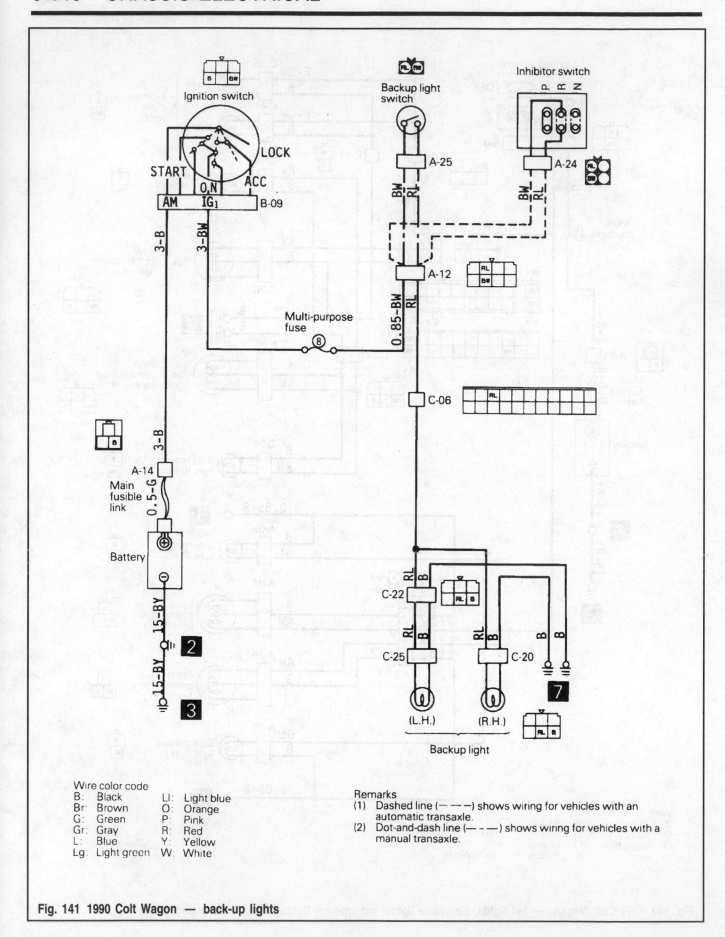

Fig. 141 1990 Colt Wagon — back-up lights

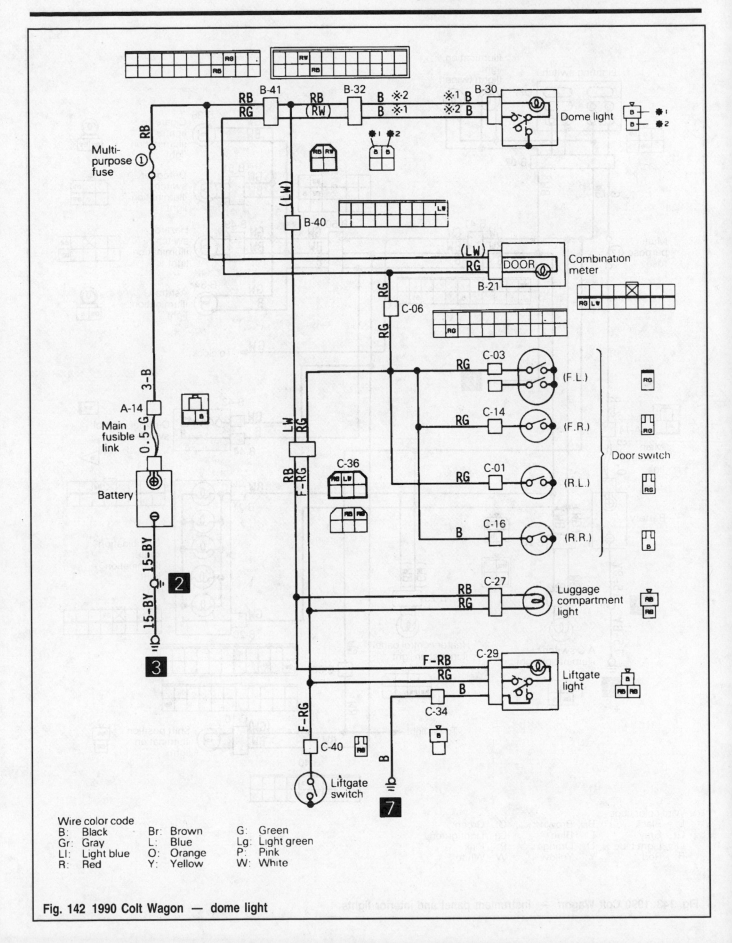

Fig. 142 1990 Colt Wagon — dome light

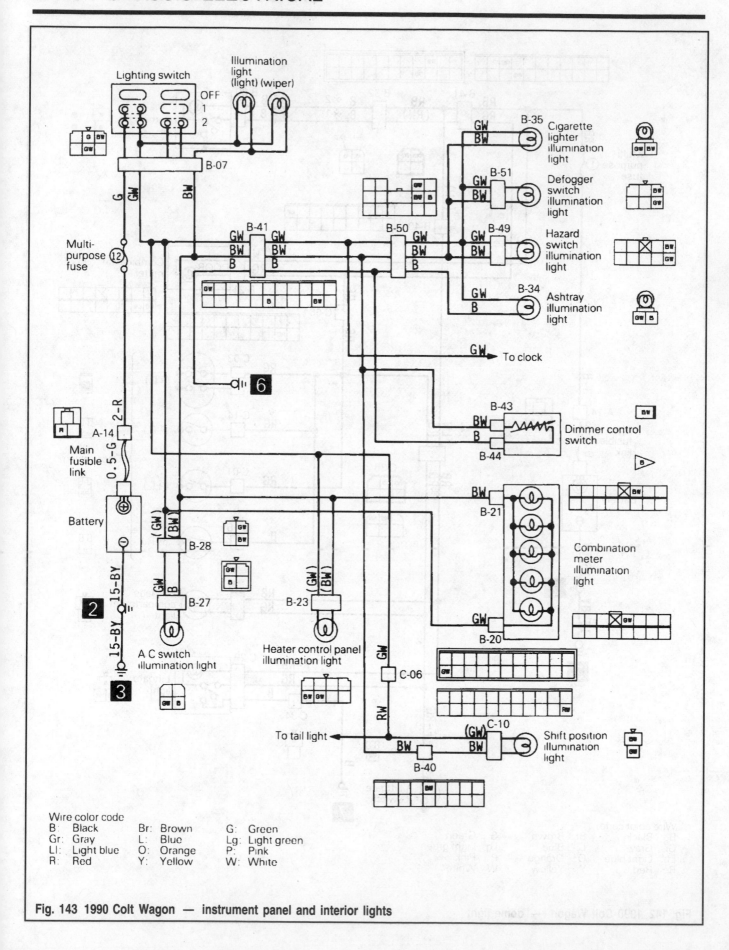

Fig. 143 1990 Colt Wagon — instrument panel and interior lights

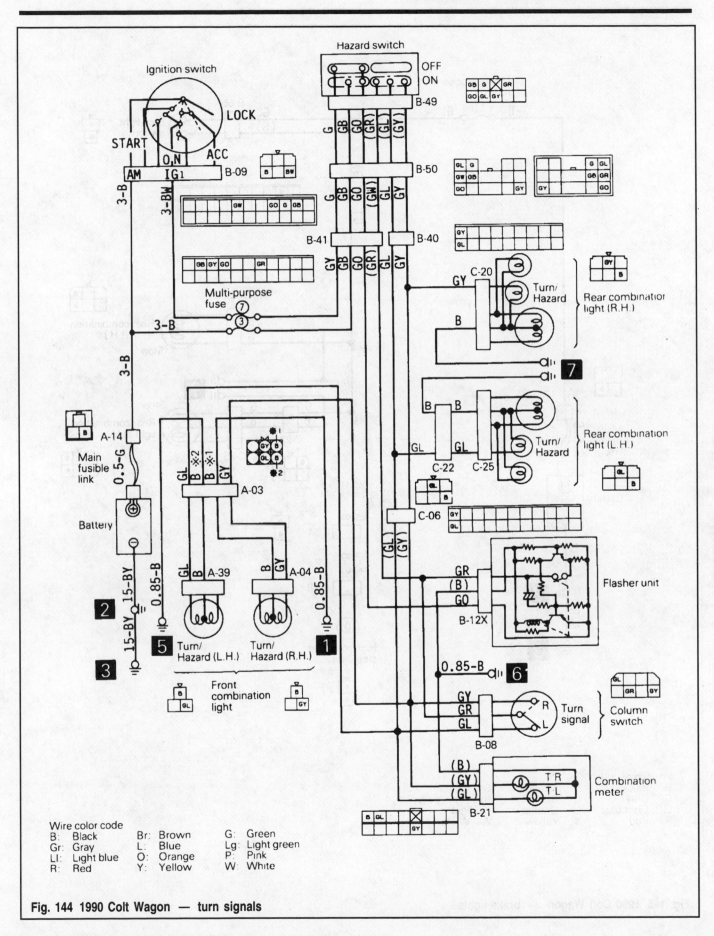

Fig. 144 1990 Colt Wagon — turn signals

Wire color code
B: Black
Gr: Gray
Ll: Light blue
R: Red
Br: Brown
L: Blue
O: Orange
Y: Yellow
G: Green
Lg: Light green
P: Pink
W: White

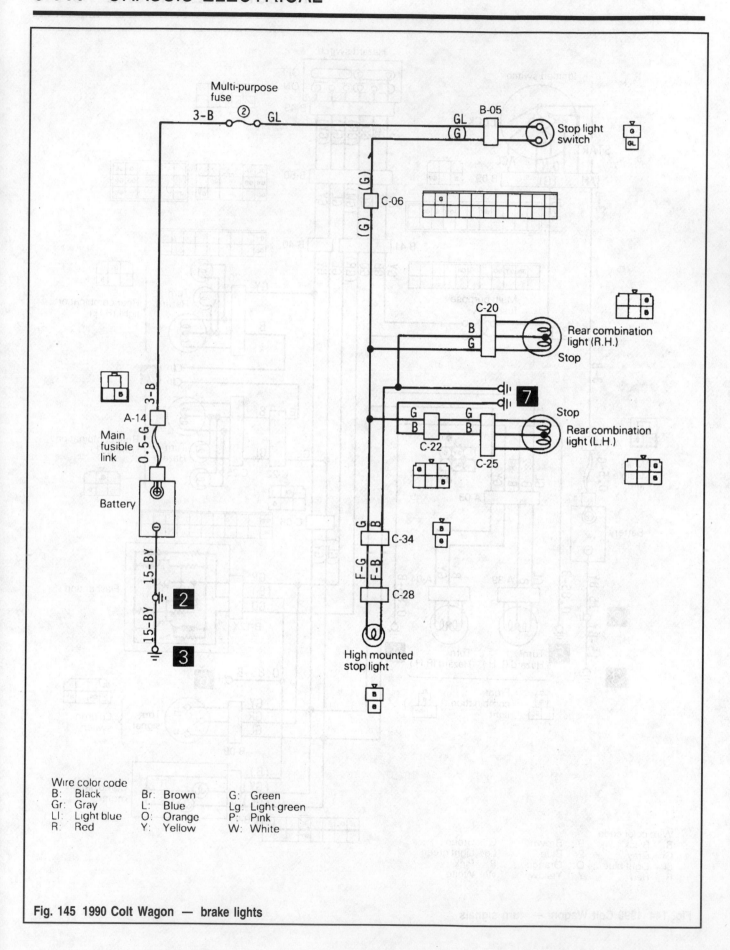

Fig. 145 1990 Colt Wagon — brake lights

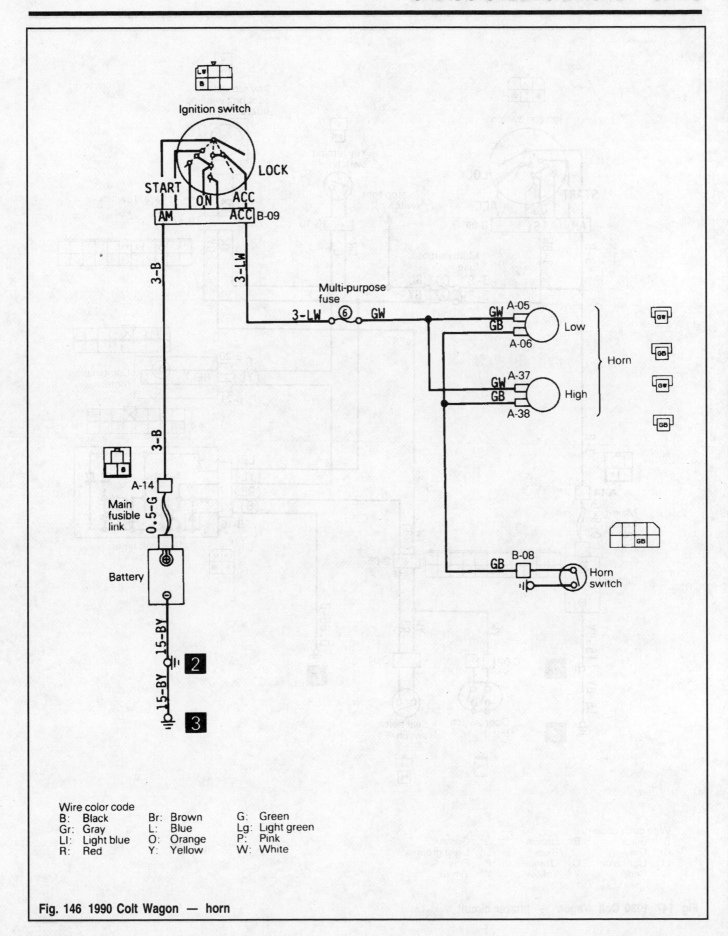

Fig. 146 1990 Colt Wagon — horn

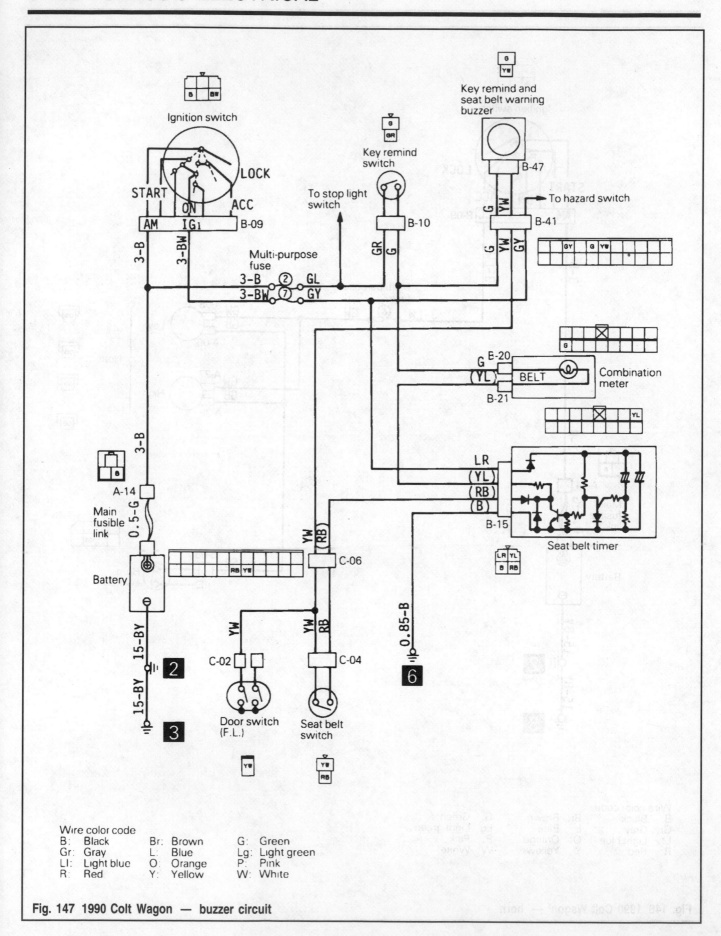

Fig. 147 1990 Colt Wagon — buzzer circuit

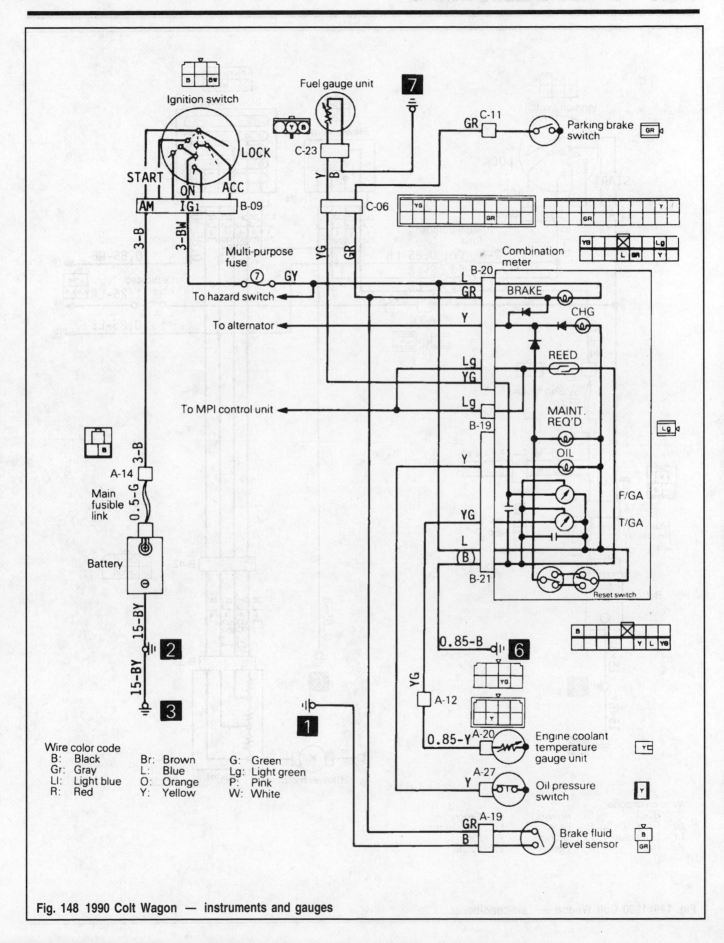

Fig. 148 1990 Colt Wagon — instruments and gauges

Wire color code
B: Black
Gr: Gray
Ll: Light blue
R: Red

Br: Brown
L: Blue
O: Orange
Y: Yellow

G: Green
Lg: Light green
P: Pink
W: White

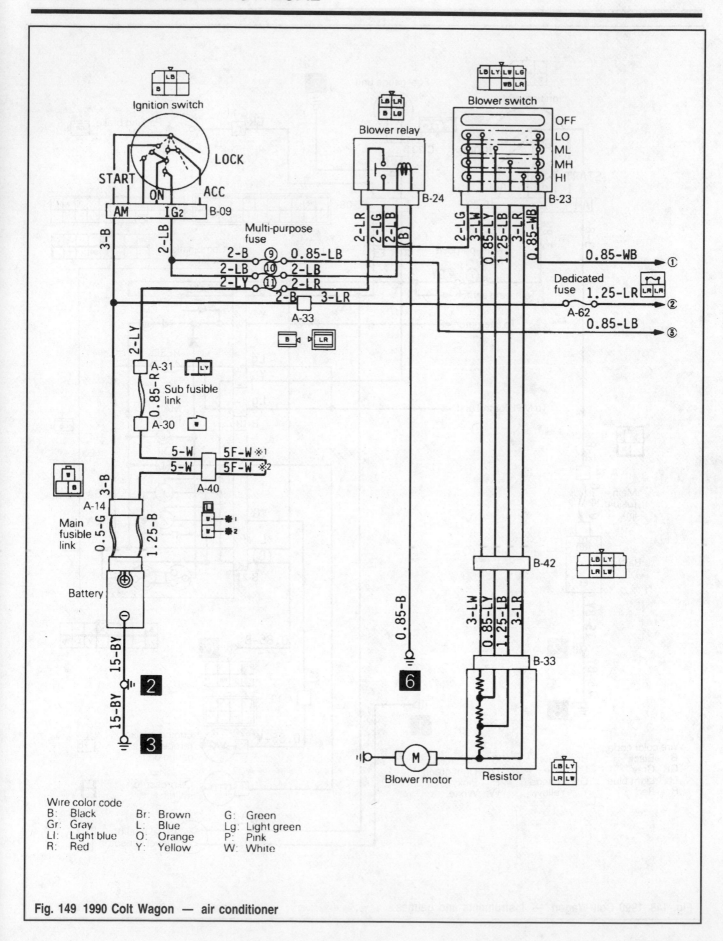

Fig. 149 1990 Colt Wagon — air conditioner

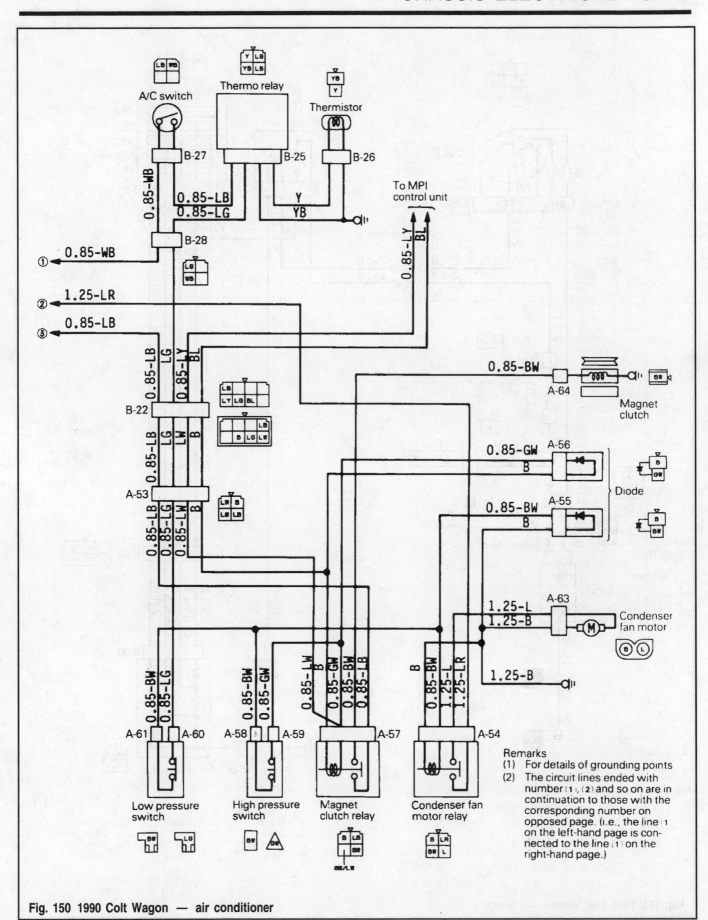

Fig. 150 1990 Colt Wagon — air conditioner

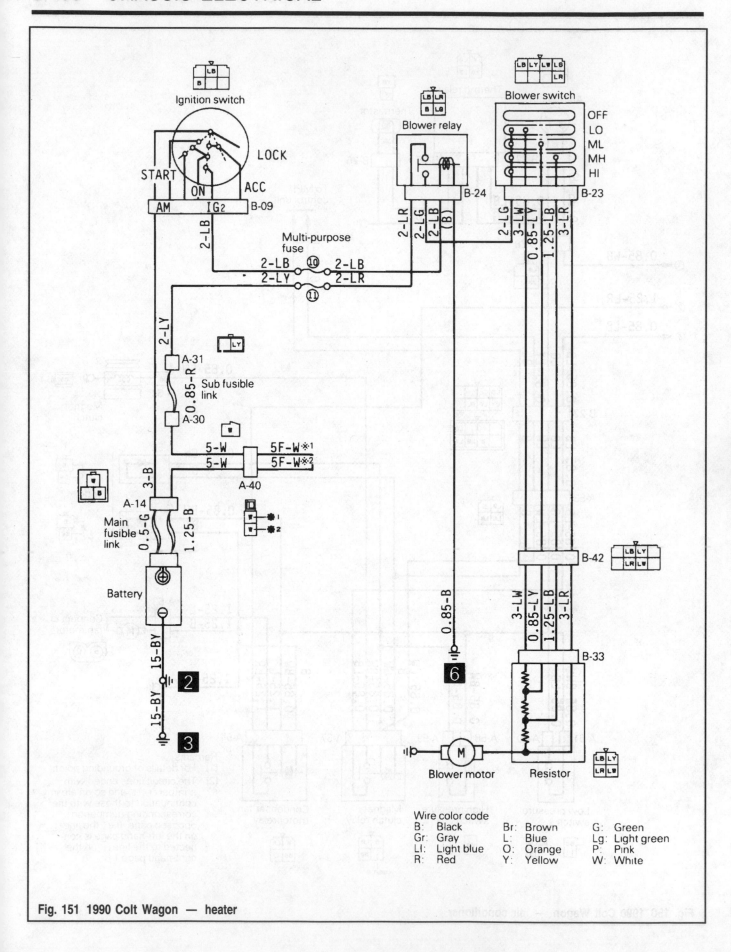

Fig. 151 1990 Colt Wagon — heater

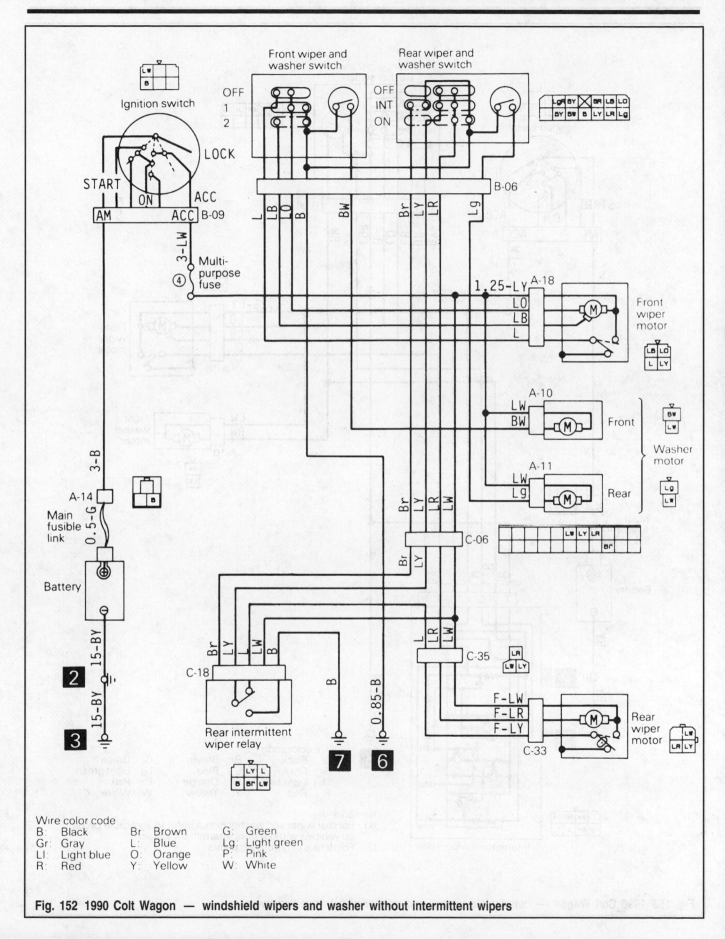

Fig. 152 1990 Colt Wagon — windshield wipers and washer without intermittent wipers

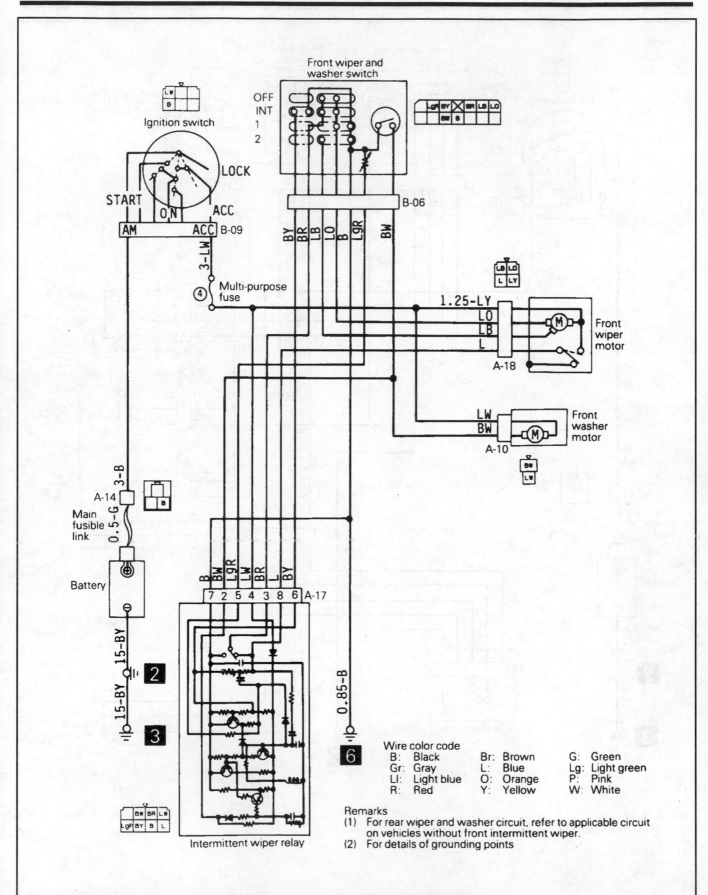

Fig. 153 1990 Colt Wagon — windshield wipers and washer with intermittent wipers

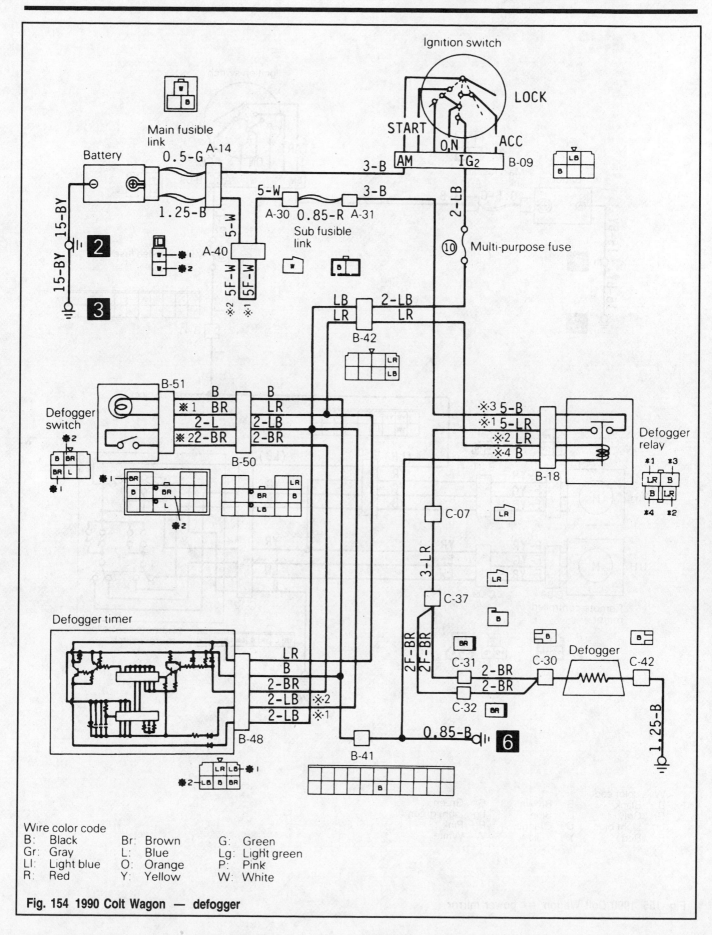

Fig. 154 1990 Colt Wagon — defogger

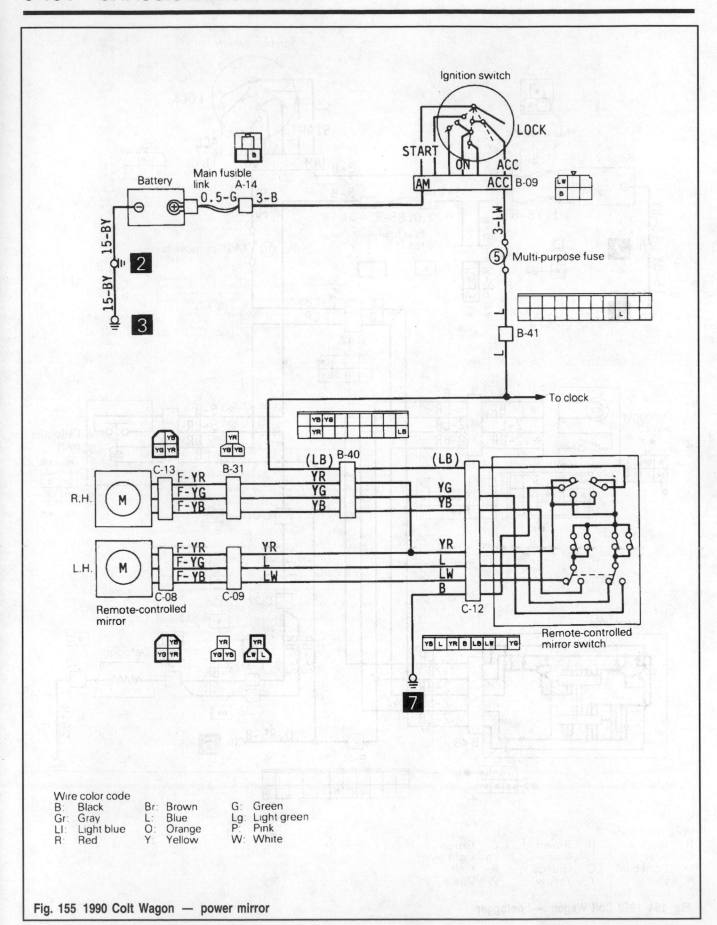

Fig. 155 1990 Colt Wagon — power mirror

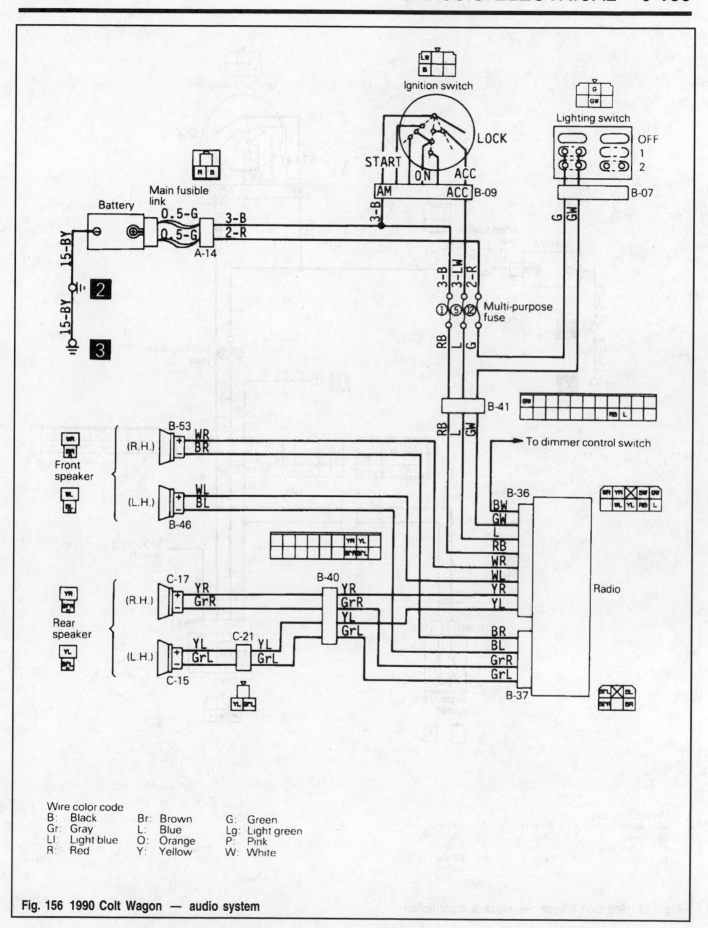

Fig. 156 1990 Colt Wagon — audio system

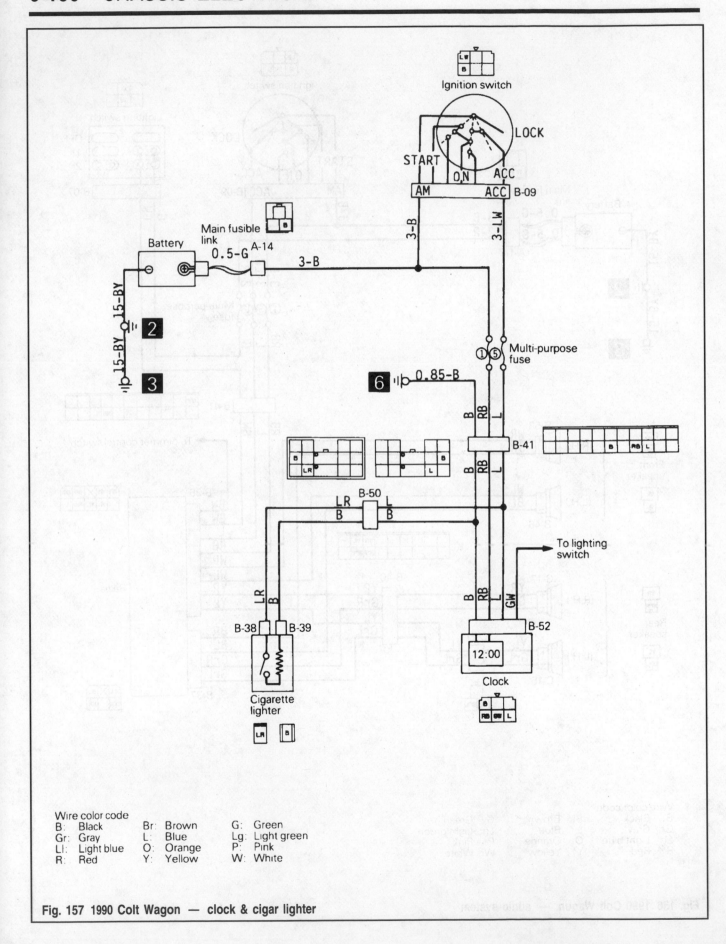

Fig. 157 1990 Colt Wagon — clock & cigar lighter

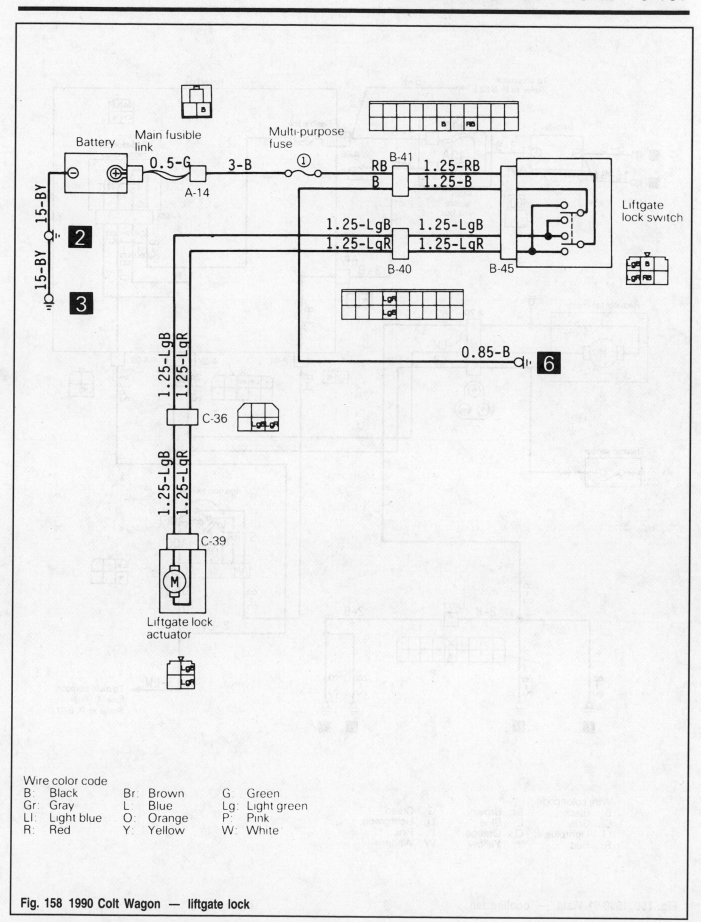

Fig. 158 1990 Colt Wagon — liftgate lock

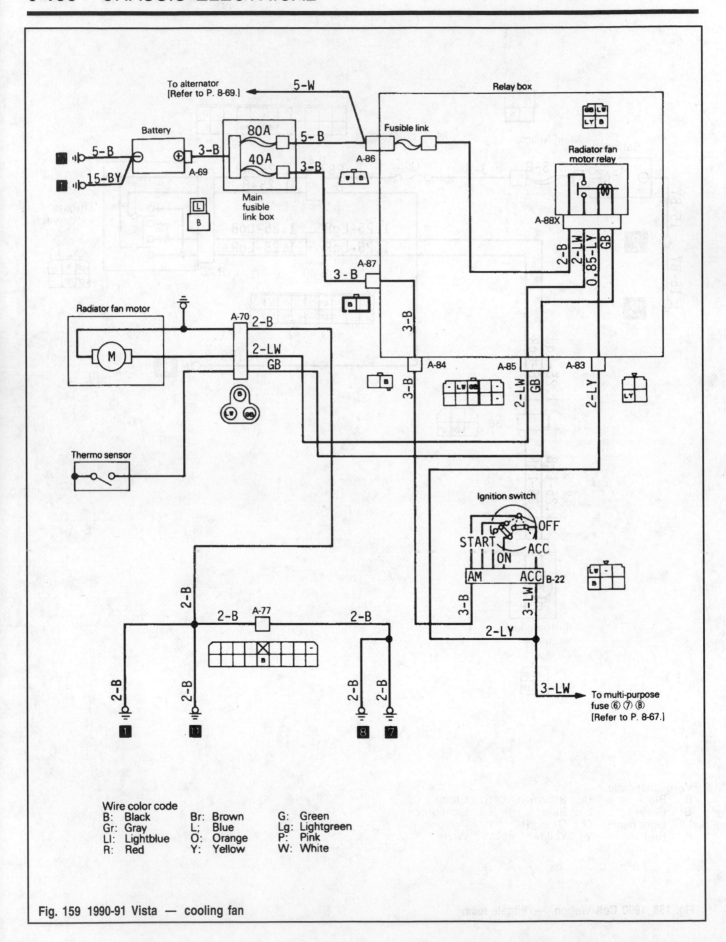

Fig. 159 1990-91 Vista — cooling fan

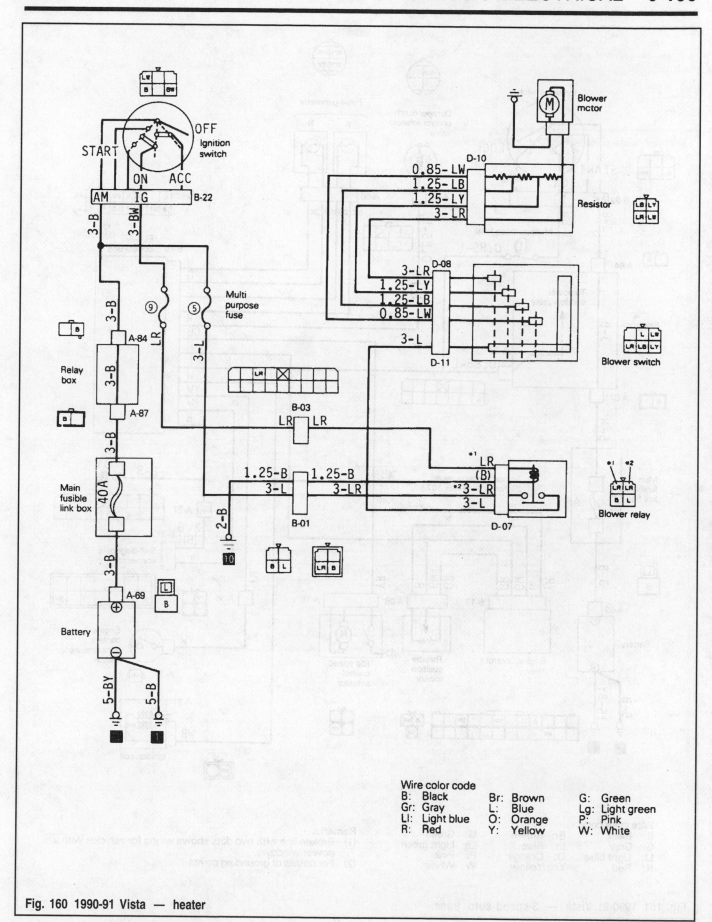

Fig. 160 1990-91 Vista — heater

Wire color code

B: Black	Br: Brown	G: Green
Gr: Gray	L: Blue	Lg: Light green
Ll: Light blue	O: Orange	P: Pink
R: Red	Y: Yellow	W: White

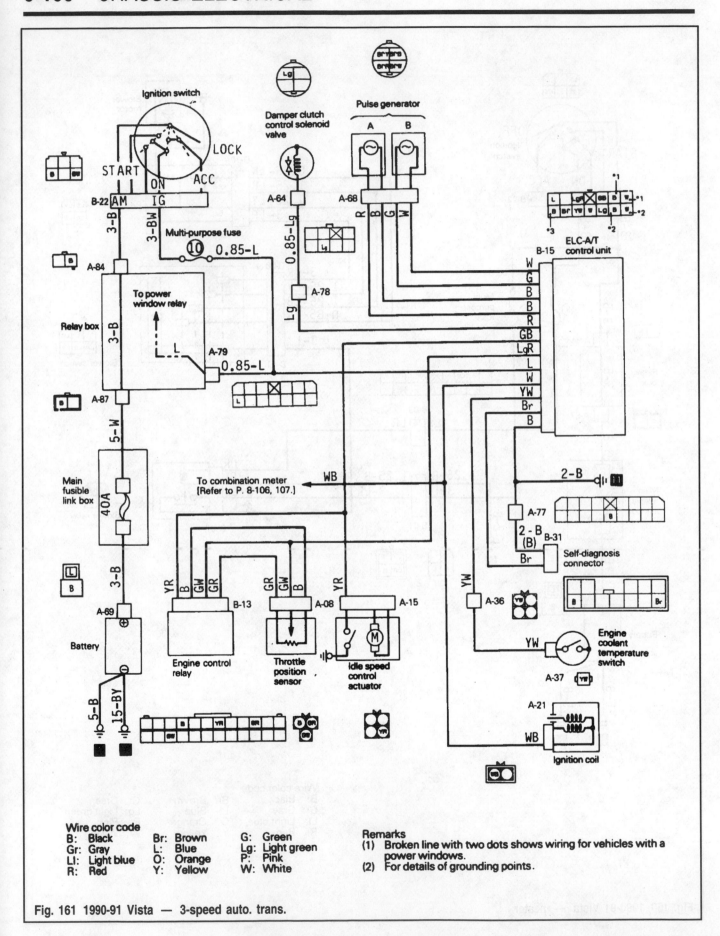

Fig. 161 1990-91 Vista — 3-speed auto. trans.

Wire color code
B: Black Br: Brown G: Green
Gr: Gray L: Blue Lg: Light green
LI: Light blue O: Orange P: Pink
R: Red Y: Yellow W: White

Remarks
(1) Broken line with two dots shows wiring for vehicles with a power windows.
(2) For details of grounding points.

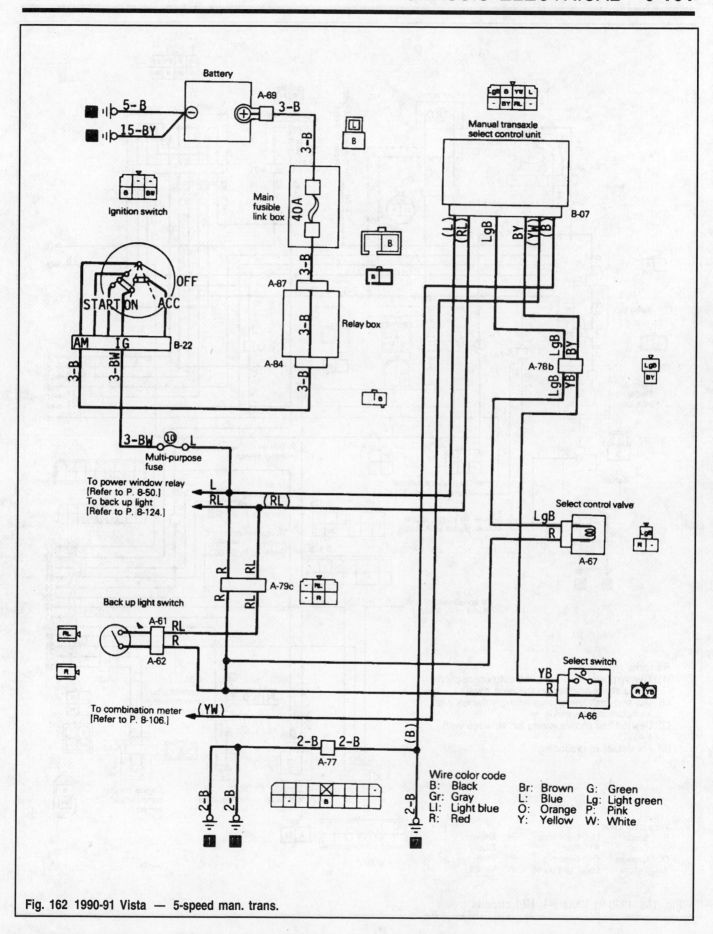

Fig. 162 1990-91 Vista — 5-speed man. trans.

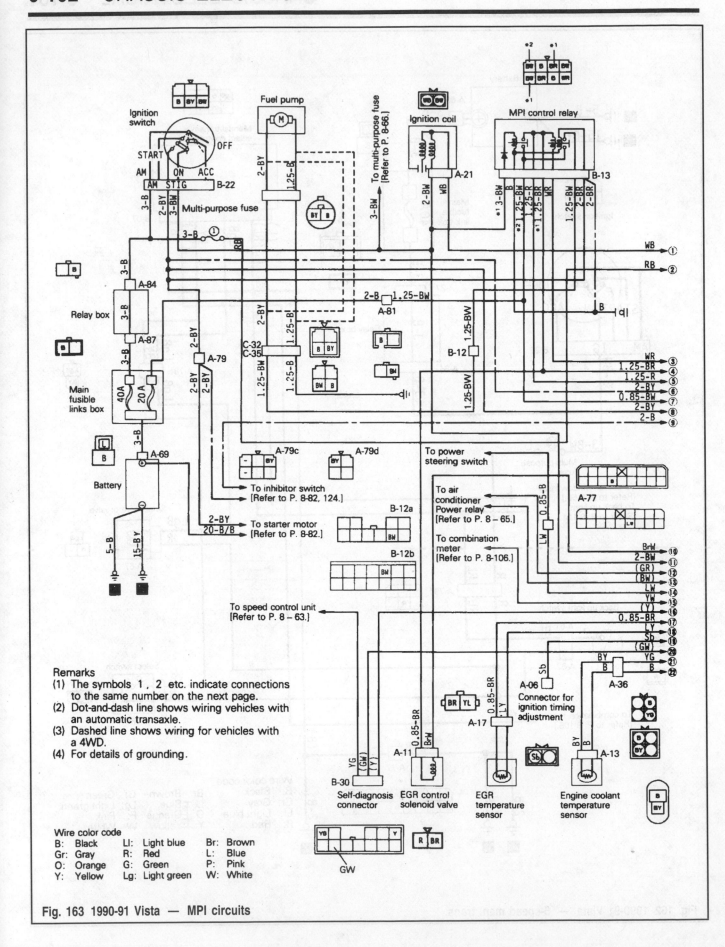

Fig. 163 1990-91 Vista — MPI circuits

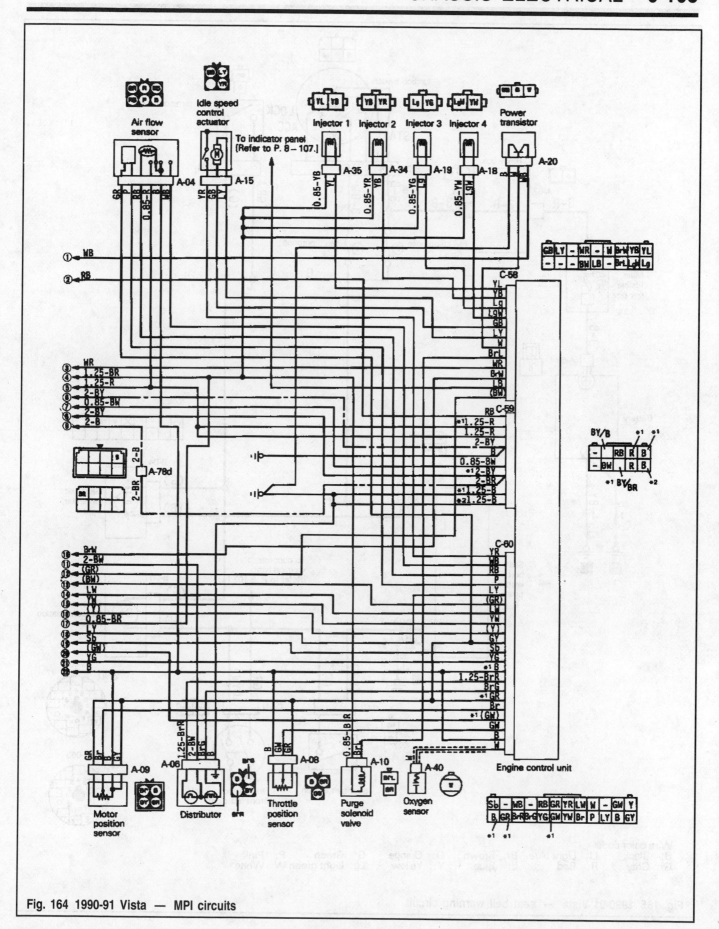

Fig. 164 1990-91 Vista — MPI circuits

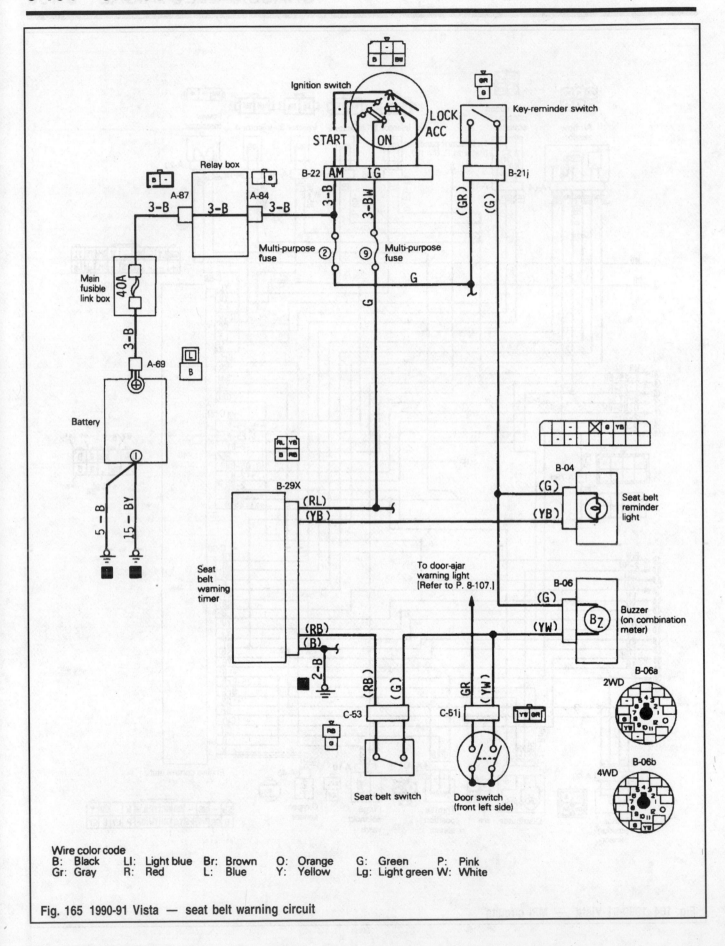

Ignition switch

LOCK
ACC
ON
START

Key-reminder switch

Relay box

Multi-purpose fuse

Multi-purpose fuse

Main fusible link box

40A

Battery

Seat belt warning timer

Seat belt reminder light

To door-ajar warning light [Refer to P. 8-107.]

Buzzer (on combination meter)

2WD

Seat belt switch

Door switch (front left side)

4WD

Wire color code
B: Black   LI: Light blue   Br: Brown   O: Orange   G: Green   P: Pink
Gr: Gray   R: Red   L: Blue   Y: Yellow   Lg: Light green W: White

Fig. 165 1990-91 Vista — seat belt warning circuit

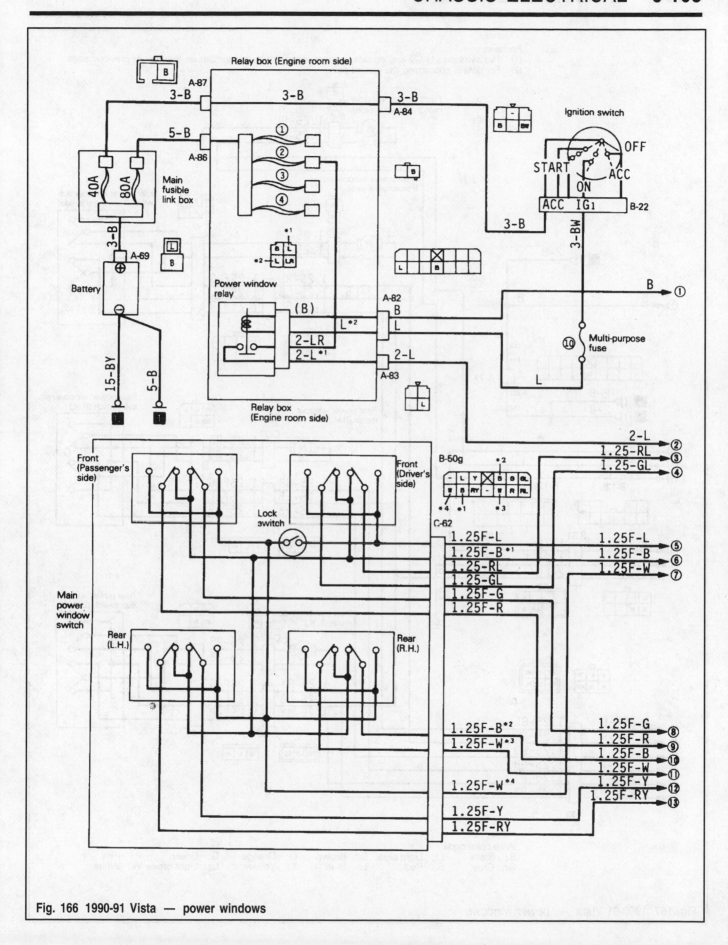

Fig. 166 1990-91 Vista — power windows

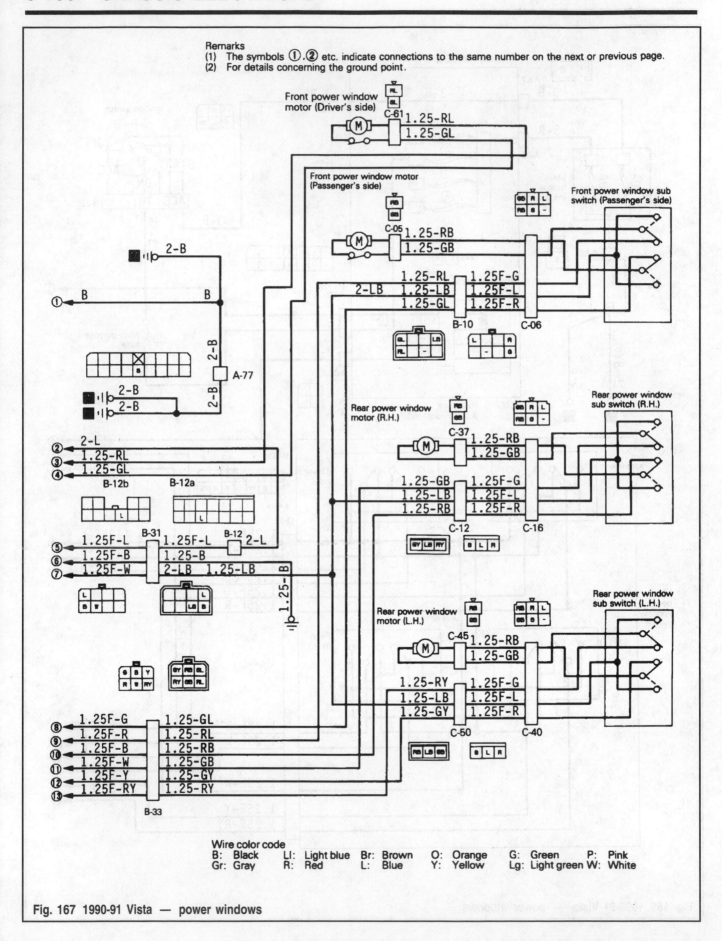

Fig. 167 1990-91 Vista — power windows

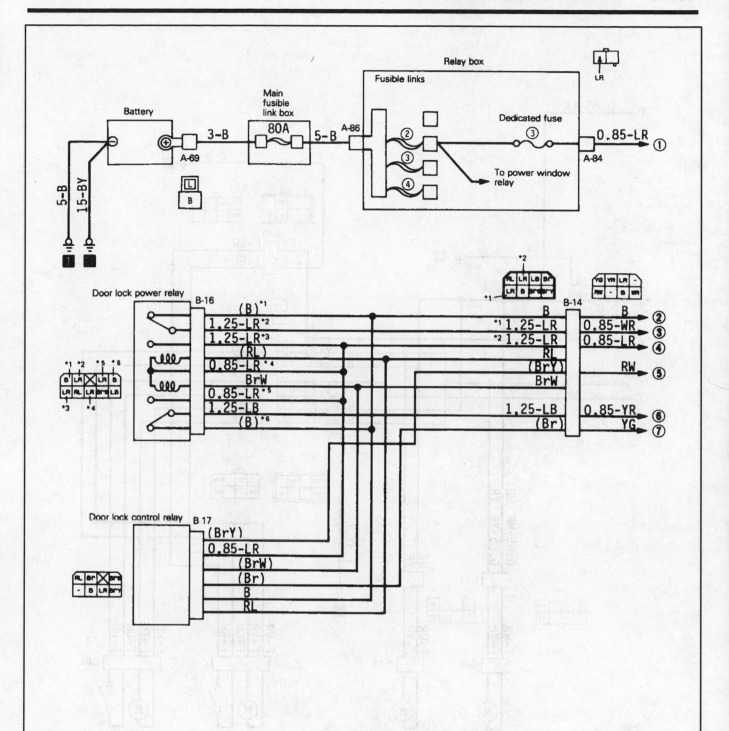

Remarks
(1) The symbols ①, ②, etc. indicate connections to the same number on the next or previous page.
(2) For details concerning the ground point.

Wire color code

B:	Black	LI:	Light blue	Br:	Brown	O:	Orange	G:	Green	P:	Pink
Gr:	Gray	R:	Red	L:	Blue	Y:	Yellow	Lg:	Light green	W:	White

Fig. 168 1990-91 Vista — power door locks

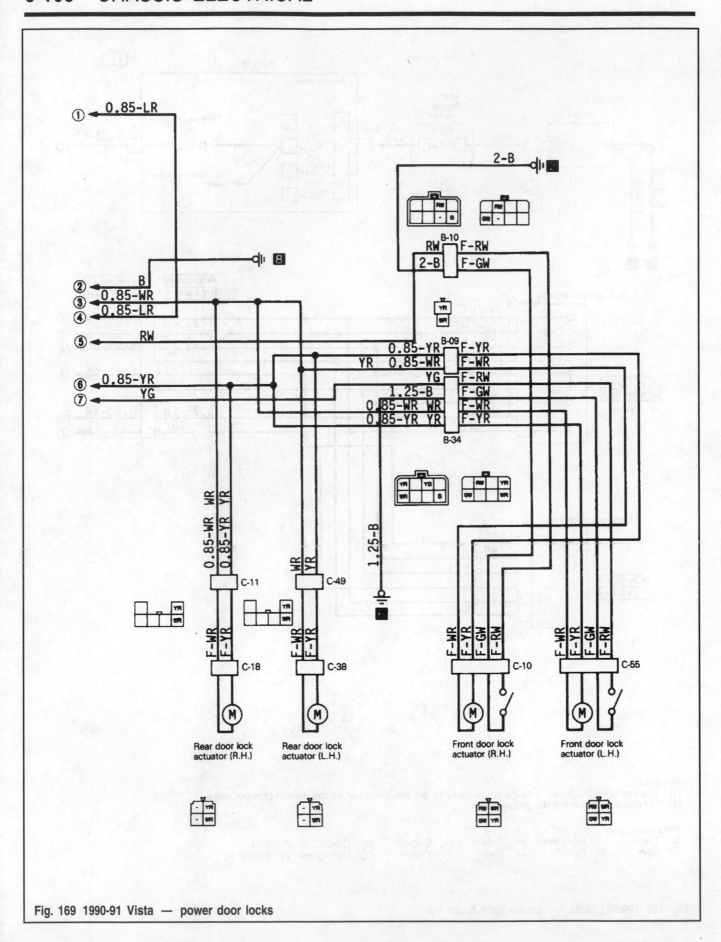

Fig. 169 1990-91 Vista — power door locks

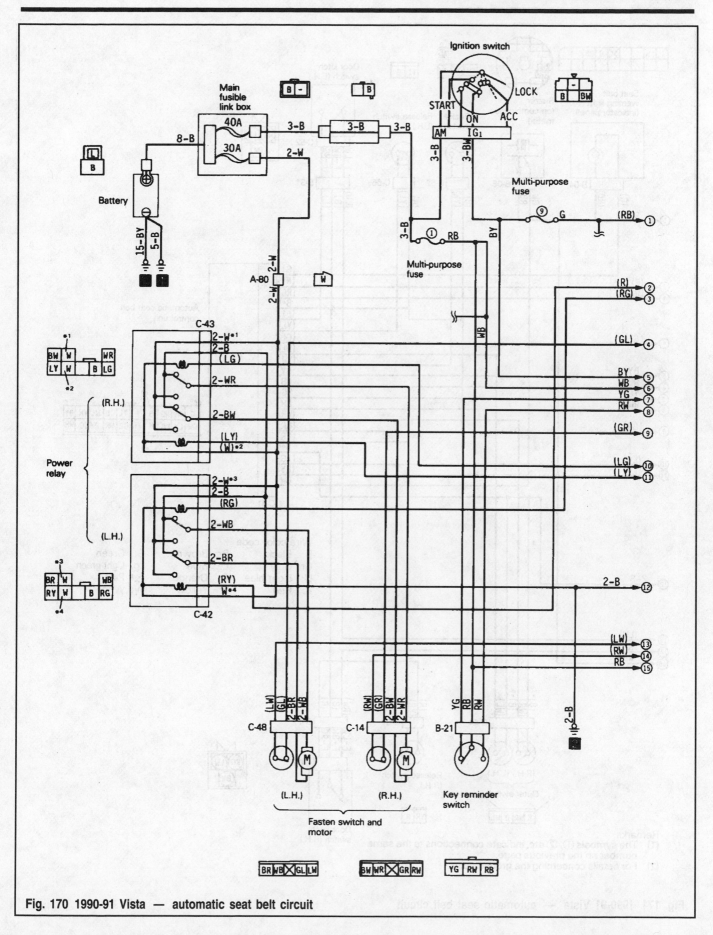

Fig. 170 1990-91 Vista — automatic seat belt circuit

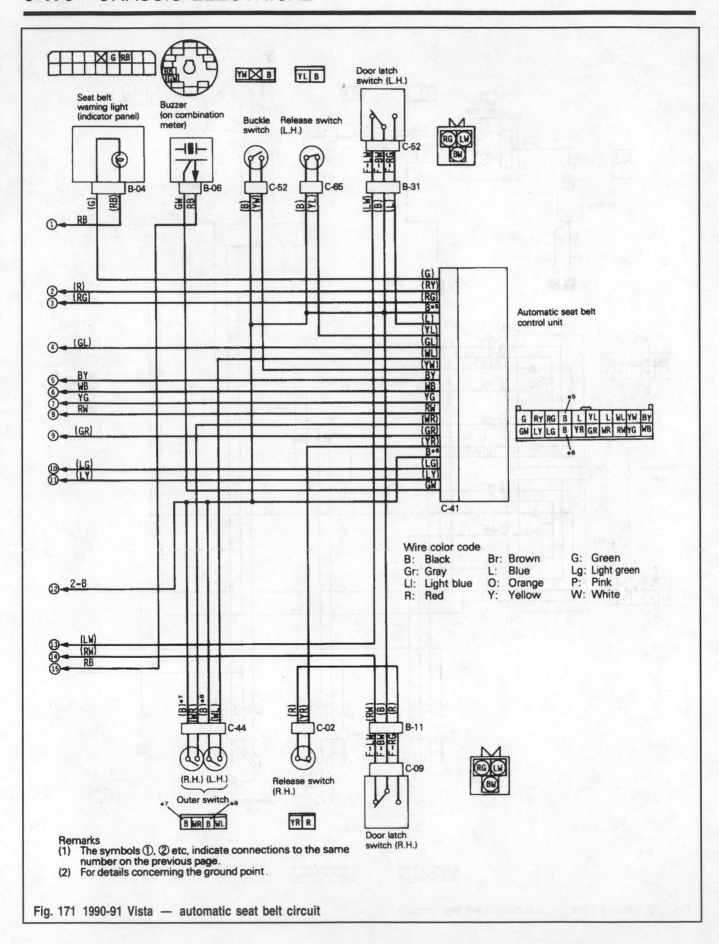

Wire color code
B:	Black	Br:	Brown	G:	Green
Gr:	Gray	L:	Blue	Lg:	Light green
Ll:	Light blue	O:	Orange	P:	Pink
R:	Red	Y:	Yellow	W:	White

Remarks
(1) The symbols ①, ② etc, indicate connections to the same number on the previous page.
(2) For details concerning the ground point.

Fig. 171 1990-91 Vista — automatic seat belt circuit

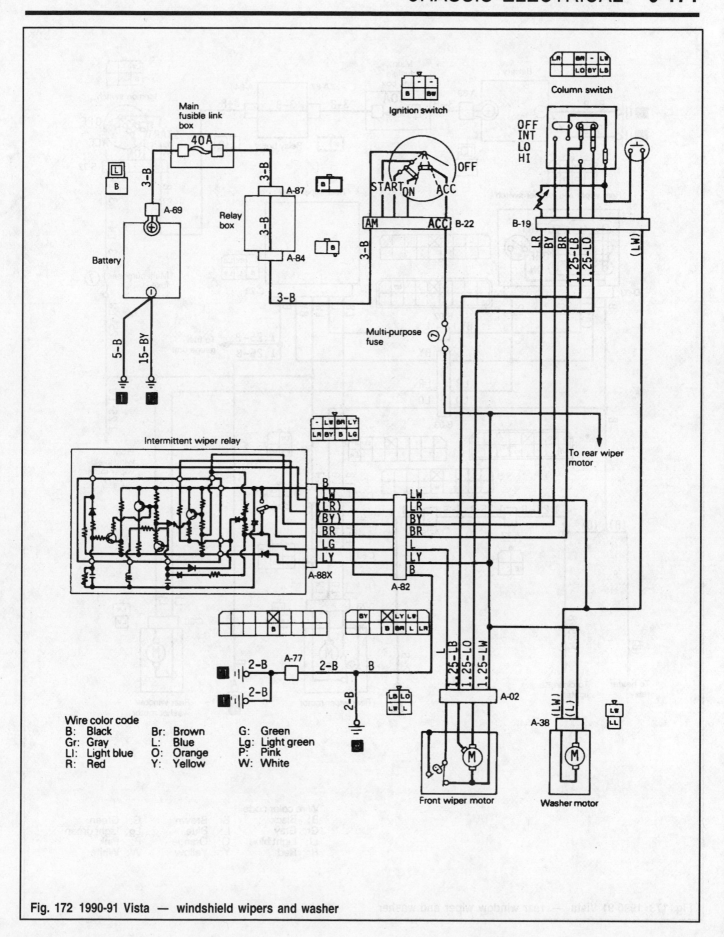

Fig. 172 1990-91 Vista — windshield wipers and washer

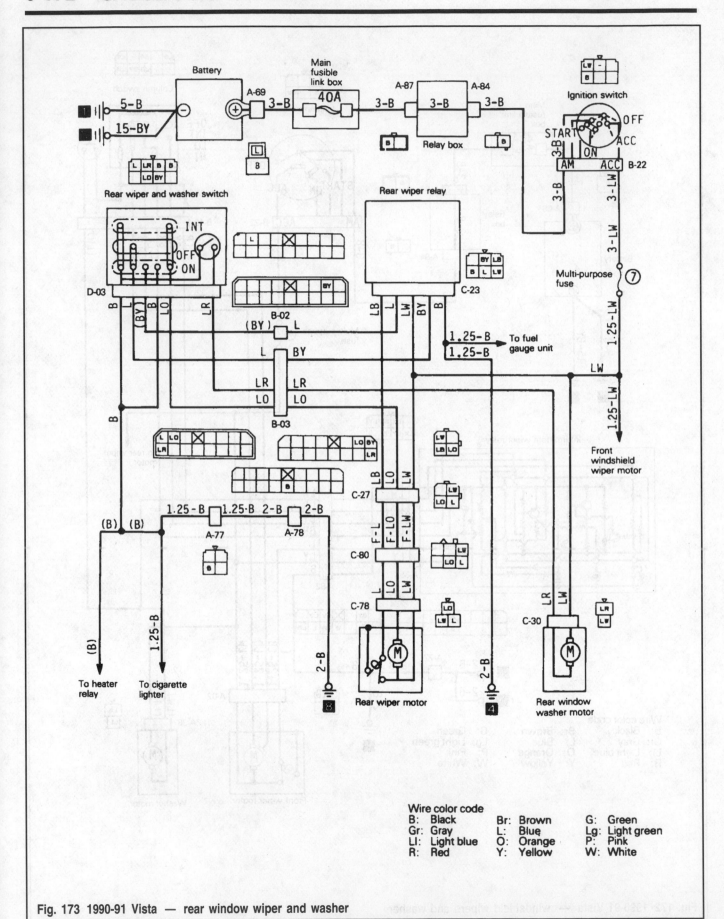

Wire color code
B: Black
Gr: Gray
Ll: Light blue
R: Red

Br: Brown
L: Blue
O: Orange
Y: Yellow

G: Green
Lg: Light green
P: Pink
W: White

Fig. 173 1990-91 Vista — rear window wiper and washer

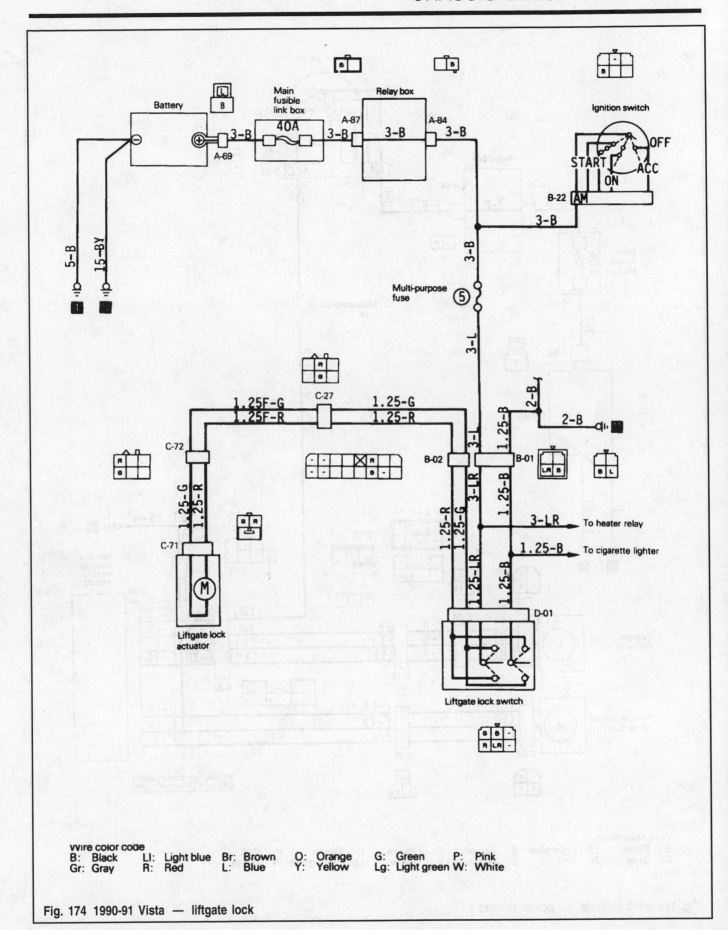

Fig. 174 1990-91 Vista — liftgate lock

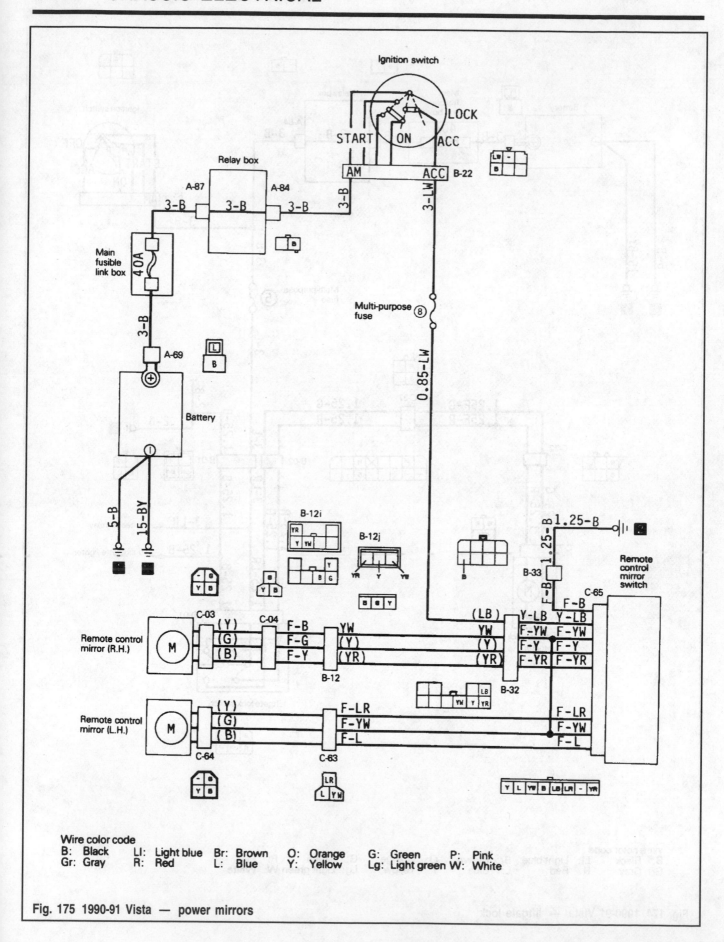

Fig. 175 1990-91 Vista — power mirrors

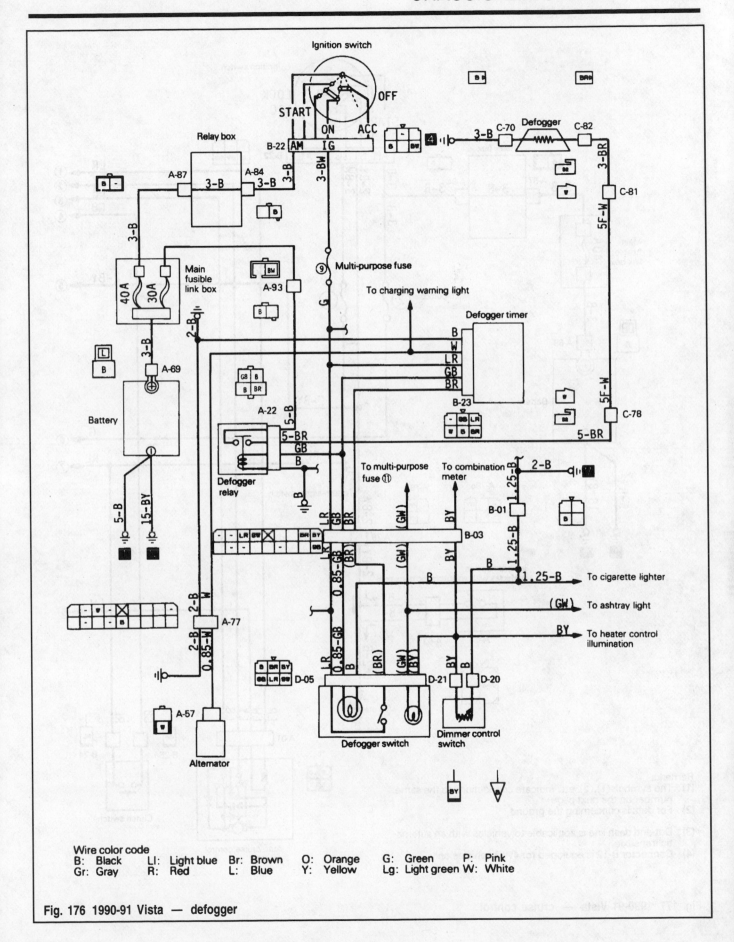

Wire color code
B: Black   Ll: Light blue   Br: Brown   O: Orange   G: Green   P: Pink
Gr: Gray   R: Red   L: Blue   Y: Yellow   Lg: Light green   W: White

Fig. 176 1990-91 Vista — defogger

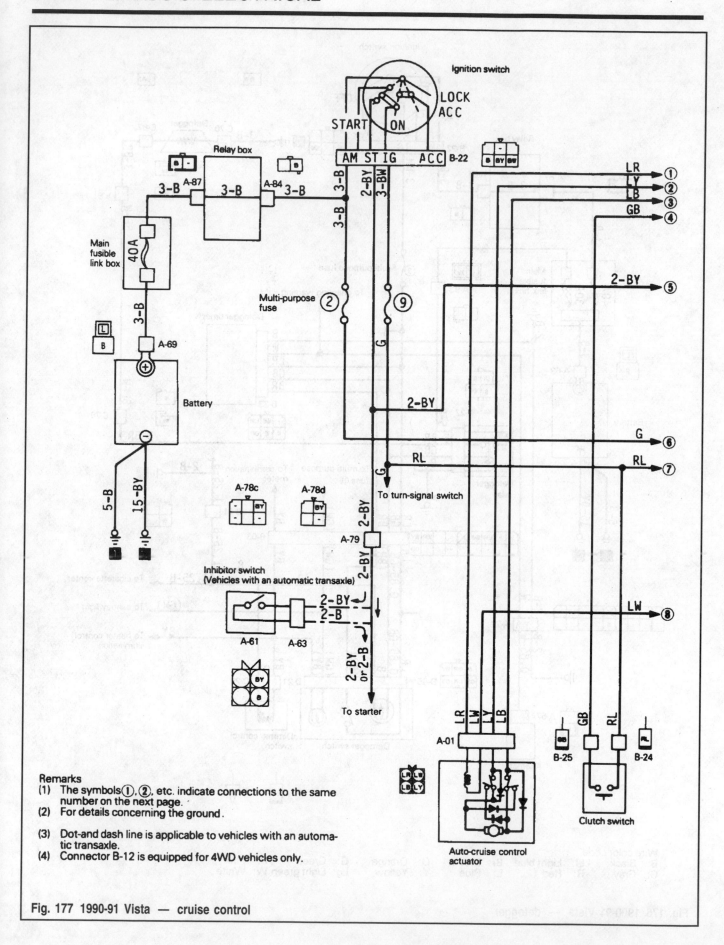

Remarks
(1) The symbols ①, ②, etc. indicate connections to the same number on the next page.
(2) For details concerning the ground.

(3) Dot-and dash line is applicable to vehicles with an automatic transaxle.
(4) Connector B-12 is equipped for 4WD vehicles only.

Fig. 177 1990-91 Vista — cruise control

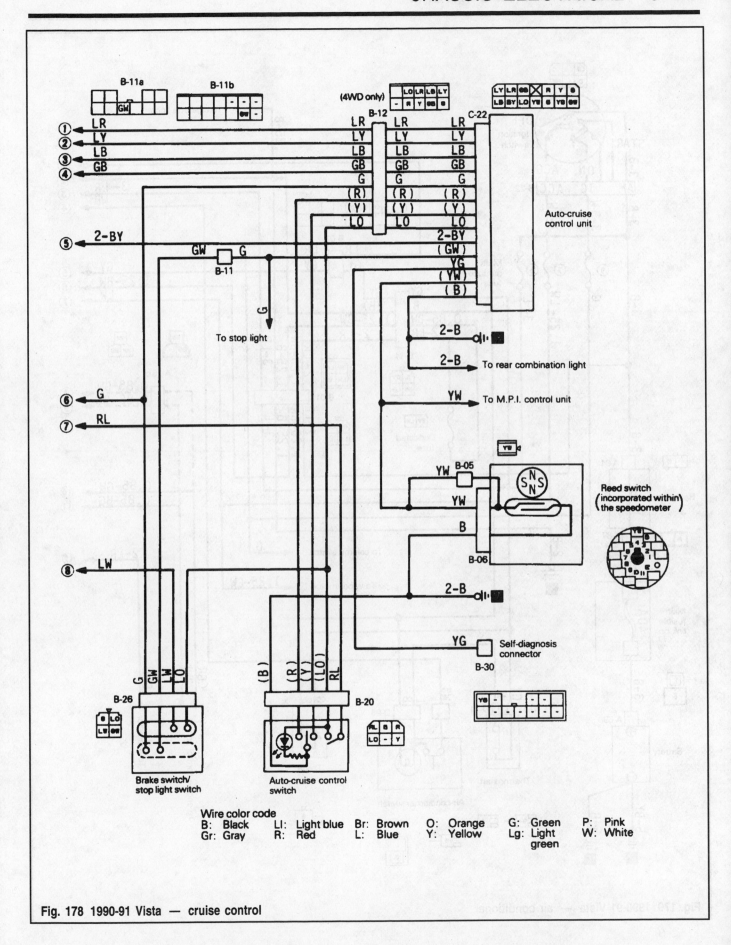

Fig. 178 1990-91 Vista — cruise control

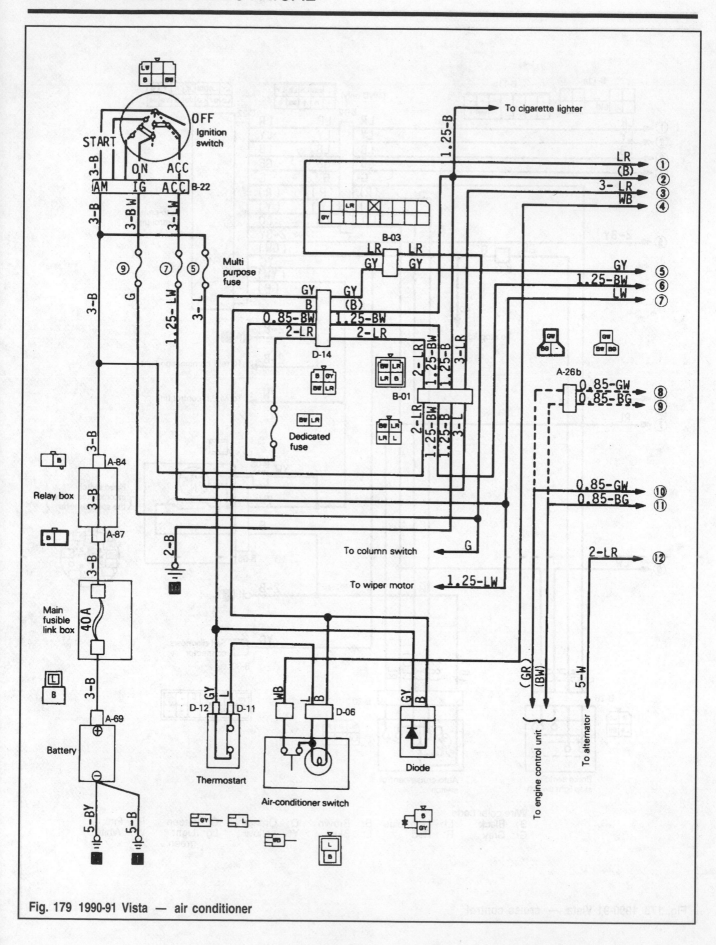

Fig. 179 1990-91 Vista — air conditioner

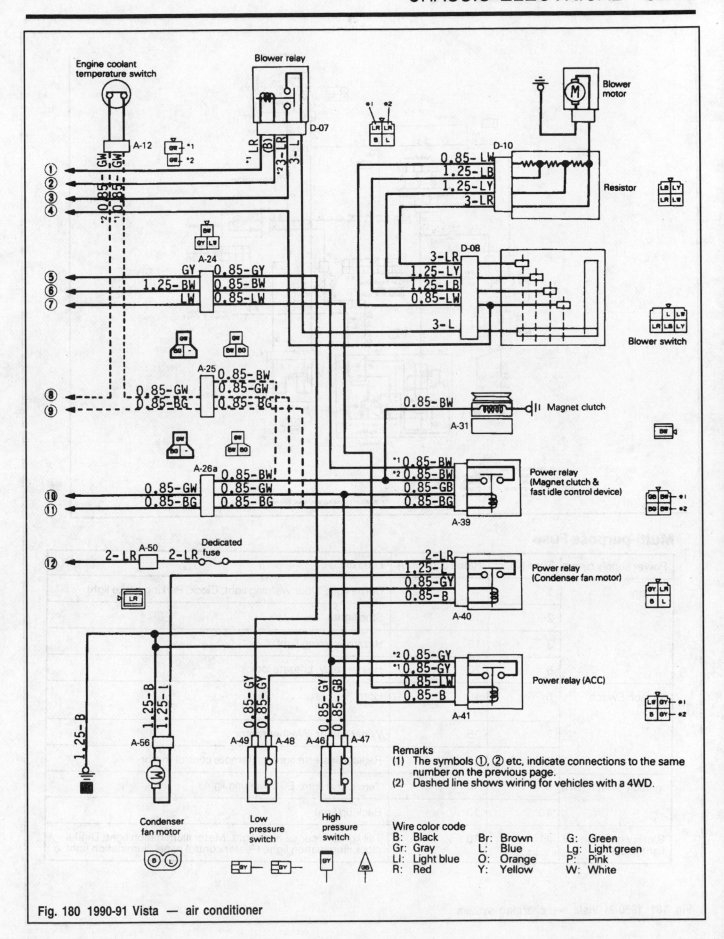

Fig. 180 1990-91 Vista — air conditioner

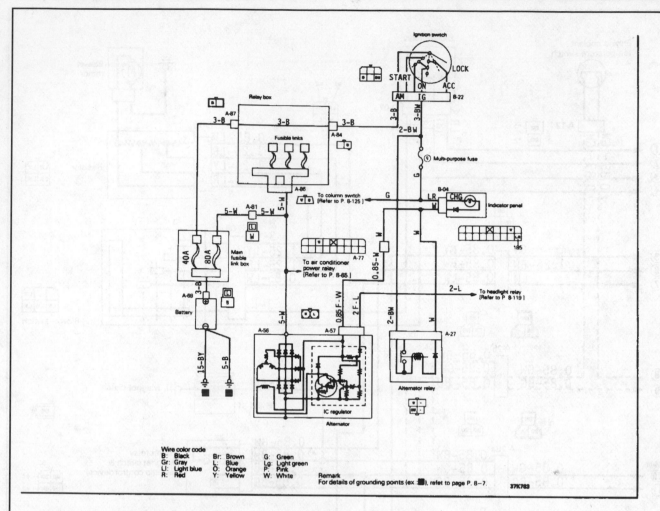

Multi-purpose Fuse

Power supply circuit	Fuse No.	Rated capacity A	Load circuit
Battery	1	10	Dome light, Door warning light, Clock, Parking brake light
	2	10	Stop lights
	3	10	Hazard warning light
	5	20	Heater relay, Liftgate lock
Ignition Switch (ACC)	6	10	Horn
	7	15	Wiper motor, Washer motor
	8	15	Radio, Cigarette lighter, Remote control mirror
Ignition Switch (ON)	9	10	Turn-signal light, EGR warning light
	10	10	Back-up light
Battery (through tail light relay)	11	10	Tail lights, License plate light, Meter illumination light, Digital clock illumination light, Heater control panel illumination light

Fig. 181 1990-91 Vista — charging system

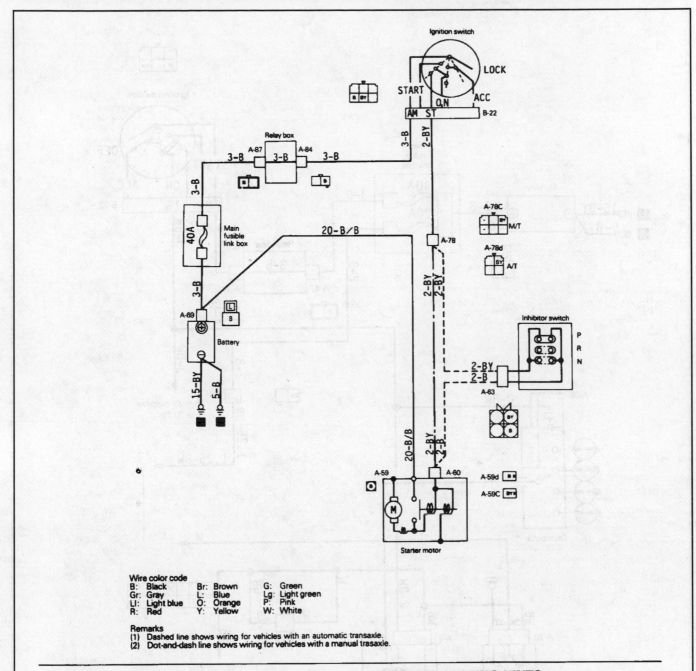

Wire color code
B: Black   Br: Brown   G: Green
Gr: Gray   L: Blue   Lg: Light green
Ll: Light blue O: Orange   P: Pink
R: Red   Y: Yellow   W: White

Remarks
(1) Dashed line shows wiring for vehicles with an automatic transaxle.
(2) Dot-and-dash line shows wiring for vehicles with a manual transaxle.

OPERATION
- When the ignition switch is turned to "START" with the inhibitor switch in "P" or "N" position (automatic transaxle vehicles), current flows through the inhibitor switch and starter coil to ground. This closes the contacts of the starter switch (magnetic switch).
- Closing the magnetic switch contacts completes the circuit from the battery to magnetic switch to starter motor and ground, so that the starter motor starts rotating.

TROUBLESHOOTING HINTS
1. Starter motor does not turn over
   1) Starter motor operating sound is heard for an instant
      - Check starter motor for condition of its magnetic switch.
   2) Starter motor does not operate at all
      - Check starter motor coils.
2. Starter motor does not stop
   - Check starter motor for condition of its magnetic switch.

Fig. 182 1990-91 Vista — starting system

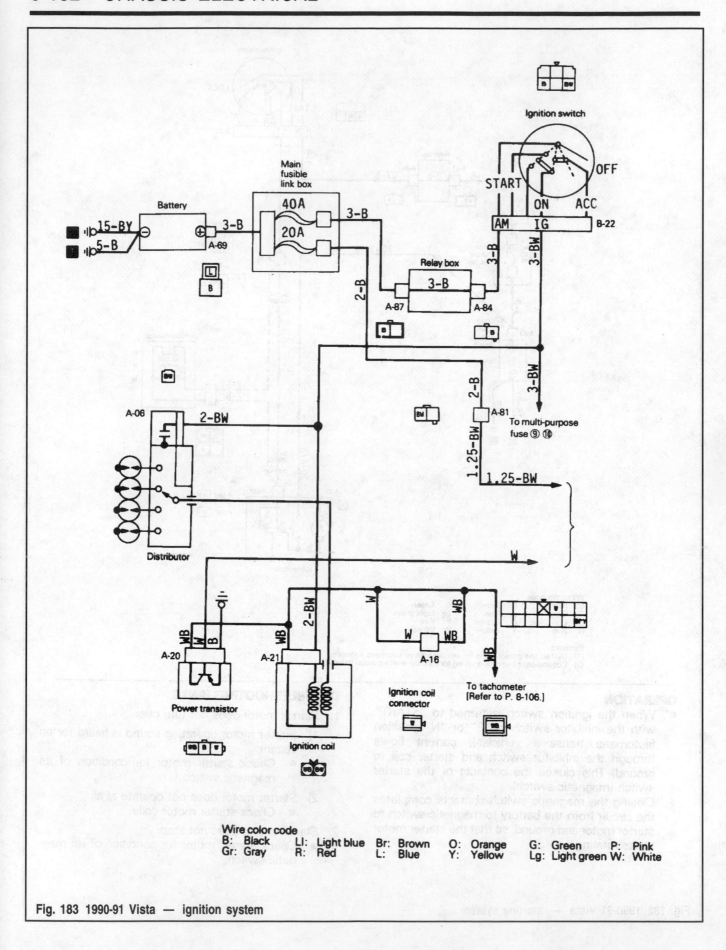

Fig. 183 1990-91 Vista — ignition system

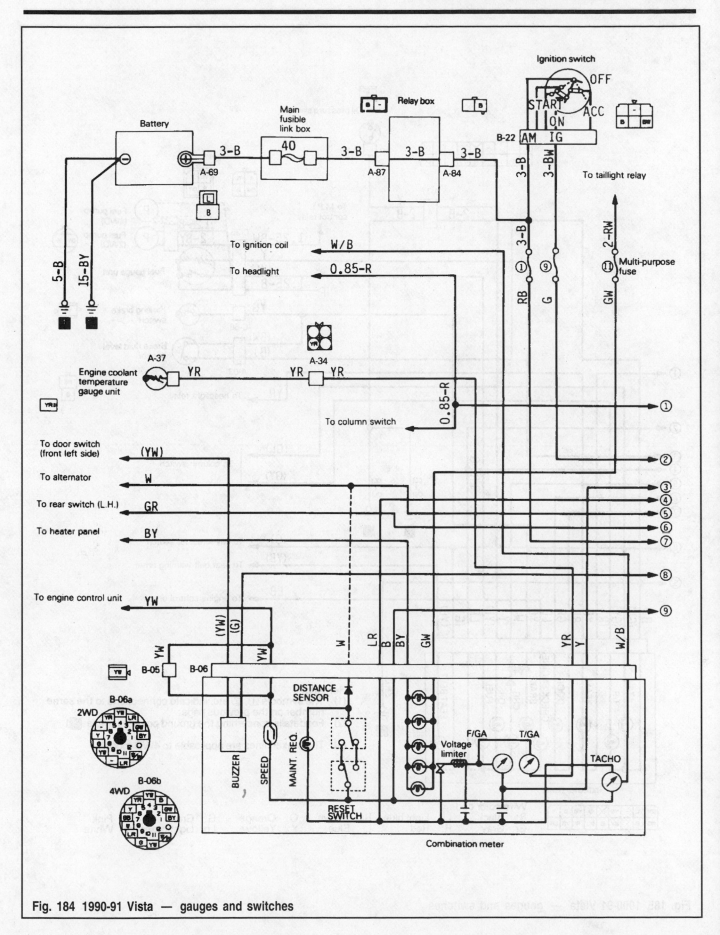

Fig. 184 1990-91 Vista — gauges and switches

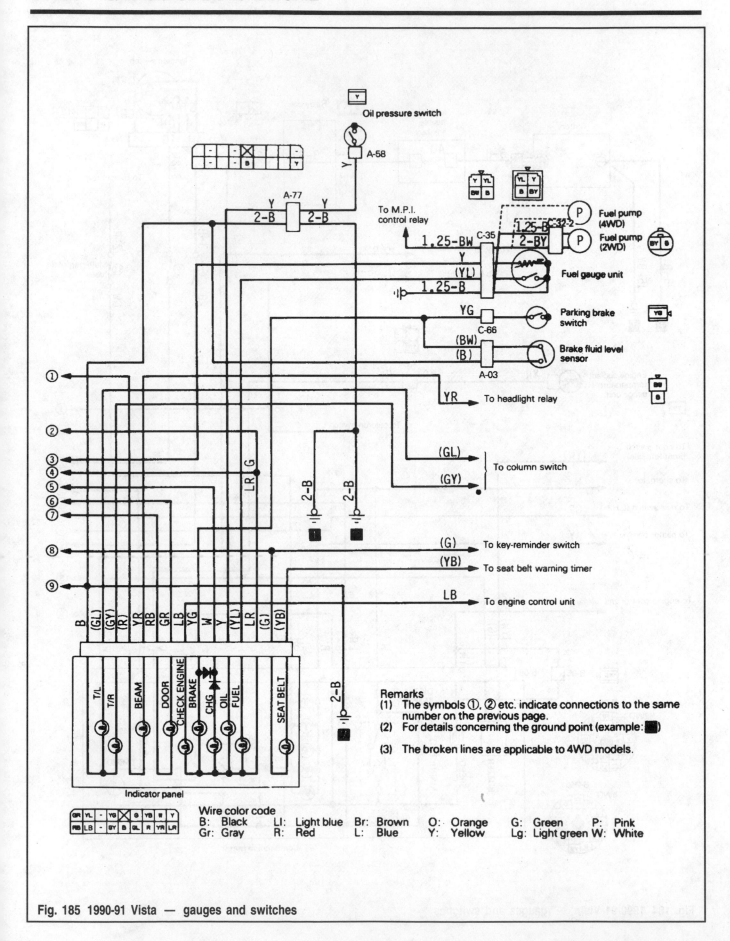

Fig. 185 *1990-91 Vista — gauges and switches*

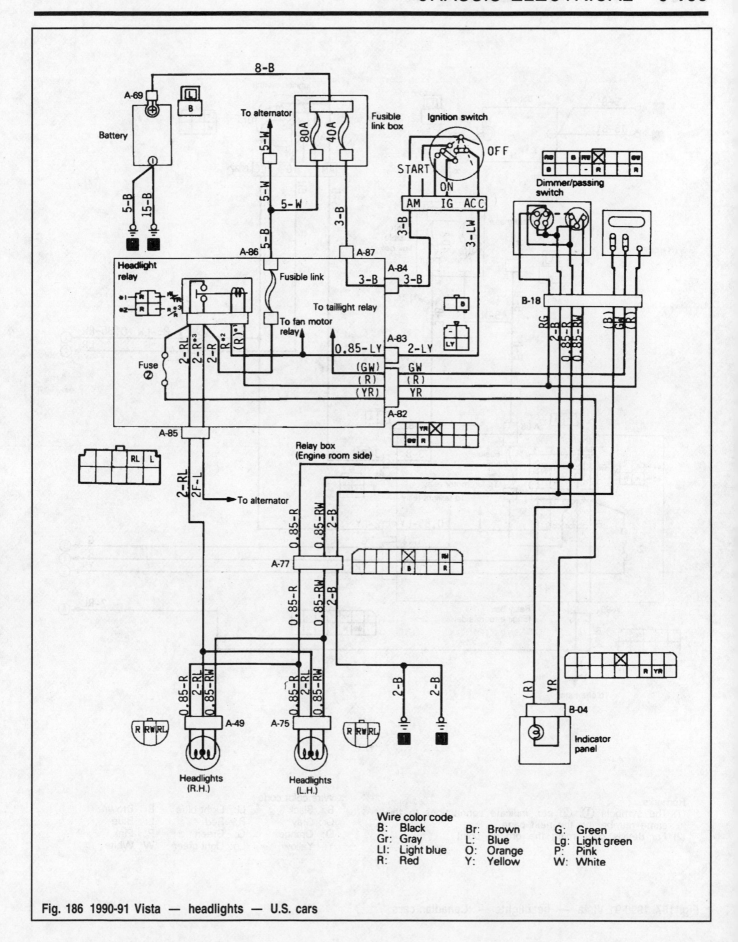

Fig. 186 1990-91 Vista — headlights — U.S. cars

Wire color code

B: Black	Br: Brown	G: Green
Gr: Gray	L: Blue	Lg: Light green
Ll: Light blue	O: Orange	P: Pink
R: Red	Y: Yellow	W: White

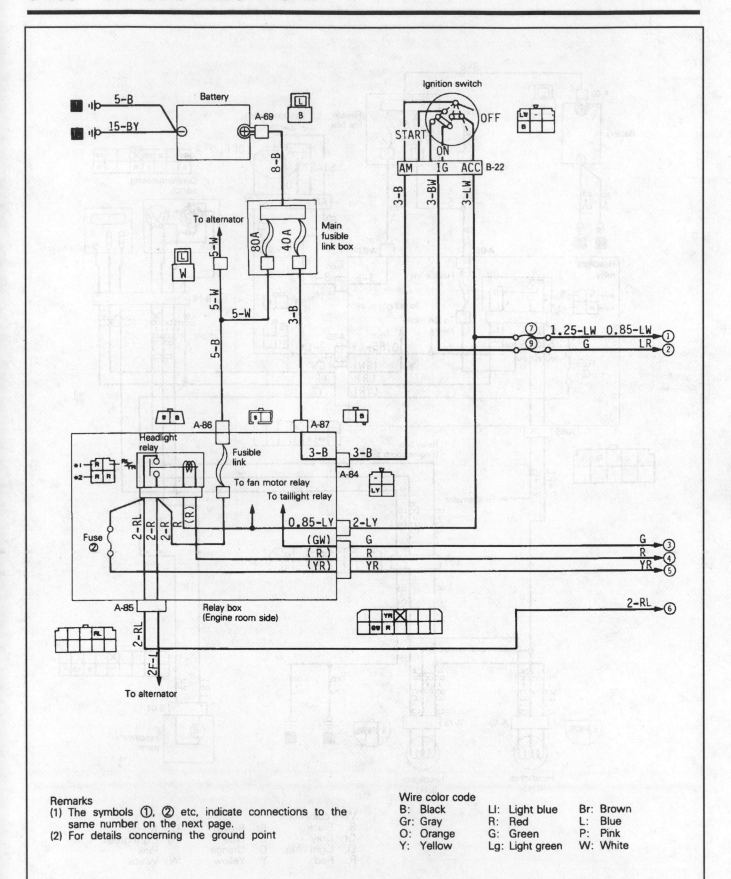

Remarks
(1) The symbols ①, ② etc, indicate connections to the same number on the next page.
(2) For details concerning the ground point

Wire color code

B: Black	LI: Light blue	Br: Brown
Gr: Gray	R: Red	L: Blue
O: Orange	G: Green	P: Pink
Y: Yellow	Lg: Light green	W: White

Fig. 187 1990-91 Vista — headlights — Canadian cars

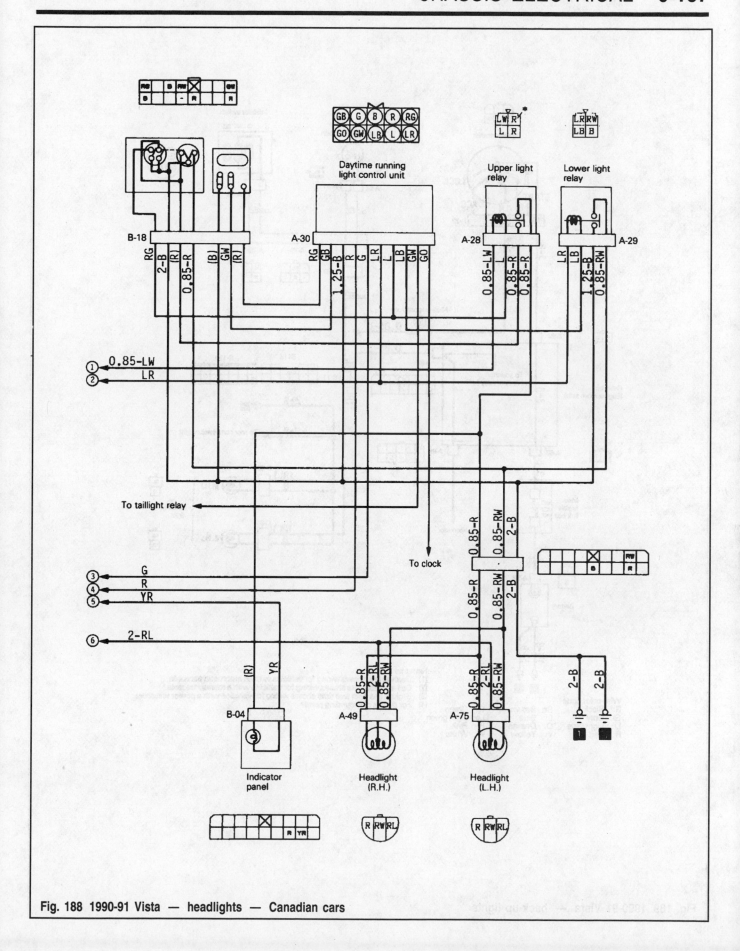

Fig. 188 1990-91 Vista — headlights — Canadian cars

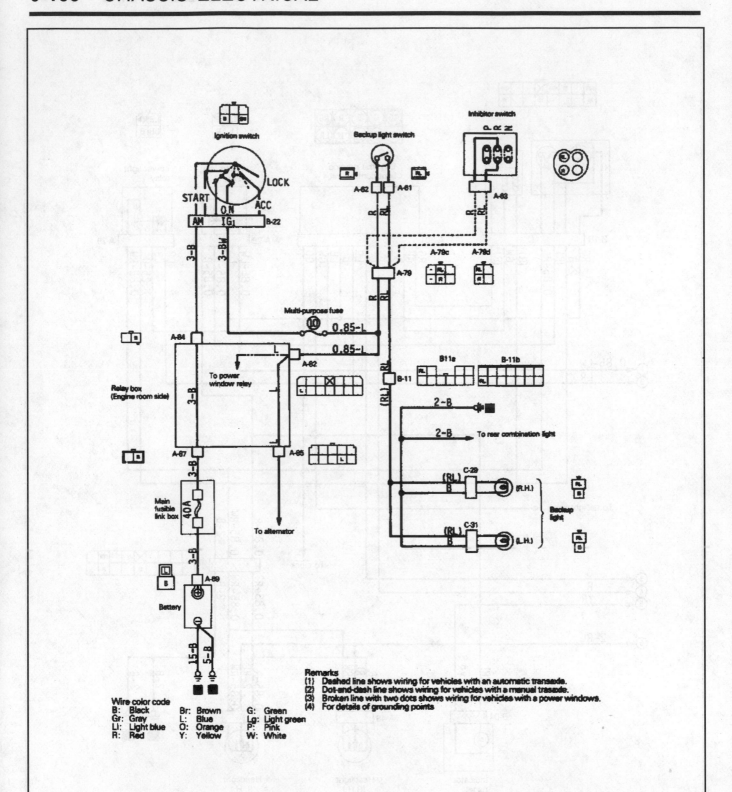

Fig. 189 1990-91 Vista — back-up lights

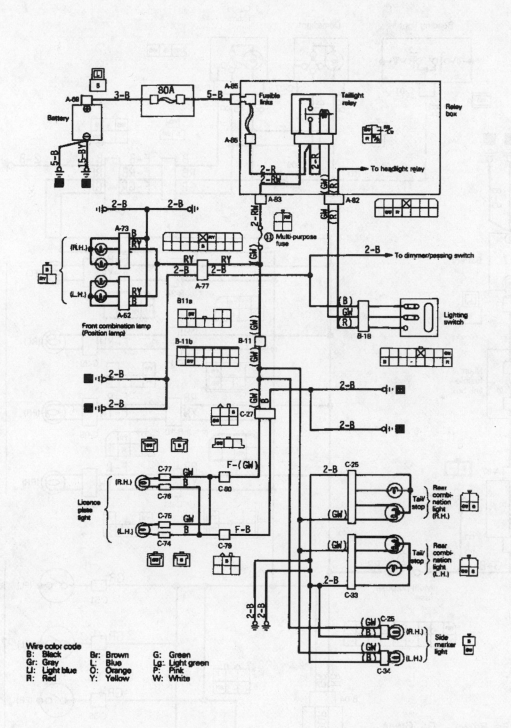

Fig. 190 1990-91 Vista — tail lights, clearance lights and license plate lights

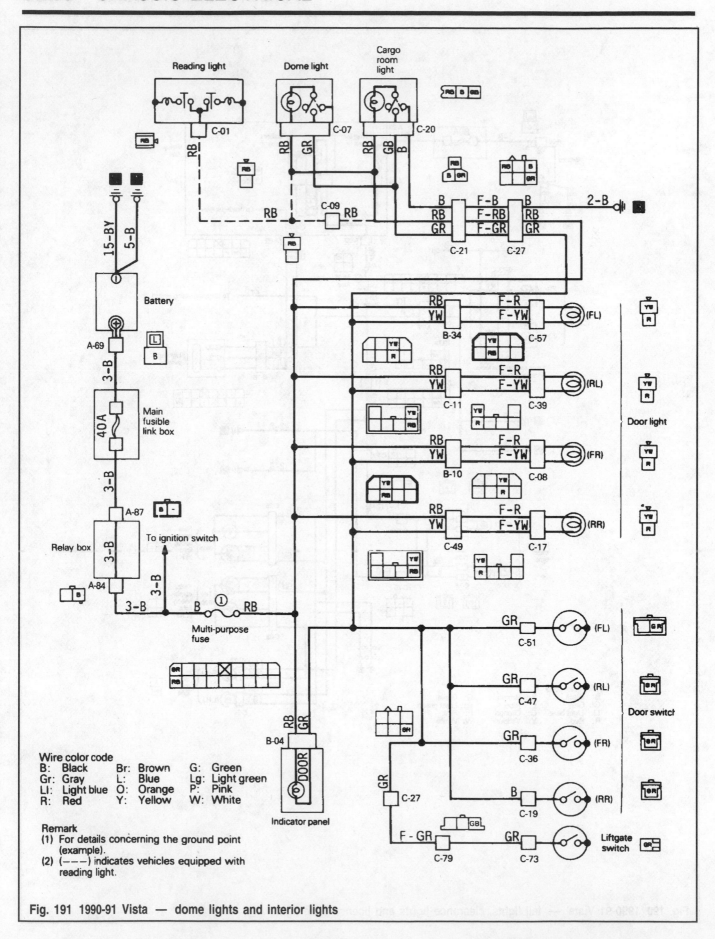

Wire color code

B:	Black	Br:	Brown
Gr:	Gray	L:	Blue
LI:	Light blue	O:	Orange
R:	Red	Y:	Yellow

G: Green
Lg: Light green
P: Pink
W: White

Remark

(1) For details concerning the ground point (example).

(2) (———) indicates vehicles equipped with reading light.

Fig. 191 1990-91 Vista — dome lights and interior lights

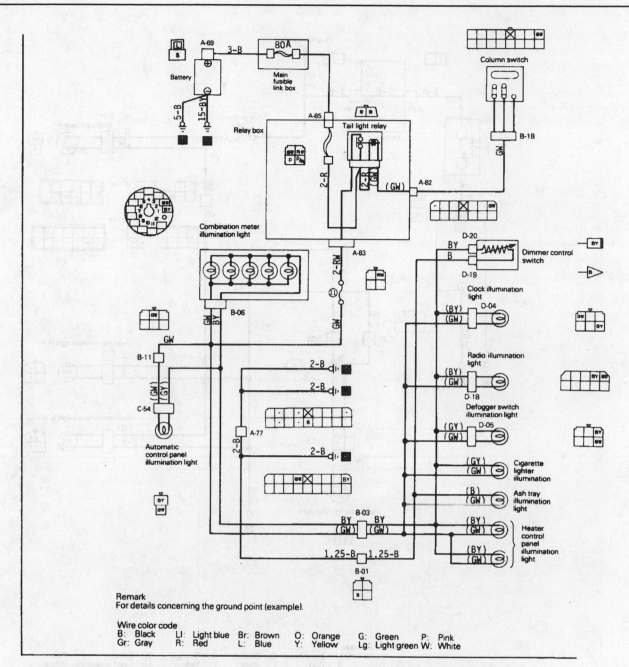

Wire color code
B: Black   Ll: Light blue   Br: Brown   O: Orange   G: Green   P: Pink
Gr: Gray   R: Red   L: Blue   Y: Yellow   Lg: Light green   W: White

OPERATION

- Voltage from the battery is normally passed to the tail light relay (connection point or coil) through the fusible link.
- Turning the lighting switch to position 1 or 2 causes current to flow through the fusible link, tail light relay (coil), the lighting switch and the ground and closes the tail light relay connection point. So, current flows through the fusible link, the tail light relay (connection point), all the lights, the rheostat and the ground causing all the lights to light.

TROUBLESHOOTING HINTS

1. 1 light does not light
   - Check the bulb.
2. Illumination cannot be adjusted
   - Check the rheostat

Fig. 192 1990-91 Vista — instrument panel lights

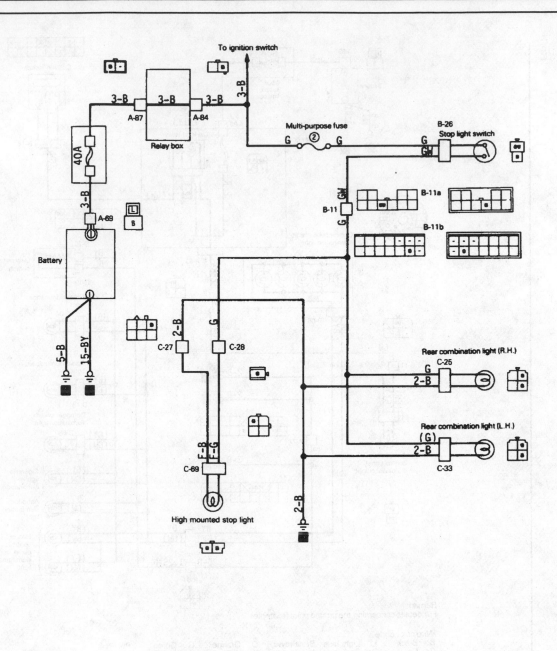

Wire color code

B: Black	Ll: Light blue	Br: Brown	O: Orange	G: Green	P: Pink
Gr: Gray	R: Red	L: Blue	Y: Yellow	Lg: Light green	W: White

OPERATION

- Battery voltage is always applied to the stop light switch through fuse No. 2.
- When the brake pedal is depressed for braking, the stop light switch contacts are closed so that current flows through fuse No. 2, stop light switch, stop lights, and ground, causing the stop lights to go on.

TROUBLESHOOTING HINTS

1. One stop light does not light
   - Check bulb.
2. Stop lights fail to go off
   - Check stop light switch.

Fig. 193 1990-91 Vista — brake lights

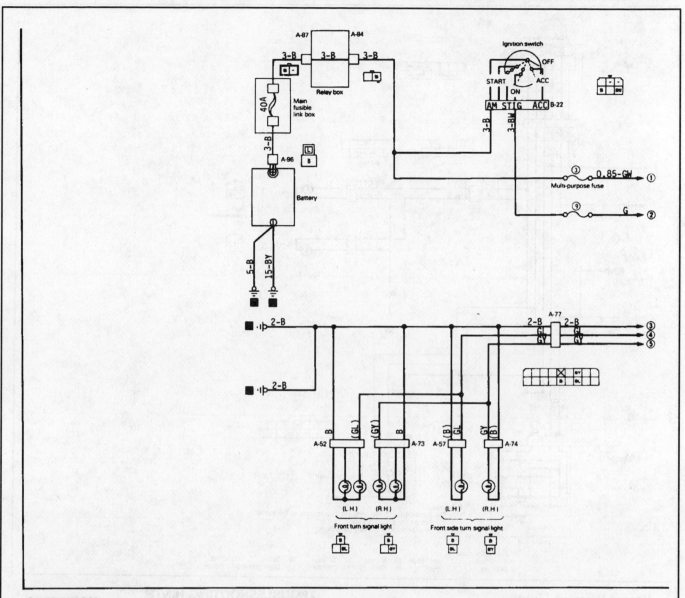

OPERATION

Turn Signal Lights

- When the turn signal light switch is at "L.H.", with the ignition switch turned to "ON", current flows through fuse No. 9, hazard warning light switch, flasher unit, and ground, causing the flasher unit to alternately close and open its contacts.
- While the flasher unit contacts are closed, current flows through the flasher unit, turn signal switch (L.H.), turn signal lights (L.H.) and ground so the turn signal lights (L.H.) go on.
- When the flasher unit contacts are open, the turn signal lights (L.H.) go off.
- This cycle is repeated to flash the turn signal lights (L.H.).
- The turn signal indicator light (L.H.) flashes at the same time as do the turn signal lights.

- When the turn signal light switch is at "R.H.", the turn signal lights (R.H.) and turn signal indicator light flash in the same way as when the switch is at "L.H.".

Remarks

If one or more turn signal light bulbs are burnt out, the flasher unit closes and opens the contacts more frequently than when normal, to warn the driver that bulb replacement is required.

Fig. 194 1990-91 Vista — turn signal and hazard lights

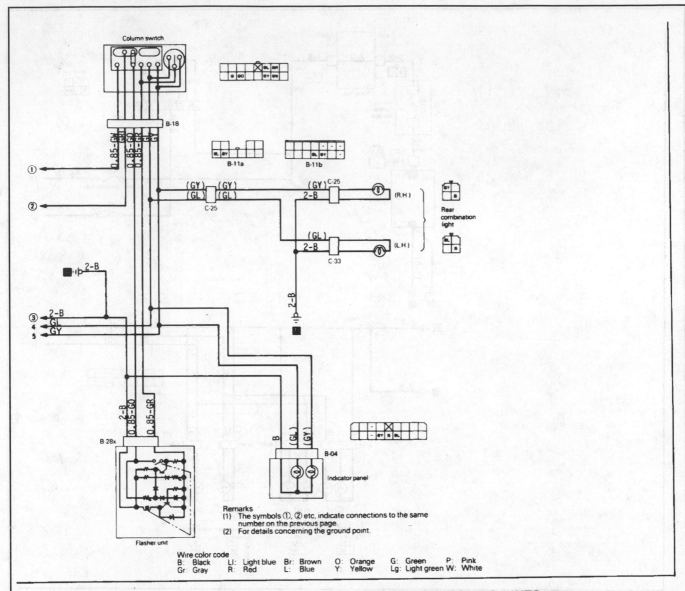

Wire color code
B: Black Ll: Light blue Br: Brown O: Orange G: Green P: Pink
Gr: Gray R: Red L: Blue Y: Yellow Lg: Light green W: White

Hazard Warning Lights

- Battery voltage is always applied to the hazard warning light switch through fuse No. 3.
- When the hazard warning light switch is turned "ON", current flows through fuse No. 3, hazard warning light switch, flasher unit, and ground, causing the flasher unit contacts to close and open repeatedly.
- While the flasher unit contacts are closed, current flows through the flasher unit, hazard warning light switch, right and left turn signal lights, and ground so all turn signal lights go on.
- When the flasher unit contacts are open, all turn signal lights go off.
- This cycle is repeated so that all turn signal lights flash simultaneously.
- Both turn signal indicator lights flash at the same time as do the turn signal lights.

TROUBLESHOOTING HINTS

1. Turn signal lights do not work neither when turn signal switch nor hazard warning light switch is operated
   - Check hazard warning light switch.

2. All turn signal lights on right or left side do not work (but all lights work when hazard warning light switch is operated)
   - Check turn signal light switch.

3. Turn signal lights flash at irregular intervals
   - Check bulbs.

4. Turn signal lights do not flash when hazard warning light switch is operated (but flash when turn signal light switch is operated)
   - Check hazard switch.

Fig. 195 1990-91 Vista — turn signal and hazard lights

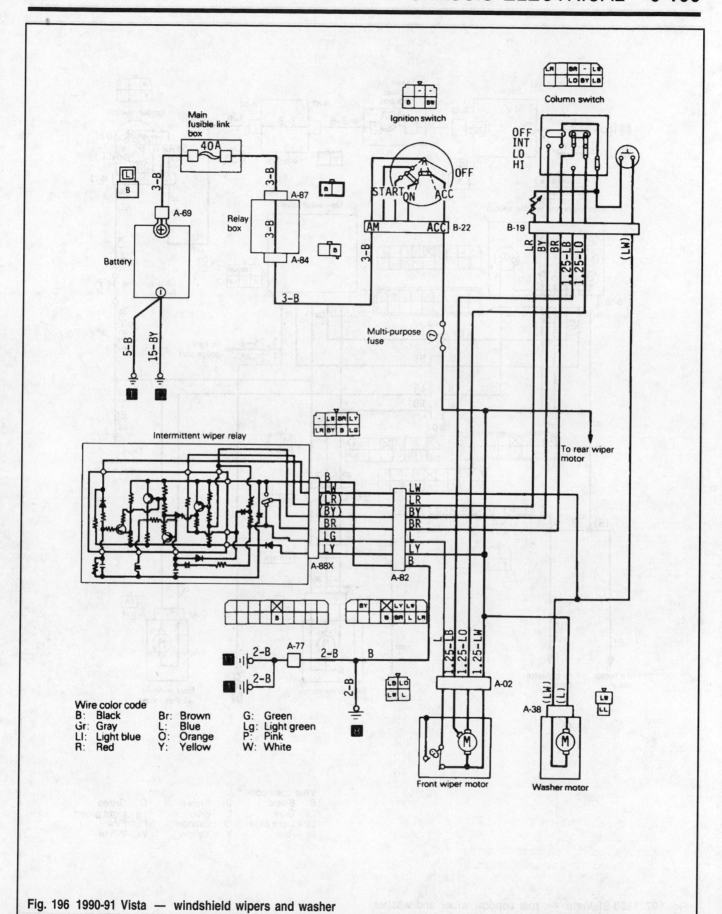

Fig. 196 1990-91 Vista — windshield wipers and washer

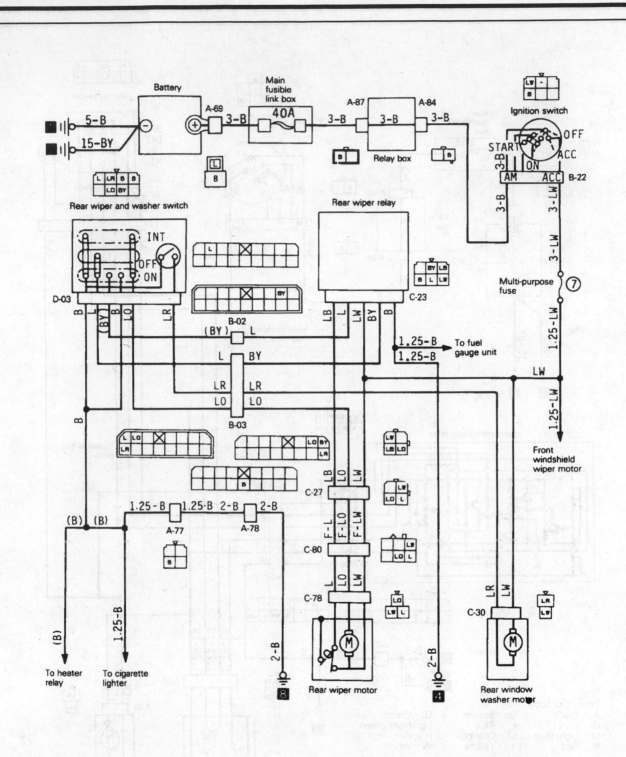

Fig. 197 1990-91 Vista — rear window wiper and washer

Wire color code
B: Black	Br: Brown	G: Green
Gr: Gray	L: Blue	Lg: Light green
Ll: Light blue	O: Orange	P: Pink
R: Red	Y: Yellow	W: White

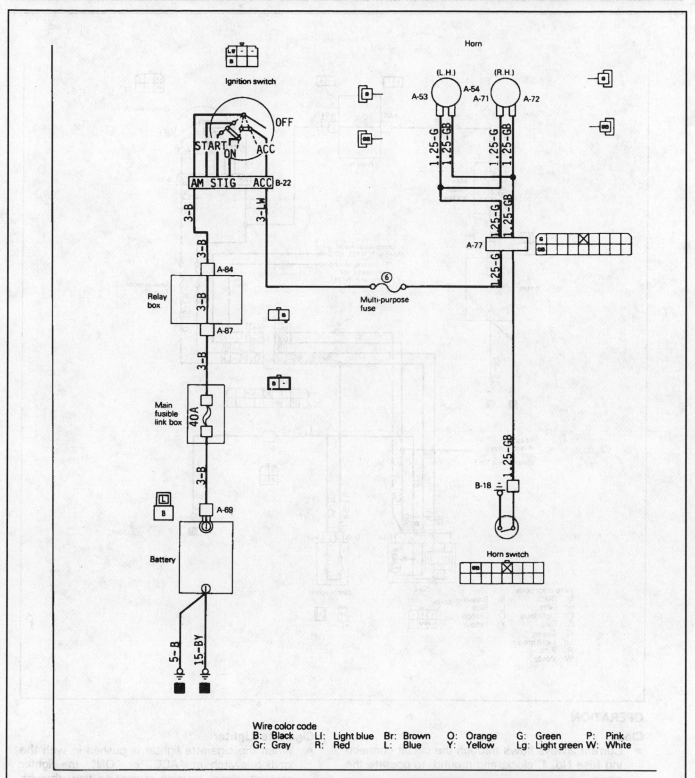

Fig. 198 1990-91 Vista — horn

OPERATION
- When the horn switch is turned on, with the ignition switch at "ACC" or "ON", current flows through fuse No. 6, horn switch, and ground, causing the horns to sound.

TROUBLESHOOTING HINTS
One or other horn does not sound
- Check horn.

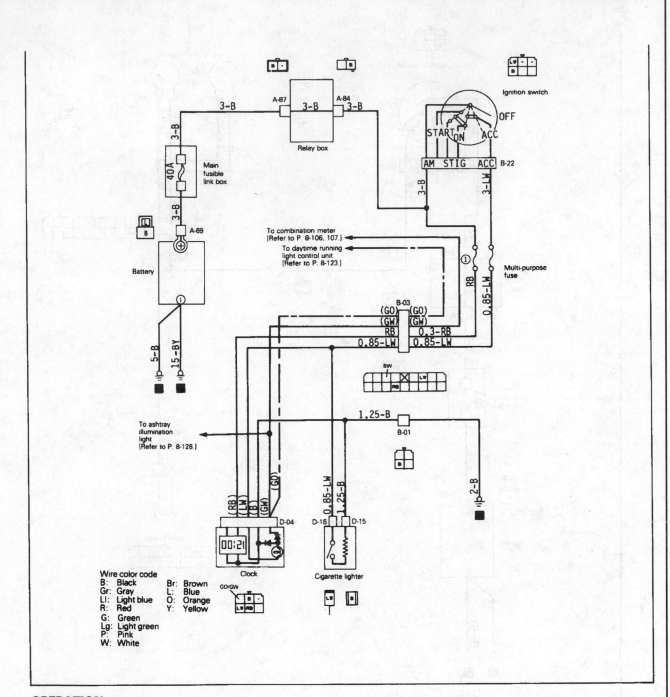

OPERATION

Clock

- Current always flows through the circuit connecting fuse No. 1, clock, and ground, to operate the clock.
- When the ignition switch is at "ACC" or "ON", current flows through fuse No. 8, clock and ground, causing the time to display on the clock.

Cigarette Lighter

- When the cigarette lighter is pushed in with the ignition switch at "ACC" or "ON", the lighter contacts close, causing current to flow through fuse No. 8, cigarette lighter, and ground, and the cigarette lighter element glows.

Fig. 199 1990-91 Vista — clock and cigar lighter

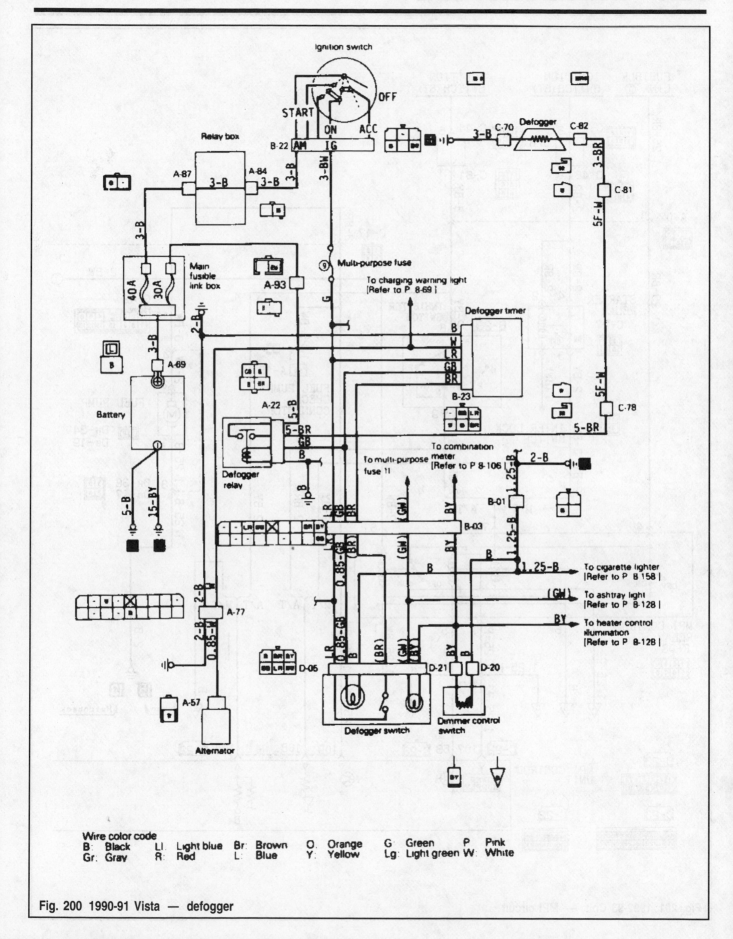

Fig. 200 1990-91 Vista — defogger

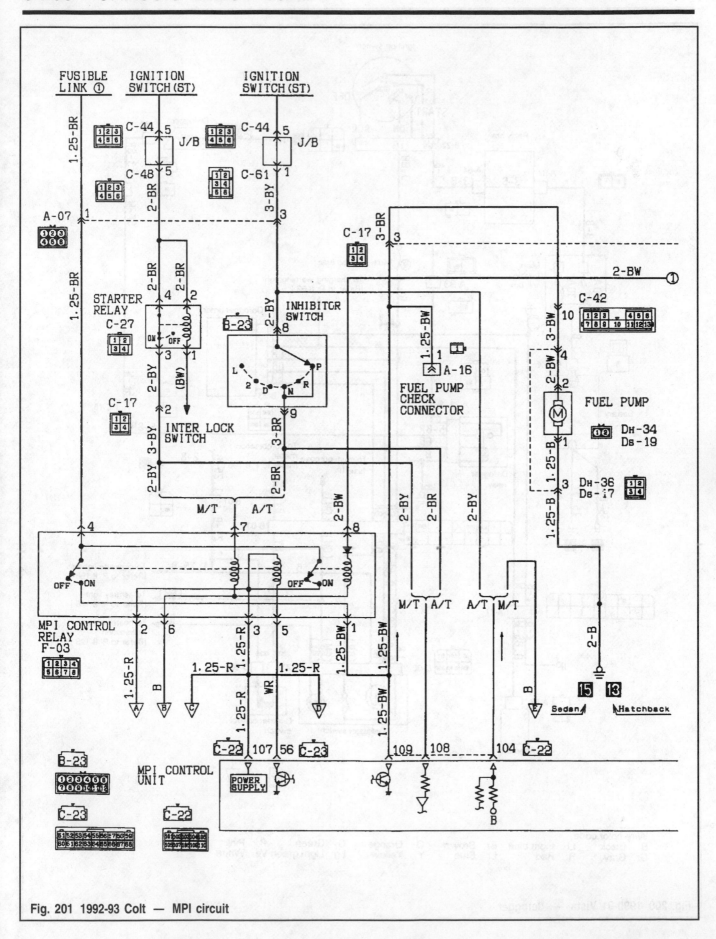

Fig. 201 1992-93 Colt — MPI circuit

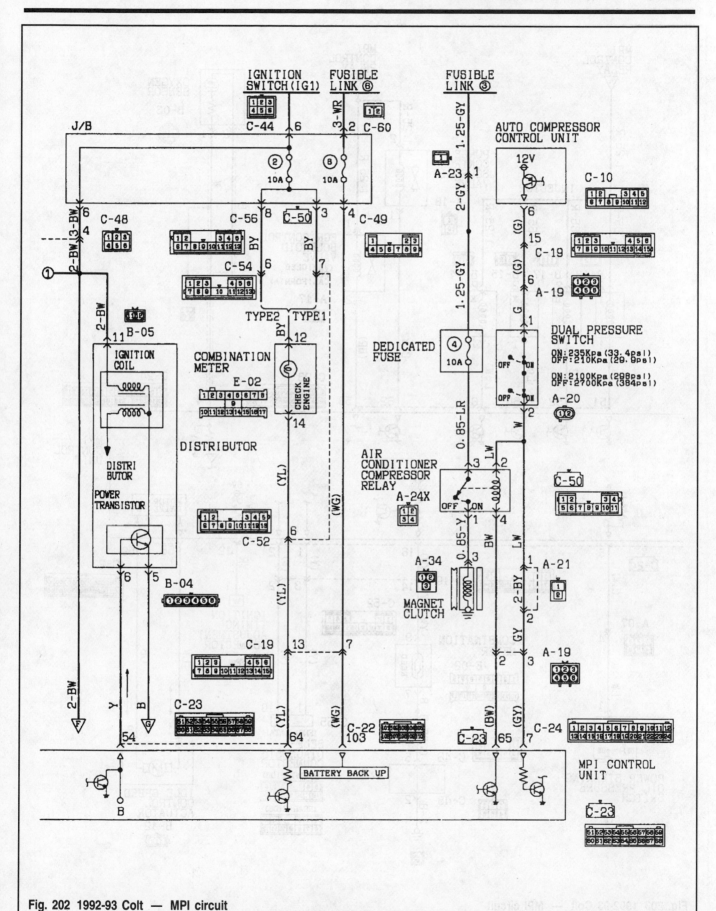

Fig. 202 1992-93 Colt — MPI circuit

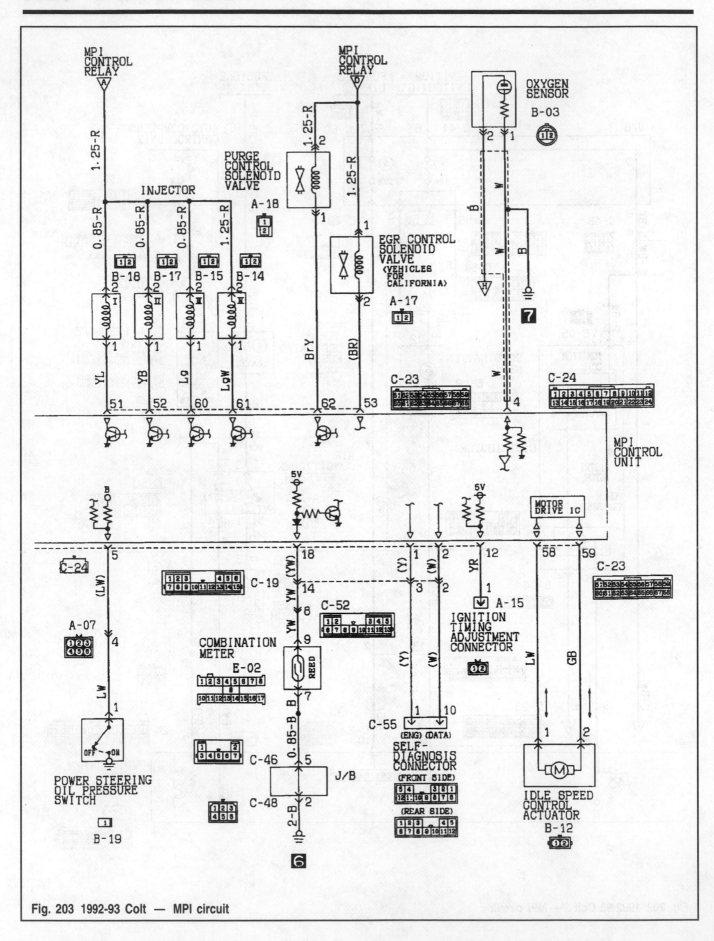

Fig. 203 1992-93 Colt — MPI circuit

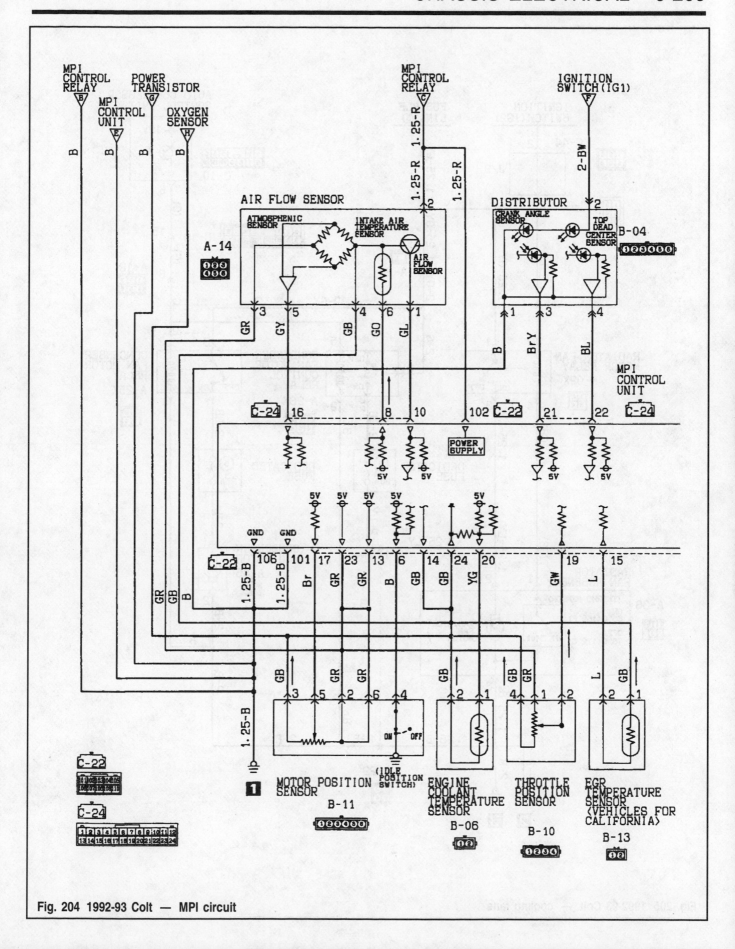

Fig. 204 1992-93 Colt — MPI circuit

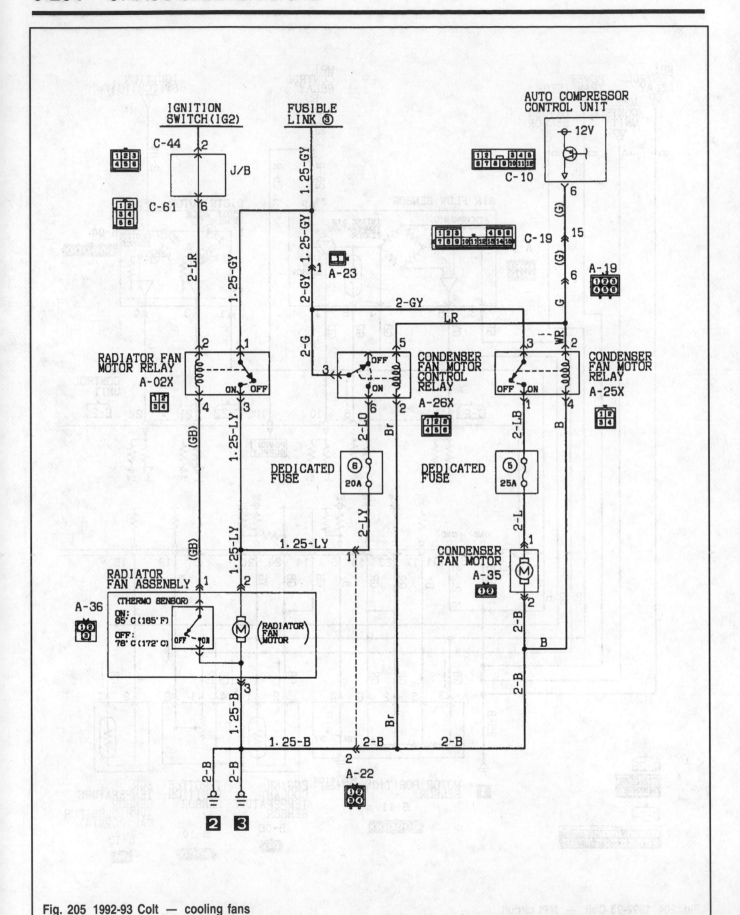

Fig. 205 1992-93 Colt — cooling fans

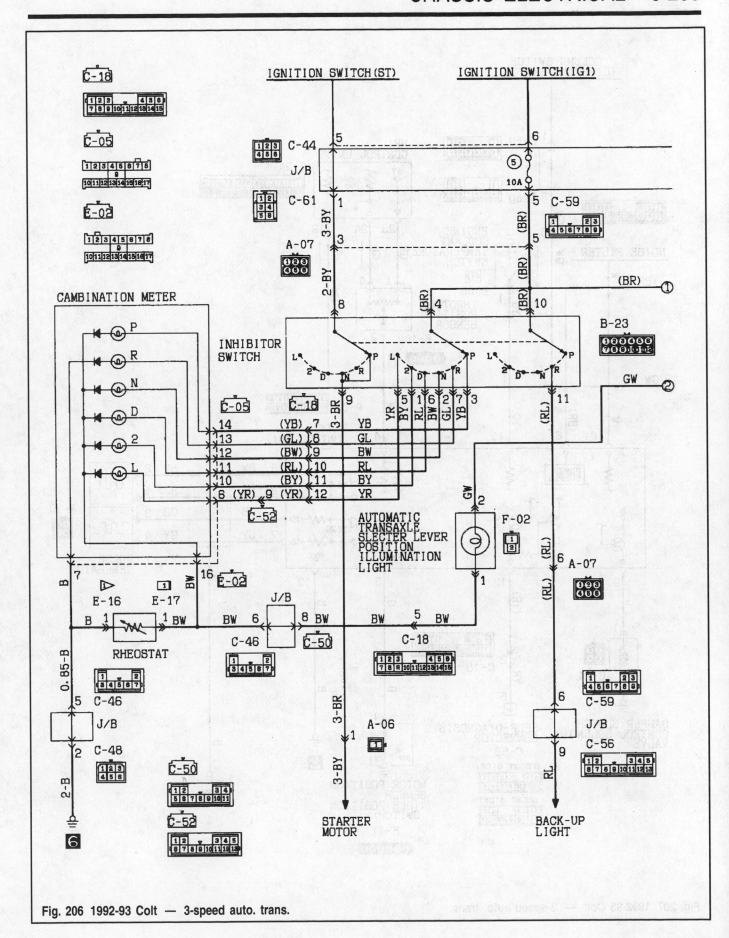

Fig. 206 1992-93 Colt — 3-speed auto. trans.

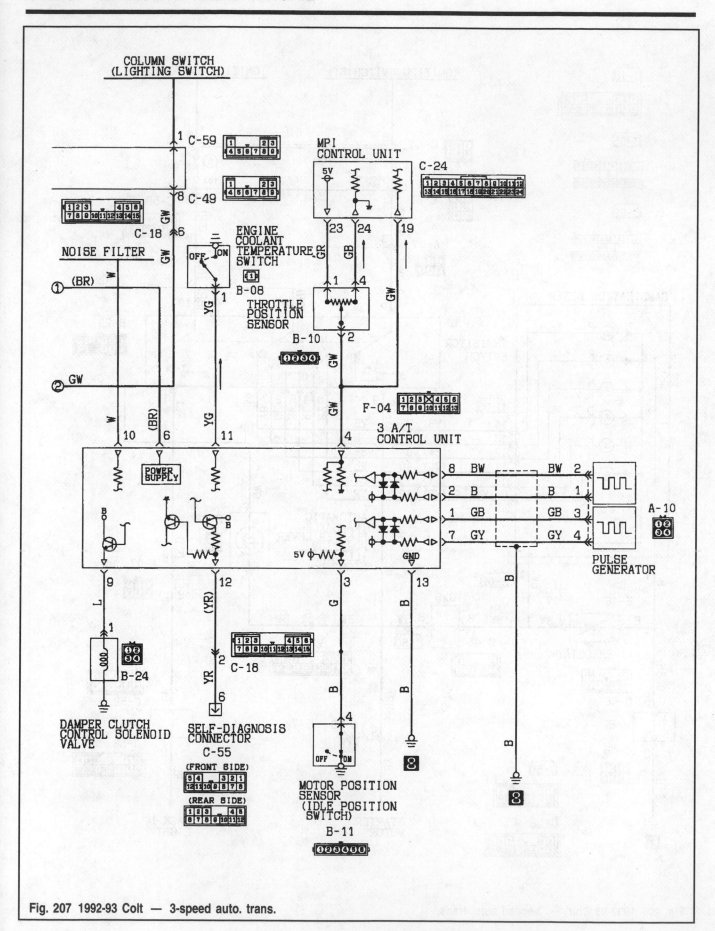

Fig. 207 1992-93 Colt — 3-speed auto. trans.

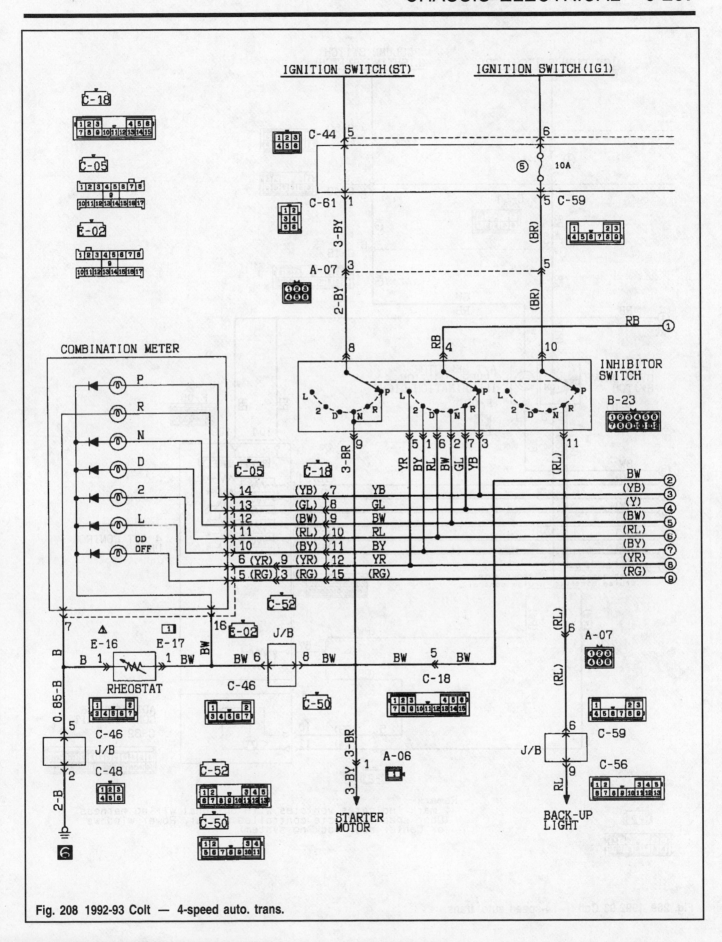

Fig. 208 1992-93 Colt — 4-speed auto. trans.

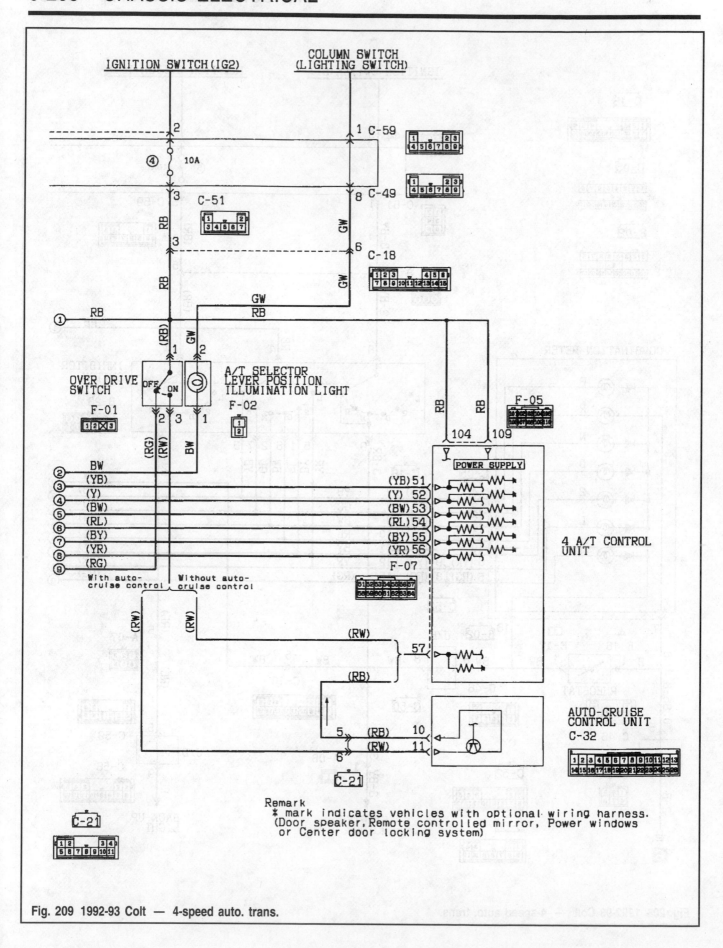

Fig. 209 1992-93 Colt — 4-speed auto. trans.

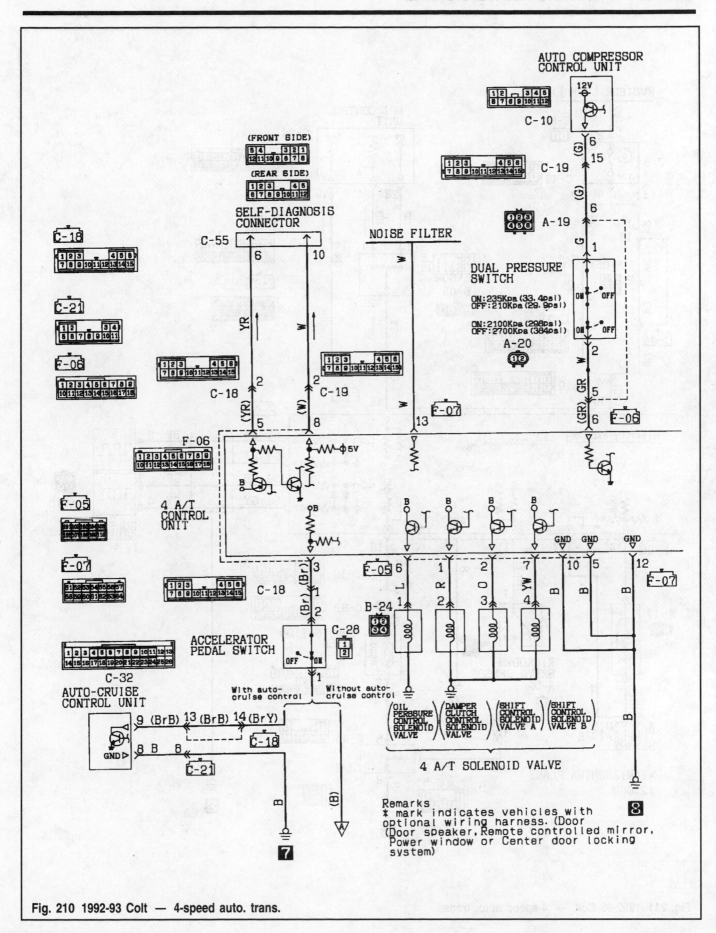

Fig. 210 1992-93 Colt — 4-speed auto. trans.

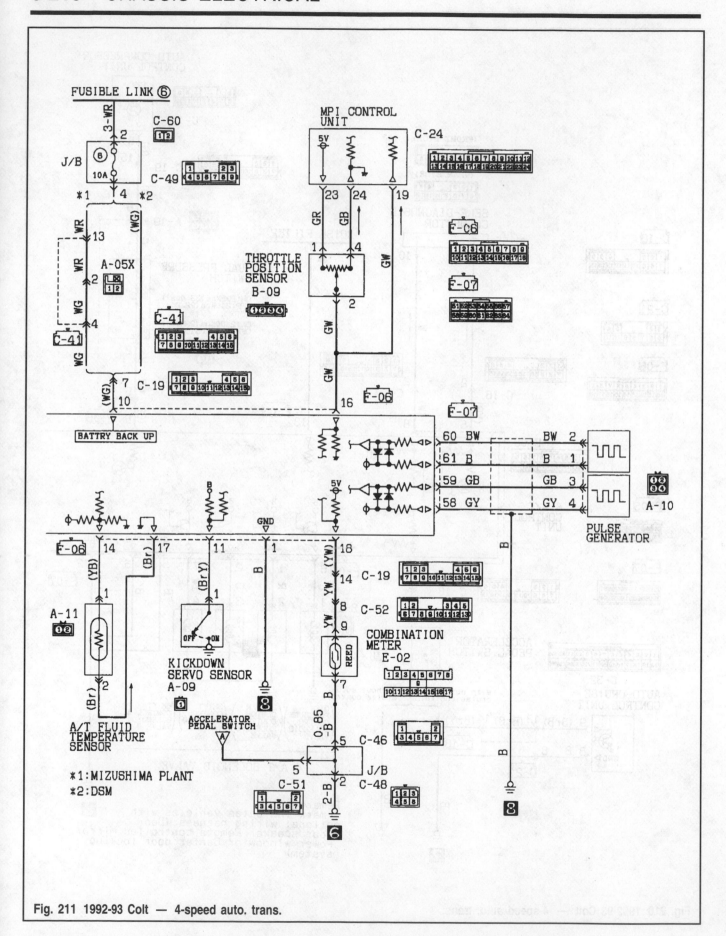

Fig. 211 1992-93 Colt — 4-speed auto. trans.

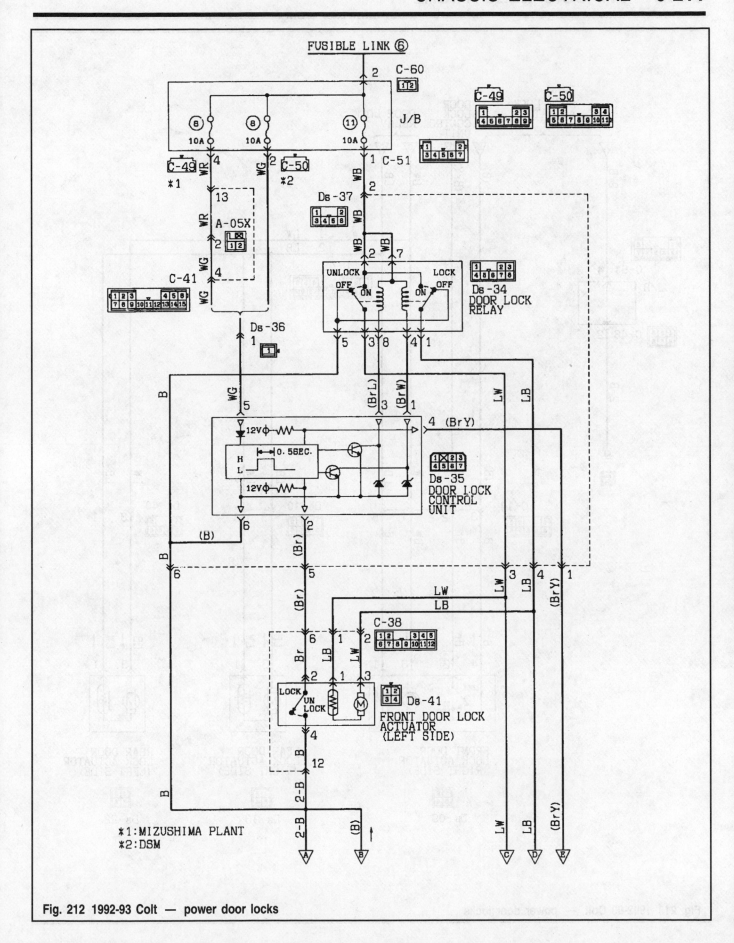

Fig. 212 1992-93 Colt — power door locks

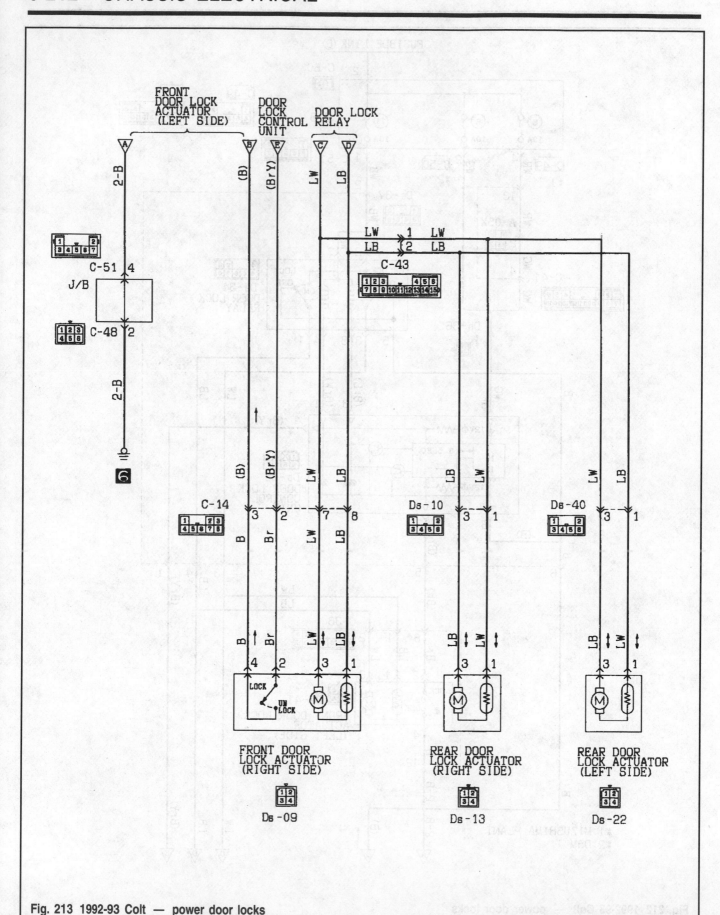

Fig. 213 1992-93 Colt — power door locks

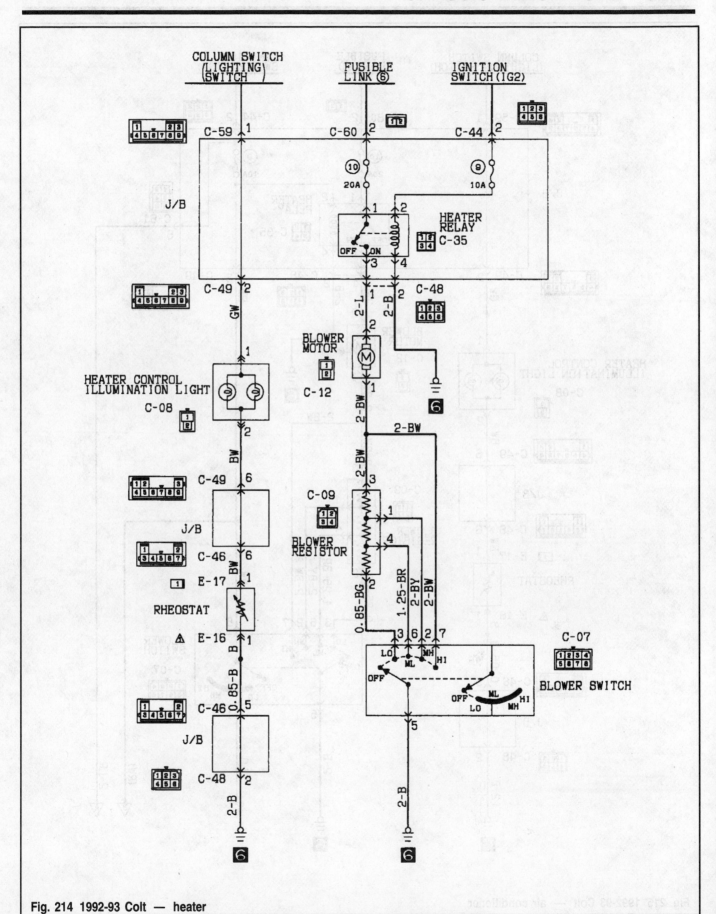

Fig. 214 1992-93 Colt — heater

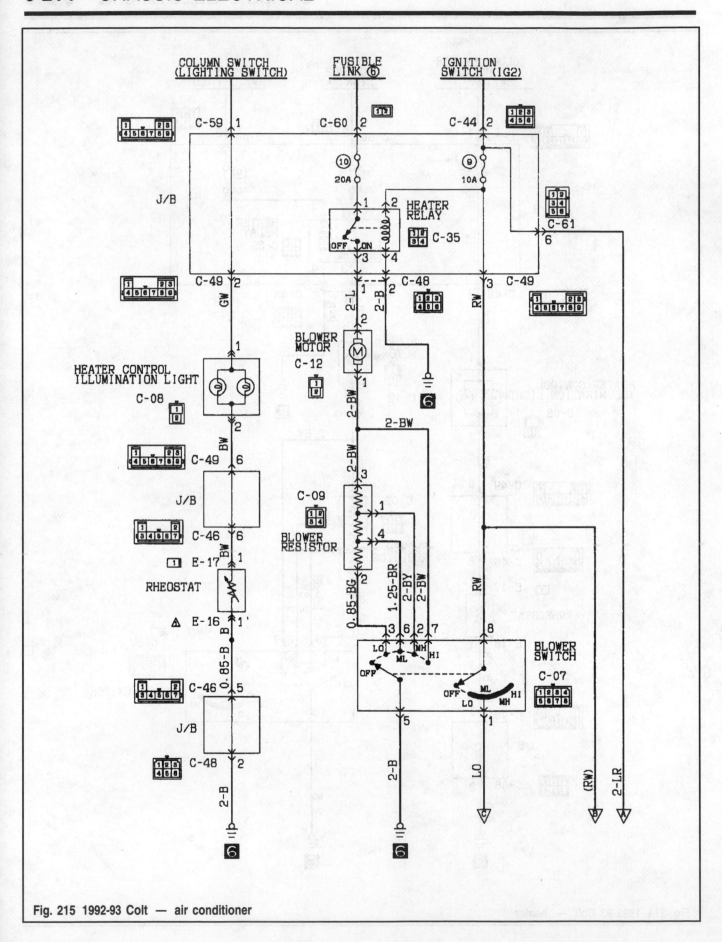

Fig. 215 1992-93 Colt — air conditioner

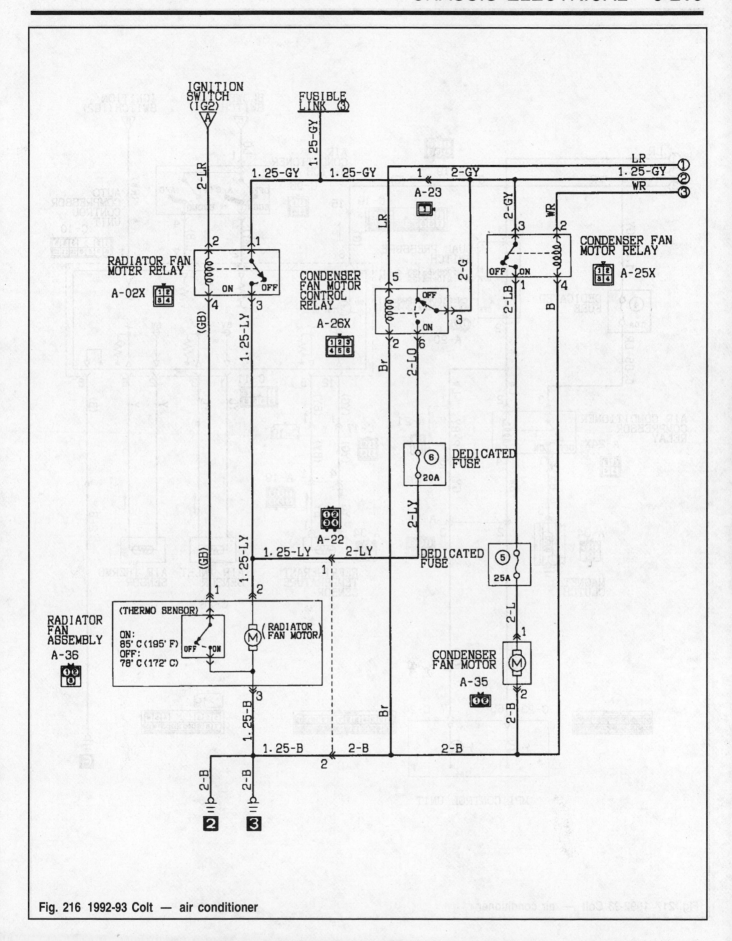

Fig. 216 1992-93 Colt — air conditioner

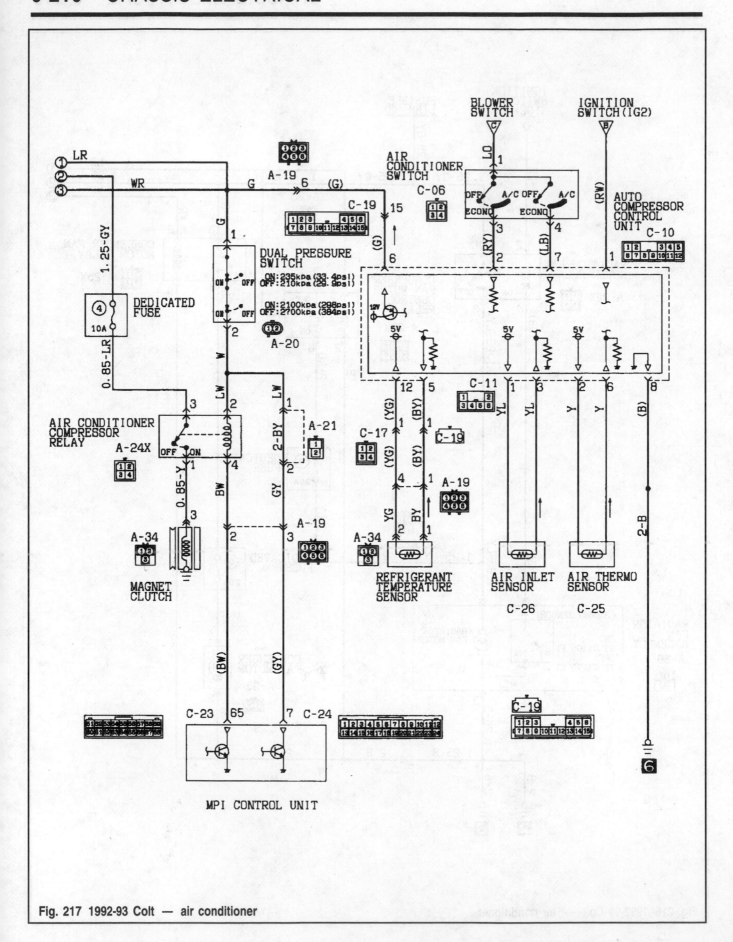

Fig. 217 1992-93 Colt — air conditioner

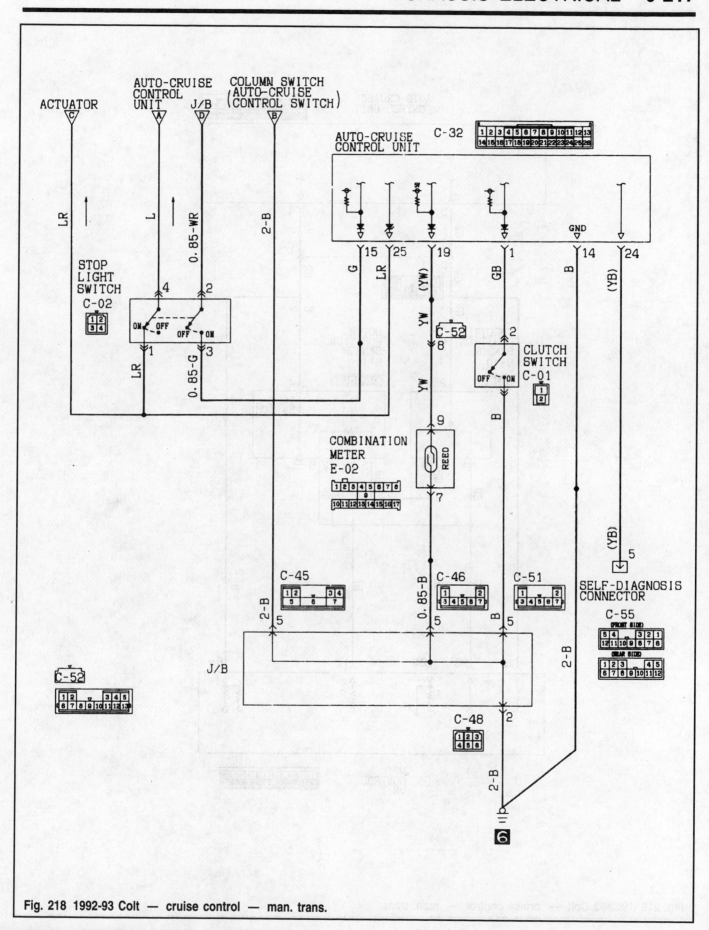

Fig. 218 1992-93 Colt — cruise control — man. trans.

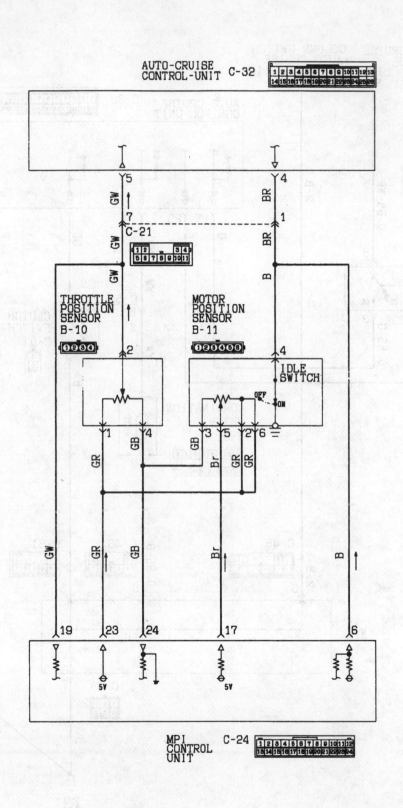

Fig. 219 1992-93 Colt — cruise control — man. trans.

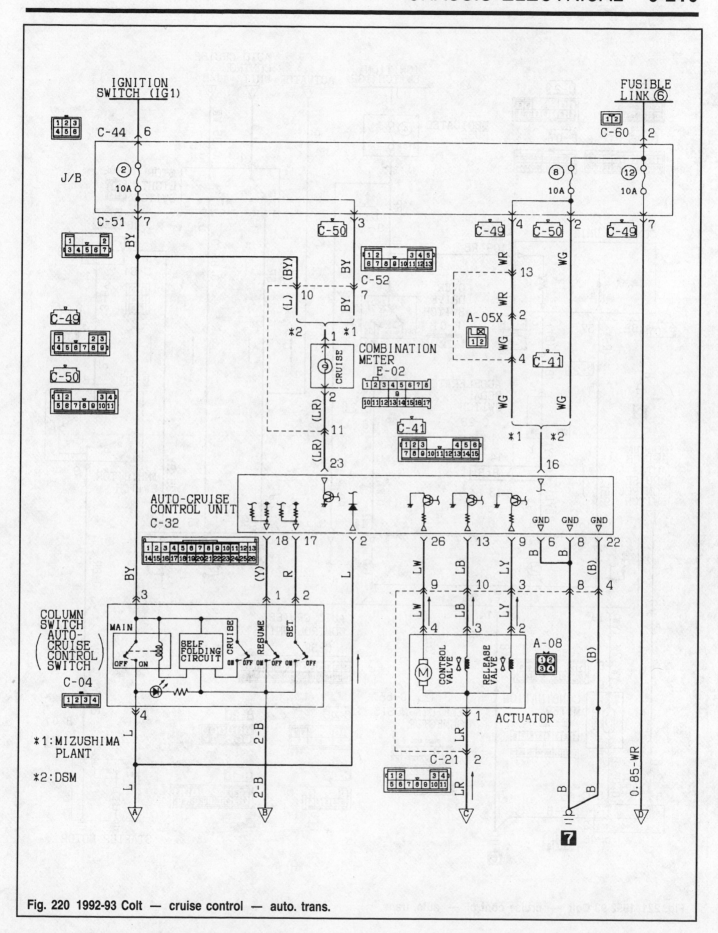

Fig. 220 1992–93 Colt — cruise control — auto. trans.

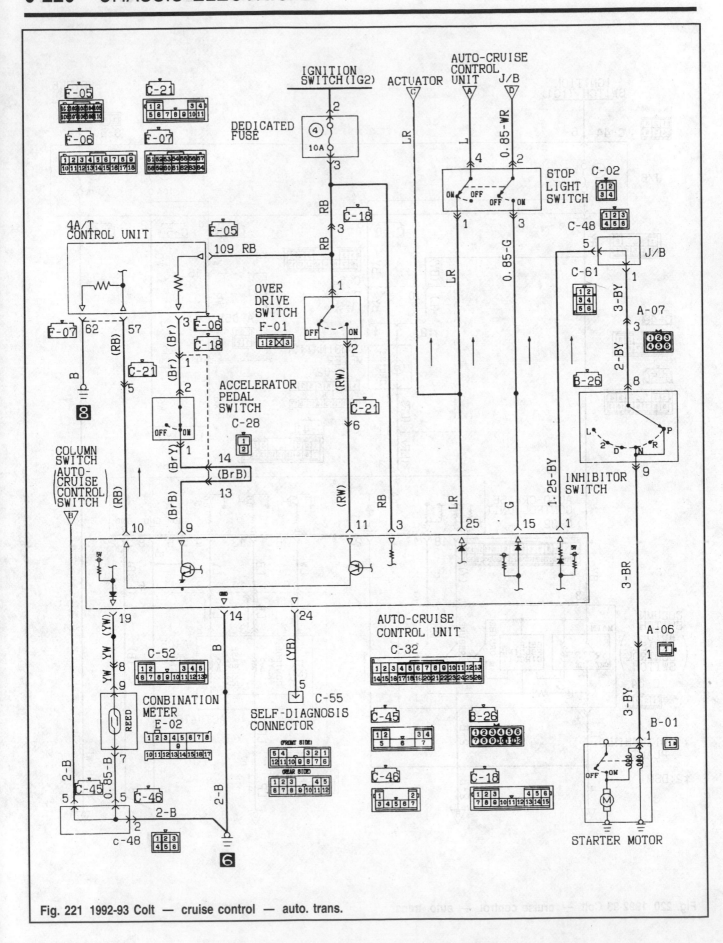

Fig. 221 1992-93 Colt — cruise control — auto. trans.

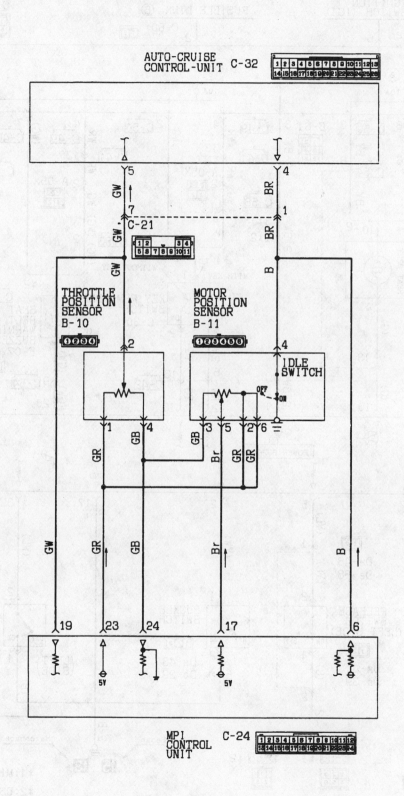

Fig. 222 1992-93 Colt — cruise control — auto. trans.

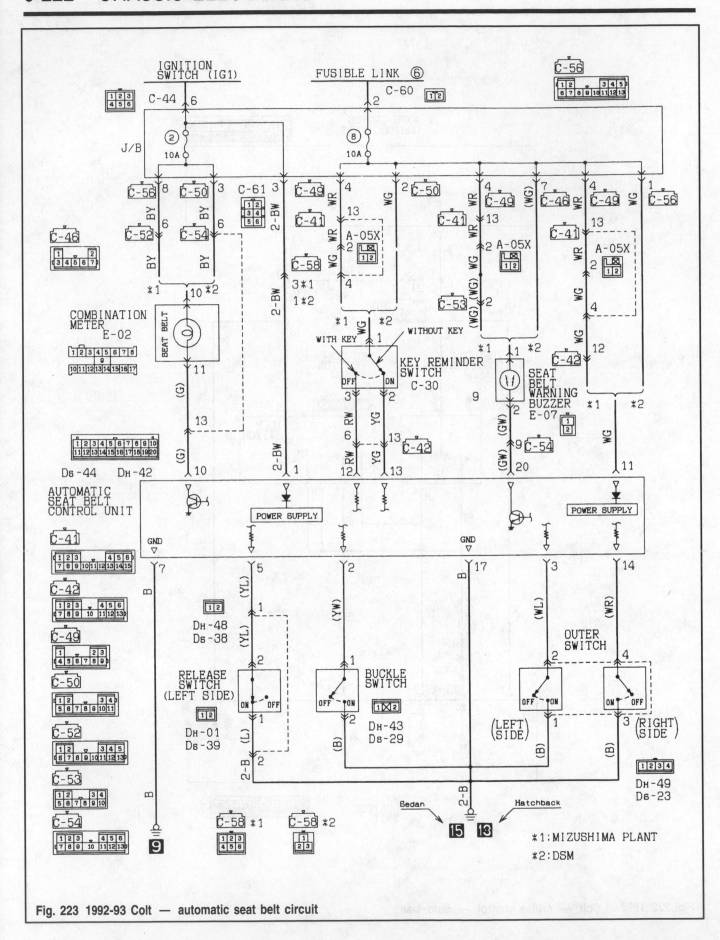

Fig. 223 1992-93 Colt — automatic seat belt circuit

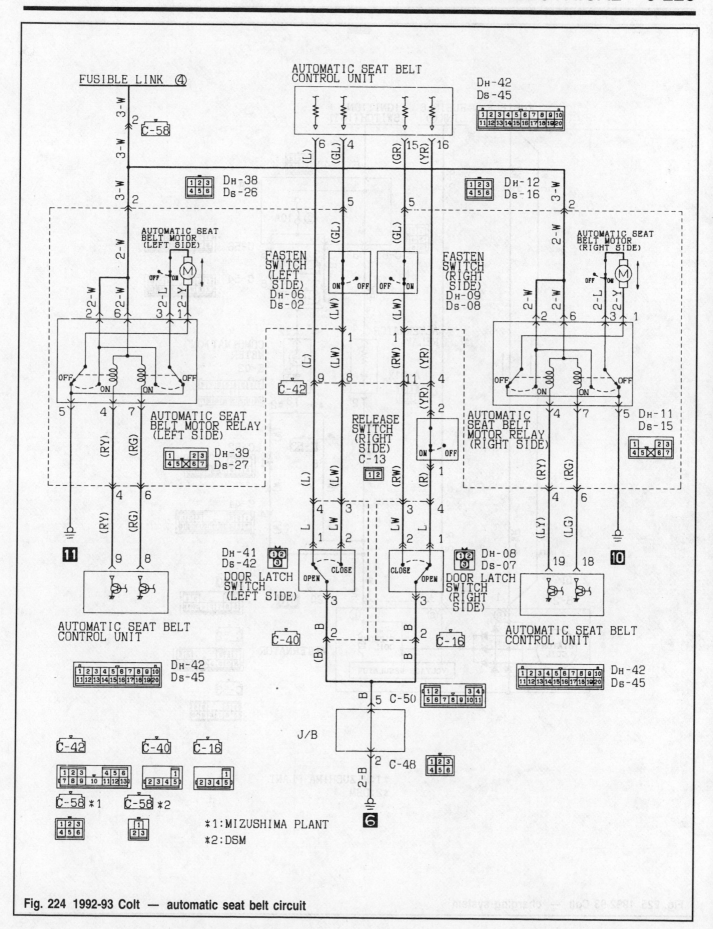

Fig. 224 1992-93 Colt — automatic seat belt circuit

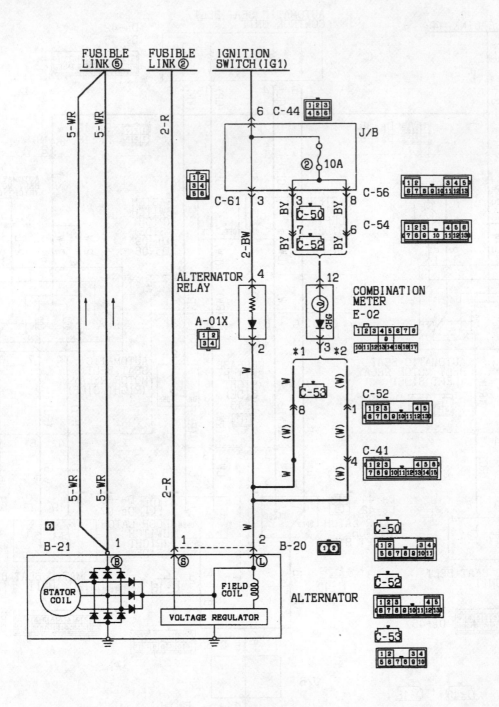

Fig. 225 1992-93 Colt — charging system

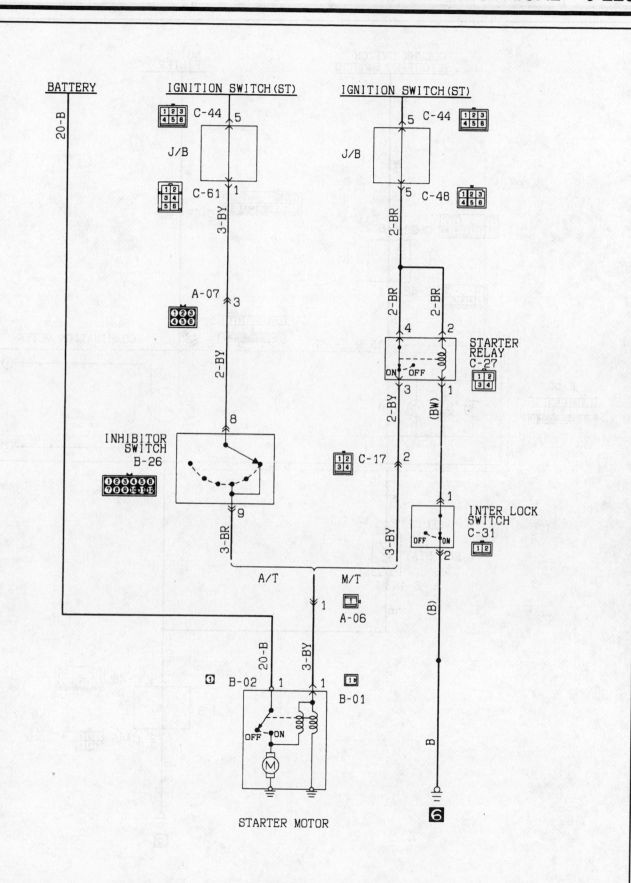

Fig. 226 1992-93 Colt — starting system

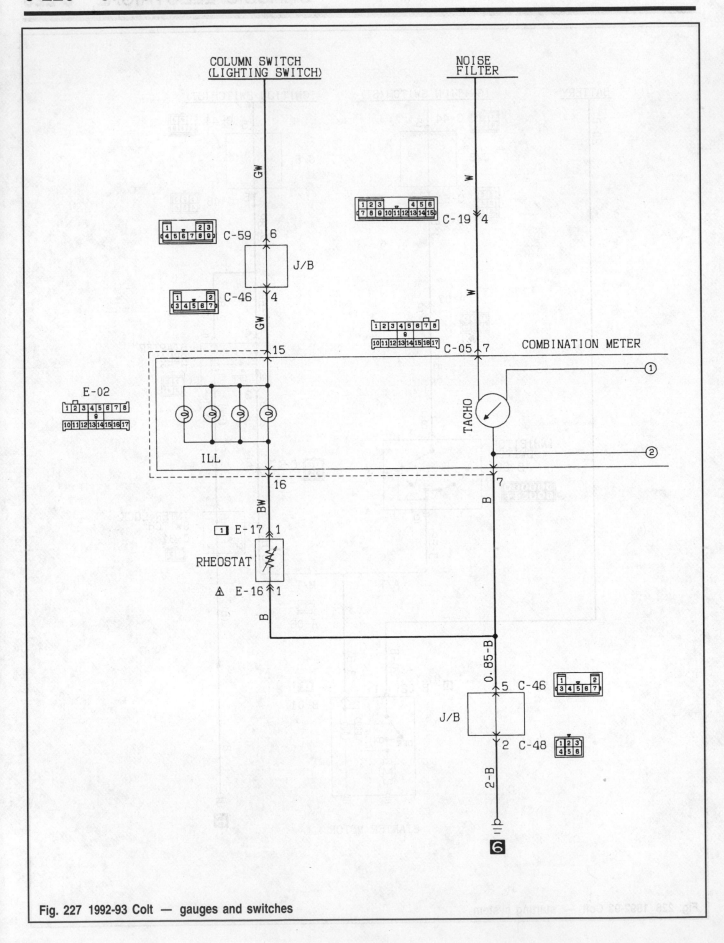

Fig. 227 1992-93 Colt — gauges and switches

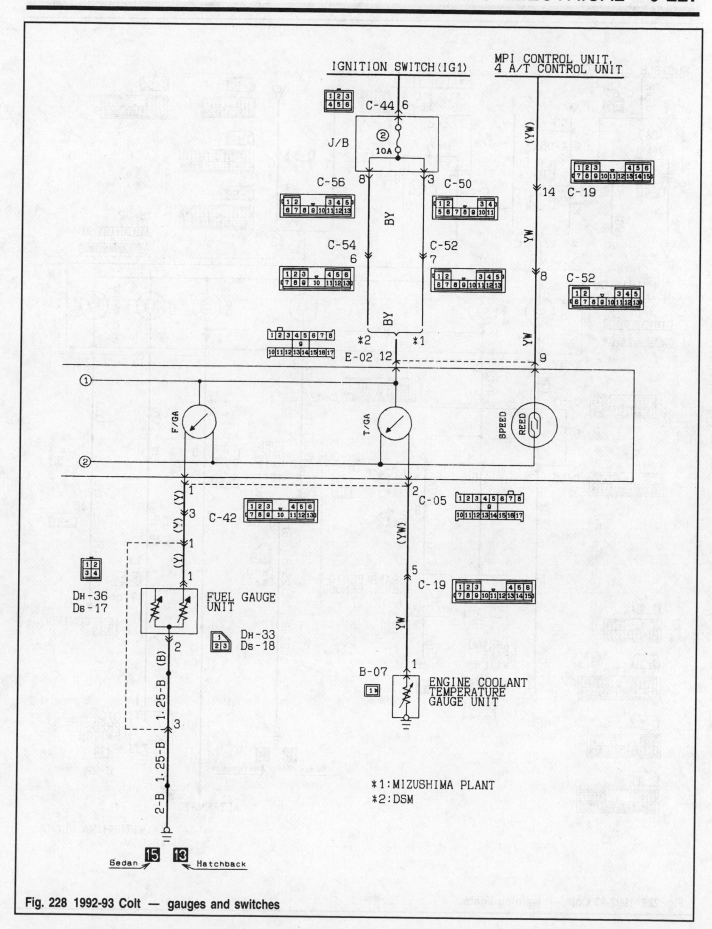

Fig. 228 1992-93 Colt — gauges and switches

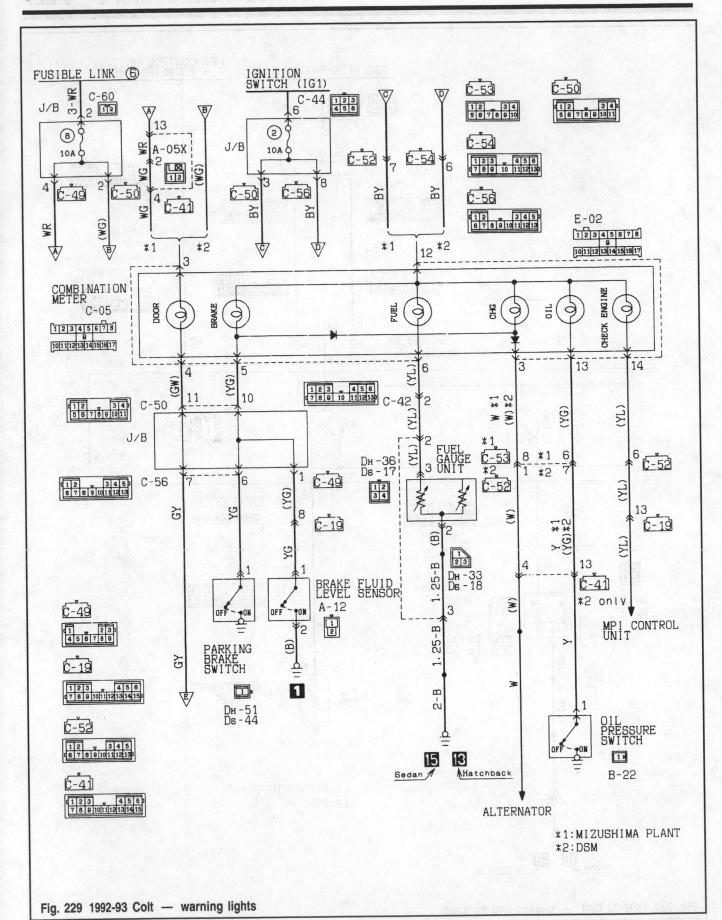

Fig. 229 1992-93 Colt — warning lights

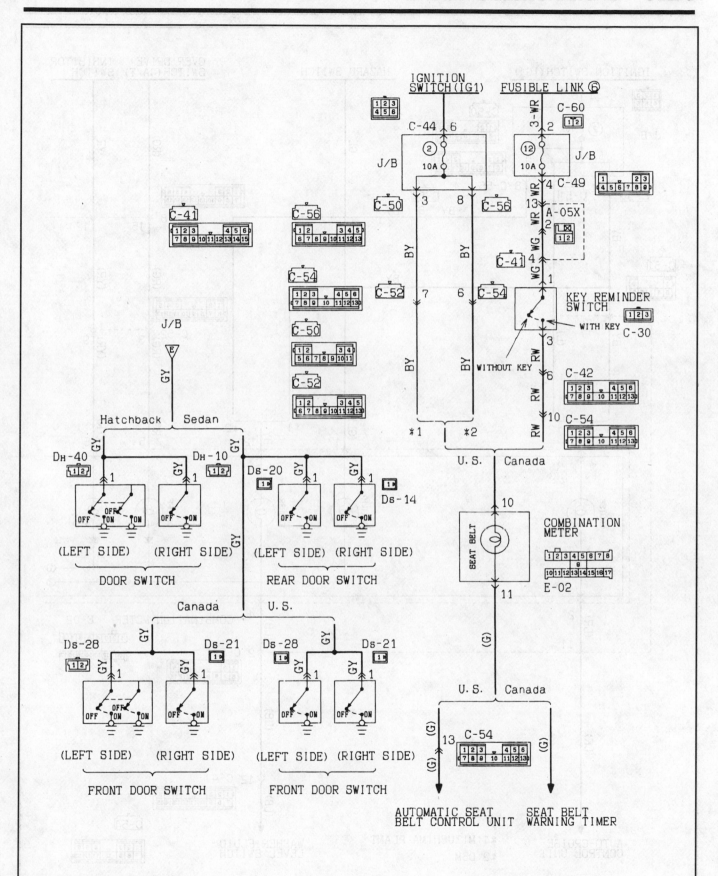

Fig. 230 1992-93 Colt — warning lights

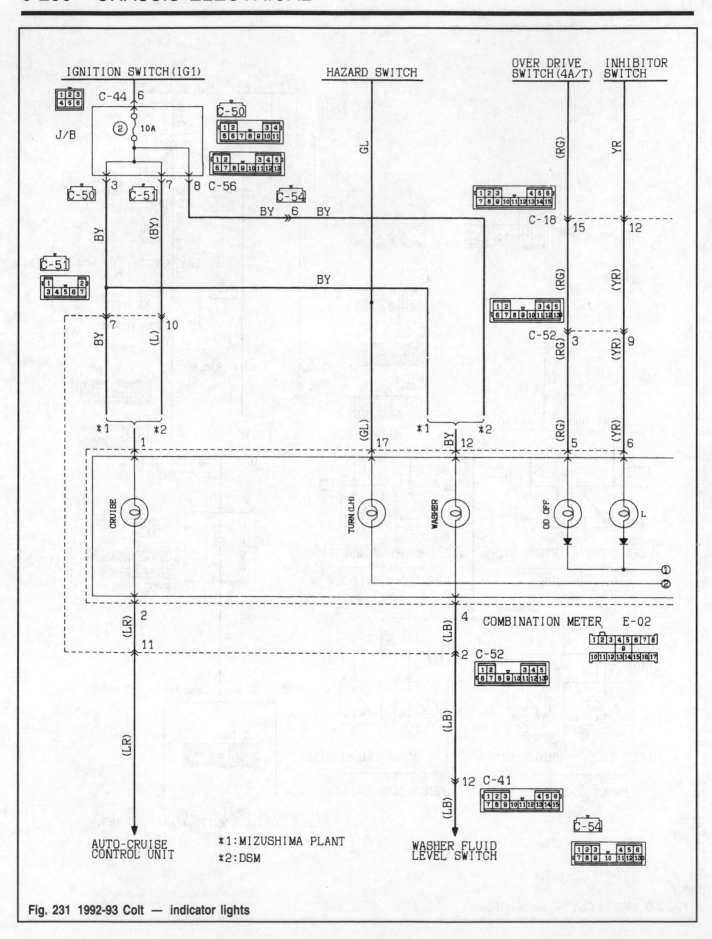

Fig. 231 1992-93 Colt — indicator lights

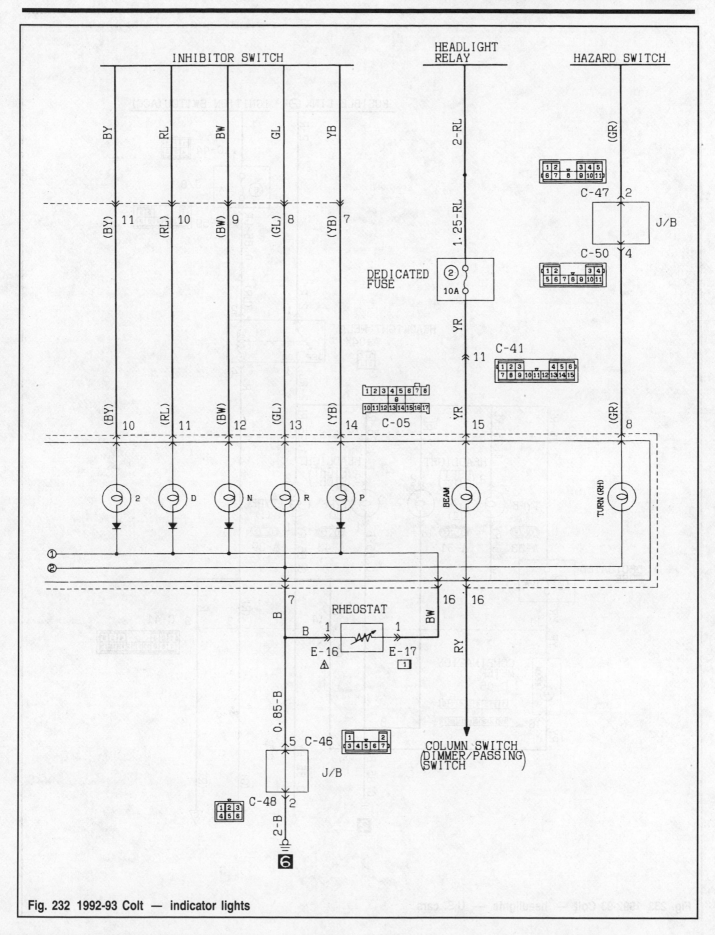

Fig. 232 1992-93 Colt — indicator lights

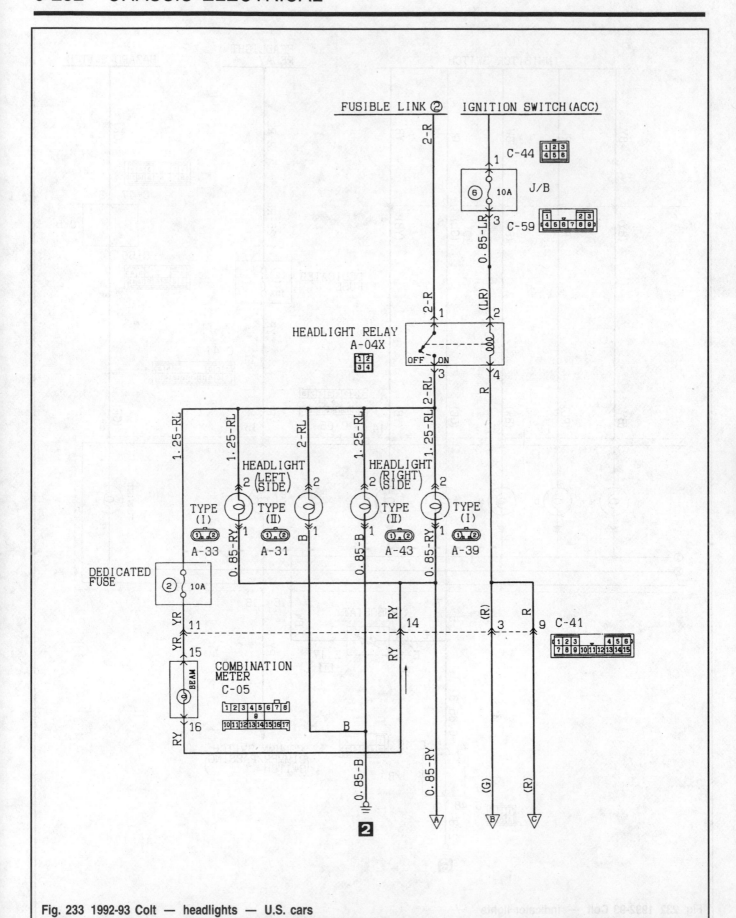

Fig. 233 1992-93 Colt — headlights — U.S. cars

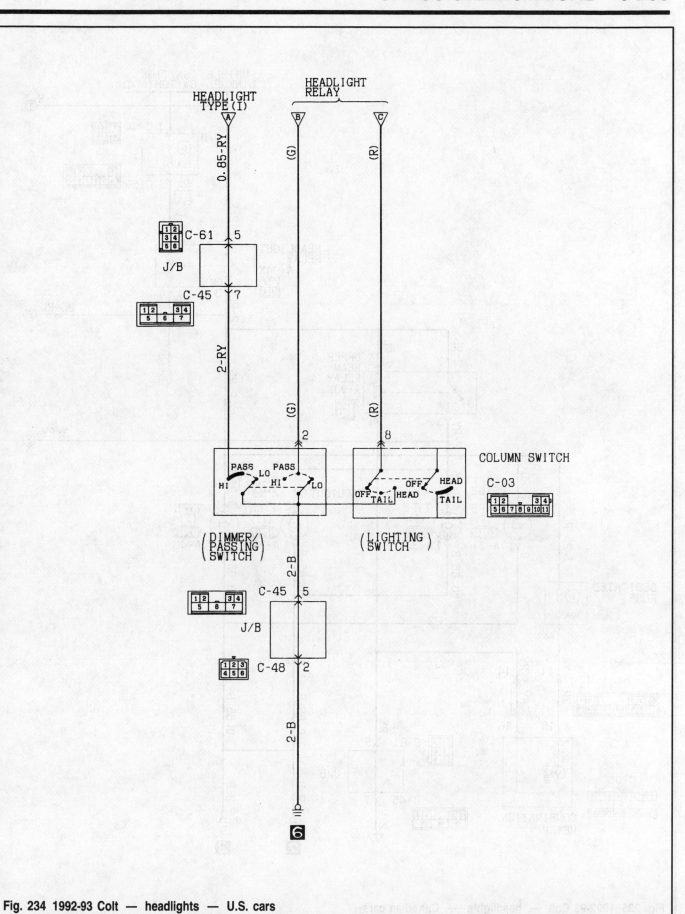

Fig. 234 1992-93 Colt — headlights — U.S. cars

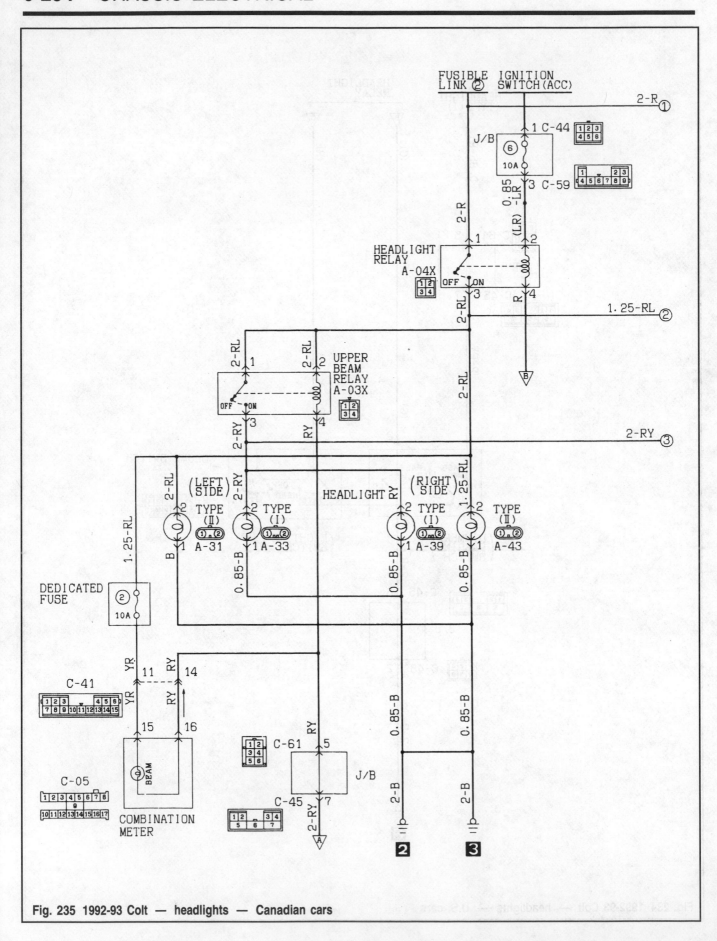

Fig. 235 1992-93 Colt — headlights — Canadian cars

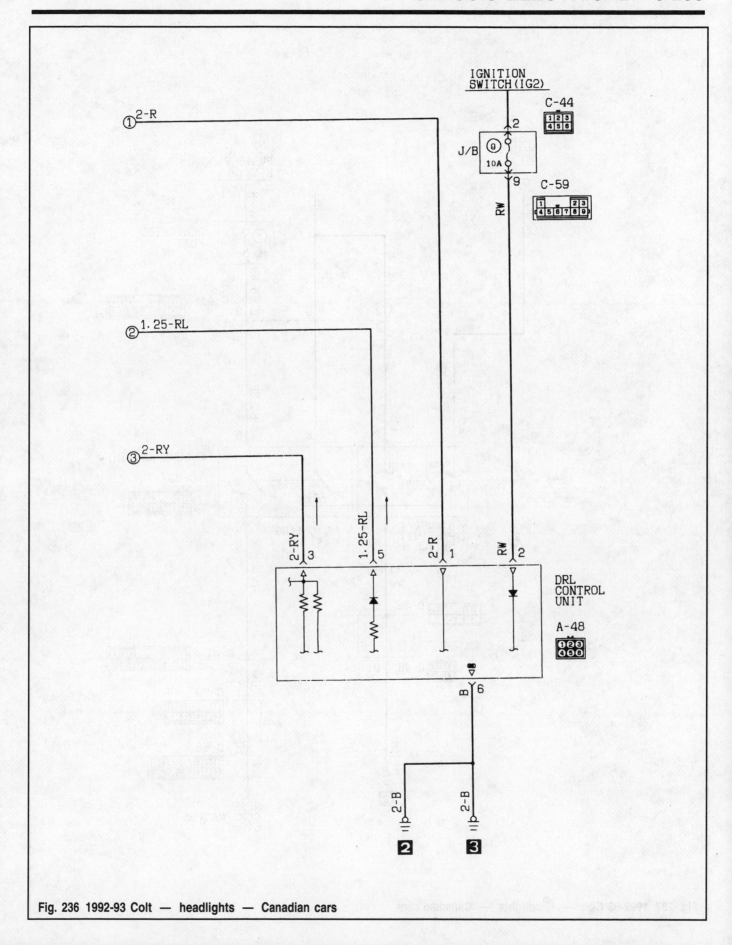

Fig. 236 1992-93 Colt — headlights — Canadian cars

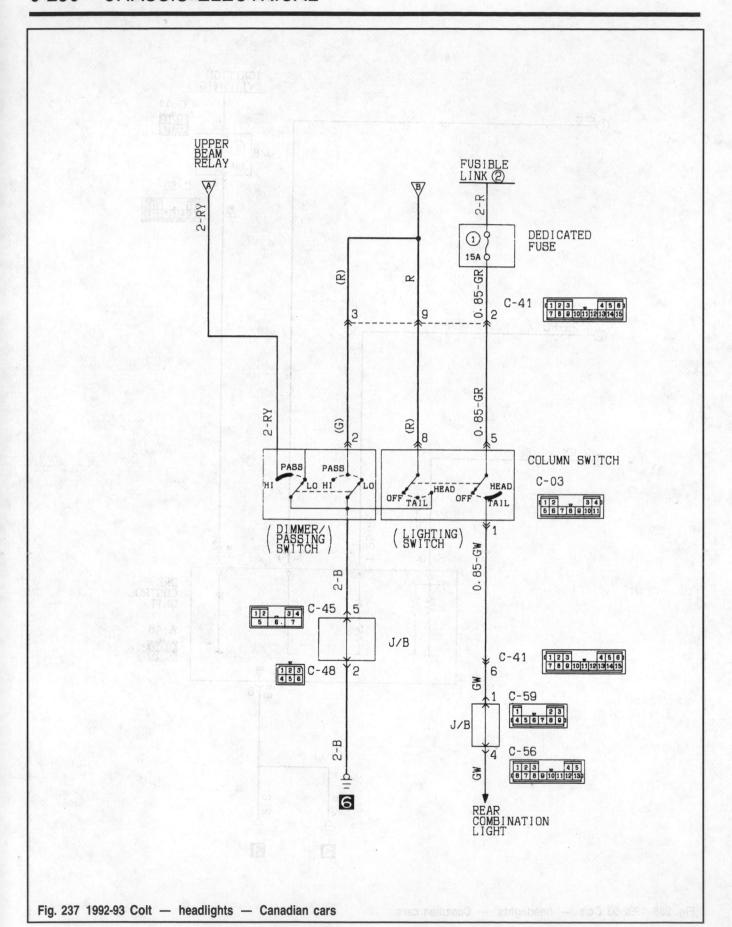

Fig. 237 1992-93 Colt — headlights — Canadian cars

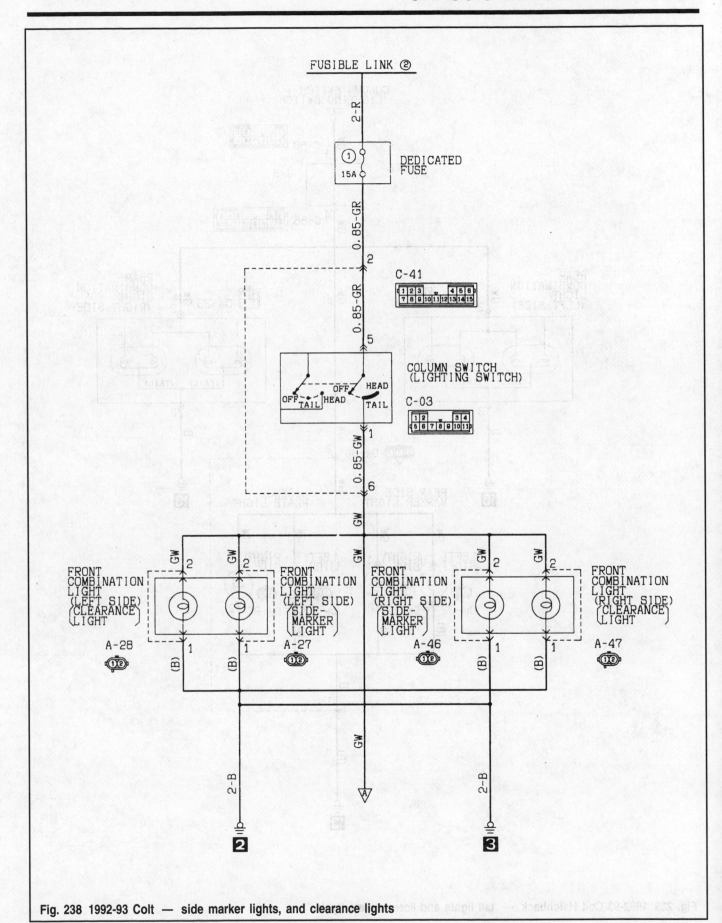

Fig. 238 1992-93 Colt — side marker lights, and clearance lights

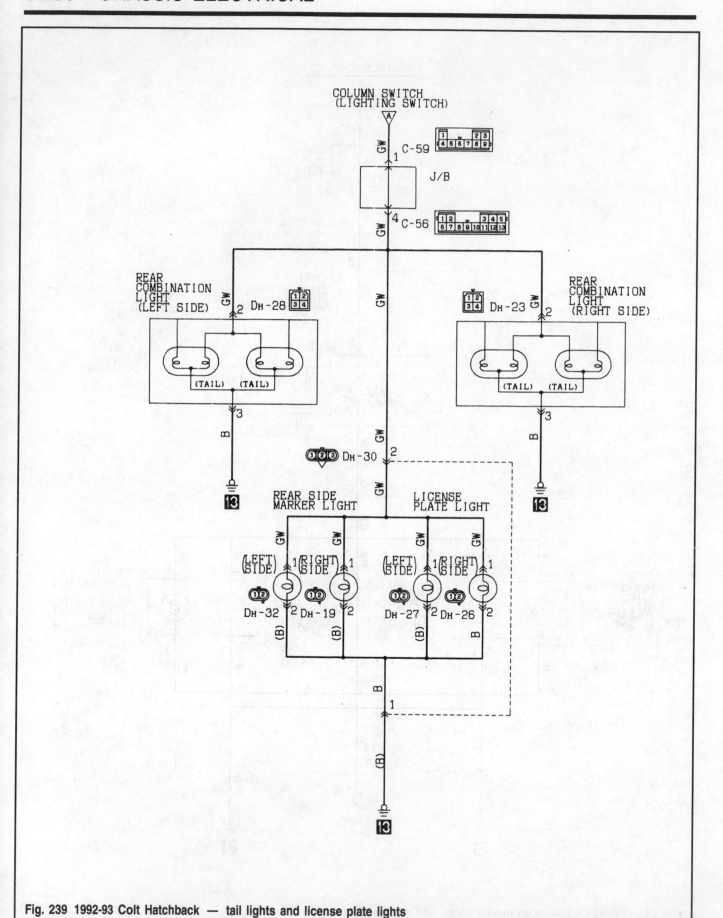

Fig. 239 1992-93 Colt Hatchback — tail lights and license plate lights

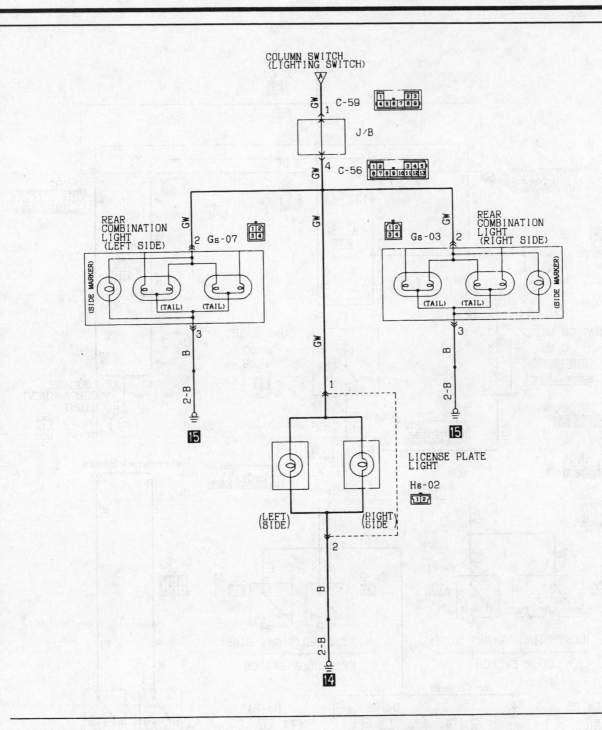

OPERATION

● When the lighting switch is set to the "TAIL" or "HEAD" position, electricity flows via dedicated fuse No. ① to each light, and each light illuminates.

TROUBLESHOOTING HINTS

1. All lights do not illuminate.
   1) The headlights also do not illuminate.
      ● Check fusible link No. ②.
   2) The headlights illuminate.
      ● Check dedicated fuse No. ①.

Fig. 240 1992-93 Colt Sedan — tail lights and license plate lights

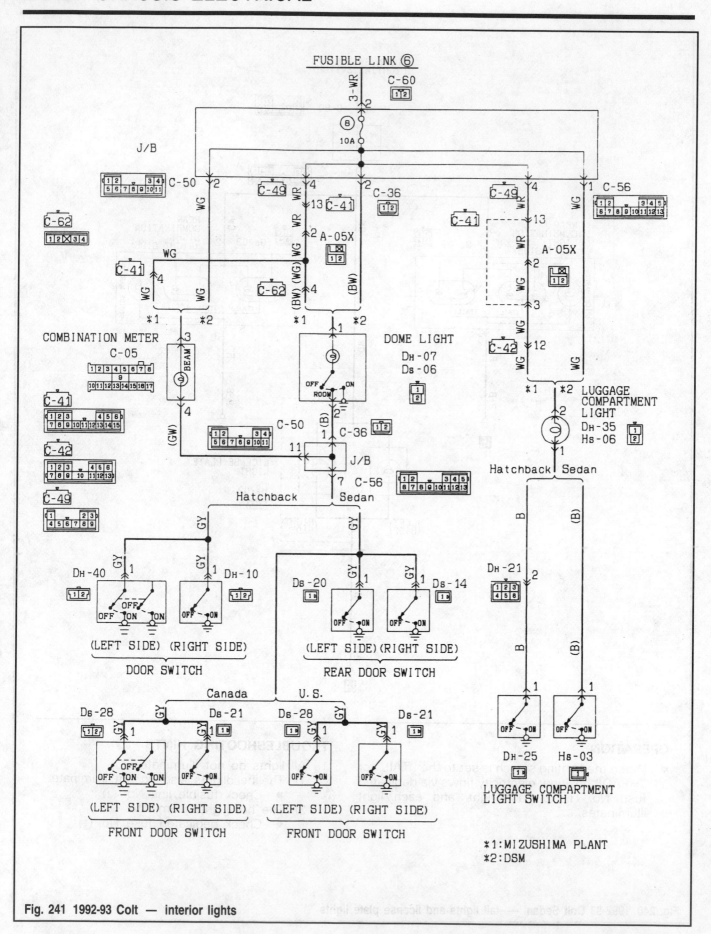

Fig. 241 1992-93 Colt — interior lights

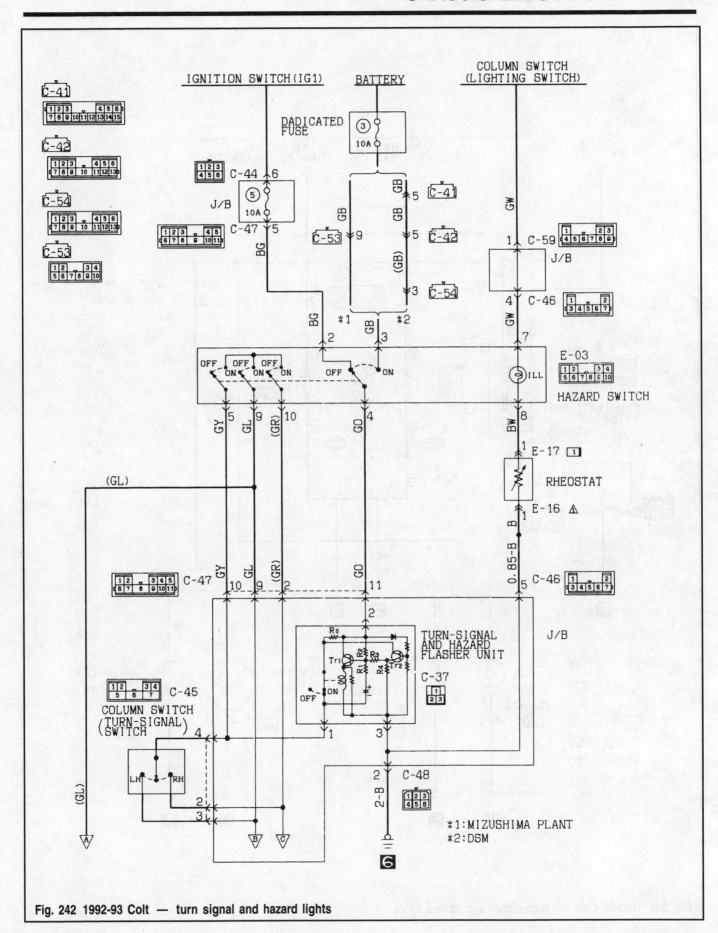

Fig. 242 1992-93 Colt — turn signal and hazard lights

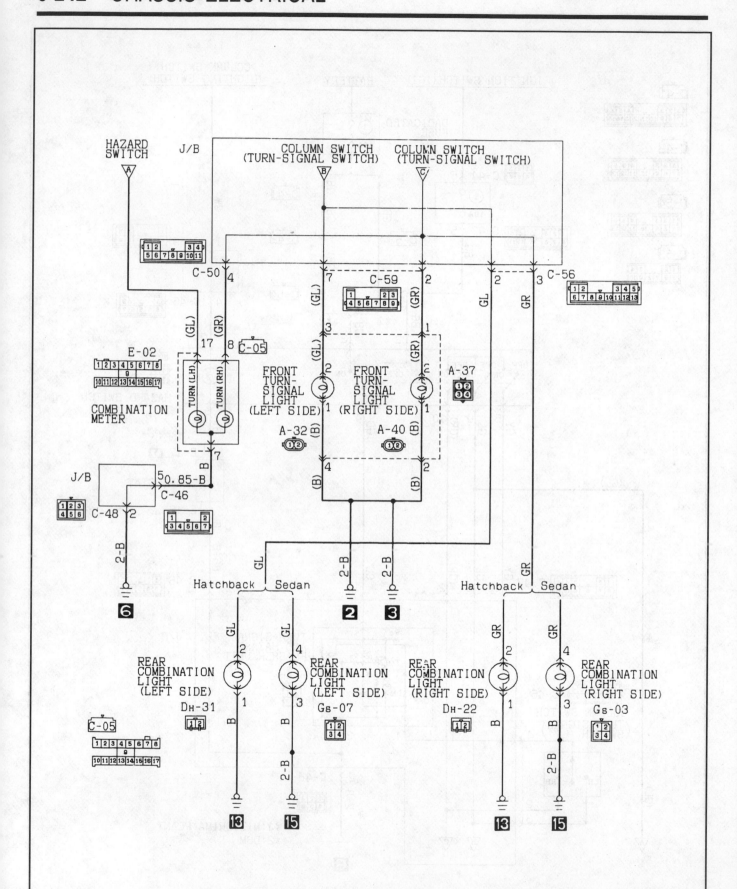

Fig. 243 1992-93 Colt — turn signal and hazard lights

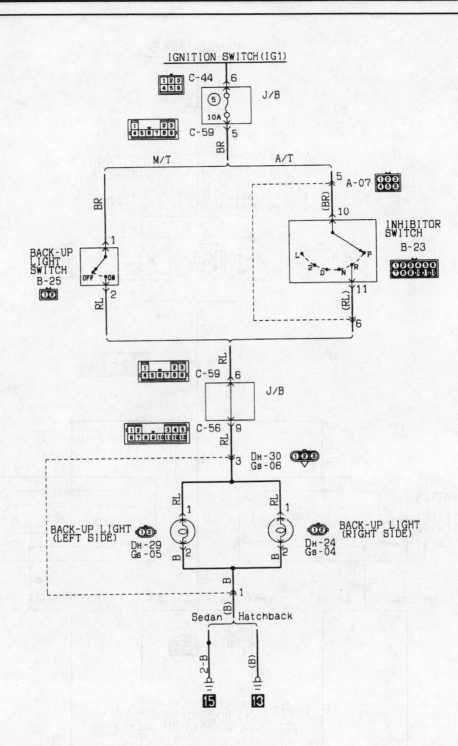

OPERATION

- When, with the ignition switch at the "ON" position, the shift lever (or the selector lever) is moved to the "R" position, the back-up light switch (M/T models) is switched ON [or the inhibitor switch (A/T models) is switched to the "R" position], and the back-up light illuminates.

Fig. 244 1992-93 Colt — back-up lights

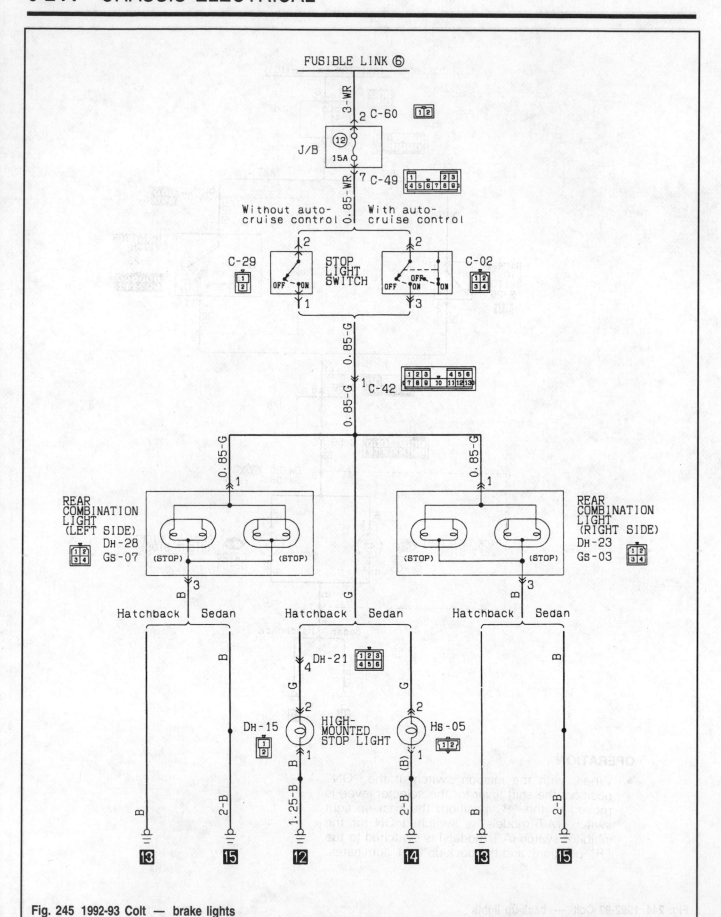

Fig. 245 1992-93 Colt — brake lights

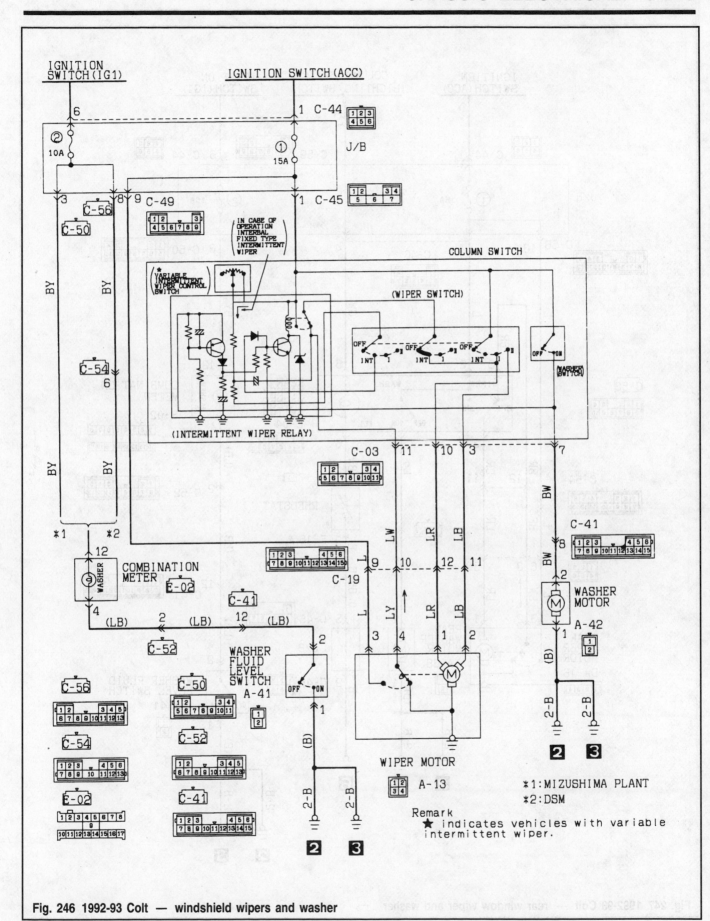

Fig. 246 1992-93 Colt — windshield wipers and washer

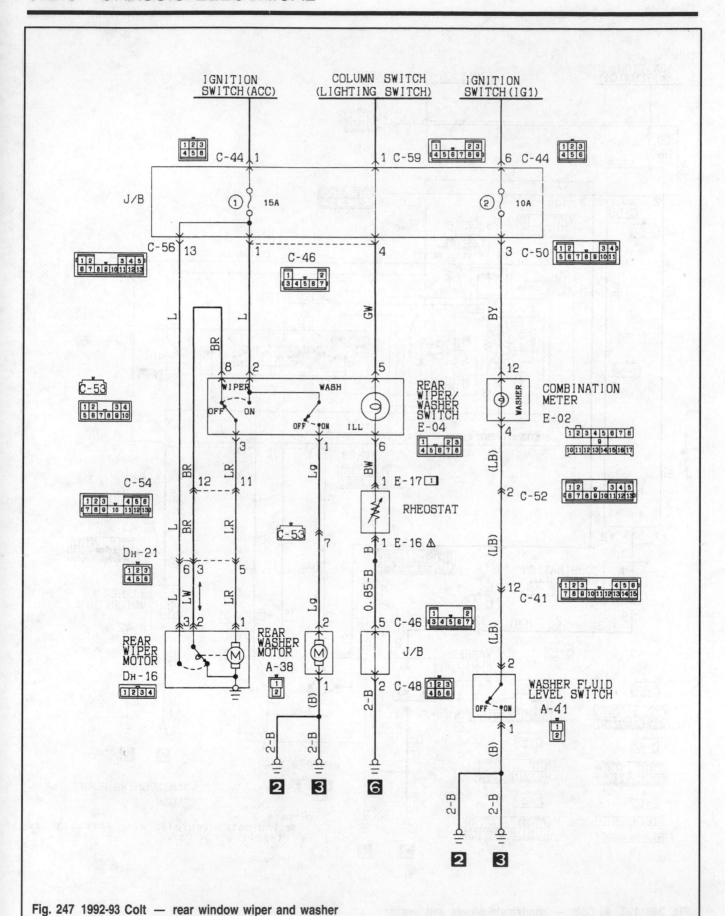

Fig. 247 1992-93 Colt — rear window wiper and washer

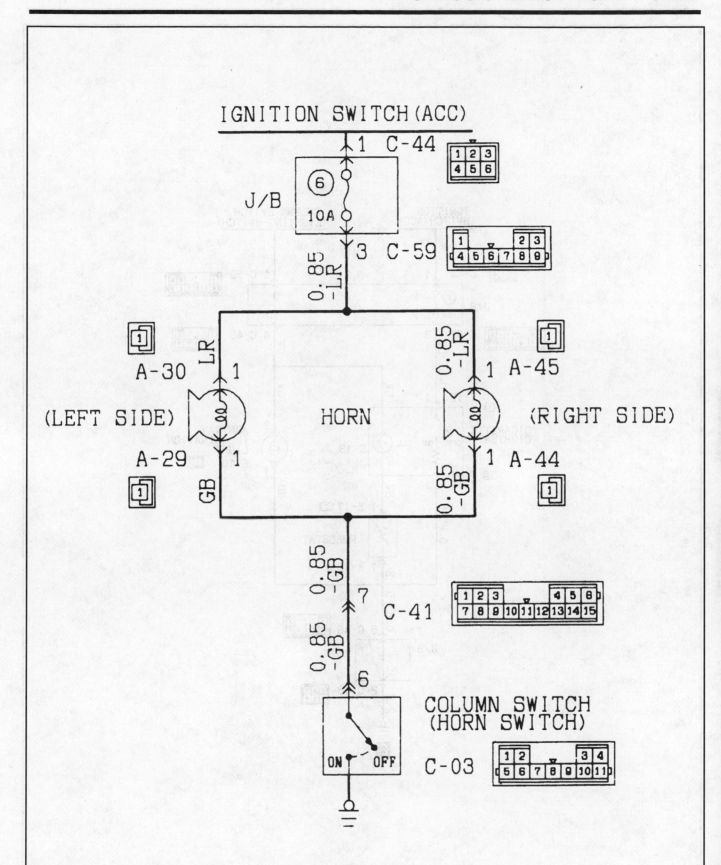

Fig. 248 1992-93 Colt — horn

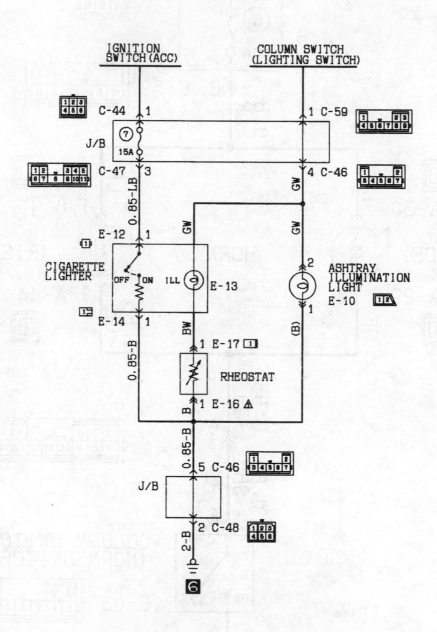

Fig. 249 1992-93 Colt — cigar lighter

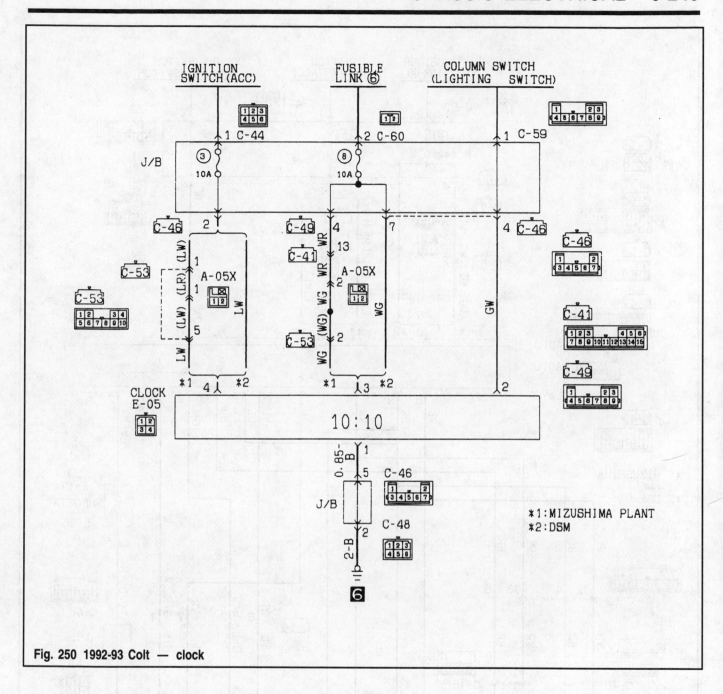

Fig. 250 1992-93 Colt — clock

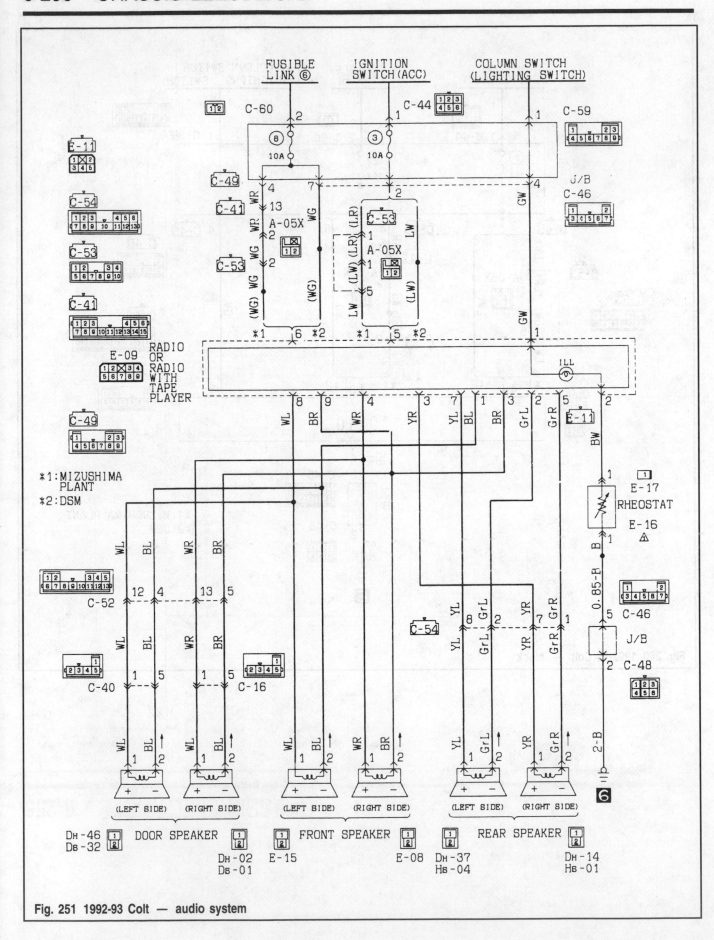

Fig. 251 1992-93 Colt — audio system

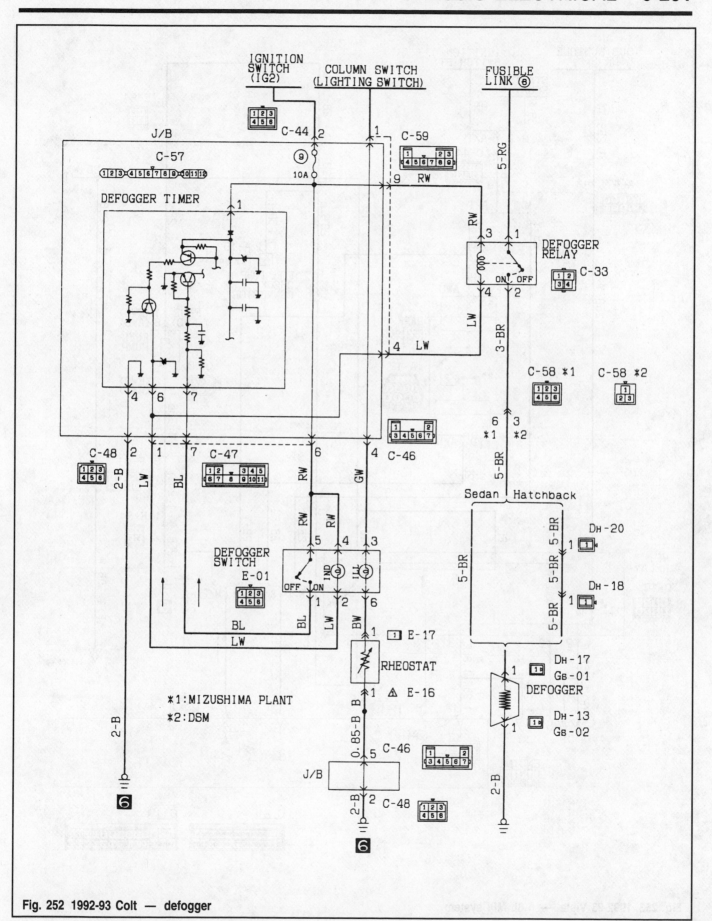

Fig. 252 1992-93 Colt — defogger

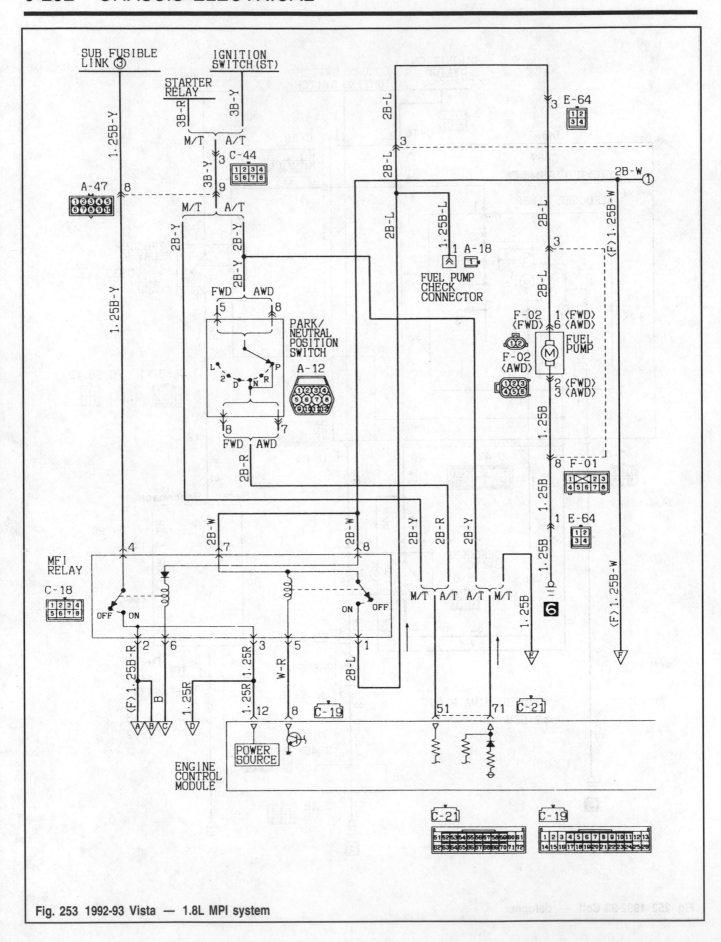

Fig. 253 1992-93 Vista — 1.8L MPI system

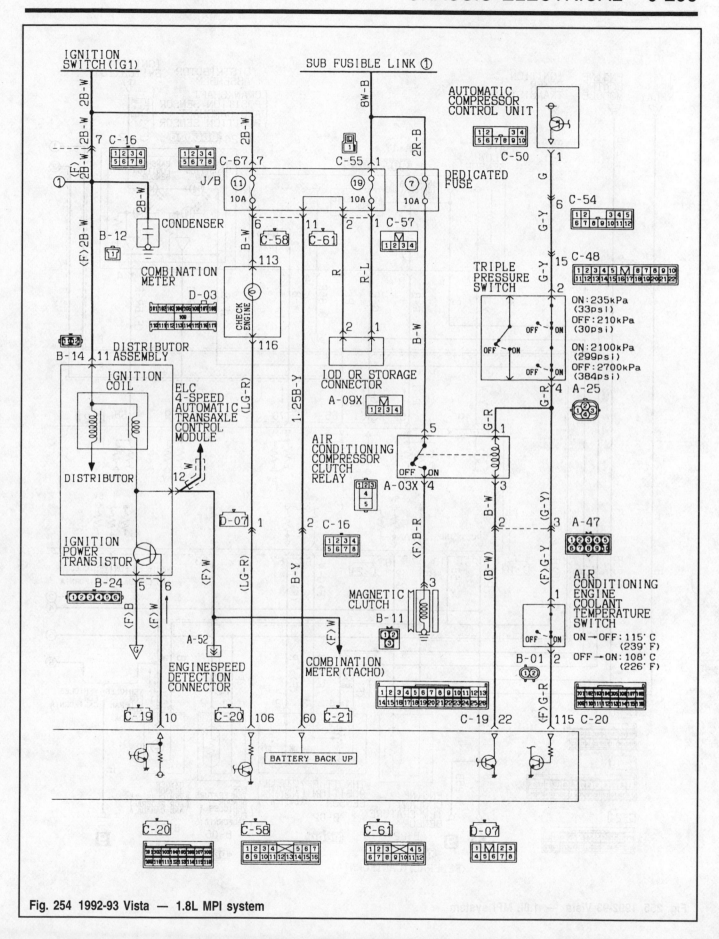

Fig. 254 1992-93 Vista — 1.8L MPI system

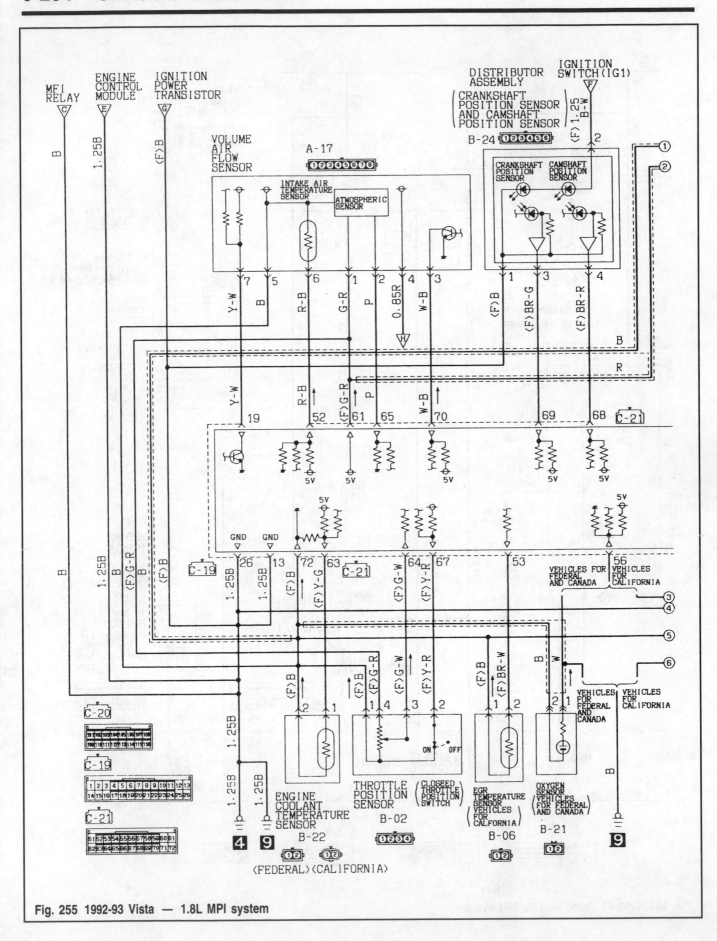

Fig. 255 1992-93 Vista — 1.8L MPI system

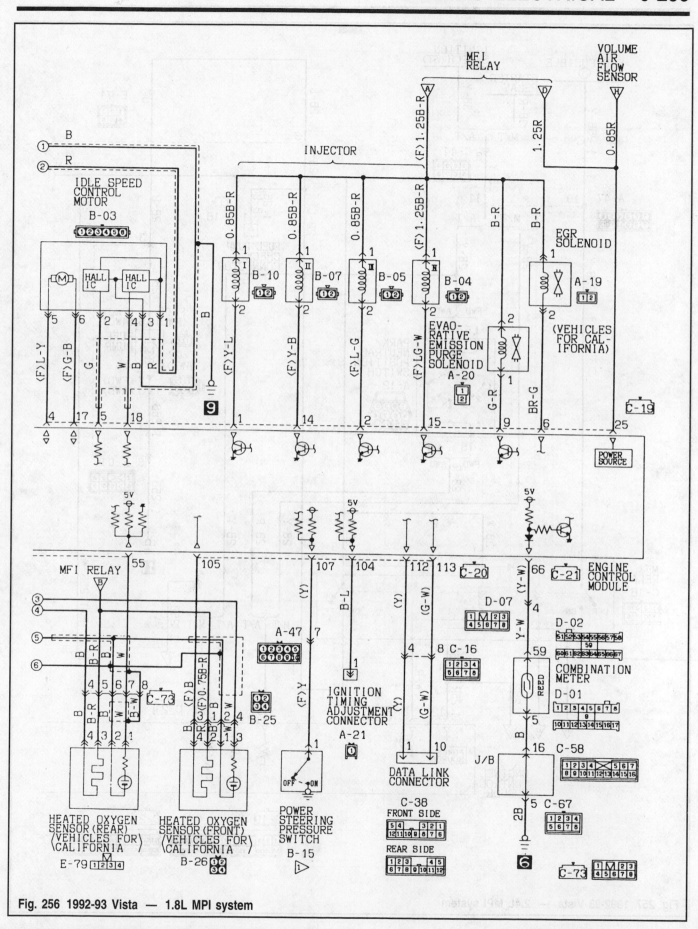

Fig. 256 1992-93 Vista — 1.8L MPI system

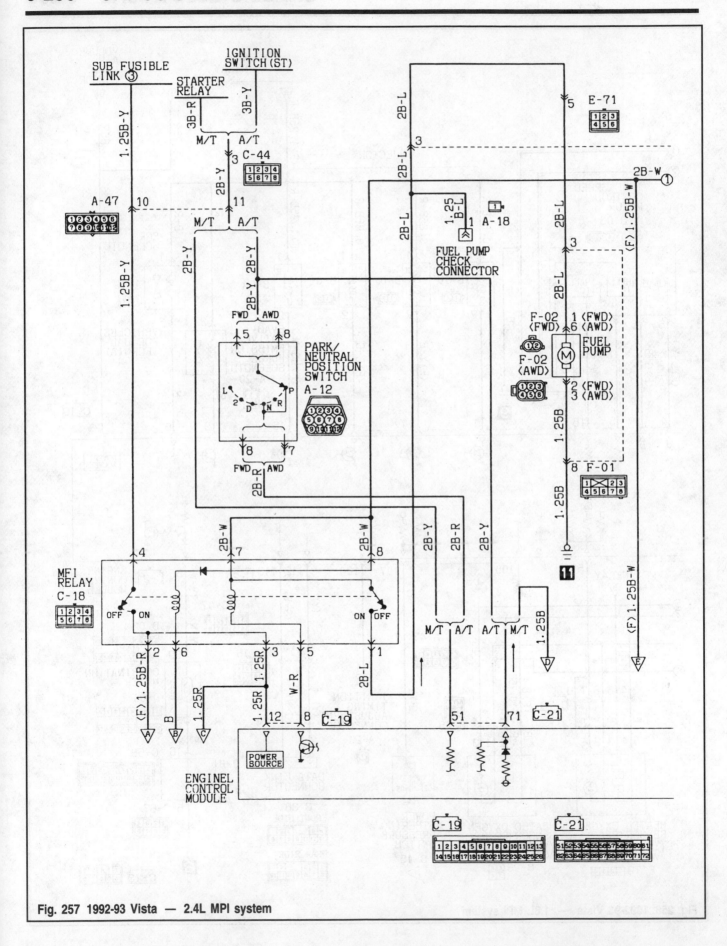

Fig. 257 1992-93 Vista — 2.4L MPI system

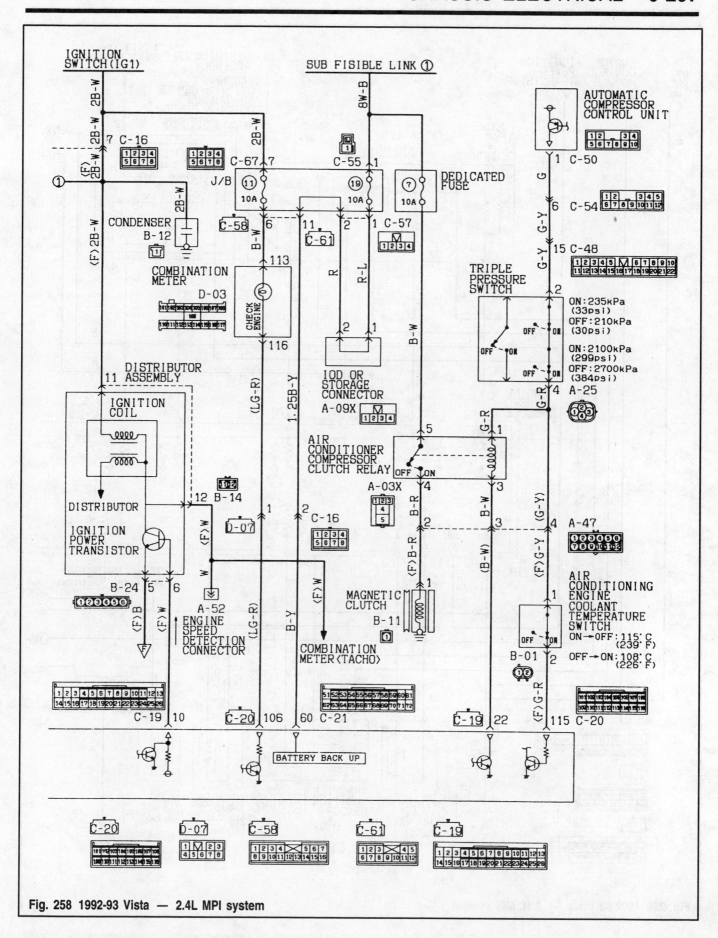

Fig. 258 1992-93 Vista — 2.4L MPI system

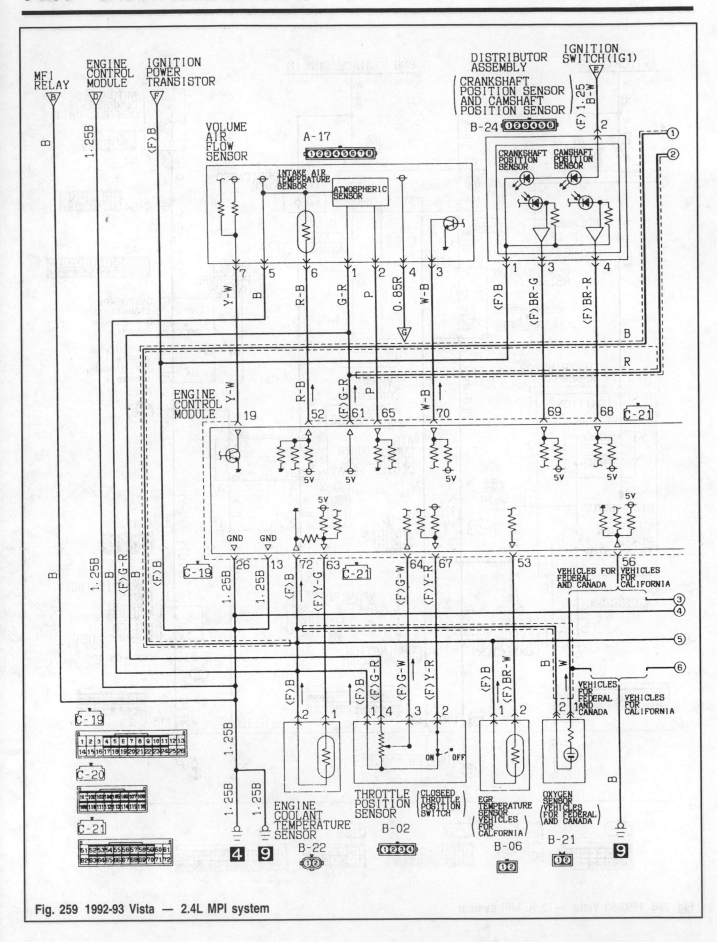

Fig. 259 1992-93 Vista — 2.4L MPI system

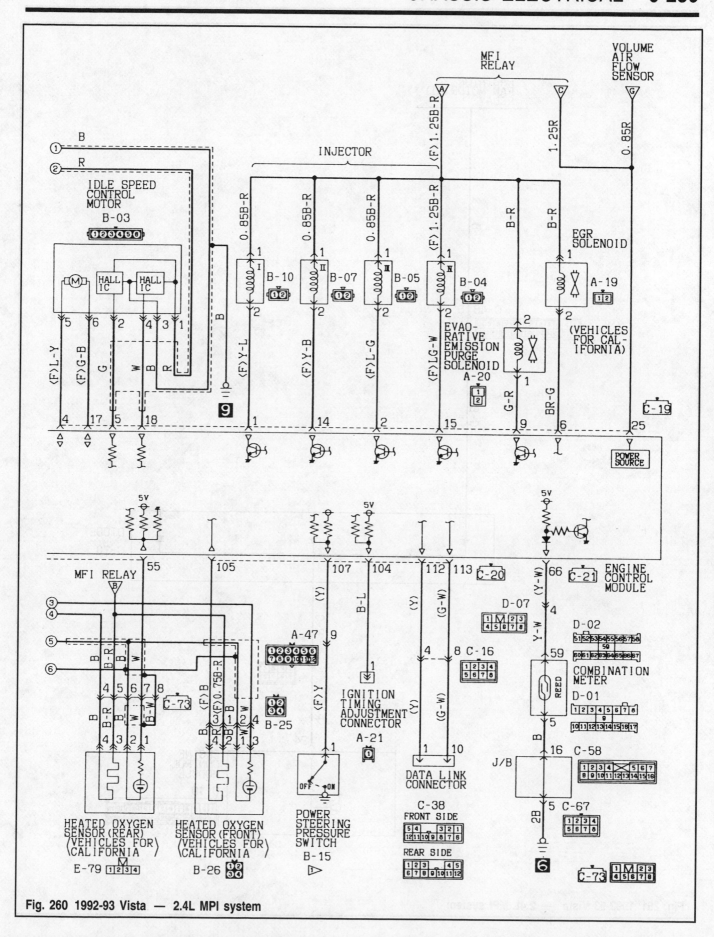

Fig. 260 1992-93 Vista — 2.4L MPI system

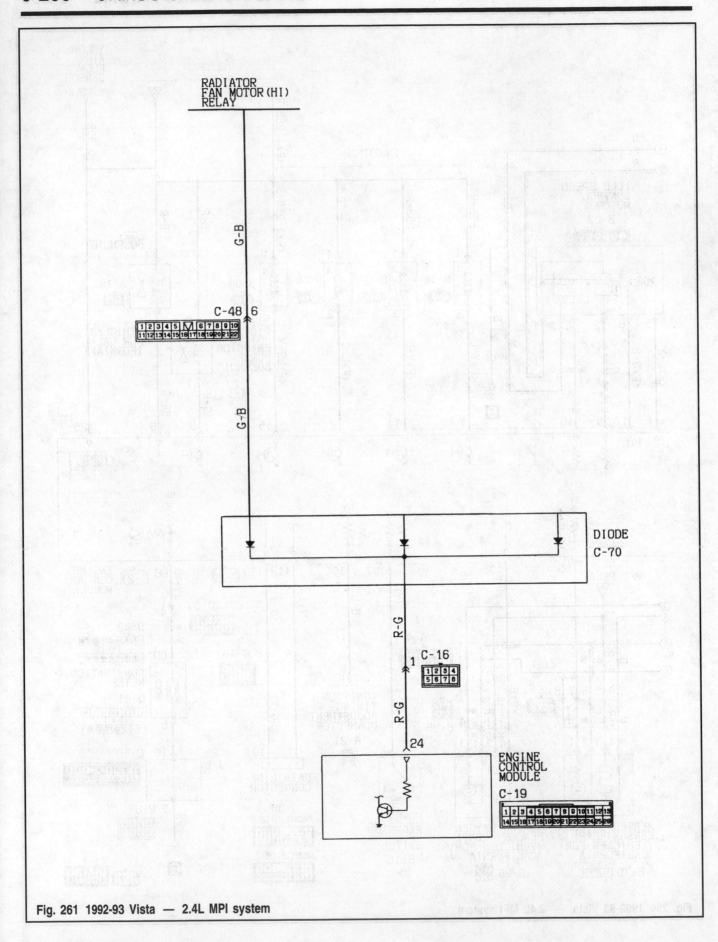

Fig. 261 1992-93 Vista — 2.4L MPI system

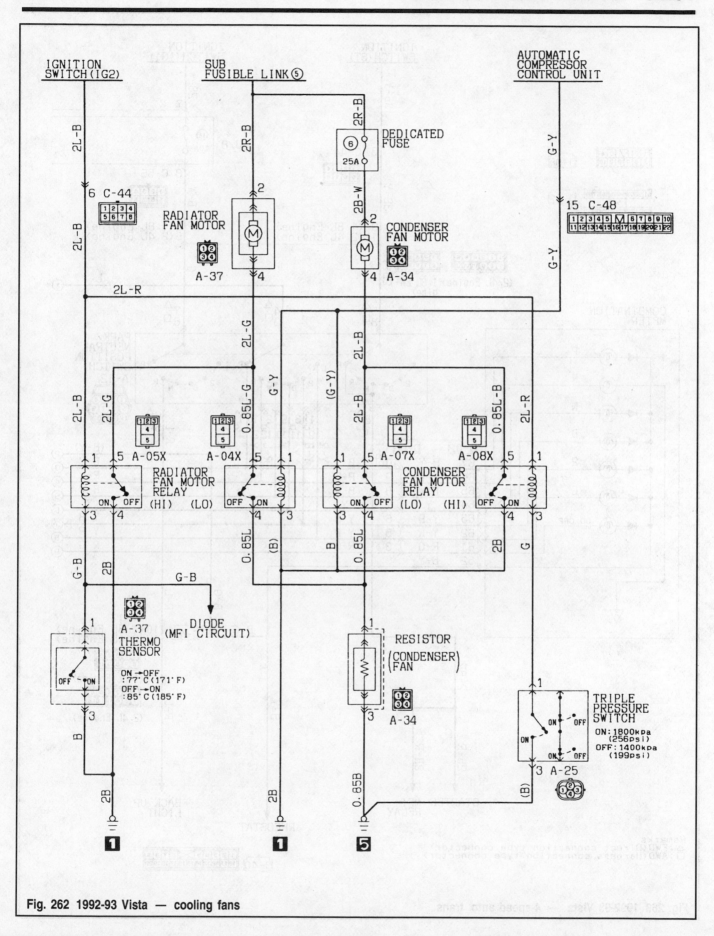

Fig. 262 1992-93 Vista — cooling fans

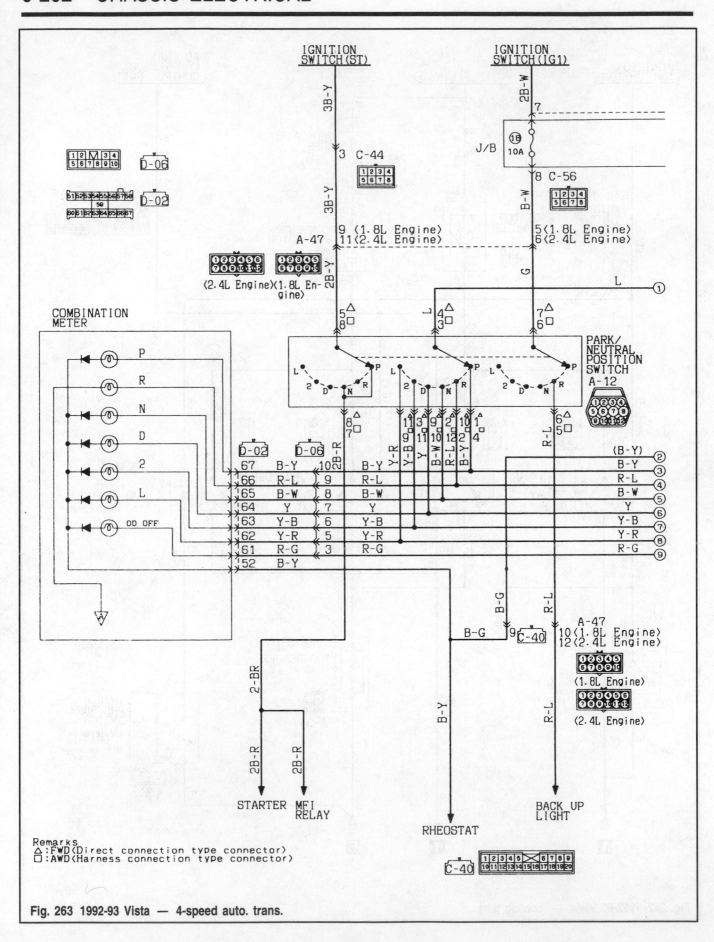

Fig. 263 1992-93 Vista — 4-speed auto. trans.

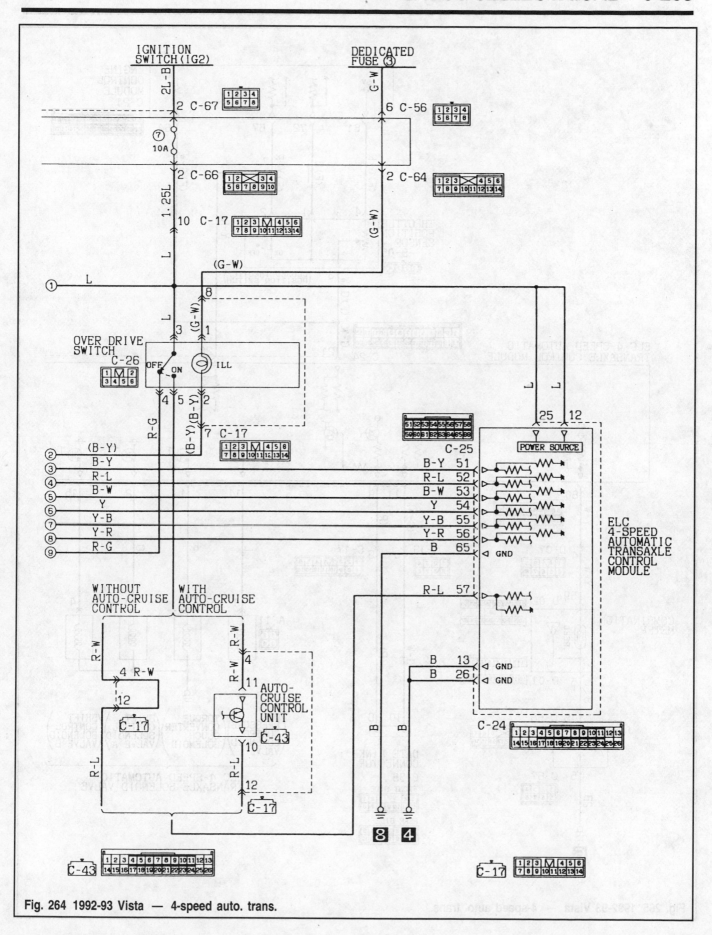

Fig. 264 1992-93 Vista — 4-speed auto. trans.

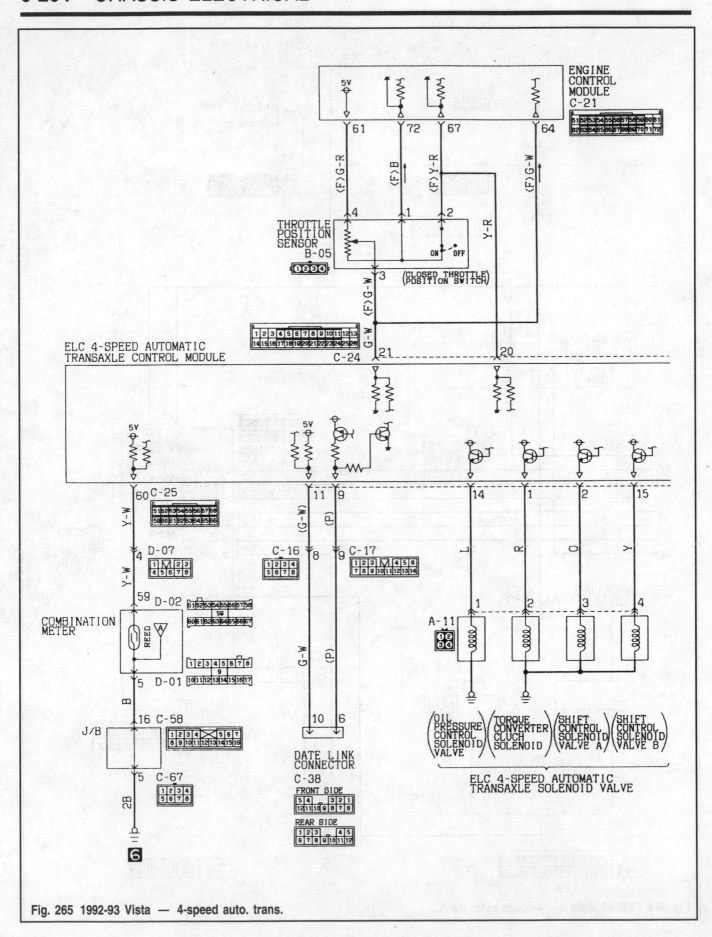

Fig. 265 1992-93 Vista — 4-speed auto. trans.

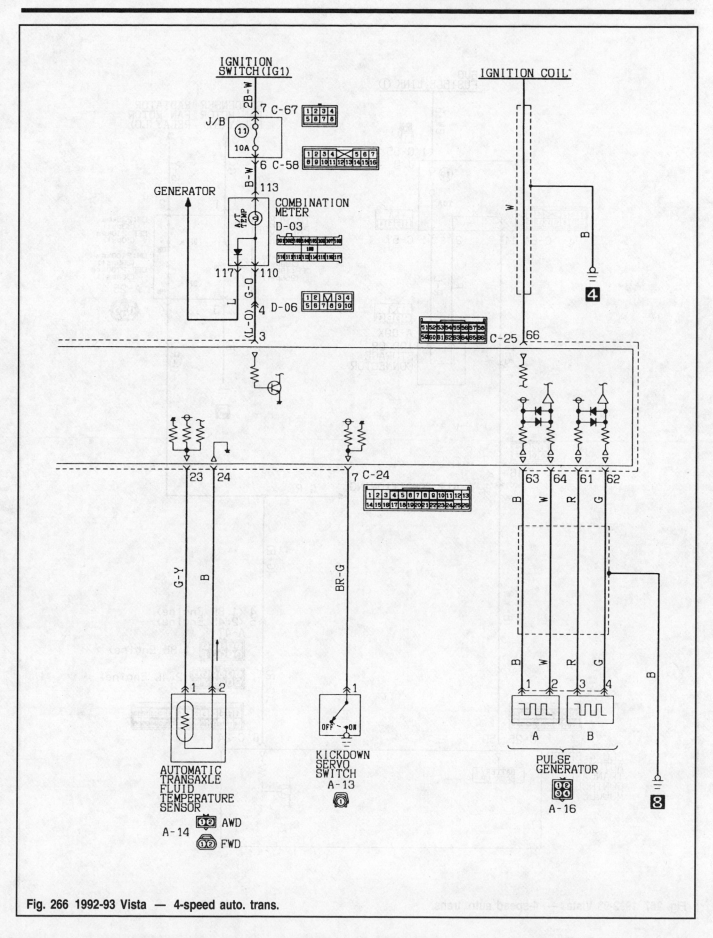

Fig. 266 1992-93 Vista — 4-speed auto. trans.

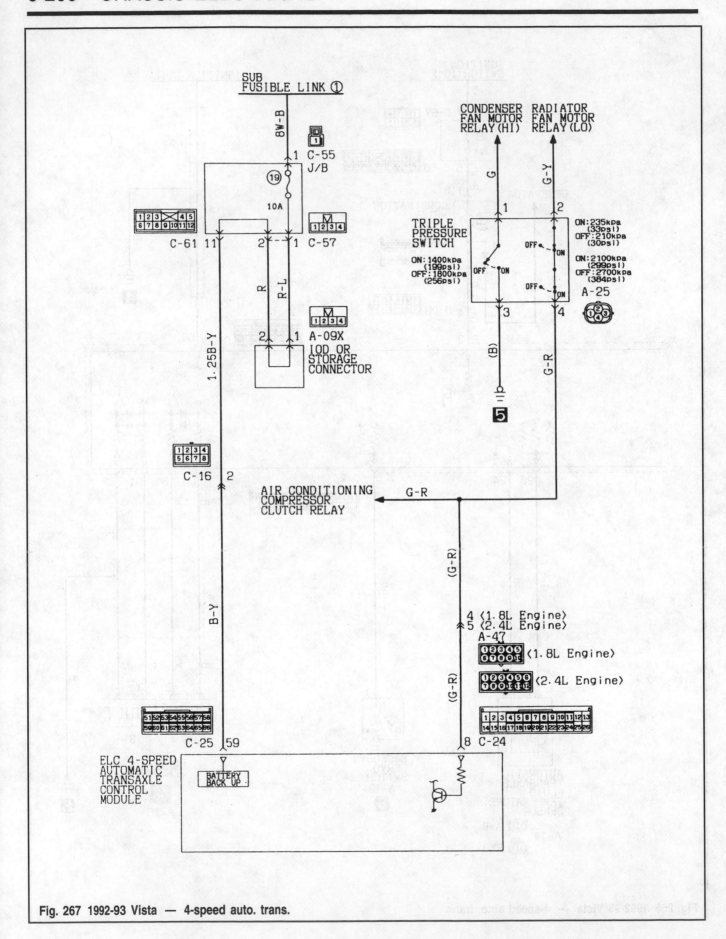

Fig. 267 1992-93 Vista — 4-speed auto. trans.

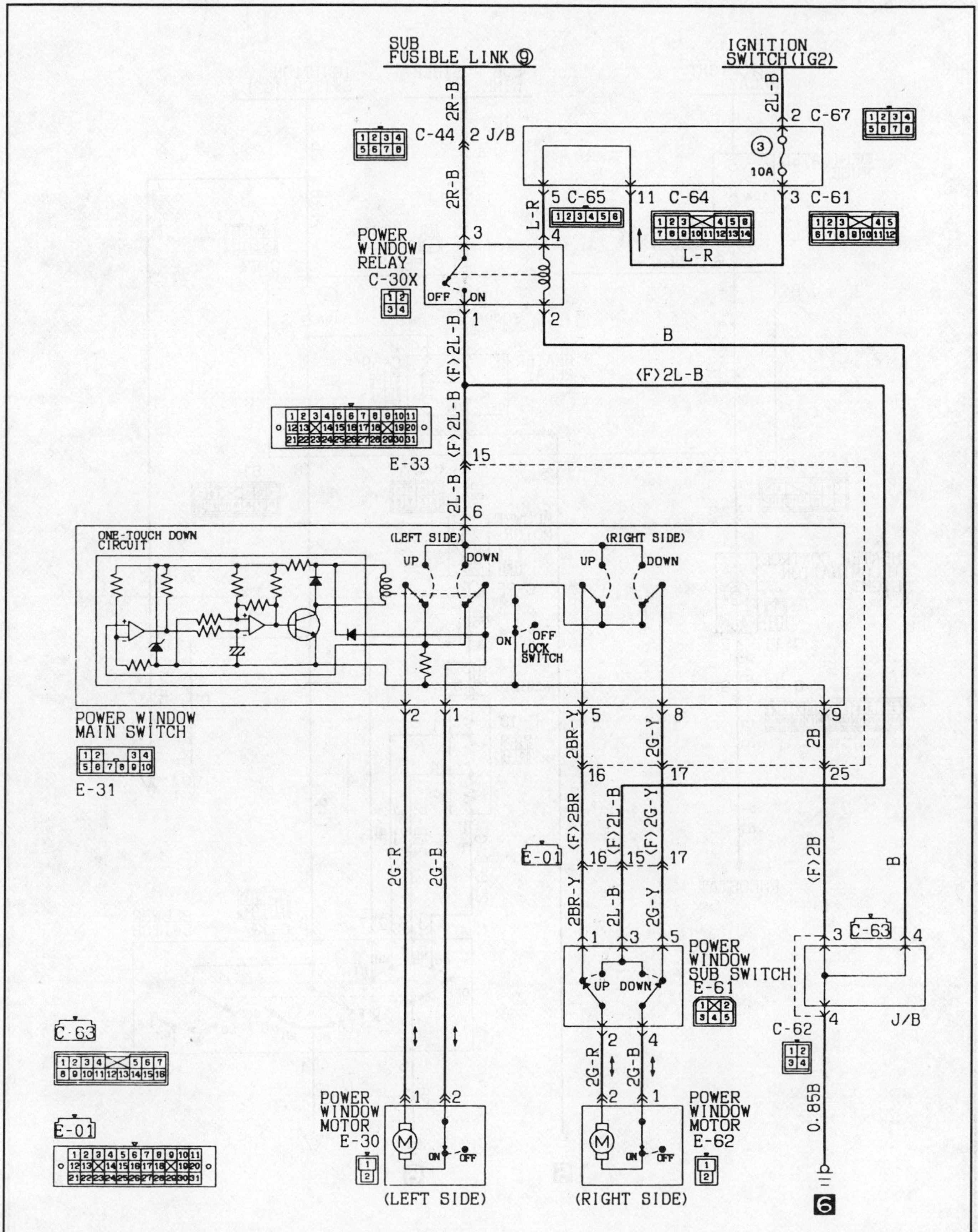

Fig. 268 1992-93 Vista — power windows

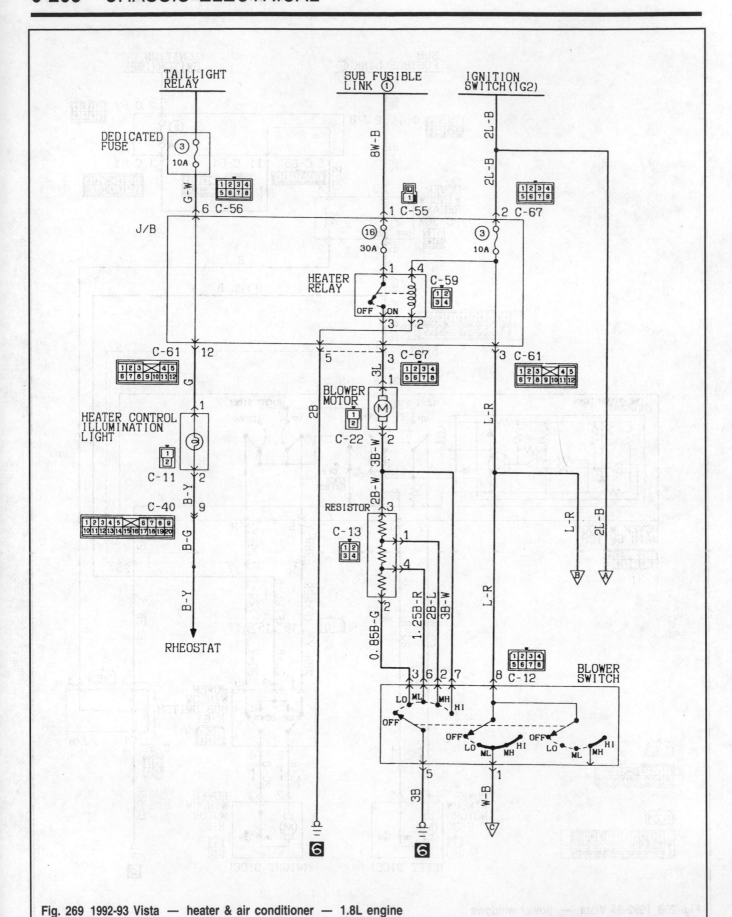

Fig. 269 1992-93 Vista — heater & air conditioner — 1.8L engine

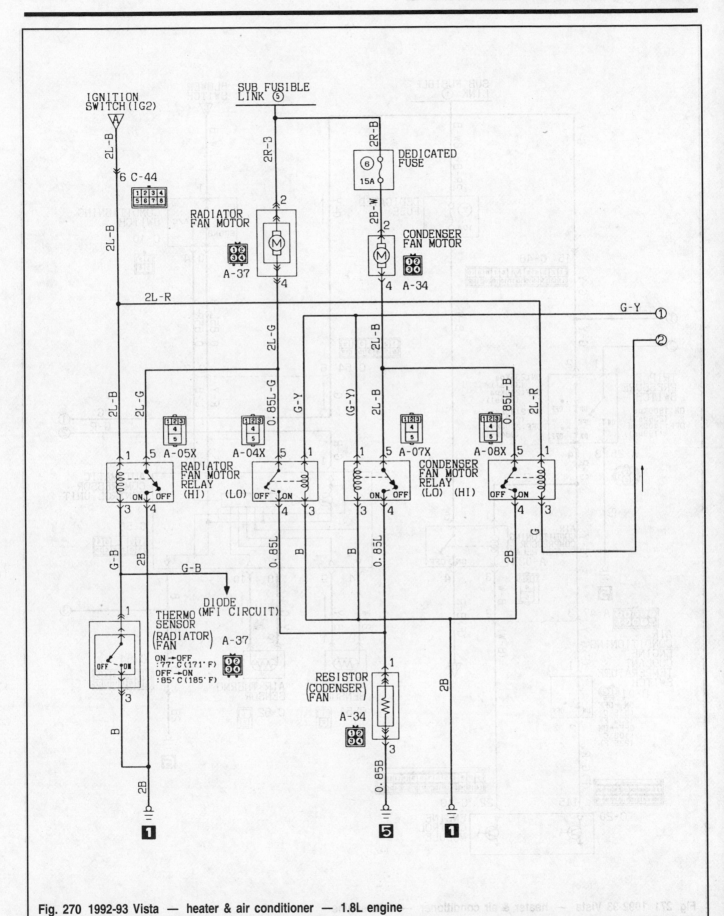

Fig. 270 1992-93 Vista — heater & air conditioner — 1.8L engine

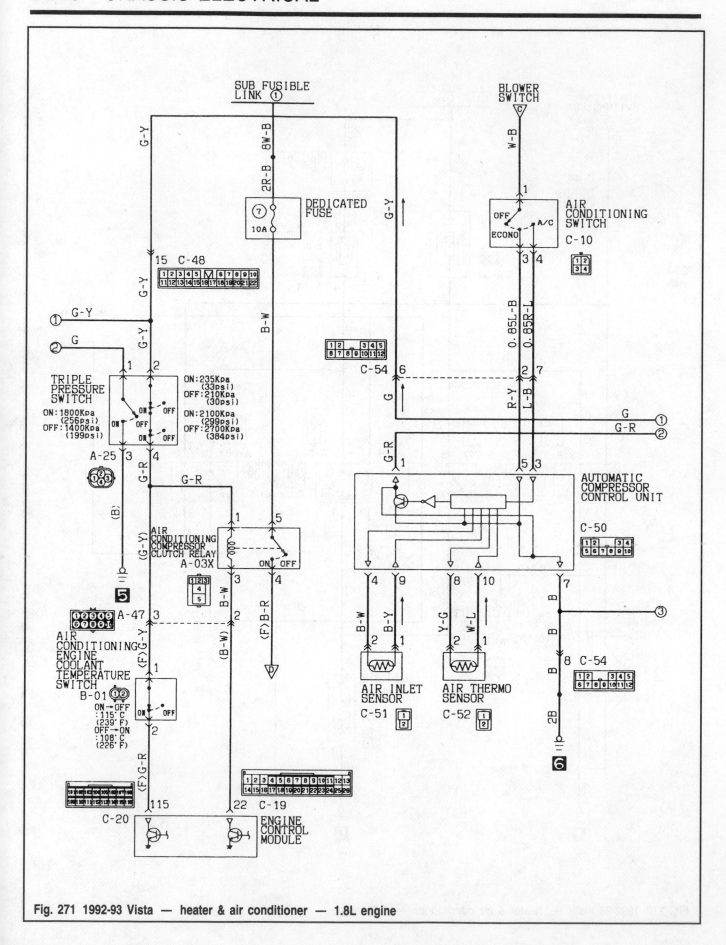

Fig. 271 1992-93 Vista — heater & air conditioner — 1.8L engine

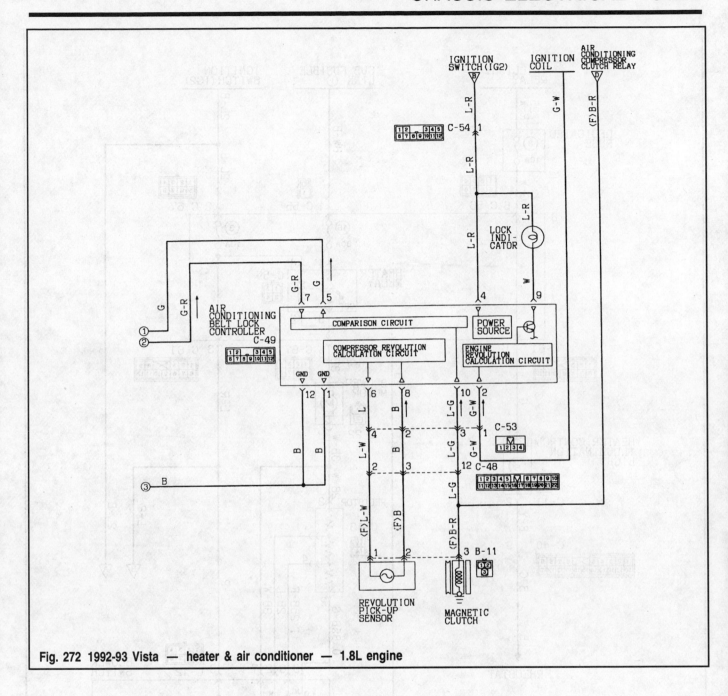

Fig. 272 1992-93 Vista — heater & air conditioner — 1.8L engine

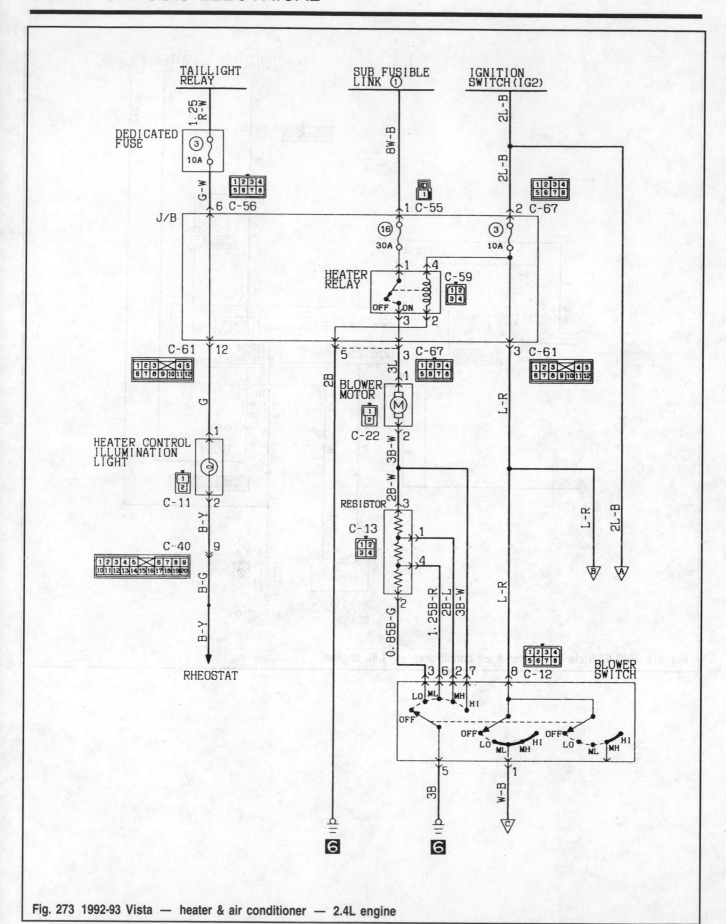

Fig. 273 1992-93 Vista — heater & air conditioner — 2.4L engine

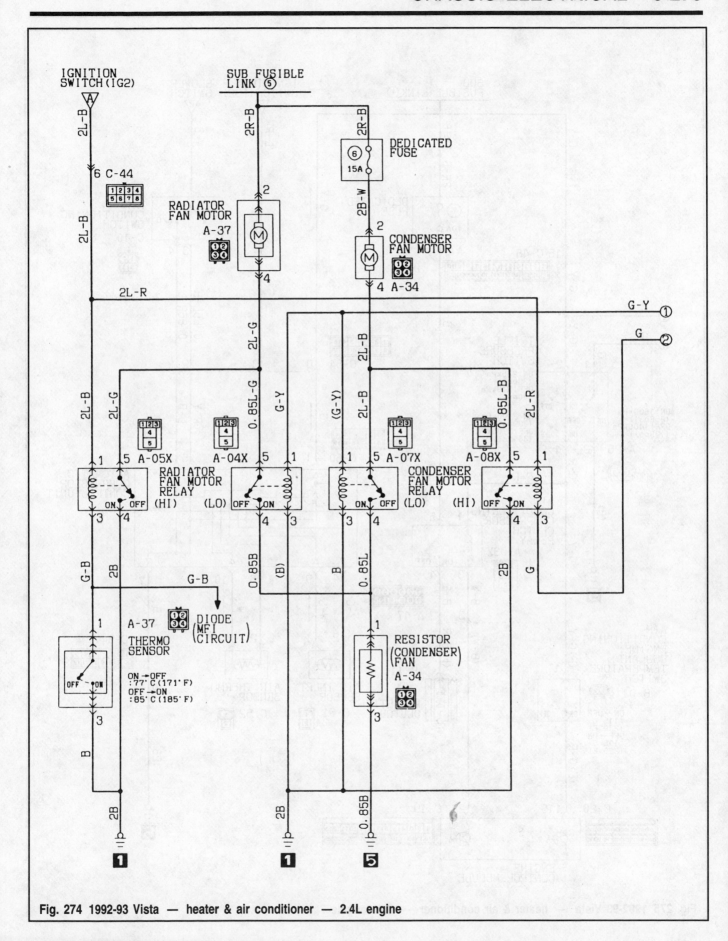

Fig. 274 1992-93 Vista — heater & air conditioner — 2.4L engine

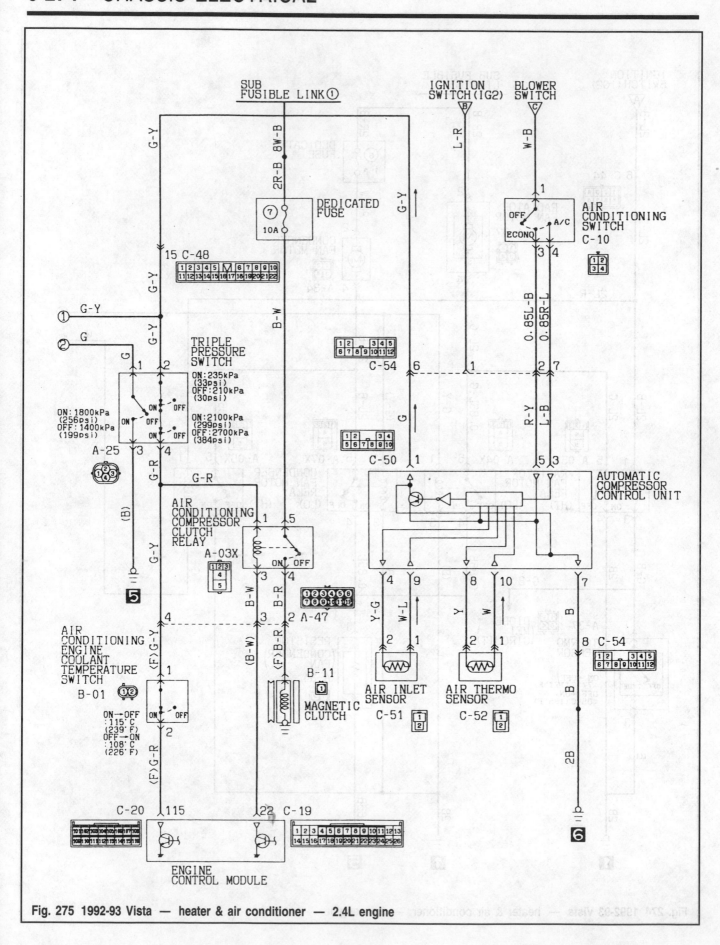

Fig. 275 1992-93 Vista — heater & air conditioner — 2.4L engine

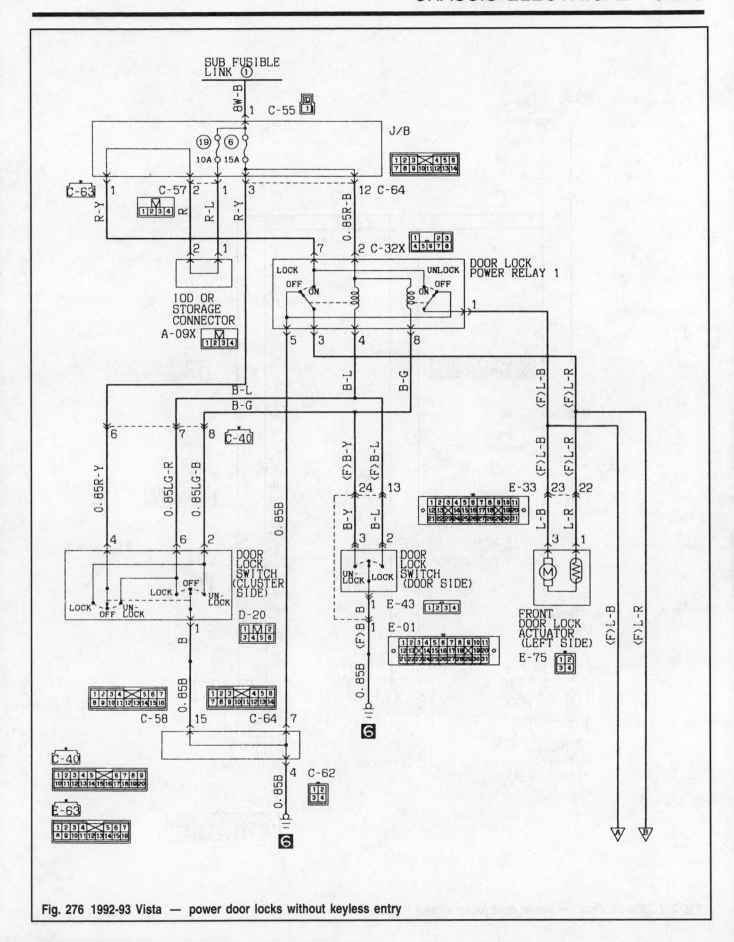

Fig. 276 1992-93 Vista — power door locks without keyless entry

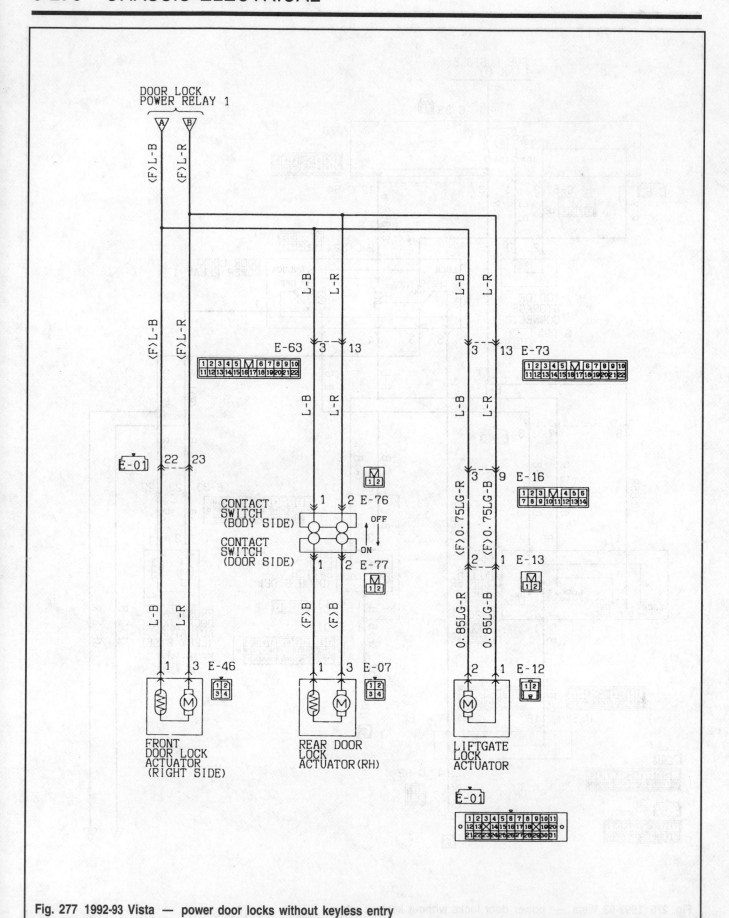

Fig. 277 1992-93 Vista — power door locks without keyless entry

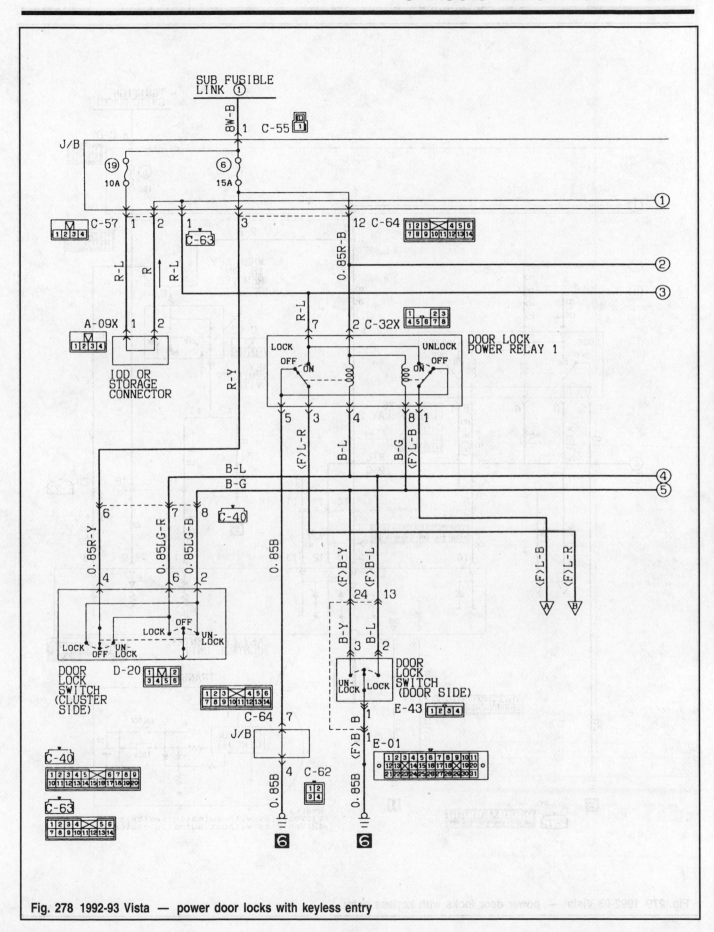

Fig. 278 1992-93 Vista — power door locks with keyless entry

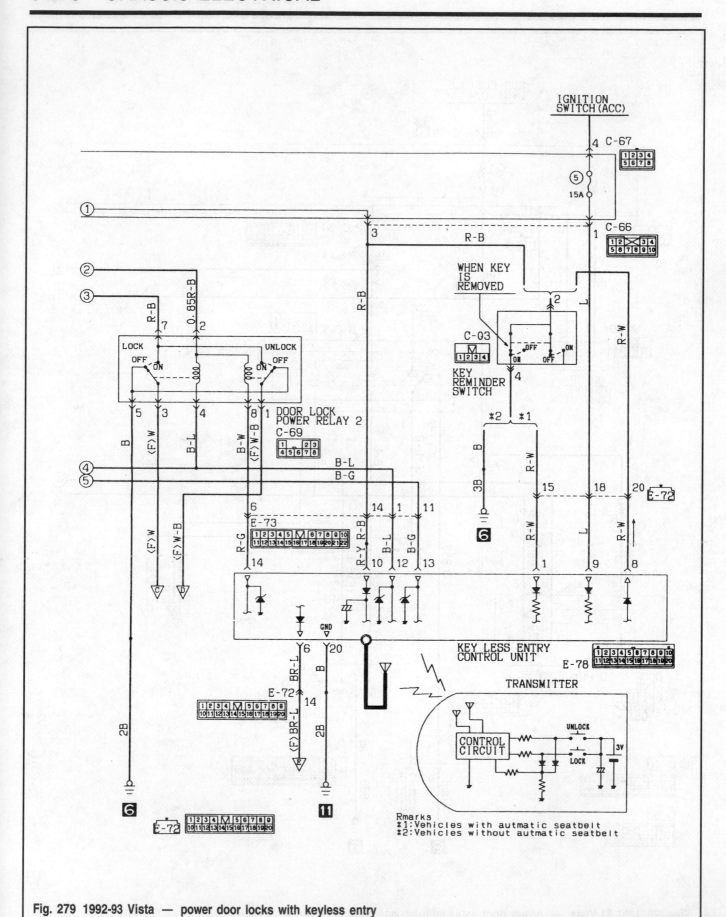

Fig. 279 1992-93 Vista — power door locks with keyless entry

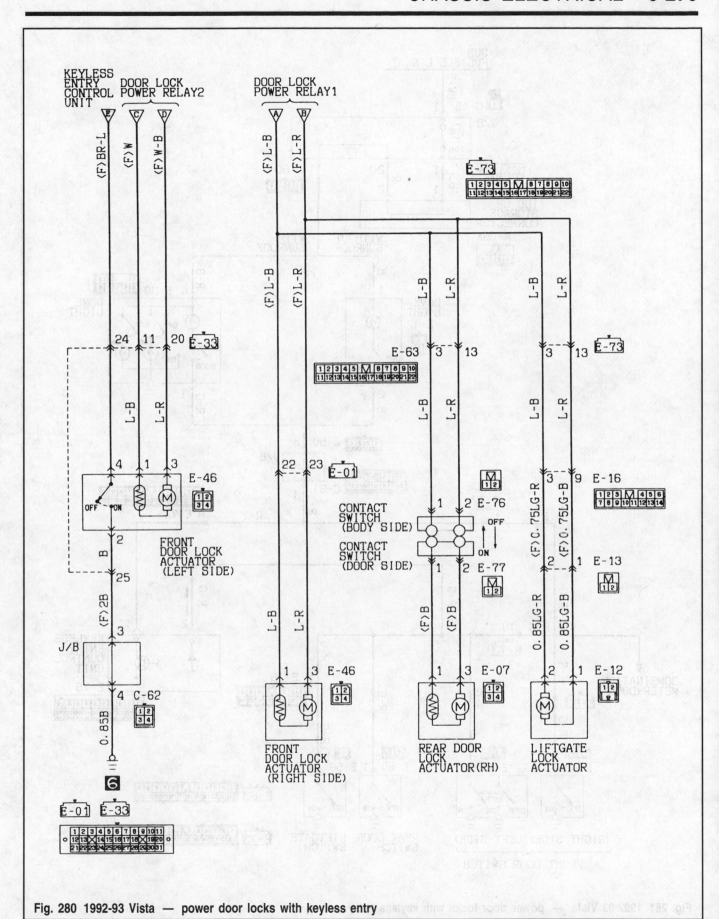

Fig. 280 1992-93 Vista — power door locks with keyless entry

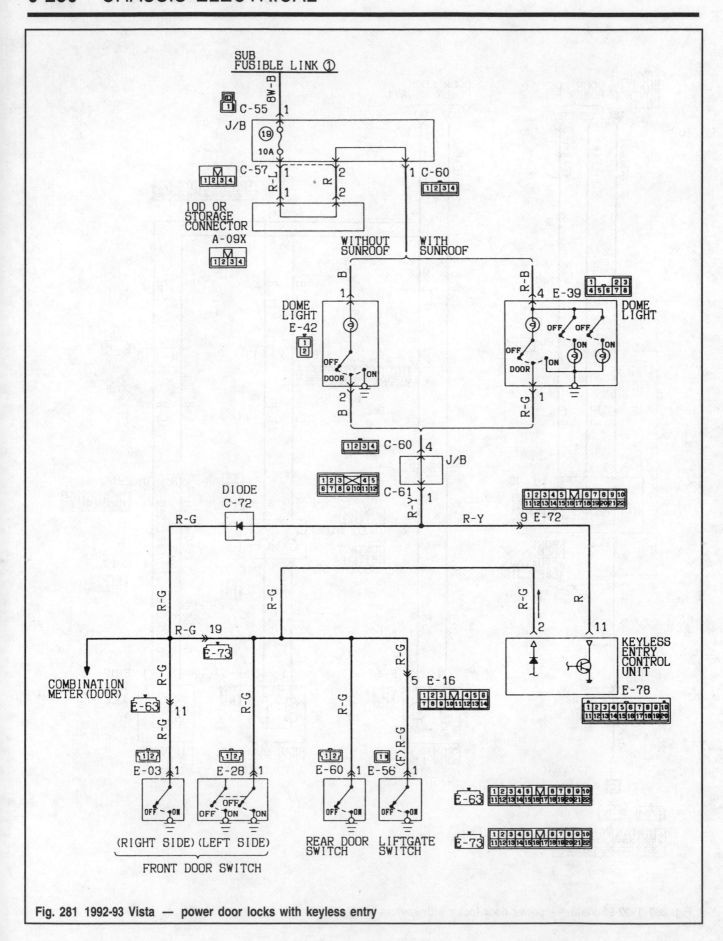

Fig. 281 1992-93 Vista — power door locks with keyless entry

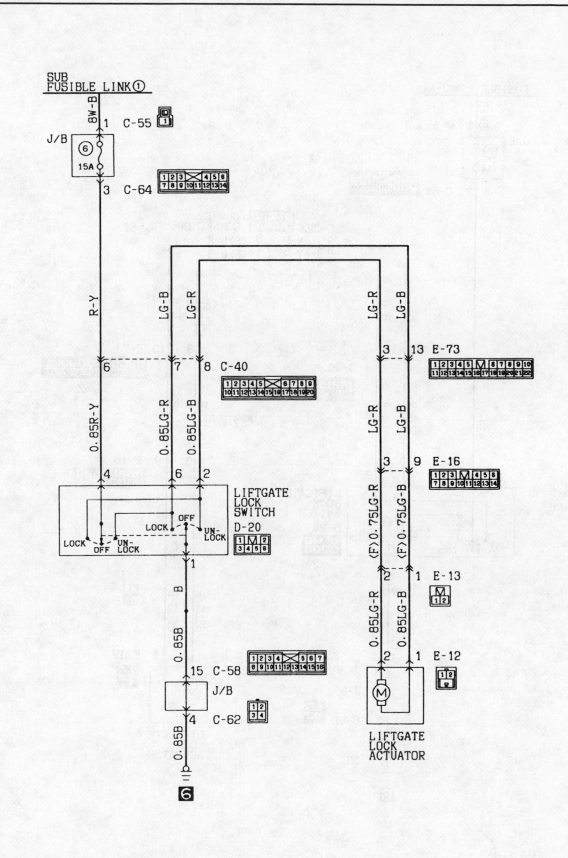

Fig. 282 1992-93 Vista — liftgate lock without keyless entry

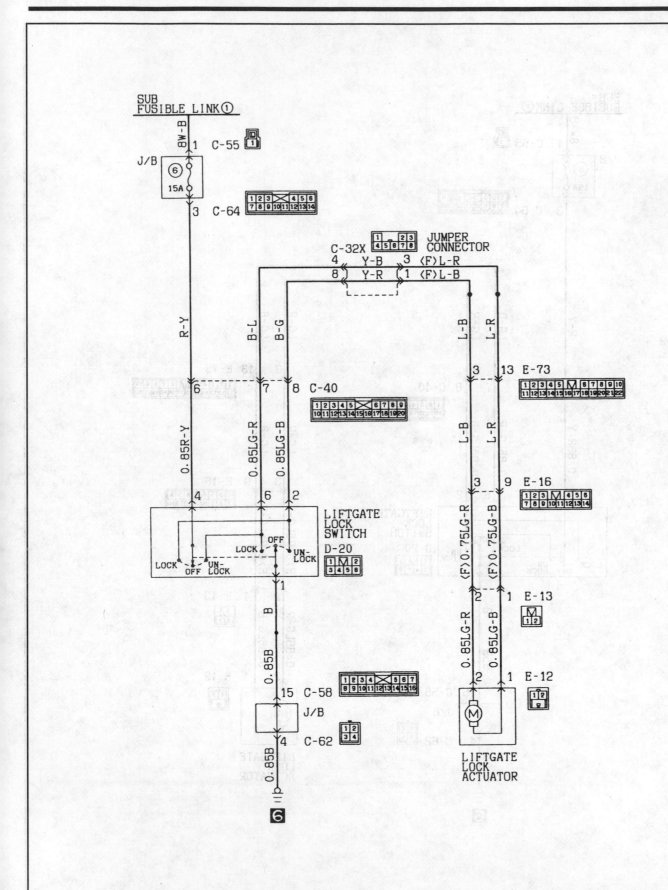

Fig. 283 1992-93 Vista — liftgate lock without keyless entry

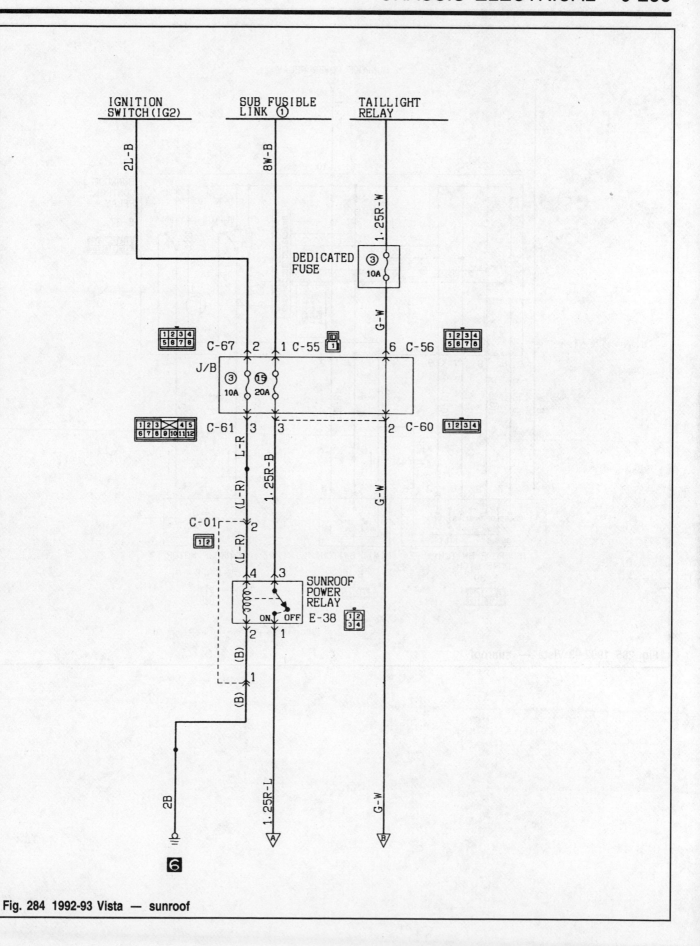

Fig. 284 1992-93 Vista — sunroof

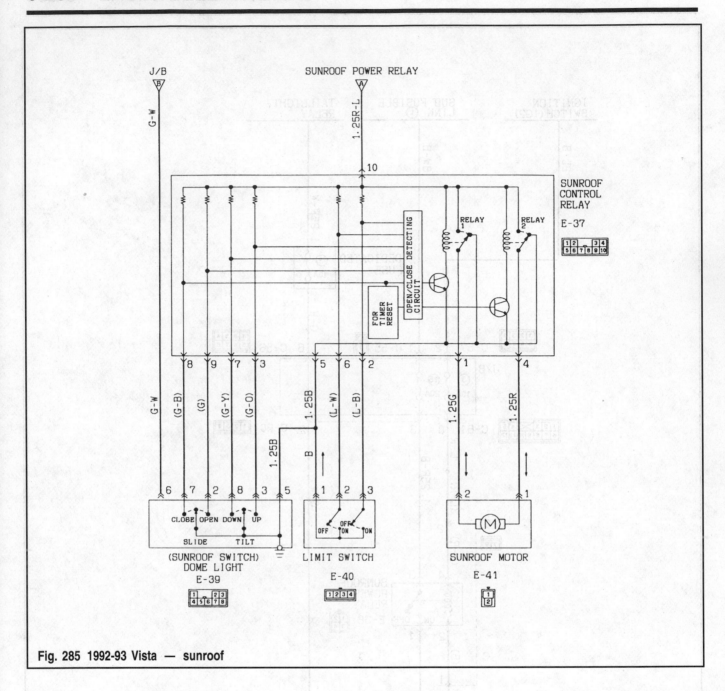

Fig. 285 1992-93 Vista — sunroof

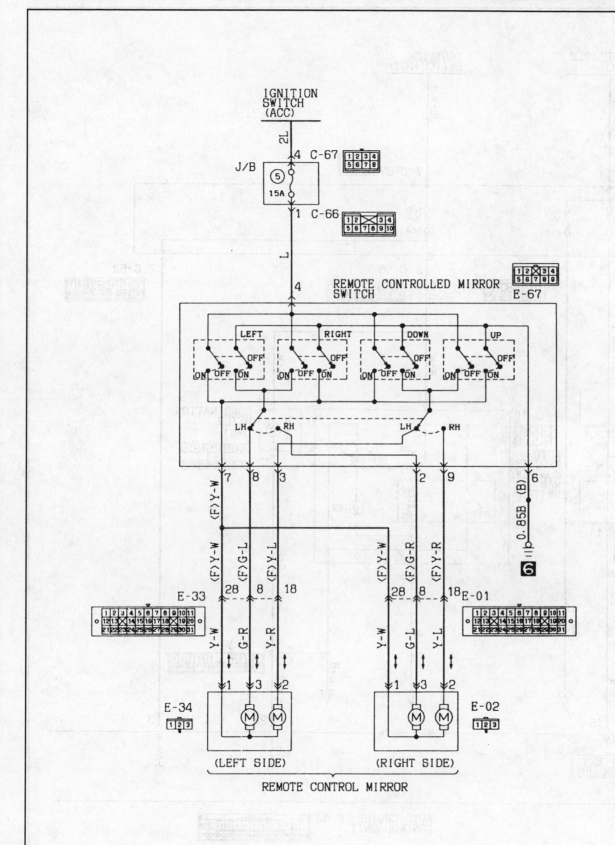

Fig. 286 1992-93 Vista — power mirrors

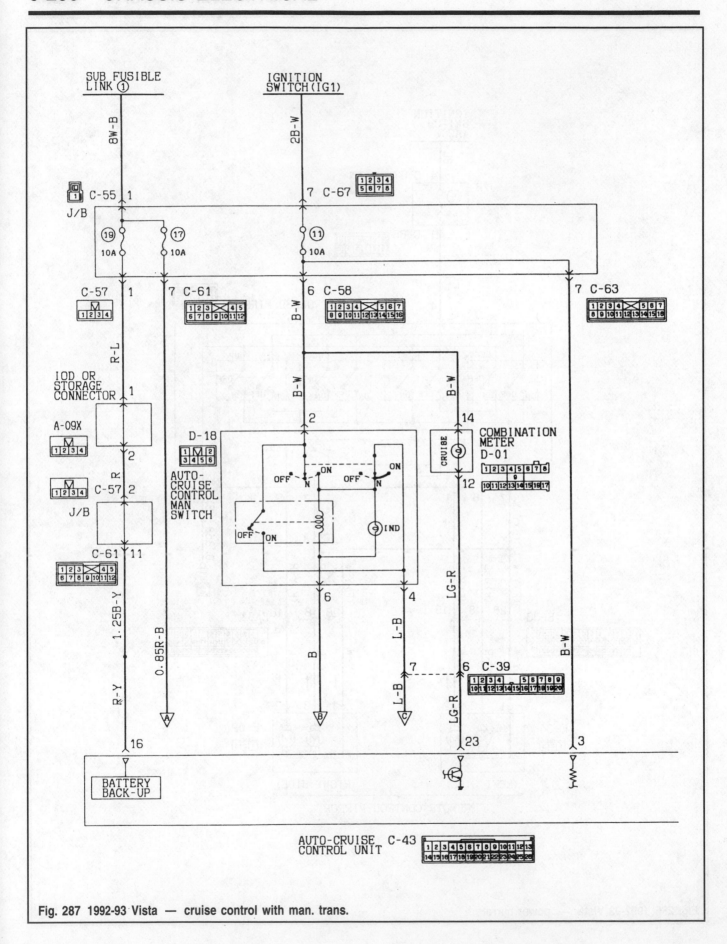

Fig. 287 1992-93 Vista — cruise control with man. trans.

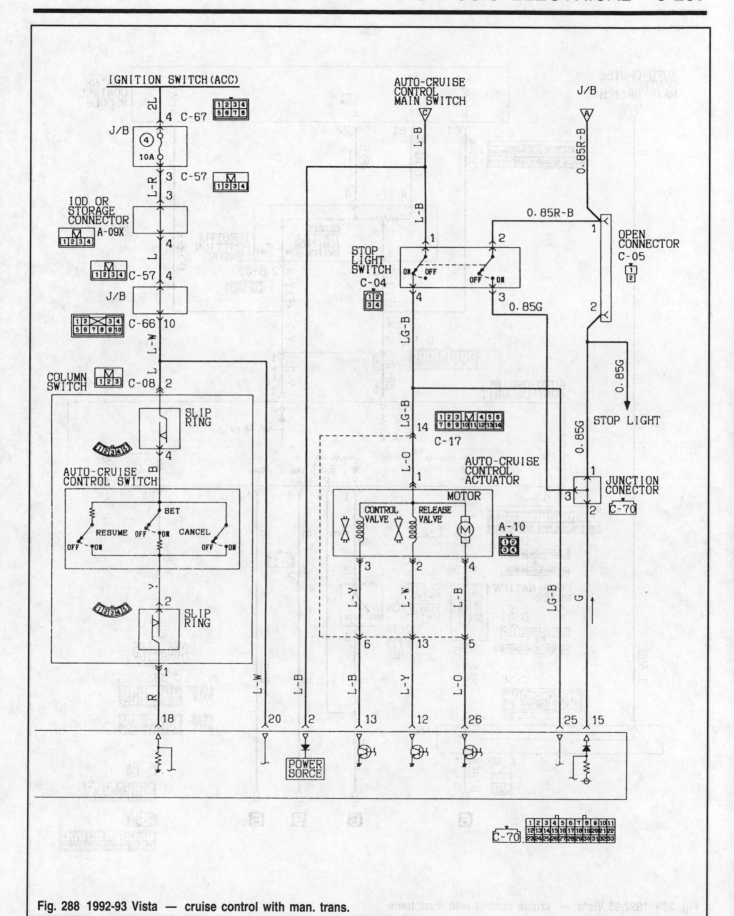

Fig. 288 1992-93 Vista — cruise control with man. trans.

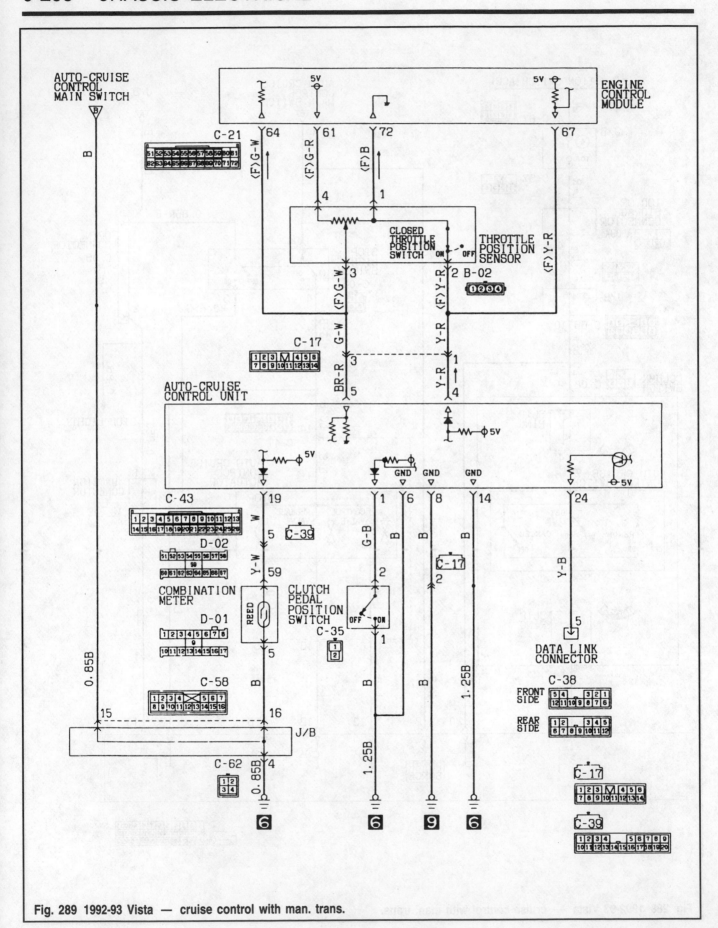

Fig. 289 *1992-93 Vista — cruise control with man. trans.*

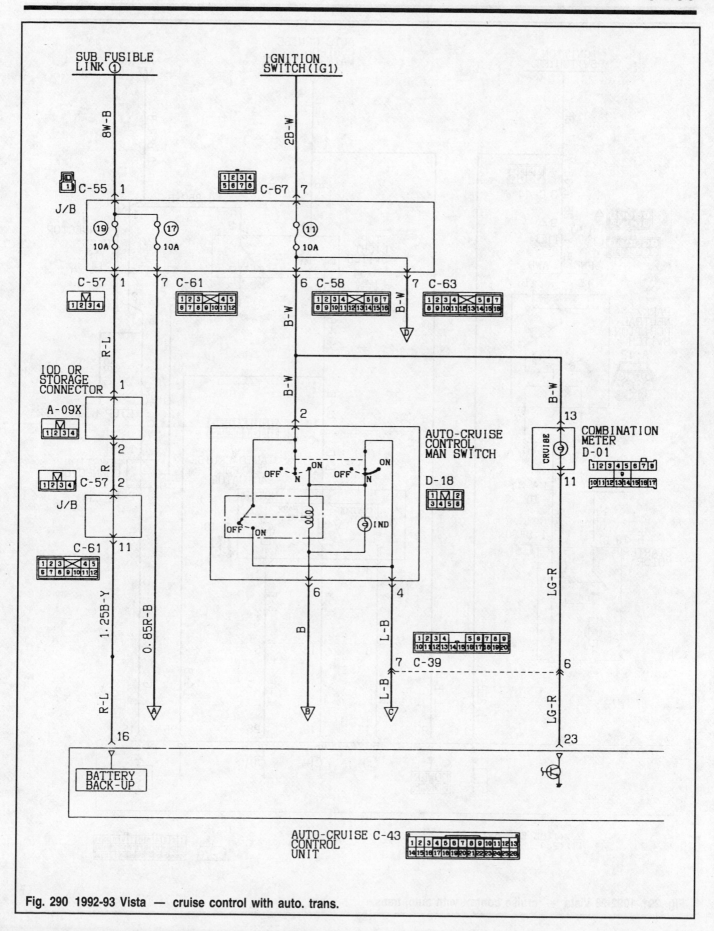

Fig. 290 1992-93 Vista — cruise control with auto. trans.

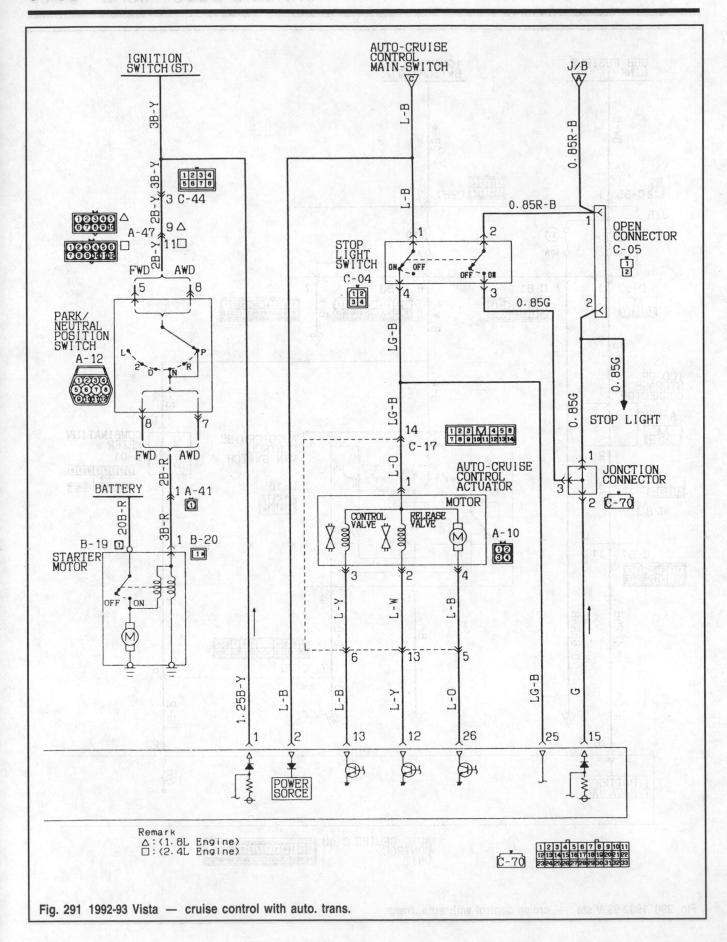

Fig. 291 1992-93 Vista — cruise control with auto. trans.

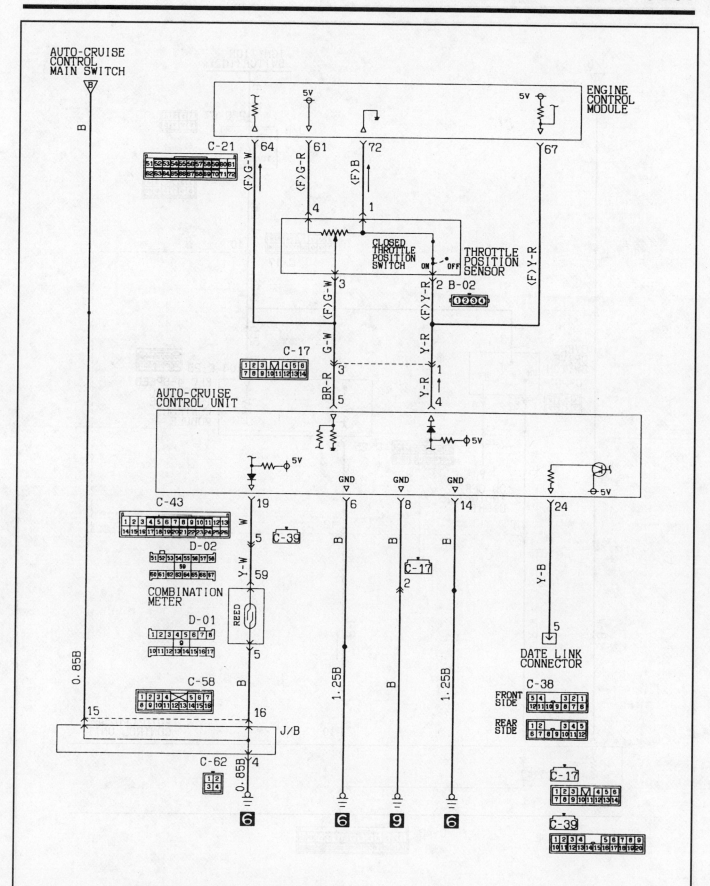

Fig. 292 1992-93 Vista — cruise control with auto. trans.

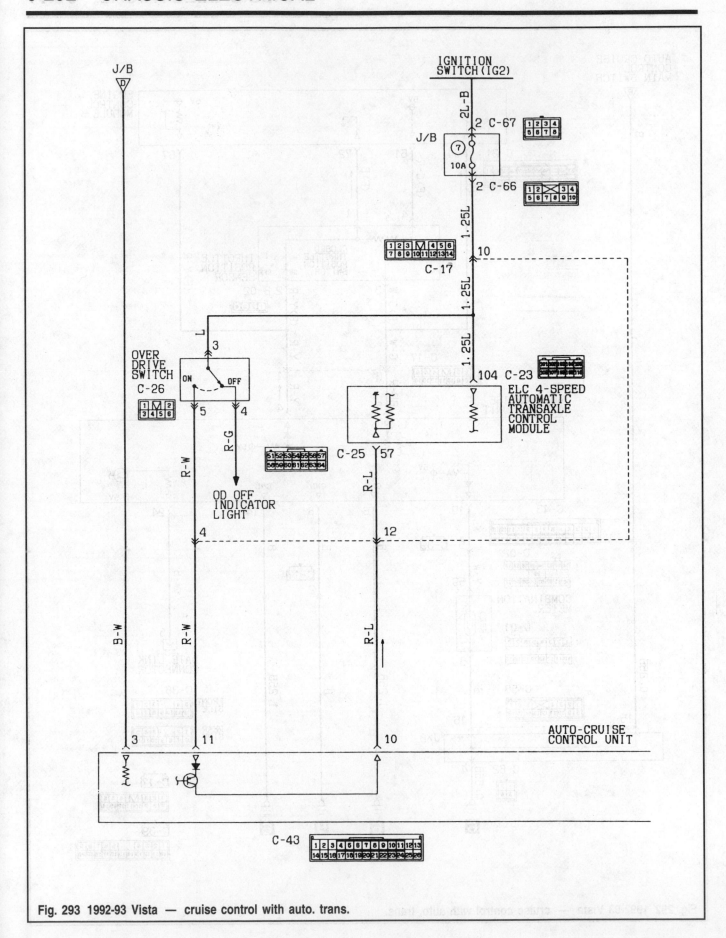

Fig. 293 1992-93 Vista — cruise control with auto. trans.

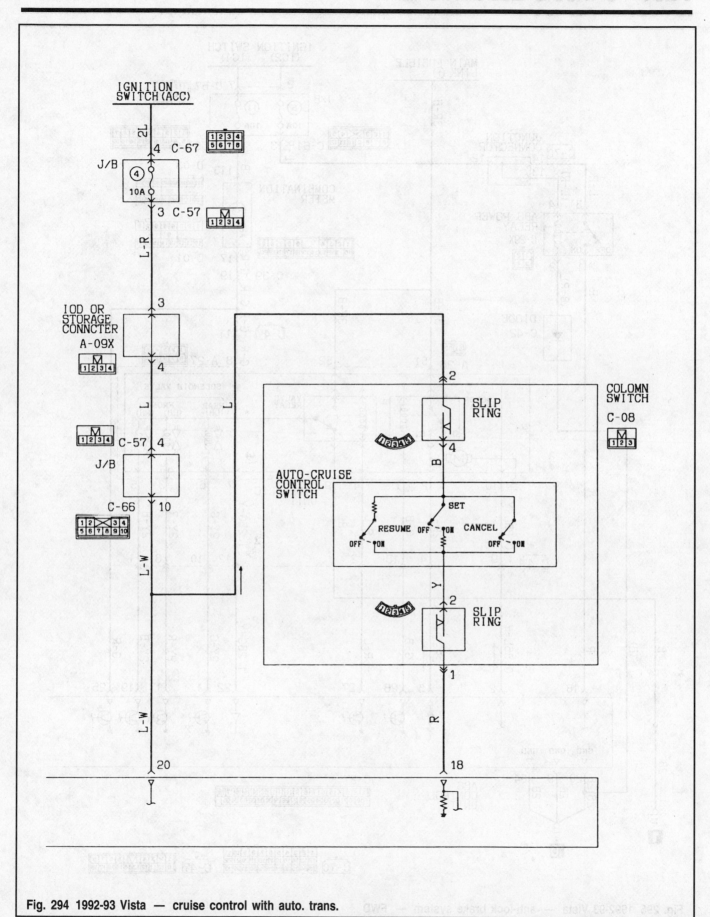

Fig. 294 1992-93 Vista — cruise control with auto. trans.

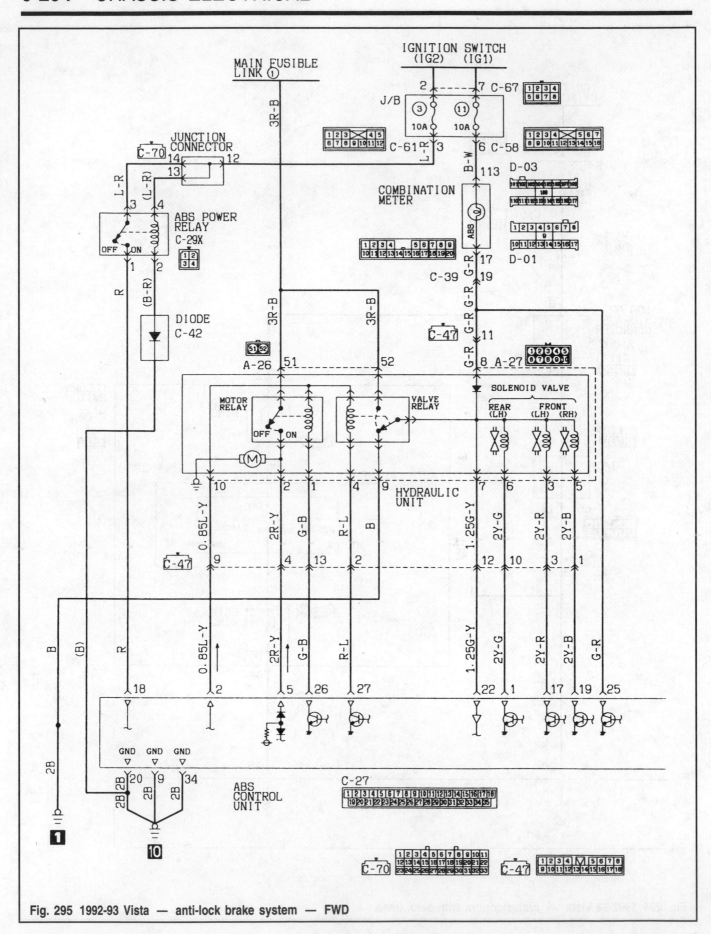

Fig. 295 1992-93 Vista — anti-lock brake system — FWD

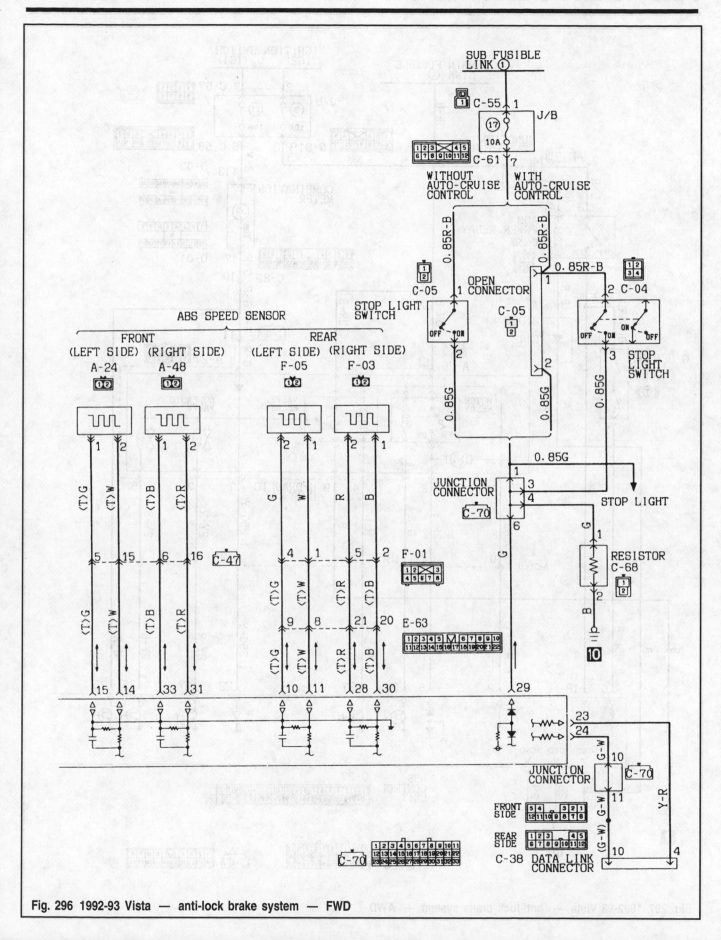

Fig. 296 1992-93 Vista — anti-lock brake system — FWD

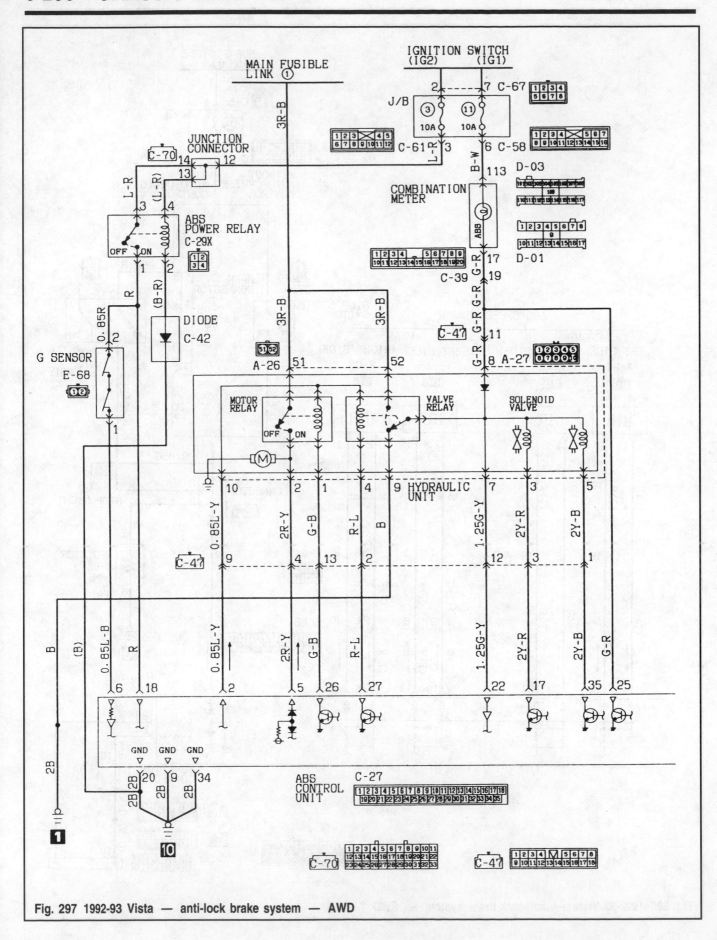

Fig. 297 1992-93 Vista — anti-lock brake system — AWD

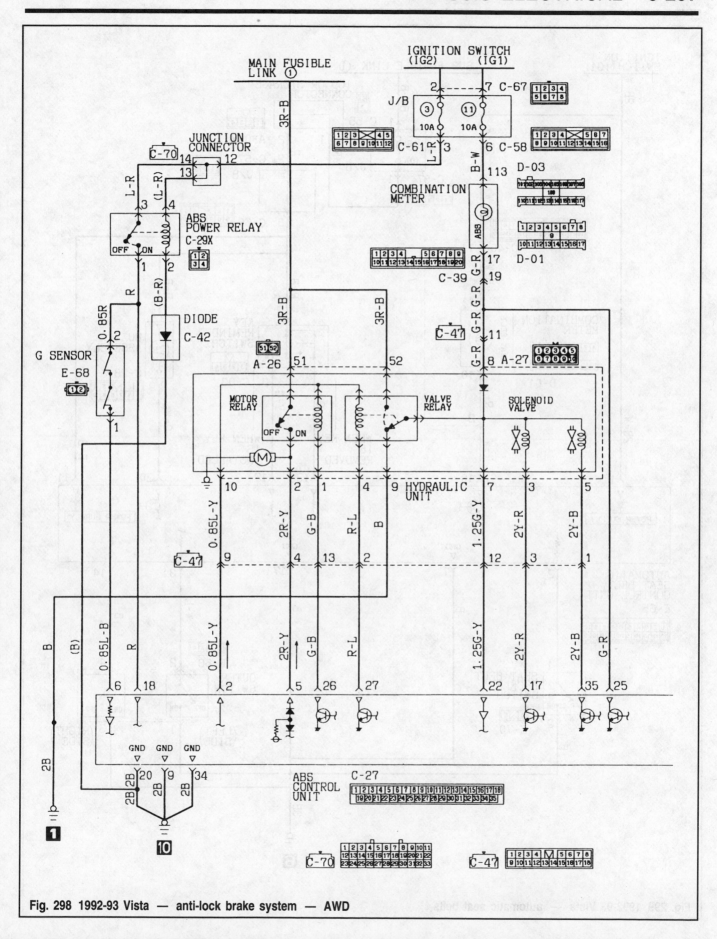

Fig. 298 1992-93 Vista — anti-lock brake system — AWD

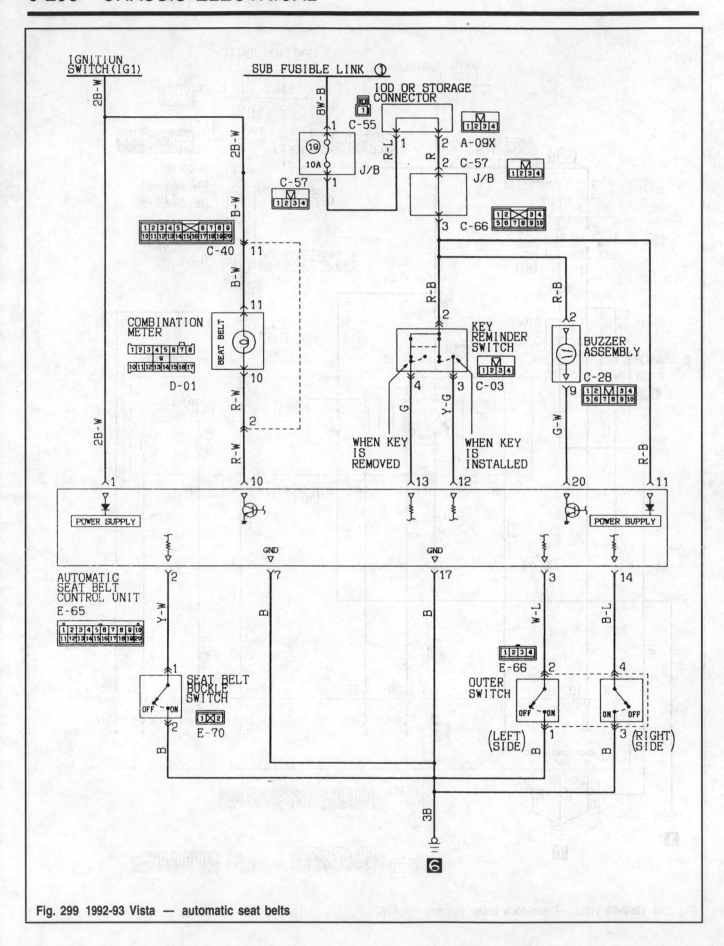

Fig. 299 1992-93 Vista — automatic seat belts

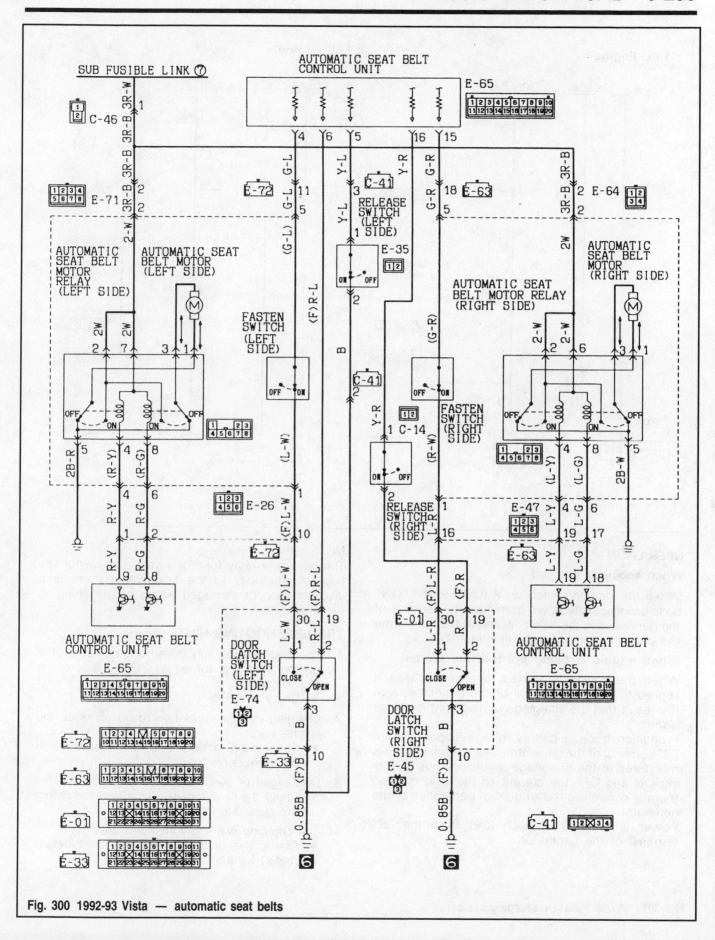

Fig. 300 1992-93 Vista — automatic seat belts

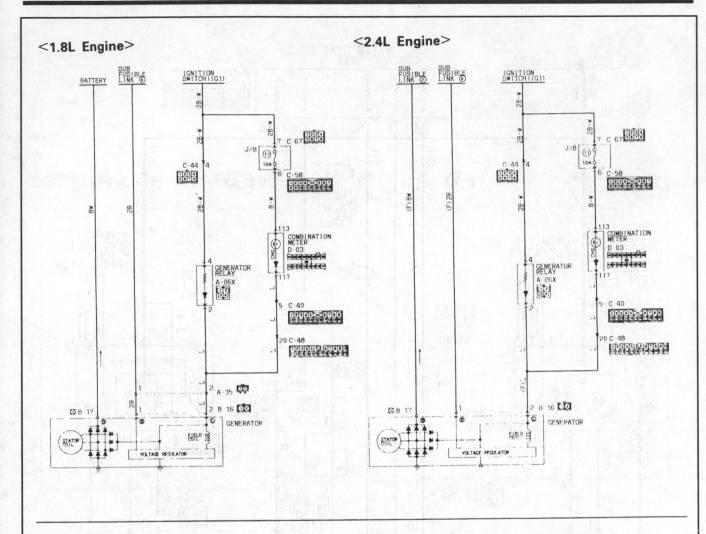

OPERATION

When engine is stopped

When the ignition switch is switched to the "ON" position, electricity flows from the "L" terminal of the generator to the field coil, and at the same time the charging warning light illuminates.

When engine is being started/has started

When the engine is started, charging voltage is applied to the "L" terminal of the generator, with the result that the charging warning light is extinguished.

In addition, because battery voltage is applied to the "S" terminal of the generator, this battery voltage is monitored at the IC voltage regulator, thus switching ON and OFF the current to the field coil and thereby controlling the amount of generation by the generator.

Power is supplied to each load from the "B" terminal of the generator.

NOTE

The generator relay functions as a back-up for the flow of electricity to the field coil if there is a disconnection or damaged wiring of the charging warning light.

TROUBLESHOOTING HINTS

1. Charging indicator light does not go on when the ignition switch is turned to "ON", before the engine starts.
   - Check the bulb
2. Charging indicator light fails to go off once the engine starts.
   - Check the IC voltage regulator (located within the generator).
3. Discharged or overcharged battery.
   - Check the IC voltage regulator (located within the generator).
4. The charging warning light illuminates dimly.
   - Check the diode (within the combination meter) for a short-circuit.

Fig. 301 1992-93 Vista — charging system

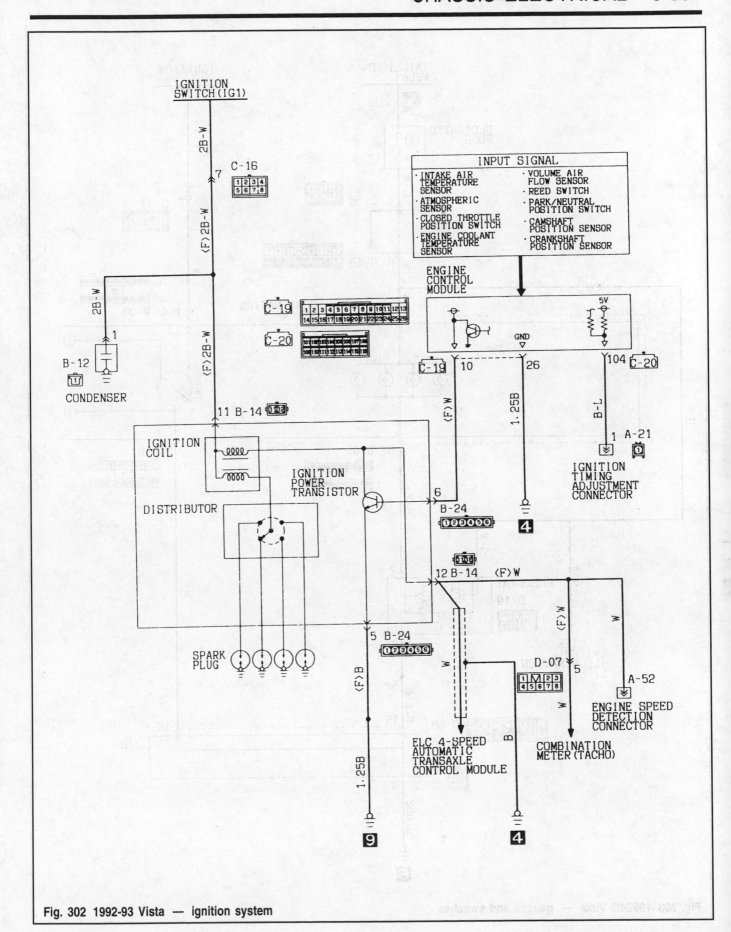

Fig. 302 1992-93 Vista — ignition system

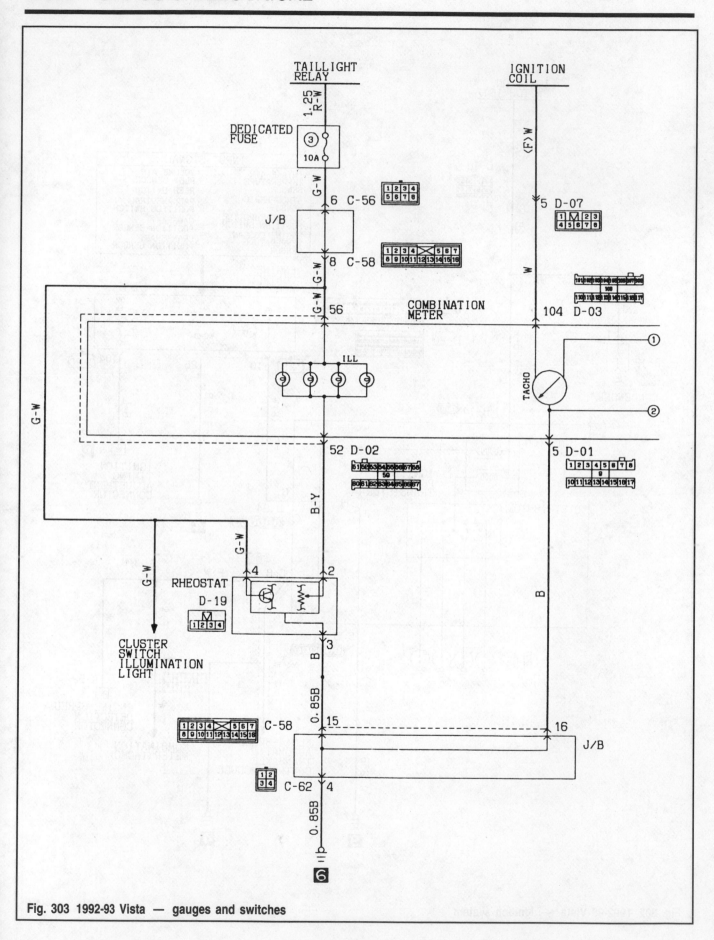

Fig. 303 1992-93 Vista — gauges and switches

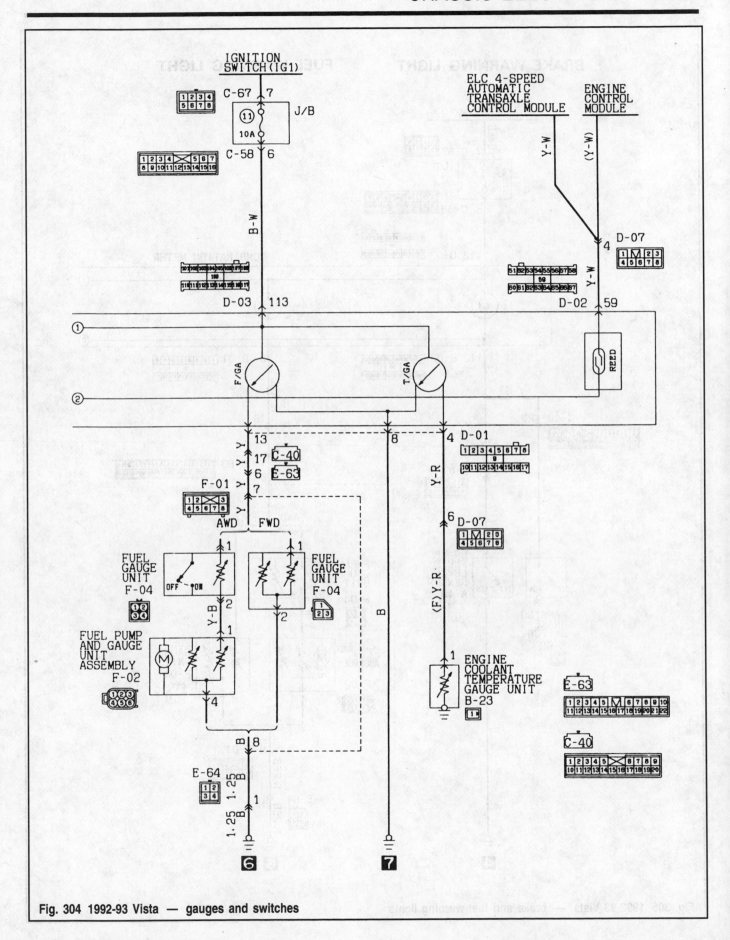

Fig. 304 1992-93 Vista — gauges and switches

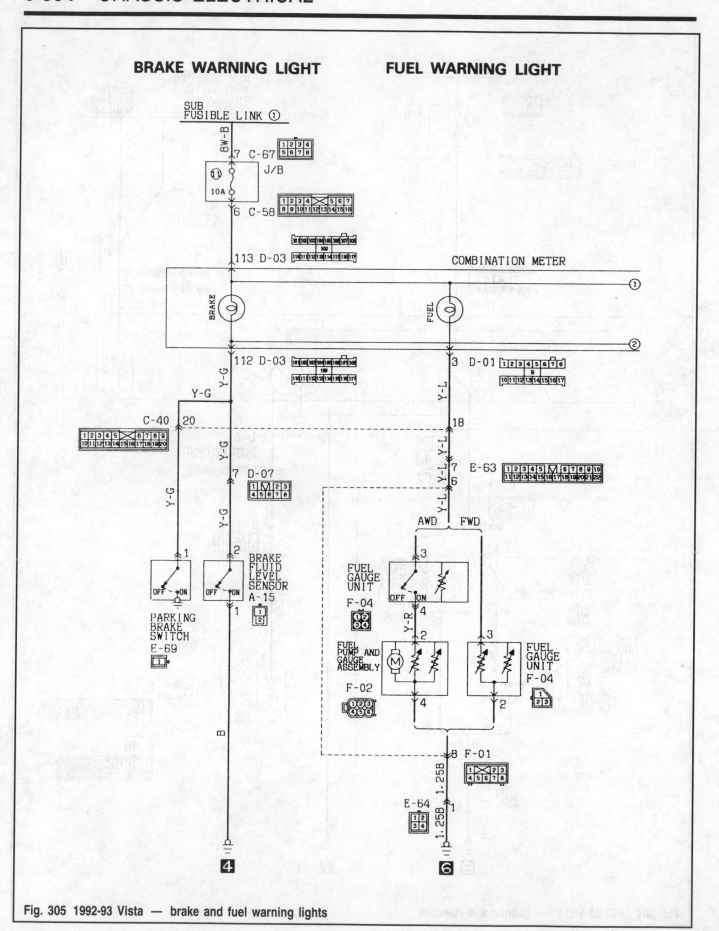

Fig. 305 1992-93 Vista — brake and fuel warning lights

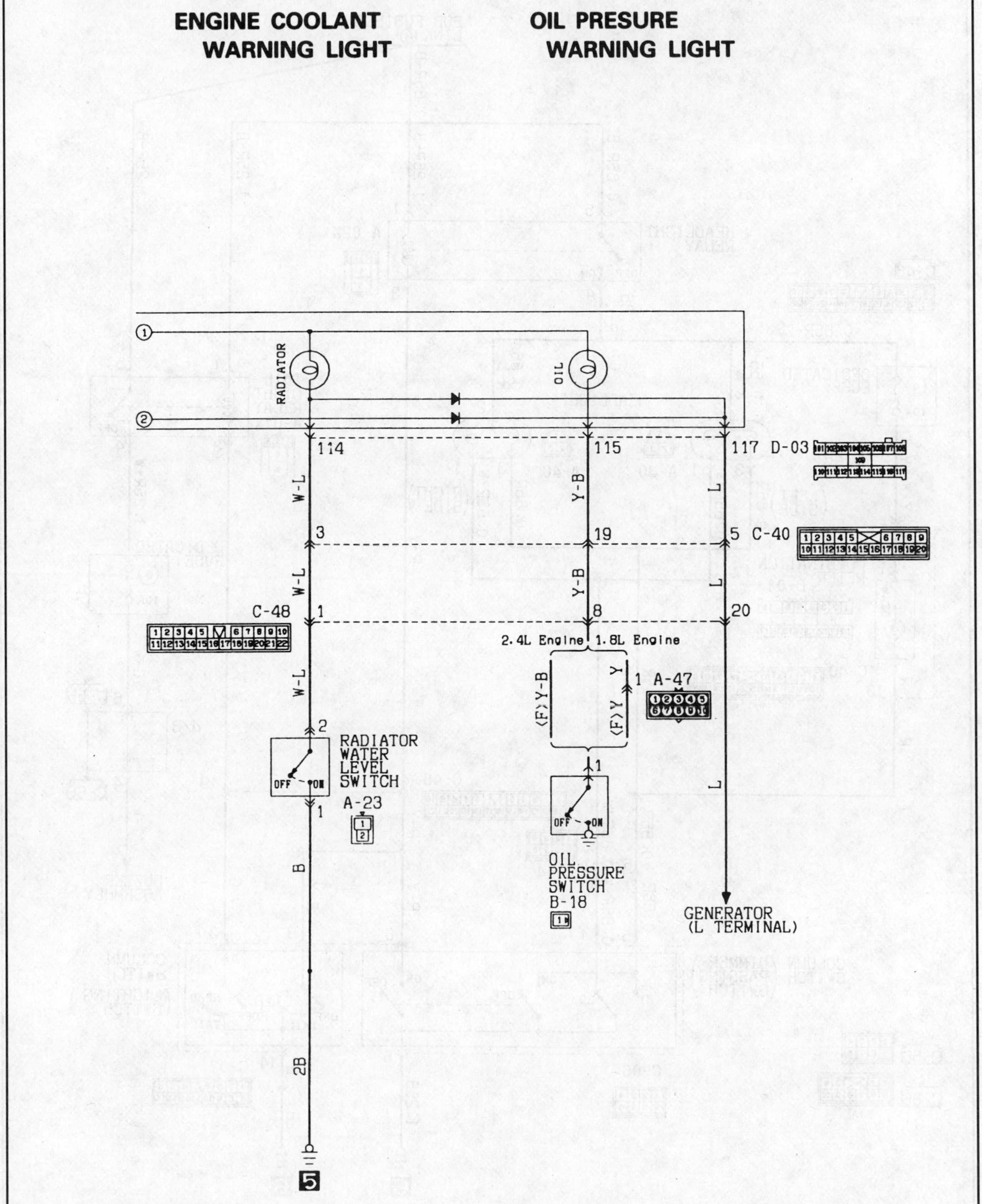

**ENGINE COOLANT
WARNING LIGHT**

**OIL PRESURE
WARNING LIGHT**

RADIATOR

OIL

①

②

114   115   117 D-03

W-L   Y-B

3   19   5 C-40

W-L   Y-B

C-48 1   8   20

W-L   2.4L Engine 1.8L Engine

⟨F⟩Y-B   ⟨F⟩Y   Y   1 A-47

2   RADIATOR
WATER
LEVEL
SWITCH
OFF ○ ON

1   A-23

B   1
OFF ○ ON

OIL
PRESSURE
SWITCH
B-18

GENERATOR
(L TERMINAL)

2B

⑤

Fig. 306 1992-93 Vista — engine coolant and oil pressure warning lights

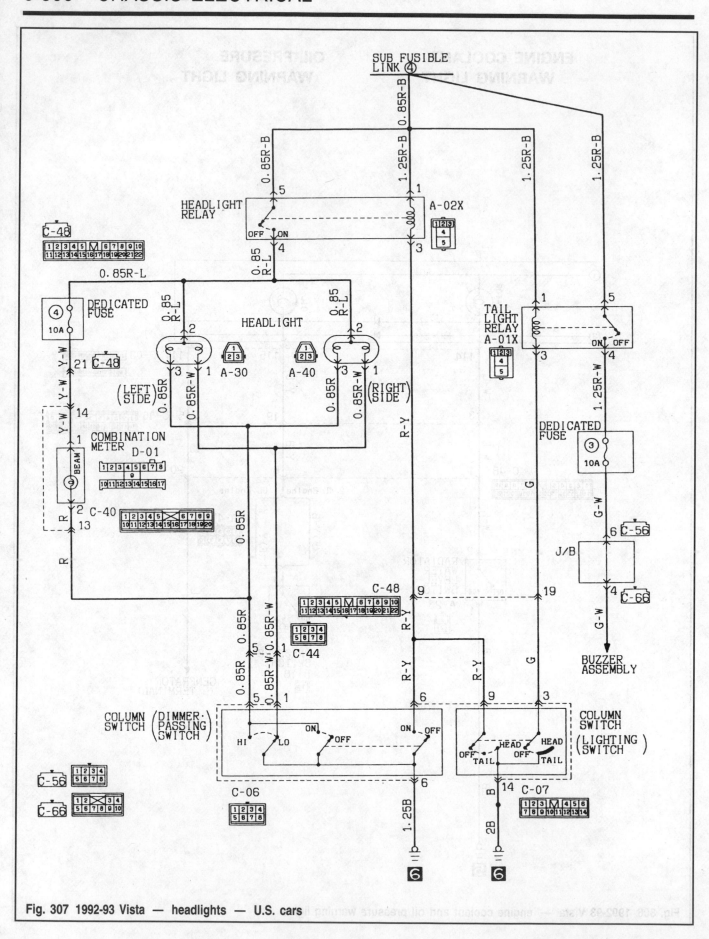

Fig. 307 1992-93 Vista — headlights — U.S. cars

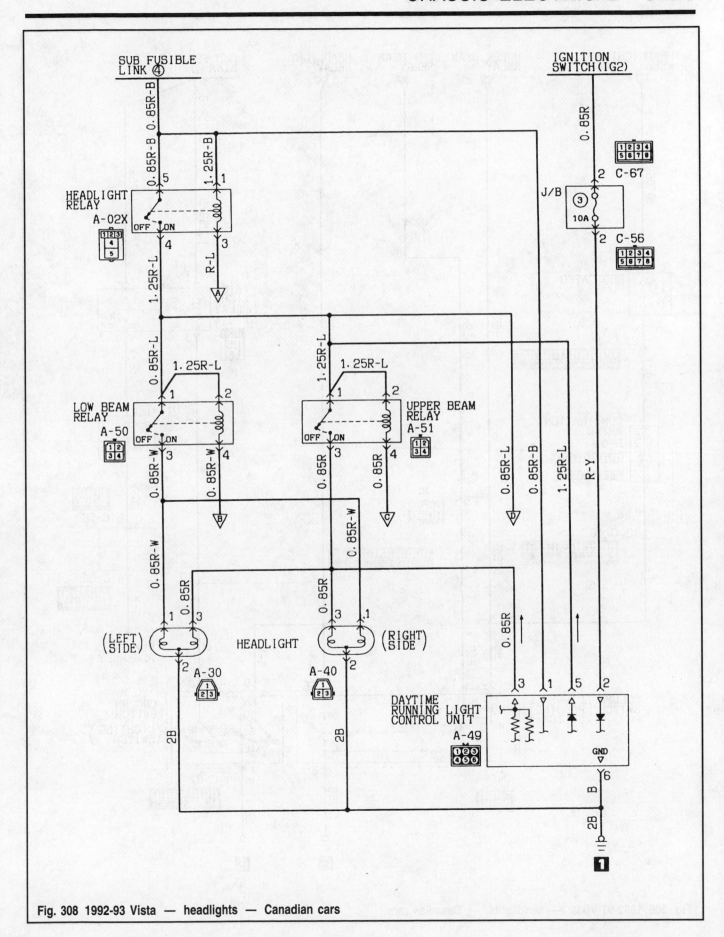

Fig. 308 1992-93 Vista — headlights — Canadian cars

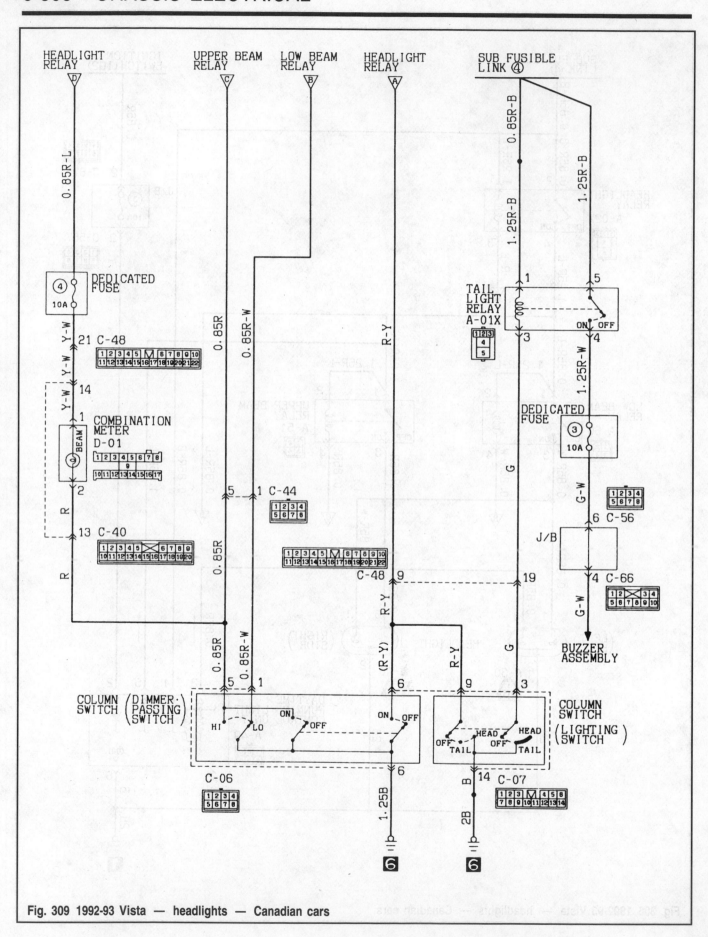

Fig. 309 1992-93 Vista — headlights — Canadian cars

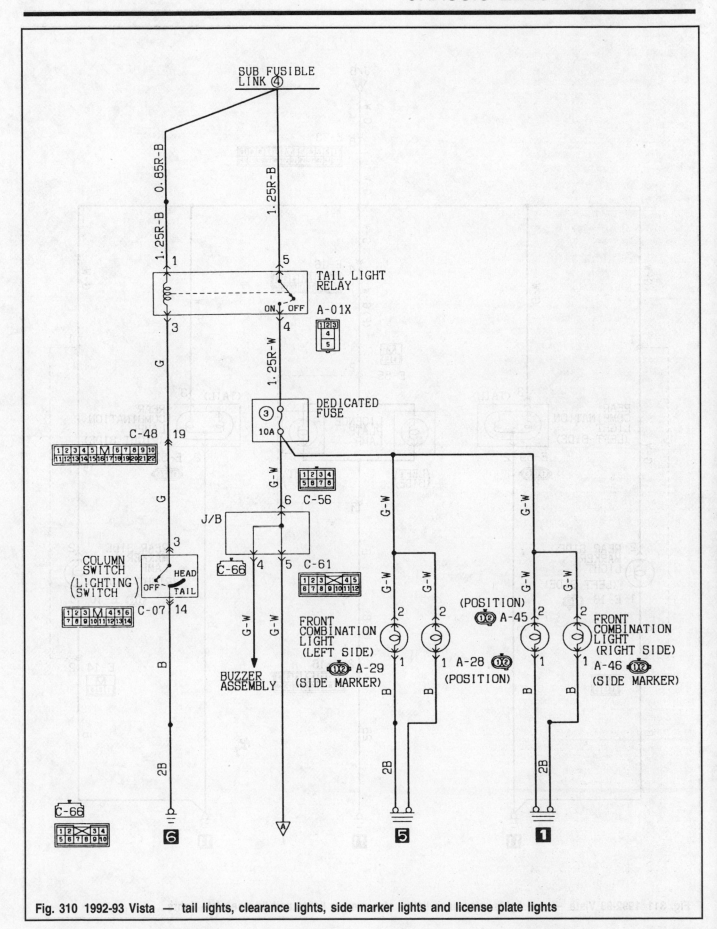

Fig. 310 1992-93 Vista — tail lights, clearance lights, side marker lights and license plate lights

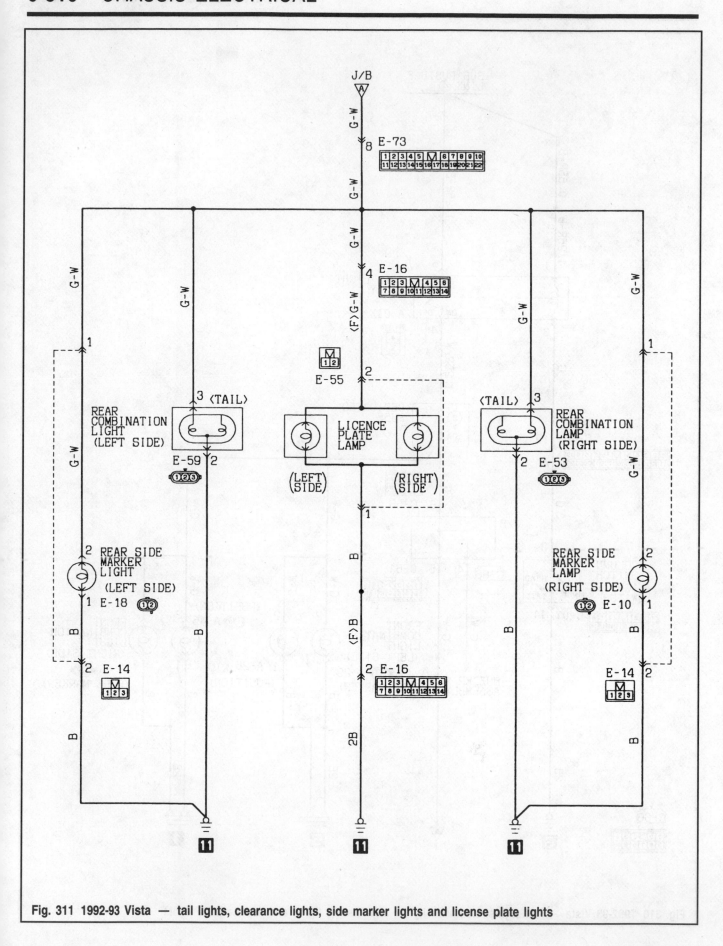

Fig. 311 1992-93 Vista — tail lights, clearance lights, side marker lights and license plate lights

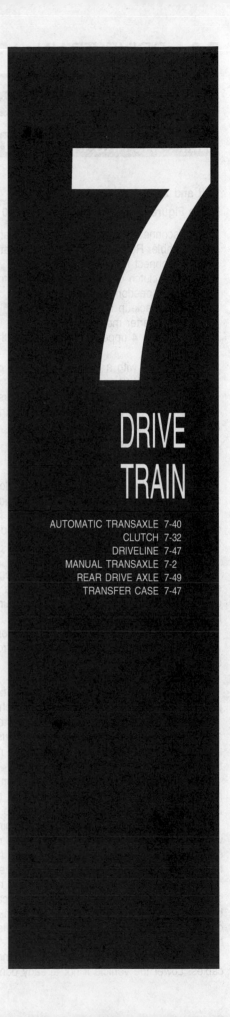

7

DRIVE
TRAIN

MANUAL TRANSAXLE

REMOVAL AND INSTALLATION

Colt and 2WD Colt Wagon

♦ See Figures 1, 2, 3, 4, 5, 6, 7, 8, 9, 10 and 11

1. Disconnect the battery ground (negative) cable and the positive cable. Remove the battery and battery tray.
2. Disconnect from the transaxle:
   a. The clutch cable or hydraulic line to slave cylinder.
   b. The speedometer cable.
   c. The back-up light harness.
   d. The starter motor.
   e. The the 4 upper bolts connecting the engine to the transaxle.
   f. On cars with a 5-speed transaxle, disconnect the selector control valve.
3. Jack up the car and support on jackstands.
4. Remove the front wheels. Remove the splash shield. Drain the transaxle fluid.
5. Remove the shift rod and extension. It may be necessary to remove any heat shields that can interfere with your progress.
6. Remove the stabilizer bar from the lower arm and disconnect the lower arm from the body side.
7. Remove the right and left halfshafts from the transaxle case. Plug the transaxle holes to prevent dirt from entering. See Halfshaft Removal.
8. Remove the engine rear cover.
9. Support the weight of the engine from above with an engine crane. Support the transaxle with a suitable floor jack or transmission jack and remove the remaining lower mounting bolts.
10. Remove the transaxle mount insulator bolt.
11. Slide the transaxle back and away from the engine, and lower the transaxle.

To install:

12. Position the transaxle on a suitable floor or transmission jack and raise it into position under the vehicle.
13. Push the transaxle towards the rear of the engine and align the mainshaft with the clutch disc. Push the transaxle into position against the engine, take care not to knock the transaxle off of the jack.
14. Install and tighten the transaxle to engine lower mounting bolts. Install the transaxle mount through bolt. Disconnect the chain hoist from the engine.
15. Install the halfshafts. Use new retaining ring circlips when installing the halfshafts. Connect the range selector cable. Connect the engine roll control bar, the lower bell housing shield, the lower arms and stabilizer bar.
16. Install the upper transaxle to engine mounting bolts, the starter motor, speedometer cable, ground cable, back-up light harness, select cable, shift cable, clutch linkage or hydraulic connection, and install the splash shield after filling the transaxle with lubricant.
17. Install the battery tray, the battery and connect the cables. Lower the vehicle if not already done.

2WD Vista

1. Disconnect the battery cables, negative cable first. Remove the battery and tray.
2. Remove the coolant reservoir.
3. Remove the air cleaner.
4. Disconnect the clutch cable, speedometer cable and backup light wiring from the transaxle.
5. Remove the upper engine-to-transaxle bolts.
6. Disconnect the select control lever and switch harness.
7. Remove the starter.
8. Disconnect and tag all wiring from the transaxle.
9. Raise and support the vehicle safely.
10. Remove the front wheels.
11. Drain the transaxle fluid.
12. Remove the extension and shift rod from the engine compartment.
13. Remove the stabilizer and strut bar from the lower control arm.
14. Remove the left and right halfshafts.
15. Support the transaxle with a suitable floor jack, taking care to avoid damaging the pan.
16. Remove the bell housing cover.
17. Remove the remaining transaxle-to-engine bolts.
18. Remove the transaxle mounting bolt.
19. Lower the jack and slide the transaxle from under the car.

To install:

20. Secure the transaxle on a transaxle jack and position it to the engine.
21. Carefully guide the transaxle input shaft into the clutch assembly. Make sure the transaxle is seated properly and is flush to the engine flange. Install 2 transaxle-to-engine bolts.
22. Install the transaxle mounting bolt. Torque the bolt to 29-36 ft. lbs. (40-50 Nm).
23. Install the lower transaxle-to-engine bolts. Torque the bolts to 32-39 ft. lbs. (43-53 Nm).
24. Remove the floor jack from the transaxle.
25. Install the left and right halfshafts.
26. Install the stabilizer and strut bar to the lower control arm.
27. Install the extension and shift rod.
28. Refill the transaxle with an approved gear oil.
29. Install the front wheels and lower the vehicle.
30. Connect all wiring to the transaxle.
31. Install the starter and mounting bolts. Torque the mounting bolts to 20-24 ft. lbs. (27-34 Nm).
32. Connect the select control lever and switch harness.
33. Install the upper engine-to-transaxle bolts. Torque the bolts to 32-39 ft. lbs. (43-53 Nm).
34. Connect the clutch cable, speedometer cable and backup light wiring to the transaxle.
35. Install the air cleaner.
36. Install the coolant reservoir and refill with coolant.
37. Install the battery tray and battery. Connect the battery cables, positive cable first.

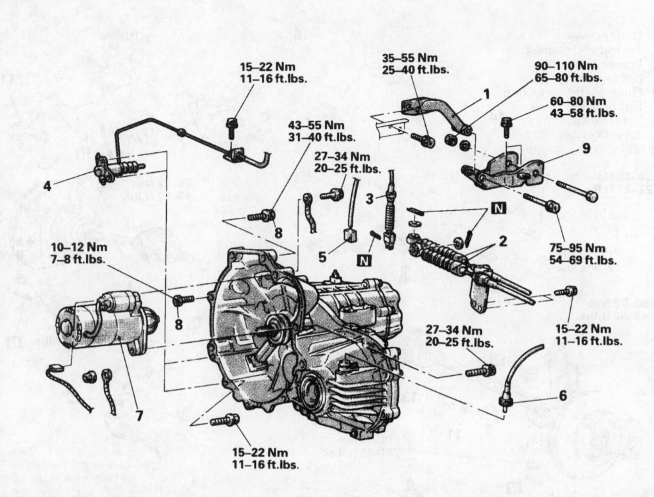

1. Tension rod <DOHC>
2. Control cable connection
3. Clutch cable connection
   <Cable control type>
4. Clutch release cylinder connection
   <Hydraulic control type>
5. Backup light switch connector connection
6. Speedometer cable connection
7. Starter motor
8. Transaxle assembly upper connecting bolt
9. Transaxle mounting bracket

Fig. 1 Remove these parts prior to transaxle removal — 1990-92 Colt hatchback or sedan

10. Under cover
11. Tie rod end connection
12. Lower arm ball joint connection
13. Drive shaft connection
14. Bell housing cover
15. Transaxle assembly lower connecting bolt
16. Transaxle assembly

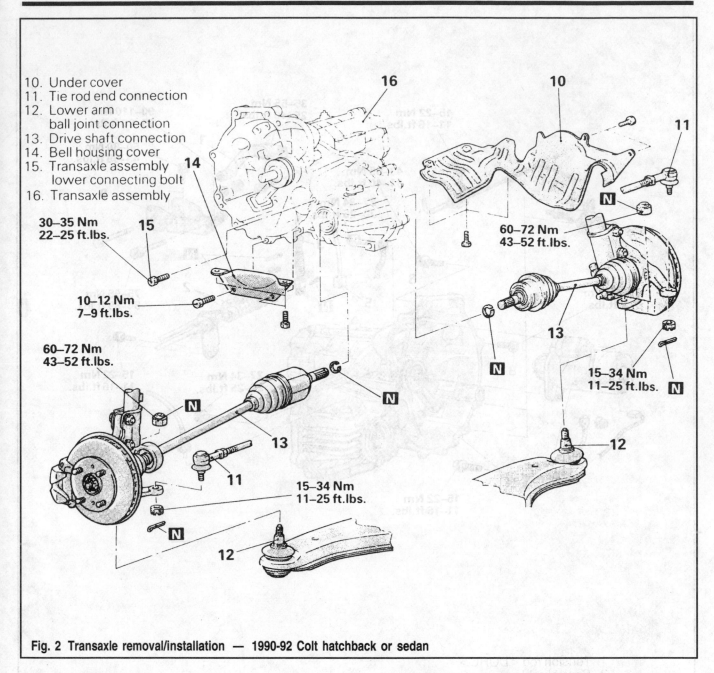

30–35 Nm
22–25 ft.lbs.

10–12 Nm
7–9 ft.lbs.

60–72 Nm
43–52 ft.lbs.

60–72 Nm
43–52 ft.lbs.

15–34 Nm
11–25 ft.lbs.

15–34 Nm
11–25 ft.lbs.

Fig. 2 Transaxle removal/installation — 1990-92 Colt hatchback or sedan

4WD Colt Wagon

▶ **See Figures 8, 9 and ?**

1. Disconnect the negative battery cable, drain the transaxle fluid and remove the under cover.
2. Remove the air cleaner, battery and battery tray.
3. Remove the split pin and disconnect the shift and select cables.
4. Disconnect the clutch cylinder line, backup light switch and speedometer cable.
5. Disconnect the stabilizer bar, tie rod ends, lower ball joint and driveshaft from the control arm and strut.
6. Remove the starter motor.
7. Place a jack under the transaxle and support the engine from above.
8. Remove the center crossmember with roll stopper bracket.

9. Remove the rear driveshaft and transfer case.
10. Remove the transaxle mount bracket and bell housing bolts.
11. Using the jack, lower the transaxle and check for interference.
To install:
12. Using the jack, raise the transaxle and check for interference.
13. Install the transaxle mount bracket and bell housing bolts. Torque the bolts to 35 ft. lbs. (47 Nm).
14. Install the rear driveshaft and transfer case. Torque the transfer bolts to 30 ft. lbs. (41 Nm).
15. Install the center crossmember with roll stopper bracket.
16. Remove the jack and engine support.
17. Install the starter motor and torque the bolts to 35 ft. lbs. (41 Nm).

13. Stabilizer bar connection
14. Lower arm ball joint connection
15. Tie rod end connection
16. Drive shaft connection
17. Bell housing cover
18. Roll rod
19. Cap
20. Transaxle mount bracket
21. Transaxle bracket
22. Transaxle assembly

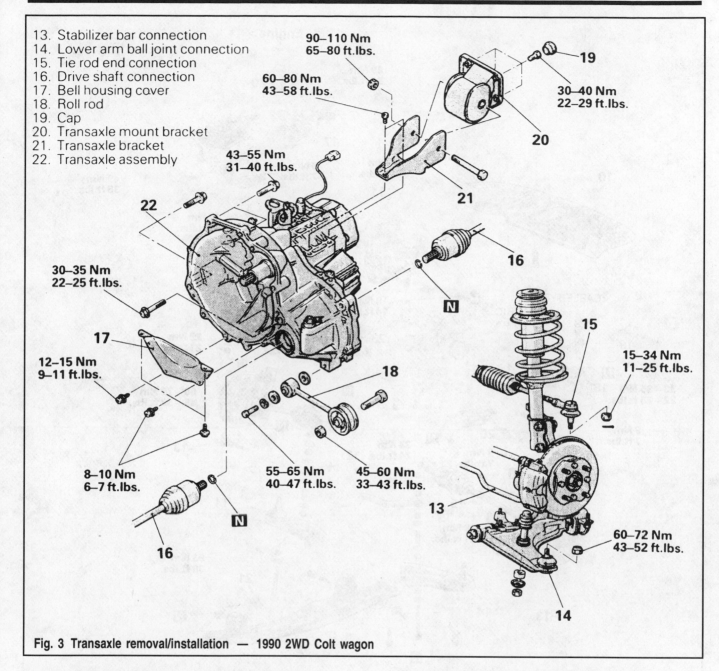

90–110 Nm
65–80 ft.lbs.

60–80 Nm
43–58 ft.lbs.

30–40 Nm
22–29 ft.lbs.

19

20

21

43–55 Nm
31–40 ft.lbs.

22

16

15

15–34 Nm
11–25 ft.lbs.

30–35 Nm
22–25 ft.lbs.

17

18

12–15 Nm
9–11 ft.lbs.

8–10 Nm
6–7 ft.lbs.

55–65 Nm
40–47 ft.lbs.

45–60 Nm
33–43 ft.lbs.

13

60–72 Nm
43–52 ft.lbs.

16

14

Fig. 3 Transaxle removal/installation — 1990 2WD Colt wagon

18. Connect the stabilizer bar, tie rod ends, lower ball joint and driveshaft to the control arm and strut.

19. Connect the clutch cylinder line, backup light switch and speedometer cable.

20. Install the split pin and connect the shift and select cables.

21. Install the air cleaner, battery and battery tray.

22. Connect the negative battery cable, refill the transaxle fluid and install the under cover.

4WD Vista

1. Disconnect the battery cables, negative cable first. Remove the battery.

2. Remove the coolant reserve tank.

3. Disconnect the speedometer cable, shift control cable and back-up light harness at the transaxle.

4. Remove the range select control valves and connectors.

5. Tag and disconnect all other wiring attached to the transaxle.

6. Remove the clutch slave cylinder.

7. Remove the vacuum reservoir tank.

8. Disconnect the starter wiring and remove.

9. Remove the upper engine-to-transaxle bolts.

10. Raise and support the vehicle safely.

11. Remove the front wheels, lower engine cover and skid plate.

12. Drain the transaxle and transfer case.

13. Remove the driveshaft.

14. Remove the transfer case extension housing.

15. Remove the left and right halfshafts.

16. Disconnect the right strut from the lower arm.

17. Remove the right fender liner.

18. Take up the weight of the transaxle with a suitable floor jack.

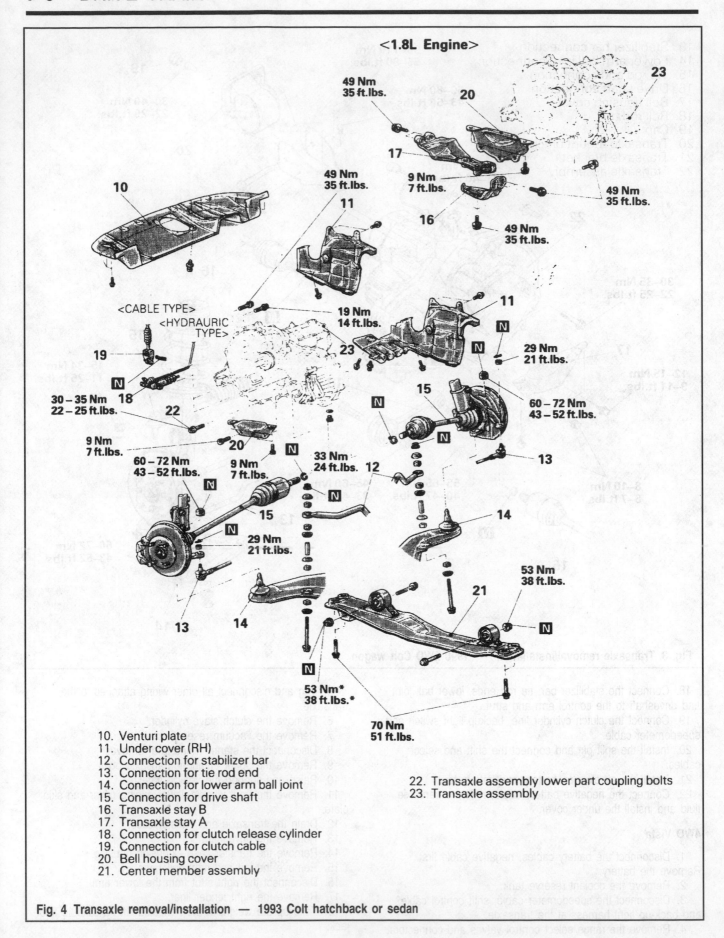

<1.8L Engine>

49 Nm
35 ft.lbs.

20

23

17

9 Nm
7 ft.lbs.

16

49 Nm
35 ft.lbs.

49 Nm
35 ft.lbs.

10

49 Nm
35 ft.lbs.

11

11

19 Nm
14 ft.lbs.

23

29 Nm
21 ft.lbs.

<CABLE TYPE>

<HYDRAURIC TYPE>

19

18

30 – 35 Nm
22 – 25 ft.lbs.

22

9 Nm
7 ft.lbs.

20

60 – 72 Nm
43 – 52 ft.lbs.

9 Nm
7 ft.lbs.

33 Nm
24 ft.lbs.

12

15

60 – 72 Nm
43 – 52 ft.lbs.

13

15

14

29 Nm
21 ft.lbs.

13

14

53 Nm
38 ft.lbs.

21

53 Nm*
38 ft.lbs.*

70 Nm
51 ft.lbs.

10. Venturi plate
11. Under cover (RH)
12. Connection for stabilizer bar
13. Connection for tie rod end
14. Connection for lower arm ball joint
15. Connection for drive shaft
16. Transaxle stay B
17. Transaxle stay A
18. Connection for clutch release cylinder
19. Connection for clutch cable
20. Bell housing cover
21. Center member assembly

22. Transaxle assembly lower part coupling bolts
23. Transaxle assembly

Fig. 4 Transaxle removal/installation — 1993 Colt hatchback or sedan

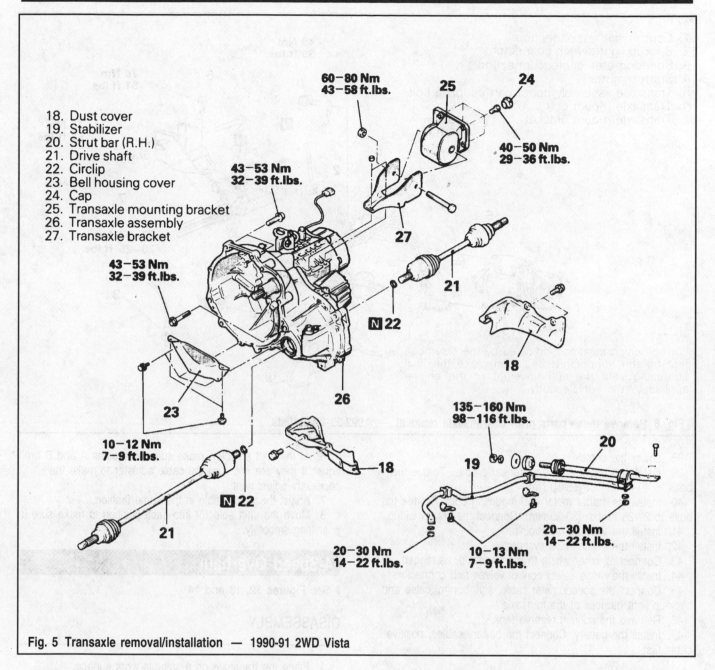

18. Dust cover
19. Stabilizer
20. Strut bar (R.H.)
21. Drive shaft
22. Circlip
23. Bell housing cover
24. Cap
25. Transaxle mounting bracket
26. Transaxle assembly
27. Transaxle bracket

60–80 Nm
43–58 ft.lbs.

40–50 Nm
29–36 ft.lbs.

43–53 Nm
32–39 ft.lbs.

43–53 Nm
32–39 ft.lbs.

10–12 Nm
7–9 ft.lbs.

135–160 Nm
98–116 ft.lbs.

20–30 Nm
14–22 ft.lbs.

20–30 Nm
14–22 ft.lbs.

10–13 Nm
7–9 ft.lbs.

Fig. 5 Transaxle removal/installation — 1990-91 2WD Vista

19. Remove the bell housing cover bolts and remove the cover.
20. Remove the remaining engine-to-transaxle bolts.
21. Remove the transaxle mount insulator bolt.
22. Remove the transaxle mounting bracket attaching bolts.
23. Move the transaxle/transfer case assembly to the right. Tilt the right side of the transaxle down, until the transfer case is about level with the upper part of the steering rack tube, then turn it to the left and lower the assembly.

To install:

24. Secure the transaxle/transfer case assembly to a transaxle jack.
25. Raise the assembly in position to the engine. It may be necessary to tilt or angle the assembly in and around the steering rack tube.
26. Once the transaxle/transfer assembly is positioned to the engine, carefully guide the input shaft into the clutch assembly.

27. Install the transaxle mounting bracket attaching bolts. Torque the bolts to 40-43 ft. lbs. (55-60 Nm).
28. Install the transaxle mount insulator bolt. Torque to 40-43 ft. lbs. (55-60 Nm).
29. Install the lower engine-to-transaxle bolts. Torque to 31-40 ft. lbs. (43-55 Nm).
30. Install the bell housing cover bolts and install the cover.
31. Remove the the floor jack from the transaxle.
32. Install the right fender liner.
33. Connect the right strut to the lower arm.
34. Install the left and right halfshafts.
35. Install the transfer case extension housing and the driveshaft.
36. Refill the transaxle and transfer case with an approved gear oil.
37. Install the front wheels, lower engine cover and skid plate.

1. Control cable connection
2. Backup light switch connector
3. Speedometer cable connection
4. Starter motor
5. Transaxle assembly upper part coupling bolt
6. Transaxle mount bolt
7. Transaxle mount bracket

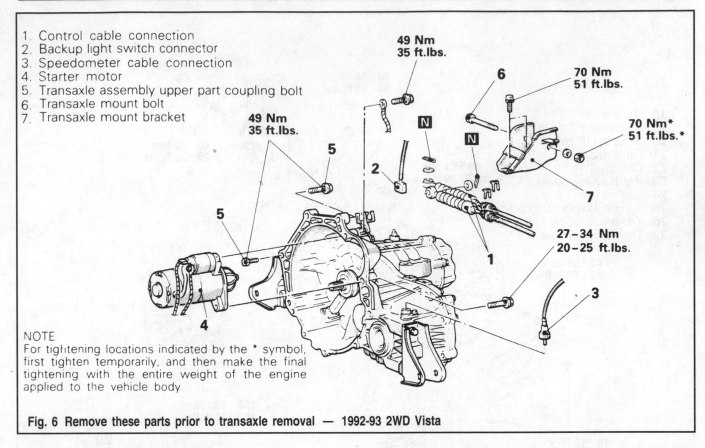

49 Nm
35 ft.lbs.

70 Nm
51 ft.lbs.

70 Nm*
51 ft.lbs.*

49 Nm
35 ft.lbs.

27–34 Nm
20–25 ft.lbs.

NOTE
For tightening locations indicated by the * symbol, first tighten temporarily, and then make the final tightening with the entire weight of the engine applied to the vehicle body.

Fig. 6 Remove these parts prior to transaxle removal — 1992-93 2WD Vista

38. Lower the vehicle.
39. Install the upper engine-to-transaxle bolts. Torque the bolts to 40-43 ft. lbs. (55-60 Nm).
40. Install the starter motor and mounting bolts. Torque the bolts to 22-25 ft. lbs. (30-35 Nm). Connect the starter wiring.
41. Install the vacuum reservoir tank.
42. Install the clutch slave cylinder.
43. Connect all other wiring to the transaxle, as tagged.
44. Install the range select control valves and connectors.
45. Connect the speedometer cable, shift control cable and back-up light harness at the transaxle.
46. Remove the coolant reserve tank.
47. Install the battery. Connect the battery cables, positive cable first.

LINKAGE ADJUSTMENT

4WD Vista

1. Disconnect the negative battery cable.
2. Remove the console assembly from the vehicle.
3. At the shift selector assembly, remove the shift cable-to-shift selector cotter pins and disconnect the shift cables from the shift selector assembly.
4. Move the transaxle shift selector and shift selector into the **N** positions.
5. If necessary, turn the shift cable adjuster to adjust the cables length to align with shift lever in the **N** position. Connect the shift cable, flange side of the resin bushing should face cotter pin side of the shift lever, with lever B and install a new cotter pin.

6. At the shift selector, make sure dimensions A and B are equal; if they are not, turn the cable adjuster to make the necessary adjustment.
7. Adjust the other cable in the same fashion.
8. Move the shift selector into each position to make sure it is shifting smoothly.

4-Speed Overhaul

▶ **See Figures 12, 13 and 14**

DISASSEMBLY

1. Place the transaxle on a suitable work surface.
2. Remove the clutch cable operating bracket and the transaxle mounting bracket.
3. Remove the backup light switch and steel ball from the case.
4. Remove the rear cover from the transaxle case. Remove the spacers from the rear of the tapered roller bearings.
5. Remove the transaxle case from the clutch housing, exposing the gear train assembly.
6. Place all shift rails in the Neutral position.

➡**The shift rails would be locked if any one of the rails are in a position other than Neutral.**

7. Remove the three poppet plugs and remove the springs and balls, from the case.

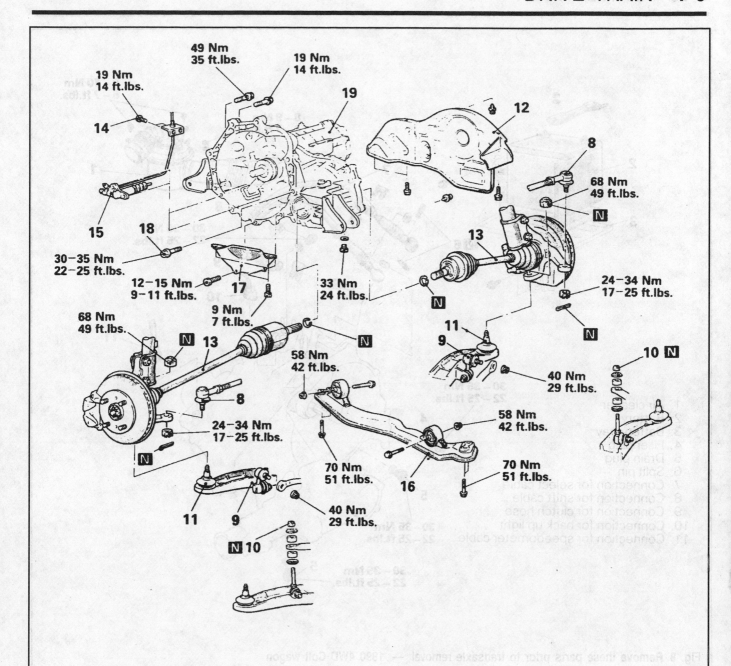

49 Nm
35 ft.lbs.

19 Nm
14 ft.lbs.

19 Nm
14 ft.lbs.

14

19

12

15

18

8

68 Nm
49 ft.lbs.

30–35 Nm
22–25 ft.lbs.

13

24–34 Nm
17–25 ft.lbs.

12–15 Nm
9–11 ft.lbs.

17

33 Nm
24 ft.lbs.

9 Nm
7 ft.lbs.

11

9

40 Nm
29 ft.lbs.

68 Nm
49 ft.lbs.

13

58 Nm
42 ft.lbs.

10

8

24–34 Nm
17–25 ft.lbs.

58 Nm
42 ft.lbs.

11

9

70 Nm
51 ft.lbs.

16

70 Nm
51 ft.lbs.

10

40 Nm
29 ft.lbs.

8. Connection for tie rod end
9. Connection for stabilizer bar <4G93 Engine>
10. Self locking nut <4G64 Engine>
11. Connection for lower arm ball joint
12. Under cover (RH)
● Draining of the transaxle oil
13. Drive shaft connection
14. Clutch oil line bracket bolt
15. Connection for release cylinder
16. Center member <4G93 Engine>
17. Bell housing cover
18. Transaxle assembly lower part coupling bolts
19. Transaxle assembly

Fig. 7 Transaxle removal/installation — 1992-93 2WD Vista

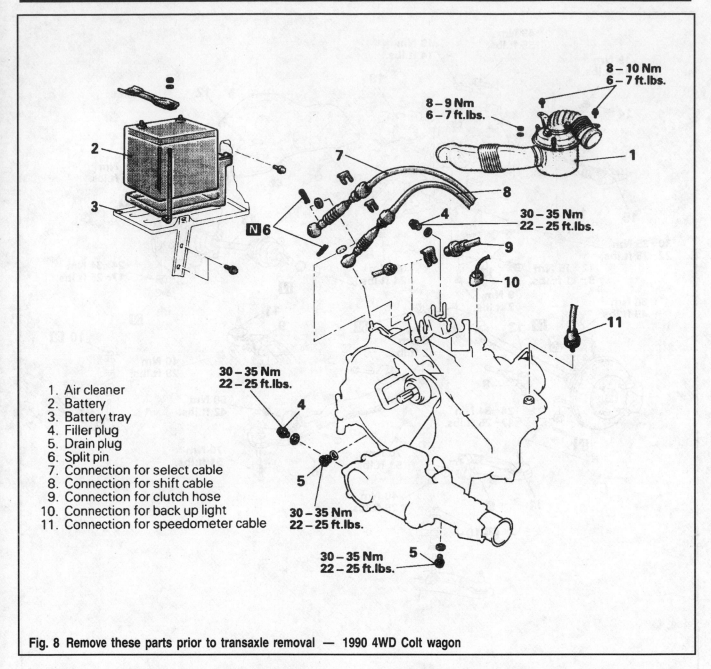

1. Air cleaner
2. Battery
3. Battery tray
4. Filler plug
5. Drain plug
6. Split pin
7. Connection for select cable
8. Connection for shift cable
9. Connection for clutch hose
10. Connection for back up light
11. Connection for speedometer cable

8 – 10 Nm
6 – 7 ft.lbs.

8 – 9 Nm
6 – 7 ft.lbs.

30 – 35 Nm
22 – 25 ft.lbs.

30 – 35 Nm
22 – 25 ft.lbs.

30 – 35 Nm
22 – 25 ft.lbs.

30 – 35 Nm
22 – 25 ft.lbs.

Fig. 8 Remove these parts prior to transaxle removal — 1990 4WD Colt wagon

8. Remove the reverse idler shaft and the reverse idler gear.

➡**The reverse idler shaft sometimes comes off with the removal of the transaxle case.**

9. Remove the reverse shift lever assembly.
10. Remove the reverse shift rail and the third/fourth shift rail spacer collar.
11. Remove the spring pins from the first/second and third/fourth shift forks using a punch and hammer. Support the shift forks before attempting to remove the spring pins
12. Pull the first/second shift rail upward from the case, sliding the rail through the shift fork. The shift rail cannot be removed until the completion of Step 13.
13. Pull the third/fourth shift rail from the case and remove the two shift rails and forks together.

14. Move the third/fourth speed synchronizer into the fourth speed position and remove the output shaft assembly.
15. Remove the differential assembly from the case.
16. Remove the bolts from the input shaft bearing retainer and remove the input shaft assembly.
17. Remove the shift shaft spring retainer and pull the spring pin with pliers.
18. Move the shift shaft towards the outside of the case by using a pin punch in the pin hole. Pull the shaft from the case and remove the control finger, two springs, spacer collar poppet spring and ball.

➡**During removal of the shift shaft from the case, the poppet ball will jump out of the control finger hole. Close the hole with an object to prevent loss of the ball.**

19. Put an identifying mark on the tapered roller bearing outer race and remove it from the case.

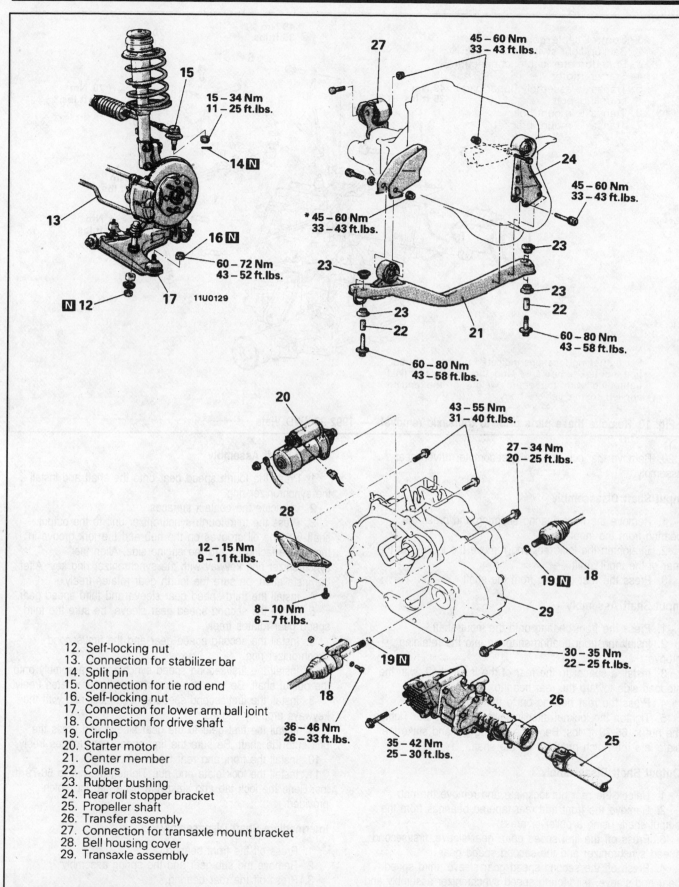

15 — 34 Nm
11 — 25 ft.lbs.

45 — 60 Nm
33 — 43 ft.lbs.

45 — 60 Nm
33 — 43 ft.lbs.

* 45 — 60 Nm
33 — 43 ft.lbs.

60 — 72 Nm
43 — 52 ft.lbs.

60 — 80 Nm
43 — 58 ft.lbs.

60 — 80 Nm
43 — 58 ft.lbs.

43 — 55 Nm
31 — 40 ft.lbs.

27 — 34 Nm
20 — 25 ft.lbs.

12 — 15 Nm
9 — 11 ft.lbs.

8 — 10 Nm
6 — 7 ft.lbs.

30 — 35 Nm
22 — 25 ft.lbs.

36 — 46 Nm
26 — 33 ft.lbs.

35 — 42 Nm
25 — 30 ft.lbs.

11U0129

12. Self-locking nut
13. Connection for stabilizer bar
14. Split pin
15. Connection for tie rod end
16. Self-locking nut
17. Connection for lower arm ball joint
18. Connection for drive shaft
19. Circlip
20. Starter motor
21. Center member
22. Collars
23. Rubber bushing
24. Rear roll stopper bracket
25. Propeller shaft
26. Transfer assembly
27. Connection for transaxle mount bracket
28. Bell housing cover
29. Transaxle assembly

Fig. 9 Transaxle removal/installation — 1990 4WD Colt wagon

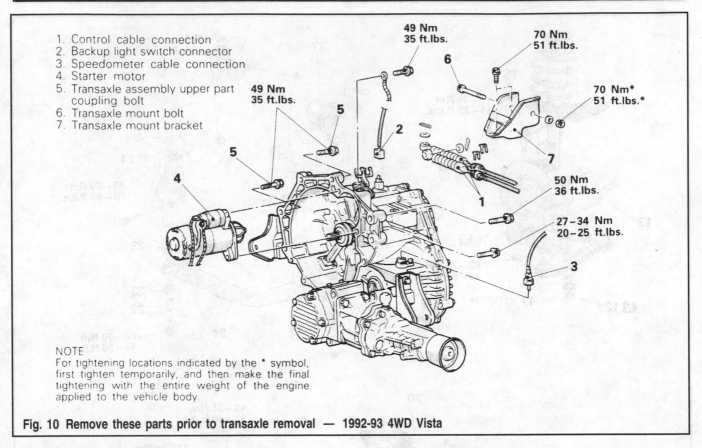

1. Control cable connection
2. Backup light switch connector
3. Speedometer cable connection
4. Starter motor
5. Transaxle assembly upper part coupling bolt
6. Transaxle mount bolt
7. Transaxle mount bracket

49 Nm 35 ft.lbs.

49 Nm 35 ft.lbs.

70 Nm 51 ft.lbs.

70 Nm* 51 ft.lbs.*

50 Nm 36 ft.lbs.

27–34 Nm 20–25 ft.lbs.

NOTE
For tightening locations indicated by the * symbol, first tighten temporarily, and then make the final tightening with the entire weight of the engine applied to the vehicle body.

Fig. 10 Remove these parts prior to transaxle removal — 1992-93 4WD Vista

20. Remove the lock and the speedometer driven gear assembly.

Input Shaft Disassembly

1. Remove the front bearing snapring and press the bearing from the input shaft.
2. Straighten the lock tab, and remove the locknut at the rear of the input shaft.
3. Press the rear bearing from the shaft.

Input Shaft Assembly

1. Press the front bearing onto the input shaft.
2. Install the front bearing snapring into the retaining groove.
3. Install a spacer to the rear of the input shaft, with the stepped side toward the rear bearing.
4. Press the rear bearing on to the input shaft.
5. Tighten the locknut after installing the lock tab. Tighten the nut to 66-79 ft. lbs. Bend the locking tab and stake the plate into the notch provided on the shaft.

Output Shaft Disassembly

1. Unlock the rear nut lockplate and remove the nut.
2. Remove the front and rear tapered bearings from the output shaft, using a puller or press.
3. Press off the first speed gear, gear sleeve, first/second speed synchronizer and the second speed gear.
4. Press off the second speed gear sleeve, third speed gear and sleeve, third/fourth speed synchronizer assembly and the fourth speed gear.

Output Shaft Assembly

1. Press the fourth speed gear onto the shaft and install the synchronizer ring.
2. Lubricate the contact surfaces.
3. Press the third/fourth synchronizer unit to the output shaft with the oil grooves on the hub and the fork groove in the sleeve facing toward the engine side. Align the synchronizer ring keyway with the synchronizer ring key. After the installation, be sure the fourth gear rotates freely.
4. Install the third speed gear sleeve and third speed gear.
5. Install the second speed gear sleeve, be sure the third speed gear rotates freely.
6. Install the second speed gear and the first/second synchronizer ring.
7. Install the first/second speed synchronizer assembly onto the output shaft. Be sure the second speed gear rotates freely.
8. Install the first/second speed synchronizer ring with the keyways properly aligned.
9. Install the first gear to the gear sleeve and press the unit onto the shaft. Be sure the first speed gear rotates freely.
10. Install the front and rear tapered bearings.
11. Install the lock plate and nut. Tighten the nut to 66-79 ft. lbs. Bend the lock tab and stake the plate into the notch provided.

Intermediate Shaft Disassembly

1. Press off the front bearing.
2. Remove the sub-gear and the spring assembly.
3. Press off the rear bearing.

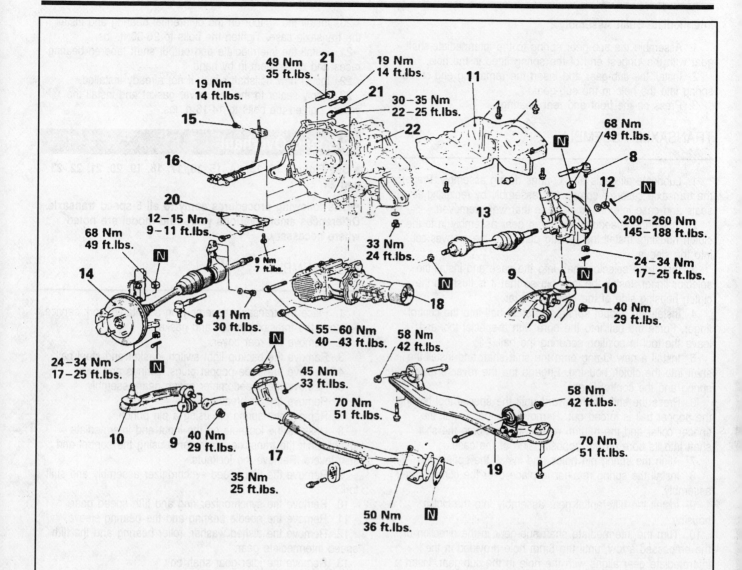

49 Nm
35 ft.lbs. **21**

19 Nm
14 ft.lbs. **11**

19 Nm
14 ft.lbs. **21**
15

30–35 Nm
22–25 ft.lbs. **22**

16

68 Nm
49 ft.lbs. **8**

20

12–15 Nm
9–11 ft.lbs.

12

200–260 Nm
145–188 ft.lbs.

68 Nm
49 ft.lbs.

9 Nm
7 ft.lbs. **14**

13

33 Nm
24 ft.lbs.

24–34 Nm
17–25 ft.lbs.

8 41 Nm
30 ft.lbs.

18

9 **10**

40 Nm
29 ft.lbs.

55–60 Nm
40–43 ft.lbs.

58 Nm
42 ft.lbs.

24–34 Nm
17–25 ft.lbs.

45 Nm
33 ft.lbs.

58 Nm
42 ft.lbs.

10 **9** 40 Nm
29 ft.lbs.

70 Nm
51 ft.lbs.

70 Nm
51 ft.lbs.

17

19

35 Nm
25 ft.lbs.

50 Nm
36 ft.lbs.

8. Connection for tie rod end
9. Connection for stabilizer bar
10. Connection for lower arm ball joint
• Draining of the transaxle oil
11. Under cover (RH)
12. Drive shaft nut (RH)
13. Drive shaft (RH)
14. Connection for drive shaft
   and inner shaft
15. Clutch oil line bracket bolts
16. Connection for clutch release
   cylinder

17. Front exhaust pipe
18. Transfer assembly
19. Center member
20. Bell housing cover
21. Transaxle assembly lower part
   coupling bolts
22. Transaxle assembly

Fig. 11 Transaxle removal/installation — 1992-93 4WD Vista

Intermediate Shaft Assembly

1. Assemble the sub-gear spring to the intermediate shaft gear with the longest end of the spring fitted in the hole.
2. Install the sub-gear and insert the remaining end of the spring into the hole in the sub-gear.
3. Press on the front and rear bearings.

TRANSAXLE ASSEMBLY

1. Lubricate all seals and O-rings during assembly. Prepare the transaxle case for component assembly by replacing all oil seals and case internal small parts that were removed.
2. Install the speedometer driven gear assembly in to the clutch housing. Install the locking plate into the grooves cot into the sleeve.
3. Install the selector shaft into the case and install the selector finger. Install the lock pin so that it is flush on the clutch housing side of the selector finger.
4. Install the poppet spring and steel ball into the control finger. Force the ball into the bore with a special tool and leave the tool in position securing the ball.
5. Install a new O-ring onto the shift shaft and install the shaft into the clutch housing. Engage the the reverse restrict spring and the control finger.
6. Press the shift shaft inward until the special tool holding the poppet ball is forced out. Remove the tool. Install the spacer collar and the neutral return spring. Force the shift shaft into its bore on the opposite side of the case.
7. Align the spring pin holes and install the spring pins
8. Install the spring retainer in place over the control finger assembly.
9. Install the differential gear assembly into the clutch housing.
10. Turn the intermediate shaft sub-gear in the direction of the embossed arrow, until the 8mm hole provided in the intermediate gear aligns with the hole in the sub-gear. Insert a snug fitting pin through the holes to hold the sub-gear in position.
11. Install the input shaft assembly and the intermediate shaft assembly into the clutch housing as a unit.
12. Install the selector shaft poppet ball. poppet spring and plug. Apply sealer to the plug and seat it flush with the housing surface.
13. Install the input shaft bearing retainer and remove the pin that secured the intermediate shaft sub-gear.
14. Install the output shaft assembly.
15. Install the interlocking plungers into the housing. Assemble the first/second and third/fourth shift rails and forks into position on the housing.
16. Install the spring pins with the split parallel with the center line of the rail.
17. Install the reverse shift rail and install the three poppet balls, springs and plugs. The poppet spring with the white paint ID must be installed in the poppet hole of the reverse shift rail. Install the small diameter ends of the springs toward the balls.
18. Install the reverse shift lever assembly, the reverse idler gear and shaft after lubricating them.
19. Apply sealer to a new gasket and install it on the clutch housing.

20. Install the spacer on the differential bearing and install the transaxle case. Tighten the bolts to 26-30 ft. lbs.
21. Install the intermediate and output shaft tapered bearing races and press them in by hand.
22. Install new halfshaft seals, if not already installed.
23. Apply sealer to the rear cover gasket and install the cover. Tighten the bolts to 14-16 ft. lbs.

5-Speed Overhaul

▶ **See Figures 12, 13, 14, 15, 16, 17, 18, 19, 20, 21, 22, 23 and 24**

➡ **The following procedures apply to all 5-speed transaxle. Differences among various years and model are noted where necessary.**

DISASSEMBLY

1. Place the transaxle assembly on a suitable work service. Remove the transaxle switch and gasket.
2. Remove the rear cover.
3. Remove the backup light switch, gasket and steel ball.
4. Remove the three poppet plugs, springs and balls.
5. Remove the speedometer driven gear assembly.
6. Remove the air breather.
7. Remove the spring pin using a pin punch.
8. Unstake the locknuts on the input and intermediate shafts. Shift the transaxle into reverse using the control and shift levers. Remove the locknuts.
9. Remove the fifth speed synchronizer assembly and shift fork.
10. Remove the synchronizer ring and fifth speed gear.
11. Remove the needle bearing and the bearing sleeve.
12. Remove the dished washer, roller bearing and the fifth speed intermediate gear.
13. Remove the idler gear shaft bolt.
14. Separate the transmission case from the clutch housing.
15. Remove the oil guide from the transmission case assembly.
16. Remove the bolt, spring washer and stopper bracket. Remove the restrictor ball assembly and gasket.
17. Remove the outer ring and oil seal from the transmission case.
18. Remove the three spacers. Remove the shift lever assembly and lever shoe.
19. Remove the reverse idler gear and shaft.
20. Remove the shift lever spring pins. Refer to the four speed transaxle procedures and remove the shift forks and rails. Remove the select spacer.
21. Remove the interlocking plungers from the clutch housing. Remove the fifth speed shift lug and select spacer.
22. Remove the output shaft assembly. Remove the deferential assembly.
23. Remove the poppet plug and the poppet spring and ball for the select shift rail.
24. Remove the input shaft front bearing retainer. Lift up the input shaft assembly together with the select shift fork and the intermediate shaft assembly.
25. Refer to the four speed procedures for component servicing and transaxle assembly.

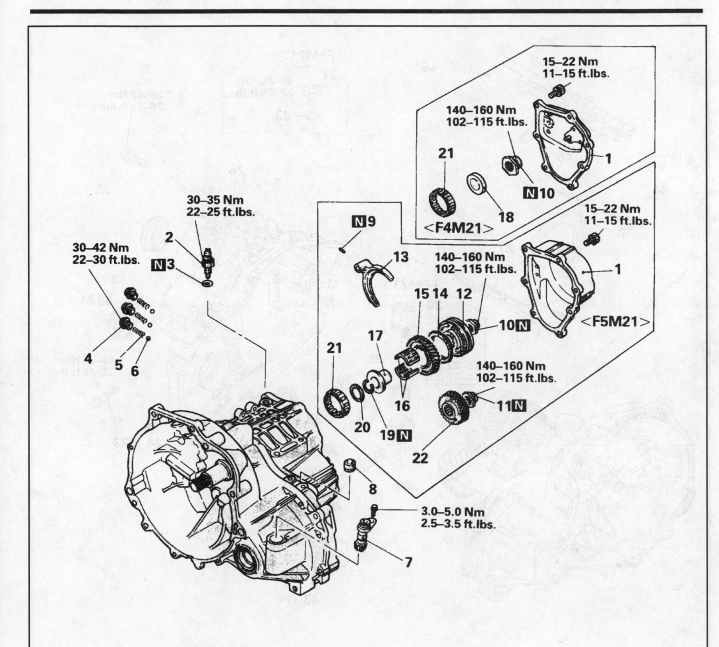

15–22 Nm
11–15 ft.lbs.

140–160 Nm
102–115 ft.lbs.

21

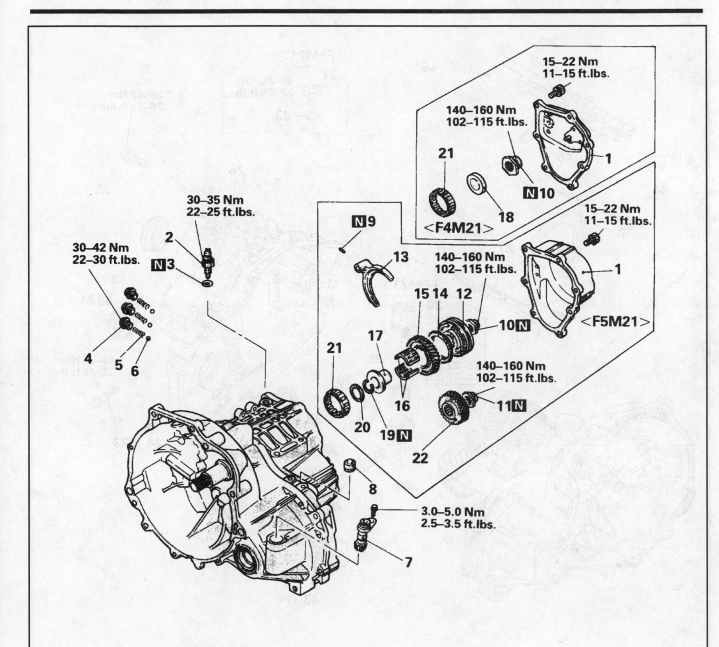 **N 10**

18

<F4M21>

N 9

30–35 Nm
22–25 ft.lbs.

2

N 3

13

30–42 Nm
22–30 ft.lbs.

N 3

140–160 Nm
102–115 ft.lbs.

15 14 12

10 N

<F5M21>

15–22 Nm
11–15 ft.lbs.

1

4 5 6

21

17

16

140–160 Nm
102–115 ft.lbs.

11 N

20

19 N

22

8

7

3.0–5.0 Nm
2.5–3.5 ft.lbs.

1. Rear cover
2. Backup light switch
3. Gasket
4. Poppet plug
5. Poppet spring
6. Poppet ball
7. Speedometer driven gear assembly
8. Air breather
9. Spring pin
10. Lock nut
11. Lock nut
12. 5th speed synchronizer assembly
13. 5th speed shift fork
14. Synchronizer ring

15. 5th speed gear
16. Needle bearing
17. Bearing sleeve
18. Dished washer
19. Snap ring
20. Spacer
21. Roller bearing
22. 5th speed intermediate gear

Fig. 12 Transaxle disassembly/assembly — F4M21 4-speed and F5M21 5-speed — 1990-93 Colt hatchback and sedan

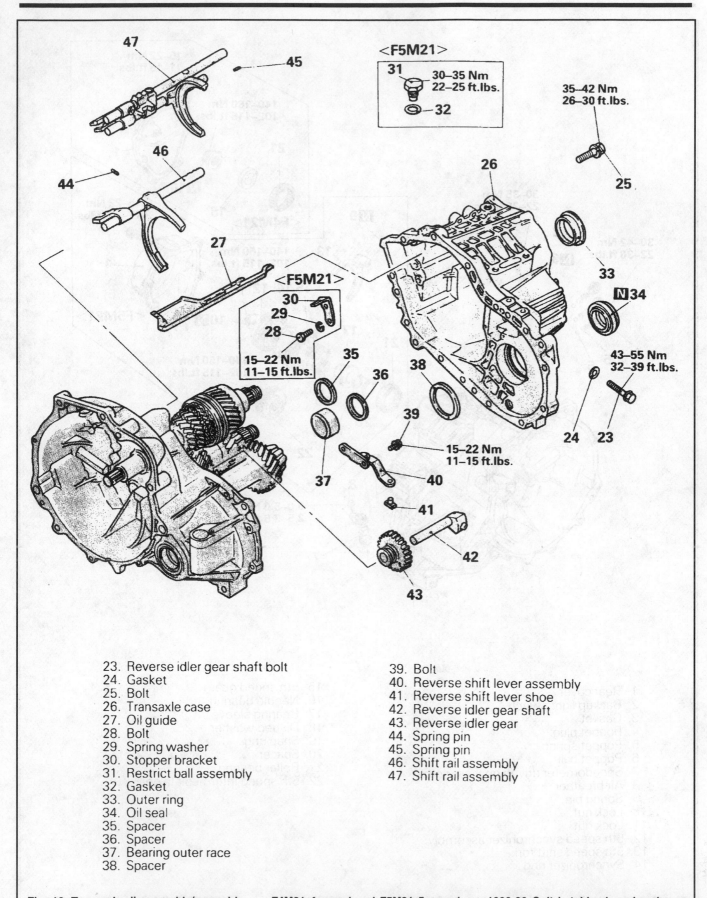

47
45
`<F5M21>`
31   30–35 Nm
22–25 ft.lbs.
32
35–42 Nm
26–30 ft.lbs.
25
46
44
26
33
N 34
27
`<F5M21>`
30
29
28
15–22 Nm
11–15 ft.lbs.
35
36
38
39   15–22 Nm
11–15 ft.lbs.
37
40
41
43–55 Nm
32–39 ft.lbs.
24   23
42
43

23. Reverse idler gear shaft bolt
24. Gasket
25. Bolt
26. Transaxle case
27. Oil guide
28. Bolt
29. Spring washer
30. Stopper bracket
31. Restrict ball assembly
32. Gasket
33. Outer ring
34. Oil seal
35. Spacer
36. Spacer
37. Bearing outer race
38. Spacer

39. Bolt
40. Reverse shift lever assembly
41. Reverse shift lever shoe
42. Reverse idler gear shaft
43. Reverse idler gear
44. Spring pin
45. Spring pin
46. Shift rail assembly
47. Shift rail assembly

Fig. 13 Transaxle disassembly/assembly — F4M21 4-speed and F5M21 5-speed — 1990-93 Colt hatchback and sedan

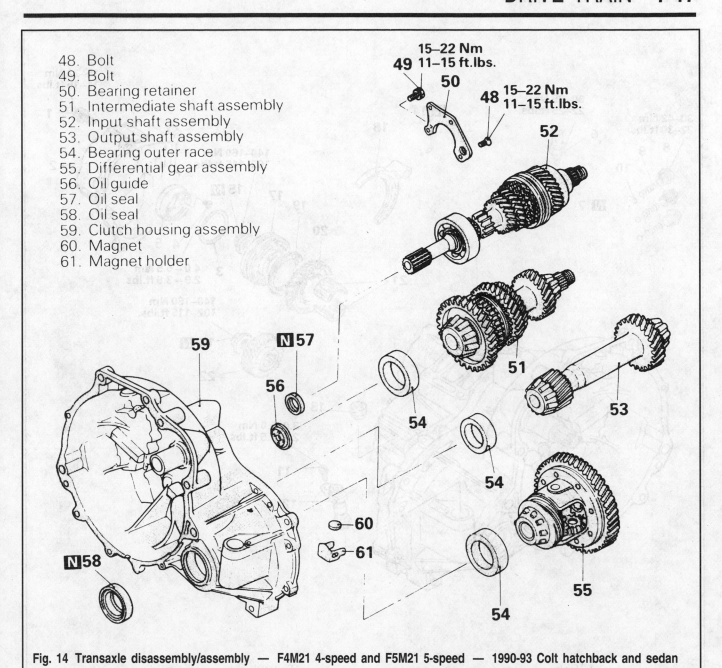

48. Bolt
49. Bolt
50. Bearing retainer
51. Intermediate shaft assembly
52. Input shaft assembly
53. Output shaft assembly
54. Bearing outer race
55. Differential gear assembly
56. Oil guide
57. Oil seal
58. Oil seal
59. Clutch housing assembly
60. Magnet
61. Magnet holder

49 15–22 Nm
11–15 ft.lbs.

50

48 15–22 Nm
11–15 ft.lbs.

52

59   **N** 57

56

54

54

54

N 58

60

61

51

53

55

Fig. 14 Transaxle disassembly/assembly — F4M21 4-speed and F5M21 5-speed — 1990-93 Colt hatchback and sedan

Input Shaft Disassembly

1. Remove the front bearing snapring and press the bearing from the input shaft.
2. Straighten the lock tab, and remove the locknut at the rear of the input shaft.
3. Press the rear bearing from the shaft.

Input Shaft Assembly

1. Press the front bearing onto the input shaft.
2. Install the front bearing snapring into the retaining groove.
3. Install a spacer to the rear of the input shaft, with the stepped side toward the rear bearing.
4. Press the rear bearing on to the input shaft.

5. Tighten the locknut after installing the lock tab. Tighten the nut to 66-79 ft. lbs. Bend the locking tab and stake the plate into the notch provided on the shaft.

Output Shaft Disassembly

1. Unlock the rear nut lockplate and remove the nut.
2. Remove the front and rear tapered bearings from the output shaft, using a puller or press.
3. Press off the first speed gear, gear sleeve, first/second speed synchronizer and the second speed gear.
4. Press off the second speed gear sleeve, third speed gear and sleeve, third/fourth speed synchronizer assembly and the fourth speed gear.

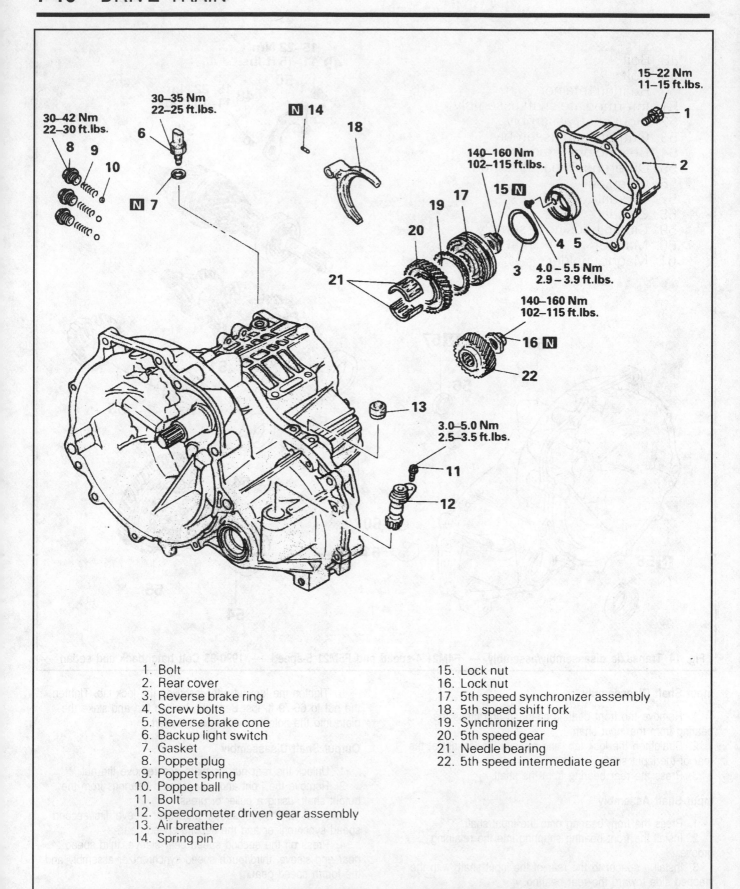

1. Bolt
2. Rear cover
3. Reverse brake ring
4. Screw bolts
5. Reverse brake cone
6. Backup light switch
7. Gasket
8. Poppet plug
9. Poppet spring
10. Poppet ball
11. Bolt
12. Speedometer driven gear assembly
13. Air breather
14. Spring pin
15. Lock nut
16. Lock nut
17. 5th speed synchronizer assembly
18. 5th speed shift fork
19. Synchronizer ring
20. 5th speed gear
21. Needle bearing
22. 5th speed intermediate gear

Fig. 15 Transaxle disassembly/assembly — F5M22 5-speed — 1990-93 Colt hatchback, sedan, 2WD wagon and 2WD Vista

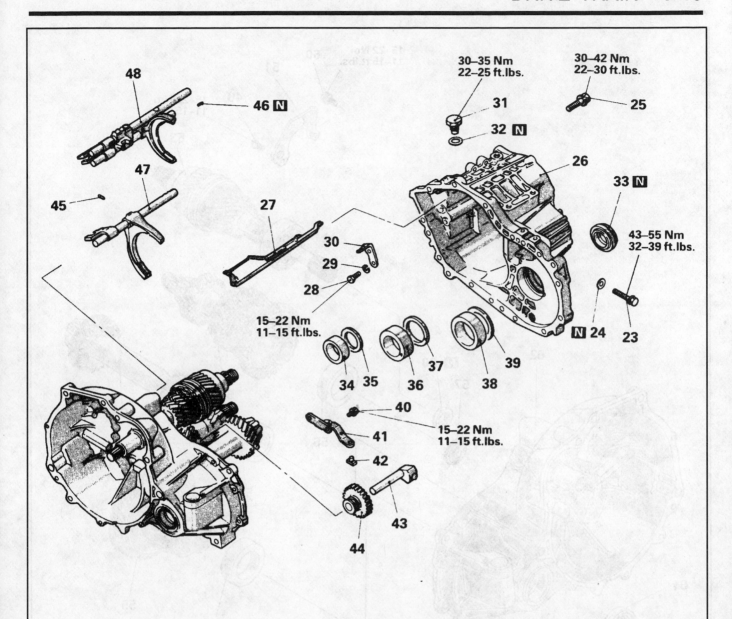

23. Reverse idler gear shaft bolt
24. Gasket
25. Bolt
26. Transaxle case
27. Oil guide
28. Bolt
29. Spring washer
30. Stopper bracket
31. Restrict ball assembly
32. Gasket
33. Oil seal
34. Bearing outer race
35. Spacer
36. Bearing outer race
37. Spacer
38. Bearing outer race
39. Spacer
40. Bolt
41. Reverse shift lever assembly
42. Reverse shift lever shoe
43. Reverse idler gear shaft
44. Reverse idler gear
45. Spring pin
46. Spring pin
47. Shift rails and forks
48. Shift rails and forks

Fig. 16 Transaxle disassembly/assembly — F5M22 5-speed — 1990-93 Colt hatchback, sedan, 2WD wagon and 2WD Vista

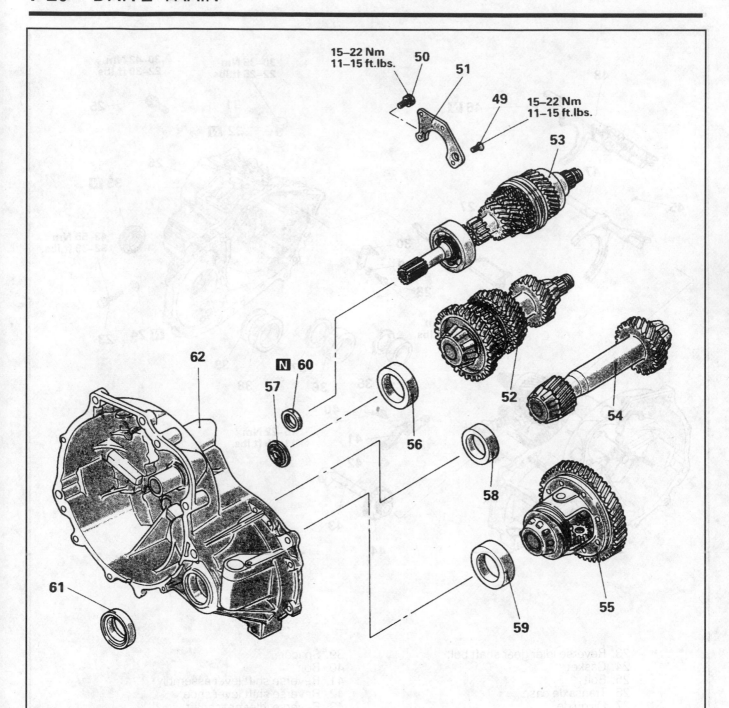

15–22 Nm
11–15 ft.lbs. 50

51

49

15–22 Nm
11–15 ft.lbs.

53

62

N 60

57

56

52

54

58

55

59

61

49. Bolt
50. Bolt
51. Bearing retainer
52. Intermediate shaft assembly
53. Input shaft assembly
54. Output shaft assembly
55. Differential gear assembly
56. Bearing outer race
57. Oil guide
58. Bearing outer race
59. Bearing outer race
60. Oil seal

61. Oil seal
62. Clutch housing assembly
63. Magnet
64. Magnet holder

Fig. 17 Transaxle disassembly/assembly — F5M22 5-speed — 1990-93 Colt hatchback, sedan, 2WD wagon and 2WD Vista

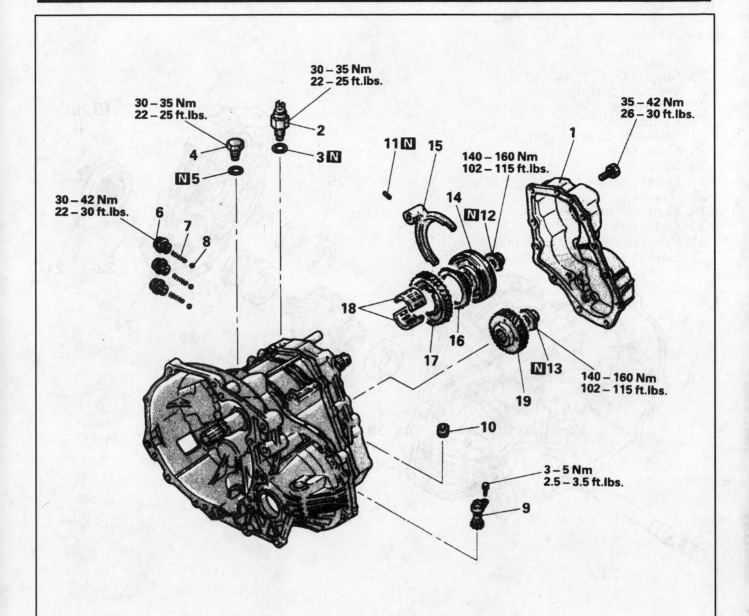

Fig. 18 Transaxle disassembly/assembly — 1990 Colt 4WD wagon and 1992-93 4WD Vista

1. Rear cover
2. Backup light switch
3. Gasket
4. Restrict ball assembly
5. Gasket
6. Poppet plug
7. Poppet spring
8. Poppet ball
9. Speedometer driven gear assembly
10. Air breather
11. Spring pin
12. Lock nut
13. Lock nut
14. 5th speed synchronizer assembly
15. Shift fork
16. Synchronizer ring
17. 5th speed gear
18. Needle bearing
19. 5th speed intermediate gear

20. Snap ring
21. Viscous coupling
22. Steel ball
23. Center shaft
24. Transaxle case adapter
25. Outer race
26. Spacer
27. Outer race
28. Spacer
29. Center differential
30. Outer race
31. Reverse idler gear shaft bolt
32. Gasket

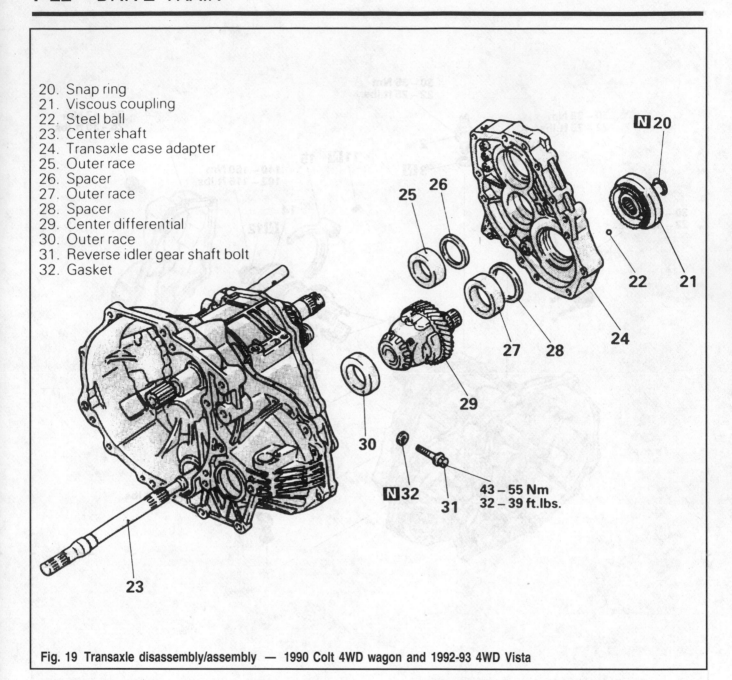

N 20

25 26

22 21

24

27 28

29

30

N 32 31 43 – 55 Nm
32 – 39 ft.lbs.

23

Fig. 19 Transaxle disassembly/assembly — 1990 Colt 4WD wagon and 1992-93 4WD Vista

Output Shaft Assembly

1. Press the fourth speed gear onto the shaft and install the synchronizer ring.
2. Lubricate the contact surfaces.
3. Press the third/fourth synchronizer unit to the output shaft with the oil grooves on the hub and the fork groove in the sleeve facing toward the engine side. Align the synchronizer ring keyway with the synchronizer ring key. After the installation, be sure the fourth gear rotates freely.
4. Install the third speed gear sleeve and third speed gear.
5. Install the second speed gear sleeve, be sure the third speed gear rotates freely.
6. Install the second speed gear and the first/second synchronizer ring.
7. Install the first/second speed synchronizer assembly onto the output shaft. Be sure the second speed gear rotates freely.

8. Install the first/second speed synchronizer ring with the keyways properly aligned.
9. Install the first gear to the gear sleeve and press the unit onto the shaft. Be sure the first speed gear rotates freely.
10. Install the front and rear tapered bearings.
11. Install the lock plate and nut. Tighten the nut to 66-79 ft. lbs. Bend the lock tab and stake the plate into the notch provided.

Intermediate Shaft Disassembly

1. Press off the front bearing.
2. Remove the sub-gear and the spring assembly.
3. Press off the rear bearing.

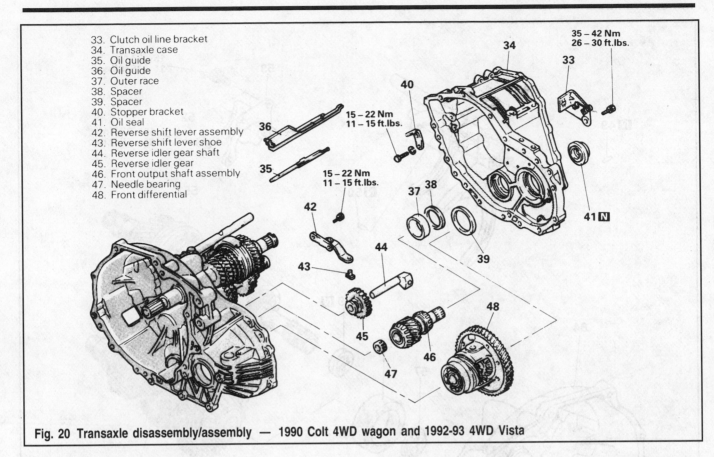

33. Clutch oil line bracket
34. Transaxle case
35. Oil guide
36. Oil guide
37. Outer race
38. Spacer
39. Spacer
40. Stopper bracket
41. Oil seal
42. Reverse shift lever assembly
43. Reverse shift lever shoe
44. Reverse idler gear shaft
45. Reverse idler gear
46. Front output shaft assembly
47. Needle bearing
48. Front differential

35 – 42 Nm
26 – 30 ft.lbs.

15 – 22 Nm
11 – 15 ft.lbs.

15 – 22 Nm
11 – 15 ft.lbs.

Fig. 20 Transaxle disassembly/assembly — 1990 Colt 4WD wagon and 1992-93 4WD Vista

Intermediate Shaft Assembly

1. Assemble the sub-gear spring to the intermediate shaft gear with the longest end of the spring fitted in the hole.
2. Install the sub-gear and insert the remaining end of the spring into the hole in the sub-gear.
3. Press on the front and rear bearings.

TRANSAXLE ASSEMBLY

1. Lubricate all seals and O-rings during assembly. Prepare the transaxle case for component assembly by replacing all oil seals and case internal small parts that were removed.
2. Install the speedometer driven gear assembly in to the clutch housing. Install the locking plate into the grooves cot into the sleeve.
3. Install the shaft into the case and install the selector finger. Install the lock pin so that it is flush on the clutch housing side of the selector finger.
4. Install the poppet spring and steel ball into the control finger. Force the ball into the bore with a special tool and leave the tool in position securing the ball.
5. Install a new O-ring onto the shift shaft and install the shaft into the clutch housing. Engage the the 5th/reverse restrict spring and the control finger.
6. Press the shift shaft inward until the special tool holding the poppet ball is forced out. Remove the tool. Install the spacer collar and the neutral return spring. Force the shift shaft into its bore on the opposite side of the case.
7. Align the spring pin holes and install the spring pins

8. Install the spring retainer in place over the control finger assembly.
9. Install the differential gear assembly into the clutch housing.
10. Turn the Intermediate shaft sub-gear in the direction of the embossed arrow, until the 8mm hole provided in the intermediate gear aligns with the hole in the sub-gear. Insert a snug fitting pin through the holes to hold the sub-gear in position.
11. Install the input shaft assembly and the intermediate shaft assembly into the clutch housing as a unit.
12. Install the selector shaft poppet ball. poppet spring and plug. Apply sealer to the plug and seat it flush with the housing surface.
13. Install the input shaft bearing retainer and remove the pin that secured the intermediate shaft sub-gear.
14. Install the output shaft assembly.
15. Install the interlocking plungers into the housing. Assemble the first/second and third/fourth shift rails and forks into position on the housing.
16. Install the spring pins with the split parallel with the center line of the rail.
17. Install the 5th/reverse shift rail and install the three poppet balls, springs and plugs. The poppet spring with the white paint ID must be installed in the poppet hole of the 5th/reverse shift rail. Install the small diameter ends of the springs toward the balls.
18. Install the 5th/reverse shift lever assembly, the 5th/reverse idler gear and shaft after lubricating them.
19. Apply sealer to a new gasket and install it on the clutch housing.

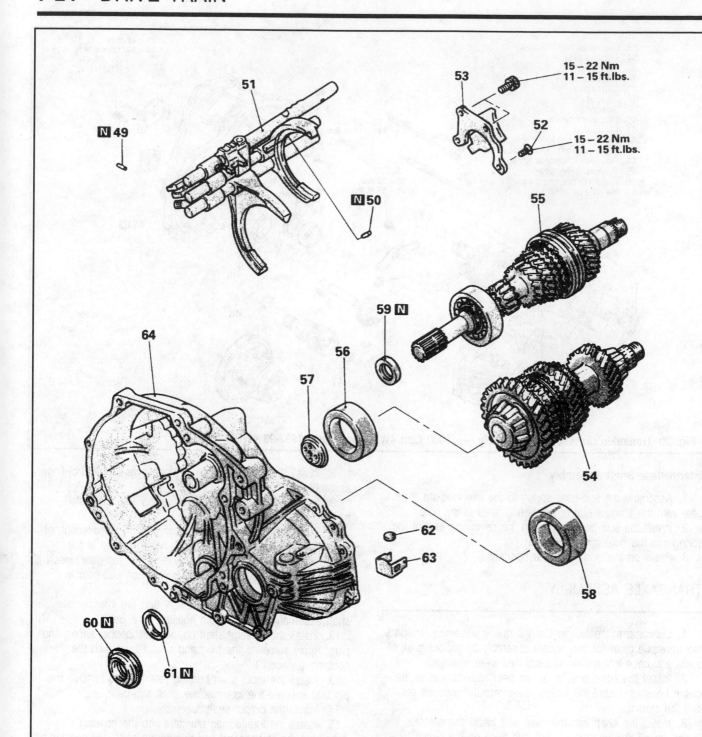

49. Spring pin
50. Spring pin
51. Shift rail assembly
52. Bolt
53. Bearing retainer
54. Intermediate gear assembly
55. Input shaft assembly
56. Outer race
57. Oil guide
58. Outer race
59. Oil seal

60. Oil seal
61. Oil seal
62. Magnet
63. Magnet holder
64. Clutch housing assembly

Fig. 21 Transaxle disassembly/assembly — 1990 Colt 4WD wagon and 1992-93 4WD Vista

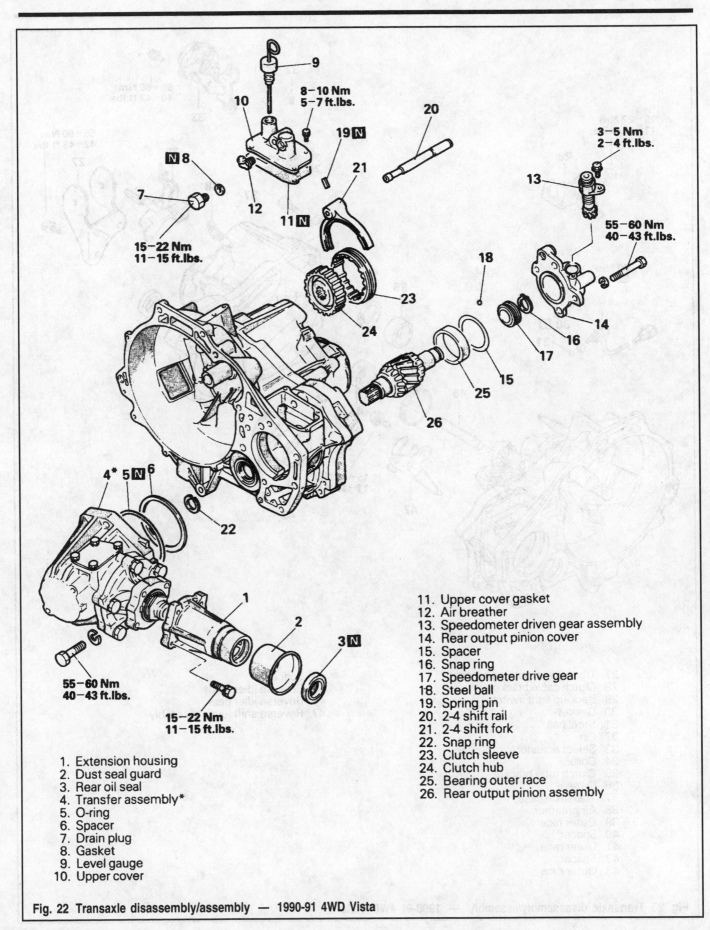

8–10 Nm
5–7 ft.lbs.

3–5 Nm
2–4 ft.lbs.

55–60 Nm
40–43 ft.lbs.

15–22 Nm
11–15 ft.lbs.

55–60 Nm
40–43 ft.lbs.

15–22 Nm
11–15 ft.lbs.

1. Extension housing
2. Dust seal guard
3. Rear oil seal
4. Transfer assembly*
5. O-ring
6. Spacer
7. Drain plug
8. Gasket
9. Level gauge
10. Upper cover

11. Upper cover gasket
12. Air breather
13. Speedometer driven gear assembly
14. Rear output pinion cover
15. Spacer
16. Snap ring
17. Speedometer drive gear
18. Steel ball
19. Spring pin
20. 2-4 shift rail
21. 2-4 shift fork
22. Snap ring
23. Clutch sleeve
24. Clutch hub
25. Bearing outer race
26. Rear output pinion assembly

Fig. 22 Transaxle disassembly/assembly — 1990-91 4WD Vista

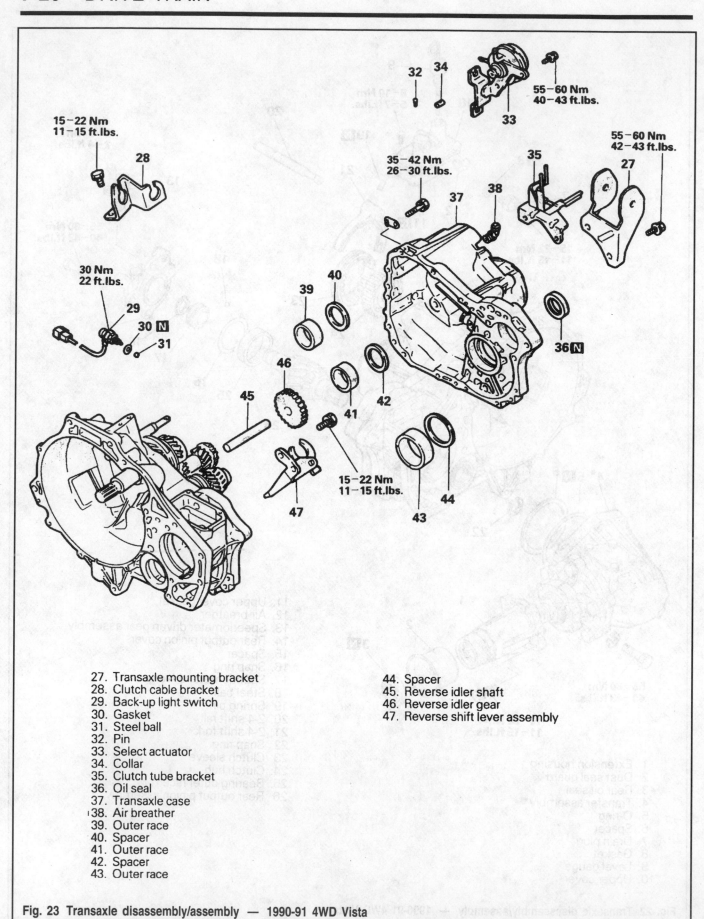

15−22 Nm
11−15 ft.lbs.

28

30 Nm
22 ft.lbs.

29

30

31

45

46

47

15−22 Nm
11−15 ft.lbs.

41

39

40

42

43

44

32 34

55−60 Nm
40−43 ft.lbs.

33

35−42 Nm
26−30 ft.lbs.

37

38

35

55−60 Nm
42−43 ft.lbs.

27

36

27. Transaxle mounting bracket
28. Clutch cable bracket
29. Back-up light switch
30. Gasket
31. Steel ball
32. Pin
33. Select actuator
34. Collar
35. Clutch tube bracket
36. Oil seal
37. Transaxle case
38. Air breather
39. Outer race
40. Spacer
41. Outer race
42. Spacer
43. Outer race

44. Spacer
45. Reverse idler shaft
46. Reverse idler gear
47. Reverse shift lever assembly

Fig. 23 Transaxle disassembly/assembly — 1990-91 4WD Vista

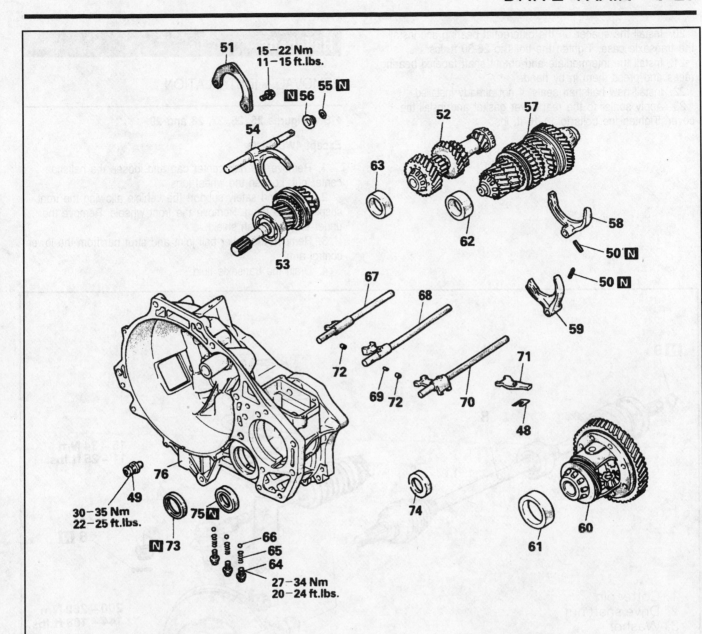

15 – 22 Nm
11 – 15 ft.lbs.

30 – 35 Nm
22 – 25 ft.lbs.

27 – 34 Nm
20 – 24 ft.lbs.

48. Select spacer
49. Restrict ball assembly
50. Spring pin
51. Bearing retainer
52. Intermediate gear assembly
53. Input shaft assembly
54. Select shift fork assembly
55. Seat
56. O-ring
57. Output shaft assembly
58. 1-2 speed shift fork
59. 3-4 speed shift fork
60. Differential assembly
61. Outer race
62. Outer race
63. Outer race
64. Poppet plug

65. Spring
66. Steel ball
67. Reverse shift rail
68. 1-2 speed shift rail
69. Interlock plunger B
70. 3-4 speed shift rail
71. 5-speed shift lug
72. Interlock plunger A
73. Oil seal
74. Outer race
75. Oil seal
76. Clutch housing assembly

Fig. 24 Transaxle disassembly/assembly — 1990-91 4WD Vista

20. Install the spacer on the differential bearing and install the transaxle case. Tighten the bolts to 26-30 ft. lbs.

21. Install the intermediate and output shaft tapered bearing races and press them in by hand.

22. Install new halfshaft seals, if not already installed.

23. Apply sealer to the rear cover gasket and install the cover. Tighten the bolts to 14-16 ft. lbs.

Halfshafts

REMOVAL & INSTALLATION

▶ **See Figures 25, 26, 27, 28 and 29**

Except 4WD Vista

1. Remove the hub center cap and loosen the halfshaft center nut. Loosen the wheel lugs.

2. Raise and safely support the vehicle allowing the front suspension to hang. Remove the front wheels. Remove the under engine splash shield.

3. Remove the lower ball joint and strut bar from the lower control arm.

4. Drain the transaxle fluid.

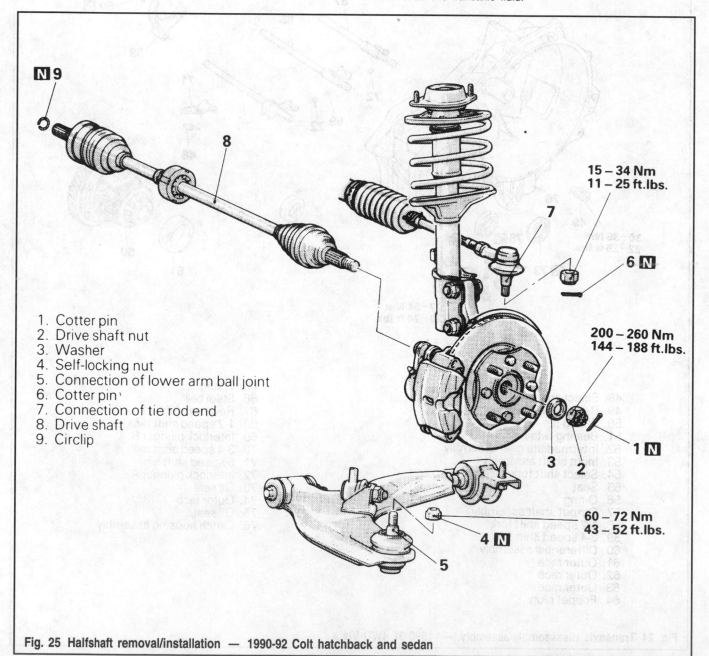

15 – 34 Nm
11 – 25 ft.lbs.

200 – 260 Nm
144 – 188 ft.lbs.

60 – 72 Nm
43 – 52 ft.lbs.

1. Cotter pin
2. Drive shaft nut
3. Washer
4. Self-locking nut
5. Connection of lower arm ball joint
6. Cotter pin
7. Connection of tie rod end
8. Drive shaft
9. Circlip

Fig. 25 Halfshaft removal/installation — 1990-92 Colt hatchback and sedan

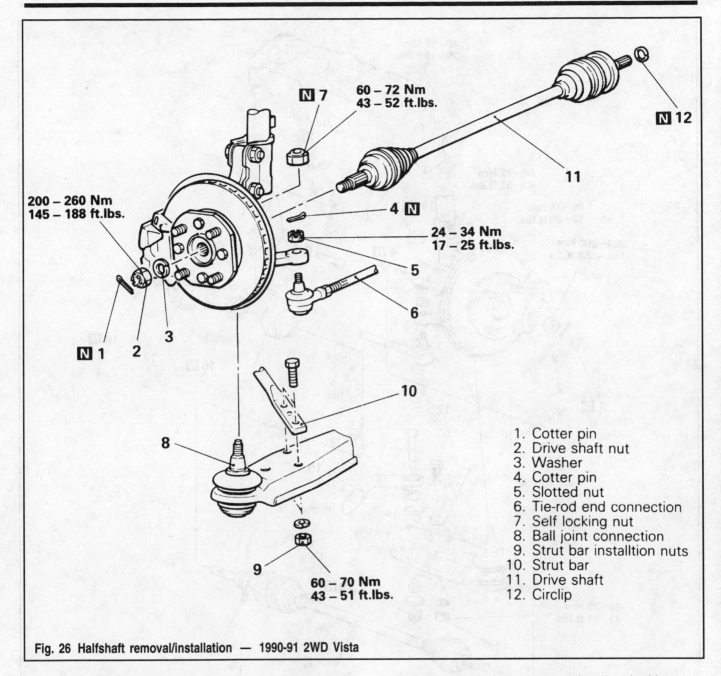

200 – 260 Nm
145 – 188 ft.lbs.

60 – 72 Nm
43 – 52 ft.lbs.

24 – 34 Nm
17 – 25 ft.lbs.

60 – 70 Nm
43 – 51 ft.lbs.

1. Cotter pin
2. Drive shaft nut
3. Washer
4. Cotter pin
5. Slotted nut
6. Tie-rod end connection
7. Self locking nut
8. Ball joint connection
9. Strut bar installtion nuts
10. Strut bar
11. Drive shaft
12. Circlip

Fig. 26 Halfshaft removal/installation — 1990-91 2WD Vista

5. On models that are equipped with a center bearing; remove the snapring or bolts that mount the center bearing/support. Insert a pry bar between the transaxle case (on the raised rib) and the halfshaft double off-set joint case (DOJ) or tripod joint (T.J.). Do not insert the pry bar too deeply or the oil seal will be damaged. Move the bar to the right to withdraw the left hand shaft; to the left to remove the right halfshaft.

➡ If the vehicle is equipped with a tripod (T.J.) Rzeppa (R.J.) joint equipped halfshaft, be sure to hold the (transaxle side) T.J. case and pull out the shaft straight. Simply pulling the shaft out of position could cause damage to the T.J. boot or the spider assembly to slip from its case.

6. Plug the transaxle case with a clean rag to prevent dirt from entering the case.

7. Use a pusher/puller tool, mounted on the wheel lugs, to push the halfshaft back and out of the drive hub. Take care to prevent the spacer from falling out of place.

8. Service the halfshaft as required. Install the halfshaft through the drive hub first, then install the transaxle side. Connect the strut bar and lower ball joint. Connect the center bearing on models equipped. ALWAYS install a new retaining circlip ring on the transaxle end when installing the halfshaft. Fill the transaxle with lubricant and install the lower splash shield. Mount the wheels and lower the vehicle. Tighten the wheel lugs, and tighten the halfshaft hub nut to 185 ft. lbs.

4WD Vista

LEFT SIDE

1. Remove the center wheel hub. Loosen the wheel lugs and the center halfshaft nut.

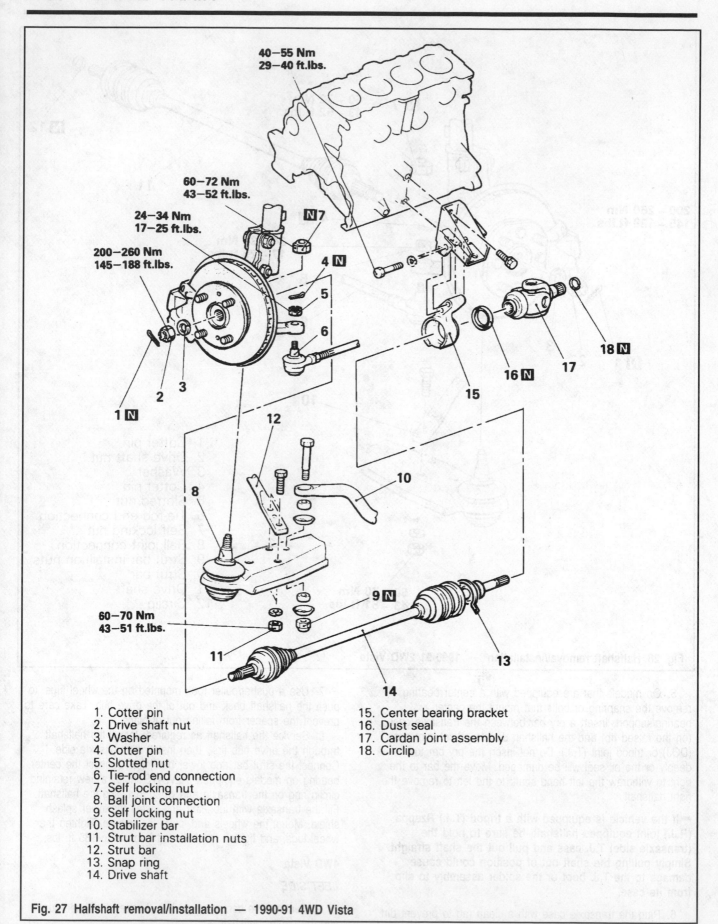

1. Cotter pin
2. Drive shaft nut
3. Washer
4. Cotter pin
5. Slotted nut
6. Tie-rod end connection
7. Self locking nut
8. Ball joint connection
9. Self locking nut
10. Stabilizer bar
11. Strut bar installation nuts
12. Strut bar
13. Snap ring
14. Drive shaft
15. Center bearing bracket
16. Dust seal
17. Cardan joint assembly
18. Circlip

Fig. 27 Halfshaft removal/installation — 1990-91 4WD Vista

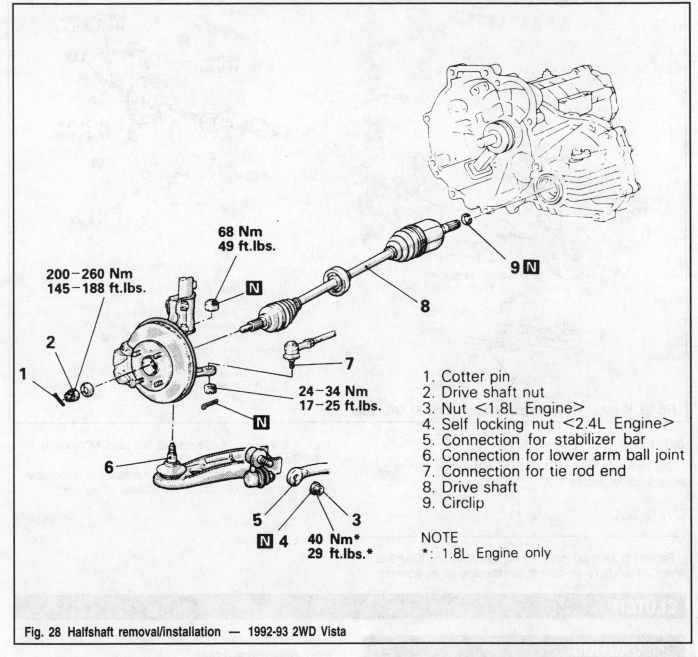

68 Nm
49 ft.lbs.

200−260 Nm
145−188 ft.lbs.

24−34 Nm
17−25 ft.lbs.

40 Nm*
29 ft.lbs.*

1. Cotter pin
2. Drive shaft nut
3. Nut <1.8L Engine>
4. Self locking nut <2.4L Engine>
5. Connection for stabilizer bar
6. Connection for lower arm ball joint
7. Connection for tie rod end
8. Drive shaft
9. Circlip

NOTE
*: 1.8L Engine only

Fig. 28 Halfshaft removal/installation — 1992-93 2WD Vista

2. Raise and safely support the front of the vehicle with the suspension hanging.

3. Remove the front wheels.

4. Drain the transaxle fluid.

5. Disconnect the lower ball joint from the steering knuckle.

6. Remove the strut bar and the stabilizer bar from the lower arm.

7. Remove the center bearing mount snapring/bolts from the bracket.

8. Lightly tap the double-offset joint outer race with a wooden mallet and disconnect the cardan joint.

9. Disconnect the halfshaft from the center bearing bracket.

10. Use a pusher/puller tool mounted to the wheel studs and press the halfshaft from the drive hub.

11. Unbolt and remove the bearing bracket.

12. Use a wooden mallet and lightly tap the cardan joint yoke and remove it from the transaxle. DO NOT pry the

cardan joint from the transaxle, damage can be caused to the joint and boot.

13. Service the halfshaft as required. Install the cardan joint.

14. Apply grease to the cardan joint contact surfaces.

15. Attach a new O-ring to the oil seal retainer.

16. Install the center bearing bracket. Torque the mounting to 40 ft. lbs.

17. Insert the center bearing into the mounting bracket, make sure it is fully seated. Secure with the snapring bolts.

18. Coat the halfshaft splines with grease and slide it into the cardan joint.

19. Slide the halfshaft into the drive hub. Install the suspension components and wheel. Lower the vehicle and tighten the wheel lugs and the center halfshaft nut. Torque the nut to 188 ft. lbs.

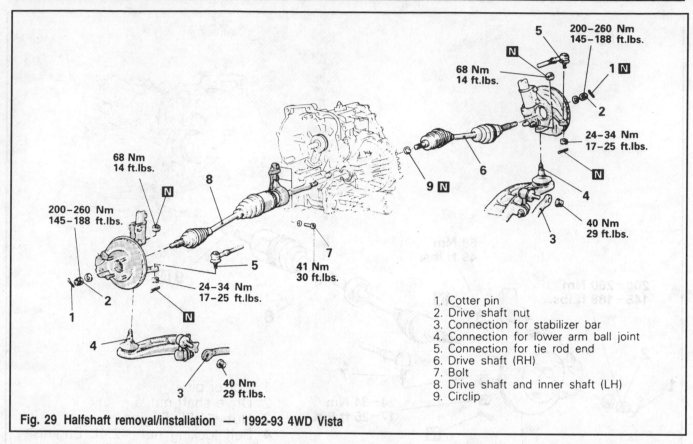

1. Cotter pin
2. Drive shaft nut
3. Connection for stabilizer bar
4. Connection for lower arm ball joint
5. Connection for tie rod end
6. Drive shaft (RH)
7. Bolt
8. Drive shaft and inner shaft (LH)
9. Circlip

Fig. 29 Halfshaft removal/installation — 1992-93 4WD Vista

RIGHT SIDE

The right side halfshaft is serviced in the same manner as those on other models.

OVERHAUL

Repair kits for most joints are not available, and those kits which are available are almost as expensive as replacement joints. It is therefore recommended that joints be replaced rather than overhauled.

Boot replacement kits are readily available and reasonably priced. Follow the kit maker's instructions.

CLUTCH

❊❊CAUTION

The clutch driven disc contains asbestos, which has been determined to be a cancer causing agent. Never clean clutch surfaces with compressed air! Avoid inhaling any dust from any clutch surface! When cleaning clutch surfaces, use a commercially available brake cleaning fluid.

The clutch assembly consists of a single dry disc and diaphragm spring pressure plate. The throwout bearing is controlled by a shaft mounted horizontally in the clutch housing. All models, except the 1991-92 4-speed Colt hatchback and 1993 Colt w/1.5L engine, are equipped with a hydraulic clutch. This system uses a master cylinder, located in the engine compartment to activate a slave cylinder located in the bell housing, which in turn moves the clutch release lever.

The 1991-92 4-speed Colt and 1993 1.5L Colt are equipped with a cable operated clutch.

Adjustments

PEDAL HEIGHT AND FREE-PLAY ADJUSTMENT

▶ See Figures 30, 31 and 32

1. Measure the distance between the floor and the top of the clutch pedal.
2. The measurement should be as follows:
   • 1990 Colt hatchback and sedan — 6.70-6.89 in. (170-175mm)
   • 1990 Colt Wagon — 6.3-6.5 in. (160-165mm)
   • 1991-92 Colt hatchback and sedan — 6.61-6.73 in. (168-171mm)

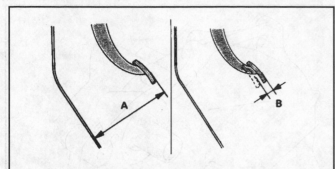

Fig. 30 Clutch pedal height measurement, left; clutch free-play measurement, right

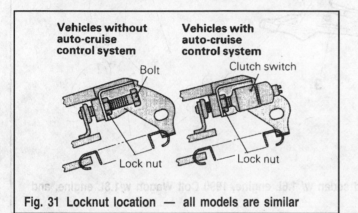

Fig. 31 Locknut location — all models are similar

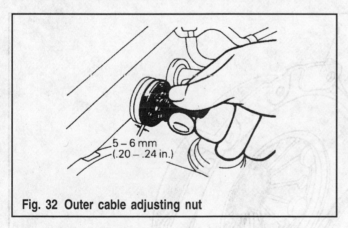

Fig. 32 Outer cable adjusting nut

- 1993 Colt hatchback and sedan — 6.38-6.50 in. (162-165mm)
- 1990-91 Vista — 7.10-7.30 in. (180-185mm)
- 1992-93 Vista — 7.68-7.87 in. (195-200mm)

3. With hydraulic clutches: if the measurement is not correct, loosen the clutch switch locknut and move the switch in or out as necessary to obtain proper height.   With cable clutches: the pedal height is not adjustable. If the height is not correct, you have bent parts or a deformed cable.

4. Check to see if the clutch pedal free-play is within specifications. Measure the distance from the top of the pedal to the distance the pedal moves before resistance is felt. On hydraulic clutches, this measurement is also adjusted at the clutch switch. On cable clutches, this measurement is adjusted

at the outer cable adjusting nut, in the engine compartment. The distance should be:

- All models w/hydraulic clutch — 0.04-0.12 in. (1-3mm)
  - 1991-92 Colt 4-speed — 0.80-1.18 in. (20-30mm)
  - 1993 Colt w/1.5L engine — 0.67-0.87 in. (17-22mm)

Driven Disc and Pressure Plate

REMOVAL & INSTALLATION

▶ See Figures 33, 34 and 35

1. Remove the transmission or transaxle as outlined.
2. Insert a pilot shaft or an old input shaft into the center of the clutch disc, pressure plate, and the pilot bearing in the crankshaft.
3. With the pilot tool supporting the clutch disc, loosen the pressure plate bolts gradually and in a crisscross pattern.
4. Remove the pressure plate and clutch disc.
5. Clean the transmission and clutch housing. Clean the flywheel surface with a non-oil based solvent. Wash your hands before installing or handling the clutch assembly parts. Hold the clutch disc by the center hub only.

➡ **Before assembly, slide the clutch disc up and down on the transmission input shaft to check for any binding. Remove any rough spots with crocus cloth and then lightly coat the shaft with Lubriplate.**

6. To remove the throwout bearing assembly: Remove the return clip and take out the throwout bearing carrier and the bearing.
7. To replace the throwout arm use a /₁₆ in. punch, knock out the throwout shaft spring pin and remove the shaft, springs, and the center lever.
8. Do not immerse the throwout bearing in solvent; it is permanently lubricated. Blow and wipe it clean. Check the bearing for wear, deterioration, or burning. Replace the bearing if there is any question about its condition.
9. Check the shafts, lever, and springs for wear and defects. Replace them if necessary.
10. If you hadn't planned on replacing the clutch disc, examine it for the following before reusing it. Loose rivets. Burned facing. Oil or grease on the facing. Less than 0.3mm left between the rivet head and the top of the facing.
11. Check the pressure plate and replace it if any of the following conditions exist: Scored or excessively worn. Bent or distorted diaphragm spring. Loose rivets.
12. Insert the control lever into the clutch housing. Install the two return springs and the throwout shaft.
13. Lock the shift lever to the shaft with the spring pin.
14. Fill the shaft oil seal with multipurpose grease.
15. Install the throwout bearing carrier and the bearing. Install the return clip.
16. Grease the carrier groove and inner surface.
17. Lightly grease the clutch disc splines.

➡ **The clutch is installed with the larger boss facing the transmission.**

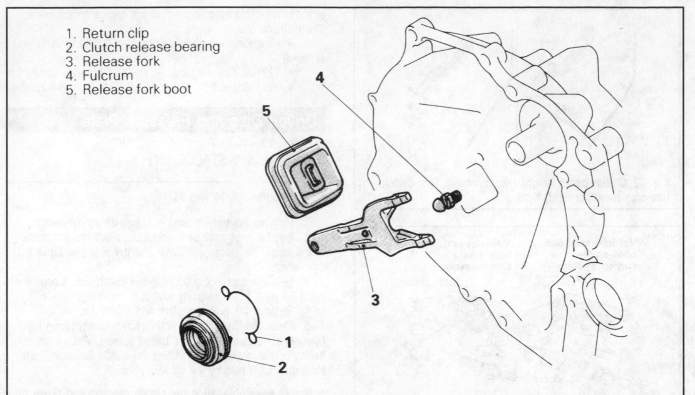

1. Return clip
2. Clutch release bearing
3. Release fork
4. Fulcrum
5. Release fork boot

Fig. 33 Clutch release bearing — 1990 Colt hatchback and sedan w/ 1.6L engine, 1990 Colt Wagon w/1.8L engine, and 1990-93 Vista

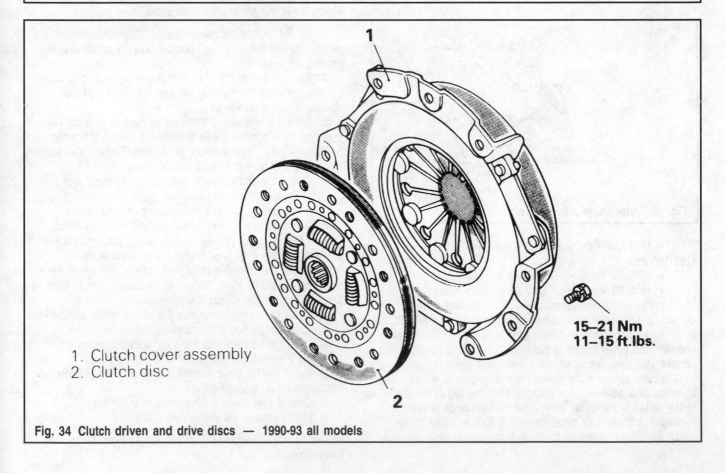

1. Clutch cover assembly
2. Clutch disc

15–21 Nm
11–15 ft.lbs.

Fig. 34 Clutch driven and drive discs — 1990-93 all models

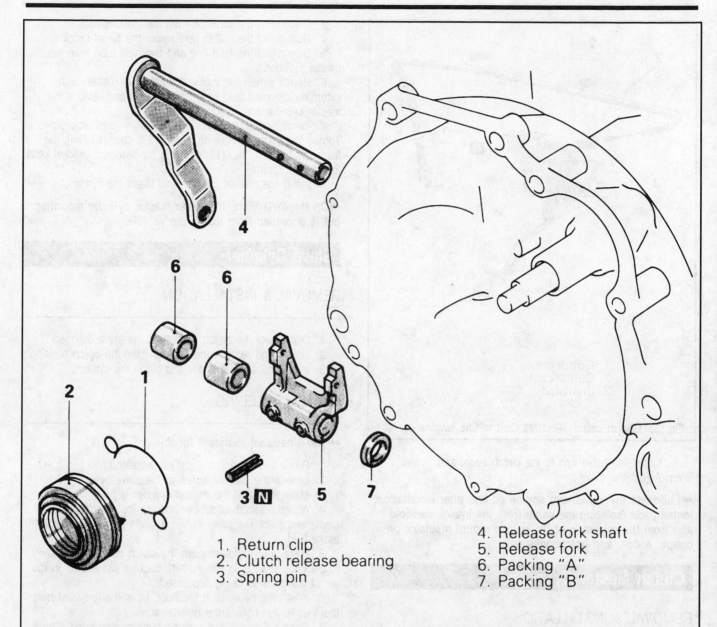

1. Return clip
2. Clutch release bearing
3. Spring pin
4. Release fork shaft
5. Release fork
6. Packing "A"
7. Packing "B"

Fig. 35 Clutch release bearing — 1990 Colt Wagon w/1.5L engine, 1991-92 Colt hatchback and sedan w/4-speed and 1993 Colt hatchback and sedan w/1.8L engine

18. Support the clutch disc and pressure plate with the pilot tool.

19. Turn the pressure plate so that its balance mark aligns with the notch in the flywheel.

20. Install the pressure plate-to-flywheel bolts head-tight. Using a torque wrench and, working in a crisscross pattern, tighten the bolts to 11-15 ft. lbs.

21. Install the transmission or transaxle as outlined.

22. Adjust the clutch as described in the following section.

Clutch Cable

REMOVAL & INSTALLATION

▶ See Figure 36

1. Loosen the cable adjusting wheel inside the engine compartment.

2. Loosen the clutch pedal adjusting bolt locknut and loosen the adjusting bolt.

3. Remove the cable end from the clutch throwout lever.

4. Remove the cable end from the clutch pedal.

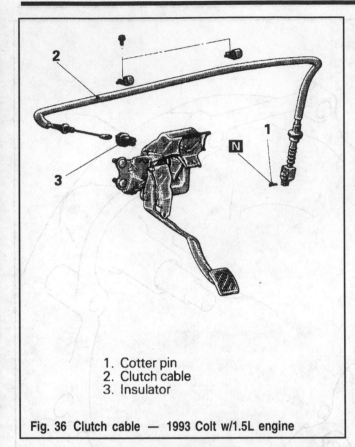

1. Cotter pin
2. Clutch cable
3. Insulator

Fig. 36 Clutch cable — 1993 Colt w/1.5L engine

5. Install the cable end to the clutch pedal and throwout lever. Adjust the clutch.

➡Lubricate the cable with engine oil and after installation, install pads isolating the cable from the intake manifold and from the rear side of the engine mount insulator on coupe, sedan, and hatchbacks only.

Clutch Master Cylinder

REMOVAL & INSTALLATION

▶ **See Figures 37, 38, 39 and 40**

1. Remove the air cleaner assembly.
2. Loosen the bleeder screw on the slave cylinder and drain the system.

3. Disconnect the pushrod from the clutch pedal.
4. Disconnect the clutch pedal from the pedal bracket.
5. Disconnect the fluid line and reservoir tube from the master cylinder.
6. Remove the reservoir and bracket on models with externally mounted fluid reservoirs. Unbolt and remove the master cylinder and remove.
7. Installation is the reverse order of removal procedures. Torque the cylinder retaining nuts to 9 ft. lbs. (13 Nm), the fluid pipe to 11 ft. lbs. (15 Nm) and the reservoir bracket bolts to 5 ft. lbs. (7 Nm).
8. Install the master cylinder and bleed the system.

➡**On the 4WD Vista, the lower master cylinder mounting nut is accessed from inside the vehicle.**

Slave Cylinder

REMOVAL & INSTALLATION

1. Disconnect the clutch hose from the slave cylinder.
2. Unbolt and remove the cylinder from the clutch housing.
3. Install the slave cylinder and bleed the system.

SYSTEM BLEEDING

➡**You'll need an assistant for this job.**

1. Raise and support the car on jackstands.
2. Loosen the bleeder screw at the slave cylinder.
3. Make sure that the master cylinder is full.
4. Attach a length of rubber hose to the bleeder screw nipple and place the other end in a glass jar half full of clean brake fluid.
5. Have your assistant push the clutch pedal down slowly to the floor. If air is in the system, bubbles will appear in the jar as the pedal is being depressed.
6. When the pedal is at the floor, have the assistant hold it there while you tighten the bleeder screw.
7. Repeat Steps 5 & 6 until no bubbles are found. Check the master cylinder level frequently to make sure that you don't run low on fluid.

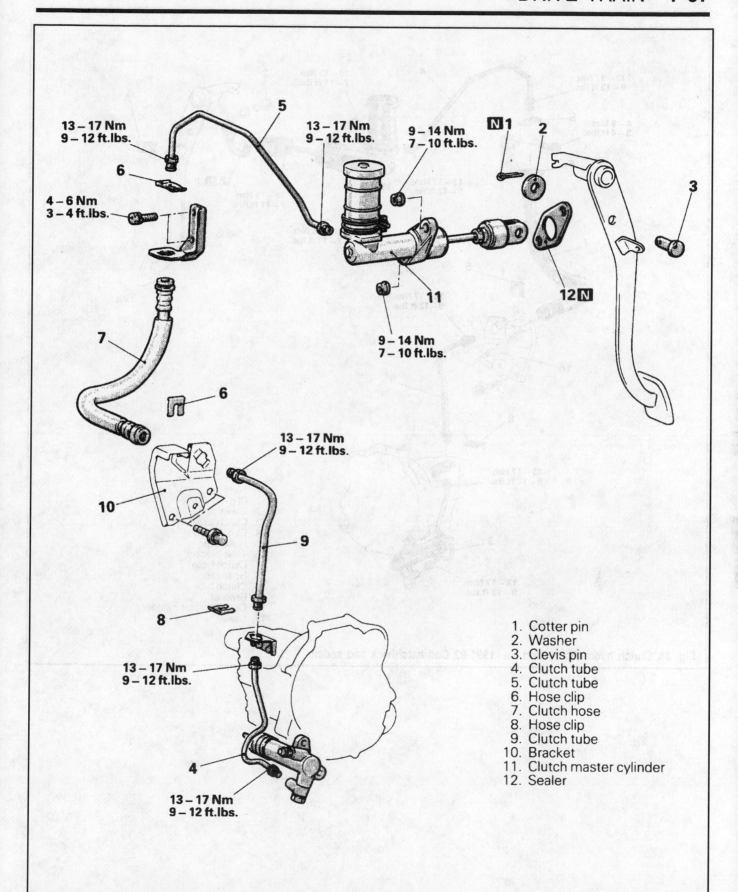

13 – 17 Nm
9 – 12 ft.lbs.

13 – 17 Nm
9 – 12 ft.lbs.

9 – 14 Nm
7 – 10 ft.lbs.

4 – 6 Nm
3 – 4 ft.lbs.

9 – 14 Nm
7 – 10 ft.lbs.

13 – 17 Nm
9 – 12 ft.lbs.

13 – 17 Nm
9 – 12 ft.lbs.

13 – 17 Nm
9 – 12 ft.lbs.

1. Cotter pin
2. Washer
3. Clevis pin
4. Clutch tube
5. Clutch tube
6. Hose clip
7. Clutch hose
8. Hose clip
9. Clutch tube
10. Bracket
11. Clutch master cylinder
12. Sealer

Fig. 37 Clutch hydraulic system — 1990 Colt hatchback and sedan

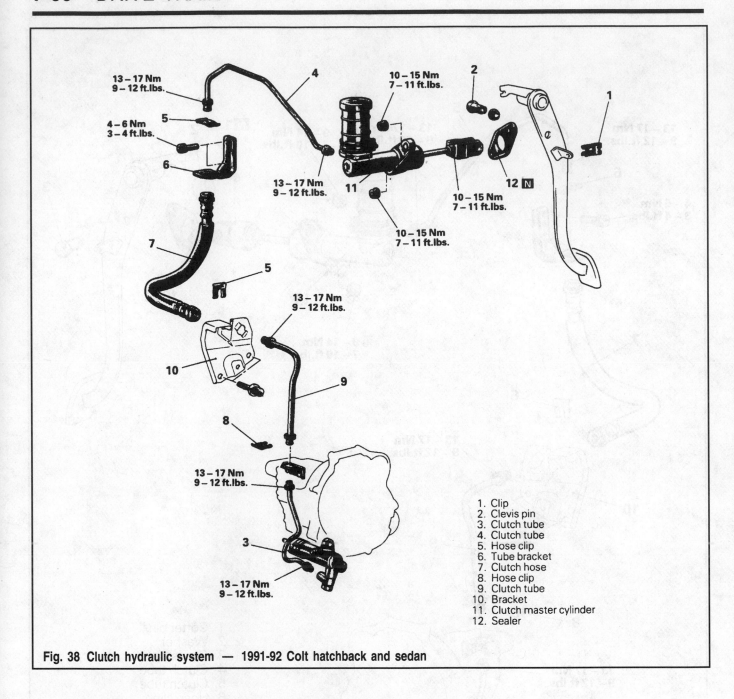

13 – 17 Nm
9 – 12 ft.lbs.

4 – 6 Nm
3 – 4 ft.lbs.

13 – 17 Nm
9 – 12 ft.lbs.

10 – 15 Nm
7 – 11 ft.lbs.

10 – 15 Nm
7 – 11 ft.lbs.

10 – 15 Nm
7 – 11 ft.lbs.

13 – 17 Nm
9 – 12 ft.lbs.

13 – 17 Nm
9 – 12 ft.lbs.

13 – 17 Nm
9 – 12 ft.lbs.

1. Clip
2. Clevis pin
3. Clutch tube
4. Clutch tube
5. Hose clip
6. Tube bracket
7. Clutch hose
8. Hose clip
9. Clutch tube
10. Bracket
11. Clutch master cylinder
12. Sealer

Fig. 38 Clutch hydraulic system — 1991-92 Colt hatchback and sedan

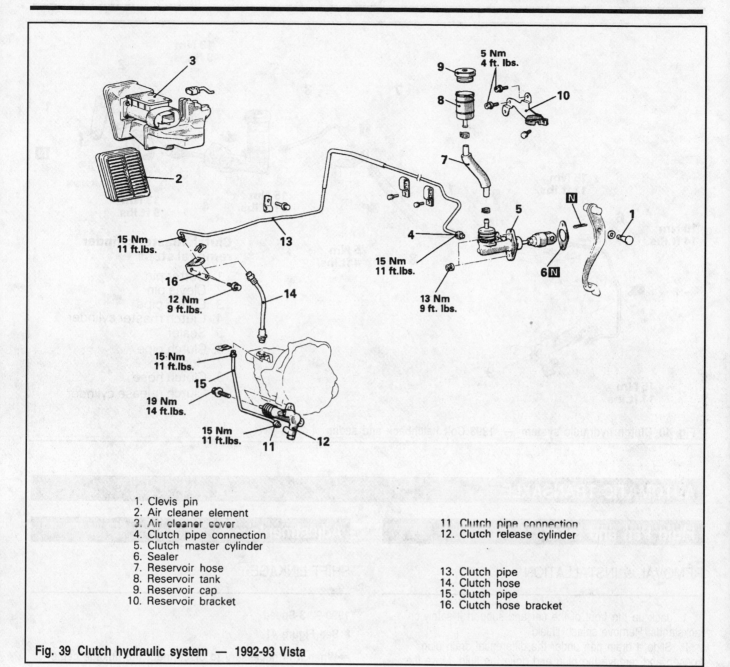

1. Clevis pin
2. Air cleaner element
3. Air cleaner cover
4. Clutch pipe connection
5. Clutch master cylinder
6. Sealer
7. Reservoir hose
8. Reservoir tank
9. Reservoir cap
10. Reservoir bracket

11. Clutch pipe connection
12. Clutch release cylinder

13. Clutch pipe
14. Clutch hose
15. Clutch pipe
16. Clutch hose bracket

Fig. 39 Clutch hydraulic system — 1992-93 Vista

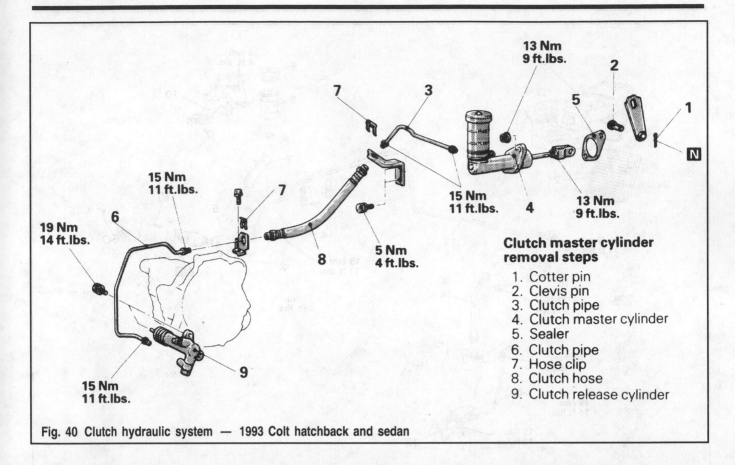

13 Nm
9 ft.lbs.

15 Nm
11 ft.lbs.

19 Nm
14 ft.lbs.

15 Nm
11 ft.lbs.

15 Nm
11 ft.lbs.

13 Nm
9 ft.lbs.

5 Nm
4 ft.lbs.

Clutch master cylinder removal steps

1. Cotter pin
2. Clevis pin
3. Clutch pipe
4. Clutch master cylinder
5. Sealer
6. Clutch pipe
7. Hose clip
8. Clutch hose
9. Clutch release cylinder

Fig. 40 Clutch hydraulic system — 1993 Colt hatchback and sedan

AUTOMATIC TRANSAXLE

Fluid Pan and Filter

REMOVAL & INSTALLATION

1. Jack up the front of the car and support it safely on jackstands. Remove splash shield.

2. Slide a drain pan under the differential drain plug. Loosen and remove the plug and drain the fluid. Move the drain pan under the transaxle oil pan, remove the drain plug (models equipped) or the oil pan and drain the fluid. The transmission fluid cannot all be drained by just draining the oil pan.

3. Remove the pan retaining evenly and allow the fluid to drain. Remove the pan.

4. The filter may be serviced at this time.

5. Use a new oil pan gasket and install the pan. Install and tighten the bolts evenly in a crisscross pattern.

6. Replace both drain plugs (if equipped). Lower the vehicle. Fill the transmission with 4.2 pts of DEXRON®II fluid. Start the engine and allow it to idle for at least two minutes. With the parking brake applied, move the selector to each position ending neutral.

7. Add sufficient fluid to bring the level to the lower mark. Check the fluid level after the transmission is up to normal operating temperature.

Adjustments

SHIFT LINKAGE

1990-92 3-Speed

▶ See Figure 41

➡When it is necessary to disconnect the linkage cable from the lever, which uses plastic grommets as retainers, the grommets should be replaced.

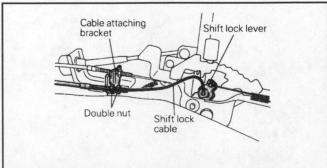

Cable attaching bracket

Shift lock lever

Double nut

Shift lock cable

Fig. 41 Shift cable adjustment points — 1990-92 Colt hatchback and sedan w/3-speed

1. Set the parking brake.

2. Move the shift lever into **P**.

3. Loosen the clamp bolt on the gear shift cable bracket.

4. Make sure the preload adjustment spring engages the fork on the transaxle bracket.

5. Pull the shift lever all the way to the front detent position **P** and torque the lock screw to 100 inch lbs. (11 Nm).

6. Check the following conditions:

a. The detent positions for **N** and **D** should be within limits of hand lever gate stops.

b. Key start must occur only when the shift lever is in **P** or **N** positions.

THROTTLE CONTROL CABLE

1990-92 3-speed

◆ See Figure 42

1. Run the engine to normal operating temperature. Shut it off and make sure the throttle plate is closed (curb idle position).

2. Raise the small cone-shaped cover on the throttle cable to expose the nipple.

3. Loosen the lower cable bracket bolt.

4. Move the lower cable bracket until the distance between the collar and the lower cover (A) directly underneath it is 0.5-1.5mm.

5. Tighten the bracket bolt to 9-11 ft. lbs.

NEUTRAL SWITCH

◆ See Figure 43

1. Place manual control lever in the Neutral position.

2. Loosen the two switch attaching bolts. Switch is located on side of transmission.

3. Turn the switch body until the flat end of the manual lever is centered over the square end of the switch body flange.

4. While keeping the switch body flange and manual lever aligned torque the two attaching bolts to 7.5-8.5 ft. lbs.

Transaxle

REMOVAL & INSTALLATION

◆ **See Figures 44, 45, 46, 47 and 48**

➡**The transaxle and converter must be removed and installed as an assembly.**

Except 1992-93 Vista

1. Disconnect the battery cables, negative first. Remove the battery and tray. Remove the air cleaner case.

2. Disconnect the throttle control cable at the carburetor. If equipped with fuel injection, disconnect the cable at the throttle body. Disconnect the manual control cable at the transaxle.

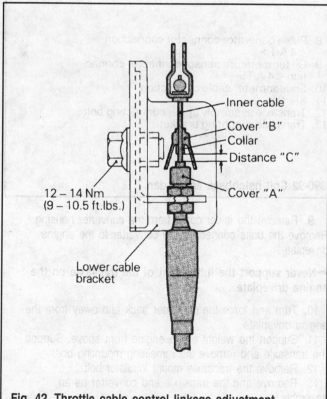

Inner cable
Cover "B"
Collar
Distance "C"
Cover "A"

12 – 14 Nm
(9 – 10.5 ft.lbs.)

Lower cable bracket

Fig. 42 Throttle cable control linkage adjustment — 3-speed

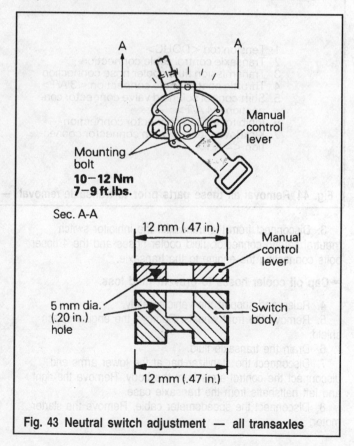

Manual control lever

Mounting bolt
**10 – 12 Nm
7 – 9 ft.lbs.**

Sec. A-A

12 mm (.47 in.)

Manual control lever

5 mm dia. (.20 in.) hole

Switch body

12 mm (.47 in.)

Fig. 43 Neutral switch adjustment — all transaxles

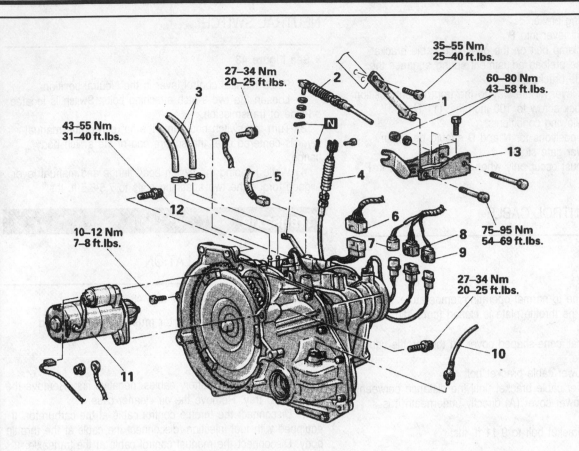

1. Tension rod <DOHC>
2. Transaxle control cable connection
3. Transmission fluid cooler hose connection
4. Throttle control cable connection <3 A/T>
5. Shift control solenoid valve connector connection <4 A/T>
6. Inhibitor switch connector connection
7. Kickdown servo switch connector connection <4 A/T>
8. Pulse generator connector connection <4 A/T>
9. Oil temperature sensor connector connection <4 A/T>
10. Speedometer cable connection
11. Starter
12. Transaxle assembly upper connecting bolt
13. Transaxle mounting bracket

Fig. 44 Removal all these parts prior to transaxle removal — 1990-92 Colt hatchback and sedan

3. Disconnect from the transaxle: the inhibitor switch (neutral safety) connector, fluid cooler hoses and the 4 upper bolts connecting the engine to the transaxle.

➡**Cap oil cooler hoses to prevent fluid loss.**

4. Raise and support the vehicle safely.
5. Remove the front wheels. Remove the engine splash shield.
6. Drain the transaxle fluid.
7. Disconnect the stabilizer bar at the lower arms and disconnect the control arms from the body. Remove the right and left halfshafts from the transaxle case.
8. Disconnect the speedometer cable. Remove the starter motor.

9. Remove the lower cover from the converter housing. Remove the bolts connecting the converter to the engine driveplate.

➡**Never support the full weight of the transaxle on the engine driveplate.**

10. Turn and force the converter back and away from the engine driveplate.
11. Support the weight of the engine from above. Support the transaxle and remove the remaining mounting bolts.
12. Remove the transaxle mount insulator bolt.
13. Remove and the transaxle and converter as an assembly.
To install:
14. Secure the transaxle to a transmission jack.

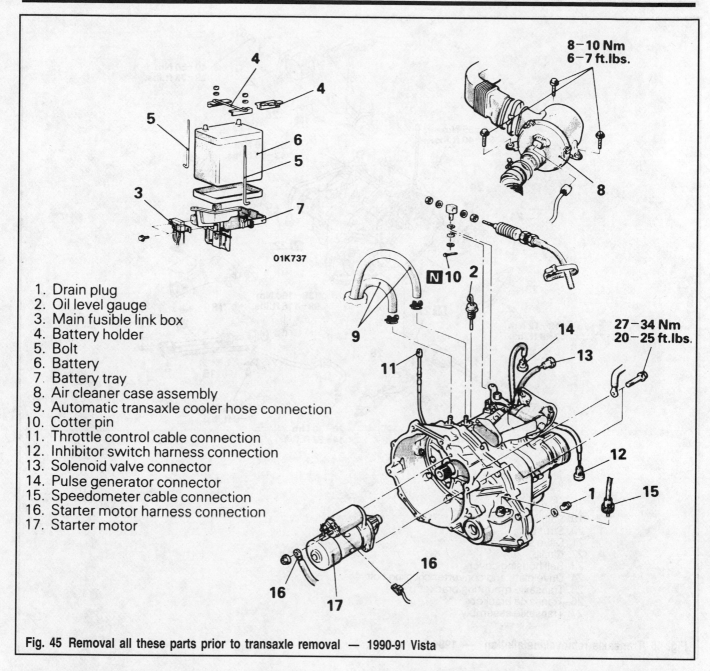

8−10 Nm
6−7 ft.lbs.

27−34 Nm
20−25 ft.lbs.

N 10

01K737

1. Drain plug
2. Oil level gauge
3. Main fusible link box
4. Battery holder
5. Bolt
6. Battery
7. Battery tray
8. Air cleaner case assembly
9. Automatic transaxle cooler hose connection
10. Cotter pin
11. Throttle control cable connection
12. Inhibitor switch harness connection
13. Solenoid valve connector
14. Pulse generator connector
15. Speedometer cable connection
16. Starter motor harness connection
17. Starter motor

Fig. 45 Removal all these parts prior to transaxle removal — 1990-91 Vista

15. Install the torque converter onto the transaxle input shaft. Make sure the converter is fully seated in to the front pump before bolting the transaxle to the engine.

16. Raise the transaxle and position it to the engine. Install the lower transmission-to-engine bolts. Torque the bolts to 31-39 ft. lbs. (43-54 Nm).

17. Install the transaxle mount insulator bolt. Torque the bolts to 31-40 ft. lbs. (43-54 Nm).

18. Install the remaining transaxle-to-engine bolts. Torque the bolts to 31-39 ft. lbs. (43-54 Nm).

19. From the converter housing, install the 3 bolts connecting the converter to the engine driveplate. Torque the bolts to 34-38 ft. lbs. (46-54 Nm).

20. Connect the speedometer cable.

21. Install the starter motor and connect the wiring to it.

22. Connect the stabilizer bar to the lower arms and connect the control arms to the body. Install the right and left halfshafts to the transaxle case.

23. Refill the transaxle fluid.

24. Install the engine splash shield. Install the front wheels.

25. Lower the vehicle.

26. Connect to the transaxle: the inhibitor switch (neutral safety) connector and the fluid cooler hoses.

27. Connect the throttle control cable to the transaxle.

28. Install the battery and tray. Connect the battery cables, positive first. If equipped with a turbocharger, install the air cleaner case.

1992-93 Vista

1. Disconnect negative battery cable.
2. Remove the air cleaner assembly.

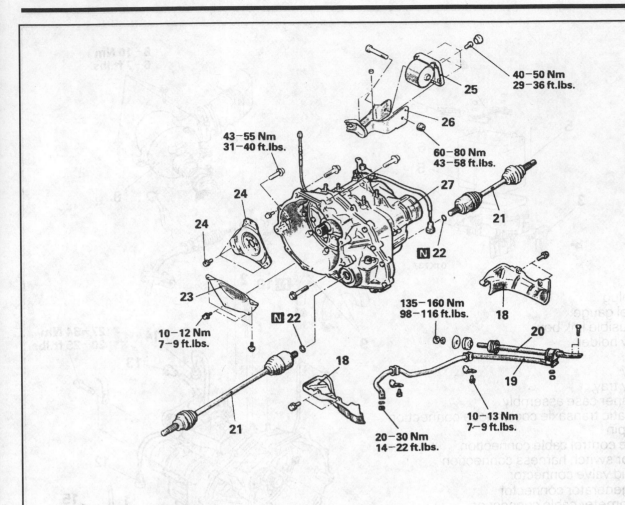

40—50 Nm
29—36 ft.lbs.

43—55 Nm
31—40 ft.lbs.

60—80 Nm
43—58 ft.lbs.

10—12 Nm
7—9 ft.lbs.

135—160 Nm
98—116 ft.lbs.

10—13 Nm
7—9 ft.lbs.

20—30 Nm
14—22 ft.lbs.

18. Dust cover
19. Stabilizer
20. Strut bar
21. Drive shaft
22. Circlip
23. Bell housing cover
24. Drive plate and converter coupling bolt
25. Transaxle mounting bracket
26. Transaxle bracket
27. Transaxle assembly

Fig. 46 Transaxle removal/installation — 1990-91 Vista

3. Disconnect the transaxle control lever. Disconnect and plug the oil cooler lines.

4. Disconnect the pulse generator connector, oil temperature connector, kickdown servo switch connector, inhibitor switch connector and solenoid valve connection.

5. Disconnect the speedometer cable connection. Remove the oil level dipstick and tube.

6. Install holding fixture to the top of the engine to support engine weight.

7. Remove the top transaxle upper coupling bolts.

8. Raise and safely support the vehicle.

9. Remove the starter motor leaving wire harness attached.

10. Remove the right side under cover. Drain the transaxle fluid.

11. Disconnect the tie rod ends, stabilizer bar and lower ball joints.

12. If equipped with 4WD, it will be necessary to remove the right driveshaft from the vehicle.

13. Except 4WD, remove the driveshafts from the transfer case, insert a pry bar between the driveshaft and the transaxle case and pry the shaft from the transaxle housing. Swing the shafts out of the way keeping the joints straight, and suspend using wire. Turn the right shaft 90 degrees toward the front of the vehicle so that it will not be a hindrance.

➡**Do not pull on the shaft during removal from the transaxle; doing so will damage the inboard joint. Do not insert the pry bar so deep as to damage the oil seal.**

14. Remove the lower bellhousing cover. Scribe a mark on the drive plate and transaxle converter face using chalk. Remove the drive plate connecting bolts while turning the crankshaft.

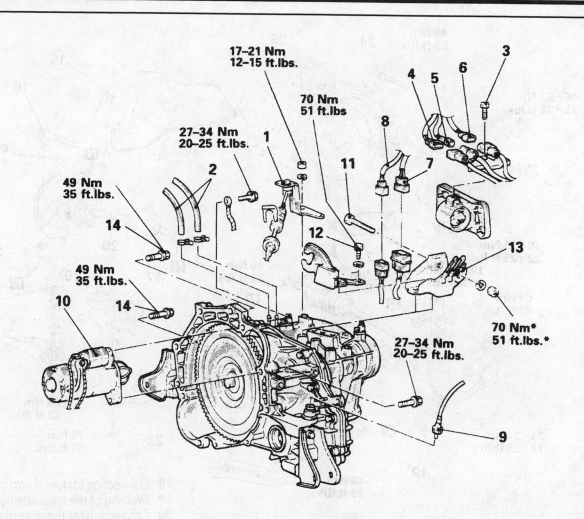

17–21 Nm
12–15 ft.lbs.

70 Nm
51 ft.lbs

27–34 Nm
20–25 ft.lbs.

49 Nm
35 ft.lbs.

49 Nm
35 ft.lbs.

70 Nm*
51 ft.lbs.*

27–34 Nm
20–25 ft.lbs.

1. Connection for manual control lever
2. Transaxle oil cooler hoses
3. Bolt
4. Pulse generator connector
5. Oil temperature connector
6. Kickdown servo switch connector
7. Inhibitor switch connector
8. Solenoid valve connector
9. Speedometer cable connection
10. Starter motor
11. Transaxle mount bolt
12. Bolt
13. Transaxle mount bracket
14. Transaxle assembly upper part coupling bolts

NOTE
For tightening locations indicated by the * symbol, first tighten temporarily, and then make the final tightening with the entire weight of the engine applied to the vehicle body.

Fig. 47 Removal all these parts prior to transaxle removal — 1992–93 FWD Vista

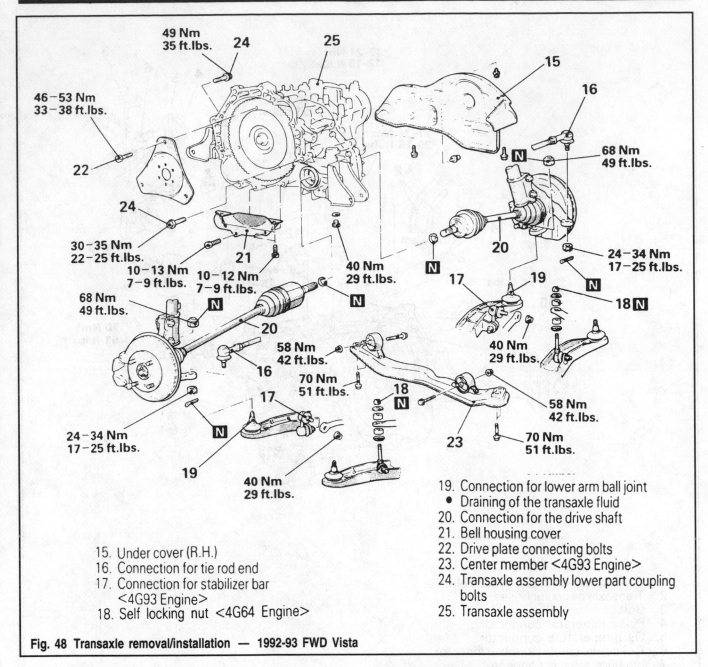

49 Nm
35 ft.lbs. **24**

25

15

16

46–53 Nm
33–38 ft.lbs.

22

68 Nm
49 ft.lbs.

24

30–35 Nm
22–25 ft.lbs.

21

10–13 Nm
7–9 ft.lbs.

10–12 Nm
7–9 ft.lbs.

20

40 Nm
29 ft.lbs.

17

19

24–34 Nm
17–25 ft.lbs.

18

68 Nm
49 ft.lbs.

20

58 Nm
42 ft.lbs.

70 Nm
51 ft.lbs.

18

16

40 Nm
29 ft.lbs.

58 Nm
42 ft.lbs.

24–34 Nm
17–25 ft.lbs.

17

19

23

70 Nm
51 ft.lbs.

19

40 Nm
29 ft.lbs.

19. Connection for lower arm ball joint
● Draining of the transaxle fluid
20. Connection for the drive shaft
21. Bell housing cover
22. Drive plate connecting bolts
23. Center member <4G93 Engine>
24. Transaxle assembly lower part coupling bolts
25. Transaxle assembly

15. Under cover (R.H.)
16. Connection for tie rod end
17. Connection for stabilizer bar <4G93 Engine>
18. Self locking nut <4G64 Engine>

Fig. 48 Transaxle removal/installation — 1992-93 FWD Vista

15. Support the transaxle using a transmission jack. Remove the center support.
16. Remove the transaxle mount bolt and bracket.
17. If equipped with 4WD, disconnect the front exhaust pipe and remove the transfer assembly.
18. Remove the lower transaxle case coupling bolts, press the torque converter towards the transfer case to prevent separation during removal and lower the transfer case from the vehicle.

To install:

19. Install the transaxle into the vehicle and secure using the lower case coupling bolts.
20. Install the transaxle mount bolt and bracket, torque through bolt nut to 51 ft. lbs. (70 Nm).
21. Align the scribe marks on the converter and the drive plate. Install the drive plate connecting bolts torquing to 33-38 ft. lbs. (46-53 Nm).

22. Install the transfer assembly and the center cross member. Remove the transmission jack.
23. Install the center exhaust pipe.
24. Install the drive axles into the transfer case taking care not to damage the oil seal lip part of the transaxle with the serrated part of the driveshaft.
25. Connect the tie rod ends, stabilizer bar and lower ball joints.
26. Install the right side under cover.
27. Lower the vehicle. Install the upper transaxle coupling bolts.
28. Connect the speedometer cable, and the electrical harness connectors disconnected during the removal procedure.
29. Install the starter motor torquing the retainer bolts to 35 ft. lbs. (49 Nm).

30. Connect the transaxle cooler hoses and the connections for the manual controls.

31. Install the air cleaner assembly and the oil level dipstick and tube.

32. Refill with Dexron II, Mopar ATF Plus type 7176, or equivalent automatic transaxle fluid.

33. Start the engine and allow to idle for 2 minutes. Apply parking brake and move selector through each gear position, ending in **N**. Recheck fluid level and add if necessary. Fluid level should be between the marks in the **HOT** range. Check operation of all gauges and meters.

Halfshafts and CV Joints

Refer to the proceeding Manual Transaxle section for service procedures.

TRANSFER CASE

REMOVAL & INSTALLATION

1. Remove the transaxle as described previously.
2. Unbolt the transfer case from the transaxle and, using a small prybar, separate the two.

3. Install the transfer case to the transaxle. Install the transaxle. The transfer case to transaxle mounting bolts are torqued to: 40-43 ft. lbs.

DRIVELINE

Driveshaft and Universal Joints

REMOVAL & INSTALLATION

▶ See Figure 49

4WD Vista

1. Raise and support the car on jackstands.

2. Drain the transfer case.
3. Matchmark the differential companion flange and the driveshaft flange yoke.
4. Unbolt the driveshaft from the differential flange.
5. Remove the two center bearing attaching nuts.

➡**Make sure you don't confuse the flat washer and the adjusting spacer. Keep them separate for assembly.**

6. Pull the driveshaft from the transfer case. Be careful to avoid damaging the transfer case oil seal.

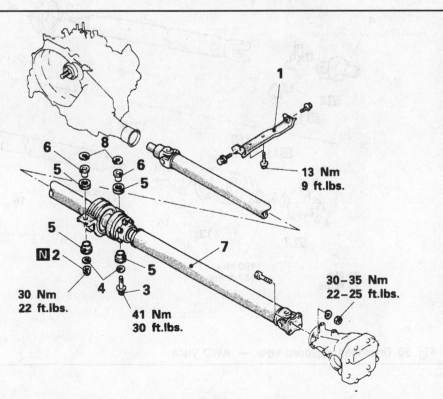

1. Center exhaust pipe bracket
2. Self-locking nut
3. Bolt
4. Washer
5. Insulator
6. Spacer
7. Propeller shaft
8. Spacer

13 Nm
9 ft.lbs.

30 Nm
22 ft.lbs.

41 Nm
30 ft.lbs.

30-35 Nm
22-25 ft.lbs.

Fig. 49 Driveshaft and U-joints — AWD Vista

7. Align the matchmarks and install the driveshaft. Torque the center bearing nuts to 25-30 ft. lbs.; the driveshaft-to-differential flange nuts to 20-25 ft. lbs.

U-JOINT OVERHAUL

▶ See Figures 50, 51 and 52

➡ Matchmark the rear yoke to shaft and/or the center yoke to yoke for proper installation reference.

1. Position the driveshaft assembly in a sturdy vise.

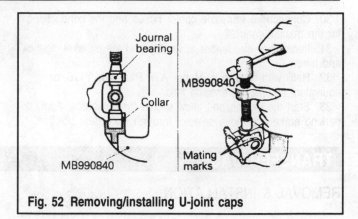

Fig. 52 Removing/installing U-joint caps

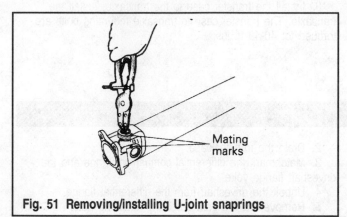

Fig. 51 Removing/installing U-joint snaprings

2. Remove the snaprings which retain the bearing caps in the slip yoke and the driveshaft.

3. Use a large punch or an arbor press and drive one of the bearing caps in toward the center of the universal joint. The joint will be forced through the opposite side of the yoke.

4. As the opposite side bearing cap is forced from the yoke, grip it with a pair of pliers and pull it, in a twisting motion, out of the yoke.

5. Press the spider cross toward the side you just pushed to force the cap back into the yoke. When the bearing cap starts to clear the yoke, pull it free with a pair of pliers. Repeat the procedure with the other side bearing caps.

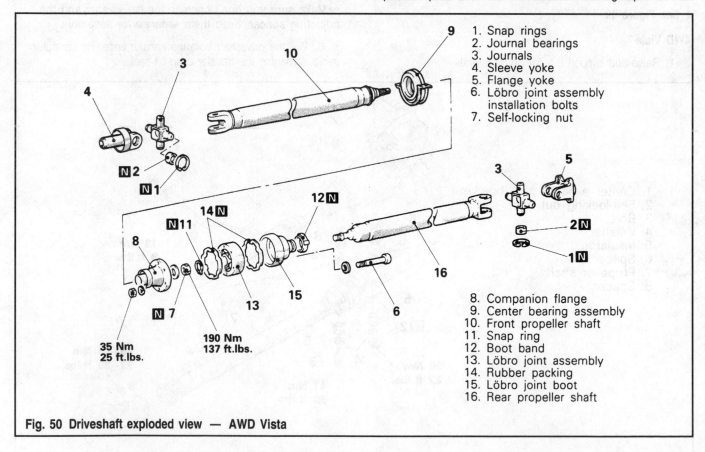

1. Snap rings
2. Journal bearings
3. Journals
4. Sleeve yoke
5. Flange yoke
6. Löbro joint assembly installation bolts
7. Self-locking nut

8. Companion flange
9. Center bearing assembly
10. Front propeller shaft
11. Snap ring
12. Boot band
13. Löbro joint assembly
14. Rubber packing
15. Löbro joint boot
16. Rear propeller shaft

35 Nm
25 ft.lbs.

190 Nm
137 ft.lbs.

Fig. 50 Driveshaft exploded view — AWD Vista

6. After removing the bearing caps, lift the bearing (spider) cross from the yoke. Thoroughly clean all dirt and foreign matter from the yoke area on both ends of the driveshaft.

➡When installing new bearing caps within the yokes, it is advisable to use an arbor press. However, if a press is not available, the bearings should be driven into position with extreme care. A heavy jolt on the needle bearing, in the cap, can easily damage or misalign them. A large vise and correct size drivers and spacers can sometimes be used, in place of a punch, to push the bearing caps in or out.

7. Start a bearing cap into the yoke bore.
8. Position the spider into the yoke and into the bearing cap. Push the cap the rest of the way into the yoke bore until it is about 6mm below the outside surface of the yoke. Install a new snapring.
9. Start a bearing cap into the yoke on the opposite side of the one just installed. Carefully press it into the yoke while aligning the spider cross with the bearing center.
10. Continue to pry the cap in until the opposite side bearing cap contacts the snapring. Install a new snapring on the side just installed. Check the clearance between the bearing cap face and the snapring. If it exceeds 0.025mm, install a thicker snapring. Check the joint for free movement. Complete the installation of the yoke and bearing caps.
11. Position the driveshaft and work on the other end if service is required.
12. After service is completed, check the assembled joints and yokes for freedom of movement. If misalignment of any part causes it to bind, a sharp rap on the side of the yoke with a brass hammer should seat the needle bearings, and provide the desired freedom of movement. Care should be exercised to firmly support the shaft end during this operation, as well as to prevent blows to the bearing caps themselves. Under no circumstances should a driveshaft be installed in a vehicle if there is any bind in the U-joints. If the binding remains, disassemble the yoke and joint a check the needle bearings for correctly vertical alignment.

REAR DRIVE AXLE

Axleshaft/Bearing

REMOVAL & INSTALLATION

4WD Vista

1. Raise and safely support the rear of the vehicle, with the suspension hanging free.
2. Remove the rear wheels.
3. Remove the brake drums.
4. Remove the bolts securing the axle flange to the intermediate shaft flange.
5. Remove the axle flange nut.
6. Use a slide hammer puller, and remove the axleshaft from the housing.

Center Bearing and Support

REMOVAL & INSTALLATION

▶ **See Figure 50**

4WD Vista

1. Remove the driveshaft and center bearing as in the above procedure.
2. Matchmark the two driveshafts with the center bearing.
3. Disassemble the universal joint connecting the center bearing with the rear driveshaft.
4. Remove and discard the self-locking nut holding the yoke half to the center bearing.
5. Pull the yoke from the center bearing.
6. Pull off the center bearing bracket.

➡**The mounting rubber is not removable from the center bearing bracket**

7. Using a two-jawed puller, remove the center bearing from the forward driveshaft.
To install:
8. Apply a coating of chassis lube to the grease holder on the center bearing and to the outer circumference of the dust boot at the point at which the shaft is inserted.
9. Install the bearing in the groove of the center bearing bracket mounting rubber. Make sure it is securely installed.
10. Install the center bearing assembly to the forward driveshaft.
11. Align the matchmarks and slide the yoke half into the center bearing. Using a new self-locking nut, seat the yoke in the center bearing. Torque the nut to 160 ft. lbs.
12. Align the matchmarks and assemble the yoke. Make sure the snaprings securing the bearings caps are installed with a clearance of 0-0.03mm between the snapring and groove in the yoke.

7. Remove the lower control arm.
8. Remove the dust cover and outer wheel bearing and seal from the axleshaft with an appropriate puller.
9. Press the inner bearing and seal from the housing. Pack the new bearing with grease and press into place.
10. Install the new inner bearing seal.
11. Install the dust cover into place evenly in the housing.
12. Coat the lip of a new seal and pack the outer bearing with grease.
13. Press in the bearing and seal.
14. Press the axleshaft into the inner arm.
15. Install the inner arm assembly.
16. Install the companion flange and nut. Torque the nut to 160 ft. lbs.
17. Connect the intermediate shaft and axleshaft. Torque the bolts to 43 ft. lbs.

Intermediate Shaft

REMOVAL & INSTALLATION

4WD Vista

1. Raise and support the rear of the vehicle with jackstands placed under the frame.
2. Disconnect the intermediate shaft and axleshaft flanges.
3. Use a small pry bar and carefully remove the intermediate shaft from the differential.
4. Service the intermediate shaft as required. Install a new seal into the differential. Install the intermediate shaft. Connect the intermediate shaft to the axleshaft. Tighten the bolts to 43 ft. lbs.

Intermediate Shaft Constant Velocity Joints

OVERHAUL

➡Two types of CV joints are used on each shaft. On the inner end of the shaft is a Birfield joint; on the outer end, a double offset joint. The DOJ can be disassembled; the Birfield joint cannot. CV joint repair kits are the only way to rebuild the joint. These kits come with a special grease. Use it.

1. Remove the boot bands.
2. Remove the circlip from the DOJ outer race.
3. Separate the intermediate shaft from the DOJ outer race.
4. Remove the balls from the DOJ cage.
5. Remove the cage from the inner race, in the direction of the Birfield joint.
6. Remove the snapring from the shaft and pull the DOJ inner race and cage from the shaft. Remove the circlip.
7. Wrap plastic tape around the splines on the shaft and slide the boots off. Pay attention to the boots, they are different from each other. Be sure to use the correct boot for each end when installing them.
8. Clean all parts in a non-flammable solvent. Check all parts for wear or damage. Replace any suspect parts. If the Birfield joint is defective, the shaft and joint must be replaced as an assembly.
9. Apply the special grease to the intermediate shaft and install the boots and bands. Be sure to install the different boots to their correct shaft end.
10. Install the cage onto the shaft, smaller end first.
11. Install the circlip.
12. Install the inner race and snapring.
13. Coat the inner race and cage with the special grease and fit them together.
14. Apply the special grease to the balls and insert them into the cage and race.
15. Apply about 2.5 ounces of the special grease to the outer race.
16. Insert the shaft into the outer race and apply another 2.5 ounces of grease on the race.

17. Install the circlip on the outer race.
18. Position the boot over the DOJ and secure it with the band.
19. Install the smaller band and position it so that 76mm exists between the two bands. Tighten the band.
20. Pack the Birfield joint with 4-5 ounces of the special grease.

Differential

REMOVAL & INSTALLATION

▶ See Figure 53

4WD Vista

1. Raise and support the rear of the vehicle with jackstand placed under the frame.
2. Drain the differential fluid.
3. Remove the intermediate shafts.
4. Matchmark and disconnect the driveshaft.
5. Take the weight off of the differential with a floor jack.
6. Remove the bolt that connects the differential front support bracket and the crossmember.
7. Remove the bolts connecting the differential rear support and the differential carrier.
8. Lower the carrier and remove it from under the vehicle. Service as required.
9. Position the differential and connect it to the supports. Connect the driveshaft and intermediate shafts. Torque the rear support to carrier bolts to 95 ft. lbs.; the front support to crossmember bolt to 101 ft. lbs.

OVERHAUL

Disassembly

▶ See Figures 54, 55, 56, 57, 58, 59, 60 and 61

1. Remove the differential cover and vent plug.
2. Remove the bearing caps.
3. Carefully lift out the differential case assembly. Take care to avoid dropping the side bearing spacers and outer races. Keep the races separate and identified.
4. Using a bearing puller, remove the side bearings.
5. If the ring gear is to be re-used, matchmark it with the case and remove it. If the gear is being re-used, remove the bolts in a crisscross sequence.
6. On conventional units, drive out the lock pin and remove the pinion gears, washers, side gears and spacers.
7. Remove the differential case assembly.
8. Hold the companion flange and remove the companion flange locknut. Discard the locknut.
9. Remove the washer.
10. Matchmark the drive pinion and companion flange, and, using a forcing tool, separate the pinion from the flange, along with the spacer and shims.
11. Using a puler, remove the pinion rear bearing.
12. Remove the pinion rear shim.
13. Remove the pinion.

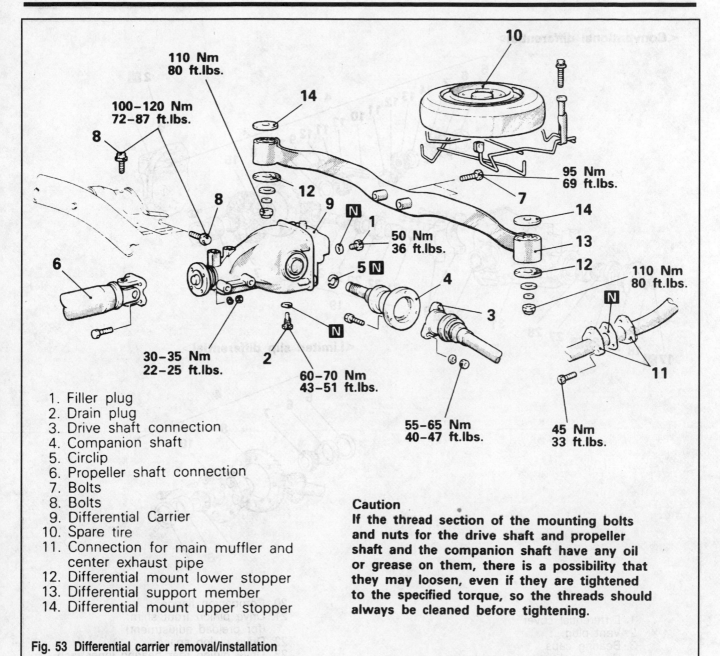

**110 Nm
80 ft.lbs.**

**100–120 Nm
72–87 ft.lbs.**

**95 Nm
69 ft.lbs.**

**50 Nm
36 ft.lbs.**

**110 Nm
80 ft.lbs.**

**30–35 Nm
22–25 ft.lbs.**

**60–70 Nm
43–51 ft.lbs.**

**55–65 Nm
40–47 ft.lbs.**

**45 Nm
33 ft.lbs.**

1. Filler plug
2. Drain plug
3. Drive shaft connection
4. Companion shaft
5. Circlip
6. Propeller shaft connection
7. Bolts
8. Bolts
9. Differential Carrier
10. Spare tire
11. Connection for main muffler and center exhaust pipe
12. Differential mount lower stopper
13. Differential support member
14. Differential mount upper stopper

Caution
If the thread section of the mounting bolts and nuts for the drive shaft and propeller shaft and the companion shaft have any oil or grease on them, there is a possibility that they may loosen, even if they are tightened to the specified torque, so the threads should always be cleaned before tightening.

Fig. 53 Differential carrier removal/installation

14. Pry out the pinion seal and remove the bearing. Drive out the bearing race.
15. Drive out the halfshaft seals.

Assembly
▶ **See Figures 62, 63, 64, 65, 66, 67, 68, 69, 70, 71, 72, 73, 74, 75, 76, 77**

1. Drive a new pinion seal into place. Oil the seal lips with chassis lube.
2. Drive a new pinion bearing race into place and install the bearing.
3. Install special tools MB990836 in the carrier along with the bearings and races. Tighten the tools until a turning torque of 8-10 inch lbs. is obtained with new, unoiled bearings, or 3-4 inch lbs. with used or new/oiled bearings is obtained. Remove the tools.

4. Position special tool MB990392 in the side bearing seat of the carrier, and select a drive pinion rear shim of a thickness that corresponds to the gap between the tools. Keep the shims to a minimum needed to fill the gap. Remove the tools.
5. Install the shims and press-fit the drive pinion rear bearing inner race.
6. Install the drive pinion front shims between the drive pinion spacer and the drive pinion front bearing.
7. Using tool MB990850, tighten the companion flange to 137 ft. lbs. Measure the turning torque. It should be equal to that recorded in Step 18. If not, add or delete shims, or change spacers.
8. Remove the companion flange and pinion. If the seal lip was damaged, replace the seal.
9. Coat the pinion and flange, and related parts with gear oil. Align the matchmarks and install the parts. Install a new

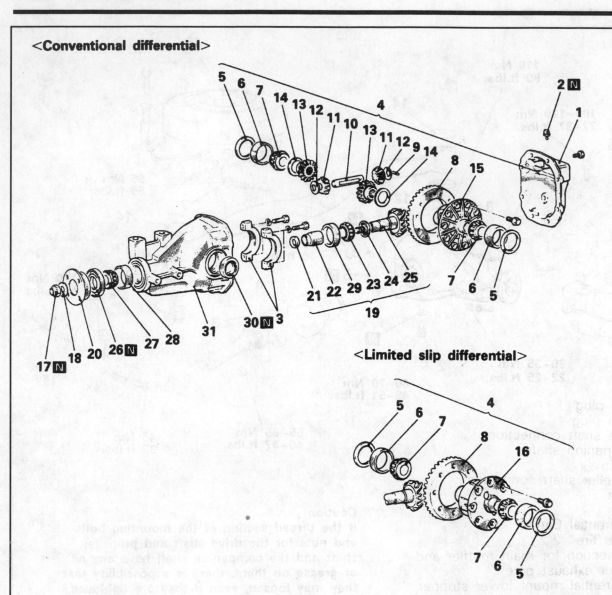

<Conventional differential>

<Limited slip differential>

1. Differential cover
2. Vent plug
3. Bearing caps
4. Differential case assembly
5. Side bearing spacers
6. Side bearing outer race
7. Side bearing inner race
8. Drive gear
9. Lock pin <for conventional differential>
10. Pinion shaft
11. Pinion gears
12. Pinion washers
13. Side gears
14. Side gear spacers
15. Differential case
16. Limited slip differential case assembly
   (Refer to P.3-40.)
17. Self-locking nut
18. Washer
19. Drive pinion assembly
20. Companion flange
21. Drive pinion front shim
   (for preload adjustment)
22. Drive pinion spacer
23. Drive pinion rear bearing inner race
24. Drive pinion rear shim
   (for pinion height adjustment)
25. Drive pinion
26. Oil seal
27. Drive pinion front bearing inner race
28. Drive pinion front bearing outer race
29. Drive pinion rear bearing outer race
30. Oil seal
31. Gear carrier

Fig. 54 Differential disassembly

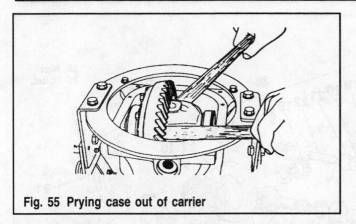

Fig. 55 Prying case out of carrier

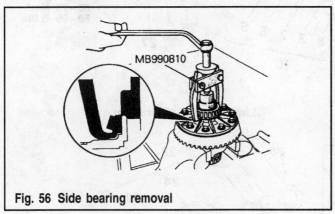

Fig. 56 Side bearing removal

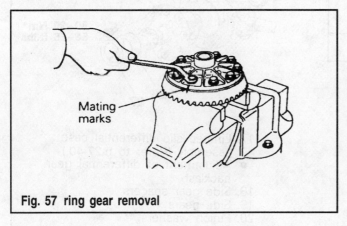

Fig. 57 ring gear removal

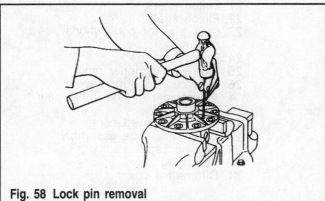

Fig. 58 Lock pin removal

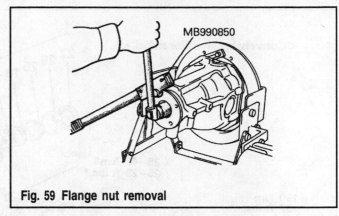

Fig. 59 Flange nut removal

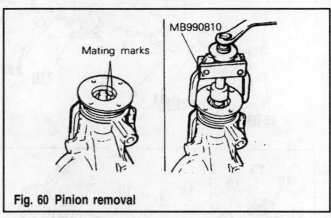

Fig. 60 Pinion removal

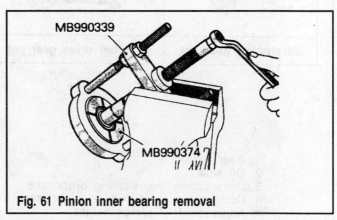

Fig. 61 Pinion inner bearing removal

nut and torque it to 137 ft. lbs. Check that the turning torque is still with specifications. If not, you'll have to find the cause and start over again.

10. Assemble the side gears, spacers, washers and pinion gears in the case. Temporarily install the pinion shaft. Adjust the differential gear backlash as follows:

    a. Lock the side gear with a wedge and measure the gear backlash with a dial indicator. Backlash should be 0-0.003 in. (0-0.76mm). The service limit is 0.008 in. (0.2mm).

    b. If backlash exceeds the limit, install thicker side gear spacers.

    c. Remeasure backlash. Adjust with shims until the backlash is correct. If backlash cannot be brought within

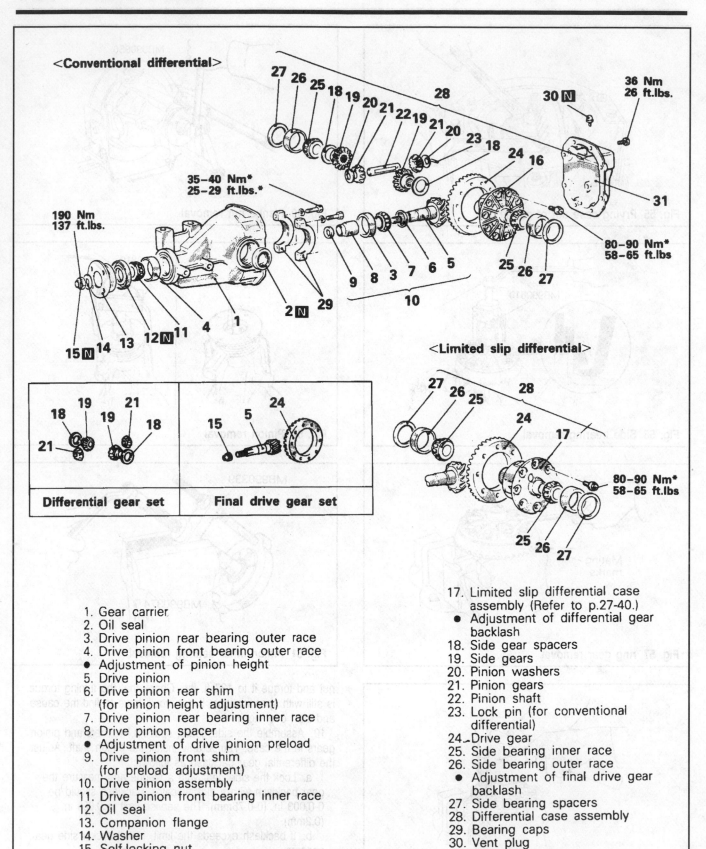

Fig. 62 Differential assembly

1. Gear carrier
2. Oil seal
3. Drive pinion rear bearing outer race
4. Drive pinion front bearing outer race
● Adjustment of pinion height
5. Drive pinion
6. Drive pinion rear shim
(for pinion height adjustment)
7. Drive pinion rear bearing inner race
8. Drive pinion spacer
● Adjustment of drive pinion preload
9. Drive pinion front shim
(for preload adjustment)
10. Drive pinion assembly
11. Drive pinion front bearing inner race
12. Oil seal
13. Companion flange
14. Washer
15. Self-locking nut
16. Differential case

17. Limited slip differential case
assembly (Refer to p.27-40.)
● Adjustment of differential gear
backlash
18. Side gear spacers
19. Side gears
20. Pinion washers
21. Pinion gears
22. Pinion shaft
23. Lock pin (for conventional
differential)
24. Drive gear
25. Side bearing inner race
26. Side bearing outer race
● Adjustment of final drive gear
backlash
27. Side bearing spacers
28. Differential case assembly
29. Bearing caps
30. Vent plug
31. Differential cover

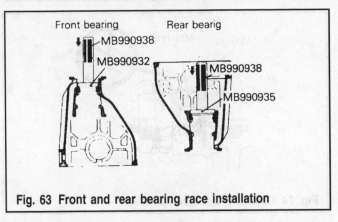

Fig. 63 Front and rear bearing race installation

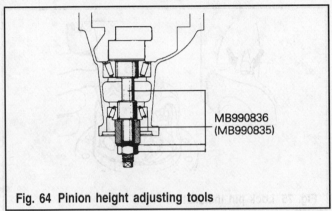

Fig. 64 Pinion height adjusting tools

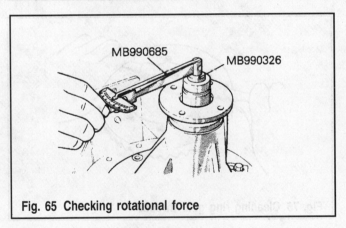

Fig. 65 Checking rotational force

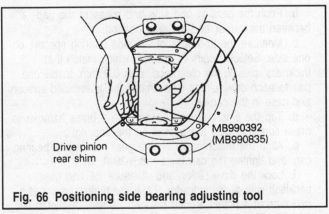

Fig. 66 Positioning side bearing adjusting tool

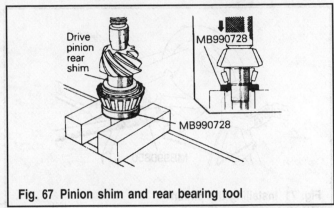

Fig. 67 Pinion shim and rear bearing tool

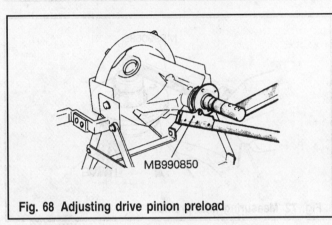

Fig. 68 Adjusting drive pinion preload

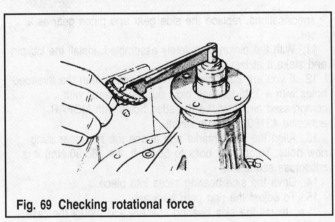

Fig. 69 Checking rotational force

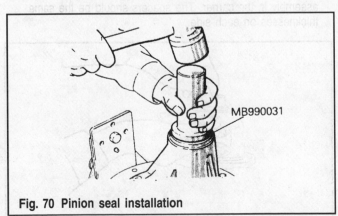

Fig. 70 Pinion seal installation

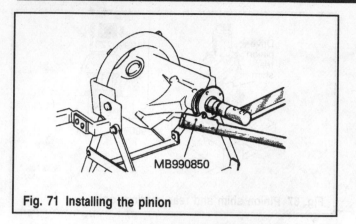

Fig. 71 Installing the pinion

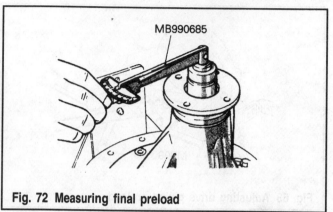

Fig. 72 Measuring final preload

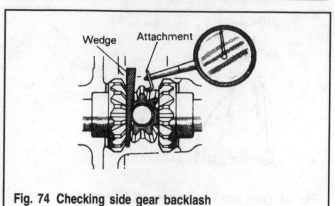

Fig. 74 Checking side gear backlash

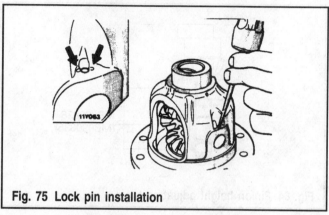

Fig. 75 Lock pin installation

specifications, replace the side gear and pinon gear as a set.

11. With the pinion completely assembled, install the lockpin and stake it at two points.

12. If you are installing a new ring gear, clean the threaded holes with a 1.25 tap and blow out the threads with compressed air. Coat the threaded holes with MOPAR adhesive 4318031 or equivalent.

13. Align the matchmarks and attach the ring gear using new bolts. Torque the bolts to 58-65 ft. lbs. (80-90 Nm) in a crisscross sequence.

14. Drive the side bearing races into place.

15. To adjust the ring gear backlash:

  a. Install the side bearing spacers and mount the case assembly in the carrier. The spacers should be the same thicknesses on each side.

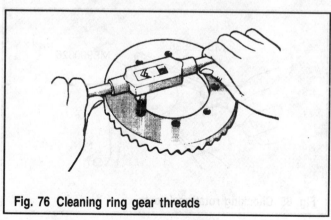

Fig. 76 Cleaning ring gear threads

  b. Push the case to one side and measure the gap between the carrier and the side bearing.

  c. Measure the thickness of the side bearing spacers on one side. Select 2 pairs of spacers which match that thickness, plus ½ the clearance, plus 0.05mm. Install one pair to each drive pinion side. Install the assembled spacers and case in the carrier.

  d. Tap the side bearing spacers with a brass hammer to make sure that they are seated on the bearing.

  e. Align the matchmarks on the gear carrier and bearing cap, and tighten the cap bolts to 25-29 ft. lbs.

  f. Lock the drive pinion and measure the ring gear backlash with a dial indicator. Take the measurement at a minimum of 4 points around the gear. Backlash should be 0.004-0.006 in. (0.11-0.16mm). If it is not correct, change the

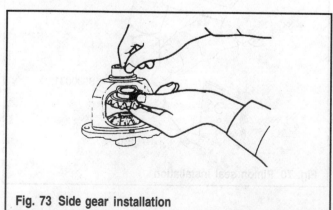

Fig. 73 Side gear installation

side bearing spacers. If you are increasing the number of spacers, use the same number for each side, using as few as possible.

g. Check the ring gear tooth contact pattern as shown in the accompanying illustration. Adjust as necessary.

h. Measure the ring gear runout at the shoulder on the reverse side of the gear. Runout limit is 0.002 in. (0.05mm). If runout is excessive, remove the ring gear from the case and reposition it.

16. If everything is assembled satisfactorily, install the cover and vent plug.

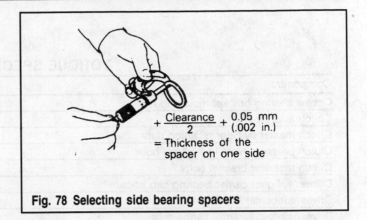

$$+ \frac{\text{Clearance}}{2} + \frac{0.05 \text{ mm}}{(.002 \text{ in.})}$$
= Thickness of the spacer on one side

Fig. 78 Selecting side bearing spacers

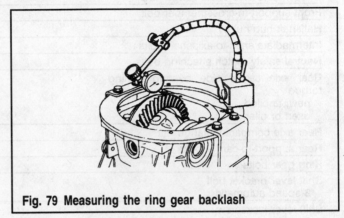

Fig. 79 Measuring the ring gear backlash

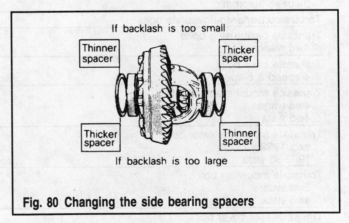

If backlash is too small

Thinner spacer | Thicker spacer

Thicker spacer | Thinner spacer

If backlash is too large

Fig. 80 Changing the side bearing spacers

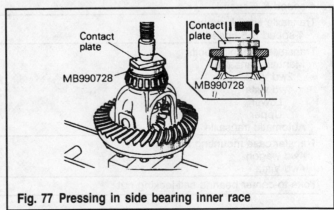

Contact plate

MB990728

Contact plate

MB990728

Fig. 77 Pressing in side bearing inner race

TORQUE SPECIFICATIONS

Component	U.S.	Metric
Center bearing bracket mounting nut	40 ft. lbs.	54 Nm
Clutch fluid pipe	11 ft. lbs.	15 Nm
Clutch master cylinder retaining nuts	9 ft. lbs.	13 Nm
Clutch pressure plate-to-flywheel bolts	11-15 ft. lbs.	15-20 Nm
Clutch reservoir bracket bolts	5 ft. lbs.	7 Nm
Differential gear carrier bearing cap bolts	25-29 ft. lbs.	34-39 Nm
Driveshaft center bearing nuts	25-30 ft. lbs.	34-38 Nm
Driveshaft-to-differential flange nuts	20-25 ft. lbs.	34-39 Nm
Front support-to-crossmember bolt	101 ft. lbs.	137 Nm
Halfshaft hub nut	185 ft. lbs.	252 Nm
Intermediate shaft-to-axleshaft bolts	43 ft. lbs.	58 Nm
Neutral safety switch attaching bolts	7.5-8.5 ft. lbs.	10-12 Nm
Rear axle carrier side bearing turning torque		
new, unoiled	8-10 inch lbs.	0.9-1.1 Nm
used or oiled	3-4 inch lbs.	0.3-0.4 Nm
Rear axle companion flange nut	160 ft. lbs.	218 Nm
Rear support-to-carrier bolts	95 ft. lbs.	129 Nm
Ring gear bolts	58-65 ft. lbs.	80-90 Nm
Shift lever bracket bolt		
3-speed automatic	9-11 ft. lbs.	12-15 Nm
Shift lever lockscrew		
3-speed automatic	100 inch lbs.	11 Nm
Torque converter-to-driveplate bolts	34-38 ft. lbs.	46-54 Nm
Transaxle bellhousing bolts		
4wd wagon	35 ft. lbs.	47 Nm
Transaxle case bolts		
4-speed & 5-speed	26-30 ft. lbs.	35-41 Nm
Transaxle mount bracket bolts		
4wd wagon	35 ft. lbs.	47 Nm
4wd vista	40-43 ft. lbs.	55-60 Nm
Transaxle mount insulator bolt		
exc. 1992-93 vista	31-40 ft. lbs.	43-54 Nm
1992-93 vista	51 ft. lbs.	70 Nm
Transaxle mounting bolt		
2wd vista:	29-36 ft. lbs.	40-50 Nm
4wd vista	40-43 ft. lbs.	55-60 Nm
Transaxle rear cover bolts		
4-speed & 5-speed	14-16 ft. lbs.	19-22 Nm
Transaxle shaft locknuts		
4-speed & 5-speed	66-79 ft. lbs.	90-107 Nm
Transaxle-to-engine bolts		
Manual Transaxle		
2wd Vista	32-39 ft. lbs.	43-53 Nm
4wd vista		
Lower	31-40 ft. lbs.	43-55 Nm
Upper	40-43 ft. lbs.	55-60 Nm
Automatic transaxle	31-39 ft. lbs.	43-54 Nm
Transfer case mounting bolts		
4wd wagon	30 ft. lbs.	41 Nm
4wd Vista	40-43 ft. lbs.	54-58 Nm
Yoke-to-center bearing self-locking nut	160 ft. lbs.	218 Nm

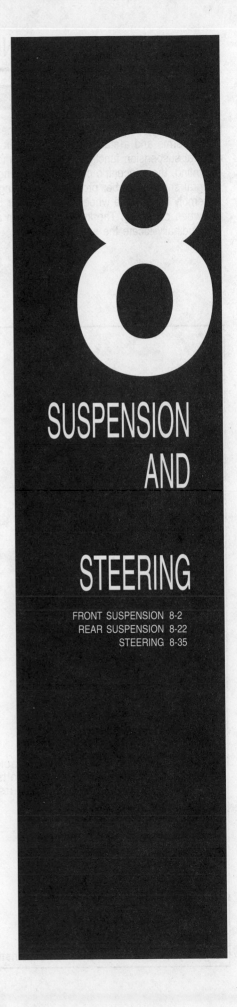

8

SUSPENSION AND STEERING

FRONT SUSPENSION

The front suspension consists of MacPherson struts, lower control arms and a stabilizer bar. The strut assembly performs several suspension functions: It provides the steering knuckle mounting, the concentric coil acts the springing medium, the integral shock absorber provides dampening and the strut assembly locates the wheel. The stabilizer bar minimizes body roll when cornering. The lower control arm acts to longitudinally locate the suspension/wheel.

MacPherson Struts

REMOVAL & INSTALLATION

Colt

▶ **See Figures 1, 2 and 3**

1. Raise and support the front of the vehicle.
2. Remove the front wheels.
3. Detach the front brake hose from the strut mounting clip.
4. Unbolt the strut from the steering knuckle.

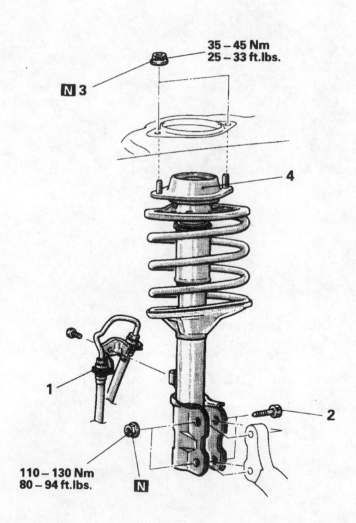

1. Brake hose and tube bracket
2. Strut lower mounting bolts
3. Strut upper mounting nuts
4. Strut assembly

Fig. 1 Front strut assembly removal/installation — 1990-92 Colt hatchback and sedan

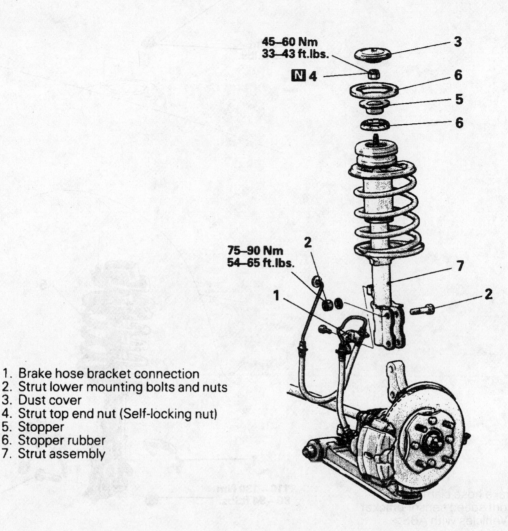

45–60 Nm
33–43 ft.lbs.

75–90 Nm
54–65 ft.lbs.

1. Brake hose bracket connection
2. Strut lower mounting bolts and nuts
3. Dust cover
4. Strut top end nut (Self-locking nut)
5. Stopper
6. Stopper rubber
7. Strut assembly

Fig. 2 Front strut assembly removal/installation — 1990 Colt Wagon

5. Remove the dust shield from the top of the fender housing mount. Insert a suitable socket (special tool MB991036, or the equivalent) into the top of the strut to loosen the gland mounting nut.

6. Insert an allen wrench through the socket, into the top of the strut shaft. Remove the mounting nut, while holding the shaft with the allen wrench.

7. Remove the strut. Service as required.

8. Mount the strut into position and secure the upper mount. Attach the lower strut bracket to the steering knuckle.

9. Torque the strut to knuckle bolts to 55-65 ft. lbs.; the upper retaining nut to 25-36 ft. lbs. Check the wheel alignment.

Vista

▶ See Figures 4 and 5

1. Raise and safely support the front of the vehicle.

2. Remove the front wheels.

3. Detach the brake hose from the clip on the strut.

4. Remove the mounting nuts that secure the upper end of the strut to the fender housing.

5. Unbolt the strut from the steering knuckle.

6. Remove the strut from the vehicle.

7. Service as required. Bolt the strut to the steering knuckle, and the upper fender mounting. Secure the brake hose to the strut mounting clip.

8. Torque the strut to knuckle bolts to 55-65 ft. lbs.; Torque the strut to fender housing bolts to 18-25 ft. lbs.

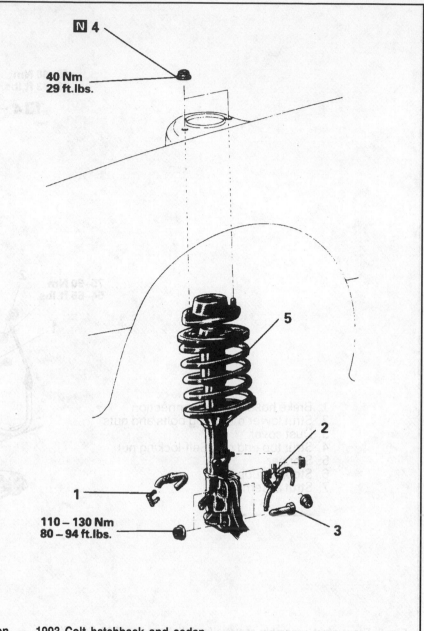

N 4

40 Nm
29 ft. lbs.

5

2

1

110 – 130 Nm
80 – 94 ft.lbs.

3

1. Brake hose clamp
2. Front speed sensor bracket
   <Vehicles with ABS>
3. Bolts
4. Flange nut
5. Strut assembly

Fig. 3 Front strut assembly removal/installation — 1993 Colt hatchback and sedan

Coil Spring

REMOVAL & INSTALLATION

Colt

▶ See Figure 6

1. Remove the strut assembly from the vehicle.

2. Using a spring compressor, fully compress the spring.

✳✳CAUTION

A compressed coil spring can release tremendous energy. Be very careful when compressing or releasing the spring. Be sure the jaws of the compressor grip the coils of the spring firmly.

3. Using special tool MB9910036, or the equivalent, and an allen wrench, remove the retaining nut.
4. Remove the rubber insulator, support, spring seat rubber bumper and spring.
5. Use a brass drift and carefully remove the bearing from the support.
6. Check all parts for wear. Service as require.

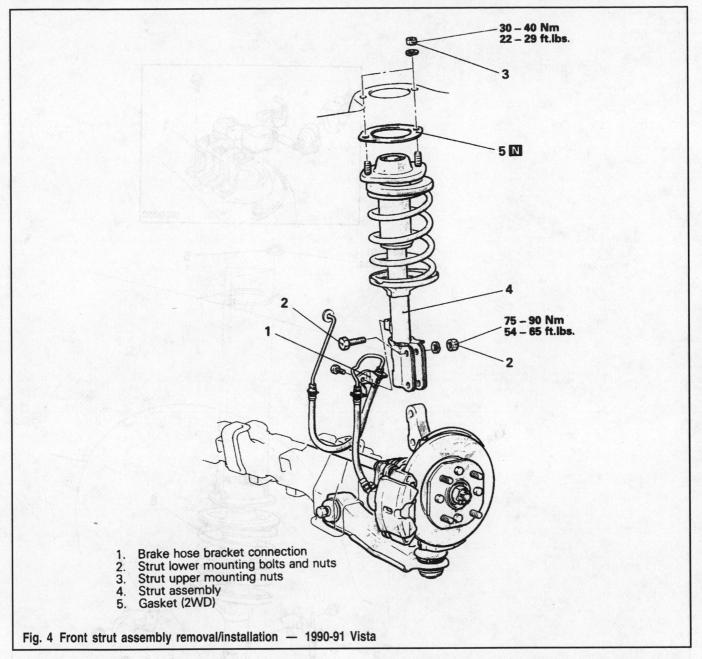

30 – 40 Nm
22 – 29 ft.lbs.

3

5 N

4

75 – 90 Nm
54 – 65 ft.lbs.

2

1. Brake hose bracket connection
2. Strut lower mounting bolts and nuts
3. Strut upper mounting nuts
4. Strut assembly
5. Gasket (2WD)

Fig. 4 Front strut assembly removal/installation — 1990-91 Vista

7. Install the bearing, spring, seat rubber bumper, support, rubber insulator and secure them with a new self-locking nut.

8. Make sure that both spring seat grooves align with the coil spring ends

➡ **Always install a new self-locking nut. DO NOT use the old nut.**

9. Tighten the gland retaining nut to 25-36 ft. lbs.

Vista

▶ **See Figures 7 and ?**

1. Remove the strut assembly as previously outlined. Clamp the strut assembly in a soft-jawed vise or wrap heavy rags around the strut before tightening the vise.

2. Install a spring compressor on the spring and tighten to compress the spring slightly. The compressor will keep the

spring compressed while the strut cover and spring seat are removed.

✳✳CAUTION

A compressed coil spring can release tremendous energy. Be very careful when compressing or releasing the spring. Be sure the jaws of the compressor grip the coils of the spring firmly.

3. Remove the upper dust cover.
4. Remove the nuts that retain the insulator to the strut. Remove the insulator.
5. Remove the spring. Service the strut as required.
6. If a new spring is to be installed, compress the spring.
7. Install the spring on the strut.
8. Fully extend the shock absorber piston rod.

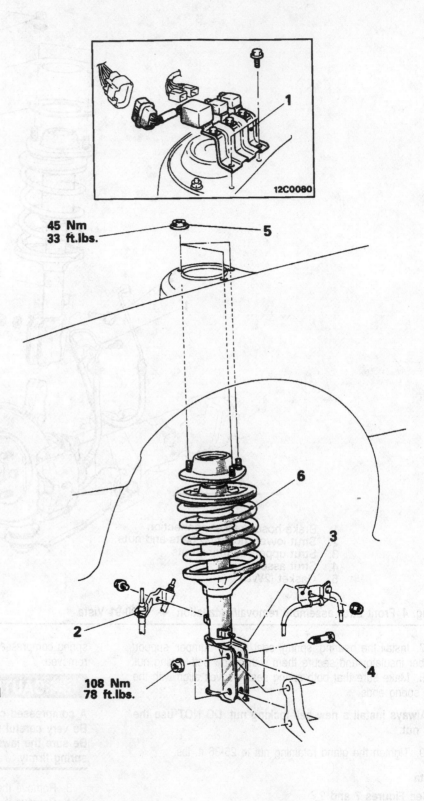

1. Daytime running lamp relay and control unit
2. Brake tube clamp
3. Front speed sensor clamp <Vehicles with ABS>
4. Bolts
5. Flange nut
6. Strut assembly

Fig. 5 Front strut assembly removal/installation — 1992-93 Vista

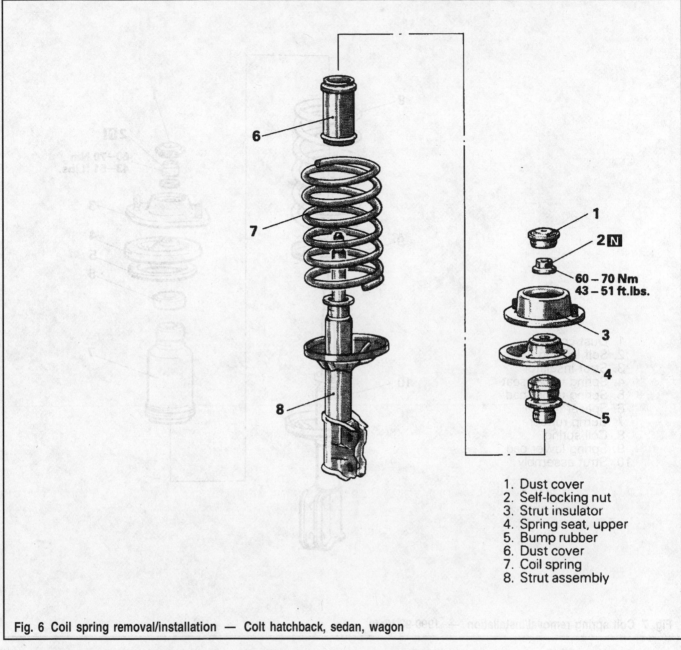

1. Dust cover
2. Self-locking nut
3. Strut insulator
4. Spring seat, upper
5. Bump rubber
6. Dust cover
7. Coil spring
8. Strut assembly

Fig. 6 Coil spring removal/installation — Colt hatchback, sedan, wagon

9. Align the spring seat upper assembly with the indent on the piston rod and the D-shaped hole.

10. Install the insulator assembly. Temporarily tighten the self-locking nut.

➡**Always install a new self-locking nut. DO NOT use the old nut.**

11. After correctly seating the upper and lower ends of the coil spring on the grooves of the upper and lower seats, release the spring compressor.

Hold the upper spring seat stationary and tighten the self-locking retaining nut. Torque the nut to 30-36 ft. lbs.

OVERHAUL

1. Remove the strut from the vehicle. Remove the coil spring from the strut.

➡**Matchmark the upper end of the coil spring and bearing plate to avoid confusion during assembly.**

2. Keep the upper mounting parts in the order of their removal, again to avoid confusion during assembly.

3. Clean the outside of the strut body, especially around the top. Use the proper size wrench to loosen the top strut body nut.

4. Remove the body nut. If a new nut came with the strut overhaul kit, discard the old nut.

5. Use a suitable tool and remove the O-ring from the top of the strut housing bore.

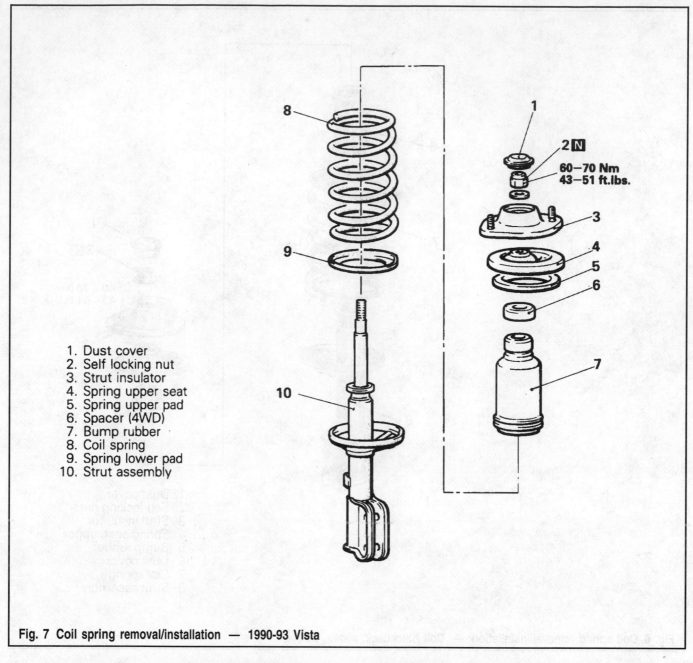

1. Dust cover
2. Self locking nut
3. Strut insulator
4. Spring upper seat
5. Spring upper pad
6. Spacer (4WD)
7. Bump rubber
8. Coil spring
9. Spring lower pad
10. Strut assembly

Fig. 7 Coil spring removal/installation — 1990-93 Vista

6. Grasp the piston rod and slowly pull the cartridge out of the housing. Remove the cartridge slowly to prevent the oil between the housing and the cartridge from splashing.

7. Pour all of the strut oil into a suitable container. Clean the inside of the housing and inspect the cylinder for dents and to insure that all loose parts have been removed from the inside of the strut body.

8. Keep the strut upright and replenish the strut cylinder with one ounce (or whatever amount is suggested by the overhaul kit instructions) of the original or fresh oil. The oil helps dissipate internal heat during operation and results in cooler strut operation. Do not put too much oil in, or the oil

may leak at the body nut when the shock heats up and causes expansion.

9. Insert the replacement cartridge into the strut body. Push the piston rod all of the way down to avoid damage if the wrench slips when installing the top nut. Carefully install the top body nut, take care not to cross-thread. Tighten the top body nut to 100 ft. lbs. (or whatever the instruction sheet calls for).

10. Install the coil spring and top parts. Pay attention to the alignment reference marks made when taking apart the strut.

11. Install the strut on the vehicle.

Lower Control Arm

REMOVAL & INSTALLATION

Colt

▶ **See Figures 8, 9 and 10**

1. Loosen the front wheel lugs. Block the rear wheels. Jack up the front of the vehicle, allowing the front suspension to hang, and safely support the vehicle on jackstands.

2. Remove the front wheels. Remove the lower engine splash shield.

3. Use a ball joint separator and disconnect the ball joint from the steering knuckle.

4. Unbolt the lower control arm from the crossmember and remove it from the vehicle.

➡ **The ball joint cannot be separated from the control arm, but must be replaced as an assembly.**

5. If the stabilizer bar is to be removed, disconnect the tie rod from the knuckle, unbolt it and remove.

6. Check all parts for wear and damage. Service as required.

7. Use an inch pound torque wrench and check the ball joint torque. Nominal starting effort should be 22-87 inch lbs. Replace the assembly if otherwise.

8. Install the stabilizer, if removed. Connect the tie rod. Position and attach the lower control arm to the crossmember. Connect the ball joint. Install the splash shield and front wheels. Lower the vehicle.

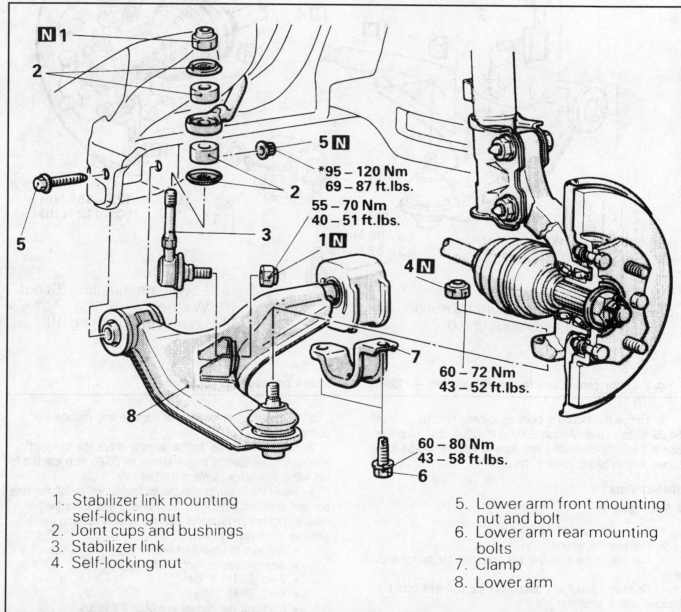

1. Stabilizer link mounting self-locking nut
2. Joint cups and bushings
3. Stabilizer link
4. Self-locking nut
5. Lower arm front mounting nut and bolt
6. Lower arm rear mounting bolts
7. Clamp
8. Lower arm

Fig. 8 Lower control arm removal/installation — 1990 Colt hatchback and sedan w/1.5L engine; all 1991-92 Colt hatchback and sedan

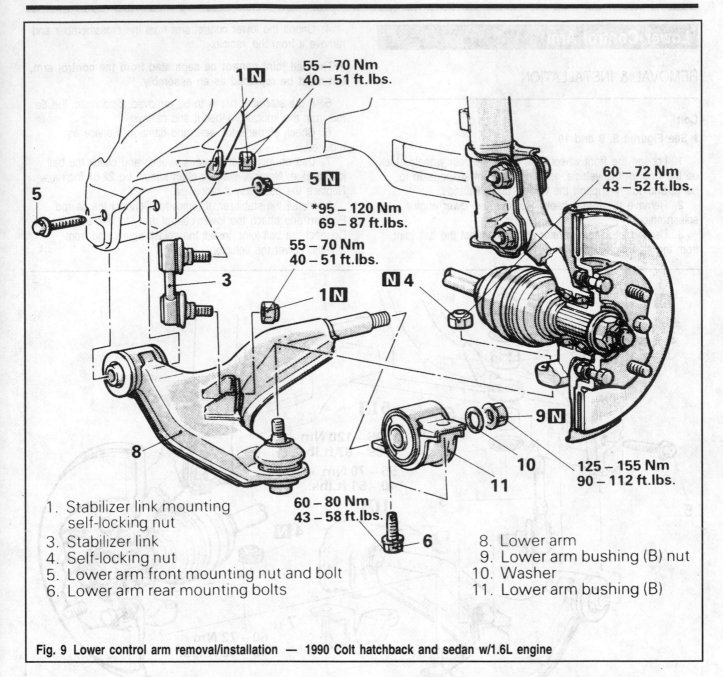

1. Stabilizer link mounting self-locking nut
3. Stabilizer link
4. Self-locking nut
5. Lower arm front mounting nut and bolt
6. Lower arm rear mounting bolts
8. Lower arm
9. Lower arm bushing (B) nut
10. Washer
11. Lower arm bushing (B)

Fig. 9 Lower control arm removal/installation — 1990 Colt hatchback and sedan w/1.6L engine

9. Torque the mounting bolts as follows: Knuckle to Strut; 54-65 ft. lbs.; Lower Arm to Body; 118-125 ft. lbs.; Stabilizer Bar to Body; 12-20 ft. lbs.; Ball Joint to Knuckle; 44-53 ft. lbs.; Lower Arm to Shaft; 70-88 ft. lbs.

1990-91 Vista

▶ See Figure 11

1. Raise and support the front end.
2. Remove the wheels.
3. Disconnect the stabilizer bar and strut bar from the lower arm.
4. Remove the nut and disconnect the ball joint from the knuckle with a separator.
5. Unbolt the lower arm from the crossmember.

6. Check all parts for wear or damage and replace any suspect part.
7. Using an inch lbs. torque wrench, check the ball joint starting torque. Starting torque should be 20-86 inch lbs. If it is not within that range, replace the ball joint.
8. Install the lower arm to the crossmember, Install the strut bar and stabilizer. Attach the front wheels and lower the vehicle. Tighten all fasteners with the wheels hanging freely. Observe the following torques:

- Ball joint-to-knuckle: 44-53 ft. lbs.
- Arm-to-crossmember: 90-111 ft. lbs.
- 2-wd: 90-111 ft. lbs.
- 4-wd: 58-68 ft. lbs.
- Stabilizer bar hanger brackets: 7-9 ft. lbs.

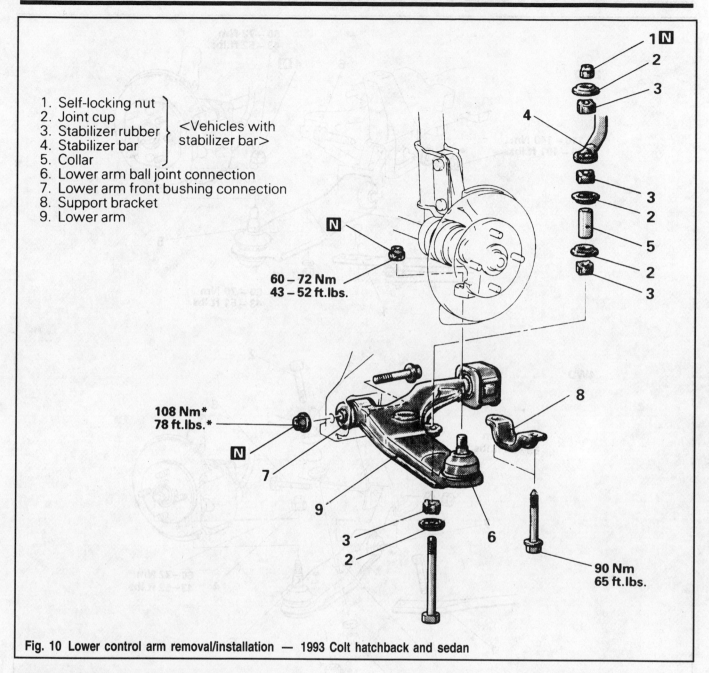

1. Self-locking nut
2. Joint cup
3. Stabilizer rubber ⎫
4. Stabilizer bar ⎬ <Vehicles with stabilizer bar>
5. Collar ⎭
6. Lower arm ball joint connection
7. Lower arm front bushing connection
8. Support bracket
9. Lower arm

60 – 72 Nm
43 – 52 ft.lbs.

108 Nm*
78 ft.lbs.*

90 Nm
65 ft.lbs.

Fig. 10 Lower control arm removal/installation — 1993 Colt hatchback and sedan

➡When installing the stabilizer bar, the nut on the bar-to-crossmember bolts and the bar-to-lower arm bolts, are not torqued, but turned on until a certain length of thread is exposed above the nut: 2WD Stabilizer Bar to Crossmember: 8-10mm; Stabilizer Bar to Lower Control Arm: 8-10mm; 4WD Stabilizer Bar to Crossmember: 8-10mm; Stabilizer Bar to Lower Arm: 13-15mm.

1992-93 Vista

▶ See Figure 12

1. Disconnect the negative battery cable.
2. Raise the vehicle and support safely.
3. Remove sway bar links from lower control arm.
4. Disconnect the ball joint stud from the steering knuckle.
5. Remove the inner mounting frame-through bolt and nut.

6. Remove the rear mount bolts. Remove the clamp if equipped.
7. Remove the rear rod bushing if servicing.
To install:
8. Assemble the control arm and bushing.
9. Install the control arm to the vehicle and install the through bolt. Replace the nut and snug temporarily.
10. Install the rear mount clamp, bolts and replacement nuts. Torque the bolts to 51 ft. lbs. (70 Nm).
11. Connect the ball joint stud to the knuckle. Install a new nut and torque to 43-52 ft. lbs. (60-72 Nm).
12. Install the sway bar and links.
13. Lower the vehicle to the floor for the final torquing of the frame mount through bolt.
14. Once the full weight of the vehicle is on the floor, torque the frame mount through bolt nuts to 75-90 ft. lbs. (102-122 Nm).

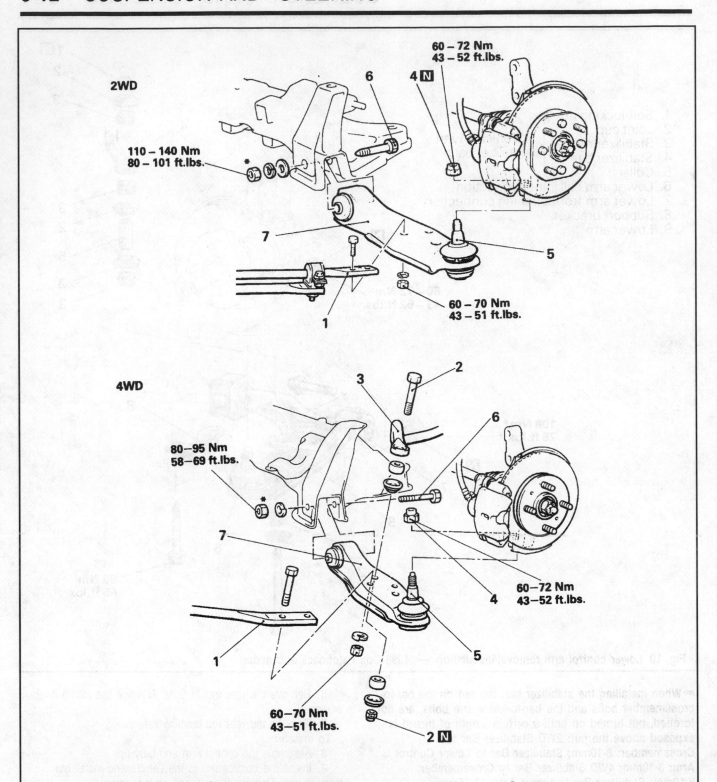

1. Strut bar
2. Stabilizer bar mounting bolt and nut
3. Stabilizer bar
4. Lower arm and knuckle coupling nut
5. Lower arm ball joint connection
6. Lower arm shaft
7. Lower arm

Fig. 11 Lower control arm removal/installation — 1990-91 Vista

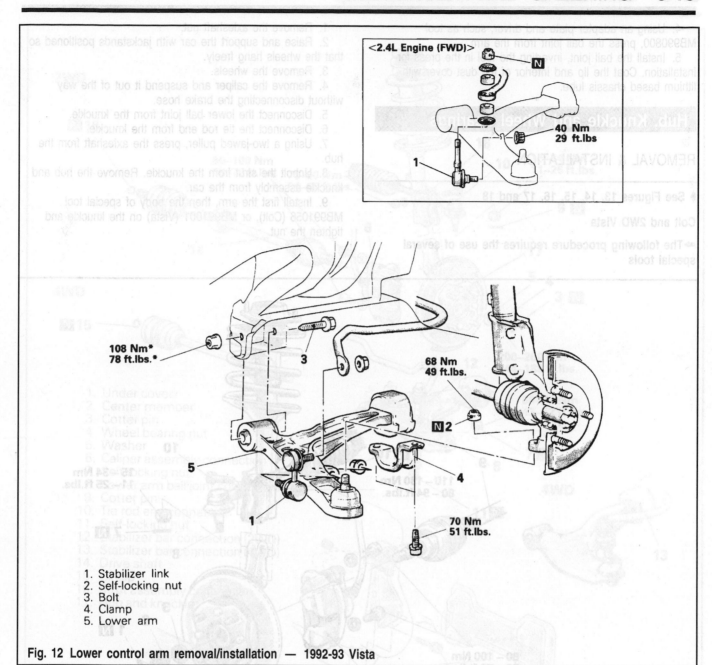

<2.4L Engine (FWD)>

40 Nm
29 ft.lbs.

108 Nm*
78 ft.lbs.*

3

68 Nm
49 ft.lbs.

N 2

5

4

1

70 Nm
51 ft.lbs.

1. Stabilizer link
2. Self-locking nut
3. Bolt
4. Clamp
5. Lower arm

Fig. 12 Lower control arm removal/installation — 1992-93 Vista

15. Connect the negative battery cable and align the front end.

Ball Joints

INSPECTION

1. Jack up the front and support the car on jackstands. There must be no weight on the front wheels.

2. Apply downward and upward pressure to the wheel avoiding any compression to the spring. If excessive play is encountered between the control arm and the steering knuckle, the ball joint probably needs replacing.

REMOVAL & INSTALLATION

▶ See Figures 8, 9, 10, 11 and 12

Colt

The ball joint is not replaceable. The ball joint and lower control arm must be replaced as an assembly.

Vista

➡ **This procedure requires a hydraulic press.**

1. See the Lower Control Arm procedure and disconnect the lower arm.

2. Remove the ball joint dust cover.

3. Using snapring pliers, remove the snapring from the ball joint.

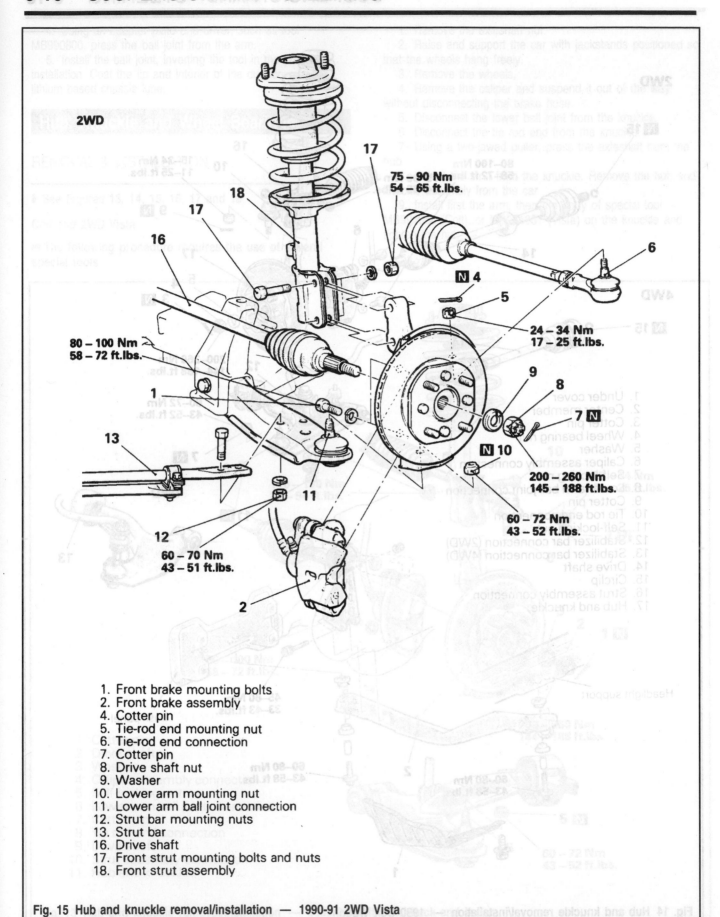

80 – 100 Nm
58 – 72 ft.lbs.

60 – 70 Nm
43 – 51 ft.lbs.

75 – 90 Nm
54 – 65 ft.lbs.

24 – 34 Nm
17 – 25 ft.lbs.

200 – 260 Nm
145 – 188 ft.lbs.

60 – 72 Nm
43 – 52 ft.lbs.

1. Front brake mounting bolts
2. Front brake assembly
4. Cotter pin
5. Tie-rod end mounting nut
6. Tie-rod end connection
7. Cotter pin
8. Drive shaft nut
9. Washer
10. Lower arm mounting nut
11. Lower arm ball joint connection
12. Strut bar mounting nuts
13. Strut bar
16. Drive shaft
17. Front strut mounting bolts and nuts
18. Front strut assembly

Fig. 15 Hub and knuckle removal/installation — 1990-91 2WD Vista

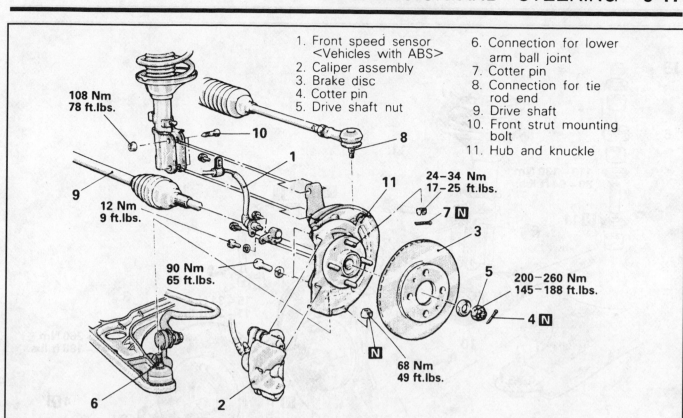

1. Front speed sensor <Vehicles with ABS>
2. Caliper assembly
3. Brake disc
4. Cotter pin
5. Drive shaft nut
6. Connection for lower arm ball joint
7. Cotter pin
8. Connection for tie rod end
9. Drive shaft
10. Front strut mounting bolt
11. Hub and knuckle

108 Nm 78 ft.lbs.

12 Nm 9 ft.lbs.

90 Nm 65 ft.lbs.

24–34 Nm 17–25 ft.lbs.

200–260 Nm 145–188 ft.lbs.

68 Nm 49 ft.lbs.

Fig. 16 Hub and knuckle removal/installation — 1992-93 Vista

10. Using special tool MB990998, separate the hub from the knuckle.

➡**Prying or hammering will damage the bearing. Use these special tools, or their equivalent to separate the hub and knuckle.**

11. Place the knuckle in a vise and separate the rotor from the hub.

12. Using special tools, C-293-PA, SP3183 and MB990781, remove the outer bearing inner race.

13. Drive the oil seal and inner bearing inner race from the knuckle with a brass drift.

14. Drive out both outer races in a similar fashion.

➡**Always replace bearings and races as a set. Never replace just an inner or outer bearing. If either is in need of replacement, both sets must be replaced.**

15. Thoroughly clean and inspect all parts. Any suspect part should be replaced.

16. Pack the wheel bearings with lithium based wheel bearing grease. Coat the inside of the knuckle with similar grease and pack the cavities in the knuckle. Apply a thin coating of grease to the outer surface of the races before installation.

17. Using special tools C-3893 and MB990776, install the outer races.

18. Install the rotor on the hub and torque the bolts to 36-43 ft lb.

19. Drive the outer bearing inner race into position.

20. Coat the out rim and lip of the oil seal and drive the hub side oil seal into place, using a seal driver.

21. Place the inner bearing in the knuckle.

22. Mount the knuckle in a vise. Position the hub and knuckle together. Install tool MB990998 and tighten the tool to 147-192 ft. lbs. Rotate the hub to seat the bearing.

23. With the knuckle still in the vise, measure the hub starting torque with an in. lb. torque wrench and tool MB990998. Starting torque should be 11.5 inch lbs. If the starting torque is 0, measure the hub bearing axial play with a dial indicator. If axial play exceeds 0.2mm, while the nut is tightened to 145-192 ft. lbs., the assembly has not been done correctly. Disassemble the knuckle and hub and start again.

24. Remove the special tool.

25. Place the outer bearing in the hub and drive the seal into place.

26. Assemble and install the knuckle.

4WD Vista

➡**The following procedure requires the use of several special tools.**

1. Remove the hub cap and halfshaft nut.

2. Raise and support the car on jackstands.

3. Remove the front wheels.

4. Drain the transaxle fluid.

5. Disconnect the lower ball joint from the knuckle.

6. Remove the strut and stabilizer bar from the lower arm.

7. Remove the center bearing snapring from the bearing bracket.

8. Lightly tap the double off-set joint outer race with a wood mallet and disconnect the halfshaft from the cardan joint.

9. Disconnect the halfshaft from the bearing bracket.

10. Using a two-jawed puller secured to the hub lugs, press the halfshaft from the hub.

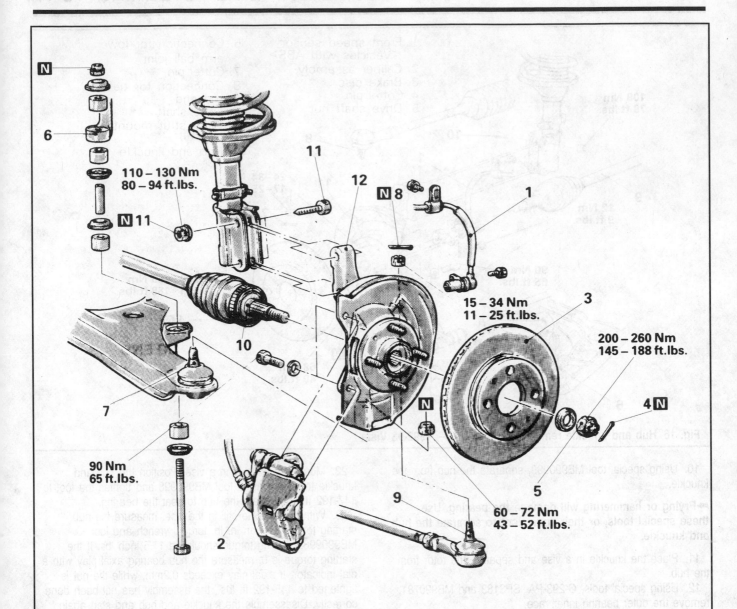

1. Front speed sensor <Vehicle with ABS>
2. Caliper assembly
3. Brake disc
4. Cotter pin
5. Drive shaft nut
6. Connection for stabilizer bar
7. Connection for lower arm ball joint
8. Cotter pin
9. Connection for tie rod end
10. Drive shaft
11. Front strut mounting bolt and nut
12. Hub and knuckle

Caution
1. **Be careful when handling the pole piece at the tip of the speed sensor and the toothed edge of the rotor so as not to damage them by striking against other parts.**
2. **For vehicles with ABS, be careful not to damage the rotors installed to the R.J. (or B.J.) outer race during removal and installation of the drive shaft.**

Fig. 17 Hub and knuckle removal/installation — 1993 Colt Hatchback and sedan

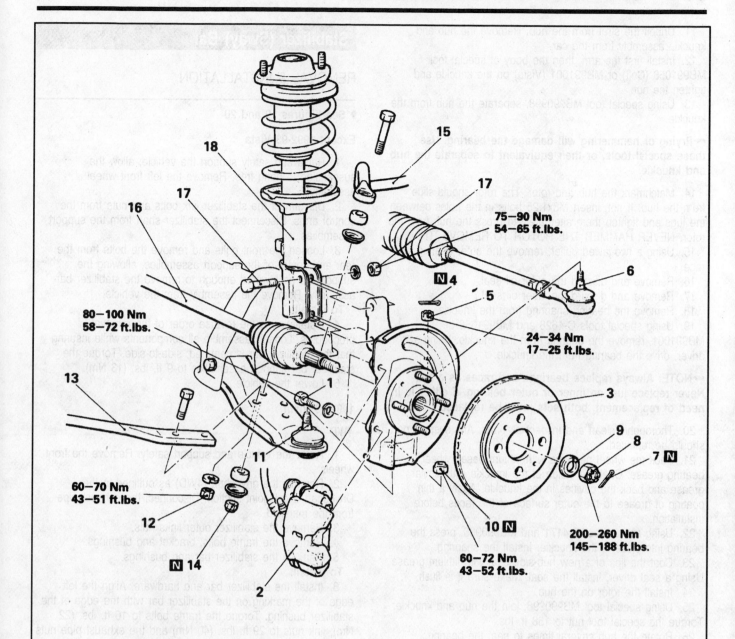

80–100 Nm
58–72 ft.lbs.

75–90 Nm
54–65 ft.lbs.

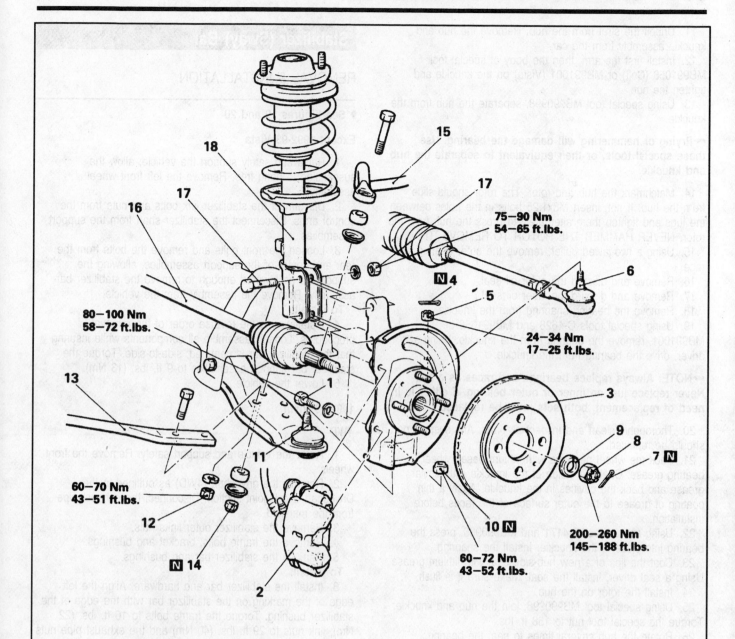 4

24–34 Nm
17–25 ft.lbs.

60–70 Nm
43–51 ft.lbs.

200–260 Nm
145–188 ft.lbs.

60–72 Nm
43–52 ft.lbs.

1. Front brake mounting bolts
2. Front brake assembly
3. Brake disc
4. Cotter pin
5. Tie-rod end mounting nut
6. Tie-rod end connection
7. Cotter pin
8. Drive shaft nut
9. Washer
10. Lower arm mounting nut
11. Lower arm ball joint connection
12. Strut bar mounting nuts
13. Strut bar
14. Stabilizer bar mounting nut
15. Stabilizer bar
16. Drive shaft
17. Front strut mounting bolts and nuts
18. Front strut assembly

Fig. 18 Hub and knuckle removal/installation — 1990–91 4WD Vista

11. Unbolt the strut from the hub. Remove the hub and knuckle assembly from the car.

12. Install first the arm, then the body of special tool MB991056 (Colt) or MB991001 (Vista) on the knuckle and tighten the nut.

13. Using special tool MB990998, separate the hub from the knuckle.

➡**Prying or hammering will damage the bearing. Use these special tools, or their equivalent to separate the hub and knuckle.**

14. Matchmark the hub and rotor. The rotor should slide from the hub. If not, insert M8x1.25 bolts in the holes between the lugs and tighten them alternately to press the hub from the rotor. NEVER HAMMER THE ROTOR TO REMOVE IT!

15. Using a two-jawed puller, remove the outer bearing inner race.

16. Remove and discard the outer oil seal.

17. Remove and discard the inner oil seal.

18. Remove the bearing snapring from the knuckle.

19. Using special tools C-4628 and MB991056 or MB991001, remove the bearing from the knuckle. Using a driver, drive the bearing from the knuckle.

➡**NOTE: Always replace bearings and races as a set. Never replace just an inner or outer bearing. If either is in need of replacement, both sets must be replaced.**

20. Thoroughly clean and inspect all parts. Any suspect part should be replaced.

21. Pack the wheel bearings with lithium based wheel bearing grease. Coat the inside of the knuckle with similar grease and pack the cavities in the knuckle. Apply a thin coating of grease to the outer surface of the races before installation.

22. Using special tool C-4171 and MB990985, press the bearing into place in the knuckle. Install the snapring.

23. Coat the lips of a new hub-side seal with lithium grease. Using a seal driver, install the seal. Make sure it is flush.

24. Install the rotor on the hub.

25. Using special tool MB990998, join the hub and knuckle. Torque the special tool nut to 188 ft. lbs.

26. Rotate the hub several times to seat the bearing.

27. Mount the knuckle in a vise. Using MB990998 and an in. lb. torque wrench, measure the turning torque. Turning torque should be 15.6 inch lbs. or less. Next, measure the axial play using a dial indicator. Axial play should be 0.2mm. If either the axial play or the turning torque are not within the specified values, the hub and knuckle have not been properly assembled. You will have to do the procedure over again. If everything checks out okay, to onto the next step.

28. Remove all the special tools.

29. Using a seal driver, drive a new seal coated with lithium grease, into place on the halfshaft side, until it contacts the snapring.

30. Assemble and install the knuckle.

Stabilizer (Sway) Bar

REMOVAL & INSTALLATION

▶ **See Figures 19 and 20**

Except 1992-93 Vista

1. Raise and safely support the vehicle; allow the suspension to hang free. Remove the left front wheel assembly.

2. Disconnect the stabilizer link bolts and nuts from the control arms. Disconnect the stabilizer shaft from the support assemblies.

3. Loosen the front bolts and remove the bolts from the rear and center of the support assemblies, allowing the supports to be lowered enough to remove the stabilizer bar assembly. Remove the assembly from the vehicle.

To install:

4. Installation is the reverse order of the removal procedures. Loosely assemble all components while insuring that the stabilizer bar is centered, side-to-side. Torque the stabilizer bar support assemblies to 9 ft. lbs. (13 Nm).

5. Lower the vehicle.

1992-93 Vista

4WD

1. Raise the vehicle and support safely. Remove the front wheels.

2. Remove the driveshaft (4WD) as outlined in the Driveshaft and U-joint section. Disconnect the exhaust pipe from the manifold.

3. Remove the stabilizer outer links nuts.

4. Remove the frame bolts, bracket and bushings.

5. Remove the stabilizer bar and bushings.

To install:

6. Install the stabilizer bar and hardware. Align the left edge of the marking on the stabilizer bar with the edge of the stabilizer bushing. Torque the frame bolts to 16 ft. lbs. (22 Nm), link nuts to 29 ft. lbs. (40 Nm) and the exhaust pipe nuts to 33 ft. lbs. (44 Nm).

7. Install the driveshaft (4WD).

2WD

1. Raise the vehicle and support safely. Remove the front wheels.

2. Remove the nut and disconnect the tie rod ends with separator tool MB991113, or equivalent.

3. Hold the link bolt still and remove the bushing nut.

4. Support the engine with a jack. Remove the center crossmember bolts and lower to gain enough run to remove the stabilizer bar.

5. Remove the frame, bolts, brackets and bushings.

6. Remove the stabilizer bar from the vehicle.

To install:

7. Install the stabilizer bar. Position the bar so that the projecting lengths of the marking from the fixture are at the measurement of 0.27 in. (7mm). Torque the bracket bolts to 16 ft. lbs. (22 Nm).

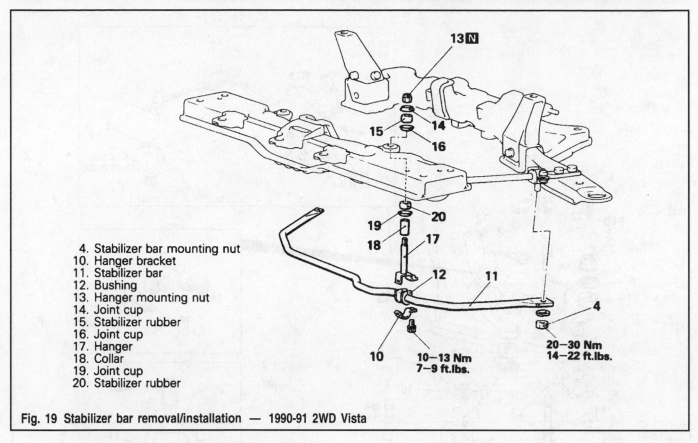

4. Stabilizer bar mounting nut
10. Hanger bracket
11. Stabilizer bar
12. Bushing
13. Hanger mounting nut
14. Joint cup
15. Stabilizer rubber
16. Joint cup
17. Hanger
18. Collar
19. Joint cup
20. Stabilizer rubber

10—13 Nm
7—9 ft.lbs.

20—30 Nm
14—22 ft.lbs.

Fig. 19 Stabilizer bar removal/installation — 1990-91 2WD Vista

8. Install the bushings, washer and nut. Torque the self-locking nut so that 0.3-0.4 in. (8-10mm) is between the washer and top of the link bolt.

9. Install the remaining components. Torque the tie rod end nut to 17-25 ft. lbs. (24-34 Nm) and the crossmember bolts to 51 ft. lbs. (70 Nm).

10. Align the front end.

Front End Alignment

CASTER AND CAMBER

Caster and camber are preset at the factory. They require service only if the suspension and steering linkage components are damaged, in which case, repair is accomplished by replacing the damaged part. Caster, however, can be adjusted slightly by moving the strut bar nut.

TOE ADJUSTMENT

Toe-in is the difference in the distance between the front wheels, as measured at both the front and the rear of the front tires.

1. Raise the front of the car so that its front wheels are just clear of the ground.

2. Use a scribing block to hold a piece of chalk at the center of each tire tread while rotating the wheels by hand.

3. Measure the distance between the marked lines at both the front and rear.

➡**Take both measurements at equal distances from the ground.**

4. Toe-in is equal to the difference between the front and rear measurements. This difference should be 2-6mm.

5. Toe-in is adjusted by screwing the tie rod turnbuckle in or out as necessary. Left side toe-in may be reduced by turning the tie rod turnbuckle toward the rear of the car. The turnbuckles should always be tightened or loosened the same amount for both tie rods; the difference in length between the two tie rods should not exceed 5mm. Tighten the locknuts to 36-40 ft. lbs.

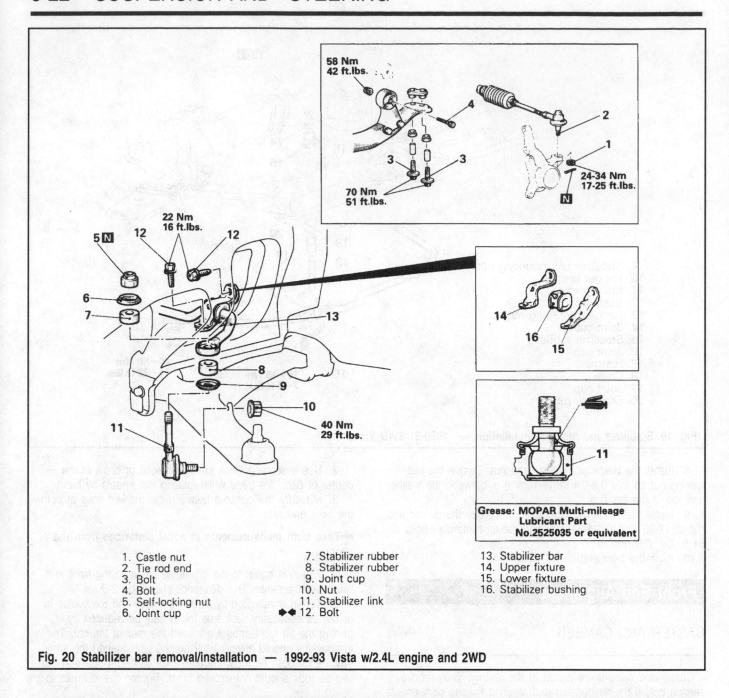

1. Castle nut
2. Tie rod end
3. Bolt
4. Bolt
5. Self-locking nut
6. Joint cup
7. Stabilizer rubber
8. Stabilizer rubber
9. Joint cup
10. Nut
11. Stabilizer link
12. Bolt
13. Stabilizer bar
14. Upper fixture
15. Lower fixture
16. Stabilizer bushing

Fig. 20 Stabilizer bar removal/installation — 1992-93 Vista w/2.4L engine and 2WD

REAR SUSPENSION

▶ **See Figures 21, 22, 23 and 24**

Coil Springs

REMOVAL & INSTALLATION

1990-91 2WD Vista

1. Raise the vehicle and support it safely. Allow the rear wheels to hang.
2. Place a suitable jack under the rear axle and remove the bottom bolts or nuts of the shock absorbers.

3. Lower the rear axle and remove the left and right coil springs.
4. Installation is the reverse order of the removal procedure.

➡**When installing the spring, pay attention to the difference in shape between the upper and lower spring seats.**

1992-93 Vista

1. Remove the rear stabilizer bar.
2. Using a jack, support the lower arm. Remove the rear shock absorber.

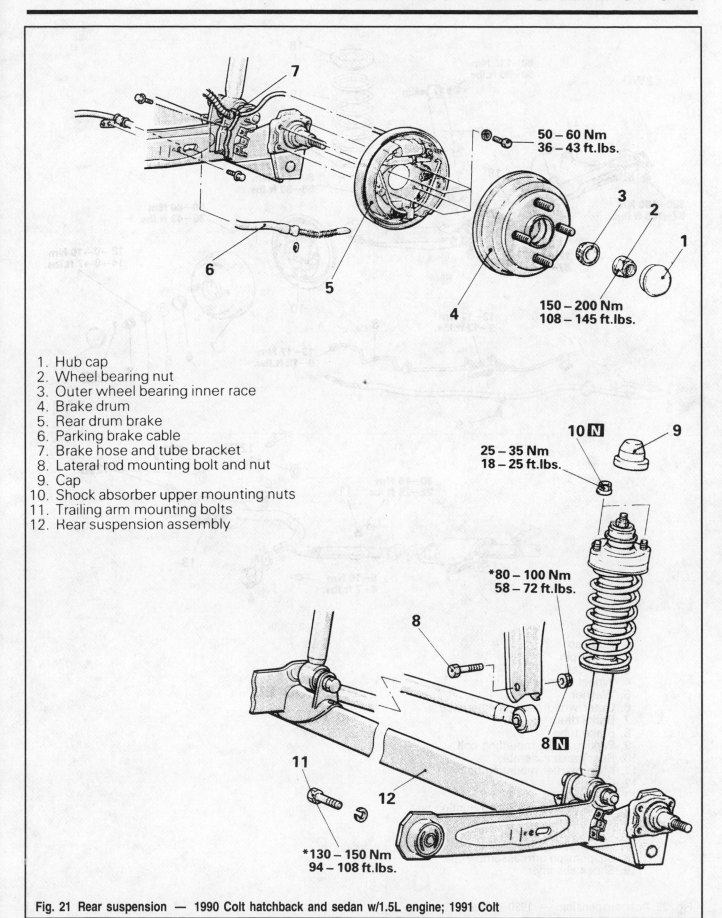

50 – 60 Nm
36 – 43 ft.lbs.

150 – 200 Nm
108 – 145 ft.lbs.

1. Hub cap
2. Wheel bearing nut
3. Outer wheel bearing inner race
4. Brake drum
5. Rear drum brake
6. Parking brake cable
7. Brake hose and tube bracket
8. Lateral rod mounting bolt and nut
9. Cap
10. Shock absorber upper mounting nuts
11. Trailing arm mounting bolts
12. Rear suspension assembly

25 – 35 Nm
18 – 25 ft.lbs.

*80 – 100 Nm
58 – 72 ft.lbs.

*130 – 150 Nm
94 – 108 ft.lbs.

Fig. 21 Rear suspension — 1990 Colt hatchback and sedan w/1.5L engine; 1991 Colt

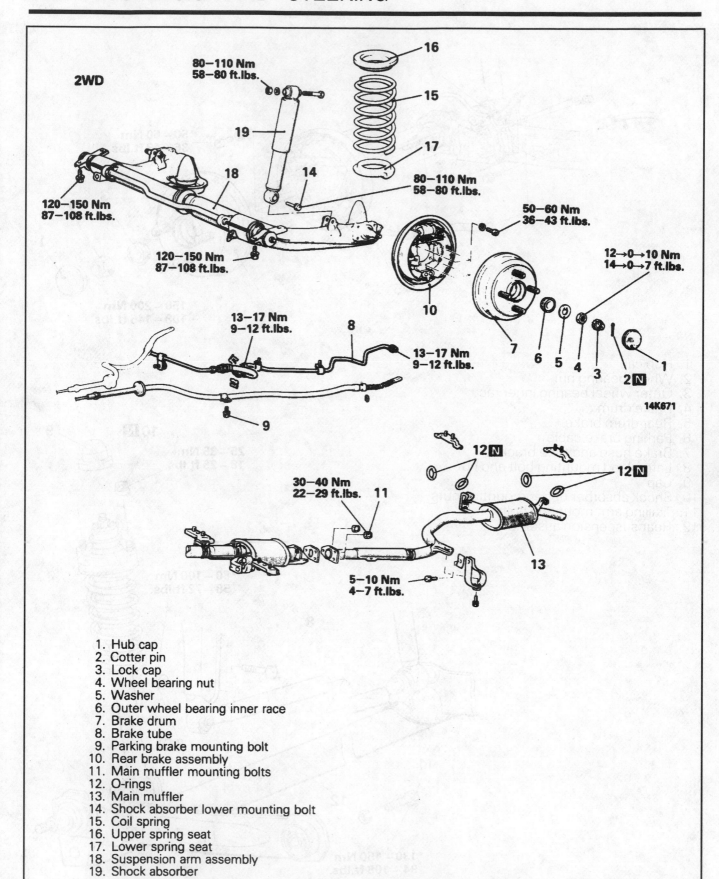

2WD

80–110 Nm
58–80 ft.lbs.

16

15

17

80–110 Nm
58–80 ft.lbs.

19

14

18

120–150 Nm
87–108 ft.lbs.

120–150 Nm
87–108 ft.lbs.

50–60 Nm
36–43 ft.lbs.

12→0→10 Nm
14→0→7 ft.lbs.

10

7   6   5   4   3   2 N   1

13–17 Nm
9–12 ft.lbs.

8

13–17 Nm
9–12 ft.lbs.

9

14K671

12 N

12 N

30–40 Nm
22–29 ft.lbs.   11

13

5–10 Nm
4–7 ft.lbs.

1. Hub cap
2. Cotter pin
3. Lock cap
4. Wheel bearing nut
5. Washer
6. Outer wheel bearing inner race
7. Brake drum
8. Brake tube
9. Parking brake mounting bolt
10. Rear brake assembly
11. Main muffler mounting bolts
12. O-rings
13. Main muffler
14. Shock absorber lower mounting bolt
15. Coil spring
16. Upper spring seat
17. Lower spring seat
18. Suspension arm assembly
19. Shock absorber

Fig. 22 Rear suspension — 1990-91 Vista

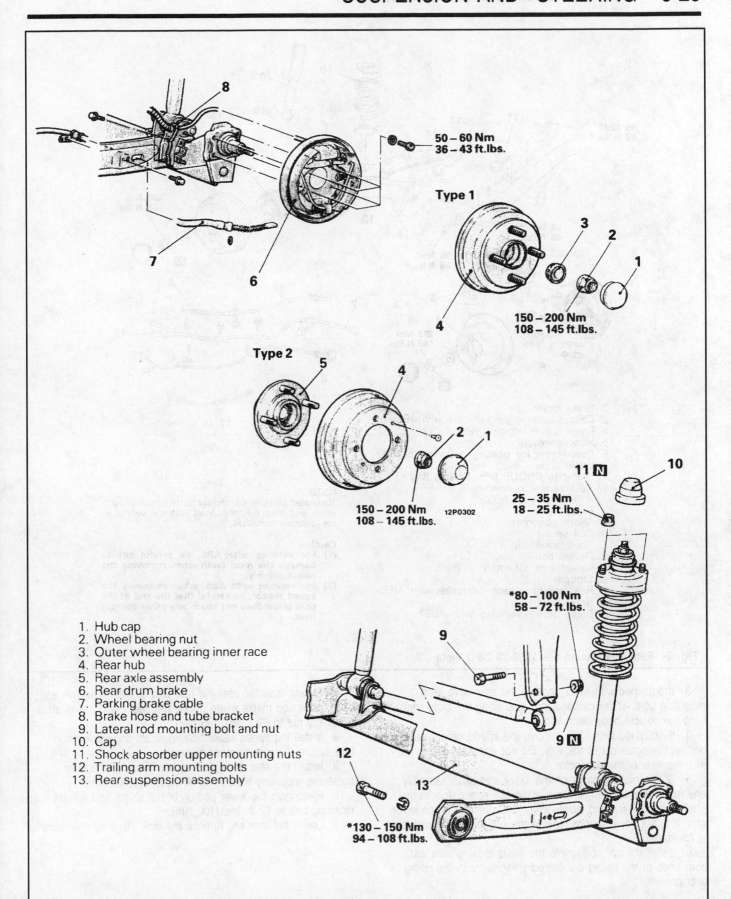

Type 1

50 – 60 Nm
36 – 43 ft.lbs.

150 – 200 Nm
108 – 145 ft.lbs.

Type 2

150 – 200 Nm
108 – 145 ft.lbs.

12P0302

25 – 35 Nm
18 – 25 ft.lbs.

*80 – 100 Nm
58 – 72 ft.lbs.

*130 – 150 Nm
94 – 108 ft.lbs.

1. Hub cap
2. Wheel bearing nut
3. Outer wheel bearing inner race
4. Rear hub
5. Rear axle assembly
6. Rear drum brake
7. Parking brake cable
8. Brake hose and tube bracket
9. Lateral rod mounting bolt and nut
10. Cap
11. Shock absorber upper mounting nuts
12. Trailing arm mounting bolts
13. Rear suspension assembly

Fig. 23 Rear suspension — 1992 Colt hatchback and sedan

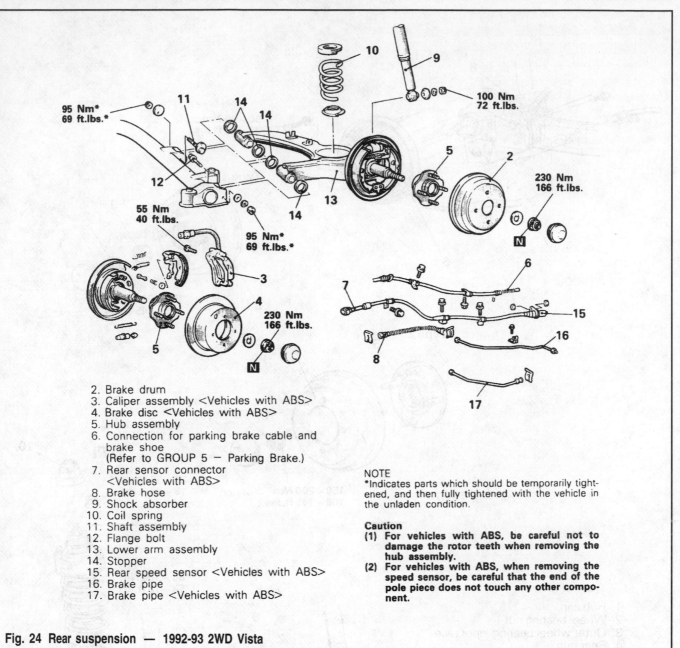

2. Brake drum
3. Caliper assembly <Vehicles with ABS>
4. Brake disc <Vehicles with ABS>
5. Hub assembly
6. Connection for parking brake cable and brake shoe
   (Refer to GROUP 5 – Parking Brake.)
7. Rear sensor connector <Vehicles with ABS>
8. Brake hose
9. Shock absorber
10. Coil spring
11. Shaft assembly
12. Flange bolt
13. Lower arm assembly
14. Stopper
15. Rear speed sensor <Vehicles with ABS>
16. Brake pipe
17. Brake pipe <Vehicles with ABS>

NOTE
*Indicates parts which should be temporarily tightened, and then fully tightened with the vehicle in the unladen condition.

Caution
(1) For vehicles with ABS, be careful not to damage the rotor teeth when removing the hub assembly.
(2) For vehicles with ABS, when removing the speed sensor, be careful that the end of the pole piece does not touch any other component.

Fig. 24 Rear suspension — 1992-93 2WD Vista

3. If equipped with 4WD, remove the rear drive shaft mounting bolts at the carrier flange and hang the drive shaft from the vehicle body using wire.

4. If equipped with ABS, remove the speed sensor clamp bolt and relocate out of the way. Do not apply tension to the wire harness of the connector.

5. Scribe mating marks on the lower arm shaft assembly and the crossmember. To remove the coil spring, loosen the shaft assembly nut and slowly lower the rear end of the lower arm. It is not necessary to remove the nut, only to loosen it.

To install:

6. Install the coil spring into the seats making sure that both ends of the spring are correctly aligned with the spring seat groove.

7. Slowly raise the rear the rear end of the lower arm and align the scribe marks made during disassembly. Tighten shaft assembly nut to 69 ft. lbs. (95 Nm).

8. Install the speed sensor clamp to its' original location and secure the wire harness making.

9. Install the rear drive shaft to the flange and secure tightening mounting bolts to 40-47 ft. lbs. (55-65 Nm).

10. Reconnect the lower portion of the shock and tighten the retaining bolt to 72 ft. lbs. (100 Nm).

11. Lower the arm and remove the jack. Align all 4 wheels.

MacPherson Strut

✳✳CAUTION

The MacPherson strut spring is under extreme pressure. Do not remove the center strut shaft nut without having the strut assembly in an approved MacPherson strut spring compressor. Severe personal injury may result if this caution is not followed.

REMOVAL & INSTALLATION

Colt

1. Raise the vehicle and support it safely. Allow the lower arms and suspension to hang. Remove the wheels.
2. Raise the axle slightly to relax the strut and to support the axle when the strut is removed. Position an additional support under the axle.
3. Take care in jacking that no contact is made on the lateral rod.
4. On hatchback, remove the trunk side trim.
5. Remove the upper dust cover cap.
6. Remove the upper mounting nuts. Remove the lower mounting bolt and nut.
7. Remove the strut from the vehicle.
8. Remove the dust cover.
9. Install a MacPherson strut spring compressor and compress the spring. Compress the spring so that the maximum length will be obtained.
10. Remove the shaft nut, strut insulator, upper spring seat and spring with the compressor installed.

To install:

11. Install the spring (with compressor), upper spring seat, insulator and shaft nut. Line up the spring end with the holes in the spring seats. Torque the shaft nut to 43-51 ft. lbs. (60-70 Nm). Remove the spring compressor.
12. Installation is the reverse order of the removal procedures. Torque the lower mounting bolt and nut to 58-72 ft. lbs. (79-98 Nm); the upper mounting nuts to 18-25 ft. lbs. (24-34 Nm).

Torsion Bar and Control Arms

▶ **See Figures 25, 26, 27, 28, 29, 30, 31, 32, 33, 34, 35 and 36**

Instead of springs, the 1990-91 4WD Vista uses transversely mounted torsion bars housed inside the rear crossmember, attached to which are inner and outer control arms. Conventional style shock absorbers are mounted on the inner arms.

REMOVAL & INSTALLATION

1. Raise and support the car with jackstands under the frame.
2. Remove the differential.
3. Remove the intermediate shafts and axleshafts.

4. Remove the rear brake assemblies.
5. Disconnect the brake lines and parking brake cables from the inner arms.
6. Remove the main muffler.
7. Raise the inner arms slightly with a floor jack and disconnect the shock absorbers.
8. Matchmark, precisely, the upper ends of the outer arms, the torsion bar ends and the top of the crossmember bracket and remove the inner and outer arm attaching bolts.
9. Remove the extension rods fixtures attaching bolts.
10. Remove the crossmember attaching bolts and remove the rear suspension assembly from the car.
11. Unbolt and remove the damper from the crossmember.
12. Remove the front and rear insulators from both ends of the crossmember.
13. Loosen, but do not remove, the lockbolts securing the outer arm bushings at both ends of the crossmember.
14. Pull the outer arm from the crossmember. Many times, the torsion bar will slide out of the crossmember with the outer arm.
15. Remove the torsion bar from either the crossmember or outer arm.
16. Inspect all parts for wear or damage. Inspect the crossmember for bending or deformation.
17. Inner arm bushings may be replaced at this time using a press. The thicker end of the bushings goes on the inner side.
18. Prior to installation note that the torsion bars are marked with an L or R on the outer end, and are not interchangeable.
19. If the original torsion bars are being installed, align the identification marks on the torsion bar end, crossmember and outer arm, install the torsion bar and arm and tighten the lockbolts. Skip Step 20. If new torsion bars are being installed, proceed to Step 20.
20. A special alignment jig must be fabricated. See the accompanying illustration for the dimension needed to make this jig. The jig is bolted to the rear insulator hole on the crossmember bracket as shown. Install the crossmember bracket as shown. Install the crossmember and inner arms. Insert the torsion bar into the outer arm, aligning the red identification mark on the torsion bar end with the matchmark made on the outer arm top side. Install the torsion bar and arm so that the center of the flanged bolt hole on the arm is 32mm below the lower marking line on the jig. Then, pull the outer arm off of the torsion bar, leaving the bar undisturbed in the crossmember. Reposition the arm on the torsion bar, one serration counterclockwise from its former position. This will make the previously measured dimension, 33mm above the lower line. In any event, when the outer arm and torsion bar are properly positioned, the marking lines on the jig will run diagonally across the center of the toe-in adjustment hole as shown. When the adjustment is complete, tighten the lockbolts. The clearance between the outer arm and the crossmember bracket, at the torsion bar, should be 5.0-7.0 mm.
21. Complete the remainder of the component parts installation. Observe the following torques:
    - Extension Rod Fixture bolts: 45-50 ft. lbs.
    - Extension Rod to Fixture nut: 95-100 ft. lbs.
    - Shock Absorber lower bolt: 75-80 ft. lbs.
    - Outer Arm attaching bolts: 65-70 ft. lbs.
    - Toe-In bolt: 95-100 ft. lbs.
    - Lockbolts: 20-22 ft. lbs.

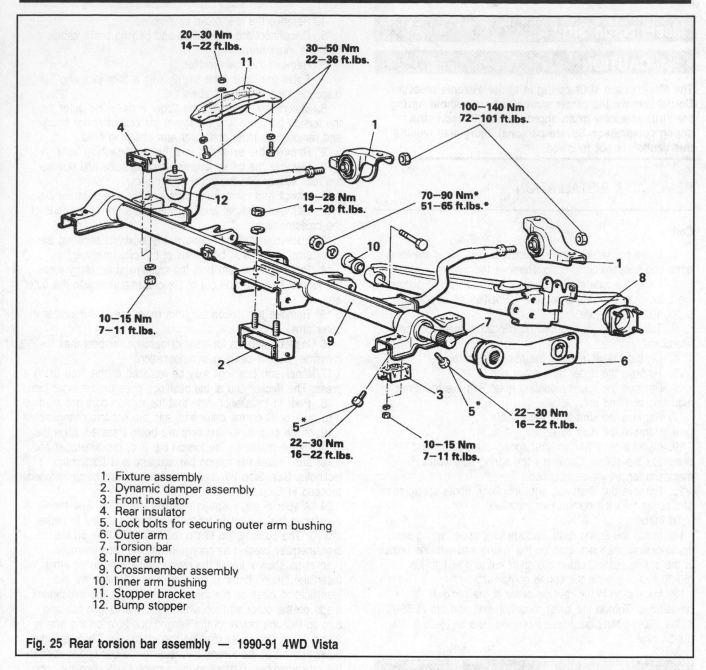

20—30 Nm
14—22 ft.lbs.

30—50 Nm
22—36 ft.lbs.

100—140 Nm
72—101 ft.lbs.

19—28 Nm
14—20 ft.lbs.

70—90 Nm*
51—65 ft.lbs.*

10—15 Nm
7—11 ft.lbs.

22—30 Nm
16—22 ft.lbs.

22—30 Nm
16—22 ft.lbs.

10—15 Nm
7—11 ft.lbs.

1. Fixture assembly
2. Dynamic damper assembly
3. Front insulator
4. Rear insulator
5. Lock bolts for securing outer arm bushing
6. Outer arm
7. Torsion bar
8. Inner arm
9. Crossmember assembly
10. Inner arm bushing
11. Stopper bracket
12. Bump stopper

Fig. 25 Rear torsion bar assembly — 1990-91 4WD Vista

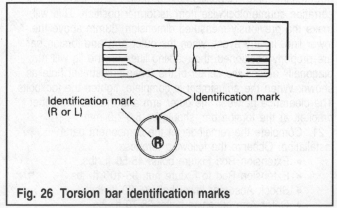

Identification mark
(R or L)

Identification mark

Fig. 26 Torsion bar identification marks

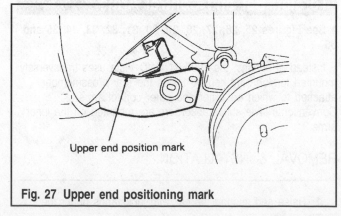

Upper end position mark

Fig. 27 Upper end positioning mark

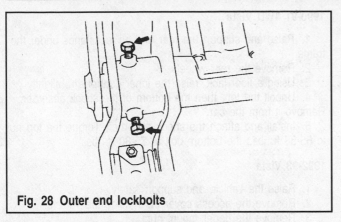

Fig. 28 Outer end lockbolts

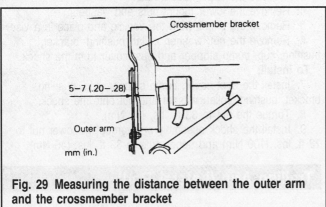

Fig. 29 Measuring the distance between the outer arm and the crossmember bracket

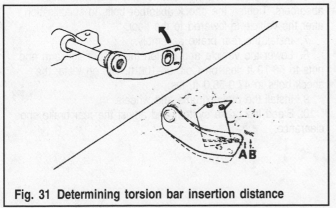

12K103

Lower side marking line

Fig. 30 Determining torsion bar insertion distance

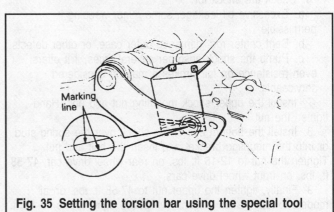

Fig. 31 Determining torsion bar insertion distance

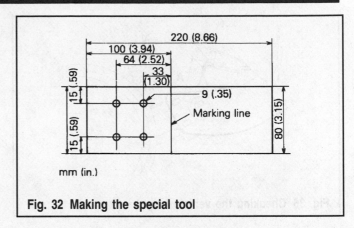

mm (in.)

Fig. 32 Making the special tool

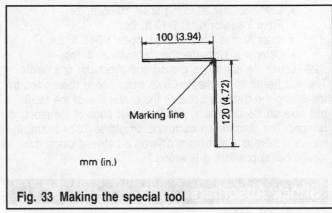

mm (in.)

Fig. 33 Making the special tool

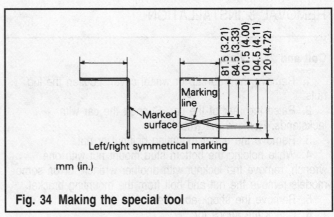

mm (in.)

Fig. 34 Making the special tool

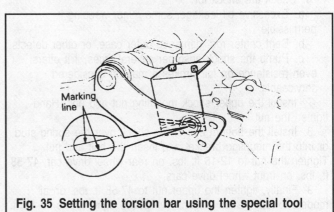

Marking line

Fig. 35 Setting the torsion bar using the special tool

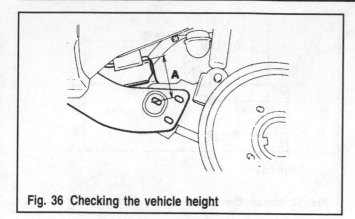

Fig. 36 Checking the vehicle height

- Crossmember attaching bolts: 80-85 ft. lbs.
- Front Insulator nuts: 7-10 ft. lbs.
- Inner Arm to Crossmember bolts: 60-65 ft. lbs.
- Damper-to-Crossmember nuts: 15-20 ft. lbs.

22. Lower the car to the ground and check the ride height. The ride height is checked on both sides and is determined by measuring the distance between the center line of the toe-in bolt hole on the outer arm, and the lower edge of the rebound bumper. The distance on each side should be 102-104mm. If not, or if there is a significant difference between sides, the torsion bar(s) positioning is wrong.

Shock Absorbers

REMOVAL & INSTALLATION

Colt and 2WD Vista

1. Remove the hub cap or wheel cover. Loosen the lug nuts.
2. Raise the rear of the car. Support the car with jackstands. Remove the wheel.
3. Remove the upper mounting bolt/nut or nut.
4. While holding the bottom stud mount nut with one wrench, remove the locknut with another wrench, or on some models remove the nut and bolt from the mounting bracket.
5. Remove the shock absorber.
6. Check the shock for:
   a. Excessive oil leakage, some minor weeping is permissible.
   b. Bent center rod, damaged outer case, or other defects.
   c. Pump the shock absorber several times, if it offers even resistance on full strokes it may be considered serviceable.
7. Install the upper shock mounting nut and bolt. Hand-tighten the nut.
8. Install the bottom eye of the shock over the spring stud or into the mounting bracket and insert the bolt and nut. Tighten the nut to 12-15 ft. lbs. on rear wheel drive car; 47-58 ft. lbs. on front wheel drive cars.
9. Finally, tighten the upper nut to 47-58 ft. lbs. on all models except station wagons, which are tightened to 12-15 ft. lbs.

1990-91 4WD Vista

1. Raise and support the rear end on jackstands under the frame.
2. Remove the rear wheels.
3. Using a floor jack, raise the inner control arm slightly.
4. Unbolt the top, then the bottom of the shock absorber. Remove it from the car.
5. Install and attach the shock absorber. Torque the top nut to 55-58 ft. lbs.; the bottom bolt to 75-80 ft. lbs.

1992-93 Vista

1. Raise the vehicle and support safely.
2. Remove the access cover from inside the vehicle.
3. Remove the upper mount nuts.
4. Remove the lower mount nuts and washers.
5. Remove the shock from the vehicle and place in a vise.
6. Remove the nut, washer, collar, bushing, bracket, bushing, cup, bump stopper and dust cover from the shock.
   To install:
7. Install the dust cover, bump stopper, cup, bushing, bracket, bushing, collar, washer and nut onto the shock.
8. Torque the nut to 33 ft. lbs. (45 Nm).
9. Install the shock assembly and torque the lower nut to 72 ft. lbs. (100 Nm) and upper nuts to 33 ft. lbs. (45 Nm).

Trailing Arm (Lateral Rod)

REMOVAL & INSTALLATION

1. Support the side frame on jack stands and remove the rear wheels. Remove the rear brake assembly.
2. Remove the muffler and jack the control arm just enough to raise it slightly. Disconnect the parking brake cable from the arm.
3. Remove the shock absorber and lower the jack. Remove the coil spring.
4. Disconnect the brake hoses at the rear suspension arms and remove the rear suspension from the body as an assembly.
5. Install the fixture to body bolts and torque to 36-51 ft. lbs. on Colt models; 51-65 ft. lbs. on Vista models.
6. Install the coil springs and loosely install the shock absorbers. Tighten the shock absorber bolts to specification after the vehicle is lowered to the floor.
7. Install the rear brake assembly.
8. Lower the vehicle and tighten the suspension arm end nuts to 56-70 ft. lbs. on Colt; 94-108 ft. lbs. on Vista; the shock bolts to 47.0-58.0 ft. lbs.
9. Install the brake drums and wheels.
10. Bleed the brake system and adjust the rear brake shoe clearance.

Rear Control Arms

REMOVAL & INSTALLATION

1992-93 Vista

1. Disconnect negative battery cable.
2. Remove the rear stabilizer bar.
3. If equipped with 4WD, remove the rear axle shaft.
4. Remove the rear brake drum.
5. If equipped with ABS, remove the rear caliper assembly and brake disc.
6. Remove the rear hub assembly. If equipped with ABS, take care not to damage the rotor teeth during hub removal.
7. Disconnect the parking brake cable from the rear brake shoe.
8. If equipped with ABS, disconnect and remove the rear wheel sensor.

➡**The speed sensor has a pole piece projecting from it. This exposed tip must be protected from impact or scratches. Do not allow the pole piece to contact the toothed wheel during removal or installation.**

9. Remove the rear shock and coil spring.
10. Remove the brake line and parking brake mounting bolts from the lower control arm.
11. Matchmark and remove the inboard lower arm pivot bolt. Remove the flange bolt and the arm from the vehicle.

To install:

12. Install the arm on the vehicle and secure with the flange bolt, temporarily tighten the nut. Install the arm pivot bolt and temporarily tighten the nut.
13. Install the rear shock and coil spring.
14. Install the brake line and parking brake mounting bolts to the lower control arm.
15. Connect the parking brake cable to the rear brake shoe.
16. Install the rear hub assembly.
17. Install the rear brake drum or, if equipped with ABS, install the rear caliper assembly and brake disc.
18. Install the rear axle shaft.
19. Install and connect the rear wheel speed sensor. Use a brass or other non-magnetic feeler gauge to check the air gap between the tip of the pole piece and the toothed wheel. Correct gap is 0.012-0.035 in. (0.3-0.9mm). Tighten the 2 sensor bracket bolts to 10 ft. lbs. (14 Nm) with the sensor located so the gap is the same at several points on the toothed wheel. If the gap is incorrect, it is likely that the toothed wheel is worn or improperly installed.
20. Lower the vehicle and tighten the lower arm flange bolt nut and the arm pivot bolt to 69 ft. lbs. (95 Nm).
21. Install the rear stabilizer bar and reconnect the negative battery cable.
22. Bleed the brake system if any lines where opened. Adjust the parking brake and perform a rear wheel alignment.

Rear Wheel Bearings

REMOVAL, INSPECTION AND INSTALLATION

➡ **NOTE:The Colt and 1992-93 Vista may be equipped with the removable tapered bearings and seal or a non-removable bearing/hub assembly. If the axle shaft is not tapered, the bearing/hub is serviced as an assembly.**

1990-91 2WD Vista

1. Loosen the lug nuts, raise the rear of the car and support it on jackstands. Remove the wheel.
2. Remove the grease cap, cotter pin, nut and washer.
3. Remove the brake drum. While pulling the drum, the outer bearing will fall out. Position your hand to catch it.
4. Pry out the grease seal and discard it.
5. Remove the inner bearing.
6. Check the bearing races. If any scoring, heat checking or damage is noted, they should be replaced.

➡**When bearings or races need replacement, replace them as a set.**

7. Inspect the bearings. If wear or looseness or heat checking is found, replace them.
8. If the bearings and races are to be replaced, drive out the races with a brass drift.
9. Before installing new races, coat them with lithium based wheel bearing grease. The races are most easily installed using a driver made for that purpose. They can, however, be driven into place with a brass drift. Make sure that they are fully seated.
10. Thoroughly pack the bearings with lithium based wheel bearing grease. Pack the hub with grease.
11. Install the inner bearing and coat the lip and rim of the grease seal with grease. Drive the seal into place with a seal driver.
12. Mount the drum onto the hub, slide the outer bearing into place, install the washer and thread the nut into place, finger-tightly.
13. Install a torque wrench on the nut. While turning the drum by hand, tighten the nut to 15 ft. lbs. Back off the nut until it is loose, then tighten it to 4 ft. lbs. If your torque wrench is not all that accurate below 10 ft. lbs. (most aren't), use an inch lbs. torque wrench and tighten the nut to 48 inch lbs.
14. Install the lock cap and insert a new cotter pin. If the lock cap and hole don't align, and repositioning the cap can't accomplish alignment, back off the nut no more than 15 degrees. If that won't align the holes either, try the adjustment procedure over again.

1992-93 2WD Vista
▶ See Figure 37

1. Raise the vehicle and support safely. Remove the tire and wheel assembly.

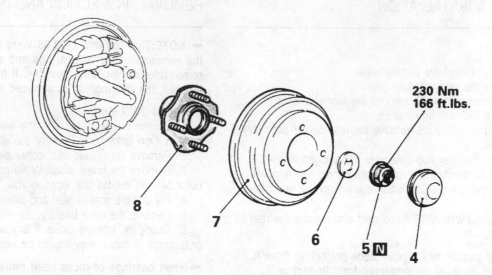

<Vehicles without ABS>

230 Nm
166 ft.lbs.

8   7   6   5 Ⓝ   4

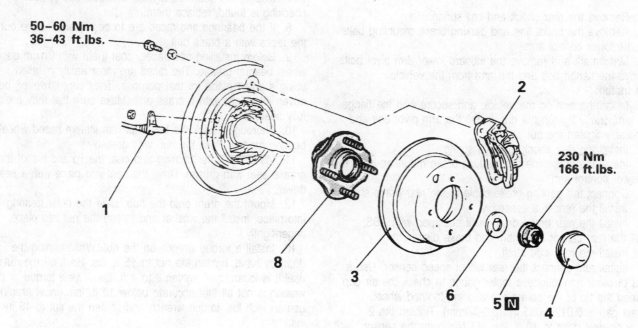

<Vehicles with ABS>

50–60 Nm
36–43 ft.lbs.

1   8   3   6   5 Ⓝ   4

2

230 Nm
166 ft.lbs.

1. Rear speed sensor ⎫
2. Caliper assembly   ⎬ <Vehicles with ABS>
3. Brake disc   ⎭
4. Hub cap
5. Flange nut
6. Tongued washer
7. Brake drum <Vehicles without ABS>
8. Rear hub assembly

Caution
The rear hub unit bearing should not be dismantled.
Care must be taken not to scratch or otherwise damage the teeth of the rotor. The rotor must never be dropped. If the teeth of the rotor are chipped, resulting in a deformation of the rotor, it will not be able to accurately detect the wheel rotation speed, and the system will not function normally.

Fig. 37 Rear wheel bearing — 1992-93 2WD Vista

2. If equipped with ABS, remove the caliper assembly, brake disc and rear wheel speed sensor from the adapter. If not equipped with ABS, remove the brake drum.

➡ **The speed sensor has a pole piece projecting from it. This exposed tip must be protected from impact or scratches. Do not allow the pole piece to contact the toothed wheel during removal or installation.**

3. Remove the dust cap, nut and washer. Do not use an air gun to remove the nut.

4. Remove the rear hub assembly taking care not to scrape or damage the teeth of the speed rotor, if equipped.

5. Inspect the hub unit bearing for wear or damage. If replacement of the bearing is required, the hub assembly and bearing is to be replaced as a unit. The rear hub unit bearing assembly should should not be dismantled.

To install:

6. Installation is the reverse of the removal procedure. Install the drum and/or hub to the vehicle. Lubricate and install the outer wheel bearing to the spindle. Torque the self-locking nut to 166 ft. lbs. (230 Nm). Stake the nut.

7. If equipped with ABS: insert a feeler gauge into the space between the speed sensor's pole piece and the toothed surface. Tighten the speed sensor at the position where the clearance at all places is 0.008-0.028 in. (0.2-0.7mm).

Colt

▶ **See Figures 38, 39 and 40**

➡**Special tools are needed for this procedure.**

1. Loosen the lug nuts. Raise the rear of the car and support it on jackstands.

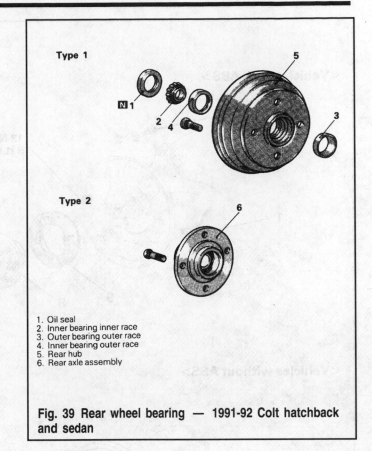

Type 1

Type 2

1. Oil seal
2. Inner bearing inner race
3. Outer bearing outer race
4. Inner bearing outer race
5. Rear hub
6. Rear axle assembly

Fig. 39 Rear wheel bearing — 1991-92 Colt hatchback and sedan

2. Remove the wheel.
3. Remove the grease cap.

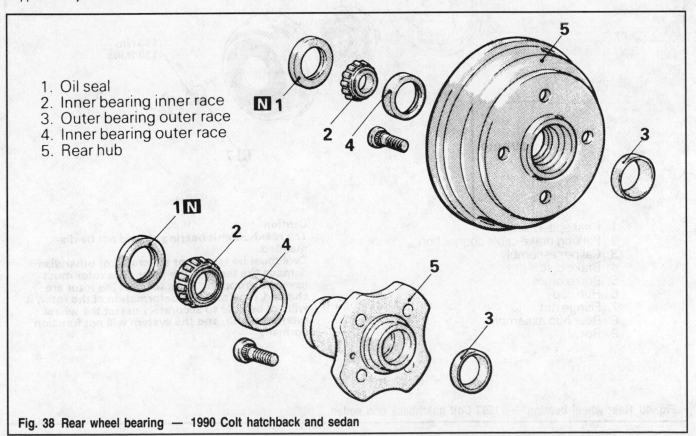

1. Oil seal
2. Inner bearing inner race
3. Outer bearing outer race
4. Inner bearing outer race
5. Rear hub

Fig. 38 Rear wheel bearing — 1990 Colt hatchback and sedan

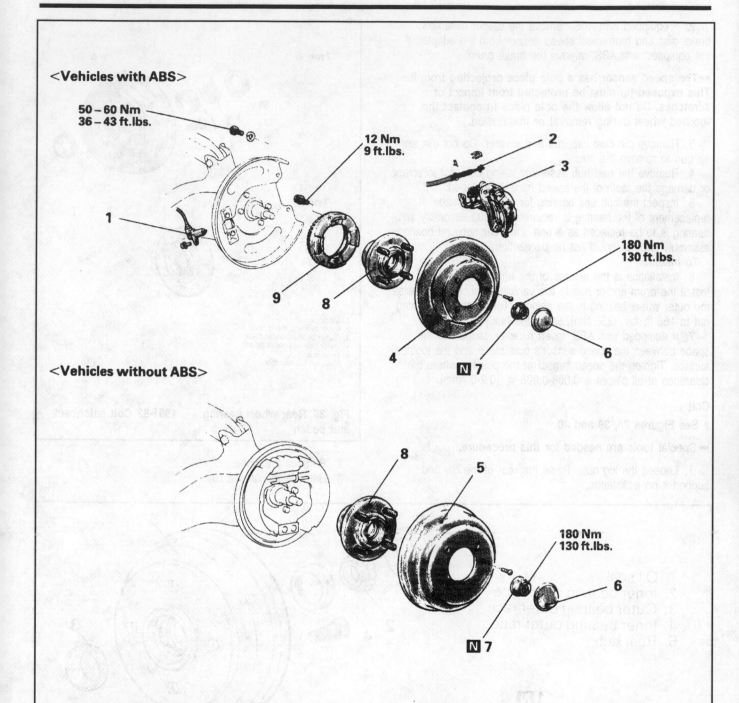

<Vehicles with ABS>

50 – 60 Nm
36 – 43 ft.lbs.

12 Nm
9 ft.lbs.

180 Nm
130 ft.lbs.

<Vehicles without ABS>

180 Nm
130 ft.lbs.

1. Rear speed sensor
2. Parking brake cable connection
3. Caliper assembly
4. Brake disc
5. Brake drum
6. Hub cap
7. Flange nut
8. Rear hub assembly
9. Rotor

Caution
The rear hub unit bearing should not be dismantled.
Care must be taken not to scratch or otherwise damage the teeth of the rotor. The rotor must never be dropped. If the teeth of the rotor are chipped, resulting in a deformation of the rotor, it will not be able to accurately detect the wheel rotation speed, and the system will not function normally.

Fig. 40 Rear wheel bearing — 1993 Colt hatchback and sedan

4. Remove the nut.

5. Pull the drum off. The outer bearing will fall out while the drum is coming off, so position your hand to catch it.

6. Pry out the oil seal. Discard it.

7. Remove the inner bearing.

8. Check the bearing races. If any scoring, heat checking or damage is noted, they should be replaced.

➡**When bearings or races need replacement, replace them as a set.**

9. Inspect the bearings. If wear or looseness or heat checking is found, replace them.

10. If the bearings and races are to be replaced, drive out the races with a brass drift.

11. Before installing new races, coat them with lithium based wheel bearing grease. The races are most easily installed using a driver made for that purpose. They can, however, be driven into place with a brass drift. Make sure that they are fully seated.

12. Thoroughly pack the bearings with lithium based wheel bearing grease. Pack the hub with grease.

13. Install the inner bearing and coat the lip and rim of the grease seal with grease.Drive the seal into place with a seal driver.

14. Mount the drum on the axleshaft. Install the outer bearing. Don't install the nut at this point.

15. Using a pull scale attached to one of the lugs, measure the starting force necessary to get the drum to turn. Starting force should be 5 lbs. If the starting torque is greater than specified, replace the bearings.

16. Install the nut on the axleshaft. Thread the nut on, by hand, to a point at which the back face of the nut is 2-3mm from the shoulder of the shaft (where the threads end).

17. Using an inch lbs. torque wrench, turn the nut counterclockwise 2 to 3 turns, noting the average force needed during the turning procedure. Turning torque for the nut should be above 48 inch lbs. If turning torque is not within 5 inch lbs., either way, replace the nut.

18. Tighten the nut to 75-110 ft. lbs.

19. Using a stand-mounted gauge, check the axial play of the wheel bearings. Play should be less than 0.2mm. If play cannot be brought within that figure, you probably have assembled the unit incorrectly.

20. Pack the grease cap with wheel bearing grease and install it.

ADJUSTMENT

Removable Bearings

COLT

1. Raise the vehicle and support it safely. Remove the rear wheel and wheel bearing cap.

2. Using an inch lb. torque wrench, turn the nut counterclockwise 2-3 turns, noting the average force needed during the turning procedure. Turning torque for the nut should be about 48 inch lbs. (5.4 Nm). If turning torque is not within 5 inch lbs. (0.5 Nm), either way, replace the nut.

3. Tighten the nut to 108-145 ft. lbs. (150-200 Nm) on 1989-93 vehicles.

4. Using a stand mounted gauge, check the axial play of the wheel bearings. Play should be less than 0.0079 in. (0.2007mm). If play cannot be brought within that figure, the unit is assembled incorrectly.

5. Pack the grease cap with wheel bearing grease and install it.

Non-Removable Bearings

Install the drum and/or hub to the vehicle. Lubricate and install the outer wheel bearing to the spindle. Torque the self-locking nut to 108-145 ft. lbs. (150-200 Nm). Stake the nut. Fill the cap with wheel bearings grease and install.

1990-91 2WD VISTA

1. Raise the vehicle and support it safely. Remove the rear wheel, wheel bearing cap and cotter pin.

2. Install a torque wrench on the nut. While turning the drum by hand, tighten the nut to 15 ft. lbs. (20 Nm). Back off the nut until it is loose, then tighten it to 7 ft. lbs. (9 Nm).

3. Install the lock cap and insert a new cotter pin. If the lock cap and hole don't align and repositioning the cap can't accomplish alignment, back off the nut no more than 15 degrees. If that won't align the holes either, try the adjustment procedure over again.

1992-93 2WD VISTA

Install the drum and/or hub to the vehicle. Lubricate and install the outer wheel bearing to the spindle. Torque the self-locking nut to 166 ft. lbs. (230 Nm). Stake the nut. Fill the cap with wheel bearing grease and install.

STEERING

Steering Wheel

REMOVAL & INSTALLATION

▶ **See Figures 41, 42 and 43**

1. Disconnect the battery ground cable. Remove the center pad retaining screws located on the back of the wheel on some models, or pull off the horn pad using steady pressure.

2. Paint or chalk matchmarks on the steering shaft and the steering wheel so that they can be correctly reinstalled.

3. Unscrew the hub nut and, using a puller, remove the steering wheel.

➡**Don't hammer or otherwise pound on the steering column, as it is collapsible.**

4. Align the matchmarks and install the steering wheel. Torque the nut to 30 ft. lbs. Install the horn pad and connect the battery cable.

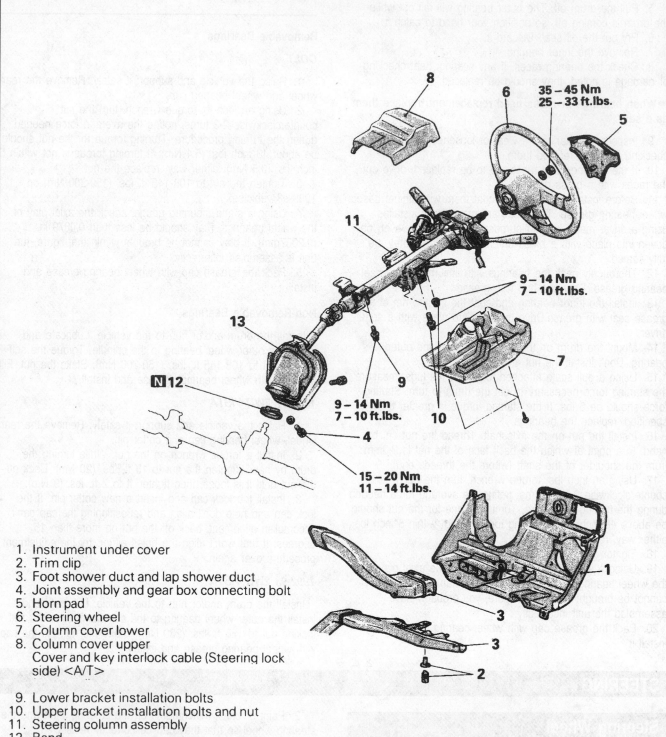

1. Instrument under cover
2. Trim clip
3. Foot shower duct and lap shower duct
4. Joint assembly and gear box connecting bolt
5. Horn pad
6. Steering wheel
7. Column cover lower
8. Column cover upper
   Cover and key interlock cable (Steering lock side) <A/T>

9. Lower bracket installation bolts
10. Upper bracket installation bolts and nut
11. Steering column assembly
12. Band
    Cable clip <A/T>
    Transaxle Control)
13. Steering joint cover

35 – 45 Nm
25 – 33 ft.lbs.

9 – 14 Nm
7 – 10 ft.lbs.

9 – 14 Nm
7 – 10 ft.lbs.

15 – 20 Nm
11 – 14 ft.lbs.

Fig. 41 Steering column and related parts — 1990-92 Colt hatchback and sedan

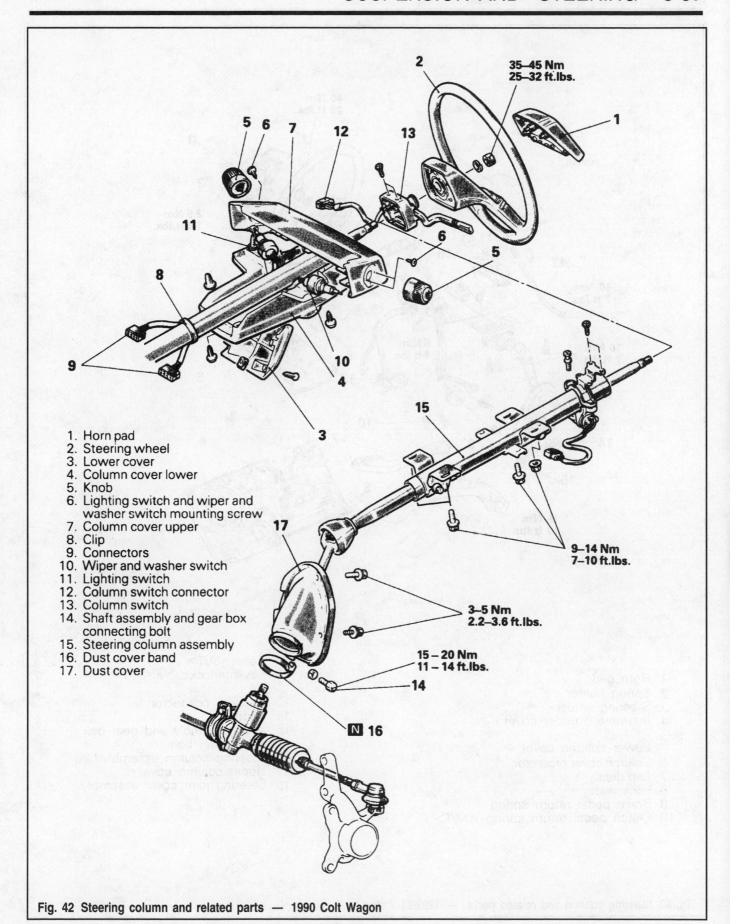

1. Horn pad
2. Steering wheel
3. Lower cover
4. Column cover lower
5. Knob
6. Lighting switch and wiper and
   washer switch mounting screw
7. Column cover upper
8. Clip
9. Connectors
10. Wiper and washer switch
11. Lighting switch
12. Column switch connector
13. Column switch
14. Shaft assembly and gear box
    connecting bolt
15. Steering column assembly
16. Dust cover band
17. Dust cover

35—45 Nm
25—32 ft.lbs.

9—14 Nm
7—10 ft.lbs.

3—5 Nm
2.2—3.6 ft.lbs.

15 — 20 Nm
11 — 14 ft.lbs.

Fig. 42 Steering column and related parts — 1990 Colt Wagon

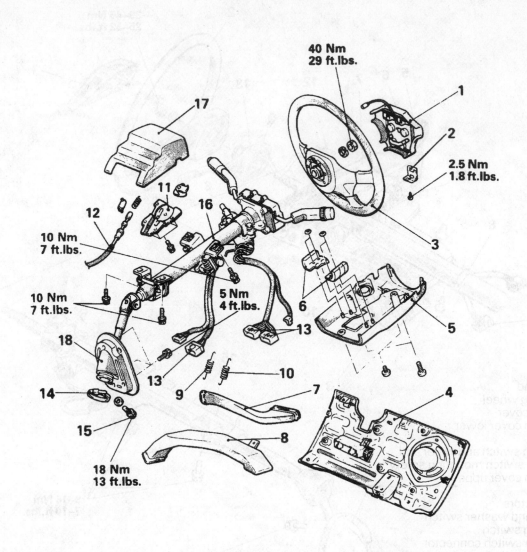

40 Nm
29 ft.lbs.

2.5 Nm
1.8 ft.lbs.

10 Nm
7 ft.lbs.

10 Nm
7 ft.lbs.

5 Nm
4 ft.lbs.

18 Nm
13 ft.lbs.

1. Horn pad
2. Spring holder
3. Steering wheel
4. Instrument under cover

5. Lower column cover
6. Column cover protector
7. Lap duct
8. Foot duct
9. Brake pedal return spring
10. Clutch pedal return spring <M/T>

11. Cover <A/T>
12. Key-interlock cable <A/T>

13. Harness connector
14. Band
15. Joint assembly and gear box
    connecting bolt
16. Steering column assembly
17. Upper column cover
18. Steering joint cover assembly

Fig. 43 Steering column and related parts — 1992-93 Vista

Turn Signal and Flasher Switch

▶ **See Figures 44 and 45**

REMOVAL & INSTALLATION

1. Remove the steering wheel.
2. Remove the lap heater duct.
3. Remove the column covers.
4. Remove the switch retaining screws, disconnect the wiring and remove the switch.
5. Install the switch. Connect the wiring. Install the column covers, heater duct and steering wheel.

Ignition Switch/Steering Lock

REMOVAL & INSTALLATION

1. Remove the turn signal switch as described above.
2. Disconnect the electrical wiring to the switch.
3. Drill out the shear bolts or cut a slot in the mounting screw heads and bracket with a hack saw and remove with a flat blade screwdriver.

➡**Use new screws and bracket when installing the switch.**

4. Remove the switch.
5. Align the column tube hole with the wheel lock guide dowel for initial assembly.

6. Insert the ignition key to make sure that the lock functions correctly.
7. Install the shear bolts. Tighten them evenly until the heads break off.
8. Complete the installation of the removed components.

Steering Column

Removal and Installation

1. Disconnect the negative battery cable. Remove the steering wheel.
2. Remove the lower column trim cover and the upper column trim cover.
3. Disconnect the light switch, wiper and washer washer switch harness connectors.
4. Matchmark the shaft and yoke. Remove shaft-to-gear retaining bolts and disconnect the shaft at the steering gear.
5. Remove both upper and lower steering column mounting bolts and remove the steering column from the vehicle.
   To install:
6. Lower the steering column through the firewall and connect the steering column to the steering gear. Install the retaining bolt. Do not tighten at this time.
7. Install both upper and lower steering column mounting bolts. Torque the mounting bolts to 7-10 ft. lbs. (9-14 Nm). Torque the column-to-steering gear bolt to 13 ft. lbs. (18 Nm).
8. Install the light switch and wiper and washer washer switch. Connect the harness connectors.
9. Install the upper column trim cover and the lower column trim cover.

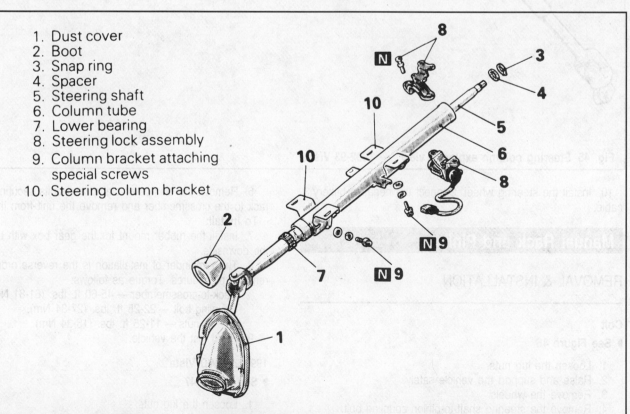

1. Dust cover
2. Boot
3. Snap ring
4. Spacer
5. Steering shaft
6. Column tube
7. Lower bearing
8. Steering lock assembly
9. Column bracket attaching special screws
10. Steering column bracket

Fig. 44 Steering column exploded view — 1990 Colt Wagon

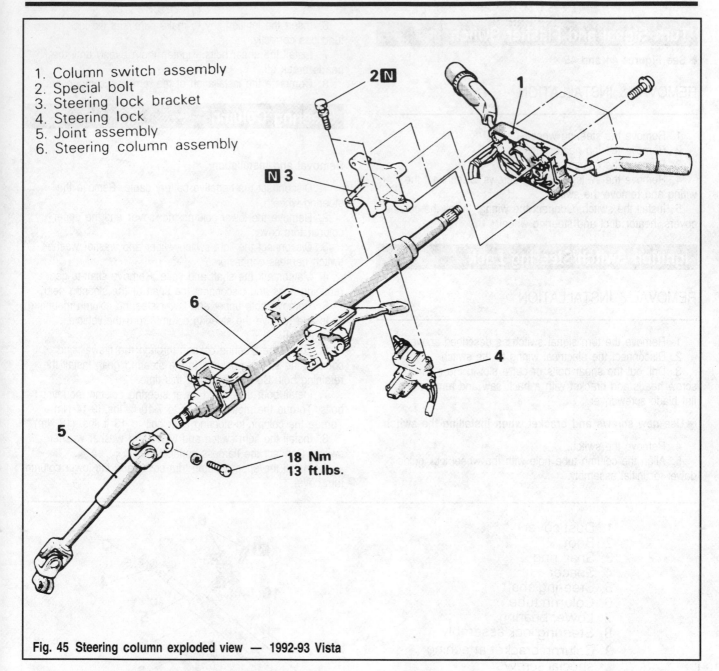

1. Column switch assembly
2. Special bolt
3. Steering lock bracket
4. Steering lock
5. Joint assembly
6. Steering column assembly

18 Nm
13 ft.lbs.

Fig. 45 Steering column exploded view — 1992-93 Vista

10. Install the steering wheel. Connect the negative battery cable.

Manual Rack and Pinion

REMOVAL & INSTALLATION

Colt

▶ **See Figure 46**

1. Loosen the lug nuts.
2. Raise and support the vehicle safely.
3. Remove the wheels.
4. Remove the steering shaft-to-pinion coupling bolt.
5. Disconnect the tie rod ends with a separator.

6. Remove the clamps or clamp and bolts securing the rack to the crossmember and remove the unit from the vehicle.
To install:
7. Install the rubber mount for the gear box with the slit on the downside.
8. The remainder of installation is the reverse order of the removal procedures. Torque as follows:
    Rack-to-crossmember — 45-60 ft. lbs. (61-81 Nm).
    Coupling bolt — 22-25 ft. lbs. (27-34 Nm).
    Tie-rod nuts — 11-25 ft. lbs. (15-34 Nm).
9. Road test the vehicle.

1990-91 2WD Vista

▶ **See Figure 47**

1. Loosen the lug nuts.
2. Raise and support the vehicle safely.

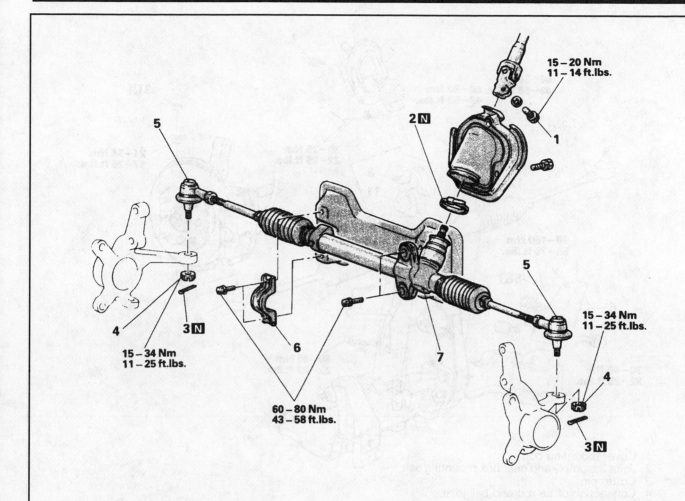

1. Joint assembly and gear box connecting bolt
2. Band
3. Split pin
4. Tie rod end and knuckle connecting nuts
5. Tie rod end
6. End housing clamp
7. Gear box assembly

Fig. 46 Manual rack and pinion assembly removal/installation — 1990-92 Colt hatchback and sedan

3. Remove the wheels.
4. Remove the steering shaft-to-pinion coupling bolt.
5. Disconnect the tie rod ends with a separator.
6. Remove the crossmember support bracket from the crossmember on the right side of the vehicle.
7. Remove the rear roll stopper-to-center member bolt and move the rear roll stopper forward.
8. Unbolt the rack from the crossmember.

➡**The rack is most easily removed using a ratchet and long extension, working from the engine compartment side.**

9. Pull the rack out the right side of the vehicle. Pull it slowly to avoid damage.

To install:

10. Installation is the reverse order of the removal procedures. Torque the rack clamp bolts to 43-58 ft. lbs.

(58-79 Nm), the tie rod nuts to 17-25 ft. lbs. (25-34 Nm) and the coupling bolt to 22-25 ft. lbs. (27-34 Nm). Fill the system and road test the vehicle.

1990-91 4WD Vista

1. Remove the steering column.
2. Raise and support the vehicle safely.
3. Remove the front wheels.
4. Using a separator, disconnect the tie rod from the knuckle.
5. Disconnect the steering shaft joint at the rack.
6. Remove the air cleaner.
7. Remove the rack attaching bolts from the rear of the No. 2 crossmember. The bolts are most easily accessed using a long extension and working from the top of the engine compartment.

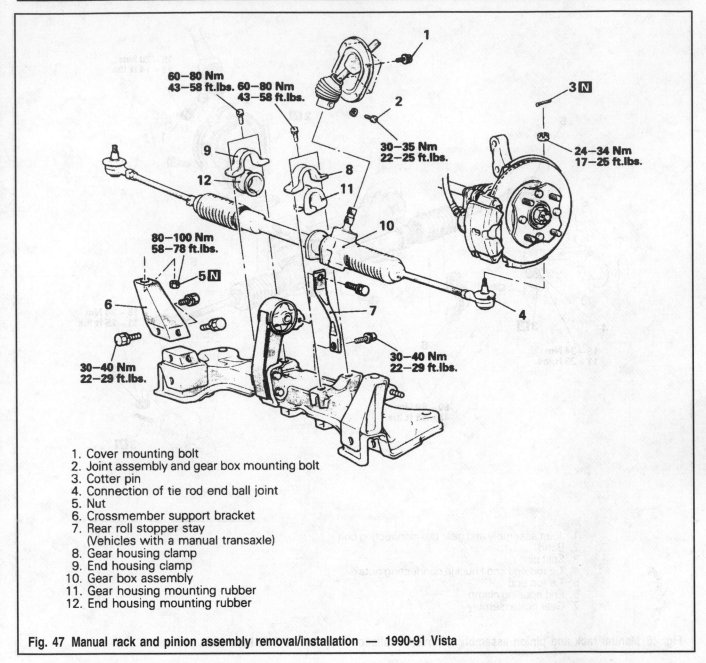

60—80 Nm
43—58 ft.lbs. 60—80 Nm
43—58 ft.lbs.

30—35 Nm
22—25 ft.lbs.

3 N

24—34 Nm
17—25 ft.lbs.

80—100 Nm
58—78 ft.lbs.

5 N

6

30—40 Nm
22—29 ft.lbs.

7

4

30—40 Nm
22—29 ft.lbs.

1. Cover mounting bolt
2. Joint assembly and gear box mounting bolt
3. Cotter pin
4. Connection of tie rod end ball joint
5. Nut
6. Crossmember support bracket
7. Rear roll stopper stay
   (Vehicles with a manual transaxle)
8. Gear housing clamp
9. End housing clamp
10. Gear box assembly
11. Gear housing mounting rubber
12. End housing mounting rubber

Fig. 47 Manual rack and pinion assembly removal/installation — 1990-91 Vista

8. Remove the rear roll stopper-to-center member bolt and move the rear roll stopper forward.

9. From under the vehicle, remove the gear box mounting bolts from the front of the No. 2 crossmember and pull out and to the left on the rack.

10. Lower the rack until the left edge of the left feed tube contacts the lower part of the left fender shield. At this point, remove the left and right feed tubes.

11. Remove the rack from the vehicle.

To install:

12. Position the rack to the No. 2 crossmember and connect the left and right feed tubes.

13. Install the rack, mounting brackets, bushing and retaining bolts. Torque the bolts to 43-58 ft. lbs. (60-80 Nm).

14. Connect the tie rods to the steering knuckle and install the retaining nuts. Torque the tie rod end retaining nuts to 17-25 ft. lbs. (24-34 Nm).

15. Install the wheel assemblies.

16. Install the steering column and connect the steering shaft joint to the rack shaft. Torque the steering shaft-to-rack bolts to 22-25 ft. lbs. (30-35 Nm).

17. Lower the vehicle. Install the air cleaner.

18. Replenish the powering fluid. Start the engine and check for leaks.

Power Rack and Pinion

ADJUSTMENT

1. Disconnect the negative battery cable.
2. Raise the vehicle and support safely.
3. Remove the steering rack assembly from the vehicle.

4. Secure the steering rack assembly in a vise. Do not clamp the vise jaws on the steering housing tubes. Clamp the vise jaws only on the housing cast metal.

5. Remove the steering gear housing end plug from the steering gear shaft bore using tool 6103 or equivalent.

6. Remove the preload adjustment cap locknut from the steering gear housing bore using tool 6097 or equivalent.

7. With rack at center position, check torque on the rack support cover to 11 ft. lbs. (15 Nm).

8. With rack at center position, rotate the shaft clockwise 1 turn in 4-6 seconds. Return the rack support cover 30-60° and adjust the total pinion torque to 5-11 inch lbs. (0.56-1.24 Nm). Set the standard value at its highest value when adjusting. Assure no ratcheting or catching when operating the rack towards the shaft direction.

9. Secure the preload adjustment cap with a new locknut using tool 6097 or equivalent. Do not allow the adjustment cap to rotate when tightening the locknut.

10. Install the end plug using tool 6103 or equivalent.

REMOVAL & INSTALLATION

Colt

▶ **See Figures 48 and 49**

1. Loosen the lug nuts.
2. Raise the vehicle and support it safely.
3. Remove the wheels.
4. Remove the steering shaft-to-pinion coupling bolt.
5. Disconnect the tie rod ends with a separator.
6. Drain the fluid.

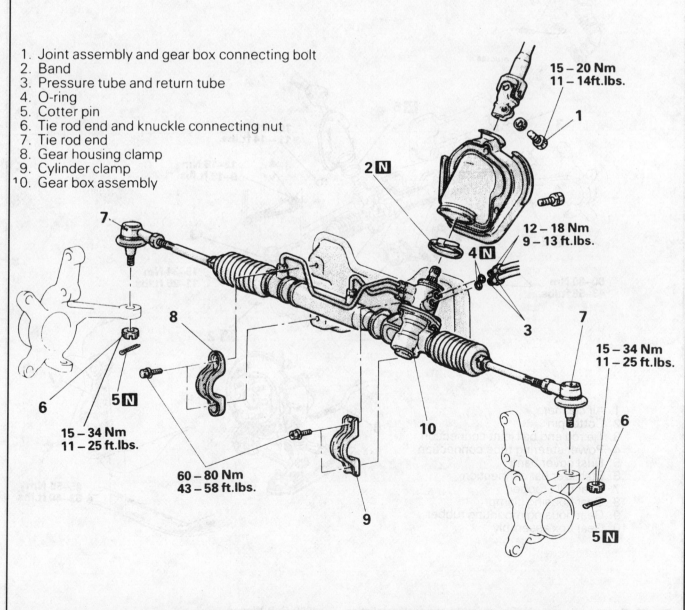

1. Joint assembly and gear box connecting bolt
2. Band
3. Pressure tube and return tube
4. O-ring
5. Cotter pin
6. Tie rod end and knuckle connecting nut
7. Tie rod end
8. Gear housing clamp
9. Cylinder clamp
10. Gear box assembly

15 – 20 Nm
11 – 14 ft.lbs.

12 – 18 Nm
9 – 13 ft. lbs.

15 – 34 Nm
11 – 25 ft.lbs.

15 – 34 Nm
11 – 25 ft.lbs.

60 – 80 Nm
43 – 58 ft.lbs.

Fig. 48 Power rack and pinion assembly removal/installation — 1990-92 Colt hatchback and sedan

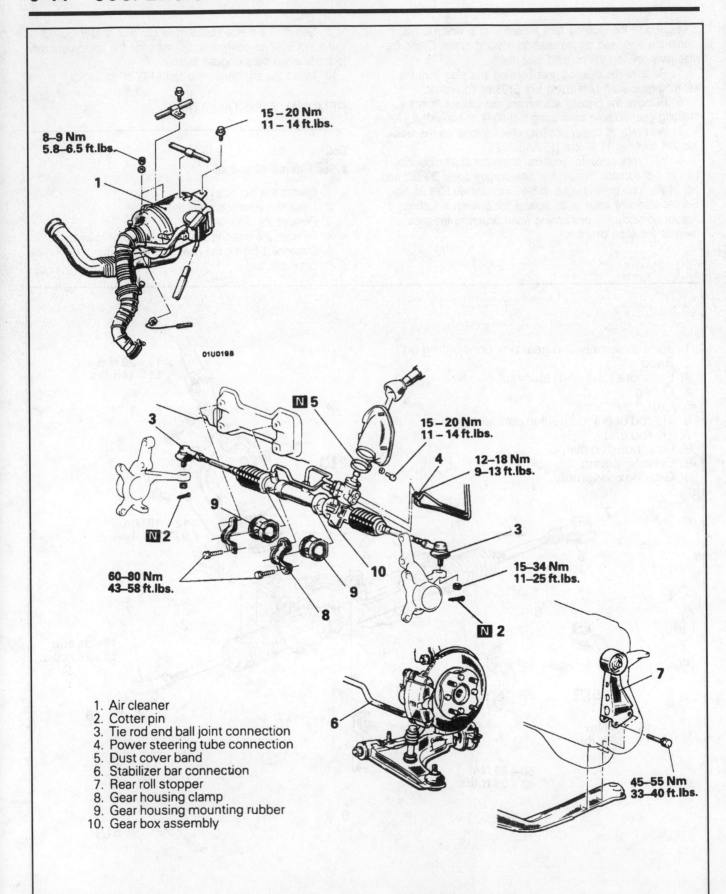

8–9 Nm
5.8–6.5 ft.lbs.

15–20 Nm
11–14 ft.lbs.

01U0198

15–20 Nm
11–14 ft.lbs.

12–18 Nm
9–13 ft.lbs.

60–80 Nm
43–58 ft.lbs.

15–34 Nm
11–25 ft.lbs.

45–55 Nm
33–40 ft.lbs.

1. Air cleaner
2. Cotter pin
3. Tie rod end ball joint connection
4. Power steering tube connection
5. Dust cover band
6. Stabilizer bar connection
7. Rear roll stopper
8. Gear housing clamp
9. Gear housing mounting rubber
10. Gear box assembly

Fig. 49 Power rack and pinion assembly removal/installation — 1990 Colt Wagon

7. Disconnect the hoses from the rack.

8. Remove the band from the steering joint cover.

9. Unbolt and remove the stabilizer bar.

10. Remove the rack unit mounting clamp bolts and take the unit out the left side of the vehicle.

To install:

11. Make sure the rubber isolators have their nubs aligned with the holes in the clamps.

12. Apply rubber cement to the slits in the gear mounting grommet.

13. Torque the clamp bolt to 43-58 ft. lbs. (58-79 Nm), the tie rod nuts to 11-25 ft. lbs. (15-34 Nm) and the coupling bolt to 22-25 ft. lbs. (29-34 Nm.

14. Fill the system and road test the car.

1990-91 2WD Vista

▶ See Figure 50

1. Loosen the lug nuts.

2. Raise and support the vehicle safely.

3. Remove the wheels.

4. Remove the steering shaft-to-pinion coupling bolt.

5. Disconnect the tie rod ends with a separator.

6. Disconnect the hoses at the rack.

7. Remove the crossmember support bracket from the crossmember on the right side of the vehicle.

8. Unbolt the rack from the crossmember.

➡The rack is most easily removed using a ratchet and long extension, working from the engine compartment side.

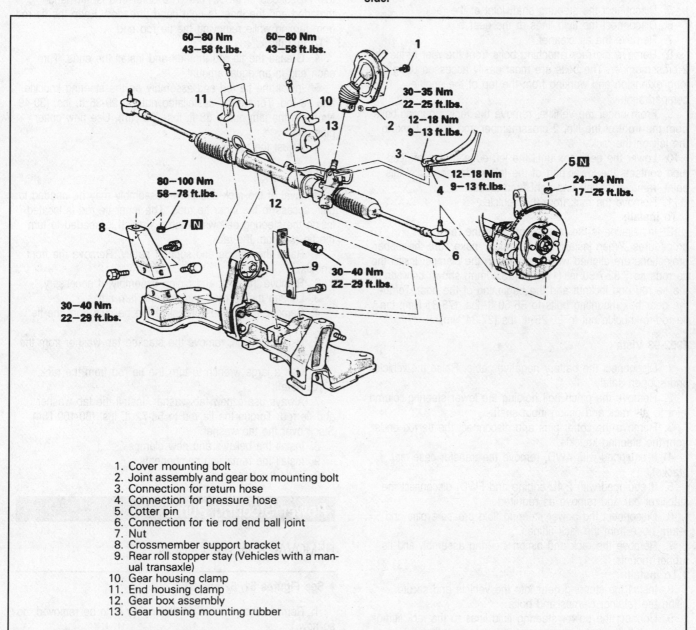

1. Cover mounting bolt
2. Joint assembly and gear box mounting bolt
3. Connection for return hose
4. Connection for pressure hose
5. Cotter pin
6. Connection for tie rod end ball joint
7. Nut
8. Crossmember support bracket
9. Rear roll stopper stay (Vehicles with a manual transaxle)
10. Gear housing clamp
11. End housing clamp
12. Gear box assembly
13. Gear housing mounting rubber

Fig. 50 Power rack and pinion assembly removal/installation — 1990-91 2WD Vista

9. Pull the rack out the right side of the vehicle. Pull it slowly to avoid damage.

To install:

10. Installation is the reverse order of the removal procedures. Torque the rack clamp bolts to 43-58 ft. lbs. (58-79 Nm), the tie rod nuts to 17-25 ft. lbs. (23-34 Nm) and the coupling bolt to 22-25 ft. lbs. (29-34 Nm). Fill the system and road test the vehicle.

1990-91 4WD Vista

1. Remove the steering column.
2. Raise and support the vehicle safely.
3. Remove the front wheels.
4. Using a separator, disconnect the tie rod from the knuckle.
5. Disconnect the steering shaft joint at the rack.
6. Disconnect the fluid lines at the gear box.
7. Remove the air cleaner.
8. Remove the rack attaching bolts from the rear of the No. 2 crossmember. The bolts are most easily accessed using a long extension and working from the top of the engine compartment.
9. From under the vehicle, remove the rack mounting bolts from the front of the No. 2 crossmember and pull out and to the left on the rack.
10. Lower the gear box until the left edge of the left feed tube contacts the lower part of the left fender shield. At this point, remove the left and right feed tubes.
11. Remove the rack from the vehicle.

To install:

12. Installation is the reverse order of the removal procedures. When installing the clamps, make sure the rubber projections are aligned with the holes in the clamps. Install the tie rods so 7.52-7.60 in. (191.00-193.00mm) shows between the tie rod end locknut and the beginning of the boot. Torque the gear box mounting bolts to 55-60 ft. lbs. (75-81 Nm); the tie rod-to-knuckle nut to 20-25 ft. lbs (27-34 Nm).

1992-93 Vista

1. Disconnect the battery negative cable. Raise the vehicle and support safely.
2. Remove the pinch bolt holding the lower steering column joint to the rack and pinion input shaft.
3. Remove the cotter pins and disconnect the tie rod ends from the steering knuckle.
4. If equipped with 4WD, remove the transfer case rear bracket.
5. If equipped with 2.4L engine and FWD, disconnect the stabilizer bar and remove as required.
6. Disconnect the power steering fluid pressure pipe and return hose from the rack fittings.
7. Remove the rack and pinion steering assembly and its rubber mounts.

To install:

8. Install the steering gear into the vehicle and secure using the retainer clamps and bolts.
9. Connect the power steering fluid lines to the rack fittings.
10. Install the stabilizer bar and rear transaxle bracket.
11. Connect the tie rod ends to the steering knuckles.
12. Connect the negative battery cable. Refill the reservoir and bleed the system.

13. Perform a front end alignment.

Tie Rod Ends

REMOVAL & INSTALLATION

Outer

1. Raise the vehicle and support it safely.
2. Remove the cotter pin and loosen the nut from the tie rod.
3. Loosen the shaft jam nut before removing the joint. Remove the tie rod ends from the knuckle with a separator tool MB990635 or MB991113. The outer end is left hand threaded and the inner is right hand threaded. Keep the tie rod from turning while removing the tie rod end.

To install:

4. Grease the tie rod threads and install the ends. Turn each end in an equal amount.
5. Install the tie rod end assembly on the steering knuckle and tie rod. Torque the castellated nuts to 29-36 ft. lbs. (39-49 Nm) and the jam nut to 38 ft. lbs. (53 Nm). Use new cotter pins.
6. Adjust the toe-in.

Inner

Removal of the rack and pinion assembly may be needed to gain access to the inner tie rods. The inner tie rod is located inside the steering bellows. A large wrench is needed to turn the tie rod from the rack.

1. Raise the vehicle and support safely. Remove the front wheels.
2. Remove the rack and pinion assembly, if necessary.
3. Loosen the tie rod-to-tie rod end jam nut.
4. Remove the clamps and slide the bellows from the tie rod.
5. Using a punch, remove the stacked tab washer from the tie rod nut.
6. Use a large wrench to turn the tie rod from the rack.

To install:

7. Always use a new tab washer. Install the tab washer and tie rod. Torque the tie rod to 58-72 ft. lbs. (80-100 Nm). Stack over the tab washer.
8. Install the bellows and new clamps.
9. Install the remaining components.
10. Align the front end.

Power Steering Pump

REMOVAL & INSTALLATION

▶ **See Figures 51, 52 and 53**

1. Remove the drive belt. If the pulley is to be removed, do so now.
2. Disconnect the pressure and return lines. Catch any leaking fluid. Remove the banjo fitting nut on later model vehicles.

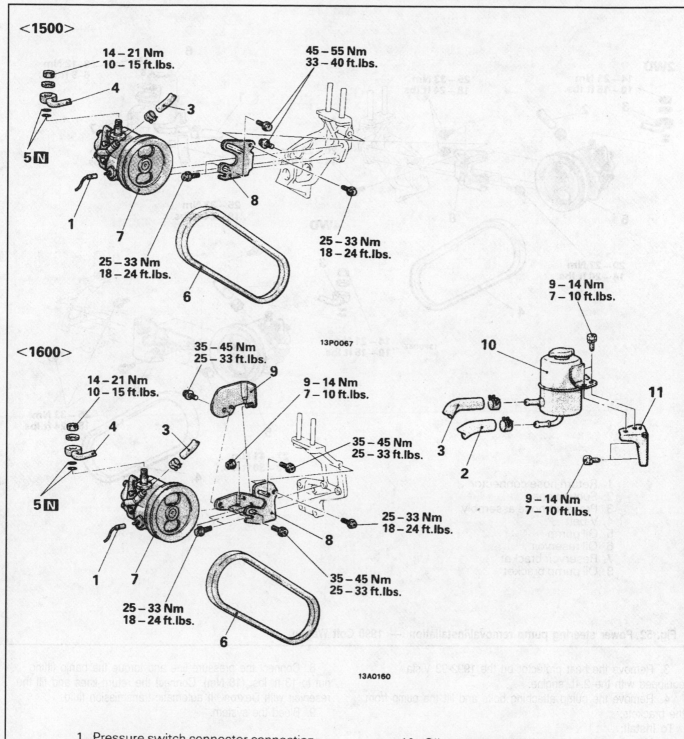

13P0067

13A0160

1. Pressure switch connector connection
2. Return hose connection
3. Suction hose
4. Pressure hose connection
5. O-ring
6. V-belt
7. Oil pump
8. Oil pump bracket
9. Heat protector <1600>

10. Oil reservoir
11. Reservoir bracket

Fig. 51 Power steering pump removal/installation — 1990 Colt hatchback and sedan

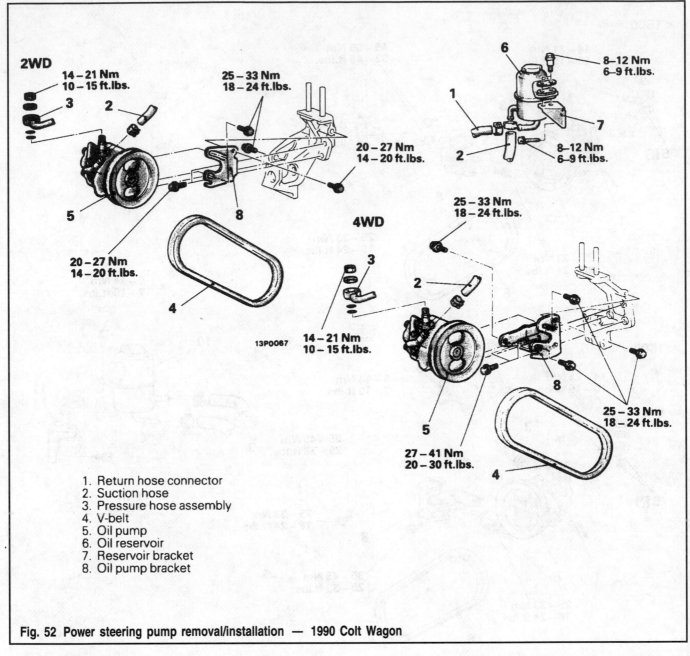

1. Return hose connector
2. Suction hose
3. Pressure hose assembly
4. V-belt
5. Oil pump
6. Oil reservoir
7. Reservoir bracket
8. Oil pump bracket

Fig. 52 Power steering pump removal/installation — 1990 Colt Wagon

3. Remove the heat protector on the 1992-93 Vista equipped with the 2.4L engine.

4. Remove the pump attaching bolts and lift the pump from the brackets.

To install:

5. Make sure the bracket-to-engine bolts are tight and install the pump to the brackets. Tighten the retaining bolts after installing the drive belt to the correct tension.

6. If the pulley has been removed, install it and tighten the nut securely. Bend the lock tab over the nut. Later model pulleys have to pressed on and off. Install the heat protector, if so equipped.

7. Install the drive belt and adjust to a tension of 22 lbs. (30 N) at a deflection of 0.28-0.39 in. (7.11-9.91mm) at the top center of the belt. Torque the pump bolts to 21 ft. lbs. (30 Nm) and hold the belt tension.

8. Connect the pressure line and torque the banjo fitting nut to 13 ft. lbs. (18 Nm). Connect the return lines and fill the reservoir with Dexron®II automatic transmission fluid.

9. Bleed the system.

BELT ADJUSTMENT

1. Press the V-belt by applying pressure of 22 lbs. (30 N) at the center of the belt.

2. Measure the deflection to confirm that it is within the standard range.

   a. Colt, standard value: 0.2-0.4 in. (6-9mm).

   b. 1990-91 Vista, standard value: 0.3-0.4 in. (7-10mm).

   c. 1992-93 Vista, standard value: 0.4-0.5 in. (9-12mm).

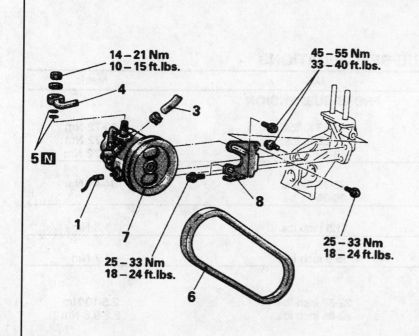

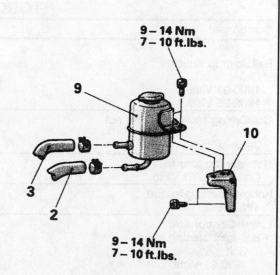

1. Pressure switch connector connection
2. Return hose connection
3. Suction hose
4. Pressure hose connection
5. O-ring
6. V-belt
7. Oil pump
8. Oil pump bracket
9. Oil reservoir
10. Reservoir bracket

Fig. 53 Power steering pump removal/installation — 1991-92 Colt hatchback and sedan

3. To adjust the tension of the belt, loosen the power steering pump mounting bolts, move the power steering pump and then retighten the bolts.

SYSTEM BLEEDING

1. The reservoir should be full of Dexron®II automatic transmission fluid.

2. Raise the vehicle and support it safely.

3. Turn the steering wheel fully to the right and left until no air bubbles appear in the fluid. Maintain the reservoir level.

4. Lower the vehicle and with the engine idling, turn the wheels fully to the right and left. Stop the engine.

5. Install a tube from the bleeder screw on the steering gear box or rack, to the reservoir.

6. Start the engine, turn the steering wheel fully to the left and loosen the bleeder screw.

7. Repeat the procedure until no air bubbles pass through the tube.

8. Tighten the bleeder screw and remove the tube. Refill the reservoir as needed and check that no further bubbles are present in the fluid. An abrupt rise in the fluid level after stopping the engine is a sign of incomplete bleeding. This will cause noise from the pump or control valve.

TORQUE SPECIFICATIONS

Component	U.S.	Metric
FRONT SUSPENSION		
Ball Joint to Knuckle		
Colt	44-53 ft. lbs.	60-72 Nm
1990-91 Vista	44-53 ft. lbs.	60-72 Nm
1992-93 Vista	43-52 ft. lbs.	60-72 Nm
Coil Spring gland retaining nut		
Colt	25-36 ft. lbs.	34-49 Nm
Vista	30-36 ft. lbs.	
Hub starting torque		
Colt and 2WD Vista	11.5 inch lbs.	1.3 Nm
Knuckle turning torque		
4WD Vista	15.6 inch lbs.	1.7 Nm
Lower Control Arm		
Ball joint starting effort		
Colt	22-87 inch lbs.	2.5-10 Nm
1990-91 Vista	20-86 inch lbs.	2.2-9.6 Nm
Lower Arm to Body		
Colt	118-125 ft. lbs.	161-170 Nm
Lower Arm to Shaft		
Colt	70-88 ft. lbs.	95-120 Nm
Lower control arm-to-crossmember		
1990-91 Vista		
2WD	90-111 ft. lbs.	122-151 Nm
4WD	58-68 ft. lbs.	79-92 Nm
Frame mount through bolt nuts		
1992-93 Vista	75-90 ft. lbs.	102-122 Nm
Rotor to hub bolts		
Colt and 2WD Vista	36-43 ft. lbs.	49-58 Nm
Stabilizer Bar to Body		
Colt	12-20 ft. lbs.	16-27 Nm
Stabilizer bar		
hanger brackets		
1990-91 Vista	7-9 ft. lbs.	10-12 Nm
Rear mount clamp		
1992-93 Vista	51 ft. lbs.	70 Nm
Support assemblies		
Except 1992-93 Vista	9 ft. lbs.	13 Nm
1992-93 Vista		
4WD		
frame bolts	16 ft. lbs.	22 Nm
link nuts	29 ft. lbs.	40 Nm
2WD		
bracket bolts	16 ft. lbs.	22 Nm
tie rod end nut	17-25 ft. lbs.	24-34 Nm
crossmember bolts	51 ft. lbs.	70 Nm
Strut-to-fender housing bolts		
Vista	18-25 ft. lbs.	24-34
Strut-to-knuckle bolts		
Colt	55-65 ft. lbs.	75-88
Vista	55-65 ft. lbs.	75-88
Strut upper retaining nut		
Colt	25-36 ft. lbs.	34-49

TORQUE SPECIFICATIONS

Component	U.S.	Metric
	REAR SUSPENSION	
Coil Springs		
1992–93 Vista		
driveshaft assembly nut	69 ft. lbs.	95 Nm
driveshaft to the flange mounting bolts	40–47 ft. lbs.	55–65 Nm
lower shock bolt	72 ft. lbs.	100 Nm
MacPherson Strut		
Colt		
Strut shaft nut	43–51 ft. lbs.	60–70 Nm
lower mounting bolt and nut	58–72 ft. lbs.	79–98 Nm
upper mounting nuts	18–25 ft. lbs.	24–34 Nm
Rear Control Arms		
1992–93 Vista		
sensor bracket bolts	10 ft. lbs.	14 Nm
lower arm flange bolt nut	69 ft. lbs.	95 Nm
arm pivot bolt	69 ft. lbs.	95 Nm
Rear Wheel Bearings		
1990-91 2WD Vista		
Hub nut		
initial torque	15 ft. lbs.	20 Nm
final torque	4 ft. lbs.	5.4 Nm
1992–93 2WD Vista		
self-locking nut	166 ft. lbs.	230 Nm
Colt		
turning torque	48 inch lbs.	5.4 Nm
hub nut final torque	108–145 ft. lbs.	150–200 Nm
Shock Absorbers		
Colt and 2WD Vista		
bottom nut	47-58 ft. lbs.	64-79 Nm
upper nut		
except station wagons	47-58 ft. lbs.	64-79 Nm
station wagons	12-15 ft. lbs.	16-20 Nm
1990-91 4WD Vista		
top nut	55-58 ft. lbs.	75-79 Nm
bottom bolt	75-80 ft. lbs.	102-109 Nm
1992–93 Vista		
lower nut	72 ft. lbs.	100 Nm
upper nuts	33 ft. lbs.	45 Nm
Suspension arm end nuts		
Colt	56-70 ft. lbs.	76-95 Nm
Vista	94-108 ft. lbs.	128-147 Nm

TORQUE SPECIFICATIONS

Component	U.S.	Metric
Torsion Bar and Control Arms		
Extension Rod Fixture bolts	45-50 ft. lbs.	61-68 Nm
Extension Rod to Fixture nut	95-100 ft. lbs.	129-136 Nm
Shock Absorber lower bolt	75-80 ft. lbs.	102-109 Nm
Outer Arm attaching bolts	65-70 ft. lbs.	88-95 Nm
Toe-In bolt	95-100 ft. lbs.	129-136 Nm
Lockbolts	20-22 ft. lbs.	27-30 Nm
Crossmember attaching bolts	80-85 ft. lbs.	109-116 Nm
Front Insulator nuts	7-10 ft. lbs.	9.5-14 Nm
Inner Arm to Crossmember bolts	60-65 ft. lbs.	82-88 Nm
Damper-to-Crossmember nuts	15-20 ft. lbs.	20-27 Nm
Trailing Arm to body bolts		
Colt	36-51 ft. lbs.	49-69 Nm
Vista	51-65 ft. lbs.	69-88 Nm
STEERING		
Manual Rack and Pinion		
Colt		
Rack-to-crossmember	45–60 ft. lbs.	61–81 Nm
Coupling bolt	22–25 ft. lbs.	27–34 Nm
Tie-rod nuts	11–25 ft. lbs.	15–34 Nm
1990-91 2WD Vista		
rack clamp bolts	43–58 ft. lbs.	58–79 Nm
tie rod nuts	17–25 ft. lbs.	25–34 Nm
coupling bolt	22–25 ft. lbs.	27–34 Nm
1990–91 4WD Vista		
rack mounting bolts	43–58 ft. lbs.	60–80 Nm
tie rod end nuts	17–25 ft. lbs.	24–34 Nm
steering shaft-to-rack bolts	22–25 ft. lbs.	30–35 Nm
Power Rack and Pinion		
Adjustments		
rack over-center torque	11 ft. lbs.	15 Nm
total pinion torque	5–11 inch lbs.	0.56–1.24 Nm
Colt		
rack clamp bolt	43–58 ft. lbs.	58–79 Nm
tie rod nuts	11–25 ft. lbs.	15–34 Nm
coupling bolt	22–25 ft. lbs.	29–34 Nm.
1990-91 2WD Vista		
rack clamp bolts	43–58 ft. lbs.	58–79 Nm
tie rod nuts	17–25 ft. lbs.	23–34 Nm
coupling bolt	22–25 ft. lbs.	29–34 Nm
1990-91 4WD Vista		
gear box mounting bolts	55–60 ft. lbs.	75–81 Nm
tie rod-to-knuckle nut	20–25 ft. lbs 27–34 Nm	
Steering Wheel nut	30 ft. lbs.	41 Nm
Tie Rod Ends		
Outer		
castellated nuts	29–36 ft. lbs.	39–49 Nm
jam nut	38 ft. lbs.	53 Nm
Inner	58–72 ft. lbs.	80–100 Nm

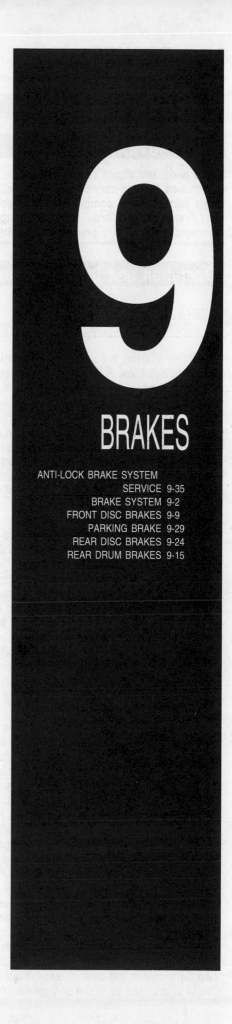

9

BRAKES

BRAKE SYSTEM

✻✻CAUTION

Brake pads and shoes contain asbestos, which has been determined to be a cancer causing agent. Never clean the brake surfaces with compressed air! Avoid inhaling any dust from brake surfaces! When cleaning brakes, use commercially available brake cleaning fluids.

Operation and System Description

HYDRAULIC SYSTEM

Hydraulic systems are used to actuate the brakes of all modern automobiles. A hydraulic system rather than a mechanical system is used for two reasons. First, fluid under pressure can be carried to all parts of an automobile by small hoses — some of which are flexible — without taking up a significant amount of room or posing routing problems. Second, a great mechanical advantage can be given to the brake pedal, and the foot pressure required to actuate the brakes can be reduced by making the surface area of the master cylinder pistons smaller than that of any of the pistons in the wheel cylinders or calipers.

The master cylinder consists of a fluid reservoir and a single or double cylinder and piston assembly. Double (or dual) master cylinders are designed to separate the front and rear braking systems hydraulically in case of a leak. The master cylinder coverts mechanical motion from the pedal into hydraulic pressure within the lines. This pressure is translated back into mechanical motion at the wheels by either the wheel cylinder (drum brakes) or the caliper (disc brakes). Since these components receive the pressure from the master cylinder, they are generically classed as slave cylinders in the system.

Steel lines carry the brake fluid to a point on the vehicle's frame near each of the vehicle's wheels. The fluid is then carried to the slave cylinders by flexible tubes in order to allow for suspension and steering movements.

Each wheel cylinder contains two pistons, one at either end, which push outward in opposite directions and force the brake shoe into contact with the drum. In disc brake systems, the slave cylinders are part of the calipers. One, two or four cylinders are used to force the brake pads against the disc, but all cylinders contain one piston only. All slave cylinder pistons employ some type of seal, usually made of rubber, to minimize the leakage of fluid around the piston. A rubber dust boot seals the outer end of the cylinder against dust and dirt. The boot fits around the outer end of either the piston or the brake actuating rod.

When at rest the entire hydraulic system, from the piston(s) in the master cylinder to those in the wheel cylinders or calipers, is full of brake fluid. Upon application of the brake pedal, fluid trapped in front of the master cylinder piston(s) is forced through the lines to the slave cylinders. Here it forces the pistons outward, in the case of drum brakes, and inward toward the disc in the case of disc brakes. The motion of the pistons is opposed by return springs mounted outside the cylinders in drum brakes, and by internal springs or spring seals, in disc brakes.

Upon release of the brake pedal, a spring located inside the master cylinder immediately returns the master cylinder piston(s) to the normal position. The pistons contain check valves and the master cylinder has compensating ports drilled within it. These are uncovered as the pistons reach their normal position. The piston check valves allow fluid to flow toward the wheel cylinders or calipers as the pistons withdraw. As the return springs force the brake pads or shoes into the released position, the excess fluid in the lines is allowed to re-enter the reservoir through the compensating ports.

Dual circuit master cylinders employ two pistons, located one behind the other, in the same cylinder. The primary piston is actuated directly by mechanical linkage from the brake pedal. The secondary piston is actuated by fluid trapped between the two pistons. If a leak develops in front of the secondary pistons, it moves forward until it bottoms against the front of the master cylinder, and the fluid trapped between the pistons will operate the rear brakes. If the rear brakes develop a leak, the primary piston will move forward until direct contact with the secondary piston takes place, and it will force the secondary piston to actuate the front brakes. In either case, the brake pedal moves farther when the brakes are applied and less braking power is available.

All dual-circuit systems incorporate a switch which senses either line pressure or fluid level. This system will warn the driver when only half of the brake system is operational.

In some disc brake systems, this valve body also contains a metering valve and, in some cases, a proportioning valve. The metering valve keeps pressure from traveling to the disc brakes on the front wheels until the brake shoes on the rear wheels have contacted the drum, ensuring that the front brakes will never be used alone. The proportioning valve controls the pressure to the rear brakes avoiding rear wheel lock-up during very hard braking.

DISC BRAKES

✻✻CAUTION

Brake pads contain asbestos, which has been determined to be a cancer causing agent. never clean the brake surfaces with compressed air! Avoid inhaling any dust from any brake surface! When cleaning brake surfaces, use a commercially available brake cleaning fluid.

Instead of the traditional expanding brakes that press outward against a circular drum, disc brake systems employ a cast iron disc with brake pads positioned on either side of it. An easily seen analogy is the hand brake arrangement on a bicycle. The pads squeeze onto the rim of the bike wheel, slowing its motion. Automobile disc brakes use the identical principal but apply the braking effort to a separate disc instead of the wheel.

The disc or rotor is a one-piece casting mounted just inside the wheel. Some discs are one solid piece while others have cooling fins between the two braking surfaces. These vented rotors enable air to circulate between the braking surfaces cooling them quicker and making them less sensitive to heat buildup and fade. Disc brakes are only slightly affected by dirt and water since contaminants are thrown off by the centrifugal action of the rotor or scraped off by the pads. Also, the equal clamping action of the two brake pads tend to ensure uniform, straight-line stops, although unequal application of the pads between the left and right wheels can cause a vicious pull under braking. All disc brakes are inherently self-adjusting. **There are three general types of disc brakes:**

The fixed caliper design uses two pistons mounted on either side of the rotor (in each side of the caliper). The caliper is mounted rigidly and does not move. This is a very efficient brake system but the size of the caliper and its mounts adds weight and bulk to the car.

The sliding and floating designs are quite similar. In fact, these two types are often lumped together. In both designs, one pad is moved into contact with the rotor by hydraulic force. The caliper, which is not held in a fixed position, moves slightly on its mount, bringing the other pad into contact with the rotor. There are various methods of attaching floating calipers. Some pivot at the bottom or top, and some slide on mounting bolts. Many uneven brake wear problems can be caused by dirty or seized slides and pivots.

DRUM BRAKES

✳✳CAUTION

Brake shoes contain asbestos, which has been determined to be a cancer causing agent. never clean the brake surfaces with Compressed air! Avoid inhaling any dust from any brake surface! When cleaning brake surfaces, use a commercially available brake cleaning fluid.

Drum brakes employ two brake shoes mounted on a stationary backing plate. These shoes are positioned inside a circular cast iron drum which rotates with the wheel. The shoes are held in place by springs; this allows them to slide toward the drum (when they are applied) while keeping the linings and drums in alignment.

The shoes are actuated by a wheel cylinder which is mounted at the top of the backing plate. When the brakes are applied, hydraulic pressure forces the wheel cylinder's two actuating links outward. Since these links bear directly against the top of the brake shoes, the tops of the shoes are then forced outward against the inside of the drum. This action forces the bottoms of the two shoes to contact the brake drum by rotating the entire assembly slightly (known as servo action). When the pressure within the wheel cylinder is relaxed, return springs pull the shoes away from the drum.

Most modern drum brakes are designed to self-adjust during application when the vehicle is moving in reverse. This motion causes both shoes to rotate very slightly with the drum, rocking an adjusting lever and thereby causing rotation of the adjusting screw via a star wheel. This on-board adjustment system reduces the need for maintenance adjustments but most drivers don't back up enough to keep the brakes properly set.

ADJUSTMENTS

All brakes used on these cars are self-adjusting. After brake shoe replacement in drum brakes, an initial adjustment must be made. See the appropriate procedure, below.

Master Cylinder

➡Be careful not to spill brake fluid on the painted surfaces of your car. Brake fluid is a great paint remover.

REMOVAL & INSTALLATION

▶ **See Figures 1, 2 and 3**

1. Disconnect the fluid level sensor.
2. Disconnect the brake tubes from the master cylinder and cap them immediately.
3. Unbolt and remove the master cylinder from the booster.
4. Install the master cylinder to the booster. Connect the brake lines and the fluid level sensor. Torque the mounting bolts to 6-9 ft. lbs. (72-108 inch lbs.).

OVERHAUL

▶ **See Figures 4, 5 and 6**

This is a tedious, time-consuming job. You can save yourself a lot of trouble by buying a rebuilt master cylinder from your dealer or a parts supply house. The small difference in cost between a rebuilding kit and a rebuilt part usually makes it more economical, in terms of time and work, to buy the rebuilt part.

1. Remove the master cylinder from the car.
2. Remove the reservoir caps and filters and drain the brake fluid. Discard this fluid.
3. Remove the piston stopper snap-ring from the open end of the master cylinder with a pair of snapring pliers, or other suitable tool.
4. Remove the stopper screw and washer (if equipped) from the bottom of the master cylinder and then remove the primary and secondary piston assemblies from the master cylinder bore.
5. Remove the caps on the underside of the master cylinder to gain access to the check valves for cleaning.

➡Do not disassemble the brake fluid level gauge, if equipped.

6. Discard all used rubber parts and gaskets. These parts should be replaced with the new components included in the rebuilding kit.

➡Do not remove the master cylinder reservoir tanks unless they are leaking.

7. Clean all the parts in clean brake fluid. Do not use mineral oil or alcohol for cleaning.
8. Check the cylinder bore and piston for wear, scoring, corrosion, or any other damage. The piston and cylinder bore can be dressed with crocus cloth, or a brake cylinder hone,

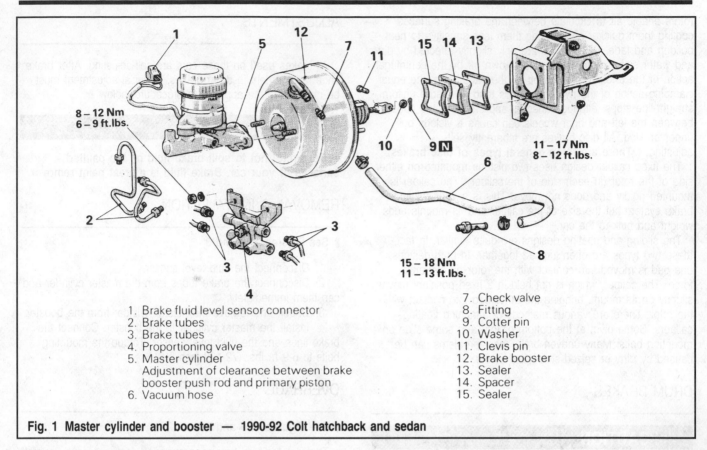

1. Brake fluid level sensor connector
2. Brake tubes
3. Brake tubes
4. Proportioning valve
5. Master cylinder
   Adjustment of clearance between brake
   booster push rod and primary piston
6. Vacuum hose

7. Check valve
8. Fitting
9. Cotter pin
10. Washer
11. Clevis pin
12. Brake booster
13. Sealer
14. Spacer
15. Sealer

Fig. 1 Master cylinder and booster — 1990-92 Colt hatchback and sedan

soaked in brake fluid. Move the crocus cloth around the cylinder bore, not in and out. Do the same to the piston, if necessary. Wash both the cylinder bore and the piston with clean brake fluid.

9. Check the piston-to-cylinder bore clearance; it should measure 0.15mm. If greater clearance exists, replace the piston, the cylinder, or both.

10. Assemble the master cylinder. Soak all of the components in clean brake fluid before assembling them.

11. Clamp the master cylinder in a vise by one of its flanges. Fill the reservoirs with fresh fluid, and pump the piston with a screwdriver until fluid squirts from the outlet ports. Install the master cylinder and bleed the system.

Power Brake Boosters

Power brakes operate just as standard brake systems except in the actuation of the master cylinder pistons. A vacuum diaphragm is located on the front of the master cylinder and assists the driver in applying the brakes, reducing both the effort and travel he must put into moving the brake pedal.

The vacuum diaphragm housing is connected to the intake manifold by a vacuum hose. A check valve is placed at the point where the hose enters the diaphragm housing, so that during periods of low manifold vacuum brake assist vacuum will not be lost.

Depressing the brake pedal closes off the vacuum source and allows atmospheric pressure to enter on one side of the diaphragm. This causes the master cylinder pistons to move and apply the brakes. When the brake pedal is released, vacuum is applied to both sides of the diaphragm, and return

springs return the diaphragm and master cylinder pistons to the released position. If the vacuum fails, the brake pedal rod will butt against the end of the master cylinder actuating rod, and direct mechanical application will occur as the pedal is depressed. The hydraulic and mechanical problems that apply to conventional brake systems also apply to power brakes, and should be checked for if the tests below do not reveal the problem. Test for a system vacuum leak as described below:

1. Operate the engine at idle with the transmission in Neutral without touching the brake pedal for at least one minute.

2. Turn off the engine, and wait one minute.

3. Test for the presence of assist vacuum by depressing the brake pedal and releasing it several times. Light application will produce less and less pedal travel, if vacuum was present. If there is no vacuum, air is leaking into the system somewhere.

4. Test for system operation as follows:

5. Pump the brake pedal (with engine off) until the supply vacuum is entirely gone.

6. Put a light, steady pressure on the pedal.

7. Start the engine, and operate it at idle with the transmission in Neutral. If the system is operating, the brake pedal should fall toward the floor if constant pressure is maintained on the pedal.

➡**Power brake systems may be tested for hydraulic leaks just as ordinary systems are tested, except that the engine should be idling with the transmission in Neutral (manual) or Park (automatic) with the wheels blocked throughout the test.**

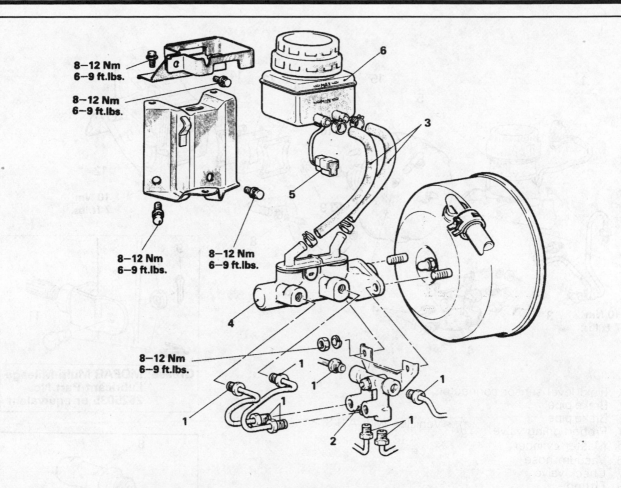

1. Brake tubes connection
2. 6 way connector (2WD) or proportioning valve (4WD)
3. Reservoir hose
   Adjusting brake booster push rod and primary piston clearance
4. Master cylinder
5. Brake fluid level sensor connector connection
6. Reservoir assembly

Fig. 2 Master cylinder and booster — 1990-91 Vista

REMOVAL & INSTALLATION

1. Remove the master cylinder.
2. Disconnect the vacuum line from the booster.
3. Remove the pin connecting the power brake operating rod and the brake lever.
4. Unbolt and remove the booster.
5. Replace the packing on both sides of the booster-to-firewall spacer with new packing.
6. If the check valve was removed, make sure the direction of installation marking on the valve is followed.
7. Install the booster and master cylinder. Torque the booster-to-firewall nuts to 6-9 ft. lbs. (72-108 inch lbs.) Torque the master cylinder-to-booster nuts to 6-9 ft. lbs.

Combination Valve or Proportioning Valve

The valve performs one or more of the following functions:
1. Controls the amount of hydraulic pressure to the rear brakes.
2. Warns of failure in the brake system (warning light on dash).
3. Inactivates rear pressure control in case of failure in the front service brake system.

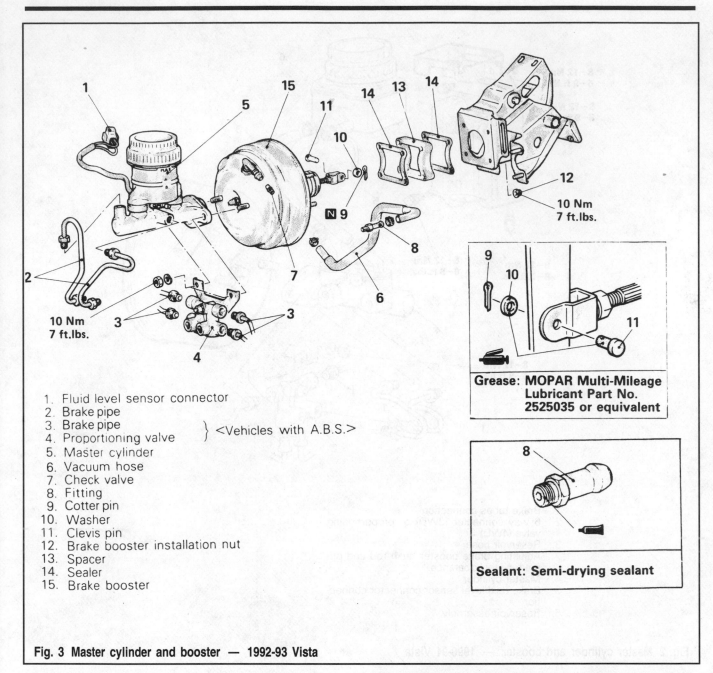

1. Fluid level sensor connector
2. Brake pipe
3. Brake pipe
4. Proportioning valve   } <Vehicles with A.B.S.>
5. Master cylinder
6. Vacuum hose
7. Check valve
8. Fitting
9. Cotter pin
10. Washer
11. Clevis pin
12. Brake booster installation nut
13. Spacer
14. Sealer
15. Brake booster

10 Nm
7 ft.lbs.

10 Nm
7 ft.lbs.

10 Nm
7 ft.lbs.

Grease: MOPAR Multi-Mileage
Lubricant Part No.
2525035 or equivalent

Sealant: Semi-drying sealant

Fig. 3 Master cylinder and booster — 1992-93 Vista

REMOVAL & INSTALLATION

1. Disconnect the brake lines at the valve.

➡**Use a flare nut wrench, if possible, to avoid damage to the lines and fittings.**

2. Remove the mounting bolts and remove the valve.

➡**Do not disassemble the valve, replace with a new one if necessary.**

3. Install the valve and connect the lines. Make sure the brake lines are tight. Fill the system with fluid and bleed the brakes.

Load Sensing Proportioning Valve

A load sensing proportioning valve (LSPV) is installed in the rear brake line on some models.

Brake fluid pressure, from the master cylinder, to the rear wheels is controlled by the LSPV according to the vehicle loading conditions, i.e., weight carried. Adjusting the pressure to the rear wheels, depending on the load, improves straight line stopping and helps prevent rear wheel lock up.

The LSPV is connected to a rear lateral rod by a link, lever, cable, and spring. The space between the vehicle floor and lateral rod determines the amount of pressure adjustment to the rear wheels. When the space is greater (light load), the spring pressure to the LSPV is light and less brake pressure is applied. As the vehicle load is increased, so is the LSPV

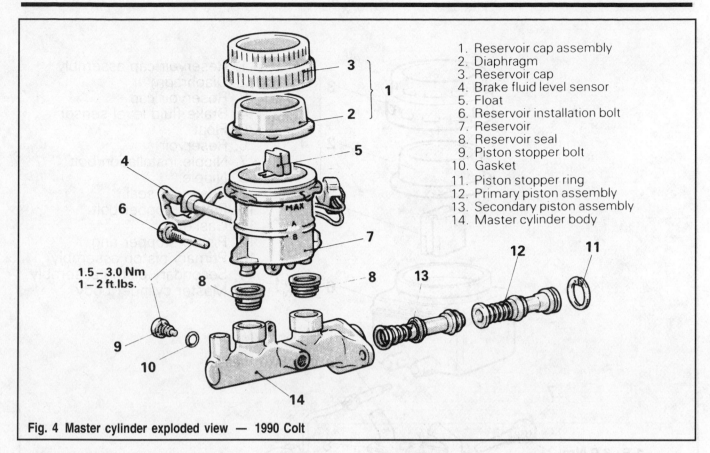

1. Reservoir cap assembly
2. Diaphragm
3. Reservoir cap
4. Brake fluid level sensor
5. Float
6. Reservoir installation bolt
7. Reservoir
8. Reservoir seal
9. Piston stopper bolt
10. Gasket
11. Piston stopper ring
12. Primary piston assembly
13. Secondary piston assembly
14. Master cylinder body

1.5 – 3.0 Nm
1 – 2 ft.lbs.

Fig. 4 Master cylinder exploded view — 1990 Colt

spring pressure and more braking pressure to the rear wheels is provided.

ADJUSTMENT

1. Park the unloaded vehicle on a level surface. Do NOT support the vehicle on a jack or other support.
2. Measure the length, of the spring, between the attaching holes in the fixed end of the LSPV and the operating lever. The length should be 89-91 mm.
3. If the length of the spring is not correct, adjust it to the correct length by turning the adjusting nut at the end of the cable located on the opposite side of the operating lever.

Brake Warning Light Switch

The warning light switch is unrepairable, and must be replaced as a unit if problems occur. The switch may be located in the combination valve, in the master cylinder reservoir or mounted in line between the master cylinder and combination/proportioning valve. Replacement is made by disconnecting the brake lines or unscrewing the switch. If the switch is located in line, the brake system will have to be bled after replacement.

Stoplight Switch

The stoplight switch is a mechanical plunger type, activated when the brake pedal is depressed. The switch is located under the dash on the brake pedal stop.

REMOVAL & INSTALLATION

Disconnect the wiring, loosen the locknut and unscrew the switch. When installing, allow about 0.5mm clearance between the top of the threads on the switch and the brake pedal arm.

Bleeding

The brakes should be bled whenever a brake line, caliper, wheel cylinder, or master cylinder has been removed or when the brake pedal is low or soft. The bleeding sequence is, left rear wheel, right front wheel, right rear wheel and left front wheel.

➡**Some models don't have a bleeder fitting on the left rear brake. Both rear brakes must be bled from the right rear.**

1. Check the master cylinder fluid level. If necessary, add fluid to bring the level up.
2. Remove the bleeder cap at the wheel cylinder or caliper. Connect a rubber hose to the bleeder and immerse the other end in a glass container half filled with brake fluid.
3. Have an assistant depress the brake pedal to the floor, and then pause until the fluid flow stops and the bleeder nipple is closed.
4. Allow the pedal to return and repeat the procedure until a steady, bubble-free flow is seen.

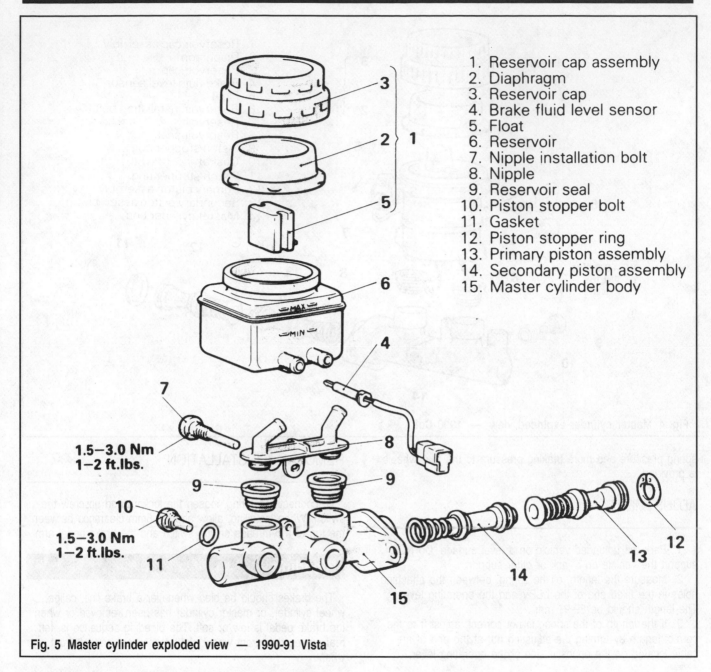

1. Reservoir cap assembly
2. Diaphragm
3. Reservoir cap
4. Brake fluid level sensor
5. Float
6. Reservoir
7. Nipple installation bolt
8. Nipple
9. Reservoir seal
10. Piston stopper bolt
11. Gasket
12. Piston stopper ring
13. Primary piston assembly
14. Secondary piston assembly
15. Master cylinder body

1.5–3.0 Nm
1–2 ft.lbs.

1.5–3.0 Nm
1–2 ft.lbs.

Fig. 5 Master cylinder exploded view — 1990-91 Vista

5. Tighten the bleeder valve and replace the cap. Move on to the next wheel in sequence.

➡Frequently check the master cylinder level during this procedure. If the reservoir goes dry, air will enter the system and it will have to be rebled.

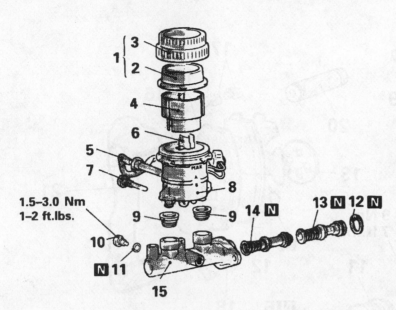

1. Reservoir cap assembly
2. Diaphragm
3. Reservoir cap
4. Filter <Vehicles with A.B.S.>
5. Brake fluid level sensor
6. Float
7. Reservoir stopper bolt
8. Reservoir tank
9. Reservoir seal
10. Piston stopper bolt
11. Gasket
12. Stopper ring
13. Primary piston assembly
14. Secondary piston assembly
15. Master cylinder body

1.5–3.0 Nm
1–2 ft.lbs.

Fig. 6 Master cylinder exploded view — 1992-93 Vista

FRONT DISC BRAKES

✳✳CAUTION

Brake pads contain asbestos fibers. Asbestos has been determined to be a cancer-causing agent. Never clean brake surfaces with compressed air! Avoid inhaling any dust from any brake surface! When cleaning brake surfaces, use a commercially available cleaning fluid.

Disc Brake Pads

INSPECTION

The brake pad thickness can usually be checked (on most models) by removing the front (or rear, models equipped) wheel, and looking a cutout at the top of the brake caliper. Replace the pads if uneven wear (inner and outer pads) is determined. Always replace the brake pads as a set (both wheels).

REMOVAL & INSTALLATION

Colt

▶ See Figures 7, 8, 9 and 10

1. Raise and support the front end on jackstands. Remove the wheels.

➡On models equipped with the PFS15 type front disc brakes; the caliper and pads are retained to the adapter by two sleeve pin bolts. Remove the pin bolts and service the assembly as required. Sleeve pin torque is 16-23 ft. lbs.

2. Remove the lower sleeve bolt from the caliper and rotate the caliper upward.

➡There is a grease coating on the bolt. Make sure that it is not removed or contaminated.

3. Support the caliper by suspending it with wire or string from a nearby suspension member.
4. Remove the inner, then outer shims from the caliper.
5. Lift out the brake pads.
6. Remove the pad liners.
7. Clean all parts in solvent made for brake parts.
8. Inspect the dust boot on the caliper piston. If it is torn or brittle, replace it. and consider rebuilding the caliper.

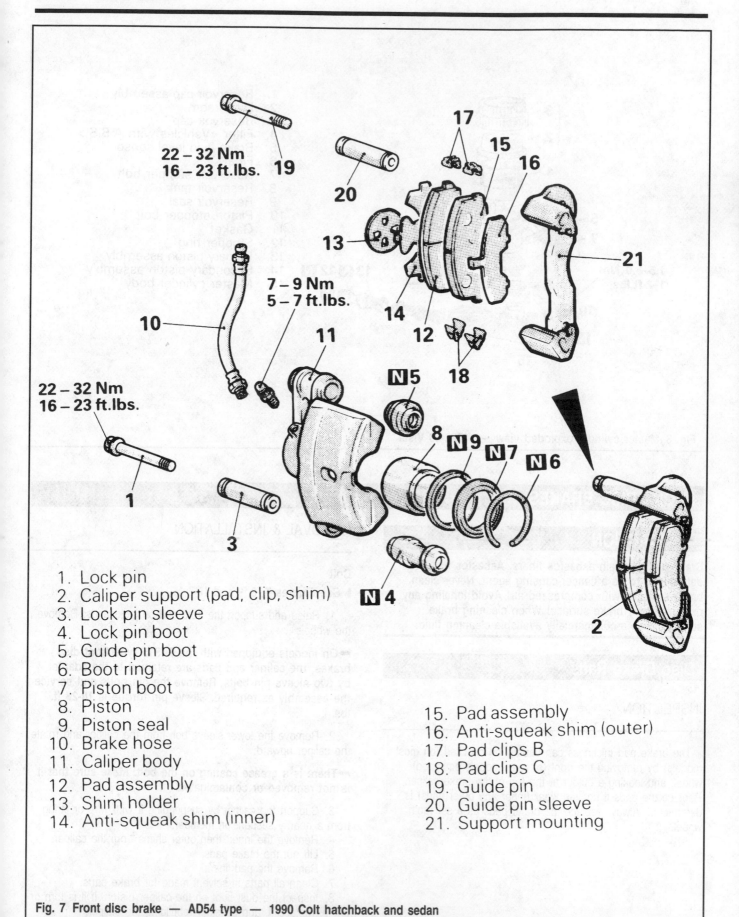

1. Lock pin
2. Caliper support (pad, clip, shim)
3. Lock pin sleeve
4. Lock pin boot
5. Guide pin boot
6. Boot ring
7. Piston boot
8. Piston
9. Piston seal
10. Brake hose
11. Caliper body
12. Pad assembly
13. Shim holder
14. Anti-squeak shim (inner)

15. Pad assembly
16. Anti-squeak shim (outer)
17. Pad clips B
18. Pad clips C
19. Guide pin
20. Guide pin sleeve
21. Support mounting

Fig. 7 Front disc brake — AD54 type — 1990 Colt hatchback and sedan

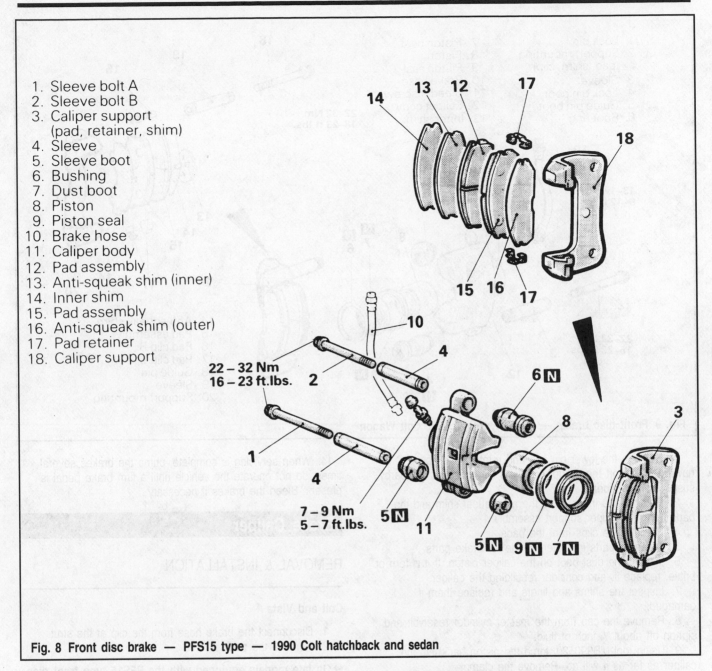

1. Sleeve bolt A
2. Sleeve bolt B
3. Caliper support (pad, retainer, shim)
4. Sleeve
5. Sleeve boot
6. Bushing
7. Dust boot
8. Piston
9. Piston seal
10. Brake hose
11. Caliper body
12. Pad assembly
13. Anti-squeak shim (inner)
14. Inner shim
15. Pad assembly
16. Anti-squeak shim (outer)
17. Pad retainer
18. Caliper support

22 – 32 Nm
16 – 23 ft.lbs.

7 – 9 Nm
5 – 7 ft.lbs.

Fig. 8 Front disc brake — PFS15 type — 1990 Colt hatchback and sedan

9. Inspect the shims and liners and replace them if damaged.

10. Remove the cap from the master cylinder reservoir and siphon off about ¼ inch of fluid.

11. Using a C-clamp, force the piston back into the caliper as far as it will go. Remove the clamp.

12. Install the liners, pads and inner, then outer shims.

➡**Never replace just one set of pads, pads should be replaced on both front wheels at the same time.**

13. Lower the caliper and install the lower sleeve bolt. Torque the bolt to 16-23 ft. lbs.

14. Start the engine and depress the brake pedal several times. Hold it depressed for about 5 seconds. Turn the engine off.

15. Rotate the brake rotor a few times. Using a spring scale hooked to one of the lugs, measure the brake drag. Remove

the pads and perform the spring scale test again. The difference between the drag test with and without the pads should not exceed 15 lbs. If the difference does exceed 15 lbs., the caliper will have to be rebuilt or replaced. Service if required. When servicing is complete, pump the brakes several times. Do not move the car until a firm brake pedal is present.

Vista

◆ **See Figures 11 and 12**

1. Raise and support the front end on jackstands. Remove the front wheels.

➡**On late models equipped with the PFS15 type front disc brakes; the caliper and pads are retained to the adapter by two sleeve pin bolts. Remove the pin bolts and service the assembly as required. Sleeve bolt torque is 16-23 ft. lbs.**

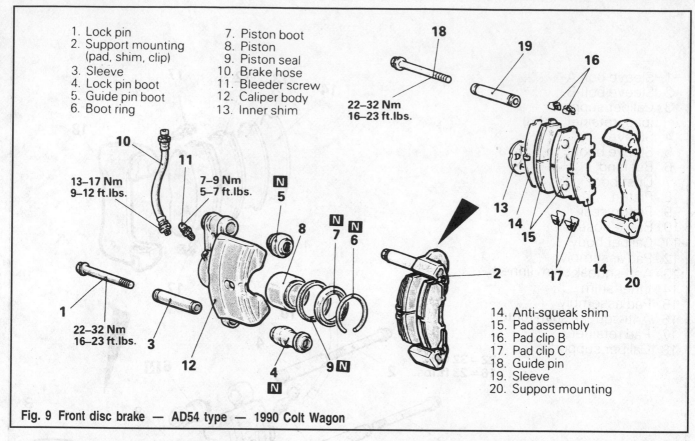

1. Lock pin
2. Support mounting (pad, shim, clip)
3. Sleeve
4. Lock pin boot
5. Guide pin boot
6. Boot ring
7. Piston boot
8. Piston
9. Piston seal
10. Brake hose
11. Bleeder screw
12. Caliper body
13. Inner shim

22–32 Nm
16–23 ft.lbs.

13–17 Nm
9–12 ft.lbs.

7–9 Nm
5–7 ft.lbs.

22–32 Nm
16–23 ft.lbs.

14. Anti-squeak shim
15. Pad assembly
16. Pad clip B
17. Pad clip C
18. Guide pin
19. Sleeve
20. Support mounting

Fig. 9 Front disc brake — AD54 type — 1990 Colt Wagon

2. Remove the lower pin bolt and rotate the caliper upwards. Support the caliper with wire or string from a nearby suspension member.

3. Remove the inner shim, the anti-squeal shim and the pads from the caliper support assembly.

4. Remove the clips from the pads.

5. Clean all parts in solvent made for brake parts.

6. Inspect the dust boot on the caliper piston. If it is torn or brittle, replace it, and consider rebuilding the caliper.

7. Inspect the shims and liners and replace them if damaged.

8. Remove the cap from the master cylinder reservoir and siphon off about ¼ inch of fluid.

9. Using tool MB990520, force the piston back into the caliper as far as it will go. Remove the clamp.

10. Install the pads with clips attached and the proper shims, in position, on the support.

➡**Never replace just one set of pads. Pads should be replaced on both front wheels at the same time.**

11. Lower the caliper and install the lower pin bolt. Torque the bolt to 16-23 ft. lbs.

12. Start the engine and depress the brake pedal. Hold it depressed for about 5 seconds. Turn the engine off.

13. Rotate the brake rotor a few times. Using a spring scale hooked to one of the lugs, measure the brake drag. Remove the pads and perform the spring scale test again. The difference between the drag test with and without the pads should not exceed 15 lbs. If the difference does exceed 15 lbs., the caliper will have to be rebuilt or replaced.

14. When servicing is complete, pump the brakes several times, do not operate the vehicle until a firm brake pedal is present. Bleed the brakes if necessary.

Brake Caliper

REMOVAL & INSTALLATION

Colt and Vista

1. Disconnect the brake hose from the clip at the strut.
2. Remove the pads.

➡**On late models equipped with the PFS15 type front disc brakes; the caliper and pads are retained to the adapter by two sleeve pin bolts. Remove the pin bolts and service the assembly as required. Sleeve bolt torque is 16-23 ft. lbs.**

3. Remove the upper pin bolt.
4. Lift off the caliper.
5. Clean all parts thoroughly.
6. Place the caliper into position and install the pin bolt. Install the brake pads and connect the brake hose. Torque the pin bolts to 16-23 ft. lbs. Bleed the system. Road test the car.

OVERHAUL

Colt and Vista

1. Remove the caliper assembly from the car.

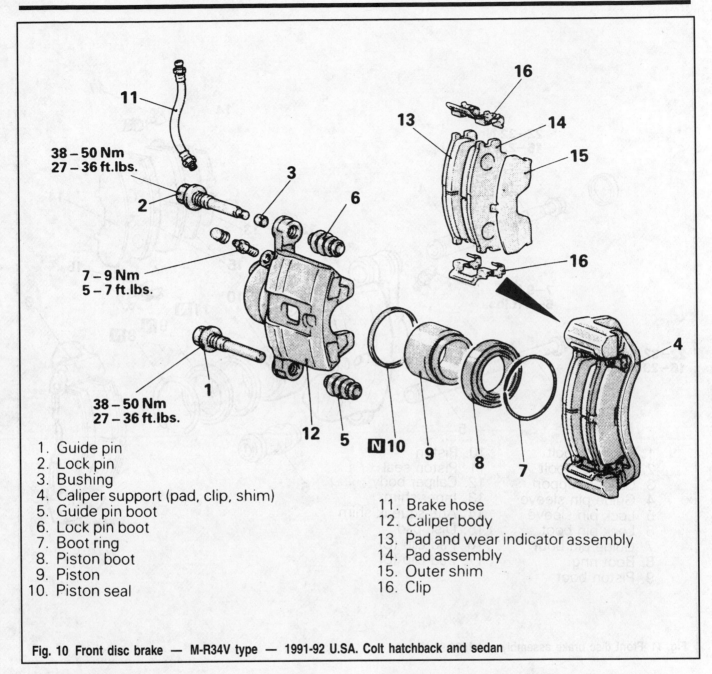

38 – 50 Nm
27 – 36 ft.lbs.

7 – 9 Nm
5 – 7 ft.lbs.

38 – 50 Nm
27 – 36 ft.lbs.

1. Guide pin
2. Lock pin
3. Bushing
4. Caliper support (pad, clip, shim)
5. Guide pin boot
6. Lock pin boot
7. Boot ring
8. Piston boot
9. Piston
10. Piston seal

11. Brake hose
12. Caliper body
13. Pad and wear indicator assembly
14. Pad assembly
15. Outer shim
16. Clip

Fig. 10 Front disc brake — M-R34V type — 1991-92 U.S.A. Colt hatchback and sedan

2. Remove the pads.

3. Remove and discard the piston dust boot.

4. Apply low pressure compressed air to the brake line hose in the caliper, and force the piston out of its bore. Keep your fingers out of the way of the piston, as it often will pop out with considerable force.

5. Remove the seal from the piston, being careful to avoid scratching the piston surface.

6. Clean all parts in alcohol. Discard all rubber parts.

7. Replace the piston if if appears worn, damaged or pitted. Replace all rubber parts.

8. Coat the piston and bore with clean brake fluid.

9. Coat the piston seal with rubber grease. Install it on the piston.

10. Insert the piston into the bore, being careful to avoid twisting the seal.

11. Apply silicone grease to the new dust boot and install it.

12. Install the caliper and brake pads. Coat the pin bolt threads with clean brake fluid on Colt; RTV silicone sealant on Vista.

Wheel Bearings/Disc Rotor

REMOVAL & INSTALLATION

Refer to the Hub, Knuckle and Rotor procedure (preceding Section) and remove the hub and knuckle assembly. This procedure also explains how to separate the rotor from the hub, and adjustment and packing of the bearings as well as bearing replacement. With the rotor removed, check for thickness and runout. See the brake specifications chart for appropriate values.

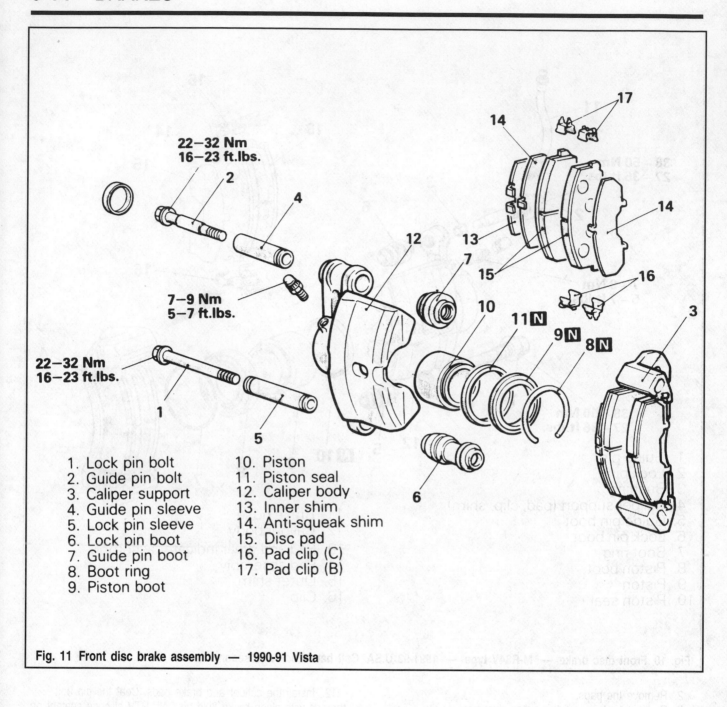

1. Lock pin bolt
2. Guide pin bolt
3. Caliper support
4. Guide pin sleeve
5. Lock pin sleeve
6. Lock pin boot
7. Guide pin boot
8. Boot ring
9. Piston boot
10. Piston
11. Piston seal
12. Caliper body
13. Inner shim
14. Anti-squeak shim
15. Disc pad
16. Pad clip (C)
17. Pad clip (B)

Fig. 11 Front disc brake assembly — 1990-91 Vista

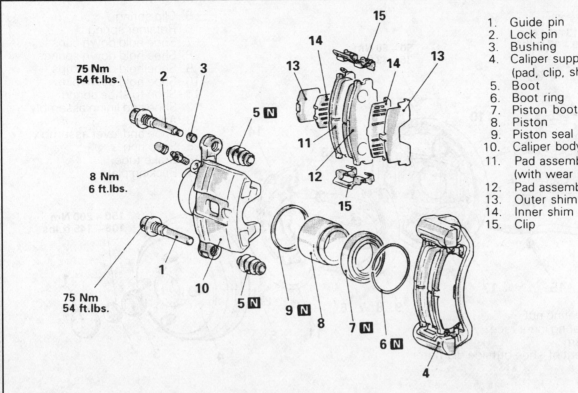

1. Guide pin
2. Lock pin
3. Bushing
4. Caliper support (pad, clip, shim)
5. Boot
6. Boot ring
7. Piston boot
8. Piston
9. Piston seal
10. Caliper body
11. Pad assembly (with wear indicator)
12. Pad assembly
13. Outer shim
14. Inner shim
15. Clip

Fig. 12 Front disc brake assembly — 1992-93 Vista

REAR DRUM BRAKES

✳✳CAUTION

Brake shoes contain asbestos, which has been determined to be a cancer causing agent. Never clean the brake surfaces with compressed air! Avoid inhaling any dust from any brake surface! When cleaning brake surfaces, use a commercially available cleaning fluid.

Brake Drum

REMOVAL & INSTALLATION

1. Remove the wheel cover and loosen the lug nuts.
2. Jack up the rear of the car and support with jackstands. Remove the lug nuts and the rear wheels.
3. Remove the hub center cap, loosen and remove the axle nut, slide the drum from the spindle (take care not to drop the axle bearing).

➡If you meet resistance while removing the drum, back off on the adjuster.

4. Inspect the drum for grooves, have it machined or replaced as necessary.
5. Install the drum and adjust the brakes. Repack the wheel bearings (refer to the bearing section in this Section).

Brake Shoes

REMOVAL & INSTALLATION

1990 Colt Hatchback and Sedan
▶ See Figure 13

1. Remove rear wheel and brake drum.
2. Remove the lower pressed metal spring clip, the shoe return spring (the large one piece spring between the two shoes), and the two shoe hold-down springs.
3. Remove the shoes and adjuster as an assembly. Disconnect the parking brake cable from the lever, remove the spring between the shoes and the lever from the rear (trailing) shoe. Disconnect the adjuster retaining spring and remove the adjuster, turn the star wheel in to the adjuster body after cleaning and lubricating the threads.
4. The wheel cylinder may be removed for service or replacement, if necessary.
5. Clean the backing plate. Install the wheel cylinder if it was removed. Lubricate all contact points on the backing plate, anchor plate, wheel cylinder to shoe contact and parking brake strut joints and contacts. Install the brake shoes after attaching the parking brake, lever and adjuster assemblies. Install the holddown and return springs.

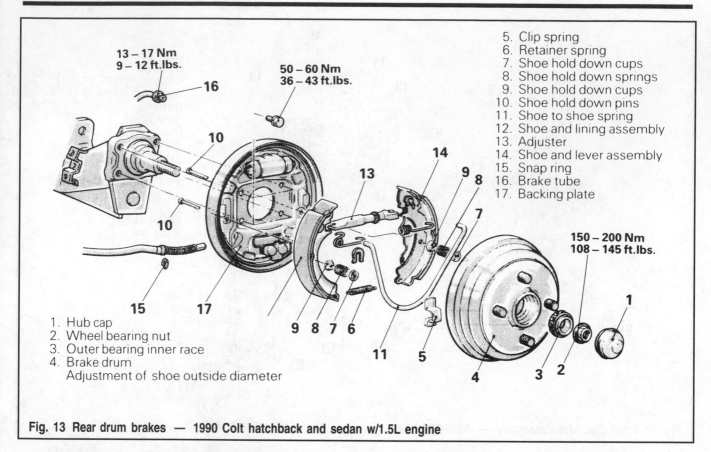

13 – 17 Nm
9 – 12 ft.lbs.

16

50 – 60 Nm
36 – 43 ft.lbs.

10

14

13

9 8

7

150 – 200 Nm
108 – 145 ft.lbs.

10

15   17

9 8 7 6

11   5

1

4   3 2

5. Clip spring
6. Retainer spring
7. Shoe hold down cups
8. Shoe hold down springs
9. Shoe hold down cups
10. Shoe hold down pins
11. Shoe to shoe spring
12. Shoe and lining assembly
13. Adjuster
14. Shoe and lever assembly
15. Snap ring
16. Brake tube
17. Backing plate

1. Hub cap
2. Wheel bearing nut
3. Outer bearing inner race
4. Brake drum
   Adjustment of shoe outside diameter

Fig. 13 Rear drum brakes — 1990 Colt hatchback and sedan w/1.5L engine

6. Pre-adjustment of the brake shoe can be made by turning the adjuster star wheel out until the drum will just slide on over the brake shoes. Before installing the drum make sure the parking brake is not adjusted too tightly, if it is — loosen, or the adjustment of the rear brakes will not be correct.

7. If the wheel cylinders were serviced, bleed the brake system. The brake shoes are then adjusted by pumping the brake pedal and applying and releasing the parking brake, Adjust the parking brake stroke. Road test the car.

1990 Colt Wagon 1991-93 Colt Hatchback and Sedan
▶ **See Figures 14, 15, 16, 17, 18, 19, 20 and 21**

1. Elevate and safely support the car on stands.
2. Remove the rear brake drums as described above.
3. Using brake spring pliers, remove the spring connecting the two shoes and the spring connecting the right side shoe to the adjuster strut.
4. Remove the shoe hold-down spring on either side by first depressing slightly and then twisting the retaining cap. (There is a common brake tool that is designed to make this almost effortless.) The tangs on the retaining post must line up with the notches in the cap; release the cap in this way and then remove the cap, spring, and spring seat. Remove shoe retaining spring with the pliers.
5. Remove the leading (right side) shoe.
6. Remove the other shoe then disconnect the parking brake cable at the shoe. It's easier to disconnect the cable with the shoe removed from the backing plate but can be done otherwise if you wish.

7. If the parking brake cable is to be removed entirely, you can now remove the snapring at the backing plate and pull the end of the cable through.

8. To install, first grease the surfaces of the shoe that will contact the backing plate (this means the side edge of the shoe, NOT the friction surface), the backing plate contact points, and the working surfaces of the anchor plate and wheel cylinder pistons. Use a silicone based grease; not all lubricants are appropriate.

9. Assemble hold down pins and springs and install the parking brake cable to the shoe. Install the shoe and secure the spring pin with the push-and-twist motion. (This can become a three-handed job; an assistant may be required.).

10. Install the other shoe and secure it.

11. Install the adjusting mechanism and springs, making sure the springs are in the correct position. It is quite possible to install the springs backwards; this will cause impaired function and noise.   When installing the shoe-to-shoe and shoe-to-strut springs, set the adjuster lever so the ratchet is locked in the fully released direction.

12. Double check the placement and installation of all components. Everything must be accurately placed and securely fastened.

13. Use the adjuster to set the brakes to the correct diameter. Use an accurate measuring device to measure the outer diameter of the brake shoes. This measurement must be set correctly; otherwise either the drum will not go over the shoes or the adjustment will be too loose. Correct measurement is 179.0-179.5mm.

14. Install the brake drum as described above.

15. Install the wheels. Make sure you depress the brake pedal repeatedly to fully adjust the self-adjusters before

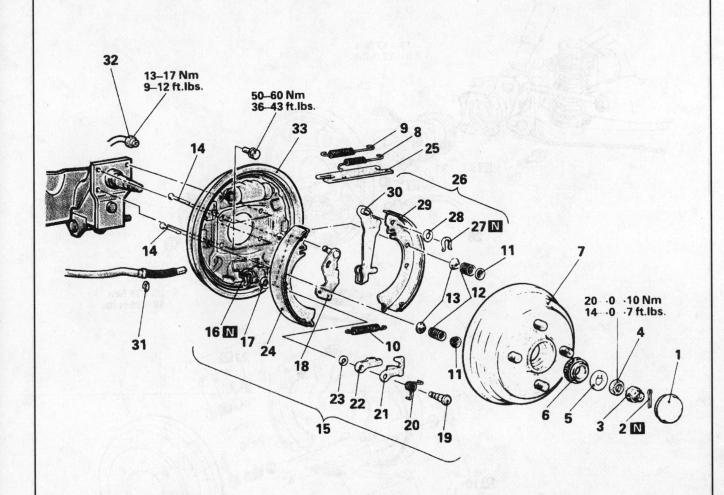

Fig. 14 Rear drum brakes — 1990 2WD Colt Wagon

1. Hub cap
2. Split pin
3. Cap
4. Wheel bearing nut
5. Tongued washer
6. Outer wheel bearing inner race
7. Brake drum
8. Shoe-to-strut spring
9. Shoe-to-shoe spring
10. Shoe retainer spring
11. Shoe hold-down cups
12. Shoe hold-down springs
13. Shoe hold-down cups
14. Shoe hold-down pins
15. Shoe (leading end) and adjuster assembly
16. Retainers
17. Washer
18. Adjuster lever
19. Pin
20. Auto adjuster latch spring
21. Stopper

22. Latch
23. Washer
24. Shoe assembly
25. Strut
26. Shoe (trailing end) and lever assembly
27. Retainer
28. Washer
29. Shoe assembly
30. Parking brake lever
31. Snap ring
32. Brake tube connection
33. Backing plate

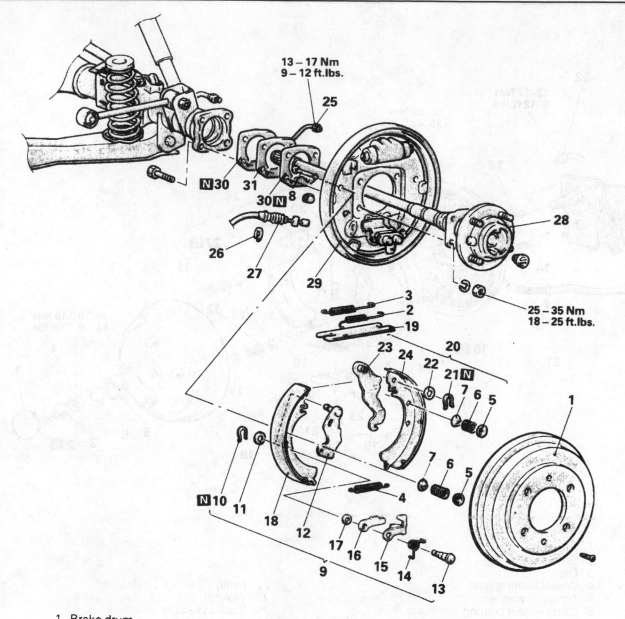

13 – 17 Nm
9 – 12 ft.lbs.

25

N30   31

30 N   8

26

27

29

28

25 – 35 Nm
18 – 25 ft.lbs.

3
2
19
20
23 24 22 21 N
7 6 5

N 10 11
18 12 17 16 15 14 13
9

4
7 6 5

1

1. Brake drum
2. Shoe-to-strut spring
3. Shoe-to-shoe spring
4. Shoe retainer spring
5. Shoe hold-down cups
6. Shoe hold-down springs
7. Shoe hold-down cups
8. Shoe hold-down pins
9. Shoe (leading end) and adjuster assembly
10. Retainers
11. Washer
12. Adjuster lever
13. Pin
14. Auto adjuster latch spring
15. Stopper
16. Latch
17. Washer
18. Shoe assembly
19. Strut

20. Shoe (trailing end) and lever assembly
21. Retainer
22. Washer
23. Parking brake lever
24. Shoe assembly
25. Brake line
26. Snap ring
27. Parking brake cable
28. Rear axle shaft assembly
29. Backing plate
30. Packing
31. Bearing retainer shim

Fig. 15 Rear drum brakes — 1990 4WD Colt Wagon

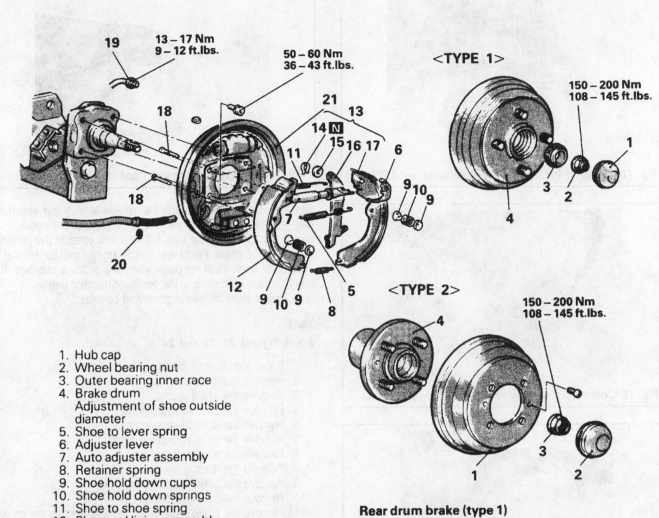

13 – 17 Nm
9 – 12 ft.lbs.

50 – 60 Nm
36 – 43 ft.lbs.

<TYPE 1>

150 – 200 Nm
108 – 145 ft.lbs.

<TYPE 2>

150 – 200 Nm
108 – 145 ft.lbs.

1. Hub cap
2. Wheel bearing nut
3. Outer bearing inner race
4. Brake drum
   Adjustment of shoe outside diameter
5. Shoe to lever spring
6. Adjuster lever
7. Auto adjuster assembly
8. Retainer spring
9. Shoe hold down cups
10. Shoe hold down springs
11. Shoe to shoe spring
12. Shoe and lining assembly
13. Shoe and lining and pin assembly
14. Retainer
15. Wave washer
16. Parking lever
17. Shoe and lining assembly
18. Shoe hold down pins
19. Brake tube
20. Snap ring
21. Backing plate

Rear drum brake (type 1)

7. Auto adjuster assembly
8. Retainer spring
9. Shoe hold down cups
10. Shoe hold down springs
11. Shoe to shoe spring
12. Shoe and lining assembly
13. Shoe and lining and pin assembly
14. Retainer
15. Wave washer
16. Parking lever
17. Shoe and lining assembly
18. Shoe hold down pins
19. Brake tube
20. Snap ring
21. Backing plate

Rear drum brake (type 2)

1. Brake drum
   Adjustment of shoe outside diameter
2. Hub cap
3. Wheel bearing nut
4. Rear hub assembly
5. Shoe to lever spring
6. Adjuster lever

Fig. 16 Rear drum brakes — 1991-92 Colt hatchback and sedan

Fig. 17 Installing trailing shoe and adjuster — 1992 Colt

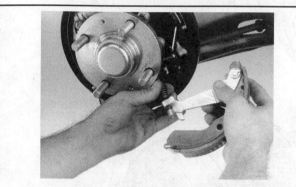
Fig. 18 Connecting parking brake cable — 1992 Colt

Fig. 19 Installing holddown spring assembly — 1992 Colt

Fig. 20 Installing lower spring — 1992 Colt

Fig. 21 Installing upper return spring — 1992 Colt

operating the vehicle. Operate the vehicle at very low speed in both forward and reverse gears, pumping the brake pedal repeatedly. Bring the car to a full stop and operate the parking brake several times. Pedal feel should be normal, but the car should roll freely (with no drag) when the pedal is released. If any condition is abnormal, the brake adjustment and/or components must be investigated and corrected.

Vista

▶ **See Figures 22, 23 and 24**

1. Raise and support the rear on jackstands.
2. Remove the wheels.
3. Remove the brake drums.
4. Remove the shoe-to-strut spring.
5. Remove the shoe-to-shoe spring.
6. Remove the shoe hold-down spring.
7. Remove the shoe retainer clip.
8. Remove the leading shoe.
9. Remove the brake cable from the lever.
10. Remove the trailing shoe.
11. Remove the brake cable snapring and remove the cable.
12. Inspect all parts for wear or damage. Heat damage is a problem common to brake systems. Sign of heat damage are bluing and cracking. It's a good idea, when replacing brake shoes, to replace all the brake hardware, i.e., springs and clips.

➡ **Never replace shoes on one side only! Replace both sets of shoes at the same time.**

13. Assembly the parking brake and adjuster assemblies on the brake shoes. Install the brake shoes and hold-downs. Connect the return springs. Apply a small amount of silicone based grease to the contact pads of the backing plate before installing the shoes. When installing the shoe-to-shoe spring and shoe-to-strut spring, set the adjuster lever all the way back against the shoe. When everything is assembled, pump the pedal several times and adjust the brakes.

Wheel Cylinders

OVERHAUL

Since the piston travel in the wheel cylinder changes when new brake shoes are installed, it is possible for previously

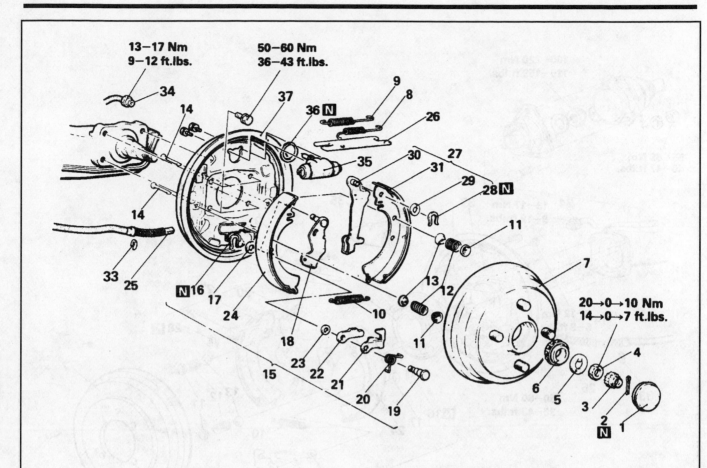

13–17 Nm
9–12 ft.lbs.

50–60 Nm
36–43 ft.lbs.

20→0→10 Nm
14→0→7 ft.lbs.

Fig. 22 Rear brake assembly — 1990-91 2WD Vista

1. Hub cap
2. Cotter pin
3. Lock cap
4. Wheel bearing nut
5. Tongued washer
6. Outer wheel bearing inner race
7. Brake drum
8. Shoe-to-strut spring
9. Shoe-to-shoe spring
10. Shoe retainer spring
11. Shoe hold-down cups
12. Shoe hold-down springs
13. Shoe hold-down cups
14. Shoe hold-down pins
15. Shoe (leading end) and adjuster assembly
16. Retainers
17. Washer
18. Adjuster lever
19. Pin
20. Auto adjuster latch spring
21. Stopper
22. Latch
23. Washer
24. Shoe assembly
25. Cable end connection
26. Strut
27. Shoe (trailing end) and lever assembly
28. Retainer
29. Washer
30. Parking brake lever
31. Shoe assembly
33. Snap ring
34. Brake tube
35. Wheel cylinder assembly
36. Gasket
37. Backing plate

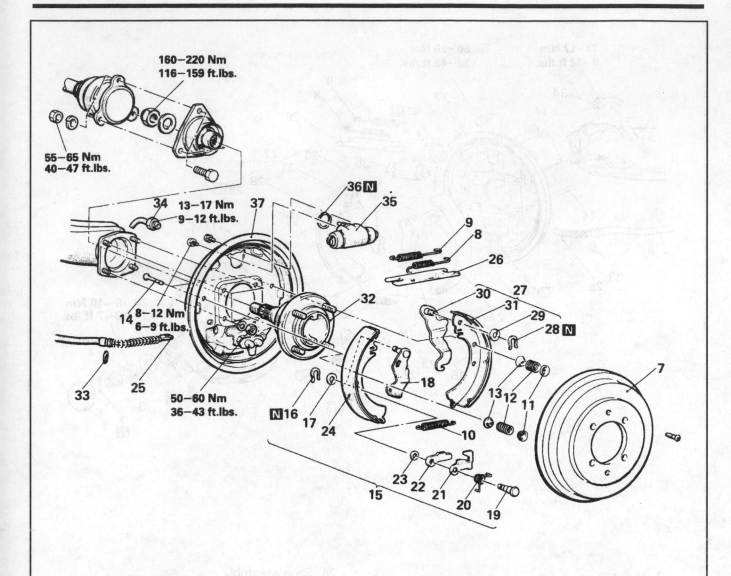

7. Brake drum
8. Shoe-to-strut spring
9. Shoe-to-shoe spring
10. Shoe retainer spring
11. Shoe hold-down cups
12. Shoe hold-down springs
13. Shoe hold-down cups
14. Shoe hold-down pins
15. Shoe (leading end) and adjuster assembly
16. Retainers
17. Washer
18. Adjuster lever
19. Pin
20. Auto adjuster latch spring
21. Stopper
22. Latch
23. Washer
24. Shoe assembly
25. Cable end connection
26. Strut
27. Shoe (trailing end) and lever assembly

28. Retainer
29. Washer
30. Parking brake lever
31. Shoe assembly
32. Rear axle shaft assembly
33. Snap ring
34. Brake tube connection
35. Wheel cylinder assembly
36. Gasket
37. Backing plate

Fig. 23 Rear brake assembly — 1990-91 4WD Vista

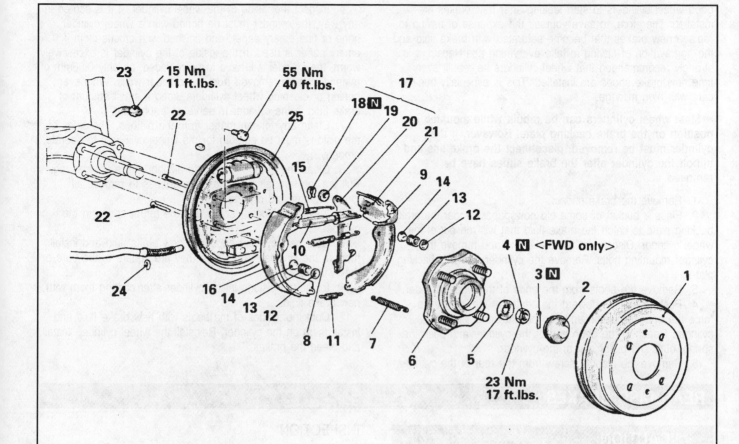

1. Brake drum
2. Hub cap <FWD>
3. Cotter pin <AWD>
4. Lock nut
5. Washer
6. Rear hub assembly
7. Lever return spring
   <AWD>
8. Shoe-to-lever spring
9. Adjuster lever
10. Auto adjuster assembly
11. Retainer spring
12. Shoe hold-down cup
13. Shoe hold-down spring
14. Shoe hold-down cup
15. Shoe-to-shoe spring
16. Shoe and lining assembly
17. Shoe and lever assembly
18. Retainer
19. Wave washer
20. Parking lever
21. Shoe and lining assembly
22. Shoe hold-down pin
23. Connection for the brake tube
24. Snap ring
25. Backing plate

Fig. 24 Rear drum brake assembly — 1992-93 Vista

good wheel cylinders to start leaking after new brakes are installed. Therefore, to save yourself the expense of having to replace new brakes that become saturated with brake fluid and the aggravation of having to take everything apart again, it is strongly recommended that wheel cylinders be rebuilt every time new brake shoes are installed. This is especially true for cars with high mileage.

➡ **Most wheel cylinders can be rebuilt while mounted in position on the brake backing plate. However, if the cylinder must be removed, disconnect the brake line and unbolt the cylinder after the brake shoes have be removed.**

1. Remove the brake shoes.

2. Place a bucket or some old newspapers under the brake backing plate to catch the brake fluid that will run out of the wheel cylinder. Disconnect the brake line and remove the cylinder mounting bolts. Remove the cylinder from the backing plate.

3. Remove the boots from the ends of the wheel cylinder.

4. Push one piston toward the center of the cylinder to force the opposite piston and cup out the other end of the cylinder. Reach in the open end of the cylinder and push the spring, cup, and piston out of the cylinder.

5. Remove the bleeder screw from the rear of the cylinder.

6. Inspect the inside of the wheel cylinder. If it is scored in any way, the cylinder must be honed with a wheel cylinder hone or fine emery paper, and finished with crocus cloth if emery paper is used. If the inside of the cylinder is excessively worm, the cylinder will have to be replaced, as only 0.08mm of material can be removed from the cylinder walls. Whenever honing or cleaning wheel cylinders, keep a small amount of brake fluid in the cylinder to serve as a lubricant.

7. Clean any foreign matter from the pistons. The sides of the pistons must be smooth for the wheel cylinders to operate properly.

8. Clean the cylinder bore with alcohol and a lint-free rag. Pull the rag through the bore several times to remove all foreign matter and dry the cylinder.

9. Install the bleeder screw and the return spring in the cylinder.

10. Coat new cylinder cups with new brake fluid and install them in the cylinder. Make sure they are square in the bore or they will leak.

11. Install the pistons in the cylinder after coating them with new brake fluid.

12. Coat the insides of the boots with new brake fluid and install them on the cylinder. Reinstall the wheel cylinder. Install and bleed the brakes.

REAR DISC BRAKES

✳✳CAUTION

Brake pads and shoes contain asbestos, which has been determined to be a cancer causing agent. Never clean the brake surfaces with compressed air! Avoid inhaling any dust from brake surfaces! When cleaning brakes, use commercially available brake cleaning fluids.

✳✳WARNING

If the car has been recently driven before repairs, all the brake surfaces and components may be very hot. Work carefully and wear gloves.

Disc Brake Pads

Wear Indicators

Some rear disc brake pads are equipped with a metal tab which will come into contact with the disc after the friction surface material has worn near its usable minimum. The wear indicators make a constant, distinct metallic sound that should be easily heard. (The sound has been described as similar to either fingernails on a blackboard or a field full of crickets.) The key to recognizing that it is the wear indicators and not some other brake noise is that the sound is heard when the car is being driven WITHOUT the brakes applied. It may or may not be present under braking during normal driving.

INSPECTION

The rear brake pads may be inspected without removal. With the rear end elevated and supported, remove the wheel(s). View the pads, inner and outer, through the cut-out in the center of the caliper. Remember to look at the thickness of the pad friction material (the part that actually presses on the disc) rather than the thickness of the backing plate which does not change with wear.

Remember that you are looking at the profile of the pad, not the whole thing. Brake pads can wear on a taper which may not be visible through the window. It is also not possible to check the contact surface for cracking or scoring from this position. This quick check can be helpful only as a reference; detailed inspection requires pad removal.

After the pads are removed, measure the thickness of the LINING portion (NOT the backing) of the pads. It must be at least 2mm. This is a factory minimum; please note that local inspection standards enforced by your state must be given precedence if they require a greater thickness.

REMOVAL & INSTALLATION

▶ **See Figures 25, 26 and 27**

➡ **NOTE:Whenever brake pads are replaced, replace them in complete sets; that is, replace the pads on both rear wheels even if only one side is worn.**

There are several combinations of shims, spacers and clips in use on these vehicles. When disassembling, work on one side at a time and pay attention to placement of these

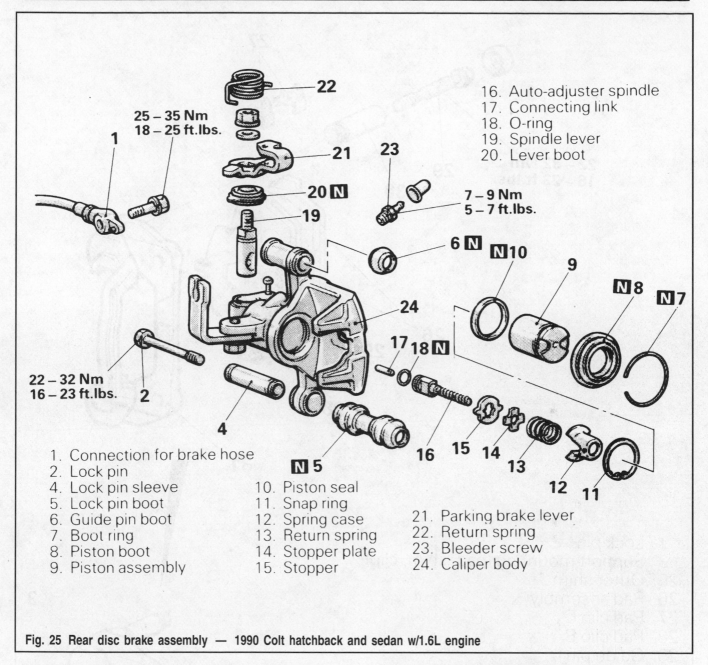

22
25 – 35 Nm
18 – 25 ft.lbs.
1
21
23
20 N
19
1
22 – 32 Nm
16 – 23 ft.lbs.
2
4
N 5

16. Auto-adjuster spindle
17. Connecting link
18. O-ring
19. Spindle lever
20. Lever boot

7 – 9 Nm
5 – 7 ft.lbs.

6 N   N 10   9   N 8   N 7

17 18 N   24

16   15   14   13   12   11

1. Connection for brake hose
2. Lock pin
4. Lock pin sleeve
5. Lock pin boot
6. Guide pin boot
7. Boot ring
8. Piston boot
9. Piston assembly

10. Piston seal
11. Snap ring
12. Spring case
13. Return spring
14. Stopper plate
15. Stopper

21. Parking brake lever
22. Return spring
23. Bleeder screw
24. Caliper body

Fig. 25 Rear disc brake assembly — 1990 Colt hatchback and sedan w/1.6L engine

components. If you become confused during reassembly, refer to the other side for correct placement.

1. Raise the vehicle and support it safely on stands.

2. Remove the rear wheels. Disconnect the parking brake cable at the caliper by removing the cotter pin and then the clevis pin and washer.

3. Unscrew and remove the lower caliper lock pin without removing its grease coating or allowing it to get dirty. Raise the caliper upward with the upper mounting pin serving as a hinge and use a piece of wire to tie or hold it in place.

4. Release the clips and then remove the pads and shims.

5. Use a tool MB990652 or an equivalent device to press the caliper piston back into the caliper. Make sure the two indentations in the caliper piston are aligned as shown. The pins on the backing plates for the pads must fit into these recesses when the pads are replaced.

6. Fit the pad and shim together and then install them into the clips and in proper relationship with the caliper piston.

7. Unwire the body of the caliper and lower it back to its normal position.

8. Install the lock pin and torque it to 27 Nm or 20 ft. lbs.

9. Reconnect the parking brake cable, using a new cotter pin.

10. Replace the wheels and lower the vehicle.

11. Make sure there is plenty of fluid in the reservoir. Pump the brake pedal repeatedly, checking the fluid level and keeping the reservoir adequately filled. Make sure the brakes actuate at the normal pedal position, indicating the fluid has pushed the pads directly against the disc before operating the vehicle.

12. Since the hydraulic system was not opened, bleeding is usually not necessary after pad replacement.

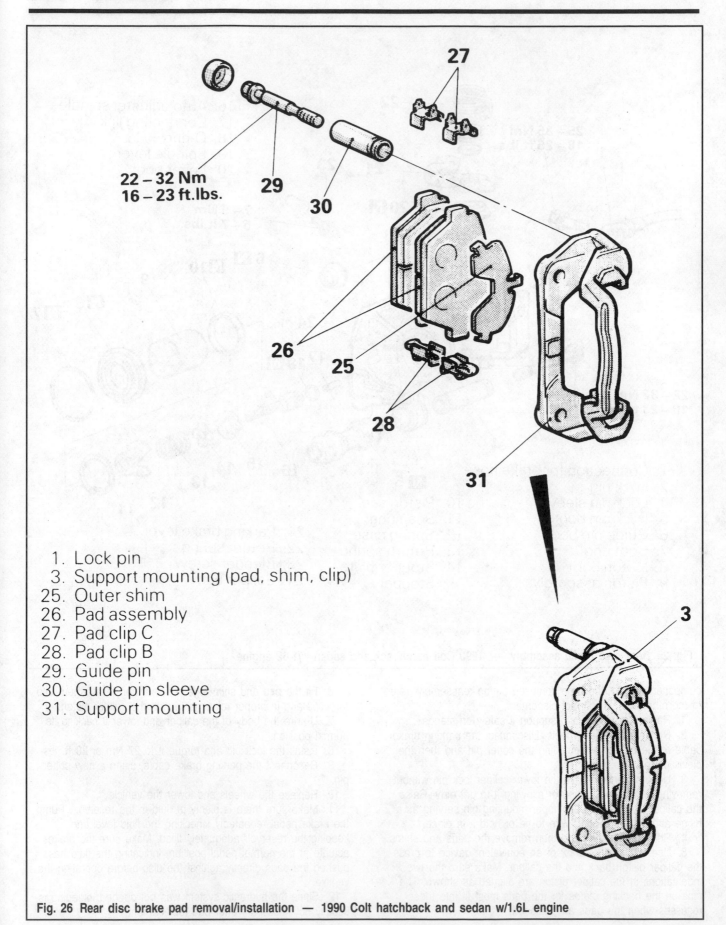

22 – 32 Nm
16 – 23 ft.lbs.

1. Lock pin
3. Support mounting (pad, shim, clip)
25. Outer shim
26. Pad assembly
27. Pad clip C
28. Pad clip B
29. Guide pin
30. Guide pin sleeve
31. Support mounting

Fig. 26 Rear disc brake pad removal/installation — 1990 Colt hatchback and sedan w/1.6L engine

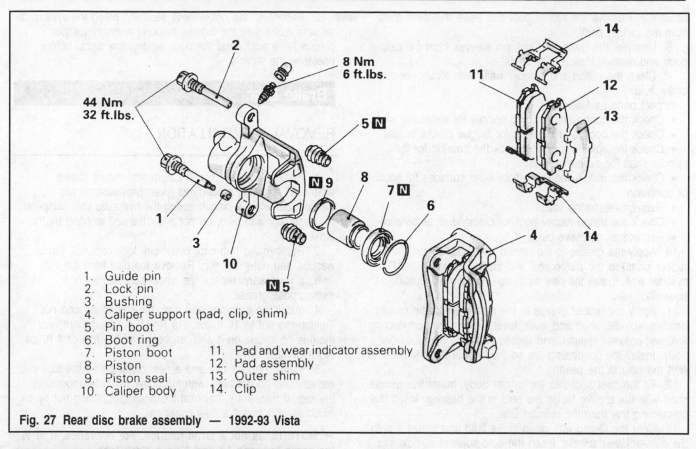

1. Guide pin
2. Lock pin
3. Bushing
4. Caliper support (pad, clip, shim)
5. Pin boot
6. Boot ring
7. Piston boot
8. Piston
9. Piston seal
10. Caliper body
11. Pad and wear indicator assembly
12. Pad assembly
13. Outer shim
14. Clip

Fig. 27 Rear disc brake assembly — 1992-93 Vista

Disc Brake Calipers

REMOVAL & INSTALLATION

1. Raise the vehicle and support it safely on stands.
2. Remove the rear wheels.
3. Disconnect the parking brake cable at the caliper by removing the special clip at the caliper and then disconnecting the fitting located on the end of the cable.
4. Place a drain pan under the work area and disconnect the brake hose at the strut. Plug the open line immediately.
5. Remove the lock (lower) pin from the caliper assembly.
6. Remove the bolts mounting the caliper support to the lower strut and remove the assembly. Remove the cap and guide pin to separate the caliper from the caliper support.
7. Assemble the complete unit before installation. Place the unit onto the car and tighten the caliper support mounting bolts to 54 Nm or 40 ft. lbs. The guide and lock pins should be tightened to 27 Nm or 20 ft. lbs.
8. Reconnect the brake line securely.
9. Connect the parking brake cable and install the clip securely.
10. Bleed the system thoroughly, keeping the master cylinder reservoir supplied with fluid during and after the procedure. Make certain the brakes have the correct feel and engagement point before lowering the car to the ground.

OVERHAUL

✳✳WARNING

The use of the correct special tools or their equivalent is REQUIRED for this procedure. Special tool MB990652 or equivalent to use in twisting the piston out of the caliper body; a steel pipe 19mm inch diameter; and special tool MB 991041 or equivalent (to remove a snapring from the caliper) will all be required.

1. Remove the caliper and support. Separate the caliper from the support.
2. With the blade of a small flat instrument, remove the boot ring from the caliper body and the pull out the piston boot.
3. Use special tool MB 990652 or equivalent to remove the piston from the caliper with a twisting motion.
4. Using a 19mm diameter steel pipe to press the spring retainer or case into the caliper body, and use MB 991041 or equivalent to remove the snapring that holds the retainer. Remove the spring case, return spring, washer, and stop from the body.
5. Remove the automatic adjuster spindle from the body and remove the connecting link. Remove the O-ring from the adjuster spindle.
6. Being careful not to scratch the cylinder wall, remove the piston seal from the caliper body using a blunt, non-metallic tool.
7. Disconnect the return spring, remove the mounting nut, and pull the parking brake actuating lever out of the caliper

assembly. Remove the rubber boot that seals the lever shaft from the caliper body.

8. Unscrew the guide and lock pin sleeves from the caliper body and remove their rubber boots.

9. Clean the piston and cylinder walls with alcohol or clean brake fluid.

Inspect parts as follows:

- Check the connecting link and spindle for excessive wear.
- Check the body of the caliper for fatigue cracks or rust.
- Check the spindle for rust. Check the bearing for the spindle shaft for excessive wear.
- Check the piston and the caliper wear surfaces for scoring or corrosion.
- Replace the piston seal.
- Check the piston rubber boot for cracking or brittleness.
- Replace all defective parts.

10. Apply the grease in the rebuild kit (specified for use on rubber parts) to the piston seal and to the groove in the cylinder wall. Install the new seal, making sure it is installed squarely.

11. Apply the proper grease in the rebuild kit to the spindle bearing, spindle, shaft and lever, lever rubber boot, connecting link, self-adjuster spindle, and related locations of the caliper body. Install the connecting link so the hole in the link lines up with the hole in the bearing.

12. Fit the dust boot into the caliper body. Insert the spindle shaft with the groove facing the hole in the bearing. Insert the connecting link from the cylinder side.

13. Coat the O-ring with clean brake fluid and mount it onto the auto-adjuster spindle. Insert the auto-adjuster spindle into the caliper.

14. Install the stop, spring washer, spring, and spring housing or case. Complete this assembly by using the steel pipe to press the spring case inward; use the special tool (used in removal) to attach the snapring to the caliper body. Make absolutely certain that the opening in the snapring faces the bleeder screw.

15. Use the special tool to twist the piston into the caliper. The cylinder is threaded so that the piston cannot move in and out of the bore without a twisting motion.

16. Apply the specified grease to the piston boot mounting grooves in the caliper body and the piston. Install the boot squarely. Carefully install the piston boot retaining ring.

17. Use the correct grease to coat the interior portion of the guide and lock pin sleeves, the threads of the caliper where the sleeves screw in, the rubber boot mounting groove, and the mounting groove for the cap. Then mount the sleeves onto the caliper and insert their respective pins.

18. With the pins, attach the caliper to the caliper support and tighten them to 27 Nm or 20 ft. lbs. Mount the caliper support to the car and tighten the bolts to 54 Nm or 40 ft. lbs.

19. Rotate the parking brake cable bracket clockwise until it contacts the caliper body and tighten the bracket in that position. Reconnect the cable to the bracket.

20. Reconnect the brake hose securely, bleed the system of air, and make sure the brakes respond normally (caliper pistons have positioned the pads against the discs) before operating the vehicle.

Brake Disc

REMOVAL & INSTALLATION

1. Remove the rear brake caliper and mount (brake assembly) following procedures given previously in this Section, but without disconnecting the hydraulic line. Suspend the assembly with wire; do not allow the unit to hang by the brake line.

2. Remove the hub cap, cotter pin, lock cap, nut, thrust washer, and outer bearing. Remove the disc from the hub.

3. If necessary, repack the wheel bearings with multipurpose grease.

4. Install the bearings and disc, thrust washer, and nut. Tighten the nut to 14 ft. lbs. (19 Nm). Loosen the nut until there is no torque on it and retighten it to 5.5 Nm or 4 ft. lbs. (48 INCH lbs).

5. Install the lock cap and a new cotter pin. If the lock cap castellations do not align with the cotter pin hole, reposition the cap. If necessary, back off the bearing retaining nut by as much as 15°. Install a new cotter pin.

➡ **NOTE:15° is not a large rotation. For reference, it is ½ the angle between 12 and 1 on a clock face.**

6. Install the hub cap.

7. Install the brake caliper and mount, following procedures given in this Section.

INSPECTION

Brake discs should be inspected for thickness at a number of spots around the braking surface with a micrometer. If the thickness is less than the minimum (refer to the Brake Specifications Chart) AT ANY POINT, the disc must be replaced. Roughness or significant grooving is also reason to replace the disc.

The disc should also be checked for runout. With the disc installed (hold it with two lug nuts if necessary), mount a dial indicator to the strut and zero it with the tip in contact with the braking surface on the disc. Rotate the disc slowly. Read the indicator; the limit for runout is 0.15mm. The disc must be replaced if runout exceeds this amount.

➡**NOTE:The condition and adjustment of the wheel bearings can affect this reading. Before replacing the disc, check the bearings for proper adjustment and lubrication.**

PARKING BRAKE

Cable

ADJUSTMENT

With Drum Brakes

1. Pull the parking brake lever up with a force of about 45 lbs. If that value cannot be determined, just pull it up as far as you can. The total number of clicks heard should be 5-7.

2. If the number of clicks was not within that range, release the lever and back off the cable adjuster locknut at the base of the lever and tighten the adjusting nut until there is no more slack in the cable.

3. Operate the lever and brake pedal several times, until no more clicks are heard from the automatic adjuster.

4. Turn the adjusting nut to give the proper number of clicks when the lever is raised full travel.

5. Raise and support the rear of the car on jackstands.

6. Release the brake lever and make sure that the rear wheels turn freely. If not, back off on the adjusting nut until they do.

With Disc Brakes

1. Pull the parking brake lever up with a force of about 45 lbs. (61 N). The total number of clicks heard should be 4-6.

2. If the number of clicks was not within that range, remove the floor console, release the lever and back off the cable adjuster locknut at the base of the lever.

3. Raise the vehicle, support safely and remove the wheel. Remove the hole plug in the brake rotor.

4. Remove the brake caliper and hang out of the way with wire.

5. Use a suitable prybar to pry up on the self-adjuster wheel until the rotor will not turn.

6. Return the adjuster 5 notches in the opposite direction. Make sure the rotor turns freely with a slight drag.

7. Install the caliper and check operation.

REMOVAL & INSTALLATION

▶ **See Figures 28, 29, 30, 31, 32 and 33**

1. Block front wheels, raise rear of car and support on jackstands.

2. Disconnect the brake cable at the parking brake lever (brakes released). Remove the cable clamps inside the driver's compartment (two bolts). Disconnect the clamps on the rear suspension arm.

3. Remove the rear brake drums and the brake shoes assemblies. Disconnect the parking brake cable from the lever on the trailing (rear) brake shoe. Remove the brake cables.

4. Install the cable and adjust.

Handbrake Warning Switch

On most models, a dash mounted warning light indicates when the hand brake is applied. The light should go on when the parking brake lever is pulled one or more notches, and go out when the lever is fully released. Adjustment is made by loosening the mounting bolt and changing the mounted positions of the switch.

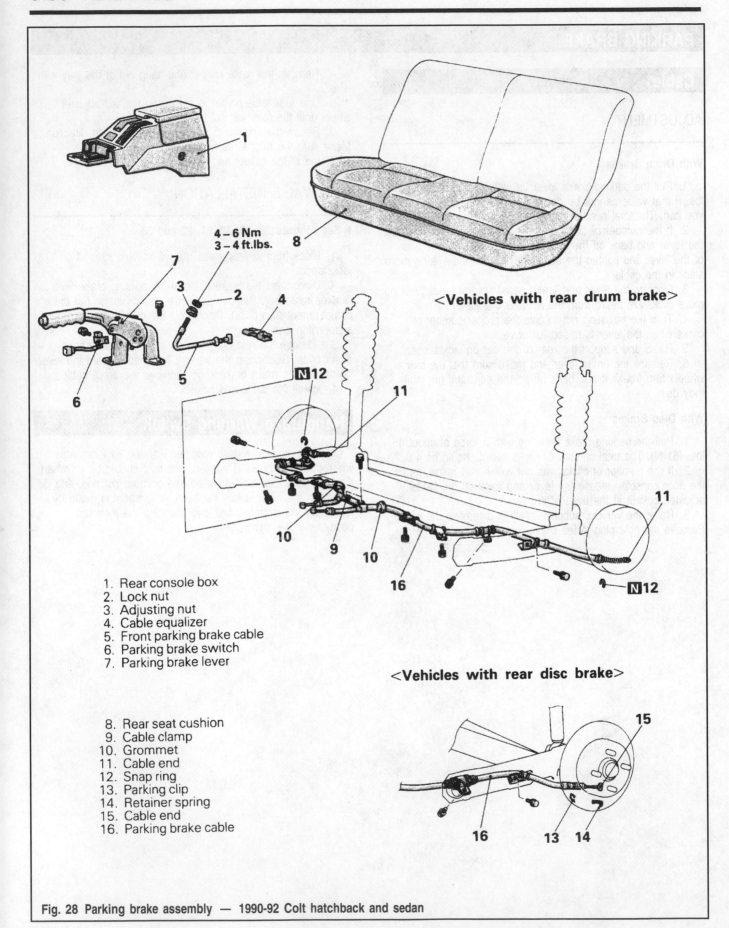

4 – 6 Nm
3 – 4 ft.lbs.

<Vehicles with rear drum brake>

<Vehicles with rear disc brake>

1. Rear console box
2. Lock nut
3. Adjusting nut
4. Cable equalizer
5. Front parking brake cable
6. Parking brake switch
7. Parking brake lever

8. Rear seat cushion
9. Cable clamp
10. Grommet
11. Cable end
12. Snap ring
13. Parking clip
14. Retainer spring
15. Cable end
16. Parking brake cable

Fig. 28 Parking brake assembly — 1990-92 Colt hatchback and sedan

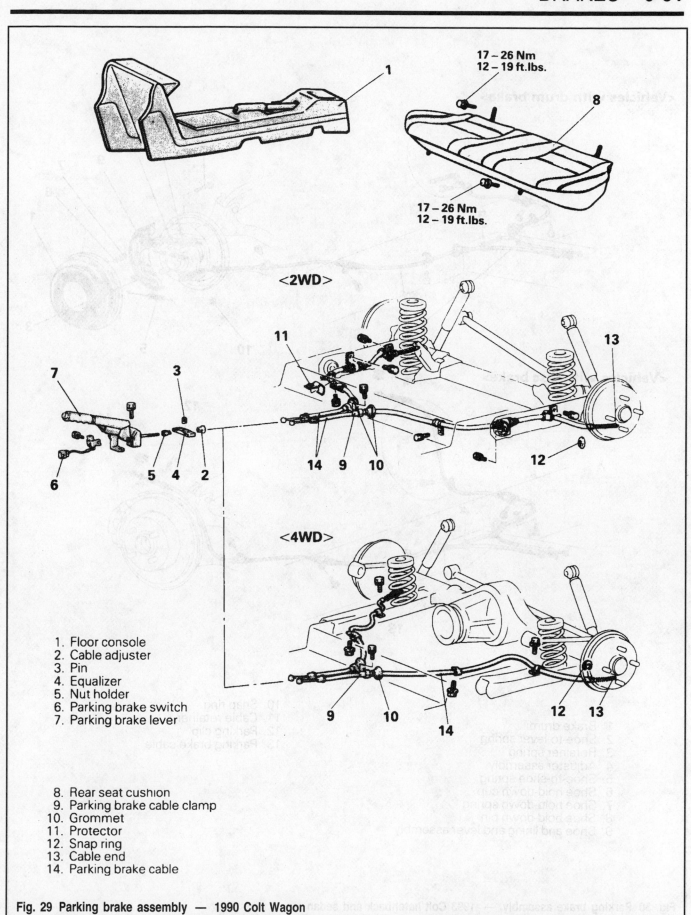

17 – 26 Nm
12 – 19 ft.lbs.

17 – 26 Nm
12 – 19 ft.lbs.

\<2WD\>

\<4WD\>

1. Floor console
2. Cable adjuster
3. Pin
4. Equalizer
5. Nut holder
6. Parking brake switch
7. Parking brake lever

8. Rear seat cushion
9. Parking brake cable clamp
10. Grommet
11. Protector
12. Snap ring
13. Cable end
14. Parking brake cable

Fig. 29 Parking brake assembly — 1990 Colt Wagon

‹Vehicles with drum brake›

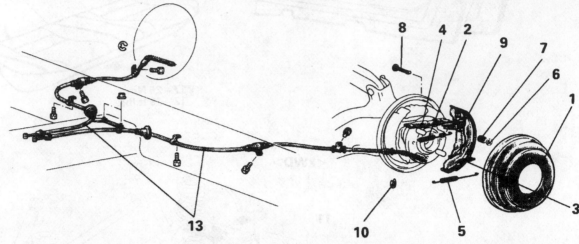

‹Vehicles with disc brake›

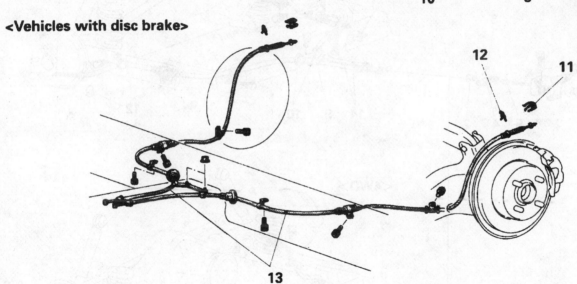

1. Brake drum
2. Shoe-to-lever spring
3. Retainer spring
4. Adjuster assembly
5. Shoe-to-shoe spring
6. Shoe hold-down cup
7. Shoe hold-down spring
8. Shoe hold-down pin
9. Shoe and lining and lever assembly

10. Snap ring
11. Cable retainer
12. Parking clip
13. Parking brake cable

Fig. 30 Parking brake assembly — 1993 Colt hatchback and sedan

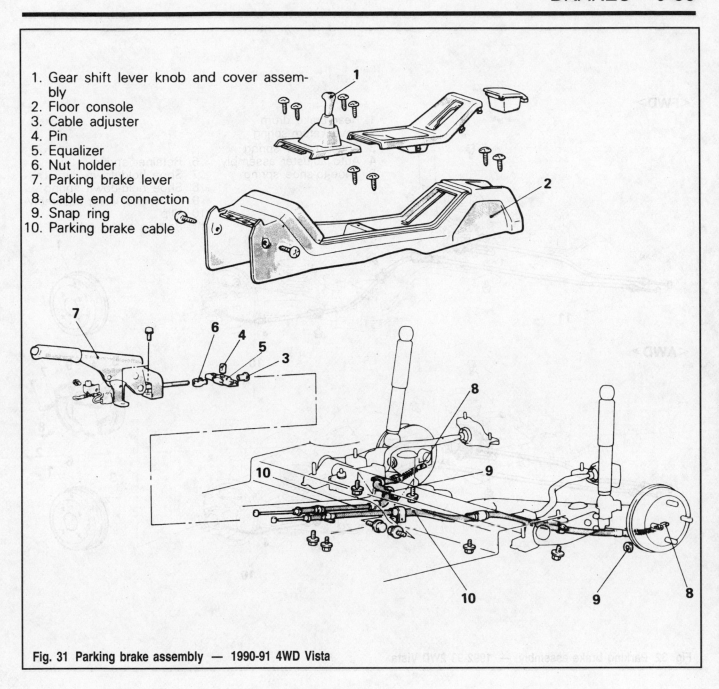

1. Gear shift lever knob and cover assembly
2. Floor console
3. Cable adjuster
4. Pin
5. Equalizer
6. Nut holder
7. Parking brake lever
8. Cable end connection
9. Snap ring
10. Parking brake cable

Fig. 31 Parking brake assembly — 1990-91 4WD Vista

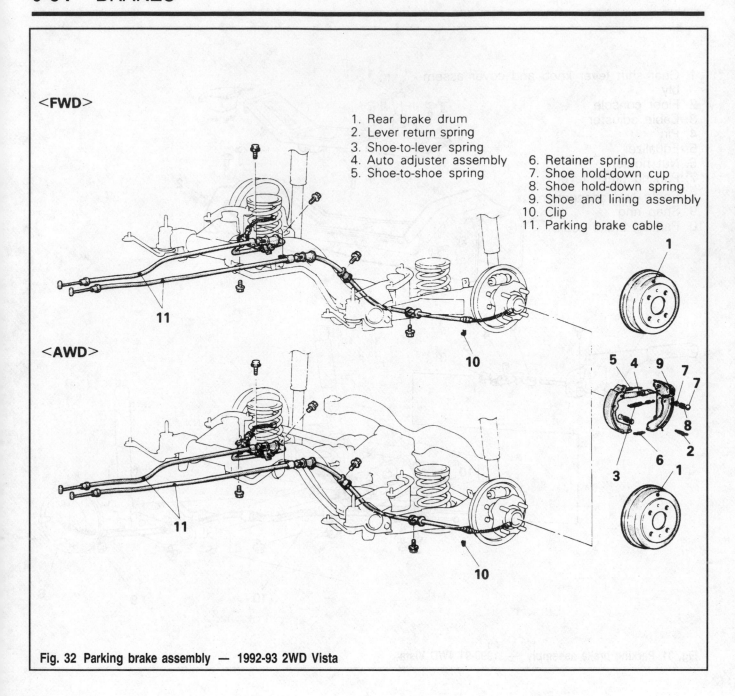

<FWD>

<AWD>

1. Rear brake drum
2. Lever return spring
3. Shoe-to-lever spring
4. Auto adjuster assembly
5. Shoe-to-shoe spring
6. Retainer spring
7. Shoe hold-down cup
8. Shoe hold-down spring
9. Shoe and lining assembly
10. Clip
11. Parking brake cable

Fig. 32 Parking brake assembly — 1992-93 2WD Vista

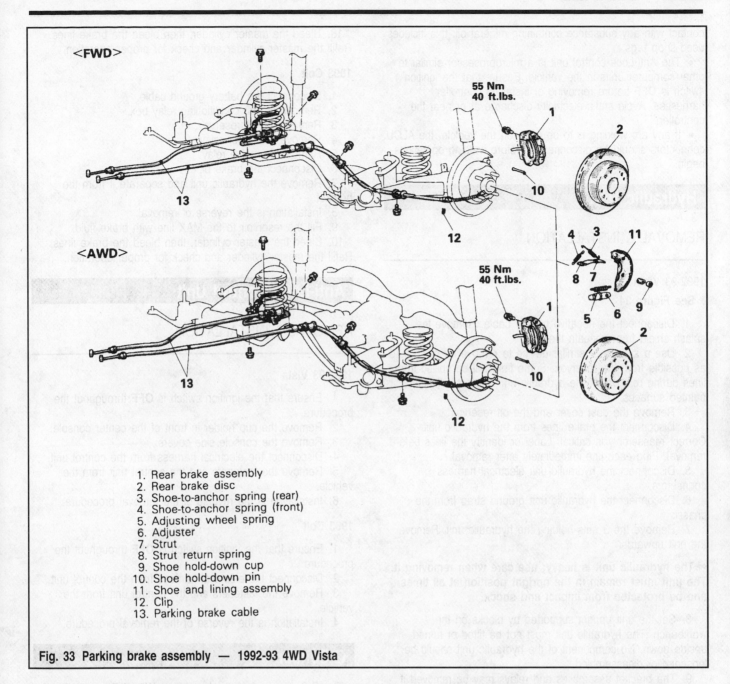

<FWD>

55 Nm
40 ft.lbs.

1

2

13

10

12

<AWD>

55 Nm
40 ft.lbs.

1

4   3   11

8   7

5   6   9

13

10

2

12

1. Rear brake assembly
2. Rear brake disc
3. Shoe-to-anchor spring (rear)
4. Shoe-to-anchor spring (front)
5. Adjusting wheel spring
6. Adjuster
7. Strut
8. Strut return spring
9. Shoe hold-down cup
10. Shoe hold-down pin
11. Shoe and lining assembly
12. Clip
13. Parking brake cable

Fig. 33 Parking brake assembly — 1992-93 4WD Vista

ANTI-LOCK BRAKE SYSTEM SERVICE

Precautions

• Certain components within the ABS system are not intended to be serviced or repaired individually. Only those components with removal and Installation procedures should be serviced.

• Do not use rubber hoses or other parts not specifically specified for the ABS system. When using repair kits, replace all parts included in the kit. Partial or incorrect repair may lead to functional problems and require the replacement of components.

• Lubricate rubber parts with clean, fresh brake fluid to ease assembly. Do not use lubricated shop air to clean parts; damage to rubber components may result.

• Use only DOT 3 brake fluid from an unopened container.

• If any hydraulic component or line is removed or replaced, it may be necessary to bleed the entire system.

• A clean repair area is essential. Always clean the reservoir and cap thoroughly before removing the cap. The slightest amount of dirt in the fluid may plug an orifice and impair the system function. Perform repairs after components have been thoroughly cleaned; use only denatured alcohol to clean components. Do not allow ABS components to come into contact with any substance containing mineral oil; this includes used shop rags.

• The Anti-Lock control unit is a microprocessor similar to other computer units in the vehicle. Ensure that the ignition switch is **OFF** before removing or installing controller harnesses. Avoid static electricity discharge at or near the controller.

• If any arc welding is to be done on the vehicle, the ALCU connectors should be disconnected before welding operations begin.

Hydraulic Unit

REMOVAL & INSTALLATION

1992-93 Vista

▶ **See Figure 34**

1. Disconnect the negative battery cable. Remove the splash shield from beneath the car.
2. Use a syringe or similar device to remove as much fluid as possible from the reservoir. Some fluid will be spilled from lines during removal of the hydraulic unit; protect adjacent painted surfaces.
3. Remove the dust cover and the oil reservoir.
4. Disconnect the brake lines from the hydraulic unit. Correct reassembly is critical. Label or identify the lines before removal. Plug each line immediately after removal.
5. Disconnect the hydraulic unit electrical harness connectors.
6. Disconnect the hydraulic unit ground strap from the chassis.
7. Remove the 3 nuts holding the hydraulic unit. Remove the unit upwards.

➡**The hydraulic unit is heavy; use care when removing it. The unit must remain in the upright position at all times and be protected from impact and shock.**

8. Set the unit upright supported by blocks on the workbench. The hydraulic unit must not be tilted or turned upside down. No component of the hydraulic unit should be loosened or disassembled.
9. The bracket assemblies and relays may be removed if desired.

To install:

10. Install the relays and brackets if removed.
11. Install the hydraulic unit into the vehicle, keeping it upright at all times.
12. Install the retaining nuts and tighten.
13. Connect the ground strap to the chassis bracket. Connect the hydraulic unit wiring harness.
14. Connect the hydraulic unit electrical harness connectors.
15. Install the dust cover and the oil reservoir.
16. Connect each brake line loosely to the correct port and double check the placement. Tighten each line to 10 ft. lbs. (13.5 Nm).
17. Fill the reservoir to the MAX line with brake fluid.

18. Bleed the master cylinder, then bleed the brake lines. Refill the master cylinder and check for proper operation.

1993 Colt

1. Disconnect the battery ground cable.
2. Remove the air conditioning relay box.
3. Remove the oil reservoir.
4. Remove the motor relay.
5. Remove the valve relay.
6. Disconnect the brake pipe.
7. Remove the hydraulic unit and separate it from the bracket.
8. Installation is the reverse of removal.
9. Fill the reservoir to the MAX line with brake fluid.
10. Bleed the master cylinder, then bleed the brake lines. Refill the master cylinder and check for proper operation.

Anti-Lock Control Unit

REMOVAL & INSTALLATION

1992-93 Vista

1. Ensure that the ignition switch is **OFF** throughout the procedure.
2. Remove the cup holder in front of the center console.
3. Remove the console side covers.
4. Disconnect the electrical harness from the control unit.
5. Remove the fasteners and the control unit from the vehicle.
6. Installation is the reverse of the removal procedure.

1993 Colt

1. Ensure that the ignition switch is **OFF** throughout the procedure.
2. Disconnect the electrical harness from the control unit.
3. Remove the fasteners and the control unit from the vehicle.
4. Installation is the reverse of the removal procedure.

G-Sensor

The G-Sensor is found only on Four Wheel Drive (4WD) vehicles.

REMOVAL & INSTALLATION

1. Disconnect negative battery cable.
2. Remove the floor console.
3. Disconnect the wiring harness connector from the sensor.
4. Remove the retaining screw and G-sensor from the mounting bracket.
5. Installation is the reverse of the removal procedure.

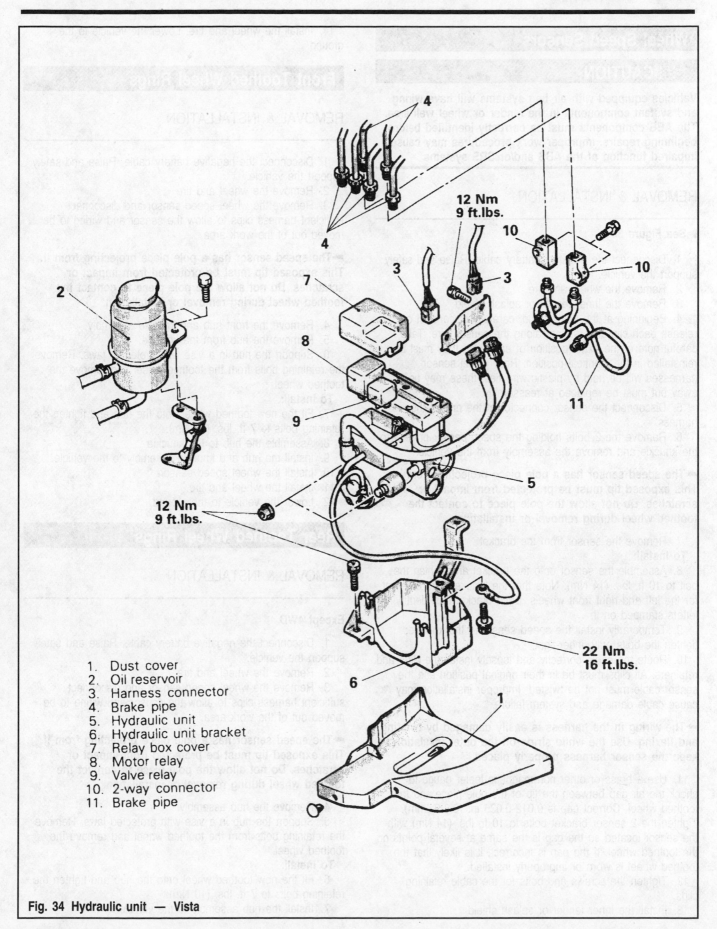

12 Nm
9 ft.lbs.

12 Nm
9 ft.lbs.

22 Nm
16 ft.lbs.

1. Dust cover
2. Oil reservoir
3. Harness connector
4. Brake pipe
5. Hydraulic unit
6. Hydraulic unit bracket
7. Relay box cover
8. Motor relay
9. Valve relay
10. 2-way connector
11. Brake pipe

Fig. 34 Hydraulic unit — Vista

Wheel Speed Sensors

❋❋CAUTION

Vehicles equipped with air bag systems will have wiring and system components in the fender or wheel well area. The ABS components must be correctly identified before beginning repairs. Improper work procedures may cause impaired function of the ABS and/or SRS systems

REMOVAL & INSTALLATION

▶ **See Figure 35**

1. Disconnect the negative battery cable. Raise and safely support the vehicle.
2. Remove the wheel and tire.
3. Remove the inner fender or splash shield.
4. Beginning at the sensor end, carefully disconnect or release each clip and retainer along the sensor wire. Take careful note of the exact position of each clip; they must be reinstalled in the identical position. Rear wheel sensor harnesses will be held by plastic wire ties; these may be cut away but must be replaced at reassembly.
5. Disconnect the sensor connector at the end of the harness.
6. Remove the 2 bolts holding the speed sensor bracket to the knuckle and remove the assembly from the vehicle.

➡**The speed sensor has a pole piece projecting from it. This exposed tip must be protected from impact or scratches. Do not allow the pole piece to contact the toothed wheel during removal or installation.**

7. Remove the sensor from the bracket.
To install:
8. Assemble the sensor onto the bracket and tighten the bolt to 10 ft. lbs. (14 Nm). Note that the brackets are different for the left and right front wheels. Each bracket has identifying letters stamped on it.
9. Temporarily install the speed sensor to the knuckle; tighten the bolts only finger-tight.
10. Route the cable correctly and loosely install the clips and retainers. All clips must be in their original position and the sensor cable must not be twisted. Improper installation may cause cable damage and system failure.

➡**The wiring in the harness is easily damaged by twisting and flexing. Use the white stripe on the outer insulation to keep the sensor harness properly placed.**

11. Use a brass or other non-magnetic feeler gauge to check the air gap between the tip of the pole piece and the toothed wheel. Correct gap is 0.012-0.035 in. (0.3-0.9mm). Tighten the 2 sensor bracket bolts to 10 ft. lbs. (14 Nm) with the sensor located so the gap is the same at several points on the toothed wheel. If the gap is incorrect, it is likely that the toothed wheel is worn or improperly installed.
12. Tighten the screws and bolts for the cable retaining clips.
13. Install the inner fender or splash shield.

14. Install the wheel and tire. Lower the vehicle to the ground.

Front Toothed Wheel Rings

REMOVAL & INSTALLATION

1. Disconnect the negative battery cable. Raise and safely support the vehicle.
2. Remove the wheel and tire.
3. Remove the wheel speed sensor and disconnect sufficient harness clips to allow the sensor and wiring to be moved out of the work area.

➡**The speed sensor has a pole piece projecting from it. This exposed tip must be protected from impact or scratches. Do not allow the pole piece to contact the toothed wheel during removal or installation.**

4. Remove the front hub and knuckle assembly.
5. Remove the hub from the knuckle.
6. Support the hub in a vise with protected jaws. Remove the retaining bolts from the toothed wheel and remove the toothed wheel.
To install:
7. Fit the new toothed wheel onto the hub and tighten the retaining bolts to 7 ft. lbs. (10 Nm).
8. Assemble the hub to the knuckle
9. Install the hub and knuckle assembly to the vehicle.
10. Install the wheel speed sensor.
11. Install the wheel and tire.
12. Lower the vehicle to the ground.

Rear Toothed Wheel Rings

REMOVAL & INSTALLATION

Except 4WD

1. Disconnect the negative battery cable. Raise and safely support the vehicle.
2. Remove the wheel and tire.
3. Remove the wheel speed sensor and disconnect sufficient harness clips to allow the sensor and wiring to be moved out of the work area.

➡**The speed sensor has a pole piece projecting from it. This exposed tip must be protected from impact or scratches. Do not allow the pole piece to contact the toothed wheel during removal or installation.**

4. Remove the hub assembly.
5. Support the hub in a vise with protected jaws. Remove the retaining bolts from the toothed wheel and remove the toothed wheel.
To install:
6. Fit the new toothed wheel onto the hub and tighten the retaining bolts to 7 ft. lbs. (10 Nm).
7. Install the hub assembly to the vehicle.

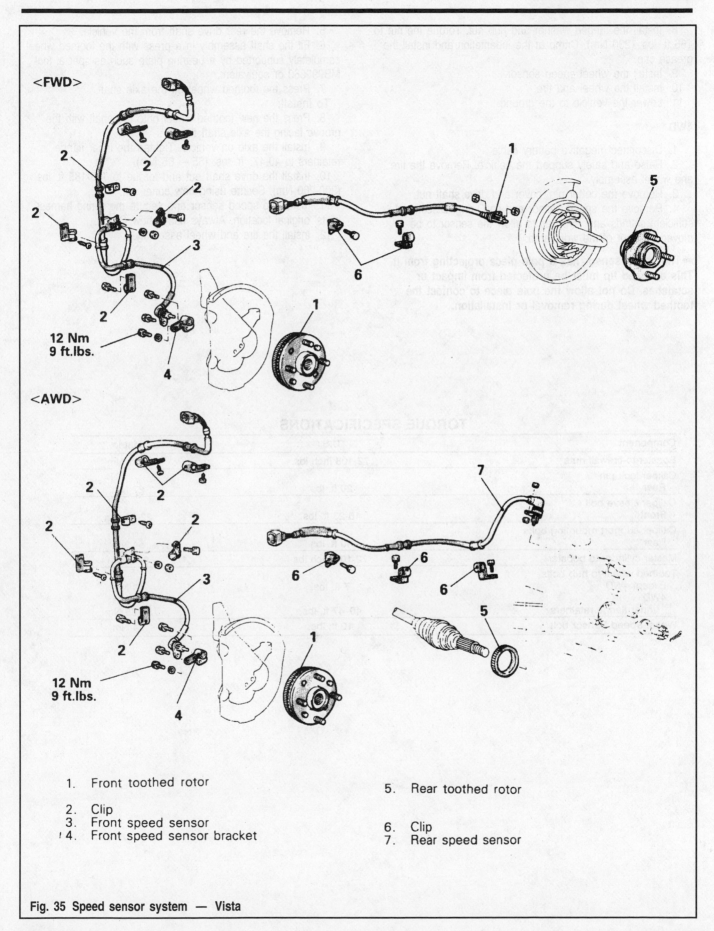

1. Front toothed rotor

2. Clip
3. Front speed sensor
4. Front speed sensor bracket

5. Rear toothed rotor

6. Clip
7. Rear speed sensor

Fig. 35 Speed sensor system — Vista

8. Install the tanged washer and hub nut. Torque the nut to 166 ft. lbs. (230 Nm). Crimp at the indentation and install the grease cap.

9. Install the wheel speed sensor.

10. Install the wheel and tire.

11. Lower the vehicle to the ground.

4WD

1. Disconnect negative battery cable.

2. Raise and safely support the vehicle. Remove the tire and wheel assembly.

3. Remove the cotter pin, cover and drive shaft nut.

4. Remove the speed sensor and its O-ring. Disconnect sufficient clamps and wire ties to allow the sensor to be moved well out of the work area.

➡ **The speed sensor has a pole piece projecting from it. This exposed tip must be protected from impact or scratches. Do not allow the pole piece to contact the toothed wheel during removal or installation.**

5. Remove the rear drive shaft from the vehicle.

6. Fit the shaft assembly in a press with the toothed wheel completely supported by a bearing plate such as special tool MB990560 or equivalent.

7. Press the toothed wheel off the axle shaft.

To install:

8. Press the new toothed wheel onto the shaft with the groove facing the axle shaft flange.

9. Install the axle on vehicle. Tighten the inner flange retainers to 40-47 ft. lbs. (55 — 65 Nm).

10. Install the drive shaft nut and torque to 145-188 ft. lbs. (200-260 Nm). Secure using new cotter pin.

11. Install the speed sensor and secure the wiring harness in its' original location. Always use a new O-ring.

12. Install the tire and wheel assembly.

TORQUE SPECIFICATIONS

Component	U.S.	Metric
Booster-to-firewall nuts	72-108 inch lbs.	8-12 Nm
Caliper lock pin Rear	20 ft. lbs.	27 Nm
Caliper sleeve bolt Front	16-23 ft. lbs.	22-31 Nm
Caliper support mounting bolts Rear	40 ft. lbs.	54 Nm
Master cylinder-to-booster	72-108 inch lbs	8-12 Nm
Toothed wheel-to-hub bolts Except 4WD 4WD	7 ft. lbs.	10 Nm
Inner flange retainers	40–47 ft. lbs.	55-65 Nm
Wheel Speed Sensor bolt	10 ft. lbs.	14 Nm

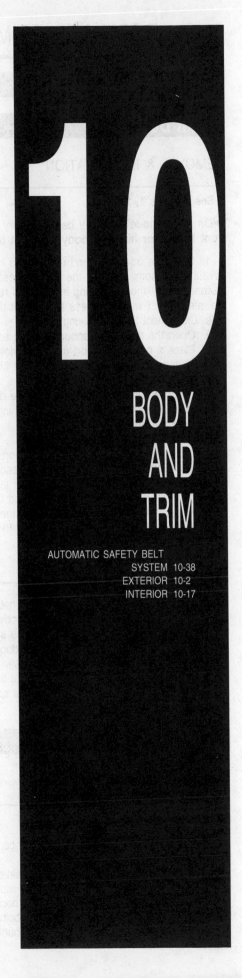

10

BODY
AND
TRIM

EXTERIOR

Front Doors

REMOVAL & INSTALLATION

▶ **See Figures 1, 2 and 3**

➡**On some models, it may be necessary to remove the front fender for hinge to body side bolt removal.**

1. Open the front door and remove the inner door panel covering. On some models, the light harness can be disconnected without requiring inner panel removal. Disconnect the interior light wiring harness and feed it through the access hole. Disconnect the door swing stop.
2. Open the door wide enough to gain access to the hinge bolts. Place a padded support under the door edge that will hold the door in a level position when the hinges have been unbolted from the frame.
3. Scribe around the door hinge on the door frame. Remove the hinge mounting bolts, lower hinge first than the upper from the door frame.
4. Remove the door.
5. Place the door on the padded support and install the hinge mounting bolts until they are snug enough to support the door, but not tight enough to prevent door adjustment. Adjust the door position until correctly aligned and tighten the hinge bolts. Adjust the striker as necessary. Connect the door stop and interior light harness. Install the inner trim panel.

ALIGNMENT

The front doors should be adjusted so that there is an even clearance all around the door edge and body. Adjust the door to position and raise or lower it so that the stamped edge line matches the body panel line. Secure the door in proper position after necessary adjustments. Loosen the door striker mounting screws to adjust the alignment of the door panel. Increase or decrease the number of shims behind the striker as required.

Hood

REMOVAL & INSTALLATION

▶ **See Figures 4 and 5**

1. Raise the hood. Scribe mark the hinge to hood panel location.
2. Place padding between the windshield/cowl and hood edge to prevent damage should the hood slip during removal.
3. Have a helper hold the front of the hood to prevent it from falling or sliding when the mounting bolts are removed.
4. Remove the hood panel to hinge mounting bolts and remove the hood.

5. Position the hood panel over the hinges and align the panel with the scribed lines. Install and tighten the mounting bolts.

ALIGNMENT

1. One, or both sets of hood hinge mounting holes or the hood panel attaching captive mounting nut locations are elongated to permit panel to fender and cowl adjustment.
2. Locate the mounting bolts that are in the elongated holes. Loosen them slightly until the hood panel position can be shifted.
3. Move the panel as required for even spacing around the hood outer edges. Tighten the bolts.
4. Adjustable (up or down) bumpers are provided, in most cases, to permit the front of the hood to be raised or lower to match the fender edges. Raise or lower the bumpers, by screwing them in or out, to adjust.

Liftgate

REMOVAL & INSTALLATION

▶ **See Figure 6**

1. Support the liftgate in the full opened position. Depending on model, remove the one piece plastic headliner if it covers the hinge mounting.
2. Scribe a mark on the liftgate to mark the hinge positions.
3. Place masking tape on the roof edge and liftgate edge to protect the paint surfaces during removal and installation.
4. Remove the liftgate prop fasteners and remove the props.
5. Have a helper on hand to support the liftgate. Remove the hinge mounting bolts and remove the liftgate.
6. Raise the liftgate into position and install the hinge mounting bolts. Tighten the bolts until they are snug, but not tight enough to prevent liftgate adjustment.
7. Shift the liftgate until the hinge scribe marks are in position and tighten the hinge mounting bolts.
8. Attach and secure the liftgate props.

Trunk Lid

REMOVAL & INSTALLATION

▶ **See Figure 7**

✳✳CAUTION

The torsion bars that keep the trunk lid in the raised position are under strong twisted pressure. When disconnecting them for their mounting holes and/or notched brackets, they may spring out and cause bodily damage. Keep fingers and face out of the way.

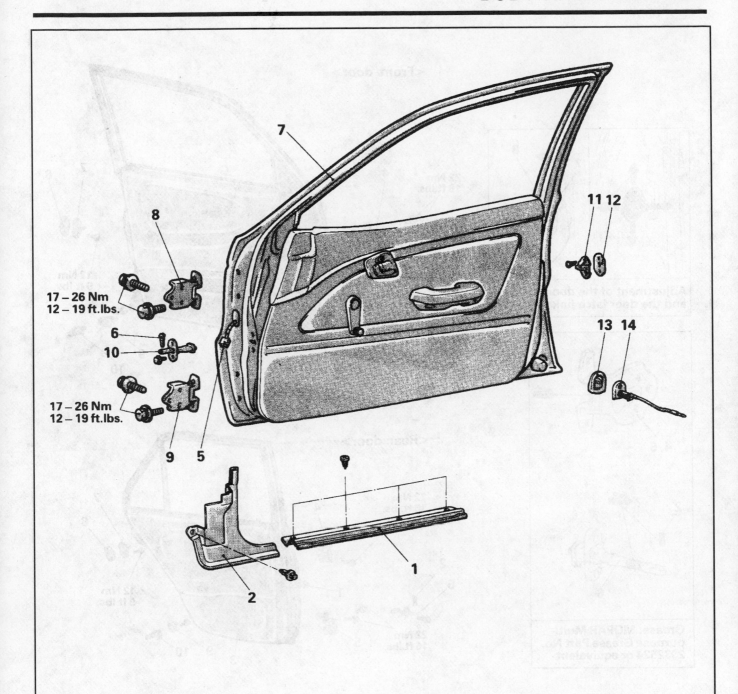

1. Front scuff plate
2. Cowl side trim
5. Connection for door wiring harness connector
6. Spring pin
7. Door assembly
8. Upper hinge
9. Lower hinge
10. Door check strap

11. Striker
12. Striker shim
13. Door switch cap
14. Door switch

17 – 26 Nm
12 – 19 ft.lbs.

17 – 26 Nm
12 – 19 ft.lbs.

Fig. 1 Door assembly — 1990-92 Colt hatchback

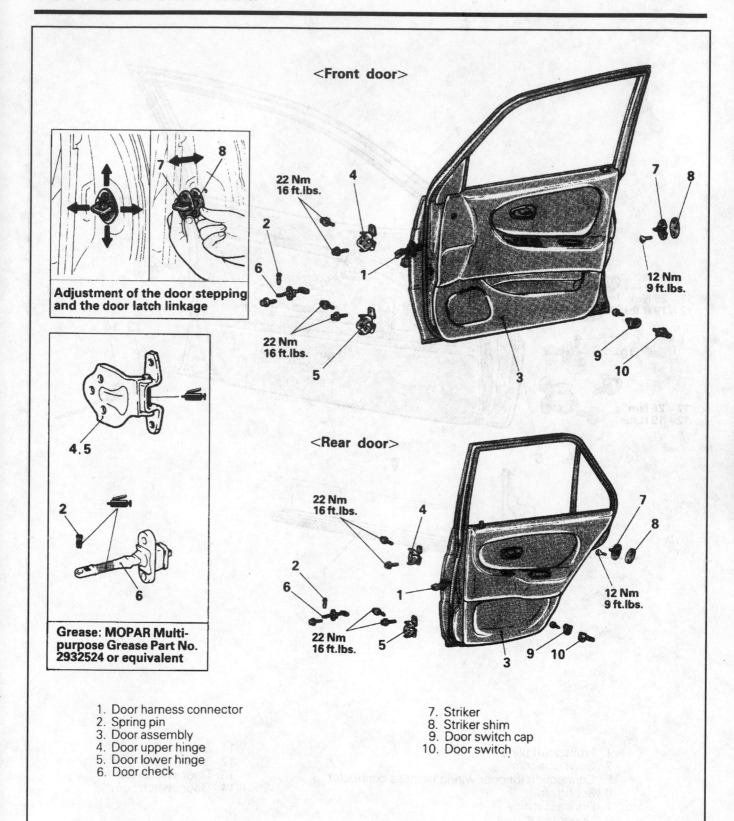

<Front door>

22 Nm
16 ft.lbs.

12 Nm
9 ft.lbs.

22 Nm
16 ft.lbs.

Adjustment of the door stepping and the door latch linkage

4.5

Grease: MOPAR Multi-purpose Grease Part No. 2932524 or equivalent

<Rear door>

22 Nm
16 ft.lbs.

12 Nm
9 ft.lbs.

22 Nm
16 ft.lbs.

1. Door harness connector
2. Spring pin
3. Door assembly
4. Door upper hinge
5. Door lower hinge
6. Door check

7. Striker
8. Striker shim
9. Door switch cap
10. Door switch

Fig. 2 Door assembly — 1993 Colt

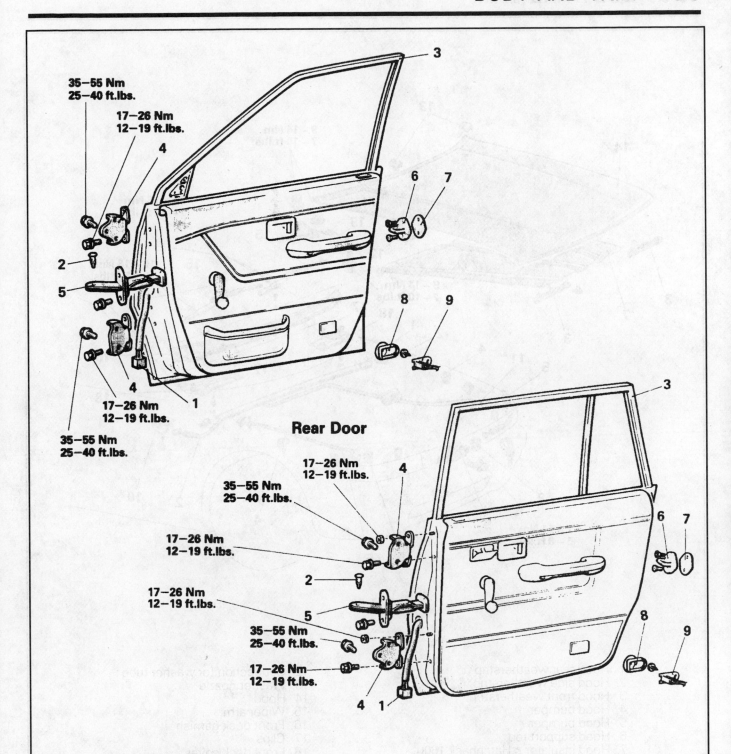

35—55 Nm
25—40 ft.lbs.

17—26 Nm
12—19 ft.lbs.

17—26 Nm
12—19 ft.lbs.

35—55 Nm
25—40 ft.lbs.

Rear Door

17—26 Nm
12—19 ft.lbs.

35—55 Nm
25—40 ft.lbs.

17—26 Nm
12—19 ft.lbs.

17—26 Nm
12—19 ft.lbs.

35—55 Nm
25—40 ft.lbs.

17—26 Nm
12—19 ft.lbs.

1. Connection of door harness connector
2. Spring pin
3. Door assembly
4. Door hinge
5. Door check
6. Striker
7. Striker shim
8. Door switch cap
9. Door switch

Fig. 3 Door assembly — 1990-91 Vista

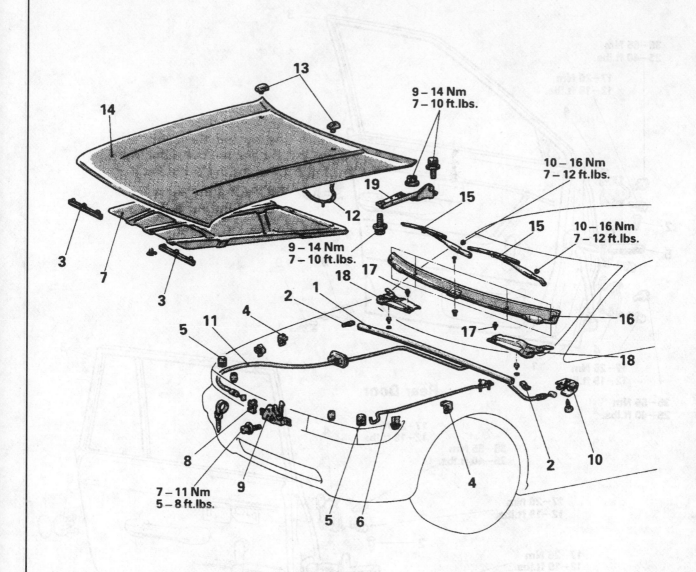

9 – 14 Nm
7 – 10 ft.lbs.

10 – 16 Nm
7 – 12 ft.lbs.

10 – 16 Nm
7 – 12 ft.lbs.

9 – 14 Nm
7 – 10 ft.lbs.

7 – 11 Nm
5 – 8 ft.lbs.

1. Hood rear weatherstrip
2. Hood side weatherstrip
3. Hood front weatherstrip
4. Hood bumper
5. Hood bumper
6. Hood support rod
7. Hood insulator <Hatchback 1600>
8. Protector
9. Hood latch
10. Hood lock release handle
11. Hood lock release cable
12. Connection for washer tube
13. Washer nozzle
14. Hood
15. Wiper arm
16. Front deck garnish
17. Clips
18. Front deck cover
19. Hood hinge

Fig. 4 Hood assembly — 1990-92 Colt hatchback and sedan

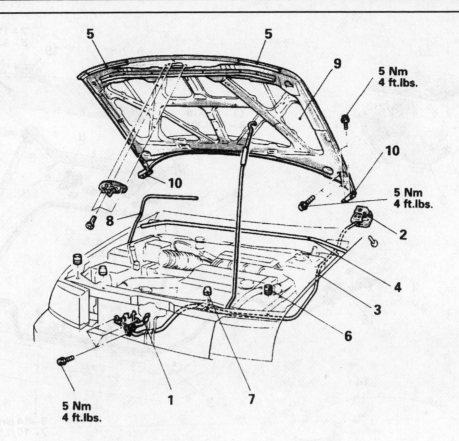

5 Nm
4 ft.lbs.

5 Nm
4 ft.lbs.

5 Nm
4 ft.lbs.

1. Hood latch
2. Hood lock release handle
3. Hood lock release cable
4. Hood weatherstrip
5. Hood front weatherstrip
6. Bumper
7. Bumper
8. Washer tube
9. Hood
10. Hood hinge

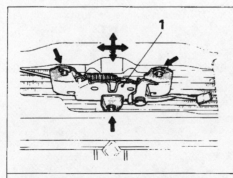

Adjustment of engine hood step and hood striker linkage

Adjustment of clearance around hood and height

Fig. 5 Hood assembly — 1992-93 Vista

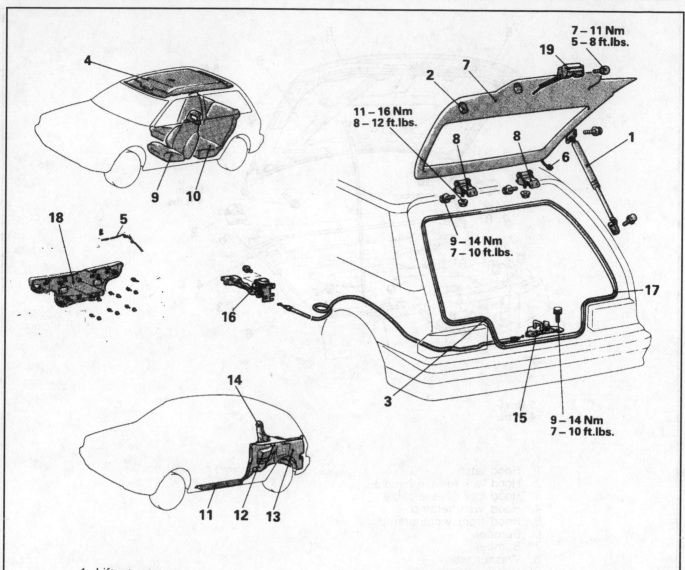

1. Liftgate stopper
2. Liftgate bumper
3. Liftgate opening weatherstrip
4. Headlining
5. Connection for rear washer tube
6. Connection for liftgate wiring harness
7. Liftgate
8. Liftgate hinge
9. Front seat (driver's side)
10. Rear seat
11. Scuff plate (driver's side)
12. Lower quarter trim (driver's side)
13. Cargo room side trim (driver's side)
14. Rear end trim

15. Liftgate striker
16. Liftgate lock release handle
17. Liftgate lock release cable
18. Liftgate trim
19. Liftgate latch

Fig. 6 Liftgate assembly — 1990-92 Colt hatchback

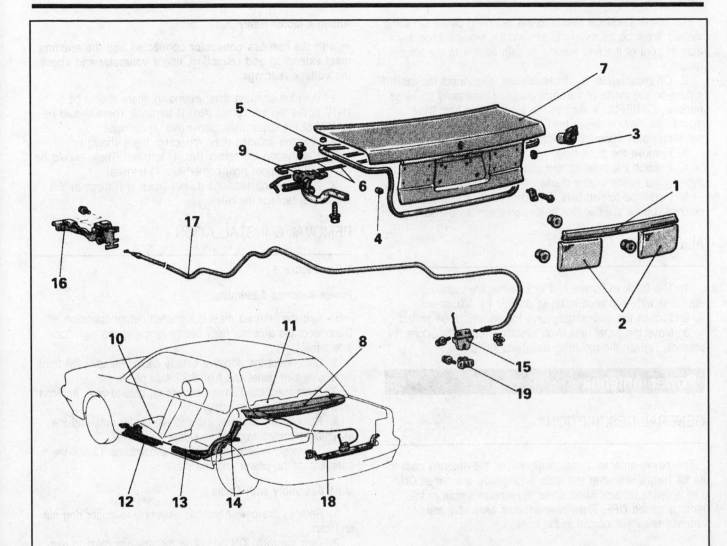

15. Deck lid latch
16. Deck lid lock release handle
17. Deck lid lock release cable
18. Rear end trim
19. Deck lid striker

1. Deck lid upper garnish
2. Deck lid lower garnish
3. Deck lid bumper (A)
4. Deck lid bumper (B)
5. Deck lid weatherstrip
6. Deck lid torsion bar
7. Deck lid
8. Rear shelf trim
9. Deck lid hinge
10. Front seat (driver's side)
11. Rear seat
12. Front scuff plate (driver's side)
13. Rear scuff plate (driver's side)
14. Rear wheel arch trim (driver's side)

Fig. 7 Trunk lid — Colt sedan

1. Scribe the hinge outline to the mounting panel. On some models it will be necessary to remove the rear package tray from in front of the rear window to gain access to the hinge mount.

2. On models with a remote release, disconnect the cable if it runs on the inside of the trunk panel. If necessary for hinge removal, CAREFULLY remove the torsion bars from their mountings. Have a helper hold the trunk lid up so that it will not slam down when the torsion bar pressure is released.

3. Remove the trunk hinge mounting bolts and the lid.

4. Position the trunk lid and install the mounting bolts after aligning the scribe locator marks.

5. Install the torsion bars, if disconnected, into their notches. Use a suitable tool to tension them while installing.

ALIGNMENT

1. The trunk lid hinges and lock striker are usually equipped with elongated holes to provide for adjustment.

2. Loosen the bolts slightly until the panel can be shifted.

3. Move the panel until even spacing around the edges is present. Tighten the mounting bolts and striker.

Power Antenna

GENERAL DESCRIPTION

The power antenna automatically raises the antenna mast to its full height whenever the radio and ignition are turned **ON**. The antenna retracts when either the ignition switch or the radio is turned **OFF**. The power antenna assembly and antenna relay are located in the trunk.

DIAGNOSIS & TESTING

Antenna Motor

➡**With the harness connector connected and the antenna mast extending and retracting, use a voltmeter and check the voltage readings.**

1. Using a 12 volt DC power supply, connect the positive lead to terminal 1 and the negative lead to terminal 2; the antenna mast should extend.

2. When the antenna is fully extended, there should be continuity between terminals 4 and 5.

3. Using a 12 volt DC power supply, connect the negative lead to terminal 1 and the positive lead to terminal 2; the antenna mast should retract.

4. When the antenna is fully retracted, there should be continuity between terminals 3 and 4.

5. During the extension and retraction process, there should be continuity between terminals 3, 4 and 5.

6. If the results do not agree with those in this procedure, replace the antenna assembly.

Antenna Motor Relay

➡**With the harness connector connected and the antenna mast extending and retracting, use a voltmeter and check the voltage readings.**

1. With the antenna mast extending, there should be (-)1-1V at the top left corner (No. 1) terminal. There should be 10-13V at the upper right corner (No. 4) terminal.

2. With the antenna mast retracting, there should be 10-13V at the top left corner (No. 1) terminal. There should be (-)1-1V at the upper right corner (No. 4) terminal.

3. If the voltage readings do not agree with those in this procedure, replace the relay.

REMOVAL & INSTALLATION

▶ **See Figure 8**

Power Antenna Assembly

Be sure the antenna mast is retracted before operation. Disconnect the antenna relay before removing the high floor side panel.

1. Disconnect the negative battery cable. Remove the trunk room side trim panel and high floor side panel.

2. Disconnect the harness connector, ground wire, antenna lead wire and the drain hose.

3. Remove the antenna assembly-to-fender nuts and the assembly from the trunk room side.

4. To install, reverse the removal procedures. Check the operation of the power antenna mast.

Mast Assembly with Cable

1. Remove the power antenna assembly-to-fender ring nut and cap.

2. Turn the radio **ON** and allow the antenna mast to rise. When the antenna is fully extended, pull the mast from the tube.

3. To install the new mast, fully extend it, straighten the rack cable (if bent), position the rack cable teeth toward the outside of the vehicle and insert the rack cable into the motor tube.

4. Once installed in the tube, turn the rack cable 90 degrees (teeth facing the front of the vehicle) to engage the gear motor.

➡**To check if the rack cable is engaged, lightly pull on the mast; if it not engaged with the gear motor, it will pull out. Straighten the rack cable and repeat the installation steps.**

5. While holding the antenna mast in an upright position, turn the radio **OFF** and all the mast retracts into the tube.

6. To complete the installation, reverse the removal procedures. Turn the radio **ON** and **OFF** to check the operation; make sure it extends and retracts smoothly.

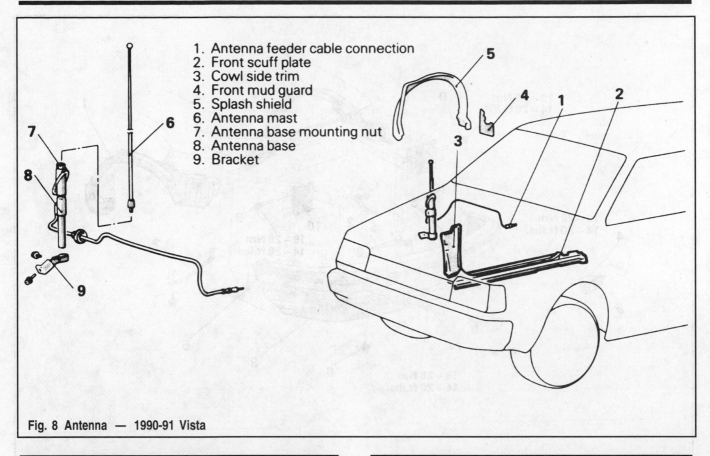

1. Antenna feeder cable connection
2. Front scuff plate
3. Cowl side trim
4. Front mud guard
5. Splash shield
6. Antenna mast
7. Antenna base mounting nut
8. Antenna base
9. Bracket

Fig. 8 Antenna — 1990-91 Vista

Bumpers

REMOVAL & INSTALLATION

▶ **See Figures 9, 10, 11, 12 and 13**

1. On models equipped: Remove the end cap to bumper mounting screw and the two end cap to fender nuts from both ends of the bumper.

2. Remove the end cap to bumper nut and remove the end cap from both ends of the bumper.

3. Support the lower edge of the bumper on a padded jack.

4. Remove the bolts that mount the bumper to the body brackets/impact absorber mount and remove the bumper.

5. Place the bumper into the proper position, use a padded jack to support the bumper, and install the bracket to bumper mounting bolts. Tighten the bolts until they are snug. but not tight enough to prevent shifting of the bumper for proper centering.

6. Adjust bumper placement as required. Tighten the mounting bolts. Install the bumper end caps.

Grille

REMOVAL & INSTALLATION

▶ **See Figures 14 and 15**

1. Remove the screws from the headlamp bezels. Remove the screws from the sides of the grille.

2. Remove the screws from the grille to center support bracket.

3. Remove the grille.

4. Place the grille into position. Install the center support screws and the outer mounting screws. Center the grille and tighten the mounting screws.

5. Install the headlamp bezel screws.

Manual Outside Mirrors

REMOVAL & INSTALLATION

1. Remove the door trim panel, or depending on model, the plastic corner trim cover at the inner front edge of the window opening in the door frame.

2. Remove the adjustment knob with an Allen wrench. Remove the screw cover plug and the mirror inner bezel mounting screws. Remove the bezel.

3. Remove the mirror mounting nuts and the mirror.

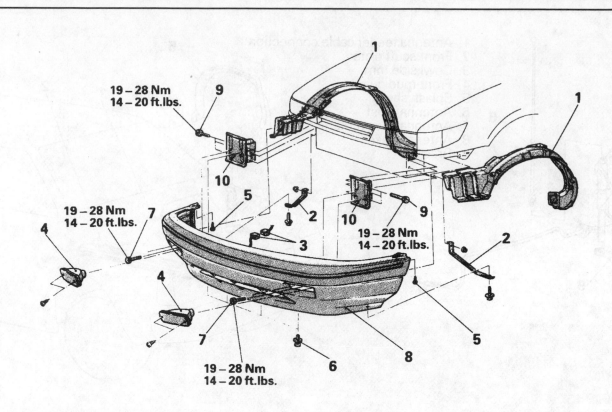

1. Splash shield
2. Side stay
3. Connection of front bumper wiring harness to front wiring harness
4. Front turn signal light
5. Front bumper face connecting screw
6. Front bumper face connecting clip
7. Front bumper reinforcement connecting bolt
8. Front bumper
9. Front bumper support connecting bolt
10. Front bumper support

Fig. 9 Front bumper — 1990-92 Colt hatchback and sedan

4. Place the mirror into position and install the mounting nuts.

5. Place the bezel into position and install the mounting screws and cover plug.

6. Install the control knob and trim panel.

Power Outside Mirrors

GENERAL DESCRIPTION

The power mirrors are controlled by a switch mounted on the door trim panel, integral of the door handle assembly on Vista series and on the center console on Colt series. Each mirror is moved by an integral set of motors; 1 motor controls the up and down motion, the other controls the left to right motion.

The mirror switch consists of a left-right change over select knob and control knobs. The switch is ready to function only when the ignition switch is in the **ACC** or **ON** position. Movement of the mirror is accomplished by the motors located in the mirror housing.

DIAGNOSIS AND TESTING

Switch

Remove the switch from the door trim panel or the console, as required. Check for continuity between the terminals in each switch position.

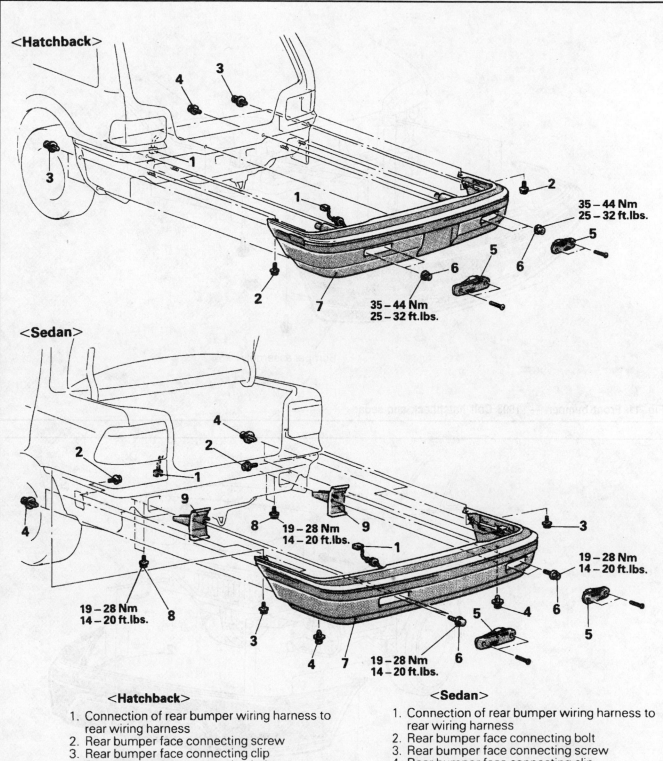

35 – 44 Nm
25 – 32 ft.lbs.

35 – 44 Nm
25 – 32 ft.lbs.

19 – 28 Nm
14 – 20 ft.lbs.

19 – 28 Nm
14 – 20 ft.lbs.

19 – 28 Nm
14 – 20 ft.lbs.

\<Hatchback\>
1. Connection of rear bumper wiring harness to rear wiring harness
2. Rear bumper face connecting screw
3. Rear bumper face connecting clip
4. Rear bumper face connecting bolt
5. Backup light
6. Rear bumper reinforcement connecting nut
7. Rear bumper assembly

\<Sedan\>
1. Connection of rear bumper wiring harness to rear wiring harness
2. Rear bumper face connecting bolt
3. Rear bumper face connecting screw
4. Rear bumper face connecting clip
5. Backup light
6. Rear bumper reinforcement connecting bolt
7. Rear bumper assembly
8. Rear bumper stay connecting bolt
9. Rear bumper stay

Fig. 10 Rear bumper — 1990-92 Colt hatchback and sedan

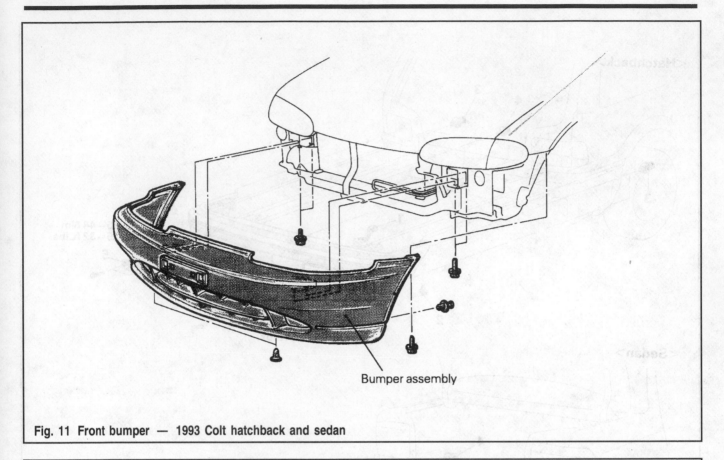

Fig. 11 Front bumper — 1993 Colt hatchback and sedan

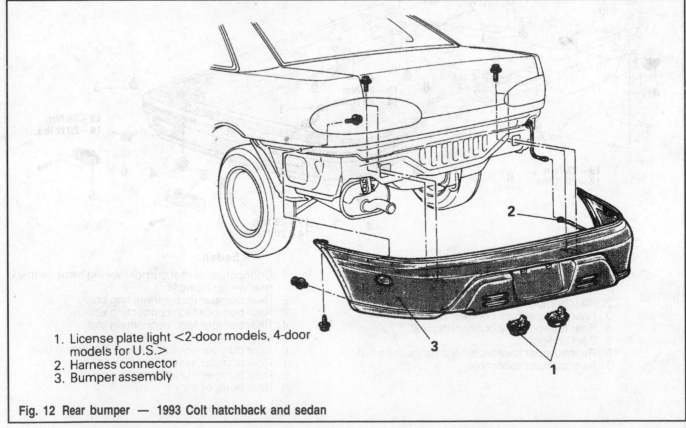

1. License plate light <2-door models, 4-door models for U.S.>
2. Harness connector
3. Bumper assembly

Fig. 12 Rear bumper — 1993 Colt hatchback and sedan

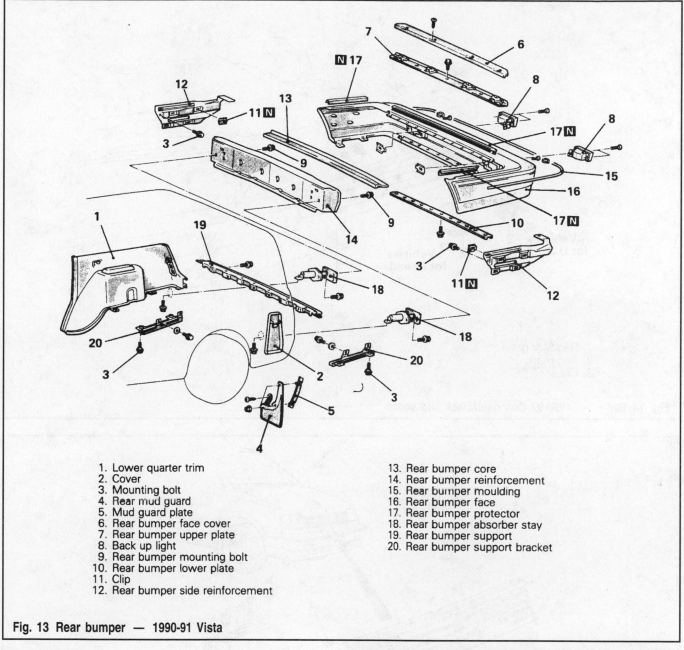

1. Lower quarter trim
2. Cover
3. Mounting bolt
4. Rear mud guard
5. Mud guard plate
6. Rear bumper face cover
7. Rear bumper upper plate
8. Back up light
9. Rear bumper mounting bolt
10. Rear bumper lower plate
11. Clip
12. Rear bumper side reinforcement

13. Rear bumper core
14. Rear bumper reinforcement
15. Rear bumper moulding
16. Rear bumper face
17. Rear bumper protector
18. Rear bumper absorber stay
19. Rear bumper support
20. Rear bumper support bracket

Fig. 13 Rear bumper — 1990-91 Vista

Mirror Assembly

1. Remove the mirror trim panel and disconnect the electrical lead to the mirror.

2. Test the mirror operation using the following procedures:

   a. Tilt up — connect a 12 volt power source to terminal 1 and ground terminal 3.

   b. Tilt down — connect a 12 volt power source to terminal 3 and ground terminal 1.

   c. Swing right — connect a 12 volt power source to terminal 3 and ground terminal 2.

   d. Swing left — connect a 12 volt power source to terminal 2 and ground terminal 3.

3. If the mirror does not operate properly in any of these tests, replace the assembly.

Fenders

REMOVAL & INSTALLATION

▶ See Figure 16

1. Clean all of the dirt from the fender mounting screws, bolts and nuts.

2. Remove the headlamp door, headlamp assembly, sidemarker lamp, or parking lamp assembly, depending on model.

3. Remove the bolt(s) attaching the rear of the front fender to the windshield cowl. This bolt is usually accessed from inside the vehicle with the door opened.

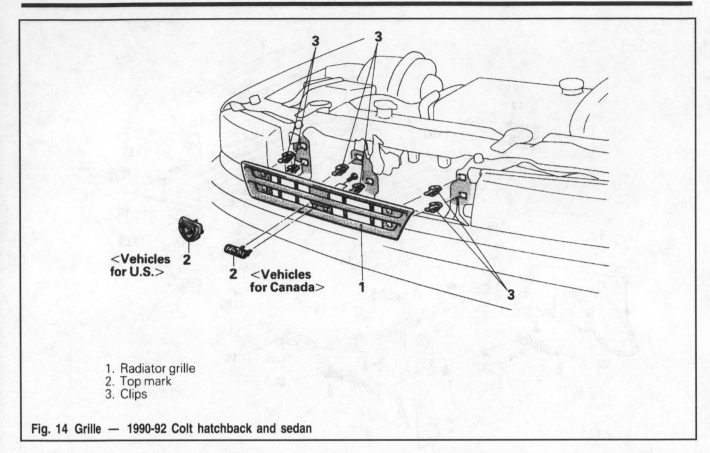

1. Radiator grille
2. Top mark
3. Clips

Fig. 14 Grille — 1990-92 Colt hatchback and sedan

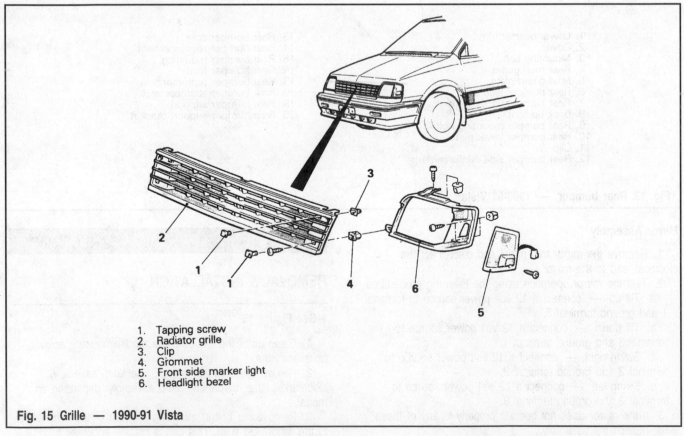

1. Tapping screw
2. Radiator grille
3. Clip
4. Grommet
5. Front side marker light
6. Headlight bezel

Fig. 15 Grille — 1990-91 Vista

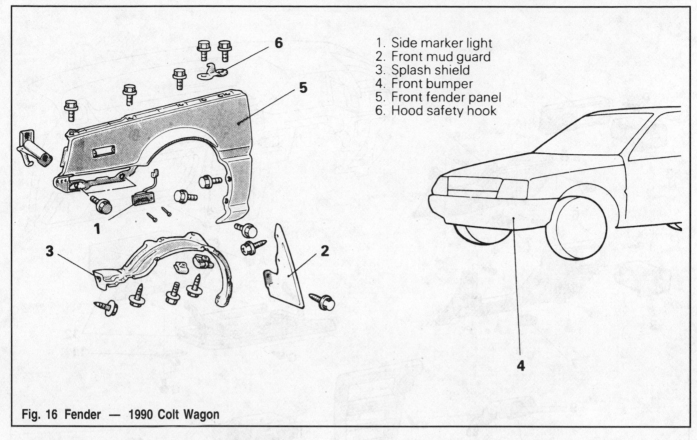

1. Side marker light
2. Front mud guard
3. Splash shield
4. Front bumper
5. Front fender panel
6. Hood safety hook

Fig. 16 Fender — 1990 Colt Wagon

4. Remove the top bolts that mount the fender to the inter-body.

5. Loosen the wheel lugs slightly. Raise and safely support the vehicle. Remove the wheel and tire assembly.

6. Remove the bolts attaching the fender brace to the body. Remove the bolts attaching the fender to the radiator support, and remove the bolts attaching the fender to the fender apron (inner splash shield).

7. Remove the bolts mounting the fender to the lower rocker sill. Check for any other mounting bolts, remove them. Remove the fender.

8. Place the fender in position and install the mounting bolts loosely. Align the lower edge of the fender to the rocker sill and secure the bolts. Align the upper edge of the fender to the cowl and tighten the bolts.

9. Tighten the remaining mounting bolts. Install the lighting equipment.

INTERIOR

Instrument Panel

REMOVAL & INSTALLATION

➡A number of pin-type fasteners are used in the installation of the instrument panel. These fasteners are called trim clips. To remove a trim clip, use a Phillips screwdriver to push the center of the pin in about 2mm, then pull the clip out. Take care to avoid pushing the center in any further, as grommet damage will occur.   When installing a trim clip, place the clip in position and push the center in flush.

1990-92 Colt Hatchback and Sedan

◗ See Figures 17 and 18

1. Remove the ashtray.
2. Remove the center panel.
3. Remove the sunglass pocket.
4. Remove the side panel — U.S. cars only.
5. Remove the left side knee protector. — U.S. cars only.
6. Remove the lower panel — Canadian cars only.
7. Remove the hood lock release handle.
8. Remove the column lower cover. See Section 8.
9. Remove the column upper cover. See Section 8.
10. Remove the radio. See Section 6.
11. Remove the glove box.
12. Remove the lower cover.
13. Remove the heater control screw.
14. Remove the gauge bezel.
15. Remove the instrument cluster. See Section 6.
16. Remove the speedometer cable adapter.
17. Remove the cluster wiring harness connectors.
18. Remove the right side speaker cover — U.S. cars only.
19. Remove the right side speaker. U.S. cars only.
20. Remove the left and right defroster grilles.
21. Remove the clock or plug.

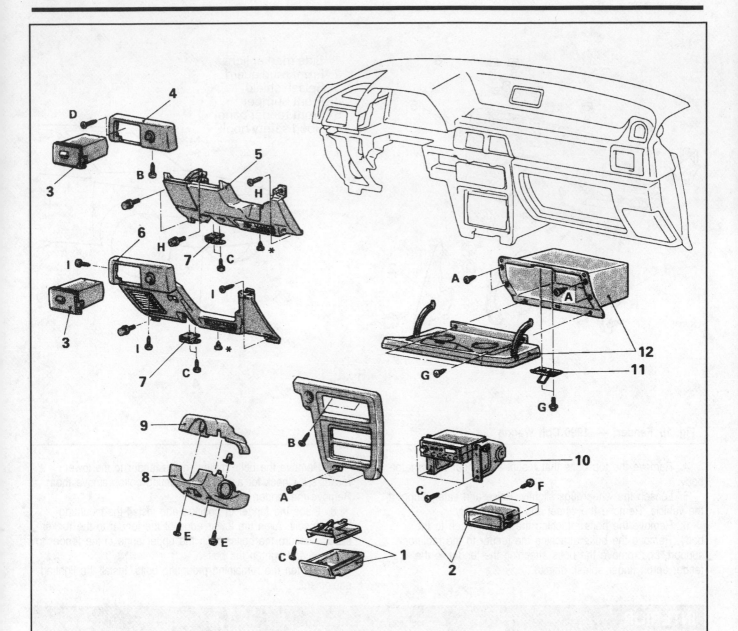

1. Ashtray
2. Center panel
3. Sunglass pocket
4. Side panel assembly <Vehicles for U.S.>
5. Knee protector assembly (L.H.) <Vehicles for U.S.>
6. Lower panel assembly <Vehicles for Canada>
7. Hood lock release handle
8. Column cover, lower
9. Column cover, upper
10. Radio
11. Striker <Vehicles for U.S.>
12. Glove box assembly <Vehicles for U.S.>

Fig. 17 Remove these parts prior to instrument panel removal — 1990-92 Colt hatchback and sedan

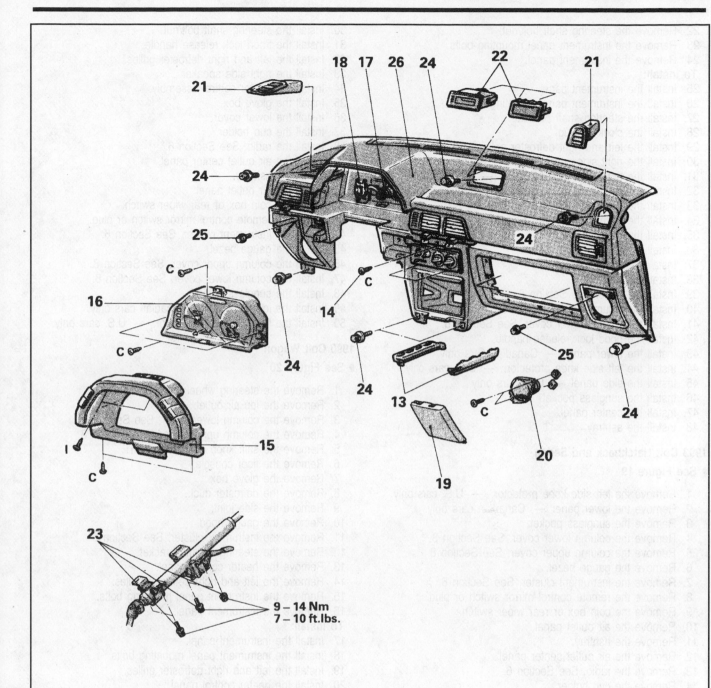

13. Instrument panel cover, lower
14. Heater control assembly installation screw
15. Meter bezel
16. Combination meter
17. Speedometer cable adapter
18. Combination meter wiring harness connector connections
19. Speaker garnish (R.H.) <Vehicles for U.S.>
20. Speaker (R.H.) <Vehicles for U.S.>

21. Side defroster grille
22. Clock or plug
23. Steering shaft mounting bolt and nut
24. Instrument panel mounting bolts
25. Instrument panel mounting bolts <Vehicles for U.S.>
26. Instrument panel assembly

Fig. 18 Instrument panel removal — 1990-92 Colt hatchback and sedan

22. Remove the steering shaft bolt/nut.
23. Remove the instrument panel mounting bolts.
24. Remove the instrument panel.

To install:

25. Install the instrument panel.
26. Install the instrument panel mounting bolts.
27. Install the steering shaft bolt/nut.
28. Install the clock or plug.
29. Install the left and right defroster grilles.
30. Install the right side speaker. U.S. cars only.
31. Install the right side speaker cover — U.S. cars only.
32. Install the cluster wiring harness connectors.
33. Install the speedometer cable adapter.
34. Install the instrument cluster. See Section 6.
35. Install the gauge bezel.
36. Install the heater control screw.
37. Install the lower cover.
38. Install the glove box.
39. Install the radio. See Section 6.
40. Install the column upper cover. See Section 8.
41. Install the column lower cover. See Section 8.
42. Install the hood lock release handle.
43. Install the lower panel — Canadian cars only.
44. Install the left side knee protector. — U.S. cars only.
45. Install the side panel — U.S. cars only.
46. Install the sunglass pocket.
47. Install the center panel.
48. Install the ashtray.

1993 Colt Hatchback and Sedan

▶ **See Figure 19**

1. Remove the left side knee protector. — U.S. cars only.
2. Remove the lower panel — Canadian cars only.
3. Remove the sunglass pocket.
4. Remove the column lower cover. See Section 8.
5. Remove the column upper cover. See Section 8.
6. Remove the gauge bezel.
7. Remove the instrument cluster. See Section 6.
8. Remove the remote control mirror switch or plug.
9. Remove the coin box or rear wiper switch.
10. Remove the air outlet panel.
11. Remove the ashtray.
12. Remove the air outlet center panel.
13. Remove the radio. See Section 6.
14. Remove the cup holder.
15. Remove the lower cover.
16. Remove the glove box.
17. Remove the heater control assembly.
18. Remove the right side speaker.
19. Remove the left and right defroster grilles.
20. Remove the hood lock release handle.
21. Remove the steering shaft bolt/nut.
22. Remove the speedometer cable adapter.
23. Remove the cluster wiring harness connectors.
24. Remove the instrument panel mounting bolts.
25. Remove the instrument panel.

To install:

26. Install the instrument panel.
27. Install the instrument panel mounting bolts.
28. Install the cluster wiring harness connectors.
29. Install the speedometer cable adapter.

30. Install the steering shaft bolt/nut.
31. Install the hood lock release handle.
32. Install the left and right defroster grilles.
33. Install the right side speaker.
34. Install the heater control assembly.
35. Install the glove box.
36. Install the lower cover.
37. Install the cup holder.
38. Install the radio. See Section 6.
39. Install the air outlet center panel.
40. Install the ashtray.
41. Install the air outlet panel.
42. Install the coin box or rear wiper switch.
43. Install the remote control mirror switch or plug.
44. Install the instrument cluster. See Section 6.
45. Install the gauge bezel.
46. Install the column upper cover. See Section 8.
47. Install the column lower cover. See Section 8.
48. Install the sunglass pocket.
49. Install the lower panel — Canadian cars only.
50. Install the left side knee protector. — U.S. cars only.

1990 Colt Wagon

▶ **See Figure 20**

1. Remove the steering wheel.
2. Remove the lap air outlet.
3. Remove the column lower cover. See Section 8.
4. Remove the column upper cover. See Section 8.
5. Remove the shift knob on cars with MT.
6. Remove the floor console.
7. Remove the glove box.
8. Remove the defroster duct.
9. Remove the side joint.
10. Remove the gauge hood.
11. Remove the instrument cluster. See Section 6.
12. Remove the steering column bracket.
13. Remove the heater control panel.
14. Remove the left and right defroster grilles.
15. Remove the instrument panel mounting bolts.
16. Remove the instrument panel.

To install:

17. Install the instrument panel.
18. Install the instrument panel mounting bolts.
19. Install the left and right defroster grilles.
20. Install the heater control panel.
21. Install the steering column bracket.
22. Install the instrument cluster. See Section 6.
23. Install the gauge hood.
24. Install the side joint.
25. Install the defroster duct.
26. Install the glove box.
27. Install the floor console.
28. Install the shift knob on cars with MT.
29. Install the column upper cover. See Section 8.
30. Install the column lower cover. See Section 8.
31. Install the lap air outlet.
32. Install the steering wheel.

1990-91 2WD USA Vista

1. Remove the lower glove box.
2. Remove the upper glove box.

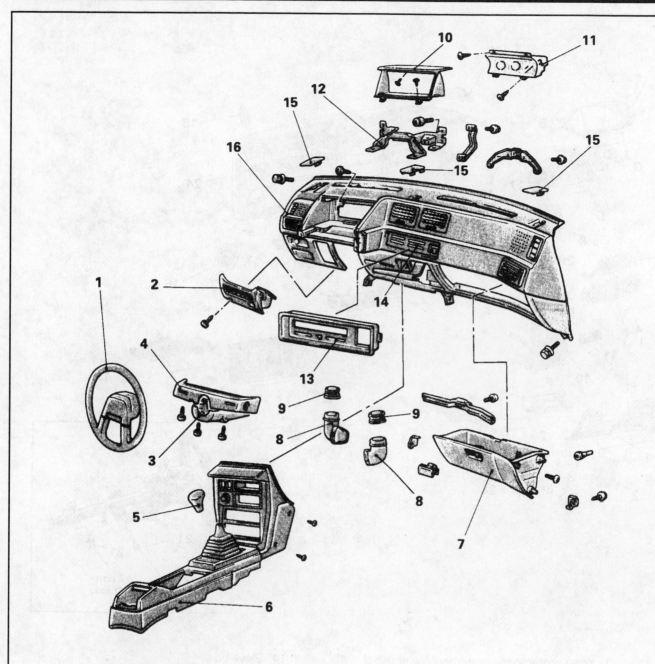

1. Steering wheel
2. Lap air outlet
3. Column cover lower
4. Column cover upper
5. Shift knob (Manual transaxle)
6. Floor console assembly
7. Glove box
8. Defroster duct
9. Side joint
10. Meter hood
11. Meter case
12. Column bracket
13. Heater control panel
14. Heater control panel assembly mounting screws
15. Cover
16. Instrument panel

Fig. 19 Instrument panel removal/installation — 1993 Colt

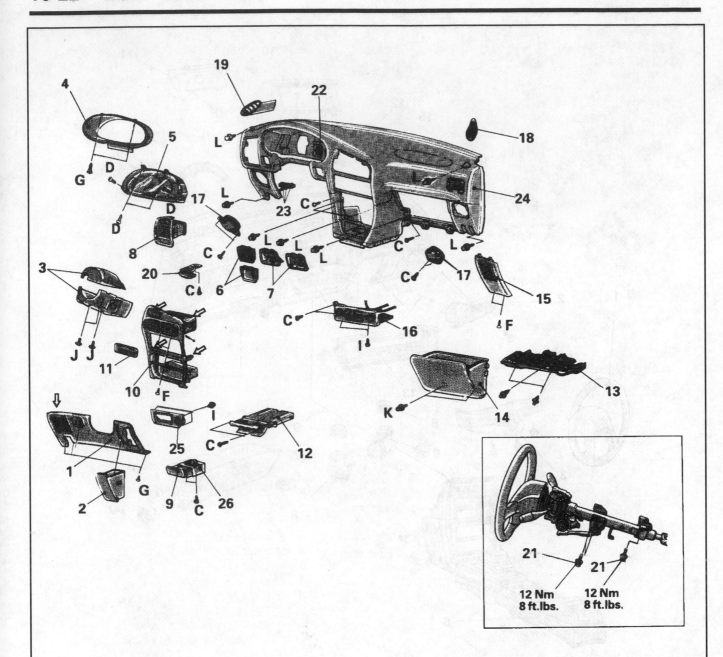

1. Knee protector or instrument lower panel assembly
2. Sunglass pocket
3. Column cover
4. Meter bezel
5. Combination meter
6. Remote control mirror switch, rheostat or plug
7. Coin box or rear wiper washer switch
8. Air outlet panel assembly
9. Ashtray
10. Air outlet center panel assembly
11. Radio plug
12. Cup holder
13. Under cover
14. Glove box
15. Corner panel
16. Heater control assembly
17. Speaker
18. Side defroster grille (RH)
19. Side defroster grille (LH)
20. Hood lock release handle
21. Steering column assembly installation bolts
22. Adapter
23. Harness connector
24. Instrument panel assembly
25. Ashtray panel
26. Ashtray bracket

Fig. 20 Instrument panel removal/installation — 1990 Colt Wagon

3. Remove the lap duct.
4. Remove the ashtray.
5. Remove the fuse box cover.
6. Remove the fuse box screws.
7. Remove the hood lock release handle.
8. Remove the gauge bezel.
9. Remove the instrument cluster. See Section 6.
10. Remove the speedometer cable adapter.
11. Disconnect the temperature control cables.
12. Remove the air duct.
13. Disconnect the blower motor.
14. Remove the upper trim covers (A & B).
15. Disconnect the antenna wire.
16. Remove the instrument panel mounting bolts.
17. Remove the instrument panel.

To install:

18. Install the instrument panel.
19. Install the instrument panel mounting bolts.
20. Connect the antenna wire.
21. Install the upper trim covers (A & B).
22. Connect the blower motor.
23. Install the air duct.
24. Connect the temperature control cables.
25. Install the speedometer cable adapter.
26. Install the instrument cluster. See Section 6.
27. Install the gauge bezel.
28. Install the hood lock release handle.
29. Install the fuse box screws.
30. Install the fuse box cover.
31. Install the ashtray.
32. Install the lap duct.
33. Install the upper glove box.
34. Install the lower glove box.

1990-91 Canadian 2WD Vista 1990-91 All 4WD Vista

1. Remove the 3 trim covers.
2. Remove the column lower cover. See Section 8.
3. Remove the lower glove box.
4. Remove the upper glove box.
5. Remove the lap duct.
6. Remove the ashtray.
7. Remove the hood lock release handle.
8. Remove the gauge bezel.
9. Remove the instrument cluster. See Section 6.
10. Remove the speedometer cable adapter.
11. Disconnect the temperature control cables.
12. Remove the air duct.
13. Disconnect the blower motor.
14. Remove the upper trim covers (A & B).
15. Disconnect the antenna wire.
16. Remove the instrument panel mounting bolts.
17. Remove the instrument panel.

To install:

18. Install the instrument panel.
19. Install the instrument panel mounting bolts.
20. Connect the antenna wire.
21. Install the upper trim covers (A & B).
22. Connect the blower motor.
23. Install the air duct.
24. Connect the temperature control cables.
25. Install the speedometer cable adapter.

26. Install the instrument cluster. See Section 6.
27. Install the gauge bezel.
28. Install the hood lock release handle.
29. Install the ashtray.
30. Install the lap duct.
31. Install the upper glove box.
32. Install the lower glove box.
33. Install the column lower cover. See Section 8.
34. Install the 3 trim covers.

1992-93 Vista

1. Install the hood lock release handle.
2. Remove the column lower cover.
3. Remove the foot duct.
4. Remove the lap duct.
5. Remove the glove box.
6. Remove the right side speaker cover.
7. Remove the glove box frame.
8. Remove the gauge bezel.
9. Remove the instrument cluster. See Section 6.
10. Remove the speedometer cable adapter.
11. Remove the ashtray.
12. Remove the center panel.
13. Remove the radio. See Section 6.
14. Remove the center air outlet.
15. Remove the heater control assembly.
16. Remove the clock or plug.
17. Remove the cluster wiring harness connectors.
18. Remove the instrument panel mounting bolts.
19. Remove the instrument panel.

To install:

20. Install the instrument panel.
21. Install the instrument panel mounting bolts.
22. Install the cluster wiring harness connectors.
23. Install the clock or plug.
24. Install the heater control assembly.
25. Install the center air outlet.
26. Install the radio. See Section 6.
27. Install the center panel.
28. Install the ashtray.
29. Install the speedometer cable adapter.
30. Install the instrument cluster. See Section 6.
31. Install the gauge bezel.
32. Install the glove box frame.
33. Install the right side speaker cover.
34. Install the glove box.
35. Install the lap duct.
36. Install the foot duct.
37. Install the column lower cover.
38. Install the hood lock release handle.

Door Panels

REMOVAL & INSTALLATION

▶ **See Figures 21, 22 and 23**

1. Lower the door glass until it is three inches from the full down position.

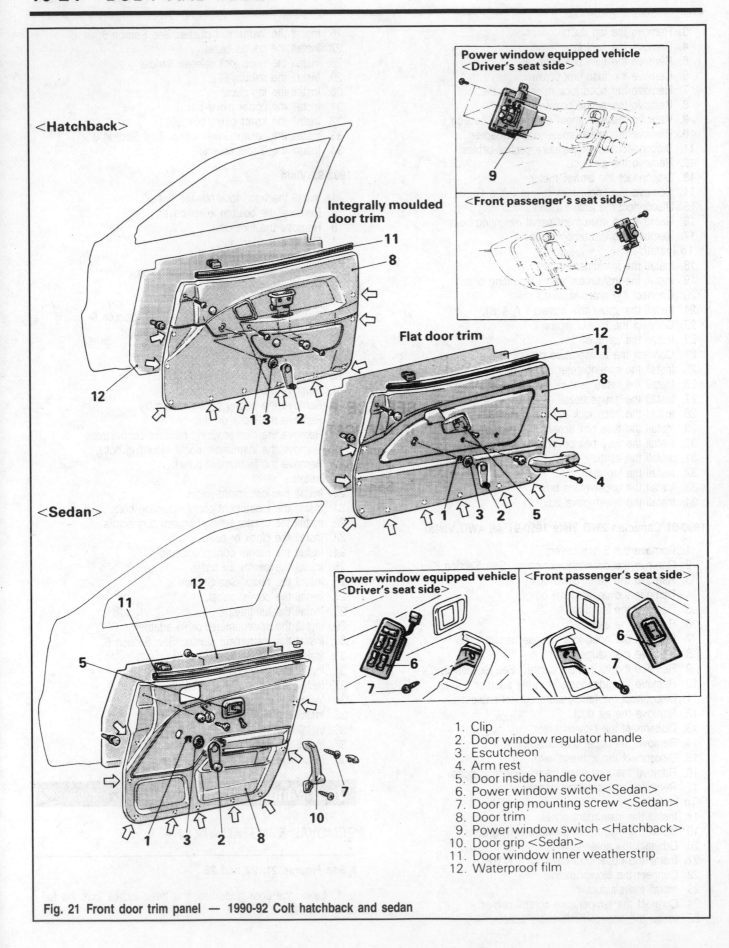

**Power window equipped vehicle
<Driver's seat side>**

9

<Front passenger's seat side>

9

<Hatchback>

**Integrally moulded
door trim**

11
8

12

1 3 2

Flat door trim

12
11
8

4

1 3 2 5

<Sedan>

12

11

5

1 3 2 8

10

**Power window equipped vehicle
<Driver's seat side>**

6

7

<Front passenger's seat side>

6

7

1. Clip
2. Door window regulator handle
3. Escutcheon
4. Arm rest
5. Door inside handle cover
6. Power window switch <Sedan>
7. Door grip mounting screw <Sedan>
8. Door trim
9. Power window switch <Hatchback>
10. Door grip <Sedan>
11. Door window inner weatherstrip
12. Waterproof film

Fig. 21 Front door trim panel — 1990-92 Colt hatchback and sedan

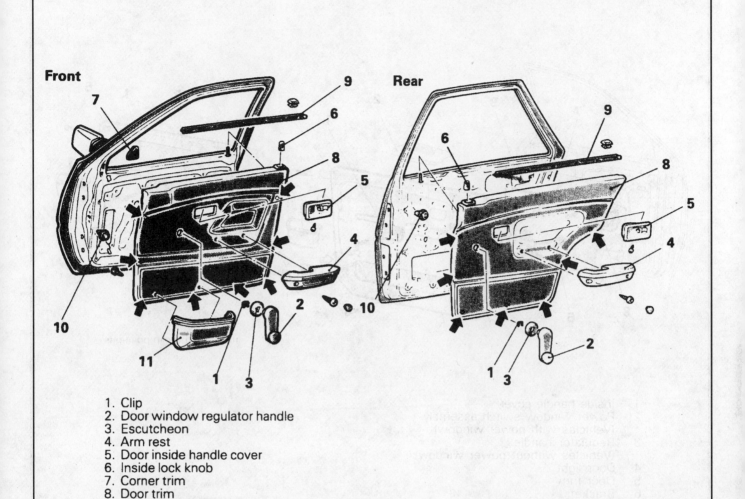

Front

Rear

1. Clip
2. Door window regulator handle
3. Escutcheon
4. Arm rest
5. Door inside handle cover
6. Inside lock knob
7. Corner trim
8. Door trim
9. Inner weatherstrip
10. Trim clip
11. Door pocket

Fig. 22 Door trim panels — 1990 Colt Wagon

2. Unlock the door and remove the remote door latch control handle bezel. On some model a screw that is hidden by a plastic hinged panel must be removed.

3. Remove the armrest mounting screws, and on models with electric controls, pry out the power window switch bezel.

4. Remove the window crank handle on models with manual window regulators.

5. Remove the two edge inserts that cover the mounting screws for the door pull strap, and remove the mounting screws and strap.

6. Insert a wide flat tool between the panel and door frame and carefully twist the tool to unfasten the retainer clips from the door.

7. If the vehicle is equipped with power locks, slide the switch bezel through the trim panel.

8. Disconnect the courtesy lamp connector. Remove the door trim panel.

9. Remove the inner plastic cover and service the components as required.

10. Place sealer along the edges of the plastic liner and put the liner onto the door frame.

11. Position the trim panel, slide the power lock bezel through the panel, connect the courtesy lamp.

12. Position the panel clips over their mounting holes and push the panel against the door frame to lock the clips.

13. Install the pull strap, the armrest, widow handle/power switch, remote latch control/bezel.

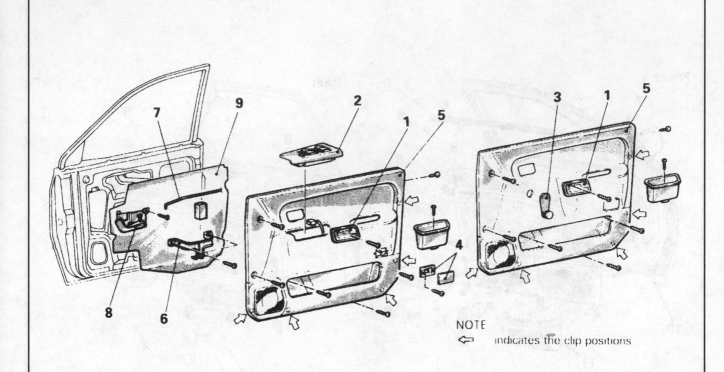

1. Inside handle cover
2. Power window switch assembly
   (Vehicles with power window)
3. Regulator handle
   (Vehicles without power window)
4. Door light
5. Door trim
6. Bracket
7. Rod
8. Inside handle
9. Waterproof film

NOTE
⇐ indicates the clip positions

Fig. 23 Front door trim panels — 1992-93 Vista

Manual Door Locks/Latch

REMOVAL & INSTALLATION

1. Remove the door trim panel and inner cover.
2. Raise the window to the full up position.
3. Disconnect all the locking clips from the remote linkage at the latch.
4. Remove the retaining screws at the door edge and remove the latch assembly.
5. Position the latch to the door frame and secure it with the retaining screws.
6. Connect all of the remote linkage to the latch levers.
7. Check latch operation. Install the inner cover and door trim panel.

Power Door Locks

GENERAL DESCRIPTION

The power door locking system consists of switches, actuators and relays. Control switches are used to operate the system. Actuators are used to raise and lower the door lock buttons. These actuators are mounted inside the door assembly and are electrically operated once the switch is depressed. A control unit or functional relay is used to allow the system to regulate current, to function and to align all the actuators and switches with one another.

Some vehicles incorporate a central unlocking system that automatically unlocks all the doors of the vehicle once the key is inserted in the door from the outside of the vehicle.

COMPONENT REPLACEMENT

▶ **See Figures 24 and 25**

Door Lock Switch

1. Disconnect the negative battery cable.
2. Remove the door trim panel and waterproof seal.
3. Disconnect the electrical connector and remove the switch.
4. Installation is the reverse of removal.

Door Lock Actuator

VISTA FRONT

1. Disconnect the negative battery cable.
2. Remove the door trim panel and waterproof seal.
3. Disconnect the rod to the door latch and the electrical connector.
4. Remove the actuator retaining screws and remove the actuator.

To install:

5. Assemble the rod holder to the lever of the door lock actuator, and install the actuator to the door panel.
6. Move the lock rod and door lock actuator to the lock position, and assemble the rod holder and lock rod.
7. Connect the electrical connector and install the door panel.

VISTA REAR

1. Disconnect the negative battery cable.
2. Remove the door trim panel and waterproof seal.
3. Disconnect the rod to the door latch and the electrical connector.
4. Remove the actuator retaining screws and remove the actuator.

To install:

5. Assemble the clamp to the lever of the door lock actuator, and install the actuator to the door panel.
6. Move the inside lock rod and door lock actuator to the unlock position, and assemble the clamp to the inside lock rod.
7. Connect the electrical connector and install the door panel.

COLT

1. Disconnect the negative battery cable.
2. Remove the door trim panel and waterproof seal.
3. Disconnect the rod to the door latch and the electrical connector.
4. Remove the actuator retaining screws and remove the actuator.
5. Installation is the reverse of removal.

Door Lock Relay and Control Unit

VISTA

1. Disconnect the negative battery cable.
2. Locate the power door lock relay and the door lock control unit, which are under the center of the instrument panel, attached to the front of the MPI and ELC-AT control units.
3. Disconnect the electrical connection and remove the retaining screw.
4. Installation is the reverse of removal.

COLT

1. Disconnect the negative battery cable.
2. Remove the left side cowl trim panel.
3. Disconnect the electrical connection and remove the door lock relay and/or control unit.
4. Installation is the reverse of removal.

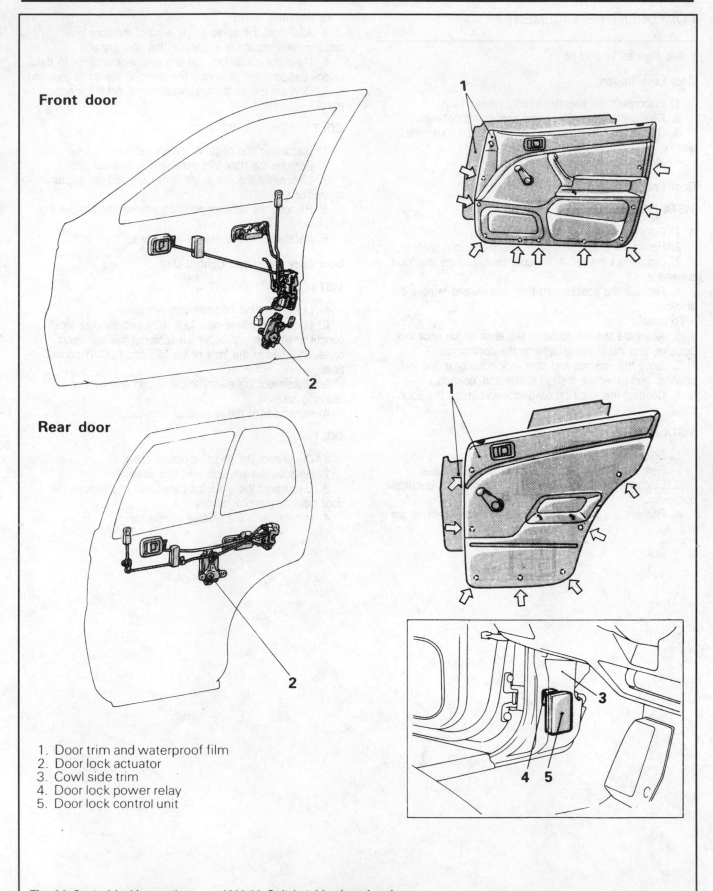

Front door

Rear door

1. Door trim and waterproof film
2. Door lock actuator
3. Cowl side trim
4. Door lock power relay
5. Door lock control unit

Fig. 24 Central locking system — 1990-92 Colt hatchback and sedan

Front Door

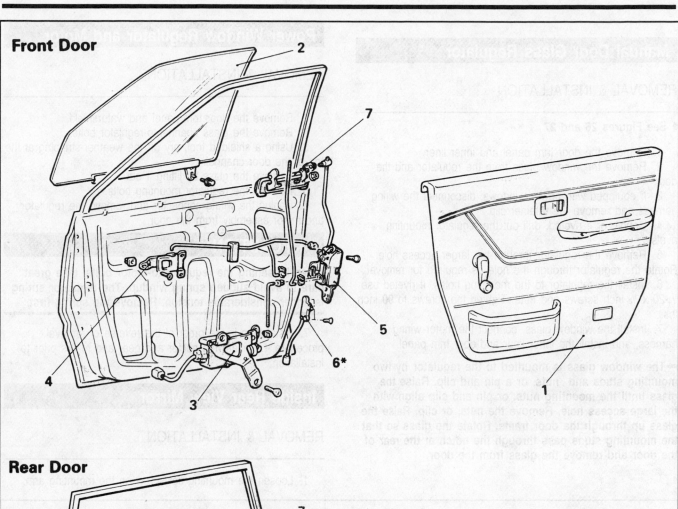

Rear Door

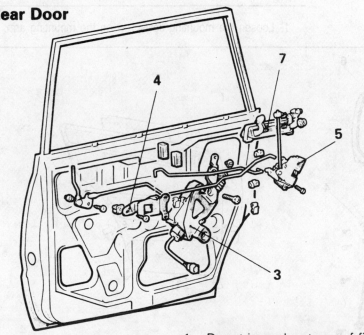

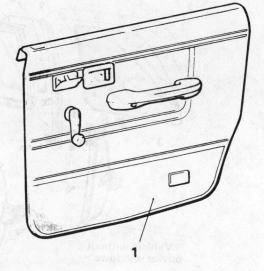

1. Door trim and waterproof film
2. Door window glass assembly
3. Door lock actuator
4. Door inside handle
5. Door latch assembly
6. Door latch switch
7. Door outside handle

Fig. 25 Door locks — 1990-91 Vista

Manual Door Glass Regulator

REMOVAL & INSTALLATION

▶ **See Figures 26 and 27**

1. Remove the door trim panel and inner liner.
2. Remove the window glass from the regulator and the door.
3. If equipped with power windows, disconnect the wiring harness and remove the retainer clip.
4. Unbolt, or if riveted, drill out the regulator mounting rivets.
5. Remove the regulator through the larger access hole. Rotate the regulator through the hole as required for removal.
6. Install the regulator to the mounting holes. If riveted use 1/4-20 x 1/2 inch screws and nuts. Tighten the screws to 90 inch lbs.
7. Install the window glass, connect the motor wiring harness, and install the inner liner and door trim panel.

➡ **The window glass is mounted to the regulator by two mounting studs and nuts, or a pin and clip. Raise the glass until the mounting nuts, or pin and clip align with the large access hole. Remove the nuts, or clip. Raise the glass up through the door frame. Rotate the glass so that the mounting studs pass through the notch at the rear of the door and remove the glass from the door.**

Power Window Regulator and Motor

REMOVAL & INSTALLATION

1. Remove the door trim panel and watershield.
2. Remove the glass channel-to-regulator bolts.
3. Using a shielded tool, pry off the weather-stripping at the top of the door channel.
4. Remove the glass by lifting it out.
5. Remove the regulator mounting bolts.
6. Unplug the wiring connector and remove the regulator and motor assembly from the door.

❈❈CAUTION

When loosening the regulator-to-motor bolts, take great care to avoid sudden spring windup. The regulator spring is under considerable tension. Remove the spring first.

7. Installation is the order of the reverse of removal procedure. Lubricate the sector and gear and rollers prior to installation.

Inside Rear View Mirror

REMOVAL & INSTALLATION

1. Loosen the mounting set screw on the mounting arm.

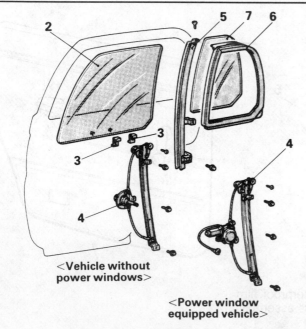

<Vehicle without power windows>

<Power window equipped vehicle>

1. Door trim and waterproof film
   Door window glass adjustment
2. Door window glass
3. Door glass holder
4. Rear window regulator assembly

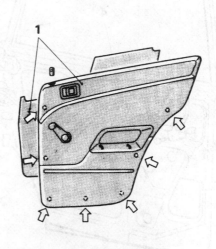

Stationary window glass removal steps

➡ 5. Rear door center sash
➡ 6. Stationary window weatherstrip
➡ 7. Stationary window glass

Fig. 26 Front door glass and regulator — 1990-92 Colt hatchback and sedan

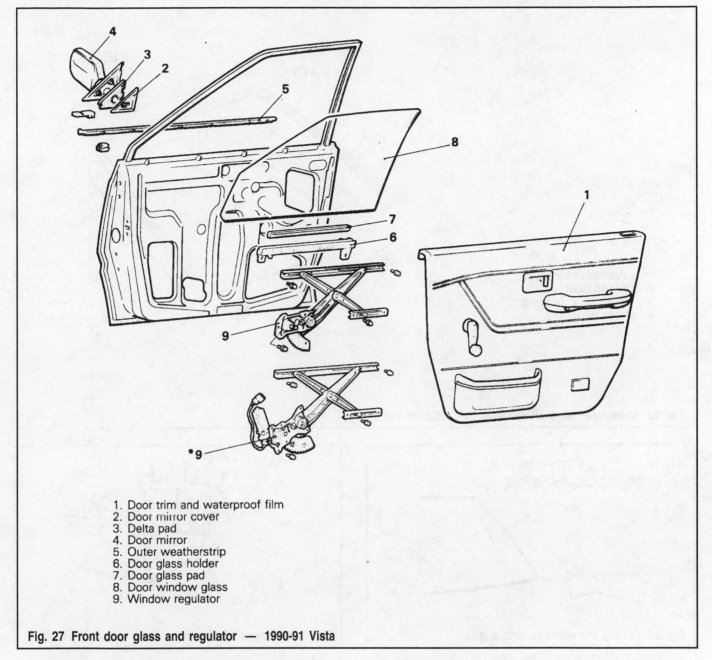

1. Door trim and waterproof film
2. Door mirror cover
3. Delta pad
4. Door mirror
5. Outer weatherstrip
6. Door glass holder
7. Door glass pad
8. Door window glass
9. Window regulator

Fig. 27 Front door glass and regulator — 1990-91 Vista

2. Slide the mirror off of the windshield mounting button.
3. Slide the mirror mounting arm over the mounting button and secure the set screw.

Windshield

REMOVAL & INSTALLATION

▶ See Figures 28, 29, 30, 31 and 32

➡You'll need an assistant for this job.   A special kit is available for replacing glass. The references to adhesives and bonding agents contained in this procedure are taking for granted that this kit is being used. Aftermarket kits are also available which contain all the necessary equipment.

1. On 1990-92 Colt hatchback and sedan models, remove the hood. Remove the wiper arms.
2. Remove the rear view mirror and front pillar trim molding.
3. Cover the sheet metal around the windshield with masking tape to protect it from scratches.
4. Remove the windshield trim molding. It's best to use a tool made for that purpose, although it can be pried off. If a special tool is not used, it's very easy to damage the molding, so be careful!
5. Drill a small hole through the rubber weather-stripping at its base. Pass a length of piano wire through the hole. Wrap each end of the wire around a wood dowel. Grip one dowel in each hand, or have your assistant take one dowel, and, using a sawing motion, pass the wire all the way around the perimeter of the weather-stripping to cut through the sealer.
6. Remove the glass.

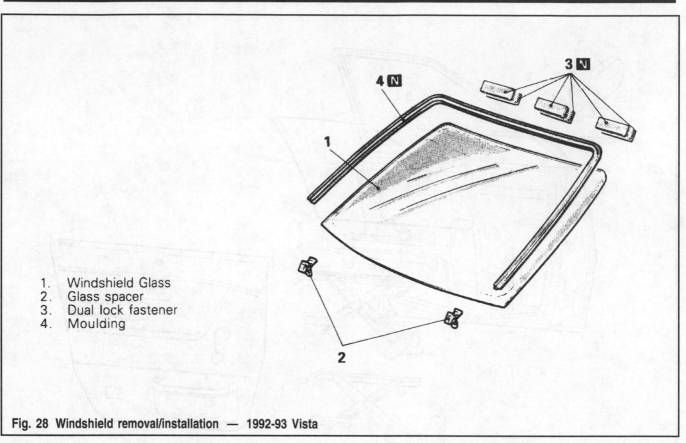

1. Windshield Glass
2. Glass spacer
3. Dual lock fastener
4. Moulding

Fig. 28 Windshield removal/installation — 1992-93 Vista

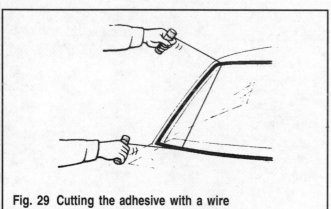

Fig. 29 Cutting the adhesive with a wire

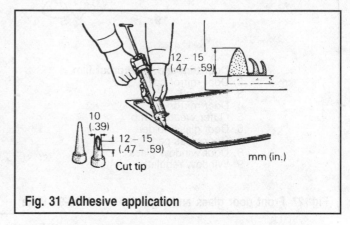

Fig. 31 Adhesive application

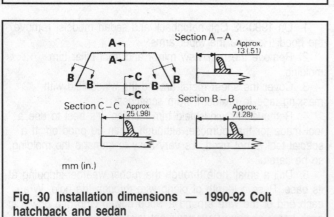

Fig. 30 Installation dimensions — 1990-92 Colt hatchback and sedan

7. Using a sharp knife, cut away the old sealer so that a 1-2mm (0.039-0.079 inch) thickness of old sealer remains around the circumference of the frame. If the old sealer comes completely off in any spot, rebuild that spot to the 1-2mm (0.039-0.079 inch) thickness with new sealer.

8. Secure a new windshield trim dam to the glass with a glass cement. The new dam should be positioned so that its outer edge is 7mm (0.276 inch) from the edge of the glass, with the lip facing outward.

9. Apply a thin coat of primer to the bonding areas of the frame and glass. Allow the primer to dry for 30 minutes. Do not allow any dirt or dust to contact the primer while it's drying. If primer gets on your hands, wash it off immediately.

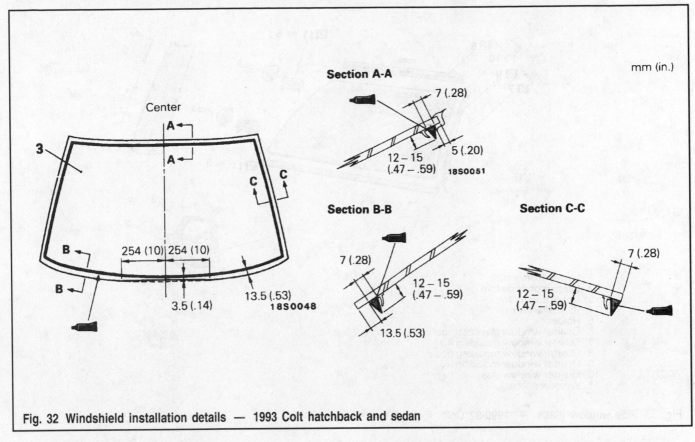

Section A-A

7 (.28)

12 – 15
(.47 – .59)   18S0051

5 (.20)

mm (in.)

Center

A

A

3

C   C

B

B

254 (10) 254 (10)

3.5 (.14)

13.5 (.53)

18S0048

Section B-B

7 (.28)

12 – 15
(.47 – .59)

13.5 (.53)

Section C-C

7 (.28)

12 – 15
(.47 – .59)

Fig. 32 Windshield installation details — 1993 Colt hatchback and sedan

10. Cement the spacers to the frame.

➡**The upper and lower spacers are different. Don't get them mixed up.**

11. Install the molding clips. If any are defective, replace them.

12. Cut the nozzle of the sealer tube as illustrated, so that it will run along the edge of the glass.

13. Apply sealer around the whole circumference so that it will fill the gap between the dam and the edge of the glass, with a bead of sealer about 8mm (0.315 inch) high. Keep the bead smooth and even, shaping it with the spatula where necessary.

14. Open the door windows. Position the glass in the frame, pushing inward lightly to compress the sealer.

15. Trim away excess sealer and fill any gaps which may have appeared. Give the sealer at least 5 hours to dry at 68°F (20°C); 24 hours at 41°F (5°C).

16. Leak test the glass.

Fixed (Stationary) Window Glass

REMOVAL & INSTALLATION

▸ **See Figure 33**

1. Carefully snap the molding from the weather-stripping.

2. Using a wood spatula, break the adhesive bond between the weather-stripping and the body flange.

3. Push out the inner lip of the weather-stripping, from inside the truck, while pushing out on the glass.

4. With the aid of an assistant, remove the glass and weather-stripping.

5. Before installing the glass, make sure that you clean all of the old adhesive from all parts.

6. Place a coat of primer in the molding. Install the weather-stripping around the glass.

7. Liberally wet the groove in the weather-stripping with liquid soap.

8. Place a string, about 4mm (0.157 inch) in diameter, in the groove all the way around the weather-stripping. Allow a good length to hang free.

9. Place the glass into position in the frame, with the free end of the string hanging inside the truck. Pull the string while pushing inward on the glass, to properly position the inner lip of the weather-stripping.

10. Go around the inner and outer sides of the weather-stripping with a thin tool to make sure that the weather-stripping is flat against the frame.

11. Using a thin coat of rubber sealer, seal the outer edge of the weather-stripping against the frame.

12. Snap the molding into place.

Seats

REMOVAL & INSTALLATION

▸ **See Figures 34, 35, 36 and 37**

1. Depending on year and model, the front seat(s) are mounted by bolts accessible from underneath the vehicle, or a combination of nuts and bolts. The nuts usually are used to

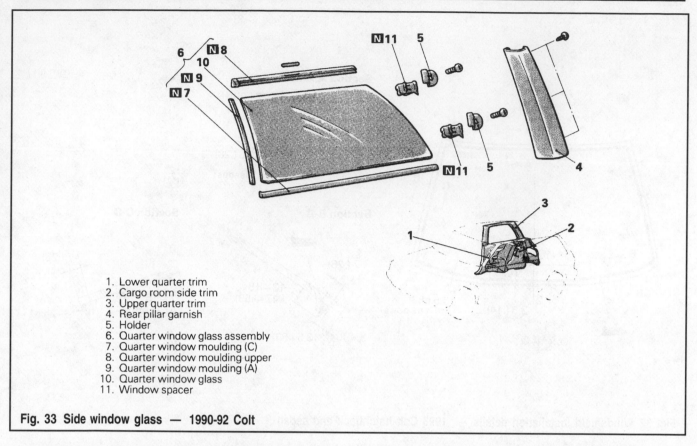

1. Lower quarter trim
2. Cargo room side trim
3. Upper quarter trim
4. Rear pillar garnish
5. Holder
6. Quarter window glass assembly
7. Quarter window moulding (C)
8. Quarter window moulding upper
9. Quarter window moulding (A)
10. Quarter window glass
11. Window spacer

Fig. 33 Side window glass — 1990-92 Colt

mount the front of the seat brackets, and are loosen from the passenger's compartment. The nuts are usually covered by a trim plug which must be removed first. The rear of the seat bracket mounting bolts are accessed from underneath the vehicle.

2. The second seat (Vista models) is mounted by nuts and bolts that can be removed from the passengers compartment.

3. Rear seats are removed by pushing the front of the seat cushion back towards the rear of the vehicle and lifting it up to free it from the mounting clips. Or, removing the bolts from the front of the seat cushion brackets. The seat back is usually retained by bolts through the floor pan that are visible after the cushion has been removed.

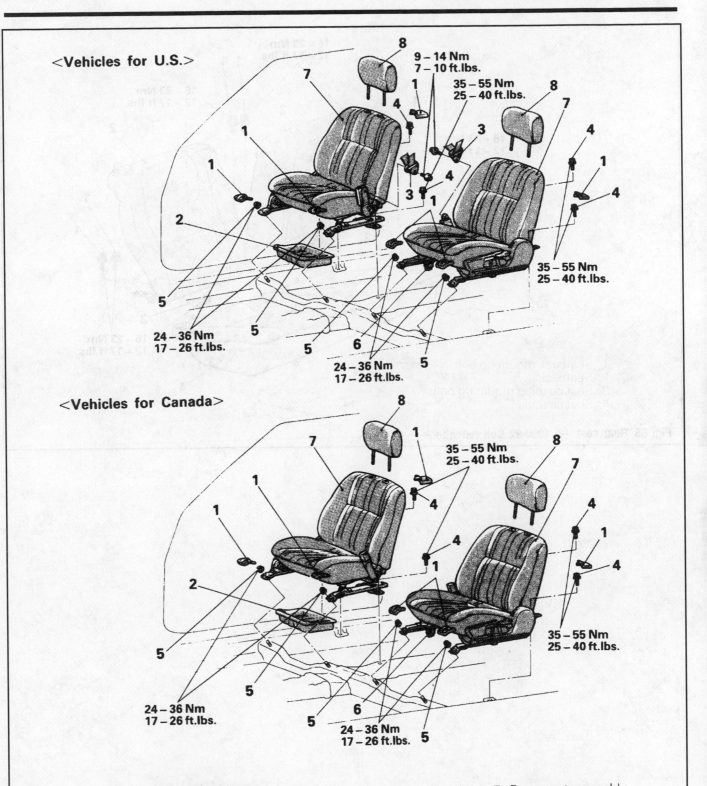

<Vehicles for U.S.>

9 – 14 Nm
7 – 10 ft.lbs.

35 – 55 Nm
25 – 40 ft.lbs.

35 – 55 Nm
25 – 40 ft.lbs.

24 – 36 Nm
17 – 26 ft.lbs.

24 – 36 Nm
17 – 26 ft.lbs.

<Vehicles for Canada>

35 – 55 Nm
25 – 40 ft.lbs.

35 – 55 Nm
25 – 40 ft.lbs.

24 – 36 Nm
17 – 26 ft.lbs.

24 – 36 Nm
17 – 26 ft.lbs.

1. Seat anchor covers
2. Seat under tray
3. Guide ring
4. Seat mounting bolts
5. Seat mounting nuts
6. Connection of seat belt switch wiring
   harness
7. Front seat assembly
8. Headrestraint

Fig. 34 Front seats — 1990-92 Colt hatchback and sedan

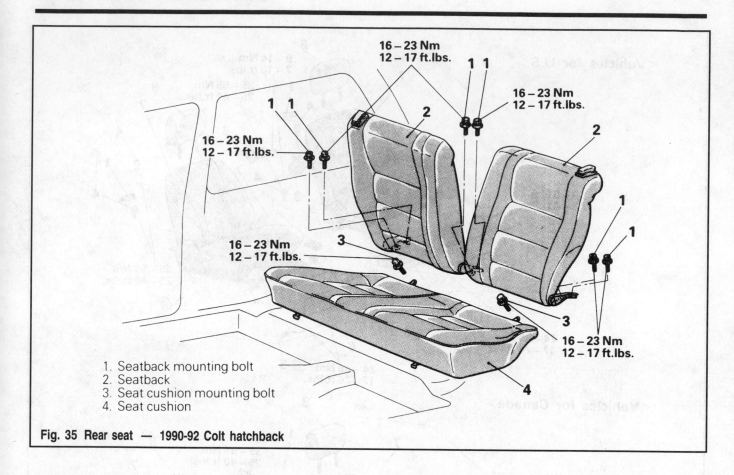

16 – 23 Nm
12 – 17 ft.lbs.

16 – 23 Nm
12 – 17 ft.lbs.

16 – 23 Nm
12 – 17 ft.lbs.

16 – 23 Nm
12 – 17 ft.lbs.

16 – 23 Nm
12 – 17 ft.lbs.

1. Seatback mounting bolt
2. Seatback
3. Seat cushion mounting bolt
4. Seat cushion

Fig. 35 Rear seat — 1990-92 Colt hatchback

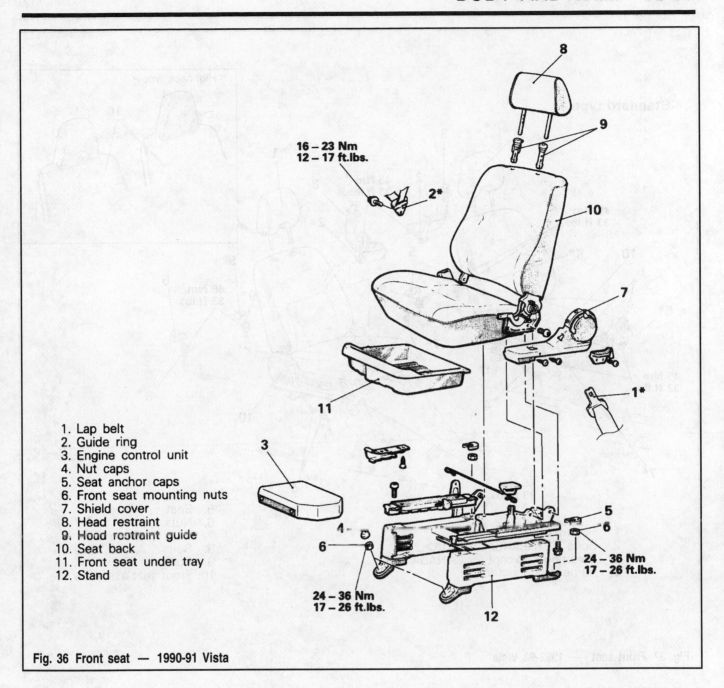

16 – 23 Nm
12 – 17 ft.lbs.

24 – 36 Nm
17 – 26 ft.lbs.

24 – 36 Nm
17 – 26 ft.lbs.

1. Lap belt
2. Guide ring
3. Engine control unit
4. Nut caps
5. Seat anchor caps
6. Front seat mounting nuts
7. Shield cover
8. Head restraint
9. Head restraint guide
10. Seat back
11. Front seat under tray
12. Stand

Fig. 36 Front seat — 1990-91 Vista

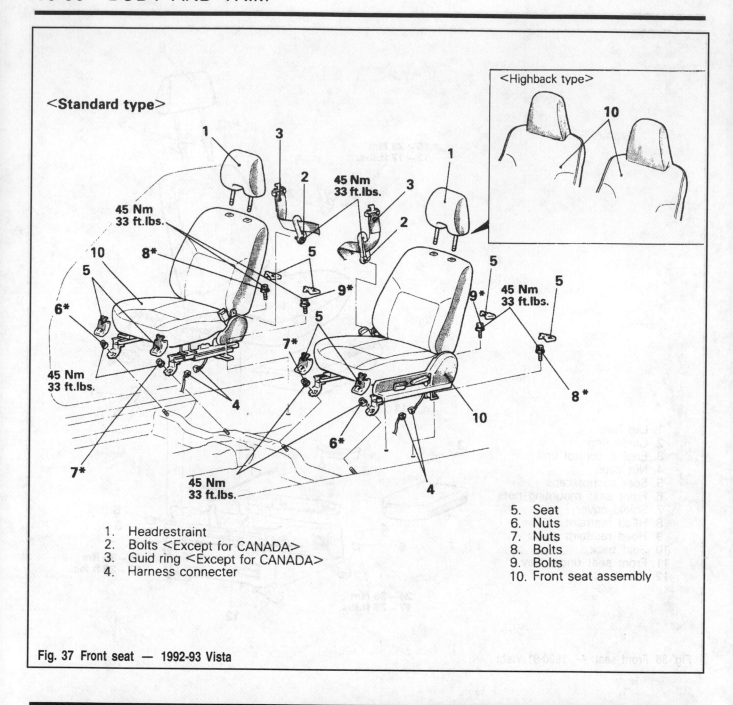

1. Headrestraint
2. Bolts <Except for CANADA>
3. Guid ring <Except for CANADA>
4. Harness connecter

5. Seat
6. Nuts
7. Nuts
8. Bolts
9. Bolts
10. Front seat assembly

Fig. 37 Front seat — 1992-93 Vista

AUTOMATIC SAFETY BELT SYSTEM

General Description

The front seats on some vehicles are equipped with an automatic seat belt system. The automatic seat belts consist of a driving device assembly, shoulder belt and manual lap belt. The system is designed to provide comfort and safety by automatically fastening and unfastening the shoulder belt as well as automatic retraction of the belts during normal vehicle operation. Sensing devices inside the belt retractor of the shoulder and lap belts are designed to lock the retractors in the event of an abrupt change in vehicle motion.

SYSTEM OPERATION

When either front door is closed and the ignition switch turned to the **ON** position, the shoulder belt automatically moves to the set (fastened) position around the occupant. When the door is opened, the shoulder belt will automatically move to the set-off (unfastened) position. The shoulder belt on the driver's side will automatically move to the set-off position when the ignition key is removed from the ignition. The belts and door for the driver's and front passenger's seats operate independently of each other.

Safety Precautions

- Keep sharp and potentially damaging objects away from the belts.
- Avoid bending or damaging any part of the buckle.
- If cleaning, use only mild soap and water. Do not use bleach or dye belt webbing.
- Do not attempt any repairs on the retractor mechanisms or covers. Always replace the defective assembly.
- If a belt becomes cut or damaged, replace it with a new one.
- Do not position any object in the trim panel that will interfere with the movement of the safety belts.

Seat Belt Motor

TESTING

1. Unplug the seat belt motor/fasten switch connector.
2. Connect a fused jumper from the positive battery terminal to terminal 3 of the motor connector, then momentarily ground terminal 4 of the motor connector. The slide anchor should go from the release position to the fasten position.

➡ **While performing this test, do not stop the slide anchor midway of the guide rail. Allow the slide anchor to move to the full fastened or released position.**

3. Connect a fused jumper from the positive battery terminal to terminal 4 of the motor connector, then momentarily ground terminal 3 of the motor connector. The slide anchor should go from the fasten position to the release position.
4. If the result is not OK, replace the seat belt motor.

Fasten Switch

TESTING

1. Disconnect the negative battery cable.
2. Unplug the seat belt motor/fasten switch connector.
3. With the slide anchor in the fasten position, check that there is continuity between terminal 1 and 2.
4. If not, replace the fasten switch assembly.

Release Switch

TESTING

1. Disconnect the negative battery cable.
2. Unplug the release switch connector.
3. With the slide anchor in the release position, check that there is continuity between terminal 1 and 2.
4. If not, replace the release switch assembly.

Motor Relay

TESTING

1. Disconnect the seat belt motor relay connector.
2. Remove the seat belt motor relay.
3. Check for continuity between terminals 1, 3 and 5 of the relay.
4. Check for continuity between terminals 4, 6 7 and 8 of the relay.
5. Applying 12 volts to terminal 6 and momentarily grounding terminal 4. Continuity should be indicated between terminals 1 and 2.
6. Applying 12 volts to terminal 7 and momentarily grounding terminal 8. Continuity should be indicated between terminals 2 and 3.
7. If the result is not OK, replace the motor relay.

REMOVAL & INSTALLATION

▶ **See Figures 38, 39, 40, 41 and 42**

1. Disconnect the negative battery cable.
2. Remove the rear console box assembly.
3. Disconnect the motor relay wiring connector.
4. Remove the relay retaining screw and remove the relay.
To install:
5. Fit the relay into position and install the retaining screw.
6. Reconnect the relay wiring connector.
7. Install the rear console box assembly.
8. Reconnect the negative battery cable.

Shoulder Belt Retractor

REMOVAL & INSTALLATION

1. Disconnect the negative battery cable.
2. Remove the shoulder belt tongue plate, guide ring and bezel.
3. Remove the rear console box assembly.
4. Disconnect the outer switch harness connector.
5. Remove the retractor assembly mounting bolts.
6. Remove the left and right retractor brackets and remove the assembly from the vehicle.
To install:
7. Fit the retractor assembly into the vehicle.
8. Fit the brackets and install the mounting bolts.
9. Reconnect the outer switch harness connector.
10. Install the rear console box assembly.
11. Install the bezel, guide ring and shoulder belt tongue plate.
12. Reconnect the negative battery cable.

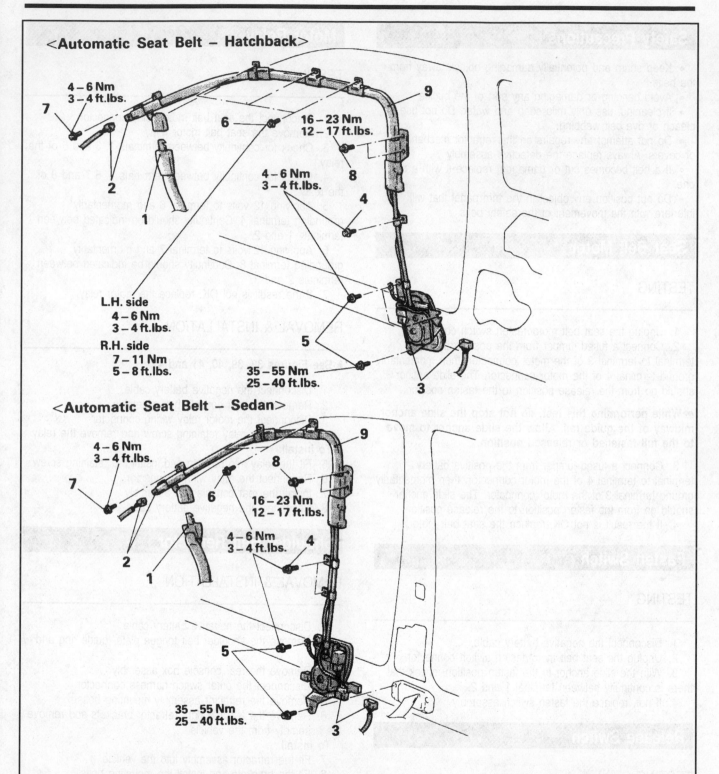

<Automatic Seat Belt – Hatchback>

4 – 6 Nm
3 – 4 ft.lbs.

7

2

1

6

16 – 23 Nm
12 – 17 ft.lbs.

8

9

4 – 6 Nm
3 – 4 ft.lbs.

4

L.H. side
4 – 6 Nm
3 – 4 ft.lbs.

R.H. side
7 – 11 Nm
5 – 8 ft.lbs.

5

35 – 55 Nm
25 – 40 ft.lbs.

3

<Automatic Seat Belt – Sedan>

4 – 6 Nm
3 – 4 ft.lbs.

7

2

1

8

6

9

16 – 23 Nm
12 – 17 ft.lbs.

4 – 6 Nm
3 – 4 ft.lbs.

4

5

35 – 55 Nm
25 – 40 ft.lbs.

3

1. Shoulder belt tongue plate
2. Release switch connector connection
3. Automatic seat belt wiring harness connector connection
4. Outer casing mounting bolts
5. Motor mounting bolts
6. Guide rail mounting bolts (A)

7. Guide rail mounting bolts (B)
8. Guide rail mounting bolts (C)
9. Driving device assembly

Fig. 38 Front seat belt retraction system — 1990-92 USA Colt hatchback and sedan

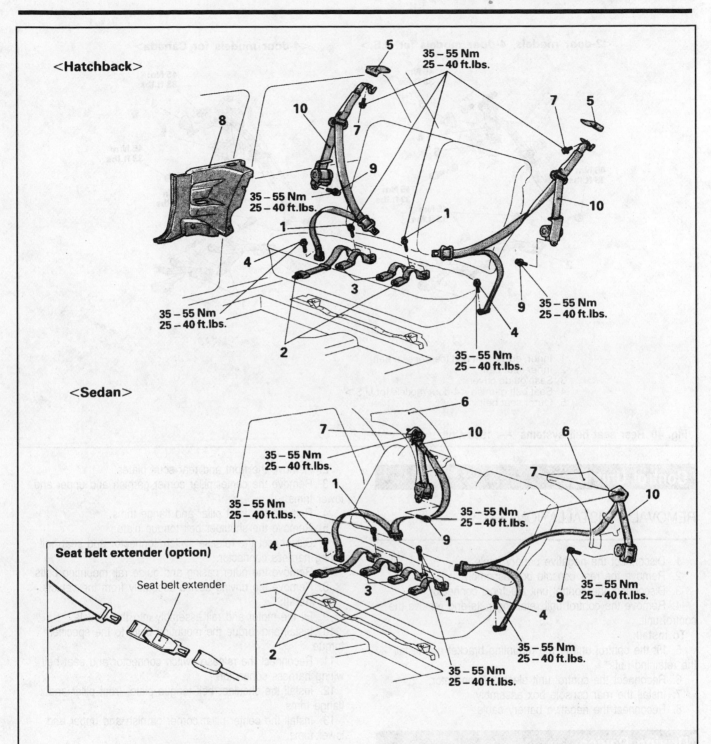

<Hatchback>

35 – 55 Nm
25 – 40 ft.lbs.

35 – 55 Nm
25 – 40 ft.lbs.

35 – 55 Nm
25 – 40 ft.lbs.

35 – 55 Nm
25 – 40 ft.lbs.

35 – 55 Nm
25 – 40 ft.lbs.

<Sedan>

35 – 55 Nm
25 – 40 ft.lbs.

35 – 55 Nm
25 – 40 ft.lbs.

35 – 55 Nm
25 – 40 ft.lbs.

35 – 55 Nm
25 – 40 ft.lbs.

35 – 55 Nm
25 – 40 ft.lbs.

Seat belt extender (option)

Seat belt extender

1. Seat belt mounting bolts
2. Rear seat belt (center)
3. Seat belt (buckle side)
4. Seat belt anchor plate attaching bolts
5. Sash guide cover <Hatchback>
6. Rear pillar trim <Sedan>
7. Sash guide attaching bolts
8. Quarter trim, lower <Hatchback>
9. Retractor bracket attaching bolts
10. Seat belt assembly (tongue side)

Fig. 39 Rear seat belts — 1990-92 Colt hatchback and sedan

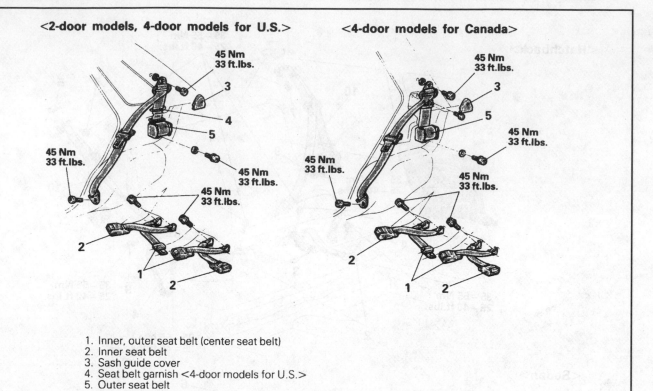

<2-door models, 4-door models for U.S.>

45 Nm
33 ft.lbs.

45 Nm
33 ft.lbs.

45 Nm
33 ft.lbs.

45 Nm
33 ft.lbs.

<4-door models for Canada>

45 Nm
33 ft.lbs.

45 Nm
33 ft.lbs.

45 Nm
33 ft.lbs.

45 Nm
33 ft.lbs.

1. Inner, outer seat belt (center seat belt)
2. Inner seat belt
3. Sash guide cover
4. Seat belt garnish <4-door models for U.S.>
5. Outer seat belt

Fig. 40 Rear seat belt systems — 1993 Colt

Control Unit

REMOVAL & INSTALLATION

1. Disconnect the negative battery cable.
2. Remove the rear console box assembly.
3. Disconnect the control unit electrical connector.
4. Remove the control unit retaining nuts and remove the control unit.
To install:
5. Fit the control unit to the mounting bracket and install the retaining nuts.
6. Reconnect the control unit electrical connector.
7. Install the rear console box assembly.
8. Reconnect the negative battery cable.

Driving Device

REMOVAL & INSTALLATION

1. Disconnect the negative battery cable.

2. Remove the front and rear scuff plates.
3. Remove the center pillar corner garnish and upper and lower trims.
4. Remove the front pillar and flange trims.
5. Remove the shoulder belt tongue plate.
6. Disconnect the release switch connector and seat belt wiring harness connector.
7. Remove the outer casing and guide rail mounting bolts.
8. Remove the driving device assembly from the vehicle.
To install:
9. Fit the motor and rail assembly into the vehicle.
10. Install and torque the mounting bolts to the specified torque.
11. Reconnect the release switch connector and seat belt wiring harness connector.
12. Install the shoulder belt tongue plate, front pillar and flange trims.
13. Install the center pillar corner garnish and upper and lower trims.
14. Install the front and rear scuff plates.
15. Reconnect the negative battery cable.

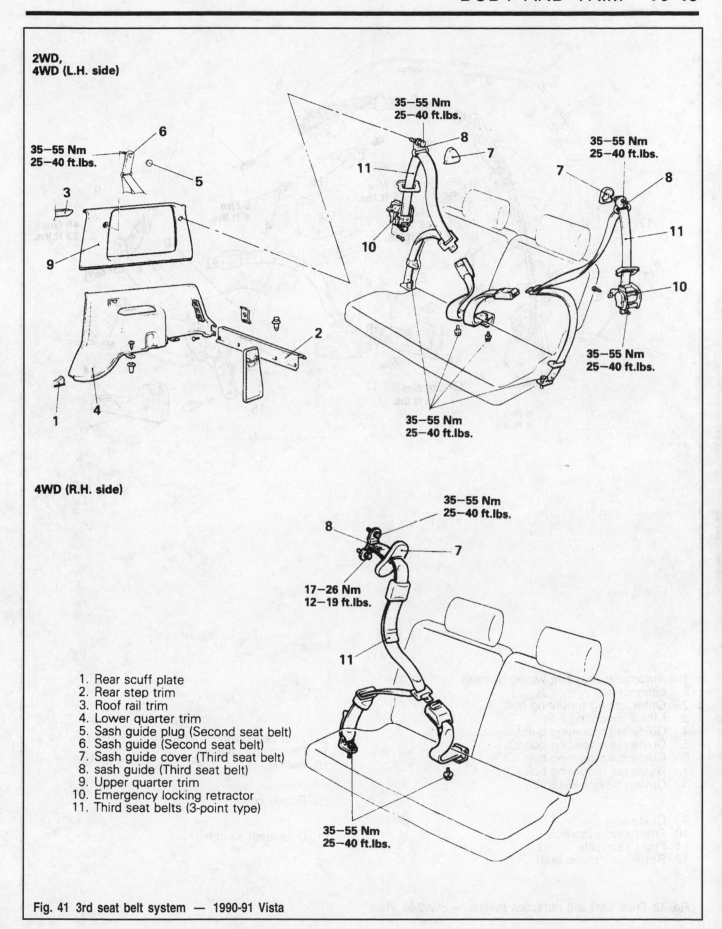

2WD,
4WD (L.H. side)

35—55 Nm
25—40 ft.lbs.

35—55 Nm
25—40 ft.lbs.

35—55 Nm
25—40 ft.lbs.

35—55 Nm
25—40 ft.lbs.

35—55 Nm
25—40 ft.lbs.

4WD (R.H. side)

35—55 Nm
25—40 ft.lbs.

17—26 Nm
12—19 ft.lbs.

35—55 Nm
25—40 ft.lbs.

1. Rear scuff plate
2. Rear step trim
3. Roof rail trim
4. Lower quarter trim
5. Sash guide plug (Second seat belt)
6. Sash guide (Second seat belt)
7. Sash guide cover (Third seat belt)
8. sash guide (Third seat belt)
9. Upper quarter trim
10. Emergency locking retractor
11. Third seat belts (3-point type)

Fig. 41 3rd seat belt system — 1990-91 Vista

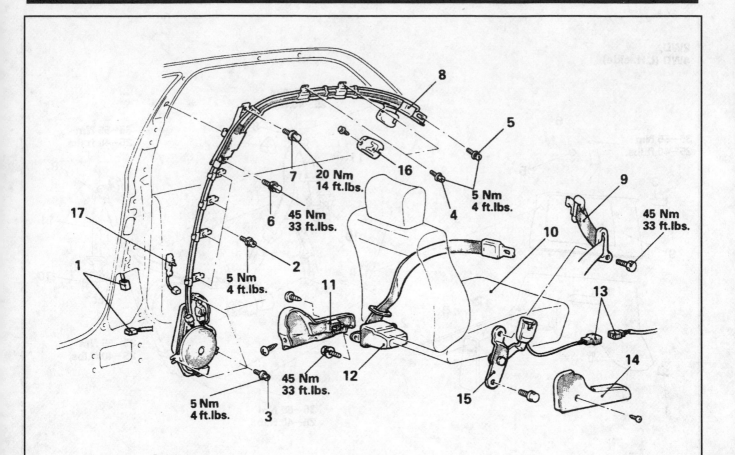

1. Automatic seat belt wiring harness
   connector
2. Outer casing mounting bolt
3. Motor mounting bolt
4. Guide rail mounting bolt (A)
5. Guide rail mounting bolt (B)
6. Guide rail mounting bolt (C)
7. Guide rail mounting bolt (D)
8. Driving device assembly

9. Guide ring
10. Front seat assembly
11. Front seat side shield
12. Retractor (for lap belt)

13. Seat belt switch connector (L.H. only)
14. Free hinge cover
15. Buckle

16. Buckle cover

17. Door latch switch

Fig. 42 Front seat belt retraction system — 1992-93 Vista

TORQUE SPECIFICATIONS

Component	U.S.	Metric
Bumper absorber nut		
Hatchback	12-16 ft. lbs.	17-22 Nm
Door hinge-to-door	12-19 ft. lbs.	17-26 Nm
Door hinge-to-body		
1990-92 Colt hatchback, sedan and Wagon	12-19 ft. lbs.	17-26 Nm
1990-91 Vista	25-40 ft. lbs.	35-55 Nm
Front bumper reinforcement bolt		
1990-92 Colt hatchback, sedan and Wagon	14-20 ft. lbs.	19-28 Nm
Front bumper support bolt		
1990-92 Colt hatchback, sedan and Wagon	14-20 ft. lbs.	19-28 Nm
Front seat mounting bolt		
1990-92 Colt hatchback and sedan	25-40 ft. lbs.	35-55 Nm
1990 Colt Wagon	12-19 ft. lbs.	17-26 Nm
Front seat mounting nut	17-26 ft. lbs.	24-36 Nm
Hood latch-to-body		
1990-92 Colt hatchback and sedan	5-8 ft. lbs.	7-11 Nm
1990 Colt Wagon	36-84 inch lbs.	4-9 Nm
1990-91 Vista	5-8 ft. lbs.	7-11 Nm
Hood hinge-to-body		
1990-92 Colt hatchback and sedan	7-10 ft. lbs.	9-14 Nm
1990 Colt Wagon	36-48 inch lbs.	4-9 Nm
Hood hinge-to-hood	7-10 ft. lbs.	9-14 Nm
Liftgate hinge-to-body	8-12 ft. lbs.	11-16 Nm
Liftgate hinge-to-liftgate		
1990-92 Colt hatchback, sedan and Wagon	7-10 ft. lbs.	9-14 Nm
1990-91 Vista	36-48 inch lbs.	4-6 Nm
Rear bumper reinforcement nut		
Hatchback	25-32 ft. lbs.	35-44 Nm
Rear bumper reinforcement bolt		
Sedan	14-20 ft. lbs.	19-28 Nm
Rear bumper stay bolt		
Sedan	14-20 ft. lbs.	19-28 Nm
Rear seatback mounting bolt		
Hatchback	12-17 ft. lbs.	16-23 Nm
1990-91 Vista	25-40 ft. lbs.	35-55 Nm
Rear seat cushion mounting bolt		
Hatchback	12-17 ft. lbs.	16-23 Nm
Rear seatback mounting nut		
Sedan	36-48 inch lbs.	4-6 Nm
Rear seat catch mounting bolt		
1990 Colt Wagon	36-48 inch lbs.	4-6 Nm
Seat belt mounting bolts		
1990-92 Colt hatchback, sedan and Wagon	25-40 ft. lbs.	35-55 Nm

GLOSSARY

AIR/FUEL RATIO: The ratio of air to gasoline by weight in the fuel mixture drawn into the engine.

AIR INJECTION: One method of reducing harmful exhaust emissions by injecting air into each of the exhaust ports of an engine. The fresh air entering the hot exhaust manifold causes any remaining fuel to be burned before it can exit the tailpipe.

ALTERNATOR: A device used for converting mechanical energy into electrical energy.

AMMETER: An instrument, calibrated in amperes, used to measure the flow of an electrical current in a circuit. Ammeters are always connected in series with the circuit being tested.

AMPERE: The rate of flow of electrical current present when one volt of electrical pressure is applied against one ohm of electrical resistance.

ANALOG COMPUTER: Any microprocessor that uses similar (analogous) electrical signals to make its calculations.

ARMATURE: A laminated, soft iron core wrapped by a wire that converts electrical energy to mechanical energy as in a motor or relay. When rotated in a magnetic field, it changes mechanical energy into electrical energy as in a generator.

ATMOSPHERIC PRESSURE: The pressure on the Earth's surface caused by the weight of the air in the atmosphere. At sea level, this pressure is 14.7 psi at 32{248}F (101 kPa at 0{248}C).

ATOMIZATION: The breaking down of a liquid into a fine mist that can be suspended in air.

AXIAL PLAY: Movement parallel to a shaft or bearing bore.

BACKFIRE: The sudden combustion of gases in the intake or exhaust system that results in a loud explosion.

BACKLASH: The clearance or play between two parts, such as meshed gears.

BACKPRESSURE: Restrictions in the exhaust system that slow the exit of exhaust gases from the combustion chamber.

BAKELITE: A heat resistant, plastic insulator material commonly used in printed circuit boards and transistorized components.

BALL BEARING: A bearing made up of hardened inner and outer races between which hardened steel balls roll.

BALLAST RESISTOR: A resistor in the primary ignition circuit that lowers voltage after the engine is started to reduce wear on ignition components.

BEARING: A friction reducing, supportive device usually located between a stationary part and a moving part.

BIMETAL TEMPERATURE SENSOR: Any sensor or switch made of two dissimilar types of metal that bend when heated or cooled due to the different expansion rates of the alloys. These types of sensors usually function as an on/off switch.

BLOWBY: Combustion gases, composed of water vapor and unburned fuel, that leak past the piston rings into the crankcase during normal engine operation. These gases are removed by the PCV system to prevent the buildup of harmful acids in the crankcase.

BRAKE PAD: A brake shoe and lining assembly used with disc brakes.

BRAKE SHOE: The backing for the brake lining. The term is, however, usually applied to the assembly of the brake backing and lining.

BUSHING: A liner, usually removable, for a bearing; an anti-friction liner used in place of a bearing.

CALIPER: A hydraulically activated device in a disc brake system, which is mounted straddling the brake rotor (disc). The caliper contains at least one piston and two brake pads. Hydraulic pressure on the piston(s) forces the pads against the rotor.

CAMSHAFT: A shaft in the engine on which are the lobes (cams) which operate the valves. The camshaft is driven by the crankshaft, via a belt, chain or gears, at one half the crankshaft speed.

CAPACITOR: A device which stores an electrical charge.

CARBON MONOXIDE (CO): A colorless, odorless gas given off as a normal byproduct of combustion. It is poisonous and extremely dangerous in confined areas, building up slowly to toxic levels without warning if adequate ventilation is not available.

CARBURETOR: A device, usually mounted on the intake manifold of an engine, which mixes the air and fuel in the proper proportion to allow even combustion.

CATALYTIC CONVERTER: A device installed in the exhaust system, like a muffler, that converts harmful byproducts of combustion into carbon dioxide and water vapor by means of a heat-producing chemical reaction.

CENTRIFUGAL ADVANCE: A mechanical method of advancing the spark timing by using flyweights in the distributor that react to centrifugal force generated by the distributor shaft rotation.

CHECK VALVE: Any one-way valve installed to permit the flow of air, fuel or vacuum in one direction only.

CHOKE: A device, usually a moveable valve, placed in the intake path of a carburetor to restrict the flow of air.

CIRCUIT: Any unbroken path through which an electrical current can flow. Also used to describe fuel flow in some instances.

CIRCUIT BREAKER: A switch which protects an electrical circuit from overload by opening the circuit when the current flow exceeds a predetermined level. Some circuit breakers must be reset manually, while most reset automatically

COIL (IGNITION): A transformer in the ignition circuit which steps up the voltage provided to the spark plugs.

COMBINATION MANIFOLD: An assembly which includes both the intake and exhaust manifolds in one casting.

COMBINATION VALVE: A device used in some fuel systems that routes fuel vapors to a charcoal storage canister instead of venting them into the atmosphere. The valve relieves fuel tank pressure and allows fresh air into the tank as the fuel level drops to prevent a vapor lock situation.

COMPRESSION RATIO: The comparison of the total volume of the cylinder and combustion chamber with the piston at BDC and the piston at TDC.

CONDENSER: 1. An electrical device which acts to store an electrical charge, preventing voltage surges.
 2. A radiator-like device in the air conditioning system in which refrigerant gas condenses into a liquid, giving off heat.

CONDUCTOR: Any material through which an electrical current can be transmitted easily.

CONTINUITY: Continuous or complete circuit. Can be checked with an ohmmeter.

COUNTERSHAFT: An intermediate shaft which is rotated by a mainshaft and transmits, in turn, that rotation to a working part.

CRANKCASE: The lower part of an engine in which the crankshaft and related parts operate.

CRANKSHAFT: The main driving shaft of an engine which receives reciprocating motion from the pistons and converts it to rotary motion.

CYLINDER: In an engine, the round hole in the engine block in which the piston(s) ride.

CYLINDER BLOCK: The main structural member of an engine in which is found the cylinders, crankshaft and other principal parts.

CYLINDER HEAD: The detachable portion of the engine, fastened, usually, to the top of the cylinder block, containing all or most of the combustion chambers. On overhead valve engines, it contains the valves and their operating parts. On overhead cam engines, it contains the camshaft as well.

DEAD CENTER: The extreme top or bottom of the piston stroke.

DETONATION: An unwanted explosion of the air/fuel mixture in the combustion chamber caused by excess heat and compression, advanced timing, or an overly lean mixture. Also referred to as "ping".

DIAPHRAGM: A thin, flexible wall separating two cavities, such as in a vacuum advance unit.

DIESELING: A condition in which hot spots in the combustion chamber cause the engine to run on after the key is turned off.

DIFFERENTIAL: A geared assembly which allows the transmission of motion between drive axles, giving one axle the ability to turn faster than the other.

DIODE: An electrical device that will allow current to flow in one direction only.

DISC BRAKE: A hydraulic braking assembly consisting of a brake disc, or rotor, mounted on an axle, and a caliper assembly containing, usually two brake pads which are activated by hydraulic pressure. The pads are forced against the sides of the disc, creating friction which slows the vehicle.

DISTRIBUTOR: A mechanically driven device on an engine which is responsible for electrically firing the spark plug at a predetermined point of the piston stroke.

DOWEL PIN: A pin, inserted in mating holes in two different parts allowing those parts to maintain a fixed relationship.

DRUM BRAKE: A braking system which consists of two brake shoes and one or two wheel cylinders, mounted on a fixed backing plate, and a brake drum, mounted on an axle, which revolves around the assembly.

DWELL: The rate, measured in degrees of shaft rotation, at which an electrical circuit cycles on and off.

ELECTRONIC CONTROL UNIT (ECU): Ignition module, module, amplifier or igniter. See Module for definition.

ELECTRONIC IGNITION: A system in which the timing and firing of the spark plugs is controlled by an electronic control unit, usually called a module. These systems have no points or condenser.

ENDPLAY: The measured amount of axial movement in a shaft.

ENGINE: A device that converts heat into mechanical energy.

EXHAUST MANIFOLD: A set of cast passages or pipes which conduct exhaust gases from the engine.

FEELER GAUGE: A blade, usually metal, of precisely predetermined thickness, used to measure the clearance between two parts.

FIRING ORDER: The order in which combustion occurs in the cylinders of an engine. Also the order in which spark is distributed to the plugs by the distributor.

FLOODING: The presence of too much fuel in the intake manifold and combustion chamber which prevents the air/fuel mixture from firing, thereby causing a no-start situation.

FLYWHEEL: A disc shaped part bolted to the rear end of the crankshaft. Around the outer perimeter is affixed the ring gear. The starter drive engages the ring gear, turning the flywheel, which rotates the crankshaft, imparting the initial starting motion to the engine.

FOOT POUND (ft.lb. or sometimes, ft. lbs.): The amount of energy or work needed to raise an item weighing one pound, a distance of one foot.

FUSE: A protective device in a circuit which prevents circuit overload by breaking the circuit when a specific amperage is present. The device is constructed around a strip or wire of a lower amperage rating than the circuit it is designed to protect. When an amperage higher than that stamped on the fuse is present in the circuit, the strip or wire melts, opening the circuit.

GEAR RATIO: The ratio between the number of teeth on meshing gears.

GENERATOR: A device which converts mechanical energy into electrical energy.

HEAT RANGE: The measure of a spark plug's ability to dissipate heat from its firing end. The higher the heat range, the hotter the plug fires.

HUB: The center part of a wheel or gear.

HYDROCARBON (HC): Any chemical compound made up of hydrogen and carbon. A major pollutant formed by the engine as a byproduct of combustion.

HYDROMETER: An instrument used to measure the specific gravity of a solution.

INCH POUND (in.lb. or sometimes, in. lbs.): One twelfth of a foot pound.

INDUCTION: A means of transferring electrical energy in the form of a magnetic field. Principle used in the ignition coil to increase voltage.

INJECTOR: A device which receives metered fuel under relatively low pressure and is activated to inject the fuel into the engine under relatively high pressure at a predetermined time.

INPUT SHAFT: The shaft to which torque is applied, usually carrying the driving gear or gears.

INTAKE MANIFOLD: A casting of passages or pipes used to conduct air or a fuel/air mixture to the cylinders.

JOURNAL: The bearing surface within which a shaft operates.

KEY: A small block usually fitted in a notch between a shaft and a hub to prevent slippage of the two parts.

MANIFOLD: A casting of passages or set of pipes which connect the cylinders to an inlet or outlet source.

MANIFOLD VACUUM: Low pressure in an engine intake manifold formed just below the throttle plates. Manifold vacuum is highest at idle and drops under acceleration.

MASTER CYLINDER: The primary fluid pressurizing device in a hydraulic system. In automotive use, it is found in brake and hydraulic clutch systems and is pedal activated, either directly or, in a power brake system, through the power booster.

MODULE: Electronic control unit, amplifier or igniter of solid state or integrated design which controls the current flow in the ignition primary circuit based on input from the pick-up coil. When the module opens the primary circuit, the high secondary voltage is induced in the coil.

NEEDLE BEARING: A bearing which consists of a number (usually a large number) of long, thin rollers.

OHM:(Ω) The unit used to measure the resistance of conductor to electrical flow. One ohm is the amount of resistance that limits current flow to one ampere in a circuit with one volt of pressure.

OHMMETER: An instrument used for measuring the resistance, in ohms, in an electrical circuit.

OUTPUT SHAFT: The shaft which transmits torque from a device, such as a transmission.

OVERDRIVE: A gear assembly which produces more shaft revolutions than that transmitted to it.

OVERHEAD CAMSHAFT (OHC): An engine configuration in which the camshaft is mounted on top of the cylinder head and operates the valve either directly or by means of rocker arms.

OVERHEAD VALVE (OHV): An engine configuration in which all of the valves are located in the cylinder head and the camshaft is located in the cylinder block. The camshaft operates the valves via lifters and pushrods.

OXIDES OF NITROGEN (NOx): Chemical compounds of nitrogen produced as a byproduct of combustion. They combine with hydrocarbons to produce smog.

OXYGEN SENSOR: Used with the feedback system to sense the presence of oxygen in the exhaust gas and signal the computer which can reference the voltage signal to an air/fuel ratio.

PINION: The smaller of two meshing gears.

PISTON RING: An open ended ring which fits into a groove on the outer diameter of the piston. Its chief function is to form a seal between the piston and cylinder wall. Most automotive pistons have three rings: two for compression sealing; one for oil sealing.

PRELOAD: A predetermined load placed on a bearing during assembly or by adjustment.

PRIMARY CIRCUIT: Is the low voltage side of the ignition system which consists of the ignition switch, ballast resistor or resistance wire, bypass, coil, electronic control unit and pick-up coil as well as the connecting wires and harnesses.

PRESS FIT: The mating of two parts under pressure, due to the inner diameter of one being smaller than the outer diameter of the other, or vice versa; an interference fit.

RACE: The surface on the inner or outer ring of a bearing on which the balls, needles or rollers move.

REGULATOR: A device which maintains the amperage and/or voltage levels of a circuit at predetermined values.

RELAY: A switch which automatically opens and/or closes a circuit.

RESISTANCE: The opposition to the flow of current through a circuit or electrical device, and is measured in ohms. Resistance is equal to the voltage divided by the amperage.

RESISTOR: A device, usually made of wire, which offers a preset amount of resistance in an electrical circuit.

RING GEAR: The name given to a ring-shaped gear attached to a differential case, or affixed to a flywheel or as part a planetary gear set.

ROLLER BEARING: A bearing made up of hardened inner and outer races between which hardened steel rollers move.

ROTOR: 1. The disc-shaped part of a disc brake assembly, upon which the brake pads bear; also called, brake disc.
2. The device mounted atop the distributor shaft, which passes current to the distributor cap tower contacts.

SECONDARY CIRCUIT: The high voltage side of the ignition system, usually above 20,000 volts. The secondary includes the ignition coil, coil wire, distributor cap and rotor, spark plug wires and spark plugs.

SENDING UNIT: A mechanical, electrical, hydraulic or electromagnetic device which transmits information to a gauge.

SENSOR: Any device designed to measure engine operating conditions or ambient pressures and temperatures. Usually electronic in nature and designed to send a voltage signal to an on-board computer, some sensors may operate as a simple on/off switch or they may provide a variable voltage signal (like a potentiometer) as conditions or measured parameters change.

SHIM: Spacers of precise, predetermined thickness used between parts to establish a proper working relationship.

SLAVE CYLINDER: In automotive use, a device in the hydraulic clutch system which is activated by hydraulic force, disengaging the clutch.

SOLENOID: A coil used to produce a magnetic field, the effect of which is produce work.

SPARK PLUG: A device screwed into the combustion chamber of a spark ignition engine. The basic construction is a conductive core inside of a ceramic insulator, mounted in an outer conductive base. An electrical charge from the spark plug wire travels along the conductive core and jumps a preset air gap to a grounding point or points at the end of the conductive base. The resultant spark ignites the fuel/air mixture in the combustion chamber.

SPLINES: Ridges machined or cast onto the outer diameter of a shaft or inner diameter of a bore to enable parts to mate without rotation.

TACHOMETER: A device used to measure the rotary speed of an engine, shaft, gear, etc., usually in rotations per minute.

THERMOSTAT: A valve, located in the cooling system of an engine, which is closed when cold and opens gradually in response to engine heating, controlling the temperature of the coolant and rate of coolant flow.

TOP DEAD CENTER (TDC): The point at which the piston reaches the top of its travel on the compression stroke.

TORQUE: The twisting force applied to an object.

TORQUE CONVERTER: A turbine used to transmit power from a driving member to a driven member via hydraulic action, providing changes in drive ratio and torque. In automotive use, it links the driveplate at the rear of the engine to the automatic transmission.

TRANSDUCER: A device used to change a force into an electrical signal.

TRANSISTOR: A semi-conductor component which can be actuated by a small voltage to perform an electrical switching function.

TUNE-UP: A regular maintenance function, usually associated with the replacement and adjustment of parts and components in the electrical and fuel systems of a vehicle for the purpose of attaining optimum performance.

TURBOCHARGER: An exhaust driven pump which compresses intake air and forces it into the combustion chambers at higher than atmospheric pressures. The increased air pressure allows more fuel to be burned and results in increased horsepower being produced.

VACUUM ADVANCE: A device which advances the ignition timing in response to increased engine vacuum.

VACUUM GAUGE: An instrument used to measure the presence of vacuum in a chamber.

VALVE: A device which control the pressure, direction of flow or rate of flow of a liquid or gas.

VALVE CLEARANCE: The measured gap between the end of the valve stem and the rocker arm, cam lobe or follower that activates the valve.

VISCOSITY: The rating of a liquid's internal resistance to flow.

VOLTMETER: An instrument used for measuring electrical force in units called volts. Voltmeters are always connected parallel with the circuit being tested.

WHEEL CYLINDER: Found in the automotive drum brake assembly, it is a device, actuated by hydraulic pressure, which, through internal pistons, pushes the brake shoes outward against the drums.

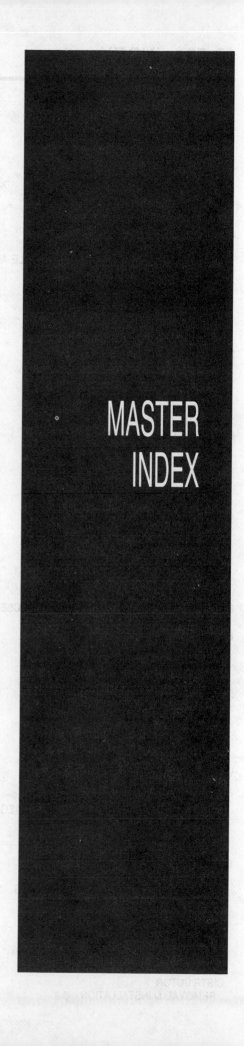

MASTER
INDEX